Frommer's®

National Parks of the American West

1st Edition

by Stephanie Avnet, T.D. Griffith,
Don and Barbara Laine,
Ed Lawrence, Jim Moore,
Matthew R. Poole, Alex Wells,
Stacey Wells, Tom Wells, and
Charles P. Wohlforth

Macmillan • USA

MACMILLAN TRAVEL
A Simon & Schuster Macmillan Company
1633 Broadway
New York, NY 10019
Find us online at **www.frommers.com**

ISBN 0-02-862067-4
ISSN 1097-783x

Editors: Douglas Stallings, Jeff Soloway, and Ron Boudreau
Production Editor: Carol Sheehan
Production Team: Eric Brinkman, David Faust, Heather Pope, and Karen Teo
Design by Paul Costello
Digital Cartography by Roberta Stockwell & Ortelius Design
Photo Editor: Richard Fox

Special Sales
Bulk purchases (10+ copies) of Frommer's and selected Macmillan travel guides are available to corporations, organizations, mail-order catalogs, institutions, and charities at special discounts, and can be customized to suit individual needs. For more information write to Special Sales, Macmillan General Reference, 1633 Broadway, New York, NY 10019.

Manufactured in the United States of America

Note: Please be advised that travel information is subject to change at any time. The publisher and the authors have endeavored to provide useful information in this publication, but we suggest that you write or call ahead for confirmation when making your travel plans. The publisher and authors cannot be held responsible for the experiences of readers while traveling. National parks are, by their very nature, potentially hazardous places. In visiting any of the places or doing any of the activities described herein, readers assume all risk of injury or loss that may accompany such activities. The publisher and the authors disavow all responsibility for injury, death, loss, or property damage that may arise from a reader's visit to any of the places or participation in any of the activities described herein, and the publisher and the authors make no warranties regarding the competence, safety, and reliability of outfitters, tour companies, or training centers described in this publication.

Color insert photo credits:
Yosemite: © Cosmo Condina/Tony Stone Images.
Crater Lake: © David Muench.
Arches, Badlands, Bryce Canyon, Canyon de Chelly, Carlsbad Caverns, Death Valley, Denali, Devils Tower, Grand Canyon, Mojave National Preserve, Mount Rainier, Mount Rushmore, Petrified Forest: © Fred Hirschmann.
Yellowstone: © Randi Hirschmann
Zion: © Scott T. Smith

Contents

Acknowledgments ix

Introduction: Enjoying the Parks Without the Crowds x

1 Just the Facts: Planning Your Trip to the National Parks of the American West 1

2 Arches National Park 9

3 Badlands National Park 27

4 Big Bend National Park 39

5 The Black Hills: Mount Rushmore National Memorial, Wind Cave National Park, Jewel Cave National Monument & Custer State Park 58

6 Bryce Canyon National Park 87

7 Canyon de Chelly National Monument 108

8 Canyonlands National Park 119

9 Capitol Reef National Park 134

10 Carlsbad Caverns National Park 148

11 Channel Islands National Park 161

12 Crater Lake National Park 179

13 Death Valley National Park 192

14 Denali National Park 208

15 Devils Tower National Monument 234

16 Glacier National Park 241

17 Glacier Bay National Park 269

18 Grand Canyon National Park 277

19 Grand Teton National Park 313

20 Great Basin National Park 343

21 Guadalupe Mountains National Park 355

22 Joshua Tree National Park 366

23 Lassen Volcanic National Park 383

24 Little Bighorn Battlefield National Monument 393

25 Mesa Verde National Park 399

26 Mojave National Preserve 410

27 Mount Rainier National Park 423

28 North Cascades National Park 446

29 Olympic National Park 465

30 Petrified Forest National Park 489

31 Point Reyes National Seashore 500

32 Redwood National & State Parks .512

33 Rocky Mountain National Park 524

34 Saguaro National Park 544

35 Sequoia & Kings Canyon National Parks 558

36 Theodore Roosevelt National Park 583

37 Yellowstone National Park 594

38 Yosemite National Park 630

39 Zion National Park 666

Appendix 690

Index 692

List of Maps

The National Parks of the American West xii
Arches National Park 11
Badlands National Park 28
Big Bend National Park 41
The Black Hills 59
Mount Rushmore National Memorial 63
Wind Cave National Park 69
Bryce Canyon National Park 89
Canyon de Chelly National Monument 109
Canyonlands National Park 121
Capitol Reef National Park 135
Carlsbad Caverns National Park 149
Channel Islands National Park 163
Anacapa Island 168
Santa Cruz Island 170
Santa Rosa Island 172
San Miguel Island 174
Santa Barbara Island 176
Crater Lake National Park 181
Death Valley National Park 193
Denali National Park 209
Devils Tower National Monument 235
Glacier National Park 243
Glacier Bay National Park 271
Grand Canyon National Park 278
Grand Canyon Village 284
Grand Teton National Park 314
Great Basin National Park 345
Guadalupe Mountains National Park 357
Joshua Tree National Park 368
Lassen Volcanic National Park 385
Little Bighorn Battlefield National Monument 394
Mesa Verde National Park 401
Mojave National Preserve 411
Mount Rainier National Park 425
North Cascades National Park 448
Olympic National Park 466
Petrified Forest National Park 491
Point Reyes National Seashore 501
Redwood National Park 514
Rocky Mountain National Park 525
Saguaro National Park 546
West Unit 548
East Unit 549
Sequoia & Kings Canyon National Parks 559
Theodore Roosevelt National Park 584
Yellowstone National Park 596
Old Faithful Area 607
Yosemite National Park 632
Yosemite Valley 636
Zion National Park 670

Authors

A native of Los Angeles and an avid traveler, **Stephanie Avnet** believes that California is best seen from behind the wheel of a red convertible. She is the author of *Frommer's Los Angeles* and *Wonderful Weekends from Los Angeles,* and a contributor to *Frommer's California.*

T.D. Griffith is the former Director of Communications for the Mount Rushmore Preservation Fund and the author of several books, including two about the memorial: *America's Shrine of Democracy* and *The Four Faces of Freedom.* A fourth-generation South Dakotan, he lives in Rapid City.

Don and Barbara Laine have written about and traveled extensively throughout the Rocky Mountains and the Southwest. They are the authors of Frommer's guides to Utah, Colorado, and Denver, Boulder & Colorado Springs, as well as a forthcoming Frommer's guide to Zion & Bryce Canyon National Parks.

An avid outdoors type—with a particular affinity for fly-fishing and skiing—Montana resident **Ed Lawrence** has written feature articles about Montana and Wyoming for dozens of outdoor and travel magazines. He is the author of *Frommer's Montana & Wyoming* and also *Frommer's Yellowstone & Grand Teton National Parks.*

Jim Moore has worked as a writer, editor, and cartographer for Frommer's. He has traveled extensively throughout the United States and Europe and now divides his time between southern California and New York.

Combining the only three things he's good at—eating, sleeping, and criticizing—**Matthew R. Poole** has found a surprisingly prosperous career as a full-time freelance travel writer. A native northern Californian and author of more than a dozen travel guides to California and Hawaii, he currently lives in San Francisco.

A resident of Park City, Utah, **Alex Wells** has written for magazines including *Conde Nast Traveler, Men's Journal,* and *Outside.* When not on assignment, he enjoys backcountry skiing and backpacking. His idea of heaven is an eternal hike through the Grand Canyon—with weekly breaks for pizza and showers. He is the author of *Frommer's Grand Canyon National Park.*

Stacey Wells is a native Californian who grew up in the foothills of the Sierra Nevada before relocating to the Bay Area. She currently lives in Oakland, where she is a newspaper reporter and freelance writer. Stacey is the author of *Frommer's Yosemite & Sequoia/Kings Canyon National Parks.*

Tom Wells is a scientist, musician, and writer who lives with his wife and three cats in the rainy Northwest and wishes only that he could get out to travel and snowboard more often than he does.

Charles P. Wohlforth is a lifelong Alaskan who has been a writer and journalist since 1986. After graduating from Princeton University, he worked as a newpaper reporter in the small town of Homer, Alaska, and then for the *Anchorage Daily News.* He has won more than 20 awards for his writing and is currently researching a new book for Frommer's on family travel to the national parks.

Acknowledgments

THE FOLLOWING INDIVIDUALS HAVE REVIEWED CHAPTERS OR HELPED THE AUTHORS in their research:

Diane Allen, **Arches;** Jane Andersen, **Mesa Verde;** Terry Baldino, **Death Valley;** Doug Ballou, **Carlsbad Caverns;** Doug Caldwell, **Rocky Mountain;** Malinee Crapsey, **Sequoia/Kings Canyon** and **Yosemite;** Tom Danton, **Saguaro;** Denny Davies, **Zion;** Anne Marie Fender, **Canyon de Chelly;** Sheri Forbes, **Mount Rainier;** Larry Frederick, **Glacier;** Paul Henderson, **Canyonlands;** Paula Hosking, **Petrified Forest;** Scott Isaacson, **Lassen Volcanic;** Beth Kaeding, **Yellowstone;** Bruce Kaye, **Theodore Roosevelt;** Peter Keller, **Redwood;** Rich McCamant, **Guadalupe Mountains;** Timothy Manns, **North Cascades;** Barbara Maynes, **Olympic;** Dave Mecham, **Bryce Canyon;** Marianne Mills, **Badlands;** Riley Ann Mitchell, **Devils Tower;** Valerie Naylor, **Big Bend;** Thea Nordling, **Capitol Reef;** Linda Olson, **Grand Teton;** Annie Hopkins Pfaff, **Great Basin;** Jim Popovich, **Mount Rushmore;** Dave Rachlis, **Zion;** Karen Rosga, **Jewel Cave;** Cheryl Schreier, **Bryce Canyon;** Ellen Seeley, **Grand Canyon;** Carol Spears, **Channel Islands;** Kirsten Talken, **Mojave;** Kent Taylor, **Crater Lake;** Ron Terry, **Wind Cave;** Joe Zarki, **Joshua Tree.**

An Invitation to the Reader

In researching this book, we discovered many wonderful places. We're sure you'll find others. Please tell us about them, so we can share the information with your fellow travelers in upcoming editions. If you were disappointed with a recommendation, we'd love to know that, too. Please write to:

Frommer's National Parks of the American West, 1st Edition
Macmillan Travel
1633 Broadway
New York, NY 10019

The following abbreviations are used for credit cards:

AE	American Express
DC	Diners Club
DISC	Discover
MC	MasterCard
V	Visa

Introduction: Enjoying the Parks Without the Crowds

The National Park Service seems to be walking a tightrope. The service really has two missions, and they sometimes seem to run in opposition to each other. Its first mission is to preserve some of America's most unique and important natural areas for future generations; the second is to make these places available for the enjoyment of all Americans. Because the number of visitors to our national parks has grown tremendously over the years, some of the busiest parks, including the Grand Canyon, Yosemite, Zion, and Yellowstone, are now searching for ways to make both these goals reality.

Park service officials have often said that the real source of congestion in the most heavily visited parks is not the numbers of people but rather the numbers of cars. (You don't go to a national park hoping to get caught up in a traffic jam, do you?) As a result, those parks with yearly attendance in the millions are now putting together plans to limit vehicle traffic within their boundaries. Yosemite is exploring several options, including having visitors leave their cars outside the park and take shuttle buses in. The Grand Canyon already bans vehicle traffic on parts of the South Rim during the busy season from mid-April through mid-October. Zion soon plans to ban vehicle traffic on its most popular scenic drive, limiting visitors to a sightseeing shuttle bus. And Yellowstone is redesigning its road system to improve traffic flow.

If all this leads you to despair that you can't have a true "wilderness" experience in one of the national parks of the American West, don't think that for a minute. Even in a park as crowded as Yosemite, there are places where you can completely escape the crowds, where you'll be able to walk among the trees and hear nothing but the sound of your own footsteps. All it takes is a little effort and planning, and that's where this book comes in handy.

Our authors have talked to the rangers, hiked the trails, and taken the tours, all the while asking, "How can our readers avoid the crowds?" In each of the following chapters, you'll find a section giving you straightforward, practical advice on just how to do this. Sure, if you're an outdoors ironman (or woman), you can avoid the crowds by taking off on the most strenuous backcountry hikes, but not everyone is made of iron. So we've searched for secluded trails that can be hiked by the average person (not just the ones you'll see on the covers of *Outside* magazine), scenic drives where you won't get caught in bumper-to-bumper traffic, and points where, with only a minimum of effort, you'll be afforded spectacular views without feeling as if you're packed into Times Square on New Year's Eve.

We've also discovered that *when* you go is as important as *where* you go. Since most of the West's national parks and monuments are busiest in July and August, you can avoid many of the people by coming in April or September,

Campground Reservations

In March 1998, a new company, Maryland-based **Biospherics, Inc.,** took over the reservations system for many of the national parks covered in this book. Though many details had not been worked out when we went to press, you should be able to make reservations though this service at **Channel Islands, Death Valley, Glacier, Grand Canyon, Joshua Tree, Mount Rainier, Rocky Mountain, Sequoia–Kings Canyon,** and **Zion** national parks by calling ☎ **800/365-CAMP** (2267). You should be able to make reservations at **Yosemite National Park** by calling ☎ **800/436-PARK** (7275). And you should be able to make cave tour reservations at **Carlsbad Caverns National Park** by calling ☎ **800/967-CAVE** (2283).

especially if you can come just before or just after the times when schools are generally out for summer vacation. Remember that most national parks are open year-round, though services are sometimes limited during the off-season. In fact, many are great places to go in winter for skiing and exploring, and these are also times when you're less likely to feel mobbed. The hoodoos of Bryce Canyon, for example, are just as strikingly beautiful when they're snow-covered, and you won't be jostling with nearly as many people at the view points.

The last thing we've discovered (though it's not a very big secret) is that there are many hidden gems among the national parks and monuments of the American West. Everyone knows about Mount Rainier and Carlsbad Caverns but not always about the less-visited parks, such as Great Basin in Nevada, Canyon de Chelly in Arizona, the Channel Islands in California, Little Bighorn Battlefield in Montana, Jewel Cave in the Black Hills of South Dakota, and the Guadalupe Mountains in Texas. These are places of great beauty or historical significance, but they're often overlooked because of their remoteness or simply because they're relatively new to the national park system.

The most important thing to remember as you make your trip is that the parks and monuments in the following chapters have been set aside and are maintained for future generations, not only our own.

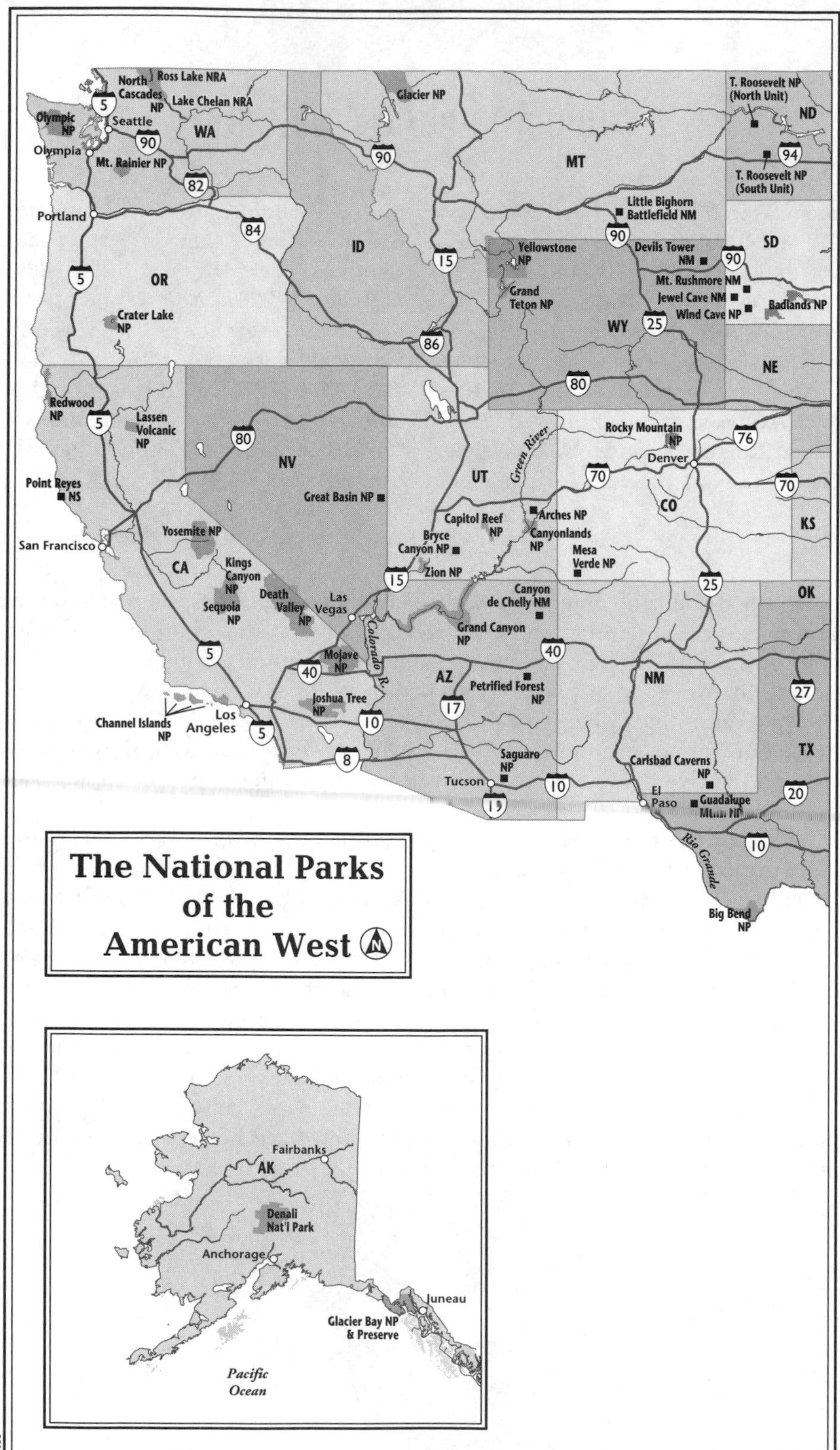

The National Parks of the American West
Ross Lake NRA
North Cascades NP
Lake Chelan NRA
Olympic NP
Seattle
Olympia
Mt. Rainier NP
WA
Glacier NP
MT
T. Roosevelt NP (North Unit)
ND
T. Roosevelt NP (South Unit)
Little Bighorn Battlefield NM
Portland
ID
Yellowstone NP
Devils Tower NM
SD
Mt. Rushmore NM
Jewel Cave NM
Wind Cave NP
Badlands NP
Grand Teton NP
WY
OR
Crater Lake NP
NE
Redwood NP
Lassen Volcanic NP
NV
Rocky Mountain NP
Denver
Green River
UT
Point Reyes NS
Great Basin NP
CO
KS
Arches NP
Capitol Reef NP
Canyonlands NP
Yosemite NP
San Francisco
Bryce Canyon NP
Mesa Verde NP
CA
Kings Canyon NP
Zion NP
Sequoia NP
Death Valley NP
Las Vegas
Canyon de Chelly NM
OK
Colorado R.
Grand Canyon NP
Mojave NP
AZ
NM
Petrified Forest NP
Joshua Tree NP
Channel Islands NP
Los Angeles
TX
Saguaro NP
Carlsbad Caverns NP
Tucson
El Paso
Guadalupe Mtns NP
Rio Grande
Big Bend NP
Fairbanks
AK
Denali Nat'l Park
Anchorage
Juneau
Glacier Bay NP & Preserve
Pacific Ocean

9-0055

1

JUST THE FACTS: Planning Your Trip to the National Parks of the American West

IN THIS CHAPTER, WE'VE TRIED TO GIVE YOU ALL THE GENERAL INFORmation you will need to plan your trip to America's national parks of the western United States. The individual park chapters that follow will be able to answer your more specific questions.

See the Parks Without the Crowds—Some General Tips

It's not easy to commune with nature when you're surrounded by hordes of fellow visitors. For each park, we've discussed the best times of year to go and listed certain areas, trails, and sites less visited than the others. Beyond that, here are a few general guidelines to follow.

◆ Try to avoid the high season; for most parks in the West, this especially means July and August, but anytime schools are not in session, parks are crowded with families on vacation. Spring and fall in many of these national parks offer mild weather, vibrant plant and animal life, and relatively empty trails and roads.

◆ Once in the park, if you find yourself in a crowd, walk away. It sounds simple, but often, while a scenic overlook is crowded, you'll find an equally good view that is completely empty just a short stretch down the road. By the same token, get off the road or the public areas completely and head down the hiking trails. More often than not, after an hour on the trail, you've left all humanity behind.

◆ Go to popular park attractions at off-peak hours, especially early in the morning or late in the afternoon. You'll be surprised at how empty the park is before 9 or 10am. Dawn and dusk are also often the best times to see wildlife.

◆ Don't forget winter. You may not see wildflowers and some roads and areas may be closed, but many national parks in the west are great places to ski, snowshoe, or even rent a snowmobile and go exploring. Lodging facilities are even open in some of them, or at least nearby.

◆ Finally, remember that some parks are rarely crowded, and we've made a special effort to include information about many of them in this book. Nearly 170 such parks are highlighted in the Park Service's booklet *Lesser Known Areas of the National Park System.* To purchase a copy, send a check or money order for $1.50 payable to the **Superintendent of Documents,** Consumer Information Center, Department 134b, Pueblo, CO 81009. The full text of this pamphlet is also available on the Park Service's Web site, which is given in the next section.

Getting Information Before Your Trip

Getting information before you go to a national park can help you make the most of your trip; it can also help you avoid the crowds. For park brochures and general planning information, write or call the **Department of the Interior, National Park Service, Office of Public Inquiries,** P.O. Box 37127, Room 1013, Washington, DC 20013-7127 (☎ **202/208-4747**), Monday to Friday, from 9am to 3pm.

The National Park Service also has a Web site at **www.nps.gov**, where each park has its own Web page that you can check out (some of these are more helpful than others—many parks in the west have expanded Web pages that have a great deal of specific information).

You can also contact each park directly (for details see "Getting Information Before Your Trip" under "Just the Facts" in each chapter).

Planning a National Park Itinerary

Even though distance seem vast in the western United States, it is possible to visit more than one of the national parks there in a single trip. In fact, people often combine visits to Yellowstone and Grand Teton, Yosemite and Sequoia, and Zion and Bryce Canyon. Utah especially is chock-full of parks in the vast area in its southern portion, in the area surrounding the new Grand Steps Escalante National Monument. Here, in addition to Zion and Bryce Canyon, you'll find Arches, Canyonlands, and Capitol Reef national parks. The parks of the California desert (Death Valley, Joshua Tree, and Mojave Preserve) can be knitted into a nice itinerary that might even leave you time to stop off in the resort town of Palm Springs. A popular trip for families is a drive through the Badlands National Park and Black Hills of South Dakota, all the way through Devils Tower to Yellowstone, not a small stretch, but doable if you have more than a week of vacation. Take a look at the map at the beginning of this chapter to see where all the parks in this guide are located as a start to planning your trip.

Fees & Permits

Though fees have gone up recently, visiting a national park is still a bargain—a steal compared to a theme park. Entry fees, ranging from nothing at Guadalupe to $20 at Grand Canyon, are usually charged per vehicle regardless of how many visitors are stuffed inside. Those arriving on foot or by bicycle, motorcycle, or public transportation pay lower per-person fees. Some parks offer passes good for unlimited visits to the same park for 12 months.

Special Passes. There are several passes that offer discounts on multiple visits to different parks. For anyone, the Golden Eagle Passport costs $50, lasts 1 year, and provides free entry to all national parks for the pass holder and any accompanying passengers in a personal vehicle. For those traveling in another manner, such as by bicycle or on foot, the pass admits free the pass holder, spouse, children, and parents. You can buy the Golden Eagle Passport at any National Park Service entry area or send a check for $60 to: Attention: Golden Eagle Passport, National Park Service, 1100 Ohio Dr. SW, Room 138, Washington, DC 20242.

The **Golden Age Passport** is a lifetime entrance pass available to those 62 years or older. It costs $10 and must be purchased in person at a National Park Service fee entry area. Be sure to bring proof of age and U.S. citizenship or permanent residency. Like the Golden Eagle, this pass admits for free the pass holder and any accompanying passengers in a personal vehicle. An additional advantage to the Golden Age Passport is that it provides a 50% discount on fees for all Park Services and facilities, such as camping, swimming, parking, boat launching, or cave tours, but not for fees charged by concessionaires.

The **Golden Access Passport** provides the same benefits as the Golden Age Passport, both free entry for the pass holder and companions and a 50% discount on fees for Park Services and facilities. It costs nothing and is available to those who are blind or permanently disabled, regardless of age. To get one, go to any park entrance fee area and show proof of disability and eligibility for receiving benefits under federal law.

Other Fees. You may also be required to pay other recreational use fees, which might be anything from $6 for a tour of Jewel Cave to $12 per night to camp in Glacier National Park. Most all the museums and exhibits you will find in park visitor centers are free, but there are many services operated by private concessionaires. So you will have to pay extra to go horseback riding in Theodore Roosevelt National Park (unless you bring our own horses) or to rent one of the audio driving tours at Yellowstone.

Backcountry Permits. At most national parks, it is necessary to obtain a backcountry permit to stay overnight in the park's undeveloped backcountry. In some parks, there are even more restrictions. To be safe, if you intend to do any backpacking, look in the individual park chapter or contact the park's backcountry office in advance. In some cases, it may be possible to obtain a permit by mail; in most cases, you must appear in person the day before your trip. Although most parks do not currently charge for backcountry permits, a few (such as Glacier) require a fee if you reserve a backcountry campsite, and some (such as Glacier Bay) restrict the number of permits issued in a given year.

Other Permits. Hunting is not allowed in national parks, but fishing often is, and you will often need a fishing permit (or a state fishing license). In some parks (Yellowstone and Grand Teton, for example), you will need a special permit to go boating. In others, such as Mount Rainier, you will need a special permit to go cross-country skiing. Check the individual park chapters for details on these and other permits that might be required.

Campground Reservations

If you plan to camp and you don't have a reservation (or aren't able to make one because the campgrounds in the park you're visiting are assigned on a first-come, first-served basis), the first thing you should do upon arrival is to make sure a site is available. Campsites at major park campgrounds fill up early in summer, on weekends, and during other peak times, such as school holidays. A reservation, or an early morning arrival at a campground (perhaps as early as 8 or 9am), is the best defense against disappointment. In each chapter, we've given an indication if a campground tends to fill up especially early.

In the camping section for each park, we've given phone numbers for campgrounds in or near the parks that take reservations. We've included National Park Service campgrounds, National Forest Service campgrounds, and those operated by private companies.

One warning: The National Park Service has recently discontinued its nationwide campground reservations system, which up until now had provided a convenient system for reservations for National Park Service campgrounds at many popular parks, including Death Valley, Grand Canyon, Joshua Tree, Rocky Mountain, Sequoia–Kings Canyon, and Yosemite. At press time, no reservations for Park Service campgrounds can be made at these parks. The Park Service hopes to have a new system in place by 1998.

You can make reservations in many **National Forest Service** campgrounds through its national reservations number (☎ **800/280-2267**). There is a fee (currently $8.25 per site) to make a campground reservation, and you must pay both this fee and your camping fee in advance (by credit card) at the time you make your reservations. It is not possible to make reservations at all these campgrounds. For more information, see the individual park chapters.

Useful Publications

It's often nice to read a little something about the place you're going in advance of your trip. If you're so inclined, many of the parks have bookstores from which you can purchase books by mail. Or you can purchase books directly from the National Park Service or other government agency.

Two useful titles are ***National Parks Visitor Facilities & Services,*** which can be purchased for $4.50 from The National Park Hospitality Association, 1331 Pennsylvania Ave. NW, Suite 724, Washington, DC 20004-1703 (☎ **202/662-7097**); and ***The Complete Guide to America's National Parks,*** published by the National Park Foundation, 1101 17th St. NW, Suite 1102, Washington, DC 20036 (☎ **202/785-4500**). The latter is available in most bookstores. The cost is approximately $14.95.

Another useful series of publications is from the National Park Service, an award-winning series of National Park Handbooks, now with more than 40 titles in print and more added yearly. These modestly priced booklets are compact introductions to the natural or historical attractions administered by the Park Service. You'll find a complete list on the Park Service's Web site. The following titles are currently available for parks covered in this guide:

- *Big Bend* by Helen Moss ($6)
- *Canyon de Chelly* by Zorro Bradley ($3)
- *Devils Tower* by Greg Beaumont ($5.50)
- *Glacier Bay* by Ruth Kirk ($6)
- *Grand Teton* by National Park Service staff ($5)
- *Little Bighorn Battlefield* by Robert Utley ($5)
- *North Cascades* by National Park Service staff ($7)
- *Saguaro* by Napier Shelton and Natt Dodge ($6.50)
- *Sequoia and Kings Canyon* by National Park Service staff ($4.50)
- *Wind Cave* by Robert Woodward and Greg Beaumont ($7.00)
- *Yosemite* by National Park Service staff ($7)

To order these by mail, send your order, along with payment, to **Superintendent of Documents,** P.O. Box 371954, Pittsburgh, PA 15250-7954, or call ☎ **202/512-1800** or fax 202/512-2250. Visa and MasterCard are accepted for phone orders.

For more information about National Park Service publications, contact Nancy McLoughlin**, Division of Publications,** National Park Service, Harpers Ferry, WV 25425-0050 (☎ **304/535-6018;** fax 304/535-6144; e-mail: Nancy_McLoughlin@nps.gov).

Maps

When you arrive at a national park site, you'll receive a large, four-color brochure that has a good map of the park on it. However, this won't always be enough if you need to do some serious hiking.

We have a few recommendations.

Though it only covers parks in California, there is a very useful series of maps by **Tom Harrison Cartography.** These maps are real works of art. Each one covers a specific area (such as Mojave National Preserve or Yosemite) and costs $5.95 or $6.95. They can be purchased in some outdoor-oriented stores, or you may be able to order them from a specialty map distributor.

Another series we like is the maps from Trails Illustrated, a company owned by National Geographic that publishes more than 50 maps of national park areas. Their maps retail for around $9 and are available in bookstores or

George Washington and Abraham Lincoln, Mount Rushmore National Memorial, South Dakota.

Thor's Hammer basking in the reflected light of a sunrise, Bryce Canyon National Park, Utah.

Spring skunk cabbage blossoms in the Carbon River Rain Forest, Mount Rainier National Park, Washington.

The ruins of the White House, an ancient cliff dwelling in Canyon de Chelly National Monument, Arizona.

Petrified logs from the Triassic Age on the Blue Mesa, Petrified Forest National Park, Arizona.

Above: *The travertine terraces of Canary Spring, Mammoth Hot Springs, Yellowstone National Park, Wyoming.*

Below: *The Devils Playground and Kelo Peak viewed from the crest of Kelso Dunes, Mojave National Preserve, California.*

The Subway in the Great West Canyon's left-hand fork in winter, Zion National Park, Utah.

The Grand Canyon viewed from just east of Yaki Point on the South Rim, Grand Canyon National Park, Arizona.

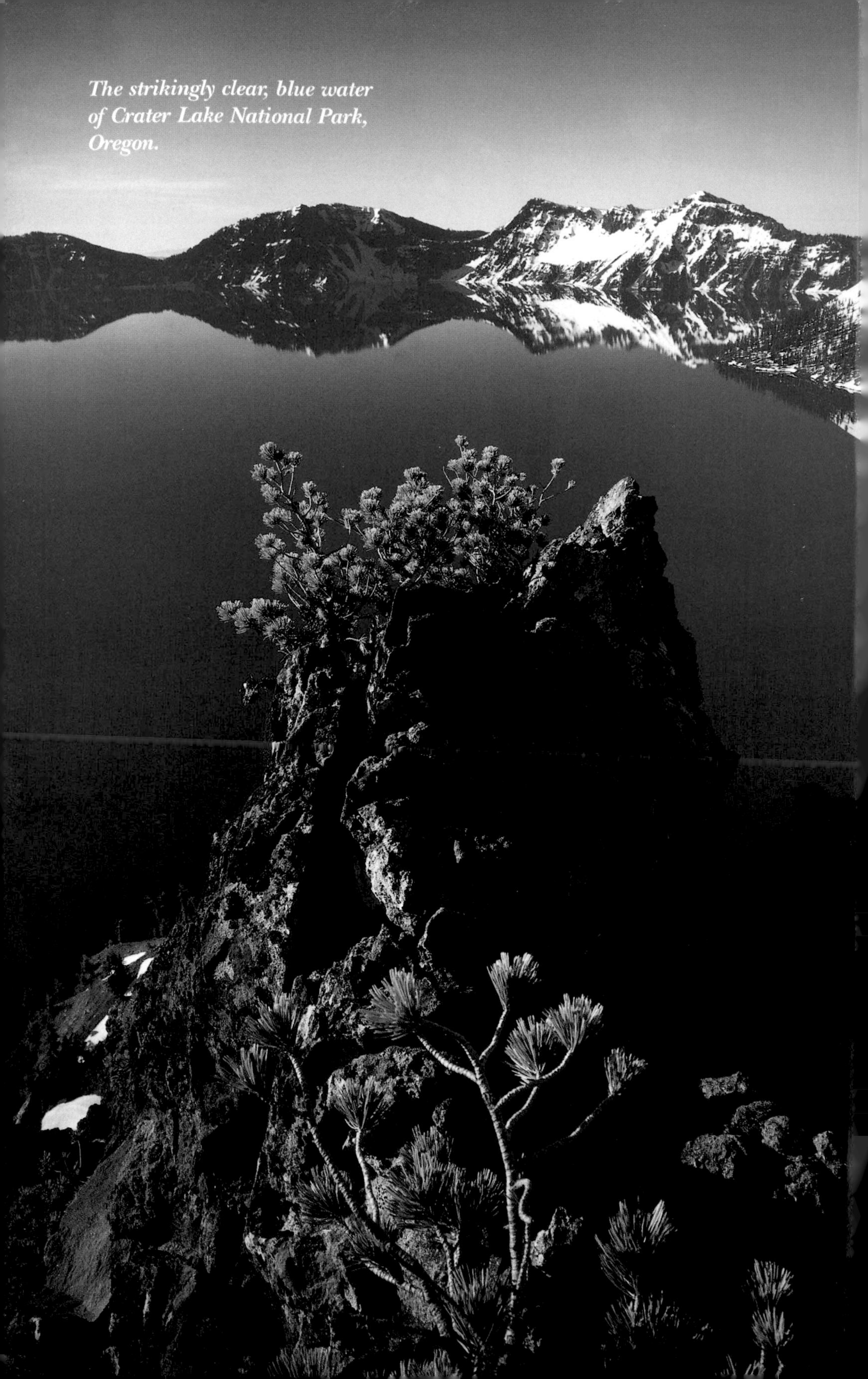

The strikingly clear, blue water of Crater Lake National Park, Oregon.

"The Totem Pole" in the Big Room, Carlsbad Caverns National Park, New Mexico.

Above: *Mt. Fellows and Pyramid Mountain are beyond a boreal forest of spruce and birch, viewed from the east end of Denali National Park, Alaska.*

Below: *The full moon at dawn, viewed across the badlands of Furnace Creek from Zabriskie Point, Death Valley National Park, California.*

Ponderosa pines frame Devils Tower, Devils Tower National Monument, Wyoming.

El Capitan enshrouded by clouds, Yosemite National Park, California.

Volcanic dust in the atmosphere casts a warm glow on Delicate Arch, Arches National Park, Utah.

Morning in Badlands National Park, South Dakota.

directly from **Trails Illustrated,** P.O. Box 4357, Evergreen, CO 80347-4357 (☎ **800/962-1643** or 303/670-3457). They have a Web site at **www.colorado.com/trails**.

If you can't find the map you want locally, you might try calling the **Adventurous Traveler Bookstore** (☎ **800/282-3963**). They carry a wide variety of hiking maps (as well as other books and maps). They have a Web site at **www2.gorp.com/atb/**. Or you can write to them to receive a printed catalog of books and maps they carry at P.O. Box 577, Hinesburg, VT 05461. Among others, they carry maps from Tom Harrison Cartography and Trails Illustrated.

Tips for RVers

Especially in the warm months, many people prefer to explore the national parks in an RV—a motor home, truck camper, or camper trailer, assuming you don't mind roughing it a bit.

One advantage to this type of travel is that early morning and early evening are among the best times to be in the parks if you want to avoid crowds and do some wildlife watching (not to mention that it's often much cooler at these times). Needless to say, it's a lot more convenient to experience the parks at these times if you're already there, staying in one of the park campgrounds. But the best reason is simply that inexplicable feeling of contentment that comes from waking up to the sound of birds singing and furry little creatures scurrying about outside your door; in other words, living the national park experience rather than just visiting, as if it were an amusement park or shopping mall.

Another reason to camp is that if you have special dietary requirements, you won't have to worry about trying to find a restaurant that can meet your needs; you'll be able to cook for yourself, either in your motor home or trailer, or on a camp stove.

There are disadvantages, of course. Small trailers and campers can be cramped, and even the most luxurious motor homes and trailers provide somewhat close quarters. Facilities in national park campgrounds are limited, although they are being upgraded to the point where camping purists are starting to complain. Even in most commercial campgrounds the facilities are less than you'd expect in moderately-priced motels, and they can be pricey. Some of the private campgrounds charge as much for an RV site with utility hookups as you'd expect to pay in a cheap motel. Coupled with the cost of gas, RV life is not always a cheaper alternative.

There are a few things that RVers might want to know. For instance, parking is often limited in the national parks of the west, especially for motor homes and other large vehicles, but most people are driving in the parks between 10am and 5pm. The solution is to head out on the scenic drives either early or late in the day, when there's less traffic. It's nicer then, anyway.

If you'll be traveling in the park in your RV and want to make it obvious that your campsite is occupied, carry something worthless to leave in it, such as a cardboard box with "Site Taken" clearly written on it. You can usually find a rock to weight it down.

Because some of the national park campsites are not level, carry four or five short boards, or leveling blocks, that can be placed under the RV's wheels. You can buy small, inexpensive levels at RV and hardware stores, and you'll discover that not only will you sleep better if your rig is level, but your food won't slide off the table and the refrigerator will run more efficiently.

Renting an RV for Your National Park Trek. If you own an RV, you're all set for a trip to the national parks, but if you don't, you might want to consider renting one.

But first, let's get one thing straight: You probably won't save a lot of money. Although it's possible to travel fairly cheaply if you limit your equipment to a tent, a pop-up tent trailer, or a small pickup truck camper, renting a motor home will probably end up costing almost as much as driving a compact car, staying in moderately priced motels, and eating in family-style restaurants and cafes. That's because the motor home will go only one-third as far on a gallon of gas as your compact car will, and they're expensive to rent—generally between $1,000 and $1,100 per week in midsummer, when rates are highest.

But carrying your house with you, like a turtle, gives you the opportunity to stay in the national park campgrounds, which many park visitors believe is one of the highlights of their trips; it lets you stop for meals anytime and anywhere you choose; and it means you won't have to worry about sleeping on a lumpy pillow. An added benefit is that you won't spend time searching for a rest room—almost all RVs have some sort of bathroom facilities, ranging from a full bath with tub/shower combination to a porta-potty that is stored under a seat.

If you're planning to fly into the area and rent an RV when you arrive, choose your starting point carefully. Not only will you want to keep the driving to a minimum—you'll be lucky to get 10 miles per gallon of gas—but rental rates vary, depending on the city in which you pick up your RV. **Cruise America,** one of the country's largest RV rental companies, quoted us a weekly rate of $1,093 for a 23-foot motor home for July 1998, with 1,000 free miles. Cruise America also rents truck campers, complete with truck. For information, contact **Cruise America** (☎ **800/327-7799;** fax 602/464-7321). The Web site is **www.cruiseamerica.com**.

Tips for Traveling with Kids

The **Junior Ranger Program** offered at most parks gives kids the chance to earn certificates, badges, and patches for completing certain projects, such as tree or animal identification, or answering questions in a workbook. It's a good way for them to learn about the national parks and the resources that the Park Service protects. Also, many parks offer special discussions, walks, and other ranger-led activities for children.

Tips for Travelers with Disabilities

There are more options and resources out there than ever before, so a disability should not stop anyone from traveling. ***A World of Options,*** a 658-page book of resources for disabled travelers, covers everything from biking trips to scuba outfitters. It costs $45 and is available from **Mobility International USA,** P.O. Box 10767, Eugene, OR 97440 (☎ **541/343-1284,** voice and TDD; Web site: www.miusa.org). For more personal assistance, call the **Travel Information Service** at ☎ **215/456-9603** or 215/456-9602 (for TTY).

Many of the major car rental companies now offer hand-controlled cars for disabled drivers. **Avis** can provide such a vehicle at any of its locations in the U.S. with 48-hour advance notice; **Hertz** requires between 24 and 72 hours of advance reservation at most of its locations. **Wheelchair Getaways** (☎ **800/873-4973;** Web site: www.blvd.com/wg.htm) rents specialized vans with wheelchair lifts and other features for the disabled in more than 100 cities across the United States.

Travelers with disabilities may also want to consider joining a tour that caters specifically to them. One of the best operators is **Flying Wheels Travel,** 143 W. Bridge (P.O. Box 382), Owatonna, MN 55060 (☎ **800/525-6790**). They offer various escorted tours and cruises, as well as private tours in minivans with lifts. Another good company is **FEDCAP Rehabilitation Services,** 211 W. 14th St., New York, NY 10011. Call ☎ **212/727-4200** or fax 212/721-4374 for information about membership and summer tours.

Vision-impaired travelers should contact the **American Foundation for the Blind,** 11 Penn Plaza, Suite 300, New York,

NY 10001 (☎ **800/232-5463**), for information on traveling with Seeing Eye dogs.

The policy of the National Park Service is to provide the highest feasible level of access for visitors with disabilities to all buildings and public use areas. Historic buildings and visitor centers are almost always wheelchair accessible, but call ahead just to make sure; you don't want to arrive at an historic park lodge only to find that your wheelchair won't allow you to go in the bathroom. Many parks have paved, wheelchair-accessible nature trails in addition to the scenic drives available to anyone in a car.

The Sierra Club publishes a useful book on the subject called ***Easy Access to National Parks: The Sierra Club Guide for People with Disabilities*** by Wendy Roth and Michael Tompane. It's available in bookstores.

And don't forget your **Golden Access Passport** (see "Fees & Permits," above). It is free and will grant you free admission to most national parks and a 50% discount on Park Services and facilities.

Tips for Travelers with Pets

As much as you may enjoy traveling with your pet, as John Steinbeck did, a better approach is this: Leave Fido home. In most parks, pets must be leashed at all times and kept off trails and out of public buildings and the backcountry. As a consequence, while you're exploring the sights and sounds of the park, Fido or Fluffy may be stuck in a stiflingly warm vehicle. And at night, though pets are usually allowed in developed campgrounds (leashed, of course), in hotels they're often at best barely tolerated or at worst completely prohibited.

Protecting Your Health & Safety

First of all, don't forget that motor vehicle accidents cause more deaths in the park every year than anything else. Scenic drives are often winding and steep; take them slowly and carefully. And no matter how stunning the snowcapped peak you may glimpse off to the side—keep your eyes on the road.

When out on the trails, even for a day hike, keep safety in mind. The wild, untouched nature of these parks is what makes them so exciting and breathtakingly beautiful—but along with wildness comes risk. The national parks are not playgrounds, nor are they zoos. The animals here are truly untamed and sometimes truly dangerous. This doesn't mean that disaster could strike any visitor at any time, but it does mean that visitors should exercise basic caution and common sense at all times, respecting the wilderness around them and always following the rules of the park.

Never feed, bother, or even approach any animals. Even the smallest among them can carry harmful, sometimes deadly, diseases, and feeding them is dangerous not only to yourself, but to the animals too, which (like us) will happily eat what their body can't handle. If you have doubts about the danger of feeding animals, just ask the Yosemite visitors whose car doors have been peeled off by bears searching for food left in trunks.

It's often a good idea to make noise as you hike, to make sure you don't accidentally stumble upon and frighten a large animal into aggression. Photographers should always keep a safe distance when taking pictures of wildlife—the best photos are shot with a telephoto lens.

It's equally important for your safety to know your limitations, to understand the environment, and to take the proper equipment when exploring the park. The visitor center should always be your stop before you hike. Park staff there can offer you advice on your hiking plans and supply you with pamphlets, maps, and information on weather conditions or any dangers, such as bear activity or flash flood possibilities on canyon hikes. Once out on the trail, hikers should always carry sufficient water and, just as important, remember to drink it. Wear sturdy shoes with good ankle support and rock-gripping souls. Always keep a close eye on any children in your group, and never let them run ahead.

Since most of us live at or near sea level, the most common health hazard is discomfort caused by **altitude sickness,** as we adjust to the parks' high elevations, a process that may take a day or more. Symptoms include headache, fatigue, nausea, loss of appetite, muscle pain, and lightheadedness. Doctors recommend that, until acclimated, the best remedy is to consume light meals and drink lots of liquids, avoiding those with caffeine or alcohol. It's a good idea to take frequent sips of water, as well.

A waterborne hazard is ***Giardia,*** a parasite that wreaks havoc on the human digestive system. If you pick up this pesky hanger-on, it may accompany you on your trip home. Untreated water from the parks' lakes and streams should be boiled for 3 to 6 minutes before consumption.

Hiking Tips

Don't venture off on any extensive hike, even a day hike, without the following gear: A compass, a topographical map, bug repellent, a whistle, and a watch. Many will also want to bring sunglasses and sunscreen. To be on the safe side, you should keep a **first aid kit** in your car or luggage, and have it handy when hiking. It should include at the least butterfly bandages, sterile gauze pads, adhesive tape, an antibiotic ointment, both children's and adult pain reliever, alcohol pads, and a knife with scissors and tweezers.

Planning a Backcountry Trip

Here are some general things to keep in mind when planning a backcountry trip:

◆ **Permits** In many parks, overnight hiking and backcountry camping requires a permit. These are often free and usually available at a visitor center.

◆ **Camping Etiquette & Special Regulations** Follow the basic rules of camping etiquette: Pack out all your trash, including uneaten food and used toilet paper. Camp in obvious campsites. If pit toilets are not available, bury human waste in holes 6 inches deep, 6 inches across, and at least 200 feet from water and creek beds. When doing dishes, take water and dishes at least 200 feet from the water source, and scatter the waste water. Hang food and trash out of reach of wildlife.

◆ **Shoes** Be sure to wear comfortable, sturdy hiking shoes that will resist water if you're planning an early-season hike.

◆ **Sleeping Bags** Your sleeping bag should be rated for the low temperatures found at high elevations. Most campers are happy to have a sleeping pad.

◆ **Water** If you're not carrying enough water for the entire trip, you'll also need a good water filter, since that seemingly clear stream is filled with a bacteria likely to cause intestinal disorders.

◆ **Your Pack** The argument rages about the merits of old fashioned external-frame packs and the newer, internal-frame models. Over the long run, the newer versions are more stable, and allow you to carry greater loads more comfortably; however, they also cost more. The key issue is finding a pack that fits well, has plenty of padding, a wide hip belt, and a good lumbar support pad.

Protecting the Environment

Many of the parks receive millions of visitors each year. Every visitor has an obligation to preserve the park for other visitors, now and in the future.

Stay on designated trails. Leave no garbage behind, even the smallest gum-wrapper. Don't disturb plants, wildlife, or archaeological resources. Don't pick flowers or collect rocks. Pay attention to trail-specific rules provided by the park rangers. Camp in designated areas only.

2

ARCHES NATIONAL PARK

by Don and Barbara Laine

NATURAL STONE ARCHES AND FANTASTIC ROCK FORMATIONS, SCULPTED as if by an artist's hand, are the defining feature of this park, and they exist in remarkable numbers and variety. Just as soon as you've seen the most beautiful, most colorful, most gigantic stone arch you can imagine, walk around the next bend and there's another—bigger, better, and more brilliant than the last. It would take forever to see them all, with more than 2,000 officially listed and more being discovered or "born" every day.

Just down the road from Canyonlands National Park in eastern Utah, Arches is much more visitor-friendly, with relatively short, well maintained trails leading to most of the park's major attractions. It's also a place to let your imagination run wild. Is Delicate Arch really so delicate? Or would its other monikers (Old Maid's Bloomers or Cowboy Chaps) really be more appropriate? And what about those tall spires? You might imagine they're castles, giant stone sailing ships, or perhaps petrified skyscrapers of some ancient city.

Exploring the park is a great family adventure. The arches seem more accessible and less forbidding than the spires and pinnacles at Canyonlands and other southern Utah parks. Some think of arches as bridges, imagining the power of water that literally cuts a hole through a solid rock. Actually, to geologists there's a big difference between arches and bridges. Bridges are formed when a river cuts a channel, while the often bizarre and beautiful contours of arches result from the erosive force of rain and snow, freezing and thawing, as it dissolves the "glue" that holds sand grains together, and chips away at the stone.

Although arches usually grow slowly—*very* slowly—something dramatic happens every once in a while. Like that quiet day in 1940 when a sudden crash instantly doubled the size of the opening of Skyline Arch, leaving a huge boulder lying at its feet. Luckily, no one (at least no one we know of) was standing underneath at the time. The same thing happened to the magnificently delicate Landscape Arch in 1991, when a slab of rock about 60 feet long, 11 feet wide, and 4½ feet thick fell from the underside of the arch. Now there's such a thin ribbon of stone that it's hard to believe it can continue hanging on at all.

Spend a day or a week here, exploring the terrain, watching the rainbow of colors deepen and explode with the long rays of the setting sun, or the moonlight glistening on ribbons of desert varnish on tall sandstone cliffs. Watch for mule deer, cottontail rabbits, and the bright green collared lizard as they go about the task of desert living. And let your own imagination run wild among the Three Gossips, the Spectacles, the Eye of the

> Ten thousand strangely carved forms in every direction, and beyond them mountains blending with clouds.
>
> —Major John Wesley Powell, 1869

Whale, the Penguins, the Tower of Babel, and the thousands of other statues, towers, arches, and bridges that await your discovery in this magical playground.

Avoiding the Crowds. This is a very popular park, and you should expect to find crowded parking areas and full campgrounds daily from March through October, with the peak month being August. The quietest times at the park are during December, January, and February, but it can be cold. Those wanting to avoid crowds might gamble on Mother Nature and visit in November or late February, when days might be delightfully sunny and just a bit cool; or bitterly cold, windy, and awful. As with most popular parks, avoid visiting during school vacations if possible.

Just the Facts

GETTING THERE & GATEWAYS

The entrance to the park is 5 miles north of Moab, Utah, on U.S. 191. To get there from Salt Lake City, about 230 miles away, follow I-15 south to Spanish Fork; then take U.S. 6 southeast to I-70; follow that east to Crescent Junction, where you'll pick up U.S. 191 south. From Grand Junction, take U.S. 70 west until you reach Crescent Junction, and then go south on U.S. 191.

The Nearest Airport. **Alpine Air** (☎ **801/575-2839**) provides daily commuter service between Salt Lake City and Moab's Canyonlands Field Airport (☎ **435/259-7421**).

The closest major airport is Walker Field in Grand Junction, Colorado (☎ **970/244-9100**), which has direct flights or connections from most major cities on **America West Express** (☎ 800/235-9292); **Delta/Skywest** (☎ 800/453-9417); **Mesa Airlines** (☎ 800/637-2247); and **United Express** (☎ 800/241-6522). From Grand Junction it's easy to rent a car and drive the 120 miles west to the park.

Renting a Car. Rentals, either standard passenger cars, vans, or four-wheel-drive Jeeps, are available in Moab from **Thrifty** (☎ **800/367-2277** or 435/259-7317), which offers a shuttle service to get you to its office from the airport. Other local companies specializing in four-wheel-drive rentals include **Farabee 4X4 Rentals** (☎ **435/259-7494**) and **Slickrock 4X4 Rentals** (☎ **435/259-5678**).

Local taxi service is provided by **West Tracks Taxi** (☎ **435/259-2294**).

GETTING INFORMATION BEFORE YOUR TRIP

For advance information on what to see in the park, plus hiking and camping, contact the **Superintendent, Arches National Park,** P.O. Box 907, Moab, UT 84532-0907 (☎ **435/259-8161,** or 435/259-5279 for TTY). It's best to write early, and specify what type of information you need. The Web site for the park is www.nps.gov/arch.

Books, maps, and videos on Arches as well as Canyonlands National Park and other southern Utah attractions can be purchased from the nonprofit **Canyonlands Natural History Association,** 3031 South U.S. 191, Moab, UT 84532 (☎ **800/840-8978;** fax 435/259-8263). Some publications are available in foreign languages, and several videos can be purchased in either VHS or PAL formats. MasterCard and Visa are accepted. Those wanting to help the nonprofit

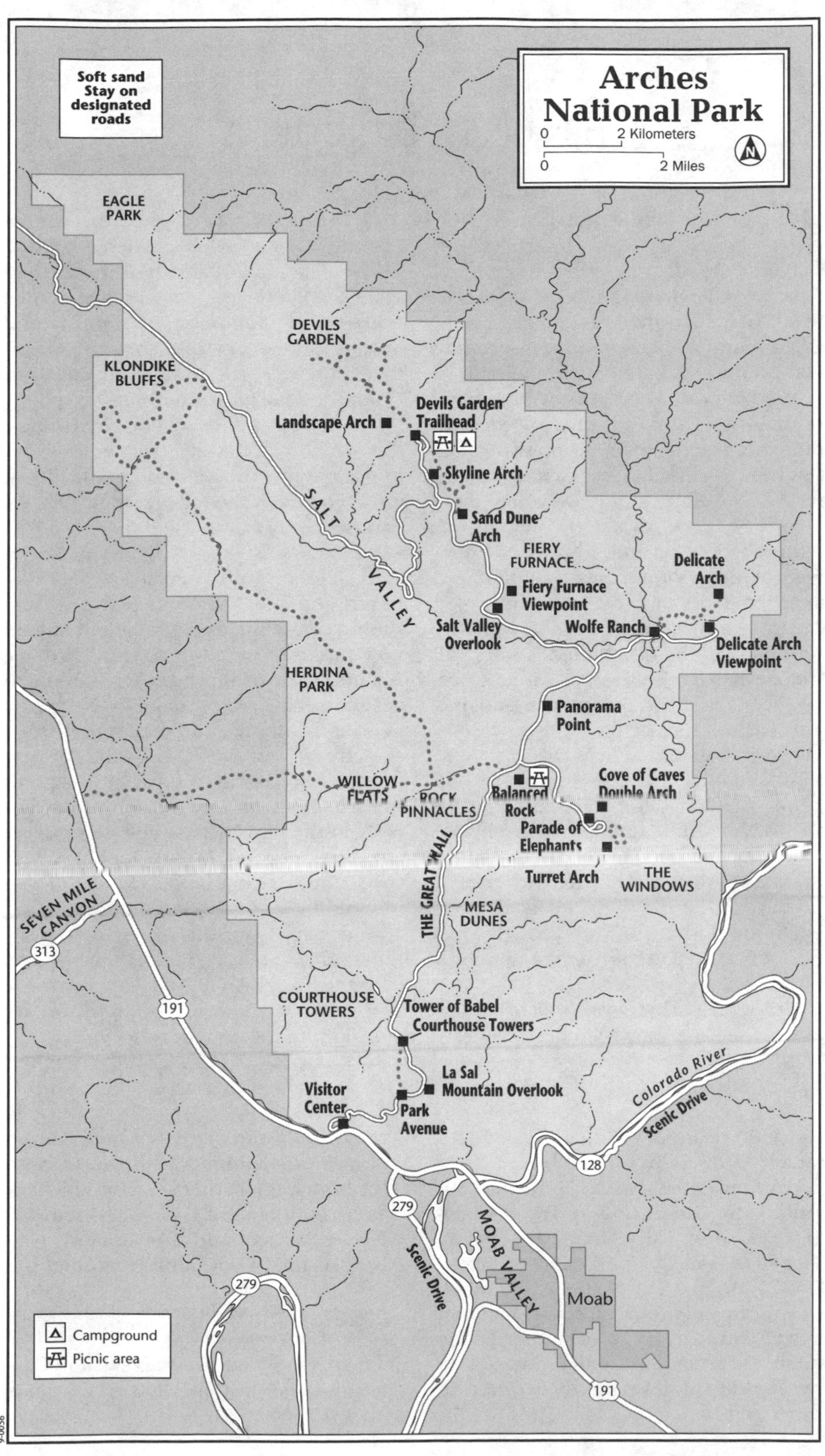

Arches
National Park
0
2 Kilometers
0
2 Miles
N
Soft sand
Stay on
designated
roads
EAGLE
PARK
DEVILS
GARDEN
KLONDIKE
BLUFFS
Landscape Arch
Devils Garden
Trailhead
Skyline Arch
Sand Dune
Arch
SALT VALLEY
FIERY
FURNACE
Fiery Furnace
Viewpoint
Salt Valley
Overlook
Delicate
Arch
Wolfe Ranch
Delicate Arch
Viewpoint
HERDINA
PARK
Panorama
Point
WILLOW
FLATS
ROCK
PINNACLES
Balanced
Rock
Cove of Caves
Double Arch
Parade of
Elephants
Turret Arch
THE
WINDOWS
THE GREAT WALL
MESA
DUNES
SEVEN MILE
CANYON
313
191
COURTHOUSE
TOWERS
Tower of Babel
Courthouse Towers
La Sal
Mountain Overlook
Visitor
Center
Park
Avenue
Colorado River
Scenic Drive
128
279
MOAB VALLEY
Scenic Drive
279
Moab
191
Campground
Picnic area
9-0056

Tips from a Park Ranger

A "good family park" is how Arches' chief of interpretation Diane Allen describes this national park. "What makes Arches special is its variety of rock formations and the ease of accessibility," she says. "You can see quite a bit even if you have only a few hours."

Allen says that 2 hours is about the minimum amount of time needed to tour the scenic drive, stopping at the viewpoints, and taking a few short walks, but 1 to $1\frac{1}{2}$ days would give you a pretty good look at the park.

She suggests starting your park experience at the **visitor center,** to find out about guided hikes and other ranger-led activities, and then getting out on the trails early in the day, while it's still cool. **The Devils Garden Trail** provides a variety of experiences, Allen says, and is a fairly easy hike to scenic **Landscape Arch.** She says that hikers need to carry and drink plenty of water—rangers recommend a gallon per person each day—because in this extremely arid climate dehydration and heat problems can be fatal. She adds that if at the end of the day you have a slight headache and feel a bit lethargic and grouchy, it's likely because you didn't drink enough water.

Although park visitors will of course want to see the park's arches—**Delicate Arch** has practically become the symbol for the state of Utah—Allen says that Arches National Park has more than arches. "There are many other formations—spires, pinnacles, a few natural bridges, and great walls," she says, adding that the park is a prime example of Colorado Plateau vegetation.

"We've got a little bit of everything," she says, "wildflowers, cactus, pinyon, juniper, a few riparian areas; and if you want to learn about geology, it's all exposed, easy to see."

The park is busiest between March and October, with August usually registering the most visitors. She says that summers are hot, and spring and fall are very pleasant. One way to avoid crowds, Allen says, is to visit in winter—"You can get fantastic hiking days in February, although you have to keep in mind that days are shorter then." The other proven way to avoid crowds, even at the height of the summer, is to get out onto the trails early in the day. "It's a much more pleasant time to be in the park," she says. "It's cooler, you have a better chance of seeing wildlife, and there are fewer people."

You can also ask rangers for suggestions on lesser-used trails. Allen says she likes the **Tower Arch Trail,** which is more of a primitive experience where you are less likely to see a lot of other hikers.

association can join ($20 annually) and get a 20% discount on purchases.

For advance area information, contact the **Grand County Travel Council,** P.O. Box 550, Moab, UT 84532 (☎ **800/635-6622** or 435/259-8825; fax 435/259-1376). The Web site for Moab is www.canyonlands-utah.com. Once you arrive, you can get information at the **Moab Information Center,** located in the middle of town at the corner of Main and Center streets. Open 8am to 9pm in the summer, with shorter winter hours, the center is staffed by Park Service, Bureau of Land Management, Forest Service, and Canyonlands Natural History Association personnel.

VISITOR CENTER

The **Arches National Park Visitor Center,** located just inside the entrance gate, has maps, brochures, and other information. A museum tells you all you need to know about arch formation and other features of the park, and there is a short orientation program in the visitor center auditorium.

ENTRANCE & CAMPING FEES & BACKCOUNTRY PERMITS

Entry into the park (for up to 7 days) costs $10 per private vehicle or $5 per motorcycle, bicycle, or pedestrian. A $25 annual pass is also available, good for both Arches and Canyonlands national parks as well as Natural Bridges National Monument. Campsites are $10 per night. Permits for overnight trips into the backcountry, available at the visitor center, are free as of this writing, but fees are anticipated.

SPECIAL REGULATIONS & WARNINGS

Backcountry hikers should practice minimum-impact techniques, packing out all trash. Of course, feeding or molesting wildlife, vandalism, and disturbing any natural feature of the park is prohibited. Wood fires are not permitted. Dogs, which must be leashed at all times, are prohibited in public buildings, on all trails, and in the backcountry.

Be aware that the desert terrain, although it appears hardy, is easily damaged. Rangers ask that hikers stay on trails, and be careful around the bases of arches and other rock formations.

SEASONS & CLIMATE

Summer days here are hot, often reaching 100°F, and winters can be cool or cold, dropping below freezing at night, with snow possible. The best time to visit, especially for hikers, is in the spring or fall, when daytime temperatures are usually between 60° and 80°F and nights are cool. Spring winds, although not usually dangerous, can be gusty, particularly as they whip through an arch, so keep hold of your hat.

SEASONAL EVENTS

An Easter sunrise service takes place annually.

USEFUL PUBLICATIONS

Those wanting more detailed descriptions of the park's hiking trails and backcountry roads than can be provided here can purchase ***Exploring Canyonlands and Arches National Parks*** (Falcon Press, 1997) by Bill Schneider, at the visitor center or by contacting the Canyonlands Natural History Association (see "Getting Information Before Your Trip," above).

Seeing the Highlights in a Day

Arches is one of the easiest national parks to see in a day if that's all you can spare. A **scenic drive** offers splendid views of countless natural rock arches and other formations, and several easy hikes open up additional scenery. The drive is 18 miles one way, plus 5 miles for a side trip to the Windows and 4.5 miles for a side trip to Delicate Arch.

Start out by viewing the short slide show at the **visitor center** to get a feel for what the park offers, and then ask rangers for their suggestions for a short hike, so you can get a close-up view of some of the arches. Possibilities include the short, easy hike to **Double Arch** and the longer and sometimes hot hike to **Delicate Arch.** If you're up for a more strenuous hike, and the timing's right, join one of the ranger-guided hikes to **Fiery Furnace,** one of the most colorful areas of the park.

Exploring the Park by Car

You can see many of the park's most famous rock formations without even getting out of your car—although we strongly urge you to get out and explore on foot. You have the option of walking short distances to a number of viewpoints, or stretching your legs on a variety of longer hikes along the way (see "Day Hikes," below). The main road is easy to navigate, even for RVs, but parking at some view points is limited. Please be considerate and leave trailers at the visitor center parking lot or in a campground.

After leaving the visitor center, drive north past the Moab Fault to the overlook parking for **Park Avenue,** a solid rock "fin" that reminded early visitors of the New York skyline. From here, your next stop is **La Sal Mountain Viewpoint,** where you look southeast to the La Sal Mountains, named by early Spanish explorers who thought the snow-covered mountains looked like huge piles of salt. In the overlook area is a "desert scrub" ecosystem, composed of sagebrush, saltbush, blackbrush, yucca, and prickly pear cactus, all plants that can survive in sandy soil with little moisture. The area's wildlife includes the kangaroo rat, black-tailed jackrabbit, rock squirrel, several species of lizards, and the coyote.

Continuing on the scenic drive, you begin to see some of the park's major formations at **Courthouse Towers,** where large monoliths such as Sheep Rock, the Organ, and the Three Gossips dominate the landscape. Leaving Courthouse Towers, watch for the **Tower of Babel** on the east (right) side of the road, then proceed past the petrified sand dunes to **Balanced Rock,** a huge boulder weighing about 3,600 tons, perched on a slowly eroding pedestal.

Continuing, you'll soon take a side road to the east (right) to **The Windows.** Created when erosion penetrated a sandstone fin, they can be seen via a short walk from the parking area. Also in this area you'll see **Turret Arch** and the **Cove of Caves.** As erosion continues in the back of the largest cave it will probably become an arch one day. A short walk from the parking lot takes you to **Double Arch,** which looks exactly like what the name implies. From the end of this trail you can also see the delightful **Parade of Elephants.**

Return to the main park road, turn north (right), and drive to **Panorama Point,** with an expansive view of Salt Valley and the Fiery Furnace, which can really live up to its name at sunset.

Next, turn east (right) off the main road onto the Wolfe Ranch Road and drive to the **Wolfe Ranch** parking area. A very short walk leads to what's left of this 100-year-old ranch. If you follow the trail a bit further, you'll see some Ute petroglyphs. More ambitious hikers can continue for a moderately difficult 3-mile round-trip excursion to **Delicate Arch,** with a spectacular view at trail's end. If you don't want to take this hike you can still see this lovely arch, albeit from a distance, by getting back in your car and continuing down the road for 1 mile and walking a short trail to the **Delicate Arch Viewpoint.**

Returning to the park's main road, turn north (right) and go to the next stop, the **Salt Valley Overlook.** The various shades and colors in this collapsed salt dome have been caused by varying amounts of iron in the rock, as well as other factors.

Continue now to the view point for **Fiery Furnace,** which offers a dramatic view of colorful sandstone fins. This is also the starting point for the ranger-guided hikes in the summer, which last $2^1/_2$ to 3 hours.

From here, drive to a pullout for **Sand Dune Arch,** located down a short path from the road, where you'll find shade and sand, a good place for kids to play, along with the arch. The trail also leads across a meadow to **Broken Arch** (which isn't broken at all, it just looks that way from a distance).

Back on the road, continue to **Skyline Arch,** which doubled in size in 1940 when a huge boulder tumbled out of it. The next and final stop is the often crowded parking area for the **Devils Garden Trailhead.** From here you can hike to some of the most unique arches in the park, including **Landscape Arch,** among the longest natural rock spans in the world.

From the trailhead parking lot, it's 18 miles back to the visitor center.

Organized Tours & Ranger Programs

From April through October, rangers lead **guided hikes** on the Fiery Furnace Trail twice daily (see "Day Hikes," below), as well as daily nature walks from various park locations. **Evening campfire programs,** also from April to October, cover topics such as rock art, geological processes, and wildlife. Check the schedule of events at the visitor center and on bulletin boards throughout the park.

Historic & Man-Made Attractions

Although few humans have left their mark in this rugged area, a few intrepid Ute Indians and pioneers have spent time here. Just off the Delicate Arch Trail is a **Ute petroglyph panel** that includes etchings of horses and bighorn sheep. Also, near the beginning of the trail is **Wolfe Ranch.** Disabled Civil War veteran John Wesley Wolfe and his son Fred moved here from Ohio in 1898, and in 1907 were joined by John's daughter Flora, her husband, and their two children. They left in 1910, after which John's cabin was destroyed by a flash flood. The cabin used by Flora's family survived and has been preserved by the Park Service. You'll see the cabin, a root cellar, and a corral.

Day Hikes

Most trails here are short and relatively easy, although because of the hot summer sun and lack of shade, it's wise to wear a hat and carry a good amount of water on any jaunt expected to last more than 1 hour. Guided hikes in Arches National Park are offered by **Dreamrides** (see "Outfitter" chart, below), at rates of about $55 for a half day and $75 for a full day.

SHORTER TRAILS

Balanced Rock Trail

0.3 mile RT. Easy. Access: Balanced Rock Parking Area on the east side of the main park road.

This short, easy walk is perfect for visitors who want to get out and stretch their legs and incidentally get a great close-up view of the huge and precariously perched Balanced Rock. The loop takes you around the formation.

Broken Arch

1 mile RT. Easy. Access: At the end of Devils Garden Campground.

This is an easy hike with little elevation change traversing sand dunes and slickrock to the arch. Watch for the rock cairns, in some places poorly defined, marking the path through the arch. A little further along there's a connecting trail to **Sand Dune Arch,** about a half mile out and back. At the end of the loop you have a 0.25 mile walk along the paved campground road back to your car.

Desert Nature Trail

0.2 mile RT. Easy. Access: Bates Wilson Memorial in front of the visitor center.

A short and easy walk following numbered posts that's a terrific introduction to the plant life you'll be seeing throughout the park. Pick up a trail guide from the brochure box at the trailhead.

Double Arch

0.25 mile one way. Easy. Access: Double Arch Parking Area, in Windows section of the park.

This easy walk, with very little elevation change, leads you to the third-largest arch opening in the park—don't be fooled by how small it looks from the parking area. Along your way look for the **Parade of Elephants,** off to the left.

Once there, you can go a little further and climb right up under the arch, being very careful not to disturb the delicate desert vegetation or natural features. To the right of Double Arch are several **caves,** which one day may become arches. If you're visiting in spring, watch for the sego lily, Utah's state flower. It has three lovely cream-colored petals with a reddish-purple spot fading to yellow at the base.

Park Avenue

1 mile one way. Easy. Access: Park Avenue or Courthouse Towers parking areas.

This is an easy downhill hike from the Park Avenue parking area. It takes you down into the canyon through groves of Utah juniper, single-leaf ash, blackbrush, and, in spring, wildflowers that sprinkle the sides of the trail with color. **Courthouse Towers, Tower of Babel, Three Gossips,** and **Organ Rock** can all be seen from the park road, but it's not nearly as awe-inspiring as actually walking among them. If you don't have a shuttle return along the park road, you might want to consider beginning the hike at the **Courthouse Towers** end and make the 320-foot climb first, so the return to your vehicle is downhill (the names of several companies that offer hiker shuttle services are given at the beginning of the section "Other Sports & Activities," below).

Sand Dune Arch

0.3 mile one way. Easy. Access: Sand Dune Arch Parking Area.

This is an easy walk through low shrubs and grasses to the arch, which is hidden among and shaded by rock walls, with a naturally created giant sandbox below. By the way, please resist the grade-school temptation to climb onto the arch and jump down into the sand—not only is it dangerous, but it can damage the arch. Just before reaching **Sand Dune Arch** there's a trail cutting off to the left that leads to **Broken Arch,** adding 1.2 miles to your hike if you decide to take it. Those who try this detour should watch for mule deer and kit foxes, which inhabit the meadow along the way.

Skyline Arch

0.2 mile one way. Easy. Access: Skyline Arch Parking Area.

This is an easy walk along a flat, well-defined trail. The feature dominating the horizon as you hike is, surprise, the Skyline Arch! On a cold November night in 1940, a large boulder fell from the opening of this arch, doubling its size.

Windows Primitive Loop

1.25-mile loop. Easy. Access: Windows Parking Area.

This easy, fairly flat hike is among the most popular in the park, but don't be put off by the number of people on the trail—the scenery is worth the lack of solitude. Hiking it early or late in the day will best minimize the numbers. On your way to **North Window,** take a short side trip to **Turret Arch.** Once you reach the Windows, take the loop around back and see for yourself why they are sometimes called Spectacles—it almost looks like a sea monster poking its large snout up into the air. And hang onto your hat, because the strong winds whipping through the arches can easily and suddenly carry it off.

LONGER TRAILS

Delicate Arch

1.5 miles one way. Moderate to difficult. Access: Wolfe Ranch Parking Area.

This hike, climbing about 480 feet, is considered by many to be the park's best and most scenic hike, though complicated by slippery slickrock, no shade, and some steep drop-offs along a narrow cliff. But your effort is rewarded with a dramatic and spectacular view of **Delicate Arch.** Along the way, you'll see the **John Wesley Wolfe Ranch** and have an opportunity to take a side trip to a **Ute petroglyph panel** that includes drawings of horses and what may represent a bighorn sheep hunt.

When you get back on the main trail, watch for **collared lizards,** bright green foot-long creatures with stripes of yellow or rust and a black collar. Feeding mostly in the daytime, they particularly enjoy insects and other lizards, and can stand and run on their large hind feet in pursuit of prey. (Didn't we see this in *Jurassic Park?*) Continuing along the trail, watch for **Frame Arch,** off to the right. Its main claim to fame is that numerous photographers have used it to "frame" a photo of Delicate Arch in the distance. Just past Frame Arch, the trail gets a little weird, having been blasted out from the cliff.

Should you opt to not take this hike, consider driving to the **Delicate Arch Viewpoint Trail,** which provides an ideal location for a photo, preferably with the arch highlighted by a clear blue sky. From the parking area it is about a 5-minute walk to the view point.

Devils Garden

7.2 miles RT. Difficult. Access: Devils Garden Parking Area.

The whole loop is a fairly long, strenuous and difficult hike, from which you can see about 15 to 20 arches and some exciting scenery. Be sure to take plenty of water, and not to hurry.

You don't have to go the entire way to see some unusual formations. Just 0.25 mile from the trailhead, a spur takes off to the right down a little hill. Here a left turn takes you to **Pine Tree Arch,** and turning right brings you to **Tunnel Arch.**

After returning to the main trail, stay to the left, and soon you'll reach the turnoff to **Landscape Arch,** a long (306 feet), thin ribbon of stone that is one of the most beautiful arches in the park. This detour is about 2 miles round-trip, but is an absolute must-see for a visit to Arches National Park. Geologically speaking, Landscape Arch is quite mature and may collapse any day. Almost immediately after your return to the main trail, look to your right for **Wall Arch.** From here the trail is less well defined but marked by cairns.

After another 0.25 mile, a side trip to the left has two spurs leading to **Partition Arch,** which you could see earlier behind Landscape Arch, and **Navajo Arch.** The spurs take you right up under the arches. Navajo Arch is shaded, providing a good spot to stop and take a breather while absorbing the view.

Once back on the main trail, which gets rougher and slicker as you hike, it's 0.5 mile to the strange **Double O Arch,** where one arch stands atop another. Now you've reached another junction, whose left spur leads to the **Dark Angel,** a dark sandstone spire reaching toward the heavens from the desert floor. The right spur takes you on to **the primitive loop,** a difficult trip through a dramatic desert environment with some drop-offs and narrow ledges. There is just one arch along this part of the trail, **Private Arch,** located on a short spur to the right. You'll have the primitive loop almost to yourself, as most people turn back at Double O Arch rather than tackle this more difficult trail.

Fiery Furnace

2 miles RT. Moderate to difficult. Access: Fiery Furnace Parking Area.

This is a difficult and strenuous ranger-led hike to some of the most colorful formations in the park. By the way, the name comes not from the summer heat, but rather from the rich reddish glow the rocks take on at sunset, resembling that of a furnace. As you hike along, a ranger describes the desert plants, points out hard-to-find arches, and discusses the geology and natural history of the area. Guided hikes are given twice daily from April to October, by reservation ($6 per adult and $3 per child over the age of 6).

You can choose to head out on your own (permits required, $2 per person) for an off-trail adventure, but special restrictions apply so you must first talk with a ranger. Trails aren't marked, so unless you are experienced in the Fiery Furnace, it's best to join a guided hike.

Tower Arch

1.2 miles one way. Difficult. Access: Follow Salt Valley Rd. for 7.1 miles, turn left toward Klondike Bluffs, and go 1.5 miles to the Tower Arch Trailhead. (Be careful not to take the left turn just before the Klondike Bluffs Rd. as it is a difficult four-wheel-drive road.)

This is a short but rugged hike on a primitive trail. It starts with a steep incline to the top of the bluff and proceeds up and down, with great views of the Klondike Bluffs to the right. From here you can see the enormous **Tower Arch** among a maze of sandstone spires. Beware of the slickrock that makes up part of the trail, and watch for the cairns leading the way. The hardest part is near the end, where you struggle uphill through loose sand. Climb up under the arch for a soothing view while you take a much-deserved break. In spring, the majestic, snow-capped **La Sal Mountains** can be seen to the east through the arch opening.

Exploring the Backcountry

There are no designated backcountry trails or campsites, and very little of the park is open to overnight camping, but backcountry hiking is permitted. Ask park rangers to suggest routes. No fires are allowed, and hikers must carry their own water and practice low-impact hiking and camping techniques. Those planning to be out overnight need to get free backcountry permits, available at the visitor center.

Other Sports & Activities

Although Arches National Park and the surrounding public lands offer plenty for the do-it-yourselfer, some 50 local outfitters offer excursions of all kinds just outside the park, from rugged mountain-bike treks to relatively comfortable four-wheel-drive adventures. You can also rent a canoe or take a guided boat trip on the Colorado River, which follows the park's southeast boundary.

The chart below lists some of the major companies that want to help you fully enjoy this beautiful country, including those that rent equipment and will shuttle you and/or your vehicle to or from trailheads. They are all located in Moab (zip code 84532). Advance reservations are often required, and it's best to check with several outfitters before

Outfitter	4X4	Bike	Boat	Horse	Rent	Shuttle
Adrift Adventures 378 Main, Box 577 ☎ 800/874-4483, 435/259-8594	Yes	Yes	Yes	Yes	Yes	Yes
Canyon Voyages River Trips 352 N. Main, Box 416 ☎ 800/733-6007, 435/259-6007	No	No	Yes	No	Yes	No
Dreamrides 96 E. Center, Box 1137 ☎ 435/259-6419	No	Yes	No	No	Yes	Yes
Kaibab Mountain Bike Tours 391 S. Main ☎ 800/451-1133, 435/259-7423	No	No	Yes	No	No	Yes

Outfitter	4X4	Bike	Boat	Horse	Rent	Shuttle
Moab Rafting Co. 4725 S. Zimmerman Lane Box 801 ☎ 800/RIO-MOAB, 435/259-RAFT	No	No	Yes	No	No	No
Navtec Expeditions 321 N. Main, Box 1267 ☎ 800/833-1278, 435/259-7983	Yes	Yes	Yes	No	No	No
Nichols Expeditions 497 N. Main ☎ 800/648-8488, 435/259-3999	No	Yes	Yes	Yes	No	No
North American River Expeditions/O.A.R.S. 543 N. Main ☎ 800/346-6277, 435/259-5865	Yes	No	Yes	No	No	No
Tag-A-Long Expeditions 452 N. Main ☎ 800/453-3292, 435/259-8946	Yes	No	Yes	No	Yes	Yes
Western River Expeditions 1371 N. U.S. 191 ☎ 800/453-7450, 435/259-7019	No	No	Yes	No	Yes	No
Western Spirit Cycling 38 S. 100 W. Box 411 ☎ 800/845-BIKE, 435/259-8732	No	Yes	No	No	Yes	No

deciding on one. When making reservations, be sure to ask about the company's cancellation policy, just in case.

Boating, Canoeing & Rafting. Although there are no bodies of water actually in Arches National Park, the Colorado River does follow the park's boundary along its southeast edge, and river-running is a wonderful change of pace from hiking over the park's dry, rocky terrain. You can travel down the river in a canoe, kayak, large or small rubber raft (with or without a motor), or in a speedy, solid jet-boat.

Do-it-yourselfers can rent kayaks or canoes for $25 to $40 for a half day and $30 to $50 for a full day, or rafts from $50 to $60 per half day and $65 to $90 for a full day. Half-day **guided river trips** cost from $25 to $35 per person, and full-day trips are usually in the $35 to $60 range. Multiday rafting expeditions, which include meals and camping equipment, start at about $300 per person. **Jet-boat trips,** which can cover a lot more river in

Especially for Kids

In the **Junior Ranger Program,** open to children from 6 to 11 years old, kids complete various projects and activities to receive a Junior Ranger badge. Participation is free.

a given amount of time, start at about $30 for a 1½-hour trip, with full-day trips about $75 per person. Children's rates are usually about 20% less.

Public boat-launching ramps are opposite Lion's Park, near the intersection of U.S. 191 and Utah 128; at Take-Out Beach, along Utah 128 about 10 miles east of its intersection with U.S. 191; and at Hittle Bottom, also along Utah 128, about 23.5 miles east of its intersection with U.S. 191. Call the Colorado Basin River Forecast Center (☎ **801/539-1311**) for recorded information on river flows and reservoir conditions statewide.

Biking. Bikes are prohibited on all trails and all cross-country travel within the national park boundaries. They are, however, permitted on the scenic drive, although you need to be aware that the 18-mile dead-end road is narrow and winding in spots, and can be crowded with motor vehicles during the summer.

Mountain bikers also have the option of tackling one of several four-wheel-drive roads (see the "Four-Wheeling" section, below). Cyclists can get information, as well as rent or repair bikes, at **Rim Cyclery,** 94 W. 100 N. (☎ **435/259-5333**); **Poison Spider Bicycle Shop,** 497 N. Main St. (☎ **800/635-1792** or 435/259-7882); **Chile Pepper Bike Shop,** 702 S. Main St. (☎ **435/259-4688**); and **Moab's Bike Service Station**, 478 Miller Creek Dr. (☎ **435/259-8732**).

Kaibab Mountain/Desert Bike Tours, 391 S. Main St. (☎ **435/259-7423**), not only rents and repairs bikes, but also offers a wide range of guide services and camping equipment rentals. Daily bike rentals are in the range of $30 to $40, including helmet. Bike shuttle services are available from **West Tracks Taxi and Shuttle** (☎ **435/259-2294**) and **Coyote Shuttle** (☎ **435/259-8656**), among others. Several local companies (see "Outfitter" chart, above) also offer multi-day mountain bike/camping tours.

Four-Wheeling. Although there aren't nearly as many four-wheel-drive opportunities here as in nearby **Canyonlands National Park,** there are a few—but check first with rangers on possible road closures and conditions that make the routes impassable. One possibility is the 17-mile road from Klondike Bluffs to Willow Flats, which is best driven from north to south because of soft sand on steep grades. Turn west off the main park road 1 mile south of Devils Garden Trailhead, and follow the road up through the Salt Valley about 7.7 miles to the turnoff for Klondike Bluffs. The next 17 miles, heading into high desert terrain, are strictly for four-wheelers, opening up panoramas of surrounding mountains and red rock formations. The route also passes Eye of the Whale Arch, views of Elephant Butte (the highest point in the park at 5,653 feet), and the imposing Courthouse Towers. Also seen along the route are drifting sand dunes and the red rock Marching Men formation. The road brings you out at the Balanced Rock Parking Area.

Local companies specializing in four-wheel-drive rentals include **Farabee 4X4 Rentals** (☎ **435/259-7494**), and **Slickrock 4X4 Rentals** (☎ **435/259-5678**). Rates are usually $75 to $90 per day.

Rock Climbing. Technical climbing is permitted in some areas of the park, but only for experienced climbers. In addition, it is prohibited on many of the park's best-known arches, as well as Balanced Rock and a few other locations. Information is available from park rangers.

Camping

INSIDE THE PARK

Located at the north end of the park's scenic drive, **Devils Garden Campground** is Arches' only developed camping area. The sites are nestled among rocks, with plenty of pinyon and juniper trees. In the summer, the campground fills early, so to get a site, it's best to get to the visitor center before 7:30am to get your registration packet for camping. Campers will find water and flush toilets in the summer; but it's all chemical toilets and no water from November through mid-March.

NEAR THE PARK

There are more than a dozen commercial campgrounds in and around Moab.

Canyonlands Campark, 555 S. Main St., Moab, UT 84532 (☎ **800/522-6848** outside Utah, or 435/259-6848), is surprisingly shady and quiet given its in-town location. This is a good choice for those with RVs or for anyone who wants a hot shower after hiking or mountain biking all day, and it's convenient to Moab's restaurants and shopping. On-site is a convenience store with food and some RV supplies.

On the north side of Moab, near the intersection of U.S. 191 and Utah 128, is **Moab Valley RV & Campark,** 1773 N. U.S. 191, Moab, UT 84532 (☎ **435/259-4469**). All sites have great views of the surrounding rock formations. The park accommodates practically any size RV in its extralarge pull-through sites, and provides maximum entertainment with cable television connections on the full RV hookups. There are trees and patches of grass for both tenters and RVers. You can refuel at the convenience store that sells propane, groceries, and RV and camping supplies. Dogs are permitted in RV sites, but not in tent sites. The park also has six comfortable cabins ($32 per night), which nonetheless still require a walk to the bathhouse.

Just south of Moab is **Spanish Trail RV Park and Campground,** 2980 S. U.S. 191, Moab, UT 84532 (☎ **800/787-2751** or 435/259-2411), with spacious sites accommodating big RVs, some shaded sites, and scenic views. It offers cable TV hookups, volleyball, and horseshoes, and a convenience store with RV supplies.

The **Moab KOA,** 3225 S. U.S. 191, Moab, UT 84532 (☎ **800/562-0372** for reservations, or 435/259-6682), is located about 3.5 miles south of Moab along U.S. 191. There are trees and all the usual KOA amenities, plus great views of the La Sal Mountains. Recreation lovers will enjoy a miniature golf course, game room, two playgrounds, and cable TV hookups; and the more practical-minded will find a convenience store with RV supplies and propane. About half of the sites are for tents only. There are also one- and two-room cabins that range in price from $33 to $37.

You'll also find campgrounds at nearby Canyonlands National Park (see "Camping" in chapter 8) and in areas under the jurisdiction of the U.S. Forest Service, Bureau of Land Management, and Utah state parks; check at the **Moab Information Center** or the **Grand Country Travel Council** (see "Getting Information Before Your Trip," above).

Accommodations

There are no lodging facilities inside the park.

NEAR THE PARK

Moab is the nearest town to Arches (5 miles south). Room rates are generally highest from mid-March through October, and sometimes drop by up to half in the winter. Rates may also be higher during special events. Room tax of about 11½% is added to all bills. Pets are not accepted unless otherwise noted.

There are several chain and franchise motels in Moab. The town's largest lodging property is the **Super 8 Motel,** on the north edge of town at 889 N. Main St.

Campground	Elev.	Total Sites	RV Hookups	Dump Station	Toilets	Drinking Water
Inside Arches						
Devils Garden	5,355	51	No	No	No	No
Inside Canyonlands						
Willow Flat	6,200	12	No	No	Yes	Yes
Squaw Flat	5,100	26	No	No	Yes	Yes
Near Canyonlands						
Dead Horse Point	5,600	21	21	Yes	Yes	Yes
Mountain View RV Park	7,000	35	29	Yes	Yes	Yes
Newspaper Rock	6,000	8	No	No	Yes	No
Watchman	4,000	231	50+	Yes	Yes	Yes
In and Near Moab						
Canyonlands Campark	4,000	113	113	Yes	Yes	Yes
Moab KOA	4,500	120	61	Yes	Yes	Yes
Moab Valley RV & Campark	4,000	130	92	Yes	Yes	Yes
Spanish Trail	4,200	81	55	Yes	Yes	Yes

(☎ **800/800-8000** or 435/259-8868; fax 435/259-8968), with 146 rooms, charging $60 to $80 double during the high season. The **Days Inn,** 426 N. Main St. (☎ **800/DAYS-INN** or 435/259-4468; fax 435/259-4018), charges $50 to $90 double in the high season. Moab has two Best Westerns: the **Best Western Canyonlands Inn,** 16 S. Main St. (☎ **800/528-1234** or 435/259-2300; fax 435/259-2301), charges $89 to $141 double, including breakfast, in the high season; and the **Best Western Greenwell Inn,** 105 S. Main St. (☎ **800/528-1234** or 435/259-6151; fax 435/259-4397), has rates of $59 to $115 double in the high season.

Archway Inn

1551 N. U.S. 191, Moab, UT 84532. ☎ **800/341-9359** or 435/259-2599; fax 435/259-2270. 90 rms, 7 suites. A/C TV TEL. Mar–Oct $79–$97 double, $140–$150 suite; lower Nov–Apr. Rates include continental breakfast. AE, DISC, MC, V.

This brand-new two-story motel, on the north edge of Moab just 2 miles from the entrance to Arches National Park, has large rooms with great views, decorated in southwestern style. Most rooms have two queen-size beds, and eight family units have two queen beds plus a queen hide-a-bed. There are also several whirlpool suites and a honeymoon suite. All units have refrigerators and microwave ovens. There's also a large outdoor heated pool, a courtyard with barbecue grills, an indoor hot tub, exercise room, bike storage room, coin-operated laundry, conference rooms, and a gift shop. Plans are underway for a restaurant and a convenience store with

Showers	Fire Pits/ Grills	Laundry	Public Phone	Reserve	Fees	Open
No	No	No	No	No	$10	Year-round
Yes	No	No	No	No	Free	Year-round
Yes	No	No	No	No	$8	Year-round
No	Yes	No	Yes	Yes	$9	Year-round
Yes	Yes	No	Yes	Yes	$10–$16	Year-round
No	Yes	No	No	No	Free	Year-round
No	Yes	No	Yes	No	$10+	Year-round
Yes	Yes	Yes	Yes	Yes	$17–$20	Year-round
Yes	Yes	Yes	Yes	Yes	$18–$24	Mar–Oct
Yes	Yes	No	Yes	Yes	$15–$22	Feb–Oct
Yes	No	No	Yes	Yes	$18–$21	Year-round

a gas station. The entire motel is non-smoking.

Bowen Motel

169 N. Main St., Moab, UT 84532. ☎ **800/874-5439** or 435/259-7132. 40 rms. A/C TV TEL. $65–$75 double. Off-season 40% less. AE, DC, DISC, MC, V.

This family owned and operated motel offers fairly large, comfortable, clean, basic rooms with one or two queen-size beds and shower/tub combos. Two family rooms sleep up to six each. The original structure dates from the 1940s; additions were made in the 1980s, and a major renovation occurred in 1993–94. Most rooms are livened up by attractive wall murals. Outside there's a heated swimming pool and locked bike storage ($2 per night extra). Several restaurants are within easy walking distance.

The Lazy Lizard International Hostel

1213 S. U.S. 191, Moab, UT 84532. ☎ **435/259-6057.** 30 dorm beds, 5 private rms, 8 cabins, 1 teepee; total capacity 65 persons. $7 dorm bed; $20 private rm; $25 and up, cabin; $5 per person teepee and camp space. Showers $2 for nonguests. Hostel membership not necessary. No credit cards.

Located on the south side of town, this hostel offers exceptionally clean, comfortable lodging at bargain rates for those willing to share. The air-conditioned main house has basic dorm rooms plus one private room. A separate building contains four additional private rooms, with fans but no air-conditioning. The best facilities are the genuine log cabins, with beds for up to six. The teepee is, well, a teepee. Guests can use a fully equipped kitchen; a living room with TV, VCR, and a collection of movies; a whirlpool tub; a self-service laundry; a gas barbecue grill; and picnic tables. If you're in a group, ask about renting the two houses nearby ($120 for the one that sleeps 20; $90 for the one that sleeps 10).

Red Stone Inn

535 S. Main St., Moab, UT 84532. ☎ **800/772-1972** or 435/259-3500; fax 435/259-2717. 50 rms. A/C TV TEL. Winter $30–$35 double; summer $50–$55 double; slightly higher in Sept and during special events. AE, DISC, MC, V.

This centrally located motel, built in 1993, is among Moab's best deals. Rooms are a bit on the small side, though spotlessly maintained, and have either one queen-size bed or two doubles. Most have kitchenettes with microwave ovens, refrigerators, sinks, and coffeemakers with coffee and other supplies. Roll-away beds are $5 extra. Three handicapped-accessible rooms have shower/tub combos, while the rest have showers only. Bring your pets for an extra charge of $5. Outside there is no swimming pool, but a picnic area has gas barbecue grills for guests' use.

Sunflower Hill Bed & Breakfast Inn

185 N. 300 E., Moab, UT 84532. ☎ **435/259-2974;** fax 435/259-3065. 11 units. A/C TV. Mar to mid-Nov and holidays $75–$150 double; mid-Nov to Feb $45–$120 double. Rates include breakfast. DISC, MC, V.

This country-style B&B, located 3 blocks off Main Street on a quiet dead-end road, offers elegant rooms and lovely outdoor areas for relaxing. The grounds are grassy and shady, and full of fruit trees and flowers. There's an outdoor hot tub (usable year-round), a picnic table, and a barbecue for guests' use. Each guest room—with names such as the Rose Room, the Sun Porch, and the Garret—has a different motif, but all are charmingly decorated with handmade quilts, matching pillow shams, and coordinated sheets.

The substantial breakfasts include homemade breads and granola, fruit juices, fresh fruits, fresh ground Colombian coffee, plus a hot entree, such as Belgian waffles.

Dining

There are no restaurants inside the park.

NEAR THE PARK

Buck's Grill House

1393 N. U.S. 191. ☎ **345/259-5201.** Reservations for 6 or more. Main courses $5.75–$19. DC, DISC, MC, V. Daily 5:30pm–closing. Closed Dec–Jan. About 1.5 miles north of town. AMERICAN WESTERN.

This popular restaurant, which many locals consider the area's best steakhouse, offers a number of choices to suit a variety of palates. The menu includes steaks, of course, plus the extremely popular prime rib, prepared fresh daily, and fresh fish. Those looking for a light (or inexpensive) meal will also find several salads and sandwiches, including a grilled buffalo meat loaf sandwich for under $6. Another especially popular dish is Buck's zucchini pie. All meats are chemical-free, vegetables are fresh, and breads and other baked items are made in-house. There is a children's menu. Buck's has full liquor service, and serves a variety of Utah microbrews.

Center Cafe

92 E. Center St. ☎ **435/259-4295.** Reservations recommended. Main courses $9–$28. DISC, MC, V. Daily 5:30–10pm. Closed Dec–Feb. About 1 block east of Main St. CONTEMPORARY AMERICAN.

Not really a cafe at all, this fine small restaurant is the place to come for innovative game and vegetarian and pasta selections. The menu changes seasonally, but might include roast pork loin with balsamic–port wine glaze; roasted eggplant lasagna layered with feta cheese and cured Moroccan olive marinara; or grilled Black Angus beef tenderloin. The restaurant has full liquor service.

Eddie McStiff's

57 S. Main St. (in Western Plaza, just south of the information center). ☎ **435/259-2337.** Reservations not accepted. Main courses $5.50–$16.50; pizza $5–$20. MC, V. Daily 3–10pm. Closed Dec–Jan. ECLECTIC.

This bustling, somewhat noisy brew pub is half family restaurant and half tavern. In the restaurant dining room, you'll find southwestern decor and paintings by local artists, while the tavern looks just like a tavern should, with a long bar, low light, and lots of wood. The menu changes seasonally, but there's always a wide range of appetizers, salads, and burgers, plus grilled steaks, pastas, and southwestern items. At least a dozen fresh-brewed beers are on tap at any time, and can also be purchased to go in 22-ounce bottles and half-gallon refillable growlers. Mixed drinks, wine, and beer are sold in the dining room with food only and beer can be purchased with or without food in the tavern. (You must be at least 21 to eat in the tavern.)

Fat City Smokehouse

36 S. 100 W. (1 block west of Main St. just south of Center St.). ☎ **435/259-4302.** Main courses $5.50–$16.50. AE, MC, V. Daily 11am–10pm. Closed Sun in winter. BARBECUE/VEGETARIAN.

Genuine Texas-style pit barbecue has made this a favorite of locals, who pile into the plain, cafe-style dining room for pork ribs, beef tips, chicken, and homemade sausage, all rubbed with a variety of seasonings, slow-smoked from 12 to 14 hours, and served with the restaurant's own sauce. Flame-grilled dinners, cooked over apple and cherry hardwoods, include fresh catfish with sweet pepper seasoning; a popular summer special is the 24-ounce T-bone. For the non–barbecue lover, there are several vegetarian sandwiches, such as the veggie club, with grilled eggplant, zucchini, onion, and green pepper on three layers of toasted nut bread, with fresh tomato pesto and a choice of cheese. Service at this casual restaurant is fast and friendly, and beer is available with meals.

Honest Ozzie's Cafe & Desert Oasis

60 N. 100 W. (1 block west of Main St. and just north of Center St.). ☎ **435/259-8442.** Breakfast items $1.50–$6.50; lunch $3.50–$6.50. MC, V. Daily 7am–3pm. Closed Nov–Feb. INTERNATIONAL/HEALTH FOOD.

This cheery little cafe recently added a waterfall and shade cloth to its garden patio—still a favorite with hummingbirds. The food is all homemade, with lots of baked items plus deli salads, daily specials, and "wraps"—a full meal all wrapped up in a large tortilla. Popular breakfasts include whole grain waffles with real maple syrup and fruit, bagels with flavored cream cheese, breakfast burritos, and bacon and eggs. For lunch, try the All American Wrap, which contains chicken-fried steak, fried potatoes, corn, cranberry sauce, and gravy. Other wraps include the Thai veggie with tofu and the Cajun catfish. The restaurant serves beer from a local microbrewery.

Moab Brewery

686 S. Main St. ☎ **435/259-6333.** Lunch $5.45–$7.95; dinner $6.45–$14.99. AE, DISC, MC, V. Daily 11:30am–10pm summer; 11:30am–9pm winter. Closed first 2 weeks Jan. ECLECTIC.

Fresh handcrafted ales brewed on-site and a wide variety of burgers, sandwiches, salads, soups, vegetarian dishes, and assorted house specialties are served at this spacious microbrewery/restaurant on the south side of town. In all, the brewery produces some 16 different ales, about half a dozen of which are available at the bar on tap at any given time. The restaurant is popular with families, who love the basic American fare, but for the adventuresome there are more exotic selections such as curried shrimp pasta and mixed sausage grill plate, as well as the spicy chicken burrito. Especially popular is the vegetarian lasagna, which is layered with four cheeses, spinach, sunflower seeds, pasta, and topped with garlic tomato-basil sauce and Parmesan cheese. The large dining room features a hang glider on the ceiling and local art work on the walls. Patio dining is also available. There is a children's menu. Beer is sold in the bar; in the restaurant diners can purchase beer, wine, or several tropical-type mixed drinks.

Moab Diner

189 S. Main St. (2 blocks south of Center St.). ☎ **435/259-4006.** Breakfast items $3.25–$5; lunch items $4.25–$5.50; main dinner courses $5–$15. MC, V. Daily 6am–10:30pm. Closes earlier in winter. AMERICAN/SOUTHWESTERN.

Late risers can get breakfast—among the best in town—all day here, with all the usual egg dishes, biscuits and gravy, six kinds of omelettes, and a spicy breakfast burrito. The decor tells you that this is definitely a diner, but it does have lots of green plants (real, not plastic). Hamburgers, sandwiches, and salads are the offerings at lunch, of course, and for dinner there's steak, shrimp, and chicken, plus liver and onions. Dinners include roll, potato, and soup or salad. In addition to ice cream, you can get sherbet, frozen yogurt, malts, and shakes, plus sundaes with seven different toppings. No alcoholic beverages are served.

Poplar Place Restaurant & Pub

11 E. 100 N. (just east of Main St., 1 block north of Center St.). ☎ **435/259-6018.** Pizza $7–$16.75; main courses $4.95–$9.95. MC, V. Daily 11:30am–11pm. Shorter hrs. in winter. MEXICAN/ITALIAN.

This two-story corner pub has been a busy lunch stop for locals since it opened in 1972, serving several microbrewed beers plus lots of pizzas, pastas, sandwiches, and Mexican dishes. The homemade pizzas, done with either a tomato or an Alfredo sauce, are probably the most popular items on the menu. Mexican selections include crab or vegetable enchiladas, a chicken burrito with green chile sauce, and what the Poplar Place calls a "faco," a cross between a fajita and taco. Dine inside or in the fresh air on their new patio. There is full liquor service.

Picnic & Camping Supplies

The best grocery store in town is City Market, 425 S. Main St. (☎ **435/259-5181**), open 24 hours a day, 7 days a week. You can pick up sandwiches from the deli, assemble your own salad at the salad bar, or choose fresh-baked items from the bakery. The store also sells hunting and fishing licenses, money orders and stamps, offers photo finishing and Western Union services, and has a pharmacy. For camping supplies and equipment for hiking, biking, and other outdoor activities, try Red Canyon Outfitters, 23 N. Main St. (☎ **435/259-3353**); or Moab Outdoors General Store, 702 S. Main St. (☎ **435/259-5731**).

Nearby Attractions

Many visitors to Arches also spend time at nearby Canyonlands National Park. There are also several excellent state parks and other attractions in the area, all described in this book's chapter on Canyonlands National Park.

3

BADLANDS NATIONAL PARK

by T.D. Griffith

IT IS A STRANGE AND SEEMINGLY WICKED PLACE. FROM THE RAGGED ridges and sawtooth spires to the wind-ravaged desolation of Sage Creek Wilderness Area, Badlands National Park is an awe-inspiring sight and an unsettling experience. Few leave here unaffectedby the vastness of this geologic anomaly, spread across 381 square miles of moonscape in western South Dakota.

Steep canyons, towering spires, and flat-topped tables are all found among Badlands buttes. Yet, despite their apparent complexity, the unusual formations of the Badlands are essentially the result of two basic geologic processes: deposition and erosion.

The layered look of the Badlands comes from sedimentary rocks composed of fine grains that have been cemented into a solid form. Layers with similar characteristics are grouped into units called formations. The bottom formation or "layer" is the **Pierre Shale,** deposited 68 to 77 million years ago during the Cretaceous period, when a shallow, inland sea stretched across the present-day Great Plains. The black mud of the sea floor hardened into shale, leaving fossil clam shells and ammonites that today confirm a sea environment. The sea eventually drained away with the uplift of the Black Hills and later, the Rocky Mountains, exposing the black shale to the air. Upper layers were weathered into a soil, now seen as yellow mounds in the park.

The **Chadron Formation,** deposited 32 to 37 million years ago during the Eocene epoch, sits above the Pierre Shale. By this time, a riverine floodplain had replaced the sea and each time the rivers flooded, they deposited a new layer of sediment on the plain. Alligator fossils indicate a lush, subtropical forest covered the region. However, mammal fossils dominate. The Chadron is best known for its large, rhinoceros-like mammals called titanotheres.

Some of the sediment carried by the rivers and by the wind was volcanic ash, the product of eruptions associated with the creation of the Rocky Mountains. The ash mixed with river and stream sediments to form clay stone, the main material from which Badlands buttes are constructed. After the Eocene epoch, the climate began to dry and cool and tropical forests gave way to open savanna. The **Brule** and **Sharps Formations** were deposited by rivers during the Oligocene epoch from 26 to 32 million years ago, and today these formations contain the most rugged peaks and canyons of the Badlands.

The serrated ridges and deep canyons of the Badlands did not exist until about 500,000 years ago when water began to

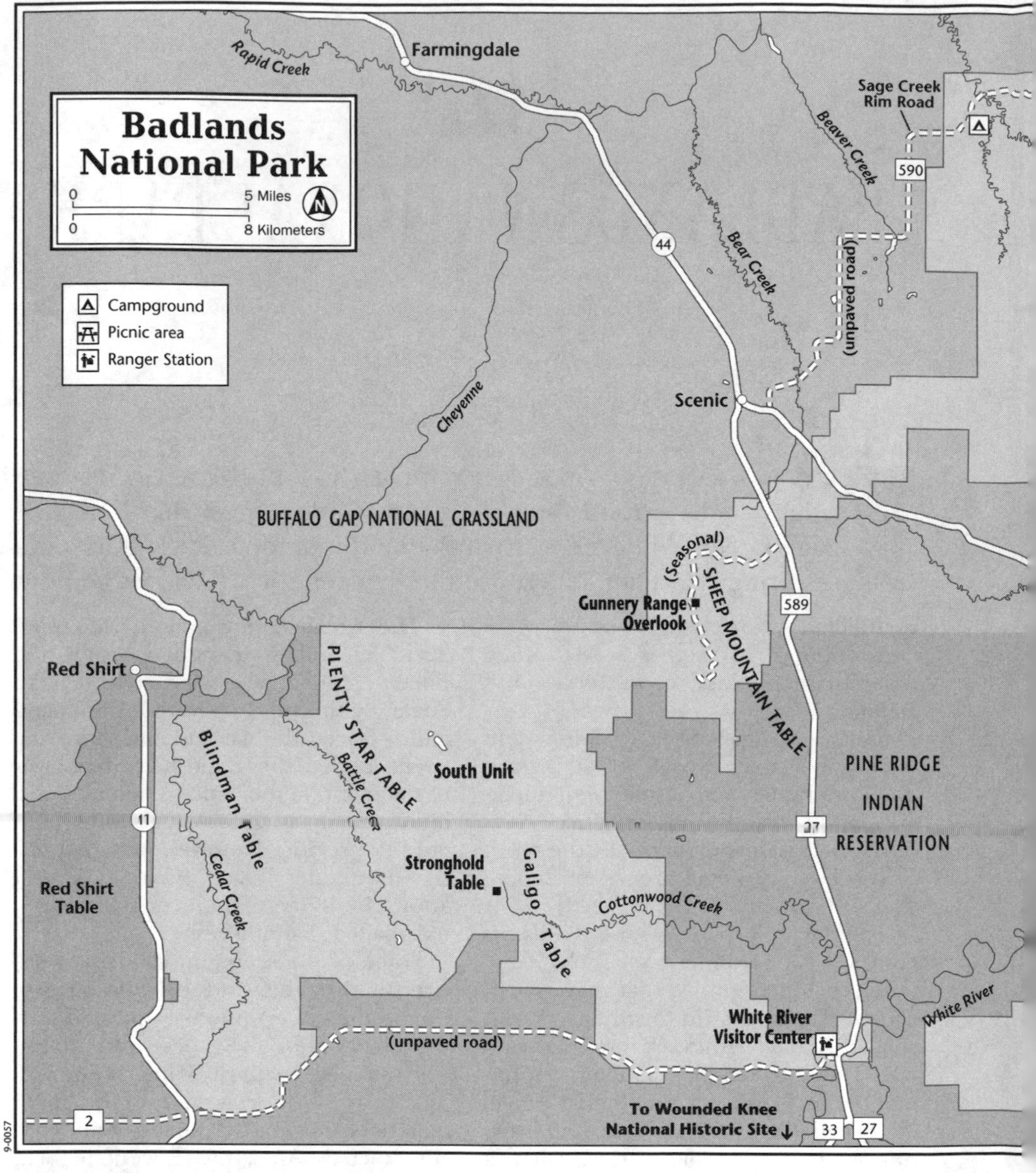

cut through the layers of rock, carving fantastic shapes into what had been a flat floodplain. Once again, the ancient fossil soils, buried for millions of years, became exposed. That erosion is ongoing. Every time it rains or snow melts in spring, more sediments are washed from the buttes in this endless work of sculpting the earth. Evidence suggests that the Badlands buttes will completely erode away in another 500,000 years. On average, the buttes erode 1 inch each year. But change can occur much slower or faster.

When buttes erode, some sediments are carried onto the prairie below. Others are passed to the White, Bad, and Cheyenne rivers. These flow into the Missouri, which drains into the Mississippi. Some Badlands sediment eventually finds its way into the Gulf of Mexico.

The Sioux Indians who once traversed this incredible landscape named it *mako sica* or "land bad." Early French-Canadian

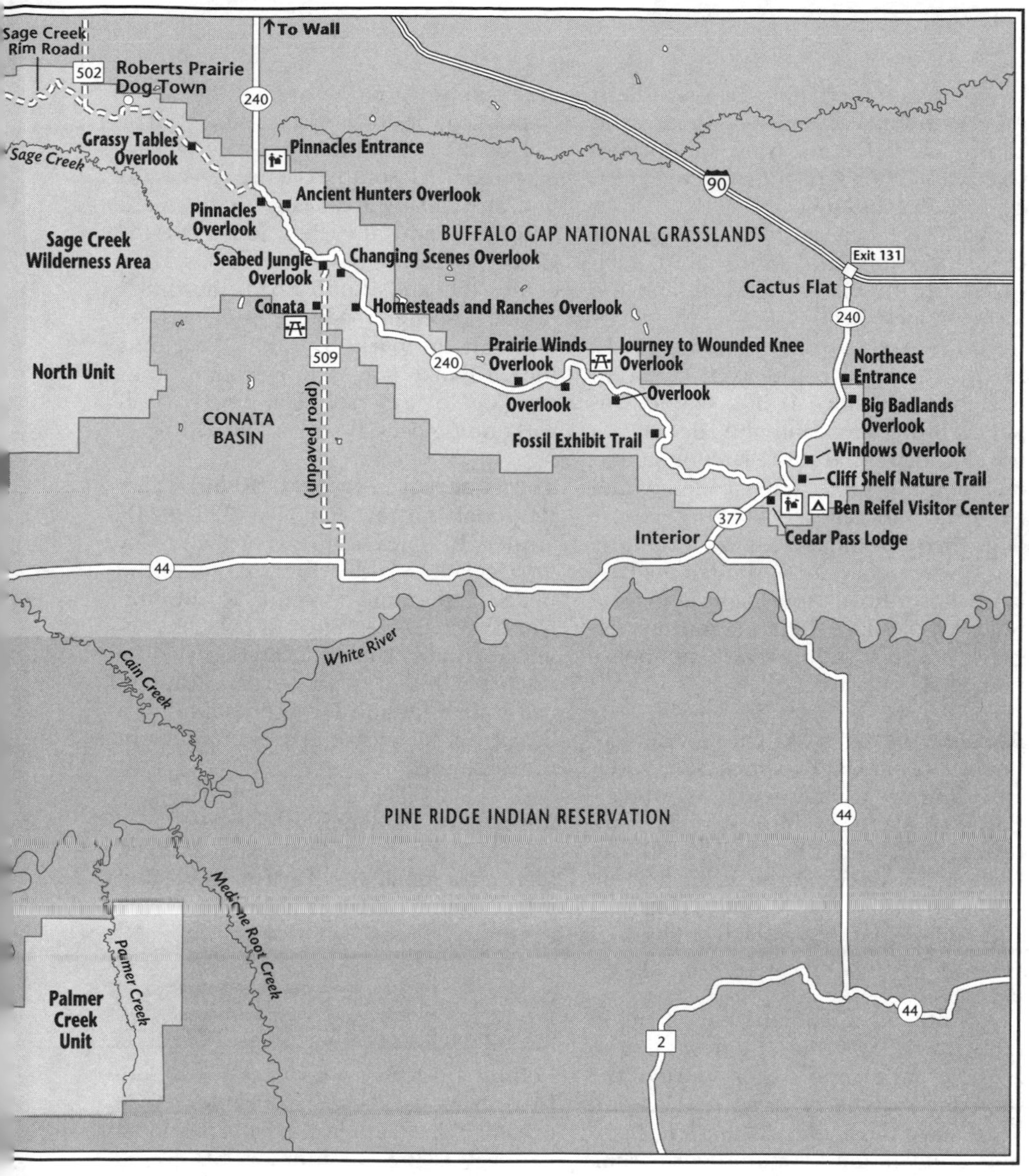

trappers labeled them *les mauvaises terres a traverser* or "bad lands to travel across."

The area was established as Badlands National Monument in 1939. Congress elevated its status to a National Park in 1978. With nearly 244,000 acres, Badlands National Park is larger than the combined areas of all of the national park units in the Midwest. The Badlands are recognized around the world as one of the richest Oligocene fossil beds known to exist. Remains of three-toed horses, dog-sized camels, saber-toothed tigers, giant pigs, and other species have been found here, all dating from 25 to 35 million years ago.

Flora & Fauna. The Badlands area represents what is called a mixed-grass prairie, and you'll find 56 different types of grasses here, most of which are native species, including green needlegrass and buffalo grass. What you won't find are many trees.

At one time, grasslands covered almost a quarter of the area of the current

United States, stretching from southern Alberta in Canada almost to Mexico and all the way to Indiana from the Rockies. Over 50% of the Badlands area is, in fact, covered by grasslands.

Wildflowers are an important part of the landscape, and you'll find such species as the Barr's milkvetch and the Visher's buckwheat.

You're likely to see bison and Rocky Mountain bighorn sheep (the native Audubon's bighorn is now extinct), as well as pronghorns and mule deer if you travel at dawn and dusk. Darting in and out of the grass, you'll see desert and eastern cottontail rabbits. And prairie dogs thrive in the area; there's a prairie dog town just beyond the end of the Badlands Loop Road. You might also see a prairie rattlesnake slithering through the grass, not to mention several nonpoisonous snake species.

Avoiding the Crowds. The vastness of Badlands National Park means that overcrowding is usually not a problem. Entrance stations, visitor centers, park concessions, and the Loop Road can become busy during the height of the summer season, especially during July and August, but most roads, trails, and services are not overtaxed any time of the year.

As with other national park units in the nearby Black Hills, those wishing to avoid crowds should stop during the shoulder seasons of April to May and September to October. If that's not possible and you must visit during the summer season, start your visit early in the day when the numbers of people are lowest and the sun hasn't begun to scorch the earth. Dawn and dusk provide ideal times to photograph the unearthly beauty of Badlands National Park.

Just the Facts

GETTING THERE & GATEWAYS

Located in extreme southwestern South Dakota, Badlands National Park is easily accessed by car either on U.S. 44 east of **Rapid City,** or off Interstate 90 at **Wall** or **Cactus Flat.** Westbound I-90 travelers take Exit 131 south (Cactus Flat) onto S. Dak. 240, which leads to the park boundary and the Ben Reifel Visitor Center at Cedar Pass. This roadway becomes Badlands Loop Road, the park's primary scenic roadway. After passing through the park, S. Dak. 240 rejoins I-90 at Exit 110 at Wall. Eastbound travelers do the reverse, beginning in Wall and ending back at I-90 at Exit 131.

The Nearest Airport. Rapid City Regional Airport (☎ **605/393-9924**), located 10 miles southeast of Rapid City on U.S. 44, provides direct access to the Black Hills and Mount Rushmore. **Northwest Airlines, Skywest** (a Delta connection), and **United Express** serve the airport with daily flights to Minneapolis, Salt Lake City, and Denver. You'll find a list of the airlines' toll-free numbers in the appendix.

Renting a Car. Rental vehicles are available at the airport from **Avis, Budget, Hertz, National,** and **Thrifty.** You'll find a list of their toll-free numbers in the appendix.

GETTING INFORMATION BEFORE YOUR TRIP

Before you leave, send away for a **Badlands National Park Trip Planner.** Write or call: Trip Planner, Badlands National Park, P.O. Box 6, Interior, SD 57750 (☎ **605/433-5361**).

For information about the area, call or write **South Dakota Tourism,** 711 E. Wells Ave., Pierre, SD 57501-3369 (☎ **605/773-3301;** fax 605/773-3256).

The park also has a Web site: **www.nps.gov/badl/** (or **www.nps.gov/badl/htmlfiles/expanded.htm** for an expanded version).

The national park is surrounded by **Buffalo Gap National Grasslands.** For information, write or call P.O. Box 425, Wall, SD 57790 (☎ **605/279-2125**).

For information about the area, contact **South Dakota Tourism,** 711 E. Wells Ave., Pierre, SD 57501-3369 (☎ **605/773-3301;** fax 605/773-3256); or the **Black Hills, Badlands & Lake Association,** 900 Jackson Blvd., Rapid City, SD 57702-2583 (☎ **605/341-1462**).

VISITOR CENTERS

Visitor centers are located at Cedar Pass and White River. The **Ben Reifel Visitor Center** at Cedar Pass is open year-round (7am to 8pm from June 10 to August 15, and 8am to 4:30pm the rest of the year) and features exhibits on the park's natural and cultural history. The nearby Cedar Pass Lodge has cabins, a gift shop, and restaurant; there's a campground here as well. The **White River Visitor Center** is open during the summer season only (late May through August) and includes exhibits about Oglala Sioux history.

ENTRANCE FEES

There is an entrance fee of $10 per passenger vehicle, which allows admission for up to 7 days. The single-person entry fee is $5 per motorcycle, bicycle, or person on foot, plus $5 for each additional passenger.

Members of the Oglala Sioux tribe pay half price.

CAMPING FEES

Camping costs $10 per site per night at the Cedar Pass Campground, with a limit of 14 nights.

SPECIAL REGULATIONS & WARNINGS

Water in the Badlands is too full of silt for humans to drink and will quickly clog a water filter. When hiking or traveling in the park, always carry an adequate supply of water. Drinking water is only available at the Cedar Pass area, the White River Visitor Center, and the Pinnacles Ranger Station. **Climbing** Badlands buttes and rock formations is allowed, but can be extremely dangerous due to loose, crumbly rock.

SEASONS & CLIMATE

Badlands weather is often unpredictable. Heavy rain, hail, and high, often damaging winds, are possible, particularly during spring and summer. Lightning strikes also are common. Summer temperatures often exceed 100°, so sunscreen, a hat, and water are essential to avoid severe sunburn, dehydration, and heat stroke. Winter travelers should beware of approaching storms and be prepared for sleet, ice, heavy snow and blizzard conditions.

USEFUL PUBLICATIONS

The National Park Service makes available a wide variety of informational brochures on topics including geology, prairie grasses, camping, backpacking, bicycling, camping, wildlife, birds, plant life, and use of horses in the park. These brochures are available at the park visitor centers and ranger stations. In addition, ***The Prairie Preamble,*** the park's official newspaper published by the nonprofit Badlands Natural History Association, provides up-to-date information on visitor center hours, park programming, camping, and hiking trails. The Association has a catalog of publications available; write to **BNHA,** P.O. Box 47, Interior, SD 57750.

ROAD CONDITIONS

Park roads are winding and steep in places, but most are paved and driving is generally a straightforward affair. Accessibility to some areas of the park is limited in the off-season due to inclement weather and poor road conditions. Unpaved roads can become dangerous in winter and during thunderstorms, when surfaces may become extremely slippery due to soil conditions.

Seeing the Highlights in a Day

It's relatively easy to examine the highlights of the North Unit of Badlands National Park in a day or less (most visitors spend an average of 3 to 5 hours in the park). A few miles south of the park's northeast entrance (the closest entrance to I-90), is the **park headquarters,** open year-round, which includes the Ben Reifel Visitor Center, Cedar Pass Lodge, and a campground, amphitheater, and dump station. After stopping at the visitor center exhibits, bookstore, information desk, and rest rooms and watching an orientation video (which we recommend), it's time to hit the trail.

The visitor center is located within 5 miles of several trailheads, scenic overlooks, and three self-guided nature trails. Each of the seven trails in the area offers an opportunity to view some of the formations for which the Badlands is famous. The **Fossil Exhibit Trail** is wheelchair accessible. The **Cliff Shelf Nature Trail** and the **Door Trail** are moderately strenuous and provide impressive glimpses of Badlands formations. But none is longer than 1 mile, and any one of them can be hiked comfortably in less than an hour. (All three trails, and several others, are described under "Day Hikes," below.)

Leading directly from the visitor center is the 30-mile long **Badlands Loop Road,** the park's most popular scenic roadway. Angling northwest toward the town of Wall, this road passes numerous overlooks and trailheads, each of which commands inspiring views of the Badlands and the prairies of the Buffalo Gap National Grassland that forms its backdrop. Binoculars will increase your chances of spotting bison, pronghorn, bighorn sheep, or coyote.

The paved portion of the Loop Road ends at the turnoff for the **Pinnacles Entrance.** Beyond this point the pavement ends and the road becomes the Sage Creek Rim Road, a 30-mile gravel road, at the end of which is the **Sage Creek Campground,** though this one is primitive and does not offer drinking water. Five miles west of the end of the pavement, a visit to the **Roberts Prairie Dog Town** gives you a chance to watch black-tailed prairie dogs "barking" their warnings and protecting their "town."

To the south, the **Stronghold Unit** is located within the Pine Ridge Indian Reservation. This unit is managed under a cooperative agreement between the National Park Service and the Oglala Lakota tribe. Since it is mainly backcountry, with no developed trails or roads, it is unlikely that you will visit this area during a 1-day stay.

BIA Highway 27 leads from the town of Scenic south to the **White River Visitor Center,** open late May through August. The visitor center has drinking water, rest rooms, information, Lakota exhibits, and a video program.

If You Have More Time

If you are able to camp or stay overnight at Cedar Pass Lodge or in the area, you'll have more opportunities to explore the park at a leisurely pace, taking advantage of some of the other trails, such as the Castle Trail, which connects the Fossil Exhibit Trail and Window Fossil Exhibit Trail and Notch Trail. You could also take advantage of some of the park's summer evening ranger programs.

Organized Tours & Ranger Programs

In addition to these suggestions, look at "Other Sports & Activities," below.

Motorcoach Tours. A number of charter bus park tours and "step-on" guide services throughout the area are available. **Gray Line of the Black Hills,** P.O. Box 1106, Rapid City, SD 57709 (☎ **800/456-4461** or 605/342-4461; fax 605/341-5152), offers bus tours of the area. Tours range in price from $15 to $40.

As does **America Tours West,** P.O. Box 867, Keystone, SD 57751-0167 (☎ **605/666-4545;** fax 605/666-4996); and **Jack**

Rabbit Charter & Tours, 301 N. Dakota Ave., Sioux Falls, SD 57104 (☎ **605/335-2290;** fax 605/336-8731). Both companies offer a range of tours in a similar price range.

Ranger Programs. A limited schedule of naturalist programs generally begins in the park in early June. Expanded opportunities for education on park resources grow with increased visitation in late June, and are carried on through the summer.

Times and topics are subject to change and many other programs are offered on a staff-available basis. Check the activities board at the Ben Reifel Visitor Center or campground bulletin boards for times, topics, and locations for these and other special ranger activities. You should expect to find among them the following:

- **Evolving Prairie Walk.** Generally conducted in the early morning and early evening, this 60-minute, 1-mile stroll introduces visitors to the paleontology, prairie, and people of the Badlands. Participants meet at the Ben Reifel Visitor Center. Sites vary and may require vehicle travel. Participants are encouraged to wear comfortable walking shoes and a hat, and to bring water and sunglasses.
- **Fossil Talk.** Generally slated for mid-morning and late afternoon, this program allows participants to meet a naturalist for a 20-minute discussion on the geologic history and fossil resources of the White River Badlands. It's wheelchair accessible and meets at the Fossil Exhibit Trail.
- **Evening Program.** Begins at 9pm in early summer, then 8:30pm starting in early August. Join a park ranger, intern, or researcher for a 45-minute in-depth examination of a topic relating to Badlands National Park. Topics will include paleontology, geology, prairie, human history, wilderness, and park management. The program is wheelchair accessible and meets at the Cedar Pass Campground amphitheater.

I've been about the world a lot and pretty much over our own country; but I was totally unprepared for that revolution called the Dakota Badlands . . . Let sculptors come to the Badlands. Let painters come. But first of all the true architect should come. He who could interpret this vast gift of nature in terms of human habitation so that Americans on their own continent might glimpse a new and higher civilization certainly, and touch it and feel it as they lived in it and deserved to call it their own. Yes, I say the aspects of the Dakota Badlands have more spiritual quality to impart to the mind of America than anything else in it made by man's God.

—Frank Lloyd Wright, in a letter to a friend following his 1935 visit to the Badlands

Day Hikes

Numerous hiking trails provide a closer look at the Badlands for those adventurous enough to leave the comforting confines of their vehicle. In fact, the entire 244,000-acre park is open to hikers. All developed trails start from parking areas within 5 miles of the Ben Reifel Visitor Center at Cedar Pass.

Fossil Exhibit Trail

0.25 mile RT. Easy. Access: The trailhead is located 5 miles northwest of the Ben Reifel Visitor Center.

An easy boardwalk loop that will give you an idea of what animal life was like 30 million years ago. A self-guided brochure can be purchased at the trailhead. Wheelchair accessible.

Tips from the Chief of Interpretation

Badlands National Park's 244,000 acres of stark scenery and barren beauty deserve special consideration on any visitor's itinerary, according to the park's chief of interpretation Marianne Mills.

"This park is larger than all of the other National Park Service units in the Midwest combined," Mills notes. "We have a great diversity of stories that converge here—the fossils and the history of fossil collecting, prairie grasses and wildlife, Lakota history, pioneer history, and homesteading. It's all here waiting to be explored."

The average visitor to the Badlands stays about 4 hours, but that probably isn't long enough to fully appreciate the vastness and diversity of this national park. Mills suggests that a 2- to 3-day stay would be best for that: "Visitors to the Badlands should at least experience a night in the park," says Mills. "The air is so clear here that the stars shine."

She also says that spring and fall are the best possible times to travel to the Badlands: "Our best weather, in my opinion, is April through the first 2 weeks of May, and September through mid-October. The grasses are just greening in spring, the birds are migrating, and the prairie animals are giving birth to their young. In the fall, the canyons and ravines are filled with beautiful golden colors, the birds are migrating on the Great Flyway, and you can enjoy an uncrowded hike, a bike ride or just a solitary experience."

Cliff Shelf Nature Trail

0.5 mile RT. Moderate. Access: The trailhead is located 0.5 mile north of the Ben Reifel Visitor Center.

A popular trail through a "slump" area where increased water retention supports an oasis of green surrounded by stark badlands formations. A self-guided brochure can be purchased on the trail. The trail has some steeper sections and boardwalk stairs. Its parking lot cannot accommodate RVs towing other vehicles.

Door Trail

0.6 mile RT. Moderate. Access: The trailhead is located 2 miles northeast of the Ben Reifel Visitor Center.

This trail winds through some of the "baddest" of the Badlands. The first 100 yards to a beautiful view at "The Door" are mostly downhill and accessible to athletic or assisted people in wheelchairs. A self-guided brochure can be purchased 100 yards up the trail. The more rugged section takes off to the right of the viewing area, and striped posts mark the way, indicating where to stop and read the trail brochure.

Window Trail

0.25 mile RT. Easy to moderate. Access: The trailhead is at the center of the Door Trail Parking Area.

A 100-yard trail leads to a spectacular view through a "window" or opening in the Badlands Wall. Wheelchair-accessible.

Notch Trail

1.5 miles RT. Moderate. The trailhead is at the north end of the Door Trail Parking Area.

This trail takes you up a drainage, then up a 45° angle cable/wood ladder. This is definitely not for those afraid of heights. Follow the drainage to the "Notch"; the payoff is a striking view overlooking the Cliff Shelf area and the White River Valley.

Castle Trail

5 miles RT. Moderate. Access: Trailheads are at the Fossil Exhibit Trail and at the Door Trail Parking Area.

Winding more than 5 miles through the mixed-grass prairie and badlands the Castle Trail is the longest developed trail in the park. The trail is fairly level and connects the Fossil Exhibit Trail and the Doors and Windows parking area. It's possible to make this a loop, if you follow the signs and turn off onto the Medicine Root Trail, which is well marked along the trail route. The Castle Trail runs parallel to some interesting Badlands formations. Since this trail is not heavily used, it offers an ideal opportunity to escape the crowds, but it can be treacherous during and just after a heavy rain.

Saddle Pass Trail

0.25 mile RT. Moderate to strenuous. Access: This trail branches off the Castle Trail just west of its intersection with the Medicine Root Trail, and leads to the Badlands Loop Rd.

In less than 0.25 mile, this trail rises steeply 200 feet from the bottom of the Badlands Wall to the top, connecting with the Castle and Medicine Root trails. It's impassable after rains, however, so be sure to ask at the visitor center.

Exploring the Backcountry

One way to escape the crowds is to hike out into the backcountry of the Badlands, which are completely open. When planning your backcountry hike, examine past, present, and forecasted weather. With even a small amount of precipitation, some trails can become slick and impassable. Carry water if you think you could be out for as little as a half hour. Cross-country hikers are encouraged to carry a map, compass, and water, and to wear or carry appropriate clothing. All overnight backcountry hikers should discuss their route with a park ranger before departure.

The park encompasses the largest prairie wilderness in the United States, where expansive grasslands make cross-country travel unique. Vast ranges of classic badlands provide rugged, challenging terrain for even skilled hikers. Wildlife is close and abundant. Best of all, the crowding that you might experience in other, more popular wild places, is unknown in Badlands National Park. Few people explore the backcountry of this park, and hikers often have hundreds of acres to themselves. No campfires are allowed in Badlands National Park.

Unlike many western national parks, the Badlands has **no formal system of backcountry permits or reservations.** Let friends and relatives know when you depart and when you expect to return. Rangers at the Ben Reifel Visitor Center can assist in planning a safe, enjoyable excursion by offering directions, safety tips, maps, and information sheets.

Spring and fall may be the best times to experience the Badlands backcountry. Days are often pleasant and nights are cool. In summer, temperatures often exceed 100° and pose health hazards. Avoid heat sickness by drinking plenty of water and avoiding the midday sun. Only the hardiest hikers attempt winter backpacking trips in the Badlands. Weather is unpredictable. Sudden blizzards can send temperatures plummeting well below zero. Severe winter temperatures coupled with strong winds make backcountry survival difficult for those unprepared. Winter hikers should speak with a ranger at the Ben Reifel Visitor Center before setting out.

Other Sports & Activities

Aerial Tours. If you want to see the Badlands from above, you have two options: helicopter or hot-air balloons. **Badger Helicopters,** which takes off from the East Entrance to Badlands National Park between mid-May and mid-September, off I-90, Exit 130. For information, write to them at 1703 W. Airport Rd., Janesville, WI 53546, or call ☎ **605/433-5322** or 608/752-4001. They offer four different aerial itineraries, starting at $12.50 per person and going up to $25 per person.

If it's a hot-air balloon adventure you're looking for, then contact **Black Hills Balloons,** P.O. Box 210, Custer, SD 57730-0210 (☎ **608/673-2520;** fax 608/673-5075). They offer flights over the Black Hills, as well as Badlands and even Devils Tower, year-round; expect to pay $165 per person for a flight.

Biking. There is no off-road biking allowed in Badlands National Park, but the park's **Loop Road** is accessible to bikes (there are even bike racks at the Ben Reifel Visitor Center). Just be aware that the road can be steep. The 22-mile route from Pinnacles Overlook to the Ben Reifel Visitor Center, is mostly downhill (though there are several steep passes to climb). Many bikers ride along **Sage Creek Rim Road,** past the prairie dog town, to spectacular views of the Badlands wilderness. During summer, though, car traffic is heavy and the temperatures hot. There are no bike rentals available in Badlands National Park.

Horse-Packing Trips. Several companies offer guided trail rides through the backcountry of the Badlands (and the Black Hills). One family-run company is **Dakota Badland Outfitters,** P.O. Box 85, Custer, SD 57730-0085 (☎ **608/673-5363;** fax 206/649-4966). They conduct 4-day horse-packing trips into the Black Hills and Badlands every week during the season for $660 to $680 per person (June through August in the Black Hills, September and October in the Badlands), or they can put together a custom Badlands trip for $250 per person per day. These costs include all meals. They will even rent you a sleeping bag or pick you up at the airport for an additional charge.

Camping

A chart summarizing facilities at campgrounds in the Badlands and Black Hills area is located in chapter 5.

INSIDE THE PARK

Camping is available inside Badlands National Park at either the Cedar Pass Campground or the Sage Creek Primitive Campground. Camping in pullouts, parking areas, picnic grounds, or in any other area not designated as a campground is not permitted in Badlands National Park. Fortunately, the park does provide two good campgrounds, as well as free permits for backcountry camping. No reservations are taken for the two campgrounds, however, so getting a good spot is a first-come first-served proposition.

Cedar Pass Campground, located just off the Loop Road, has 110 sites suitable for tents or RVs, as well as an amphitheater, rest rooms, drinking water, shaded tables, trash containers, pay phone, campground host, dump station, and Night Sky Interpretive Area; however, there are no RV utility hookups, showers, or laundry. The campground is $10 per site per night in summer, with a 14-day maximum stay, and $8 per site per night in winter. Campfires are not allowed in the park.

Sage Creek Primitive Campground, which is also open year-round, has picnic tables and pit toilets. However, access may be limited in winter months due to impassable roads; the campground is located at the end of Sage Creek Rim Road, a gravel road that begins at the point where the park's Loop Road turns toward the Pinnacles Entrance. The campground is free, with a 14-day maximum stay (there are 15 sites). Water is not available.

NEAR THE PARK

There is one commercial campground near Badlands National Park. Others are located closer to the Mount Rushmore area and are listed in chapter 5.

Badlands Ranch Resort is much more than a campground. In addition to 35 sites with full RV hookups (which rent for $20 per night), you can pitch a tent on the grounds for $12 a night; you'll find a barbecue area with gas grills, a

The Famous Wall Drug Store

You'll see the signs offering "free ice water" at the Wall Drug Store at 510 Main St. in Wall, which is about 9 miles north of Badlands National Park on S.D. 240. And you'll see them almost everywhere you go throughout the Black Hills region, all of them telling you how many miles it is to the small town of Wall and the eponymous drugstore (there are now over 3,000 of these signs, all over the world). The advertising gimmick saved what used to be a small-town drugstore in an isolated community from bankruptcy during the Great Depression. But Dorothy and Bill Hustead's gimmick also turned their little establishment into a block-long Old West emporium that now draws crowds from all over the United States and the world. You can buy pancakes or donuts (some of the best in the state, in fact), Native American crafts, books, jewelry, western apparel, or you can just watch the animated "cowboy band" perform every 15 minutes. Do you want a "genuine" jackalope? Yes, they've got those too. Oh, and the ice water is still free.

pool, showers, Jacuzzi, laundry facilities, playground for the kids, good fishing, rock hunting, and trail rides. For more information, see the "Accommodations" section, below.

Accommodations

INSIDE THE PARK

Cedar Pass Lodge Cabins

In Badlands National Park, P.O. Box 5, Interior, SD 57750. ☎ **605/433-5460;** fax 605/433-5560. 24 cabins. A/C TEL. $42–$60 double. AE, DISC, MC, V. Closed late Oct to mid-Apr.

The Cedar Pass Lodge, adjacent to the Ben Reifel Visitor Center, offers air-conditioned cabins. Because the best light in the Badlands is found at daybreak and dusk, visitors are encouraged to stay a night in the cabins or in the park's campgrounds and experience the best the Badlands has to offer.

NEAR THE PARK

The communities of Wall, north of the park, and Rapid City, 55 miles to the west on I-90, offer hundreds of hotel and motel rooms, as well as quaint bed-and-breakfast establishments. Establishments in Wall are listed here; those in Rapid City and the Mount Rushmore area are listed in chapter 5. Rates vary by season, but are modest.

IN INTERIOR

Badlands Ranch Resort

S. Dak. 44, Interior, SD (HCR 53, P.O. Box 3, Interior, SD 57750). ☎ **605/433-5599.** 7 cabins, 4 motel units, B&B space for up to 25. A/C TV. $30–$68 cabin, $30–$50 motel rm, $68–$100 B&B rm; rates are negotiable during winter months. Breakfast is included in the B&B rates only. AE, DISC, MC, V. From the park, head west on S. Dak. 44 approximately 6 miles toward Interior; when you go past the KOA Campground, look for the marked turnoff that leads to the resort's grounds.

This new, year-round resort, which opened in July 1997, is located on 200 picturesque acres with views of the Badlands and plenty of wildlife for watching. In addition to the several accommodations options, there are also RV and tent camping sites (see "Camping," above). There are a pool and hot tub for all guests to use, not to mention nightly bonfires and cookouts with entertainment, two lakes for fishing, and horseback trails (moonlight trail rides can also be arranged). If you wish, the owners can also help you arrange guided tours of the area's attractions and the adjoining Indian reservation. Rooms in the B&B are more plush; the three floors will accommodate couples or groups of up to 25. Its top-floor honeymoon suite has a sunroom, whirlpool, and views of the Badlands. This is a very friendly place.

IN WALL

Super 8 Motel

711 Glenn St. (2 blocks north of I-90 at Exit 110), Wall, SD 57790. ☎ **800/800-8000** or 605/279-2688. 29 rms. A/C TV TEL. $35–$70 double. AE, MC, V. Open year-round.

Here you'll find clean rooms and reasonable rates. The motel is close to the Badlands and the world famous Wall Drug Store.

Best Western Plains Motel

712 Glenn St. (2 blocks north of I-90 at Exit 110), Wall, SD 57790. ☎ **800/279-2145** or 605/279-2145. 29 rms. A/C TV TEL. $45–$90 double. AE, DISC, MC, V. Closed Dec–Feb.

This is another reliable motel in Wall, a short drive from Badlands National Park. There's an outdoor pool, game room, gift shop, and in-room coffee. It's near all local restaurants and the Wall Drug Store.

Dining

INSIDE THE PARK

Cedar Pass Lodge Restaurant

In Badlands National Park. ☎ **605/433-5460.** Main courses $5–$9. AE, DISC, MC, V. Open daily for all meals. Closed late Oct to mid-Apr.

Located near the Ben Reifel Visitor Center in the park's North Unit, the Lodge's restaurant (the only dining choice inside the park) has a full menu ranging from buffalo burgers to steaks and trout, as well as ice-cold soft drinks, beer, and wine for superb after-hike refreshments.

NEAR THE PARK

In Interior, the **Wooden Knife Drive-Inn,** at the junction of U.S. 44 and S. Dak. 377, on Interior's east side (☎ **605/433-5463**), is home to the world-famous Wooden Knife Frye Bread Mix, burgers, chicken, trademark Indian tacos, ice cream, and refreshments. It's an inexpensive place to stop for a quick bite.

There are other eating places in the communities surrounding Badlands National Park, including Wall and Interior. Establishments in Rapid City and the communities surrounding Mount Rushmore are listed in chapter 5.

Picnicking in the Park

Badlands National Park has two designated picnic areas, though you're likely to see people munching at nearly every overlook and trailhead in the park.

Conata Picnic Area is located on Conata Road, just south of Dillon Pass and the Badlands Loop Road in the North Unit. It has tables, trash cans, and pit toilets. Camping and fires are not allowed, and there is no drinking water.

Big Foot Picnic Area is located near Big Foot Pass on the Badlands Loop Road in the North Unit, about 7 miles northwest of the Ben Reifel Visitor Center. It also has tables, trash cans, and pit toilets but not drinking water. Camping and fires are not allowed.

Nearby Attractions

Beyond the boundaries of Badlands National Park are several other areas and sites that you may wish to visit. These include Mount Rushmore National Memorial, Wind Cave National Park, Jewel Cave National Monument, Black Hills National Forest, Custer State Park, and Crazy Horse Memorial, each of which is located south of Rapid City; Buffalo Gap National Grasslands borders the park, and Wounded Knee, South Dakota, is 25 miles south of the White River Visitor Center.

4

BIG BEND NATIONAL PARK

by Don and Barbara Laine

VAST AND WILD, BIG BEND NATIONAL PARK IS A LAND OF EXTREMES, diversity, and a few contradictions. Its rugged terrain harbors thousands of species of plants and animals—some seen practically nowhere else on earth. A visit to the park can be a hike into the sun-baked desert, a float down a majestic river through the canyons, or a trek among high mountains where bears and mountain lions rule.

Geologists tell us that millions of years ago an inland sea covered this area. As it dried up, sediments of sand and mud turned to rock, and then came the creation of mountains and roar of volcanoes until, finally, millions of years of erosion produced the delightful canyons and rock formations we marvel at today. These rock formations—with their wonderful hues of red, orange, yellow, white, and brown—have created a unique and awe-inspiring world of immensity and rugged beauty. This is not a fantasyland of delicate shapes and intricate carvings, such as Bryce Canyon in Utah, but a powerful and dominating landscape. Although the greatest natural sculptures can be seen in the park's three major river canyons—the Santa Elena, Marsical, and Boquillas—all throughout Big Bend you can find spectacular and majestic examples of what nature can do with this mighty yet malleable building material we call rock.

Visitors to Big Bend National Park encounter not only a geologic wonder, but also a wild, rugged wilderness, populated by a myriad of desert and mountain plants and animals, ranging from box turtles and black-tailed jackrabbits to funny-looking javelina and powerful black bears and mountain lions. The park is considered a birders' paradise, with more bird species than at any other national park. It's also a wonderful spot to see wildflowers and the delightfully colorful display of cactus blooms.

For hikers, there's a tremendous variety of trails, from easy walks to rugged backcountry routes that barely qualify as trails at all. There are also opportunities to let the Rio Grande do the work as it carries rafts, canoes, and kayaks through canyons carved through 1,500 feet of solid rock. Drivers of 4X4s will also enjoy exploring the backcountry roads, and history buffs will find a number of interesting historical attractions and cultural experiences.

Avoiding the Crowds. Average annual visitation at Big Bend National Park is about 287,500. Although the park is relatively uncrowded much of the year, there are several periods when lodging and campgrounds are full: spring break (usually the second or third week in March), Easter weekend, Thanksgiving weekend,

Tips from a Park Ranger

"This park has something for everyone," says Valerie Naylor, Big Bend's chief of interpretation and visitor services. One of the park's assets, she says, is its variety of activities, including both easy day hikes and extended backpacking trips, great bird watching, wildlife viewing, and camping.

Big Bend is not a good choice for a quick visit, and Naylor recommends that people spend at least 3 days. "Be prepared for long distances, and don't expect all the amenities you might find in other places," she says.

Although the park usually receives fewer than 300,000 visitors each year, making Big Bend one of America's lesser-used national parks, Naylor says that it does get busy occasionally, particularly during spring break time, usually March and early April, when college students arrive in mass to hit the trails. The hottest months at the park are May and June, she says, adding that the heat of July and August is usually tempered by afternoon thunderstorms. September is among the slowest times in the park, and it can be very nice, although still hot. "October is a great time, still quiet and a bit cooler," she says.

Naylor says that those visiting in summer will want to avoid hiking in the desert, but can still get out on the trails by going up into the Chisos Mountains, where it can be 20° cooler than on the river. She also recommends hiking into the high country from October through December to see the beautiful fall colors.

and the week between Christmas and New Year's Day. Park visitation is generally highest in March and April, and lowest in August and September.

But although the park's visitor centers, campgrounds, and other developed facilities may be taxed during the busier times, visitors can still be practically alone simply by seeking out lesser-used hiking trails. Big Bend is simply a physically big park. Those seeking solitude should discuss their hiking skills and expectations with rangers, who can offer advice on the best areas to get away from the crowd.

Just the Facts

GETTING THERE & GATEWAYS

Big Bend National Park is not really close to anything except the Rio Grande and Mexico. There is no public transportation to or through the park, so to get to the park you'll need a personal vehicle.

Park headquarters is 108 miles southeast of the town of Alpine via Tex. 118 and 69 miles south of Marathon via U.S. 385. There is train and bus service to Alpine, where the nearest hospital is located.

From El Paso, 323 miles northwest of the park, take I-10 east 121 miles to Exit 140, follow U.S. 90 southeast 99 miles to Alpine, then turn south on Tex. 118 for 108 miles to park headquarters.

The Nearest Airports. The nearest airport is **Midland-Odessa** (☎ **915/560-2200**), 225 miles north, serviced by **Continental, American,** and **Southwest Airlines.** From the airport take I-20 west about 50 miles to Exit 80 for Tex. 18, which you follow south about 50 miles to Fort Stockton. There take U.S. 385 south 125 miles through Marathon to park headquarters.

The nearest major airport is **El Paso International** (☎ **915/772-4271**) in central El Paso just off I-10, with service from

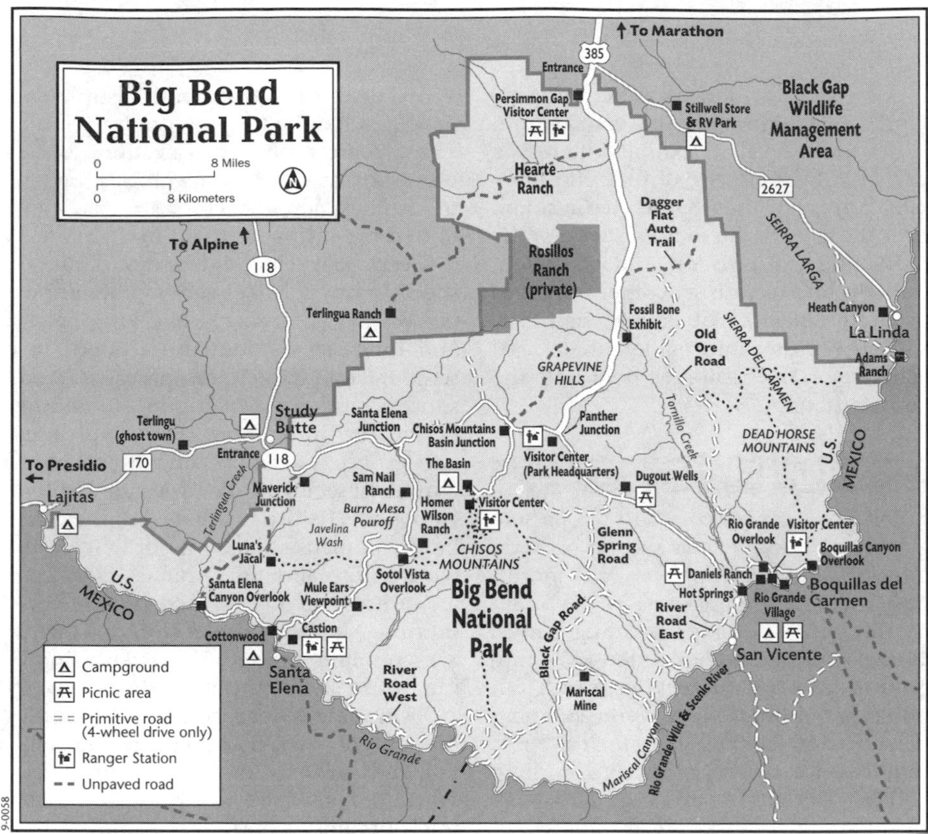

American, America West, Continental, Delta, Southwest, Frontier, and Aero Litoral (☎ **800/237-6639**).

Renting a Car. Car rental agencies at the El Paso airport include **Advantage, Alamo, Avis, Budget, Dollar, Hertz,** and **National.**

Toll-free reservations numbers for all the airlines and car-rental agencies listed in this section are given in the appendix.

GETTING INFORMATION BEFORE YOUR TRIP

For advance information about the park and its facilities, services, programs, and recreational opportunities, contact the **Superintendent, Big Bend National Park,** TX 79834 (☎ **915/477-2251**). It's a good idea to write early and specify the kind of information you need. The Web site for the park is **www.nps.gov/bibe**.

Books, maps, and videos on Big Bend are available from **Big Bend Natural History Association,** P.O. Box 196, Big Bend National Park, TX 79834 (☎ **915/477-2236**), which will send you a catalog. Those wanting to help the nonprofit association can join ($25 annually) and get a 15% discount on purchases.

The park is open 24 hours a day, year-round.

VISITOR CENTERS

There are four visitor centers in the park. **Panther Junction Visitor Center** (open year-round daily 8am to 6pm) is centrally located at park headquarters; **Persimmon Gap Visitor Center** (open most of the year; hours vary) is at the North Entrance to the park on U.S. 385; **Rio Grande Village Visitor Center** (open November through April; hours vary) is on the river in the eastern part of the park; and **Chisos Basin Visitor Center** (open year-round; hours vary) is in the Chisos Mountains in the middle of the park, at 5,401 feet in elevation.

All visitor centers provide information, backcountry permits, books, and maps, and also have exhibits; there is a particularly impressive display on mountain lions at Chisos Basin. At **Castolon,** near the river in the southwest end of the park, there is a visitor contact station. Bulletin boards with schedules of ranger programs, notices of animal sightings, and other visitor information are located at each of the visitor centers and the contact station.

ENTRANCE & CAMPING FEES

Entry into the park costs $10 per passenger vehicle, and $5 per person on foot, motorcycle, bicycle, or bus. A 12-month pass is $20. Camping costs $7 per night in the three developed campgrounds. There's a concession-operated RV campground at Rio Grande Village with full hookups, costing $14.50. A free camping permit, available at any visitor center, is required for all backcountry camping; and free permits are also required for all river-float trips (see "Camping" and "River Running," below).

SPECIAL REGULATIONS & WARNINGS

The maximum speed limit inside the park is 45 m.p.h., with lower limits posted frequently at curves and near intersections or parking pullouts. Watch for wild animals along the roads, particularly javelina, deer, and rabbits, especially at night when they may be blinded by your vehicle's headlights and stunned into standing still in the middle of the road. Of course, feeding wildlife is prohibited, not only to minimize the risk of injuries to park visitors, but also because it's bad for the animals.

The Basin Road Scenic Drive into the Chisos Mountains has some sharp curves and steep grades and is not recommended for trailers longer than 20 feet or RVs longer than 24 feet. The **Ross Maxwell Scenic Drive** to Castolon is okay for most RVs and trailers but can present a problem for those with insufficient power to handle the steep pull back up. These roads require extra caution by all users—drivers of motor vehicles, pedestrians, and bicyclists. Horses are not permitted on any paved roads in the park.

Desert heat can be dangerous. Hikers should carry at least 1 gallon of water per person per day; wear a hat, long pants, and long sleeves; and use a good sunscreen. Don't depend on springs as water sources, and avoid hiking in the middle of the day in summer. Early mornings and evenings are best for both comfort and sight-seeing. Talk to rangers about your plans before heading out; they can help you plan a hike in accordance with your ability and time frame. They can also advise you on expected weather conditions—sudden summer thunderstorms are common and can cause flash flooding in usually dry washes and canyons.

Swimming is not recommended in the Rio Grande, even though it may look tantalizingly inviting on a hot summer day. Waste materials and waterborne microorganisms have been found in the river, and can cause serious illness. Also, strong undercurrents, deep holes, and sharp rocks in shallow water are common. Should you decide to swim in spite of these warnings, be sure to wear a life jacket.

Wood or ground fires are prohibited in the park, and caution is advised when using camp stoves, charcoal grills, and cigarettes. Smoking is prohibited on all trails. Check at the visitor centers for current drought conditions, and any special restrictions that may be in effect when you visit.

SEASONS & CLIMATE

Weather here is generally mild to hot, although because of the vast range of elevations—from about 1,800 feet at the eastern end of Boquillas Canyon to 7,825 feet on Emory Peak in the Chisos Mountains—conditions can vary greatly throughout the park at any given time. Essentially, the higher you go, the cooler

Keeping the Wild in Wildlife, or How to Avoid an Unpleasant Encounter

“The signs and warnings are everywhere: “This is bear and mountain lion country,” and although one of the thrills of visiting Big Bend National Park is the opportunity to see wildlife, for the safety of both the human visitors and the park’s wildlife, these animals should always be viewed from a distance. Rangers say that since the 1950s there have been more than 1,000 sightings of mountain lions in the park, and numerous sightings of black bears. While the vast majority have been relatively uneventful—although definitely something to tell the neighbors about when you get home—two people have been attacked by mountain lions in the park. Fortunately, both recovered from their injuries; unfortunately, in both cases it was considered necessary to kill the mountain lions.

Hikers, especially in the Chisos Mountains, should be especially careful to minimize the danger of an encounter. First, discuss your hiking plans with park rangers to see if there have been any recent mountain lion sightings where you plan to hike. Don’t hike alone, especially at dawn or dusk. Watch children carefully—never let them run ahead. If you do end up face-to-face with a mountain lion, rangers offer these tips: Don’t run, but stand your ground, shout, wave your arms, and try to appear as large as possible. If you have children with you, pick them up. If the mountain lion acts aggressively, throw stones, and try to convince it that not only are you not prey but that you may be dangerous yourself. Then report the incident to a ranger as soon as possible.

The other animal you may see is one of the estimated 15 to 20 black bears that currently live in the Chisos Mountains. Bears are attracted to food, and the best way to avoid an unwanted encounter with a bear is to keep a clean camp. Park rangers recommend that you store all foodstuffs, cooking utensils, and toiletries in a hard-sided vehicle. Food storage lockers are available for hikers and campers in the Chisos Mountains. Always dispose of garbage properly in the receptacles provided. If you do see a bear, keep a safe distance; do not approach or follow it, and of course, never attempt to feed a bear. If a bear approaches you, scare it away by shouting, waving your arms, or throwing rocks or sticks. Watch for cubs—you never want to be between a mother bear and her cubs. Report any sightings of bears to a ranger.

Bears and mountain lions aren’t the only wild animals in the park. Many visitors see javelinas (officially known as collared peccaries), which look a bit like pigs and are very near-sighted. A group of 10 to 20 are often seen in and near Rio Grande Village Campground, and some of them have learned to recognize the crinkling sound of potato chip bags, and will run toward the sound in hopes of a snack. Although javelina are not aggressive, they are easily frightened, and could inflict some damage with their javelin-sharp tusks, for which they’re named.

Also deserving of mention are the park’s poisonous snakes, scorpions, spiders, and centipedes, which are most active during the warmer months. Rangers advise that you watch carefully where you put your feet and hands, and use flashlights at night. Hikers may want to consider wearing high boots or protective leggings. It’s also a good idea to check your shoes and bedding before use.

and wetter you can expect it to be, although no section of the park gets a lot of precipitation.

Summers here are hot, often well over 100°F in the desert in May and June, and afternoon thunderstorms are common from July through September. Winters are usually mild, although temperatures occasionally drop below freezing, and light snow is possible, especially in the Chisos Mountains. Fall and spring are usually warm and pleasant.

SEASONAL EVENTS

Annual events within the **International Good Neighbor Day Fiesta,** on the third Saturday in October, are designed to promote international friendship and understanding with music, dancing, food, and cultural demonstrations.

USEFUL PUBLICATIONS

The free newsprint handout, ***The Big Bend Paisano,*** published seasonally by the park service, is a great source of current information on seminars, new or special publications, suggested hikes, kids' activities, and local facilities, with telephone numbers inside and outside the park.

The ***Official Big Bend National Park Handbook*** (Washington, D.C.: Department of the Interior, 1983) by the Division of Publications, National Park Service, is a good introduction to the what and why of the park, describing in detail the terrain, flora, fauna, and human history of the area. There are also several booklets detailing improved and unimproved roads and hiking trails, produced by the park service. A particularly good hiking guide is ***Hiking Big Bend National Park*** (Helena, Montana: Falcon Press, 1996) by Laurence Parent. Those planning backpacking trips will also want to get the appropriate topo maps, which, along with the publications discussed above, are available at the park's visitor centers or by mail from the **Big Bend Natural History Association** (see "Getting Information Before Your Trip," above).

Seeing the Highlights in a Day

Big Bend National Park is huge, and you can't hope to see all of it in 1 day or even 2. It's best to allow at least 3 days, essentially devoting 1 day each to the desert, river, and mountains. However, if you have a limited amount of time in the park, the best choice is to first head up to the **Chisos Basin** and see the mountains in the middle of the park. Take the short, easy **Window View Trail,** a self-guided nature trail (see "Day Hikes," below) that discusses the flora and fauna of the Chisos Mountains. Then head back down and drive the **Ross Maxwell Scenic Drive** (see "Exploring the Park by Car," below) through the Chihuahuan Desert to the Rio Grande. If time allows, hike into **Santa Elena Canyon** (see "Day Hikes," below), one of the most beautiful canyons in the park. Finally, take in a ranger program at one of the park amphitheaters.

Exploring the Park by Car

There are several paved roads in the park—one goes through and others take you to different parts of the park. In addition, there are several unimproved roads requiring high clearance or 4X4 vehicles (see "Backcountry Driving," below).

There are two scenic drives in the park, both with sharp curves and steep inclines and not recommended for certain RVs and trailers (see "Special Regulations & Warnings," above).

The 7-mile **Chisos Basin Drive** climbs up Green Gulch to Panther Pass before dropping down into the Basin. Near the pass there are some sharp curves, and parts of the road are at a 10% grade. The views are wonderful any time of the year, and particularly when the wildflowers dot the meadows, hills, and roadsides with color. The best month for wildflowers is usually October, after the summer rains.

When you've breathed your fill of clear mountain air, head back down and turn west toward the **Ross Maxwell Scenic Drive** through the Chihuahuan Desert and finally to the Rio Grande. This drive winds through the desert on the west side of the Chisos Mountains, giving you a different perspective of them. Afterwards, it passes through Castolon, and then continues along and above the river to **Santa Elena Canyon.** Here you should park and hike the trail, which climbs above the river, offering great views into the steep, narrow canyon and back toward the road (see "Day Hikes," below).

Another worthwhile drive, recommended for all vehicles, begins at **Panther Junction Visitor Center** and goes to Rio Grande Village. From the visitor center head southeast through the desert toward the high mountains that form the skyline in the distance. The first half of the drive passes through desert grasses, finally making a comeback after severe overgrazing in the decades before the establishment of the park in 1944. Recovery is slow in this harsh climate, but it is beginning to revegetate.

As the elevation gradually decreases, you progress further into the desert, and the grasses give way to lechugilla and ocotillo stalks, cacti, and other arid-climate survivors. Off to the south is the long, rather flat **Chilicotal Mountain,** named for the chilicote, or Mescal-bean bushes, growing near its base. The chilicote's poisonous red bean is used in Mexico to kill rats. Several miles further the River Road turns off and heads southwest toward Castolon, more than 50 miles away. This is a primitive road for high-clearance vehicles only.

If you are in a car or truck and feel adventuresome, take the **Hot Springs** turnoff about a mile beyond the Tornillo Creek Bridge. It follows a rough wash to a point overlooking the confluence of Tornillo Creek and the Rio Grande. A trail along the river bank leads to several springs. The foundation of a bathhouse is a remnant of the town of Hot Springs, which thrived here about 20 years before the park was established, and continued as a concession for another 10 years.

Back on the paved road, you'll soon pass through a short tunnel in the limestone cliff, after which is a parking area for a short trail to a view point overlooking **Rio Grande Village.** At the view point you'll find a marker identifying the various peaks and other features that can be seen. It's just a short drive from here to Rio Grande Village, your destination, where you can take a 0.25-mile nature trail ending at a high point above the Rio Grande, offering terrific views up and down the river.

Organized Tours & Ranger Programs

Park naturalists offer a variety of programs year-round. Illustrated evening programs take place at the 5,400-foot **Chisos Basin amphitheater** in summer. From November through April, evening programs are offered regularly in the amphitheater at **Rio Grande Village** and occasionally in the Chisos Basin and at Cottonwood Campground. Subjects include the park's geology, plants, animals, and human history. Rangers also offer guided **nature walks,** usually between 0.5 mile and 5 miles, and occasionally lead driving tours. Workshops are also planned, on subjects such as adobe construction or photography. Look for weekly schedules on the bulletin boards scattered about the park.

The **Big Bend Natural History Association** (see "Getting Information Before Your Trip," above) offers a variety of seminars, ranging from 1-day workshops, starting at $40, to multiday programs starting at $80. Subjects could include black bears, archaeology, bats, birds, cacti, and wildflowers. A 1-day introductory overview covers the plants, animals, geology, and history of the park. In recent years there have also been multiday photography workshops by noted nature photographer Jim Bones.

Historic & Man-Made Attractions

There is evidence that both prehistoric Indians and later Apaches, Kiowas, and Comanches occupied this area. Throughout the park you can find **petroglyphs, pictographs,** and other signs of early human presence, including ruins of **stone shelters.** Ask rangers for directions to the various rock art and ruin sites—there are pictographs along the Hot Spring Trail (see "Day Hikes," below)—and along the river. Watch for **mortar holes** scattered throughout the park, sometimes a foot deep, where American Indians would grind seeds or mesquite beans.

Also within the park boundaries are the remains of several early 20th-century communities, a mercury mine, and projects by the Civilian Conservation Corps.

The **Castolon Historic District,** located in the southwest section of the park just off the Ross Maxwell Scenic Drive, includes the remains of homes and other buildings, many stabilized by the park service, that were constructed in the early 1900s by Mexican–American farmers, Anglo settlers, and the U.S. Army. The first is the **Alvino House,** the oldest surviving adobe structure in the park, dating from 1901. Nearby is **La Harmonia Store,** built in 1920 to house cavalry troops during the Mexican Revolution, but never actually used by soldiers because the war ended. The building was then purchased by two civilians, who converted it into a general store, calling it *La Harmonia* for the harmony and peaceful relations they hoped to encourage among area residents. The store continues to operate, selling snacks, groceries, and other necessities.

The village of **Glenn Springs,** located in the southeast section of the park and accessible by dirt road off the main park highway, owes its creation to having a reliable water source in an otherwise arid area. It was named for a rancher called H.E. Glenn, who grazed horses in the area until he was killed by Indians in the 1880s. By 1916 there were several ranches, a factory that produced wax from the candelilla plant, a store, a post office, and a residential village divided into two sections—one for the Anglos and the other for the Mexicans. But then Mexican bandit-revolutionaries crossed the border and attacked, killing and wounding a number of people, looting the store, and partially destroying the wax factory. Within 3 years the community was virtually deserted. Today, the spring still flows, and you can see the remains of several adobe buildings and other structures.

Remains of a small health resort can be seen at the **Hot Springs,** accessible by hiking trail or dirt road, along the Rio Grande west of Rio Grande Village in the park's southeast section. Construction of the resort was begun by J.O. Langford in 1909, who was forced to leave during the Mexican Revolution. However, Langford returned and completed the project in the 1920s, advertising the Hot Springs as "The Fountain of Youth that Ponce de León failed to find." Today you can see the ruins of a general store/post office, other buildings, and a foundation that fills with natural mineral water, at about 105°, creating an almost natural hot tub.

To get to the **Marsical Mine** you will likely need a four-wheel-drive or high-clearance vehicle. Located in the south-central part of the park, it is most easily accessed by River Road East, which begins 5 miles west of Rio Grande Village. The mine operated on and off between 1900 and 1943, producing 1,400 76-pound flasks of mercury, which was almost one-quarter of the total amount of mercury produced in the United States during that time. Mining buildings, homes, the company store, a kiln, foundations, and other structures remain, in what is now a National Historic District.

Also in the park you can see some excellent examples of the work done by the **Civilian Conservation Corps** in the 1930s and early 1940s. These include stone culverts along the Basin Road, the Lost Mine Trail, and several buildings, including some stone-and-adobe cottages that are still in use at the Chisos Mountain Lodge.

Day Hikes

SHORTER TRAILS

Panther Path

50 yards RT. Easy. Access: Panther Junction Visitor Center.

This is a short walk through a garden of cacti and other desert plants. A booklet discussing the park's plant life is available at the trailhead.

Window View Trail

0.3 mile RT. Easy. Access: Chisos Basin Trailhead.

Level, paved, and wheelchair-accessible, this self-guided nature trail (a brochure is available at the trailhead) runs along a low hill and offers beautiful sunset views through the Window, a V-shaped opening in the mountains to the west.

Chihuahuan Desert Nature Trail

0.5 mile RT. Easy. Access: Dugout Wells Picnic Area, 5.9 miles east of Panther Junction.

A good introduction to the flora of the Chihuahuan Desert, this is an easy stroll along a relatively flat gravel path with signs describing the plants you see along the way.

Rio Grande Village Nature Trail

0.75 mile RT. Easy. Access: Southeast corner of Rio Grande Village Campground, across from site 18.

A good choice for sunrise and sunset views, this self-guided loop nature trail (booklet available at the trailhead) climbs from the surprisingly lush river floodplain about 125 feet into desert terrain and up a hilltop that offers excellent panoramic views.

Tuff Canyon

0.75 mile RT. Easy. Access: Ross Maxwell Scenic Drive, 5 miles south of Mule Ears Overlook access road.

This easy trail leads into a narrow canyon, carved from soft volcanic rock called tuff, with several canyon overlooks.

Santa Elena Canyon

0.8 mile one way. Moderate. Access: End of Ross Maxwell Scenic Drive.

You may get your feet wet crossing a broad creek on this trail, which also takes you up a series of steep steps. But it's one of the most scenic short trails in the park, leading along the canyon wall, with good views of rafters on the Rio Grande, and down among the boulders along the river. Interpretive signs describe the canyon environment. Beware of flash flooding as you cross the Terlingua Creek, and skip this trail if the creek is running swiftly.

Burro Mesa Pour-Off

1 mile RT. Easy. Access: Parking area at the end of Burro Mesa spur road, about 11.5 miles down the Ross Maxwell Scenic Drive on the west (right).

This short hike takes you to the bottom of a desert pour-off. The beginning of the trail is a well-marked path, but as you turn into Javelina Wash it becomes less obvious so watch for the lines of rocks pointing the way. The trail has an elevation gain of about 60 feet. The pour-off is a long, narrow chute that is usually dry, but the extensive cut gives testimony to the power of rushing water after a heavy summer rain. Don't attempt to climb to the top from here; it is quite hazardous. There is an easier way for those with good route-finding skills: See "Top of Burro Mesa Pour-Off," below.

Boquillas Canyon Trail

1.4 miles RT. Moderate. Access: End of Boquillas Canyon Rd.

This hike begins by climbing a low hill and then drops down to the Rio Grande, ending near a shallow cave and huge sand dune. There are good views of the scenic canyon and the Mexican village of Boquillas, across the Rio Grande.

Chisos Basin Loop Trail

1.6-mile loop. Easy. Access: Chisos Basin Trailhead.

This fairly easy walk climbs about 350 feet into a pretty meadow and leads to an overlook that offers good views of the park's mountains, including Emory Peak, highest point in the park at 7,825 feet.

Top of Burro Mesa Pour-Off

1.8 miles one way. Moderate. Access: Trailhead parking about 7 miles down the Ross Maxwell Scenic Drive on the west (right).

This moderate hike takes you through some narrow rocky gorges to the top of the Burro Mesa Pour-Off. The trail may not be well-marked, so it's a good idea to carry a topographical map and compass. As you hike along the now-dry washes you'll realize that the rock cairns marking the trail are quickly scattered when water floods through them. There is a gradual decline of about 525 feet to the top of this desert waterfall, where the drainage drops suddenly and precipitously from the wash where you stand to the one below. Do not chance this hike in stormy weather, as you might get washed away with the rock cairns.

Hot Springs Trail

1 mile RT. Easy. Access: End of improved dirt road to Hot Springs, off road to Rio Grande Village.

An interpretive booklet available at the trailhead describes the sights, including a historic health resort and homestead (see "Historic & Man-Made Attractions," above), along this easy loop. Fairly substantial ruins remain of a general store/post office, other buildings, and a foundation that fills with natural mineral water, at about 105°, creating an inviting hot tub. Also along the trail are pictographs left by ancient Indians, and panoramic views of the Rio Grande and Mexico.

LONGER TRAILS

Grapevine Hills Trail

2.2 miles RT. Easy. Access: 6 miles down the unpaved Grapevine Hills Rd.

An easy walk, this trail follows a sandy wash through the desert, among massive granite boulders, ending at a picturesque balancing rock. There is an elevation change of about 240 feet.

Mule Ears Spring Trail

3.8 miles RT. Moderate. Access: Mule Ears Overlook Parking Area, along the Ross Maxwell Scenic Drive.

This relatively flat desert trail crosses several arroyos and then follows a wash most of the way to Mule Ears Spring. It offers great views of unusual rock formations, such as the Mule Ears, and ends at a historic ranch house and rock corral.

Pine Canyon Trail

4 miles RT. Moderate. Access: End of unpaved Pine Canyon Rd. (check on road conditions before going).

With a 1,000-foot elevation gain, this trail takes you from desert grasslands, dotted with sotols, into a pretty canyon with dense stands of pinyon, juniper, oak, and finally bigtooth maple and ponderosa pine. At the higher elevations of this trail you'll also see Texas madrones—evergreen trees with smooth reddish bark shed each summer. At the end of the trail is a 200-foot cliff, which becomes a picturesque waterfall after heavy rains. At the cliff's base you're likely to see columbine, a member of the buttercup family, which has delicate yellow flowers.

Chimneys Trail

4.8 miles RT. Moderate. Access: Ross Maxwell Scenic Drive, 1.2 miles south of the Burro Mesa Pour-Off access road.

This flat trail through the desert follows an old dirt road to a series of chimney-shaped rock formations. American Indian petroglyphs can be seen on the southernmost chimney, and nearby are ruins of rock shelters. Those who want to extend this hike can continue, although the trail is difficult to follow after the Chimneys and a topographical map is highly recommended.

Lost Mine Trail

4.8 miles RT. Moderate. Access: Chisos Basin Rd. at Panther Pass.

A moderately difficult self-guided nature trail (a booklet is available at the trailhead), this is a popular mountain hike that climbs about 1,100 feet. It was built in the early 1940s by the Civilian Conservation Corps—evidence of their rock work can still be seen. Along the way, the trail climbs through forests of pinyon, juniper, and oak, and offers splendid views. Those with limited time or ambition don't have to hike all the way—some of the trail's best views are about 1 mile from the trailhead, from a saddle where you can look out over a pretty canyon to the surrounding mountains and even deep into Mexico.

Window Trail

5.2 miles RT. Moderate. Access: Chisos Basin Trailhead.

A scenic trail through Oak Creek Canyon, this hike involves descending about 800 feet to the base of the Window, a V-shaped opening in the mountains that frames panoramic desert scenes. Following the Oak Creek drainage, it provides a good chance to see deer, javelina, rock squirrels, and a variety of birds.

Slickrock Canyon

10 miles RT. Moderate. Access: Main Park Rd., about 12 miles west of Panther Junction, at Oak Creek Bridge.

This hike follows Oak Creek northwest to a small, scenic canyon, passing along the south edge of Slickrock Mountain. This is not a marked trail, but rather a route through sand and gravel washes, and a topographical map is helpful. Hikers in this deep canyon will find desert plants such as mesquite and creosote bush, and possibly tracks of coyotes, javelinas, and mountain lions.

Exploring the Backcountry

There are numerous possibilities for backpacking in the park, both on established and marked hiking trails and on relatively unmarked hiking routes following washes, canyons, or abandoned rough dirt roads dating from the late 1800s. In all there are more than 150 miles of designated trails and routes. Cross-country hiking is also permitted. Rangers advise that because many trails and hiking routes are hard to follow, hikers should carry detailed 7.5-minute topographical maps and compasses. Maps and hiker's guidebooks can be purchased at the visitor centers or in advance from the **Big Bend Natural History Association** (see "Getting Information Before Your Trip," above).

Campers can use numerous designated backcountry campsites in the park, and are also allowed to camp in desert areas. The required free permits must be obtained in person, no more than 24 hours in advance. In the high Chisos Mountains, backcountry campers must stay at designated campsites and carry special permits, available on a first-come, first-served basis. These Chisos Mountains campsites are often difficult to obtain during the park's busiest times—Thanksgiving and Christmas holidays and college spring break season, usually in March or early April.

Ground fires are prohibited throughout the park. Rangers warn that backcountry water availability is spotty and changeable, and say that all backpackers should carry enough water for their entire trip.

Other Sports & Activities

Backcountry Driving. There are a number of unimproved roads in Big Bend requiring high clearance vehicles and sometimes four-wheel-drive. Many have roadside campsites. Get details on current road conditions from rangers before setting out and pick up the useful backcountry road guide, available at visitor centers. All overnight trips require backcountry permits.

Horseback Riding. Horses are permitted on most dirt roads and many park trails (check with rangers for specifics), and may be kept overnight at many of the park's primitive road campsites, although not at the developed campgrounds. The **Government Springs Campsite,** located 3.5 miles from Panther Junction, is a primitive campsite with a corral that accommodates up to eight horses. It can be reserved up to 10 weeks in advance (☎ **915/477-2251,** ext. 158). Those riding horses in the park must get free stock use permits, which should be obtained in person up to 24 hours in advance at any of the park's visitor centers.

Although there are no commercial outfitters offering guided rides in the park as of this writing, there are opportunities for rides just outside the park on private land, at nearby Big Bend Ranch State Park, and across the river in Mexico. **Big Bend Stables,** P.O. Box 6, Terlingua, TX 79852 (☎ **800/887-4331** or 915/371-2212), and **Lajitas Stables,** Star Route 70, Box 380, Terlingua, TX 79852 (☎ **888/508-7667** or 915/424-3238), offer a wide variety of trail rides, lasting an hour to all day to several days. Some trips follow canyon trails; others visit ancient Indian camps, ghost towns, or abandoned mines. They can also take you to see pictographs, fossils, and petrified wood. Both stables are under the same management. Rates are about $20 per hour for the first hour and $10 per hour after that; multiday trips are usually about $100 per day. Novice riders and children four and up are welcome.

Mountain Biking. Bikes are not permitted on hiking trails, but are allowed on the park's many established dirt roads. Mountain bikes are available for rent from **Desert Sports,** P.O. Box 448, Terlingua, TX 79852 (☎ **888/989-6900** or 915/371-2727; fax 915/371-2726), located on FM 170, 4 miles west of the junction of FM 170 and Tex. 118. Rates are $25 per day, $125 for 5 to 7 days, and $15 for each additional day after 7. The company also offers multiday guided trips, including a combination mountain-biking and float trip in the park—3 days for $350.

River Running. The Rio Grande follows the southern edge of the park for 118 miles, and extends another 127 miles downstream as a designated Wild and Scenic River. The river offers mostly fairly calm float trips, but does have a few sections of rough white water during high-water times. It can usually be run in a raft, canoe, or kayak. You can either bring your own equipment, or rent equipment near the park (none is available in the park), or take a trip with one of several river guides approved by the National Park Service.

Those planning trips on their own must obtain free permits at a park visitor center, in person only, no more than 24 hours before the trip. Permits for the lower canyons of the Rio Grande Wild and Scenic River are available at the **Persimmon Gap Visitor Center,** when it's open, and a self-serve permit station located at **Stillwell Store and RV Park,** 7 miles from the park's North Entrance on FM 2627. Permits for the section of river through Santa Elena Canyon can also be obtained at a self-serve permit station at the Barton Warnock Environmental Education Center in the community of Lajitas, Texas, west of the park. Park rangers, however, strongly advise that everyone planning a river trip check with them beforehand to get the latest river conditions. A river-running booklet, with additional information, is available at park visitor centers and from the **Big Bend Natural History Association** (see "Getting Information Before Your Trip," above).

Rafts, inflatable kayaks, and canoes can be rented from **Desert Sports,** P.O. Box 448, Terlingua, TX 79852 (☎ **888/989-6900** or 915/371-2727; fax 915/371-2726), which is located on FM 170, 4 miles west of the junction of FM 170 and Tex. 118. Rafts cost $20 per person per day (with a three-person minimum) with discounts for trips longer than 4 days; inflatable kayaks cost $30 per day for one person and $40 per day for two people; and canoes cost $40 per day, with discounts for multiday rentals. The company also provides shuttle services, and offers a wide variety of multiday canoe and raft trips, where you can either grab a paddle and take an active role, or sit back and let your boatman and the river do the work. Typical prices are $750 for 7 days on the river, floating from Castolon along the southern edge of the park to Marsical Canyon; and $1,400 for 12 days on the Rio Grande Wild and Scenic River, downriver from the national park.

Desert Sports also offers a number of trips that combine a float trip with hiking or mountain biking. Prices start at $240 for a 2-day trip that includes a 6- to 8-hour hike in a particularly scenic area on the Mexican side of the border, and then a boat trip through the national park's beautiful Santa Elena Canyon. Also see "Mountain Biking," above. Most trips are offered from September through May only.

Another company that offers guided trips on the Rio Grande is **Big Bend River Tours,** P.O. Box 317, Lajitas, TX 79852 (☎ **800/545-4240** or 915/424-3219), which has raft trips daily year-round. Trips range from a half-day float for about $50 per person to 10-day excursions for about $1,000 per person. Among the most popular trips is the 19-mile float through beautiful Santa Elena Canyon, which can be done as a day trip (about $100 per person), a 2-day trip (about $215 per person), or a 3-day trip (about $310 per person), with rates varying somewhat based on the number of people making the trip. The canyon offers spectacular scenery and wonderful serenity, plus the excitement of a challenging section of rapids called the Rockslide. There are often opportunities to see javelinas, coyotes, beavers, wild burros, golden eagles, and peregrine falcons. The longer trips include a stop in a side canyon with waterfalls and peaceful swimming holes.

Also offering raft trips year-round, at similar rates, are **Far Flung Adventures,** P.O. Box 31, Terlingua, TX 79852 (☎ **800/359-4138** or 915/371-2489), and **Texas River Expeditions,** P.O. Box 583, Terlingua, TX 79852 (☎ **800/839-7238** or 915/371-2633).

Wildlife Viewing & Bird Watching There is an absolutely phenomenal variety of wildlife at Big Bend National Park. About 450 species of birds will be found here over the course of the year—that's more than at any other national park and nearly half of all those found in North America. At latest count there are also about 75 species of mammals, close to 70 species of reptiles and amphibians, and more than three dozen species of fish.

This is the only place in the United States where you'll find the Mexican long-nosed bat, listed by the federal government as an endangered species. Other endangered species that make their homes in the park include the black-capped vireo, the peregrine falcon, and a tiny fish—the Big Bend gambusia, whose favorite food is mosquito larvae.

Birders consider Big Bend National Park a key bird-watching destination, especially for those looking for some of

Especially for Kids

Big Bend National Park has a **Junior Ranger Program** for children of all ages. Kids learn about the park through a variety of activities, and earn stickers, certificates, badges, and patches. Pick up Junior Ranger Activity Books ($1) at any visitor center. Park rangers also present programs on a variety of topics for children, most taking place from November through April. Advance registration is usually required. Check at the visitor center for information on upcoming programs.

America's more unusual birds. Among the park's top bird-watching spots are the Rio Grande and Cottonwood campgrounds, the Chisos Basin, and the Hot Springs. Species to watch for include the colorful golden-fronted woodpecker, which can often be seen year-round among the cottonwood trees along the Rio Grande; and the rare colima warbler, whose range in the United States consists solely of the Chisos Mountains at Big Bend National Park. Among the hundreds of other birds that call the park home, at least part of the year, and are seen fairly frequently, are scaled quail, spotted sandpipers, white-winged doves, greater roadrunners, lesser night-hawks, white-throated swifts, black-chinned hummingbirds, broad-tailed hummingbirds, acorn woodpeckers, northern flickers, western wood-pewees, ash-throated flycatchers, tufted titmice, bushtits, cactus wrens, canyon wrens, loggerhead shrikes, Wilson's warblers, and Scott's orioles.

Mammals you may see in the park include desert cottontails, black-tailed jackrabbits, rock squirrels, Texas antelope squirrels, Merriam's kangaroo rats, coyotes, gray foxes, raccoons, striped skunks, mule deer, and white-tailed deer. There are occasional sightings of mountain lions, usually called panthers here, in the Green Gulch and Chisos Basin areas. Two attacks on humans have occurred (see the special section titled "Keeping the Wild in Wildlife, or How to Avoid an Unpleasant Encounter," above). Black bears, which were frequently seen in the area until about

Campground	Elev.	Total Sites	RV Hookups	Dump Station	Toilets	Drinking Water
In the park						
Chisos Basin	**5,401**	**63**	**No**	**Yes**	**Yes**	**Yes**
Cottonwood	**2,169**	**31**	**No**	**No**	**Yes**	**Yes**
Rio Grande Village	**1,850**	**100**	**No**	**Yes**	**Yes**	**Yes**
Rio Grande Village Trailer Park	**1,850**	**25**	**25**	**No**	**Yes**	**Yes**
Nearby						
Terlingua Oasis RV Park	**2,480**	**175**	**125**	**Yes**	**Yes**	**Yes**
Stillwell Store and RV Park	**2,600**	**80+**	**80**	**Yes**	**Yes**	**Yes**

1940, were mostly killed off by area ranchers who saw them as a threat to their livestock. However, with the protection provided by national park status, they began to return in the mid-1980s, and have by now established a small population.

There are a number of reptiles in the park, including some poisonous snakes, such as diamondback, Mojave, rock, and black-tailed rattlesnakes, plus the trans-pecos copperhead (see "Keeping the Wild in Wildlife, or How to Avoid an Unpleasant Encounter," above). Fortunately, it is unlikely you will see a rattler or copperhead, since they avoid both the heat of the day and busy areas. You are more apt to encounter nonpoisonous western coachwhips, which are often seen speeding across trails and roadways. They're reddish, sometimes bright red, and among America's fastest snakes, sometimes called "red racers." Other nonpoisonous snakes that inhabit the park include Texas whipsnakes, spotted night snakes, southwestern black-headed snakes, and black-necked garter snakes.

Among the lizards you may see scurrying along desert roads and trails is the southwestern earless lizard—adult males are green with black and white chevrons on their lower sides, and often curl their black-striped tails over their backs. You'll also see various whiptail lizards in the desert, but in the canyons and higher in the mountains, watch for the crevice spiny lizard, which is covered with scales and has a dark collar. Although rare, there are also western box turtles in the park, as well as several types of more common water turtles.

Camping

A free camping permit, available at any visitor center, is required for use of the primitive backcountry roadside and backpacking campsites.

INSIDE THE PARK

There are three developed campgrounds run by the park service plus an RV park run by a concessionaire.

Rio Grande Village Campground is the largest. It has numerous trees, many with prickly pear cacti growing up around them, and thorny bushes everywhere. Sites are either graveled or paved and are nicely spaced for privacy. They often fill up by 1pm in winter (the high season). One area is designated a "No Generator Zone." Separate but within walking distance is **Rio Grande Village**

Showers	Fire Pits/ Grills	Laundry	Public Phone	Reserve	Fees	Open
No	**Yes**	**No**	**Yes**	**No**	**$7**	**Year-round**
No	**Yes**	**No**	**No**	**No**	**$7**	**Year-round**
No	**Yes**	**No**	**No**	**No**	**$7**	**Year-round**
Yes	**No**	**Yes**	**Yes**	**No**	**$14.50**	**Year-round**
No	**Yes**	**Yes**	**Yes**	**No**	**$6.50–$14.50**	**Year-round**
Yes	**No**	**No**	**Yes**	**Yes**	**$8–$13**	**Year-round**

Trailer Park, a concessionaire-operated RV park with full hookups. It looks like a parking lot in the midst of grass and trees, fully paved with curbs and back-in sites (no pull-throughs). Tents are not permitted. The small store has limited camping supplies and groceries, a coin-operated laundry, showers for a fee, propane, and gasoline.

Chisos Basin Campground, although not heavily wooded, has small pinyon and juniper trees and well-spaced sites. The campground is nestled around a circular road in a bowl below the visitor center. The access road to the campground is steep and curved, so take it slowly.

Cottonwood Campground is named for the huge old cottonwood trees that dominate the scene. Sites in this rather rustic area are gravel and spacious, within walking distance to the river. There are pit toilets.

NEAR THE PARK

About 7 miles east of the North Entrance to the park on FM 2627 is **Stillwell Store and RV Park,** HC 65, Box 430, Alpine, TX 79830 (☎ **915/376-2244**), a casual RV park in desert terrain. There are two areas across the road from each other. The south side has full hookups, while the north only has water and electric, but the north also features horse corrals and plenty of room for horse trailers. There is also almost unlimited space for tenters, who are charged $4 per person. The park office is at the Stillwell Store, where you can get groceries, limited camping supplies, and gasoline. There is also a small museum (donations accepted), with exhibits from the Stillwell family's pioneer days.

About 3 miles from the West Entrance to the park is **Terlingua Oasis RV Park,** part of the Big Bend Motor Inn complex at the junction of Tex. 118 and FM 170 (P.O. Box 336, Terlingua, TX 79852; ☎ **800/848-BEND** or 915/371-2218). This park offers both 30- and 50-amp electric service, pull-through and back-in sites, grassy tent areas, gas and diesel fuel, a restaurant (see "Dining," below), a convenience store, and a gift shop. If you don't have a tent or camper, you can rent a camping cabin or even a teepee for $18.50.

Accommodations

INSIDE THE PARK

Chisos Mountain Lodge

Chisos Basin, Big Bend National Park, TX 79834-9999. ☎ **915/477-2291;** fax 915/477-2352. 72 units. $67–$73 double. AE, DC, DISC, MC, V.

The lodge offers a variety of accommodations from simple motel rooms to historic stone cottages. Pets are accepted. Motel rooms are small and simply decorated but well-maintained. They have two double beds, air-conditioning, tub/shower combo, and terrific views of the Chisos Mountains, but they don't have telephones or TVs. The Casa Grande Motor Lodge, part of the Chisos Mountain Lodge, offers somewhat larger motel rooms, attractively furnished, with a tiled bath, tub/shower combo, and most have two beds. Each room has a private balcony and air-conditioning.

Built by the Civilian Conservation Corps in the 1930s, the six delightful stone cottages are very popular, with stone floors, front patio, wooden furniture, three double beds, and shower only. Book as far in advance as possible.

The lodge units are the least expensive accommodations and are a bit more rustic. They have one double and one single bed, a tiled bath, tub/shower combo, wood furnishings, painted brick walls with western and/or southwestern art, and good views.

NEAR THE PARK

Big Bend Motor Inn

Junction of Tex. 118 and FM 170 (P.O. Box 336), Terlingua, TX 79852. ☎ **800/848-BEND** or 915/371-2218; fax 915/371-2555. 86 rms. A/C TV TEL. $65–$72 double; $105–$125 duplex. DISC, MC, V.

About 3 miles from the West Entrance to the park, this motel offers simple but comfortable rooms, most with one king bed or two queen-size beds. Some have kitchenettes, and two units each have a bedroom, a living room, and a kitchen. There are also a few smaller rooms with one queen bed.

Chisos Mining Co. Motel

On FM 170 about 3.4 miles west of Tex. 118 (P.O. Box 228), Terlingua, TX 79852. ☎ **915/371-2254.** 28 units including 8 cabins. A/C. $35–$45 double. MC, V.

This is an attractive, homey, well-maintained motel. The motel units have tub/shower combos, and some have TVs. Cabins have showers only and a kitchen, but no TV. There's a curio shop on the premises.

Mission Lodge

Junction of Tex. 118 and FM 170 (P.O. Box 169), Terlingua, TX 79852. ☎ **915/371-2555.** 24 rms. A/C TV TEL. Mar–June $55 double; July–Apr $45–$50. DISC, MC, V.

Located across the street from the Big Bend Motor Inn, and owned by the same people, the Mission Lodge is smaller, simpler, and less expensive, but still clean and well-maintained. Rooms have one queen-size bed and a tub/shower combo.

Dining

INSIDE THE PARK

Chisos Mountain Lodge Restaurant

Chisos Basin, Big Bend National Park. ☎ **915/477-2291.** Breakfast $3.80–$6.50; lunch and dinner $6.25–$14. AE, DC, DISC, MC, V. Daily 7am–8pm. AMERICAN.

The dining room is simply but attractively decorated, with good views from the large windows. The menu changes but generally includes steak, pork chops, roast turkey, and baked trout, plus specials such as chicken fajitas, lasagna, and a vegetarian dish. Children's portions and a sandwich menu are available. No alcohol is served. Hikers and others on the move can order a "traveler's lunch" to be picked up the next morning.

NEAR THE PARK

Big Bend Motor Inn Restaurant & Convenience Store

Junction of Tex. 118 and FM 170, Terlingua. ☎ **915/371-2218.** $4–$11. DISC, MC, V. Daily 6am–10pm. MEXICAN/AMERICAN.

This is a simple restaurant offering basic Mexican and American fare such as sandwiches and burgers, burritos and tacos.

Picnic & Camping Supplies

Inside the park there are limited groceries and camping supplies available at Chisos Basin, Rio Grande Village, Castolon, and Panther Junction; and there is a gift shop in the lodge at the Basin. Gasoline is available at Castolon, Rio Grande Village, and Panther Junction only, so check your gas gauge before heading out, as everything in this park is pretty far from everything else. Minor car repairs are available at Panther Junction.

Outside the North Entrance to the park, southeast about 7 miles on FM 2627, is **Stillwell Store and RV Park** (☎ **915/376-2244**), where you'll find groceries, limited camping supplies, and gasoline. Just outside the West Entrance to the park, in Study Butte/Terlingua, the **Roadrunner Deli** (☎ **915/371-2364**) has a good selection of sandwiches to eat in or take out, for about $4. It may be closed in summer. Nearby are two gas stations, a convenience store, and liquor store. Also in the Study Butte/Terlingua area is **Desert Sports** (☎ **888/989-6900** or 915/371-2727), on FM 170, 4 miles west of the junction of FM 170 and Tex. 118, with rental equipment, bike and boat parts and supplies, maps, and guidebooks.

Nearby Attractions

A QUICK TRIP TO MEXICO

You can turn your national park visit into an international excursion by visiting Santa Elena or Boquillas, two dusty little border towns just across the Rio Grande from the park. Many park visitors make the quick trip into Mexico for lunch and a walk around; for more information, pick up the park service pamphlet regarding visiting the two towns. The restaurants serve good Mexican dishes such as enchiladas and tacos, in the $3 to $5 range. U.S. dollars are welcome. The menus are in English, although few people in the villages speak English.

To reach either village you'll pay about $2 (round-trip) for a short trip across the river in the rowboat operating as a ferry. Though the trip is legal, these are not official ports of entry and you will usually see no border guards or customs officials. Those with concerns about leaving the United States in such an informal manner may want to discuss the trip with Big Bend National Park rangers before going.

Boquillas is home to about 25 families. It has one restaurant (Falcon's), a bar, and several stores. The town has no electricity, telephone service, or medical facilities. The river crossing is located just downstream of Rio Grande Village. Once you cross the river you need to either walk, or rent a burro, or use the "truck taxi": a pickup truck that usually takes visitors into the village for a small fee. The village of **Santa Elena** is about the same size as Boquillas, but has electricity. There are two restaurants—Enadina's and Maria Elena's—plus a small museum containing fossils and other items, a small grocery store, and a curio shop. The river crossing is southwest of Cottonwood Campground.

A NEARBY STATE PARK

Perhaps even more remote and rugged than Big Bend National Park is **Big Bend Ranch State Park,** P.O. Box 2319, Presidio, TX 79845 (☎ **915/229-3416**), which covers some 277,000 acres of Chihuahuan Desert wilderness along the Rio Grande west of the national park. Purchased by the state of Texas from private owners in 1988, this mostly undeveloped park contains two mountain ranges, extinct volcanoes, scenic canyons, and a wide variety of plants and animals. There is also a small herd of Texas longhorn cattle, a reminder of the property's ranching days. Several outfitters offer river trips as well as mountain-biking and hiking excursions in the state park. See "Other Sports & Activities," above.

A 35-mile well-maintained gravel road (FM 170) provides a wonderful scenic drive along the Rio Grande, and also offers access to several put-in and take-out points for rafts and canoes. The park has several miles of designated four-wheel-drive roads, and about 30 miles of hiking and backpacking trails, with trailheads along FM 170. There are also about 14 miles of trails open to mountain bikes. The park has a number of primitive camping areas; no water or other facilities are available.

There is no state park office as of this writing. Those planning trips into the park can get permits and information at Barton Warnock Environmental Education Center (see below) or **Fort Leaton State Historical Park,** 4 miles east of Presidio on FM 170 (☎ **915/229-3613**). Entrance fees are $3 for adults, $2 for senior citizens, and free for children under 13. There is also a $3 per person fee for some activities, such as camping, boat launching, and fishing.

While you're in the neighborhood, consider an hour or two at **Barton Warnock Environmental Education Center,** 1 mile east of Lajitas on FM 170 (☎ **915/424-3327**). The center contains a museum on the Big Bend area with exhibits on its geology, archaeology, human history, and wildlife. There are also 2.5 acres of desert gardens with a self-guided walk among the various plants of the Chihuahuan Desert, and a gift shop and bookstore. Gates are open daily year-round from 8am to 4:30pm; admission costs $3 for adults and $1.50 for children 6 to 12 years old.

5

THE BLACK HILLS:
Mount Rushmore National Memorial, Wind Cave National Park, Jewel Cave National Monument & Custer State Park

by T.D. Griffith

CHISELED IN GRANITE HIGH ON A PINE-CLAD CLIFF IN SOUTH DAKOTA'S fabled Black Hills, just 2 hours west of the desolate Badlands, are the portraits of four of America's greatest leaders. For more than 57 years, George Washington, Thomas Jefferson, Abraham Lincoln, and Theodore Roosevelt have quietly gazed across the Great Plains and a land they did so much to mold, drawing 2.5 million visitors a year.

Most people spend but a short hour or two gazing at the memorial, maybe eating a sandwich, then going on their way to Yellowstone or their next destination. Those with the time and inclination will find much to occupy their time. Within an hour's drive of Mount Rushmore, you will find not only Wind Cave National Park and Jewel Cave National Monument, but also Custer State Park, one of the best and largest state parks in the country, as well as the Crazy Horse Memorial, a work in progress that will be far larger than Mount Rushmore. And if you are willing to get off the beaten path—something that relatively few visitors do—you will find a backcountry dotted with trails through the region's pine forests, a virtually untrammeled wilderness where you can escape the crowds for days, or perhaps just an hour.

Geologists predict the presidents will continue their earthly vigil at **Mount Rushmore National Memorial** for many centuries, eroding at the petrified pace of only a quarter inch every 10,000 years. But, while major changes aren't predicted for the giant faces anytime soon, visitors to the base of the mountain will discover a new experience beginning in June 1998.

Thanks to the Mount Rushmore Preservation Fund—one of the most successful public-private fundraising partnerships for the National Park Service to date—$56 million in improvements await travelers at the base of the sculpture, including new theaters, viewing terraces, interpretive exhibits, walking trails, and concession facilities.

There is little doubt that, had some thoughtful South Dakota leaders not preserved 83 square miles of the Black Hills as **Custer State Park** more than 75 years ago, it would have become a national park. The area has too many incredible

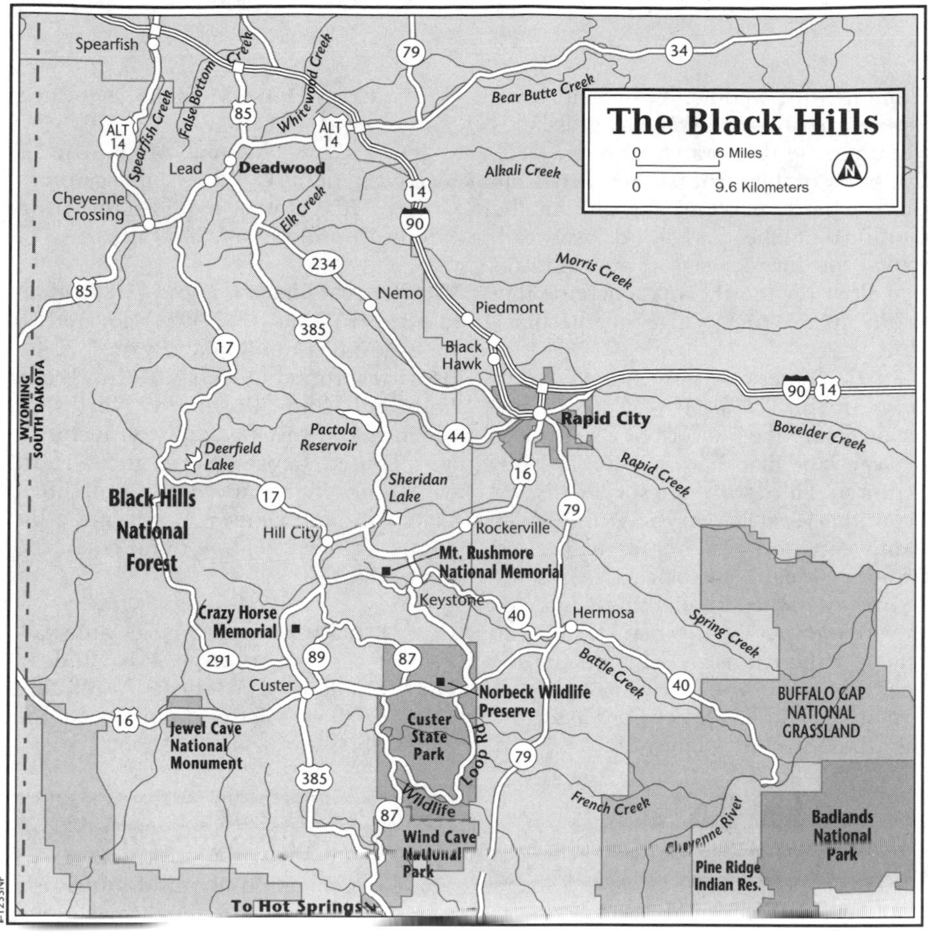

natural attractions and recreational opportunities to be dismissed, or missed on a visit to the area.

As the "crown jewel" of South Dakota's state park system, Custer State Park offers 73,000 acres of prime Black Hills real estate, the largest and most diverse population of wildlife, the best accommodations and facilities, and the most memorable natural resources of any park in the state.

Located east of the town of Custer, the park is home to four distinctive resorts, fishing lakes, wildlife loops, campgrounds, scenic drives, and granite spires so impressive that they make you want to get out of the car and walk the forest floor. Alternating between rolling meadows and foothills, pine forests, and the giant fingerlike granite spires of the Needles, Custer State Park is a must on any Black Hills itinerary.

With 81 miles of mapped passageway, Wind Cave is one of the longest caves in the world. And, with each succeeding expedition, the interconnecting network of known passages continues to grow, sometimes by a few paces, other times by several hundred feet. Even after more than 100 years, there is still something to discover in the darkened depths of **Wind Cave National Park.** Barometric wind studies conducted by the U.S. Geological Survey estimate that approximately 5% of the total cave has been discovered.

But there's a great deal more to Wind Cave than just its underground geological wonders. Aboveground, 28,295 acres of rolling prairie and ponderosa pine forests are littered with wildflowers and teeming with wildlife. Bison and antelope graze on the park's lush grasslands while prairie dogs watch from the relative safety of their "towns." In the fall, elk can be herd "bugling" throughout the confines of the park, and overhead, watch for hawks, eagles, and vultures that float on the thermal currents that rise from the rocky ridges of the Black Hills.

In the limestone labyrinth that rests below the Black Hills, Jewel Cave is a mysterious mazelike network of caverns and passageways that have yet to be fully explored. Filled with rare specimens and beautiful jewel-like crystals, this dark, damp cave may well represent the last frontier for earthly explorers.

In a time when satellites have mapped the topography of the planet, and can read the license plate of a car or the headline of a newspaper lying on a park bench, places like **Jewel Cave** truly are the "underground wilderness."

Just the Facts

GETTING THERE & GATEWAYS

Rapid City is the most popular gateway to the Black Hills and its bountiful selection of national and state parks, monuments, and memorials.

The most direct route to the Black Hills by car is I-90. To reach **Mount Rushmore,** take Exit 57 to U.S. 16 (Mount Rushmore Road) and continue approximately 23 miles southwest of Rapid City to the memorial entrance.

Custer State Park is accessible via S. Dak. 79 and S. Dak. 36 from the east, U.S. 16A from the north and west, and S. Dak. 87 from the north and south. It's located right between Mount Rushmore and Wind Cave.

Wind Cave National Park is best accessed via U.S. 385 north of Hot Springs, South Dakota, or S. Dak. 87 from Custer State Park, which shares its southern boundary with Wind Cave's northern perimeter. It's about an hour's drive south from Mount Rushmore.

The **Crazy Horse Memorial** is located 5 miles north of Custer on U.S. 16/385.

Jewel Cave National Monument is located right off U.S. 16, 13 miles west of Custer. It's almost equidistant from Mount Rushmore or Wind Cave.

The Nearest Airport. **Rapid City Regional Airport** (☎ **605/393-9924**), located 10 miles southeast of Rapid City on U.S. 44, provides direct access to the Black Hills and Mount Rushmore. **Northwest Airlines, Skywest** (a Delta connection), and **United Express** serve the airport with daily flights to Minneapolis, Salt Lake City, and Denver. You'll find a list of the airlines' toll-free numbers in the appendix.

Renting a Car. Rental vehicles are available at the airport from **Avis, Budget, Hertz, National,** and **Thrifty.** You'll find a list of their toll-free numbers in the appendix.

GETTING INFORMATION BEFORE YOUR TRIP

To get information about Mount Rushmore, contact the **Superintendent, Mount Rushmore National Memorial,** P.O. Box 268, Keystone, SD 57751-0268 (☎ **605/574-2523**). Mount Rushmore has a page on the National Park Service Web site at **www.nps.gov/moru**.

To get information about **Custer State Park,** contact the park directly at HC83, Box 70, Custer, SD 57730-9705 (☎ **605/255-4515**); or the **Division of Parks and Recreation,** Department of Game, Fish and Parks, 523 E. Capitol Ave., Pierre, SD 57501-3182 (☎ **605/773-3391**). The park has a Web site at **www.state.sd.us/state/executive/tourism/sdparks/custer/custer.htm**.

To get information about Wind Cave, contact the Superintendent, **Wind Cave National Park,** RR1, P.O. Box 190-WCNP, Hot Springs, SD 57747-9430 (☎ **605/745-4600**). Wind Cave has a page on the National Park Service Web site at **www.nps.gov/wica**.

To get info about Jewel Cave, contact the **Superintendent, Jewel Cave National Monument,** RR1, Box 60 AA, Custer, SD 57730 (☎ **605/673-2288**). Jewel Cave has a page on the National Park Service Web site at **www.nps.gov/jeca**.

To get information about Crazy Horse, contact the **Crazy Horse Memorial,** Avenue of the Chiefs, Custer, SD 57730-9506 (☎ **605/673-4681**).

For information about the entire area, contact **South Dakota Tourism,** 711 E. Wells Ave., Pierre, SD 57501-3369 (☎ **605/773-3301;** fax 605/773-3256); or the **Black Hills, Badlands & Lake Association,** 900 Jackson Blvd., Rapid City, SD 57702-2583 (☎ **605/341-1462**).

SEASONS & CLIMATE

Summer daytime temperatures in the Black Hills average around 80°F and higher, so comfortable clothing, a hat, and sunscreen are advised. Temperatures often drop rapidly after sunset, particularly in the mountains. In the fall, sunny skies and crisp temperatures can make for pleasant traveling conditions, though snowstorms may occur as early as September in higher elevations.

Winter temperatures average 40° to –20°F. Beware of icy road conditions and limited services during winter. Plan accordingly. Even in spring, weather can often be cold and wet. Pack warm clothing and rain gear.

Visiting Mount Rushmore National Memorial

Widely regarded as one of the man-made wonders of the world, Mount Rushmore is as much a work of art as it is an engineering marvel. Its creator, Gutzon Borglum, wanted to symbolize in stone the very spirit of a nation and, through four of its most revered leaders, its birth, growth, preservation, and development. A half century after its completion, Mount Rushmore remains one of America's most enduring icons.

> **. . . Let us place there, carved high, as close to heaven as we can, the words of our leaders, their faces, to show posterity what manner of men they were. Then breathe a prayer that these records will endure until the wind and the rain alone shall wear them away.**
>
> **—Gutzon Borglum, sculptor of Mount Rushmore**

In 1924, the renowned sculptor Gutzon (pronounced *Gut*-zun) Borglum visited the Black Hills, ready to carve a lasting legacy for himself and the nation he had come to love. Supported by state historian Doane Robinson and U.S. Sen. Peter Norbeck, Borglum surveyed the Harney Range of the Black Hills and its 17 peaks exceeding 7,000 feet. The artist hoped to locate a mountain with a suitable mass of stone, as well as a southeasterly exposure which would take advantage of the sun's rays for the greatest portion of the day. He decided on a rock outcropping named Mount Rushmore.

Progress on the memorial was frequently stalled by inclement weather and lack of funds. All told, the monument was completed at a cost of about $1 million during 6½ years of work that occurred over a 14-year period.

Plaster Portraits. Having studied under master sculptor Auguste Rodin in Paris, Borglum understood art. When he arrived at Rushmore ready to create his life's work in 1925, Borglum was 58 years old and already had created a full roster of memorials to famous Americans, including Gen. Philip Sheridan, Gen. Robert E. Lee, and Abraham Lincoln. Relying on his independent study of the four presidents, as well as life masks, paintings, photographs and descriptions of others, Borglum created plaster sketches of the four presidents. These sketches became the models for the memorial, and copies of each president's likeness were always on display on the mountain as a guide for the workmen.

Using a method of measurement called "pointing," Borglum taught his crews to measure the models, multiply by 12, and transfer the calibrations to the mountain carving. Using a simple ratio of 1:12, 1 inch on the model would equal 1 foot on the mountain.

Borglum and his dedicated crew used dynamite to carve more than 90% of the memorial. Powdermen became so skilled in the use of dynamite that they could grade the contours of the cheeks, chin, nose, and eyebrows to within inches of the finished surface. Skilled drillers used bumper bits and pneumatic drills to complete each portrait, leaving the surfaces of the presidents' faces as smooth as a concrete sidewalk. Up close, the pupils of each of the presidents' eyes are actually shallow recessions with projecting shafts of granite. From a distance, this unlikely shape makes the eyes sparkle. Several men were injured while working at Mount Rushmore, but miraculously, no one was killed during its construction.

As work neared completion in March 1941, Borglum died in a Chicago hospital at age 74. His son, Lincoln, carried on the work for another 6 months, but that work was soon interrupted by the winds of war. On October 31, as war clouds rumbled over Europe, the younger Borglum and his crew turned off the drills and removed the last scaffolding from the sculpture, returning the mountain to the eternal silence from which they had awakened it in 1927.

The untiring effort of the Borglums and their determined cadre of influential supporters resulted in a work of art for the ages. Washington, the most prominent figure in the group, symbolizes the birth of a republic founded on the principle of individual liberty; Jefferson, who managed to fund the Louisiana Purchase and balance the federal budget, signifies the growth of the United States; Lincoln, the Great Emancipator, imparts the strength of character responsible for preserving the union in the throes of its most bloody Civil War; and Theodore Roosevelt, the "Trust Buster" and friend of the common man who completed the Panama Canal and asserted America's role in the world.

Avoiding the Crowds. Peak visitation at Mount Rushmore occurs during the traditional family vacation months of June, July, and August. In the early 1990s, annual visitation exceeded 2.7 million, overtaxing facilities designed and constructed in the late 1950s to accommodate 1 million visitors per year; that problem should be alleviated with the expanded visitor facilities due to open in 1998.

When travel patterns and weather are considered, the ideal times to visit Mount Rushmore are April and May, as well as September and October. Although spring months can be wet and cold, Fall visits can be ideal due to the Hills' dry weather patterns. The varied mix of trees and plant life found in the alpine meadows and creek-carved canyons also makes the Black Hills a popular destination for avid "leaf-peepers."

The ideal time to view the sculpture is daybreak, when the golden orb of the sun crawls out of the morning mist of the Badlands—80 miles east of Mount Rushmore—and slaps its warm blanket around the wakened images of the four presidents. Few vacationers are awake at sunrise, making it among the best times to enjoy a more contemplative and less crowded experience at Mount Rushmore. And, there may be no finer setting for breakfast than the park's Buffalo Dining Room, which affords a commanding view of the presidents.

ESSENTIALS

Visitor Center. Mount Rushmore is open 24 hours a day, year-round. The **Information Center,** located just inside the entrance to the memorial, is open every day of the year (except December 25) from 8am to 5pm in winter, and 8am

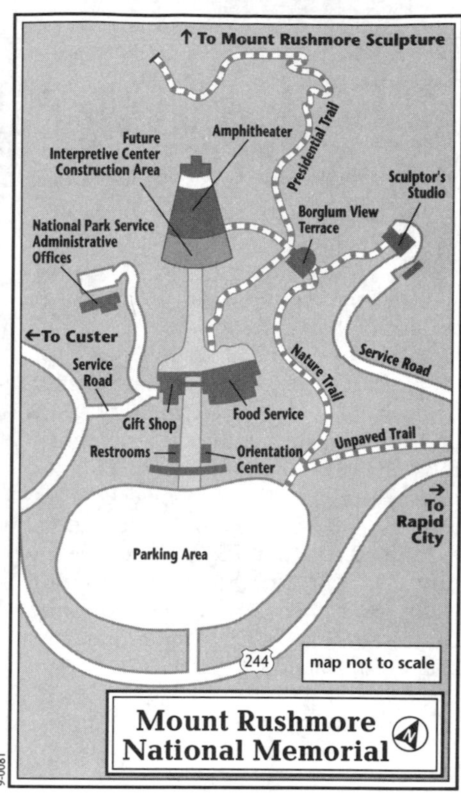

to 10pm in summer. The new **Visitor Center and Museum,** which opens in mid-June 1998, will maintain the same hours.

Entrance Fees. Mount Rushmore remains one of the few popular parks that's managed to avoid an entrance fee. However, there is a $5 fee for parking, which is funding new parking structures at the memorial. Limited free parking is available across from the main parking lot as you arrive at Rushmore from Keystone. Expect a short walk if you elect to park free.

Special Regulations & Warnings. All pets, including dogs and cats, must be under physical control of the owner, whether leashed or caged. All visitors to Mount Rushmore must stay on designated trails. Rock climbing is prohibited in the memorial without a permit. Visitors who attempt to climb the rock-talus slope at the base of the carving will be arrested and are subject to fines and jail sentences. Rangers also discourage feeding of the many squirrels, chipmunks, and birds that inhabit the park.

Useful Publications. The National Park Service makes available a number of informational pamphlets and other materials at the Information Center as you enter the memorial. A variety of books, maps, and videos are sold in the bookstore of the memorial's new Museum/Interpretive Center. All proceeds from the bookstore—operated by the non-profit Mount Rushmore History Association—are dedicated to the Park Service's interpretive programs at the memorial.

SEEING THE HIGHLIGHTS IN A DAY

Unlike many of the larger national park units in the country, a complete visit to Rushmore may be accomplished in 2 to 3 hours. Even with a new repertoire of interpretive exhibits, trails, and theaters (all of which are described below), the park can be thoroughly explored and fully appreciated in a fraction of the time of many of its western counterparts.

Particularly in the high-visitation summer months, the park is best placed at the beginning or end of a visitor's daily itinerary. Excellent light at daybreak, coupled with its scenic setting and great breakfasts in the Buffalo Dining Room, makes Mount Rushmore hard to beat for the first stop of the day. The patriotic ranger program and dramatic lighting ceremony, held nightly at 9pm from mid-May through September, also make the memorial memorable at night.

EXPLORING THE PARK BY CAR

While Mount Rushmore is best enjoyed on foot, many visitors overlook an impressive view of the sculpture that is best reached by car. After leaving the park's parking lot, turn right on S. Dak. 244 and proceed west then northwest around the memorial. Less than a mile from the parking lot you'll discover the proud profile of George Washington in the upper right corner of your windshield. While

Tips from the Park Superintendent

After a dozen years at Mount Rushmore National Memorial, Superintendent Dan Wenk will see the massive mountain memorial in an entirely new light when expanded facilities open in June 1998. So will more than 2 million foreign and domestic visitors. "The old experience was basically a 13-minute movie and a quick look at the mountain carving. The new experience includes two new theaters, 21 new interpretive and educational exhibits, a Presidential Trail, new restaurant and gift areas, and more importantly, a richer and more profound understanding of the forces that have shaped this nation."

The list of improvements that awaits visitors in 1998 is impressive: A $10 million concession facility, a $4 million Visitor Center and Museum, a $3.5 million amphitheater, a $2 million Information Center, and a $500,000 trail.

The improvements are the result of the Mount Rushmore Preservation Fund, a nationwide campaign that has raised $25 million to preserve the sculpture, stage its formal dedication, and enhance the interpretive opportunities at the memorial. Contributions have been used to fund the first structural stability study in the memorial's history and revamp aging facilities designed to accommodate half of current visitation.

surveying the scene, keep an eye out for Rocky Mountain goats that frequent the memorial and the Black Elk Wilderness Area to the west.

ORGANIZED TOURS & RANGER PROGRAMS

Mount Rushmore is home to some of the most heavily attended interpretive programs in the national park system. Offerings include a variety of walks, talks, films, and special programs, including the following:

◆ A 30-minute **Nature Walk** leads to the Sculptor's Studio, with frequent stops to discuss the area's flora, fauna, and geology. The walking tour ends at the historic studio in time for the Studio Talk.

◆ The 15-minute **Studio Talk** (open summer only) at the 1939 Sculptor's Studio examines techniques used by the artist to carve the memorial, as well as the original tools and actual plaster models employed in its construction.

◆ **Amphitheater Programs** are extremely popular and often patriotic. Depending on the timing of your visit, you could be treated to a solemn ceremony, a full-fledged celebration, or an exciting musical presentation. The amphitheater has hosted a wide array of activities, including a concert by the Mormon Tabernacle Choir, the taping of daytime soap operas such as *General Hospital,* a reading by the late Jimmy Stewart, naturalization ceremonies for new U.S. citizens, and dozens of speeches by world leaders, including Presidents Franklin Roosevelt, Eisenhower, and Bush, and former Canadian Prime Minister Brian Mulroney.

◆ There is a regular **30-minute program** at the amphitheater that includes a talk and a movie about the memorial, which coincides with its dramatic lighting ceremony. The program begins at 9pm from mid-May through September and at 8pm in the spring and fall months. Visitors are encouraged to bring a light coat or sweater because even summer evenings in the Black Hills can be chilly.

◆ The sculpture is **illuminated** nightly for 1 to 2 hours all year long.

◆ A **13-minute film** narrated by noted newsman and South Dakotan

Tom Brokaw is shown continuously at the Visitor Center and Museum. Painting a broad overview of the memorial's history, construction, and subjects, the movie gives visitors a greater understanding of the colossal carving.

HISTORIC BUILDINGS & OTHER ATTRACTIONS

The 1939 **Sculptor's Studio** played an important role in the final years of the construction of Mount Rushmore. Today, the spacious studio and the artist's models it houses are integral to understanding how Borglum and his drill-dusty crew carved the sculpture from Black Hills granite. Rangers offer talks on the tools and techniques that contributed to progress on the work. Check the Information Center for scheduled programs.

After a 3-year absence, the popular **Avenue of Flags** makes its return to Mount Rushmore in 1998. Located on the walkway between the Concession Building and the new Visitor Center and Museum, the avenue features the official flags of all U.S. states, territories, districts, and commonwealths, arranged in alphabetical order.

DAY HIKES

The new **Presidential Trail** begins near the main viewing terrace, then proceeds west through the ponderosa pines to the talus slope at the base of the sculpture. It's 0.5 mile and rated easy. When completed, the improved boardwalk will circle the southeastern slope of the mountain before arriving at the Sculptor's Studio. In addition to decreasing crowding on the memorial's viewing terraces, this new wheelchair-accessible trail takes visitors into the woods and affords new vantage points from which to view the four presidents.

Visiting Custer State Park

Despite its size (as one of the largest state parks in the Lower 48), Custer State Park can become crowded. Its unique historical, cultural, and natural resources attract throngs of visitors in the summer months, who tend to crowd scenic drives, lakeshores, campgrounds, stores, and resorts.

The best times to visit the park are from April to May and September to October. Spring offers a reawakening of the grasslands and the birth of cinnamon-colored bison calves, as well as elk, deer, antelope, and other wildlife. Fall beckons the change of colors in every canyon and ravine, as well as the bugling of bull elk as they search for mates.

ESSENTIALS

Visitor Centers. The **Peter Norbeck Visitor Center,** located between the State Game Lodge and the Coolidge Inn Store on U.S. 16A, offers informational brochures, interpretive exhibits, and a variety of educational items which explore the park and its resources.

The **Wildlife Station Visitor Center** is located on the southeast part of the Wildlife Loop, and offers shade, information, and exhibits.

Entrance & Camping Fees. An annual park pass is $20; a temporary license (valid for 7 days) is $3 per person or $8 per vehicle; an off-season temporary license is $2 per person or $5 per vehicle; and a motor coach license is $1 per person per visit.

Modern campsites are $13 per unit per night; semi-modern campsites are $10; basic campsites are $6; and firewood may be purchased for $2 per cubic foot.

Special Regulations & Warnings. The park's biggest attraction may be its 1,500 head of bison. Remember that all animals in the park are wild and sometimes dangerous. In particular, despite their size and apparent calm, bison are extremely fast and can be lethal if provoked, so give them plenty of space. Campers and hikers should never drink water from lakes, streams, or springs.

Crazy Horse Memorial

Known by locals as the "Fifth Face" in the Black Hills, the sculpture of the legendary Lakota leader Crazy Horse has come to life.

Carving began with the dedication of the work on June 3, 1948. A half century later, work continues on what will be the world's largest work of art. Begun by the late sculptor Korczak Ziolkowski (Jewel-*cuff*-ski), and carried on by his widow and children, the mountain sculpture is dedicated to all Native Americans.

"My fellow chiefs and I would like the white man to know the red man has great heroes, too," Sioux Chief Henry Standing Bear wrote Ziolkowski in 1939, inviting him to carve the mountain memorial in the Black Hills. Seven years later, the sculptor agreed and began carving the colossal work.

When completed, Crazy Horse will sit astride his mount, pointing over his stallion's head to the sacred Black Hills. So large is the sculpture (563 feet high) that the four presidents on Mount Rushmore would fit in the horse's head.

Visitors driving by the site on U.S. 16/385, 5 miles north of the town of Custer, often hear dynamite blasts, a surefire signal that work on the mountain carving is progressing. When night blasts are detonated, they tend to be among the most impressive events in the Black Hills.

In addition to viewing the carving in progress and watching an audiovisual display about the work, visitors may stop in at the **Indian Museum of North America at Crazy Horse,** which is home to one of the most extensive collections of Native American artifacts in the country. The museum's gift shop features authentic Native American–made items.

Useful Publications. The South Dakota Game, Fish and Parks Department provides a number of helpful brochures for the park, each of which is available at the Peter Norbeck Visitor Center and at park headquarters. In addition, the park's newspaper, ***Tatanka,*** provides information on the park's resorts and activities. The newspaper is available at each park entrance station, the visitor center, and the park headquarters.

SEEING THE HIGHLIGHTS IN A DAY

Of all the state and federal parks in South Dakota, Custer State Park may be the most difficult to see in only a day. Three trademark scenic drives, numerous hiking trails and nature walks, historic sites, wildlife loops, resorts, and some of the most spectacular scenery in the West tend to slow down all travelers in the park.

If you only have a day, try the 18-mile **Wildlife Loop** (described in the next section). The observation deck of the **Mount Coolidge Fire Tower** and also the historic **Gordon Stockade** are also popular draws. If you have time, take a hike, perhaps on the popular trail to the **Cathedral Spires.**

EXPLORING THE PARK BY CAR

When you're driving Custer State Park, it's important that you keep an eye on the road and not your watch. Winding roads make travel through the park much slower than in other areas of the state. So please plan travel accordingly.

For a first-class sightseeing excursion, pick any of the park's three scenic drives: the Needles Highway, the Wildlife Loop Road, or the Iron Mountain Road. Each of these winding drives is enjoyed at a slower pace—generally 25 m.p.h. or slower.

Needles Highway. This is a 14-mile mesmerizing journey through pine and spruce forests, meadows surrounded by birch and quaking aspen, and giant granite spires that reach to the sky. Visitors pass the picturesque waters of Sylvan Lake, through tunnels, and near a unique rock formation called the "Needle's Eye."

Wildlife Loop Road. An 18-mile drive through open grasslands and pine-clad hills—an area that is home to most of the park's wildlife. Count pronghorn, bison, white-tailed deer and mule deer, elk, coyote, begging burros, prairie dogs, eagles, hawks, and other birds. The best wildlife viewing time is early morning and evening, when animals are most active. Stop by the Wildlife Station Visitor Center on the southeast part of the loop for information and interesting exhibits.

Iron Mountain Road. Although only a portion of this scenic roadway rests in Custer State Park, it ranks as a must-see on any South Dakota visit. The winding road runs between Mount Rushmore and the junction of U.S. 16A and S. Dak. 36. Along the route are wildfire exhibits, wooden pig-tail bridges, pullouts with wonderful views, and tunnels that frame the four presidents at Mount Rushmore.

Be Aware: Tunnels on Iron Mountain Road (U.S. 16A) are 12 feet, 6 inches high and 13 feet, 6 inches wide. Tunnels on the Needles Highway/Sylvan Lake Road (S. Dak. 87) are as low as 10 feet, 8 inches and as narrow as 8 feet, 7 inches.

DAY HIKES

Custer State Park is home to a wide variety of hiking experiences, ranging from short nature walks to backcountry treks through some of the grandest scenery anywhere. A 22-mile segment of the South Dakota Centennial Trail, the **Harney Peak Summit Trail,** extends through Custer State Park. The **Cathedral Spires Trail** is also a popular choice. Be aware that most trails are open to mountain bikers, too.

Visiting Wind Cave National Park

For several centuries, Native Americans have told stories of holes in the Black Hills through which the wind would blow and howl. But the first recorded discovery of Wind Cave came in 1881 when brother Jesse and Tom Bingham were lured to the cave by a whistling noise. As the legend goes, the wind was rushing from the cave entrance with such force that it blew Tom's hat right off his head.

A few days later, when Jesse returned to the cave to show this phenomenon to friends, he was surprised to find that the wind had shifted directions and his hat was sucked into the cave. A hundred years later, we know that the direction of the wind is related to the difference in atmospheric pressure between the cave and the surface.

J.D. McDonald was the first person to attempt to establish a tourist attraction at Wind Cave, complete with stagecoach transportation, a hotel, and gift shop. He did this primarily because there were no valuable mineral deposits in the cave to mine. But "ownership" of the cave came into question, and the matter soon entered a courtroom. The controversy caught the attention of the Department of the Interior, which decided in December 1899 that no party had a claim to Wind Cave. In 1901, the department

> **. . . we made our way down the stairway against the very strong wind and then began our descent proper, into the wonderful, indescribably wonderful cave—down, down into the very bowels of the earth.**
>
> **—An early explorer at Wind Cave**

Tips from the Park Superintendent

Wind Cave National Park Superintendent Jimmy Taylor loves where he works.

"This is truly an amazing park," says Taylor, who moved to southwestern South Dakota 5 years ago from Colorado National Monument. "You can see and hear wildlife here. We have 300 to 400 head of elk, 300 bison, 125 antelope, two highways, and two all-weather gravel roads that make this park very accessible and suitable to the family sedan."

Wind Cave is "an intimate park" where road-weary travelers can put the brakes on and enjoy plant and animal life at its best, Taylor says. Visitors often settle back and just watch prairie dogs build their colony-like "towns" or bison graze on the prairie grasses. In fall, Taylor says there's nothing quite like the sound of a lonely bull elk bugling from a rocky ridge in the park.

And beneath this remarkable place, says Taylor, is an underground wilderness whose depths have only been guessed at, and whose complexity we are only beginning to understand.

"Imagine," the superintendent says, "that only a few hundred feet underground there are spaces people have never seen, and perhaps, may never see. Think, that every time someone crawls through a hole or peaks into the next opening, they may literally be the first person in the history of mankind who has ever seen it."

withdrew all the land around the cave from homesteading.

On January 9, 1903, Pres. Theodore Roosevelt signed the bill that established Wind Cave as the seventh national park in the country, and the first one created to protect the underground resources of a cave. In 1913 and 1914, the American Bison Society assisted in reestablishing a bison herd at Wind Cave through the donation of 14 head from the New York Zoological Society. Also arriving in the park were 21 elk from Wyoming and 13 pronghorn antelope from Alberta, Canada. Today, Wind Cave is home to 350 bison, as well as large herds of elk and antelope.

Avoiding the Crowds. With more than 28,000 acres, two paved highways, two all-weather gravel roads, eight excellent trails, backcountry camping, and plenty of room to roam, avoiding the crowds in Wind Cave National Park is almost as easy as smiling.

July and August are the busiest months at Wind Cave. Annual visitation at the park averages 700,000, while about 100,000 people participate in a cave tour each year. When planning daily itineraries, include Wind Cave in either the early morning or late afternoon, when visitation is lowest and wildlife is most active.

ESSENTIALS

Visitor Center. The visitor center (located right off U.S. 385), which is open year-round (except Thanksgiving and Christmas), has books, brochures, exhibits, and slide programs about the cave and other park resources. Cave tour information and tickets also are available, and schedules of activities, including talks and nature walks, are posted. There are vending machines for snacks and soft drinks.

Entrance & Camping Fees. Wind Cave National Park does not charge an entrance fee. It does, however, charge a fee for cave tours, ranging from $4 ($1 with a Golden Age Passport) for a simple

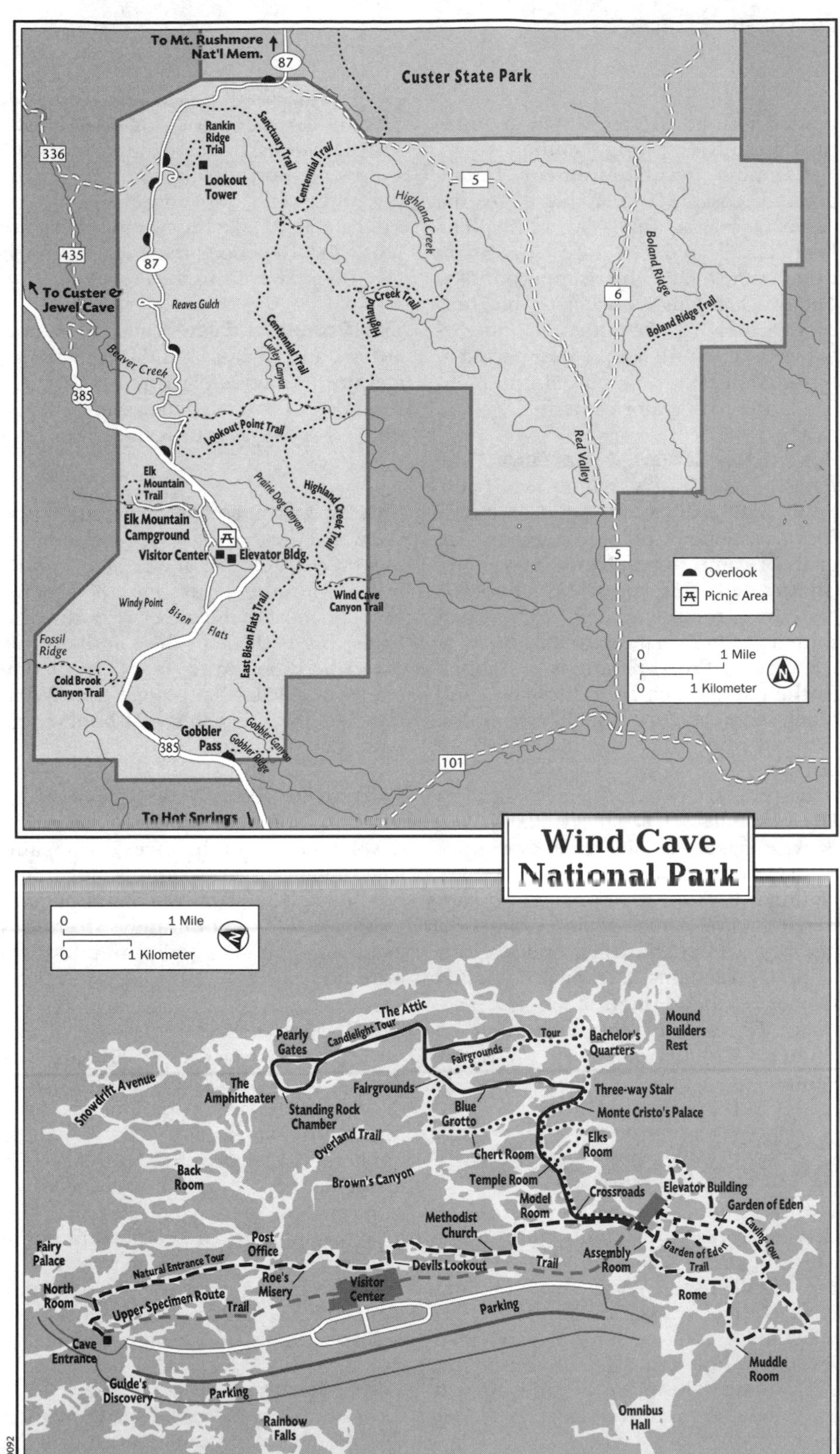

To Mt. Rushmore Nat'l Mem.
87
Custer State Park
Rankin Ridge Trial
Lookout Tower
Sanctuary Trail
Centennial Trail
336
5
Highland Creek
Boland Ridge
435
87
To Custer & Jewel Cave
Reaves Gulch
Highland Creek Trail
6
Boland Ridge Trail
Centennial Trail
Curley Canyon
Beaver Creek
385
Lookout Point Trail
Red Valley
Elk Mountain Trail
Prairie Dog Canyon
Highland Creek Trail
Elk Mountain Campground
Visitor Center
Elevator Bldg.
5
Overlook
Picnic Area
Windy Point
Bison
Flats
Wind Cave Canyon Trail
East Bison Flats Trail
Fossil Ridge
Cold Brook Canyon Trail
0
1 Mile
0
1 Kilometer
Gobbler Pass
Gobbler Canyon
Gobbler Ridge
385
101
To Hot Springs
Wind Cave National Park
0
1 Mile
0
1 Kilometer
The Attic
Candlelight Tour
Pearly Gates
Tour
Bachelor's Quarters
Mound Builders Rest
Fairgrounds
Snowdrift Avenue
The Amphitheater
Fairgrounds
Three-way Stair
Standing Rock Chamber
Blue Grotto
Monte Cristo's Palace
Overland Trail
Elks Room
Chert Room
Back Room
Brown's Canyon
Temple Room
Crossroads
Elevator Building
Model Room
Garden of Eden
Methodist Church
Caving Tour
Fairy Palace
Post Office
Assembly Room
Garden of Eden Trail
Natural Entrance Tour
Devils Lookout
Trail
Roe's Misery
Visitor Center
North Room
Upper Specimen Route
Trail
Rome
Parking
Cave Entrance
Muddle Room
Guide's Discovery
Parking
Omnibus Hall
Rainbow Falls
9-0092

guided tour to $15 for a 4-hour introduction to basic caving techniques.

Camping in Elk Mountain Campground costs $10 per night in the summer season (mid-May to September), and is reduced to $5 per night other times that the campground is open; all camping is on a first-come, first-served basis. Backcountry camping is allowed at Wind Cave; a free permit is required and must be picked up in person at the park visitor center.

Special Regulations & Warnings. The danger of wildfire at Wind Cave is generally high year-round. Build fires only in the campground and only in fire grills or camp stoves. Never leave a fire unattended. Pets must be physically restrained at all times. Pets are not permitted in buildings, the backcountry, or the cave. Off-road driving is prohibited in the park. Watch for rattlesnakes and black widow spiders, which favor prairie dog burrows and may strike without warning.

Useful Publications. The National Park Service makes available a wide variety of informational handouts at Wind Cave National Park on topics including park history, cave tours, hiking, camping, geology, wildlife, bird life, prairie grasses and ecosystems, and environmental concerns. In addition, the park produces ***Passages,*** a free visitor guide to Wind Cave that is available at the visitor center.

SEEING THE HIGHLIGHTS IN A DAY

Even with more than 44 square miles of flowing forest, grasslands, and quiet canyons, visitors can appreciate most of the highlights of Wind Cave National Park in a day or less. You'll have time to take both a cave tour, most of which take less than 2 hours, and a drive around the park to view the bison and elk. If you have time, then get out on one of the park's hiking trails.

ORGANIZED CAVE TOURS

The park offers five cave tours during the summer season and one tour the remainder of the year. More adventurous cavers will be able to take the two tours that are limited to 10 people; these will definitely take them away from the crowds.

The Garden of Eden Tour. This tour enters and leaves Wind Cave by an elevator and takes participants past representative features of the cave. With 150 stairs, this 1-hour tour is the park's least strenuous.

Natural Entrance Tour. Beginning at the walk-in entrance to the cave and leaving by elevator, this moderately strenuous 75-minute tour has 300 stairs (though most of the these are down) and leads visitors through the middle of the cave where box work, made up of thin blades of calcite that project from Wind Cave's walls and ceiling in a honeycomb pattern, is abundant.

Fairgrounds Tour. This tour includes some of the larger rooms found in the developed area of the cave. Participants view many cave formations, including box work. The tour enters and exits by elevator. This moderately strenuous excursion has 450 stairs and lasts 90 minutes.

Candlelight Tour. This is one of the most popular tours, especially for children over 8. Trekking through a less-developed, unlighted part of the cave, tour participants each carry a candle bucket and experience the cave by candlelight. Shoes with nonslip soles are required; no sandals are allowed. This tour is limited to 10 people (minimum age is 8). This strenuous tour covers 1 mile of rugged trail and lasts 2 hours. Reservations, available up to 1 month before the tour, are strongly advised.

Caving Tour. You can also explore Wind Cave away from the established trails. On this 4-hour adventure, visitors will be

Deadwood: The Wildest & Woolliest Town in the West

There was a time when it wasn't safe to walk the cobblestone streets of the Black Hills' original sin city. But that was a thousand gunfights and barroom brawls ago, when Deadwood was known as the wildest, wickedest, woolliest town in the West, where Wild Bill Hickok was gunned down and where Calamity Jane Canary claimed she could out-drink, out-swear, and out-spit any man.

Today, the sounds of slot machines and street-side barkers have replaced the sporadic gunshots, crunching blows, and general rowdiness of a century ago, where miners, gamblers, and painted ladies all searched for their pot of gold. They found gold, of course, but seldom did they retain it.

The city's merchants, bankers, and saloon-keepers, however, cleverly invested their money in beautiful Victorian buildings and residences that today stand as testament to a richer time.

Although Deadwood was labeled "a disaster" by historic preservation officials less than 10 years ago, it's alive and kicking today. This is due to a great extent to limited stakes gaming, approved by South Dakota voters in 1989 to generate revenues that would then be dedicated to restoring and preserving this mile-high community.

Just 8 years (and $85 million) later, state and national historic preservation officials call Deadwood's metamorphosis "a miracle." Brick streets, period lighting, and colorful trolleys greet visitors, who spend hours ducking in doorways and trying their luck in the town's 80—yes *80*—gaming halls. In addition to gaming action, Deadwood is known to have many of the finest restaurants and hotels in the state.

For more information on accommodations, walking tours, museums, attractions, special events, and gaming packages, contact the **Deadwood Chamber of Commerce & Visitor Bureau** (☎ **888/433-2396**), or stop by the **History and Information Center** in the classic train depot at 3 Siever St.

introduced to basic, safe caving practices. You need to wear old clothes and gloves, since much of the tour is spent crawling. Long pants, long-sleeve shirts, and sturdy, lace-up boots or shoes with nonslip soles are a must. The park provides hard hats, lights, and kneepads. Do not bring jewelry, watches, or other valuables on this tour. This tour is limited to 10 people and the minimum age is 16. (Signed consent forms from a parent or guardian are required for 16- and 17-year-olds.) Reservations, which are available 1 month before the tour, are required.

For People With Disabilities. The visitor center and the cave are accessible to people with limited mobility. Call ahead (☎ **605/745-4600**) to make special arrangements or inquire about a special tour at the information desk. Some areas of the cave are accessible to wheelchairs. Fees are charged for special services.

EXPLORING THE PARK BY CAR

The rolling prairies of western South Dakota run smack into the ponderosa pine forests of the Black Hills in Wind

Cave National Park. The park's highways and backcountry roads provide the scenic backdrop for some of the best wildlife viewing opportunities in the region. Bison, pronghorn, elk, and other wildlife abound in this rugged preserve, and you'll be able to see many of them as you drive down through Custer State Park on S. Dak. 87 to Wind Cave. Several scenic roadways lead through the Black Hills to Wind Cave. Roadside sightseers will find the **Wildlife Loop Road, Iron Mountain Road,** and the **Needles Highway** particularly enjoyable. All of these are in Custer State Park, just north of Wind Cave National Park and are described in the preceding section.

One warning: Tunnels on Iron Mountain Road (U.S. 16A) are 12 feet, 6 inches high and 13 feet, 6 inches wide. Tunnels on the Needles Highway/ Sylvan Lake Road (S. Dak. 87) are as low as 10 feet, 8 inches and as narrow as 8 feet, 7 inches.

RANGER PROGRAMS

Park rangers provide a number of special talks and programs at Wind Cave. Topics range from local wildlife, plants and geology to area history and spelunking and cave surveying. Campfire programs are conducted most evenings during the summer months. There is usually a ranger-guided **prairie hike** conducted a 9am daily during the summer months, which leaves from the visitor center and lasts about 2 hours; since the location and time of this hike change fairly often, you should check with the visitor center for specific times, and also for the times and topics of other ranger talks and programs.

DAY HIKES

More than 30 miles of trails crisscross the backcountry of Wind Cave National Park. Several can be combined to create interesting round-trip hikes in the park. Or, you may want to leave the trails and hike a ridgeline, through a canyon, or across an open prairie bordered by ponderosa pine. Backcountry camping is permitted in the northwestern portion of the park with a free permit that may be obtained at the visitor center or either of the Centennial trailheads.

Park handouts also provide information on more than a half-dozen other trails ranging from 1.4 miles to 8.6 miles.

Centennial Trail

6 miles one way. Moderate. Access: The trailhead is located on S. Dak. 87, 0.7 mile north of its intersection with U.S. 385.

Wind Cave provides the southern terminus for the 110-mile-long Centennial Trail, built in honor of South Dakota's centennial in 1989. The trail leads through the heart of the Black Hills before ending at Bear Butte State Park near Sturgis. Wind Cave hosts a 6-mile section of the Centennial Trail, where hikers can explore the diversity of the park. The trail crosses the prairie, climbs the foothills and forested ridges, then examines the wetter, riparian habitat of Beaver Creek.

Rankin Ridge Nature Trail

0.75 mile RT. Easy. Access: The trailhead is located at the Rankin Ridge Parking Lot.

This loop trail leads to the highest point in the park, and is one of Wind Cave's most popular. You can stop at the lookout tower, about halfway around the loop. Booklets are available at the trailhead.

Elk Mountain Nature Trail

0.5 mile one way. Easy. Access: The trailhead is located at the Elk Mountain Campground.

This interpretive trail explores an ecotone, or meeting zone, where prairie and forest converge. Booklets are available at the trailhead. It's a short, easy hike.

Visiting Jewel Cave National Monument

The exploration of Jewel Cave began about 1900 when two South Dakota prospectors, Frank and Albert Michaud, and a companion, Charles Bush, happened to hear wind rushing through a hole in the rocks in Hell Canyon. After enlarging the hole, they discovered a cave full of sparkling crystals. The entrepreneurs filed a mining claim on the "Jewel Lode," but they uncovered no valuable minerals, so they attempted to turn the cave into a tourist attraction instead. The business was never a success, but the cave's uniqueness did attract attention, and in 1908 Pres. Theodore Roosevelt established Jewel Cave National Monument to protect the small but remarkable cave.

A half century later, exploration of the cave intensified. Led by the husband and wife team of Herb and Jan Conn, spelunkers discovered new wonders and explored and mapped many new miles of passageway. Today, the cave is among the longest on earth and its distinct and rare formations rank it as a world-class cave.

When first asked to consider a trek below the surface, the Conns were reluctant. But after their first excursion into the underworld, the couple could not be turned away. In more than 2 decades of spelunking in Jewel Cave, the Conns logged 708 trips into the cave and 6,000 hours of exploration and mapping. Their efforts proved that Jewel Cave was among the most extensive and complex cave ecosystems in the world, filled with scenic and scientific wonders.

The explorers discovered chambers with exquisite calcite crystals and other rare specimens. One room mapped by the Conns, the **Formation Room,** is now a highlight of the scenic tour conducted by National Park Service rangers. They also found rooms as large as 150 by 200 feet, passageways as long as 3,200 feet, and a place where the cave wind blows at speeds of 32 miles per hour. In 1980, after discovering more than 65 miles of passageways, the Conns retired, and a new generation of spelunkers pushed the known boundaries of the cave to well over 110 miles.

When the Conns said, "We are still just standing on the threshold," they could not have known how accurate they were. Studies by the U.S. Geological Survey have since attempted to determine the amount of passageway in the cave by measuring the volume of air leaving or entering the cave, depending on the barometric pressure outside. Conclusions of those studies indicate that known passageways at Jewel Cave constitutes less than 5% of what actually exists in the quiet darkness below the Black Hills.

Only Mammoth Cave in Kentucky and Optimisticeskaja in the Ukraine are longer than Jewel Cave. Explorations of Jewel Cave in 1997 moved the cave from fourth- to third-longest, surpassing Holloch Cave in Switzerland.

Known for its calcite nailhead and dogtooth spar crystal, intricately constructed box work and delicate decorations known as frostwork, Jewel Cave also is home to some extremely rare and unusual specimens. The Cave's hydromagnesite "balloons," fragile silvery bubbles that look as if they might pop any minute, have been found in just a handful of other caves. Scintillites, reddish rocks coated with sparkling clear quartz crystals, were unknown until they were discovered in Jewel Cave. One particularly intriguing mineral, gypsum, combines with time and the ceaseless presence of seeping water in the cave to assume the shape of flowers, needles, spiders, and cottony beards that sway from the heat of an explorer's lamp.

Avoiding the Crowds. The highest visitation at Jewel Cave occurs in the

> **The excitement of discovery, the elation and despair. The thrill of pushing forward to discover what is there.**
>
> **—Jan Conn, Jewel Cave Explorer, 1975**

Tips from the Chief of Interpretation

Fall, winter, and spring are ideal times to visit Jewel Cave National Monument, according to Chief of Interpretation Karen Rosga. Even with arctic blasts on the surface, temperatures within the cave are constant at 49°, with humidity averaging 88% to 90%.

"In the middle of winter, it can actually be quite pleasant in the cave," says Rosga, who worked as a seasonal ranger for 8 years before becoming a permanent National Park Service employee a decade ago. She said annual visitation at the monument averages 150,000 people.

"To this point, we have been very successful in developing a visitor experience that allows people to enjoy the cave in a relatively pristine state," Rosga adds. "Jewel Cave is one of the most structurally complex caves in the world and it is still being explored. This is not a cave that has been fully mapped and it's probable that it will not be fully explored in any of our lifetimes."

For travelers with children over 6, Rosga is quick to recommend the "adventurous experience" of a candlelight tour into the cave, the park's **Junior Ranger Program,** and the variety of surface programs that augment the cave tours. In spring, the park is a popular field trip destination for area schools, she noted.

traditional summer season of June, July, and August. With 1,274 acres above the surface and annual visitation of approximately 150,000, Jewel Cave is rarely overcrowded, even at the height of the tourist season. However, because space on some scenic tours is limited and 92,000 park visitors participate in a cave tour annually, visitors should anticipate a wait as long as 90 minutes to be able to enter the cave. If you want to keep your wait to a minimum, arrive early in the morning or late in the day.

ESSENTIALS

Visitor Center. The park visitor center has information on all aspects of Jewel Cave National Monument. Various books and brochures are available, and park rangers are on duty and eager to assist travelers with planning their visit, pointing out special interpretive programs, and answering any questions about the cultural, historical, and geologic resources within the park. Up-to-date cave information and tour tickets also are available at the visitor center, which is open daily from 8am, throughout the year. It closes at 4pm from October through April and has extended hours from May through September.

Entrance Fees. There is no entry fee for the national monument, but you'll pay a fee for cave tours. The **Scenic** and **Historic** tours are $6 ($3 for children under 16); the **Spelunking** tour is $18. Golden Age and Golden Access Passport-holders pay reduced tour fees.

Special Regulations & Warnings. Low-heeled, rubber-soled shoes are highly recommended because trails can be slippery; some stair-climbing is required on each tour. A jacket, sweater, or sweatshirt will keep you comfortable in the 49° year-round temperature of the cave. Persons with respiratory or heart problems, who have been recently hospitalized, or have a fear of heights or confined spaces should talk with a park ranger before selecting a tour. Damaging or even touching cave formations is prohibited due to the fragile and irreplaceable nature of the formations. Pets and smoking are not allowed in the cave. Cameras are permitted on cave tours, but tripods are not.

Useful Publications. The National Park Service makes available brochures covering a wide variety of topics at the Jewel Cave Visitor Center. Among them are pamphlets exploring bats, birds, wildflowers, surface trails, spelunking tours, and the history and exploration of the cave.

SEEING THE HIGHLIGHTS IN A DAY

There are only 2 square miles of aboveground real estate at Jewel Cave National Monument, so exploring the highlights is possible in a fraction of a day. Visitors should allocate 2 to 3 hours for a trip to the visitor center, a scenic cave tour, and a walk on one of the monument's surface tours.

CAVE TOURS

Visitors can have an adventure in Jewel Cave by taking any of the park's ranger guided cave tours. Tickets for the Scenic Tour must be purchased at the visitor center on the day of the tour. Tickets for the Historic Candlelight Tour can be purchased at the Historic Ranger Cabin, 1 mile west of the visitor center. Reservations for the Spelunking Tour are strongly encouraged and can be made up to 30 days in advance by calling, writing, or stopping by the visitor center (the number to call is ☎ **605/673-2288**). For your convenience, call the monument before visiting to determine whether special hours, activities, or tour schedules are being observed.

Scenic Tour. This 0.5-mile, 75-minute tour visits chambers decorated with calcite crystals and colorful stalactites, stalagmites, and draperies. The loop tour begins at the visitor center with an elevator ride into the cave. Tour participants take a paved, lighted path and climb up and down more than 700 stairs on this moderately strenuous journey into the underground wilderness. The tour,which is offered year-round, is conducted several times daily from May to September and is limited to 30 persons.

Historic Tour. This 0.5-mile, 105-minute tour follows in the footsteps of early Jewel Cave explorers. Tour participants see the cave's calcite-coated passageways lighted by old-style candle lanterns. This round-trip tour starts at the cave's historic entrance in Hell Canyon. Moderately strenuous with many steep stairs, this tour requires much bending and stooping. Long pants and sturdy, closed-toe shoes are highly recommended. The tour is offered several times daily from mid-June through late August and is limited to 25 persons (definitely call ahead to find out if it will be offered when you are in the area). Children under age 6 are not allowed on the Historic Tour.

Spelunking Tour. This physically and mentally challenging 0.5-mile, 4-hour tour gives participants a taste of modern-day cave crawling in a wild, undeveloped portion of Jewel Cave. The round-trip tour begins at the visitor center with an elevator ride into the cave. Old clothes, kneepads, and gloves are recommended; ankle-high laced boots with lug soles are required. The park supplies hard hats and headlamps. To qualify for the tour, participants are required to crawl through an 8½-by-24-inch concrete block tunnel. This tour is offered daily (12:30pm) from mid-June through mid-August; the limit is 10 persons (here's your chance to avoid the crowds). Children 15 years of age and younger are not allowed on the Spelunking Tour; 16- and 17-year-olds must have a parent or guardian's written permission. You can (and should) reserve your place on a tour up to 30 days in advance).

RANGER PROGRAMS

During the summer season, a number of special interpretive programs take place in the visitor center on the surface, including ranger talks, demonstrations, and guided walks. Check the visitor center for specific times, topics, and tours available during your visit.

DAY HIKES

Travelers to Jewel Cave should also take the time to experience life in the world above the cave. In the park above Jewel Cave, visitors can take a nature hike (there are two hiking trails), have a picnic, or enjoy some of the plants and wildlife that inhabit the rugged hills and canyon country of the Black Hills.

In the stillness of the ponderosa pine forest that blankets the park live mule deer, white-tailed deer, elk, porcupines, coyote, squirrels and chipmunks, marmots, and several species of birds, including golden eagles and hawks. Plants of both the prairie and the hills grow here, and in summer, wildflowers paint the landscape.

Walk on the Roof

0.25 mile RT. Easy. Access: The trail begins and ends at the visitor center.

While visiting the "roof" of Jewel Cave on this self-guided interpretive walk, you'll learn how the monument's surface and sub-surface resources interact. Interpretive trail guides for this walk are available at the information desk in the visitor center.

Canyons Trail

4 miles RT. Easy to moderate. Access: The trailhead is located at the visitor center.

This 4-mile loop trail provides the opportunity to become more familiar with surface resources and geologic features of the monument. The trail winds past several natural attractions entrusted to the National Park Service, including the limestone palisades of Hell Canyon and Lithograph Canyon, as well as the deer, birds, and wildflowers that live in the ponderosa pine forest through which the trail winds. If you want to experience a part of the Canyon Trail without going the entire distance, you might try the 1.5-mile round-trip between the visitor center and the historic area of the cave.

Guided Tours

A number of charter bus park tours and "step-on" guide services throughout the area also are available. **Gray Line of the Black Hills**, P.O. Box 1106, Rapid City, SD 57709 (☎ **800/456-4461** or 605/342-4461; fax 605/341-5152), offers bus tours of the area. Tours range in price from $15 to $40.

As does **America Tours West,** P.O. Box 867, Keystone, SD 57751-0167 (☎ **605/666-4545;** fax 605/666-4996); and **Jack Rabbit Charter & Tours,** 301 N. Dakota Ave., Sioux Falls, SD 57104 (☎ **605/335-2290;** fax 605/336-8731). Both companies offer a variety of tours in a similar price range.

Sports & Activities

Aerial Tours. If you want to see the Black Hills from above, then contact **Black Hills Balloons,** P.O. Box 210, Custer, SD 57730-0210 (☎ **605/673-2520;** fax 605/673-5075). They offer flights over the Black Hills, as well as Badlands National Park and even Devils Tower National Monument, year-round; expect to pay $165 per person for a flight.

Biking. There are more than 6,000 miles of fire trails, logging roads, and other undeveloped roads throughout the Black Hills region, so this is quickly becoming a top spot for mountain biking. Custer State Park is a prime spot for mountain biking since most park trails and roads are open to bikers. (The **Legion Lake Resort** in Custer State Park rents mountain bikes; see the complete listing under "Accommodations," below, for more information.) You can also rent a mountain bike year-round at **Golden Circle Tours,** P.O. Box 454, Custer, SD

57730 (☎ **605/673-4349;** fax 605/673-5338). Its office is located on U.S. 16A, 1 mile east of Custer. The company offers guided van tours of the area as well (see "Guided Tours," above).

Fishing. **Horsethief Lake,** below Mount Rushmore, where there is a nice National Forest Service campground (see "Camping," below, for complete information), is stocked with rainbow trout. **Center and Stockade lakes** in Custer State Park are also good fishing spots. You'll need a nonresident fishing license, which you can buy at any sporting-goods store and at many convenience stores. But many streams in this area, including **Grizzly Bear Creek,** which is behind Mount Rushmore, are full of brook trout.

Horse-Packing Trips. Several companies offer guided trail rides through the backcountry of the Black Hills. One family-run company is **Dakota Badland Outfitters,** P.O. Box 85, Custer, SD 57730-0085 (☎ **605/673-5363;** fax 206/649-4966). It conducts 4-day horse-packing trips into the Black Hills and Badlands every week during the season for $660 to $680 per person (June through August in the Black Hills, September and October in the Badlands National Park), or it can put together a custom Badlands trip for $250 per person per day. These costs include all meals. The company will even rent you a sleeping bag or pick you up at the airport for an additional charge.

Snowmobiling. There are hundreds of miles of groomed snowmobile trails in the upper Black Hills, and many guest ranches and resorts in the area rent snowmobiles to their guests. **Deadwood Gulch Resort** (see "Accommodations," below) rents snowmobiles. You can get more information on trails and companies that rent snowmobiles from **South Dakota Tourism,** 711 E. Wells Ave., Pierre, SD 57501-3369 (☎ **605/773-3301**).

Camping

While there are no campgrounds within the boundaries of Mount Rushmore National Memorial or Jewel Cave National Monument, there are several campgrounds in Custer State Park and another campground in Wind Cave National Park, not to mention privately operated campgrounds in the area and those operated by Black Hills National Forest.

The Black Hills has enough campsites to accommodate 25,000 overnight guests. Many campgrounds offer free shuttle services, nightly entertainment, pools, recreation areas, convenience stores, and horseback riding. Reservations are recommended. Choice spots are often filled by midmorning, so arriving at popular campgrounds early in the day is advised.

For more information on camping opportunities, contact **Camp South Dakota,** South Dakota Tourism, 711 Wells St., Pierre, SD 57501-3369 (☎ **605/773-3301**). For information on camping in South Dakota's state parks, contact the **Department of Game, Fish, and Parks,** 523 E. Capitol, Pierre, SD 57501-3182 (☎ **605/773-3718**). For information on National Forest Service campgrounds, contact the **Superintendent, Black Hills National Forest,** RR2, P.O. Box 200, Custer, SD 57783 (☎ **605/673-2251**).

IN WIND CAVE NATIONAL PARK

Located in the pine forests 1 mile north of the park visitor center, **Elk Mountain Campground** has 75 sites for tents and recreational vehicles. The campground is open April through October on a first-come, first-served basis; no reservations are accepted. Campers find picnic tables, fire grills, drinking water, and rest rooms. The campground fee is $10 per night per site mid-May through mid-September and $5 per night per site the remainder of the year. Park rangers give campfire programs at the amphitheater in the

Campground	Total Sites	RV Hookups	Dump Station	Toilets	Drinking Water
In Badlands National Park					
Cedar Pass	110	No	Yes	Yes	Yes
Sage Creek	15	No	No	Yes	No
Near Badlands National Park					
Badlands Ranch Resort	35	Yes	No	Yes	Yes
In Wind Cave National Park					
Elk Mountain	75	No	No	Yes	Yes
In Custer State Park					
Blue Bell	35	No	No	Yes	Yes
Center Lake	70	No	No	Yes	Yes
Game Lodge	55	No	Yes	Yes	Yes
Grace Coolidge	26	No	No	Yes	Yes
Legion Lake	25	No	No	Yes	Yes
Stockade Lake	85	No	No	Yes	Yes
Sylvan Lake	40	No	No	Yes	Yes
Black Hills National Forest					
Horsethief Lake	36	No	No	Yes	Yes
Roubaix Lake	56	No	No	Yes	Yes
Private Campgrounds in the Black Hills					
American Presidents	40	Yes	No	Yes	Yes
Berry Patch	130	Yes	Yes	Yes	Yes
Big Pine	85	Yes	No	Yes	Yes
Deadwood Gulch	107	Yes	Yes	Yes	Yes
Miners	28	Yes	No	Yes	Yes
Mount Rushmore KOA	500	Yes	Yes	Yes	Yes
Rapid City KOA	200	Yes	Yes	Yes	Yes

summer. Campers taking advantage of the backcountry are encouraged to practice low-impact camping and hiking techniques. The campground host, who can answer questions and provide assistance, resides at site no. 22 at the entrance to A Loop.

IN CUSTER STATE PARK

None of the campgrounds at Custer State Park have RV hookups. All of the campgrounds require park entrance as well as camping permits.

Each campsite at Custer State Park has a gravel or paved camping pad, a fire

Showers	Fire Pits/ Grills	Laundry	Public Phone	Reserve	Fees	Open
No	No	No	Yes	No	$10	Year-round
No	No	No	No	No	Free	Year-round
Yes	Yes	Yes	Yes	Yes	$12–$20	May 1–Sept 20
No	Yes	No	Yes	No	$10	Apr–Oct
Yes	Yes	Yes	Yes	Yes	$13	May 1–Sept 15
No	Yes	No	No	Yes	$10	May 1–Sept 15
Yes	Yes	Yes	Yes	Yes	$13	May 1–Sept 15
No	Yes	No	No	Yes	$13	May 1–Sept 15
Yes	Yes	No	Yes	Yes	$13	May 1–Sept 15
No	Yes	No	No	Yes	$13	May 1–Sept 15
Yes	Yes	Yes	Yes	Yes	$13	May 1–Sept 15
No	Yes	No	No	Yes	$14–$16	Year-round
No	Yes	No	Yes	Yes	$12	Year-round
Yes	Yes	Yes	Yes	Yes	$17–$21	May 15–Oct 1
Yes	Yes	Yes	Yes	Yes	$17.25–$23.50	Apr 1–Nov 1
Yes	Yes	Yes	Yes	Yes	$13–$17.50	May 10–Oct 1
Yes	Yes	Yes	Yes	Yes	$21	Apr 15–Oct 1
Yes	Yes	Yes	Yes	Yes	$16.50	Apr 15–Oct 15
Yes	Yes	Yes	Yes	Yes	$20.95–$28.95	May 1–Oct 1
Yes	Yes	Yes	Yes	Yes	$19.45–$25.95	Apr 15–Oct 15

grate, and a picnic table. Electric hookups are not available. About 200 campsites throughout the park may be reserved beginning January 2 for the entire season, while other sites are available on a first-come, first-served basis. The cost is $13 per night for all campgrounds, except for those at Center Lake, which cost $10 per night.

Campsites range from modern and semimodern sites, to primitive campsites located in natural areas of the park. Group camping is available at two campgrounds and the French Creek Horse

Camp is designated specifically for campers with horses.

For information or to make reservations contact **Custer State Park,** HC 83, Box 70, Custer, SD 57730 (☎ **800/710-2267** or 605/255-4515).

Blue Bell Campground, with 35 sites, is located in a mature stand of ponderosa pine near French Creek in Custer State Park, not far from the site where Lt. Col. George Armstrong Custer and his 7th Cavalry discovered gold in the Hills in 1874. There are rest rooms and showers as well as easy access to the Wildlife Loop Road, horseback riding, stream fishing, and fabulous hiking.

Game Lodge Campground is another of Custer State Park's fine campgrounds with 30 sites. This one was designed for larger RVs, but tenters will find cool, shady sites and an occasional bison along the banks of Grace Coolidge Creek. Conveniently located near the Park's Peter Norbeck Visitor Center and the State Game Lodge, where Pres. Calvin Coolidge spent his 3-month summer vacation in 1927.

Legion Lake Campground, with 25 sites, is centrally located in Custer State Park, with easy access to Harney Peak, Sylvan Lake, the Wildlife Loop, and fishing, boating, and hiking opportunities. Historic sites are within walking distance, as is the Legion Lake Resort across the highway.

You'd probably have to camp in Yosemite Valley to get a better view than the one at **Sylvan Lake Campground.** This mountain retreat is located near Harney Peak, at 7,242 feet, the highest point between the Rockies and the Swiss Alps, and affords visitors the best in Black Hills hiking, mountain climbing, and mountain biking. Just off the incredible Needles Highway. Its 40 spots fill fast, so scope out yours early in the day, pitch a tent, and go exploring.

There are also three other campgrounds in the park with more primitive facilities (no laundry, no flush toilets). These are **Center Lake,** with 70 sites, 5 miles northeast of the junction of U.S. 16A and S. Dak. 87; **Grace Coolidge,** with 26 sites, 13 miles east of Custer on U.S. 16A, just inside the park's eastern boundary; and **Stockade Lake,** with 85 sites, located just inside the park's western boundary on U.S. 16.

IN THE BLACK HILLS NATIONAL FOREST

It's possible to reserve a National Forest Service campsite, but there is a $8.65 charge for making the reservation. Contact the **National Recreation Reservation Center,** P.O. Box 900, Cumberland, MD 21501-0900 (☎ **800/280-2267;** fax 301/722-9802), or you can do it online at nrrc.com. Per night camping fees are $12 to $15 a night.

Horsethief Lake Campground, only a mile west of the four faces of freedom on Mount Rushmore, may be one of the Black Hills best-kept secrets. All 36 sites are adjacent to picturesque Horsethief Lake, where then-Pres. George Bush filled his creel with trout in 1991. At a 5,000-foot elevation, 28 sites are for tents, travel trailers, and RVs, while eight sites are for tents only. Well, to be honest, it's not exactly a secret any more, and the spaces not already reserved (up to 50% can be reserved) fill fast. Claim yours early in the day. There is a 3-day limit, and sites cost $14 per night in the RV/tent loop, $16 per night on the lakefront.

Roubaix Lake Campground, located off U.S. 385 on FDR 255, has 56 campsites nestled in a ponderosa pine forest and located next to scenic Roubaix Lake, which offers great fishing and swimming at a 4,700-foot elevation. The campground accommodates tents, travel trailers, and RVs and is popular with local residents. Spaces fill fast and can't be reserved. Claim yours early in the day. There is a 10-day limit, and sites cost $12 per night.

PRIVATE CAMPGROUNDS

American Presidents Campground, P.O. Box 446, Custer, SD 57730 (☎ **605/673-3373**), is a perfect spot for touring the southern Black Hills. Its 40 sites are located on 20 acres. The campground's 40-by-60-foot heated pool is popular, as are its free miniature golf and horseshoes. The campground also has a store, free showers, and a laundry. Fishing nearby. A 10% discount is offered on reservations made before May 15.

Berry Patch Campground, 1860 E. North St., Rapid City, SD 57701 (☎ **800/658-4566** or 605/341-5588), is the easiest campground to reach on and off I-90; it's also clean and friendly. Full hookups and drive-throughs complement its heated pool, laundry facilities, groceries, and game room. By the time you leave, you'll claim owners Chuck and Holly Bossen among your friends.

Big Pine Campground, P.O. Box 52, Custer, SD 57730 (☎ **605/673-4054**), secluded from traffic noises, offers 85 level, naturally shaded sites, hookups, flush toilets, hot showers, fireplaces, and wood, as well as a store, game room, playground, hiking, and horseshoes.

Deadwood Gulch RV Resort & Campground, P.O. Box 643, Deadwood, SD 57732 (☎ **800/695-1876** or 605/578-1294), has a first-rate shower house, sports court, swimming pool, convenience store, and creekside restaurant greeting guests at this spacious family fun park and resort. There's never a dull moment as adults enjoy 24-hour casino action, while the kids score with an 18-hole miniature golf course, bumper boats, batting cages, go-carts, and a giant arcade. The trail ride and ranch breakfast high atop the Hills may be the region's best.

Miners RV Park, P.O. Box 157, Keystone, SD 57751 (☎ **605/666-4638**), in the heart of the former mining town of Keystone, is close to numerous attractions and only a stone's throw from Mount Rushmore National Memorial. The campground and its adjacent motel offer cool shade and a gurgling brook, as well as a store, gas, ice, laundry, gifts, restaurant, heated pool and hot tub, and a fun walk down Keystone's Main Street.

Mount Rushmore KOA, P.O. Box 295, Hill City, SD 57745 (☎ **800/562-8503**), attached to the Palmer Gulch Resort, is among the best in region, if not the largest. With 450 sites and 50 camping cabins, two pools and spas, water slide, Indian dancers, movies, miniature golf, fishing, hayrides, restaurant, tours, and car rental, this is what most campgrounds want to be when they grow up.

Rapid City KOA, P.O. Box 2592, Rapid City, SD 57709 (☎ **800/KOA-8504** or 605/348-2111), is conveniently located on Rapid City's eastern flank. This KOA also is large with 200 sites and cabins. It offers a free pancake breakfast, and a grand pool and spa. Bus tours and car rentals are available, and great shopping, sightseeing, and Rushmore Plaza Civic Center are nearby.

Accommodations

There are no accommodations at Mount Rushmore, Wind Cave, or Jewel Cave, but inns, hotels, motels, lodges, and bed-and-breakfasts are plentiful in nearby Black Hills communities and parks. However, there are four popular lodges in Custer State Park. Reservations are strongly recommended, particularly in summer months. For some popular destinations such as Custer State Park, it's best to call 6 months to a year in advance of your visit. In addition to the places listed below in Rapid City, Nemo, and Deadwood, you'll find accommodations in Keystone and Hill City (especially convenient to Mount Rushmore), as well as in Custer and Hot Springs (more convenient to Jewel Cave and Wind Cave, respectively). If you're continuing west, you might also consider Newcastle, Wyoming, which is 25 miles west of Jewel Cave National Monument as a place to stay; there are several accommodation choices there.

For information on accommodations and camping in the Black Hills, contact the **South Dakota Department of Tourism,** 711 Wells, Capitol Lake Plaza, Pierre, SD 57501 (☎ **605/773-3301**); or the **Black Hills, Badlands and Lakes Association,** 900 Jackson Blvd., Rapid City, SD 57702-2583 (☎ **605/341-1462**).

IN RAPID CITY

Audrie's Bed & Breakfast

23029 Thunderhead Falls Rd., Rapid City, SD 57702. ☎ **605/342-7788.** 9 units, all with private bath. TV TEL. $95–$145. Prices include full breakfast. Couples only. Personal checks or cash only (no credit cards). Open year-round. Located 6 miles west of town on U.S. 44.

This place combines an old-world charm with a Black Hills flair. Antiques, fireplaces, and hot tubs grace every suite and cottage. Set on the banks of a rippling trout stream, Audrie's is ideally situated to explore the wonders of the national parks, monuments, and memorials in the Black Hills. And you won't go away hungry. This is a nonsmoking establishment.

Hotel Alex Johnson

523 Sixth St., Rapid City, SD 57701. ☎ **800/888-2539** or 605/342-1210; fax 605/342-7436. 143 rms and suites. A/C TV TEL. May 15–Oct 15 $85–$115 double; Oct 16–May 14 $45–$85 double. AE, DC, DISC, MC, V.

This is a finely restored hotel listed on the National Historic Register. You will find an Irish pub, gift shop, Jacuzzi suites, and a restaurant on the premises. It's Germanic Tudor mixed with Lakota Sioux atmosphere on the inside with a Germanic Tudor exterior. The furniture was handcrafted in Rapid City to replicate the hotel's original furnishing in 1928. The hotel has a highly recommended restaurant, The Landmark, that is open for breakfast, lunch, and dinner.

Rushmore Plaza Holiday Inn

505 N. Fifth St., Rapid City, SD 57701. ☎ **800/465-4329** or 605/348-4000; fax 605/348-9777. 205 rms and suites. A/C TV TEL. Jan 4–June 6 $79–$99 double; June 7–Jan 3 $108–$147. AE, DC, DISC, MC, V.

This eight-story atrium hotel with a pool and waterfall also has a nice piano lounge, exercise facilities, and a car-rental desk. It's a great place to stay when you don't feel the need to go outdoors and is close to downtown shopping, dining, and entertainment.

IN NEMO

Twin Peaks Ranch

17 miles west of Sturgis Rd. on Nemo Rd., 2 miles past Nemo in Paradise Valley (P.O. Box 80, Nemo, SD 57759). ☎ **605/578-2771;** Web site: twinpeaks.nemo.sd.us. Main Ranch House (accommodates up to 14 persons) plus 3 cabins. Ranch House: May 15–Sept 15 $395; Sept 16–May 14 $375. Cabin: May 15–Sept 15 $98; Sept 16–May 14 $80. Discounts available for more than 4 nights' lodging. MC, V.

Nestled in the scenic valley carved by Box Elder Creek and surrounded by the grandeur of Black Hills National Forest, Twin Peaks' 6,700-square-foot log house is ideal for group gatherings and family reunions, while the cabins provide the setting for a quiet hideaway. Favored activities include trout fishing, hiking, rock climbing, mountain biking, horseback riding, and bird watching. Horse boarding is available.

IN DEADWOOD

The Bullock Hotel

633 Historic Main St., Deadwood, SD 57732. ☎ **800/336-1876** or 605/578-1745; fax 605/578-1382. 36 rms and suites. A/C TV TEL. $35–$155 double. AE, DISC, MC, V.

This is the finest hotel in South Dakota. You'll find turn-of-the-century surroundings complemented by modern amenities, a perfect combination. There's also 24-hour gaming, a full-service bar, and a quaint restaurant called Bully's. For a special treat, try one of the Jacuzzi suites. Keep an eye out for the hotel's namesake, legendary lawman Seth Bullock, whose ghost has a habit of reappearing here.

Deadwood Gulch Resort

U.S. 85 S., 1 mile from Historic Main St. (P.O. Box 643, Deadwood, SD 57732). ☎ **800/695-1876** or 605/578-1294; fax 605/578-2505. 100 rms. A/C TV TEL. Oct 1–June 15 $62–$75 double; June 16–Sept 5 $99; Sept 6–30 $65–$75. AE, DISC, MC, V.

With a clean hotel, three casinos, a convention center, bars, creekside restaurant, convenience store and gas station, amusement park, arcade, campground, spa, and heated pools, this ranks as South Dakota's only true resort. There's trolley service to historic Main Street. In the summer, the resort has mountain-bike rentals and horseback rides; in the winter, you can rent snowmobiles, and there are special events year-round.

IN CUSTER STATE PARK

Custer State Park is home to four rustic resorts that offer lodging, dining, and a wealth of recreational opportunities in the heart of the Black Hills.

The **State Game Lodge & Resort,** located on U.S. 16A near the park's main visitor center, served as the "Summer White House" for Pres. Calvin Coolidge in 1927 and was visited by Pres. Dwight Eisenhower. The stone and wood lodge features stately rooms, motel units, and pine-shaded cabins, as well as meeting and banquet facilities. The Lodge offers an excellent Buffalo Jeep Safari Ride into the backcountry.

The **Sylvan Lake Resort,** on S. Dak. 87 in the northeast corner of Custer State Park, overlooking scenic Sylvan Lake and the Harney Range, features cozy lodge rooms and rustic family cabins. The lodge also is close to a number of outdoor activities, including hiking, mountain biking, swimming, fishing, boating, and rock climbing.

The **Blue Bell Lodge & Resort,** located on S. Dak. 87, just before the turnoff for the Wildlife Loop Road (if you are traveling south), is among western South Dakota's best-kept secrets. The retreat has a western guest ranch flavor, with handcrafted log cabins scattered around a lodge with dining room, lounge, and meeting room. A general store, gift shop, and gasoline station are located on-site, and fishing is available nearby. The resort also offers hayrides, chuck-wagon cookouts, and trail rides through some of the park's magnificent backcountry.

The **Legion Lake Resort,** located near the junction of the Needles Highway (S. Dak. 87 and U.S. 16A), dates from 1913 and features cottages nestled in the pines on the lakeshore. A dining room, store, paddleboats, and mountain bikes are available at the resort, and the 110-mile Centennial Trail passes through the Legion Lake area.

Rates at these lodges range from around $65 for a sleeping cabin at Legion Lake in the high season, to $300 for a four-bedroom cabin at the State Game Resort. The more facilities and amenities, the more you will pay. Most of the resorts open in late April or May and close down in September or October; a few cabins are kept open for winter sports aficionados, however. These fill up quickly, and some people call 6 months in advance for reservations.

For more information or to make reservations at any of Custer State Park's resorts, call ☎ **605/255-4521.**

Dining

Dining in the Black Hills tends to be a casual affair. Few restaurants take reservations, and ties and jackets are seldom required. But the selection can be excellent, ranging from homemade pies and ranch-raised buffalo to hearty steaks and succulent pheasant. "Summer" means Memorial Day through Labor Day.

In the Parks. The only national park in the Black Hills with full-service dining for all meals is at **Mount Rushmore** (the Buffalo Dining Room is described below). At **Wind Cave,** you'll find only vending machines. At **Jewel Cave,** you'll find only snack vending machines in the visitor center. The resorts at **Custer State Park** offer dining facilities, which nonguests may enjoy as well (see the individual resort descriptions under "Accommodations," above).

We've recommended several places, from Deadwood south to Hot Springs. In addition to those in Rapid City, the largest city in the area, you'll find dining possibilities in Keystone, Hill City, Custer, and Hot Springs.

In addition to the places listed below, you might consider two modest restaurants in Custer, which is east of Jewel Cave National Monument, west of Custer State Park, and northwest of Wind Cave National Park. The **Bavarian Inn,** at the junction U.S. 385 and U.S. 16 (☎ **605/673-4412**), serves American and German dishes at reasonable prices. **The Chief Restaurant,** 140 Mount Rushmore Rd. (☎ **605/673-2318**), offers family-style dining, with choices ranging all the way from prime rib to pizza.

AT MOUNT RUSHMORE NATIONAL MEMORIAL

Buffalo Dining Room

At Mt. Rushmore National Memorial. ☎ **605/574-2515.** No reservations. AE, DISC, MC, V. Summer daily 7am–8pm; other times of the year daily 8am–4pm (though hrs. can vary during the off-season according to visitation patterns). Breakfast items $3–$6.50; lunch entrees $6–$8; dinner entrees $6–$8. AMERICAN.

Every day, visitors to the Black Hills dine with presidents at Mount Rushmore's fabled Buffalo Dining Room. Operated by AmFac Parks and Resorts, the memorial's concessionaire, the dining room serves a wide array of fare year-round in one of the world's most famous settings. Scrambled eggs, hash browns, homemade biscuits and sausage gravy, country-fried steak with coffee, tea, or milk costs $2.99, a good price. What's especially nice about the place is that most choices retain a homemade taste, not something you can say about all national park fare. Buffalo stew is excellent; you'll also find burgers, hot dogs, chicken dishes, pot roast, spaghetti, baked fish, ham steaks, great pies and fudge, and monumental scoops of ice cream.

IN KEYSTONE

The Ruby House Restaurant and Red Garter Saloon

Main St., Keystone. ☎ **605/666-4404.** Breakfast items $2–$6; lunch entrees $5–$9; dinner entrees $6.50–$14. DISC, MC, V. Summer daily for all meals, but hrs. can vary, so call ahead if you're coming at an off time. STEAK/SEAFOOD.

Steaks, seafood, and other specialties are served in a richly appointed Victorian dining room. This is a quiet stop in a tumultuous town.

IN HILL CITY

The Alpine Inn

Main St., Hill City. ☎ **605/574-2749.** Reservations not accepted. Lunch choices $2–$5, dinner entrees $6–$8. No credit cards. Summer Mon–Sat 11am–2:30pm and 5–10pm; other times 11am–2:30pm and 5–9:30pm. Closed Sun. STEAKS.

The Alpine Inn remains a favorite among most locals and all carnivores. If you're a vegetarian, this might not be the ideal spot for you. Lack of wide selection on entrees is mitigated by a choice of more than 30 desserts, most of which are homemade and all of which are delectable.

IN RAPID CITY

1915 Firehouse Brewing Co.

610 Main St., Rapid City. ☎ **605/348-1915.** Reservations accepted for parties of 6 or more only. Lunch entrees $5–$8; dinner entrees $5 $16. AE, DC, DISC, MC, V. Summer Sun–Thurs 11am–10pm, Fri–Sat until midnight;

other times of the year Sun–Thurs 11am–9pm, Fri–Sat until 10pm. CONTINENTAL/EUROPEAN PUB FARE.

The entire brewing process is visible behind glass in this classic, renovated fire station. Brats, burgers, buffalo, and chicken wings round out the hearty microbrews of the Firehouse. Among the most popular selections are its Reuben sandwich, the bean soup offered in fall, and the desserts, such as the Big Cookie, a freshly baked white and dark chocolate mix that fills a dinner plate, then is topped with two large scoops of French vanilla ice cream and served with melba sauce on the side. Live entertainment is offered on a large, heated patio Friday and Saturday nights from Memorial Day through Labor Day.

Botticelli Ristorante Italiano

523 Main St., Rapid City. ☎ **605/346-0089.** Reservations for parties of 20 or more only. Lunch entrees $4.25–$9; dinner entrees $8.50–$15.50. MC, V. Mon–Fri 11am–3pm; Mon–Thurs and Sun 5–9pm; Fri–Sat 5–10pm; closed for lunch Sat–Sun. ITALIAN.

Although it's among the region's newest restaurants, Botticelli has quickly become a culinary hot spot. Featuring a wide selection of creamy pastas and delightful chicken and veal dishes, the fare smacks of Northern Italy. Even though they set up shop in the middle of cattle country, owners/chefs Luigi Turletti and Dino Faryat may have struck a gold mine.

Fireside Inn

On U.S. 44, 7 miles west of Rapid City. ☎ **605/342-3900.** Reservations for parties of 6 or more only. Lunch entrees $5–$6; dinner entrees $12–$35. AE, DISC, MC, V. Summer daily 11am–9pm, other times of the year 4–9pm. ITALIAN/STEAKS.

Bean soup is a greater starter, but this place has made a name for itself from its excellent prime rib and intimate fireside setting. Relax with refreshments on a spacious new patio before checking out the 20-ounce Cattlemen's Cut. Or you might want to sample the fresh salmon or an indescribable Chicken Wellington. The New York steak is still among the best in the business.

Golden Phoenix

2421 W. Main St., Rapid City. ☎ **605/348-4195.** Reservations accepted. Lunch entrees $4.50–$4.75; dinner entrees $5–$9. AE, DC, DISC, MC, V. Daily 11am–10pm. CHINESE.

There is a wide selection of Chinese dishes, but it's hard to beat the Mongolian beef, the sesame chicken, or the Hunan shrimp. A relaxed atmosphere with great prices, quick service, and convenient parking make this a good choice in Rapid City.

IN ROCKERVILLE

The Gaslight Restaurant

Main St., Rockerville, 10 miles south of Rapid City on U.S. 16. ☎ **605/343-9276.** Lunch entrees $4–$9; dinner entrees $7–$17. AE, DISC, MC, V. Summer daily 11am–10pm; other times of the year Wed–Sun 11am–9pm. STEAKS/PASTA.

The Gaslight brings fun to family dining in an Old West saloon setting with an antique soda fountain, great steaks, a candy counter, and homemade ice cream. The hand-cut steaks are lean and tasty, and the restaurant also offers seafood and pasta dishes in a relaxed setting. It's a very casual place.

IN PIEDMONT

Elk Creek Steakhouse & Lounge

I-90 at Exit 46, north of Rapid City. ☎ **605/787-6349.** Dinner entrees $4.50–$29. AE, DISC, MC, V. Mon–Thurs 5–10pm, Fri–Sat 5–11pm, Sun 4:30–10pm. STEAKS.

Steak's the thing at Elk Creek, and its new buffalo cuts are excellent. The special duchess potatoes are to die for, and the chef's special—a rib eye served on an English muffin, topped with broccoli, mock crab, and a hollandaise-cheese sauce—is wicked. The lounge features a live band on Saturday night and home-grown country music talent on Sunday afternoon.

NEAR HOT SPRINGS

Dakota Rose Restaurant

Jct. U.S. 18/385 and S. Dak. 79, 5 miles southeast of Hot Springs. ☎ **605/745-6447.** Reservations not accepted. Lunch entrees $4–$8; dinner entrees $5–$15. MC, V. Summer daily 6am–10pm; other times of the year 8am–9:30pm. AMERICAN.

Here you'll find family style dining, plus a soup and salad bar in a covered wagon. Chicken-fried steaks, prime rib, and homemade soups are the most popular dishes. But there is a wide selection of dishes with reasonable prices, as well as a new bar and lounge.

IN DEADWOOD

Deadwood Social Club

On the 2nd floor of Saloon No. 10, 657 Main St. ☎ **800/952-9398.** Reservations appreciated but not necessary. Lunch entrees $4–$7; dinner entrees $5.50–$14. AE, MC, V. Summer daily 11am–10pm; other times of the year Tues–Sun 11am–9pm. STEAKS/PASTA.

A warm atmosphere made even cozier with light jazz and blues in the background and one of South Dakota's largest wine selections in the cellar. The tenderloin and rib eye are each served with grilled vegetables and roasted New England potatoes, then topped with a special demiglace. Pasta dishes, such as the popular rigatoni con pollo, are exquisite. On the lighter side, Mother's Enchiladas are a favorite. After lunch or dinner, browse through the art gallery on the same floor.

Jakes

Upstairs from the Midnight Star, Main St., Deadwood. ☎ **800/999-6482** or 605/578-1555. Reservations recommended. Dinner entrees $14–$23. AE, DC, DISC, MC, V. Summer Mon–Thurs 5–10pm, Fri–Sat 5–11pm; other times of the year Mon–Thurs 5:30–9:30pm, Fri–Sat 5–10pm. STEAKS/PASTAS.

Before dining, browse handsomely displayed costumes worn by Kevin Costner in most of his feature films, including *JFK, Dances With Wolves,* and *Waterworld.* Kevin and his brother Dan own the place, which features some of the most unusual food in the region. Sample seasonal dishes including salmon, elk, chicken, duck, lamb, and buffalo. The 16-ounce grilled pork porterhouse, a center cut smothered with brandy pear sauce, melts in your mouth. Or try the pan-seared buffalo rib eye. A different pasta feature and wild game entree are featured each night. Appetizers include escargot, steamed mussels, and smoked ruby trout. There is also an excellent wine list.

6

BRYCE CANYON NATIONAL PARK

by Don and Barbara Laine

WELCOME TO A MAGICAL LAND, A PLACE OF INSPIRATION AND spectacular beauty where thousands of intricately shaped hoodoos stir the imagination as they stand together in silent watch over the canyon.

Hoodoos, geologists tell us, are simply pinnacles of rock, often oddly shaped, left standing by the forces of millions of years of water and wind erosion. But perhaps the truth really lies in a Paiute legend. These American Indians, who lived in the area for several hundred years before being forced out by Anglo pioneers, told of a "Legend People" who lived here in the old days; for their evil ways they were turned to stone by the powerful Coyote, and even today they remain frozen in time.

Whatever the cause, Bryce Canyon is unique. Its intricate and often whimsical formations are smaller and on a more human scale than the impressive rocks seen at Zion, Capitol Reef, and Canyonlands national parks. And it's far easier to explore than the huge and sometimes intimidating Grand Canyon. Bryce is comfortable and inviting in its beauty; we feel we know it simply by gazing over the rim.

Although the colorful hoodoos are the first things to grab your attention, it isn't long before you notice the deep amphitheaters that enfold them, with their cliffs, windows, and arches—all colored in shades of red, brown, orange, yellow, and white—that change and glow with the rising and setting sun. Beyond the rocks and light are the other faces of the park: three separate life zones, each with its own unique vegetation, changing with elevation; and a kingdom of animals, from the busy chipmunks and ground squirrels to stately mule deer and their archenemy, the mountain lion.

Human exploration of the Bryce area likely began with the Paiutes, and it's possible that trappers, prospectors, and early Mormon scouts may have visited here in the early to mid-1800s, before Maj. John Wesley Powell conducted the first thorough survey of the region in the early 1870s. Shortly after Powell's exploration, Mormon pioneer Ebenezer Bryce and his wife, Mary, moved to the area and tried raising cattle. Although they stayed only a few years before moving to Arizona, Bryce left behind his name and his oft-quoted description of the canyon as "a helluva place to lose a cow."

Tips from a Park Ranger

"A lot of people think this is one of America's prettiest parks," says ranger Dave Mecham, who has spent about 10 years at Bryce Canyon National Park. "The hoodoos are what people come to see—that's what made Bryce famous—and it's the most popular thing."

"But living here, it's not my favorite aspect of the park," Mecham says. "I enjoy the long-distance views from the rim; that's what really inspires me at this point." The ranger adds, "Looking out from the rim of Bryce, across the hoodoos, it seems you can see forever. The atmospheric conditions are almost ideal, and you get the feeling that you're looking at a piece of America that's still pretty wild, and just hasn't changed much through time."

Bryce Amphitheater has the best scenery in the park, in Mecham's opinion.

"It's the place in the park where everything's coming together geologically to carve hoodoos at their best," he says. He particularly enjoys the **Rim Trail** that runs along the edge of the canyon, and highly recommends the section between Inspiration and Bryce points, with perhaps the very best view from a section known as **Upper Inspiration Point,** which is 300 to 400 yards south of Inspiration Point.

Among Mecham's favorite trails is the **Fairyland Loop,** which takes about 4 hours. "I think it's a fantastic trail," he says. To get the best views, he advises, start at Sunrise Point, go down past Tower Bridge and back up through Fairyland Canyon to Fairyland Trailhead, and then take the Rim Trail back to Sunrise Point. "It's 5 miles below the rim and then 3 miles of rim trail. Fairyland Canyon is beautiful, the highlight of that loop, and as you come around the bend, you're hiking straight toward a really beautiful backdrop. If you're going the opposite direction you have to keep stopping to look over your shoulder."

Mecham calls Bryce Canyon a "morning park," because the views are much better illuminated by early morning light than at any other time of day. He recommends spending at least 1 night at or near the park.

"If you're spending the night close by, I think it would be a big mistake to miss sunrise—in the middle of the summer that's getting up before six," he says. "I would definitely tell people that near the top of their list for their Bryce visit is seeing the sunrise here."

Getting up early is also the best way to avoid crowds, according to Mecham, since most people don't get to the view points or out onto the trails until about 10am. The other way to avoid crowds is to walk away from them. Mecham says that you're likely to not see anyone at all on the park's two backcountry trails at the south end of the park, but avoiding crowds even in the park's most popular areas often takes only a short walk.

"Sunset Point is the busiest place in the park, especially in midsummer at midday," he says. "You finally get a parking spot, then walk out to a very crowded view point, where you're standing shoulder to shoulder—it's real hectic—but if you take a 5-minute walk south along the rim trail towards Inspiration Point, you'll leave the people immediately—they just cluster at those views."

Mecham says September and October are probably the best times to visit. "It's still busy," he says, "but less crowded on trails." However, if you really want to avoid people, you'll feel you have the park all to yourself if you visit midweek in the middle of the winter. "We plow the roads so people can drive to the view points and photograph the canyon with snow on it, and the people that ski or snowshoe will enjoy it the most," he says, adding, "Skiing is at its best in January and February, when it's really cold."

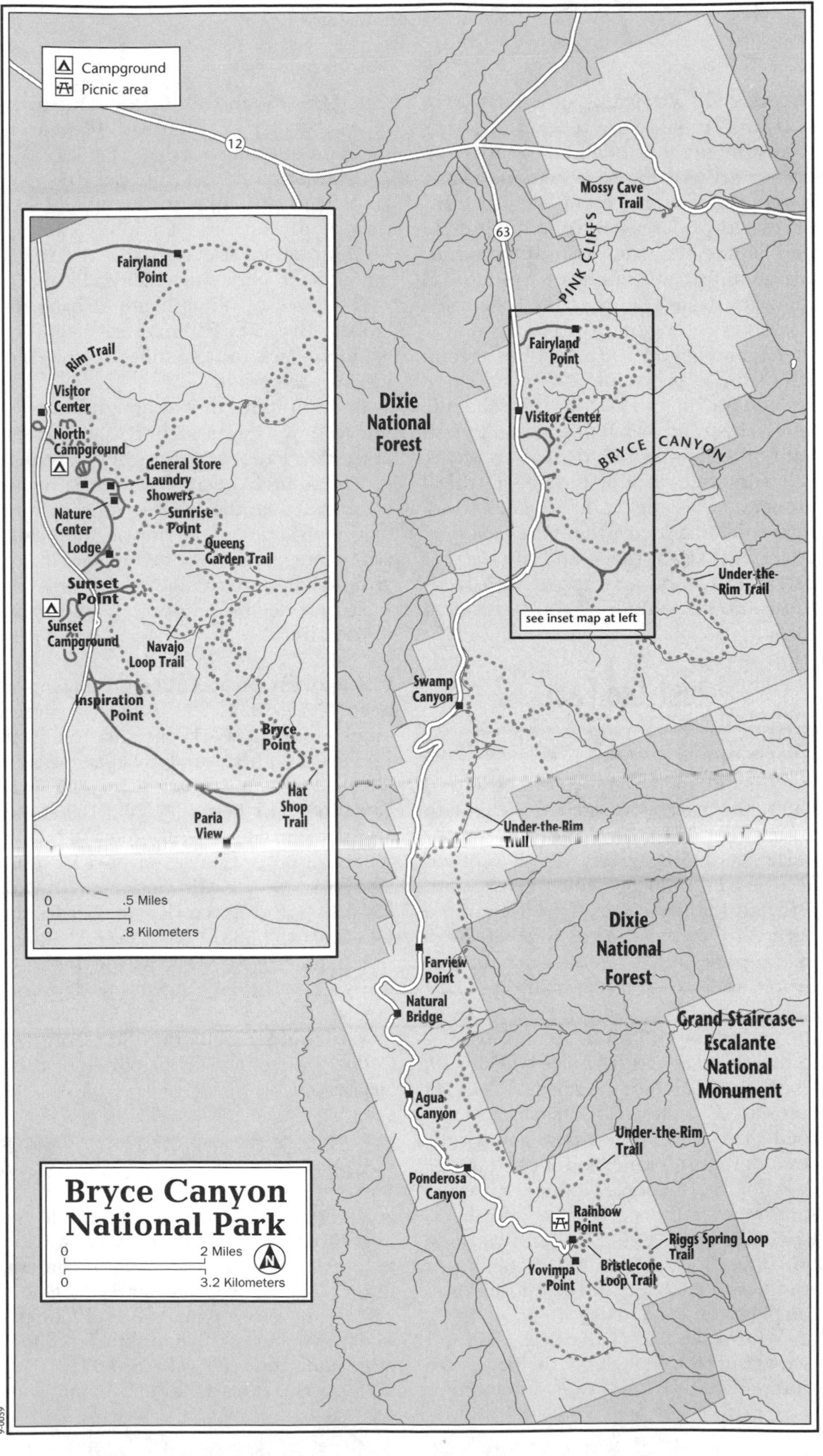
Campground
Picnic area
12
63
Mossy Cave Trail
PINK CLIFFS
Fairyland Point
Visitor Center
BRYCE CANYON
Under-the-Rim Trail
see inset map at left
Dixie National Forest
Swamp Canyon
Under-the-Rim Trail
Farview Point
Natural Bridge
Agua Canyon
Ponderosa Canyon
Dixie National Forest
Grand Staircase-Escalante National Monument
Under-the-Rim Trail
Rainbow Point
Riggs Spring Loop Trail
Yovimpa Point
Bristlecone Loop Trail
Fairyland Point
Rim Trail
Visitor Center
North Campground
General Store
Laundry
Showers
Nature Center
Sunrise Point
Lodge
Queens Garden Trail
Sunset Point
Sunset Campground
Navajo Loop Trail
Inspiration Point
Bryce Point
Hat Shop Trail
Paria View
0 .5 Miles
0 .8 Kilometers
Bryce Canyon National Park
0 2 Miles
0 3.2 Kilometers
N
9-0059

Avoiding the Crowds. Although Bryce Canyon National Park receives only two-thirds the number of annual visitors that pour into nearby Zion National Park, Bryce can still be crowded, especially during its peak season from mid-June to mid-September, when the campgrounds are often full by 2pm. If you have to visit then, try to hike some of the lesser-used trails (ask rangers for recommendations), and get out onto the trails as soon after sunrise as possible.

A better time to visit, if your schedule allows, is spring or fall. If you don't mind a bit of cold and snow, the park is practically deserted in the winter—a typical January sees some 22,000 to 25,000 visitors, while in August there are well over 10 times that number—and the sight of bright red hoodoos capped with fresh white snow is something you won't soon forget.

Just the Facts

GETTING THERE & GATEWAYS

Situated in the mountains of southern Utah, the park is crossed from east to west by Utah 12, with the bulk of the park, including the visitor center, accessed by Utah 63, which turns south off Utah 12 into the main portions of the park. U.S. 89 runs north to south, west of the park, and Utah 12 heads east to Tropic and eventually Escalante.

From Salt Lake City, it's 260 miles to the park. Take I-15 south about 200 miles to Exit 95, head east 13 miles on Utah 20, south on U.S. 89 for 17 miles to Utah 12, and east 17 miles to the park entrance road. The entrance station and visitor center are just 3 miles south of Utah 12.

From St. George, about 126 miles southwest of the park, travel north on I-15 10 miles to Exit 16, then head east on Utah 9 for 63 miles to U.S. 89, north 43 miles to Utah 12, and east 17 miles to the park entrance road.

From Cedar City (I-15 exits 57, 59, and 62), about 80 miles west of the park, take Utah 14 west 41 miles to its intersection with U.S. 89 and follow that north 21 miles to Utah 12, then east 17 miles to the park entrance road.

From Capitol Reef National Park, take Utah 24 west 10 miles to Torrey, and then turn southwest onto Utah 12 (through Boulder and Escalante) for about 110 miles to the park entrance road.

A couple of other handy driving distances: Bryce is 83 miles east of Zion National Park and 245 miles northwest of Las Vegas, Nevada.

Keep in mind that although most visitors to Bryce have cars or RVs, this is one of the few national parks where a vehicle isn't absolutely necessary, at least in the summer. A **shuttle bus** operates in summer with stops at all major trailheads, view points, the visitor center, and campgrounds. Stop in the lobby of Ruby's Inn (just outside the entrance to the park) for details.

The Nearest Airport. Bryce Canyon Airport (☎ **435/834-5239**) is located several miles from the park entrance on Utah 12. Direct flights from Las Vegas, Nevada, are provided by **Scenic Airlines** (☎ **702/739-1900**), **Air Vegas** (☎ **702/795-7144**), and **Air Nevada** (☎ **702/736-2702**). Car rentals at Bryce Canyon Airport are available from **Bryce Air Service** (☎ **435/834-5208**) and **Bryce Canyon Car Rental** (☎ **800/432-5383** or 435/834-5200), which also has a desk in the lobby of Ruby's Inn (See "Accommodations," below).

You could also fly into St. George or Cedar and rent a car at either of their airports.

GETTING INFORMATION BEFORE YOUR TRIP

For advance information on what to see in the park, hiking trails, camping, and lodging, write to the **Superintendent, Bryce Canyon National Park,** P.O. Box 170001, Bryce Canyon, UT 84717, or call weekdays between 8am and 4:30pm mountain time (☎ **435/834-5322**). It's best to write at least a month before your planned visit, and ask for a copy of the national park newspaper ***Hoodoo,*** which contains a map of the park, plus information on hiking trails, services, weather, ranger-conducted activities, and current issues such as road construction in the park. The Web site for the park is **www.nps.gov/brca**.

If you want even more details to help plan your trip, you can order books, maps, posters, and videos from the nonprofit **Bryce Canyon Natural History Association,** Bryce Canyon, UT 84717 (☎ **435/834-4602;** fax orders 888/362-2642 or 435/834-4102). The association publishes a number of excellent books, and offers a special trip-planning packet that includes a driving and hiking guide, a natural history guide, and a descriptive and photographic guide to both Bryce and Zion national parks, all for a package price of about $9. Several videos are available, both in VHS and PAL formats.

VISITOR CENTER

Located at the north end as you enter the park, the visitor center has exhibits on the geology and history of the area and presents a short introductory slide show. Rangers can answer your questions and provide backcountry permits. You can also pick up several free brochures, and buy books, maps, videos, postcards, and posters. The visitor center is open daily year-round except Thanksgiving, Christmas, and New Year's days.

ENTRANCE & CAMPING FEES

Entry into the park (for up to 7 days) is $10 per private vehicle or $5 per motorcycle, bicycle, or pedestrian. A $20 annual pass is also available. Campsites cost $10 per night.

Permits, which cost $5 and are available at the visitor center daily until 8pm, are required for all overnight trips into the backcountry. Backcountry camping is permitted on only two trails, with details at the visitor center.

SPECIAL REGULATIONS & WARNINGS

While most visitors to Bryce Canyon enjoy an exciting vacation without serious mishap, accidents can occur. The most common injuries by far are sprained, twisted, and broken ankles, possibly because of the nature of the trails. Park rangers strongly recommend that hikers, even those just out for short day hikes, wear sturdy hiking boots with good traction and ankle support.

Another concern in the park in recent years has been **bubonic plague,** which, contrary to popular belief, is treatable with antibiotics if caught early. The bacteria that causes bubonic plague has been found on fleas in prairie dog colonies in the park, so you should avoid contact with wild animals, especially prairie dogs, chipmunks, ground squirrels, and other rodents. Those taking pets into the park should dust them with flea powder. Avoiding contact with infected animals will greatly minimize the chances of contracting this holdover from the Dark Ages, but caution is still necessary. Symptoms, which generally occur from 2 to 6 days after exposure, may include high fever, headache, vomiting, diarrhea, and swollen glands. Anyone showing these symptoms after visiting the park should get medical attention immediately—the plague can be fatal if not treated promptly.

Backcountry hikers should practice minimum-impact techniques and carry their own water. Bicycles are not allowed in the backcountry or on the trails. Lighting fires, feeding or molesting wildlife, and disturbing any natural feature of the park are all prohibited. Dog-owners should keep their pets leashed at all times, and may not take them on the trails, in the backcountry, or in public buildings.

SEASONS & CLIMATE

With elevations ranging from 6,000 to 9,000 feet, Bryce Canyon is cooler than southern Utah's other, lower elevation parks. From May through October, daytime temperatures are pleasant—usually from the low 60s to the upper 80s—while nights are cool, dropping into the 40s even at the height of summer. Afternoon thunderstorms are common in July and August. During winter, days are generally clear and crisp, with high temperatures often reaching the 40s, while nights are cold, usually in the single digits or teens, or even dipping well below zero. Snow is common in winter, but park staff plow the roads to the view points.

SEASONAL EVENTS

In addition to the nightly campfire/amphitheater programs, once each month astronomers from Hansen Planetarium in Salt Lake City present a **starwatching program.** Check at the visitor center for the current schedule.

USEFUL PUBLICATIONS

A particularly useful book for serious hikers is ***Hiking Zion & Bryce Canyon National Parks*** (Helena, Mont.: Falcon Publishing Co., 1997) by Erik Molvar and Tamara Martin. It's available from the **Bryce Canyon Natural History Association** (see "Getting Information Before Your Trip," above).

Seeing the Highlights in a Day

It would be easy to spend a week in Bryce Canyon, starting with the visitor center, then moving along to the scenic drive, a few short walks, and then advancing to more serious hikes. But what makes this park so attractive to many visitors is that there are ways to see a good deal of Bryce in a short amount of time.

Start at the **visitor center** and watch the short slide show that explains some of the area's geology. Then either drive the 18-mile (each way) dead end **park road,** stopping at view points to gaze down into the canyon (see "Exploring the Park by Car," below), or hop on the **Bryce Tours van** for a 2-hour guided tour, complete with lively commentary (see "Organized Tours & Ranger Programs," below).

Whichever way you choose to get around, make sure you spend at least a little time at **Inspiration Point,** which offers a splendid (and yes, inspirational) view into **Bryce Amphitheater** and its hundreds of statuesque pink, red, orange, and brown hoodoo stone sculptures. After seeing the canyon from the top down, it's time to get some exercise, so walk at least partway down the **Queen's Garden Trail.** If you can spare 3 hours, hike down the Navajo Loop and return to the rim via Queen's Garden Trail (see "Day Hikes," below). Those not willing or physically able to hike into the canyon can enjoy a leisurely walk along the **Rim Trail,** which provides spectacular views down into the canyon, especially about an hour before sunset. That evening, try to take in the **campground amphitheater program.**

Exploring the Park by Car

The park's **18-mile scenic drive** (one way) follows the rim of Bryce Canyon, offering easy access to a variety of views into the fanciful fairyland of stone sculptures below. Trailers, not allowed on the road, must be left at several parking lots. Because all overlooks are on your left as you begin your drive, it's best to avoid crossing traffic by driving all the way to the end of the road and stopping at the overlooks on your return. Allow 1 to 2 hours.

After leaving the visitor center, drive the length of the 18 mile road to **Yovimpa and Rainbow Point overlooks,** which offer expansive views of southern Utah, Arizona, and sometimes even New Mexico. From these pink cliffs you can look down on a colorful platoon of stone soldiers, standing at eternal attention. A short loop trail from Rainbow Point leads to an **1,800-year-old bristlecone pine,** believed to be the oldest living thing at Bryce Canyon.

From here, drive back north to **Ponderosa Canyon Overlook,** where you can gaze down from a dense forest of spruce and fir at multicolored hoodoos, and then continue to **Agua Canyon Overlook,** with some of the best color contrasts you'll find in the park. Looking almost straight down, watch for a hoodoo known as **The Hunter,** with a hat of green trees.

Now continue on to **Natural Bridge,** actually an arch carved by rain and wind, spanning 85 feet. From here, continue to **Fairview Point,** where there's a panoramic view to the distant horizon and the Kaibab Plateau at the Grand Canyon's North Rim. Next, pass through **Swamp Canyon,** and continue until you hit a turnoff from the main road on the right.

This turnoff leads to three view points, the first of which is **Paria View,** looking off to the south of the White Cliffs, carved into light-colored sandstone by the Paria River. To the north of Paria View, you'll find **Bryce Point,** a splendid stop for seeing the awesome **Bryce Amphitheater,** the largest natural amphitheater in the park, as well as distant views of the Black Mountains to the northeast and Navajo Mountain to the south. From here it's just a short drive to **Inspiration Point,** which offers views similar to those at Bryce Point plus the best view in the park of the **Silent City,** a sleeping metropolis of stone.

Now return to the main road and head north to **Sunset Point,** where you can see practically all of Bryce Amphitheater, including the aptly named **Thor's Hammer** and the 200-foot-tall cliffs of **Wall Street.**

Continue north to a turnoff for your final stop at **Sunrise Point,** where there's an inspiring view into Bryce Amphitheater. This is the beginning of the **Queen's Garden Trail,** an excellent choice for even a quick walk below the canyon's rim.

Organized Tours & Ranger Programs

Park rangers present a variety of free programs and activities. **Evening programs,** which may include a slide show, take place most nights at campground amphitheaters. Topics vary, but could include such subjects as the animals and plants of the park, geology, and man's role in the park's early days. Rangers also give **half-hour talks** on similar subjects several times daily at various locations in the park, and lead **hikes and walks,** including a moonlight hike (reservations required) and a wheelchair-accessible 1-hour canyon rim walk. Schedules are posted on bulletin boards at the visitor center, general store, campgrounds, and Bryce Canyon Lodge.

Once or twice a week spring through fall, usually in the evening, a **talk** is given on the patio of Bryce Canyon Lodge. Topics covered include lodge history, the geology of the area, and discussion of some trails. These talks are free of charge. Check at the lodge for the current schedule.

Bryce Canyon Scenic Tours & Shuttles (☎ **800/432-5383** or 435/834-5200) offers 2-hour tours year-round, leaving several times daily from Ruby's Inn just outside the park entrance. The cost is $18 for adults and $9 for youths 14 and younger. Watch out for specialized sunrise, sunset, and wildlife tours, call for details.

Getting a Bird's-eye View of the Park. For an unforgettable view of the canyon and its numerous formations, contact **Bryce Canyon Helicopter Scenic Flights** (ask for the flight desk at Ruby's Inn, ☎ **435/834-5341**). Tours last from 17 minutes to more than an hour, the longer trips including the entire park plus surrounding attractions of Kodachrome Basin State Park and a nearby ghost town. Go in the morning for the clearest air and best lighting, and try to make reservations a day ahead. Prices start at $55 for a 17-minute flight over the northern section of the park, and range up to $225. Anyone weighing less than 100 pounds is charged half.

Scenic Airlines (☎ **800/634-6801**) offers combination air tours over Bryce Canyon and Zion national parks plus the North Rim of Grand Canyon national park. Tours are given year-round, with prices starting at $275 for adults and $225 for children.

Historic & Man-Made Attractions

Although early Indians and 19th-century pioneers spent some time in what is now Bryce Canyon National Park, they left disappointingly little evidence. The park's main historic site is the handsome sandstone and ponderosa pine **Bryce Canyon Lodge,** built by the Union Pacific Railroad and opened in 1924. Much of it has been faithfully restored to its 1920s appearance.

Day Hikes

One of the wonderful things about Bryce Canyon is that you don't have to be an advanced backpacker to really get to know the park.

All trails below the rim have at least some steep grades, so you should wear hiking boots with a traction tread and good ankle support to avoid ankle injuries, the most common accidents in the park. During the hot summer months you'll want to hike either early or late in the day, always keeping in mind that it gets hotter the deeper you go into the canyon. Bryce's rangers have recently stopped rating hiking trails as to their difficulty, saying that what is easy for one person may be difficult for another. Ratings here are provided by the authors and other experienced hikers, and are entirely subjective.

SHORTER TRAILS

Bristlecone Loop

1 mile RT. Easy. Access: Rainbow Point Parking Area at the end of the scenic drive.

An easy walk entirely above the canyon rim, traversing a subalpine fir forest. Here you'll find more Bristlecone pines than along the other park trails. It takes just ¾ to 1 hour to complete the loop, which has an elevation change of 100 feet.

Hat Shop Trail

3.8 miles RT. Difficult. Access: Bryce Point Overlook.

This is a strenuous hike with a 900-foot elevation change. Leaving the rim, you'll drop quickly to the Hat Shop, so-named because it consists of hard gray "hats" perched on narrow reddish brown pedestals. The trail offers close-up views of gnarled ponderosa pine and Douglas fir, as well as distant panoramas across the Aquarius Plateau toward the Grand Staircase–Escalante National Monument. This trail is also the beginning of the Under the Rim Trail (see "Exploring the Backcountry," below).

Mossy Cave Trail

0.8 mile RT. Easy. Access: Along Utah 12, about 3.5 miles east of the highway's intersection with Utah 63.

This often-overlooked trail located outside the main part of the park offers an easy and picturesque 45-minute walk. The trail follows an old irrigation ditch up a short hill to a shallow cave, where seeping water nurtures the cave's moss. Just off the trail you'll also see a small waterfall. Elevation gain is 150 feet. Hikers will usually get their feet wet, and should be careful when crossing the ditch.

Navajo Loop Trail

1.4 miles RT. Moderate. Access: Trailhead signpost at the central overlook point at Sunset Point.

This trail descends from the rim 521 feet to the bottom of the canyon floor and back up again, and is considered moderately strenuous. It crosses graveled switchbacks, and affords terrific views of several impressive formations.

A great choice for getting down into the canyon and seeing the most with the least amount of sweat is to combine Navajo Loop with the **Queen's Garden**

Trail (see below). The total distance is just under 3 miles, with a 521-foot elevation change. Most hikers take from 2 to 3 hours. It's best to start at the Navajo Loop Trailhead at Sunset Point and leave the canyon on the less steep Queen's Garden Trail, returning to the rim at Sunrise Point, 0.5 mile to the north. Along the Navajo Loop section you'll pass Thor's Hammer (why hasn't it fallen?), view the awesome Twin Bridges, and gaze at the towering skyscrapers of Wall Street. Turning onto the Queen's Garden Trail you'll see some of the park's most fanciful formations, including majestic Queen Victoria herself, for whom the trail was named, as well as the Queen's Castle and Gulliver's Castle.

Queen's Garden Trail

0.9 mile one way. Easy to moderate. Access: South side of Sunrise Point.

This short, moderately easy trail takes you down into Bryce Amphitheater, with rest benches near the formation called Queen Victoria. It drops 320 feet below the rim. Combining the Queen's Garden Trail with the Navajo Loop Trail (see above) is a great way to see some magnificent hoodoos.

LONGER TRAILS

Fairyland Loop

8 miles RT. Difficult. Access: Fairyland Point Overlook, off the park access road north of the visitor center; also accessible from Sunrise Point.

From Fairyland Point this strenuous but little-traveled trail descends into Fairyland Canyon, then meanders up, down, and around Boat Mesa, crosses Campbell Canyon, passes Tower Bridge junction—a short 200-yard side trail takes you to the base of Tower Bridge—and begins a steady climb to the Chinese Wall. About halfway along the wall, the trail begins the serious ascent back to the top of the canyon, finally reaching it near Sunrise Point. To complete the loop follow the Rim Trail back through juniper, manzanita, and Douglas fir to Fairyland Point. The loop has an elevation change of 900 feet.

Peekaboo Loop

6.8 miles RT. Difficult. Access: Bryce Point Overlook Parking Area.

This trail, open to hikers, mules, and horses, winds among hoodoos below Bryce and Inspiration points, and is considered strenuous, with an elevation change of 800 feet. There are several fairly steep inclines and descents, but the views make all the effort worthwhile. You can see far to the east beyond Bryce Canyon toward the Aquarius Plateau, Canaan Mountain, and the Kaiparowits Plateau; or enjoy the closer prospect of the Wall of Windows, the Three Wisemen, the Organ, or the Cathedral. Various connecting trails make Peekaboo easily adaptable.

Rim Trail

5.5 miles one way. Easy to moderate. Access: North trailhead is at Fairyland Point, south trailhead is at Bryce Point; also accessible from Sunrise, Sunset, and Inspiration points, and numerous other locations in between.

The Rim Trail, which does not drop into the canyon but offers splendid views from above, meanders along the rim for over 5 miles, with a total elevation change of 550 feet. It includes a 0.5-mile section between two overlooks—Sunrise and Sunset—that is suitable for wheelchairs. Overlooking Bryce Amphitheater, the trail offers excellent views almost everywhere, and is a good choice for an early morning or evening walk, when you can watch the changing light on the rosy rocks below.

Sheep Creek Trail

3 to 5 miles one way. Easy to moderate. Access: Trailhead sign and parking area 5 miles south of the visitor center.

This trail takes you down into the canyon bottom, and if you try the extension, right out of the park into the Dixie National Forest. The first mile is on the rim, but then the trail descends the Sheep Creek draw below pink limestone cliffs toward the canyon bottom, traversing part of the Under the Rim Trail along its way. Watch signs carefully; the route can be confusing. The trail has up to a 1,250-foot elevation change.

Exploring the Backcountry

For diehard hikers who don't mind rough terrain, Bryce has two backcountry trails, usually open in the summer only. The truly ambitious can combine the two trails for a weeklong excursion. Permits, which cost $5 and are available at the visitor center, are required for all overnight trips into the backcountry.

Riggs Spring Loop

8.8-mile loop. Moderate to difficult. Access: South side of parking area for Rainbow Point.

This hike can be completed in 4 or 5 hours, or can be more comfortably done as a relaxing overnight backpacking trip. The trail goes through a deep forest, but also provides breath-taking views of the huge Pink Cliffs at the southern end of the plateau. It has an elevation change of 1,675 feet.

Under the Rim Trail

22.6 miles one way. Moderate. Access: Eastside of the parking area for Bryce Point Overlook.

This moderately strenuous trail runs between Bryce and Rainbow points, and furnishes the full spectrum of views of Bryce Canyon's scenery. Since the trail runs below the rim, it is full of steep inclines and descents, with an overall elevation change of 1,500 feet. Allow 2 to 3 days to hike the entire length. There are five camping areas along the trail, plus a group camp area.

Other Sports & Activities

Horseback Riding. To see Bryce Canyon the way early pioneers did, you need to look down from a horse or mule. **Canyon Trail Rides** (☎ **435/679-8665**), with a desk inside Bryce Canyon Lodge, offers a close-up view of Bryce's spectacular rock formations from the relative comfort of a saddle. A 2-hour ride to the canyon floor and back costs $26.50 per person (no one under 5 years old), and a half-day trip further into the canyon costs $40 per person (no one under 8 years old). Prices include tax. Riders for both trips cannot weigh over 220 pounds, and rides are offered, weather permitting, from April through October. First-time riders are welcome.

Guided rides are also provided by **Ruby's Scenic Rim & Outlaw Trail Rides** (☎ **800/679-5859** or 435/679-8761), at Ruby's Inn, with similar rates and restrictions. Ruby's also offers a full-day ride with lunch for $75. Ruby's will also board your horse, if you happen to have one. Reservations are recommended for both companies.

Biking & Mountain Biking. *Cyclists beware:* Bikes are prohibited on all trails, as well as forbidden for travelling cross-country within the national park boundaries. Only the park's established scenic drive is open to cyclists, but keep in mind that the 18-mile road through the park is narrow and winding, and can be crowded with motor vehicles during the summer.

Because mountain bikers are not welcome on national park hiking trails, you'll have to leave Bryce in search of trails. Fortunately, you won't have to go far. The **Dave's Hollow Trail** starts at the Bryce Canyon National Park boundary sign on Utah 63, the park entrance road, about a mile south of Ruby's Inn. The double-track trail goes west for about 0.5 mile before connecting with F.S. 090, where you turn south and ride for about 0.75 mile before turning right onto an easy ride through Dave's Hollow to the Dave's Hollow Forest Service Station on F.S. 087.

From there you can retrace your route for an 8-mile round-trip ride; for a longer 12-mile trip, turn right on F.S. 087 to

Utah 12 and then right again back to Utah 63 and the starting point. A third option is to turn left on F.S. 087 and follow it to Tropic Reservoir (see "Fishing," below). For further information, contact the **Dixie National Forest,** 82 N. 100 E., Cedar City, UT 84720 (☎ **435/865-3700**).

Mountain bikes can be rented across the street from **Ruby's Inn** (☎ **435/834-5341**) for $5 an hour or $15 for up to 4 hours. They also do repairs.

Fishing. The closest fishing hole to the park is at **Tropic Reservoir,** a large lake in a ponderosa pine forest. From the intersection of Utah 63 (the park entrance road) and Utah 12, drive west about 3 miles to the unpaved F.S. 087, and then drive about 7 miles south. There at the reservoir you will find a forest service campground open in the summer, a boat ramp, and fishing for rainbow, brook, and cutthroat trout. Locals say fishing is sometimes better in streams higher up than in the reservoir itself. For further information, contact the **Dixie National Forest,** 82 N. 100 E., Cedar City, UT 84720 (☎ **435/865-3700**).

Wildlife Watching. The park has a variety of wildlife, ranging from mule deer, which seem to be almost everywhere, to the often seen golden-mantled ground squirrel and Uinta chipmunk. Also in the park are black-tailed jackrabbits, coyotes, striped skunks, and deer mice. Occasionally visitors catch a glimpse of a mountain lion, most likely on the prowl in search of a mule deer dinner; and elk and pronghorn may also be seen at higher elevations.

The Utah prairie dog, now listed as a threatened species, is actually a rodent. It inhabits park meadows in busy colonies, and can be fascinating to watch. However, be sure to keep your distance, because its fleas may carry disease (see "Special Regulations & Warnings," earlier in this chapter).

Of the many birds in the park, you're bound to hear the rather obnoxious call of the Steller's jay. Other birds often seen include violet-green swallows, common ravens, Clark's nutcrackers, American robins, red-shafted flickers, dark-eyes juncos, and chipping sparrows. Watch for white-throated swifts as they perform their exotic acrobatics along cliff faces. The park is also home, at least part of the year, to peregrine falcons, red-tailed hawks, golden eagles, bald eagles, and great horned owls.

The Great Basin rattlesnake, although pretty, should be given a wide berth. Sometimes growing to more than 5 feet long, this rattler is the park's only poisonous reptile. Fortunately, like most rattlesnakes, it is just as anxious as you are to avoid a confrontation. Other reptiles you may see in the park are the mountain short-horned lizard, the tree lizard, the side-blotched lizard, and the northern sagebrush lizard.

Winter Sports & Activities

Bryce is beautiful in the winter, when the white snow settles over the red, pink, orange, and brown statues standing proudly against the cold winds. A limited number of **snowshoes** are loaned free of charge at the visitor center, and may be used anywhere in the park except on cross-country ski tracks.

Cross-country skiers, meanwhile, will find several marked, ungroomed trails (all above the rim), including **The Fairyland Trail,** which leads 1 mile through a pine and juniper forest to the Fairyland Point Overlook. From here you can take the 1-mile **Forest Trail** back to the road, or continue north along the rim for

Especially for Kids

During the summer, children 12 and younger can join the **Junior Rangers,** participate in a variety of programs, and earn certificates and patches. Pick up Junior Ranger booklets at the visitor center.

another 1.2 miles to the park boundary. There are also connections to ski trails in the adjacent national forest.

Although the entire park is open to cross-country skiers, rangers warn that it's impossible to ski the steep trails leading down into the canyon. Stop at the visitor center for additional trail information, and go to **Ruby's Inn,** just north of the park entrance (☎ **435/834-5341**), for information on cross-country ski trails and snowmobiling opportunities outside the park. Ruby's grooms over 50 kilometers of ski trails, and also rents cross-country ski equipment starting at $7 for a half day.

Camping

INSIDE THE PARK

Typical of the West's national park campgrounds, the two facilities at Bryce offer plenty of trees with a genuine "forest camping" experience and easy access to trails, but limited facilities. **North Campground** has 105 sites; **Sunset Campground** has 111 sites. North Campground is closer to the Rim Trail, making it easier to rush over to catch those amazing sunrise and sunset colors.

Try to get to the park early to claim a site (usually by 2pm in the summer). Showers ($2 in quarters) are located at a general store in the park, although it's a healthy walk from either campground. A section of North Campground is open year-round for off-season visitors, but Sunset Campground is open May through September only. The Park Service also operates an RV dump station ($2 fee) in the summer.

The general store near the Sunrise point parking area has a coin-operated laundry and a snack bar, plus bundles of firewood, food and camping supplies, and souvenirs. There are tables on a covered porch along one side of the building.

NEAR THE PARK

Just outside the park is **Ruby's Inn RV Park & Campground,** Utah 63 (P.O. Box 22), Bryce, UT 84764 (☎ **435/834-5301** or 435/834-5341; fax 435/834-5481; credit cards accepted), with shuttle bus service into the park during July and August. Cool off in one of the many shaded campsites, or wander over to the adjacent lake and horse pasture. There is also a game room, horseshoes, and a store with groceries and RV supplies.

Bryce Pioneer Village, 80 S. Main St. (Utah 12) (P.O. Box 119), Tropic, UT 84776 (☎ **800/222-0381** or 435/679-8546; fax 435/679-8607; credit cards accepted), is a small motel/cabins/campground combination in nearby Tropic, with easy access to several restaurants. Showers are available to

Campground	Elev.	Total Sites	RV Hookups	Dump Station	Toilets	Drinking Water
North	7,700	105	No	No	Yes	Yes
Sunset	8,000	111	No	No	Yes	Yes
Bryce Pioneer Village	7,600	15	15	Yes	Yes	Yes
King's Creek (USFS)	8,000	34	No	Yes	Yes	Yes
Red Canyon (USFS)	7,400	36	No	No	Yes	Yes
Ruby's Inn RV Park	7,600	227	127	Yes	Yes	Yes
Kodachrome Basin SP	5,800	24	No	Yes	Yes	Yes

noncampers for $2, and there's a dump station charging $3.

King's Creek Campground, in the Dixie National Forest (mailing address 82 N. 100 E., Cedar City, UT 84720; ☎ **435/865-3700**) is located above Tropic Reservoir, with graded gravel roads and sites nestled among tall ponderosa pines. The reservoir has two boat ramps (see "Fishing," earlier in this chapter). To get there from the park, head west on Utah 12 about 2.5 miles to the access road, turn south (left) and follow signs to Tropic Reservoir for about 7 miles to the campground.

About 9.5 miles west of the park is another Dixie National Forest campground, **Red Canyon Campground** (contact the Dixie National Forest, 82 N. 100 E., Cedar City, UT 84720; ☎ **435/865-3700**). Set among the trees along the south side of Utah 12, it offers terrific views of the red rock formations across the highway, although there is a bit of road noise.

Kodachrome Basin State Park, about 22 miles southeast of Bryce park, has an attractive campground with sites scattered among unusual rock "chimneys" and pinyon and juniper trees.

Accommodations

Room taxes add about 9% to the total cost. Pets are not accepted unless otherwise noted.

INSIDE THE PARK

Bryce Canyon Lodge

Bryce Canyon National Park, UT. ☎ **435/834-5361.** Information and reservations: AmFac Parks & Resorts, 14001 E. Iliff Ave., Suite 600, Aurora, CO 80014. ☎ 303/29-PARKS; fax 303/338-2045. 114 units in motel rms and cabins; 3 suites and 1 studio in lodge. TEL. $83–$90 motel double; $93–$105 cabin; $115–$120 lodge unit. AE, DISC, MC, V. Closed Nov–Mar.

Location is what you're buying here, and there's no denying that this is the perfect place to stay while seeing Bryce Canyon National Park, allowing you to watch the play of changing light on the rock formations throughout the day. The handsome sandstone and ponderosa pine lodge, which opened in 1924, contains desks in the lobby for horseback riding and other activities, and a gift shop that offers everything from postcards and souvenirs to a fine selection of Indian pawn jewelry. The luxurious lodge suites are wonderful, with white wicker furniture, ceiling fans, and separate sitting rooms. The guest units, on the other hand, are simply pleasant, modern motel rooms, with two queen-size beds and either a balcony or a patio. The best choice is one of the cabins. They're not large, but have high ceilings, stone (gas-burning) fireplaces, and log beams—you might call the

Showers	Fire Pits/ Grills	Laundry	Public Phone	Reserve	Fees	Open
No	Yes	No	No	No	$10	Year-round
No	Yes	No	No	No	$10	May–Sept
Yes	Yes	No	Yes	Yes	$10–$15	Mid-Apr to Oct
No	Yes	No	No	No	$8	Mem Day–Labor Day
No	Yes	No	No	No	$9	Apr–Oct
Yes	Yes	Yes	Yes	Yes	$14–$22	Apr–Oct
No	Yes	No	No	Yes	$10	Year-round

ambience "rustic luxury." There is no swimming pool. Try to reserve 4 to 6 months in advance.

NEAR THE PARK

Best Western Ruby's Inn

Utah 63 at the entrance to Bryce Canyon (P.O. Box 1), Bryce, UT 84764. ☎ **800/528-1234** or 435/834-5341; fax 435/834-5265. 369 units including 60 suites. A/C TV TEL. June–Sept $85–$110 double, $120–$125 suite; Apr–May and Oct $60–$92 double, $100–$115 suite; Nov–Mar $44–$70 double, $80 suite. AE, DC, DISC, MC, V.

This large Best Western provides most of the beds for tired hikers and canyon gazers visiting the park. The lobby is among the busiest places in the area, with an ATM, a small liquor store, car rentals, a beauty salon, a 1-hour film processor, and tour desks where you can arrange excursions of all sorts, from horseback and all-terrain vehicle rides to helicopter tours. Near the lobby is a restaurant; a Western art gallery; a huge general store that sells souvenirs, cowboy hats, camping supplies, and groceries; and a U.S. post office. Outside there are two gas stations.

Spread among nine separate buildings, the modern motel rooms contain art depicting scenes of the area, wood furnishings, and shower/tub combos. Some even have whirlpools. Services include a concierge and courtesy transportation from the Bryce Airport; and facilities include two indoor pools, one indoor and one outdoor whirlpool, a sundeck, bicycle rental, nature and cross-country ski trails, a game room, and two coin-operated laundries. Your pets are welcome.

Bryce Pioneer Village

80 S. Main St. (Utah 12; P.O. Box 119), Tropic, UT 84776. ☎ **800/222-0381** or 435/679-8546; fax 435/679-8607. 47 motel rms, 20 cabins. A/C TV TEL. Cabin $39–$85; rm $60–$85 double. DISC, MC, V.

The small, no-frills motel rooms here have showers only (no tubs), but they're clean and completely adequate for those seeking a night's rest at a reasonable rate. The cabins, which were relocated from inside the national park, are more interesting. Most lack tubs and are small but cute; several others, renovated within the past few years, are much larger, with two queen beds, attractive floral-print wallpaper, and bathrooms with shower/tub combinations. There are also two rooms with three queen beds. There's no pool to cool off in, but there is a whirlpool, two hot tubs, a picnic area, and a small curio shop. Just outside the motel office you can see the cabin where Ebenezer and Mary Bryce, for whom the national park is named, lived in the late 1870s. The motel accepts pets. Check on possible winter closure.

Bryce Point Bed & Breakfast

61 N. 400 W. (P.O. Box 96), Tropic, UT 84776-0096. ☎ **435/679-8629.** 5 rms, 1 honeymoon cottage. TV. $70 double; $90–$120 honeymoon cottage. Rates include full breakfast. MC, V.

Each room in Lamar and Ethel LeFevre's bed-and-breakfast is named for and decorated in the style of one of the couple's children. For instance, son Les is a firefighter, so the Les and Dela room contains firefighting memorabilia and photos; son Lynn is in the airline industry, so you'll find airplane mementos in Lynn and Karen's room. In addition to memorabilia, most rooms offer beautiful views of Bryce Point through large picture windows. All rooms have queen beds and private baths (showers only); and all have TV/VCR combos, with free use of the LeFevre's video collection. Breakfasts are full and satisfying, with selections such as bacon and eggs with pancakes and apple cider syrup. The honeymoon cottage is beautifully furnished in country style, with a gas fireplace in the living room, full kitchen, washer and dryer, and king bed in the spacious bedroom. The B&B is entirely nonsmoking.

Canyon Livery Bed & Breakfast

50 S. 660 W. (P.O. Box 24), Tropic, UT 84776-0024. ☎ **888/889-8910** or 435/679-8780. Call for fax. 5 rms. A/C. Apr–Oct $70–$75 double; Nov–Mar $60 double. No credit cards.

The rooms in this delightful bed-and-breakfast are ultrasimple but come with beautiful handmade quilts on the queen beds. Two are dedicated to women pioneers and have brass beds, two have handmade wooden beds and are dedicated to male pioneers, and the fifth is western, with a wonderful high arched window providing terrific views of the night sky. Breakfasts are continental, with fresh homemade bread, fresh fruits (often from the B&B's own trees), juice, and coffee. All rooms have their own entrances and windows facing the national park; the three upstairs rooms have private balconies. There's even a corral if you happen to bring your horse. Smoking is not permitted.

Foster's

Utah 12 (mailing address: Star Rte., Panguitch, UT 84759), Bryce, UT. ☎ **800/475-4318** or 435/834-5227; fax 435/834-5304. 52 units. A/C TV TEL. Winter $49.95 double; summer $59.95 double. AE, DISC, MC, V.

You'll find clean, quiet, and economical lodging at Foster's, located 1.5 miles west of the Bryce Canyon National Park access road turnoff. Also on the grounds is a restaurant (see "Dining," below) and a grocery store (open 7am–8pm, closed December and January) with a decent bakery. The small rooms in this modular unit are decorated with posters showing scenery of the area and contain either one queen-size or two double beds. Bathrooms have showers only.

World Host Bryce Valley Inn

200 N. Main St., Tropic, UT 84776. ☎ **800/442-1890** or 435/679-8811; fax 435/679-8846. 65 rms. A/C TV TEL. Apr–Oct $60–$75 double; Nov–Mar $30–$45 double. AE, DISC, MC, V.

Located 8 miles east of the park entrance road, these basic motel rooms offer a clean, economical choice for park visitors. Rooms, all of which have shower/tub combos, are furnished with either one or two queen beds. There's one suite with two queens and a hide-a-bed, and one handicapped-accessible room. The motel has an outdoor whirlpool tub (but no pool), and a 24-hour coin-operated laundry. At The Hungry Coyote Restaurant & Saloon (see "Dining," below) you can fill up on American and Mexican cuisine, and then get dessert at the separate ice cream parlor. A gift shop on the premises offers a large selection of American Indian arts and crafts, handmade gifts, rocks, and fossils. Pets are accepted for an additional fee.

Dining

INSIDE THE PARK

Bryce Canyon Lodge

Bryce Canyon National Park. ☎ **435/834-5361.** Reservations required for dinner. Breakfast $2.75–$6.25; lunch $[illegible]–$[illegible]; dinner $10.50–$15.95. AE, DC, DISC, MC, V. Daily 6:30am–4:30pm, and 5:30–9:30pm. Closed Nov–Mar. AMERICAN.

It's worth coming here just for the mountain lodge atmosphere, with two large stone fireplaces, American Indian weavings and baskets, a huge 45-star 1897 American flag, and large windows looking out on the park. But the food's pretty good, too, and reasonably priced considering that this is the only real restaurant actually in the park. House specialties at dinner include an excellent slow-roasted prime rib au jus and broiled chicken breast. We also recommend the fresh mountain trout. Vegetarians should try the grilled polenta or the vegetarian lasagna. Afterwards, ask about the lodge's specialty desserts, such as the exotic and very tasty wild "Bryce-berry" crumb cake. At lunch you'll find the trout, plus burgers, sandwiches, and salads; breakfasts offer all the usual American selections. Service is very attentive and friendly, although a bit too speedy at dinner. The restaurant will even pack lunches to go for hikers, and offers a children's menu and full liquor service.

NEAR THE PARK

Canyon Diner

Just north of the park entrance on Utah 63, in the Ruby's Inn complex, Bryce Canyon. ☎ **435/834-5341.** Most items $2–$6.50. AE, DISC, MC, V. Daily 6:30am–10pm. AMERICAN.

This fast-food restaurant adjacent to the Best Western Ruby's Inn is a great place to fill up the kids without going broke. Breakfasts include several egg croissants; for lunch and dinner you can get hoagies, burgers, hot dogs, stuffed potatoes, pizza, fried chicken, and lots of salads, including a good crab salad. On a hot day, try a basic salad complemented by a filling malt or milkshake. No alcohol is served.

Foster's Family Steak House

Utah 12 about 1.5 miles west of the Park Entrance road. ☎ **435/834-5227.** Reservations not accepted. Breakfast and lunch items $1.75–$5.99; main dinner courses $8.99–$18.99. AE, DISC, MC, V. Mar–Nov daily 7am–10pm; Dec–Feb daily 5–10pm. STEAK/SEAFOOD.

The simple western decor here provides the appropriate atmosphere for a family steak house, popular among locals for its slow-roasted prime rib and steamed Utah trout. Foster's also offers several steaks (including a 14-ounce T-bone), sandwiches, a soup of the day, and homemade western-style chile with beans. All the pastries, pies, and breads are baked on the premises. For the kids, there's a children's menu; for adults, there's bottled beer available with meals. All menu items can be ordered to go.

Hungry Coyote Restaurant & Saloon

200 N. Main St. (Utah 12; 8 miles east of the park entrance road), at the World Host Bryce Valley Inn, Tropic. ☎ **435/679-8822.** Main breakfast courses $3.95–$6.95; dinner $4.95–$20.75. AE, DISC, MC, V. Daily 6–11am and 5–11pm; shorter hrs. in winter. AMERICAN/MEXICAN.

The Old West is still king here; look around at the rough wood walls, old ranch tools, kerosene lanterns, and warnings that patrons must "check your gun with the waitress." Beef eaters will savor the thick 20-ounce T-bone, the most expensive item on the menu, while Mexican food lovers might opt for the fajitas. You can also get pork chops, grilled chicken breast, or trout. The restaurant has a full liquor license as well.

Ruby's Inn Cowboy's Buffet and Steak Room

Ruby's Inn complex, Bryce. ☎ **435/834-5341.** Breakfast buffet $7 adults, $6 children 3–12; lunch buffet $9 adults, $7 children 3–12; main courses breakfast and lunch $3–$13.50; dinner buffet $14.50; main dinner courses $5.50–$19.50. AE, CB, DC, DISC, MC, V. Summer daily 6:30am–9:30pm; winter daily 6:30am–8:30pm. STEAK/SEAFOOD.

The busiest restaurant in the Bryce Canyon area, Ruby's moves 'em through with buffets at every meal plus a well-rounded menu and friendly service. The breakfast buffet offers the usual family restaurant staples of scrambled eggs, fresh fruit, several breakfast meats, potatoes, and cereals; you can also get omelettes and eggs cooked to order. At the lunch buffet you'll find country-style ribs, fresh fruit, salads, soups, vegetables, and breads. The dinner buffet features slow-roasted beef and other meats, pastas, potatoes, and salads. Regular menu dinner entrees include prime rib, huge ribs, breaded-and-grilled southern Utah rainbow trout, broiled chicken breast, burgers, and salads. Full liquor service is available.

Picnic & Camping Supplies

There is a small store inside the national park with a few groceries and camping supplies, plus snacks, and all at surprisingly low prices. Just outside the park entrance, the huge general store in Ruby's Inn (see "Accommodations," above) offers camping supplies, groceries, western clothing, and souvenirs. Also on the property is an ATM machine and a 24-hour gas station and auto repair.

Nearby Attractions

North of Ruby's Inn, **Bryce Canyon Country Rodeo** has bucking broncos, bull riding, calf roping, and all sorts of rodeo fun in a 1-hour program from Memorial Day to August, Monday to Saturday evenings at 7:30pm. Admission is $7 for adults and $4 for children under 12.

Directly across Utah 63 from the motel are **Old Bryce Town Shops,** open from mid-May through September, where you'll find a rock shop, souvenir shops, a Christmas store, and an opportunity to buy that genuine cowboy hat you've been wanting. Next to the shops is a children's petting farm (free admission), with performing horses and a cowboy poet; you can also try your hand at gold-panning ($4 pan rental).

Nearby, **Bryce Canyon Country Rodeo** has bucking broncos, bull riding, calf roping, and all sorts of rodeo fun in a 1-hour program from Memorial Day through August, Monday through Saturday evenings at 7:30pm. Admission is $7 for adults and $4 for children under 12.

A New National Monument

GRAND STAIRCASE-ESCALANTE NATIONAL MONUMENT

Covering some 1.7 million acres, this vast area of red-orange canyons, mesas, plateaus, and river valleys became a national monument by presidential proclamation on September 18, 1996. Known for its rugged beauty, it contains a combination of geological, biological, paleontological, archaeological, and historical resources. In announcing the creation of the monument, President Clinton proclaimed, "This high, rugged, and remote region was the last place in the continental United States to be mapped; even today, this unspoiled natural area remains a frontier, a quality that greatly enhances the monument's value for scientific study."

Under the jurisdiction of the Bureau of Land Management, the monument is expected to remain open for grazing and possible oil and gas drilling under existing leases (although no new leases will be issued), as well as hunting, fishing, hiking, camping, and other forms of recreation. A management plan is expected to be completed by late 1999.

Unlike most other national monuments, almost all of this vast area is undeveloped—there are few all-weather roads, only one maintained hiking trail, and two developed campgrounds. But for the adventurous there are miles upon miles of dirt roads and practically unlimited opportunities for hiking, horseback riding, mountain biking, and camping.

The national monument can be divided into three distinct sections: The Grand Staircase of sandstone cliffs—including five life zones from Sonoran Desert to coniferous forests—is the southwest section; the Kaiparowits Plateau, a vast, wild region of rugged mesas and steep canyons, is the center section; and the Escalante River Canyons, a delightfully scenic area containing miles of interconnecting river canyons, is the northern section.

JUST THE FACTS

Getting There

The national monument takes in a large region of southern Utah, covering an area almost as big as the states of Delaware and Rhode Island combined. Bryce Canyon National Park is to the west; Capitol Reef National Park is on the northeast edge; and Glen Canyon National Recreation Area lies along the east and part of the south sides.

Access is via Utah 12 along the monument's northwest edge, from Kodachrome Basin State Park and the communities of Escalante and Boulder; and via U.S. 89 to the southern section of the monument, east of the town of Kanab.

Information & Visitor Centers

Contact the **Escalante Interagency Office** on the west side of Escalante at 755 W. Main St. (Utah 12), P.O. Box 246, Escalante, UT 84726 (☎ **435/826-5499**); or the **Bureau of Land Management** office at 318 N. First E. St., Kanab, UT 84741 (☎ **435/644-2672**). These offices have maps, a handsome color brochure, and handouts on a variety of activities.

Fees, Regulations & Safety

There is no charge to enter the monument; those planning overnight trips into the backcountry should obtain permits (free at this writing) at either of the offices listed above. Regulations are similar to those on other public lands, and particularly forbid damaging or disturbing archaeological and historic sites in any way.

Water is the main safety concern here, whether there's too little or too much. This is generally very dry country, so those going into the monument should carry plenty of drinking water. However, thunderstorms can turn the monument's dirt roads into impassable mud bogs in minutes, stranding motorists; and potentially fatal flash floods through narrow canyons can catch hikers by surprise. Everyone planning trips into the monument should check first with one of the offices listed above (see "Information & Visitor Centers," above) on current and anticipated weather and travel conditions.

SPORTS & ACTIVITIES

Hiking, Mountain Biking & Horseback Riding. Located about 15 miles northeast of Escalante via Utah 12, the **Calf Creek Recreation Area** has a campground (see "Camping," below) and a picnic area with fire grates, tables, trees, drinking water, and flush toilets. Well shaded, it lies along a creek at the bottom of a narrow, high-walled rock canyon.

The best part of the recreation area is the moderately strenuous 5.5-mile round-trip hike to **Lower Calf Creek Falls.** A sandy trail leads along **Calf Creek,** past beaver ponds and wetlands, to a beautiful waterfall cascading 126 feet down a rock wall into a tree-shaded pool. You can pick up an interpretive brochure at the trailhead.

Even though the Calf Creek Trail is the monument's only officially marked and maintained trail, there are numerous unmarked cross-country routes ideal for hiking, mountain biking, and horseback riding. We strongly recommend that hikers stop at the Interagency Office in Escalante or the Bureau of Land Management office in Kanab to get recommendations on hiking routes and to purchase topographical maps.

Hikers need to remember that this is wild country, and it can be hazardous. Rangers recommend carrying at least 1 gallon of water per person per day and warn that all water from streams should be treated before drinking. Flooding is always a danger. Hikers should check with the BLM before attempting to hike through the monument's narrow slot canyons, where a sudden rainstorm miles away can cause a **flash flood,** trapping hikers without escape. Other unpleasant hazards include poison ivy in the wetter areas and poisonous snakes and scorpions. Last but not least, the trails, many of them over smooth slickrock, can be slippery, so hikers should wear sturdy hiking boots with good soles.

Among the popular and relatively easy-to-follow hiking routes is the footpath to **Escalante Natural Bridge,** which repeatedly crosses the river, so be prepared to get wet up to your knees

A National Monument is Born in Controversy

In a move hailed by environmentalists but condemned by developers and others, President Clinton on September 18, 1996, took the country and especially the state of Utah by surprise when he announced that by presidential proclamation he was creating a new national monument. At 1.7 million acres, the Grand Staircase–Escalante National Monument covers almost 2,700 square miles in southern Utah, a huge tract that includes some of the West's most rugged and scenic terrain, but is also an area rich in coal, oil, and gas.

While the president's election-year timing may have been political, there is little doubt that he was convinced that this vast chunk of real estate must be protected. In his proclamation, Clinton stated, "The Grand Staircase–Escalante National Monument's vast and austere landscape embraces a spectacular array of scientific and historic resources."

However, Utah's political leaders and many of its citizens did not take kindly to the president's "protection." Utah Sen. Orrin Hatch denounced Clinton's action as "the mother of all land-grabs." In mid-1997, a Utah government agency and the state's association of counties filed lawsuits against the federal government, claiming that Clinton exceeded his authority.

Although part of the controversy has to do with states' rights—Utah has traditionally been opposed to federal government intervention in what it considers its own business—the main reason people in Utah are upset is probably money. The monument contains more than 60 billion tons of coal. Developers claim that, because of the president's proclamation, a planned mine had to be scrapped, costing the area up to 900 jobs, plus royalties of about $1 billion over the next 50 years. However, supporters of the national monument designation say that the only real change is that no new mining claims can be made. The president's proclamation specifically states that existing permits and leases are not affected.

occasionally. The easy 2-mile (one way) hike begins at a parking area at the bridge that crosses the Escalante River near Calf Creek Recreation Area, 15 miles northeast of the town of Escalante. From the parking area, hike upstream to Escalante Natural Bridge, on the south side of the river. The bridge is 130 feet high and spans 100 feet. From here you can continue upstream, exploring the side canyons, or turn around and head back to the parking lot.

Also starting at the Utah 12 bridge parking area is a hike downstream to **Phipps Wash.** Mostly moderate, this hike goes about 1.5 miles to the mouth of Phipps Wash, which enters the river from the west. On a north side drainage of Phipps Wash you'll find Maverick Natural Bridge; by climbing up the south side you can get to Phipps Arch.

Hiking the national monument's **slot canyons** is very popular, but we can't stress too strongly that you need to check on flood potentials before starting out. One challenging and very strenuous slot canyon hike is through **Peek-a-boo and Spooky canyons,** which are accessed from the Hole-in-the-Rock Road (see "Sightseeing & Four-Wheeling," below). Stop at the Escalante Interagency Office for precise directions.

Sightseeing & Four-Wheeling. Since this is one of America's least-developed large sections of public land, it offers a wonderful opportunity for exploration by the adventurous. Be aware, though, that

> On this remarkable site, God's handiwork is everywhere.
>
> —Pres. Bill Clinton, September 18, 1996

roads inside the monument are dirt that becomes mud, and impassable, when it rains.

One particularly popular road is the **Hole-in-the-Rock Scenic Backway,** which is partly in the national monument and partly in the adjacent Glen Canyon National Recreation Area. Like most roads in the monument, this should be attempted in dry weather only. Starting about 5 miles northeast of Escalante off Utah 12, this clearly marked dirt road travels 57 miles (one way) to the Hole-in-the-Rock, where Mormon settlers, in 1880, cut a passage through solid rock and used ropes to lower their wagons down a 1,200-foot cliff to the canyon floor and Colorado River below.

About 12 miles in, the road passes by the sign to **Devil's Rock Garden,** an area of classic red rock formations and arches, where you'll also find a picnic area (about 1 mile off the main road). The road continues across a plateau of typical desert terrain, ending at a spectacular scenic overlook of Lake Powell. The first 35 miles of the scenic byway are relatively easy (in dry weather) in a standard passenger car, but then it gets a bit steeper and sandier, and the last 6 miles of the road require a high clearance 4X4 vehicle. Allow about 6 hours round-trip, and make sure you have plenty of fuel and water.

Another recommended drive in the national monument is the **Cottonwood Canyon Road,** which runs from Kodachrome State Park south to U.S. 89, along the monument's southern edge, a distance of about 46 miles. The road is sandy and narrow, and washboard in places, but usually passable for passenger cars in dry weather. It mostly follows Cottonwood Wash, with good views of red rock formations plus distant panoramas from hilltops. Unfortunately, views through the canyon are marred by two power lines, which make photography a challenge—though in all fairness, we should acknowledge that the road would not exist at all if not for the power lines.

About 10 miles east of Kodachrome Basin State Park is a short turnoff from Cottonwood Canyon Road that leads to **Grosvenor Arch.** This magnificent stone arch, with an opening 99 feet wide, was named for National Geographic Society founder and editor Gilbert H. Grosvenor, and is well worth the trip.

Wildlife Viewing & Bird Watching. The isolated and rugged terrain offers good habitat for a number of species, such as desert bighorn sheep and mountain lions. As for birds, more than 200 species have been spotted, including bald eagles, golden eagles, Swainson's hawks, and peregrine falcons. The best areas for seeing wildlife are along the Escalante and Paria rivers and Johnson Creek.

CAMPING

Backcountry camping is permitted in most areas of the monument with a permit (free at this writing), available at the Interagency office in Escalante and BLM office in Kanab. There are also two designated campgrounds. **Calf Creek Recreation Area,** about 15 miles northeast of the town of Escalante via Utah 12, has about a dozen sites and a picnic area. Open year-round, the tree-shaded campground is in a scenic, steep canyon along Calf Creek, surrounded by high rock walls. Campers can enjoy the volleyball court and the nearby interpretative hiking trail (see "Hiking, Mountain Biking & Horseback Riding," above). Be advised that though the campground has modern rest rooms and drinking water, it does not have showers, RV hookups, an RV dump station, and garbage removal.

In addition, from November through March water is turned off and only vault toilets are available. To reach the campground vehicles must ford a shallow creek, a task not recommended for vehicles over 25 feet long. Campsites cost $7 per night; day use is $2 per vehicle.

The national monument's other designated campground is **Deer Creek,** located 6 miles east of the town of Boulder along the scenic Burr Trail Road. Here there are four primitive sites and no drinking water or other facilities—but at least the camping is free.

7

CANYON DE CHELLY NATIONAL MONUMENT

by Alex Wells

CANYON DE CHELLY, WHOSE NAME DERIVES FROM A NAVAJO WORD FOR "rock canyon," is a special place, as significant for its natural beauty as for its archaeological treasures. For the most part, this is a place for learning about *peoples,* notably the ancestral Pueblo people, whose remarkable dwellings and rock art grace the alcoves under the canyon's massive sandstone overhangs, and the Navajo, whose rich culture still flourishes here today. The monument's two scenic drives provide access to view points above some of the most remarkable archaeological sites in the park as well as some of the canyon's most distinctive geology, but you will only be able to see all of this up close by hiking, riding a horse, or taking a Jeep tour into the canyon with a Navajo guide.

At the mouth of the canyon, Chinle Wash, a seasonal creek that drains the 9,500-foot-high Chuska Mountains to the east, trickles out from between two rock walls and into the town of Chinle, Arizona. Upstream from here, the canyon's sheer walls rise quickly and dramatically; from 30 feet high at the mouth, they climb to 1,000 feet only 18 miles to the east. Streaked black in places by mineral deposits known as Desert Varnish, the red walls stunningly contrast the lush cottonwood trees and checkerboard plots of farmland below.

Like mirror images of Canyon de Chelly, two significant canyons, del Muerto (Spanish for "of the dead") and Monument, branch off from the 27-mile-long main canyon at different points upstream. All three canyons follow sharply winding paths that seasonal creeks first etched into rock some 50 million years ago. These creeks gradually sawed down through sandstone, undercutting the rock in places to form towering amphitheaters and deep alcoves.

These overhangs, together with abundant water and relatively fertile ground, have made these canyons sacred places to Native Americans, who have occupied them almost continuously for the past 2,000 years. The ancestral Pueblo peoples tilled the soil here from near the time of Christ through about A.D. 1300. The 100 ancient dwellings here reflect the developments in their culture, as the Puebloans progressed from building small pit houses of sticks and mortar to multistoried cliff houses of impressive masonry.

Their descendants, the Hopi, farmed here intermittently from around 1400 to

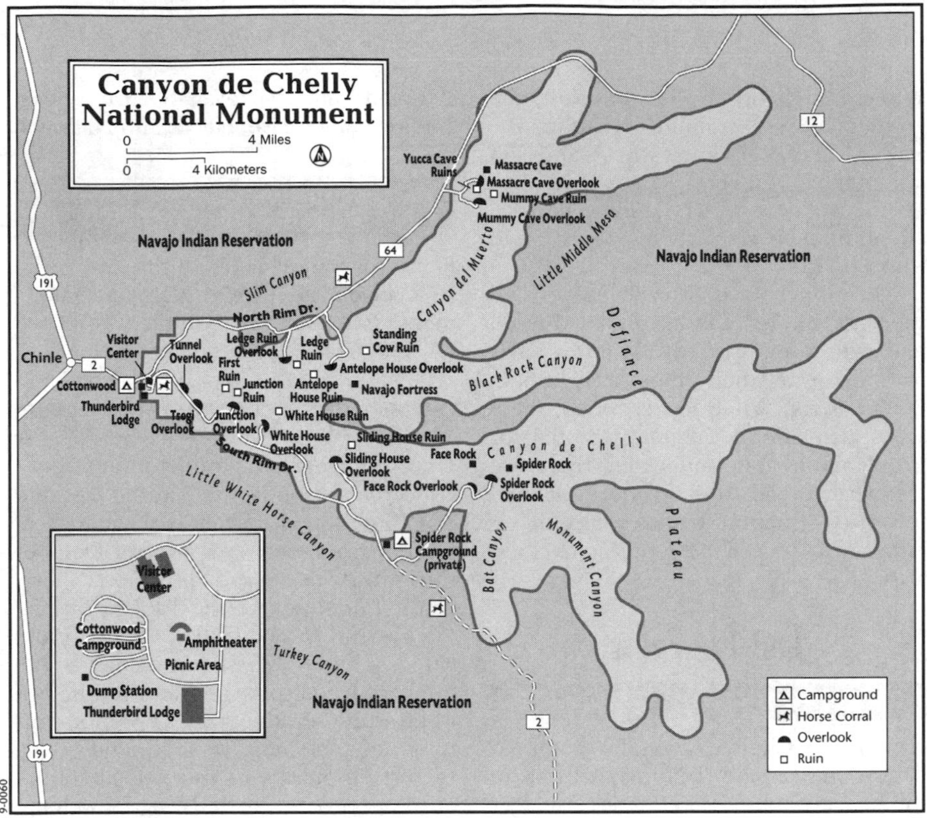

1800, planting peach orchards in many of the side canyons. At least a few of the Hopi mixed with the Navajo, a tribe of seminomadic shepherds and raiders who first moved into the these canyons in the 1700s. This blending of cultures is reflected in similar religious beliefs, farming techniques, and clan systems. More than 200 Navajo families live inside the canyons today, some in the traditional hexagonal or octagonal structures known as hogans. Many more dwell on the canyon rims.

Long a place of human life, Canyon de Chelly has also seen conflict and unnatural death. Many Navajo died in battles with Spanish soldiers in the early 1800s, and more perished in the 1860s, when the U.S. Army drove the tribe from northern Arizona to a temporary settlement in New Mexico. In recognition of the history, natural beauty, and archaeological resources of the canyon, President Hoover declared Canyon de Chelly a national monument in 1931. The Park Service operates the monument through a partnership with the Navajo Tribal Council.

Avoiding the Crowds. If your goal is to avoid people altogether, don't come to Canyon de Chelly. Although beautiful, it is far from pristine, with working farms covering much of its 131 square miles. As at any park, however, distancing yourself from large groups of tourists will bring rewards. It will give you chances to learn about the canyon's occupants, and to listen for the echoes of Ancestral Pueblo life.

The single best way to lose the crowds, according to the national monument's superintendent, Anna Marie Fender, is to "take off with a Navajo guide and hike in the canyon."

"The guides," she says, "can take people on trails that are different from the routes the Jeeps take. Even the popular places like Antelope House are accessible by trails [down side canyons]."

When hiking off the beaten path, the guide takes responsibility for finding the way. "Most of them know what is and isn't acceptable," Ms. Fender says. "And most of them know which landowners will allow them to cross their property and who won't."

The upper parts of each canyon are the least traveled. In Canyon del Muerto, few visitors venture above Mummy Cave; in Canyon de Chelly, most turn back at Spider Rock. While less crowded, these areas also offer a greater potential for problems, as the landowners there are less accustomed to—and more inclined to resist—visitation. Unless your guide is either savvy or well-liked, problems could arise.

Just the Facts

GETTING THERE & GATEWAYS

Canyon de Chelly National Monument begins on west side of Chinle, Arizona, in the heart of the Navajo Reservation, 222 miles northwest of Flagstaff, Arizona, and 89 miles northeast of Gallup, New Mexico.

From Flagstaff, the easiest route to the park is to take I-40 east to U.S. 191 north to Ganado. (If you're coming from Gallup, you'll also be taking I-40 to U.S. 191; you'll just be coming from the opposite direction.) At Ganado, drive west on Ariz. 264 and then pick up U.S. 191 again heading north to Chinle.

The name *Chinle* derives from a Navajo word for the place where water flows out of a canyon. The town, which originated as a trading post in 1882, now boasts a large grocery store, a hospital, schools, three hotels, and numerous restaurants.

Navajo Transit (☎ **520/729-4002**) offers bus service between Gallup, New Mexico, and Chinle.

The Nearest Airport. Flagstaff's **Pulliam Airport** is served by America West Express. The airport is located 3 miles south of town off I-17.

Car rentals are available from **Avis, Budget, Enterprise, Hertz,** and **National.**

GETTING INFORMATION BEFORE YOUR TRIP

For information before you leave, write to **Canyon de Chelly National Monument,** P.O. Box 588, Chinle, AZ 86503 (☎ **520/674-5500**).

VISITOR CENTER

Upon arriving, head for the monument's visitor center on Route 7 at the east end of Chinle, open daily May through September from 8am to 6pm, and October through April from 8am to 5pm. Here, you'll find interpretive displays on the Pueblo and Navajo Indians. A 22-minute video, *Canyon Voices,* complements the interpretive displays. When you're finished with the video, take a few moments to watch a Navajo silversmith craft jewelry, or step outside to visit a hogan, a traditional log-and-earth Navajo dwelling, which is open to visitors.

ENTRANCE & CAMPING FEES

Park admission is free, as is camping at Cottonwood Campground. There is an additional fee to hire a Navajo guide (which is a requirement for hiking into the canyon); various guide services are outlined in "Guide Services," below.

SPECIAL REGULATIONS & WARNINGS

Because families live here, and because the canyon is subject to natural dangers such as flash floods, any visitor who wants to venture into the canyon must hire a Navajo guide or run the risk of being charged with trespassing. (The one exception to this rule is the **White House Trail,** on which no guide is required.) In addition to respecting private property, please don't violate the privacy of canyon residents, many of whom are offended by having their pictures taken. As a gesture of goodwill, avoid photographing them without their permission, even from a distance.

Visitors are sometimes cited for possession of alcohol, which is illegal in the Navajo Nation. If you're caught with alcohol anywhere on the reservation (including the national monument and its campground), you'll be subject to fines starting at $50.

Vehicle break-ins are common at the overlooks. If you can't leave your valuables at home, stow them in your trunk, or leave them in the hotel safe.

Also, exercise caution when camping inside the canyon—a few visitors have been assaulted during overnight stays in the canyon. Those who insist on spending the night are urged to travel in groups.

The walls of these canyons, while not as high as those at Grand Canyon, are no less deadly. Be cautious around the rims. During monsoon season, lightning frequently strikes the rims. Move away from these exposed areas when a storm approaches. Finally, avoid driving across the reservation at night. In daylight, the open rangeland and bumpy roads are easy to navigate. At night, however, travel becomes risky.

Time Zones. The Navajo Reservation, unlike the rest of Arizona, observes daylight saving time. During months when daylight saving time is in effect, the time here is an hour later on the reservation than in the rest of Arizona.

SEASONS & CLIMATE

With elevations ranging from 5,500 feet at the visitor center to 7,000 feet on the rim above Spider Rock, Canyon de Chelly National Monument is cooler than many visitors expect. On winter nights, when cold air sinks to the canyon floor, lows can dip into the teens. Snow falls both inside the canyon and on the rim, and it often sticks at the higher elevations and on the north-facing slopes. Winter highs generally average in the 40s and 50s. Spring tends to be breezy, dry, and pleasant, with highs ranging from the 60s to the 80s. During April and May, runoff from the Chuskas fills the creeks in del Muerto and de Chelly canyons, making them especially pretty. In summer the red rocks heat up, and July brings many days of 100° or more. In late July and August, afternoon monsoons send waterfalls cascading off the rocky rims and down into the canyon. Many people love to visit the canyon after the monsoons end in fall, when the temperatures have cooled and the deciduous vegetation begins to change color.

USEFUL PUBLICATIONS

For a comprehensive look at the cultural history of Canyon de Chelly, pick up ***Canyon de Chelly: Its People and Rock Art,*** by Campbell Grant (Tucson, Ariz.: University of Arizona Press) in the visitor center bookstore. In addition to describing the canyon's ruins and rock art, Grant links the history of those sites to the migrations and cultural changes among the peoples of the Southwest.

A less-detailed but pretty book is ***Canyon de Chelly: The Story Behind the Scenery,*** by Charles Supplee, Douglas Anderson, and Barbara Anderson. Part of a series on the national parks, this 48-page book mixes spectacular color photographs with a general discussion of the history of Canyon de Chelly.

You can order any of these books from the park **bookstore.** Just call the visitor center (☎ **520/674-5500**). They accept Visa and MasterCard.

When you arrive you may also want to pick up a copy of the park newspaper, ***Canyon Overlook,*** which has useful information about the park and a map.

Seeing the Highlights in a Day

If you only have a day to see the park, take the **North Rim Drive** in the morning, when the sun illuminates the many ruins along it. Drive back for lunch at **Thunderbird Lodge,** then travel along the **South Rim** in the afternoon. On the way, plan to make a 2-hour round-trip hike to **White House.**

If you have 2 days to see the park, take the scenic drives and the White House Ruin hike on the first day. On the second day, sign up for a **guided Jeep, horse,** or **hiking tour.** Since you've already seen White House up close, you may wish to travel the length of **Canyon del Muerto** on the second day, ending with a close-up view of **Mummy House.**

Exploring the Park by Car

The monument's two scenic drives provide access to view points above some of the most remarkable archaeological sites in the park. The North Rim Drive, 34 miles round-trip, features four overlooks located off spur roads from Ariz. 64. Three open onto Canyon del Muerto. The South Rim Drive, 37 miles round-trip, travels near the rim of Canyon de Chelly and has six view points, the last above Spider Rock, where an 800-foot-high rock spire marks the confluence of Canyon de Chelly and Monument Canyon. On both drives, binoculars are useful for viewing archaeological sites.

NORTH RIM DRIVE

As you drive west from the visitor center, the first stop on the **North Rim Drive** is the **Ledge Ruin Overlook.** From the parking area here, the 0.25-mile trail to the right ends at an overlook of Ledge Ruin, an Ancestral Puebloan dwelling perched on a shelf 100 feet above the canyon floor. From the same parking area, the 0.25-mile trail to the left leads to an overlook of two small dwellings in side-by-side alcoves just above the floor of the canyon. In the alcove to the right is a square-walled *kiva*—an Ancestral Puebloan dwelling that may have been rebuilt by the Navajo. In the alcove to the left is an even smaller Ancestral Puebloan structure, which some Navajo say was occupied by one of their medicine men during the 1800s. Although the Navajo respect the dead and have traditionally shied away from using the ruins of other tribes, many had no choice but to occupy Ancestral Puebloan structures after their own dwellings were destroyed in the U.S. Army's campaign against them.

Your next stop is **Antelope House Overlook.** The trail that goes to the right from the parking area undulates for 0.25 mile across sandstone to a vantage point above Antelope House, the ruin of a village that housed from 20 to 40 people between A.D. 700 and 1250. Most of the structures that remain today were completed after 1050. The ruin takes its name from four Navajo paintings of antelopes on the wall to the east of it. These lovely yellow-and-white images date from the 1830s. The white pictographs nearby are older, Ancestral Puebloan art.

The trail to the left travels to an overlook of **Fortress Rock,** a butte that divides del Muerto and Black Rock canyons. For at least 100 years, the Navajo hid from their enemies atop this rock, using wood ladders to climb from ledge to ledge, then pulling the ladders up behind them. The practice ended in the 1863, when U.S. Army Col. Kit Carson gave up chasing the Navajo, opting instead to destroy their crops, livestock, and dwellings. Carson's infamous slash-and-burn campaign ended with the surrender of most of the tribe in 1864. After their surrender, the army drove the Navajo 400 miles on foot from Ft. Defiance, Arizona, to Bosque Redondo, New Mexico, with thousands dying on the way. Four years later, the Navajo returned, virtually empty-handed, to the lands around Canyon de Chelly.

The next stop is at the **Mummy Cave Overlook.** From here, you'll see what many believe to be the most spectacular ruins in the canyon. Mummy Cave consists of two deep alcoves connected by a narrow ledge, all under a 150-foot sandstone overhang. The overhang shelters the largest set of dwellings in the national monument, with 55 rooms in the eastern alcove, 20 in the western alcove, and 15 on the ledge. The sites in the alcoves are oldest. Each features the alternating layers of thin and wide stones that are typical of Kayenta-style masonry of the 1100s. One part of the dwelling in the western alcove has been tree-ring dated from A.D. 306.

The site on the ledge is more recent. Its three-story tower dates from 1284, making it the last ancestral Pueblo structure constructed in what is now the national monument. This ruin, built around a large boulder, consists of the shaped rectangular blocks typical of Mesa Verde–style masonry. The construction date dovetails with a large exodus from Mesa Verde, raising the possibility that a number of people may have migrated here at that time.

The final and certainly saddest stop on the North Rim Drive is at the **Massacre Cave Overlook.** The path that forks to the left takes you to a view point above Massacre Cave, where Spanish troops led by Lt. Antonio Narbona in 1804 killed roughly 120 Navajos, most of them women and children, according to Navajo accounts. Massacre Cave is the ledge and shallow cave 200 feet below the overlook and about 600 feet above the floor of the canyon. While easily visible from the rim, this ledge cannot be seen from below, and the Navajos had successfully hidden there during a number of conflicts. On the morning of the massacre, however, their location was revealed. Some say a Navajo man angry with his clan led the troops to the location; others maintain that a Navajo woman who had once been enslaved by the Spanish scoffed at them as they passed by on the valley floor. After discovering the hiding place, the troops launched a daylong assault, firing more than 10,000 rounds and killing most of the people on the ledge.

By taking the trail that forks right, you'll reach the **Yucca Cave Overlook,** which affords views of archaeological sites in two small alcoves just below the overlook. The one on the right, Yucca Cave, houses one of the oldest ruins in the park, dating from perhaps A.D. 200. The flat stones laid on edge at the base of this structure are characteristic of Basket Maker (early Pueblo) sites, where stones such as this were used to seal the dirt walls of pit houses and storage cists.

Now, you double back along the same route, perhaps stopping for lunch at the Thunderbird Lodge. You can do the South Rim Drive in the afternoon.

SOUTH RIM DRIVE

Your first stop is at **Tunnel Overlook,** where a short walk takes you to the head of a side canyon of Canyon de Chelly. The Ancestral Puebloans, who hunted first with spears and later with bow and arrow, needed to close in on large game to have a chance of killing it. To do this, they frequently trapped animals at the end of box canyons such as the one below this overlook.

At your next stop, the wheelchair-accessible **Tsegi Overlook,** you'll have a long view east down Canyon de Chelly at the patchwork of corn and alfalfa fields. Through these fields, and flanked by cottonwood and Russian Olive trees, the sandy riverbed known as Chinle Wash carves a serpentine path. Before the Civilian Conservation Corps (CCC) planted these trees for floodbank control, the river frequently changed its course and the lay of the land on the canyon floor. For the Ancestral Puebloan, the only safe and practical place to live was above the floor.

From **Junction Overlook,** you'll see First Ruin, the remains of 22 rooms and two kivas in a 150-foot-high alcove on the opposite wall of the canyon. Junction Ruin, named for its location near the junction of de Chelly and del Muerto canyons, is visible in an alcove a few hundred yards to its right. A small clan probably built and lived in each of these enclaves during the classic Pueblo period (A.D. 1100–1300). As you look at Junction Ruin, note the small (2½ by 2 feet) doorway near the center of the structure. The Ancestral Pueblo Indians, most of whom stood between 5 feet and 5 feet, 4 inches in height, made the outside doorways small so that during inclement weather the openings could be sealed with sandstone slabs.

Don't miss the wheelchair-accessible **White House Overlook.** Here you can look 600 feet down to two ruins—one on the valley floor and the other on a ledge 35 feet above it. Archaeologists believe that the lower ruin once had 60 rooms and four kivas. At four or five stories high, it reached to the ledge on which the upper one, with 10 rooms, was located. The White House is named for an interior wall of the upper ruin that is plastered with white gypsum clay. The Ancestral Pueblo people commonly used clay such as this to cover soot from fires. Today, graffiti left by 19th-century travelers mars the wall. The trail from here down to the ruin is the only place where you can enter the canyon without a guide or ranger (see "Day Hikes," below for a description; you'll need 2 hours to make this hike).

Your next stop, **Sliding House Overlook,** sits above a ruin of between 30 and 50 rooms occupied from A.D. 900 to 1200. In spite of the excellent engineering skills of the Ancestral Pueblo Indians, who frequently used retaining walls and fill dirt to create platforms on uneven ground, the ruin is now slipping down the slope upon which it was constructed.

At **Face Rock Overlook,** a view-finder will help you locate four Ancestral Puebloan ruins scattered around the canyon. Because these ruins are small, you'll probably need binoculars to see them well. Once spotted, their precipitous locations may surprise you.

You won't need a view-finder once you've walked the 200 yards from the **Spider Rock Overlook** parking area to the overlook itself. Here, the view is dominated by the 800-foot-high Spider Rock—two spires of rock, joined at the bottom, that separate Monument and de Chelly canyons. This stunning natural landform is named for Spider Woman, the deity who taught weaving to the Navajo and who the Navajo believe makes her home at the rock. Canyon de Chelly is roughly 1,000 feet deep here.

GUIDE SERVICES

If you'd like to tour the inner canyon with a guide, you can go by jeep, horseback, or on foot. All guides working at the canyon have completed a 5-day course on guiding provided by the Park Service. Several guide companies work at the canyon.

Guided Jeep Tours. **Thunderbird Lodge Canyon Jeep Tours,** P.O. Box 548, Chinle, AZ 86503 (☎ **800/679-2473** or 520/674-5841), offers half- and full-day tours of the canyon in four- and six-wheel-drive trucks, each of which seats 20 or more passengers in open, unshaded flatbeds (unofficially known as "Shake-and-Bakes.") The **half-day tours,** which cost $35 for adults and $26 for kids 12 and under, travel to Standing Cow Ruin in Canyon del Muerto, then to White House Ruin in Canyon de Chelly before returning to the lodge (a 3½-hour round-trip). The **full-day tours,** which cost $57 per person and include a bag lunch, go to Mummy Cave in Canyon del Muerto and to Spider Rock in Canyon de Chelly. Call or write the company for more information or reservations.

If you'd like to stop the Jeep at your leisure, **DeChelly Tours,** P.O. Box 2539, Chinle, AZ 86503 (☎ **520/674-3772** or 520/674-5433), rents out Jeep Wranglers and Jeep Scramblers for $100 and $150, respectively, for 3 hours. Each additional hour for either vehicle costs $30. The rate includes a guide, who will tailor a tour to your wishes.

Guided Hikes. If you're interested in hiking into the canyon (or if you're eager to test your own four-wheel-drive vehicle in the 30-foot-deep sand of Chinle Wash), guides are available through the **Tsegi Guide Association,** P.O. Box 588, Chinle, AZ 86503 (☎ **520/674-5500**), for $10 an hour. For that rate, the guide will guide a group of 1 to 15 people (or 1 vehicle) into the canyon. For each additional vehicle (up to a total of 5), add $1 per hour to the rate. These guides, who can be hired at the Canyon de Chelly Visitor Center, also negotiate fees for overnights in the canyon. Contact the association for more information.

Ernest Jones of **Canyon Hiking Service,** P.O. Box 2832, Chinle, AZ 86503 (no phone), leads group hikes into the canyon from a designated meeting place near Cottonwood Campground. The meeting times are posted on the sign there. Minimum cost is $12 per person. Write to him for more information.

Guided Horseback Tours. Three companies offer horseback tours in the national monument. **Justin's Horse Rental,** P.O. Box 881, Chinle, AZ 86503 (**☎ 520/674-5678**), is closest to the visitor center, off the South Rim Drive near the mouth of Canyon de Chelly. Justin's offers half-day rides that go either to Sliding Rock or Antelope House, or vehicle-assisted full-day rides that start on the rim near Spider Rock or Mummy Cave, drop into the canyon, then travel downstream to the mouth of Canyon de Chelly. Cost is $8 per hour per person, plus $8 per hour for the guide.

Located 8 miles north of the visitor center on the North Rim Drive, **Twin Trails Tours,** P.O. Box 3068, Chinle, AZ 86503 (**☎ 520/674-8425**), travels into Canyon del Muerto. Their 3-hour tours (cost: $45 per person) go as far as Blue Bull Cave, while their full-day tours (cost: $70 per person) go to either Antelope House or Mummy Cave. Two-hour rim rides ($35 per person) are also available.

Tohtsoni Ranch (**☎ 520/755-6209**), located 1.25 miles beyond where the pavement ends on the South Rim Drive, offers a 4-hour round-trip ride to Spider Rock for $8 per hour per person, plus an $8 hourly charge for the guide.

Ranger Programs

Sunset interpretive discussions are offered several nights a week from during high season at the amphitheater at Cottonwood Campground. Topics include geology, archaeology, and history of the native peoples of the Southwest. Other talks with rangers or members of the **Tsegi Guide Association** are scheduled regularly. Ranger programs are somewhat more limited at Canyon de Chelly than at other parks in the national park system, so you'll need to consult the bulletin board at the visitor center for a specific schedule of programs when you arrive.

Day Hikes

White House Trail

1.25 miles one way. Moderate. Access: The trailhead is located at the White House Overlook.

This trail to the 70-room White House Ruin is the only place you can enter the canyon without a guide. After traversing the rim to the east for about 1,000 feet, the trail drops 600 vertical feet into the canyon in a series of long, gradual switchbacks, slanting sideways where it passes over cross-bedded layers of sandstone. In many spots, the trail skirts boulders that have fallen from the rim. Tamarisk, recognizable by its feathery leaves, and Russian Olive trees, characterized by blue-green leaves and spiky branches, flourish in the sandy areas around the river. The trail travels along the valley floor for about a quarter of a mile before crossing a bridge over Chinle Wash to the ruin itself. Navajo vendors from inside the canyon frequently sell cold drinks and jewelry in a shady area near the ruin. Pit toilets can be found here. (For more on White House ruin, turn to the driving tour.)

Camping

There are only two options for camping in and around Canyon de Chelly. One campground is operated by the National Park Service (which is free); one is a commercial campground. Camping is not allowed in the backcountry.

For **group camping reservations,** contact Canyon de Chelly National Monument, P.O. Box 588, Chinle, AZ 86503. The group sites, which are for tent-camping only, are on a loop at the north end of the Cottonwood Campground.

These are the only camping sites that can be reserved.

Cottonwood Campground

Located 0.5 mile southwest of visitor center off the South Rim drive. No phone. 96 sites, no RV hookups. Free. Reservations not accepted. Open year-round, but water is seasonal.

This first-come, first-served Park Service campground would be a desirable spot even if it weren't free. (You can make reservations for groups.) Bent like dancers, cottonwood trees shade its three loops, two of which are open to RVs. Although no sites stand out as quietest, most are peaceful enough to afford a good night's sleep, and the tenting is generally good on the campground's sandy floor. The rest rooms tend to be fairly clean, and the amphitheater is a short walk away. (In winter, no water is available, and portable toilets take the place of flush toilets.)

Because the entrance gate is unmanned, panhandlers from town occasionally wander the area. The campground often fills up, and dispersed camping is forbidden on the Navajo Reservation. So be sure to get here early in the day to claim a site.

Amenities: Dump station, public toilets, drinking water (except in winter), fire pits/grills, public phones located at the nearby Thunderbird Lodge; no showers or laundry facilities.

Spider Rock RV Park and Camping Too

10 miles east of the visitor center on South Rim Dr. (P.O. Box 666), Chinle, AZ 86503. ☎ **520/ 674-8261.** 42 sites, all with RV hookups. $10 per night; use of solar showers $2. Reservations not accepted. May close seasonally (call ahead to determine availability, especially in winter months).

At this primitive campground, $10 per night buys a dusty pull-off with a stone fire ring, a rickety homemade picnic table, and the use of a chemical toilet. It also buys the company of pinyon and juniper trees, sagebrush, and the vast desert silence. A 1.5-mile nature trail takes off from the campground, which is smaller and quieter than Cottonwood.

Amenities: Public toilets, solar showers (for an additional fee), fire pits/grills; no drinking water, laundry facilities, or public phones.

Accommodations

No accommodations are located inside the national monument boundaries, but Thunderbird Lodge is located just outside, only 0.5 mile from the park's visitor center.

Best Western Canyon de Chelly

3 miles west of the Canyon de Chelly Visitor Center on Ariz. 7, (P.O. Box 295), Chinle, AZ 86503. ☎ **800/327-0354** reservations only, or 520/674-5875; fax 520/674-3715. 99 rms. A/C TV TEL. May–Oct $112 double; Mar 16–Apr $85 double; Nov–Mar 15 $66 double. AE, DC, DISC, MC, V.

The biggest attraction of this motel, during summer at least, is the outdoor deck next to its indoor swimming pool, where bathers sprawl across lawn furniture and absorb the late afternoon sun. The rooms, which open onto the parking area, are fairly standard, with sloping ceilings, stucco walls, and a Southwestern motif, as well as coffeemakers in the bathrooms. Those furthest from Ariz. 7 are quietest, although all seem solid enough to offer a good night's rest.

Holiday Inn Chinle

0.3 mile west of Canyon de Chelly Visitor Center on Ariz. 7 (P.O. Box 1889), Chinle, AZ 86503. ☎ **520/674-5000;** fax 520/674-8264. 108 rms. A/C TV TEL. Apr–Oct $109 double; Nov–Mar $69 double. AE, DC, DISC, MC, V.

The newest hotel in Chinle looks and feels like a resort. Stone paths wend through landscaped courtyards to an outdoor swimming pool. On summer evenings a chef cooks ribs, steaks, and chicken on an outdoor grill. The rooms themselves are the most pleasant in the area; decorated in rich colors, each has one glass wall that opens onto a patio or balcony. Room service is available.

Rainbow Inn at Tsaile

At Dineh College, 26 miles northeast of Chinle on Ariz. 64. (Mailing address: Rainbow Inn, Dineh College, Tsaile, AZ 86556.) ☎ **888/464-2648** or 520/724-6830; fax 520/724-3327. 8 rms. TV. $52.82 double. MC, V.

Dineh College recently converted some of its surplus student housing into a motel. Although the conversion did little to disguise the fact that these are dorm rooms (the cinder-block walls, tile floors, twin beds, and plastic chairs will remind you), the rooms are quiet enough and clean enough to make this viable lodging. Less expensive than the motels in Chinle, the Rainbow Inn has the added advantage of being off the tourist-trampled path and within walking distance of a cultural hub of the Navajo people: the Ned A. Hatathill Cultural Center. (Admission to this museum, which houses an impressive collection of classic and contemporary Navajo art, is free. Students at the college guide complimentary tours when school is in session.)

Thunderbird Lodge

Off the South Rim Dr., 0.5 mile from the Canyon de Chelly Visitor Center (P.O. Box 548), Chinle, AZ, 86503. ☎ **800/679-2473** or 520/674-5841; fax 520/674-5844. 71 rms, 1 suite. A/C TV TEL. Apr–Nov 15 $83 double; Nov 16–Mar $67 double. AE, DC, DISC, MC, V.

Built on the grounds surrounding an 1896 trading post (now the restaurant), Thunderbird Lodge is a pleasant retreat within walking distance of the national monument. The rooms, most of which are in red, pueblo-style buildings, have ceiling fans and mission-style furniture. If you don't mind double beds, ask for the De Chelly units, which cost about $5 less the newer Adobe rooms and open onto a grassy courtyard instead of the parking lot. Four other rooms are housed in stone buildings nearly as old as the trading post. These "Lodge" rooms cannot be reserved over the phone and are available on a first-come, first-served basis. With just one double bed in each room, they cost about $10 less than the others and are a nice reward for those lucky enough to find one vacant.

A UNIQUE OPTION

Coyote Pass Hospitality

P.O. Box 91, Tsaile, AZ 86556. ☎ **520/724-3383** or 520/787-2295. Hogan rates: $85 for first person; $10 for each additional person (up to 15 total). Rates include breakfast. No credit cards.

At Coyote Pass Hospitality, host Will Tsosie, Jr. will lodge you in one of several dirt-floored hogans scattered across his clan's traditional sheep-grazing lands east of Canyon de Chelly. Accommodations are very rustic, without running water or (in all but one case) electricity, and with wood stoves for heat. In the morning, after stepping into the sunlight that warms the east-facing door of your abode, you'll be served a traditional Navajo breakfast. Because Tsosie entertains only those who are genuinely interested in Native American culture, he may decline to host some people or may assign readings to be done as homework to others. Most stays last more than 1 night and include tours that are tailored to the interests of each client.

Dining

There are no dining facilities within the boundaries of Canyon de Chelly National Monument, but there are several recommendable options in Chinle, and the Thunderbird Lodge is just outside the monument itself.

Garcia's Restaurant

At Holiday Inn Canyon de Chelly, 0.3 mile west of the Canyon de Chelly Visitor Center on Ariz. 7.

☎ **520/674-5000,** ext. 511. Reservations not accepted. Breakfast courses $1.95–$8.50; lunch entrees $5.95–$7.95; dinner entrees $5.95–$17.95. AE, DC, DISC, MC, V. Apr–Oct 6:30am–10pm; Nov–Mar 7–11am and 5–9pm. NATIVE AMERICAN/SOUTHWESTERN.

When looking for a restaurant in Chinle, don't blow past the Holiday Inn, which has the best in town but no sign announcing its presence. Garcia's occupies a pleasant room with hanging plants, Southwestern furniture, and sandstone-colored walls decorated with fake pictographs. On summer evenings, when the desert air cools to that perfect temperature, Garcia's deck is even nicer than the seating inside. The regular menu features Navajo, traditional American, and southwestern dishes, including some especially good fajitas. On summer nights it also includes barbecued chicken or steaks. In the morning, you can browse at a full breakfast buffet or order courses such as breakfast burritos, buckwheat pancakes, and huevos rancheros. Garcia's also prepares box lunches with made-to-order sandwiches. The full lunch menu, which includes a variety of salads and custom-made burgers, is available only during high season.

Junction Restaurant

At the Best Western Canyon de Chelly, on Ariz. 7, 3 miles west of the Canyon de Chelly Visitor Center. ☎ **520/674-8443.** Reservations not accepted. Breakfast courses $1.50–$6.50; lunch $3.95–$7.25; dinner $4.50–$15.95. AE, DISC, MC, V. May–Sept 6:30am–10pm; Oct–Apr 6:30am–9pm. AMERICAN/SOUTHWESTERN.

Like most restaurants with revolving pie display cases, this one seems best in the morning. The breakfasts, which include southwestern dishes such as breakfast burritos and huevos rancheros and American fare such as pork chops and pancakes, should please most diners. The seasonal fresh-fruit bowl really does have fresh fruit (capped with a maraschino cherry). Lunches include an appetizing selection of Navajo tacos, stew, and fry bread, as well as a variety of burgers and hot and cold sandwiches. Steaks—chicken-fried, hamburger, top sirloin, and T-bone—dominate the menu at dinnertime, when the lighting might remind you of your college library.

Thunderbird Cafeteria

At Thunderbird Lodge, off South Rim Dr., 0.5 mile from the Canyon de Chelly Visitor Center. ☎ **520/674-5841,** ext. 195. Breakfast $1.25–$5.75; lunch $2.65–$5.60; dinner $2.65–$5.60. Summer 6:30am–9pm; rest of the year 6:30am–8pm. AMERICAN CAFETERIA.

Hundreds of Native American artifacts blanket the walls of this cafeteria, recalling the days when the building served as a trading post. Ideally, they'll distract you from the food, some of which seems nearly as old as the building (1896). The best choices are the casseroles and the made-to-order dishes such as eggs, burgers, and steaks. (If all else fails, load up on french fries, which are quite good.) In addition to steaks, dinner selections include chicken fillets, tamales, and beef stew.

Picnic & Camping Supplies

Located on U.S. 191 just north of Route 7, **Basha's** (☎ **520/674-3464**) carries everything you'll need for picnicking. If you're missing an item for your car or campsite, Chinle's **General Store** (☎ **520/674-5486**), which shares the same parking lot with Basha's, might have it.

8

CANYONLANDS NATIONAL PARK

by Don and Barbara Laine

UTAH'S LARGEST NATIONAL PARK, CANYONLANDS IS A RUGGED HIGH desert of rock, with spectacular formations and gorges carved out over the centuries by the park's primary architects, the Colorado and Green rivers. This is a land of extremes: vast panoramas, dizzyingly deep canyons, dramatically steep cliffs, broad mesas, and towering red spires.

The most accessible part of Canyonlands is the Island in the Sky District, in the northern section of the park between the Colorado and Green rivers, where a paved road leads to sites such as Grand View Point, overlooking some 10,000 square miles of rugged wilderness. Island in the Sky also has several easy to moderate trails offering sweeping vistas of the park. A short walk provides views of Upheaval Dome, which resembles a large volcanic crater but may actually have been created by the crash of a meteorite. For the more adventurous, the 100-mile White Rim Road takes experienced mountain bikers and those with high-clearance four-wheel-drive vehicles on a winding loop tour through a vast array of scenery.

The Needles District, in the park's southeast corner, offers only a few view points along the paved road, but numerous possibilities for hikers, backpackers, and those with high-clearance 4X4s. Named for its tall, red-and-white striped rock pinnacles, this diverse district is home to impressive arches, including the 150-foot-tall Angel Arch, as well as grassy meadows and the confluence of the Green and Colorado rivers. Backcountry visitors to the Needles District will also find ruins and rock art left by prehistoric Indians some 800 years ago.

Most park visitors don't get a close-up view of the Maze District, but instead see it off in the distance from Grand View Point at Island in the Sky, or Confluence Overlook in the Needles District. That's because it's inhospitable and practically inaccessible, lying on the west side of the Green and Colorado rivers. You'll need a lot of endurance and at least several days to see even a few of its sites, such as the appropriately named Lizard Rock and Beehive Arch. Hardy hikers can visit Horseshoe Canyon in 1 day, where they can see the Great Gallery, an 80-foot-long rock art panel.

The park is also accessible by boat, which is how explorer Maj. John Wesley Powell first saw the canyons in 1869,

Tips from a Park Ranger

"A wilderness of rock," is how Paul Henderson, Canyonlands's chief of interpretation, describes the park, adding that it contains some of the most remote country left in the lower 48 states, with premier backcountry and river-running possibilities. "There's some wonderful opportunities here to find solitude that don't exist in too many other places," Henderson says.

Canyonlands is essentially chopped into three pieces by the Colorado and Green rivers, which come together near the middle of the park. According to Henderson, the districts are in many ways quite different.

"Island in the Sky District receives the highest visitation and has the most extensive front-country road system, so it's a place where folks that aren't equipped for a backcountry adventure can still get a good feeling for what this park is all about," he says. "There's a paved road system with scenic overlooks and short trails, and you can have a really good experience in half a day," he says.

However, Henderson says that Island in the Sky is not only for the pavement-bound. "The premier opportunity at Island in the Sky is the White Rim Road," he says, "a network of old mining roads and cowboy trails that make about a 100-mile trip—it's one of the premier mountain-biking trips in the country."

The Needles District, he says, is not a good place to cycle, but it has absolutely first rate options for hiking, backpacking, and four-wheeling. "Needles is pretty rough country, with some classic four-wheel-drive roads that for the most part are not for novice four-wheel-drivers," Henderson says. He adds that there are also some fairly easy 4X4 roads in the district. Those planning to drive into the backcountry, particularly novices, would be wise to discuss their plans with rangers before they set out. "I cringe when I see somebody in a brand-new $35,000 rig and it's probably the first time they've locked it into four wheel drive," he says. "Needles isn't the place to start."

The park's third district, the Maze, is very rough backcountry, Henderson says, and certainly not for everyone. It is, however, a good place to go if you don't want to see many people. "In August 1997, we had about 40,000 people at Island in the Sky, about 20,000 at Needles, and we had 546 at the Maze."

Another way to avoid crowds is to visit in winter, when you'll practically have the park to yourself, according to Henderson, and even in fall things are quieting down. "From mid-October to mid-November it's starting to get chilly at night, the temperature will probably hit freezing a couple of times, but you have the potential for just gorgeous fall weather, and the crowds have really dwindled," he says.

Because of the especially rugged nature of Canyonlands's terrain, advance planning is the key to a rewarding experience. "The better planning they can do, the better prepared they can be, the better experience they're going to have here," Henderson says, adding, "We really try to work with folks to match their experience and their desires with the appropriate places to go in the park."

when he made his first trip down the Green to its confluence with the Colorado, and then even further downstream, eventually to the Grand Canyon. River access is from the towns of Moab and Green River; local companies there offer boat trips of various duration.

You'll find a fascinating mixture of mountain and desert animals in Canyonlands, depending on the time of year and

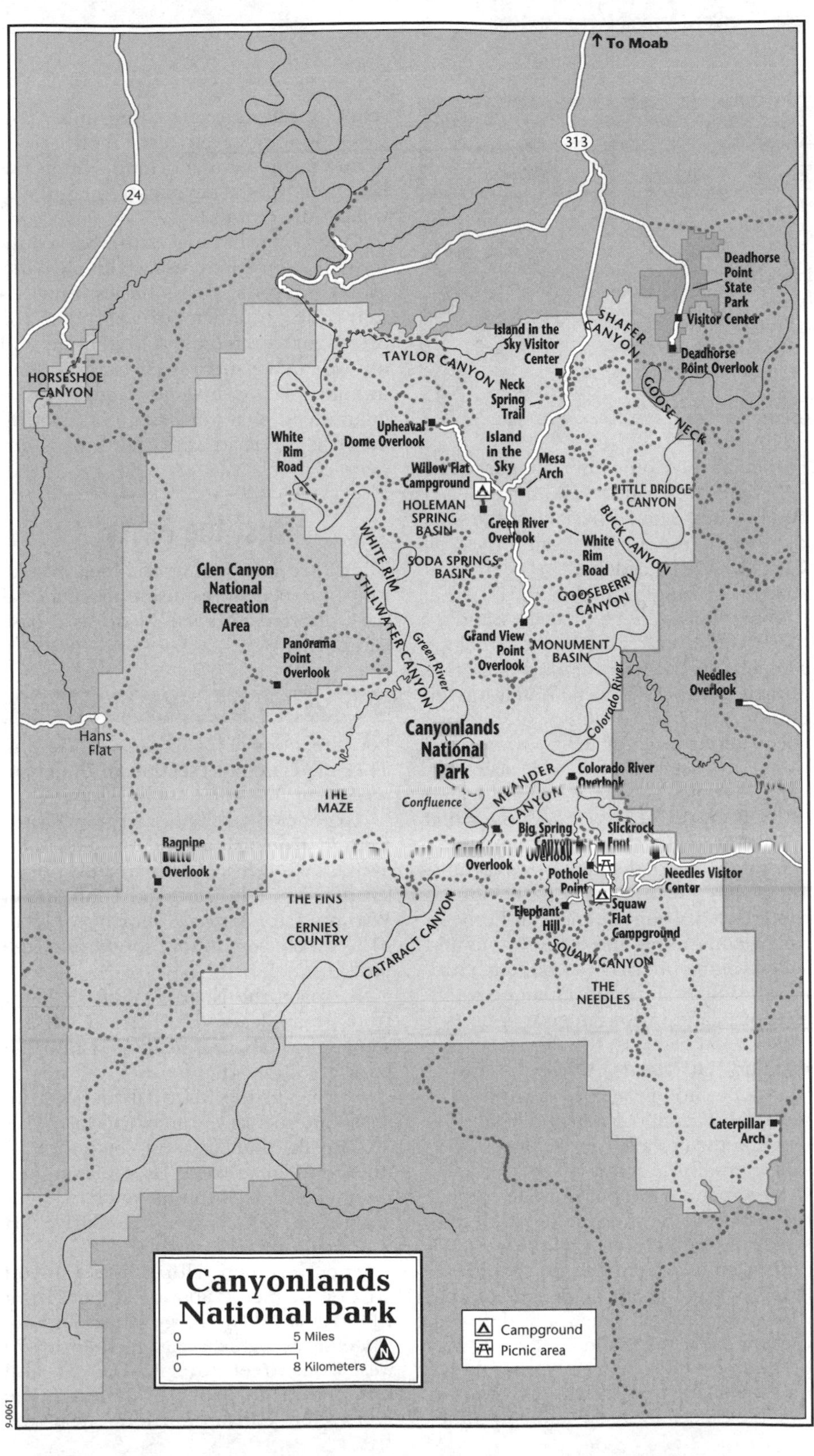
To Moab
313
24
Deadhorse
Point
State
Park
Visitor Center
Deadhorse
Point Overlook
SHAFER
CANYON
Island in the
Sky Visitor
Center
TAYLOR CANYON
Neck
Spring
Trail
GOOSE NECK
HORSESHOE
CANYON
Upheaval
Dome Overlook
White
Rim
Road
Island
in the
Sky
Mesa
Arch
Willow Flat
Campground
LITTLE BRIDGE
CANYON
HOLEMAN
SPRING
BASIN
Green River
Overlook
White
Rim
Road
BUCK CANYON
WHITE RIM
SODA SPRINGS
BASIN
Glen Canyon
National
Recreation
Area
GOOSEBERRY
CANYON
STILLWATER CANYON
Grand View
Point
Overlook
MONUMENT
BASIN
Green River
Panorama
Point
Overlook
Needles
Overlook
Colorado River
Hans
Flat
Canyonlands
National
Park
MEANDER
CANYON
Colorado River
THE
MAZE
Confluence
Big Spring
Slickrock
Bagpipe
Overlook
Pothole
Point
Needles Visitor
Center
Squaw
Flat
Campground
Elephant
Hill
THE FINS
ERNIES
COUNTRY
CATARACT CANYON
SQUAW CANYON
THE
NEEDLES
Caterpillar
Arch
Canyonlands
National Park
0
5 Miles
0
8 Kilometers
N
Campground
Picnic area
9-0061

> We glide along through a strange, weird, grand region. The landscape everywhere, away from the river, is of rock.
>
> —Maj. John Wesley Powell, during his 1869 boat trip down the Green and Colorado rivers.

particular location within the park. The best times to see most wildlife are early and late in the day, especially in the summer when the midday sun drives all Canyonlands residents in search of shade. Throughout the park you'll probably hear, if not see, coyotes, and it's likely you'll spot white-tailed antelope squirrels and other rodents scampering among the rocks as well. Watch for the elusive and rather antisocial bighorn sheep along isolated cliffs, where you might also see a golden eagle or turkey vulture soaring above the rocks in search of food. In the little pools of water that appear in the slickrock after rainstorms, you're likely to see tadpole shrimp—1-inch-long crustaceans that look as though they would be more at home in the ocean. Among the cottonwoods and willows along the rivers you'll find a variety of wildlife: deer, beaver, an occasional bobcat, and various migratory birds.

Avoiding the Crowds. Although Canyonlands does not get nearly as crowded as most other national parks in Utah, the more popular trails can be busy at certain times. Spring and fall see the most visitors at the park, but summer too has recently become more popular, despite scorching temperatures. Those who seriously want to avoid humanity should visit from November through mid-March, when the park is practically deserted, though some trails and 4X4 roads may be inaccessible. College spring break time—usually mid-March and April—can be especially busy, and any other school vacation usually brings more visitors as well. But even in the high season, hiking in the early morning—often the best time to hike anyway—is a good way to beat the crowds.

One thing that makes the backcountry experience here especially pleasant, even during the park's busiest times, is that the number of permits for overnight trips is limited (and often sold out well in advance), so if you're willing to hike, bike, or drive far enough you're guaranteed that you won't be sharing the trail or road with a lot of other people.

Just the Facts

There are no lodging facilities, restaurants, or even stores inside the national park. Most visitors use Moab as a base camp.

GETTING THERE & GATEWAYS

For directions to Moab, see the "Getting There & Gateways" section of the chapter 2.

To get to the Island in the Sky Visitor Center from Moab (about 34 miles away), take U.S. 191 (which runs north-south through eastern Utah from Wyoming to Arizona) north to Utah 313, which you follow south into the park.

To reach the Needles Visitor Center from Moab, leave U.S. 191 at Utah 211 south of Moab, and head west into the park. It's about 75 miles.

Getting to the Maze District is a bit more interesting. From Moab take U.S. 191 north, then go west for about 11 miles on I-70, crossing Green River, and then take Utah 24 south. Watch for signs and follow two- and four-wheel-drive dirt roads east into the park.

The detached Horseshoe Canyon area of the park is about 120 miles from Island in the Sky. To get there by two-wheel-drive vehicle, again follow I-70 west from Green River to U.S. 24, and then go south about 24 miles to the Horseshoe Canyon turnoff (near the

"Watch for Sand Drifts" sign), where you turn left. Follow this maintained dirt road for about 30 miles to the canyon's west rim, where you can park. This is the trailhead for the hike to the Great Gallery (see "Day Hikes," below).

The Nearest Airport/Renting a Car. See the "The Nearest Airport" and "Renting a Car" sections in chapter 2.

GETTING INFORMATION BEFORE YOUR TRIP

For advance information on what to see and do in the park, contact the **Superintendent, Canyonlands National Park,** 2282 SW Resource Blvd., Moab, UT 84532-8000 (☎ **435/259-7164**). It's best to write at least a month before your planned visit, and specify what type of information you need. The Web site for the park is **www.nps.gov/cany**.

For more advance information and advice when you arrive, contact the **Canyonlands Natural History Association** and the **Moab Information Center** (see the "Getting Information Before Your Trip" section of chapter 2).

VISITOR CENTERS

Canyonlands National Park operates two visitor centers: **Island in the Sky Visitor Center,** in the northern part of the park, and **Needles Visitor Center,** in the southern section. In both, you can get advice from rangers as well as maps and free brochures on hiking trails.

ENTRANCE & CAMPING FEES & BACKCOUNTRY PERMITS

Entry into the park (for up to 7 days) costs $10 per private vehicle or $5 per motorcycle, bicycle, or pedestrian. A $25 annual pass is also available.

The **camping fee** at Squaw Flat Campground in the Needles District is $8; camping at Willow Flat Campground in the Island in the Sky District is free.

Backcountry permits, available at either visitor center, are required for all overnight stays in the park, except at the two established campgrounds. Permit reservations can be made in advance (☎ **435/259-4351**). Permits for overnight four-wheel-drive and mountain-bike trips are $25, while those for overnight backpacking trips are $10. The permit for white-water boating through Cataract Canyon is $25; flat-water boating costs $10.

There is also a $5 day-use fee for those visitors bringing motor vehicles, horses, or mountain bikes on roads into Salt Creek/Horse Canyon and Lavender Canyon in the Needles District.

SPECIAL REGULATIONS & WARNINGS

Backcountry hikers should practice minimum-impact techniques, including packing out all trash. Vandalism, feeding or molesting wildlife, and disturbing any natural feature of the park are all prohibited, as are wood fires.

Canyonlands National Park is not a good place to take pets. Dogs, which must be leashed at all times, are prohibited in public buildings, on all trails, and in the backcountry. This includes four-wheel-drive roads—dogs are not permitted even inside your vehicle.

It cannot be stressed too strongly that the terrain at Canyonlands can be brutal, and it's important that you know not only your own limitations, but also the limitations of your vehicle and other equipment. Due to the extreme variety of terrain, the main safety problem at Canyonlands is that people underestimate the hazards. Rangers warn hikers to carry at least 1 gallon of water per person per day, to be especially careful near cliff edges, to avoid overexposure to the intense sun, and to carry maps when going off into the backcountry. During lightning storms, avoid lone trees, high ridges, and cliff edges. Four-wheel-drive vehicle operators should be aware of their vehicles' limitations and carry extra food and emergency equipment. Also, everyone going into the backcountry should let someone know where they're going and when they plan to return. Traveling alone in Canyonlands is not the best idea.

SEASONS & CLIMATE

Summers here are hot, with temperatures sometimes exceeding 100°F. Winters can be cool or cold, dropping well below freezing at night. The best time to visit, especially for hikers, is in the spring or fall, when daytime temperatures are usually from 60° to 80°F, and nights are cool. Late summer and early fall visitors should be prepared for afternoon thunderstorms.

USEFUL PUBLICATIONS

Canyonlands Natural History Association offers a number of helpful books and maps for sale (see the "Getting Information Before Your Trip" section of chapter 2). A couple of very good guides to hiking and off-roading are ***Exploring Canyonlands and Arches National Parks*** (Helena, Mont.: Falcon Press, 1997) by Bill Schneider, and ***Canyon Country Off-Road Vehicle Trails, Canyon Rims and Needles Areas*** (Moab, Utah: Canyon Country Publications, 1990) by F.A. Barnes.

Seeing the Highlights in a Day

Canyonlands is not an easy place to see in a short period of time. In fact, if your schedule permits only a day or less, skip the Needles and Maze districts entirely, and drive directly to the **Island in the Sky Visitor Center.** After looking at the exhibits, drive to several of the overlooks, stopping along the way for a short hike or two. Make sure you get to the **Grand View Point Overlook,** at the south end of the paved road. Among the best trails for this quick trip are the **Grand View Trail,** which starts at the overlook and is especially scenic in late afternoon. Allow about 1½ hours for this easy 2-mile walk. Also recommended is the **Upheaval Dome Overlook Trail,** which should take about a half hour, and brings you to a mile-wide crater of mysterious origins.

Perhaps a better choice for a quick visit to the park, especially for those with a bit of extra cash, is to take a guided trip by four-wheel-drive vehicle or raft. See the "Organized Tours & Ranger Programs" and "Outfitters Based in Moab" sections, below.

Exploring the Park by Car

No driving tour has yet been designed to show off Canyonlands National Park. The Island in the Sky District has about 20 miles of paved highway, some gravel roads accessible to two-wheel-drive vehicles, and several view points. The Needles District only has 8 miles of paved roads. Many (but not all) of Needles's view points and trailheads are accessible only by high-clearance four-wheel-drive vehicles or plain old foot power. The Maze District has only two main roads, neither of them paved. Both lead to trailheads.

Of course, if your "car" happens to be a serious 4X4, and if you are equally serious about doing some hard-core four-wheeling, this is the park for you. See the "Other Sports & Activities" section, below. Due to constantly changing conditions of dirt roads, we strongly suggest that you discuss your plans with rangers before setting out.

Organized Tours & Ranger Programs

In summer evenings, rangers offer **campfire programs** at Squaw Flat Campground in the Needles District. Short morning talks are presented frequently during the summer at the Island in the Sky Visitor Center.

Canyonlands by Night (☎ **435/259-5261**) is an evening river trip, operating May through October, that combines a sunset boat ride with stories of outlaws, discussions of rock formations, and a show of colored lights on the canyon walls. The office and dock are just north of Moab at the Colorado River Bridge. The trip is $20 for adults, $10 for children 6 to 12, and free for children under 6. Reservations are recommended.

FLYING TOURS

Many of Canyonlands's most spectacular sections are difficult to get to, to say the least. One solution is to take to the air. **Redtail Aviation,** P.O. Box 515, Moab, UT 84532 (☎ **800/842-9251** or 435/259-7421), based at Moab's Canyonlands Field Airport, has been flying sightseeing tours over southeastern Utah since 1978, and offers several easy ways to see the most of Canyonlands and surrounding areas. A 1-hour flight covers all three of the park's districts plus Dead Horse Point State Park, at about $60 per person. A 2-hour, $130 flight explores the same areas plus Capitol Reef National Park, Lake Powell, and Robber's Roost, where outlaw Butch Cassidy is said to have hidden out.

Slickrock Air Guides of Moab (☎ [illegible] or 435/259-[illegible], fax 435/259-2226) offers a 1-hour scenic flight over Canyonlands National Park and Dead Horse Point State Park for about $70 per person. A 3-hour flight that takes in Canyonlands, Lake Powell, Capitol Reef, and goes all the way to the edge of the Grand Canyon, costs about $200 per person.

Historic & Man-Made Attractions

This land was once the domain of prehistoric Indians, who constructed their buildings out of the region's rock, hunted deer and bighorn sheep, and left numerous drawings on rock walls. Most of the park's archaeological sites are in the Needles District. They include the well-preserved cliff dwelling called **Tower Ruin,** high on a cliff ledge in Horse Canyon; and an easy-to-get-to **ancient granary,** near the Needles Visitor Center, accessible on the short self-guided Roadside Ruin Trail. Throughout the park you'll also find evidence of more modern peoples—the trappers, explorers, and cowboys of the 19th century.

In Horseshoe Canyon, a separate and remote section of the park on the west side of the Green River, you'll find the **Great Gallery,** one of the most fantastic rock art panels in the Southwest. More than 80 feet long, the panel contains many red and white paintings of what appear to be larger-than-life human figures, most without distinguishable arms and legs. The paintings are believed to be at least 2,000 years old.

Day Hikes

On these trails with little shade, no reliable water sources, and temperatures soaring to over 100°F in the summer, rangers strongly advise that hikers carry at least 1 gallon of water per person per day, along with sunscreen, a hat, and all the usual hiking and emergency equipment. Actually, if you expect to do some serious hiking, try to plan your trip for the spring or fall, when conditions are much more hospitable.

All hikers should be careful on the many trails that cross slickrock, a general term for any bare rock surface. As the name implies, it can be slippery, especially when wet. Also, because some of the trails may be confusing, hikers attempting the longer ones should bring good topographical maps, available at park visitor centers and at stores in Moab.

Guided hikes in the park are available from **Dreamrides** (see "Outfitters Based in Moab," below), with full-day trips ranging from $95 to $115.

The following are some of the many park's many hiking possibilities, arranged by district; check with rangers for other suggestions.

ISLAND IN THE SKY DISTRICT

SHORTER TRAILS

Grand View Trail

1 mile one way. Easy. Access: Grand View Point Overlook at south end of paved road.

At the trailhead, stop and read the sign that points out all the prominent features you can see, such as the Totem Pole, the confluence of the Colorado and Green rivers, and the White Rim Trail. Although this is a fairly flat and easy trail to hike, it can seem obscure in places—watch carefully for the cairns, since some are on the small side. And remember to stay back from the cliff edge. This trail is especially beautiful at sunset, when the panorama seems to change constantly with the diminishing angle of sunlight.

Mesa Arch Trail

0.5 mile RT. Easy. Access: The trailhead is along a paved road about 6 miles south of the visitor center.

This is an easy self-guided nature walk through an area of pinyon and juniper trees, mountain mahogany, cactus, and a plant called Mormon Tea, from which Mormon pioneers made their hot drinks. The trail's main scenic attraction is the Mesa Arch, made of Navajo sandstone. It hangs precariously on the edge of a 500-foot cliff, framing a spectacular view of nearby mountains.

Upheaval Dome Overlook

0.5 mile one way. Moderate. Access: The trailhead is at the end of the Upheaval Dome Rd.

This hike to the overlook has a few steep inclines. Upheaval Dome doesn't fit with the rest of the Canyonlands's terrain—it's the result not of gradual erosion like the rest of the park, but rather of a dramatic deformity in which rocks have been pushed into a domelike structure. At one time it was theorized that the dome was formed by a hidden volcano, but now experts say the cause may have been a meteorite that struck the earth some 60 million years ago. Hiking another 0.5 mile takes you to a second overlook, closer to the Dome, but with a less panoramic view.

Whale Rock Trail

0.5 mile one way. Moderate. Access: The trailhead is about 4 miles down the Upheaval Dome Rd.

This trail gives the hiker breathtaking 360° views of the entire Island in the Sky District. It's a climb of 300 feet up a slickrock trail with handrails. Wander around on top a bit and study the varied formations; to those with some imagination, the outcrop you just climbed resembles a whale.

LONGER TRAILS

Gooseberry Trail

3 miles one way. Moderate. Access: Island in the Sky Picnic Area, about 11 miles south of the visitor center.

Although the beginning of this trail is so steep it looks like a cliff, don't be deterred. True, it drops 1,400 feet over the course of the hike, and most of that (1,300 feet) in the first 1.5 miles. But the trail is well made, and with a little care is quite safe. As you gingerly hike down the switchbacks—be careful of the loose sand—you get superb views of the White Rim Country. Once down in Gooseberry Canyon, it's nearly a level walk out to the road. When you decide you're ready to face the climb back to the top, remember you can take lots of rest stops to admire the varying scenery.

Lathrop Trail

5 miles one way. Difficult. Access: The trailhead is about 1.5 miles south of the visitor center along paved road.

The first 2.5 miles of this trail is on top of the mesa, but then it meanders down into the canyon, descending about 1,600 feet to the White Rim Road. This strenuous hike traverses steep terrain and loose rock—and remember, you have to climb back up to your car, unless you have been able to arrange for someone to meet you at the road. As you hike down the slope, you get grand views of Lathrop Canyon, and occasional glimpses of the Colorado River. It is possible to continue down to the river from the road (another 4 miles each way), but check with rangers about the feasibility of this overnight trip before attempting it.

Neck Spring Trail

5 miles RT. Moderate to difficult. Access: The trailhead is about 0.5 mile south of the visitor center along paved road.

This fairly strenuous hike follows the paths that animals and early ranchers created to reach water at two springs. You'll see water troughs, hitching posts, rusty cans, and the ruins of an old cabin. Because of the water source, you'll encounter types of vegetation not usually seen in the park, such as maidenhair ferns and gamble oak. The water also draws wildlife, including mule deer, bighorn sheep, ground squirrels, and hummingbirds. Climbing to the top of the rim, you get a beautiful view of the canyons and even the Henry Mountains, some 60 miles away.

Syncline Loop Trail

8 miles RT. Difficult. Access: Upheaval Dome Picnic Area at the end of Upheaval Dome Rd.

This is a long, hot day hike over one of the only three loop trails in the Island in the Sky District. Be sure to start early and bring plenty of water. The trail drops 1,300 feet, and is best hiked clockwise so you take the steepest part going down, into Upheaval Canyon. Along the way, you'll follow dry washes, climb small hills and steep canyon sides, cross part of the Syncline Valley, pass Upheaval Dome, traverse some slickrock, and finally hit an area of lush vegetation.

NEEDLES DISTRICT

Hiking trails here are generally not too tough, but keep in mind that slickrock can live up to its name and that there is generally little shade.

SHORTER TRAILS

Roadside Ruin Trail

0.3 mile RT. Easy. Access: The trailhead is just over 0.5 mile west of the visitor center along paved road.

This self-guided nature walk leads to an ancient granary, probably used by the early Puebloans some 700 to 1,000 years ago to store corn, nuts, and other foods. For 25¢ you can get a brochure at the trailhead that discusses the native plants along the trail. Although flat, this trail can be muddy when wet.

Slickrock Foot Trail

2.4 miles RT. Moderate. Access: The trailhead is about 6.5 miles from the visitor center, almost at the end of the road.

This moderate trail leads to several view points. View points show off the stair-step topography of the area, from its colorful canyons and cliffs to its flat mesas and striped needles. Beware careful on the slippery slickrock.

LONGER TRAILS

Elephant Hill–Druid Arch Trail

5.4 miles one way. Moderate. Access: Elephant Hill Trailhead at end of graded gravel road, drivable in most 2-wheel-drive passenger cars, although those in large vehicles such as motor homes will want to avoid it.

There are a number of interconnecting trails leading into the backcountry from this trailhead. The hike to Druid Arch, though not difficult, challenges hikers with steep drop-offs, quite a bit of slickrock, and a 1,000-foot increase in elevation. But the effort is worth the views, as you hike through narrow rock canyons, past colorful spires and pinnacles, and up the steep climb to the bench just below the huge Druid Arch, its dark rock somewhat resembling the stone structures at Stonehenge, England.

Confluence Overlook Trail

5.5 miles one way. Moderate to difficult. Access: Big Spring Canyon Overlook.

This hike has steep drop-offs and little shade, but it's worth the effort—it shows off splendidly the many colors of the Needles District, and also offers excellent views into the Maze District of the park. The climax is a spectacular view overlooking the confluence of the Green and Colorado rivers in a 1,000-foot-deep gorge. This hike can be done as a day hike (allow 4 to 6 hours) or quite pleasantly as an overnight hike.

Squaw Canyon–Big Spring Canyon Loop

7.5-mile loop. Difficult. Access: Squaw Flat Campground.

This difficult hike over steep slickrock winds through woodlands of pinyon and juniper, offering views along the way of the Needles rock formations for which the district is named, plus nearby cliffs and mesas as well as distant mountains. Watch for wildflowers from late spring through summer. The hike can be completed in about half a day, but there are also several backcountry campsites making it available to overnighters.

MAZE DISTRICT

To get to the trailheads in the Maze District involves serious four-wheel-drive roads, and few people attempt it. The 3-mile **Maze Overlook Trail** is not for beginning hikers or anyone with a fear of heights, and is quite steep in places, requiring the use of your hands for safety. At the trailhead you get a fine view of the many narrow canyons that create the image that has given this district its name; then the trail descends 600 feet to the canyon bottom.

The 12-mile **Harvest Scene Loop** (12-mile loop, difficult, 7 to 10 hours or overnight) leads over slickrock and along canyon washes—watch for the cairns to be sure you don't wander off the trail—to a magnificent example of rock art. Trailheads for other trails lie in what is known as the Doll House Area. Check with a ranger for current trail conditions and difficulty.

HORSESHOE CANYON

This detached section of the park was added to Canyonlands in 1971 mainly because of its **Great Gallery,** an 80-foot-long rock art panel with larger-than-life human figures, believed to be at least several thousand years old. Horseshoe Canyon Unit is some 120 miles (one way) from Island in the Sky, and there's only one road in (see "Getting There & Gateways," above). From the parking area it's a 6.5-mile round-trip hike to see the rock art. The hike begins with a 1.5-mile section down an 800-foot slope to the canyon floor, where you then turn right and go 1.75 miles to the Great Gallery. There is no camping in Horseshoe Canyon, but just outside the park boundary primitive camping is available on Bureau of Land Management property on the rim.

Exploring the Backcountry

There are many opportunities for backpacking in Canyonlands National Park, although hikers will often be sharing trail/road combinations with four-wheel-drive vehicles and mountain bikes. Additional information is provided below.

Other Sports & Activities

Canyonlands is a park that begs to be explored—if you've come to Utah for mountain biking, hiking, four-wheeling, or rafting, this is the place. The region holds a few surprises, too, from ancient Native American dwellings and rock art to dinosaur bones.

Unlike most national parks, the backcountry at Canyonlands is not only the domain of backpackers. Here, rugged four-wheel-drive and mountain-bike roads, as well as rivers navigable by boat, journey to some of the park's most scenic areas. Primitive campsites, strategically located throughout the backcountry, are available to all visitors, regardless of their mode of transport. Just be sure to make your backcountry campsite reservations well in advance—up to a year ahead for the more popular areas. You can get reservation forms and detailed information by mail, phone, or from the park's Web site (see "Getting Information Before Your Trip," above).

OUTFITTERS BASED IN MOAB

Although Moab offers plenty for the do-it-yourselfer, some 50 local outfitters offer excursions of all kinds, from lazy canoe rides to hair-raising jet-boat and four-wheel-drive adventures. The chart below lists some of the major companies that want to help you fully enjoy this beautiful country. They are all located in Moab (zip code is 84532). Advance reservations are often required, and it's best to check with several outfitters before deciding on one. In addition to asking about what you'll see and do and what it will cost, it doesn't hurt to make sure the company is insured and has the proper permits with the various federal agencies. Also ask about its cancellation policy, just in case.

Boating, Canoeing & Rafting. After spending hours in the blazing sun looking at mile upon mile of huge red sandstone rock formations, it's easy to get the idea that Canyonlands National Park is a baking, dry, rock-hard desert. Well, it is. But both the Colorado and Green rivers run through the park, and one of the most exciting ways to see the park and surrounding country is from river level.

You can travel into the park in a canoe, kayak, large or small rubber raft (with or without motor), or speedy, solid jet-boat. Do-it-yourselfers can rent kayaks or canoes for $25 to $40 for a half day and $30 to $50 for a full day, or rafts from $50 to $60 per half day and $65 to $90 for a full day. Half-day guided river trips cost from $25 to $35 per person, and full-day trips are usually in the $35 to $60 range. Multiday rafting expeditions, which include meals and camping equipment, start at about $300 per person. Jet-boat trips, which can cover a lot more river in a given amount of time, start at about $30 for a 1½-hour trip, with full-day trips costing about $75 per person. Children's rates are usually about 20% less. Some companies also offer sunset or dinner trips. Sheri Griffith Expeditions even offers a 4-day, 3-night "Expedition in Luxury," at about $900 per person, complete with gourmet food served with white tablecloths, wineglasses, and candles; and your every need anticipated. See "Outfitters Based in Moab," above.

The Colorado and Green rivers meet in the park, and both are fairly calm before the confluence. However, after the confluence the Colorado becomes serious white water, where you will most likely want to be on a guided raft trip.

One fantastic canoe trip is along the Green River. Canoeists usually start in or near the town of Green River (put in at Green River State Park or at Mineral Bottom, just downstream) and spend about 2 days to get to the Green's confluence with the Colorado, where they can arrange to be picked up by a local outfitter.

Public boat-launching ramps in the Moab area are opposite Lion's Park, near the intersection of U.S. 191 and Utah 128; at Take-Out Beach, along Utah 128 about 10 miles east of its intersection with U.S. 191; and at Hittle Bottom, also along Utah 128, about 23.5 miles east of its intersection with U.S. 191. Recorded information on river flows and reservoir conditions statewide can be obtained from the **Colorado Basin River Forecast Center** in Salt Lake City (☎ **801/539-1311**).

Four-Wheeling. Unlike most national parks, where all motor vehicles and mountain bikes must stay on paved roads, Canyonlands has miles of rough, four-wheel-drive roads where mechanized

Outfitter	4X4	Bike	Boat	Horse	Rent	Shuttle
Adrift Adventures 378 Main, Box 577 ☎ 800/874-4483, 435/259-8594	Yes	Yes	Yes	Yes	Yes	Yes
Canyon Voyages River Trips 352 N. Main, Box 416 ☎ 800/733-6007, 435/259-6007	No	No	Yes	No	Yes	No
Dreamrides 96 E. Center, Box 1137 ☎ 435/259-6419	No	Yes	No	No	Yes	Yes
Kaibab Mountain Bike Tours 391 S. Main ☎ 800/451-1133, 435/259-7423	No	Yes	No	No	Yes	No
Lin Ottinger Tours 600 N. Main ☎ 435/259-7312	Yes	No	No	No	No	No
Moab Rafting Co. 4725 S. Zimmerman Lane Box 801 ☎ 800/RIO-MOAB, 435/259-RAFT	No	No	Yes	No	No	No
Navtec Expeditions 321 N. Main, Box 1267 ☎ 800/833-1278, 435/259-7983	Yes	Yes	Yes	No	No	No
Nichols Expeditions 497 N. Main ☎ 800/648-8488, 435/259-3999	No	Yes	Yes	Yes	No	No
North American River Expeditions/O.A.R.S. 543 N. Main ☎ 800/346-6277, 435/259-5865	Yes	No	Yes	No	No	No
Pack Creek Ranch U.S. 191, south of Moab P.O. Box 1270 ☎ 435/259-5505	No	No	No	Yes	No	No
Red River Canoe Co. 497 N. Main ☎ 435/259-7722	No	No	Yes	No	Yes	Yes

Outfitter	4X4	Bike	Boat	Horse	Rent	Shuttle
Rim Tours 1233 S. U.S. 191 ☎ 800/626-7335, 435/259-5223	No	Yes	No	No	Yes	No
Sheri Griffith Expeditions 2231 S. U.S. 191 Box 1324 ☎ 800/332-2439, 435/259-8229	No	No	Yes	No	No	No
Tag-A-Long Expeditions 452 N. Main ☎ 800/453-3292, 435/259-8946	Yes	No	Yes	No	Yes	Yes
Tex's Riverways 691 N. 500 W. Box 67 ☎ 435/259-5101	No	No	Yes	No	Yes	Yes
Western River Expeditions 1371 N. U.S. 191 ☎ 800/453-7450, 435/259-7019	No	No	Yes	No	Yes	No
Western Spirit Cycling 38 S. 100 W. Box 411 ☎ 800/845-BIKE, 435/259-8732	No	Yes	No	No	Yes	No

transport is king. Keep in mind that we're talking serious four-wheeling here, where most roads require high-clearance short-wheelbase vehicles. Many of these roads also require the skill that comes only from experience, so it's usually a good idea to discuss your plans with rangers before putting your high-priced vehicle on the line. Four-wheelers must stay on designated 4X4 roads, but here the term *road* can mean anything from a graded, well-marked two-lane gravel byway to a pile of loose rocks with a sign that says "that-a-way." Many of the park's Jeep roads are impassable during heavy rains and for a day or 2 after.

Local companies specializing in four-wheel-drive rentals include **Farabee 4X4 Rentals** (☎ **435/259-7494**) and **Slickrock 4X4 Rentals** (☎ **435/259-5678**). Rates are usually $75 to $90 per day. Pets are not permitted in the backcountry, even inside vehicles, and backcountry permits are needed for all overnight trips. (See "Entrance & Camping Fees & Backcountry Permits," above.)

The best four-wheel-drive adventure in Canyonlands's Island in the Sky District—some say this is also among the top mountain-biking routes in America—is the **White Rim Road,** which runs some 100 winding miles and affords spectacular and ever-changing views, from broad panoramas of rock and canyon to close-ups of red and orange towers and buttes. A high-clearance 4X4 is essential. Expect the journey to be slow, lasting 2 to 3 days, although with

Especially for Kids

Youngsters from 6 to 12 years old can join the **Junior Rangers,** participate in a variety of programs, and earn badges.

the appropriate vehicle it isn't really difficult. There are primitive campgrounds along the way, but reservations on this popular route should be made well in advance.

Four-wheeling on one of many exciting routes in the Needles District can be an end in itself or simply a means to get to some of the more interesting and remote hiking trails and camping spots. Four-wheelers will find one of their ultimate challenges on the **Elephant Hill Jeep Road,** which begins at a well-marked turnoff near Squaw Flat Campground. Although most of the 10-mile trail is only moderately difficult, the stretch over Elephant Hill itself near the beginning can be a nightmare, with steep, rough slickrock, drifting sand, loose rock, and treacherous ledges. Coming down the hill there is one switchback that requires you to back to the edge of a steep cliff before continuing ahead. This is also a favorite of mountain bikers, although bikes will have to be walked on some stretches over an abundance of sand and rocks. The route offers views of numerous rock formations, from striped needles to balanced rocks, plus steep cliffs and rock "stairs." Side trips can add another 30 miles. Allow from 8 hours to 3 days.

For a spectacular view of the Colorado River, the **Colorado River Overlook Road** can't be beat. This 14-mile round-trip is popular with four-wheelers, backpackers, and mountain bikers. Considered among the park's easiest 4X4 roads, the first part is very easy indeed, accessible by high-clearance two-wheel-drives, but the second half has a few rough and rocky sections that require four-wheel-drive. Starting at the Needles Visitor Center parking lot, the trail takes you past numerous panoramic vistas to a spectacular 360° view of the park and the Colorado River some 1,000 feet below.

Biking. Road bikes are of little use in Canyonlands, except for getting to and from trailheads, view points, visitor centers, and campgrounds in the Island in the Sky and Needles districts. Although bikes of any kind are prohibited on hiking trails and cross country in the backcountry, they are permitted on designated two- and four-wheel-drive roads. This means that **mountain bikers** have a great many possibilities here, although they will find themselves sharing dirt roads with motor vehicles of every size, plus occasional hikers. Since some of the four-wheel-drive roads have deep sand in spots, which can turn into quicksand when wet, mountain biking, while certainly a challenge, may not be as much fun as you'd expect. It's wise to talk with rangers about conditions on specific roads before setting out.

Among rides that are popular with mountain bikers are the Elephant Hill and Colorado River Overlook Jeep roads, both in the Needles District. The 100-mile White Rim Road, in the Island in the Sky District, also makes a great mountain-bike trip (allow at least 4 days), especially for bikers who can arrange for an accompanying 4X4 vehicle to carry water, food, and camping gear. See the "Four-Wheeling" section, above. For information on where to get advice, bike rentals and repairs, equipment, and bike shuttle services, see the "Biking" section in chapter 2.

Camping

INSIDE THE PARK

There are two developed campgrounds in the park, both with limited facilities. In the Island in the Sky District, **Willow**

Flat Campground has no water; in the Needles District, **Squaw Flat Campground** has trucked-in water in the summer, but no water in the winter. Primitive campsites are also available throughout the park for four-wheelers, boaters, mountain bikers, and backpackers (see "Exploring the Backcountry," above).

NEAR THE PARK

Near Island in the Sky, the campground at **Dead Horse Point State Park (☎ 435/259-2614)** has electric hookups; while the BLM's **Newspaper Rock Campground** (☎ **435/587-2141**), along the road to the Needles District, offers primitive camping. Additional camping facilities are available on nearby public lands administered by the Bureau of Land Management and U.S. Forest Service; check at the **Moab Information Center,** located in Moab at the corner of Main and Center streets (☎ **435/259-3911**). Those heading north to the community of Green River will find additional camping at two state parks. There are also over a dozen commercial campgrounds in and around Moab; for information on these, see the "Camping" section in chapter 2.

Those visiting the Needles District of the park will find several commercial campgrounds in the town of Monticello, along U.S. 191, about 15 miles south of the intersection of U.S. 191 and the park entry road. These include **Mountain View RV Park,** along the north edge on Monticello at 632 N. Main St. (P.O. Box 910), Monticello, UT 84535 (☎ **435/587-2974**), a well-maintained campground with grassy sites, some trees, and cable TV hookups.

For more details on these campsites as well as those in Moab, see the "Campground" chart in chapter 2.

Accommodations, Dining, & Picnic & Camping Supplies

There are no facilities for lodging, dining, or buying supplies inside Canyonlands National Park. The nearest town to the park is Moab. For information on restaurants, hotels, and supply stores in Moab, see the "Accommodations," "Dining," and "Picnic & Camping Supplies" sections in chapter 2.

9

CAPITOL REEF NATIONAL PARK

by Don and Barbara Laine

RELATIVELY UNKNOWN, CAPITOL REEF NATIONAL PARK IS ONE OF those undiscovered gems, quietly going about its business of protecting and interpreting its various natural wonders and historic sites, and drawing far fewer visitors than its more famous neighbors, Bryce Canyon and Zion. But when people do stumble across this park, they are often amazed—Capitol Reef not only offers more of that spectacular southern Utah scenery, but has a unique twist and a personality all its own.

The geologic formations here are downright peculiar. This is a place to let your imagination run wild, where you'll see the appropriately named Hamburger Rocks, sitting atop a white sandstone table; the tall, bright-red Chimney Rock; the silent and eerie Temple of the Moon; and the commanding Castle. The colors of Capitol Reef's canyon walls come from a spectacular palette, which is why the Navajos called the area "The Land of the Sleeping Rainbow."

But unlike some of southern Utah's other parks, Capitol Reef is more than brilliant rocks and barren desert. Here the Fremont River has helped create a lush oasis in an otherwise unforgiving land. Cottonwood, willow, ash, and other trees fill its banks. In fact, 19th-century pioneers found the land so inviting and the soil so fertile that they established the community of Fruita, planting orchards that have been preserved by the National Park Service.

Because of differences in elevation and water availability in different sections of the park, you'll find a variety of ecosystems and terrain, along with a variety of possible activities. There are trails for hiking, mountain biking, and four-wheeling; lush fruit orchards; rich, green cottonwood groves and desert wildflowers; an abundance of songbirds; and a surprising amount of wildlife, from lizards and snakes to the bashful ring-tailed cat (which isn't a cat at all, but a member of the raccoon family). You'll also find thousand-year-old petroglyphs left behind by the ancient Fremont and Anasazi peoples, and other traces of the past left by the relatively modern Southern Paiutes. This was both a favorite hideout for Wild West outlaws, and a home for industrious Mormon pioneers, who planted orchards while their children learned the three Rs and studied the Bible and the Book of Mormon in the Fruita Schoolhouse.

The name Capitol Reef conjures up images of a tropical shoreline—it seems

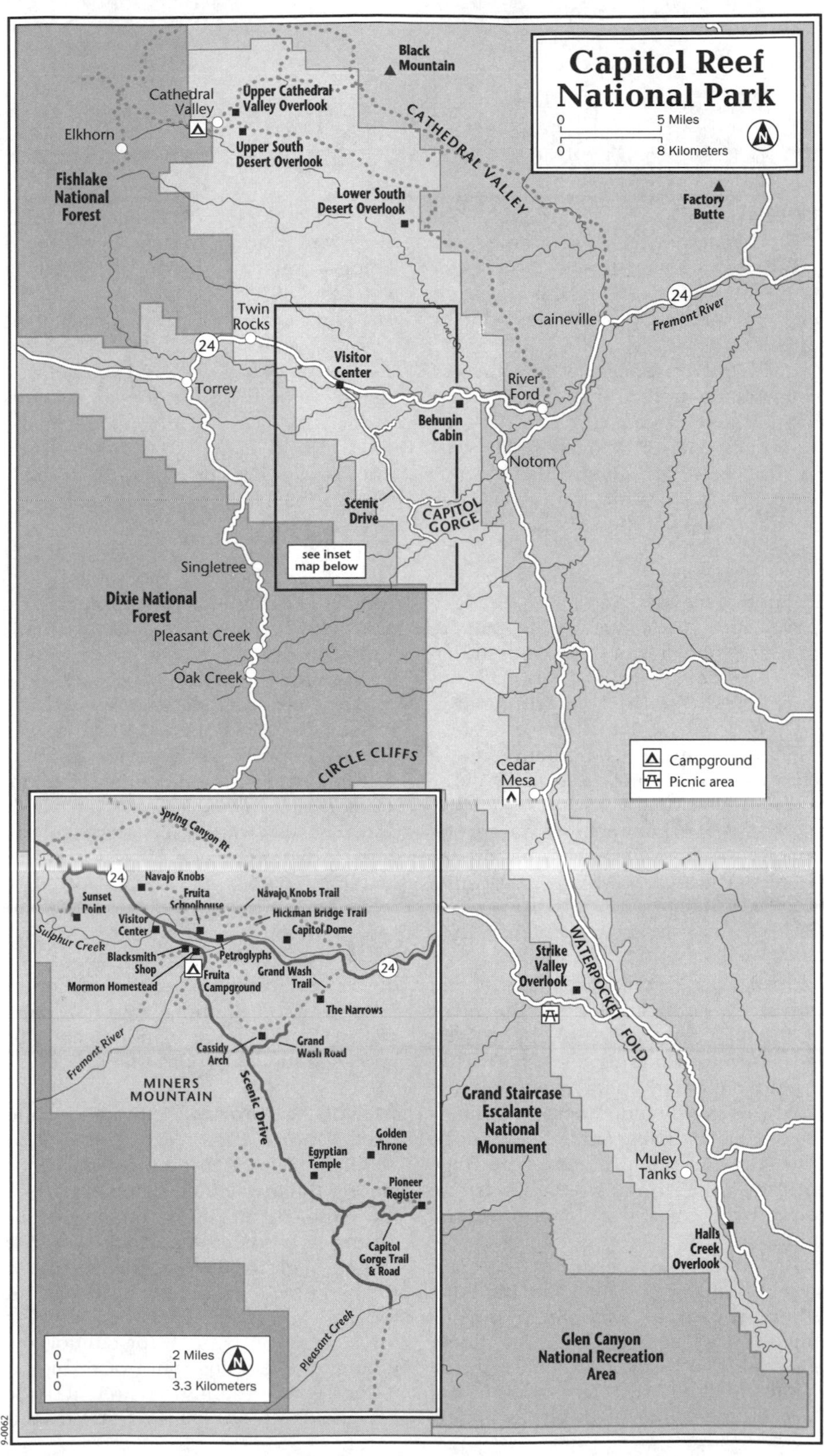

Capitol Reef National Park
0
5 Miles
0
8 Kilometers
Black Mountain
Cathedral Valley
Upper Cathedral Valley Overlook
Elkhorn
Upper South Desert Overlook
Fishlake National Forest
CATHEDRAL VALLEY
Lower South Desert Overlook
Factory Butte
Twin Rocks
24
Caineville
Fremont River
Visitor Center
Torrey
River Ford
Behunin Cabin
Notom
Scenic Drive
CAPITOL GORGE
see inset map below
Singletree
Dixie National Forest
Pleasant Creek
Oak Creek
CIRCLE CLIFFS
Cedar Mesa
Campground
Picnic area
Strike Valley Overlook
WATERPOCKET FOLD
Grand Staircase Escalante National Monument
Muley Tanks
Halls Creek Overlook
Glen Canyon National Recreation Area
Spring Canyon Rt
Navajo Knobs
Sunset Point
Fruita Schoolhouse
Navajo Knobs Trail
Hickman Bridge Trail
Visitor Center
Capitol Dome
Sulphur Creek
Blacksmith Shop
Petroglyphs
Fruita Campground
Grand Wash Trail
Mormon Homestead
The Narrows
Cassidy Arch
Grand Wash Road
Fremont River
MINERS MOUNTAIN
Scenic Drive
Golden Throne
Egyptian Temple
Pioneer Register
Capitol Gorge Trail & Road
Pleasant Creek
0
2 Miles
0
3.3 Kilometers
9-0062

Tips from a Park Ranger

Thanks to the geography of the Waterpocket Fold, there's a lot of variety in the park—in elevation, landscape, and terrain, according to Thea Nordling, Capitol Reef's chief of interpretation.

"This tilted layer cake of geologic strata formed a variety of different microhabitats as it eroded," she says. "There's an immense desert wilderness, but within that you've got perennial rivers that have created a very rich river-based habitat, where prehistoric and historic people settled."

Capitol Reef is still relatively unknown, she says, and hasn't changed much since *Outside* magazine sang its praises as one of America's eight undervisited national parks—"parks as they were meant to be." Nordling says, "When people stop at Capitol Reef on their way to one of Utah's better-known national parks, they're usually pleasantly surprised."

The park is known for its wonderful colors, and Nordling says you can see them practically everywhere. "At sunset along Utah 24 and along the scenic drive you'll find a brilliant spectrum of colors—you can see them right from your car."

"The Frying Pan Trail is one of my favorite hikes," she says. "It's well marked, easy to get to, and you get wonderful views from the top as you hike along the crest of the Waterpocket Fold." Nordling adds that an added benefit to the trail is that it provides access to the spectacular spur trail to Cassidy Arch.

The dirt roads in the park can be a bit rugged, but most are accessible by two-wheel-drive, high-clearance vehicles, she says. However, Nordling advises that a four-wheel drive vehicle makes exploring the remote areas of the park easier and less worrisome in bad weather.

Nordling says that given a choice, she would probably visit in the spring or fall, because it's a bit cooler for hiking then. But, she adds, "summer's beautiful too, because wildflowers are in bloom and the orchards are open for fruit picking."

odd for a park composed of cliffs and canyons in landlocked Utah. But many of the pioneers who settled the West were former seafaring men, and they extended the traditional meaning of the word *reef* to include these seemingly impassable rock barriers. They added *Capitol* to the name because the huge round white domes of sandstone reminded them of the domes of capitol buildings.

Actually, to be accurate, the park should probably be called The Big Fold. When the earth's crust uplifted some 65 million years ago, creating the Rocky Mountains and Colorado Plateau, most of this uplifting was relatively even. But here, through one of those fascinating quirks of nature, the crust wrinkled into a huge fold. Running for 100 miles, almost all within the national park, it's known as the Waterpocket Fold.

Avoiding the Crowds. Although Capitol Reef National Park receives only about 700,000 visitors annually—making it among the least-visited national parks in the West—it can still be busy, especially during its peak season, which lasts from May through September. For this reason, the best time to visit is fall; particularly in October and November, when temperatures are warm enough for comfortable hiking and camping, but not so high as to send you constantly in search of shade. You also don't have to be as worried about flash floods through narrow canyons as you do during the July-through-September thunderstorm season.

Just the Facts

GETTING THERE & GATEWAYS

Capitol Reef National Park is 121 miles northeast of Bryce Canyon National Park, 204 miles northeast of Zion National Park, 224 miles south of Salt Lake City, and 366 miles northeast of Las Vegas, Nevada.

The park straddles Utah 24, which connects with I-70 both to the northeast and northwest. Coming from the east along I-70, take Exit 147 and follow Utah 24 southwest to the park. Traveling from the west along I-70, there are two options: Exit 48 for Sigurd and follow Utah 24 east to the park; or Exit 85 for Fremont Junction, take Utah 72 south to Loa, where you pick up Utah 24 east to the park.

Those coming from Bryce Canyon National Park can follow Utah 12 northeast to its intersection with Utah 24 at the small town of Torrey, and turn right (east) to Capitol Reef. If you're approaching the park from Glen Canyon National Recreation Area, take Utah 276 (from Bullfrog Basin Marina) or Utah 95 (from Hite Crossing) north to the intersection with Utah 24, and follow that west to the park.

The Nearest Airport. The closest major airport is **Walker Field** in Grand Junction, Colorado (☎ **970/244-9100**), which has direct flights or connections from most major cities on **America West Express, Delta/Skywest, Mesa Airlines,** and **United Express.**

Renting a Car. Car rentals are available in Grand Junction in the airport area from **Avis, Hertz, National, Sears,** and **Thrifty.**

Toll-free reservations numbers for all the airlines and car-rental agencies listed in this section are given in the appendix.

GETTING INFORMATION BEFORE YOUR TRIP

For advance information on what to see in the park, hiking trails, and camping, contact the **Superintendent, Capitol Reef National Park,** Torrey, UT 84775 (☎ **435/425-3791**). The Web site is **www.nps.gov/care**. Books and maps are also available by mail from the nonprofit **Capitol Reef Natural History Association,** Capitol Reef National Park, HC 70, Box 15, Torrey, UT 84775-9602 (☎ **435/425-3791,** ext. 113).

VISITOR CENTER

The small visitor center is located on the park access road at its intersection with Utah 24. A path connects it to the campground, passing the historic blacksmith shop of Fruita, orchards, and a lovely shaded picnic ground. The visitor center has exhibits on the geology and history of the area and presents a short introductory slide show on the park. Rangers there can answer questions and provide backcountry permits. You can also pick up several free brochures, and buy books, maps, videos, postcards, and posters. The visitor center is open daily year-round.

ENTRANCE & CAMPING FEES

Entry into the park (for up to 7 days) costs $4 per vehicle or $2 per motorcycle, bicycle, or pedestrian. Camping in the main campground near the visitor center costs $8 per night; the two primitive campgrounds are free.

Free permits, available at the visitor center, are required for all overnight trips into the backcountry.

SPECIAL REGULATIONS & WARNINGS

Bicycles are prohibited in the backcountry and on all hiking trails. Feeding or molesting wildlife, vandalism, and disturbing any natural feature of the park are all prohibited. Because skunks refuse to follow park rules regarding wildlife diet, campers should be especially careful of where they store food, and dispose of garbage promptly. Dogs, which must be leashed at all times, are prohibited on all trails and public buildings, and must not be taken more than 100 feet from any road.

While most visitors to the park enjoy a wonderful vacation without mishap, problems can occur. Hikers need to carry plenty of water, especially in midsummer, and watch out for rattlesnakes. The midget faded rattlesnake is only 12 to 18 inches long; its larger cousin, the Great Basin rattlesnake, can grow to 2 feet in length. Both will try to avoid you, but will strike if cornered.

The other major concern is the weather: Afternoon thunderstorms during July, August, and September can bring flash floods, which fill narrow canyons suddenly without warning. Steep-walled Grand Wash and Capitol Gorge can be particularly hazardous, and should be avoided whenever storms are threatening.

SEASONS & CLIMATE

Because of its higher elevation, Capitol Reef doesn't get as hot as some of the other southwestern parks do, even in the middle of summer. But winters, when visitation is low, can also be very pleasant. Snow falls sometimes, but it doesn't usually last, and temperatures are often in the 50s. Late winter and spring can be windy.

Depending on weather, the scenic drive sometimes closes, most frequently in late summer during flash flood season, but occasionally in winter due to snow. When closed, you can still access a network of trails from Utah 24 and also get down into the picnic area and campground.

SEASONAL EVENTS

Usually scheduled for the third Friday in September, **Harvest Homecoming** celebrates the annual fall fruit harvest and the area's pioneer legacy. Activities and exhibits may include demonstrations of pioneer crafts and skills, such as candle making, quilting, ham smoking, sorghum processing, soap making, and sheep shearing.

Seeing the Highlights in a Day

Because Capitol Reef is such a compact park, it's fairly easy to see a lot in a short amount of time. Although the ideal situation would be to have 2 to 3 days in the park, spending about 1½ days out on the trails, it is quite possible to have an enjoyable time with just half a day or so. Because there are no food services in the park (except fruit in season), you'll want to pack a picnic lunch.

Start at the **visitor center,** and watch the short slide show explaining the park's geology and early history. Then head out on the paved 25-mile round-trip **scenic drive** (described below), stopping along the way for a short hike, perhaps the easy walk up the Grand Wash with a strenuous side trip to Cassidy Arch. Drive to the historic pioneer community of **Fruita,** near the beginning of the scenic drive, and wander through the orchards, where you're likely to see deer. Then visit the historic **Gifford Farmhouse,** where you can get a taste of the daily life of Fruita's Mormon settlers and purchase replicas of pioneer era household items and crafts. You can then hike one of the shorter trails in the Fruita area before going to see the Fruita Schoolhouse and some of the park's **petroglyphs.** In the evening, try to take in a ranger conducted program at the amphitheater.

Exploring the Park by Car

Capitol Reef is relatively easy to see from the comfort of your automobile. From the visitor center, a **scenic drive** leads about 12.5 miles south into the park, offering good views of the dramatic canyons and rock formations that comprise Capitol Reef. Pick up a copy of the free scenic drive brochure at the entrance station, then set out, stopping at view points to gaze up and out at the array of colorful cliffs, monoliths, and commanding rock formations.

If the weather is dry, drive down the gravel **Capitol Gorge Road** at the end of the paved scenic drive for a look at what many consider the best scenery in the park. It's a 5-mile round-trip drive. If you're up for a short walk, the relatively flat 2-mile (round-trip) **Capitol Gorge Trail,** which starts at the end of Capitol Gorge Road, takes you to the historic **Pioneer Register,** a rock wall where traveling pioneers "signed in" (see "Day Hikes," below).

Another dry-weather driving option is the **Grand Wash Road,** a maintained dirt road that is subject to flash floods, but in good weather offers an easy route into spectacular backcountry. Along the 2-mile round-trip you'll see Cassidy Arch, where famed outlaw Butch Cassidy is said to have hidden out.

Utah 24, which crosses Capitol Reef from east to west, also has several view points offering a good look at some of the park's best features, such as the monumental **Capitol Dome,** which resembles the dome of a capitol building; the striking **Chimney Rock** formation; the aptly named **Castle** formation; the historic **Fruita Schoolhouse;** and some roadside **petroglyphs** left by the prehistoric Fremont people (see "Historic Attractions," below).

Organized Tours & Ranger Programs

Park rangers present a variety of free programs and activities from the spring through fall. **Campfire programs** take place most evenings at the outdoor amphitheater near Fruita Campground. Topics vary, but could include the animals and plants, geology, and human history of the area. Rangers also lead hikes and walks, and give short talks on history at the pioneer Fruita Schoolhouse and the Gifford Farmhouse. Schedules are posted on bulletin boards at the visitor center and Fruita Campground.

Historic Attractions

Throughout the park you'll find evidence of human presence here through the centuries. The Fremont people lived along the river as early as A.D. 700, staying until about A.D. 1250. Primarily hunters and gatherers, the Fremonts also grew corn, beans, and squash to supplement their diet, leaving little behind when they abandoned the area. Their dwellings were pit houses, which were dug into the ground and surrounded with boulders that supported the roof. The remains of one can be seen from the **Hickman Bridge Trail.** Many of the Fremont's petroglyphs (images carved into rock) and some pictographs (images painted on rock) are still visible on the canyon walls. If we could read them, they might tell us why these early Americans left the area, a puzzle that continues to baffle historians and archaeologists. One easily accessible site is located 1 mile east of the visitor center along Utah 24. There is a sign near the parking area and a short path to the petroglyph panel, which contains some of the most interesting images in the park.

Prospectors and other travelers passed through the **Capitol Gorge** section of the park in the late 1800s, leaving their names on the Pioneer Register. You can reach the **Pioneer Register** via a 2-mile loop (see "Day Hikes," below).

Mormon pioneers established the aptly named community of **Fruita** (now an historic district listed on the National Register of Historic Places) when they discovered that this was a good area for growing fruit. The orchards those settlers planted continue to flourish, tended by park workers who invite you to sample the "fruits" of their labor. Nearby is the historic Fruita blacksmith shop. The tiny **Fruita Schoolhouse,** built in 1896, was a church, social hall, and community meeting hall in addition to a one-room schoolhouse. The school closed in 1941, but was carefully restored by the National Park Service in 1984. It is authentically furnished with old wood and wrought-iron desks, a wood stove, chalk board, and textbooks. The handbell used to call students to class still rests on the corner of the teacher's desk.

Also in the Fruita district, the **Gifford Farmhouse,** built in 1908, is typical of rural Utah farmhouses of the early 1900s. Renovated and furnished by the Capitol Reef Natural History Association, the home is located off the scenic drive about 1 mile south of the visitor center, and is open from April through September. The home's former kitchen is used as a gift shop by the natural history association; it sells reproductions of the household tools and utensils used by Mormon pioneers, plus various crafts, jams and jellies, dried fruits, historic postcards, and books.

Day Hikes

Trails through Capitol Reef National Park offer sweeping panoramic views of colorful cliffs and soaring spires, eerie journeys through desolate, steep-walled canyons, and cool walks along the tree-shaded Fremont River. Watch carefully for petroglyphs and other reminders of this area's first inhabitants. This is also the real Wild West, little changed from the way cowboys, bank robbers, settlers, and gold miners found it in the late 1800s. One of the best things about hiking here is the combination of scenic beauty, Native American art, and Western history you'll discover.

> **The colors are such as no pigments can portray. They are deep, rich, and variegated; and so luminous are they, that light seems to flow or shine out of the rock.**
>
> **—Geologist C.E. Dutton, 1880**

Among the last areas in the continental United States to be explored, many parts of Capitol Reef National Park are still practically unknown, perfect for those who want to see this rugged country in its natural state. Several local companies offer guide and shuttle services, including **Wild Hare Expeditions,** P.O. Box 750194, Torrey, UT 84775 (☎ **888/304-HARE** or 435/425-3999). In addition to the treks discussed below, Wild Hare offers photo tours, cross-country ski tours, and snowshoe tours, and also rents snowshoes ($7 per day). The company's guided hikes and backpacking trips range from 2-hour hikes starting at $20 per person to multiday backpacking trips, with meals and equipment provided, starting at about $150 per person. Most groups are small, although large groups can be accommodated. Rates are lower for children.

SHORTER TRAILS

Capitol Gorge Trail

1 mile one way. Easy. Access: End of the Capitol Gorge dirt road.

This is a fairly easy, mostly level walk along the bottom of a narrow canyon. Looking up at the tall, smooth walls of rock conveys a strong sense of what the pioneers must have seen and felt 100 years ago when they moved rocks and debris to haul their wagons up this canyon. The trail leads past the Pioneer Register, where prospectors and other early travelers carved their names. The earliest legible signatures were made in 1871 by J.A. Call and "Wal" Bateman.

Fremont River Trail

1.25 miles one way. Easy to moderate. Access: Fruita Campground.

This self-guided nature trail is quite easy (and wheelchair accessible) for the first 0.5 mile as it meanders through the orchards along the river, but becomes increasingly strenuous thereafter. The path climbs up through orchards to overlook the lovely valley. Parts of the trail are steep; other parts are a long steady incline.

Goosenecks Trail

0.1 mile one way. Easy. Access: Goosenecks Parking Area on Utah 24 west of the visitor center.

This short walk affords great views of Sulphur Creek Canyon. It's a particularly good trail for those with a short amount of time because it offers both sweeping panoramic views of the geology of Waterpocket Fold and close-ups of interesting rock formations.

Hickman Bridge Trail

1 mile one way. Moderate. Access: Hickman Bridge Parking Area on Utah 24 east of the visitor center.

Starting at the Fremont River, this self-guided nature trail heads into the desert, ascending some steep grades to the Hickman Natural Bridge, which has an opening 133 feet wide and 125 feet high. The trail has a 400-foot elevation gain.

Sunset Point Trail

0.3 mile one way. Easy. Access: Goosenecks Parking Area on Utah 24 west of the visitor center.

A short easy trail over fairly level ground, this hike affords panoramic views of cliffs and domes. The vistas are most dramatic around sunset.

LONGER TRAILS

Cassidy Arch Trail

1.75 miles one way. Difficult. Access: Off Grand Wash dirt road.

This strenuous trail offers spectacular views as it climbs steeply from the floor of Grand Wash to high cliffs overlooking the park. From the trail you'll also get several perspectives of Cassidy Arch, a natural stone arch named for outlaw Butch Cassidy, who is believed to have occasionally used the Grand Wash as a hideout.

Chimney Rock Trail

3.5 miles RT. Moderate to difficult. Access: Chimney Rock Parking Area on Utah 24 west of the park access road.

This trail begins with a strenuous climb up switchbacks to the more moderate loop trail on top. It affords views of Chimney Rock from both below and above, plus panoramic views of the surrounding areas once on top.

Cohab Canyon Trail

1.75 miles one way. Moderate to difficult. Access: Fruita Campground.

After the first 0.25 mile, which is rather strenuous, this trail evens out a bit and has fewer steep grades. It climbs to a hidden canyon above the campground, and has short side trails leading to overlooks. From the overlooks you get good views of the Fremont River, historic Fruita, and the campground.

Fremont Gorge Overlook Trail

2.25 miles one way. Difficult. Access: Blacksmith shop.

A strenuous climb to 1,000 feet above the Fremont River, this trail rewards you with a great view into the Fremont Gorge at the end. The middle of the hike, across Johnson Mesa, is fairly easy. The trail also affords good views of Fruita and the Wingate Escarpment.

Frying Pan Trail

3 miles one way. Difficult. Access: Fruita Campground or Grand Wash Parking Area.

This strenuous but scenic trail links Cohab and Cassidy Arch trails on the summit. It follows the ridge of the Capitol Reef escarpment, with a number of climbs up and down canyons, over slickrock. You'll get good views of Miners

Mountain to the southwest, rugged canyons to the side, and the Grand Wash below at the end of the trail.

Golden Throne Trail

2 miles one way. Difficult. Access: Capitol Gorge Parking Area.

A strenuous climb from the bottom of the gorge to the top of the cliffs at the base of the Golden Throne, this trail provides panoramic vistas whenever you stop to catch your breath. The Golden Throne is a large formation of Navajo sandstone that glows golden yellow in the light of the setting sun.

Grand Wash Trail

2.25 miles one way. Easy. Access: Grand Wash Parking Area.

This is a relatively easy hike along a narrow wash bottom with sheer rock walls on both sides. The trail shows the phenomenal power of water, as it winds between tall polished walls of stone, scoured smooth by the force of flash floods.

Navajo Knobs Trail

4.5 miles one way. Difficult. Access: Hickman Bridge Parking Area on Utah 24 east of the visitor center.

Beginning with a look at Hickman Natural Bridge, this strenuous hike then climbs up 1,000-foot cliffs for a view of the Fruita Orchard and campground. Afterwards, it continues several miles to Navajo Knobs for a spectacular 360° panoramic view of the park.

Old Wagon Trail

3.5 miles RT. Difficult. Access: West side of scenic drive near end.

This 1,000-foot climb up the east flank of Miners Mountain is certainly strenuous, but it affords unusual views of the Wingate Escarpment and Navajo Domes, plus panoramic views of the Waterpocket Fold.

Rim Overlook Trail

2.25 miles one way. Difficult. Access: Hickman Bridge Parking Area on Utah 24 east of the visitor center.

After a strenuous climb up 1,000-foot cliffs, hikers are rewarded with good views of the Fruita Orchards, the campground, and vistas to the south.

Exploring the Backcountry

The park offers a variety of backpacking opportunities, including the 16-mile round trip **Upper Muley Twist** route, which follows a canyon through the Waterpocket Fold and offers views of arches and narrows and a panoramic vista of Waterpocket Fold from an overlook; and the 22-mile round-trip **Halls Creek Narrows,** which follows Halls Creek through a beautiful slot canyon (where you'll have to wade or swim). A number of backcountry routes are discussed in a park hiking map and guide, available at the visitor center. **Free backcountry permits** (also available at the visitor center) are required for all overnight hikes. Backcountry hikers should discuss their plans with rangers before setting out, since many of these routes are prone to flash floods.

Other Sports & Activities

Four-Wheeling & Mountain Biking. As in most national parks, bikes and four-wheel-drive vehicles are restricted to established roads, but Capitol Reef has several such "established" roads—actually little more than dirt trails—that provide exciting opportunities for those using 4X4s or pedal-power.

The only route appropriate for road bikes is the 25-mile round-trip scenic drive, described above, but both the Grand Wash and Capitol Gorge roads (see "Exploring the Park by Car," above), plus three much longer dirt roads, are open to mountain bikes as well as four-wheel-drive vehicles. Be aware that rain can make the roads impassable, so it's best to check on current conditions with park rangers before setting out.

One recommended trip is the **Cathedral Valley Loop.** It covers more than 60 miles on a variety of road surfaces, including dirt, sand, and rock, and requires the fording of the Fremont River, where water is usually 1 to 1½ feet deep. The rewards are beautiful, unspoiled scenery, including bizarre sandstone monoliths and majestic cliffs, in one of the park's most remote areas. On the way, there's a small primitive campground in Cathedral Valley (see "Camping," below). Access to this loop is from Utah 24, just outside the park, 11.7 miles east of the visitor center via the River Ford Road, or 18.6 miles east of the visitor center on the Caineville Wash Road.

Mountain bike and four-wheel-drive tours into the national park and surrounding areas are provided by **Wild Hare Expeditions** (see address and phone under "Day Hikes," above). Full-day tours, including lunch, cost $60 to $75. The also company offers a variety of other guided trips, including multiday excursions, and rents mountain bikes, at $20 for a half day and $30 for a full day, with discounts for those taking guided tours and for multiday rentals.

Four-wheel-drive tours are also available from **Hondoo Rivers & Trails** in Torrey (☎ **800/332-2696** or 435/425-3519), with similar rates. Those wanting to go four-wheeling on their own can rent a 4X4 for about $75 per day, at Thousand Lakes RV Park & Campground (see address and telephone under "Camping," below).

Horseback Riding. Horses are welcome on some park trails but prohibited on others; check at the visitor center. **Pleasant Creek Trail Rides,** P.O. Box 102, Bicknell, UT 84715 (☎ **800/892-4597** or 435/425-3315; fax 435/425-3806), offers a variety of rides in the area, ranging from 1 hour to 6 days. A 1-hour ride costs $15; a full-day ride through the national park, including lunch, costs about $90. Also providing horseback trips is **Hondoo Rivers & Trails** (☎ **800/332-2696** or 435/425-3519).

Especially for Kids

Children from 6 to 12 can become **Junior Rangers,** and receive a cloth patch for their efforts, by purchasing a booklet in the visitor center and completing a variety of projects. Kids from third through eighth grades can become **Junior Geologists** by joining a ranger on a field trip (usually held once each week in summer). Families are invited to borrow a **Family Fun Pack** at the visitor center. The pack contains park-related games and activities.

Wildlife Viewing. Summer in Capitol Reef is hot and sometimes stormy, but it's a good season for wildlife viewing. In particular, many species of lizards make their home in the park; you will probably catch a glimpse of one warming itself on a rock. The western whiptail, eastern fence, and side-blotched lizards are the most common, but the loveliest is the collared lizard, dark in color but with light speckles that allow it to blend easily with lava rocks and become almost invisible to its foes.

Watch also for deer and marmots throughout the park, especially along the path between the visitor center and Fruita Campground. This area is also where you're likely to see chipmunks and antelope ground squirrels. Although they're somewhat shy and only emerge from their dens at night, the ring-tailed cat, a member of the raccoon family, also calls the park home; as do the seldom-seen bighorn sheep, bobcat, cougar, fox, and coyote.

If you keep your eyes to the sky you may see a golden eagle, sharp-shinned hawk, or any of the many other types of birds attracted by the park's variety of habitats. Year-round residents include chukars, common flickers, yellow-bellied sapsuckers, horned larks, canyon wrens, rock wrens, American robins, ruby-crowned kinglets, starlings, and American kestrels. In warmer months you're also likely to see yellow warblers, red-winged blackbirds, western tanagers, northern orioles, violet-green swallows, white-throated swifts, and black-chinned hummingbirds. Bird watching is particularly good along the Fremont River in the spring and early summer.

Camping

INSIDE THE PARK

The 71-site **Fruita Campground,** located along the main park road, 1 mile south of the visitor center, has trees and deer, and is within walking distance of the Fruita School and other historic attractions. There are also modern rest rooms, but water may be turned off in the winter, leaving only pit toilets.

Capitol Reef also has two primitive campgrounds. **Cedar Mesa Campground,** in the southern part of the park, is about 8 miles down unpaved Notom-Bullfrog Road, which heads south off Utah 24 just outside the East Entrance to the park (the road may be impassable in wet weather). **Cathedral Valley Campground** is in the northern part of the park. To get there from Utah 24, turn north on unpaved Cathedral Valley Road (about 5 miles east of the park), and go about 30 miles. Be advised that this road requires a high-clearance or four-wheel-drive vehicle at all times and may be completely inaccessible in bad weather.

Backcountry camping is permitted in much of the park with a free permit, available at the visitor center.

WEST OF THE PARK

There are several commercial campgrounds and an attractive U.S. Forest Service campground in the community of Torrey, about 5 miles west of the park entrance.

At **Sandcreek RV Park & Hostel,** 540 Utah 24 (P.O. Box 750276), Torrey, UT 84775 (☎ **435/425-3577**), you'll find RV sites with full hookups, plus grassy tent sites, not to mention great views in all directions. Trees have been planted and will provide shade as they grow, and a swimming pool is also planned. There is already a gift shop and espresso bar.

Also in Torrey is **Thousand Lakes RV Park & Campground,** Utah 24 (P.O. Box 750070), Torrey, UT 84775 (☎ **800/355-8995** for reservations, or 435/425-3500). In addition to the usual amenities, this campground offers good views of surrounding rock formations, plus some shade trees. RV sites are gravel; tent sites are grass. The campground also has four cabins, which rent for $26 to $29. Campers can rent 4X4s for $75 a day, and can feast on western dinners Tuesday through Saturday. There is also

Campground	Elev.	Total Sites	RV Hookups	Dump Station	Toilets	Drinking Water	Showers
Fruita	5,500	71	0	Yes	Yes	Yes	No
Cedar Mesa	5,400	5	0	No	Yes	No	No
Cathedral Valley	7,000	5	0	No	Yes	No	No
Sandcreek	6,840	24	12	Yes	Yes	Yes	Yes
Singletree	8,200	31	31	Yes	Yes	Yes	No
Sleepy Hollow	4,600	36	36	No	Yes	Yes	Yes
Thousand Lakes	6,840	67	58	Yes	Yes	Yes	Yes

a convenience store, horseshoes, and barbecues.

In addition to the two commercial campgrounds discussed above, **Austin's Chuck Wagon Lodge and General Store** in Torrey has a half dozen RV sites. See the "Accommodations" section, below.

Those looking for a forest camping experience on the west side of the national park will like **Singletree Campground,** located on Utah 12 about 16 miles south of Torrey (Teasdale Ranger District of the Dixie National Forest, Box 99, Teasdale, UT 84773; ☎ **435/425-3702**). Located in a forest of tall pines, this campground has standard individual campsites plus five multiple-family sites. All sites are paved, and many offer distant panoramic views of the national park. Near two of the large multiple-family sites, you'll find a horseshoe pit and volleyball court. Multiple-family units cost $16 to $24.

EAST OF THE PARK

Located along Utah 24 about 15 miles east of the park is **Sleepy Hollow Campground,** HC 70, Box 40, Caineville, UT 84775 (☎ **435/456-9130**). Although the terrain is generally desert, the tent sites are nicely shaded, and there are also a few trees in the RV area. There's a convenience store with beverages, snack items, film, ice, and souvenirs. An attractive one-bedroom apartment at the back of the store sleeps up to four, with rates from $60 for two.

Accommodations

There are no lodging facilities in the park itself, but the town of Torrey, just west of the park entrance where Utah 12 meets Utah 24, can take care of most needs. Remember that room tax adds about 9% to lodging bills. Pets are generally not accepted, unless otherwise noted. Also see the Sleepy Hollow Campground listing in the "Camping" section, above.

NEAR THE PARK

There is an attractive **Days Inn,** 675 E. Utah 24 (at its intersection with Utah 12), Torrey, UT 84775 (☎ **800/DAYS-INN** or 435/425-3111; fax 435/425-3112). It charges $59 to $79 for two in summer, with lower rates the rest of the year.

Austin's Chuck Wagon Lodge & General Store

12 W. Main St. (P.O. Box 750180), Torrey, UT 84775. ☎ **800/863-3288** or 435/425-3335; fax 435/425-3434. 20 rms, 1 family suite. A/C TV. Newer units $58 double, older units $39 double, family suite $80 double plus $5 for each additional person. AE, MC, V. Closed Dec–Feb.

This attractive and nicely landscaped motel contains both newer modern motel rooms, with telephones, satellite TV, and two queen-size beds; and also older units, which have knotty pine walls, one queen bed, and no phones.

Fire Pits/ Grills	Laundry	Public Phone	Reserve	Fees	Open
Yes	**No**	**Yes**	**No**	**$8**	**Year-round**
Yes	**No**	**No**	**No**	**Free**	**Year-round**
Yes	**No**	**No**	**No**	**Free**	**Year-round**
No	**Yes**	**Yes**	**Yes**	**$9–$18**	**Mid-Mar to mid-Oct**
Yes	**No**	**No**	**Yes**	**$8**	**Memorial Day to mid-Sept**
No	**No**	**No**	**Yes**	**$12–$15**	**Apr–Sept**
Yes	**Yes**	**Yes**	**Yes**	**$9–$17**	**Apr–Oct**

There is also a family suite, which sleeps six in three bedrooms and has a large living room and a fully equipped kitchen. Guests have access to an outdoor pool and whirlpool, and free movies in the newer rooms. On the property there is also a grocery store/bakery, coin-operated laundry, and hair salon. An attached RV park has six sites, with full hookups, at $15 each per night including tax.

Best Western Capitol Reef Resort

2600 E. Utah 24 (P.O. Box 750160), Torrey, UT 84775. ☎ **800/528-1234** or 435/425-3761; fax 435/425-3300. 50 units. A/C TV TEL. June–Sept $75–$85 double; Oct–May $47–$75 double; $90–$125 suite. AE, DC, DISC, MC, V.

Located a mile west of the national park entrance, this attractive Best Western provides an excellent location for park visitors. Try to get a room on the back side of the motel; you'll be rewarded with fantastic views of the area's red rock formations. Standard rooms have two queen-size beds, white stucco walls, and southwestern-style scenic prints. A restaurant serves three meals daily year-round. Bonuses include the outdoor heated pool, whirlpool, and sundeck, all out back away from road noise, with glass wind barriers and spectacular views.

Boulder View Inn

385 W. Main St. (Utah 24), Torrey, UT 84775. ☎ **800/444-3980** or 435/425-3800. 12 rms. A/C TV TEL. $52 double. Rates include continental breakfast. AE, DISC, MC, V.

Located just 1 mile west of the junction of Utah highways 12 and 24, this is an attractive modern motel with a southwestern motif. Rooms are large and comfortable, containing tub/shower combos, queen or king beds, and a table with two chairs. Swimmers and smokers are out of luck—there is no swimming pool and no smoking permitted in any of the rooms. Several restaurants are within walking distance.

Capitol Reef Inn & Cafe

360 W. Main St. (Utah 24), Torrey, UT 84775. ☎ **345/425-3270**. 10 rms. A/C TV TEL. $42 double. DISC, MC, V. Closed Nov–Mar.

This is a small, beautifully landscaped Western-style motel, set back from the road. Rooms are large, homey, and comfortable, with either two queen beds or one queen and a double; only one room has a tub/shower combo, others have showers only. Furniture is handmade solid wood. Fun-loving guests enjoy a playground, trampoline, and 10-person whirlpool. Adjacent, under the same ownership, is an excellent restaurant (see "Dining," below), and a gift shop with American Indian crafts, guidebooks, and maps. Pets are accepted.

Skyridge Bed & Breakfast Inn

On Utah 24, just east of its intersection with Utah 12 (P.O. Box 750220), Torrey, UT 84775. ☎ **435/425-3222.** 6 rms. TV TEL. $82–$120 double. Rates include breakfast and evening hors d'oeuvres. MC, V.

This combination bed-and-breakfast and art gallery offers a delightful alternative to the standard motel. The three-story contemporary inn has six distinctive rooms. Each comes with private bath and VCR, and each is decorated with an eclectic mix of antiques, collectibles, folk sculpture, and contemporary art, including at least one piece by innkeeper/artist Karen Kesler. One room also has a private deck with a hot tub, and another has a two-person whirlpool tub. The shared gallery/living room has an impressive fireplace, plus books, games, and a collection of classic and contemporary movies available for guest use. A new outdoor hot tub has been added as well. The inn is located on 75 acres, with its own hiking and biking trails and spectacular views of the national park and Boulder Mountain.

Wonderland Inn

At the junction of Utah 24 and 12 (P.O. Box 67), Torrey, UT 84775. ☎ **800/458-0216** or 435/425-3775. 50 rms, 2 suites. A/C TV TEL.

Summer $58–$80 double; winter $40–$60 double. AE, DC, DISC, JCB, MC, V.

This modern motel, built in 1990, is on a hill set back from the highway, making it very quiet and peaceful. Built, owned, and managed by Ray and Diane Potter and family, the property is especially well kept. The motel has a combination indoor/outdoor heated swimming pool, tanning room, whirlpool, and even a beauty salon. A restaurant serves three meals daily year-round, with a popular breakfast buffet in the summer.

Dining

There are no dining facilities in the park itself, but the town of Torrey, just west of the park entrance, offers several options.

NEAR THE PARK

Brink's Burgers Drive-In

165 E. Main St., Torrey. ☎ **435/425-3710.** Most items $1–$4.50. MC, V. Daily 11am–8pm. Closed in winter. BURGERS/SANDWICHES.

This nonfranchise fast-food restaurant serves great burgers and English-style chips in a cafelike decor, or you can take your food outside to picnic tables. In addition to much better than average burgers, choices include chicken and fish selections, cheese sticks, onion rings, zucchini sticks, and spicy potato wedges. The restaurant also offers wagon rides complete with Dutch oven dinners ($15 for adults, $7.50 for children 10 and under). Milk shakes and ice-cream cones are also available; no alcohol is served.

Cafe Diablo

599 S. Main St., Torrey. ☎ **435/425-3070.** Main courses $12.95–$16.95. MC, V. May–Oct 15, daily 4–10pm. Closed Oct 16–Apr. SOUTHWESTERN.

Looks are deceiving. What appears to be a simple small-town cafe in a converted home is in fact a very fine restaurant, offering innovative beef, pork, chicken, and seafood selections, many created with a southwestern flair. The menu varies, but could include pumpkinseed-crusted local trout, served with cilantro-lime sauce and rice pancakes; polenta lasagna, which is layers of polenta, ricotta, and grilled vegetables, with salsa and mozzarella cheese; or a simple charbroiled New York steak. Pastries, all made on the premises, are spectacular, and beer—both microbrewed and mainstream—is available.

Capitol Reef Inn & Cafe

360 W. Main St. ☎ **435/425-3271.** Breakfast $4.25–$7.50; main courses $5–$16. DISC, MC, V. Daily 7–11am and 5–9pm. Closed Nov–Mar. ECLECTIC/VEGETARIAN.

A local's favorite, this restaurant offers fine, fresh, and healthful dining, among the best you'll find in Utah. Famous for its locally raised trout, it is equally well-known for its ten-vegetable salad, which is served with all dinner entrees. Vegetables are all grown locally. Several dishes, such as spaghetti, fettuccine primavera, and shish kebab can be ordered vegetarian or with various meats or fish. Portions are large and prices reasonable, and there's live music to boot most evenings. The atmosphere is comfortable and casual, with many diners gazing out the large windows at the magnificent scenery beyond. There's also children's menu, domestic and imported beers, and an extensive wine list.

Picnic & Camping Supplies

In addition to groceries, **Austin's Chuck Wagon Lodge & General Store,** at 12 W. Main St. in Torrey (☎ **435/425-3335**), has a bakery, a coin-operated laundry, and a hair salon. Austin's is closed December through February.

10

CARLSBAD CAVERNS NATIONAL PARK

by Don and Barbara Laine

ONE OF THE LARGEST AND MOST SPECTACULAR CAVE SYSTEMS IN THE world, Carlsbad Caverns National Park comprises some 80 known caves that snake through the porous limestone reef of the Guadalupe Mountains. Fantastic and grotesque formations fascinate visitors, who find every shape imaginable (and unimaginable) naturally sculpted in the underground—from frozen waterfalls to strands of pearls, soda straws to miniature castles, draperies to ice-cream cones.

Formation of the caverns began some 250 million years ago, when a huge inland sea covered this part of America. A reef formed, and then the sea disappeared, leaving the reef covered with deposits of salts and gypsum. Eventually uplifting and erosion brought the reef back to the surface, and then the actual cave-building began. Rainwater slowly seeped through cracks in the earth's surface, dissolving the limestone and leaving hollows behind. With the help of sulfuric acid, created by gases released from oil and gas deposits further below ground level, the cavern passageways grew, sometimes becoming huge rooms.

Once the caves were hollowed out, nature became artistic, decorating the rooms with a vast variety of fanciful formations. Very slowly, water dripped down through the rock into the caves, dissolving more limestone and absorbing the mineral calcite and other materials on its journey. Each drop of water then deposited its tiny load of calcite, gradually creating the cave formations that lure hundreds of thousands of wide-eyed visitors to Carlsbad Caverns National Park each year.

Although American Indians had known of Carlsbad Cavern for centuries, it was not discovered by settlers until ranchers in the 1880s were attracted to it by sunset flights of bats emerging from the cave. The first reported trip into the cave was in 1883, when a man supposedly lowered his 12-year old son into the cave entrance. A cowboy named Jim White, who worked for mining companies that collected bat droppings for use as a fertilizer, began to explore the main cave in the early 1900s. Fascinated by the cave formations, White shared his discovery with others, and soon word of this magical belowground world began to spread.

Carlsbad Cave National Monument was created in October 1923. In 1926, the first electric lights were installed, and in 1930 Carlsbad Caverns gained national park status.

Underground development at the park has been confined to the famous

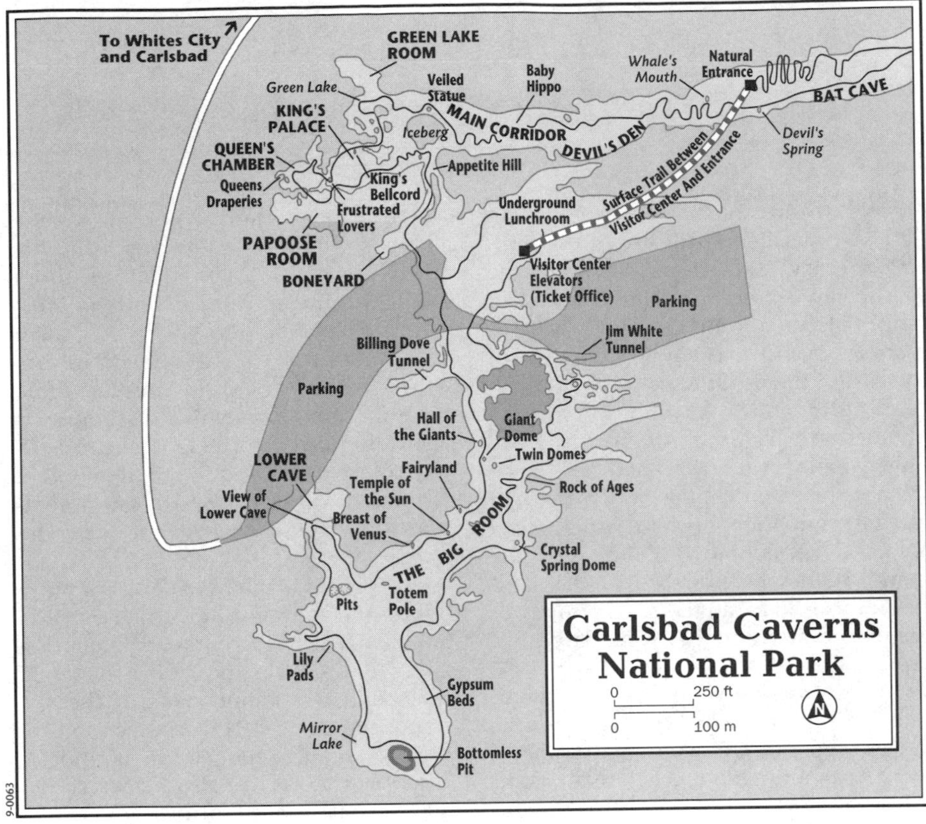

Big Room, one of the largest and most easily accessible of the caverns, with a ceiling 25 stories high and a floor large enough to hold 14 football fields. Visitors can tour parts of it on their own, aided by a new state-of-the-art CD-ROM portable audio guide, and explore other sections and several other caves on guided tours. The cave is also a summer home to about 1 million Mexican free-tailed bats, which hang from the ceiling of Bat Cave during the day, but put on a spectacular show each evening as they leave the cave in search of food and again in the morning when they return for a good day's sleep.

In addition to the fascinating underground world, the national park has a scenic drive, interpretative nature trail, and backcountry hiking trails through the Chihuahuan Desert.

Avoiding the Crowds. Carlsbad Caverns National Park is open year-round. Crowds are thickest in summer, and on weekends and holidays year-round, so visiting on weekdays between Labor Day and Memorial Day is the best way to avoid them. January is the quietest month.

Visiting during the park's off-season is especially attractive because the climate in the caves doesn't vary regardless of the weather on top, where the winters are generally mild and summers warm to hot. The only downside to an off-peak visit is that you won't be able to see the bat flights. The bats head to Mexico when the weather starts to get chilly, usually by late October, and don't return until May. There are also fewer guided cave tours off-season, although those tours will have fewer people. The best time to see the park might well be September, when you can still see the bat flights but there are fewer visitors than during the peak summer season.

Tips from a Park Ranger

"Caves are not familiar to the human experience—they're unknown, scary," says Douglas Ballou, the park's cave supervisor. "Here, under the guise of an adventure, we're helping people gain a greater appreciation of caves and the world of caving."

Visitors actually see only a few of the many caves that are in the park, according to Ballou, who says that of the park's 80-plus caves only 10 are open for wild caving, and then only to experienced cavers. Most people, of course, visit the park's namesake, Carlsbad Cavern, and some also take ranger-guided tours of nearby Slaughter Canyon Cave and Spider Cave.

"If you can only see one thing here, see the Big Room in Carlsbad Cavern," advises Ballou. "Allow an hour, and if you have more time and are in good physical condition, take the Natural Entrance Route into the cave, which has a 750 foot descent and is a bit strenuous."

The scientific potential from caves is tremendous, Ballou says, adding that research is underway in one of the park's caves that may eventually provide a cure for certain types of cancer. "They're collecting microscopic life forms—bacteria that survive without sunlight and secrete an enzyme that appears to be able to kill breast cancer cells without harming healthy human cells." While park visitors usually don't have the opportunity to see scientists at work, they can get a feel for what it's like to explore caves, and to see the pools of water and other isolated environments that allow these microscopic life-forms to exist.

He says that many park visitors miss out on the aboveground attractions, and he particularly recommends that they take the 9.5-mile scenic drive, which provides fine panoramic views of the surrounding desert. "Late afternoon or early evening is best, when it's not so hot," Ballou says. He also suggests a picnic at Rattlesnake Springs, a "birders' paradise," he calls it, and adds that those who want to experience the Chihuahuan Desert without any crowds should consider hiking the park's backcountry, which is done by less than 1% of the park's visitors.

Just the Facts

GETTING THERE & GATEWAYS

The main section of the national park, with the visitor center and entrance to Carlsbad Cavern, the park's main cave, is located about 30 miles southwest of the city of Carlsbad via U.S. 62/180 and N. Mex. 7. From Albuquerque drive east on I-40 for 59 miles to Clines Corners, and turn south on U.S. 285 for 216 miles to the city of Carlsbad. For the caverns continue southwest 23 miles on U.S. 62/180 to White's City, and go about 7 miles on N. Mex. 7, the park access road, to the visitor center. From El Paso drive east 150 miles on U.S. 62/180 to White's City, and then 7 miles on N. Mex. 7 to the visitor center. Visitor services are sometimes limited in the area, especially on the drive from El Paso, so plan accordingly.

The Nearest Airport. Air travelers can fly to **Cavern City Air Terminal** (☎ **505/885-5236**), 4 miles south of the city of Carlsbad, which has commercial service from Albuquerque. Taxi service is available at the airport.

The nearest major airport is **El Paso International** (☎ **915/772-4271**) in central El Paso just off I-10, with service from **American, America West, Continental, Delta, Southwest, Frontier,** and **Aero Litoral** (☎ **800/237-6639**).

Renting a Car. Car-rental agencies at the El Paso airport include **Advantage, Alamo, Avis, Budget, Dollar, Hertz,** and **National.**

Toll-free reservations numbers for all the airlines and car-rental agencies listed in this section are given in the appendix.

GETTING INFORMATION BEFORE YOUR TRIP

For a copy of the park's brochure and other information, contact the **Superintendent, Carlsbad Caverns National Park,** 3225 National Parks Hwy., Carlsbad, NM 88220 (☎ **505/785-2232,** or 505/785-2107 for recorded information). The Web site is **www.nps.gov/cave**.

Books and maps can be ordered in preparation for your trip from the **Carlsbad Caverns–Guadalupe Mountains Association** (see address in "Visitor Center," below). Those arriving in the city of Carlsbad before going to the park can get brochures, maps, and other information at the National Park Service's administrative office and bookstore, at 3225 National Parks Hwy. (at its intersection with West Pecan Street). It's open Monday through Friday from 8am to 4:30pm.

VISITOR CENTER

The visitor center at the park is open daily 8am to 7pm from Memorial Day to mid-August. Self-guided cave tours are available from 8:30am to 5pm. The rest of the year the visitor center is open from 8am to 5:30pm, and self-guided cave tours are available from 8:30am to 3:30pm. The park is closed on Christmas Day. Plan to arrive early in the day for maximum options.

At the visitor center are displays depicting the geology and history of the caverns, bats and other wildlife, and a three-dimensional model of Carlsbad Cavern. You can also get information about the tours available and other park activities, both below- and aboveground. There is a well-stocked bookstore, operated by the **CarlsbadCaverns–Guadalupe Mountains Association,** P.O. Box 1417, Carlsbad, NM 88221-1417 (☎ **505/785-2232,** ext. 481), whose Web site is www.caverns.com/~ccgma. An annual family membership in the nonprofit association costs $25, and provides a 15% discount at this and many other park bookstores.

Attached to the visitor center is a family-style restaurant (see "Dining," below) and a gift shop (☎ **505/785-2281**) that offers the usual souvenir items such as postcards and sweatshirts, plus film and a variety of gift items including handmade American Indian crafts. Another gift shop is located in the Underground Rest Area (see "Dining," below).

ENTRANCE FEES

Admission to the visitor center and aboveground sections of the park is free. The basic cavern entry fee, which is good for 3 days and includes self-guided tours of the Natural Entrance and Big Room, is $6 for adults, $3 for children 6 to 15, and free for children under 6. The entrance fee for those with Golden Age and Golden Access passports is $3; Golden Eagle Passports are not valid for cave entrance or tours. An excellent audio tour of the two self-guided routes is available for a $3 rental fee.

A general cave admission ticket is required in addition to tour fees for all guided cave tours except those to Slaughter Canyon Cave and Spider Cave. Reservations are required for all guided tours. Holders of Golden Age and Golden Access passports receive 50% discounts on tours. The King's Palace guided tour costs $5 for adults, $2.50 for children 6 to 15, and is free for children aged 4 and 5 with an adult—younger children are not permitted. Guided tours of Left Hand

Tunnel, limited to those 6 and older, cost $5 for adults and $2.50 for children 6 to 15. Guided tours of Spider Cave, Lower Cave, and Hall of the White Giant are limited to those 12 and older, and cost $15 for adults and $7.50 for youths 12 to 15. Slaughter Canyon Cave tours, for those 6 and older, cost $10 for adults and $5 for children 6 to 15.

You can make reservations for cave tours up to 3 months in advance by calling ☎ **800/967-CAVE** (2283) in the U.S., or 301/722-1257. Payment can be made by DISC, MC, or V, and by check or money order. The reservations number is available 7 days a week from 10am to 10pm EST.

SPECIAL REGULATIONS & WARNINGS

As you would expect, damaging the cave formations in any way is prohibited. What some people do not understand is that they should not even touch the formations, walls, or ceilings. This is not only because many of the features are delicate and easily broken, but also because skin oils will both discolor the rock and disturb the mineral deposits that are necessary for growth.

Smoking and any other kind of tobacco use are prohibited underground. In addition, food, drinks, candy, and chewing gum are not allowed on the underground trails. Those making wishes should not throw coins or other objects into the underground pools.

Cave explorers should wear flat shoes with rubber soles and heels, because of the slippery paths, and a light sweater or jacket for comfort in the constant underground temperature of 56°. Children under 16 must remain with an adult at all times while in the caves. Although strollers are not allowed for younger children, child backpacks are a good idea, but beware of low ceilings and doorways along the pathways.

Pets are not permitted in the caverns, on park trails, or in the backcountry, and because of the hot summer temperatures pets should not be left unattended in vehicles. There is a kennel (☎ **505/785-2281**) available at the visitor center. It has cages in an air-conditioned room, but no runs, and is primarily used by pet owners for periods of 3 hours or so while they are on cave tours. Pets are provided with water, but not food, and there are no grooming or overnight facilities. Reservations are not necessary; cost is $3.75 per pet.

SEASONS & CLIMATE

The climate aboveground is warm in the summer, with highs often in the 90s and sometimes exceeding 100°F, and evening lows in the mid-60s. Winters are mild, with highs in the 50s and 60s in the day and nighttime lows usually in the 20s and 30s. Summers are known for sudden intense afternoon and evening thunderstorms; August and September see the most rain. Underground it's another story entirely, with a year-round temperature that varies little from its average temperature of 56°, making a jacket or sweater a welcome companion on your cave visit.

SEASONAL EVENTS

On the second Thursday in August (usually), a "bat flight breakfast" from 5 to 7am encourages visitors to watch the bats return to the cavern after their night of insect-hunting. Park rangers cook a special breakfast for early morning visitors for a small fee and then join them to watch the early morning return flight. Call the park for details.

USEFUL PUBLICATIONS

Because the park's backcountry trails may be hard to follow, rangers strongly recommend that those planning any serious aboveground hiking obtain topographical maps. An excellent book for hikers is ***Hiking Carlsbad Caverns and***

Guadalupe Mountains National Parks (Helena, Mont.: Falcon Press, 1996) by Bill Schneider, which was published in partnership with the Carlsbad Caverns–Guadalupe Mountains Association and is keyed to the Trails Illustrated topographical map of the park. Both are available at the visitor center's bookstore or from the Carlsbad Caverns–Guadalupe Mountains Association (see "Visitor Center," above).

Seeing the Highlights in a Day

Those with only 1 day to spend at Carlsbad Caverns National Park can see quite a bit if they organize their time well. First stop at the **visitor center** to look at the exhibits and check out that day's guided tour offerings and ranger programs. If you would like to take any guided tours later in the day, it's best to buy tickets now. Then head into the main cave through the steep **Natural Entrance Route,** and continue on a self-guided tour of the **Big Room,** which is 750 feet below the ground. For those not wishing to follow the steep switchback trail into the Natural Entrance, and anyone with health concerns, an elevator is also available in the visitor center that will deliver you easily and safely to the Big Room.

You'll finish your Big Room tour at the elevators near the **Underground Rest Area,** so pick up a sandwich there or take the elevator up to the surface, where you can dine in the restaurant at the visitor center or drive out to Rattlesnake Springs for a picnic lunch. After lunch, take the **King's Palace Guided Tour** (for which you wisely purchased tickets earlier). Then walk the nature trail outside the visitor center and drive the 9.5-mile **Walnut Canyon Desert Drive.** If possible, try to get back to the amphitheater at the cave's Natural Entrance by dusk to see the nightly **bat flight** (mid-May through October only), when thousands of bats leave the cave for a night of insect-hunting.

Exploring the Park by Car

No, you can't take your car into the caves, but it won't be totally useless here, either. For a close-up as well as panoramic view of the Chihuahuan Desert, head out on the **Walnut Canyon Desert Drive,** a 9.5-mile loop. You'll want to drive slowly on the one-way gravel road, both for safety and to thoroughly appreciate the dramatic scenery. Passenger cars can easily handle the tight turns and narrow passage, but the road is not recommended for motor homes and cars pulling trailers. Pick up an interpretive brochure for the drive at the visitor center bookstore.

Organized Tours & Ranger Programs

In addition to the cave tours, which are discussed below, rangers give a talk on bats at sunset each evening from May to October at the cavern's Natural Entrance (times change; check at the visitor center). Rangers also offer a variety of demonstrations, talks, guided nature walks, and other programs daily. Especially popular are the climbing programs, where rangers demonstrate caving techniques. In recent years there have also been a series of stargazing programs presented by graduate students from New Mexico State University. A schedule of ranger-led activities is posted at the visitor center.

Historic & Man-Made Attractions

While this park is devoted primarily to the work of nature, observing human activities in the caves is also part of the Carlsbad Caverns National Park experience. Throughout the main cavern you'll see evidence of humans' use (and misuse) of the caves. Those taking the guided Lower Cave tour will see historical artifacts left by early cave explorers, including members of a 1924 National Geographic Society expedition.

Cave Exploration

Carlsbad Cavern (the park's main cave), Slaughter Canyon Cave, and Spider Cave are open to the general public. Experienced cavers with professional-level equipment can request permission to explore ten of the park's other caves.

Most park visitors head first to Carlsbad Cavern, which has elevators, a paved walkway, and an Underground Rest Area. A 1-mile section of the Big Room self-guided tour is accessible to those in wheelchairs (no wheelchairs are available at the park), though it's best to have another person to assist. Pick up a free accessibility guide at the visitor center.

MAIN CARLSBAD CAVERN ROUTES

Most visitors see Carlsbad Cavern by taking the following three trails, all of which are lighted, paved, and have handrails. However, the Big Room is the only one of the three that's considered easy (most of it is wheelchair accessible).

The formations along these trails are strategically lit to display them at their most dramatic. This also means that today's visitors can see much more of the cave than early explorers, who were limited by the weak light produced by their lanterns. The odd tints of green and yellow that may appear in your photos are caused by the various types of electric lighting used, and not by your film processor.

Big Room Self-Guided Tour

1.25-mile loop. Easy. Access: Visitor center elevator to Underground Rest Area or via the Natural Entrance Route (see below).

Considered the one thing that all visitors to Carlsbad Caverns National Park must do, this easy trail meanders through a massive chamber—it isn't called the Big Room for nothing—where you'll see some of the park's most spectacular formations and likely be overwhelmed by the enormity of it all. Allow about 1½ hours.

Natural Entrance Route

1.25 miles. Moderate to difficult. Access: Outside the visitor center.

This fairly strenuous hike takes you into Carlsbad Cavern on the same basic route used by its early explorers. You leave the daylight to enter a big hole, and then descend more than 750 feet into the cavern on a steep and narrow switchback trail, moving from the "twilight zone" of semidarkness to the depths of the cave, which would be totally black without the electric lights conveniently provided by the Park Service. The self-guided tour takes about 1 hour and ends near the elevators, which can take you back to the visitor center. However, it is strongly recommended that from here you proceed on the Big Room Self-Guided Tour, which is described above, if you have not already been there.

King's Palace Guided Tour

0.75-mile loop. Moderate. Access: Visitor center elevator to Underground Rest Area.

This ranger-led walk wanders through some of the cave's most scenic chambers, where you'll see wonderfully fanciful formations in the King's Palace, Queen's Chamber, and Green Lake Room. Watch for the delightful Bashful Elephant formation between the King's Palace and Green Lake Room. Along the way, rangers discuss the geology of the cave and early explorers' experiences. Although the path is paved, there is an 80-foot elevation change.

Caving Tour Programs in Carlsbad Cavern

Ranger-led tours to these less-developed sections of Carlsbad Cavern provide more of the experience of exploration and genuine caving than the above tours over well-trodden trails. These caving tours vary in difficulty, but all include a period of absolute darkness or "blackout," which can make some people uncomfortable. Because some tours involve walking or crawling through tight spaces, people who suffer from claustrophobia should discuss specifics with rangers before purchasing tickets.

See below for age requirements and required equipment, which can include AA batteries, gloves, and knee pads. Rangers provide headlamps and helmets on some tours. All tours must be reserved and have individual fees in addition to the general cave entry fee. Tours are popular and are sometimes fully booked weeks in advance, so reserve early.

Left Hand Tunnel

0.5 mile one way. Easy. Access: Starts at the visitor center near the elevator.

The easiest of the caving tours, in this one you actually get to walk (rather than crawl) the entire time! Hand-carried lanterns (provided by the Park Service) light the way and the trail is dirt but relatively level. You'll see a variety of formations, fossils from Permian times, and pools of water. Open to those 6 and older. The tour takes about 2 hours.

Lower Cave

1 mile RT. Moderate. Access: Starts at the visitor center near the elevator.

This 3-hour trek involves descending or climbing over 50 feet of ladders, and an optional crawl. It takes you through an area that was explored by a National Geographic Society expedition in the 1920s, and you'll see artifacts from that and other explorations. In addition, you'll encounter a variety of formations, including cave pearls, which look a lot like the pearls created by oysters and can be as big as golf balls. Open to those 12 and older only. Four AA batteries are required for the provided headlamp; sturdy hiking boots and gloves are recommended.

Hall of the White Giant

0.5 mile one way. Difficult. Access: Starts at the visitor center.

If you want a strenuous, 3- to 4-hour trip where you crawl through narrow, dirty passageways and climb up slippery rocks, this tour is for you. The highlight is, of course, the huge formation called the White Giant. Only those in excellent physical condition should consider this tour; children must be at least 12. Four AA batteries for the provided headlamp and sturdy hiking boots are required; and knee pads, gloves, and long pants are strongly recommended.

OTHER CAVING TOURS

It takes some hiking to reach the other caves in the park, so carry drinking water, especially on hot summer days. All children under 16 must be accompanied by an adult; other age restrictions apply as well. Each tour includes a period of true and total darkness or "blackout." There are tour fees for both, but a general cave admission ticket is not required. Tours are popular and are frequently fully booked, so call a few months ahead for reservations.

Slaughter Canyon Cave

1.25 miles RT (plus 0.5-mile hike to and from cave). Moderate. Access: The cave is about a 45-min. drive from Carlsbad and is reached via U.S. 62/180, going south 5 miles from White's City, to a marked turnoff that leads 11 miles to a parking lot. Tours meet and depart from the cave entrance located 0.5 mile west of the parking lot.

Discovered in 1937, this cave was mined for bat guano (used as fertilizer) until the 1950s. It consists of a corridor 1,140 feet long with many side passageways. This highly recommended guided tour lasts about 2½ hours, plus at least another half hour to hike up the steep trail to the cave entrance. No crawling is involved, although the smooth flowstone and old bat guano on the floor can be slippery, so good hiking boots are recommended. You'll see a number of wonderful cave formations, including the crystal-decorated Christmas Tree, the Teardrop, the 89-foot-high Monarch, and the menacing Klansman. Open to children 6 and older. Participants must take D battery flashlights.

Spider Cave

1-mile loop (plus 0.5-mile hike to and from cave). Difficult. Access: Meet at the visitor center and follow a ranger to the cave.

Very strenuous, this tour is ideal for those who want the experience of a rugged caving adventure as well as some great underground scenery. Highlights include climbing down a 15-foot ladder, squeezing through very tight passageways, and climbing on slippery surfaces. All this after a fairly tough 0.5-mile hike to the cave entrance. But it's worth it. The cave has numerous beautiful formations—most much smaller than those in the Big Room—and picturesque pools of water. Children must be at least 12 years old. Participants need four AA batteries for the provided headlamps and good hiking boots. Knee pads, gloves, and long pants are strongly recommended.

WILD CAVING

Experienced cavers with the proper gear can request special permits from the park's **Cave Resources Office (☎ 505/785-2232**, ext. 363 or 368) to enter one of several undeveloped caves in the park on their own. There is also one cave, Ogle Cave, that is open to experienced vertical cavers on a ranger-led trip. Applications should be submitted at least 1 month ahead of time. There is a $12 fee for entry into Ogle Cave; permits for other caves are free. Further information is available from the Cave Resources Office.

Other Sports & Activities

Hiking & Backpacking. Most of the hiking here is done underground, as discussed above, but there are opportunities for hiking on top of the earth's surface as well. The park's busiest trail is the **Nature Trail,** a fairly easy, 1-mile paved loop that begins just outside the visitor center and has interpretative signs describing the various plants of the Chihuahuan desert.

About a half dozen other trails wander through the park's 30,000 acres of designated wilderness. These **backcountry trails** are generally poorly marked—rangers strongly recommend that hikers carry topographical maps, which can be purchased at the visitor center. Be careful of rattlesnakes, especially in warmer months. Lighting fires and entering backcountry caves without permits are both prohibited. Free permits, available at the visitor center, are required for all overnight hikes.

Backcountry trails include the 3.5-mile (one way) Guano Road Trail, with an elevation change of 710 feet; the 6-mile (round-trip) Rattlesnake Canyon Trail, with an elevation change of 670 feet; the 6-mile (one way) Slaughter Canyon Trail, which has an elevation change of 1,850 feet; the 11-mile (one way) Yucca Canyon Trail, with a 1,520-foot elevation change; the 11.8-mile (one way) Guadalupe Ridge Trail, with an elevation change of 2,050 feet; the 3.5-mile (one way) Juniper Ridge Trail, with an 800-foot elevation change; and the 1.5-mile (one way) Ussery Trail, which has an elevation change of 2,500 feet. Backcountry camping is permitted (with a free permit) on all of the above trails except Guano Road. Additional trail information is available from park rangers.

Horseback Riding. Most of the backcountry trails are open to those on horseback. A small corral is available for equestrians' use, with advance arrangements. Contact the park **Resource**

Management Office (☎ **505/785-2232,** ext. 363 or 368) for details.

Wildlife Viewing & Bird Watching. At sunset, from mid-May through October, a crowd gathers at the Carlsbad Cavern Natural Entrance to watch hundreds of thousands of bats take off for the night. All day long the Mexican free-tailed bats, which spend their winters in Mexico, sleep in the cavern, and then strike out on an insect hunt each night. An amphitheater in front of the Natural Entrance provides seating, and ranger programs are held each evening (exact times vary, check at the visitor center) during the bat's residence at the park. The most bats will be seen in August and September, when baby bats born earlier in the summer join their parents, along with migrating bats from the north, on the nightly forays. Early risers can also see the return of the bats just before dawn. Flash photography is not permitted, as it may disturb the bats.

However, bats aren't the only wildlife at Carlsbad Caverns. The park has a surprising number of **birds**—more than 300 species—many of which have been seen in the Rattlesnake Springs area. Among species you're likely to see are turkey vultures, red-tailed hawks, scaled quail, killdeer, mourning doves, lesser nighthawks, black-chinned hummingbirds, vermilion flycatchers, canyon wrens, northern mockingbirds, black-throated sparrows, and western meadowlarks. In addition, each summer several thousand cave swallows usually build their mud nests on the ceiling just inside the Carlsbad Cavern Natural Entrance (the bats make their home further back in the cave).

Among the park's **larger animals** are mule deer and raccoons, which are sometimes spotted near the Natural Entrance at the time of the evening bat flights. The park is also home to porcupines, hognosed skunks, desert cottontails, black-tailed jackrabbits, rock squirrels, and the more elusive ringtails, coyotes, and gray fox. These are sometimes seen in the late evenings along the park entrance road and the Walnut Canyon Desert Drive. In recent years there have also been a few sightings of mountain lions and bobcats.

Especially for Kids

Children usually love the self-guided walk through the main cavern's **Big Room,** with its many bizarre and beautiful shapes, especially when they're encouraged to let their imaginations run wild. Younger children, however, are often bored on the **King's Palace Guided Tour** because it has several stops, and everyone must remain with the group. (Children under 4 are not permitted on the King's Palace tour.) Families with children at least 6 years old (and preferably a bit older) usually enjoy the **Slaughter Canyon Cave** tour, which has some spectacular formations and gives the feeling of exploring a wild cave.

The park also offers a **Junior Ranger Program,** in which kids can earn badges by completing various activities. Details are available at the visitor center.

Camping

There are no developed campgrounds or vehicle camping of any kind in the national park. Backcountry camping, however, is permitted in some areas (see "Backcountry Trails" under "Hiking & Backpacking," above). Pick up free permits at the visitor center.

NEAR THE PARK

The closest camping is **White's City RV Park,** 17 Carlsbad Cavern Hwy. at N. Mex. 7 (P.O. Box 128), White's City, NM 88268

(☎ **800/CAVERNS** or 505/785-2291), located in the White's City complex at the east edge of the park boundary, about 7 miles east of the visitor center. In addition to RV sites with hookups and shade shelters, the campground has practically unlimited tent camping in a grassy area with picnic tables and some trees. Because the campground is part of the White's City complex, with its motels, restaurants, and other services, campers have access to facilities such as the motel pool, an ATM, convenience store, liquor store, post office, gift shop, and museum.

A good choice in the city of Carlsbad is **Carlsbad RV Park,** 4301 National Park Hwy., Carlsbad, NM 88220 (☎ **888/8RV-PARK** or 505/885-6333). Sites are mostly pull-throughs and are large enough to accommodate big rigs with slide-outs. Some sites have cable TV hookups. This tree-filled park has a game room, a playground, and a meeting room. A convenience store sells groceries, gifts, and RV supplies.

Those who will be exploring the city of Carlsbad and other area attractions may want to use as a base camp **Brantley Lake State Park,** P.O. Box 2288, Carlsbad, NM 88221 (☎ **505/457-2384**). Located 12 miles north of the city of Carlsbad via U.S. 285, and then 4.5 miles northeast on Eddy County Road 30, this quiet and relaxing park is almost 40 miles from the Carlsbad Caverns Visitor Center. Boating, swimming, and fishing on the 2,800-acre lake are all on offer here, as well as good bird watching. In addition to the developed campsites with hookups, there is primitive camping along the lakeshore for 20 to 50 RVs or tents, depending on the lake level. The park also has boat ramps, picnic tables, two playgrounds, and exhibits on the 19th-century community of Seven Rivers, considered one of the West's wildest towns, which now lies at the bottom of the lake.

Accommodations

There are no accommodations within the park. The closest are at White's City, which contains a variety of businesses under one management, including lodging, dining, shops, a museum, gas station, and an RV park.

The next closest services are in and near the city of Carlsbad. Here you'll find several chain and franchise motels. Those located on the southwest edge of the city, on the road to Carlsbad Caverns, include **Days Inn of Carlsbad,** 3110 National Parks Hwy., Carlsbad, NM 88220 (☎ **800/325-2525** or 505/887-7800; fax 505/885-9433), with rates for two of $50 to $60; **Motel 6,** 3824 National Parks Hwy., Carlsbad, NM 88220 (☎ **505/885-0011;** fax 505/887-7861), which charges $32 for two people; **Quality Inn,** 3706 National Parks Hwy. (P.O. Box 5037), Carlsbad, NM 88220 (☎ **800/228-5150** or 505/887-2861; fax 505/887-2861), with rates for two of $54 to $89; and **Super 8 Motel,** 3817 National Parks Hwy., Carlsbad, NM 88220 (☎ **800/800-8000** or 505/887-8888; fax 505/885-0126), charging $46 to $53 for two. For additional information on area lodging contact the **Carlsbad Chamber of Commerce,** P.O. Box 910 Dept. B, Carlsbad, NM 88221-0910 (☎ **800/221-1224** or 505/887-6516).

Campground	Elev.	Total Sites	RV Hookups	Dump Station	Toilets	Drinking Water
Carlsbad RV Park & Campground	3,110	136	95	Yes	Yes	Yes
Brantley Lake State Park	3,300	51+	51	Yes	Yes	Yes
White's City RV Park	3,630	80+	80	Yes	Yes	Yes

Best Western Cavern Inn

17 Carlsbad Cavern Hwy. at N. Mex. 7, White's City, NM 88268. ☎ **800/CAVERNS** (direct), 800/528-1234, or 505/785-2291; fax 505/785-2283. 105 rms. A/C TV TEL. May 15–Sept 15 $60–$85 double; Sept 16–May 14 $55–$75 double. AE, DC, DISC, MC, V.

This motel and its associated properties are the most convenient places to stay while visiting Carlsbad Caverns. Rooms are spacious, with southwestern decor and either two queen-size beds or one king. About half have whirlpool tubs. Most folks dine and drink at the complex's Velvet Garter Saloon and Restaurant or pick up a quick meal at nearby Fast Jack's (see "Dining," below). The White's City arcade contains a post office, a small grocery store, a gift shop, a museum, and a theater for weekend melodramas. Between the Cavern Inn and its neighbor properties, there are two swimming pools, two hot tubs, and a tennis court.

Best Western Motel Stevens

1829 S. Canal St., Carlsbad, NM 88220. ☎ **800/730-2851** (direct), 800/528-1234, or 505/887-2851, fax 505/887-6338. 202 rms, 15 suites. A/C TV TEL. $55–$65 double; $65 and up suite. AE, DC, DISC, MC, V.

Well-landscaped gardens surround this handsome property, composed of several buildings spread across spacious grounds. All the rooms have southwestern decor and most have two queen beds. Some units, with peaked ceilings to make them feel even larger, also have back-door patios. You can save money on dining by renting a microwave/refrigerator combo ($5), or by using the kitchenettes in the suites. There are some wheelchair-accessible rooms with roll-in showers. The motel has a restaurant (see "Dining," below), room service, a courtesy car, guest laundry, 24-hour front desk, swimming and wading pools, and a playground.

Holiday Inn

601 S. Canal St. (P.O. Box 128), Carlsbad, NM 88220. ☎ **800/742-9586,** 800/HOLIDAY, or 505/885-8500; fax 505/887-5999. 100 rms. A/C TV TEL. $86–$96 double. AE, DC, DISC, MC, V.

A handsome New Mexico Territorial-style building houses this first-rate full-service hotel in downtown Carlsbad. Guests can frolic in an attractive outdoor heated swimming pool, sauna, and whirlpool. There's also an exercise room and playground, and a self-service laundry. Some wheelchair-accessible rooms have roll-in showers. The hotel has two restaurants: Ventana's offers fine dining and serves steaks, prime rib, seafood, and pastas; the Phenix Bar and Grill serves Italian cuisine and steaks.

Dining

INSIDE THE PARK

There are two concessionaire-operated restaurants at the park (☎ **505/785-2281**). A family style full-service restaurant at the **visitor center** serves three meals daily. It offers standard breakfasts such as bacon and eggs, hot cakes, sweet rolls, and Spanish omelettes. For lunch and dinner you'll find a variety

Showers	Fire Pits/ Grills	Laundry	Public Phone	Reserve	Fees	Open
Yes	Yes	Yes	Yes	Yes	$15–$19	Year-round
Yes	Yes	No	Yes	No	$7–$11	Year-round
Yes	Yes	Yes	Yes	Yes	$15–$20	Year-round

of sandwiches, beef burgers, a veggie burger, and a few Mexican food items. The menu also includes chicken-fried steak, a garden salad with breast of chicken, grilled marinated breast of chicken, and daily specials. Prices are in the $2 to $7 range. The restaurant is open 8:30am to 4:30pm most of the year, with extended hours from Memorial Day through mid-August.

The **Underground Rest Area,** located inside the cavern 750 feet below ground, contains a cafeteria-style eatery offering fast food such as sandwiches, pizza, and burritos. Prices range from $2.50 to $6. There is also a gift shop, with a variety of items including postcards, sweatshirts, and film. Concession hours are coordinated with cave hours.

NEAR THE PARK

The Flume

Best Western Motel Stevens, 1829 S. Canal St., Carlsbad. ☎ **505/887-2851.** Reservations recommended for dinner. Lunch $4–$8; dinner $7–$16. AE, DC, DISC, MC, V. Mon–Sat 6am–10pm, Sun 6am–9pm. AMERICAN.

This relatively elegant restaurant has comfortable seating, candlelight, wall sconces, and chandeliers. For breakfast and lunch you can choose from a good selection of American favorites. The dinner menu includes a variety of steaks, seafood such as the New Orleans shrimp plate, and chicken, including a house specialty: teriyaki chicken breast. Lighter dinners for light eaters are also available.

Larez Restaurant

1524 S. Canal St., Carlsbad. ☎ **505/885-5113.** Main courses $3–$9. AE, DISC, MC, V. Mon–Fri 11am–2pm and 4–9pm. MEXICAN.

Real Mexican food prepared personally by restaurant owner Dora Larez is what you'll get here, and be prepared to wait a little for it, since items are prepared from scratch. Decor is unpretentious—cafe-like, simple, and clean. The food is tasty, but not excessively spicy. Try the guacamole salad with homemade chips for an excellent appetizer. The menu also includes a good selection of enchiladas, tacos, burritos, and other Mexican standards, plus a few lesser-known dishes such as the asada plate, chunks of pork with red chile sauce. A good choice is the Larez special, which includes two enchiladas, a taco, Spanish rice, beans, a guacamole salad, and a chile relleno. American dishes include chicken-fried steak, pork chops, and hamburgers. All menu items can be prepared for take-out.

Velvet Garter Saloon and Restaurant

26 Carlsbad Hwy., White's City. ☎ **505/785-2291.** Reservations recommended in summer. Main courses $7–$13. AE, DC, MC, V. Daily 4–9pm. AMERICAN.

This comfortable family style restaurant, with a separate saloon, has two beautiful stained-glass windows portraying the caverns and the Guadalupe Mountains, as well as other works of western art and assorted Old West touches. The menu includes steaks, chicken, and fish; there's also a salad bar and full liquor service. Nearby, Fast Jack's serves three meals daily, with various breakfast items, burgers, sandwiches, and a few full meals, with prices from $1 to $6.

Picnic & Camping Supplies

The closest grocery store to the national park is the convenience store located at the **Texaco gas station** in the White's City complex, at the intersection of U.S. 62/180 and N. Mex. 7, about 7 miles from the visitor center. You'll find a good variety of stores in the city of Carlsbad, including an **Albertson's grocery store** at 808 N. Canal St., at its intersection with West Church Street (☎ **505/885-2161**). It has a well-stocked deli and bakery, and is open daily 6am to 11pm.

11

CHANNEL ISLANDS NATIONAL PARK

by Jim Moore

A RUSTED WINDMILL STILL WATCHES OVER SCORPION RANCH ON THE eastern end of Santa Cruz Island, a reminder of man's indelible impact upon even our wildest places. But the Channel Islands are still places defined more by the wind and the sea. On land, the dry grasses and shrubs remain constantly in motion, mimicking the whitecapped water of the Santa Barbara Channel separating the islands from the mainland. In the waters surrounding the islands lives a diversity of life matched by few places on earth.

Even though it is one of the less visited national parks in the system, without the awe-inspiring scenery of Yosemite or Grand Teton, there is plenty to keep visitors coming back to the Channel Islands, much of it underwater. Opportunities for sea kayaking and hiking are many; and despite the islands' isolation, the opportunities to get away from the crowds abound. You'll find plants and animals here that live nowhere else, as well as archaeological remains of long-vanished cultures. It's a draw for underwater explorers from all over (twice as many people come here to explore the waters around the islands than ever set foot on the shore); you'll be able to go underwater without leaving the comfort of the main visitor center or the Anacapa landing dock (by video at least), when you watch rangers with video cameras explore the kelp forest twice a week.

Channel Islands National Park encompasses the five northernmost islands of an eight-island chain: Santa Barbara, Anacapa, Santa Cruz, Santa Rosa, and San Miguel. (Santa Catalina, San Clemente, and San Nicolas are not included in the park.) Not limited to the islands themselves, the park also encompasses 1 nautical mile of ocean around each island, and the 6 nautical miles around each island have been designated a national marine sanctuary. The smallest of the park's islands, tiny Santa Barbara, lives a solitary existence. The four northern islands are clustered in a 40-mile-long chain—though during the last ice age, before the continental ice sheets melted, raising the level of the seas, these islands were actually connected, forming one huge island geologists call Santarosae.

The four northern islands in the park are actually an extension of the Santa Monica Mountains; fossil records indicate that Santa Cruz, Santa Rosa, and

San Miguel were actually connected to the mainland at one point, but massive geological turmoil pushed them seaward some 600,000 years ago. Only Anacapa and Santa Barbara began their existence as islands (though some geologists argue that Santa Cruz was also never attached to the mainland)—both were formed by underwater volcanic activity.

Flora & Fauna. The isolation of the Channel Islands, which have been separated from the mainland for thousands of years, has allowed a diverse array of life to develop and evolve, prompting some biologists to dub them the "North American Galapagos." Most of the differences from mainland species are in size, shape, or color variation. Perhaps the most curious of the islands' inhabitants was the pygmy mammoth, only 4 to 6 feet tall, that roamed over Santarosae during the Pleistocene era—fossilized remains have been found on San Miguel and Santa Rosa.

Other island species, however, have survived. Like the mammoth, the Santa Cruz gopher snake, island spotted skunk, and island fox have all evolved to be smaller than their mainland relatives. Weighing just 4 pounds, the island fox is actually the smallest fox species in North America. Like Darwin's finches in the Galapagos, the islands native birds also show marked adaptation: The Santa Cruz Island scrub jay displays "gigantism"—it is one-third larger and deeper blue than mainland jays, and the orange-crowned warbler and rufous-sided towhee have oversize body parts.

The diversity of animal life on the islands is outdone only by the vast array of native plant life. One of the most spectacular of the islands' plants is the yellow coreopsis, or "tree sunflower," which can be found on all five islands as well as the mainland. Other species of plants live nowhere else on earth—the islands support 43 endemic varieties of plants. Some are prehistoric species that vanished from the mainland thousands of years ago—the ironwood has lived only on these islands for the past 3 million years. Like the pygmy mammoth, Santa Rosa's endemic Torrey pine population dates from the Pleistocene era, though a remnant mainland subspecies survives at Torrey Pines State Reserve north of La Jolla, California.

Marine life around the islands, however, easily wins the diversity award. The islands are the meeting point of two distinct marine ecosystems: The cold, nutrient-rich waters of northern California swirl together with the warmer, clearer currents of Baja California. Everything from microscopic plankton to the largest creature ever to live on earth, the blue whale, calls these waters home. Orcas and great white sharks, anemone and abalone, lobsters and starfish, plus dozens of varieties of fish, live in the tide pools, kelp forests, and waters surrounding the islands. Six varieties of seal and sea lions beach themselves on San Miguel, five of which breed here, making it the largest seal and sea lion breeding colony in the United States. The islands are also the most important seabird nesting area in California.

Some History. Thousands of years before Europeans discovered these islands, Native Americans crossed the channel in *tomols,* seaworthy plank canoes waterproofed with tar from oil seeps. All four of the northern islands were inhabited by the Chumash, or "island people," who first crossed the channel between 11,000 and 30,000 years ago. They supported themselves both through hunting and gathering and through their extensive trade network with the mainland communities.

In 1542 the Portuguese explorer Juan Rodriguez Cabrillo, sailing for Spain, became the first European to see the islands. While Cabrillo is probably better remembered for discovering California than this island chain, he died here as a result of a fall while wintering on an island he referred to as San Lucas (believed to be San Miguel or possibly Santa Rosa). Though his grave has never been discovered, historians believe him

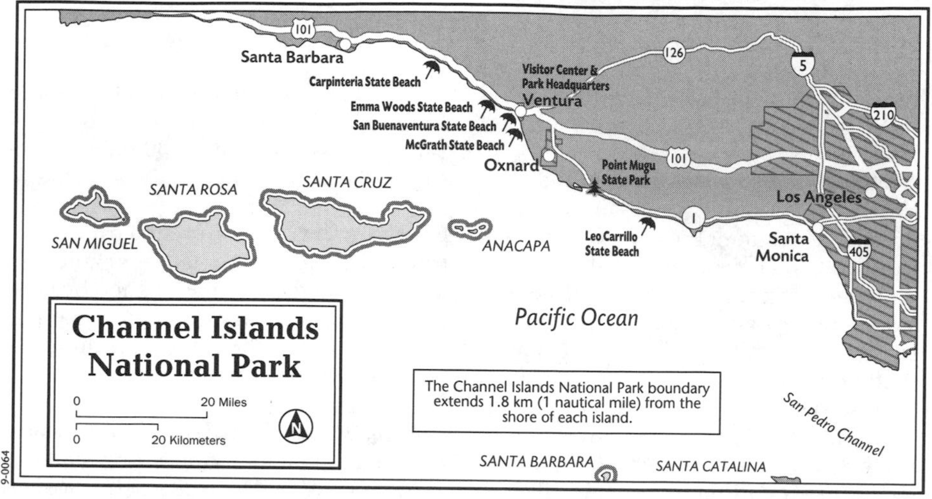

to have been buried here—a monument dedicated to him stands on San Miguel. While other explorers passed the islands over the next 2 centuries, it was 250 years before English Capt. George Vancouver fixed the present names of the islands on nautical charts in 1793.

During the late 1700s and early 1800s the islands and their surrounding waters were extensively trapped and hunted by fur traders and whalers. Prized for its valuable pelt, the sea otter was hunted to near extinction. When otters became scarce, hunters turned their attention to seals and sea lions who were valued for their fur and oil, nearly decimating their populations as well.

In the early 1800s the indigenous populations of Chumash were relocated to mainland missions, and by the mid-1800s ranching became the dominant economic mainstay of the islands: Santa Cruz supported working cattle and sheep ranches into the 1970s; **Vail and Vickers Company** still operates its cattle stocking operations from Santa Rosa; Anacapa, San Miguel, and Santa Barbara were also heavily grazed or cultivated. Today the impact of these ranches is blatantly evident, particularly on Santa Cruz and Santa Rosa. The rolling grasslands that cover much of the island terrain are predominantly fennel and other non-native grasses imported for grazing fodder for the cattle and sheep raised here.

Government presence has been felt here since the early part of this century. The U.S. Coast Guard (then known as the U.S. Lighthouse Service) first moved onto Anacapa in the early 1900s—an operational lighthouse still watches over the eastern edge of the island. In 1938 Anacapa and Santa Barbara were declared a national monument by Pres. Franklin D. Roosevelt. In 1980 the national monument was upgraded to a national park, adding Santa Cruz, Santa Rosa, and San Miguel.

While the National Park Service maintained control of the islands, ownership was still not that simple. The U.S. Navy has owned San Miguel since before World War II. Santa Rosa was still privately owned until December 1986, and to make things even more complicated the former owners, Vail and Vickers Company, have leased the island back from the Park Service in 5-year special-use permits for their cattle stocking operations, though visitation is allowed. Until February 1997, when the last member of the Gherini family sold the Park Service his portion of the 6,000-acre sheep ranch on the eastern end of Santa Cruz, all of Santa Cruz was still privately owned. Today the National Park Service owns and manages the eastern ten percent, while a private nonprofit organization, the Nature Conservancy, owns and manages the western 90% of the island. In 1987 Dr. Cary Stanton bequeathed his share of the island to the Nature Conservancy largely to keep it out of the hands of the government and Park Service, many of whose policies he did not agree with.

Avoiding the Crowds. Unlike at many of the more popular (and more easily accessible) national parks, crowds are rarely a problem on any of the islands. (In a given year, about 220,000 people stop in at the park visitor center; 200,000 go into the park waters, but only about 60,000 actually travel to the islands themselves.) While visitors rarely number above 80 a day to any given island, the open section of Anacapa is so small that it may be difficult, though still possible, to completely separate yourself from the flock. As for the other four islands in the park, you should have no trouble finding a secluded picnic spot or overlook. The relative difficulty of reaching the islands makes it easy to find a secluded spot without too much effort or advance preparation. Santa Barbara Island is the most distant and least crowded in the chain; San Miguel is the wildest and offers wonderful, solitary backcountry hiking possibilities. But even Anacapa, the closest and most heavily visited island, will afford you opportunities for solitude if you just walk away from the crowds.

Just the Facts

GETTING THERE & GATEWAYS

Most people travel to the islands by boat from **Ventura,** but even though there are no park fees, unless you have your own boat, getting there is expensive—anywhere from $32 to $120 per person, the higher price being for a trip by air to Santa Rosa. If you fly, you may leave from the **Camarillo** airport. Anacapa, 14 miles out, is closest to the mainland, about a 1-hour boat ride.

The Nearest Airport. The closest major airport to the Channel Islands is **Los Angeles International Airport (LAX).** It's served frequently by all the major airlines, with connections to almost anywhere in the world you might want to go (check our list of toll-free numbers in the appendix). LA is 96 miles southeast of Santa Barbara, Ventura is 30 miles southeast of Santa Barbara.

Renting a Car. You can rent a car at LAX from all major car-rental companies. In fact, Los Angeles is one of the cheapest places in the country to rent a car. Major companies and their toll-free numbers are listed in the appendix.

Getting to the Islands by Boat. Island Packers, next door to the visitor center at 1867 Spinnaker Dr. (recorded information ☎ **805/642-7688,** or 805/642-1393 for reservations), is one of the park's two concessionaires for boat transportation to and from the islands. They will take you on a range of regularly scheduled boat excursions, from 3½-hour nonlanding tours of the islands ($21 per person) or full-day tours of individual islands led by naturalists ($49 per person) to 2-day excursions to two islands ($245). Island Packers is also a great source of information about specialty trips to the islands—diving, sea kayaking, and so on. Private yachts and commercial dive and tour boats from all over southern California also visit the park on a regular basis. The new, second boat concessionaire, leaving from **Santa Barbara Harbor** is Truth Aquatics (☎ **805/962-1127**). They charge $70 for a 1-day round-trip to either San Miguel or Santa Rosa. The trips take 3 hours each way.

If You Have Your Own Boat. If you want to take **your own boat** out, check with the mainland visitor center. Access to the islands is prohibited in some places and difficult in others—to go ashore often requires a skiff, raft, or small boat:

- You may land without a permit on east Anacapa, Santa Barbara, and east Santa Cruz between Chinese Harbor and Sandstone Point.
- West Anacapa, except the beach at Frenchy's Cove, is closed to the public to protect nesting brown pelicans.
- Access to Middle Anacapa requires a ranger escort.

◆ Landings on Santa Rosa and San Miguel do not require a permit for beach use; to go inland on either island free permits, available at the visitors center, are necessary.

◆ To land on the private western portion of Santa Cruz, boaters must obtain a permit from the **Nature Conservancy,** Santa Cruz Island Preserve, P.O. Box 23259, Santa Barbara, CA 93121 (☎ **805/694-7839**). A fee is charged, no overnight stays are permitted, and it may take 10 or 12 days to process the request. Applications are available from the mainland visitor center or by contacting the Nature Conservancy directly.

Getting to the Islands by Air. If you want to get to Santa Rosa in a hurry, **Channel Islands Aviation,** 305 Durley Ave., Camarillo, CA 93010 (☎ **805/987-1678**), will fly you there in one of its small, fixed-wing aircraft.

GETTING INFORMATION BEFORE YOUR TRIP

If you want to get information about the Channel Islands before you leave, contact the **Superintendent, Channel Islands National Park,** 1901 Spinnaker Dr., Ventura, CA 93001 (☎ **805/658-5730;** fax 805/658-5799).

You can get information on the Web at the Channel Islands page on the National Park Service Web site: **www.nps.gov/chis**.

For information on Ventura, try the **Ventura Visitors & Convention Bureau,** 89-C S. California St., Ventura, CA 93001 (☎ **800/333-2989** or 805/648-2075). Their Web site is **www.ventura-usa.com**.

VISITOR CENTERS

The main visitor center for the islands is actually on the mainland, in Ventura Harbor, where you'll also find the park headquarters. Visit the **Channel Islands National Park Headquarters and Visitor Center,** 1901 Spinnaker Dr., Ventura, CA 93001 (☎ **805/658-5700**), to get acquainted with the various programs and individual personalities of the islands through maps and displays. It's open from 8:30am to 4:30pm weekdays, 8am to 5pm weekends; hours are slightly extended (a half hour on each end) during the "busier" summer season between Memorial Day and Labor Day.

Anacapa and **Santa Barbara** islands also have smaller visitors centers.

Rangers run interpretive programs both on the islands and at the mainland visitor center year-round.

ENTRANCE & CAMPING FEES

There are neither entrance nor camping fees for the islands, but you should consider the cost of getting to the islands when planning your budget. **Permits** are required for camping on all five islands; while they are free, you must make reservations by calling the park visitor center permits line (☎ **805/658-5711**).

SPECIAL REGULATIONS & WARNINGS

The relative inaccessibility of these islands compared to other national parks makes preplanning a must. The boat concessionaires are often booked up a month or so in advance, so be sure to make reservations. Also, remember that once on the islands, you can't go back to your car, so be sure to bring anything you might need (including water, food, and equipment if you're camping). If you're camping, bring a good tent—if you don't know the difference between a good and a bad tent, the island wind will gladly demonstrate it for you. And don't forget to reserve a camping permit.

SEASONS & CLIMATE

While the climate is mild with little variation in temperature year-round, the weather on the islands is always unpredictable. Thirty-mile-an-hour winds can blow for days, or sometimes a fog bank will settle in and smother the islands for weeks at a time. Winter rains can turn island trails into mud baths. In general, plan on wind, lots of sun (bring sunscreen), cool nights, and the possibility of hot days. Water temperatures are in the 50s and 60s year-round. Also be aware that inclement weather or sea conditions can cause concessionaires to cancel trips on the day of the excursion, so it's a good idea to have a plan B just in case.

SEASONAL EVENTS

From **January through March,** gray whales can be viewed as they pass by on their annual 10,000-mile migration from their warmer breeding grounds off the coast of Baja California to their cold water feeding grounds in the Arctic Ocean.

Blue and humpback whales can sometimes be seen in the waters off the islands between **June and October.**

USEFUL PUBLICATIONS

While a wide variety of publications dealing specifically or tangentially with the park, islands, and waters is available in the mainland visitor center, among the most helpful are the free handouts focusing on the individual islands. The park's Web site (www.nps.gov/chis) is also helpful in that it is updated more often than some of the printed materials.

Exploring the Islands

Each of the five islands is relatively distinct and difficult to reach. **If you only have a day,** Anacapa and east Santa Cruz are the closest to the mainland and the easiest to get to. The bad side: They're the most crowded (though *crowded* is a relative term here). Even if you have a few days to visit the Channel Islands, odds are you're only going to visit one or two islands on a given trip, so it's a good idea to study your options before going.

EXPLORING ANACAPA

Sitting only 14.5 nautical miles off the Ventura coast, tiny Anacapa is easily the most visited of the park's islands. Referring to Anacapa as an island, however, is somewhat misleading—it is actually a chain of three small islets—East, Middle, and West Anacapa—inaccessible to each other except by boat. Seen from shore, the flat landscapes of East and Middle Anacapa stand out in sharp contrast to West Anacapa's twin peaks. In his log in 1769, the Spanish explorer Portola referred to Anacapa as *Las Mesistas* (or "little tables").

Anacapa is the only island in the chain to keep anything resembling its original name—Anacapa is actually a corruption of the Chumash word *Eneepah,* meaning island of deception or mirage, and on a foggy or hot day it is easy to see why: Tricks of light seem to make the island's cliff walls seem enormous at times or almost nonexistent at other; 40-foot-high **Arch Rock,** a natural offshore bridge, can seem to dominate the eastern end of the island or barely emerge from the water.

At only 1.1 square miles, Anacapa is probably not the best choice for people who need a lot of room to roam around. To cramp things even more, only East Anacapa is completely open to the public. Visitors to Middle Anacapa must be accompanied by a park ranger.

Visitors interested in seeing the island's marine life up close may want to opt for a trip to **Frenchy's Cove** on West Anacapa instead of visiting East Anacapa. Unlike most of the tide pools on the mainland, the island's tide pools remain in pristine condition, housing thriving marine communities. Only the beach at Frenchy's Cove is open to visitors, though. The rest of West Anacapa is closed to protect the nesting areas of the endangered brown pelican—the islet houses the largest breeding rookery for the bird on the West Coast.

Seabirds are easily the island's most abundant wildlife. Because of the island's relative lack of predators, thousands of birds nest on the island, including the endangered brown pelican and western gulls. Cormorants, scoter ducks, and black oystercatchers can also be

Which Island Should You Visit?

Since you will probably only make it to one or two of the islands during your visit, figuring out which islands to devote your time to is probably a more important question than how to avoid the crowds. When I asked the rangers this question, the answer was pretty much a universal: "It depends on what you want to do."

ANACAPA. Families with children will probably want to start with Anacapa. There are more organized activities here than on the other islands, and the crossing to Anacapa is the shortest—an important consideration when dealing with potentially seasick youngsters. If you're interested in sea kayaking, Anacapa's scores of sea caves also make it your best bet. Though much smaller than its huge neighbor Santa Cruz, Anacapa has several times more caves, many of which can be entered by kayak.

SANTA CRUZ. Even with fewer caves than Anacapa, Santa Cruz is still a good choice for sea kayakers—the island's Painted Cave is the largest and deepest sea cave in the world. This is the largest of the islands, but most of it is owned by the **Nature Conservancy,** and you must apply for permission to visit the portions of the island they manage.

SANTA ROSA. This is probably your best bet if you want to visit one of the islands for more than a day (it's relatively big, so there's more to explore). Those interested in ranching history and *vaquero* (Mexican cowboy) culture will probably want to visit Santa Rosa. Vail and Vickers still operates a working cattle ranch on the island, and except for the advent of motor vehicles, things are pretty much run the way they have been for the past century. Santa Rosa's hundreds of undisturbed archaeological sites (please leave them undisturbed) also may attract anthropology buffs and others interested in Chumash culture. Those interested in endemic plant life will probably also enjoy a visit to Santa Rosa. Though a century of ranching has wreaked havoc on the island's traditional landscape, the prehistoric stand of Torrey pines is spectacular—this particular species grows in only one other spot on earth. (It grows in a small area near San Diego.)

SAN MIGUEL. If backcountry hiking is what you're after, the choice is pretty simple: The 15-mile trek to Point Bennet offers the most visible wildlife and greatest diversity of scenery among the park's hikes. San Miguel is also your best choice if you want to observe wildlife—as many as 35,000 seals and sea lions can gather at Point Bennet; Prince Island in the mouth of Cuyler Harbor is an important seabird nesting area, and the park's largest land mammal, the diminutive island fox, roams the island.

SANTA BARBARA. This is the smallest of the island chain, not to mention the most distant. After a 3-hour boat trip, though, you'll be as alone as you might ever care to be, and completely free to hike all around this tiny island in almost-solitude.

seen plying the air and waters above and around the island.

The island also harbors a community of California sea lions and harbor seals. The animals rest and breed on Anacapa's rocky shores and feed in the kelp forests surrounding the island. Overlooks at **Cathedral Cove, Pinniped Point,** and **Inspiration Point** offer visitors excellent views of the animals.

While most of the year the island is covered with scrubby brownish vegetation, winter rains bring the island's vegetation to vibrant life—the bright

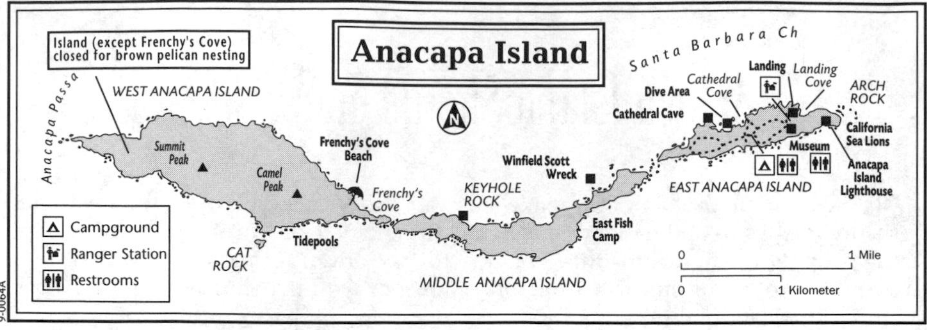

blossoms of the yellow coreopsis, or "tree sunflower," are often so numerous that they can be seen from the mainland.

Organized Tours & Ranger Programs. Despite its confines, Anacapa is the most visitor-friendly island in the park: Rangers lead guided nature walks daily during the summer, and self-guided trail booklets are available at the visitor center on the island.

Every Tuesday and Thursday from Memorial Day through Labor Day, rangers plunge into the kelp forest off the island with a video camera. The rangers allow visitors to view the undersea world in the monitor on the island's landing dock (or on a large screen in the mainland visitor center).

Historic & Man-Made Attractions. In 1853, the steamer ***Winfield Scott*** grounded and sank off the coast of Middle Anacapa (remains of the wreck can still be seen off the north coast of the islet), prompting the government to build a 50-foot tower supporting an acetylene beacon.

In 1932, the U.S. Lighthouse Service replaced the tower with the present **lighthouse** and facilities on East Anacapa. The fully automated lighthouse still used the original handmade Fresnel lens until 1990, when a more modern lighting system was installed—the original lead crystal lens is now on display in the island's visitor center. The lighthouse is still operated by the U.S. Coast Guard, but visitors are warned not to approach the building—the foghorn can leave permanent hearing damage. Special ranger-led tours are available.

Today the other lighthouse service buildings house the visitor center and ranger residences. The churchlike building actually houses two 55,000-gallon water tanks that supply freshwater for the residences and fire fighting. The building was designed to resemble a Spanish mission to discourage snipers who used to take pot shots at the wooden tanks.

Day Hikes. The 2-mile, figure-eight **Loop Trail** on East Anacapa serves up plenty of great views and is a good introduction to the island's natural history. A pamphlet describing the island's most significant features is available in the small visitors center. Rangers also lead guided nature walks daily during the summer.

Camping. Camping is allowed on East Anacapa year-round, but don't bring more than you can carry up the 154-stair, half-mile trail from the landing cove. The campground has seven sites and a capacity of 30 people. The campsites are primitive; there is no shade, and food and water are not available. Pit toilets are provided. No fires are allowed, but cooking is permitted on enclosed, backpack-type stoves. Bring earplugs and steer clear of the foghorn, which can leave permanent hearing damage. There is no charge for camping, but a permit is required. Permits can be obtained at the park visitor center or by calling ☎ **805/658-5711;** campground reservations fill up quickly, so be sure to call in advance.

EXPLORING SANTA CRUZ

By far the biggest of the islands—nearly 100 square miles—Santa Cruz is also the most diverse. It has huge canyons, year-round streams, beaches, cliffs, the highest mountain in the Channel Islands (2,400 feet), abandoned cattle and sheep ranches, and Native American Chumash village sites—2,000 Chumash were probably living on the island when Cabrillo first visited in 1542, many of them producing "shell-bead-money," a major barter item for tribes throughout California.

The pastoral **central valley** that separates the island's two mountains is still being created by a major earthquake fault. The island also hosts seemingly endless displays of flora and fauna, including 650 species of plants, nine of which are endemic; 140 land bird species; and a small group of other land animals, including the island fox. Lying directly between cold northern and warm southern waters, the waters off the island host a marine community representing 1,000 miles of coastline.

Originally called *Limuw* by the Chumash, the island gained its present moniker after a priest's staff was accidentally left on the island during the Portola expedition of 1769. A resident Chumash found the cross-tipped staff and returned it to the priest, inspiring the Spaniards to dub the island *La Isla de Santa Cruz,* or the Island of the Sacred Cross.

Most of the island is still privately owned: The **Nature Conservancy** holds the western nine-tenths. On February 10, 1997, the Park Service took over the eastern end from the Gherini family, which had operated a sheep ranch here. Most visitors come to **Scorpion Ranch** and **Smuggler's Ranch** on the Park Service's land. Unfortunately, the island's ranching heritage has left its mark on the land—the island has been badly overgrazed by feral sheep. Much of the most beautiful land is on the Nature Conservancy property, which includes Santa Cruz's lush Central Valley and the islands' highest peaks.

It's difficult, but not impossible, to get access to the Conservancy land; Island Packers runs occasional trips to **Prisoner's Harbor.** At one point, it was possible to arrange stays at Christy Ranch on the windswept west end of the island and visits to the Main Ranch in the Central Valley, but at press time the ranches were under restoration, and access was restricted. Contact the **Nature Conservancy** (☎ **805/962-9111**) for up-to-date information.

Valdez Cave (also known as Painted Cave for its colorful rock types, lichens, and algae) is the largest and deepest known sea cave in the world. The huge cave stretches nearly a quarter of a mile into the island and is nearly 100 feet wide. The entrance ceiling rises 160 feet, and in the spring, a waterfall tumbles over the opening. Located on the northwest end of the island, the cave can only be entered via dinghy or kayak. Information on sea kayaking trips is under "The Extra Mile: Exploring the Coastline & Waters Off the Channel Islands," below.

Historic & Man-Made Attractions. After over a century of ranching, Santa Cruz has acquired its fair share of historic buildings, including adobe ranch houses, barns, blacksmith and saddle shops, wineries, and a chapel. The ranch house and adobe bunkhouse at **Scorpion Ranch** are now used as the ranger residence and headquarters. All around Scorpion Ranch fascinating ranch and farm implements, some dating back decades, speckle the landscape. The Park Service has plans to include some in a visitor center on the island. Also planned is an interpretive center in the historic buildings.

Day Hikes. Most hikes in the national park land of Santa Cruz begin at Scorpion Ranch. The easiest and shortest hike is the **Historic Ranch Walk.** The ranch area is visible from the beach, so it shouldn't prove too hard to find. This hike is basically the beginning leg of all the hikes described below, so if you are

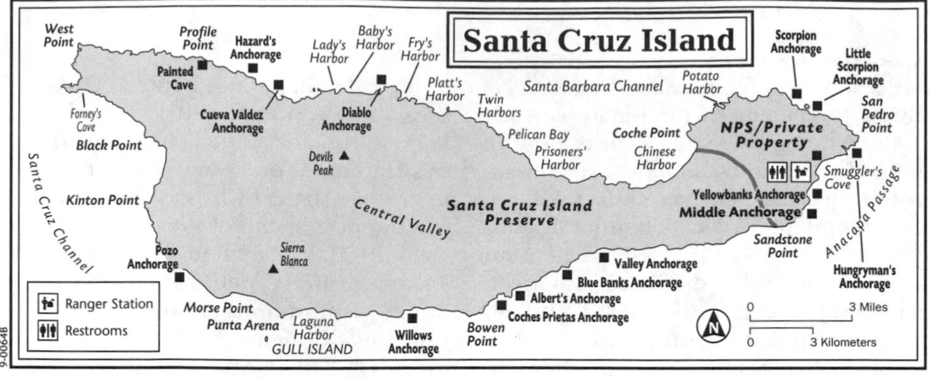

planning to take one of those, you don't really need to allocate much additional time for this hike.

The hike up to **Cavern Point** leads you up to the bluffs northwest of Scorpion Harbor, providing spectacular views of the north coast of the island. Between December and February, this is an excellent vantage from which to spot migrating gray whales. Follow the main trail from the beach through the ranch area. Just past the ranch look for the first side canyon on your right (west). Follow the trail through the cypress grove and up the side of the canyon to Cavern Point. Avoid the unstable cliff ledges at the top and return the way you came. At 2 miles round-trip, the hike is ranked moderate to difficult due to a 200-yard uphill climb, uneven terrain, and loose rock.

A little longer than the Cavern Point Hike, the hike up to the **Potato Harbor Overlook** also provides magnificent coastal views. Head past the ranch about 0.75 mile until you come to a big break in the eucalyptus trees. A trail sign marks the spot. Follow the old road on the right (west) up to the dirt airstrip. Walk around the airstrip (be aware of aircraft operations) to the northwest side until you reach the bluff trail to Potato Harbor Overlook. Avoid cliff edges, and return the way you came. The trip is 4 miles round-trip and is ranked moderate due to a 1-mile uphill climb.

For another coastal view, you can head up to **Scorpion Bluffs.** Approximately 100 feet past the ranch area, before the eucalyptus grove, head left (east) on the road/trail across the streambed to the base of Smugglers Road. At the top of the road, follow the trail that goes along the bluffs. Avoid cliff ledges, and return the way you came. The round-trip is 2 miles and is ranked moderate for its 300-foot elevation gain.

Your best chance to see the endemic island jay is to head up **Scorpion Canyon.** Follow the main road/trail though the ranch area and into the eucalyptus grove. The trail will eventually wind in and out of an old streambed before reaching the first oak tree after approximately 1.5 miles. You may continue up the streambed, but the terrain is rocky and uneven.

For those with a little more time to spend, the hike to **Smugglers Cove** is a nice way to spend a day. At 7 miles round-trip, though, it is not recommended for day visitors with time constraints. Easy to follow, the hike follows Smugglers Road all the way from Scorpion Ranch to the white sand and cobblestone beaches of Smugglers Cove. If the Park Service has not removed them by your visit, you may see groups of feral sheep or horses left over from the island's ranching days. Due to the 600-foot elevation gain over many uphill sections, the hike is ranked strenuous.

There are also numerous hikes through the Nature Conservancy property, many beginning at Pelican Bay. Often the hikes are led by a Nature Conservancy naturalist who will point out natural and historical highlights. For more information contact the **Nature Conservancy** at ☎ **805/962-9111.**

Camping. Camping is allowed at the Scorpion Ranch Campground on the east end of Santa Cruz year-round. All gear must be carried 0.5 mile to the numerous unshaded and many shaded sites, curiously littered with rusted, abandoned ranch implements and vehicles. At press time the Park Service was planning to haul most away, though some may be included in a planned ranch implement museum. The campsites are primitive; there is plenty of shade, but food and water are not available. Pit toilets are provided. Cooking is permitted on enclosed backpack-type stoves, and open fires are allowed in specified locations. There is no charge for camping, but a permit is required and can be obtained at the park visitor center or by calling ☎ **805/658-5711.** There is no camping allowed on Nature Conservancy land (the western 90% of the island).

EXPLORING SANTA ROSA

Windy Santa Rosa was California's only singly owned, private island until it was purchased by the Park Service for $30 million in the 1980s from the Vail and Vickers ranching company. As part of the purchase agreement, the Vails are allowed to ranch the island until 2011. Close to 6,500 cattle still call the 54,000-acre island home.

The second largest island in the park, Santa Rosa displays widely different landscapes: After decades of ranching, rolling nonnative grasslands cover about 85% of the island, but columnar volcanic formations and high mountains with deep canyons are also present. A unique **coastal marsh** on the east end of the island is among the most extensive freshwater habitat found on any of the Channel Islands.

As with Santa Cruz, the island's size allows for a fantastic variety of life. While the impact of ranching has been severe, native plant species still survive, primarily in the rocky canyons and upper slopes. Santa Rosa is home to a large concentration of endangered plant species, 34 of which occur only on the islands. **Torrey Pines** grow only in two places. One is on Santa Rosa, in two ancient groves near Bechers Bay. (They also grow on the mainland near San Diego.) The island's vast grasslands provide prime habitat for 195 bird species; shore birds and waterfowl prefer the marshy terrain on the island's eastern tip.

Santa Rosa is also home to the diminutive island fox, a tiny cousin of the gray fox that has become nearly fearless as it has evolved in the predator-free island environment. They'll walk right through your camp if you let them. In all the world, the rarely seen spotted skunk lives only here and on Santa Cruz.

The **kelp beds** that surround the island function as an invaluable nursery for the sea life that feeds the Channel Islands' marine mammals and seabirds.

The Chumash lived on *Wima* (their name for the island) until they were moved to mainland Missions in approximately 1820. Through radiocarbon dating, scientists have been able to date human use of the island back 11,000 years, making Santa Rosa an invaluable archaeological resource. Over 500 largely undisturbed **archaeological sites** have been recorded. In 1959 archaeologist Philip Orr discovered an individual we now refer to as Arlington Woman. Lacking evidence of a traditional burial site, scientists believe she was killed accidentally some 10,000 years ago, possibly while gathering food.

The island also provides an important fossil record. A fossilized pygmy mammoth skeleton carbon-dated at 12,000 years old was discovered on the island in 1994. It is the most complete specimen ever discovered.

Historic & Man-Made Attractions. While visitors are warned not to disturb Chumash archaeological sites, the island does provide insight into another more modern culture: Until their lease is up,

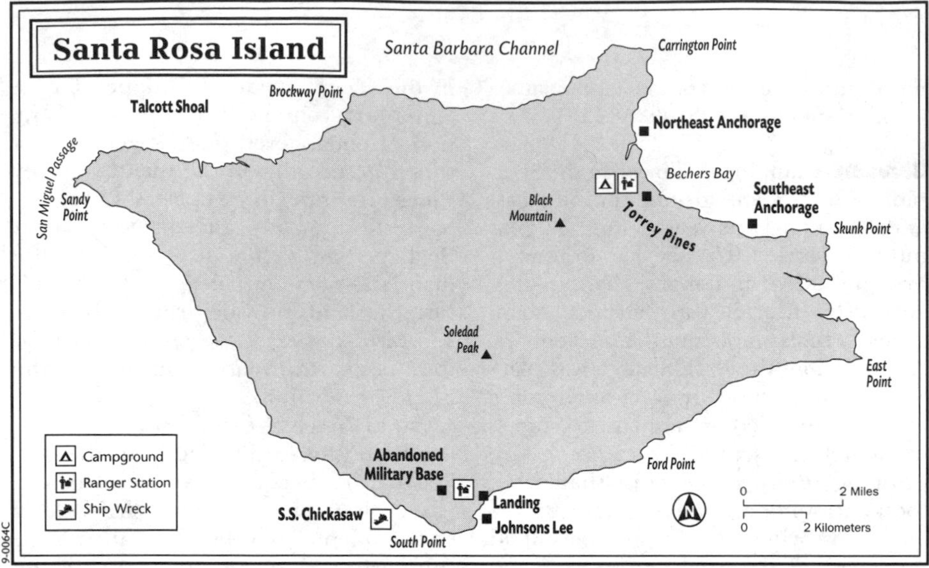

or until they choose to stop, Vail and Vickers Company will continue to operate a working cattle ranch on the island. Except for the addition of modern-day vehicles, the ranch's operation has changed little since its beginning in 1902. While visitors are not allowed into the main ranch areas out of respect for the ranch personnel's privacy, the flavor of traditional *vaquero* (Mexican cowboy) lifestyle is still evident.

Day Hikes. Because of its large size, Santa Rosa offers a diverse array of possible hikes. The shortest and easiest is probably the **East Point Trail.** At only 1 mile round-trip the hike provides rare glimpses of the island's endemic stand of Torrey pines, as well as the brackish marsh on the island's east end.

The **Cherry Canyon Trail** provides excellent opportunities to see inland island wildlife. There are also sweeping views of the interior of the island. The trail is 4 miles round-trip and is ranked moderate.

The **Lobo Canyon Trail** descends through Lobo Canyon to a Chumash Village site—be sure not to disturb this or any of the island's other archaeological sites—and then on to an excellent tide-pooling area. Unlike most mainland tide pools, the Channel Islands' intertidal zones have not been destroyed by man's impact on their fragile habitats. The hike is 5 miles round-trip and is ranked moderate.

Camping. Camping is allowed in the old ranch compound in Water Canyon on Santa Rosa's northeast end year-round. All gear must be carried a mile and a half from the pier on Bechers Bay. The campground is provided with water, chemical toilets, and each of the 15 sites has its own picnic table and windbreak. If you're lucky, you might see the Vail and Vickers cowboys working the herd, just as they have for more than 100 years. A fence around the campground keeps the cattle out, but foxes will still sneak in and steal food scraps; store food appropriately.

Beach camping is also permitted on a limited number of beaches around the island at certain times of the year. While the winds will definitely test your tent, this is a good option for sea kayakers and divers who don't want to lug their equipment all the way into Water Canyon.

There is no charge for camping anywhere on the island, but a permit is required. Permits can be obtained at the park visitor center or by calling ☎ **805/658-5711.**

EXPLORING SAN MIGUEL

People often argue about what's the wildest place left in the Lower 48. They bat around names like Montana, Colorado, and Idaho. Curiously, no one ever thinks to consider San Miguel, the farthest west of the Channel Islands. They should, for this 9,500-acre island is a wild, wild place. Lying west of the influence of Point Conception, the wind blows constantly here, and the island can be shrouded in fog for days at a time. Human presence is definitely not the status quo here.

Visitors land at **Cuyler Harbor,** a half moon–shaped cove on the island's east end. Arriving here is like arriving on earth the day it was made: Perfect sand, outrageously blue water; seals basking on the offshore rocks. The island's caliche forest appears otherworldly. Created by caliche (calcium carbonate) sandcastings of a once-living forest, today all that remains are these natural stone sculptures.

As it did on most of the other islands in this chain, a rich history of ranching nearly destroyed native vegetation. The removal of the imported grazing animals, though, has given the island's recovery a major boost. Today many native species are reclaiming their ancestral lands.

Though widely hunted during the 19th century, the island's pinniped (seals and sea lions) population has clearly recovered. At certain times of the year 35,000 animals can occupy the beach at **Point Bennet,** including California sea lions, northern elephant seals, and northern fur seals, making it one of the largest concentrations of wildlife in the world. The Guadalupe fur seal and Stellar sea lion, former island residents, are also occasionally spotted. Harbor seals haul out on other island beaches.

Prince Island, just outside the mouth of Cuyler Harbor, is an important nesting area for western gulls, brown pelicans, cormorants, and Cassin's auklets. And San Miguel's inland bird species can once again count the peregrine falcon among their number. After years of decimation by the pesticide DDT, the former resident has been reintroduced to the island and is now nesting successfully.

The waters around San Miguel are the richest yet most dangerous of all the islands, as it is exposed to wave action from all sides. Harsh sea conditions have resulted in a fair number of shipwrecks in the surrounding waters. Among the most scenic wrecks is the *Cuba,* which went under on September 8, 1923. (Everyone on board the Pacific Mail luxury liner was rescued along with $2,500,000 in gold and silver bullion.)

Swimming among the wrecks are a wide variety of sea mammals: In addition to the pinnipeds, dolphins, porpoises, gray whales, orcas, and even blue whales can sometimes be seen off the island's shore.

The boat concessionaires' schedule to San Miguel is sporadic in summer and almost nonexistent in winter, so call ahead.

Historic & Man-Made Attractions. Like Santa Rosa, San Miguel has more than 500 **Chumash archeological sites** visitors are warned not to disturb them.

The island also holds the remains of the earliest modern structure on any of the islands. In 1850s Capt. George Nedever established a sheep, cattle, and horse ranch on the island. The **adobe** he built is barely visible today.

In the 1930s, Herbert and Elizabeth Lester became the island's caretakers. During his time on the island Herbert became known as "the King of San Miguel." After being asked to leave the island during World War II by the navy, which owned San Miguel, Herbert committed suicide in 1942. Both he and Elizabeth are buried on San Miguel. Today the location of the **Lester Ranch Complex** is only marked by a few fence posts and small piles of rubble near the trail. Technically the navy still owns San Miguel, though it is managed by the Park Service.

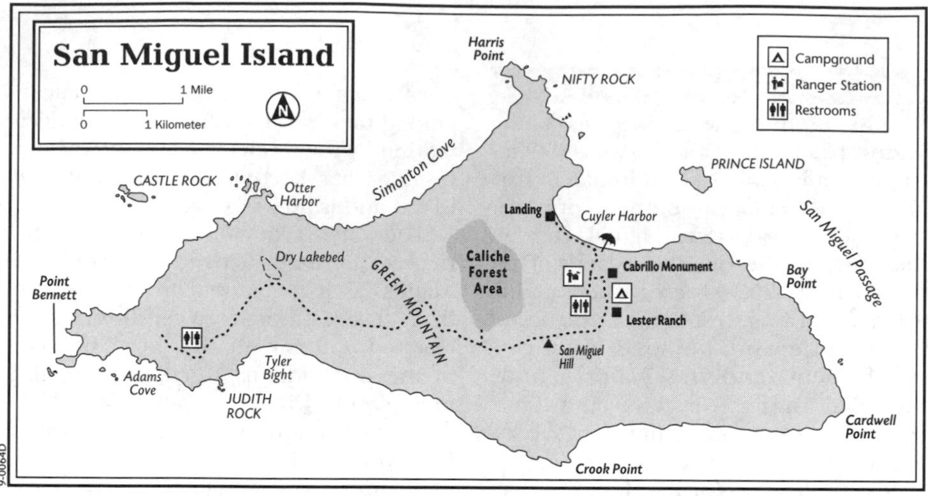

Day Hikes. Outside of the Cuyler Harbor/Lester Ranch Area, hikes on San Miguel must be led by a ranger. There are three trails on San Miguel, all of which meet at Lester Ranch. Due to terrain, length, and the tiring effects of walking in all that wind, all three San Miguel hikes are ranked moderately strenuous.

If you don't feel up to a serious trek, you can still make the relatively easy walk from the landing at Cuyler Harbor to Cabrillo Monument and Lester Ranch, the starting point for the three official hikes.

The first trail heads north to **Harris Point,** allowing marvelous views of Prince Island to the east and Simonton Cove to the west. Taking the trail southeast from Lester Ranch will lead you to **Cardwell Point.**

San Miguel's most popular hike, though, is the 7-mile round-trip trek along the **Point Bennet Trail** to the aforementioned caliche forest.

For those with more time, consider following the trail all the way to Point Bennet, a 15-mile round-trip. You cannot camp along the trail! The diversity of scenery and wildlife on view is seemingly endless for those hikers hardy enough to endure the wind and weather. After crossing San Miguel Hill, the trail passes the caliche forest. From the caliche forest, the trail heads west to Point Bennet, passing south of the island's other peak, Green Mountain. At the end of the trek, the barking of sea lions will signal your arrival at Point Bennet, where as many as 35,000 pinnipeds can congregate.

Note: San Miguel Island was used as a bombing range for the U.S. Navy between 1948 and 1970. Live ordnance is still occasionally uncovered by shifting sand, so it is extremely important to stay on established trails.

Camping. Camping is allowed on San Miguel year-round, though camping dates are subject to the availability of the San Miguel Island ranger. Located 1 mile south of Cuyler Harbor, between Cabrillo Monument and the old Lester Ranch complex, the campground has nine primitive sites and a capacity of 30 people. The second half of the hike-in is a steep climb up Nidever Canyon—keep this in mind before packing your accordion. There is a pit toilet and basic wind shelter at each site, but food and water are not available. No fires are allowed, but cooking is permitted on enclosed backpack-type stoves. Be sure to bring a strong tent, sleeping bag, and waterproof clothes—the wind is often fierce and damp fog can set in for days.

There is no charge for camping, but a permit is required. Permits can be obtained at the park visitor center or by calling ☎ **805/658-5711;** campground reservations fill up quickly, so be sure to call in advance.

EXPLORING SANTA BARBARA

Lonely, lonely Santa Barbara. As you come upon Santa Barbara Island after a typical 3-hour crossing, you'll think that someone took a single, medium-size, grassy hill, ringed it with cliffs, and plunked it down in the middle of the ocean. When you drop anchor, you'll realize that your initial perception is basically on target. Landwise, there's just not a lot here. Even the Chumash eschewed residing on the island for its lack of fresh water. But the upside is that, of all the islands, Santa Barbara gives you the best sense of what it's like to be stranded on a desert isle. Being on Santa Barbara, far enough out to sea so that the mainland is almost invisible, gives you an idea of just how immense the Pacific really is.

The deserted appearance of Santa Barbara is somewhat misleading, though. During the 1920s, farming, overgrazing, intentional burning by island residents, and the introduction of rabbits all but destroyed the island's native vegetation. To survive the island conditions, plants must be tolerant of salt water and wind—and unfortunately, perfectly suited to this type of environment is the Santa Barbara ice plant.

Originally imported from South Africa in the early 1900s, the non-native ice plant survives by capturing moisture from sea breezes and subsequently leaches salt into the soil, raising the soil's salt concentration and making it difficult for native species to survive. Like the infamous story of Australia's imported rabbits (or the not-so-famous story of Santa Barbara's imported rabbits), the ice plant has wreaked havoc on the natural ecosystem, virtually taking over much of the island and pushing out native species. Through their resource management program, however, the Park Service is taking steps to eradicate non-native species from the islands. With the rabbits now removed, the giant coreopsis is once again thriving, blanketing the island in gold every spring.

Other than the **landing cove,** there's no access to the water's edge. (The snorkeling in the chilly cove is great.) You can hike the entire 640-acre island in a few hours; then it's time to stare out to sea. You won't be let down. The cliffs and rocks are home to elephant seals and sea lions who feed in the kelp forests surrounding the island. Weighing up to 6,000 pounds, the once threatened elephant seal is appropriately named; and because of the island's small size, the barking of sea lions can be heard almost everywhere. The **Sea Lion Rookery, Webster Point,** and **Elephant Seal Cove** all provide excellent overlooks from which to observe the animals. Be sure to stay at least 100 yards away from the animals, particularly from January through July during pupping time—young animals may become separated from their mothers if disturbed.

Santa Barbara's cliffs and rocks are also home to swarms of seabirds such as you'll never see on the mainland, including western gulls, endangered brown pelicans, and the world's largest colony of xantus murrelets. Inland species include the horned lark, orange-crowned warbler, and house finch, all endemic subspecies found only on Santa Barbara Island.

There's also a tiny **museum** chronicling island history. Island Packers and Truth Aquatics only schedules boats to Santa Barbara between April and November.

Day Hikes. Hiking the short **Canyon View Nature Trail** is a good introduction to Santa Barbara, but since it's the smallest of the Channel Islands, it's not all that difficult to hike all three of the island's main trails (they only come to 5.5 miles combined). All trails begin and end at the campground and visitor center.

The **Elephant Seal Cove Trail** heads southwest from the visitor center to the west coast of the island, and then heads up by Webster Point, a favorite beach for sea lions and elephant seals, and then up to Elephant Seal Cove.

The **Arch Point Loop Trail** heads north from the visitor center to Arch

Point, the northernmost tip of the island. It then turns south, following the island's northwestern bluffs before turning inland and crossing the Elephant Seal Cove Trail. Once across the Elephant Seal Cove Trail, the trail becomes the **Signal Peak Loop Trail** and continues southwest and up Signal Peak. It then follows the bluffs around the southern portion of the island, cutting inland briefly to bypass Cat Canyon. Once on the southeastern side of the island, the trail heads up to Sea Lion Rookery where it heads inland to the middle of the island and then north back to the visitor center.

Camping. Camping is allowed on Santa Barbara year-round. Note, though, that all gear must be carried up the 131 steps to the campground, located approximately 0.25 mile inland. The eight campsites are primitive; there are pit toilets, but food, water, and shade are not available. No fires are allowed, but cooking is permitted on enclosed backpack-type stoves. There is no charge for camping, but a permit is required. Permits can be obtained at the park visitor center or by calling ☎ **805/658-5711;** campground reservations fill up quickly, so be sure to call in advance.

The Extra Mile: Exploring the Coastline & Waters Off the Channel Islands

Sea Kayaking. One of the best ways to explore the fascinating coastline of the islands is by kayak. Warren Glaser of **OAARS** (Outdoor and Aquatic Recreation Specialists), P.O. Box 1416, Ventura, CA 93001 (☎ **805/642-2912**), leads small group tours by sea kayak to all five Channel Islands. The trips allow you to explore sea caves and rock gardens. Channel crossing by charter boat, brief lessons, and lunch are included. Fares generally run $125 per person. Three-day adventures to Santa Rosa, with meals, campsite, and guide included are offered for $295.

Aqua Sports (☎ **805/968-7231**) and **Paddle Sports** (☎ **805/899-4925**), both also headquartered in Ventura, also lead similar trips, or trips can be arranged through Island Packers.

Diving. A good portion of Channel Islands National Park is underwater. In fact, twice as many visitors come annually to dive the waters than ever set foot on the islands. Scuba divers come here from all over the globe for the chance to explore stunning kelp forests, shipwrecks, and underwater caves, all with the best visibility in California. Everything from sea snails and urchins to orcas and great white sharks call these waters home.

Truth Aquatics in Santa Barbara (☎ **805/962-1127**) is the best provider of single- and multiday dive trips to all the islands.

Ventura Dive & Sport (☎ **805/650-6500**) also leads trips, including their "Discover Program," which allows novice and uncertified divers to explore the waters accompanied by an instructor.

Channel Islands Scuba (☎ **805/644-3483**) and **Pacific Scuba** (☎ **805/984-2566**) also lead regular trips, as do boats from San Pedro and other southern California ports.

Accommodations in Ventura

While there are no accommodations other than camping available on any of the islands, there are lots of options in Ventura, the launching point for most island trips. The Nature Conservancy used to allow stays at Christy Ranch on the windswept west end of Santa Cruz, but at press time the ranch was under restoration and access was restricted. Contact the **Nature Conservancy** (☎ **805/962-9111**) for up-to-date information.

In addition to the places listed below, there are also a number of chain motels in the area including the **Best Western,** 708 E. Thompson Blvd. (☎ **805/648-3101**); **Motel 6,** 2145 E. Harbor Blvd. (☎ **805/643-5100**); and **Vagabond Inn,** 756 E. Thompson Blvd. (☎ **805/648-5371**).

Bella Maggiore Inn

67 S. California St. (½ block south of Main St.), Ventura, CA 93001. ☎ **800/523-8479** or 805/652-0277. 24 rms and suites. TV TEL. $75–$150 double; $100–$130 suite. Extra adult $10, extra child (under 12) $5. Rates include full breakfast and afternoon refreshments and appetizers. AE, DISC, MC, V.

The Bella Maggiorc is an intimate Italian-style inn whose simply furnished rooms (some with fireplaces, balconies, or bay window seats) overlook a romantic courtyard or roof garden. Complimentary breakfast is served each morning around the patio fountain, an intimate spot known to non-guests as Nona's Courtyard Cafe. Nona's also serves dinner on Friday and Saturday nights. A kind of European elegance pervades all but the reasonable rates here; and be sure to ask about midweek specials.

The Country Inn at Ventura by the Sea

298 Chestnut St. (½ block south of Thompson), Ventura, CA 93001. ☎ **800/44-RELAX** or 805/653-1434. 120 rms, 2 suites. $74–$99 double; $129–$199 suite. Extra adult $10, extra child (under 12) free. Rates include full breakfast and afternoon cocktails and appetizers. AE, DISC, MC, V.

Set within walking distance of the beach and Ventura pier, the Country Inn is a good choice for families. It pleasantly blends the convenience of a chain hotel (the Country Inns are operated by the Comfort Inn chain) with the perks of a bed-and-breakfast. All rooms come with a microwave and refrigerator, and for an additional $10, you can add a canopy bed and fireplace. Try and get a room facing away from the highway—the traffic can get pretty loud.

La Mer European Bed & Breakfast

411 Poli St. (west of City Hall), Ventura, CA 93001. ☎ **805/643-3600.** 5 rms, 4 with private entrance. $105–$155 double. Rates include full breakfast and complimentary wine in room. No children. MC, V.

Perfect for a romantic getaway, La Mer is a 1890 Cape Cod–style home with a spectacular view of the ocean from the parlor and two of the five guest rooms, each of which is furnished in a different international style. Whether you choose the "Madame Pompadour" French chamber with wood-burning stove, the "Vienna Woods" Austrian hideaway with sunken bathtub, or one of three other rooms, you'll love this cozy little cottage. They offer generous midweek packages for couples, which can include gourmet candlelit dinners, cruises to Anacapa Island, country carriage rides, therapeutic massages, or all of the above!

Dining in Ventura

There is no food available on any of the islands in the national Park; however, there are several recommendable places in Ventura.

Andria's Seafood Restaurant and Market

1449 Spinnaker Dr. (in Ventura Harbor Village). ☎ **805/654-0546.** Main courses $6–$30.

Sun–Thurs 11am–9pm; Fri–Sat 11am–10pm. No credit cards; ATM cards accepted. SEAFOOD.

Set aside your inevitable reservations at seeing the fast-food decor of this place and proceed to the counter to place your order—Andria's has been voted Ventura County's best seafood restaurant for 11 years running. Doubling as a fresh seafood market and restaurant, the fish here goes basically from the ocean, into the deep-fat fryer (charbroiled selections are also available), and onto your plate, with only a short stint on the boat in between. The food isn't fancy, but it's fresh, and the outdoor harborside seating is pleasant.

Rosarito Beach Cafe

692 E. Main St. (at Fir St.). ☎ **805/653-7343.** Main courses $10–$19. Tues–Sat 11:30am–2pm; Tues–Thurs and Sun 5:30–9pm, Fri–Sat 5–10pm. AE, DISC, MC, V. MEXICAN.

Four year-old Rosarito Beach Cafe really packs them into this 1938 Aztec revival moderne building and its welcoming outdoor patio. Diners in the know bring their palates for superb Baja-style cuisine whose tangy elements are borrowed from the Caribbean, not to mention the delicious handmade tortillas. This place has a culinary sophistication rare in modest Ventura.

The Sportsman

53 California St. (½ block south of Main). ☎ **805/643-2851.** Main courses $4–$14. Mon–Fri 11am–10pm, Sat 9am–2pm and 5–10pm, Sun 9am–2pm and 4–10pm. AE, MC, V. AMERICAN.

You might walk right by the inconspicuous facade of Ventura's oldest (since 1950) restaurant. Like the intriguingly retro lettering on its awning, the interior hasn't changed a lick since then: plush leather booths, brass lamps, wood-paneled bar, giant trophy swordfish on the back wall, and light kept at dimness levels normally reserved for planetariums. The Sportsman looks "fancy" but is quite affordable (especially at breakfast and lunch), and they serve up fine hearty breakfasts, burgers, steaks, and other grilled items. Or you can wet your whistle with $2.50 well drinks from the bar.

Yolie's Fresh Mex Grill

26 S. Garden St. (corner of Main, west of Mission). ☎ **805/652-0338.** Main courses $5–$13. Mon–Thurs 11am–9pm, Fri–Sat 11am–10pm, Sun 10am–9pm. AE, DISC, MC, V. MEXICAN.

This colorful cantina's funny moniker is a nickname of the proprietor, Yolanda, and the place is better than its nondescript business-park exterior leads you to believe. Yolie's offers an impressive fresh salsa bar (authentic and delicious) as well as an admirable beer, margarita, and tequila menu. The patio and dining room are festooned with rainbow *serapes* and *sombreros*; the kitchen quickly sends out traditional combination plates (as well as lighter and/or vegetarian adaptations).

Picnic & Camping Supplies

Since there is no food available on any of the islands, make sure to bring a picnic lunch and water for day trips and enough food and water (1 gallon a day per person) if you are camping. Picnic supplies can be bought at the **Von's** grocery store at 2433 E. Harbor Blvd. (☎ **805/642-6761**) in Ventura; the **Village Market** (☎ **805/644-2970**) in Ventura Harbor Village is another source.

The **Sports Chalet** in Oxnard, 1885 Ventura Blvd. (☎ **805/405-5222**), is the best area choice for picking up any camping essentials you forgot to pack.

12

CRATER LAKE NATIONAL PARK

by Tom Wells

TO THE VAST MAJORITY OF PEOPLE, INCLUDING PLENTY OF OREGOnians and most out-of-staters, southern Oregon means one thing: Crater Lake. Even if it weren't the deepest lake in the country, its astounding beauty would be undeniable. Visitors to the area have not even the slightest hint of the awesome grandeur that lies ahead as they approach the rim of the caldera, which makes the lake's stunning appearance 1,000 feet below all the more astounding.

"I came, I saw, I left," might be the motto of most of the 500,000 visitors each year, who, from mid-June to mid-September, ride dutifully around the Rim Road and then move on. If you're looking to interact with the landscape on a more personal level, however, there are options, such as road biking around the Rim Road, and day hiking to the summits of several peaks, including that of 764-foot Wizard Island in the middle of the lake, not to mention superb cross-country skiing and snowshoeing in winter.

Southern Oregon has some of the most complex geography in the state. It is here that the Cascade Range, Coast Range, and Siskyou Mountains all come together in a jumble of peaks and valleys. However, the lack of high peaks deceives many into thinking this region is not as wild as more mountainous areas to the north and south. It is partly this perception that kept the region relatively unexplored by Europeans until the late 1800s.

With Mount Shasta, Mount Lassen, the Trinity Alps, and the Marble Mountains just to the south of the border in California, it is hard to get excited about the low peaks of southern Oregon. Here, signs of past volcanic activity are less vertical, yet more dramatic. **Mount Mazama,** now known as Crater Lake, once stood as tall as its neighbors to the south, but 7,700 years ago it erupted with almost unimaginable violence. When it had finished erupting, this volcano collapsed in on itself, forming a vast caldera 6 miles wide and almost 4,000 feet deep. Over the millennia, the caldera slowly filled with water to become today's Crater Lake. The sapphire-blue lake's surface is at the base of 1,000- to 2,300-foot cliffs that rise to a total elevation of more than 8,000 feet.

Rising up from the middle of the lake is 764-foot high **Wizard Island,** which can be visited on informative boat tours that start from the Cleetwood Cove on the Lake's north shore. The high elevation of the caldera rim and heavy winter snowfalls mean that the summer season here is short (and packed with people).

The lake was first encountered by whites when, in 1853, gold prospectors searching for a lost gold mine stumbled upon the lake's rim. The Indian tribes of the region, which held the lake as sacred, had never mentioned its existence to the first explorers and settlers who arrived in this region. But, by 1886, explorers had made soundings and established its depth at 1,996 feet, making it the deepest lake in the United States. Sonar soundings later set the depth at 1,932 feet. In 1902, the lake was designated a national park.

The lake has no inlet or outlet streams and is instead fed solely by springs, snowmelt, and rainfall. Evaporation and ground seepage keep the lake at a nearly constant level. Because it is so deep, it rarely freezes entirely over, despite the long, cold winters at this elevation. The last time it froze completely was in 1949.

The Pacific Crest Trail passes through the park, though at a distance from the lake's rim. There are even fish to be caught in the lake. Wildlife is mostly limited to the lowlands surrounding the crater, although at the summit you can see hawks, eagles, and many types of birds and small mammals. In addition, the forester's dreaded nemesis, the spotted owl, has been found nesting within the park boundaries. The forested slopes provide refuge for deer, elk, porcupine, and rabbit.

Avoiding the Crowds. It's hard to avoid crowds here. Given the area's harsh winters, most visitors come during the relatively short "summer" season between mid-June and the end of September. Our best advice is to give yourself more than single day that 90% of the visitors d at the park. Once you've seen and iated the lake (appreciate the lake rly before the crowds form), go off and hike some of the less-trampled paths. Several of the longer trails will lead you to fabulous and relatively uninhabited view points. We especially recommend the **Dutton Creek, Garfield Peak,** and **Mount Scott trails,** all of which are described in "Day Hikes," below.

Just the Facts

GETTING THERE & GATEWAYS

There are three ways into Crater Lake National Park, the most convenient being from the west and south on Ore. 62, which runs through the southwest corner of the park.

To get to the park's West Entrance, drive northeast from **Medford** on Ore. 62; the distance is 75 miles.

To get to the park's South Entrance from **Klamath Falls,** travel north on U.S. 97, then northwest on Ore. 62; the total distance is 61 miles.

To get to the park's North Entrance from **Roseburg,** take Ore. 138 east; the total distance to Rim Drive is approximately 90 miles (this entrance is closed in winter).

If You're Driving in Winter. Call the **Crater Lake National Park Headquarters** for road information (☎ **541/594-2211, ext. 402**). In the wintertime, access to the park by the northern route is frequently limited by snow, so expect delays from October to May.

The Nearest Airports. If you need to fly into the Crater Lake area, you have two options.

Rogue Valley International Airport, which is located in Medford, is served by **Horizon Air** and **United Airlines.** You can rent a car here from **Avis, Budget, Hertz,** and **National** (their telephone numbers are given in the appendix). It's a 75-mile drive from here.

Somewhat farther away is **Eugene,** which has an airport 9 miles northwest of downtown, off Ore. 99 West. It is served by **Alaska Airlines, Horizon, Skywest,**

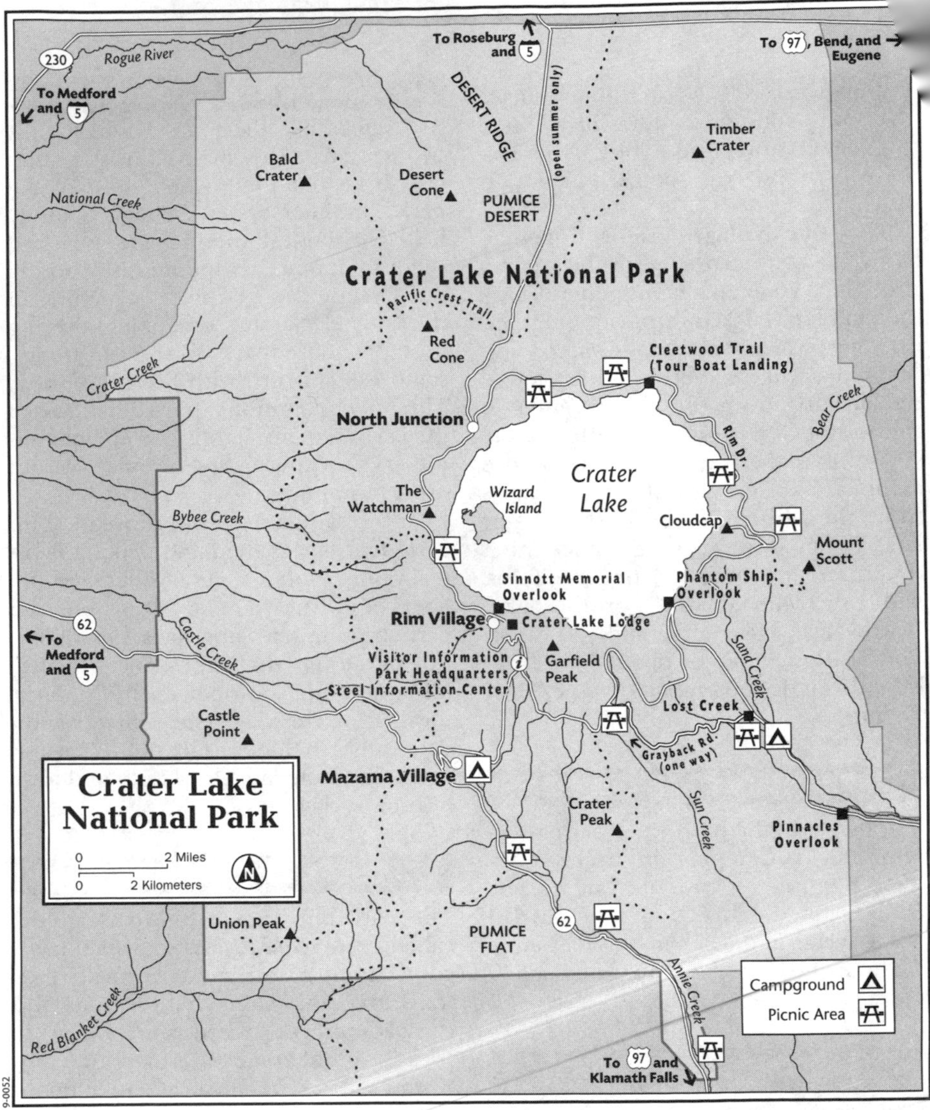

United, and **United Express.** You can rent a car here from **Avis, Budget, Hertz,** and **National** (the telephone numbers are given in the appendix). It's a 71-mile drive south from Eugene to Roseburg on I-5, then another 93 miles east to Crater Lake on Ore. 138.

GETTING INFORMATION BEFORE YOUR TRIP

Contact the park headquarters for up-to-the-minute information. Write to **Crater Lake National Park,** P.O. Box 7, Crater Lake, OR 97604, or call (☎ **541/594-2211,** ext. 400).

VISITOR CENTERS

The park has two visitor centers. **Steel Information Center,** is south of the lake, off the Ore. 62 and open daily (from 9am to 5pm) year-round. The National Park Headquarters is here. You won't be able to get coffee and muffins, but yo can talk to a ranger and find out ab local weather forecasts and general information, purchase books, p and maps, as well as watch the requisite 18-minute educational film. In addition to a general store, where you can buy gas, there are also rest rooms and a post office here.

The **Rim Village Visitor Center** is along the southern edge of the caldera rim. Here you can obtain general park information, backcountry camping permits, and educational books, videos, and maps. In addition, there is a short, paved trail leading from the visitor center to the Sinnot Overlook, which offers a fine view of the lake and several interpretive exhibits. To the east, about 200 yards from the visitor center is the Crater Lake Lodge, with guest amenities and a restaurant featuring Northwest cuisine and unparalleled views of the lake. Nearby are a cafeteria and gift shop. The visitor center is open daily from June through September (from 8:30am to 6pm).

ENTRANCE & CAMPING FEES

Entrance into the park is $10 per passenger vehicle. Camping in backcountry areas requires registration, but no fee. Camping in Mazama Campground is $13 per tent site, and $14 per RV site. Camping in the Lost Creek Campground is $10 per site.

SPECIAL REGULATIONS & WARNINGS

No, you may not climb into the caldera. The only access to the lake is through the Cleetwood Cove Trail. Believe me, after getting a view at some of the steep and sharp-looking volcanic boulders lining the trip down, you won't want to try.

Bicycles are not allowed on park trails, and neither are your pets. In addition, don't think of shortcutting on trails.

Even more importantly, fire preven- [illegible] is of such a concern in this park that [illegible] ng on the trails is prohibited, [illegible] s building a fire any-where other [illegible] pits at the designated camp-

SEASONS & CLIMATE

At Crater Lake there are basically only two seasons. The main tourist season lasts from mid-June, when most of the park's facilities open, through September. The busiest months are July and August. Summer temperatures in southern Oregon can get pretty scorching in the lower elevations, sometimes hovering near the 100°F mark, so you can understand the concern with fire prevention. The upper elevations (including most of the park) remain slightly cooler, but even the lake's rim can get pretty hot and dusty in summer.

In the winter, excessive snowfall of up to 44 feet buries the park, making it virtually impassable to everyone save the skiers and snowshoers, for whom the park becomes a snow-lover's paradise. Roads along the lake rim are left unplowed and are open to the non-car travelers exclusively. The winter season generally includes fall and spring, stretching from late October to mid-June or even early July.

USEFUL PUBLICATIONS

The park publishes a free park guide, called ***Crater Lake Reflections,*** which has a good summary of most of the park's trails, accommodations, and seasons. You can obtain a copy when you contact the park for other visitor information.

You can also obtain a catalog of books and maps about the park by writing to the **Crater Lake Natural History Association,** P.O. Box 157, Crater Lake, OR 97604.

Seeing the Highlights in a Day

This is one park that is accessible by car and open to the day trip.

Most people arriving from the gateway communities of Medford and Klamath Falls—or farther south from the California hinterlands—enter the park's West and South entrances on Ore. 62. Bypass the **Mazama Village** area unless you need to load up on snacks, and stop in at the

Steel Information Center, if you want to get a preview of what you're about to see.

At this point, provided you have the stamina to hike down to the lakeshore, it might be a good idea to head for the requisite **boat trip** to Wizard Island before it gets too late in the day, and consequently, too crowded at the boat dock (the first boat leaves at 10am).

Drive north, clockwise around the rim from the Rim Village entrance, to the Cleetwood Cove Trailhead (the only trail in the park that leads to the lakeshore), approximately 5 miles past the junction of the northern route to the Pumice Desert.

The trip down **Cleetwood Cove Trail** to the cove is for the muscles in the front of your thighs, and the trip back is for your calves. It's a steep, strenuous trail, equal to a climb of 65 flights of stairs, or an elevation change of about 700 feet over 1 mile's distance. Consider carefully whether you are in good enough shape to make the 1-mile climb back up before you head down to the boat dock. There are benches along the way, if you have to rest (you will). At the trailhead is a concessionaire who sells tickets for the guided boat ride, which runs regularly nine times a day from July through early September, from 10am until a final 4:30pm departure time. The cost is $12.50 for adults and $7 for children. (Bring your own water, some sunscreen, and a jacket. You never know what kind of weather is going to happen.) The tour will take approximately 1³/₄ hours before you arrive safely back to shore, provided that you don't layover on Wizard Island when the boat stops there during the tour.

It's perfectly fine to hang out and explore **Wizard Island** for awhile, climbing the 700 feet to its summit on the **Wizard Island Trail,** and then catching the next boat back. (As if the 700 feet you're going to climb on the Cleetwood Trail on the way back isn't enough.) You might want to eat lunch on the beach at Cleetwood Cove before you head back up the trail. After all, this is the only area of the park where you can get next to the water, so why not take advantage?

Nevertheless, doing the boat ride early in the day is getting a lot done. Now you're free to **drive the rim** to your heart's content, as it's pretty much the only other thing to do, unless you plan to hike out and do some backcountry camping, or spend the night at one of the two campgrounds. If that's not the case, drive clockwise toward the **Cloudcap Overlook** turnoff, for a brief drive to the 2,000-foot views of the lake and, farther off on the horizon to the south, Mt. Scott and Mt. Shasta.

Keep heading clockwise along the rim drive. You'll eventually approach a turnoff to view **The Pinnacles,** an area of unique rock formations. These spires are the remnants of fumaroles that formed in hot volcanic debris from the great eruption of Mount Mazama.

The road back to the rim terminates at a junction with another great view point, the **Phantom Ship Overlook.** The "ship" is an ornate piece of eroded basalt jutting up from the lake that sometimes seems to be sailing when the wind is whipping up the water just right. Then again, you might want to skip this if you got the up-close look on your boat ride.

Return to the **Rim Village,** where you started your clockwise journey along the rim, for a last stop of the day, a little walk to the **Rim Village Visitor Center,** where a ranger will answer the questions you're sure to have built up during the day. Or ignore the ranger altogether and head down the path to the **Sinnot Overlook,** which has exhibits that tell you about the names and histories of the many peaks that may now be lit by the late-day sun.

You can get a cup of coffee for the road on a quick visit to the Rim Village Cafeteria, or sit back and watch the sun go down with a meal at the **Crater Lake Lodge** (see "Accommodations," below), which is about 200 feet to the east of th visitor center. (Be sure to call ahead reservations. Way ahead.)

The Crater Lake Rim Drive

Henry Ford could have invented this park, at least in the summertime. Exploring the park by car is de rigueur for most people. There are 33 miles of the famous Rim Drive, with more than 30 overlooks lining this summertime-only two-lane road, and a couple of spur roads that lead you to spectacular spots in the southeastern section of the park. Allow 2 hours to complete the drive, and allow even more time to enjoy any of the many trails and overlooks that are accessible from the Rim Drive. Gasoline is available only at Mazama, and then only in the summertime from late May to mid-October. Otherwise, gasoline should be purchased in Medford, Roseburg, or any of the other outlying communities.

If you decide to skip the boat ride, you'll have time for a short hike. Two of the easy, short trails in the park are the **Annie Creek Canyon and Godfrey Glen trails,** which begin around Mazama Village. A third is the **Castle Crest Wildflower Trail,** which begins at the Steel Information Center. None of these trails are over 2 miles (they're all described in the "Day Hikes" section, below).

If You Have More Time

If you're out for something a little more strenuous than the Rim Drive, strap on the pack and head for the **Pacific Crest Trail.** The Crater Lake section of this famous trail will take you south from the northern section of the park to the Dutton Creek area. From there, you can head back along the trail section that parallels the Rim Drive to your original connecting point, some 2.5 miles out toward the North Entrance Station.

Even though most summer visitors come into the park's West or South entrances, you can still access Crater Lake from the north. And it's a shame to miss [illegible]limpse of these northern perimeter [illegible] as the vast purplish sands of the [illegible] **Desert** are rather otherworldly [illegible]lowers are scattered in isolated [illegible] its flat canvas. If you have the time, it might be worthwhile to detour north when driving in from the south, just to see this area. From the South Entrance, it adds only an extra 15 miles or so, depending on how far out toward the North Entrance Station you want to drive. And since most folks are spending their time coming to drive the Rim Drive, it's possible to put a little space between yourself and everyone else, even in the middle of a summer day at the height of the season. Bring plenty of water, though; it gets dusty out there.

Organized Tours & Ranger Programs

There are many ranger-led programs and tours in the summer. From the Rim Village, there are 15-minute geology talks given daily at the **Sinnot Memorial Overlook** (below the visitor center) from 10am to 5pm, on the hour. There is also a guided afternoon hike up **Garfield Peak** that meets at the flagpole in front of the visitor center, as well as a tour of the **Crater Lake Lodge** and Village that meets at the same spot at 1pm daily.

From the Mazama Campground, there are evening programs at an outdoor amphitheater on a variety of topics posted daily at the visitor centers.

The talks start at 9pm from June 29 to July 31 and at 8:30pm from August 1 to Labor Day.

Of course, the most famous Crater Lake tour is the **guided boat tour** that leaves the Cleetwood Cove every 45 minutes or so, daily from late June through mid-September, from 10am to the last shove-off at 4:30pm. Remember, there is a steep trail down to the boat landing. The tour glides past the Phantom Ship and docks briefly at Wizard Island, before heading back to the Cleetwood Dock. Tickets can be purchased at the trailhead. Tickets are $12.50 for adults, $7.50 for children.

Sometimes the wait for the ride can be as long as 1½ hours. Purchase your ticket and then go off and do some hiking. Come back, and your boat will be waiting when you make it to the dock. Also, keep in mind that if you do get off the boat on Wizard Island, you might have to wait until somebody gets off the next boat arriving, so you can get on for the return trip. Boat capacity is limited, and people have on occasion been stuck on the island for several hours. So, be forewarned! Luckily, you can hike the 2-mile **Wizard Island Trail** (described under "Day Hikes," below).

Historic & Man-Made Attractions

Aside from the **Crater Lake Lodge,** which you might want to take a look at even if you don't spend the night (or take the tour described in the previous section), there are few man-made attractions per se in Crater Lake National Park. But there is evidence of past travels through, and visits to, this area by numerous people over the last 150 years. If you're lucky, you might be able to find some **wagon trails,** whose faint impressions can be found here and there throughout the outer perimeters of the park. Ask the helpful rangers at the visitor center to suggest trails where you might be able to see them.

Day Hikes

SHORTER TRAILS

Annie Creek Canyon

1.7 miles RT. Easy. Access: Reach the trailhead via the Mazama Campground Trailhead, between the D and E loops of the campground.

This is a short, scenic walk through an old-growth forest and wildflower meadows, which serves as a nice little breather to all the ancient volcanic starkness going on up at the rim. There is an elevation gain of about 200 feet.

Castle Crest Wildflower Trail

1 mile RT. Easy. 100-foot elevation gains. Access: The trailhead is at park headquarters in Mazama Village, Crater Lake National Park.

Summer is short on the rim of Crater Lake, so when the snow finally melts, wildflowers burst forth with nearly unrivaled abandon. This short trail meanders through one of the best displays of wildflowers in the park. Late July and early August are the best wildflower periods.

Cleetwood Trail

2.2 miles RT. Moderate. 675-foot elevation gains. Access: The trailhead is on the north side of the lake, 4.5 miles east of the North Junction.

This is the only trail down to the shore of Crater Lake, and it stays busy with those who just want to get to the water and those who are headed to Cleetwood Cove to take the boat tour described above. Because the trail leads downhill, many visitors are lured into thinking that this is an easy trail. It's not! The climb back up from the water to the rim is strenuous and steep, though luckily it goes on for only a mile.

Godfrey Glen

1 mile RT. Easy. Access: The trailhead is 1.5 miles past the Mazama Village Entrance, on right side of the road.

This trail is a very easy walk through old-growth forest and alpine meadows overlooking the Annie Creek Valley. You'll cross Munson Creek at Duwee Falls before you head back to the car. It's a good walk for the kids, with lots of possibilities to see deer, elk, rabbits, or grouse.

The Watchman

1.4 miles RT. Moderate. 655-foot elevation gain. Access: The trailhead is 3.7 miles northwest of Rim Village on West Rim Dr.

With a historic fire lookout perched on its summit, the Watchman is one of the high points on the rim of the caldera. A short but steep trail leads to the top for an outstanding view of the lake with the conical Wizard Island rising from the deep blue of the foreground. This is the shortest climb you can do along the rim of the caldera.

Wizard Island

2 miles RT. Easy to moderate. 765-foot elevation gains. Access: Take the Cleetwood Trail (see above) and then a boat tour around the lake, disembarking on the island.

Though it is small, Wizard Island is a great temptation to many Crater Lake visitors. The island, with its steep volcanic cone rising from the deep, is fun to explore for a few hours, and this trail goes to the island's summit. To spend some time here, take an early boat tour, get off on the island, and arrange to come back on a later boat. Because most of the hiking is on jagged lava rock, be sure to wear sturdy boots.

LONGER TRAILS

Bald Crater/Boundary Springs

20 miles RT. Easy to moderate. Few elevation gains. Access: Via the Rim Dr. to northwest of [illegible]e Rim Village area; continue to the Northern [illegible]Junction of the Rim Dr. and the northern [illegible]road; from here, it's 3 miles down the [illegible]ccess road to the trailhead on the

This trail gives you plenty of chances to contemplate the past and present of the surrounding areas. The ashy, flat, and rolling Pumice Desert stretches to the north along the trail as you travel some 3-odd miles toward the 8,763-foot summit of the Red Cone, a miniature Mount Mazama before it collapsed and created the caldera that holds the lake. The plains give way to ancient forests interspersed with fields of wildflowers. At the junction of the Pacific Coast Trail and the Bald Crest Trail, turn right to head for another miniature Mount Mazama experience: Bald Crater Peak. The peak is about 2 miles south of some fine campsites at the end of the Bald Crater Trail, along Boundary Springs, near the headwaters of the beautiful Rogue River.

Crater Peak

5 miles RT. Easy to moderate. Access: From park headquarters, head east around the Rim Dr. The trailhead is approximately 1.5–2 miles east from the Steel Information Center.

Volcanoes, volcanoes, volcanoes! Here's another one, or the leftovers of another one. This beautiful little walk takes you to a peak that is both a peak and a crater. How? The summit of this hike is the rim of yet another little volcanic cone to the south of the once huge Mount Mazama.

The trail begins with an uphill stroll through 2 miles of alpine forest and meadow, before reaching the steep final 0.5 mile to the summit of Crater Peak, with its full panoramic vistas of Sun Mountain, Maklaks, and Scoria to the south, and the rim of Crater Lake to the north. To the west lies Arant Point, near Mazama, and to the east the Grayback Ridge. All of them combine to form an incredible view. There are plenty of wildlife opportunities here, too. Early in the morning or late in the evening, you may see deer or elk.

Discovery Point

2.6 miles RT. Easy to moderate. Access: Get to the trailhead from the west end of the Rim Village Parking Lot.

This trail, like most trails around the rim, provides brilliant views of the vast lake and Wizard Island below, ending after a short climb at an overlook where John Hillman, one of the first European explorers of the area, first witnessed the beauty of Crater Lake in 1853. The spot is known as Discovery Point.

Dutton Creek

4.8 miles RT. Easy to moderate. Access: Via the trailhead at the west end of the Rim Village Parking Lot.

If you think the whole volcano experience is about ash and pumice, check out the old-growth forest of hemlocks, fir, and pine located on the sometimes vertiginous Dutton Creek Trail. This is also the section of the Pacific Crest Trail that leads the long-distance hiker up to the rim. But for short-timers heading south, it provides an opportunity to get away from the crowds and see something besides a volcano's mouth. That something might be a deer or an elk as you hike down this narrow, heavily forested valley along Dutton Creek, before reaching the junction with the Pacific Crest Trail and getting ready for the climb back the way you came.

Garfield Peak

3.4 miles RT. Moderate. 1,010-foot elevation gain. Access: The trailhead is at the east end of Rim Village Parking Lot.

Sure the view from the Rim Village borders on sublime, but the parking lot full of cars, families wandering along the rim trail, and general national park see-it-all-without-leaving-your-car atmosphere just doesn't do this natural wonder justice. You'll leave most of the crowds behind, get in a good hike, and treat yourself to an even more breathtaking (literally, since the hike starts above 7,000 feet) view of the lake by hiking to the summit of 8,054-foot Garfield Peak, which lies just east of the Rim Village. The route gains all its elevation in a short 1.5 miles of nearly constant switchbacks. From the summit, the entire lake is visible below, including the island called Phantom Ship, which is hard to see from the Rim Village. To the south, Mount Shasta can be seen.

Mount Scott

5 miles RT. Strenuous. 1,480-foot elevation gains. Access: The trailhead is 14 miles east of park headquarters on East Rim Dr. and across the road from Cloudcap Junction.

If the trail to Garfield Peak had a few too many other hikers on it for your tastes, try this trail to the top of 8,929-foot Mount Scott. This is the highest point within Crater Lake National Park, and the trail is longer, steeper, and entails more elevation gain than the trail up Garfield Peak. These factors tend to weed out those folks who just aren't serious about their views. Needless to say, the views from the summit are the most far-reaching in the park, encompassing not only the entire lake but such surrounding peaks as Mount Thielsen, Mount Shasta, and Mount McLoughlin, as well as the vast expanse of Klamath Lake to the south.

Pacific Crest Trail Section

33 miles one way. Moderate to strenuous. Access: Via Mazama Village. Approximately 1 mile west of the village, the trailhead is on the right.

For those who want to chalk up this particular section of the Pacific Crest Trail, there's a lot to chalk up. The trail essentially bisects the park, with only one section that follows the rim for views of the lake. Otherwise, you're pretty much out there in the flatlands.

From the trailhead, the path follows the base of the mountain's curve to the west for nice views of the mountain's slow climb to its rim to your right, and the rolling high desert plains to your left. At the northern end of the walk, before crossing into the vast Pumice Desert, there is an opportunity to circle back to the rim at North Junction.

Pumice Flat

6 miles RT. Easy to moderate. Access: Join the trailhead 3 miles south of Mazama Village on Ore. 62.

This is the southern equivalent of the park's northern Pumice Desert area. This dusty trail takes you through gently rolling pumice and ash plains, littered with sharp volcanic rocks, before intersecting the Pacific Crest Trail for the loop to Mazama. You can also simply return on the shorter route back to the trailhead where you started.

Stuart Falls

11 miles RT. Easy to moderate. Access: The trailhead is 3 miles south of the Mazama Village park entrance on Ore. 62.

Well, Stuart Falls are really outside the park's boundaries, but the trailhead isn't, so what can you do? Enjoy, I guess. It's a nice contrast as you climb down to the dusty and volcanically beautiful Pumice Flats before heading into the Red Blanket Valley after the junction with the Pacific Crest Trail. You'll begin to notice a bare trickle of water turning into a creek turning into a much bigger creek that ends up as a fine crashing mist of spray known as Stuart Falls. Folks have been known to take a rest in Stuart Fall's fine white spray before heading back up the steep and often parched trail.

Other Summer Sports & Activities

Biking. The 33-mile circuit of Crater Lake is one of the most popular road-bike trips in the state, despite the heavy car traffic with which riders must share the road. Although it would seem at first that this would be an easy trip, numerous ups and downs (especially on the east side of the lake) turn it into a very demanding ride. Also keep in mind that not only are there more hills on the east side, but there are also fewer views, which makes that side of the lake a bit tedious. A more view-packed alternative would be to do the 21-mile out and back ride from the Rim Village to the Cleetwood Cove Trailhead (and maybe add on a boat tour of the lake). There are no bike rentals available in the park, but Diamond Lake Resort rents them in the summer. (See the "Accommodations" section, below, for details on the resort.) Bikes are not allowed on park trails.

Swimming. Although Crater Lake is too deep to ever reach a truly comfortable temperature (even in the summer), plenty of people take the plunge each summer and do a few quick strokes to cool down after hiking the Cleetwood Cove Trail or after exploring Wizard Island. Remember, there is no other access point to the lake in the park. You can also swim on Wizard Island, as well, and many do. But there are no facilities in either place as this is a very informal thing.

Other Winter Sports & Activities

Cross-Country Skiing. The **Diamond Lake Nordic Center,** located 4 miles north of the park on Ore. 138 (☎ **800/733-7593**), offers Crater Lake ski tours that include a snowcat ride to the North Rim Ski Trail. Tours are $35/person, but they operate only if there are at least 10 people going. They also rent cross-country skis. Maps of ski areas are available at the Steel Information Center at park headquarters.

Without a doubt, the rim of Crater Lake National Park offers some of the best cross-country skiing in the country. Not only are there numerous views of sapphire-blue Crater Lake 1,000 feet below you, but the views to the west and south take in Mount McLoughlin, Mount Shasta and countless ridges and seemingly endless forest vistas as well.

The ultimate ski tour, of course, is the 30- to 33-mile circuit of the lake. Although this route has been done in a single day by racers, most skiers take 3 days and enjoy the views along the way. Because the weather is better and there's still plenty of snow, March and April are the most popular months to do this trip. The route is very straightforward, although you may have to do some route finding on the northeast side of the lake.

The **West Rim Trail** is the most popular day skiing area. The trail follows Rim Drive, which in summer is always clogged with cars circumnavigating the lake. However, by winter the road is unplowed and the snow cover turns it into an excellent trail, which requires a little climbing. The West Rim Trail is best done in good weather and good snow conditions. Consult with a ranger in the Steel Information Center at park headquarters for snow conditions before heading out.

The **East Rim Trail** is not nearly as popular as the West Rim Trail for the simple reason that it is between 4.25 and 5.4 miles to the first view of the lake (depending on where you start). This trail also has a lot more ups and downs. So, why would you want to start on this section at all? To stay out of the wind, that's why. If, after driving all the way up here there's a gale-force wind blowing up the west slopes, you really don't have much choice. Never set out, though, without checking with the rangers at park headquarters to find out about avalanche conditions and other dangers.

Snowmobiling. During winter months snowmobiling is allowed in the park, but only on the North Entrance road and then only up to its junction with Rim Drive (snowmobiles are not allowed on Rim Drive). You cannot drive snowmobiles on any park trails, either. It's possible to rent snowmobiles from **Diamond Lake Resort** during the winter months. You'll find the prices high—up to $125 per day per person, depending on whether you're just renting or going on a resort-led snowmobile tour. Full details for Diamond Lake Resort are given in the accommodations section.

Snowshoeing. With its jewel of a lake for a centerpiece and views that extend all the way to Mount Shasta in California, Crater Lake National Park is a natural magnet for snowshoers. Though the **West Rim Trail** is the most popular route (just as it is for cross-country skiing), snowshoers have the advantage of being able to go where few skiers dare to go: up the slopes of Garfield Peak. This craggy summit rises 1,000-feet above the Rim Village just east of Crater Lake Lodge. Before you head out, discuss possible routes with the rangers and ask about avalanches and other potential dangers.

If you've never snowshoed before, you can give it a try at **Rim Village,** where 90-minute guided snowshoe hikes are offered on winter weekends (November 25 through March). Hikes start at 1pm.

Camping

Within Crater Lake National Park, there are only two campgrounds—one large and one small. You can make campground reservations up to 3 months in advance by calling ☎ **800/365-CAMP** (2267). Payment must be made at the time you make the reservation.

Mazama Village Campground ($13 per tent and $14 per RV per night) has 198 sites available, with drinking water, disposal station, rest rooms, a public phone, and fire pits at all sites. It is located at Mazama Village off Ore. 62. There is also a general store and post office adjacent to the campground. It's open from June through mid-October.

Lost Creek Campground ($10 per night) has 16 sites for tents only. It is located on the southeastern section of the park, on the spur road to The Pinnacles. It's open from mid-July to mid-September.

Accommodations & Dining

INSIDE THE PARK

Aside from the Crater Lake Lodge Dining Room, which is moderate in price, places to eat in the park are limited to the snack bar at the Rim Village Cafeteria and Gift Shop, as well as the grocery store in the Mazama Village.

Crater Lake Lodge

Mailing address: 1211 Ave. C, White City, OR 97503. ☎ **541/830-8700;** fax 541/830-8514. 71 rms. $110–$150 double. MC, V. Closed mid-Oct to mid-May.

Perched on the edge of the rim overlooking Crater Lake, this lodge was completely rebuilt in 1995 and has since become the finest national park lodge in the Northwest. Not only are the views breathtaking, but the amenities are modern without sacrificing the rustic atmosphere that visitors expect in a mountain lodge. Among the lodge's few original features are the stone fireplace and ponderosa pine–bark walls in the Great Hall. Slightly more than half the guest rooms overlook the lake, and although most of the rooms have modern bathrooms, there are eight rooms with claw-foot bathtubs. The very best rooms are the corner rooms on the lake side of the lodge. As at other national park lodges throughout the country, reservations here are hard to come by. Plan as far in advance as you can.

The lodge's **dining room** serves creative Northwest cuisine and provides a view of both Crater Lake and the Klamath River basin.

Mazama Village Motor Inn

Mailing address: 1211 Ave. C, White City, OR 97503. ☎ **541/830-8700;** fax 541/830-8514. 40 rms. $78.25 double. MC, V. Closed Nov–May.

Though the Mazama Village Motor Inn isn't on the rim of the caldera, it's just a short drive away. The modern motel-style guest rooms are housed in 10 steep-roofed buildings that look much like traditional mountain cabins. A laundry, gas station, and general store make Mazama Village a busy spot in the summer.

NEAR THE PARK

Since the park is so isolated, there are few dining options in the small, surrounding communities for dining outside of the following places.

Diamond Lake Resort

Diamond Lake, OR 97731. ☎ **800/733-7593** or 541/793-3333; fax 541/793-3309. 40 rms, 10 studios, 42 cabins. TV. $70 double; $75 studio for 2; $100–$155 cabin. MC, V.

Located on the shores of Diamond Lake near the North Entrance to the national park, this resort has long been a popular family vacation spot, and with Mounts Thielsen and Bailey flanking the lake, this is one of the most picturesque settings in the Oregon Cascades. The variety of accommodations provides plenty of choices, but our favorites are the lakefront cabins, which are large enough for a family or two couples. These have great views of the lake and mountains. If you want to do your own cooking, you'll find kitchenettes in both the cabins and studios. Unfortunately, this resort has gotten fairly run down in recent years. The lodge also offers several dining options, though most visitors opt to cook their own meals. Boat, mountain-bike, and horse rentals are available, and there's a small sandy beach and a bumper-boat area. In winter the resort is most popular with snowmobilers but also attracts a few cross-country skiers, as well as downhillers here to snowcat ski on Mount Bailey.

Prospect Historical Hotel and Motel

391 Mill Creek Dr., Prospect, OR 97536. ☎ **800/944-6490** or 541/560-3664; fax 503/560-3825. 23 rms. $60–$80 double. DISC, MC, V.

This hotel, located in the tiny hamlet of Prospect, 30 miles from Crater Lake's Rim Village, is a combination of an 1889 vintage hotel and a modern motel. The old hotel is a big white building with a wraparound porch on which are set several bent-willow couches. The small rooms in the historic hotel have few furnishings, but they do have a country styling that gives them a bit of charm. If you stay in one of these rooms, a continental breakfast is included. The motel rooms are much larger and have TVs and telephones, and some of these rooms also have kitchenettes. The elegant **dining room** is well known for its excellent meals, with main courses such as rack of lamb, and shrimp scampi ranging in price from $10 to $16. Sunday brunch is particularly popular.

Steamboat Inn

42705 N. Umpqua Hwy., Steamboat, OR 97447-9703. ☎ **800/840-8825** or 541/498-2230; fax 541/498-2411. 8 rms, 2 suites, 5 cottages, 4 houses. $125 double; $160 cottages and houses; $235 suite. MC, V.

Located roughly midway between Roseburg and Crater Lake, this inn on the bank of the North Umpqua River is by far the finest lodging on the North Umpqua. While the lodge appeals primarily to anglers, the beautiful gardens, luxurious guest rooms, and gourmet meals also attract a fair number of people looking for a quiet getaway in the forest and a base for hiking and biking. If you aren't springing for one of the suites, which have their own soaking tubs overlooking the river, your best bet will be stream-side rooms, which are referred to as cabins but really aren't. These have all been recently renovated, have gas fireplaces, and open onto a long deck that overlooks the river. The hideaway cottages are more spacious but don't have river views and are 0.5 mile from the lodge (and the dining room). Dinners are multicourse affairs served in a cozy **dining room,** and breakfast is available all day. There's also a fly-fishing shop on the premises.

Union Creek Resort

56484 Ore. 62, Prospect, OR 97536. ☎ **541/560-3565.** 9 rms, 14 cabins. $38–$48 double; $50–$85 cabin for 2 to 6 people. MC, V.

Located almost across the road from the Rogue River Gorge, this cabin resort has been catering to Crater Lake visitors since the early 1900s and is listed on the National Register of Historic Places. Tall trees shade the grounds of the rustic resort, which is right on Ore. 62 about 23 miles from Rim Village. Accommodations include both lodge rooms and very basic cabins (many of which have kitchenettes), and most have been updated in recent years. Across the road from the cabins and lodge building is Beckie's Café, which serves home-style meals and is best known for its pies. This is your best and closest option outside the Crater Lake National Park on the west side.

13

DEATH VALLEY NATIONAL PARK

by Stephanie Avnet

In 1994, Death Valley National Monument became Death Valley National Park. The forty-niners, whose suffering gave the valley its name, would've howled at the notion. Death Valley National *Park* seems a contradiction in terms, an oxymoron of the great outdoors. To them, other four-letter words would've come to mind: gold, mine, heat, lost, dead. And the four-letter words shouted by the teamsters who drove the 20-mule-team borax wagons need not be repeated.

Americans looking for gold in California's mountains in 1849 were forced to cross the burning sands here to avoid the severe snowstorms in the nearby Sierra Nevada. Some perished along the way, and the land became known as Death Valley. Not much about the valley's essence has changed. Its mountains stand naked, unadorned. The bitter waters of saline lakes evaporate into bizarre razor-sharp crystal formations. Jagged canyons jab deep into the earth. The ovenlike heat, the frigid cold, and the driest air imaginable combine to make this one of the world's most inhospitable locations.

Death Valley is raw, bare earth, the way things must've looked before life began. Here earth's forces are exposed to view with dramatic clarity; just looking out on the landscape, you'll find it impossible to know what year, or century, it is. It's no coincidence that many of Death Valley's topographical features are associated with hellish images: Funeral Mountains, Furnace Creek, Dante's View, Coffin Peak, and Devil's Golf Course. But the valley can be a place of serenity as well.

Human nature being what it is, it's not surprising that people have long been drawn to challenge the power of Mother Nature, even in this, her "home court." The area's first foray into tourism was in 1925, a scant 76 years after the forty-niners' harrowing experiences (which would've discouraged most sane folks from ever returning). It probably would've begun sooner, but the valley had been consumed with lucrative borax mining since the late 1880s.

In one of his last official acts, Pres. Herbert Hoover signed a proclamation designating Death Valley a national monument in February 1933. With the stroke of a pen he not only authorized the protection of a vast and wondrous land but also helped to transform one of the earth's least hospitable spots into a popular tourist destination.

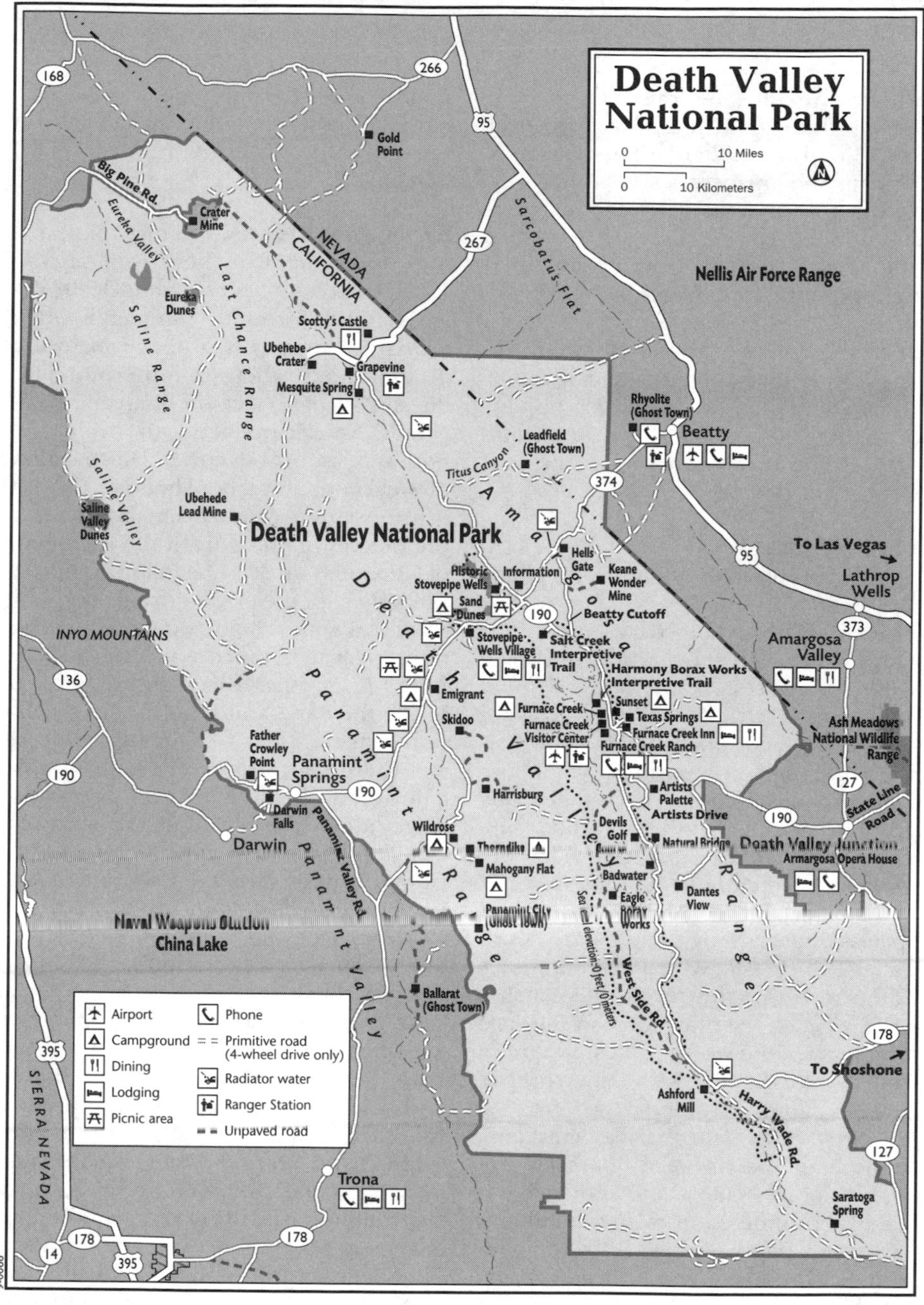

The naming of Death Valley National Monument came at a time when Americans were discovering the romance of the desert. Land that had previously been considered hideously devoid of life was now being celebrated for its spare beauty; places that had once been feared for their harshness were now being admired for their uniqueness.

In 1994, when President Clinton signed the California Desert Protection Act, Death Valley National Park became the largest national park outside Alaska, with more than 3.3 million acres.

Though remote, it's one of the most heavily visited, and you're likely to hear less English spoken than German, French, and Japanese.

Today's visitor drives in air-conditioned comfort, stays in comfortable hotel rooms or well-maintained campgrounds, orders meals and provisions at park concessions, and even quaffs cold beer at the local saloon. He or she may take a swim in the Olympic-size pool, tour a Moorish castle, shop for souvenirs, and enjoy the desert landscape while hiking along a nature trail with a park ranger.

Flora & Fauna. Most of Death Valley's climate zones are harshly limiting to plants and animals, but they're nevertheless diverse. Within the park, elevations range from 282 feet below sea level (Badwater, the lowest point in the United States) to 11,049 feet above sea level (Telescope Peak, blanketed by snow during winter and early spring). At the lowest elevations is little sign of life; any groundwater is highly saline and supports only algae and bacteria. One notable exception is the unique and endangered **desert pupfish,** an ancient species that's slowly adapted to Death Valley's increasingly harsh conditions. You can see the tiny fish in the marshes of Salt Creek, halfway between Furnace Creek and Stovepipe Wells, where a boardwalk lined with interpretive plaques allows you an up-close look.

Hardy desert shrubs like **mesquite, creosote,** and **arrowweed** flourish at the mouths of canyons, where enough fresh water is channeled from the mountains to support these miserly plants. You have to look closely to discern the surprising number of small mammals and birds that live at the lower elevations (sea level to 4,000 feet); **rabbits, rodents, bats, snakes, roadrunners,** and even **coyotes** all get by on very little water. At the higher elevations, where **pinyon pine** and **juniper** woodlands blanket the slopes, animals are more plentiful and can also include **bobcats** and the elusive **bighorn sheep.** Over 8,000 feet, look for small stands of **bristlecone pine,** the planet's longest-lived tree; some specimens on Telescope Peak are more than 3,000 years old.

Avoiding the Crowds. You may think that no one would plan their vacation in a 120°F–plus remote desert, but Death Valley is full year-round. Summer is when primarily Europeans visit, and many are disappointed when the thermometer doesn't soar to record-breaking heat. North Americans tend to avoid the hottest season and crowd Death Valley on weekends and school holidays the rest of the year. December and January are the quietest months (with the exception of Christmas week). The following advice will help ease the crush during your visit:

- Make all accommodations reservations as far in advance as you can, at least 2 or 3 months. Facilities are limited inside the park, and Death Valley's isolation make it time consuming to locate elsewhere. Since none of Death Valley's campgrounds is currently accepting reservations, those planning to set up in one of the "first come, first served" camping areas should try to claim a site between 9am and noon.
- Try to avoid visiting on weekends and during school vacation periods, like Easter week.
- Plan to enjoy the most popular activities (Scotty's Castle tours, designated scenic drives and overlooks, Borax and Eagle mine sites, easy interpretive hikes) early in the day, since crowds start building up around 10am. An alternative, particularly on summer days, is to wait until crowds dissipate around 4pm. Remember the sun doesn't set until after 7pm between June and September.
- The best way to gain real solitude is to come with a four-wheel-drive vehicle with high road clearance—you'll find a whole world that's inaccessible to most of Death Valley's visitors. There are hidden valleys and ghost towns, mountainous sand dunes, and remote canyons to explore. Check the Park Service's official map, where roads are clearly marked according to degree of passability.

Just the Facts

GETTING THERE & GATEWAYS

There are several routes into the park—all involve crossing one of the steep mountain ranges that isolate Death Valley. The most common access route from Los Angeles and points south is via Calif. 127 from I-15 at the town of Baker; from Death Valley Junction, Calif. 190 leads to the park's center. Perhaps the most scenic entry is via Calif. 190 from the west, reached from Calif. 14 and U.S. 395 by taking Calif. 178 from Ridgecrest. To access the same route from the north, pick up Calif. 190 directly from U.S. 395 at Olancha. You can also approach the park from Nevada, by taking Nev. 374 from Beatty, located on U.S. 95.

The Nearest Airport. The nearest airport is Las Vegas's **McCarran International Airport,** 5757 Wayne Newton Blvd. (☎ **702/261-5743**). Most airlines have regularly scheduled flights into Vegas: Air Canada, Alaska Airlines, American/American Eagle, America West, American Trans Air, Canadian International, Condor, Continental, Delta/Skywest, Frontier, Hawaiian, Kiwi, Midway, Midwest Express, Northwest, Reno Air, Southwest, Sun Country, TWA, United, US Airways, and Western Pacific. See the appendix for these airlines' phone numbers.

Renting a Car. All the major car-rental companies are represented in Las Vegas at the airport. National companies with outlets here are **Alamo, Avis, Budget, Dollar, Enterprise, Hertz, National,** and **Thrifty.** See the appendix for their phone numbers. **Allstate** (☎ **800/634-6186** or 702/736-6148) is a local rental company that also rents four-wheel-drive vehicles.

It's a 2.5-hour drive from Vegas to Death Valley. A four-wheel-drive vehicle is recommended for backcountry travel, and you'll need one to access 2 of the 10 campgrounds (see "Entrance Fees" and "Camping Fees," below).

Taking a Bus. Las Vegas's **Express Tours** (☎ **702/739-8120**) offers a shuttle service leaving the Best Value Inn on East Tropicana Avenue daily at 8am and 1pm for Furnace Creek Ranch in Death Valley. The return trips from Furnace Creek to Las Vegas are at 10:25am and 3:50pm. The cost is $25. For a complete schedule, call the number above.

GETTING INFORMATION BEFORE YOUR TRIP

Contact the **Superintendent, Death Valley National Park,** Death Valley, CA 92328 (☎ **760/786-2331**).

The park has a web page on the National Park Service's Web site at **www.nps.gov/deva**.

VISITOR CENTERS

Park headquarters are at the **Furnace Creek Visitor Center** (☎ **760/786-2331**) in Furnace Creek, 15 miles inside the eastern park boundary on Calif. 190. You'll find well-done interpretive exhibits and an hourly slide program as well as an extensive bookstore operated by the Death Valley Natural History Association. It's open daily from 8am to 7pm in winter and from 8am to 5pm in summer.

There's also a museum, a bookshop, and an information center at **Scotty's Castle** (☎ **760/786-2313**), open daily from 9am to 5pm (see "Historic & Man-Made Attractions," below).

There is a ranger station that collects fees and can provide you with information at **Stovepipe Wells** (☎ **760/786-2342**).

ENTRANCE FEES

You'll be required to pay a $10 per car entrance fee, valid for 7 days. Pay at the Furnace Creek Visitor Center or at ranger stations at Stovepipe Wells and Scotty's Castle; be sure to keep the receipt handy for the duration of your stay, since you'll be required to show it when passing the entry checkpoint near Scotty's Castle.

CAMPING FEES

There are 10 campgrounds within park boundaries, 2 of which, Thorndike and Mahogany Flat, are reachable only with a four-wheel-drive vehicle. These and two others are free; overnight fees elsewhere range from $10 to $16. Only four campgrounds are open year-round—see "Camping" for details.

SPECIAL REGULATIONS & WARNINGS

It isn't called Death Valley for nothing, but there's little chance that you'll encounter any life-threatening situations, especially if you carefully follow some commonsense safety tips. You'll find these and many more hints in brochures available at the park's visitor centers.

◆ Dehydration is your most urgent concern, particularly in summer, when temperatures routinely reach 120°F and higher at the arid lower elevations. Always carry a supply of water for everyone, including your car. Recommended minimum amounts are 1 gallon per person per day and twice that if you're planning strenuous activity. It's a good idea to stow several gallons for the car, even though radiator water is available from tanks placed at strategic points (uphill climbs) along the main roads.

◆ Always carry sunscreen and protective clothing, including a wide-brimmed hat and sunglasses. Drink often, whether you feel thirsty or not, and be alert for the signs of dehydration: dizziness, headache, and cold, clammy skin.

◆ When driving, turn off your air-conditioning on uphill grades to lessen engine strain and prevent overheating. In the event that your car does overheat, keep the engine running and turn the car into the breeze. While the car idles, pour sufficient water over the radiator to cool it before removing the cap and refilling the radiator water.

◆ What's the number-one cause of death in Death Valley? Single-car accidents, which can happen in summer or winter, daylight or nighttime. There are many long miles of roads through the park; though well paved, they often have sharp curves, dips, and steep downhill grades. Be alert for wildlife on the road and don't let yourself be distracted by the scenery. If your tires wander off the edge of the pavement at high speed, don't jerk the wheel, which can cause you to skid out of control. Instead, gradually slow down until it's safe to bring all four tires back onto the road.

SEASONS & CLIMATE

Although Death Valley is undeniably one of the world's driest deserts, altitudes range from 282 feet below sea level to over 11,000 feet above; therefore, "desert" doesn't always equal "hot." From June to September, temperatures in the valley can soar above 120°F, making the mountain sections of the park a welcome relief with temperatures in the 70s and 80s. But in November to February, when valley temperatures are comfortable in the 60s and 70s, many higher areas are frigid and snowy. But there's something for everyone, making Death Valley a year-round national park.

SEASONAL EVENTS

The weeklong **Death Valley 49'ers Encampment** is held in the second week in November. It features a fiddlers' contest, a burro flapjack race, square dancing, special tours, a Western art show, and a golf tournament. For more details, contact the park headquarters (see above).

USEFUL PUBLICATIONS

Be sure to pick up the official ***Guide for the Visitor,*** a newspaper-style free handout listing most of the park basics. It's available at ranger stations and the Furnace Creek Visitor Center. Also see if they're still distributing a little orange folder called ***Hot Weather Hints.*** In addition to providing a wealth of information on avoiding heat exhaustion and on high-temperature auto care, the pamphlet has amusing ca. 1960 illustrations.

You may also want to check out Cliff Lawson's *A Traveler's Guide to Death Valley National Park* (Los Olivos: Cachuma Press/Death Valley Natural History Association, 1996), or John Krist's *50 Best Short Hikes in California Deserts* (Berkeley: Wilderness Press, 1995).

The **Death Valley Natural History Association,** P.O. Box 188, Death Valley, CA 92328 (☎ **760/786-3285;** fax 760/786-2236), operates the park's bookstores; contact them for their latest publications list and catalog.

Seeing the Highlights in a Day

The distances inside Death Valley National Park are prohibitive, so the following is merely a guideline. If there's a destination you don't want to miss (for example, the Wildrose Charcoal Kilns), you'll have to pass up some of the more popular sites in the interest of time.

If you have only 1 day and want to get a sampling of the park's best-loved spots, start at the **Furnace Creek Visitor Center,** located at the center of the action in Furnace Creek (see "Visitor Centers," above). View either the **slide show** or the **short film** (shown continuously) for an overview of the park and a taste of the things you won't get a chance to see. This advice holds even for visitors with several days; there's *always* something you'll have to miss. Step over to the center's museum for a look at the 10-by-20–foot **relief map** of the entire park, which will give you a feel for where your destinations are in the context of the whole region, including the all-important elevation factor. If you have time, check out the tiny **Borax Museum,** housed in an old miners' boardinghouse at nearby Furnace Creek Ranch. Admission to the museum is free.

Scotty's Castle is a "must-see" for most people, but you need to plan ahead due to the popularity of ranger-guided house tours. Even if you want to explore only the grounds, remember that the castle is 53 miles north of Furnace Creek, an hour's drive each way. A good plan is to make the castle your first activity after breakfast, avoiding the crowds and freeing up the afternoon for seeing other sites or squeezing in an easy half-hour hike. Easily reached spots are **Artists Palette, Harmony Borax Works, Badwater, Devil's Golf Course, Zabriskie Point,** and **Dante's View.**

If the weather is fine, replace one or two of these attractions with a short hike (like **Mosaic Canyon, Sand Dunes,** or the **Salt Creek Nature Trail**)—for details, see "Day Hikes," below. Just after the junction where Calif. 190 turns west toward the Sand Dunes and Stovepipe Wells, you'll pass the **Devil's Cornfield,** where arrowweed bushes grow in unusual clumps resembling corn stalks. There's a turnout where you can park to explore this strange landscape and plant, which was named for the way Native Americans fashioned arrow shafts from the stalks.

Because each gateway to Death Valley has its own features, visitors with time limitations can maximize their experience by choosing a different entrance and exit route. If you drove in on Calif. 127 through Death Valley Junction, try leaving via the scenic route west through the Panamint Valley. If you entered from the Panamint side, try following Calif. 178 south from Furnace Creek, across the Black Mountains and Greenwater Valley, to pick up Calif. 127 at Shoshone.

Exploring the Park by Car

Death Valley National Park is crisscrossed by a network of roads, ranging from washboard remnants of old mining days to well-maintained highways built during the 1930s. You'll find that most of the popular destinations, as well as the five major entry routes, have superior-quality roads suitable for all passenger vehicles as well as trailers and motor homes. One exception is the Emigrant/Wildrose Canyon pass between Calif. 190 and Calif. 178, sections of which are rough, narrow, and winding; vehicles over 25 feet are prohibited at all times, and other drivers may want to consult the ranger about current road conditions before attempting the unpaved section south of Wildrose.

The park is ideal for viewing by car. Conservationists are adamant that the parade of vehicles detracts from the valley's natural beauty and preservation, but this feature does help make the park more accessible to those with limited time to traverse the vast distances involved (and limited ability to withstand the often grueling weather). Some of the most beautiful sites have handy access roads, vista turn-outs, or loop drives to facilitate viewing. These include **Artists Palette,** where the 8-mile one-way Artists Drive takes you through a colorful display hidden from the main road. Over millions of years, mineral deposits have created brilliant swaths of color across the low, rocky hills. There's a scenic overlook at the beginning of the drive as well as a parking area farther ahead in case you want to stop and scramble amid the pink, blue, red, orange, and green patches.

South of Artists Drive, Calif. 178 takes you past several of Death Valley's highlights, which best illustrate this environment of low-elevation extremes. **Devil's Golf Course,** accessible by a short spur of graded dirt road, sets your car right in the middle of a forbidding landscape created by salt and erosion on a lake bed that dried up about 2,000 years ago. The results are spikes, pits, craters, and jagged ridges stained brown and smoothed by human feet near the parking area; walk just 2 minutes in any direction and you'll see the salty white surface in its natural state.

About 5 miles south of this is **Badwater,** whose simple name indicates the lowest, hottest, and (curiously) wettest spot on the valley floor. At 279 feet below sea level, Badwater is the lowest spot in the park accessible by auto and marked by permanent spring-fed pools. The water at first seemed like relief to early travelers—until they tasted the amounts of chloride, sodium, and sulfate. More than a few must've sputtered "Bad water!" It isn't poisonous, however, and is home to beetles, soldier fly larvae, and a soft-bodied saltwater snail that slowly adapted to these conditions.

A similar site is 25 miles north on Calif. 190: **Salt Creek,** home to the **Salt Creek pupfish,** found nowhere else on earth. You can glimpse this little fish, which has made some amazing adaptations to survive in this arid land, from a wooden boardwalk nature trail. In spring, a million pupfish might be wriggling in the creek; but by summer's end only a few thousand remain.

Your car will also take you all the way to two of the best lookout points around, both along Calif. 190 southeast of Furnace Creek. Before sunrise, photographers set up their tripods at **Zabriskie Point,** 5 miles southeast of Furnace Creek off Calif. 190, and aim their cameras down at the pale mudstone hills of Golden Canyon and the great valley beyond. The panoramic view is magnificent.

Another grand park vista is at **Dante's View,** located 25 miles south of Furnace Creek via Calif. 190 and Dante's View Road, a 5,475-foot point looking out over the shimmering Death Valley floor backed by the high Panamint Mountains.

Nearly everyone takes the scenic drive up Scotty's Castle Road to visit the park's major man-made attraction, **Scotty's Castle** (see below), and while you're there it's worth taking the 15-minute drive to **Ubehebe Crater,** 9 miles west of the Castle, the otherworldly pockmark from a volcanic explosion 3,000 years ago. You'll know that you're close when the landscape begins to darken from layers of cinders spewn from the half-mile crater, and a convenient loop road takes you up to the most scenic lip. A few explanatory signs grace the parking area, and there's a hiking path (for those willing to brave the often-gusting winds) to an even more dramatic overlook and a field of smaller craters.

Organized Tours & Ranger Programs

In addition to providing hourly **Scotty's Castle** "Living History" tours (see below), Death Valley rangers keep busy giving lectures, group discussions, and film presentations to help acquaint visitors with this unusual area. The topics are varied, including learning about the desert tortoise or roadrunner; the pioneer disaster of 1849 that gave Death Valley its name; video of the elusive bighorn sheep; secrets of 500-million-year-old fossil beds; and explanations of some geological oddities that puzzle park visitors. For those eager to get their shoes dusty, several hikes and guided walks are conducted seasonally, with themes like Moonlight Meander and Canyon Secrets. Contact park headquarters for a seasonal schedule of day and evening events; nearly all programs (except for year-round Scotty's Castle tours) cease between mid-May and early October.

Historic & Man-Made Attractions

Scotty's Castle, the Mediterranean hacienda in the northern part of the park, is unabashedly Death Valley's premier attraction. Visitors are wowed by the elaborate Spanish tiles, well-crafted furnishings, and innovative construction that included solar water heating. Even more compelling is the colorful history of this villa in remote Grapevine Canyon, brought to life by park rangers dressed in 1930s clothing. Don't be surprised if the castle cook or a friend of Scotty's gives you a special insight into castle life.

Construction of the "castle"—more officially, Death Valley Ranch—began in 1924. It was to be a winter retreat for eccentric Chicago millionaire Albert Johnson. The insurance tycoon's unlikely friendship with prospector/cowboy/spinner-of-tall-tales Walter Scott put the $2.3 million structure on the map and captured the public's imagination. Scotty greeted visitors and told them fanciful stories from the early hard-rock-mining days of Death Valley.

The 1-hour guided tour of Scotty's Castle is excellent, both for its inside look at the mansion and for what it reveals about the eccentricities of Johnson and Scotty. Tours depart every 20 minutes from 9am to 5pm; they fill up quickly, so arrive early for the first available spots (there's an $8 fee). During busy periods, you may have to wait an hour or more, perusing the gift shop or relaxing in the snack bar. There's also a self-guided walking tour (excluding the interiors); the pamphlet *A Walking Tour of Scotty's Castle* leads you on an exploration from stable to pool, from bunkhouse to powerhouse. **Organized groups** (only) can reserve tour times by calling ☎ **760/786-2392.**

For another side of the human experience here, visit the **Harmony Borax Works,** located 2 miles south of Furnace Creek off Calif. 190 and then a short spur road—a rock-salt landscape as tortured as you'll ever find. Death Valley prospectors called borax "white gold," and though it wasn't exactly a glamorous substance, it was a profitable one. From 1883 to 1888, more than 20 million pounds of it were transported from the Harmony Borax Works, and borax mining continued in Death Valley until 1928. A short trail with interpretive signs leads past the ruins of the old borax refinery and some outlying buildings.

Transport of the borax was the stuff of legends, too. The famous 20-mule teams hauled the huge loaded wagons 165 miles to the rail station at Mojave. (To learn more about this colorful era, visit the Borax Museum at Furnace Creek Ranch, near the park visitor center). Other remnants of human industry are the **Eagle Borax Works** ruins, 20 miles south of Furnace Creek via Badwater Road and the unpaved dirt West Side Road, and the **Wildrose Charcoal Kilns,** 39 miles south of Stovepipe Wells off Emigrant Canyon Road, where vast amounts of charcoal were manufactured for use on the lucrative silver mining in neighboring Panamint Valley. Located near the Wildrose Ranger Station and campground, the road to the kilns is paved but precariously twisted, and vehicles over 25 feet are prohibited.

Day Hikes

There are trails to suit all levels of expertise and at varying elevations. Wherever you hike, never forget to bring enough water; even in seemingly mild weather conditions, hikers can become easily dehydrated. Park rangers can provide topographical maps, current weather conditions, and detailed directions to each trailhead.

SHORTER TRAILS

Borax Flats

1 mile RT. Easy. Access: The trailhead is at the parking area for the Harmony Borax Works, 2 miles north of Furnace Creek off Calif. 190, then down a short spur road.

At the borax works, an old boiler, tanks, and mule-drawn wagons preserve the early history of lucrative borax refining in Death Valley. At the parking area, a paved trail with interpretive signs encircles the relics; leaving the paved loop, it descends to the dry lake bed and crusty salt marshes where Chinese laborers once gathered the precious substance. The salt flats can be muddy and very hot, so watch your footing and always carry water.

Eureka Dunes

1 mile RT. Easy. Access: The trailhead is well marked in the Eureka Sand Dunes National Natural Landmark Area, at the end of South Eureka Rd.

This area is approachable only from the remote north end of the park and by rutted dirt and gravel roads subject to washout, so travel to this area requires a sturdy vehicle in good condition. The dunes, however, are magnificent, the tallest and oldest in North America. The whole family will enjoy romping here, spotting dune grass and wildflowers or the tracks of lizards and rodents. The view from atop the highest dune (700 feet) takes in the splendid contrast of creamy sand against the layer-cake band of nearby rock, and small avalanches of sand create the trademark "singing" peculiar to such dunes.

Keane Wonder Mine

2 miles RT. Strenuous. Access: The trailhead, which is marked, is located past the parking area and the old mill site; the mine is 20 miles north of Furnace Creek via Daylight Pass Cutoff and then after 3 miles of graded dirt road.

A rocky mountainous trail climbs steeply to the site of this successful gold mine, passing along the way the solid, efficient wooden tramway that carried ore out of the mountain. The trail obeys an old miner's adage that the best way up a mountainside is the straightest, even if the most strenuous—but you'll be rewarded with spectacular views of the park and substantial artifacts from the mining operation. The many mine tunnels and shafts are fascinating though potentially deadly; cave-ins, rattlesnakes, poisonous gases, and abandoned explosives lead the list of reasons to keep your distance. If this hike is beyond your fitness level, try the Keane Wonder Spring, below.

Keane Wonder Spring

2 miles RT. Easy. Access: The trailhead leads away from the Keane Wonder Parking Area in a northerly direction, away from the steeper mine hike.

This trail undulates gently across an alluvial fan and follows the pipeline from the spring that supplied water for the gold-mining operation. The smell of sulfur and piping calls of birds signal your arrival at the spring, which lies slightly uphill of the trail. A short walk beyond leads to cabin ruins and a mine shaft.

Mosaic Canyon

2.4 miles RT. Easy. Access: The trailhead is located at the end of a short, graded dirt road just east of Stovepipe Wells via Calif. 190.

This easy stroll requires a bit of rock scrambling into a canyon where water has polished the marble rock into white, gray, and black mosaics. The first mile is very easy, suitable for every skill level, and children will love running their hands over the water-smoothed rock walls. More adventurous climbers can continue up a series of chutes and dry waterfalls in the latter half of the hike.

Natural Bridge

1 mile RT. Moderate. Access: Located 15 miles south of Furnace Creek via Badwater Rd. and a 2-mile unpaved spur road suitable for passenger vehicles.

This short walk takes you into a colorful narrow canyon. The loose gravel underfoot makes for a tiring walk, but it's less than half a mile to the distinctive formation that gives the canyon its name: a rock bridge overhead, formed when rushing waters cut through the softer underlayer of rock.

Salt Creek Nature Trail

0.5 mile RT. Easy. Access: Salt Creek is located 14 miles north of Furnace Creek via Calif. 190 or 13 miles east of Stovepipe Wells, then down a 1-mile graded dirt spur road. Closed in summer.

A guided hike (leaflets are available for 50¢ from a stand at the trailhead) on a wooden boardwalk leads you along the unique salt marshes, pointing out unusual plants along the way. Watch also for the amazingly adaptive Salt Creek pupfish flashing about in the shallow water.

Sand Dunes

2 miles RT. Easy. Access: The trailhead is located 3 miles west of the Calif. 190 junction; it's indicated with a signed turnoff and has picnic tables and a rest room.

While not as majestic as the remote Eureka Dunes in northern Death Valley, these golden mounds off Scotty's Castle Road are easy to reach and fun to romp around on. There's no formal trail—simply explore to your heart's content; kids especially will enjoy a barefoot romp on the fine sand dotted with stands of mesquite. Don't forget an adequate supply of water; in the midday sun, the dunes get very hot.

Titus Canyon

3 miles RT. Easy. Access: The trailhead is up a signed dirt road off Scotty's Canyon Rd. (about 15 miles north of Calif. 190) that leads to the mouth of Titus Canyon, where a road for four-wheel-drive vehicles continues through to Nev. 374; the trail begins at the point where the road becomes one way coming toward you (from Nevada). Closed in summer.

As you hike, watch for vehicle traffic coming one way from the other direction. The canyon's rock walls are an amateur geologist's dream—layers of orange and black volcanic sediment streaked with threads of gleaming white calcite. Though you can augment this easy hike by continuing through the canyon, there's a broad pullout from the road at 1.5 miles; it's a good place to enjoy the view, and perhaps a picnic, before returning the way you came.

Ubehebe Crater

1.5 miles RT. Moderate. Access: The trailhead leads up from the parking area for Ubehebe Crater, which is 7 miles northwest of the Grapevine Ranger Station.

You get to the crater via a steep but plain trail that leads from the parking area, up to the crater's lip, around some of the contours, and past to several lesser craters. Black cinders and volcanic fragments cover the desolate countryside surrounding Ubehebe Crater, which erupted as recently as 1,000 years ago. Fierce winds can hamper your progress, but you'll get an exhilarating feeling, as though you're visiting another planet.

High-top boots or shoes are recommended for the pebbly path.

LONGER TRAILS

Golden Canyon

4.6 miles RT. Easy to moderate. Access: The trailhead is located at the parking lot for Golden Canyon along Calif. 178, about 2 miles south of the Furnace Creek Inn.

This trail's proximity to Furnace Creek, plus its varying degrees of difficulty, make it popular. Start by hiking along the once-paved route that allowed cars to drive into the canyon but was destroyed by flash flooding. Soon you'll be scrambling around the "badlands," yellowed hills of mud and silt deposited by ancient lakes. Those with more stamina can continue past towering Manly Beacon (a sandstone formation), across gullies and washes, and then steeply up to Zabriskie Point for panoramic views of the forbidding badlands.

Grotto Canyon

4 miles RT. Moderately difficult. Access: The trailhead is located 2.5 miles east of Stovepipe Wells on Calif. 190.

This trail is marked by deep "grottoes" in the rocks (smooth hollows formed by erosive floodwaters). The first mile follows a rugged gravel road up the canyon's alluvial fan; if you have an off-road vehicle, drive this portion as far as the wash. Continue on foot from there, as the canyon narrows and you begin to encounter the grottos, beyond which waterfalls trickle. The cool hidden grottos are a nice place to stop for a snack, sheltered from the sun.

Jayhawker Canyon

4.2 miles RT. Moderate. Access: The trailhead from Calif. 190, just west of the Emigrant Ranger Station.

This route follows the path of a desperate group of pioneers attempting to find a way out of Death Valley in 1849. The footing is treacherous in this debris-filled canyon, and several forks and tributaries can distract you from staying in the main wash. At the end of the trail lies a spring marking the Jayhawkers' camp, also a popular stopping place for the native Shoshone. Boulders in the area are marked with petroglyphs depicting bighorn sheep, along with the initials of several pioneers scratched into the rocks.

Telescope Peak

14 miles RT. 8,130 feet to 11,049 feet. Strenuous. Access: The trailhead is located at the Mahogany Flat Campground past the Wildrose Charcoal Kilns (only experienced drivers with high-clearance 4-wheel-drive vehicles should attempt the road).

A grueling 3,000-foot climb ultimately leads to the 11,049-foot summit, where you'll be rewarded with the view described thusly by one pioneer; "You can see so far, it's just like looking through a telescope." Snow-covered in winter, the peak is best climbed from May to November. Consult park rangers for current conditions and detailed advice—and *never attempt this climb alone.*

Wildrose Peak

8.4 miles RT. 6,890 feet to 9,060 feet. Strenuous. Access: The trailhead for this steep and strenuous climb is located at the Wildrose Charcoal Kilns, a historic point usually accessible by passenger vehicles (check with park rangers for road conditions before departing).

Mostly comprised of steady and unrelenting ascents, this hike has several level portions for rest stops. And you'll need them since you'll be climbing over 2,000 feet on the way to the 9,060-foot summit. Plants along the way include sage, ephedra, pinyon pines, and junipers; marvelous views take in the Panamint and Death Valleys as far as the Sierra. The windy peak is marked by a bronze USGS survey marker and a climbing register signed by other successful hikers. It's unwise to attempt this hike in winter or without obtaining a topographical map from the ranger station.

Especially for Kids

As in most national parks, Death Valley offers a **Junior Ranger Program** to help acquaint youngsters with the park's history, natural attractions, and desert safety. Booklets of educational puzzles, quizzes, and drawing exercises are available at all ranger stations; your kids can return them filled out and receive an official Junior Ranger badge.

Other Sports & Activities

Biking. Because 94% of the park is federally designated wilderness, cycling is allowed only on roads used by autos and not on hiking trails. Weather conditions between May and October make bicycling at the lower elevations ill-advised at times other than early morning.

There are no bike rentals available in the park, and given the park's isolation, the only practical option is to bring your own bike. You'll need a pretty rugged mountain bike to do most of these routes.

Good routes for bikers are **Racetrack** (28 miles, mainly level), **Greenwater Valley** (30 miles, mainly level), **Cottonwood Canyon** (20 miles), and **West Side Road** (40 miles, fairly level with some washboard sections). **Artists Drive** is 8 miles long, paved, with some steep uphills. A favorite is **Titus Canyon** (28 miles on a hilly road—it's highly recommended that you make this a one-way descent).

Camping

Death Valley offers little variety to those seeking conventional accommodations, but campers (tent, trailer, and RV) can expect to find more comforts than at most other desert parks. You should take special care, however, when selecting a campground. While most locations are closed seasonally to protect visitors from the harshest elements (only four campgrounds are open year-round), there's always a risk of unseasonably hot temperatures at the largely unshaded campgrounds on the valley floor, as well as early or late snow at remote mountain sites. Always inquire with the park ranger about current conditions before setting up camp.

Also remember that two campgrounds, Thorndike and Mahogany Flat, are reachable only with a four-wheel-drive vehicle. These (plus Emigrant and Wildrose) are free; overnight fees elsewhere range from $10 to $16. The only RV hookups are at Stovepipe Wells and at the Panamint Springs Resort (a commercial campground). There are no laundry facilities in the park.

Emigrant Campground, located 9 miles south west of Stovepipe Wells on Calif. 190, has 10 sites open from April through October. There are toilets and drinking water but few other facilities (there is a public telephone). This campground is free.

Furnace Creek Campground, located just north of the Furnace Creek Visitor Center, has 136 sites. Showers are available nearby (for a fee). There are no RV utility hookups, but there is a dump station. This campground is open year-round and charges $16 per site per night.

Mahogany Flats Campground, 38 miles south of Stovepipe Wells, off Trona-Wildrose Road, is only reachable by four-wheel-drive vehicle and open only from April through November. It has 10 spaces and charges no fee. There are pit toilets but no other facilities (including drinking water).

Mesquite Spring Campground, with 30 spaces, is 5 miles south of Scotty's Castle on Grapevine Road It charges $10 per night. There are flush toilets, an RV dump station, and drinking water, but no other facilities. It is open year-round.

The **Panamint Springs Resort** (☎ **702/482-7680**), located 30 miles west of Stovepipe Wells on Calif. 190, operates a campground with 40 spaces (12 with RV utility hookups) for $15 per night for the RV hookups, $8 for just a tent campsite.

There are flush toilets, drinking water, and showers. There is no RV dump station, however. It is open year-round. With Destinet out of the picture and no replacement chosen, this is the only campground in the park where you can currently reserve a space.

Stovepipe Wells Campground, has 200 spaces. There are 15 RV hookups and a dump station. You'll find flush toilets, drinking water, and nearby showers (for a fee). The campground charges $10 for a campsite, $15 if you want an RV utility hookup. It is open from October through April only.

Sunset Campground, located just 0.25 mile east of the Furnace Creek Ranch, has 1,000 spaces. There are toilets, drinking water, and nearby showers (for a fee). There is an RV dump station but no hookups. The fee is $10; it is open only from December through April.

Texas Spring, in the same area as the Sunset Campground, has 92 sites and 2 group sites. There are toilets, drinking water, and nearby showers (for a fee). There is a nearby RV dump station but no hookups. The fee is $10 per site for an individual site, $40 for a group site.

Thorndike Campground, which is 37 miles south of Stovepipe Wells, off the Trona-Wildrose Road, is reachable only by four-wheel-drive vehicle. It has eight primitive campsites with pit toilets but no other facilities, not even drinking water. It's open from March through November and is free.

Wildrose Campground, located 30 miles south of Stovepipe Wells off the Trona-Wildrose Road, has 30 sites. The campground has pit toilets and drinking water (from April to November only). The campground, however, is open year-round.

Reservations. Reservations for Furnace Creek and the group sites at Texas Spring can be made by calling the **National Park Reservation Service** at ☎ **800/365-CAMP** (2267). Payment can be made by DISC, MC, V, check, or money order. For reservations at privately owned **Panamint Springs,** call ☎ **702/482-7680.**

Accommodations

INSIDE THE PARK

Furnace Creek Inn

On Calif. 190, 1 mile south of the Furnace Creek Visitor Center (P.O. Box 1, Death Valley,

Campground	Elev.	Total Sites	RV Hookups	Dump Station	Toilets	Drinkin[g] Water
Emigrant	2,100	10	No	No	Yes	Yes
Furnace Creek	–196	136	No	Yes	Yes	Yes
*Mahogany Flat**	8,200	10	No	No	Yes	No
Mesquite Spring	1,800	30	No	Yes	Yes	Yes
Panamint Springs Resort	N/A	40	12	No	Yes	Yes
Stovepipe Wells	sea level	200	15	Yes	Yes	Yes
Sunset	–190	1,000	No	Yes	Yes	Yes
Texas Spring	sea level	94	No	Yes	Yes	Yes
*Thorndike**	8,200	8	No	No	Yes	No
Wildrose	4,100	30	No	No	Yes	Yes†

* Road not passable for trailers, campers, or motor homes. Passenger cars not advised; four-wheel-drive vehicle may be necessary.

CA 92328). ☎ **760/786-2345.** 66 units. A/C TV TEL. Oct–May $220–$300 double; June–Sept $140–$200 double. AE, DC, DISC, MC, V.

The Furnace Creek Inn is exceptional and exceptionally expensive, a 1930s resort whose charm has been successfully preserved. Like an oasis in the middle of stark Death Valley, the inn's red-tiled roofs and sparkling, spring-fed pool hint at the elegance within, where 66 deluxe rooms and suites have every modern amenity. Stroll the lush palm-shaded gardens before sitting down to a meal in the elegant dining room, where the food is excellent but the formality a bit out of place. Tennis on lighted courts and nearby golf and horseback riding are available; they even run a shuttle from the Furnace Creek private airstrip for well-heeled guests. *Reserve early:* The inn is booked solid year-round with American and European guests who appreciate a little pampering after a day spent in the park.

Furnace Creek Ranch

On Calif. 190, 1 mile south of the Furnace Creek Visitor Center (P.O. Box 1, Death Valley, CA 92328). ☎ **760/786-2345;** fax 760/686-9945. 224 units. A/C TEL. $85–$125 per unit. AE, DC, DISC, MC, V.

Though the Furnace Creek Ranch is run by the same folks who maintain the "swell-egant" Inn up the hill, the ranch is more down to earth, with 224 air-conditioned rustic cottages great for families. Though the setting feels like a summer camp, the amenities are complete, including a spring-fed pool, an 18-hole golf course, lighted tennis courts, and a selection of dining options (see below). Year-round rates depend on cabin size and placement.

Panamint Springs Resort

Calif. 190, 30 miles west of Stovepipe Wells (P.O. Box 395, Ridgecrest, CA 93556). ☎ **702/482-7680.** 14 rms. A/C. $50–$95. AE, MC, V.

The only lodging within the park not operated by the official concessionaire is the Panamint Springs Resort, across the Panamint Range and about a 45- to 60-minute drive west from Furnace Creek. A welcome change from the furious consumerism of Death Valley, this truly charming rustic motel has plain but clean rooms as well as a no-frills indoor/outdoor cafe and snack shop.

Showers	Fire Pits/ Grills	Laundry	Public Phone	Reserve	Fees	Open
No	No	No	Yes	No	Free	Apr–Oct
Nearby (fee)	Yes	Nearby	Yes	Yes	$16	Year-round
No	Yes	No	No	No	None	Mar–Nov
No	Yes	No	No	No	$10	Year-round
Yes	Yes	No	Nearby	Yes	$8/$15	Year-round
Nearby (fee)	Yes	No	Yes	No	$10/$15	Dec–Apr
Fee	No	No	No	No	$10	Dec–Apr
Fee	Yes	No	No	No**	$10/$40	Dec–Apr
No	Yes	No	No	No	No	Mar–Nov
No	Yes	No	No	No	No	Year-round

** Groups (only) may make reservations.
† April–November only.

The rooms have swamp coolers and can accommodate up to six.

Stove Pipe Wells Village

On Calif. 190 at Stovepipe Wells (Calif. 190, Death Valley, CA 92328). ☎ **760/786-2387;** fax 760/786-2389. 83 rms. A/C. $53–$76 double. AE, DC, DISC, MC, V.

The truly budget-conscious opt for Stove Pipe Wells Village, where 83 modest air-conditioned motel rooms surround a small pool. About 23 miles northwest of Furnace Creek, Stovepipe Wells has a general store, saloon, and dining room (see below). The rates are the same year-round, and all have two twin beds, two double beds, or one king.

NEAR THE PARK

Because accommodations in Death Valley are both limited and expensive, you might consider the money-saving (but inconvenient) option of spending a night in one of the two gateway towns: **Lone Pine** on the west side of the park, and **Baker** on the south. **Beatty, Nevada,** which has inexpensive lodging, is slightly more than an hour's drive from the park's center. Accommodations are limited to unremarkable motels. In Death Valley Junction, the restored **Amargosa Hotel** (☎ **760/852-4441**) offers 14 air-conditioned rooms in a historic out-of-the-way place, 40 minutes from Furnace Creek. Credit cards (MC, V) are accepted, and room rates are $35 to $55 for a double.

Dining

INSIDE THE PARK

Face it, you're a captive audience; there aren't many dining options inside the park, and most are run by the same concessionaire anyway. Here's a rundown of your choices.

There are three dining options at the **Furnace Creek Ranch,** all are relatively informal. The best and most economical is the **49'er Cafe,** a diner with better-than-average food and a widely varied menu. It's open daily from 7am to 9pm. The adjacent **Wrangler Steakhouse** offers an all-you-can-eat buffet for breakfast (6 to 9am), lunch (11am to 2pm), and dinner (3:30 to 5:30pm). The prices are higher than average, but the buffet is a wise choice for families with hearty eaters. From 6:30 to 9:30pm, the Wrangler reverts to table service, grilling steaks, ribs, and other satisfying specialties; the servings are generous, but the dinners pricey. All these places accept major credit cards (AE, DC, DISC, MC, V).

The **dining room** at the **Furnace Creek Inn** (☎ **760/786-2345**) is formal and expensive; the menu is varied, featuring elements of several continental and regional cuisines. While many travelers' budgets preclude splurging on such a meal, the peaceful setting and attentive service can be a welcome treat during otherwise exhausting travels through the park; it's also a nice excuse to see the inn's immaculate grounds. Breakfast, lunch, and dinner are served. The Sunday buffet brunch is truly an orgy of food. Reservations are necessary. Jackets are suggested for men at dinner. The dining room serves breakfast, lunch, and dinner, but closes from 2:30 to 5:30pm daily. Major credit cards (AE, DC, DISC, MC, V) are accepted.

There's a restaurant at **Stovepipe Wells,** kind of a cross between a camp dining room and a casual cafe. Plan carefully, because it closes between posted meal hours, leaving hungry travelers to scrounge at the convenience store across the street. It does accept the major credit cards (AE, DC, DISC, MC, V).

Other choices are a **snack bar** at **Scotty's Castle** and a rustic (and affordable) burgers-and-beer **cafe** at **Panamint Springs.**

Helpful hint: Meals and groceries are exceptionally costly inside the park due to the remote location. If possible, consider bringing a cooler with some snacks, sandwiches, and beverages to last the duration of your visit. Ice is easily obtainable, and you'll also be able to keep water chilled.

NEAR THE PARK

Too far away for a round-trip excursion once you're in Death Valley, **The Mad Greek** (☎ **760/733-4354**) in Baker is simply a must on the way there or home. Literally at the junction of I-15 and Calif. 127, this roadside treasure is an ethnic surprise beloved by many. White tiles and Aegean-blue accents complement a menu of traditional Greek specialties like souvlaki, spinach-and-feta spanikopita, stuffed grape leaves, green salad with tangy feta, exquisite pastries, and even Greek beer. The mile-long menu also includes traditional road fare, like hamburgers and hot sandwiches. The food is the main attraction, but travelers also know to "hold it" until they reach the Mad Greek's sparkling-clean rest rooms. Credit cards (AE, DISC, MC, V) are accepted.

Picnic & Camping Supplies

Within park boundaries are two sources of supplies. **Furnace Creek Ranch** has a market carrying a fairly wide selection of groceries and ice; propane gas is available at the adjacent service station. **Stovepipe Wells** offers ice, limited groceries, propane gas, and white gas.

Outside the park, if you want to stock up before entering, groceries and supplies are available in the towns of **Baker, Beatty, Shoshone,** and **Ridgecrest.** For visitors approaching on U.S. 395 from the south, Ridgecrest is your best choice—it's a sizable city with chain grocery stores, fast-food restaurants, and a selection of gas stations.

14

DENALI NATIONAL PARK

by Charles P. Wohlforth

DENALI (PRONOUNCED DEN-*al*-EE) NATIONAL PARK CONTAINS Mount McKinley, at 20,320 feet the tallest mountain in North America, but you don't need to go to the park to see the mountain, and most people don't see it even when they do go. And Denali encompasses a broad expanse of alpine tundra and taiga populated by bears, wolves, Dall sheep, caribou, moose, eagles, fox, beavers, and small mammals, but that's typical of much of interior and Arctic Alaska. And in and around the park, opportunities exist for river rafting, "flightseeing," hiking, and tourist activities—but again, you don't have to go to the park for that.

What makes Denali National Park a unique place to visit is the human management of the wilderness—in Denali, anyone, even for modest expense, can get into a pristine natural environment and see wildlife in its natural state. A single National Park Service decision makes that possible: The only road through the park is closed to the public. This means that to get into the park, you must ride a crowded bus over a dusty gravel road hour after hour, but it also means that the animals are still there to watch and their behavior remains essentially normal. From the window of the bus, you're likely to see grizzly bears doing what they would be doing even if you weren't there. It may be the only $20 safari in the world.

What's even more unique is that you can get off the bus pretty much whenever you want to and walk away from the road across the tundra, out of sight of the road, and be alone in a primeval wilderness utterly undisturbed by human development. Most anywhere else, it costs a lot of money or requires a lot of muscle and outdoors skill to get to places where you can do that. Unfortunately, most Denali visitors never take advantage of the opportunity. Being alone under God's big sky makes many people nervous, perhaps because most of us never have been really away from other people, much less apart from anything people have made. But that's the essence of Alaska—learning, deep down, how big creation is and how small you are, one more mammal on the tundra under the broad sky. Uniquely at Denali, you can be there, and then, when you're ready to return to civilization, you can just walk to the road and catch the next bus—they come every half hour.

It's little wonder that Denali is so popular when it offers such a valuable experience at such a low cost—or at least it wouldn't be a wonder if that were why it

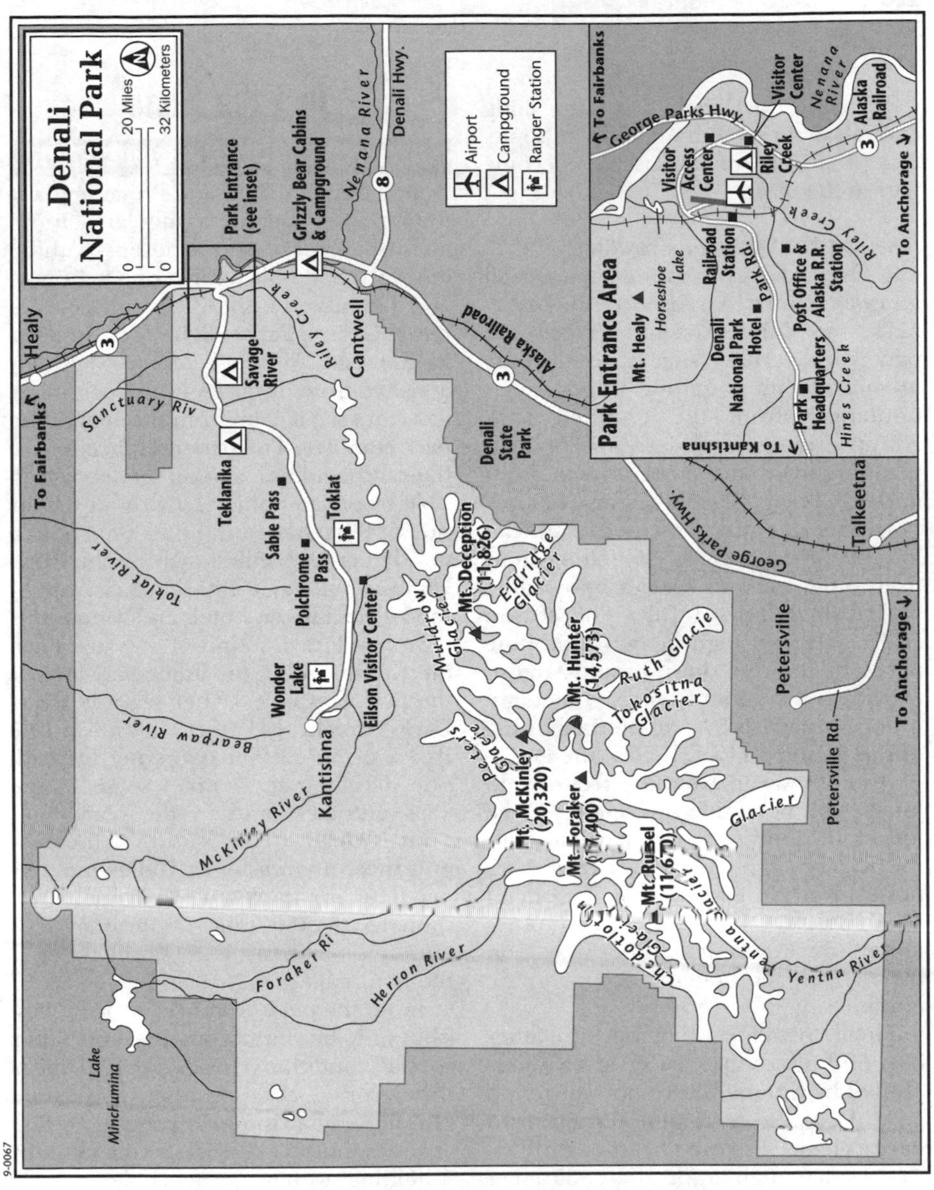

is so popular. As it happens, mass marketing may be the real reason. More than half a million visitors go annually during a 3-month season, many on package tours that rush them through so quickly the park becomes more a picture outside a window rather than an experience. Denali has become a thing people feel they must do, and seeing Mount McKinley is a thing they must do when they visit Denali. Since the mountain is usually shrouded in clouds, the chance that they'll succeed in that mission is probably less than one in three. So why spend so much money to stay at the ticky-tacky roadside development at the park's entrance and then to ride on a bus over a bumpy road for most of a day? A friend swears she overheard a tourist ask, as she boarded the train leaving Denali, "Why did they put the park way out here in the boondocks?"

Do come to Denali, but come long enough to do something, to learn something, and, in some sense, to become part of the place.

Avoiding the Crowds. Crowding is relative. Once you're out in the park, Denali is never crowded. A transportation bottleneck, the shuttle system, protects the park from overuse. What makes the busy season difficult is getting through that bottleneck from the crowded park entrance into the wilderness. For that, planning to avoid the busy season, from mid-May to mid-September, may help.

During the visitor season, you can improve your chances of getting away from others of your species by avoiding the peak month of July. The season really gets into high gear in mid-June and starts to wind down in mid-August, providing a month of relative quiet and often reduced prices at the beginning of the season and another at the end.

Another way to avoid the crowds is to book a stay in a wilderness lodge. Three lodges in Kantishna, listed below, have the right to carry clients to their businesses over the park road in buses and vans. Outside the park, several other lodges fly in clients. Either way, you bypass the bottleneck at the park entrance.

Finally, remember that there are other beautiful places that are relatively unexploited by visitors. You're not obliged to go to Denali to see alpine terrain or to have a chance of seeing bears or caribou. The Denali Highway, leading 135 miles east through the Alaska Range from Cantwell, 30 miles south of the park entrance, is in some ways more spectacular than the park road. Wrangell–St. Elias National Park, the nation's largest park, is barely used. The Richardson Highway and Steese Highway cross areas of broad, Arctic tundra with limitless vistas similar to those found in the park. The vast Arctic contains many more remote and inspiring vistas, if you can afford a flight to the North or a drive up the Dalton Highway, through the Brooks Range.

Just the Facts

GETTING THERE & GATEWAYS

Denali National Park and Preserve is a 6-million-acre, roughly triangular polygon about the size of Massachusetts, with an entrance 230 miles north of Anchorage and 120 miles south of Fairbanks on the paved **George Parks Highway** or the **Alaska Railroad.** Although Mount McKinley is visible from as far away as Anchorage, you can't see it at all from the area of the **park entrance.** The park entrance, site of the railroad depot and all services accessible by private vehicle, stands on the far side of the park from the mountain, in a wooded area. A mile north on the Parks Highway, along a cliff-sided canyon of the **Nenana River,** hotels and restaurants have developed a kind of seasonal town on private land in the immediate area of the park entrance. Other services are at **Carlo Creek,** 14 miles south on the Parks, or at another gathering of roadside development 7 miles south of the park entrance, and in the year-round town of **Healy,** 10 miles north of the park entrance. Increasingly, **Talkeetna** has become an alternative gateway, even though it's 150 miles from the park entrance by car, as it is physically closer to the mountain.

From the park entrance, a road accessible only by shuttle bus (except under special conditions) leads west 90 miles through the park, past a series of campgrounds and a visitor center, and ending at the **Kantishna district,** a collection of inholdings with wilderness lodges.

The Nearest Airports. **Anchorage** is the main entry hub for Alaska. It's served by several major carriers, primarily with connections through Seattle, including **United, Delta,** and **Alaska** airlines, the primary carrier to Alaska. You can also fly into **Fairbanks** on Alaska Airlines. You'll find toll-free numbers for all of these in the appendix.

Renting a Car. All the major car rental companies have outlets at the **Anchorage**

Airport (their names and toll-free numbers are given in the appendix). In **Fairbanks,** Avis and Hertz have outlets at the airport. Just expect to pay over $55 a day for your car rental.

By Car. Renting a car and driving from Anchorage will prove cheaper than taking the train for most parties. The drive is about 4½ hours from Anchorage, 2½ hours from Fairbanks, on a good two-lane highway. Many of the views along the Parks Highway are equal to the views on the train, but large stretches, especially in the Matanuska and Susitna valleys, near Anchorage, have been spoiled by ugly roadside development, which you don't see on the train. A long but spectacular detour around the mess leads through Hatcher Pass on a mountainous gravel road open only in the summer. Further north from Anchorage, the Parks Highway passes through Denali State Park. If the weather's clear, you can see Mount McKinley from the pullouts here. The state park also contains several campgrounds and hiking trails and a veterans memorial.

By Rail. The most popular way to get to Denali National Park is by train. The **Alaska Railroad,** P.O. Box 107500, Anchorage, AK 99510-7500 (☎ **800/544-0552** or 907/265-2494; Web site **www.alaska.net/~akrr**), which pioneered tourism to the park before the George Parks Highway was built in 1972, has daily service in the summer from Anchorage and Fairbanks. Trains leave both cities at 8:15am, arriving at the park from Anchorage at 3:45pm and from Fairbanks at noon, crossing and going on to the opposite city for arrival at 8:15pm in each. The fare from Anchorage to Denali is $99 one way. The full train runs only from mid-May to mid-September, with slightly lower fares in May and September than during the summer. During the winter, the Alaska Railroad runs a single passenger car from Anchorage to Fairbanks and back once a week. If you're here, ride it one way—it's a truly spectacular, truly Alaskan experience.

The advantages of taking the train to Denali are that it's a historic, unspoiled route through beautiful countryside; there's a good chance of seeing moose and caribou; it's fun and relaxing; there's commentary along the way; and the food on any of the three sets of cars is good. There are disadvantages, too. The train is more expensive. You can rent a car for 4 days and drive up for the same price as two one-way tickets on the train. It's slow, adding 3 hours to a trip from Anchorage to the park, and when it's late, it can be very late. And, once you arrive, you have to rely on shuttles and courtesy vans to get around outside the park—not a big drawback, since shuttles are frequent.

The Alaska Railroad's locomotives also pull two sets of cars with full domes owned by **Princess Cruises and Tours,** 2815 Second Ave., Suite 400, Seattle, WA 98121-1299 (☎ **800/835-8907**), and **Holland America–Westours/Gray Line of Alaska,** 300 Elliot Ave. W., Seattle, WA 98119 (☎ **907/277-5581**). Each provides separate, distinct service and operates independently, as described below. You can't walk from one kind of car to another. Fares are $129 on the Princess cars, and $125 on the Holland America–Westours cars; lodging packages are available.

The Princess and Holland America–Westours cars cater primarily to their cruise-ship and package customers, but do sell tickets to independent travelers. They offer a luxurious but controlled experience wherein each passenger has his or her own dome-car seat on a unique, beautifully appointed railroad car. You're expected to stay in your assigned seat and eat during a scheduled dining seating, and you may have to ride backward or sideways in cars designed with tables and living room–style furniture, and spend almost 8 hours sitting across a table from strangers whom you may or may not like.

The Alaska Railroad cars, on the other hand, are traditional railroad cars, with seats facing forward, and you can sit anywhere you want, move between cars and stand in the breezeway between cars, and eat when you want to. The food is not the luxurious fare the cruise lines strive for, but it's still quite good, served in an old-fashioned dining car with table cloths and flowers. A couple of dozen dome-car seats are available, with a 20-minute limit on staying in them—not the dome-to-yourself arrangement of the cruise-line cars. Well-trained guides provide intermittent commentary and answer questions in each car. Children will enjoy the Alaska Railroad cars more; adults can judge for themselves which approach is more appealing.

Between the two cruise-line car offerings, Princess's Midnight Sun Express Ultra Dome Rail Cars appeared clearly preferable to me. The decor was fresher and better maintained than in the Holland America–Westours cars, there was more headroom in the upstairs dome area, and rear platforms allowed passengers to get out of their seats and enjoy the fresh air. However, my personal preference would be the Alaska Railroad cars. Even if you can't sit in a dome the whole way, the windows still are large and clean, and I think half the fun of riding on a train is moving around and meeting a variety of people.

By Bus. Several van and bus services inexpensively connect Anchorage and Fairbanks to Denali. Most will carry bikes and other gear for an additional fee. **Alaska Direct Busline** (☎ **800/770-6652** or 907/277-6652) charges $45 from Anchorage to Denali and $25 from Fairbanks to the park. The **Alaska Backpacker Shuttle** (☎ **800/266-8625** or 907/344-8775) carries passengers from Anchorage in a van that leaves from the hostel at 700 H St., downtown. The fare is $35 one way, $60 round-trip. **Fireweed Express** (☎ **888/505-8267** or 907/452-0521) offers van service starting from Fairbanks for $25 one way, $40 round-trip, picking up at the visitor center, among other places.

GETTING INFORMATION BEFORE YOUR TRIP

To get information before you leave, write the **Superintendent, Denali National Park,** P.O. Box 9, Denali Park, AK 99755 (☎ **907/683-2294**).

The National Park Service's Web site (**www.nps.gov/dena/**) provides a free map and lots of information.

For general information on traveling to Alaska, contact the **Alaska Division of Tourism,** Dept. 801 (P.O. Box 110801), Juneau, AK 99811-0801 (☎ **907/465-2010**), which will send you a free *Official State Guide and Vacation Planner* with information on traveling to all parts of Alaska, including advertising from many tourism-related businesses.

VISITOR CENTERS

The **park visitor center,** to the right less than a mile from the Parks Highway intersection, is the place to pick up bus tickets and campground permits from a desk staffed by ARA employees (the company that handles all Denali reservations). There's usually a long line for walk-in purchases, but a will-call desk speeds things up if you have reservations. Rangers roving the center and at an information desk can answer questions before you waste a lot of time in line; they also provide rudimentary information on local businesses other than ARA. The visitor center is open from 7am to 8pm daily.

Inside the park, there is a visitor center at **Eielson** (at 66 miles) and ranger stations at **Toklat** (53 miles) and **Wonder Lake** (95 miles).

You can also get questions answered at the interagency **Alaska Public Lands Information Center** (☎ **907/271-2737** in Anchorage, or 907/456-0527 in Fairbanks). The visitor center also has an auditorium showing a slide show and a bookstore with maps and publications. There's a neat little area for kids. Rangers staff a backcountry permit desk (see below for information).

ENTRANCE FEES

The Park Service charges an entrance fee to come into Denali National Park, but there is no gate, and no one collects the fee or asks for a ticket or receipt to show you've paid it. When you book a campground site or a bus ride, the fee is automatically added to your bill. Individual fees are $5, $10 for families, and they're good for 7 days. Annual passes are available, but are unlikely to be worthwhile unless you're planning more than three visits, each separated by more than a week.

Fees for the various bus trips are described in "Regular Shuttles: A Summary," below.

CAMPING PERMITS & FEES

Each Park Service campground has different fees, regulations, and access limitations. All sites must be reserved, except the Morino Backpacker Campground, which has a self-registration system and is only for people without vehicles. The Sanctuary and Igloo campgrounds can be reserved only in person and sites may not be available when you arrive, so it's wise to at least start your stay with reservations at another campground.

There's a one-time reservation fee of $4 per campground in addition to the campground permit fees. Canceling or changing camping reservations carries a fee of $6 per site and is possible only up to 2 days before the reservation. When you make your reservation, you'll receive a confirmation in the mail or by fax. Take that document to the visitor center to pick up your camping permit.

The visitor center is open 7am to 8pm. If you won't make it by 8pm you must call ☎ **907/683-1266** to avoid losing your site. Fees and regulations for individual campgrounds are in the "Campground" chart, below. Descriptions are in the Camping section, below. Reservation procedures are given above. To get beyond the 14-mile checkpoint, you need to ride on the camper bus or go by bicycle. The camper bus fare is $15.

WHO CAN DRIVE THE PARK ROAD

Lodges in Kantishna can use the park road to bring in customers, but everyone else is under strict controls. You can drive past Mile 14 on the park road only under certain circumstances: (1) You have a 3-day camping permit at Teklanika Campground (you must remain parked at the campground for the entire 3 days); (2) you are a credentialed professional photographer or researcher with a special permit; or (3) it is the last few days in September and you have won a permit in a lottery that allows 1,600 cars free passage on the road. After the 4 days of permit driving are over, the road is open to anyone as far as Mile 30 until the snow flies; then it's maintained only as far as the headquarters, 3 miles from the entrance.

SEASONS & CLIMATE

The park is populated by people beginning in mid-May, when there still is some snow; the humans migrate south again in mid- to late September, when winter is closing in. In the off-season only a few dozen residents remain—caretakers who watch over the hotels and other buildings and sled-dog-driving rangers who patrol the backcountry.

May is iffy at Denali, but fall is a wonderful time to go. The weather gets nippy at night and there can be surprise snowfalls, but rain is less likely and the trees and tundra turn wonderful colors. By early September, visitors are so few that the park no longer takes telephone reservations. By mid-September, private cars can drive on the park road for 4 days—the Park Service holds a lottery to determine who will get that treat.

USEFUL PUBLICATIONS

You may want a copy of Kim Heacox's worthwhile booklet ***Denali Road Guide,*** available for $5 at the visitor center bookstore, published by the **Alaska Natural History Association,** 401 W. First Ave.,

First to the Top

On September 27, 1906, renowned world explorer Dr. Frederick Cook announced to the world by telegraph that he had reached the summit of Mount McKinley after a lightning-fast climb, covering 85 miles and 19,000 vertical feet in 13 days with one other man, a blacksmith, at his side. On his return to New York, Cook was lionized as a conquering explorer and published a book of his summit diary and photographs. Even today, the Frederick Cook Society meets regularly to memorialize and celebrate the deed.

They spend even more effort trying to convince the rest of the world that it wasn't just a huge hoax.

In 1909, Cook again made history, announcing that he had beat Robert Peary to the North Pole. Both returned to civilization from their competing treks at about the same time. Again Cook was the toast of the world. Then his Eskimo companions mentioned that he'd never been out of sight of land, and his story began to fall apart. After being paid by Peary to come forward, Cook's McKinley companion also recanted. (It turns out Peary probably also faked his pole discovery.) A year later, Cook's famous summit photograph was re-created on a peak 19 miles away and 15,000 feet lower than the real summit.

In 1910, four prospectors from Fairbanks took a more Alaskan approach to the task. Without fanfare, they marched up the mountain carrying a large wooden pole they could plant on top to prove they'd made it. But on arriving at the top, they realized that they'd climbed the slightly shorter north peak. Weather closed in, so they set up the pole there and descended. Then, when they got back to Fairbanks, no one could see the pole and they were accused of trying to pull off another hoax. In 1913, Episcopal missionary Hudson Stuck was the first to reach the real summit—and reported he saw the pole on the other peak.

Since then, some 18,000 climbers have attempted McKinley, around 10,000 have made the summit, and more than five dozen climbers have died trying. Hundreds more try every year, flying to the Kahiltna Glacier from Talkeetna and then taking about a month to reach the top and get back down. Altitude and weather are the primary killers and deterrents to those who don't reach the summit.

No one has managed to re-create the feat Frederick Cook claimed to his death to have accomplished. But the 150 members of the Frederick Cook Society, based in New York, fight on to clear his name and establish Cook as the first to the Pole and the top of North America's tallest mountain. And they continue to gather evidence to discredit Peary, charging that Cook's difficulties were caused by a conspiracy of Peary supporters. As recently as 1994, the society funded an expedition to retrace part of Cook's route and validate his photographs and diaries.

Ninety years after Cook's telegram, the world isn't listening anymore.

(I am indebted to Dermot Cole's article on Cook in the April 1995 issue of *Alaska* magazine.)

Anchorage, AK 99501 (☎ **907/274-8440**). It provides a milepost commentary you can follow as you ride the shuttle bus.

The same firm publishes guides to Denali birds, mammals, geology, and trails. Most shuttle-bus drivers do a good job of providing commentary, too. If you'll be doing any extensive day hiking, you may also want to bring a detailed topographical map printed on waterproof plastic (available for $8.99

from the visitor center) and a compass; if you're just going to walk a short distance off the road you won't need such preparations.

PLANNING A VISIT TO DENALI

I have always enjoyed traveling without an itinerary, so you can believe me when I say that you *must* plan a trip to Denali National Park and reserve all accommodations, campsites, and trips into the park well in advance—for mid-July peak travel, make reservations by May. The park hotel is sometimes booked up by December for midsummer. Travelers who just show up at the visitor center without any reservations often have to spend at least a day, and probably 2, outside the park before they can get a seat on a shuttle bus, a campground site, or a backcountry permit. It's quite a letdown to arrive at the park for a wilderness experience and have to spend the first few hours standing in line at the always-crowded visitor center trying to buy a bus ticket for 2 days later. Since it can be difficult to know before you've been there exactly what you want to do, I've tried to help by preparing some sample plans for visitors with different budgets and degrees of "roughing it."

If you intend to do backcountry camping and exploring on your own, be sure to check out "Exploring the Backcountry," below for essential information.

CHOOSING AN ITINERARY

Pampered Exploration. Arrive by train at the park, checking into accommodations either at the park, a mile north, or in Healy—shuttles and courtesy vans will get you around. Attend a ranger talk, the *Cabin Nite* dinner-theater show, or go on a short nature walk around the park hotel in the evening. Get to bed early, and the next morning take a shuttle bus before 7am into the park, riding to the Eielson Visitor Center to see the terrain and animals, and possibly to get a view of the mountain, arriving there in late morning. Now ride partway back toward the entrance before getting off the bus at a place of your choosing for a walk and to eat the bag lunch you've brought along with you (pack all trash out, of course), or take one of the Park Service guided walks. After enjoying the wilderness for a few hours, head back on the bus, finishing a long day back at the hotel. Next day try a rafting ride, flightseeing trip, or other activity near the entrance to the park before reboarding the train.

Family Camping & Exploring. Arrive at the park entrance by car with your camping gear and food for a couple of nights. Camp that evening at the Riley Creek Campground near the visitor center and enjoy the evening ranger program or the lecture at the park hotel, or take one of the short hikes near the park entrance. Next day, catch a shuttle bus or camper bus into the park to one of the campgrounds there—either set up camp early at the eastern end of the park and then ride west for sightseeing, or ride the bus all the way to the Wonder Lake Campground. Hike around the campground, or take the bus to one of the broad vistas of alpine tundra and explore. Next day, take the bus ride through the park to see the wildlife, hike the backcountry, then head back to the campground for another night. Your final evening, spend the night at a hotel in Healy for a shower and a rest. Add a day outside the park, if you want, for rafting or horseback riding.

Outdoors Adventure. Arrive by train, bus, or car with your backpack, camping gear, and food for at least several days' hiking. Go immediately to the visitor center to orient yourself to the backcountry-permit process, buying the information you need for your trek (see "Exploring the Backcountry," later in this chapter) and choose the unit area that looks most promising. Backcountry permits cannot be reserved in advance, only in person for the next day, and they go fast. If you're lucky, permits will be left for the day after you arrive; more likely, you'll need to camp at the Morino Backpacker

Campground, 1.9 miles on the park road from the highway, and arrive at the visitor center by the 7am opening to get your permit for the following day. Now you've got another day to wait; if you've reserved a shuttle-bus seat, you can get a preview of the park and see some wildlife, or outside the park, go on a rafting trip. The next morning you can start your backcountry hike, taking the camper bus to your unit, then traveling for up to 2 weeks in a huge area of wilderness reserved almost exclusively for your use.

Wilderness Lodges. For those who can afford it, this may be the best way to see Denali. The lodge will fly you out—or, if it's in Kantishna, drive you through the park—and you'll immediately be away from the crowds in remote territory. The lodges all have activities and guides to get you out into the wilderness. If you're not staying in Kantishna, you may want to schedule a day to ride the shuttle bus into the park to see the mountain and wildlife anyway, with an evening in a hotel near the park or in Healy.

The Talkeetna Option. Drive only as far as Talkeetna, about 110 miles north of Anchorage, and board a flightseeing plane from there to the park, perhaps landing on a glacier on Mount McKinley itself. You'll stand a better chance of seeing the mountain than anyone else, since the weather tends to be better on the south side and you won't have to go on a certain, prearranged day when the weather may be poor. You'll also save yourself hours of driving to the park and the bus ride into the park. But you'll miss the wildlife-viewing opportunities that can be had only on the ground in the park. See the Talkeetna section at the end of this chapter.

Climbing Mount McKinley. McKinley, because of its altitude and weather, is among the world's most challenging climbs. Every year experienced climbers die—most years, several. If you're looking here for advice, you're certainly not up to an unguided climb. A guided climb is a challenging and expensive month-long endeavor for experienced climbers in excellent condition. Climbs generally start with a flight from Talkeetna to a Kahiltna Glacier base camp. You must preregister at least 60 days before your departure with the Park Service's **Talkeetna Ranger Station,** P.O. Box 588, Talkeetna, AK 99676 (☎ **907/733-2231**). It also can provide names of qualified guides. There's a $150-per-climber fee to help cover the cost of administering the mountaineering program.

MAKING RESERVATIONS

Most of the Park Service's dealings with the public are handled by **ARA's Denali Park Resorts,** P.O. Box 87, Denali Park, AK 99755, or 241 W. Ship Creek Ave., Anchorage, AK 99501 (☎ **800/622-7275** or 907/272-7275; fax 907/264-4684). ARA also operates the buses and handles reservations for seats, for sites at the Park Service campgrounds (except the self-serve Morino Backpacker Campground), and for the only hotel within the park, as well as reserving rooms in its two other hotels outside the park and booking rafting trips and a dinner-theater show.

Destinations in Travel, P.O. Box 76, Denali National Park, AK 99755 (☎ **800/354-6020** or 907/683-1422), takes care of reservations for independent travel at Denali as well as arranging park and outdoor-oriented trips all over the state.

If you have limited time, plan your visit around your bus and campground reservations, making them well in advance. Hotel reservations, while also tight, are easier to get and less important to the purpose of your visit. Space loosens up considerably in the early and late season.

How the System Works. Here's the system for reservations: 40% of the available shuttle-bus seats and campsites (except at Morino, Sanctuary River, and Igloo Creek campgrounds) are available for reservation by fax or mail starting December 1 the preceding year, and by phone daily between 7am and 5pm Alaska time, starting sometime in February. Some years, this number has been perpetually busy. Fax requests, which can be sent 24 hours a day until 2 days before the reservation, may be your best shot. The Web site has a fax form, or make your own, including the dates, times, and campgrounds you want, alternative dates, names and ages of the people in your party, entrance fees (see above), $4 reservation fee, and an American Express, Discover, MasterCard, or Visa card number, with expiration. You don't have to figure out the total. You can pay by check as well if reserving by mail. A confirmation is sent by mail or fax within 2 days.

Beginning 2 days in advance, the remaining 60% of the shuttle and campground spots are available in person only, at the visitor center, and are quickly booked up. When you get to the front of the line, if there's still a night available 2 days hence, you can book that night and book up to 14 continuous nights afterward at that campground or any other. (A backcountry permit qualifies to keep the 14 days continuous, but 14 days of camping or backcountry time is all you can have all year, total.) Sometimes less desirable shuttle times, with departures later in the day, remain available even until the day of departure.

The doors of the visitor center open at 7am, and in the peak season the line is already in place when they do, forming as early as 6am.

Under this system, if you arrive without reservations, you must get to the visitor center early and take what you can get. Even then, you may have to wait 2 days before staying at a park campground or riding the bus. That means spending your time outside the park in private accommodations.

The Park Service has worked on improving the process, but still it's basically a rationing system to allocate a scarcity of seats and sites. Those who make reservations get first dibs, and the rest are weeded out according to their level of their desire through the frustration and delays of the system.

On (& Off) the Bus

Your visit to Denali will likely revolve around your ride on the shuttle bus into the park to see the wildlife and get out for a walk in the wilderness. Some planning will make it a more comfortable ride.

ABOUT THE SHUTTLES

If you drive to the park, you'll still need to take the shuttle bus, described below, to get into its heart.

If you take the train or bus, you'll find that virtually all accommodations have arrangements to get you around, although this becomes less convenient as you get farther from the park entrance. If your hotel doesn't have a courtesy van of its own, there usually is a scheduled shuttle. ARA operates a bus that carries guests from its Denali Park Resort hotels, a mile north and 7 miles south of the park, to the park entrance. You can use the bus even if you're not staying at an ARA hotel—have the desk at your hotel call for a pickup. You can also get around on a rented bike. See "Other Sports & Activities," below.

For a summary of the kinds of bus trips and fares available in Denali, see "Regular Shuttles: A Summary," below.

PLANNING FOR YOUR SHUTTLE TRIP

You can buy shuttle tickets to the Toklat (pronounced *toe*-klat) River, 53 miles into the park; the Eielson (*aisle*-son) Visitor Center at 66 miles; Wonder Lake at 85 miles; or Kantishna, at about 95 miles. Of course, you have to go both ways unless you have a campground reservation, a backcountry permit, or accommodations in Kantishna—which means that you're in for a long drive.

If you don't get off the bus along the way, the round-trip takes 6½ hours to Toklat, 8 hours to Eielson, and 11 hours to Wonder Lake. The Park Service shuttles don't make 1-day round-trips to Kantishna.

In choosing your destination, you need to balance your stamina, your desire to save time for a day hike, and your desire to see wildlife. In the early morning, people often see moose and black bear on the first part of the road. In the summer, brown bear are seen most in the higher country, beyond Toklat, which also is the best area for caribou, but in the fall berry season, the grizzlies show up all along the drive. The best views of McKinley show up after Mile 61, also beyond Toklat. The mountain is most likely to be visible in the morning, as clouds often pile up during the day. Going beyond Eielson to Wonder Lake provides more amazing views, including a land-covered glacier and many classic images of Mount McKinley.

In general, however, I think Eielson is the best destination for most people, offering both the chance to see the mountain and some wildlife while leaving some time to get out and walk.

Reserve your shuttle ticket for as early as you can stand to get up in the morning. This strategy will give you more time for day hikes and enhance your chances of seeing the mountain and wildlife. Many animals are more active in the morning, especially on hot days. The first bus leaves the visitor center at 5am, the next at 6am, and then every half hour until the 2:30pm bus, which gets back at 10:30pm. By taking an early bus, you can get off along the way for a hike, then walk back to the road and get the next bus that comes along with a spare seat. If you were to take the 5am bus, you'd have 9½ hours of slack time before you'd have to catch the last bus heading east. (To be on the safe side, don't push it to the very last bus.) The sun won't set until after 11pm May to July, so there'll be plenty of light. If you need to get back to the park entrance at a certain hour, leave yourself plenty of time, because after getting off your eastbound bus, you can't reserve seats going back the other way, and you may have to wait for a bus with room to take you.

Here's the hard part for families: Young children will go nuts on an 8-hour bus ride, and often can't pick out the wildlife—this isn't a zoo, and most animals blend into their surroundings. Older children also have a hard time keeping their patience on these trips, as do many adults. The only solution is to get off the bus and turn your trip into a romp in the heather. When you've had a chance to revive, catch the next bus. Besides, just because you buy a ticket to Eielson doesn't mean that you have to go that far. Young children need car seats, which you can borrow from the Park Service.

Shuttle-bus tickets can be canceled only with 2 days' advance notice, and then at a cost of $6 each. The weather is unpredictable that far in advance. If it's rainy, your chances of seeing wildlife are reduced and your chance of seeing Mount McKinley nil. Don't lose hope, however, as the park is large and the weather can be different at the other end of your long drive; besides, there's nothing you can do about it. Dry, overcast weather is best for wildlife watching.

SHUTTLE ADVICE

Before you leave for the visitor center to get on your shuttle bus, you need a packed lunch and plenty of water; you should be wearing sturdy walking shoes and layers of warm and cooler clothing with rain gear packed; you should have binoculars or a spotting scope at the ready; and you should have insect repellent handy.

There are no reserved seats on the bus. The left side has the best views on the way out.

Shuttle-bus etiquette is to yell out when you see wildlife. The driver will stop and everyone will rush to your side of the bus. After you've had a look, give

Regular Shuttles: A Summary

◆ The **ARA courtesy shuttle** links hotels (1 mile north, 7 miles south, and within the park) to the park entrance. It operates on a continuous loop and is free. It requires no ticket or reservations.

◆ The **Front-country shuttle** links facilities within park to the entrance area. The route includes the main visitor center, Riley Creek Campground, train depot, and Park Hotel. It operates on a continuous loop and is free, requiring no ticket or reservations.

◆ The **Camper shuttle** provides access to campgrounds beyond the park entrance. The route operates from the main visitor center to Wonder Lake Campground, 85 miles into the park. It runs several times a day, but check with the park for an exact schedule. The cost is $15 adults, $7.50 children 13 to 16, free children 12 and under.

◆ The **Backcountry shuttle** (or just "the shuttle") provides general access to the park and wildlife viewing; there is limited commentary, depending on the driver; no food service is available. The route goes from the main visitor center as far as Kantishna, 95 miles away through the park. The shuttle runs every 30 minutes to **Eielson Visitor Center,** every hour to **Wonder Lake,** less frequently to **Kantishna.** The cost is $20 to Eielson, $26 to Wonder Lake, $30 to Kantishna; children 13 to 16 are half price, children 12 and under free.

someone else a chance to look out your window or to get a picture. Try to be quiet and don't stick anything out of the bus, as that can scare away the animals. Of course, you have to stay on the bus when animals are present. Most buses will see grizzly bears, caribou, Dall sheep, and moose, and occasionally wolves, but, as one driver said, the animals aren't union workers, and it's possible that you won't see any at all.

THE SHUTTLE ROUTE

Here are some of the highlights along the road (check the visitor center or the Park Service information handouts to confirm times of the guided walks):

Mile 9. In clear weather, this is the closest spot to the park entrance with a view of Mount McKinley. This section also is a likely place to see moose.

Mile 14. The end of the paved road at the Savage River Bridge. This generally is as far as private vehicles can go. A Park Service checkpoint stops anyone who doesn't have a proper permit. A good picnic spot.

Mile 17. The Park Service discourages hiking here due to damage to the ground cover, but Primrose Ridge is an attractive spot for a walk. The portable toilets are as far as the Natural History Tour bus goes.

Mile 30. A large rest stop overlooking the Teklanika River has flush toilets, the last until the Eielson Visitor Center. The Teklanika, like many other rivers on Alaska's glacier-carved terrain, is a braided river—a relatively small stream wandering in a massive gravel stream bed. It's thought that the riverbed was created by water from fast-melting glaciers at the end of the last ice age.

Mile 33. Craggy Igloo Mountain is a likely place to see Dall sheep. Without binoculars, they'll just look like white dots. Heathery, open terrain suitable for an outing.

Mile 37.5. Tattler Creek, a good place for a steep day hike to see sheep and maybe bears.

Miles 38–43. Sable Pass, a critical habitat area for bears, is closed to people. A half-eaten sign helps explain why. Bears show up here mostly in the fall. This is the start of the road's broad alpine vistas.

Mile 46. The top of 5-mile-wide Polychrome Pass, the most scenic point on the ride. Caribou sometimes pass in a great valley framed by mountains of colored rock—they look the size of ants from the mountainside rest stop. Another toilet break.

Mile 53. The Toklat River, another braided river, is a flat plain of gravel with easy walking. The river bottom is habitat for bears, caribou, and wolves. A ranger leads a hike here of up to 2 hours, the Toklat Trek—check the visitor center for times.

Mile 58. Highway Pass, the highest point on the road. In good weather, dramatic views of Mount McKinley start here. The alpine tundra to the Eielson Visitor Center is inviting for walking.

Mile 64. Thorofare Pass, where the road becomes narrow and winding, is a good area to look for bear and caribou. Bus drivers know best where the animals are on any particular day; they exchange information among themselves.

Mile 66. The Eielson Visitor Center, the end of most bus trips, has flush toilets, a covered picnic area, and a small area of displays where rangers answer questions. Among the displays is one explaining why you probably can't see the mountain from this best of vantage points, just 33 miles from its summit. Mount McKinley creates its own weather, and is visible about a third of the time in the summer. Starting late in June, a ranger-guided tundra walk occurs daily at 1:30pm, lasting no more than an hour. If you leave the bus here for a hike, you can get a ride back later by signing up on the standby list kept by a ranger.

Mile 68.5. The incredibly rugged terrain to the north is the earth and vegetation covering Muldrow Glacier. The road comes within a mile of its face, then continues through wet, rolling terrain past beaver ponds, and finally descends into a small spruce patch near Mile 82.

Mile 86. Wonder Lake Campground, the closest road point to Mount McKinley, 27 miles away. Some buses continue another half hour to Kantishna.

Organized Tours & Ranger Programs

BUS TOURS

In addition to the park shuttles, ARA also operates narrated bus tours, booked mostly with package visitors.

The Natural History Tour provides just a taste of the park, going 17 miles down the park road. It's a 3-hour guided bus tour, leaving from the visitor center. It operates three times daily and costs $34 for adults, half price for children.

The Wildlife Tour goes to Toklat when the mountain is hidden by clouds, and 8 miles farther, to Highway Pass, when it is visible. Food is provided, but you can't get off the bus along the way, and the route skips the beautiful grizzly and caribou habitat toward the Eielson Visitor Center. The tour lasts 7 hours and leaves from the visitor center twice daily. The cost is $58 for adults, half price for children.

Also, the Kantishna Roadhouse (listed below under "Wilderness Lodges") offers a 190-mile, 1-day marathon with lunch and a dogsled and gold panning program at the halfway mark, at the lodge. It's well done, with commentary, but you can't get off the bus along the way, and the return trip may be too rushed to stop for all wildlife sightings.

They are not affiliated with the park or the main concessionaire, ARA, so you have to book directly through the lodge. The cost is $99.

FLIGHTSEEING

Getting a good, close look at Mount McKinley itself is best accomplished by air. Frequently, when you can't see McKinley from the ground, you can see it from above the clouds. It's an impressive mountain, standing huge and white far above most of the surrounding terrain. The best flights take at least 90 minutes and circle McKinley.

Denali Air (☎ **907/683-2261**) has an office in the Nenana Canyon and flight operations at Mile 229.5 of the Parks Highway. An hour-long flight going within a mile of the mountain costs $150. **Denali Wings** (☎ **907/683-2245**), operating out of Healy, has similar rates, and is half price for kids 14 and under with an adult.

Era Helicopters (☎ **800/843-1947** or 907/683-2574; e-mail fltsg@era-aviation.com) has hourly flights for $179, including van pickup from the hotels. The drawback of a helicopter is you can't get near wildlife because the aircraft is so noisy. They also offer guided hiking with a helicopter drop-off outside the park boundaries for $265. See the end of this chapter for flightseeing from Talkeetna.

GUIDED HIKES

The Park Service offers several guided hikes out in the park, beyond the 14-mile checkpoint. The daily Discovery Hike lasts 4 hours and goes somewhere different every day. You need to wear hiking shoes or boots and bring food, water, and rain gear. A special bus carrying the hikers leaves the visitor center at 8am, starting in mid-June. Reserve a place in advance. The Toklat Trek is an irregularly scheduled ranger-led walk in the Toklat River stream bed. The Tundra Walk, at 1:30pm daily starting in late June, is a short guided stroll from the Eielson Visitor Center, at Mile 66 on the park road. Check in at the visitor center for late word on all the hikes before heading out on a long bus trip.

Ranger Programs & Activities

The Park Service offers lectures, guided hikes (see the section above), and a sled-dog demonstration at the park entrance to keep you entertained and interpret the park while you wait for a bus or permit. Pick up a copy of the park newspaper, *Denali Alpenglow,* at the visitor center for current offerings and times.

Dogsled Demonstration. In the winter, rangers patrol the park by dogsled, as they have for decades. In the summer, to keep the dogs active and amuse the tourists, they run a sled on wheels around the kennel and a ranger gives a talk two to three times a day. Although there's no substitute for seeing dogs run on snow, this is as close as you'll get in the summer. It was the highlight of my 3-year-old's trip to Denali. A free bus leaves the visitor center for each show, at the kennels near the headquarters at Mile 3.4 on the park road. Or you can join a guided 2-mile hike at the visitor center, which heads up the Rock Creek Trail to arrive at the kennels for each dogsled show.

Hotel & Visitor Center Programs. Rangers offer a talk and film at 1:30pm daily, and a lecture, possibly with slides, at 8pm, in the auditorium at the park hotel. There are ranger talks at the visitor center auditorium at 11am, 1:30pm, and 8pm.

Day Hikes

The Park Service is making a concerted effort to discourage the making of trails in the tundra or taiga of the park proper, but there are six easy, well-maintained trails around the park entrance area, the longest of which is the Mount Healy Overlook, a 5-mile round-trip. The others are strolls of 2 miles or less. A trail guide of sorts is printed in the *Denali Alpenglow* park newspaper, handed out by the Park Service; "The Nature of Denali," available at the visitor center, is a natural-history guide to the trails.

Exploring the Backcountry

Trekking the backcountry on a multiday backpacking journey is challenging and rugged, but also the most authentic way to see the park and understand its meaning. Only people with strong outdoor skills who are in good physical condition should attempt a strenuous backcountry overnight, however, as there are no trails or other people to guide you. For this reason, I haven't included a list of needed gear and supplies.

You must be flexible about where you're going and be prepared for any kind of terrain, because you can't choose the backcountry unit you will explore until arriving at the backcountry desk at the visitor center and finding out what's available. This information, and a map of the units, is posted on a board behind the desk. Groups of four or more may have a hard time finding a place to hike, but there's almost always *somewhere* to go. A couple of rangers are there to help you through the process.

The alpine units are most popular. That's where you get broad views and can cross heathery valleys walking in any direction. But to go far, you'll also have to be ready to climb over some rugged, rocky terrain, and the tundra itself is deceptively difficult walking—it's soft and hides ankle-turning holes. The wooded units are least popular, since bushwhacking through overgrown land is anything but fun. The best routes for making time here and anywhere in the Alaska Bush are along the braided river valleys and stream beds. You need to be ready for a lot of stream crossings.

You can only reserve permits 1 day in advance, but you can reserve permits for continuation of your trip for up to 14 days at the same time. Units that aren't contiguous to the park road are more likely to be available, because you can't expect to make it that far on the first night of a hike. Because of the way the system is set up, the first night of a trip is the hard one to get; after that, each night gets progressively easier. You'll have to take the camper bus to get to your backcountry unit.

Before you decide to go to Denali, however, you may want to broaden your thinking—if you're up to a cross-country hike without a trail, there are tens of millions of acres in Alaska available for backpacking that don't require a permit. Check with the Alaska Public Lands Information Center in Anchorage or Fairbanks for ideas about road-accessible alpine wilderness in Gates of the Arctic National Park, on the Denali Highway; in Wrangell–St. Elias National Park; and elsewhere.

BACKCOUNTRY PERMITS

The permit system for staying overnight in the undeveloped backcountry is onerous enough to weed out those who aren't serious about a wilderness experience.

Permits are free, but can be obtained only 24 hours in advance and only in person at the backcountry desk in the visitor center. Since the unit areas book up quickly during the summer season, you may have to wait outside the park before you can start your hike. Camping at the Morino Backpacker Campground during the wait is a good, inexpensive choice that doesn't require advance reservations.

The park is divided into 43 backcountry units, 29 of which are accessible from the park road. For your first night, you have to stay in one of these 29, as it isn't practical in 1 day to get into the park and hike across a roadside unit to camp in a unit that's off the road. Each unit generally has only a few permits available. You can reserve up to 14 days in the backcountry during the summer, planning a route from one unit to another and getting all the permits at the start. Because of this regulation, you may find the units you're most interested in already booked, even if you're first in line on the first morning they become available. Have second and third choices ready.

Before venturing into the backcountry, everyone is required to watch an orientation film called the *Backcountry Simulator.* The Park Service will provide bear-resistant food containers in which you are required to carry all your food. Guns are not permitted in the park; a pepper spray for self-defense is a good idea and proper camping etiquette essential to avoid attracting bears.

USEFUL PUBLICATIONS

At the visitor center bookstore, buy the $8.99 *Denali National Park and Preserve* topographical map, published by Trails Illustrated, P.O. Box 4357, Evergreen, CO 80437-4357 (☎ **800/962-1643** or 303/670-3457; fax 303/670-3644; Web site www.colorado.com/trails). Printed on plastic, it includes the boundaries of the 43 backcountry units and much other valuable information.

Also, you'll want to consult *Backcountry Companion,* by Jon Nierenberg, a book selling for $8.95 that describes each of the units. Published by the Alaska Natural History Association, 401 W. First Ave., Anchorage, AK 99501 (☎ **907/274-8440**), it's for sale at the visitor center, or you can look at a well-thumbed copy kept at the backcountry desk.

Other Sports & Activities

Biking. A bicycle provides special freedom in the park. Bicyclists can ride past the checkpoint where cars have to turn back, at Mile 14 on the park road. Park campgrounds have bike stands, and you can take a bike on the shuttle or camper bus. The longest stretch on the park road between campgrounds is 52 miles. On the downside, the buses kick up a lot of dust, and bikes may not go off-road. Pick up a copy of the bicycle rules from the backcountry desk before you start.

Denali Mountain Bike, P.O. Box 448, Denali National Park, AK 99755 (☎ **907/683-2453** summer, 907/457-2453 winter), rents bikes, including helmets and gear, for $25 a day. They also lead extended guided trips on the Denali and Elliott highways and are the only bike-repair shop in 130 miles (Fairbanks is the next closest).

Rafting & Boating. Floating the swift, glacial water of the Nenana River Canyon as it passes the park entrance has become a major activity at the park, because it's convenient and fun. The entire trip is outside the park. Several companies compete for your business, most offering a choice of slow, Class II water, suitable for children as young as age 5, or a white-water trip with numerous Class III and IV rapids, with minimum ages around 12. Each trip takes 2 to 2½ hours and costs around $50, or floating through both costs around $70 and takes twice as long. Most of the companies fit you out with rain gear for the white-water trips, but you get soaked to the skin anyway; afterward, you'll need a shower, as the glacial silt sticks to your skin and hair.

The **Denali Outdoor Center** (☎ **907/683-1925**) supplies dry suits to white-water passengers, so they remain warm and dry, and offers runs where clients help paddle. Their office is on the right across from the McKinley Chalet Hotel as you head north on the Parks Highway through the business area nearest the park. The cooperative of five guides also offers inflatable kayak schools and tours. **Denali Park Resorts** (☎ **800/276-7234**), the park concessionaire, also does a fine job (but no dry suits), and allows children as young as age 5 on the slow-water version of its raft trips with a half-off discount to kids 11 and under.

Horseback Riding. There is no riding in the park itself, but there are several opportunities in similar terrain outside its boundaries. **Beaver Lake Trail Rides,** P.O. Box 107, Denali National Park, AK 99755 (☎ **800/893-6828** or 907/683-1699), offers rides in groups of up to six in the Healy Valley. Trips range from 1 hour for $60 to 4 hours for $125, leaving several times a day. **Wolf Point Ranch,** P.O. Box 127, Cantwell, AK 99729 (☎ and fax **907/768-2620**), offers 4- and 6-day pack trips for $910 or $1,350 per person, respectively.

Camping

The park has eight campgrounds. Recreational vehicles can find a place, as can tent campers who want to be away from people out in the wilderness. Fees for each campground are listed in the campground chart. Here I aim to give you a feel for what each is like so you can choose which you'd prefer. For private campgrounds see "Accommodations," later in this chapter.

To get to campgrounds beyond Mile 14 on the park road, you have to take the $15 camper bus (unless you're staying 3 days or more at Teklanika). If it seems expensive, consider this: The ticket is a free pass to travel all over the park, which would cost as much as $11 more if bought for the shuttle.

Campground Programs. The Riley Creek, Savage River, Teklanika, and Wonder Lake campgrounds have ranger programs almost nightly.

Supplies. Convenience stores with limited camping supplies, are located near the park hotel and at the gas station near the large hotels a mile north of the park entrance.

Riley Creek is the traditional family campground in the woods right at the entrance to the park. With 100 sites, paved roads, flush toilets, and a sewage dump station, it's far from wilderness; but it is readily accessible, easy to get a permit, and young children won't care if it's not exactly the backcountry. For more ambitious campers, Riley Creek is a good stop for your first night in the park, when you need time to get your bearings before heading to a more remote area. The front-country shuttle bus stops in the parking lot, where there's a single pay phone. Riley Creek is a roaring tributary of the Nenana, running just below the campground; the best sites back onto the creek. Riley is the only campground open year-round, although the water is off in the winter.

Morino Backpacker Campground, set aside for walk-in campers, is especially attractive for backcountry travelers

Campground	Total Sites	RV Hookups	Dump Station	Toilets	Drinking Water
Inside the Park					
Riley Creek	**100**	**No**	**Yes**	**Yes**	**Yes***
*Morino Backpacker***	**60**	**No**	**No**	**Yes**	**Yes**
Savage River	**33 sites**	**No**	**No**	**Yes**	**Yes**
Savage Group	**3**	**No**	**No**	**Yes**	**Yes**
*Sanctuary River***	**7**	**No**	**No**	**Yes**	**No**
Teklanika River	**53**	**No**	**No**	**Yes**	**Yes**
*Igloo Creek***	**7**	**No**	**No**	**Yes**	**No**
*Wonder Lake***	**28**	**No**	**No**	**Yes**	**Yes**

* No water in winter.
** Tent sites only.
† Reservations must be made in person (not in advance of your park trip).

waiting for their permits. It is essentially just a wooded area about a mile from the visitor center where backpackers can put up their tents and use portable outhouses. Sites are designated by stakes and are self-registered. There is no parking area.

Savage River, just a mile short of the park road checkpoint beyond which vehicles cannot go, is both easily accessible and relatively remote, 13 miles from the park entrance. It's the best choice for car or RV campers who want to get away from the park entrance but don't have 3 days to spend camping at Teklanika. There are 33 sites. The bathrooms have flush toilets. Savage Group is the nearby group camping area. The taiga (sparsely wooded tundra) is good for exploring, and there's a decent chance of seeing moose and possibly black bear.

Sanctuary River is a small, primitive campground with seven tent sites is 9 miles beyond the road checkpoint. There are chemical toilets. The campground is in the woods near a ranger station.

Teklanika River, at Mile 29 on the park road, is the only campground for car or RV camping beyond the checkpoint. There is no RV dump station. You can drive in if you agree not to move your vehicle for at least 3 days. You'll also need a special $20 shuttle pass, good for the duration of your stay, which allows free exploration of the park. With 53 sites, it's a large campground, but the sites are adequately separated by trees. It has flush toilets.

Igloo Creek, the last campground for 52 miles, is a primitive tent camp with seven sites near a ranger station. It's the closest campground to the open terrain of alpine tundra.

The 28 tent-camping sites at Wonder Lake, near the end of the park road, are in high demand, next to placid Wonder Lake and with spectacular views of Mount McKinley. Despite the remote location, it has flush toilets and a ranger station is only 2 miles away. Winter stays late at this end of the park, and the campground doesn't open until sometime in June.

Accommodations

Patterns of land ownership and the furious pace of development around Denali have led to a hodgepodge of roadside hotels, cabins, lodges, campgrounds, and

Showers	Fire Pits/ Grills	Laundry	Public Phone	Reserve	Fees	Open
No	Yes	No	Yes	Yes	$12	Year-round
No	Yes	No	Yes	No	$6	Late May to Sept
No	Yes	No	No	Yes	$12	Late May to Sept
No	Yes	No	No	Yes	$40	Late May to Sept
No	No	No	No	Yes†	$6	Late May to Sept
No	Yes	No	No	Yes	$12	Late May to Sept
No	No	No	No	Yes†	$6	Late May to Sept
No	No	No	No	Yes	$12	June–Sept

restaurants in pockets arrayed along more than 20 miles of the Parks Highway. There are rooms of good quality in each of the pockets, but the going rates vary widely. The most expensive rooms, and the first booked, are in the immediate area of the park entrance. Next are the hotels south of the park. Both these areas are entirely seasonal. The best deals are in Healy, 10 miles north of the park, where you can find a room for $50 less than a comparable room near the park entrance. Of course, if you don't have a car it's most convenient to stay in or near the park. The other choices are to stay in Talkeetna, the back door to the park, described below; at a lodge in the Kantishna inholding within the park; or at a remote wilderness lodge. I've listed each of the choices separately. Despite their high prices, rooms can be hard to find in the high season and it's wise to book well ahead. If you don't mind gambling, however, you can often get great last-minute deals from hotels that have had large cancellations from their package tour clients.

The local **bed tax** is 7%.

NEAR THE PARK

This area, sometimes known as Denali or Nenana Canyon, extends about a mile north of the park entrance on the Parks Highway, including the park hotel, which is 1.5 miles within the park. Two huge hotels that primarily serve package tour passengers dominate the area: the **Denali Princess Lodge,** Mile 238.5, Parks Highway (P.O. Box 110), Denali National Park, AK 99755 (☎ **800/426-0050;** fax 206/443-1979), and the **McKinley Resorts Chalets,** Mile 238.5, Parks Highway (mailing address: 241 W. Ship Creek Ave., Anchorage, AK 99501; ☎ **800/276-7234** or 907/276-7234; fax 907/258-3668). If they have a cancellation, you may be able to get attractive rooms at one of these places at the last minute for a fraction of their astronomical rack rates. The McKinley Resorts Chalets also is a good place to book activities.

In addition to those I've listed, you'll find good rooms at **Sourdough Cabins,** Mile 238.5, Parks Highway (P.O. Box 118), Denali, AK 99755 (☎ **907/683-2773**), which has comfortable little cabins in the woods below the highway in the $120 to $130 range; and at **Denali River View Inn,** Mile 238.4, Parks Highway (P.O. Box 49), Denali National Park, AK 99755 (☎ **907/683-2663;** fax 907/683-7433), with 12 good standard rooms for $134 double. All of the hotels in this area are open only during the tourist season, roughly May 15 to September 15.

Denali Bluffs Hotel

Mile 238.4, Parks Hwy. (P.O. Box 72460), Fairbanks, AK 99707. ☎ **907/683-7000;** fax 907/683-7500. 112 rms. TV TEL. High season $179 double. Low season $126 double. $10 each additional person. AE, DISC, MC, V.

A series of buildings, brand new in 1996, look down from the mountainside above the highway. Most of the light, tastefully decorated rooms have balconies, two double beds, coffeemakers, and small refrigerators, and those on the upper floor have vaulted ceilings. A courtesy van will take you anywhere in the area, and a coin-op laundry is available.

Denali Crow's Nest Cabins

Mile 238.5, Parks Hwy. (P.O. Box 70), Denali National Park, AK 99755. ☎ **907/683-2723;** fax 907/683-2323. 39 cabins. High season $139 cabin for 2. Low season $89. Additional person in cabin $10 extra. MC, V.

Perched in five tiers on the side of a mountain above the Nenana Canyon area, looking down on Horseshoe Lake and the other (big) hotels, the cabins are large and comfortable, especially those on the 100 and 200 level. A log cabin and the warmth of the Crofoot family create more of an appropriate, Alaskan feeling than the modern, standard rooms that have filled the canyon. You spend a lot of time climbing stairs, however, and despite the great views and the price, the cabins are simple, not luxurious. They book tours and offer a courtesy van, free coffee, and an outdoor Jacuzzi. The restaurant, **The Overlook,** is recommended separately under "Dining," later in this chapter.

Denali National Park Hotel

Mile 1.5, Denali National Park Rd. (P.O. Box 87), Denali National Park, AK 99755. (For reservations, contact Denali Park Resorts, 241 W. Ship Creek Ave., Anchorage, AK 99501; ☎ **800/276-7234.**) 100 rms. High season $147 double. Low season $109 double. Additional person in rm $10 extra. AE, DISC, MC, V.

The only hotel within the park burned down in 1972; this "temporary" structure, cobbled together from old railroad cars and modular housing units, has served ever since, gaining an oddly historic feel of its own. The park hotel is a center of park activities, with hiking trails out the back door, and has more character than the other big hotels, but it needs remodeling and the rooms have no views. There's a courtesy shuttle, coffee in the rooms, and a tour desk.

The attractive **dining room** serves large portions. The lounge, in a pair of railroad cars, has a good, campy feel. Smoking is permitted in only one of the two rail cars it occupies, a fair arrangement for both sides of that debate. For fast food, the snack bar is quite adequate, and probably the best place for take-out in the area. The gift shop has reasonable prices, regulated by the Park Service.

Denali Windsong Lodge

Mile 238.6, Parks Hwy. (P.O. Box 31), Denali National Park, AK 99755. (Winter P.O. Box 2210011, Anchorage, AK 99522.) ☎ **800/208-0200** or 907/683-1240; Web site www.alaskalodges.com. 48 rms. TV. High season $149 double. Low season $99–$129 double. $10 each additional person. AE, DISC, MC, V.

Two-story, wooden buildings sit in a quiet area back in the trees behind the Princess Lodge near an appealing little campground. The proximity to the big lodge means a variety of restaurants are within easy walking distance. The good standard rooms, with exterior entries, have two double beds, satellite TV, coffeemakers, and views from the top of a bluff. A free shuttle is provided to the train station.

IN HEALY

Healy is 10 miles north of the park entrance, but a world away. It's a year-round community with an economy based primarily on a large coal mine and only secondarily on the park. There are a number of hotels and bed-and-breakfasts with rooms that cost from $20 to $90 less than those near the park. They say the water tastes better, too.

Besides my two favorites listed below, you'll find hundreds of small, serviceable rooms with twin beds at a converted pipeline camp, the **Denali North Star Inn,** Mile 248.5, Parks Highway (P.O. Box 240), Healy, AK 99743 (☎ **800/684-1560** or 907/683-1560; fax 907/683-4026), for $110 double. Across the highway, the **Stampede Lodge,** Mile 248.8, Parks Highway (P.O. Box 380), Healy, AK 99743 (☎ **907/683-2242;** fax 907/683-2243), has attractively decorated rooms, on the small side, in a renovated 1946 railroad building. They charge $90, double, in the summer. There's a reasonably priced restaurant inside serving three meals a day.

Motel Nord Haven

Mile 249.5, Parks Hwy. (P.O. Box 458), Healy, AK 99743. ☎ **800/683-4501** in Alaska only, or 907/683-4500. 24 rms. TV TEL. High season $108–$117 double. Winter $70 double. AE, MC, V.

This fresh, new little hotel has large, immaculate rooms with one or two queen-size beds. They're equal to the best standard rooms in the Denali Park area and a lot less expensive. Bill and Patsy Nordmark offer free newspapers, coffee, tea, and hot chocolate, and a sitting room with a collection of Alaskan books. The rooms have interior entrances, and some have kitchenettes. All have been nonsmoking since construction. Up to four people can stay in the rooms with two beds for the price of a double.

White Moose Lodge

Mile 248, Parks Hwy. (P.O. Box 68), Healy, AK 99743. ☎ **800/481-1232** or 907/683-1233. 9 rms. TV. $85 double. Rates include coffee, tea, and pastry breakfast. Additional adult in rm $10 extra, additional child $5 extra. AE, DC, DISC, MC, V. Closed Oct to mid-May.

This old, low-slung building among stunted black spruce contains an unlikely find—comfortable, cheerfully decorated rooms with flower boxes, plus a hospitable host, former wildlife photographer and New Zealander Kirsty Knittel. It's a good value for a basic room.

SOUTH OF THE PARK

There are several groups of accommodations south of the park. I've listed just a few. You may also want to try **McKinley Creekside Cabins**, 13 miles south at Mile 224, Parks Highway (P.O. Box 89), Denali National Park, AK 99755 (☎ **907/683-2277;** fax 907/683-1558), which has cabins with private or shared baths starting at $99 double, including a hot breakfast.

Denali Cabins

Mile 229, Parks Hwy. (P.O. Box 229), Denali National Park, AK 99755. ☎ **907/683-2643;** fax 907/683-2595. (In winter, 200 W. 34th Ave., Suite 362, Anchorage, AK 99503; ☎ **907/258-0134;** fax 907/243-2062.) 41 rms, 2 suites. High season $124 cabin for 2; $159 suite. Additional person in rm $10 extra. Low season $84 cabin for up to 4. MC, V. Closed mid-Sept to mid-May.

These roomy cedar cabins, arranged around a grassy compound with a pair of hot tubs, are a good choice for families. The kids may find someone their own age to play with on the boardwalks or lawns. Also, with a cabin you don't worry as much about noise. There's a scheduled courtesy van and free coffee.

Denali River Cabins

Mile 231, Parks Hwy. (mailing address: P.O. Box 81250, Fairbanks, AK 99708). ☎ **800/230-7275** or 907/683-2500; fax 907/456-5212; Web site www.denaliirivercabins.com. High season $140–$150 cabin for 2. Low season $95–$105 cabin for 2. Additional person in rm $10 extra. MC, V.

These cedar cabins along boardwalks above the Nenana River feel fresh and luxurious. The sauna has a picture window on the river, there's a Jacuzzi, free coffee and newspapers, a van to the train station, and bicycle rentals. They'll even throw a wine and cheese party with advance notice. But the cabins have shower stalls, not tubs, and for the rate you may be expecting something more. The 17 cabins on the river, with decks over the water, are $10 more.

The Perch

Mile 224, Parks Hwy. (P.O. Box 53), Denali National Park, AK 99755. ☎ and fax **907/683-2523.** 11 cabins, 4 with bath. $65–$95 cabin for 2. Additional person in cabin $10 extra. AE, MC, V. Closed Sept 15–May 16.

In the trees along rushing Carlo Creek, 13 miles south of the park entrance, a variety of cabins range from duplexes with large, modern rooms with private baths to adorable little A-frames with lofts that share a bathhouse. There's a sense of privacy and of being out in the woods along the wooden walkways. It's an exceptional value. Atop a steep hill the **restaurant and bar,** one of my favorites in the area, provides reason for the name. It's a friendly, light place with solid meals of fish, beef, and bread ranging in price from $14 to $40. In summer they're open for three meals a day, in winter only on weekends.

PRIVATE CAMPGROUNDS

McKinley Kampground, Mile 248.5, Parks Highway (P.O. Box 340), Healy, AK 99743 (☎ **800/478-2562** in Alaska, or 907/683-2379), is the best private campground in the Denali area. The campsites are surrounded by birch trees. There's a coin-op laundry and other facilities. Basic tent sites are $16.75 to $19.25, $27.50 for full hookups. **Denali Grizzly Bear Cabins and Campground,** Mile 231, Parks Highway (P.O. Box 7), Denali National Park, AK 99755-9998 (☎ **907/683-2696**), has some wooded campsites and some in a gravel lot, for $16. Cabins are for rent too, starting at $21.50 for a small tent cabin. Cabins with their own bathrooms are $92.

WILDERNESS LODGES

For those who can afford it, there's no better way to be in the wilderness without giving up civilized comforts than to book a few days at a wilderness lodge. The first three establishments I've listed are in the Kantishna district, an area of park inholdings near McKinley, reached by bus or van 95 miles over the park road. Once there, you can explore the park using a special pass for shuttle rides starting in Kantishna, which costs $15.

Camp Denali/North Face Lodge

Kantishna District (P.O. Box 67), Denali National Park, AK 99755. ☎ **907/683-2290** or 907/683-1568. 17 cabins, none with bath (Camp Denali); 15 rms with bath, (North Face Lodge). $315 per person per night, double occupancy, all inclusive. Minimum stay 3 nights in cabin, 2 nights in rm. No credit cards. Closed early Sept to early June.

Uniquely at this pioneering ecotourism establishment, you can wake to the white monolith of Mount McKinley filling your window. Also uniquely, the naturalist guides here have the right to use the park road free of the shuttle system for hikes, biking, lake canoeing, bird watching and photography sessions, and other outdoor learning activities. During some sessions, nationally reputed academics and other experts lead the program. All arrivals and departures are on fixed session dates and start with a picnic on the park road on the way out. The lovely Camp Denali cabins each have their own outhouse and share a central bathhouse and wonderful shared lodge rooms—it would be my first choice for anyone who can stand not having his own flush toilet. North Face Lodge has traditional rooms with private baths. A conservation ethic pervades the operation, from the home-grown vegetables to the proprietors' efforts to preserve the natural values of private land in the park.

Denali Backcountry Lodge

Kantishna District (P.O. Box 189), Denali National Park, AK 99755. ☎ **800/841-0692** or 907/683-2594; fax 907/783-1308; e-mail denalibl@alaska.net. (In winter: P.O. Box 810, Girdwood, AK 99587; ☎ 907/783-1342.) 30 cabins. $285 per person per night, double occupancy, all inclusive. MC, V.

Thirty comfortable, modern cedar cabins sit in rows on a deck next to babbling Moose Creek and a two-story lodge building. Guests can sit in a screened porch away from the mosquitoes and watch the day go by, or join a choice of guided hikes, natural history programs, or other activities around the lodge each day. To go out into the park, you're on your own, either on a lodge mountain bike or the shuttle, although the ride in from the entrance is treated as a safari. Stay at least 2 nights. It's run by Alaska Wildland Adventures, which offers a variety of well-regarded ecotourism packages all over the state.

Kantishna Roadhouse

Kantishna District, Denali National Park (mailing address: P.O. Box 81670, Fairbanks, AK 99708). ☎ **800/942-7420** or 907/683-1475; fax 907/683-1449. 28 rms. $550 double, all inclusive. AE, DISC, MC, V.

This well-kept property of many buildings along Moose Creek in the old Kantishna Mining District trades on both the mining history and outdoors opportunities of the area. Some rooms are large and luxurious, while others are in smaller single cabins with lofts. The log central lodge has an attractive lobby with people coming and going—it's got more of a hotel feel, and might be more attractive to an older, less active set than the other lodges in the Kantishna District. Daily activities include guided hikes, wagon rides, biking, and gold panning, and there's an excellent dogsled demonstration that coincides with a $99 day trip that comes out for the bus ride and lunch only.

Denali Wilderness Lodge

Wood River (mailing address: P.O. Box 50, Denali National Park, AK 99755). ☎ **800/541-9779** year-round, or 907/683-1287; fax 907/479-4410; Web site www.AlaskaOne.com/dwlodge. (In winter: P.O. Box 71784, Fairbanks, AK 99707; ☎ 907/479-4000.) 23 rms and cabins. $290 per person per night, double occupancy, all inclusive. AE, DISC, MC, V.

The extraordinary log buildings were built by the late big-game guide Lynn Castle along the Wood River, and his amazing collection of mounted exotic animals from all over the world is in a sort of museum room. They don't kill the animals anymore: Now they're more valuable to look at alive, and the lodge has become an ecoestablishment, flying guests in for as little as a half day for flightseeing, horseback riding, hiking, and talks by naturalists and the like. But stay at least a couple of days to really experience the place. The 25-horse stable is the unique centerpiece, and this is the best place for riders. The cabins, while not luxurious, are quite comfortable and have private bathrooms. The food is terrific. The location is distant from Mount McKinley, in a remote valley 30 miles east of the park entrance.

Dining

The large hotels all have fine dining and casual restaurants. The restaurants at the Denali Princess Lodge have beautiful dining rooms with great views. The **Chalet Center Cafe** at the McKinley Resorts Chalets is one of my favorites for an inexpensive meal. It's a cafeteria serving good sandwiches and healthy dishes, in a large, light room. See **The Perch,** listed above under "Accommodations," for another good choice.

Lynx Creek Pizza

Mile 238.6, Parks Hwy. ☎ **907/683-2547.** All items $3.25–$22.95. AE, DISC, MC, V. Daily 11am–11:30pm. Closed late Sept to early May. PIZZERIA.

This ARA-managed pizza restaurant is a center of activity for the less well heeled visitors to Denali, as it's the only place to get a slice and a cheap beer. The food isn't anything special and there often are lines to order, but the dining room is a low-key, relatively nontouristy place to meet young people.

The Overlook Bar and Grill

Mile 238.5, Parks Hwy., up the hill above the Denali Canyon area. ☎ **907/683-2641.** Main courses lunch $9–$15; dinner $9–$25. MC, V. 11am–11pm. Closed mid-Sept to mid-May. BURGERS/STEAK/SEAFOOD.

This fun, noisy place has the feeling of a classic bar and grill. The dining room, with woodsy lodge decor, looks out on a spectacular view of the Nenana Canyon. The salmon and filet mignon were well seasoned and done to a turn and the service was friendly and jocular. The lunch menu seemed a bit high. A huge variety of craft beers is available, with nine on tap. Full liquor license.

Denali in the Evening

The main evening event is the concessionaire's **Cabin Nite Dinner Theater,** at the McKinley Resorts Chalets (☎ **800/276-7234**), a professionally produced musical revue about a gold rush–era woman who ran a roadhouse in Kantishna. You can buy the $35 tickets, half price under age 11, virtually anywhere in the area. The actors, singing throughout the evening, stay in character to serve big platters of food to diners sitting at long tables, doing a good job of building a rowdy, happy atmosphere for adults and kids. You go for the show, not the all-you-can-eat salmon and ribs—they try to make up for the quality with quantity. Princess Cruises and Tours puts on a similar evening show, **Mt. McK's Roadhouse Review,** in a big wall tent at the Denali Princess Lodge. The food is basically the same, too. Tickets are for sale at the hotel's tour desk (☎ **800/426-0500**) for $35, or $14 for the show without the meal. The **Northern Lights Theater and Gift Shop,** across the Parks Highway from the McKinley Resorts Chalets (☎ **907/683-4000**), shows the *Northern Lights Photosymphony,* a music-accompanied slide show on a 34-foot-wide screen. Admission is $6.50. It's also a good gift shop, with a mixture of the usual T-shirts and higher-quality gifts.

Talkeetna: Back Door to Denali

Talkeetna, a historic and funky little town with a sense of humor but not much happening, slept soundly from its decline around World War I until just a few years ago. Now there are paved streets (both of them), a new National Park Service building of stone, a new railroad depot, and a large new luxury hotel north of town. It seems that while Talkeetna slumbered in a time capsule, an explosion of visitors was happening at the Denali National Park. Now, not entirely voluntarily, Talkeetna finds itself enveloped in that boom.

As a threshold to the park, Talkeetna has significant pros and cons that you must take into account. On the positive side, it's closer to Anchorage; the development is much more interesting and authentic than at the park entrance; there's lots to do in the outdoors and great views of the mountain, less frequently obscured by clouds. On the negative side, a big minus: You can't get into the park from here. That means you miss the dramatic scenery, easy backcountry access, and unique wildlife viewing of the park road.

The town itself dates from the gold rush, and there are many charming log and clapboard buildings. You can spend several hours looking at two small museums and meeting people in the 2-block main street, then go out on the Talkeetna or Susitna River for rafting, a jet-boat ride, or fishing, or take a flightseeing trip to the national park.

GETTING THERE

By Car. Talkeetna lies on a 13-mile spur road that branches from the Parks Highway 99 miles north of Anchorage and 138 miles south of the park entrance.

By Train. The Alaska Railroad serves Talkeetna daily on its runs to Denali National Park during the summer, and weekly in the winter. See the listing earlier in this chapter.

By Van. The **Talkeetna Shuttle Service,** P.O. Box 468, Talkeetna, AK 99676 (☎ **907/733-2222** or 907/355-1725), runs back and forth to Anchorage, for $40 to $90 per person, depending on the size of your group.

ESSENTIALS

Visitor Information. The commercially operated **Denali/Talkeetna Visitor Center** is at the intersection of the Parks Highway and Talkeetna Spur Road (☎ **907/733-2688** summer; 907/733-2499 winter), open in summer, daily from 8am to 7:30pm; in winter, Monday through Friday from 9am to 4pm. A new $1.5 million **Talkeetna Ranger Station,** P.O. Box 588, Talkeetna, AK 99676 (☎ **907/733-2231**), primarily serves people who aim to climb Mount McKinley, but will answer other's questions, too.

Orientation. This town of 600 doesn't take long to figure out. Just drive the spur road till you hit the historic area on Main Street, then explore on foot. Turn right across the railroad tracks as you get into town for the **Talkeetna State Airport,** campground and boat launch, and some businesses.

Getting Around. You can walk everywhere in Talkeetna, but there are good **mountain-biking** routes, too. **CGS Bicycles,** on Main Street (P.O. Box 431), Talkeetna, AK 99676 (☎ **907/733-1279**), rents mountain bikes for $18 a day and leads trail tours starting at $20 per person.

Some Fast Facts. A 2% **sales tax** applies. At this writing there is **no bank** or **ATM,** the nearest being in Wasilla, an hour south on the Parks Highway. In **emergencies** dial ☎ **911.** The **Alaska State Troopers** (☎ **907/733-2256**), at Mile 97.8 on the Parks Highway, are just south of the intersection with the spur road, next to the **Denali Medical Center** (☎ **907/733-1833**), which has a 24-hour emergency room.

Special Events. The **Talkeetna Moose Dropping Festival,** over a weekend in mid-July, is a community fair to raise money for the Talkeetna Historical Society (☎ **907/733-2487**). The main event doesn't involve dropping moose, as an aggrieved animal lover once complained, but dropping moose droppings.

IN TOWN

Talkeetna is famous for its laid-back atmosphere and outdoors, not for activities, but there are two small museums. The **Talkeetna Historical Society Museum,** on the Village Airstrip a half block south of Main Street (☎ **907/733-2487**), contains artifacts and displays on the local mining history, including photographs and biographies of individual characters. It's also a good place to get community information, open daily in summer, 10am to 6pm. The **Museum of Northern Adventure** is a wax museum of Alaska scenes and memorabilia, on the east end of Main Street (☎ **907/733-3999**). It's funny and corny, and great for children. Admission is $2.50 for adults, $1.50 for children.

GETTING OUTSIDE

The only way you'll get into the park from Talkeetna is by **flightseeing** with one of the glacier pilots who supports McKinley climbs, which typically begin with a flight from here to Kahiltna Glacier. **K2 Aviation,** a renowned McKinley expedition operator with a main office at Talkeetna State Airport (P.O. Box 545-B), Talkeetna, AK 99676 (☎ **800/764-2291** or 907/733-2291; Web site www.alaska.net/~flyk2), also has a booking office on the Parks Highway. They offer a flightseeing tour that circles the mountain and shows it off from every angle, and even lands on a glacier on the mountain itself (possible from November to mid-July). Depending on the length of the tour, prices range from $85 to $175 per person; add $40 to land on a glacier. **Doug Geeting Aviation,** at the state airport (P.O. Box 42), Talkeetna, AK 99676 (☎ **800/770-2366** or 907/733-2366; Web site www.alaska.net/~airtours/), is another well-regarded mountain flying operation, with a flight that lands on two different glaciers, and even an acrobatic flight in a two-seat biplane. Prices range from $65 to $250 per person.

Talkeetna is at the confluence of the wild Talkeetna and Susitna rivers. **Mahay's Riverboat Service,** P.O. Box 705, Talkeetna, AK 99676 (☎ **907/733-2223**), is a top guide, with 5-hour jet-boat charters for $115 per person, operating from a dock near the public boat launch on the Talkeetna River. Owner Steve Mahay is legendary, the only person ever to shoot Devil's Canyon in a jet boat. Besides **fishing,** Mahay offers **river tours** ranging from 20 minutes to 5 hours, concentrating on sightseeing and natural history; prices start at $19.95 per person. For a quieter look at the river, **Talkeetna River Guides,** on Main Street (P.O. Box 563), Talkeetna, AK 99676

(☎ **800/353-2677** or 907/733-2677; Web site www.alaska.net/~trg/trg_dir/), offers a 2-hour wildlife **river rafting** tour on the Talkeetna three times a day for $39 adults, $15 children. They also offer guided fishing.

ACCOMMODATIONS & DINING

The beautiful new **Mt. McKinley Princess Lodge,** Mile 133.1, Parks Highway, Denali State Park, AK 99755 (☎ **800/426-0500** or 907/733-2900; fax 907/733-2904), finished in 1997 by the Princess cruise line, capitalizes on a striking view of the mountain, only 42 miles away as the crow flies. The hotel isn't really near anything, 100 miles south of the park entrance and about 45 road miles from Talkeetna, but the operator puts on a full set of activities. Standard rooms are $175 a night in the high season. They're open mid-May to mid-September.

In Talkeetna itself, the choices are more modest but perfectly adequate. **Swiss-Alaska Inn,** near the boat launch (P.O. Box 565), Talkeetna, AK 99676 (☎ **907/733-2424**), is a friendly family business with good, reasonably priced meals, specializing in German dishes, and large, attractive rooms in the newer of its buildings, which rent for $100 a night. The **Talkeetna Motel,** at the west end of Main Street (P.O. Box 115), Talkeetna, AK 99676 (☎ **907/733-2323**), has clean, basic rooms for $80 double. There are other lodgings and several B&Bs available for booking through the visitor center. **Latitude 62,** on the right as you come into town (☎ **907/733-2262**), serves good food in a roadhouse vein. A couple of fun little places on Main Street serve lunch.

15

DEVILS TOWER NATIONAL MONUMENT

by T.D. Griffith

RISING 1,270 FEET ABOVE THE FOREST FLOOR AND THE VALLEY OF the Belle Fourche River, the stone stump of Devils Tower greets visitors miles before they arrive at the nation's first national monument. Established in 1906 by Pres. Theodore Roosevelt in the first use of the new Antiquities Act, Devils Tower may rest off the beaten path in extreme northeast Wyoming, but it's well worth an excursion. It is probably best remembered as the site of an alien spaceship landing in the movie *Close Encounters of the Third Kind.*

Col. Richard I. Dodge, who commanded a military escort to a U.S. Geological Survey party that visited the Black Hills in 1875, is credited with giving the formation its name. In his book *The Black Hills,* which was written the year after his journey, Dodge described Devils Tower as "one of the most remarkable peaks in this or any other country."

The steep-sided mass of igneous rock rises abruptly from the grasslands and pine forests, and remains one of the Black Hills most conspicuous geologic features. Devils Tower National Monument covers an area of about 2 square miles (1,347 acres).

Geology. While the 53 million-year-old Tower itself is composed of hard igneous rock, much of the remaining exposed rock within the monument boundaries is composed of soft sediments from the warm shallow seas of the Mesozoic Era. These colorful bands of rock encircling the igneous core include layers of sandstone, shale, mudstone, siltstone, gypsum, and limestone.

The story of Devils Tower's geology is but one chapter in the geologic history of the Black Hills. Unfortunately, even after extensive studies and detailed geologic mapping, the definitive chapter explaining the origins of Devils Tower has yet to be written.

There are several theories which attempt to explain the formation of Devils Tower. The theory most often used suggests that the Tower is the eroded remnant of an ancient volcanic feature forming from a mass of molten rock that cooled slowly deep below the surface. Over the 53 million subsequent years, the erosion of thousands of feet of overlying sediments exposed the granite-like monolith. Much of the original igneous formation has peeled off as well, leaving an apron of rubble all around the Tower.

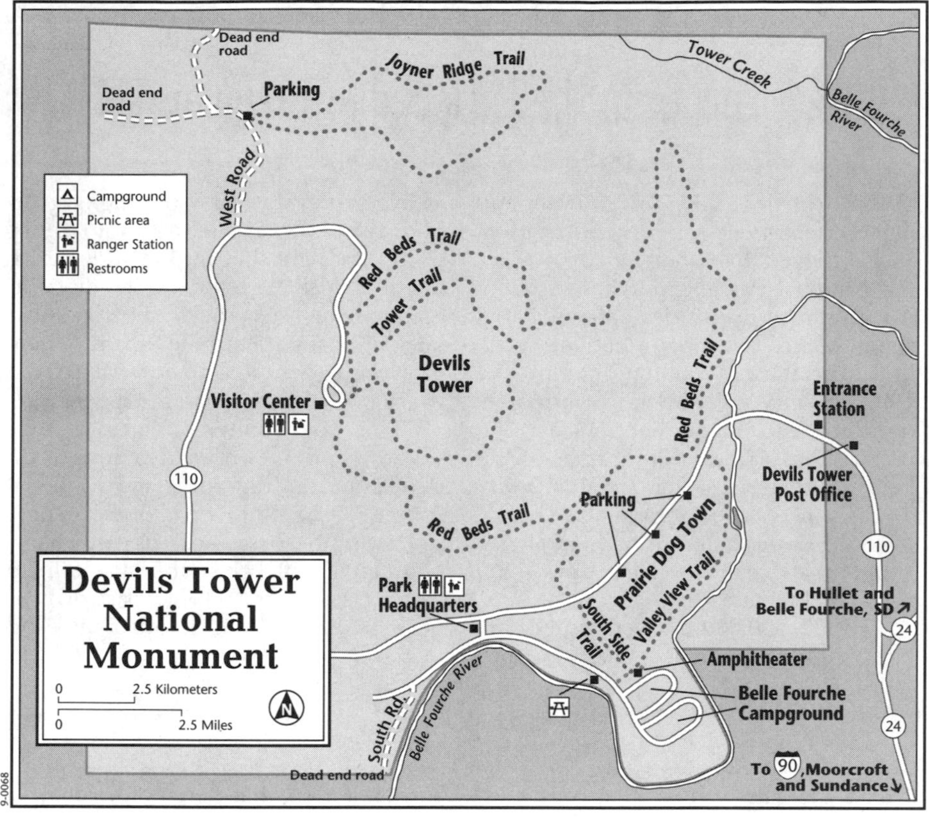

The formation of the Tower occurred in the early Tertiary period some 60 million years ago. Scientists believe that a mass of molten rock forced its way upward through miles of rock, forming an inverted, cone-shaped structure under layers of sedimentary rock that form what is now northeastern Wyoming. As the molten rock slowly cooled, it cracked and fractured, creating one of the most striking features of the monument, its polygonal columns. Most of the columns are five-sided, but some are four- and six-sided. The largest columns measure 6 feet to 8 feet in diameter at their base and taper gradually upward to about 4 feet in diameter at the summit.

Over centuries, the gentle waters of the Belle Fourche River carried away sedimentary layers, leaving the more erosion-resistant igneous rock behind. Today the Tower appears to sit quietly on the crest of a wooded hill. But the Tower's base is actually the bottom of the unexposed magma which is covered with fallen columns and soil.

> **"A dark mist lay over the Black Hills, and the land was like iron. At the top of the ridge I caught sight of Devils Tower upthrust against the gray sky as if in the birth of time the core of the earth had broken through its crust and the motion of the world was begun. There are things in nature that engender an awful quiet in the heart of man; Devils Tower is one of them."**
>
> **—N. Scott Momaday**

Tips from the Park Superintendent

Former Devils Tower National Monument superintendent Deb Liggett has seen much of what the National Park Service has to offer. After a stint at Everglades National Park, she moved to the superintendent's post in northeastern Wyoming. Then in late 1997, the career Park Service employee transferred to Alaska. She says her 3½ years at Devils Tower will always stay with her: "I have a friend who says that Devils Tower is like a piece of sculpture—perfect in every light and from every angle. I think that's really true. The Tower can be quite dramatic."

In 1997, 450,000 travelers visited this National Monument—as many people as live in the state of Wyoming. Liggett said visitors, particularly photo buffs, prefer the light they find in early morning or at dusk. With the surrounding forest and decreased crowds, she noted that fall can be a perfect time to visit. Whenever you choose to stop at Devils Tower, you'll probably be pleased, Liggett said.

"The Tower often creates its own shadows and its own weather, with terrific thunder and lightning storms in the summer," she said. "People often come to Devils Tower as a lark—as a quick trip between Rushmore and Yellowstone. I think they have a classic park experience. They are definitely pleasantly surprised by their discovery."

Indian Legend. Native Americans have their own name for Devils Tower. They call it *Mateo Tepee,* or Grizzly Bear Lodge. Descendants of several of the Indian nations of the Great Plains share similar legends of how the prominent butte was formed.

According to one version of the legend, seven sisters watch with horror as their brother is turned into a bear. The sisters run away from him, to the stump of a large tree, which beckons them to climb on. (In other versions, they run to a large, flat stone.) When they do, the stump rises up into the sky, and the bear, unable to climb up the stump to kill the sisters, scores it with its claws. The sisters are then raised up into the sky, becoming the seven stars of the Big Dipper.

What inspired the imagination of Native Americans more than 100 years ago also attracts their reverence. In deference to the religious significance of the Tower to many American Indian tribes, the National Park Service has requested that climbing of the Tower be voluntarily suspended so that ceremonies may be conducted without interference.

First Ascent. As the battle to preserve the monument from commercial encroachment was being waged in 1893, two local ranchers decided it was time someone made the first recorded climb to its summit.

William Rogers and Willard Ripley planned for months before making their first attempt on the southeast face on July 4, 1893. As the date approached, the pair began distributing handbills offering such amenities as ample food and drink, daily and nightly dancing, and plenty of grain for horses. The flyers also touted the feat as the "rarest sight of a lifetime."

Rogers and Ripley used a wooden stake ladder they had built that summer for the first 350 feet of the climb. As more than 1,000 spectators watched, the pair made the harrowing climb in about an hour, raised Old Glory, then sold pieces of it as mementos of the occasion. Thereafter, the Tower became a popular place for Independence Day family gatherings. At the annual affair in 1895, Mrs. Rogers used her husband's ladder to become the first woman to reach the summit.

On Top of the Tower. From its base, most visitors would surmise that the top of Devils Tower is a flat, barren pinnacle. As over 5,000 climbers who made it to the peak in 1997 will attest, the top of the Tower isn't that much different than the countryside that surrounds it—except, perhaps, that five states are visible from the top of the rock.

The summit is actually slightly domed with a few small outcroppings and covered with prairie grasses, prickly pear cactus, currant and gooseberry bushes, and native big sage, thanks to prairie falcons and turkey vultures that nest in the Tower's columns and deposit seeds on top. A number of animals also have been spotted on the crown of Devils Tower, including rattlesnakes, pack rats, and red squirrels that have slithered and scampered up the cracks and fissures.

At the top, climbers may sign a register and record any unusual aspect or oddity of their adventure. More than 28,000 signatures have been gathered since records of Tower climbs were first kept in 1937. In that time, climbers have used more than 220 routes to the top; in 1941 world-record holding parachutist George Hopkins jumped from an airplane to the cap of the Tower, then lost his escape rope and was stranded on top for 6 days until rescued.

Avoiding the Crowds. It's relatively easy to avoid the crowds at Devils Tower National Monument—simply because there aren't too many days each year when congestion is a problem. Traffic patterns at the monument are similar to those of national park areas throughout the West. Expect the highest visitation from June through August, lower visitation in the shoulder months of April to May and September to October; and the lowest visitation during the remaining winter months.

If you must visit during the summer, stop at the Tower early in the day, or take in a fireside ranger talk when crowds have thinned in the evening.

Just the Facts

GETTING THERE & GATEWAYS

Because of its remote location, Devils Tower is best accessed by private vehicle. The entrance to the monument is 33 miles northeast of Moorcroft, Wyoming, and 27 miles northwest of Sundance, Wyoming, via U.S. 14 (you travel to the immediate area on I-90). Scheduled airlines service Gillette, Wyoming (regional commuter service), and Rapid City, South Dakota, where cars may be rented. For information on the Rapid City airport and rental car options, please see chapter 3.

GETTING INFORMATION BEFORE YOUR TRIP

If you would like to receive information about Devils Tower before you leave, you can contact **Devils Tower National Monument,** P.O. Box 10, Devils Tower, WY 82714 (☎ **307/467-5283**).

You can get information on the Web at **www.nps.gov/deto**.

VISITOR CENTER

While the park is open year-round, the monument's **Visitor Center** is located 3 miles from the entrance. Open seasonally (April through October), the center offers exhibits about the Tower's history and geology. Hours are 8:30am to 5pm in the Spring, 8am to 7:30pm in the summer (Memorial Day through Labor Day). Activities are offered during the summer. Parking is limited in summer.

ENTRANCE FEES

There is an entrance fee of $8 per vehicle or $3 per person (on a motorcycle or bicycle, or on foot).

CAMPING FEES

Camping costs $12 per site per night; for group sites, the fee is $3 per person, for up to 20 persons in a group.

SPECIAL REGULATIONS & WARNINGS

Do not feed, chase, or disturb prairie dogs. They bite and may carry diseases. Abandoned prairie dog holes are often homes to black widow spiders and rattlesnakes. Obey all posted signs. All resources within the monument are protected by law. Disturbing animals or gathering items such as rocks or flowers is strictly prohibited. Pets must be on a leash at all times and are not permitted on trails in the monument.

SEASONS & CLIMATE

The monument is open year-round. The climate and seasons at Devils Tower echo those in the Black Hills region. Summer days can be hot and dry; evenings and early mornings damp and cool. Spring weather is often chilly and wet, while fall storms are not uncommon. Winter weather is commonly cold, but snow and sunlight can combine to create incredible pictures of the landmark.

USEFUL PUBLICATIONS

The **Devils Tower Natural History Association** operates a bookstore at the monument's Visitor Center. For publications information, write the association at P.O. Box 37, Devils Tower, WY 97214-0037.

Seeing the Highlights in a Day

It's easy to experience all that Devils Tower has to offer in less than a day. Rangers recommend that you allow 2 to 4 hours to visit the monument, walk a trail, stop at the visitor center, and view the prairie dogs. Because of its isolation, you might also wish to camp at the park's campground or stay in the surrounding area, especially if you want to take advantage of some of the summer ranger talks.

Surrounded by ponderosa pines and bathed in blue sky, the towering rock obelisk visible for many miles, it's easy to imagine the reaction of the first lonely Indian scouts and French fur trappers who stumbled upon this stunning geologic anomaly a few centuries ago. As they did, you will wonder.

Home to whole towns inhabited by the feisty black-tailed prairie dog, the grounds of Devils Tower National Monument are perfect for picnicking and viewing wildlife. You can watch the sociable prairie dogs in their colony, or "town," just inside the park's East Entrance station. The critters excavate elaborate networks of underground passageways, then guard their burrows with warning "barks" when predators such as hawks, eagles, bullsnakes, coyote, red fox, and mink come too close. Walk the leisurely 1-mile **Valley View Trail** or savor a picnic lunch among the wildflowers at the monument's picnic area on the banks of the sleepy Belle Fourche River.

Climbing the Tower

Climbers must register with a ranger prior to starting their climb and on their return, otherwise there are no permits or requirements for climbing the Tower. Be prepared for sudden storms; carry rain gear and a flashlight. Rockfall is common, so climbing helmets are advised. Ask a ranger for additional safety and climbing information. A voluntary climbing ban is observed each June out of respect for Native American beliefs about the monument. Experienced climbers might wish to consult *Devils Tower National Monument: A Climber's Guide,* by Steven Gardiner and Dick Guilmette (Seattle: The Mountaineers, 1986), before attempting a climb; the book can be purchased by mail from the Devils Tower Natural History Association (the address is in "Useful Publications," above).

Organized Tours & Ranger Programs

Interpretive Talks. Meet a park ranger in front of the Visitor Center from mid-June through Labor Day for bear tales and interpretive talks about the region's geology and Tower trivia. These short programs explore the cultural and natural history of the monument. Programs last about 15 minutes and are wheelchair accessible. Check at the Visitor Center for scheduled times.

Tower Walk. Meet a park ranger in front of the Visitor Center at 9:30am daily mid-June through Labor Day, and enjoy a lively walk as the sun rises above the Tower. Good walking shoes and water are recommended. These guided walks last about an hour and end on the Tower Trail. Allow 10 minutes to return to the Visitor Center. If you wish to continue your trek and complete the 1.3-mile Tower Trail, allow an additional 30 minutes.

Climbing Demonstrations. Join a park ranger at the climbing kiosk, located in the middle of the Visitor Center parking lot, from July 1 through Labor Day, for a climbing demonstration. Learn more about technical rock climbing at Devils Tower during this 30-minute demonstration. Check at the Visitor Center for scheduled times.

Evening Programs. Learn more about America's first national monument by the glow of a campfire. Join a park ranger in the monument's amphitheater each evening from Memorial Day through Labor Day. Topics will vary, so check with the Visitor Center or campground host for topics. Programs are weather-dependent and during inclement weather, programs may be moved to the picnic shelter.

Cultural Program Series. During the summer season, Devils Tower plays host to numerous cultural demonstrators who bring their expertise to the monument. Among the guests are Native American storytellers, musicians, historians, impersonators, photographers, poets, and astronomers. Check the Visitor Center or campground host for special guests and schedules.

Day Hikes

Devils Tower will announce itself (through your windshield) miles before you arrive at the entrance to the monument. In fact, you may drive to within a few hundred yards of the Tower. But the real highlight of any visit to Devils Tower is the park's trails. So get out and enjoy them. Pets are not allowed on trails.

The paved **Tower Trail,** at 1.3 miles, goes all the way around the Tower, offering close-up views of the Tower on fairly level ground, while wayside exhibits tell the Tower's story. It's considered an easy trail, and most visitors walk it.

There are several other trails: Red Beds Trail 3 miles; Southside Trail 0.6 mile; Joyner Ridge Trail 1.5 miles; Valley View Trail 0.6 mile. Since none of the trails get very crowded, these are a good way to examine the terrain around the monument, including the pine forest and the prairie dog town, and avoid some of the summer crowds, especially if you have more than a couple of hours to spend at the park.

Camping

A campground is located just a mile from the monument's headquarters. The adjacent Valley View Trail skirts a giant prairie dog town, and the campground's amphitheater offers excellent interpretive ranger programs. Open seasonally (April to October), the 55 sites at this campground accommodate RVs and tents on a first-come, first-served basis, but there are no utility hookups or dump station; each site costs $12 per night. The campground has three group sites, which cost $3 per person per night, for up to 20 persons in a group. Each campsite has a cooking grill, table, and nearby drinking water. Rest rooms are accessible for persons with disabilities. There are no hookups, showers, or laundry facilities in the monument. A post office and full services are found within 1 mile of the campground and in nearby communities.

Accommodations & Dining

There are no accommodations or dining within the monument boundaries. However, there are options in the surrounding communities of Sundance and Hulett.

NEAR THE PARK

In Sundance, we recommend the **Bear Lodge Motel,** 218 Cleveland St., on Wyo. 14 at Business Loop I-90 (mailing address: P.O. Box 912, Sundance, WY 82729; ☎ **800/341-8000** or 307/283-1611). A double room will cost around $50 per night during the summer and fall, less during the winter and spring; major credit cards (AE, DISC, MC, V) are accepted. A 32-ton native stone fireplace greets guests in the western style lobby, where you can have free coffee. Its location in the center of town, across the street from two restaurants and the community's museum, is convenient.

In Hulett, we recommend the **Motel Pioneer,** 3 blocks north of downtown on Wyo. 24 (mailing address: P.O. Box 389, Hulett, WY 82720) (☎ **800/231-6335** or 307/467-5656). Several of the units come with kitchenettes or refrigerators. Rates are $49 per night from May 1 to November 30, $39 per night from December 1 to April 30; major credit cards (AE, DISC, MC, V) are accepted. Two rooms are large family units. The rooms are nice and clean. Public tennis courts are next door, and there is a golf course across the highway if you are feeling active. It's 9 miles to the national monument entrance from here.

16

GLACIER NATIONAL PARK

by Ed Lawrence

GLACIER NATIONAL PARK WAS NAMED TO DESCRIBE THE 48 SLOW-moving glaciers that carved awe-inspiring valleys throughout this expanse of nearly 1 million acres. It exists because of the efforts of George Bird Grinnell, a 19th-century magazine publisher and cofounder of the Audubon Society. Following a pattern established with Yellowstone and Grand Teton, Grinnell lobbied for a national park to be set aside in the St. Mary region of Montana, and in May 1910 his efforts were rewarded. Just over 20 years later, it became, with its northern neighbor Waterton Lakes National Park in Canada, Glacier-Waterton International Peace Park—a gesture of goodwill and friendship between the governments of two countries.

Glacier National Park is conspicuously different than those parks to the south. With spewing geysers and wildlife, Yellowstone attracts travelers that crowd, and almost clutter, its narrow roads. Grand Teton entrances visitors with revered, cathedral-like spires that grasp the sky overhead. Glacier beckons with equally stunning though somewhat smaller peaks (many covered year-round with glaciers), verdant mountain trails that cry out for hikers, and the sheer diversity of its plant and animal life.

Majestic and wild, this vast preserve continues to overwhelm visitors as much as any other national park in the Lower 48. Every spring, Glacier is a postcard that comes to life: Wildflowers carpet its meadows; bears emerge from months of hibernation; and moose, elk, and deer again play out the drama of birth, life, and death in the wilderness. The unofficial mascot in these parts is the grizzly, a refugee from the high plains that now inhabits the Montana mountains.

Man has left his imprint on the park, of course—the patter of feet has taken an environmental toll. But park management continues to successfully maintain the delicate balance between tourism and preservation. Nature is at work as well: The glaciers are receding (the result of global warming, some say) and avalanches have periodically ravaged Going-to-the-Sun Road, the curving, scenic 50-mile road that bisects the park. For the time being, the park is intact and very much alive, a treasure in a vault that is open to visitors.

If your time is limited, simply motor across Going-to-the-Sun Road, viewing the dramatic mountain scenery. Longer-term visitors will find diversions for both families and hard-core adventurers; while some hiking trails are suitable for tikes, many more will challenge those

Tips from the Park Superintendent

Visitors wishing to escape the crowds of summer will find September and October to be excellent times to visit. In late September and throughout the month of October the fall colors in the park highlight its quieter nature during this time of year.

A highlight of the fall color season is the display put on by the larch trees throughout the western portions of the park. Entire hillsides will turn a bright yellow and fade to a dull orange glow as the month of October wanes. Larch are one of the only two deciduous coniferous species in the United States, and many visitors are shocked to see such dramatic color in the western mountains.

determined to conquer and scale the park's tallest peaks. Glacier's lakes, streams, ponds, and waterfalls are equally engaging. Travelers board cruise boats to explore the history of the area; recreational types fish, row, and kayak.

To truly experience Glacier requires slightly more effort, interest, and spunk than you'd expend at, say, drive-through Yellowstone. Sure, you can glimpse her sights from behind the windshield—but abandon the pavement for even the easiest and shortest of the hundreds of hiking trails, and you'll find a window into her soul.

Avoiding the Crowds. The simplest way to accomplish this task is to travel in the off-season, before mid-June, when the park begins to fill, and after Labor Day, when families traveling with youngsters have returned home. (August is the busiest month in *all* of the parks hereabouts.) If that's not possible, consider the following: Since most people congregate in close proximity to the major hotels, find a trailhead that is equidistant from two major points and head for the woods. If you must drive, to make the trip more enjoyable (and traffic-free), journey across the Going-to-the-Sun Road before 8:30am; you'll be astounded at the masterful job Mother Nature does of painting her mountains. You can always see more wildlife in the early morning (or just before dark). At the very least, to avoid restaurant lines, plan on eating an hour earlier, or later, than standard dining hours.

Just the Facts

GETTING THERE & GATEWAYS

Glacier National Park is located in the northwest corner of Montana, on the Canadian border. The closest cities to the park with airline service are Kalispell, 29 miles southwest of the park, and Great Falls, 143 miles southeast of the park. If you're driving, the easiest ways to reach the park are from U.S. 2 and U.S. 89.

There are six entrances to Glacier National Park: at West Glacier; Camas Road; St. Mary; Many Glacier; Two Medicine; and Polebridge. Access is primarily at either end of Going-to-the-Sun Road: at West Glacier on the southwest side and St. Mary on the east.

From the park's western boundary, you may enter at Polebridge to access Bowman and Kintla lakes or take Camas Road to Going-to-the-Sun Road.

The following east-side entrances are primarily designed to access specific places and may not necessarily take you into the heart of the park: Essex, East Glacier, Two Medicine, Cut Bank, and Many Glacier.

Visitor entrance passes are sold at the West Glacier, Two Medicine, Many Glacier, Polebridge, and St. Mary park

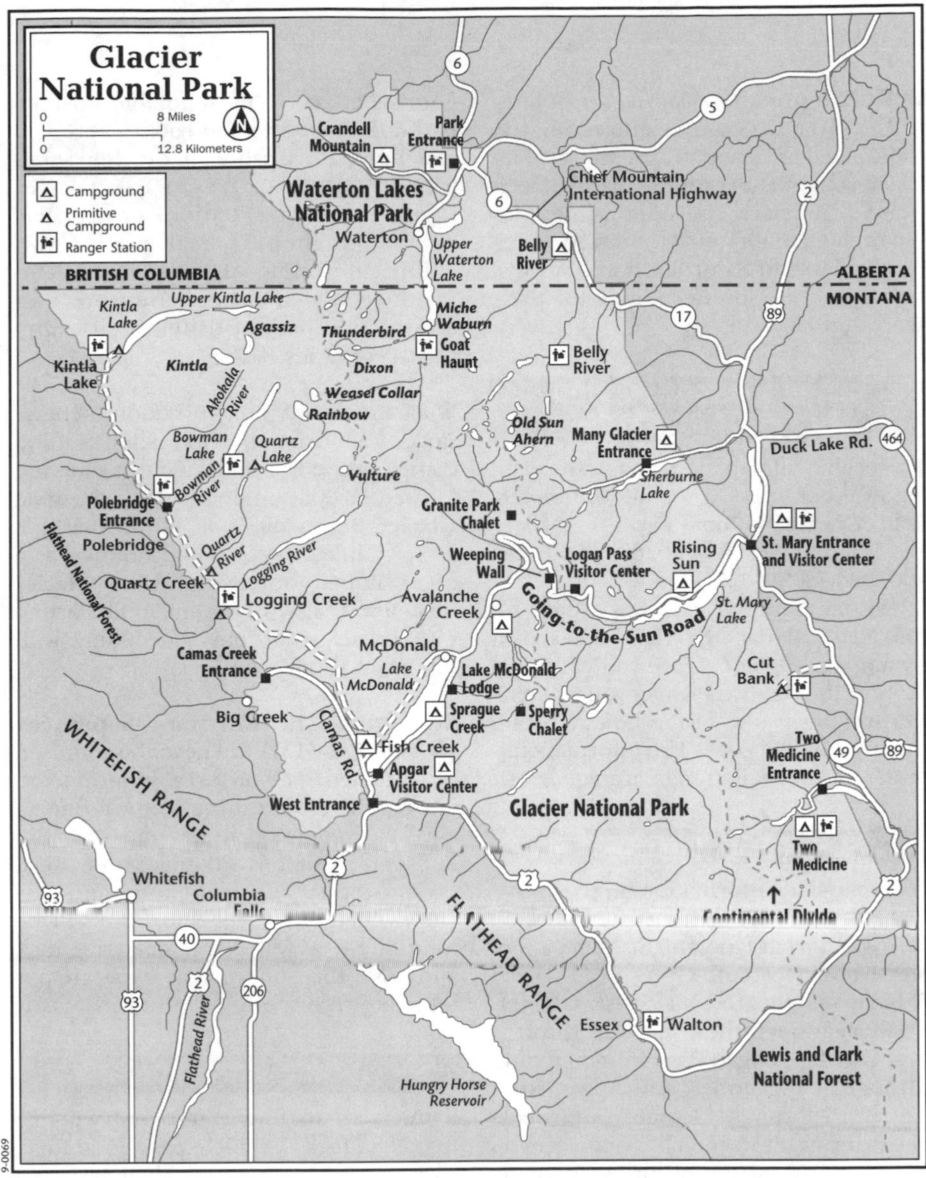

entrances. Entrance is severely restricted during winter months when most of Going-to-the-Sun Road is closed. (See "Seasons & Climate," below, for more information.)

The Nearest Airports. **Glacier Park International Airport,** north of Kalispell at 4170 U.S. 2 (☎ **406/257-5994**), is serviced by **Northwest, Delta,** and **Horizon.**

Great Falls International Airport (☎ **406/727-3404**) has daily service on **Delta, Northwest,** and **Horizon.**

Toll-free numbers for all of these airlines can be found in the appendix.

Renting a Car. Rental cars are available in Kalispell, Great Falls, Whitefish, East Glacier, Essex, and West Glacier. **Avis, Budget, Hertz,** and **National** all have counters at Kalispell's airport. **Hertz, Avis,** and **National** have counters at Great Falls International Airport. Toll-free reservations numbers for all these car rental companies are given in the appendix.

By Rail. **Amtrak**'s *Empire Builder* (☎ **800/872-7245**), a Chicago Seattle round-trip route, makes stops seasonally at East Glacier and year-round at West Glacier when the park is open (mid-May through October) on Monday, Wednesday, Friday, and Saturday. It also stops at Essex, near the southern tip of the park, year-round.

GETTING INFORMATION BEFORE YOUR TRIP

To receive information about the park before your trip, write the **Superintendent, Glacier National Park,** West Glacier, MT 59936 (☎ **406/888-7800;** fax 406/888-7808).

Glacier National Park has a page on the National Park Service Web site at **www.nps.gov/glac/**. Once you've looked around the site for a while, you will realize that this is one of the best Web sites for any national park. The information is much more detailed than average.

VISITOR CENTERS

For up-to-date information on park activities, check in at visitor centers located at Apgar, Logan Pass, and St. Mary; a center manned by info-givers from Travel Alberta is located at West Glacier. **St. Mary** is open from mid-May through mid-October; **Logan Pass,** from mid-June through mid-October; and **Apgar,** from late April through October (and weekends during the winter). Visitor centers are open 8am to 5pm during the early part of the season (mid-May through the end of June), and hours are extended during July, August, and the first half of September. Park information may also be obtained from the **Two Medicine, Polebridge,** and **Many Glacier Ranger Station** or park headquarters.

ESSENTIAL SERVICES

East Glacier. The **Glacier Park Trading Company** (☎ **406/226-4433**), on U.S. 2, has a limited supply of fresh and canned goods. Perhaps its most notable attribute is the deli shop in the back, where you can purchase freshly made deli sandwiches. Other services at East Glacier include a service station, post office, several gift shops, a small market with a limited supply of fresh meats and produce as well as beer and wine, and a modest supply of fishing and camping accessories.

West Glacier. A service station, general store, Laundromat, photo shop, rafting companies, post office, and gift shop are located in this compound, as is the **West Glacier Bar,** a dimly lit four-seater that serves adult beverages and doubles as a retail liquor store. The **West Glacier Restaurant** serves ho-hum food starting with breakfast at 7am and ending with dinner at 10pm.

St. Mary. The **St. Mary Supermart** (☎ **406/732-4431**) will never be confused with a metropolitan area supermarket, but it's the closest thing you will find in any of the park gateway cities except Kalispell, which is 80 miles due west. Fresh produce, canned goods, and beverages including beer and wine will be found here, as will a large magazine rack and post office, but you can expect to pay tourist-town prices.

ENTRANCE & CAMPING FEES

Rangers are on duty at most entry points to collect fees. A **vehicle pass** good for 7 days costs $10. An **individual pass** for walk-ins and bicycle and motorcycle riders, also good for 7 days, is available for $5. A **season pass** may be purchased for $20 that allows unlimited entry to Glacier National Park for 1 year. A separate entrance fee is charged for visitors to Waterton Lakes National Park.

The **camping** fees are $10 to $12 per night at 1 of the regular park campgrounds. Most campgrounds are available on a first-come, first-served basis. Fish Creek and St. Mary campgrounds may be reserved ahead of time, starting

March 15, 1998, through the National Park Service Reservation System by calling ☎ **800/365-CAMP.** Campsites are limited to eight people and two vehicles per site. Most campgrounds have drinking water, rest rooms with flush toilets, and cold running water. Utility hookups are not provided.

Visitors planning to camp overnight in Glacier's backcountry must stop at a visitor center or ranger station and obtain a Backcountry Use Permit. Backcountry permits may be reserved in advance, in person, or by mail. Permits are limited to 6 nights, with no more than 3 nights allowed at each campground. Certain campgrounds have a 1-night length of stay limit. There are separate fees for advance reservations and backcountry camping. For information on backcountry camping, contact: **Glacier National Park,** West Glacier, MT 59936 (☎ **406/888-7800**).

Backcountry camping permits may be obtained in person from the visitor centers at Apgar, Waterton Townsite, and St. Mary, or the ranger stations at Many Glacier, Two Medicine, and Polebridge. During summer months permits may be obtained no earlier than 24 hours before your trip. Due to lower demand in winter, camping permits are available up to 7 days in advance. There are a few rules that do take effect beginning each November 20, so double-check at visitor centers for details.

SPECIAL REGULATIONS & WARNINGS

The following regulations apply to visitors.

Biking. Bikes are restricted to established roads, bike routes, or parking areas, and are not allowed on trails. Restrictions apply to the most hazardous portions of Going-to-the-Sun Road during peak travel times from around mid-June to Labor Day; call ahead to find out when the road will be closed to bikers. During low-visibility periods caused by fog or darkness, a white front light and a back red reflector are required.

Boating. While boating is permitted on some of Glacier's lakes, motor size is restricted to 10 horsepower on most. A detailed list of other regulations is available at park headquarters and staffed ranger stations. Park rangers may inspect or board any boat to determine regulation compliance.

Camping. Camping is permitted only at designated locations, even in the backcountry, and is strictly prohibited on the roadside.

Fishing. Anglers may be surprised to know that a fishing license is not required within the park's boundaries; however, there are guidelines, so check with rangers at visitor centers or ranger stations for regulations. Also, keep in mind since the eastern boundary of the park abuts the Blackfeet Indian Reservation, you may find yourself fishing in their territorial waters. To avoid a problem, purchase a $10 use permit from businesses in the gateway towns; the permit covers fishing, hiking, and biking in the reservation. Fishing outside the park in Montana waters requires a state license; check in at a local fishing shop to make certain you are legal.

Horses. While visitors may bring their own horses and pack animals into the park, restrictions apply to private stock. A free brochure detailing regulations regarding horseback riding is available from the Park Service.

Pets. All pets must be on a leash no longer than 6 feet, and under physical restraint or caged while in the park. Pets are not allowed indoors at any of the park's gift shops, restaurants, or visitor centers, or on any trails.

Vehicles. Before planning your drive through Glacier, RVers should know that there are vehicle size restrictions for

Going-to-the-Sun Road. Park regulations prohibit vehicles over 21 feet on the 24-mile stretch of Going-to-the-Sun Road between Avalanche Campground and Sun Point on St. Mary Lake.

SEASONS & CLIMATE

Glacier is magnificent at any time of the year, but some roads are closed and park access is limited in the winter. By far the most popular time to visit is during the summer, when Going-to-the-Sun Road is fully open; during summer months sunrise is around 5am, and sunset at nearly 10pm, so there's plenty of time for exploring. The shoulder seasons of spring and fall are equally magnificent with budding wildflowers and variegated leaves and trees, but these sights can only be viewed from the park's outer boundaries and a limited stretch of the scenic highway.

In winter, Glacier shuts itself off from much of the motorized world. The Going-to-the-Sun Road is usually plowed from West Glacier to the head of Lake McDonald. U.S. 89 provides access to the St. Mary area. The North Fork Road from Columbia Falls is open for winter travel to the North Fork area and the Polebridge Ranger Station. Snowmobiles, which are allowed in Yellowstone, are forbidden here. All unplowed roads become trails for snowshoers and cross-country skiers, who rave about the vast powdered wonderland that exists here. Guided trips into the backcountry are a great way to experience the park in winter, or you can strap on a pair of snowshoes and explore it on your own. Temperatures sometimes plummet to –30°F, so appropriate dress for those conditions is essential.

USEFUL PUBLICATIONS

The Glacier Natural History Association offers a vast array of publications that are sold throughout the park; for a catalog, contact **Glacier Natural History Association,** Historic Depot, Department W, P.O. Box 428, West Glacier, MT 59936 (☎ **406/888-5756;** fax 406/888-5271) or on the Web at **www.nps.gov/glac/gnha3.htm**.

Seeing the Highlights in a Day

If you have a limited amount of time to spend in Glacier, the best way to experience the full gamut of the park's beauty is to drive Going-to-the-Sun Road, the 50-mile road that bisects the park between West Glacier and St. Mary. Points of interest are clearly marked along this road by interpretive signage and correspond to the park brochure ***Points of Interest Along the Going to the Sun Road,*** which is available at visitor centers. You may need several rolls of film to make the journey. (All hiking trails mentioned below are described in more detail in the "Day Hikes" section.)

Remember that the road gains more than 3,400 feet in 32 miles, and is very narrow in places. Visitors with a fear of heights may consider taking a cruise in a guided coach (see "Organized Tours & Ranger Programs," below). And because of the road's narrowness, oversized vehicles and trailers must use U.S. 2; see "Special Regulations & Warnings," earlier in this chapter, for information on vehicle restrictions.

Just a short drive from West Glacier is **Lake McDonald,** the largest body of water in the park; numerous turnouts along the way present opportunities to photograph the panoramic views of the lake with its mountainous backdrop. **Sacred Dancing Cascade** and **Johns Lake** are visible by taking an easy 0.5-mile hike from the roadside through a red cedar/hemlock forest, often with views of moose and waterfowl. The **Trail of the Cedars** is a short, wheelchair-accessible boardwalk trail thickly carpeted in vibrant, verdant hues. Almost exactly halfway along Going-to-the-Sun is the **Loop,** an excellent vantage point for views of **Heaven's Peak.** Just 2 miles farther is the **Bird Woman Falls Overlook,** an outlook for falls located across the valley. The **Weeping Wall,** a wall of rock which does, in fact, weep profusely in

Picnicking Tips

The best picnicking spot on the Going-to-the-Sun Road is at **Sun Point,** which is also the trail-head for the 1.6-mile round-trip to Baring Falls, a trail that follows the shoreline of the lake. From the picnic area, however, the views across the lake to the mountains are unrivaled in the park. Even better: Be there at sunrise.

the summer, is a popular subject for photographers.

At the 32-mile mark from West Glacier is **Logan Pass,** one of the park's most highly trafficked areas and the starting point for the hike to **Hidden Lake,** one of the park's most popular. There's a visitors center here, atop the Continental Divide.

As you head downhill, you'll reach the turnout for **Jackson Glacier,** the most easily recognizable glacier in the entire park; followed by **Sunrift Gorge** and **Sun Point,** which are accessible via two short trails that present opportunities to view wildlife.

Exploring the Park by Car

Because of the massive mountains that surround the visitor to Glacier National Park, it is impossible to drive through the park without drawing comparisons to Grand Teton. Perhaps the most significant difference is that here one drives among the mountain peaks, which envelop a visitor; at Teton the mountains are viewed from a distance, unless you're willing to head for the hiking trails.

Going-to-the-Sun Road is by far the most driver-friendly avenue in which to enjoy the park and see some of the more spectacular views if you don't want to actually get out of the car. Consult the previous section, "Seeing the Highlights in a Day," for an idea of what you'll see along this road.

Circumnavigating the lower half of the park is easily accomplished in 1 long day, without traveling at warp speed, during which you'll experience Glacier's splendor and get a bird's-eye view of Big Sky country in the process. After a leisurely breakfast in West Glacier, you'll be in East Glacier in plenty of time for lunch at the Glacier Park Lodge (see "Accommodations," below) and at St. Mary or Many Glacier for dinner. To complete a counterclockwise loop from West Glacier, hop onto U.S. 2 and head along the park's southern boundary to Essex and East Glacier, then north to St. Mary.

The **road between West Glacier and East Glacier,** which is approximately 57 miles, is a well-paved, two-lane affair that winds circuitously around the western and southern edges of the park and follows the Middle Fork of the Flathead River. In the summertime, the fluorescent orange blobs you'll see on the river below are inner tubes and white-water rafts filled with the hordes who travel the river every summer. As you descend to the valley floor, you'll travel through beautiful, privately owned Montana ranch- and farmland. Shortly after entering the valley, look to the north and admire the park's massive peaks—spires as beautiful as any on the planet. The **Goat Lick** parking lot, on U.S. 2 just east of Essex, gets you off the beaten path and provides a view down into a canyon carved by the Flathead River; if you have time, take the short hike down to the stream.

Beyond East Glacier, as you head northwest on Mont. 49 and west towards Two Medicine, you'll notice that the earth appears to fall off. The contrast is inescapable—mountains tower in the west, but to the east the Hi-Line begins, sporting a horizon that extends so far and so flat as to seemingly lend credence and legitimacy to the Flat Earth Society. But round a corner on the Two Medicine Road and suddenly you'll find yourself faced with three mountains (Appistocki Peak, Mount Henry, and Bison Mountain) bare of vegetation but as red as their Southwest counterparts.

Photo Tips

The adventurous shutterbug will find that the best photo ops occur early in the morning, regardless of location. Near bodies of water, the sunrise provides an unrivaled multitude of oranges, blues, and yellows. Then, as the earth warms, lakes are transformed to fog-covered valleys, creating a mystical photographic opportunity.

One of the most picturesque spots is the **west end of St. Mary Lake;** not only does it paint the lake orange and yellow, it paints the mountains red and orange. A close runner-up is the view looking west from an overlook across St. Mary Lake to see Goose Lake in the foreground and the peaks and glaciers at the west end of the lake. These are the views from which postcards are made.

The difference here is that the crevasses are filled with snow, even in mid-August. Ten miles later, continuing the route northward on U.S. 89, you'll come across a wide panorama of mountain peaks, valleys, ridges, and forested mountains that truly characterize Glacier's personality. Conclude the bottom half of your long loop by winding downward from these high elevations to the village of St. Mary. Not a bad day's drive!

There are two ways to see the park's western boundary and to access the **Polebridge area,** in the north; one is slow and uncomfortable, the other slightly faster and *less* uncomfortable. The **North Fork Road** (Mont. 486) from Columbia Falls takes about an hour to negotiate. It's a sometimes-paved (mostly gravel and pothole-filled) stretch that follows the North Fork of the Flathead River; spectacular views ameliorate the condition of the drive. Not much is there besides water and scenery, but the area around Polebridge is a popular spot for the outdoor crowd—an excellent location to experience Montana's natural beauty without modern-day distractions like telephones and TVs.

The **Inside North Fork Road,** just north of Apgar, also runs to Polebridge. However, it's totally unpaved, takes an hour longer, and is much harder on driver, passenger, and equipment. Unless you are a glutton for punishment, I suggest you take the faster route and spend that extra hour relaxing on a riverbank.

Organized Tours & Ranger Programs

Ranger-guided activities and evening campfire and slide-show programs are offered daily throughout the park. The park's ***Nature with a Naturalist*** publication—free upon entering the park and also available at visitor centers—is a thorough source for days, times, and locations of various educational programs. During campfire chats rangers discuss a variety of topics related to the park. Local tribal members provide programs highlighting Native American culture and history. Most programs are free, although those including boat trips may include a minimal charge.

Narrated boat tours from Lake McDonald, St. Mary, Two Medicine, and Many Glacier are offered daily from mid-June to mid-September by **Glacier Park Boat Co.** These "scenicruises" combine the comfort of an hour-long lake cruise with a short hike or picnic to create an unforgettable Glacier experience. Spectacular views of Lake McDonald sunsets, the awe-inspiring Grinnell Glacier, and the panoramic rugged cliffs ringing St. Mary Lake are just a few of the possible photo opportunities you may have while enjoying a cruise. The boats typically depart every other hour, usually five times each day, although schedules are subject to change in late season or if the weather is inclement. For a

> **Give a month to this precious reserve. The time will not be taken from the sum of your life. Instead of shortening, it will indefinitely lengthen it and make you truly immortal.**
>
> **—John Muir, naturalist and conservationist**

complete listing of departure times and dates, contact **Glacier Park Boat Co.,** P.O. Box 5262, Kalispell, MT 59903 (☎ **406/257-2426**). Listed below are seasonal phone numbers for cruises at the following locations: **Lake McDonald** (☎ **406/888-5727**), **Many Glacier** and **Two Medicine** (☎ **406/732-4480**), and **St. Mary** (☎ **406/732-4430**).

Unique **coach tours** are given aboard a scarlet 1936 "Jammer" coach—so-named because of its standard transmission—along Going-to-the-Sun Road and north to Waterton. These coaches, with their roll-back tops, are an ideal means of transportation along this scenic route: their drivers provide insightful commentary about the park and its history and you don't have to worry about how close you may be to the edge of the often-precipitous road! The tours are conducted by **Glacier Park;** current coach schedules can be requested directly from them at VIAD Corp. Center, Phoenix, AZ 85077-0928 (☎ **602/207-6000**).

Interpretive van tours of the Going-to-the-Sun Road conducted by Native American guides originate from East Glacier, Browning, and St. Mary. Contact **Sun Tours** (☎ **800/SUN-9220** or 406/226-9220).

Scenic helicopter tours of Glacier are offered by **Eagle Aviation** (☎ **406/387-4160**), **Glacier Heli Tours** (☎ **800/879-9310**), and **Kruger Helicopters** (☎ **406/387-4565**). Prices range from $60 to $90 for 1- to 2-hour tours, depending on your destination. All are located within 2 miles of West Glacier off U.S. 2.

The **Glacier Institute** conducts field classes each summer that examine Glacier's cultural and natural resources. These 1- to 8-day courses are open to anyone and include instruction, transportation, park fees, and college credit. Instructors are highly skilled in their area of expertise, bringing to each course an intimate knowledge of the region and their subject matter. The classroom is Glacier National Park and the Flathead National Forest. Previous courses have covered alpine wildflowers, Glacier's grizzlies, weather systems, and nature photography. Contact the institute for a copy of their current catalog at 137 Main St., P.O. Box 7457, Kalispell, MT 59904 (☎ **406/755-1211**). Prices range from $40 to $600 per session.

Finally, **Glacier Wildnerness Guides,** P.O. Box 535, West Glacier, MT 59936 (☎ **800/521-7238** for reservations, or 406/387-5555; fax 406/387-5656), organizes backpacking trips into the Glacier National Park backcountry. They have recently been named the exclusive backpacking guide service in the park. See "Exploring the Backcountry," below, for more information on this company and their trips.

Day Hikes

With more than 700 miles of maintained trails, hiking is the best way to truly explore the park in depth. Clearly, the joy is in getting from point A to point B, since accommodations are pretty sparse once you arrive. Since most of these trails are rather short (indeed some of the nature trails are quite short), you might also wish to look in "Exploring the Backcountry," below; many of the longer trails described there can be done fully (or at least partially) in a day and are likely to take you farther off the beaten path (and away from the crowds).

Trail maps are available at outdoor stores in Whitefish and Kalispell as well as at visitor centers and the major ranger stations at each entry point.

Before striking off into the wilderness, however, check with the nearest visitor center or ranger station to determine the accessibility of your destination, trail conditions, and recent bear sightings. This may save you a lot of headache (even in the summer months) if you're planning a high-country hike and 10 miles into the trip a ranger turns you back.

The Park Service asks you to stay on trails to keep from eroding the fragile components of the park. Also, snowbanks shouldn't be traversed, especially the steeper ones. You should have proper footwear and rain gear, enough food, and, most important, enough water, before approaching any trailhead. A can of pepper spray can also come in handy when you're in grizzly habitat. *Note:* If you're planning on hiking in Canada, be sure to purchase the pepper spray that can be transported across the border; there *is* a difference. Contact Canadian Customs at ☎ 800/320-0063 for regulations. See "Exploring the Backcountry," below, for further relevant information.

LAKE MCDONALD AREA

Trail of the Cedars Nature Trail

0.25 mile RT. Easy. Access: The trailhead is located across from the Avalanche Campground Ranger Station.

This easy, level trail, consisting of a wheelchair-accessible boardwalk, offers a respite from the crowds in forested area. There are interpretive signs along the way.

Trout Lake

8.4 miles RT. Moderate. Access: The trailhead is located at the north end of Lake McDonald, 1.5 miles west on Lake McDonald Rd.

This is a good workout if you're moping around Lake McDonald Lodge sipping coffee and skipping rocks off the lake. This hike is straight up and straight down. The trail to the foot of Trout Lake and back is a little more than 8 miles and begins from the north end of Lake McDonald.

LOGAN PASS AREA

Hidden Lake Nature Trail

1.5 miles one way. Easy. Access: The trailhead is at the Logan Pass Visitor Center.

This trail climbs 460 feet and requires more spunk than others in the area, yet it's still not too hard. It's a popular trail, but if you hike all the way to the lake, you'll be able to avoid some of the crowds. Since it's an interpretive nature trail, there are several signs along the way that point out what you are seeing.

Sun Point Nature Trail

1.4 miles RT. Easy. Access: The trailhead is located 9 miles west of St. Mary at Sun Point Parking Area.

This is an easy walk on gentle slopes away from the road that presents commanding views of Baring Falls.

The Loop

7 miles RT. Easy to moderate. Access: The trailhead is located on Going-to-the-Sun Rd., about halfway between Avalanche Campground and Logan Pass Visitor Center.

Not considered easy mainly on account of its length, The Loop is the popular hiking trail that winds up to Granite Park Chalet and back. Many people use it as a continuation of the Highline Trail, but this is the section to do if you're not quite so adventurous (the Highline Trail is almost 12 miles long). If you want to spend the night in the chalet, contact **Glacier Wilderness Guides** for reservations (☎ **800/521-7238**). (See the descriptions of the chalets under "Camping," below.)

MANY GLACIER AREA

Swiftcurrent Lake Nature Trail

2.4 miles RT. Easy. Access: The trailhead is located at the picnic area 0.5 mile west of the hotel turnoff.

This is a fun hike because it's along the shore, through the woods, and near a marsh, so you may see deer and birds. Keep an eye out for Blue grouse, too. If you have time, continue on the trail as it circles Lake Josephine, another easy hike, adding 2.8 miles to the trip.

TWO MEDICINE AREA

Running Eagle Falls

0.3 mile one way. Easy. Access: The trailhead is located 1 mile west of the Two Medicine Entrance.

Hardly even a hike, the easiest trail in the area is to Running Eagle Falls along a ⅓-mile trail that winds through a heavily forested area to a large, noisy waterfall.

Appistoki Falls

1.2 miles RT. Easy. Access: The trailhead is the same as the Mt. Henry Trailhead.

This easy trail, with an elevation gain of only 260 feet, is an ideal spot for an early morning cup of coffee or midday repast.

Twin Falls Trail

3.8 miles one way. Easy. Access: The trailhead is located at the Two Medicine Campground.

The most popular hiking path in this area is the one to Twin Falls, which originates at the campground. Hikers may walk the entire 3.8-mile distance to Twin Falls on a clearly identified trail, or boat across Two Medicine Lake to the foot of the trailhead, and hike the last mile.

Exploring the Backcountry

Depending upon your point of view, negotiating the backcountry may translate to a leisurely stroll, or a tortuous experience in the high country. Choices range from 4-mile day hikes to multi-day treks, so you'll need to consider your experience and fitness level before heading into the underbrush. Then, locate a park map that presents trails and campsites in their proximity to one another.

Backcountry campgrounds have maps at the entrance to show you the location of each campground, the pit toilet, food preparation areas, and, perhaps most important, food storage areas. If you fish while camping, it's recommended you exercise catch-and-release to avoid attracting wildlife in search of food. If you eat the catch, be certain to puncture the air bladder and throw the entrails into deep water at least 200 feet from the nearest campsite or trail. When backpacking in Glacier, especially in the high country, it's important to remember to pack as lightly as possible and make sure you're aware of the degree of the ascent your particular trail may have. And remember the cardinal rule: Pack it in, pack it out. No exceptions.

Wherever you decide to go, remember that you must secure a backcountry permit before your trip.

A Guided Backcountry Trip. Many folks like to stand back and let someone else make all the arrangements, leaving themselves free to concentrate on the hiking experience itself. If this seems like your kind of trip, then you may wish to consider the services of **Glacier Wilderness Guides,** the exclusive backpacking guide service in Glacier National Park. For a price, they will put together any kind of trip; but they have several regularly scheduled throughout the season, from the end of June through the beginning of September. These include a 3-day "taste" of the park for $120 per person per day, and an entire week in the wilderness for $570 per person. Add $10 per day to these prices if you want them to provide your equipment (backpack, tent, sleeping bag, and pad). They'll even organize a trip where you spend the day hiking and the night cuddled in a comfy inn inside the park or in the Granite Park Chalet (described in more detail under "Camping," below).

They are based in West Glacier, their main office located 1.5 miles west of West Glacier on U.S. 2 (a second office is in West Glacier itself, behind the Glacier Highland Motel, across from the Amtrak depot). For a complete list of their trips, more information, or to make reservations, contact the company at P.O. Box 535, West Glacier, MT 59936 (☎ **800/521-7238** for reservations, or 406/387-5555; fax 406/387-5656). Or they have a Web site at **www.gorp.com/glacierwg/default.htm**.

KINTLA LAKE AREA

Kintla Lake to Upper Kintla Lake

12 miles one way. Moderate. Access: The trailhead is located at the Kintla Lake Campground.

This 12-mile hike skirts the north shore of Kintla Lake above Polebridge for about 7 miles before climbing a couple hundred feet. This stretch of the Boulder Pass hike is a breeze. However, once you hit Kintla Creek you may want to reconsider going any farther. With 12 miles under your belt at this point, climbing 3,000 feet may not seem like a great idea. The trail, once it breaks into the clear, offers views of several peaks, including Kinnerly Peak to the south of Upper Kintla Lake.

POLEBRIDGE AREA

Bowman Lake

71 miles one way. Moderate. Access: The trailhead is located at the Bowman Lake Campground; follow Glacier Rte. 7 to Bowman Lake Rd., just north of Polebridge, then follow the signs to Bowman Lake Campground.

This trail (14 miles to Brown Pass) is similar to the Kintla Lake hike in difficulty, and, like the Kintla Lake Trail, passes the lake on the north. After a hike through the foliage, the trail climbs out of reach of anyone in bad shape, then ascends 2,000 feet in less than 3 miles to join the Kintla Lake Trail at Brown Pass. A left turn takes you back to Kintla Lake (23 miles), a right takes you to Goat Haunt at the foot of Waterton Lake (9 miles).

Quartz Lake

12 miles RT. Moderate. Access: The trailhead is located near the Quartz Creek Campground; cross the bridge over Bowman Creek and you're on your way.

The loop is 12 miles and runs up and over a ridge and down to the south end of Lower Quartz Lake. From there it's a level 3-mile hike to the west end of Quartz Lake, then it's 6 miles back over the ridge farther north (and higher up) before dropping back to Bowman Lake. An interesting aspect of this trail is evidence of the Red Bench Fire of 1988, which took a chunk out of the North Fork area.

LOGAN PASS AREA

Highline Trail

11.9 miles one way (including The Loop). Moderate. Access: The trailhead is located at the Granite Park Chalet.

This relatively easy hike, which gains a mere 200 feet in elevation over 7.6 miles, begins at the Logan Pass Visitor Center and skirts the Garden Wall at heights of over 6,000 feet to Granite Park Chalet. Keep an eye on your watch to be certain you'll have enough time for the return hike to Logan Pass. You can continue on from the chalet to the Loop, the aptly-named section of Going-to-the-Sun Road, rather than retracing your steps. The trail actually terminates here (an additional 3.5 miles), although you'll need to plan for a shuttle back to your car. (It's also possible to continue all the way to Upper Waterton Lake, but if you do this, you should allow 3 days for the trip.)

TWO MEDICINE AREA

Pitamakan Pass Trail

8.8 miles one way. Moderate. Access: The trailhead is located at the Two Medicine Campground.

This trail presents several options: 1 or 2 long day hikes, or you can use it as the jumping-off point for an extended trip. From the trailhead, the path winds to Old Man Lake, and a campground and then on to Pitamakan Pass. At this point, your options are to return via the same trail or to continue to **Dawson Pass,** through Twin Falls, then back to the campground, which adds 10 miles to the trip and completes the 18.8-mile loop. Alternately, you could head north on the **Cut Bank** or **Nyack Creek trails,** which will add days to your trip.

Other Summer Sports & Activities

Boating. With all of this water around, it only makes sense that boat rentals would also be available, as they are. At **Apgar** and **Lake McDonald** you will find kayaks, canoes, rowboats, and motorboats; gas-powered outboard motors of 10 horsepower or less are permitted at Two Medicine Lake and Bowman Lake. You can also rent kayaks, canoes, rowboats, and electric motorboats at Two Medicine. At **Many Glacier** you can rent kayaks, canoes and rowboats. For details call **Glacier Park** (GPI) at ☎ **406/257-2426**

Fishing. The crystal-clear mountain streams and lakes of Glacier are home to many native species of trout. Anglers looking to hook a big one should try the North Fork of the Flathead for cutthroat and any of the three larger lakes in the park (Bowman Lake, St. Mary Lake, and Lake McDonald) for lake trout and cutthroat. For sound equipment, sage advice, or to schedule a guided foray, contact **Lakestream Flyshop** in Whitefish (☎ **406/862-1298**).

Kayaking. Most kayaking in the park involves passages across lakes; the most popular are Bowman Lake and Lake McDonald. Inquire at any ranger station for details and conditions (for information on kayak rentals, see "Boating," above).

Horseback Riding. One alternative to overstressing your muscles on hiking trails is to saddle up Old Paint and take an Old West approach to transportation.

Horseback riding at East Glacier is provided by **Two Medicine River Outfitters** (☎ **406/226-4408**), located a stone's throw from the front door of the lodge; they offer hourly and half-day rides into the nearby wilderness. **Mule Shoe Outfitters** (☎ **406/888-5121**), offers similar rides from corrals at Lake McDonald and the Many Glacier Corral.

Mountain Climbing. The peaks of Glacier Park rarely exceed elevations of 10,000 feet, but don't let the surveyors' measurements fool you. Glacier has some incredibly difficult climbs, and you must inquire at a visitor center or ranger station regarding climbing conditions and closures. Climbers are lost here every summer; in general, the peaks are unsuitable, except for experienced climbers or those traveling with experienced guides.

Rafting & Float Trips. Though the waters that are actually in the park don't lend themselves to white-water rafting, the boundary forks of the Flathead River are some of the best in the northwest corner of the state. For just taking it easy and floating on your back in the summer sun, the North Fork of the Flathead River stretching from Polebridge to Columbia Falls and into Flathead Lake is ideal. Portaging in Polebridge can be difficult if there's not a good sport waiting for you downstream, however. The same may be said for the Middle Fork of the Flathead, which forms the southern border of the park, as well.

For white-water voyagers, the North Fork of the Flathead River (Class II and III) and the Middle Fork (Class III) are the best bets. Inquire at any ranger station for details and conditions, since flow rates change dramatically as snow melts or storms move through the area.

The Middle Fork is a little more severe and isn't the sort of river you enjoy with an umbrella drink in your hand. The names of certain stretches of the Middle Fork are terror-inspiring in themselves (the Narrows, Jaws, Bonecrusher) and to assuage that terror, several outfitters offer expert and sanctioned guides to

Tame Ways to See Wild Animals

If you've done all this traveling, and still haven't seen a live bear, check out the **Great Bear Adventure,** 10555 U.S. 2 E., in Coram, just a stone's throw from West Glacier. This 10-acre compound is the home of four healthy, free-roaming black bears, including one 750-pounder that is the largest in the state. The path you drive through the compound—actually, it's a private residence with a backyard full of bears—is approximately a mile long and presents unlimited viewing opportunities of active critters foraging for food. Because of the unscheduled and nonpatterned manner of feeding they are constantly foraging for food just as they do in the wilderness.

If you haven't been to any "wildlife museums," which are essentially stuffed-animal displays, the **Wildlife Museum** at 10780 U.S. 2 E., West Glacier (☎ **406/387-5800**), may be worth a look. Here you'll find, preserved in something akin to their natural state, most of the animals indigenous to this area, including grizzlies and black bears, deer, elk, caribou, moose, mountain lions, and several bird species. The museum is closed in winter.

make sure you're not floating downstream facedown in the river of life.

Several outfitters based in Whitefish and Kalispell organize such trips. One to contact is **Rising Sun Outdoor Adventures,** 501 S. Karrow, Whitefish, MT 59937 (☎ **406/862-5934**). The company organizes sailing adventures on Flathead Lake, custom horseback and float trips on nearby rivers, and mountain-biking and hiking tours.

Montana Raft Company, P.O. Box 535, West Glacier, MT 59936 (☎ **800/521-7238** for reservations, or 406/387-5555; fax 406/387-5656), part of Glacier Wildnerness Guides, also offers rafting trips through Glacier and the area. They offer trips through-out the season ranging from 2-day trips for $250 per person, to 3½-day trips for $420 per person; all trips include a day hike in Glacier National Park. Their prices include all necessary equipment and food. For more information on this company, see "Exploring the Backcountry," above.

Winter Sports & Activities

Snowshooing & Cross-Country Skiing. Glacier has an abundance of cross-country ski trails, the most popular of which is the **Upper Lake McDonald Trail** to the Avalanche picnic area. This 8-mile trail offers a relatively flat route up Going-to-the-Sun Road with views of McDonald Creek and the mountains looming above the McDonald Valley.

For the advanced skier, the same area presents a more intense trip that heads northwest in a roundabout fashion to the **Apgar Lookout.** This 10½-mile trip may be a little more than the beginner bargains for.

The most popular trail on the east side is **the Autumn Creek Trail** near Marias Pass. However, avalanche paths cross this area, so the prudent skier will inquire about current weather conditions.

Yet another popular spot is in **Essex** along the southern boundary of the park at the Izaak Walton Inn.

Winter Road Conditions. Going-to-the-Sun Road is open seasonally, usually from early June to mid-October, although it may be open earlier or later, depending upon weather conditions. Call the park (☎ **406/888-7800**) to find out when tentative openings and closings are scheduled. During the winter, you may drive Going-to-the-Sun Road for 10 miles from West Glacier along Lake McDonald to the road closure; this is a popular destination for cross-country skiers.

Camping

INSIDE THE PARK

Two of the ways to spend your evenings at the park are from inside the hotel lounge looking across a martini at the folks in the campground, and vice versa. For those who prefer the latter, Glacier offers campers 10 campgrounds, 7 of which are accessible by paved road. Though utility connections are not provided at these sites, fireplaces, picnic tables, washrooms, and cold running water are located at each campground. The nightly fees run $10 to $12. Most campgrounds are available on a first-come, first-served basis. Fish Creek and St. Mary campgrounds may be reserved ahead of time, starting March 15, 1998, through the National Park Service Reservation System by calling ☎ **800/365-CAMP**. Campsites are limited to eight people and two vehicles per site. Most campgrounds have drinking water, rest rooms with flush toilets, and cold running water. Utility hookups are not provided. Stop at any ranger station for information on closures and availability, or consult the campground chart.

Backcountry Camping. If it's the backcountry you're bent on seeing, Glacier has 66 backcountry campgrounds. Fortunately, many are at lower elevation, so inexperienced backpackers have an opportunity to take advantage of them. For an accurate depiction of your itinerary's difficulty, and advice on what may be needed, check with rangers in the area you are contemplating visiting. One of the main sources of danger is running into a bear. Visitors planning to camp overnight in Glacier's backcountry must stop at a visitor center or ranger station and obtain a Backcountry Use Permit. Backcountry permits may be reserved in advance, in person, or by mail. Permits are limited to 6 nights, with no more than 3 nights allowed at each campground. Certain campgrounds have a 1-night length of stay limit. There are separate fees for advance reservations and backcountry camping. For information on backcountry camping, contact **Glacier National Park,** West Glacier, MT 59936 (☎ **406/888-7800**).

Winter Camping. Though snow camping isn't the activity for everyone, it's a great way to see the park in winter, and to complement a winter excursion. Permits are required for all overnight trips but there is no fee to reserve one up to 7 days in advance.

Fish Creek is on the west side of Lake McDonald; **Many Glacier** is in the northeast part of the park; **Rising Sun** is on the north side of St. Mary Lake; **St. Mary** is on the east side of the park; and **Two Medicine** is at the southeast part of the park near East Glacier. Sprague Creek, near the West Glacier Entrance, offers a paved road but does not allow towed vehicles or vehicles longer than 21 feet.

Despite its proximity to the center of the hotel and motel activity, the **Many Glacier Campground** is a well-forested, almost secluded campground that provides as much privacy in a public area as we've seen anywhere. The campground has adequate space for recreational vehicles and truck/camper combinations, but space for trucks pulling trailers is limited. It is a veritable mecca for tent campers.

Apgar Campground is located at the bottom of Lake McDonald, near the West Glacier Entrance and the Apgar Visitor Center. You'll find 196 sites with flush toilets and an RV dump station.

The **Avalanche Campground** area may be the nicest of all because it is situated in the bottom of the valley, 4 miles north of Lake McDonald on Going-to-the-Sun Road in a heavily treed area that is also immediately adjacent to the river and all that portends. Of its 87 sites, 50 are suitable for RVs.

Bowman Lake Campground is located at the end of a primitive dirt road in the northwest section of the park (accessed through the Polebridge entrance. Its 48 sites aren't recommended for RVs, and they're relatively primitive (no flush toilets or dump station).

The bad news about the **Cut Bank Campground** road is that it's not paved. The good news is it's only 5 miles from the pavement of U.S. 89 to the ranger station and campground, which are located in the southeast portion of the park between St. Mary and Two Medicine. Still more good news is that the unpaved aspect of the road deters many from heading into the outback to this campground, which sits in the shadow of Bad Marriage and Medicine Wolf mountains. The campground was only recently reopened after having been rebuilt, so is still relatively undiscovered; the road, and campground, are best suited to recreational vehicles 21 feet or shorter.

Fish Creek Campground is located 2 miles from Apgar, on the western shore of Lake McDonald. Its 180 sites are served by flush toilets and have a dump station.

Kintla Lake Campground is located in the northwest section of the park, reached by primitive dirt roads through the Polebridge entrance station, so it is not recommended for RVs. There are 13 sites, pit toilets, and no dump station.

Logging Creek is another primitive campground reached by dirt roads, just beyond Quartz Creek.

Quartz Creek is another primitive campground, accessed by primitive dirt roads through the Polebridge entrance.

Campground	Total Sites	RV Hookups	Dump Station	Toilets	Drinking Water
In the Park					
Apgar	196	No	Yes	Yes	Yes
Avalanche	87	No	Yes	Yes	Yes
*Bowman Lake**	48	No	No	Yes	Yes
*Cut Bank**	19	No	No	Yes	Yes
Fish Creek	180	No	Yes	Yes	Yes
*Kintla Lake**	13	No	No	Yes	Yes
*Logging Creek**	8	No	No	Yes	Yes
Many Glacier	110	No	Yes	Yes	Yes
*Quartz Creek**	7	No	No	Yes	Yes
Rising Sun	83	No	Yes	Yes	Yes
Sprague Creek	25	No	No	Yes	Yes
St. Mary	148	No	Yes	Yes	Yes
Two Medicine	99	No	Yes	Yes	Yes
Near the Park					
Y Lazy R	40	Yes	Yes	Yes	Yes
Johnson's of St. Mary	115	Yes	Yes	Yes	Yes
Glacier Campground	160	Yes	Yes	Yes	Yes
Lake Five Resort	35	Yes	Yes	Yes	Yes

* Campground accessible only by narrow dirt roads. RVs not recommended.
** Public showers located nearby, for a fee.

Rising Sun Campground, located 6 miles west of St. Mary, has 83 sites, flush toilets, and a disposal station. There are also public showers at the Rising Sun Motor Inn, which is nearby.

Sprague Creek Campground is located on the eastern shore of Lake McDonald. It has 25 sites, flush toilets, but no dump station. Also, no towed trailers or vehicles longer than 21 feet are allowed.

St. Mary Campground, just outside the town of St. Mary, has 148 sites with flush toilets and a dump station.

The **Two Medicine Campground** is situated in the shadows of major mountains near three lakes and a stream. It is a forested area that has 99 beautiful sites, plenty of shade, and opportunities to wet a fishing line or dangle your feet in cool mountain water. There are flush toilets and a dump station.

Chalets. Two of the park's most popular destinations, Granite Park and Sperry chalets, are National Historic Landmarks built by the Great Northern Railway between 1912 and 1914. They were closed in 1993 because of substandard sewage and water systems. Each is the subject of an extensive restoration project; the **Granite Park Chalet** has reopened, but as a hiker's shelter only. Guests must bring their own food, water, cooking and eating utensils, flashlights, and sleeping bags. Rooms and beds are provided, as are a kitchen with a cooking stove and dining room. No public water is available, so bring your own. The

Showers	Fire Pits/ Grills	Laundry	Public Phone	Reserve	Fees	Open
No	Yes	No	Yes	No	$12	mid-May to Oct
No	Yes	No	No	No	$12	mid-June to Labor Day
No	Yes	No	No	No	$10	mid-May to Labor Day
No	Yes	No	No	No	$10	June–Sept
No	Yes	No	Yes	Yes	$12	Late June to Labor Day
No	Yes	No	No	No	$10	mid-May to Labor Day
No	Yes	No	No	No	$10	July–Labor Day
Yes**	Yes	No	Yes	No	$12	mid-June to mid-Sept
No	Yes	No	No	No	$10	July–Labor Day
Yes**	Yes	No	Yes	No	$12	mid-June to mid-Sept
No	Yes	No	No	No	$12	mid-May to late Sept
No	Yes	No	Yes	Yes	$12	Late May to early Sept
No	Yes	No	Yes	No	$12	mid-May to early Sept
Yes	Yes	Yes	Yes	Yes	$10/$15	June to mid-Sept
Yes	Yes	Yes	Yes	Yes	$12/$15/$16	Apr–Oct
Yes	Yes	Yes	Yes	Yes	$15/$18	mid-May to Sept
Yes	Yes	Yes	Yes	Yes	$16/$20	mid-May to Sept

chalet has 12 rooms (all single bunk beds), and sleeps two to six per room.

According to park officials, Sperry Chalet will open in 1998, though the park promised a similar opening in 1997. For more information contact **Glacier Wildnerness Guides/Montana Raft Company** (☎ **800/521-7238** or 406/387-5555). This company handles the reservations for Granite Park Chalet as well as operates guided hikes into the Glacier backcountry (see "Exploring the Backcountry," above, for more information). The chalets are pricey if you just stay overnight ($60 per person per night, with an additional $10 per person linen charge; there's no running water or other facilities); you may get better value by going on an organized trip.

NEAR THE PARK

IN EAST GLACIER

Y Lazy R

P.O. Box 146, East Glacier, MT 59434. ☎ **406/226-5573.** 10 tent sites, 30 RV sites. $10 tent, $15 full hookup.

Situated just off U.S. 2, this campground is conveniently located within walking distance of East Glacier and is the closest to town with laundry facilities. Plan to arrive early if you want to snag one of the few sites with trees. This place is a great value and an ideal place to plant the RV before heading off to explore the region.

IN ST. MARY

Johnson's of St. Mary

St. Mary, MT 59417. ☎ **406/732-5565.** 50 tent sites, 65 RV sites. $12 tent; $15 RV with electricity and water only, $16 full hookup.

From April through September (depending on the weather) this is where you want to camp if you can get a spot. With showers ($2) and a Laundromat, campers both inside the park and out come to St. Mary for ablutions and a good meal.

IN WEST GLACIER

Glacier Campground

P.O. Box 447, 12070 U.S. 2, West Glacier, MT 59936. ☎ **406/387-5689.** 80 tent sites, 80 RV sites. $15 tent; $18 RV; $30–$40 cabin.

One mile west of West Glacier on U.S. 2 is the closest campground outside the park. Set amid a forested area overgrown with evergreens, it's a quiet, comfortable place to retreat under the shade of the trees, especially on hot summer days. Most sites have water and electric hookups; the balance are perfect for tent camping. Five rather primitive cabins are also available, but furnishings are modest: sleeping beds with mattresses, electricity, but no plumbing or kitchen facilities. Recreational facilities include volleyball, horseshoes, and a basketball court; also on the premises are a Laundromat and teensy general store that has little to offer except a fresh quart of milk or a T-shirt.

Lake Five Resort

540 Belton Stage Rd., West Glacier, MT 59936. ☎ **406/387-5601.** 9 cabins, 35 sites (14 of which have trailer hookups). $70–$98 cabin; $16–$20 site.

Located 3 miles west of West Glacier and approximately 1 mile from U.S. 2 is this cabin and campground arrangement, an alternative to potentially crowded park campgrounds. Situated on a 235-acre lake surrounded by private homes and summer cottages, the resort is far from the maddening crowd (though still close to the park itself). Seven of the nine cabins are on the lakefront, all of them equipped with baths and showers. The only distraction may be the sound of powerboats.

Accommodations

IN THE PARK

With only one exception, Glacier Park (GPI) operates all of the hostelries in

Glacier National Park, which fall into two different categories. Lake McDonald Lodge, Glacier Park Lodge, and Many Glacier Hotel are first-tier properties that have been popular destinations since early in the century; Swiftcurrent Motor Inn is typical of the casual motel-style properties at the other end of the spectrum that provide good accommodations for less money. Although the lodges have a certain stately charm, don't expect in-room hot tubs or even air--conditioning. For example, the structures may have been constructed to withstand natural disasters, but little thought was given to interior soundproofing. So if you're an eavesdropper, you'll be in heaven; if you're a light sleeper, bring earplugs. While all of the lodges are adequately comfortable, their greatest attribute, aside from the architecture, may be their location in one of the most stunning natural settings in the world.

Reserve well in advance; July and August dates may fill before the spring thaw. For more information on the following properties or to make a reservation contact **Glacier Park,** VIAD Corp. Center, Phoenix, AZ 85077-0928 (☎ **602/207-6000**).

Apgar Village Lodge

Apgar Village, Box 398, West Glacier, MT 59936. ☎ **406/888-5484.** 28 cabins, 20 motel rms. TV. $69–$210 cabin; $57–$86 motel rm. DISC, MC, V. Closed mid-Oct to Apr.

The Apgar Village Lodge is located on the south end of Lake McDonald and is one of two lodgings located in Apgar Village. A less expensive alternative to the park's GPI-owned properties, the log and frame cabins have a rustic charm but lack in-room amenities.

Glacier Park Lodge

Glacier National Park, MT 59936. ☎ **602/207-6000.** 154 rms. TEL. $114–$160 lodge; $206 suite. AE, DISC, MC.

Conveniently located just inside the Southeast Entrance at East Glacier, this is the flagship inn of the park, an imposing timbered lodge that stands as a stately tribute to the Great Northern Railroad and its early attempts to lure tourists to Glacier. The carefully manicured lawn and ever-blooming wildflowers frame the grounds in colors spectacular enough to rival the mountain backdrop. The interior features massive Douglas fir pillars, some 40 inches in diameter and 40 feet tall. In fact, stand in the middle of the lobby and look up—you'll discover beams carved from massive trees that are the structural supports for the entire building. Skylights, massive wrought iron chandeliers, and a desk hewn from a 36-inch-diameter log add to the Old West flavor of the room.

Rooms are well furnished, but showers are elbow-banging small, and sinks are significantly smaller than those found in today's modern hotels and motels. A wooden deck outside the lounge provides an excellent spot for cocktails, reading, or a late-afternoon snooze. A glass-enclosed breezeway connects the main building to the annex; the oak chaise lounges found there are the ideal spot from which to watch sunrise. There's even an immaculately groomed executive-style nine-hole golf course. The Native American Trading Post offers traditional souvenirs, as well as nicely crafted Native American artwork and clothing.

While here, plan to spend an evening around the fireplace as Native Americans recount the history and culture of the Blackfeet Tribe.

Lake McDonald Lodge

Glacier National Park, MT 59936. ☎ **602/207-6000.** 62 rms in lodge and motel, 38 cottage rms (some without private bath). TEL. $113 lodge rm; $75 motel unit; $64–$113 cottage. AE, DISC, MC, V.

The Lake McDonald Lodge *feels* like a lodge, perhaps because that's how it began its life. This two-story building doesn't have the same towering ceilings and open spaces as other park hotels, but it has a warm, cozy feeling inspired by its construction. Situated on the shore of the park's largest lake, it provides a marvelous central base for exploring the western part of the park. The lodge is a center for boating activity; scenic cruises depart daily and canoe rentals are popular. Rooms in the Stewart Annex and well-preserved cabins are comfortable, but less desirable; be sure to inquire as to whether yours has a private bath. Common lounging areas are furnished with heavy couches, sofas and chairs that surround a stone fireplace. The lodge houses a dining room, gift shop, and lounge; a coffee shop, post office, and sundries store are also on the grounds.

Many Glacier Hotel

Glacier National Park, MT 59936. ☎ **602/207-6000.** 208 rms. TEL. $91–$113 lodge rm; $174 suite. AE, DISC, MC, V.

This alpine-style hotel may be the most photographed building in the park. When you arrive at Many Glacier after driving along the park's interior road from Babb, it comes slowly into view, as picturesque as a Swiss chalet and almost as inviting as the turquoise blue waters of Swiftcurrent Lake. Built in 1915 by the Great Northern Railway, this is the largest lodging in the park and among the most popular. Its chalet-style architecture fits right in with the alpine environment that surrounds it. In August, after the huckleberries ripen, you can almost count on seeing grizzly bears on the slopes of the mountain across the road from the hotel—they are easy to find, just look for the crowds.

Rooms are located in the main lodge around the balconies overlooking the lobby or in the adjoining annex. A dining room, coffee shop, gift shop, and lounge are all located in the hotel; nightly cabaret performances begin midsummer.

Rising Sun Motor Inn

Glacier National Park, MT 59936. ☎ **602/207-6000.** 63 rms. TEL. $72–$75 motor inn unit; $64 cottage unit. AE, DISC, MC, V.

Located 6.5 miles from St. Mary, just off Going-to-the-Sun Road, the Rising Sun is a complex made up of a restaurant, a motor inn, cottages, a camp store, a gift shop, and a service station. While the rooms are comfortable enough, the lake is across the street, and you'll be ideally located to explore the eastern side of the park from Going-to-the-Sun. The Rising Sun is considerably lacking in appeal. There's a lot of asphalt and plain brown buildings here, along with 28 motel rooms, 9 of which are located in the same building as the camp store, and 35 rooms in duplex cottages. It's still a convenient place to be, though, especially if you plan to take a scenic cruise or rent a boat.

Swiftcurrent Motor Inn

Glacier National Park, MT 59936. ☎ **602/207-6000.** 88 rms and cabins (most cabins without private bath). TEL. $66–$75 motor inn unit; $29–$49 cabin. AE, DISC, MC, V.

The appeal here is for those satisfied with modest prices and decor—primarily active types interested in spending lots of time exploring the backcountry trails. Like Many Glacier, which is just up the street, the inn is set against a mountain backdrop in what is considered a hiker's paradise. There are 42 motor inn rooms, 20 motel rooms, and 26 cabins. Each of the motel units includes a private bath; cabins are outfitted with kitchenettes, one or two bedrooms, and *perhaps* a bath (public facilities are nearby if you don't get a private bath). There's also a coffee shop/restaurant on the premises. Actually, with the money you'll save by staying here instead of in the more posh Many Glacier, you might just be able to afford dinner in the hotel dining room.

Village Inn

Glacier National Park, MT 59936. ☎ **602/207-6000.** 36 rms. $80–$105 double; $124 suite. AE, DISC, MC, V.

Not to be confused with Apgar Village Lodge (see above), the Village Inn is the smallest of the properties operated by

GPI in Glacier. Located in Apgar Village, the inn is convenient to the general store, cafes, and boat docks. Like its counterparts throughout the park, the Village Inn is comfortably outfitted with modest furnishings, making it a cozy and convenient place to set up camp: all 36 rooms are located on 2 floors of the inn and 12 of them are outfitted with kitchenettes. Second-level rooms have the same lake views as those downstairs, but have less people traffic. Though you also won't find a dining room on the property, the restaurants of Lake McDonald and Apgar are all close by. Close to the Apgar corral and the docks of Lake McDonald, not to a plethora of hiking trails, Apgar Village bustles with activity during the summer and is a great choice for families.

NEAR THE PARK

If the convenience of staying on Glacier's back porch is important to you, the following places are your best bets. However, in surrounding communities not necessarily classified as gateway towns, you'll find a greater variety of accommodations, especially if you're willing to travel as far as Whitefish, Kalispell, or Columbia Falls. These places might be more in line with your needs if the park is merely a 1- or 2-day part of your vacation.

IN EAST GLACIER

Backpacker's Inn

P.O. Box 94, East Glacier, MT 59434. ☎ **406/226-9392.** 3 cabins, sleeping 20 people. $10 per person. DISC, MC, V. Closed mid-Oct to Apr.

This dorm-style hostel consists of three cabins—one for men, one for women, and one coed—each sleeping up to six people (the coed cabin sleeps eight). At $10 per person, the price is right, but don't expect the rooms to include much more than a bed.

Brownies Grocery and AYH Hostel

P.O. Box 229, East Glacier, MT 59434. ☎ **406/226-4426** or 406/226-4456. 10 rms, 2 family rms (all with shared bath). AYH members $10–$15 or $30 family rm; nonmembers $13–$23 or $35 family rm. MC, V. Closed Oct to early May, depending on the weather.

Reservations are recommended at this popular combination grocery store/hostel, which offers comfortable rooms at extremely affordable prices. Dorm and family rooms are located on the second floor of a rustic, older log building with several common rooms for guests to share, including a porch, kitchen, bathrooms, and laundry.

Mountain Pine Hotel

Mont. 49, East Glacier, MT 59434. ☎ **406/226-4403.** 25 units. TV TEL. $50–$66 double. DISC, MC, V.

This property is a one-story, '50s-type motel that provides clean, well-furnished rooms equipped with cable TV, in a shaded, timbered area on the main highway. Most standard rooms have two queen-size beds, reading chairs and table, chest, and bathrooms with tub-shower combinations. Considering the fact that rooms here are about a third as expensive as at the park hotels, this is an excellent alternative.

Jacobson's Cottages

P.O. Box 216, East Glacier, MT 59434. ☎ **406/226-4422.** 12 cottages. $50–$60 cottage. AE, DISC, MC, V. Closed Nov–Apr.

Located in a nicely wooded area, these quaint cottages are small but comfortable. And while they aren't equipped with either TVs or kitchens (with one exception), entertainment and good food are short walks away with the Restaurant Thimbleberry a half block down the street and Two Medicine a mere 4-mile drive. The cottages are available seasonally, and reservations are recommended.

IN ESSEX

Izaak Walton Inn

P.O. Box 653, Essex, MT 59916. ☎ **406/888-5700.** 30 rms, 3 suites, 4 caboose cottages. $95 double; $146 suite; $475 caboose (3-night minimum). MC, V.

Built in 1939 by the railway, this historic Tudor lodge once served as living quarters for rail crews who serviced the railroad. Located just off U.S. 2 on the southern boundary of Glacier Park, the Izaak Walton is now extremely popular with tourists and locals alike, many of whom choose to travel via train, which arrives a mere 50 feet from the front door of the lodge. During winter months this inn is a popular jumping-off spot for cross-country skiers.

IN POLEBRIDGE

North Fork Hostel and Square Peg Ranch

P.O. Box 1, Polebridge, MT 59928. ☎ **800/775-2938** or 406/888-5241. 15 bunks, 2 log homes, 2 cabins. $12 bunk; $40 log home; $25 cabin. AE.

Formerly called the Quarter Circle MC Ranch and located inside the park, this lodge was moved to its present location near Polebridge in the late 1960s, and is probably best suited to the back-to-nature traveler. It now sits within a stone's throw of the North Fork of the Flathead River. The lodge features complete kitchen facilities for the do-it-yourselfer, as do the log homes, each with three double beds, a fireplace, and a refrigerator, which is powered by a generator.

Polebridge Mercantile and Cabins

P.O. Box 42, Polebridge, MT 59928. ☎ **406/888-5105.** 4 cabins, 1 tepee. $30–$35 cabin; $20 tepee. Children stay free. MC, V.

If you can make the trek up the gravelly North Fork Road, then give these bare-bones cabins a try. There is no electricity and no running water, let alone bedding—it's bring your own sleeping bag at the Merc. However, each cabin has propane cooking stoves and lights, and the views out over the west side of Glacier National Park make the $35 price tag a steal, especially if you brought the kids. This may sound like an adventure in hell, but Polebridge is a happening spot in the summer when all the river rats and seasonal residents converge for whopping good times and tall tales about the rapids they've run and their mountaineering adventures.

IN ST. MARY

St. Mary Lodge

U.S. 89 and Going-to-the-Sun Rd., St. Mary, MT 59417. ☎ **800/452-7275** or 406/363-3689. 57 rms, 19 cottages. $88 rm; $250 cottage. AE, DISC, MC, V.

Situated at the St. Mary end of Going-to-the-Sun Road, this lodge is another member of the minority of properties that aren't managed by GPI. The main lodge and attendant rooms are standard Montana fare, with tasteful western lodgepole furniture and furnishings. Lodging is in three different areas in close proximity to the center of the complex; lodge and motel rooms are nicely done motel-style units that may be furnished with two single beds or a queen. Rooms are tiny but are furnished with stylish lodgepole pine beds, tables, and brass reading lamps. Baths are small, self-contained units with showers. Nicer units are in the Glacier cabins, which boast living areas with dining tables, kitchenettes with microwaves and minifridges, and queen beds in a separate sleeping area. The most expensive units here are the Pinnacle Cottages, newly constructed cabins perched on a bluff across the highway from the main complex that afford views of Going-to-the-Sun Road and St. Mary Lake.

IN WEST GLACIER

Great Northern Chalets

12127 U.S. 2, West Glacier, MT 59936. ☎ **800/387-5340.** 6 rms. $95–$105. DISC, MC, V.

This small, family oriented resort located near West Glacier offers log chalets that have balconies facing landscaped flower gardens and a pond, with mountain views in the distance. A 16-foot indoor hot tub spa is on the property, as are a volleyball court that doubles as a sandbox for children, and a pond that is used for fly-fishing instruction. Two types of chalets are offered, the largest being a beautifully furnished two-story, two-bedroom unit with three queen beds, a full bathroom upstairs, and half bath downstairs. Smaller chalets have one large upstairs bedroom with two queen beds, and a downstairs level with a full-size sleeper sofa and a kitchen with service for six.

West Glacier Motel

200 Going-to-the-Sun Rd., West Glacier, MT 59936. ☎ **406/888-5662.** 32 rms. $59 single or double. DISC, MC, V.

Formerly the Riverbend Motel, this property has two locations. Half of the units are in West Glacier on the Going-to-the-Sun Road, about 1 mile from the park entrance, and a second set of units is 1 mile away on a forested piece of ground that presents panoramic views of the park. This 1950s-style motel, in addition to its location and property, boasts having TV sets despite the fact that there is virtually no reception unless it happens to be your lucky day. However, the prices can't be beat during peak season, and rates drop dramatically the week before Labor Day. Cabins are better suited to family use, since they come with two or three queen beds, kitchens completely equipped for cooking, and a dishwasher.

Glacier River Ranch Bed & Breakfast

P.O. Box 176, Coram, MT 59913. ☎ **406/387-4151.** 5 rms, 1 suite. TEL. $85–$110 double; $405 suite. Three-night minimum stay. MC, V. Rates include continental breakfast.

This 40-acre ranch, bordered by the Flathead River, 7 miles north of the West Glacier Entrance to the park, offers a framed lodge with five bedrooms, a TV room (with cable, no less), a hot tub, and a main room. In short, all the creature comforts are at your disposal. The flavor of the West is evident in the no-pets rule, which allows all domesticated animals *except* the horse. (Overnight horse accommodations are available.) A trout pond is located on the property for anglers who don't feel a compunction to walk to the river. We wouldn't call the breakfast a full breakfast, but the selection of baked items, fruits, cereals, and coffee is adequate.

Glacier Wilderness Resort

P.O. Box 295, West Glacier, MT 59936. ☎ **406/888-5664.** 10 lodges. TEL. $130–$150 per lodge per night. Five-night minimum stay. MC, V.

Surrounded by Forest Service lands, the lodges at this year-round resort are as private as you can get. Each lodge is a "home," complete with a stereo, VCR, and a hot tub on the front porch. Families will find the two-bedroom lodges to their liking, and kids can play outdoors during the day (there are 23 undeveloped acres) and at the Recreation Center, with diversions like foosball, pool, and video games. Hiking trails abound and some even come up on some surprising waterfalls. For a summer stay, reservations should be made before March.

Mountain Timbers

P.O. Box 94, West Glacier, MT 59936. ☎ **800/841-3835** or 406/387-5830. 7 rms (4 with private bath). $55–$85 double with shared bath; $95–$125 double with private bath. AE, MC, V.

Tucked away on the other side of the Flathead River near the south side of the park is this cozy B&B. Situated on 260 acres, the beautiful 5,000-square-foot lodge offers easy access to the park and more than 10 miles of gorgeous hiking and biking trails of its own. It's an excellent spot for avoiding park crowds. After days spent in the outdoors, evenings may be spent soaking in the hot tub or lounging in the library. During winter months the lodge is transformed into an excellent base for cross-county skiers, with more than 10 miles of well-groomed trails that are even good enough for the locals.

Vista Motel

P.O. Box 98, West Glacier, MT 59936. ☎ **406/888-5311.** 26 rms. TV. $60–$140 double. AE, DISC, MC, V. Closed Nov–Feb.

Perched atop a hill at the West Entrance to Glacier National Park, the Vista boasts tremendous views of the mountains, but there is one catch: You'll have to visit from March through October to see them. Accommodations are not memorable, but rooms are clean and comfortable, and there's an outdoor heated pool.

Dining

INSIDE THE PARK

Food options inside the park are primarily limited to dining rooms operated by **GPI** that, regrettably, are overpriced and unimaginative more often than not. A constant turnover of chefs at the park's lodges makes it difficult to sustain a high level of quality from season to season. The dining rooms are convenient, however, and you're almost always assured of friendly service from a staff of twentysomething college students from around the country. Credit cards accepted at all GPI properties include Discover, MasterCard, and Visa; traveler's checks are also accepted but personal and business checks are not.

You'll find above-average food served at above-average prices in the dining rooms at the major properties. **Glacier Park Lodge** has the Goatlick Steak & Rib House and the Teepee Room; **Lake McDonald Lodge** has the Cedar Dining Room and Lounge; **Many Glacier Hotel** has the Ptarmigan Dining Room. The dining rooms open with the park and close sometime in September, depending on the facility. At each dining room, breakfast is served from 6:30 to 9:30am; lunch from 11:30am to 2pm; and dinner from 5:30 to 9:30pm. Coffee and snack shops open either at 7 or 8am and close at 9pm.

The alternatives include second-tier restaurants in close proximity to the hotels, most of which are comparable to chain restaurants. The coffee shop at the **Rising Sun Motor Inn** serves "hearty American fare"; the **Swiftcurrent Motor Inn** restaurant is the Italian Garden, which serves meals from 6am to 10pm. Breakfast prices range from $4 to $7; lunch and dinner feature combinations of salads, sandwiches, pasta dishes, and lasagna or "create your own" pizza. At **Apgar** you'll find the Cedar Tree Deli, which specializes in sandwiches, ice cream and cold drinks, and Eddie's Cafe, a family dining arrangement. The restaurant at **Lake McDonald** is Trail's End, where you'll find Continental breakfast ($5) and a full buffet breakfast ($8.25). Lunch is sandwiches and soup ($6 to $9); among items on the dinner menu are beef tenderloin, roast duckling, seared mountain trout, roast turkey, Alaskan salmon, pasta, chicken, and steaks ($12 to $20).

NEAR THE PARK

The gateway cities aren't exactly a culinary wasteland, but for *really* good food head for Whitefish or Kalispell.

IN EAST GLACIER

Whistle Stop, 1020 Mont. 49 (☎ **406/206-4426**), may serve up the very best breakfasts in the area. Omelettes are a specialty; they come in seven different styles, including a Spanish omelet with chorizo sausage, lots of peppers, tomatoes, onions, and spinach. Definitely an eye-opener.

The Snow Goose Grill, located in St. Mary Lodge Resort, is the high-priced alternative. Breakfasts start at $4.50 for a stack of flapjacks and run to $7 for steak and eggs. The ambience is upscale for these parts—a glass-enclosed dining room with views of the mountains and the creek. Luncheon entrees include typical restaurant sandwiches with fancy names like the "Garden Wall," filled with such diverse items as turkey and buffalo steak; prices range from $5 to $9. The dinner menu features Montana ground buffalo steak ($27), lake whitefish ($12), and prime rib ($18).

The **Park Cafe** (☎ **406/732-4482**), only 1½ blocks away on U.S. 89, is a cozier, less-pretentious, home-style restaurant in an old house that presents an excellent alternative to resort and patio dining. The food's good, prices are moderate, and it's not as crowded.

Glacier Village Restaurant

304–308 Mont. 2, East Glacier. ☎ **406/226-4464.** Reservations accepted. Breakfast items $3–$5; lunch $4–$7; main courses dinner $8–$17. MC, V. Daily 6am–10pm. Closed Oct–Apr. AMERICAN.

This family owned, seasonal restaurant is one of the few full-service joints in the area that serves three meals, starting with breakfast at 6am. It's actually two in one: a cafeteria on one side and a full-service restaurant on the other. Portions are healthy and prices are moderate, but don't expect anything too exotic. The cafeteria half dishes up great home style food with standards like yummy waffles and pancakes made from homemade batter, as well as a hearty chicken potpie. The restaurant side is impressive with a menu that includes medallions of pork with raspberry sauce and a succulent smoked chicken breast spinach salad.

Restaurant Thimbleberry

112 Park Dr., East Glacier. ☎ **406/226-5523.** Breakfast items $5–$6; lunch $5–$7; main courses dinner $9–$15. No credit cards. Daily 7am–9:30pm. Closed Oct–Apr. AMERICAN.

Locally famous for their incredible pies—the lemon meringue and raspberry are both excellent choices—the Thimbleberry serves a great veggie omelette for breakfast, sandwiches and salads for lunch, and an excellent cornmeal-dusted St. Mary's Lake whitefish for dinner. This is a good choice for vegetarians looking for something other than a Montana steak or hamburger, and the calorie-conscious will find several fat-free choices. If you've never had frybread, then this is the place to try it.

Serrano's

29 Dawson Ave., East Glacier. ☎ **406/226-9392.** Reservations recommended. Main courses $8–$10. DISC, MC, V. May to mid-Oct daily 5–10pm; closed mid-Oct to Apr. MEXICAN.

Perhaps the area's best restaurant, except for the hotels, is Serrano's Mexican Restaurant, which is just off the highway at the center of town. Serrano's has an outstanding local reputation, so don't be surprised if you encounter masses of people during the height of summer. You can expect hearty portions of Americanized Mexican food if you make this your dining stop. On top of that, the restaurant also has an ample selection of imported beers and microbrews.

IN POLEBRIDGE

Northern Lights Saloon

Polebridge. ☎ **406/888-5669.** Reservations not accepted. Main courses $5–$9. No credit cards. Daily 4pm–midnight. Closed Labor Day to Memorial Day. AMERICAN.

When people don't mind traveling over 30 miles of bumpy gravel road, when they don't blink an eye as they hit yet another gaping pothole and lose a hubcap or bend a rim, you've got to realize that they must know something you don't about wherever it is they're going: in this case, the Northern Lights Saloon. This small restaurant, located squarely in the middle of nowhere, boasts summer crowds that often have to wait patiently outside for a table to clear. Picnic tables, a volleyball net, and the peaks of Glacier Park are there to make the wait as painless as possible. Seating choices are uncomplicated: Take a seat at one of the five tables, or find a spot at the bar. You won't find a place with more character or with friendlier staff and customers, and you don't need a tie.

IN WEST GLACIER

Heaven's Peak Restaurant

12130 Mont. 2, West Glacier. ☎ **406/387-4754.** Lunch $6–$8, main dinner courses $9–$15. DISC, MC, V. Daily 11am–10pm. AMERICAN.

West Glacier's newest eating facility is in a massive log building right off the highway within footsteps of town. A massive deck overlooks a beautiful sculpted rock garden and manicured lawns grounds and provides comfortable seating but, alas, also provides road noise. The chef is proud of the fact there is no deep fryer on the property, nor are anything except fresh ingredients used in meal preparation. The luncheon menu includes several salads as well as various sandwich dishes($6 to $8); dinners include fresh fish as well as pasta, chicken, and beef ($13 to $15); a children's menu is also available. However, as of this writing, you'll have to bring your own wine if you want to imbibe during your meal.

Glacier Highlander Restaurant

U.S. 2, West Glacier. ☎ **406/888-5427.** Reservations accepted. Breakfast $3–$5; lunch $5–$7; dinner $7–$14. DISC, MC, V. Daily 7am–9pm. Closed Nov 2–Mar 31. AMERICAN.

This may be the spot to satisfy the sweet tooth; a baker is on hand, so the pies are well worth the stop, and the cinnamon rolls are breakfast giants. The Highland Burger is, by any standard, a great hunk of beef, and the fresh trout is a dinner specialty.

A Side Trip into Waterton Lakes National Park

It's worth finding the time to explore the upper regions of this area. From St. Mary, head north to visit **Waterton Lakes National Park,** Glacier's northern, Canadian counterpart. you'll be rewarded with different yet equally beautiful scenery and a touch of European culture.

Waterton is considered the place where the Canadian mountains meet the rolling prairies; at this juxtaposition there is a more diverse variety of flowers and animals than is found in most national parks in this region. As you travel along the high ridge you'll see meadows and boggy areas that are ideal habitat for moose; later you'll find yourself surrounded by lakes, as the Canadian Rockies fill the horizon. The area is also a haven for elk, mule deer, and bighorn sheep, and both grizzly and black bears are found in the park.

JUST THE FACTS

Getting There. From the Eastern Entrance of Glacier National Park at St. Mary, drive north through Babb, which is barely a whistle-stop, until you reach the intersection of Mont. 17—it's very well marked. Head northwest to the Canadian border, where Mont. 17 becomes Canada Highway 6 (remember, you need proof of citizenship—and a driver's license doesn't always work). Head down into the valley until you reach the park entrance on your left.

Visitor Information. The park's only **Visitor Reception Centre** is just inside the park, on the same road you used coming in (☎ **403/859-5133**).

A BRIEF HISTORY

Compared to its counterparts in the Lower 48, Waterton is a tiny park; the total size is only 203 square miles. However, the park has great historical significance; based on more than 200 identified archaeological sites, historians think that Aborigines first populated the area 11,000 years ago.

In modern times, after Canada's first oil well was drilled here and the park was about to become an oil field, it was set aside as a national park, thanks to the efforts of a local rancher. Then in 1932, following an initiative by the Rotary Clubs of Alberta and Montana, Waterton Lakes and Glacier national parks were designated the world's first International Peace Park, and have since come to represent the need for cooperation between nations where sharing resources and ecosystems is possible. The areas were designated Bio-Sphere Reserves by the UNESCO Man and Bio-Sphere Program, in order to provide information about the relationships between people and the environment.

EXPLORING THE PARK

Unlike most "park centers"—essentially a smattering of restaurants, souvenir shops, and gas stations clustered around the primary lodging—Waterton Village actually *is* a village. As you cruise the perimeter of the lake headed for Waterton Village, you'll pass three large lakes, the habitat of bald eagles that are often seen perched atop the snags of dead trees. The park bears a striking resemblance to Teton in that its attractions spread out across a narrow valley floor; however, the valley is narrower and three-fourths of it is surrounded by peaks, so the overall effect is cozier and equally dramatic.

By most standards, it's also windier here, though locals say that they don't acknowledge the wind unless there are whitecaps in the rest room toilets at the Prince of Wales Hotel (see "Accommodations," below).

Hiking, cruising the lake, or just doing nothing are ideal pastimes in this neck of the woods. Most of the 191 miles of trails are easily accessible from town and range in difficulty from short strolls to steep treks for overnight backcountry enthusiasts. Hiking permits may be obtained at the visitor reception center up to 24 hours in advance of your trip, or reserved by calling ☎ **403/859-5133.**

DAY HIKES

The park is a popular destination for European, Canadian, and American hiking fanatics. For nearly 20 years, the 10.8-mile **Crypt Lake hike** has been rated as one of Canada's best hikes—except for those prone to seasickness, since the trailhead is reached by taking a 2-mile boat ride across Upper Waterton Lake. After that, the trail leads past Hellroaring Falls, Twin Falls, and Burnt Rock Falls before reaching Crypt Falls, and a passage through a 60-foot rock tunnel. The elevation gain is 2,300 feet, but veterans say the whole hike is doable in 3 hours.

A second extended tour is from the marina and heads south across the international boundary to **Goat Haunt,** Montana, an especially popular trip because of the sightings of bald eagles, bear, bighorn sheep, deer, and moose, as well as numerous unusual geologic formations. For details regarding the boat shuttle, call ☎ **403/859-2362.**

The **International Peace Park Hike** is a free guided trip held on Saturdays from the end of June through the end of August. Participants meet at the Bertha Trailhead at 10am and spend the day on an 8.5-mile trail that follows Upper Waterton Lake. At the end of the trail, hikers return via boat to the main dock. Adult fare is C$10 (U.S.$7); children's fare C$5 (U.S.$3.60).

CAMPING

There are 15 designated wilderness campgrounds with dry toilets and surface water, some of which have shelters.

At the west end of the village is **Townsite Campground,** a Canada Park Service–operated facility with 235 sites that's an especially popular jumping-off spot for campers headed into the park's backcountry. Prices range from C$15 to C$21 (U.S.$11 to U.S.$15); half of the sites have electricity and sewage disposal; also available on the premises are kitchen shelters, washrooms, and shower facilities. The site is perched right on the lake, so views are excellent and trails await evening strollers.

ACCOMMODATIONS

For complete lodging information contact **central reservations** for the Waterton area (☎ **800/215-2395**).

While the **Prince of Wales Hotel** (see below) is clearly the flagship in these woods, alternate arrangements can be made at **Kilmore Lodge** (☎ **403/859-2334**). This cozy country inn on Emerald Bay, at the north end of the lake, has an antique decor. Bedrooms have down comforters and the dining room and lounge are on premises. Waterton's newest property is the **Lodge at Waterton Lake** (☎ **888/985-6343** or 403/859-2150), which opened in July 1997. In the heart of Waterton Village, the lodge offers lake and mountain views; some rooms have fireplaces, whirlpool tubs, and kitchenettes. Other facilities include a health center spa and indoor pool.

The Prince of Wales Hotel

Waterton Lakes National Park, AB TOK 2M0. ☎ **403/859-2231** or 602/207-6000 in the off-season. 87 rms. TEL. C$180–C$235 (U.S.$127–U.S.$165) double, C$360 (U.S.$254) suite. MC, V. Closed Oct–Apr.

The Prince of Wales compares to the finest park hostelries in Montana and Wyoming. Built in 1927 by the Great Northern Railway, the hotel boasts soaring roofs, gables, and balconies that convey the appearance of a giant alpine chalet. The lobby, like many of the old railroad hotels, is wood, wood, and more wood—in this case accented by tufted furniture and carpeting. Two-story-tall windows overlook the lake and village, only minutes away by footpath. Rooms, though small, have aged well, with dark-stained high-paneled wainscoting and heavily upholstered chairs. Baths are European-style tubs with wrap-around curtains; one look at the size of the wash basins, and you'd surmise guests were Lilliputian-size when the hotel was first constructed.

If you don't spend the night, at least stop in for a traditional British high tea, served afternoons at 3pm for C$14 (U.S.$10). All in all, the experience is very European—even the gift shop sells china and crystal.

DINING

All of the village's restaurants and retail outlets are within a 4-block area on Waterton Avenue (which the locals call Main Street). So despite the fact that many buildings aren't numbered, you'll have no problem finding places to eat or shop.

Waterton Park Family Cafe (no phone) has indoor dining on plastic chairs and tables and is organized for the family looking for a modestly priced meal; breakfast prices average C$4 to C$7 (U.S.$2.85 to U.S.$5), and dinner runs C$10 to C$13 (U.S.$7 to U.S.$9). Just up the street, **Zum's** (☎ **403/859-2388**) is another family oriented restaurant with a comparable menu but lower prices. More luxurious surroundings, and slightly higher prices, are the order of the day at **Kootenai Brown Dining Room** (☎ **403/859-2211**) at the Bayshore Inn, considered the luxury spot on the lake. The order of the day is steaks, chicken, rack of lamb and the occasional seafood entree; prices range from C$13 to C$19 (U.S.$9 to U.S.$14).

New Frank's Restaurant (☎ **403/859-2240**) serves both conventional Western fare that includes beef, chicken, and spaghetti—with prices ranging from C$8 to C$13 (U.S.$5.70 to U.S.$9)—as well as a Chinese menu that includes an all-you-can-eat evening buffet for C$10 (U.S.$7).

17

GLACIER BAY NATIONAL PARK

by Charles P. Wohlforth

GLACIER BAY IS A WORK IN PROGRESS; THE BOAT RIDE TO ITS HEAD IS a chance to see creation fresh. The bay John Muir discovered in a canoe in 1879 didn't exist a century earlier. Eighteenth-century explorers had found instead a wall of ice a mile thick where the entrance to the branching, 65-mile-long fjord now opens to the sea. Receding faster than any other glacier on earth, the ice melted into the ocean and opened a spectacular and still-unfinished land. The land itself is rising 1½ inches a year as it rebounds from the weight of now-melted glaciers. As your vessel retraces Muir's path—and then probes northward in deep water where ice stood in his day—the story of this new world unravels in reverse. The trees on the shore get smaller, then disappear, then all vegetation disappears, and finally, at the head of the bay, the ice stands at the water's edge surrounded by barren rock, rounded and scored by the passage of the ice and not yet marked by the waterfalls cascading down out of the clouds above. It's often windy and cold at the head of the bay, near the glaciers. Precipitation and cold add up to glaciers. Be prepared, and try to enjoy the beauty of the mist and rain—at times the smooth, silver water, barren rock, white clouds, and ice create an ethereal study in white.

Glacier Bay, first set aside by Pres. Calvin Coolidge in 1925, is managed by the National Park Service, which has the difficult job of protecting the wilderness while showing it to the public. This is a challenge, since this rugged land the size of Connecticut can be seen only by boat or plane, and the presence of too many boats threatens the park (plus, the whales appear to be sensitive to the noise of vessels). Since the 1970s, when in 1 year only a single whale returned, the Park Service has used a permit system to severely limit the number of ships that can enter the bay. With Alaska tourism booming, the state's powerful congressional delegation pushed for more cruise-ship permits for the bay. The Park Service agreed to an increase to take effect in 1997, and was sued by the National Parks and Conservation Association. Already, any tour boat sees several other ships on a day's journey up the bay, but how much it bothers the whales really can't be proved. As for the visitors, they seem happy: In 1996, *Consumer Reports* readers voted this the best of all the national parks to visit.

If you go, you'll either be on one of those vessels or in an aircraft. There really is no cheap way to visit Glacier Bay. The uniqueness of the glaciers of Glacier Bay lies in their size and geological activity, in their number, and in the opportunity to see them fairly close-up in a remote setting. On a Glacier Bay boat ride you'll also see wildlife—sea lions and eagles almost certainly, and possibly humpback whales. But there are other places in Southeast rich with marine wildlife, so don't feel compelled to go.

Avoiding the Crowds. This won't be a problem on our visit to Glacier Bay. Probably the best way to see the park and avoid the crowds is simply to travel there independently. If you're not on a big cruise ship (the way most people see the park), you'll have an opportunity to hike the trails at Barlett Cover and to take a guided boat or plane ride with only a few other passengers. You'll have the opportunity to stay in the Glacier Bay Lodge or in nearby Gustavus, which has some of the most attractive accommodations in Alaska. And you'll see the glaciers up close and personal. Glacier Bay is not a cheap destination, nor is it very easy to get to. But if you want to avoid the crowds, this is one of the places you can really do it.

Just the Facts

GETTING THERE & GATEWAYS

Gustavus is the gateway to Glacier Bay. Unless you're on a cruise ship, you'll fly or take a passenger ferry to Gustavus, then take a van to the park headquarters. The vans meet the planes and boats and cost $10 to make the 10-mile trip to the park.

By Boat. The *Auk Nu* passenger ferry (☎ **800/820-2686** or 907/586-8687) leaves Juneau's Auke Bay Harbor from 11789 Glacier Hwy. at 11am daily May through September. The fare is $45 one way, $85 round-trip. The *Auk Nu* lands at the Gustavus dock at 1:15pm, goes on an afternoon whale-watching cruise, then leaves for Juneau at 5:45pm, arriving at 8pm.

There is a multiday boat excursion into the park from Juneau; it's described under "Seeing the Park," below.

By Air. Various commuter carriers serve Gustavus from the nearby towns, including **L.A.B. Flying Service** (☎ **800/426-0543** or 907/766-2222). Five daily flights from Juneau are $60 one way.

It's possible to take a flightseeing trip to Glacier Bay from Haines; details are given under "Seeing the Park," below.

GETTING INFORMATION BEFORE YOUR TRIP

To get information about Glacier Bay before your trip, contact the park headquarters at **Glacier Bay National Park and Preserve,** Gustavus, AK 99826 (☎ **907/687-2230**, or e-mail the park at **GLBA_Administration@nps. gov**). Be sure to ask for the Directory of Commercial Services.

The park's main concessionaire, **Glacier Bay Tours,** however, operates most of the activities. They can be reached at 520 Pike St., Suite 1400, Seattle, WA 98101 (☎ **800/451-5952** or 206/623-2417; fax 206/623-7809; Web site **www.glacierbaytours.com**) or, locally, in the summer only, at P.O. Box 199, Gustavus, AK 99826 (☎ **907/697-2226;** fax 907/697-2408).

You can see information on the park on the National Park Service Web site at: **www.nps.gov/glba/**.

Be aware that there are no public buildings in **Gustavus** because there is no government: Only the community association and the state government hold sway. **Puffin Bed and Breakfast,** P.O. Box 3, Gustavus, AK 99826 (☎ **800/478-2258** in Alaska only, or 907/697-2260; e-mail 73654.550@compuserve.com), has a booking agency. Generally, you'll rely on your host at the inn or B&B for information. Be certain you reserve a place to stay before showing up in Gustavus.

VISITOR CENTER

The Park Service interprets the park mainly by placing well-prepared rangers on board all cruise and tour vessels entering the bay, but they also maintain a modest **Visitor Center** with displays on the park on the second floor of the concessionaire's lodge at Bartlett Cove. The park's offices, a free campground, a backcountry office, a few short hiking trails, a dock, and other park facilities also surround the lodge in a wooded setting.

ENTRANCE & CAMPING FEES

There are no fees to visit or camp in Glacier Bay National Park and Preserve (or at least you don't have to pay them directly). The fees to use the park are included in the price of any activity you do pay for (your boat trip around the bay, your lodge room).

SPECIAL REGULATIONS & WARNINGS

◆ Visitors are urged not to eat mussels and clams from Glacier Bay because a naturally occurring neurotoxin that causes **paralytic shellfish poisoning** has been found in high concentrations in the area's shellfish. **Giardia** has also been a problem in park waters; all water should be boiled or treated before drinking.

◆ **Firearms are prohibited** in Glacier Bay National Park and must be secured at the Visitor Information Station for the duration of your stay if you bring them into the park boundaries.

◆ **Sportfishing** is allowed in Glacier Bay, but you will need to purchase an Alaska state fishing license (available at the Glacier Bay Lodge during summer months).

◆ Entrance into the park and preserve by **private boat** requires a permit between June 1 and August 31. Permits are limited and may be reserved (call the park's main number for information).

◆ **Campers** should obtain a permit at the park's Visitor Information Station, but these are not limited and need not be reserved. **Backcountry permits** are required for overnight backcountry travel.

SEASONS & CLIMATE

The travel season to Glacier Bay generally lasts between mid-May and September (when most of the area's accommodations shut down for the winter and when the Visitor Center closes). Rain and long periods of cool, overcast weather are common in the area, with daytime temperatures ranging from 45° to 65°F. You should bring a hat, gloves, rain gear, and waterproof footwear. Most boat service into Gustavus is suspended except during summer, but you can still fly in. However, weather conditions occasionally cause flight cancellations, so it's a good idea to have some room in your schedule to accommodate these.

USEFUL PUBLICATIONS

You can purchase books on the natural and cultural history of Glacier Bay and of Alaska from the Alaska Natural History Association. Write or call the park headquarters for a catalog and order form; you can also request the catalog by e-mail (send your request to **Melody_Jamieson @nps.gov**).

If You Only Have 1 Day

Because of its isolation, Glacier Bay cannot be seen easily in a day trip, though it is possible. If you only have 1 day, you can fly to the park via **Haines Air** (☎ **907/789-2336**) from Juneau, Haines, or Skagway, and then take the *Spirit of Adventure* tour boat (the boat trip is described below). But it makes for a long day—you have to board the plane at 5:30am in Juneau—and the schedule leaves no time in Glacier Bay for anything but the boat trip. The package fare from Juneau is $329.50. A better choice is to spend the night before the boat trip in Gustavus or at the lodge. The overnight lodge package is $342.50 to $411.50. You can book either package through the park's concessionaire, Glacier Bay Tours and Cruises (details in the next section).

Seeing the Park

BY BOAT

The ***Spirit of Adventure*** tour boat is the main way for independent travelers to see the park. It is operated by park concessionaire **Glacier Bay Tours and Cruises,** 520 Pike St., Suite 1400, Seattle, WA 98101 (☎ **800/451-5952** or 206/623-2417; fax 206/623-7809; Web site www.glacierbaytours.com), or, locally, in the summer only, P.O. Box 199, Gustavus, AK 99826 (☎ **907/697-2226;** fax 907/697-2408). The fast, quiet tour boat carries up to 250 passengers in upper and lower lounges in a comfortable, table-oriented seating configuration. Bring heavy rain gear, as the windows can fog up and you'll want to spend as much time as possible outside. There's a snack bar and a simple lunch is provided. Bring binoculars or rent them on board for $2; they're a necessity. The boat leaves Bartlett Cove at 7am for a 9-hour cruise, for $153.50.

If your budget allows, there may be no better way to see Glacier Bay than on a small cruise ship on an excursion of a couple of days or more. Glacier Bay

Tours and Cruises' ***Wilderness Explorer*** and the larger ***Wilderness Adventurer*** get you out into the park in a pampered outdoors experience. Leaving Juneau on trips of varying lengths, passengers hike, kayak, or boat in the bay during the day and sleep and eat in comfort on board at night. The trips range in length from 2 to 6 days and in price from $549 to $2,300.

Smaller operators based in Gustavus also do these trips. If you have a large group, you can have a boat and guide to yourself. Mike Nigro, a former backcountry ranger and 25-year resident, takes groups of 4 to 6 for $1,400 to $1,650 per day on a 42-foot yacht. **Gustavus Marine Charters** is reached at P.O. Box 81, Gustavus, AK 99826 (**☎ 907/697-2233;** fax 907/697-2414).

BY AIR

The other way to get into the park is by flightseeing. **Frontier Air,** P.O. Box 1, Gustavus, AK 99826 (**☎ 907/697-2386**), offers flights from the Bartlett Cove Visitor Center. Other companies offer tours from various towns, Haines being the closest, served by **L.A.B. Flying Service** (**☎ 800/426-0543** or 907/766-2222). You'll see the incredible rivers of ice that flow down into the bay, and may even see wildlife. What you give up is a lingering, up-close look and the awesome sense of having all that ice and rock above you.

Exploring the Backcountry

It is possible to explore the undeveloped areas of the park by sea kayak or by foot and to camp on your own, but this is recommended only for experienced outdoor types. The *Spirit of Adventure* will drop you off at one of several designated points (they change each year, and there is an additional fee for this service).

Backcountry permits have been required since summer 1997 and may be limited in summer 1998 (be sure to call ahead to the park if you are seriously considering this option). They are free, however, and there is a **camper orientation** program offered twice daily at the Bartlett Cover Visitor Information Station; all campers in Glacier Bay are strongly urged to attend this program.

Ranger Programs

During the season, there are several daily programs in Bartlett Cover, including twice-daily **films;** a 3-hour, guided **morning hike;** a guided walk through the **Forest Loop** (described under "Day Hikes," below); and a twice-nightly **evening program.**

Day Hikes

There are three hiking trails, right at the Bartlett Cove compound. A free trail guide is available at the visitor center.

The **Forest Loop** is an easy trail about 1 mile long, beginning at the Glacier Bay Lodge.

After a half-mile trip through a forest of spruces and hemlocks, the trail winds down to the beach, bringing you near the dock. The best months for wildflower-viewing on the trail are June and July; the best months for bird watching are May and June (when the bird migration is at its peak).

The **Bartlett River Trail** is a 4-mile round-trip; it's an easy to moderate trail that often has a few muddy spots. The endpoint is the Bartlett River Estuary, where you can see a concentration of waterfowl, especially during migrations and molting season.

The **Bartlett Lake Trail** branches off the Bartlett River Trail after about 0.25 mile. The 6-mile round-trip is through a rain forest, ending in Bartlett Lake; it's not a loop, so you must double back on the return.

Other Sports & Activities

Hiking & Biking in Gustavus. Gustavus offers delightful opportunities for both informal hiking and biking. There are few cars in and around the town because they have to be hauled here on a barge, but most inns in Gustavus provide bikes. The roads are fun to explore, and the sandy beaches, accessed from the town dock, are a great place for a walk and a picnic. It's 14 miles from Good River Road along the shore around Point Gustavus to the Bartlett Cove National Park Center, 7 miles from the town dock along the beach to the airport.

Sea Kayaking. The great majority of people see the park on cruise ships or on one of the tour boats described above. A sea kayak is the outdoors way. I can only imagine what it's like to see humpback whales from a kayak. Most kayakers go to see the glaciers up the protected eastern fjords after being carried part of the way by the *Spirit of Adventure,* or stay in the Beardslee Islands, near the Bartlett Cove lodge, where there are no glaciers. The *Spirit of Adventure* beaches at several prearranged spots to put kayakers and hikers ashore. Make sure you calibrate the length of your trip to your outdoors experience—this is remote territory, and you can't just leave once you're out there. Also, everyone going into the backcountry is required to check in with the backcountry office by the lodge for orientation.

Glacier Bay Sea Kayaks, P.O. Box 26, Gustavus, AK 99826 (☎ **907/697-2257;** fax 907/697-3002; Web site www.he.net/~kayakak/), is the Park Service concessionaire, operating May 1 to September 30. They offer instruction and rentals for $50 a day, and drop-offs up the bay are $174.50 round-trip.

In Gustavus, 7 miles away from the park, **Sea Otter Kayak,** P.O. Box 228, Gustavus, AK 99826 (☎ **907/697-3007**), rents kayaks on Dock Road.

For guided kayak trips, **Alaska Discovery,** 5449 Shaune Dr., Suite 4, Juneau, AK 99801 (☎ **907/780-6226;** fax 907/780-4220; Web site www.gorp. com/akdisc.htm), offers trips ranging from 6 hours to 7 days. A 6-hour guided paddle around Bartlett Cove and the Beardslees is $119; a 7-day tour, $1,890; they offer a 3-day, 2-night kayaking expedition among the whales for $600 per person. They take a boat to a base camp, then kayak among the whales from there.

Whale Watching. While much of the whale watching doesn't take place in Glacier Bay National Park proper, you have several opportunities from nearby Gustavus. Whale-watching trips aboard the ***Auk Nu*** leave the town dock for Point Adolphus every day at 2pm. Icy Strait, where the vessel cruises, is the most reliable place in the state to see humpbacks in summer. They come here because a swirl of currents makes it a rich feeding ground. The fare for the 3-hour cruise is $78, and you get your money back if you don't see whales.

Other, smaller operators will provide a more intimate experience on smaller boats. They'll also combine the trip with superb halibut and salmon fishing. Your inn host in Gustavus can make the arrangements. A boat typically charters for $200 or more per person for a full day.

Alaska Seair Adventures, P.O. Box 299, Gustavus, AK 99826 (☎ **907/697-2215**), is a family offering their Grumman Widgeon flying boat, a 73-foot yacht, and a comfortable lodge for guided packages starting at about $2,900 for 5 days.

Gustavus-based **Spirit Walker Expeditions,** P.O. Box 240, Gustavus, AK 99826 (☎ **800/KAY-AKER** or 907/697-2266; fax 907/697-2701; Web site www.he.net/~kayak), leads guided 1- to 7-day trips to the whale-watching grounds and beyond. The 1-day trip is $115; 7 days, $1,850.

Camping

There is a **free campground,** located about 0.25 mile by trail from the main dock, with bear-resistant food caches, firewood, chemical toilets, and a warming hut. You must do all your cooking and eating in the intertidal zone, where there is a designated fire ring. Group camping is permitted for groups of 12 or more. You cannot make reservations. The park strongly urges all campers to attend a twice-daily **camper orientation program,** given in the Bartlett Cover Visitor Information Station.

Accommodations & Dining

INSIDE THE PARK

Glacier Bay Lodge

Bartlett Cove (P.O. Box 199), Gustavus, AK 99826. ☎ **800/451-5952** or 907/697-2226; fax 206/623-7809 or 907/697-2408. 56 rms. TEL. $156 double. Additional person in rm $9 extra. Hostel bunks $28 per person. MC, V. Closed Sept 22–May 4.

Operated by park concessionaire Glacier Bay Tours and Cruises, this is the only place to stay in the park, although Gustavus, 10 miles down the road, has some of the most attractive accommodations in Alaska, some for the same price or less. The lodge rooms are comfortable but, for the price, nothing special. They're in buildings accessed from the main lodge by boardwalks. Laundry facilities arc available. The restaurant has great views of Bartlett Cove. There are inexpensive main courses on the dinner menu, but mainly it's a fine-dining establishment with dishes in the $20 range. Breakfast is available as early as 5:45am and dinner as late as 10pm. There is no bar. For those on a budget, there are bunk rooms with six beds each for men and women. The lodge also provides showers for the free Park Service campground.

NEAR THE PARK

There are a surprising number of good places to stay in Gustavus. In addition to the places listed below, I can also recommend the motel-style **Growley Bear Inn,** Dock Road (P.O. Box 246), Gustavus, AK 99826 (☎ **907/697-2730**), and **Good River Bed and Breakfast,** Good River Road (P.O. Box 37), Gustavus, AK 99826 (☎ and fax **907/697-2241;** Web site http://thor.he.net/~river), a cozy but rustic homestay B&B back in the woods next to a creek. A new luxury inn, **Glacier Bay's Bear Track Inn,** 255 Rink Rd. (☎ and fax **907/697-3017**), was opening as this went to press.

There isn't much of a choice for food. There's a small store and there's a restaurant on Dock Road that isn't always open. The full-service restaurant at the Glacier Bay Lodge is open all summer, and the inns that serve meals to their guests will sometimes make room for you if you call ahead.

Annie Mae Lodge

2 Grandpa's Farm Rd. (P.O. Box 80), Gustavus, AK 99826. ☎ **907/697-2346;** fax 907/697-2211; e-mail mnimaka@sprynet.com. 11 rms, 9 with bath. $80 double without bath or meals; $215 double with bath and all meals; $90 per additional person in rm. AE, DC, MC, V.

The lodge of big logs, with porches that wrap around, is secluded down a dirt side road overlooking a field of wildflowers through which runs a little creek. The cozy decor is country-style, with family pictures and memorabilia on the walls and a friendly dog. The set menu emphasizes seafood. They have a courtesy car and free bicycles, but no liquor license.

Glacier Bay Country Inn

Tong Rd. (P.O. Box 5), Gustavus, AK 99826. ☎ **907/697-2288;** fax 907/697-2289; Web site www.glacierbayalaska.com. 6 rms, 3 cabins. $260 double; $276 cabin. Rates include all meals. Additional adult in rm $75 extra; additional child under 12 $54 extra. Closed Oct–Apr.

Set on a 160-acre former agricultural homestead well back in the woods, this inn is renowned for its food and service. The quaint and quirky lodge building has lots of places to sit and watch the passing wildlife. Ponch and Sandi Marchbanks also operate Grand Pacific

Charters, with three boats for fishing and whale watching, and **Whalesong Lodge,** P.O. Box 389, Gustavus, AK 99826 (☎ **907/697-2741**), which has a three-bedroom apartment and B&B accommodations, as well as a lodge package with meals at the Glacier Bay. Nonguests are welcome for dinner, too, if there's room, but must call ahead. A van to the airport, laundry, free bicycles, and car rentals are available. There is no smoking inside and no liquor license.

Gustavus Inn at Glacier Bay

Gustavus Rd. (P.O. Box 60), Gustavus, AK 99826 (in winter, 7920 Outlook, Prairie Village, KS 66208). ☎ **800/649-5220** or 907/697-2254; fax 907/697-2255 in summer, 913/649-5220 in winter. 9 rms, 2 suites. $270 double. Additional person in rm $135 extra; children under 12 half price. AE, MC, V. Closed Sept 16–May 15.

This is the original and still the best of the Gustavus inns—although that's a fine point, as several of them are extraordinarily good. Occupying an old homestead farmhouse at the center of the community, the inn offers lovely rooms in a pastoral setting with overflowing hospitality and superb, plentiful food. The Lesh family, running the inn since 1965, has published a cookbook, and people come just to eat. The inn is unique in having a bar with beer and wine for guests. Fishing, touring, and kayaking packages are available, as is a courtesy car, free bikes, and laundry service.

A Puffin's Bed and Breakfast

Rink Creek Rd. (P.O. Box 3), Gustavus, AK 99826. ☎ **907/697-2260;** fax 907/697-2258; e-mail 73654.550@compuserve.com. 3 cabins, 1 house. $85 cabin for 2, $125 house for 2. Additional adult in rm $20 extra; additional child (up to 12 years old) in rm $10 extra. MC, V.

The cabins are set among the trees, connected by paths to a central building where breakfast is served in a big room with a cathedral ceiling. The two-bedroom house with a complete kitchen and laundry facilities is a good choice for families; it does not include breakfast. The proprietors also run a full-service travel agency, offering a multitude of packages for visiting Gustavus and Glacier Bay, and have a shop selling gifts, ice cream, and Mexican food. A courtesy car, free bikes, and a coin-op laundry are available.

18

GRAND CANYON NATIONAL PARK

by Alex Wells

THE FIRST THING YOU MAY NOTICE ABOUT THE GRAND CANYON IS ITS size. At 277 river miles long, roughly 5,000 feet deep, and an average of 10 miles across, it's so big that even the breezes seem to draw a deep breath at the rims. In the past 6 million years, while the Colorado River was carving the main canyon, runoff from the rims cut hundreds of side canyons draining into the larger one. Separating these side canyons, buttes and mesas rise thousands of feet from the its floor. Early cartographers and geologists noticed similarities between these terraced buttes and some of the greatest works of human hands. They began calling them temples, and named them after Far Eastern deities such as Brahma, Vishnu, and Shiva.

The canyon not only inspires reverence but tells the grandest of stories. Half the earth's history is represented in its rocks. The oldest and deepest rock layer, the Vishnu Schist, began forming 2 billion years ago, before aerobic lifeforms even existed. The different layers of sedimentary rock that piled up atop the Schist tell of landscapes that changed like dreams. They speak of mountains that really did move, eroding away into nothingness. Of oceans that poured forth across the land before receding. Of deserts, swamps, and rivers the size of the Mississippi—all where the canyon now lies. The very evolution of life is illustrated by the fossils in these layers.

Many of the latest products of evolution—more than 1,500 plant and 400 animal species—still survive at the canyon today. If you include the upper reaches of the Kaibab Plateau (on the canyon's North Rim), this small area of northern Arizona includes zones of biological life comparable to ones found as far south as Mexico and as far north as Alaska. The species come in every shape, size, and temperament, ranging from tiny ant lions dwelling on the canyon floor to 1,000-pound elk roaming the rims. And for every species there is a story within the story. Take the Douglas fir, for example. Once part of a forest that covered both rims and much of the canyon, this tree has endured since the last ice age on shady, north-facing slopes beneath the South Rim—long after the sun-baked rim itself became too hot and inhospitable.

A number of different tribes have lived in or around the canyon, and the Navajo, Havasupai, Paiute, Hopi, Zuni, and Hualapai tribes still live in this area.

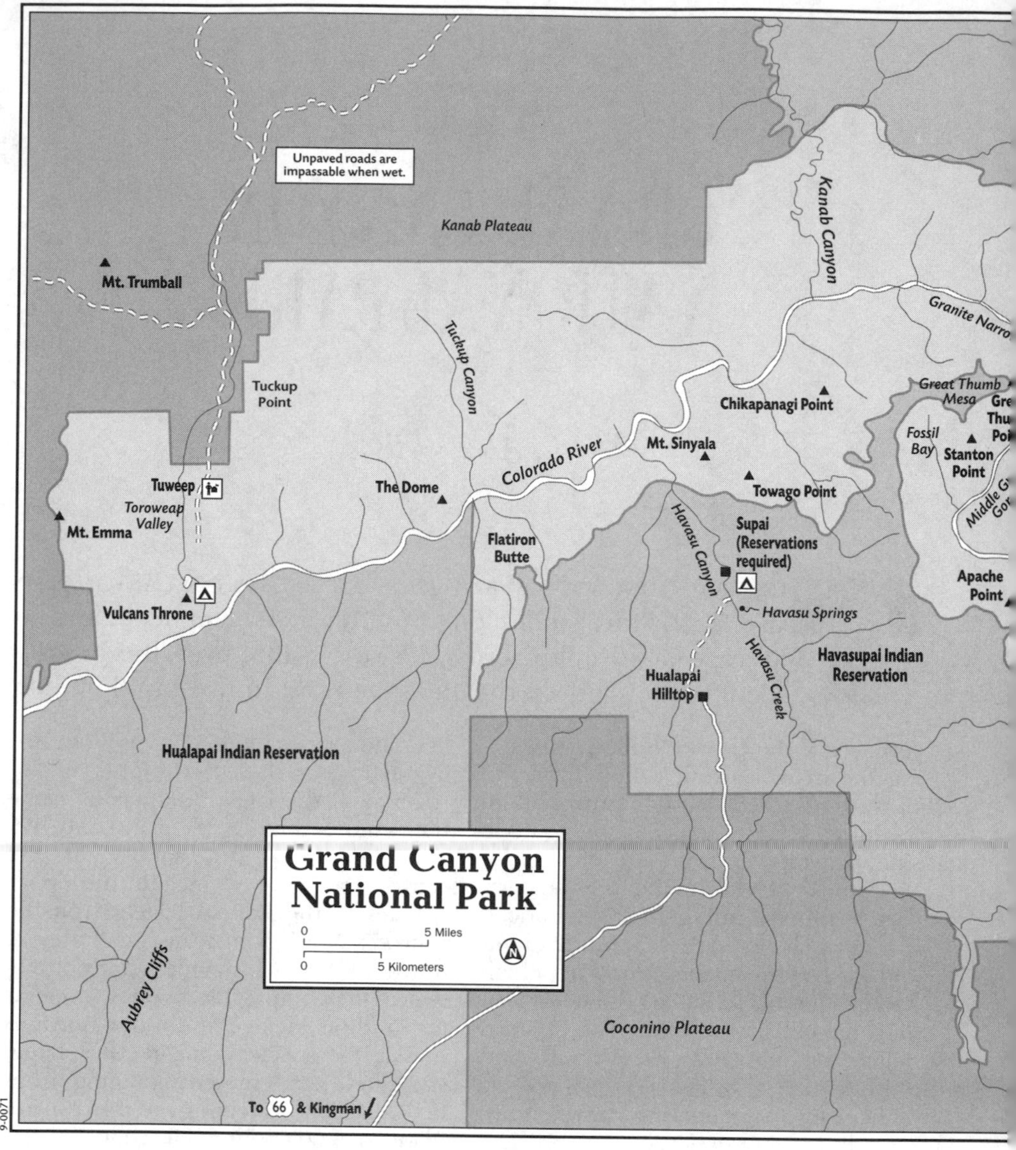

Before whites arrived, they awakened to the colors of the canyon, made their clothes from its plants and animals, smelled it, touched it, tasted it, and felt it underfoot. The Hopi still regard the canyon as their place of emergence and the place to which their dead return. Their predecessors left behind more than 3,000 archaeological sites and artifacts as old as 10,000 years.

In the 1500s Spanish missionaries and gold-greedy explorers passed through the area, but it wasn't until the 1800s that white people began settling here. Prospectors clambered through the canyon in search of precious minerals, and some of them stayed after their mines, plagued by high overhead, shut down. The first tourists followed, and began flooding the area after the railroad linked Grand Canyon Village to Williams, Arizona, in 1901. The canyon attracted and inspired icons like Mary Colter, the brilliant architect who obsessed over creating buildings that blended with the landscape, and

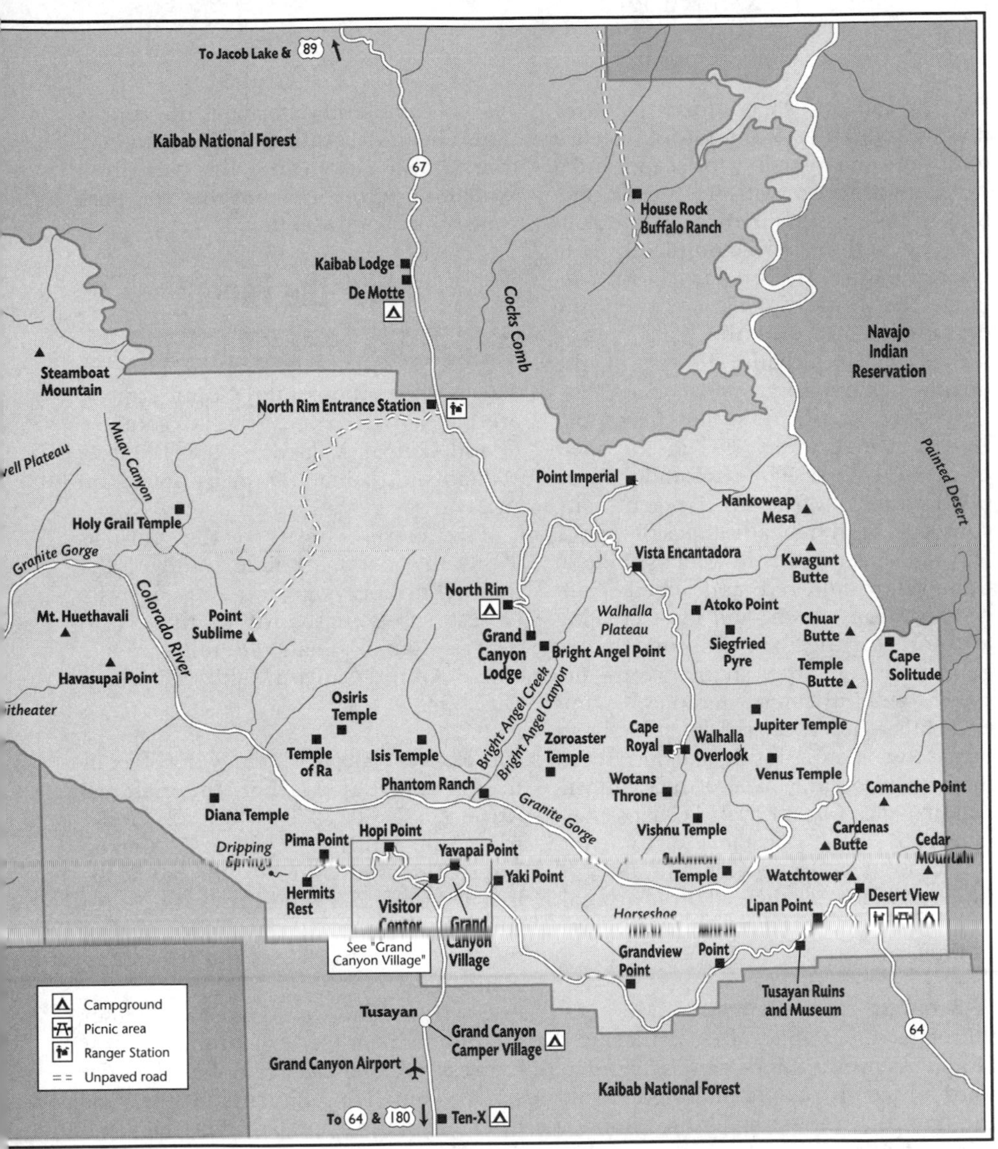

Georgie White, who began her illustrious river-running career by *swimming* 60 miles down the Colorado River in the western canyon. The list of people who have done amazing things here seems nearly as long as the river.

When Theodore Roosevelt visited here in 1903, the canyon moved him to say, "Leave it as it is. You cannot improve on it. The ages have been at work on it, and man can only mar it. What you can do is to keep it for your children, your children's children . . . as the one great sight which every American . . . should see." Roosevelt did his part to back up his words, using the Antiquities Act to declare Grand Canyon a national monument in 1908. Congress established Grand Canyon National Park in 1919.

Although Congress called it a "park," Grand Canyon still has a daunting, even ominous side. Visitors, no matter how many times they enter it, must negotiate with it for survival. One look at the clenched jaw of a boatman as he or she rows into Lava Rapids will remind you that the canyon exacts a heavy price for mistakes, the most common of which is to underestimate it. Try to escape, and it becomes a prison, with walls 5,000 feet high. The canyon's menace reminds us that we still haven't completely conquered nature. It even has its own symbols: the rattlesnake's warning; the elegant symmetry of the black widow; the seductive, lilylike flower of the deadly sacred datura.

Clearly, you can suffer here, but reward is everywhere. It's in the spectrum of colors: The Colorado River, filled with runoff from a recent rain, runs blood red beneath slopes of orange Hakatai shale; cactus flowers explode in pink, yellow, and red; and lichens paint rocks orange, green, and gray, creating art more striking than the works in any gallery. It's in the shapes, too—the spires, amphitheaters, temples, ramps and cliffs—and in the shadows that bend across them before lifting like mist. It's in the myriad organisms and their individual struggles for survival. Perhaps most of all, it's in the constancy of the river, which, even as it cuts closer to a beginning, reminds us that all things break down, wash away, and return to the earth in time.

Avoiding the Crowds. Maureen Oltrogge, the public affairs officer for Grand Canyon, offers this straightforward advice for people wanting to avoid the crowds at the park: "Prime season is July and August. Try to visit at another time. If you can't come during the off-season, we recommend that you come before 10am or after 2pm, so that you can avoid both the lines at the entrance gates and the parking problems inside the park."

The advice holds true for both rims. Oltrogge points out that because the North Rim lacks facilities for large numbers of people, it sometimes feels as crowded as the South Rim, in spite of having roughly one-eighth the visitation.

Although mass transit won't help you avoid the crowds, it might make those crowds more bearable, says Oltrogge. "We recommend alternate transportation. There's a shuttle from Tusayan, and there's also a train into the park from Williams. We recommend that you park your vehicle and use these."

Just the Facts

GETTING THERE & GATEWAYS

The nearest cities to the Grand Canyon are Flagstaff, Arizona, 78 miles south of Grand Canyon Village on U.S. 180; and Williams, Arizona, 59 miles south on Ariz. 64.

The closest town to the park is Tusayan, Arizona, 1 mile south of the South Entrance gates on Ariz. 64. The closest substantial town to the North Rim is Kanab, Utah, 78 miles northwest of Grand Canyon National Park on U.S. 89A.

The Nearest Airports. Many travelers fly to **Phoenix/Sky Harbor International Airport** (☎ **602/273-3300**), 220 miles from the South Rim, or to **McCarron International Airport** (☎ **702/261-5743**) in Las Vegas, 263 miles from the North Rim. Both these airports are served by the major airlines and car-rental companies.

For those who would like to fly closer than Phoenix or Las Vegas, **America West Express** (☎ **800-235-9292**) has daily jet service connecting Phoenix/Sky Harbor International Airport and **Flagstaff Pulliam Airport.** Closer still is **Grand Canyon National Park Airport** (☎ **520/638-2446**) in Tusayan, 1.5 miles outside the park entrance. **Air Nevada** (☎ **800/634-6377** or 702/736-8900), **Eagle Canyon Airlines** (☎ **800/446-4584** or 702/740-8300), and **Scenic Airlines** (☎ **800/634-6801** or 520/638-2436) offer daily service between Las Vegas and **Grand Canyon National Park Airport** in Tusayan. Air Nevada and Scenic both fly out of North Las Vegas Airport, while Eagle Canyon flies from McCarron International Airport. Meanwhile, **Temple Air** (☎ **800/933-7590**) offers daily service between Flagstaff and Tusayan.

By Rail. Amtrak (☎ **800/872-7245** or 520-774-8679) regularly stops in downtown Flagstaff, where lodging, rental cars, and connecting bus service are available. The **Historic Grand Canyon Railway** (☎ **800/843-8724**) offers daily service linking Williams and Grand Canyon Village. Pulled by a historic steam engine in summer, the train leaves Williams in the morning and returns in late afternoon.

By Bus. **Nava-Hopi Tours** (☎ **800/892-8687**) has bus service linking Grand Canyon National Park with Williams and Flagstaff. To reach those cities by bus, call **Greyhound** (☎ **800/231-2222**). Daily bus service between the North and South rims is available on the **Trans-Canyon Shuttle** (☎ **520/638-2820**).

Renting a Car. At Grand Canyon National Park Airport in Tusayan, car rentals are available through **Budget** (☎ **520/638-9360**). Most major car-rental companies have offices in Flagstaff.

Exploring the Park Without a Car. **Canyon Airport Shuttle** (☎ **520/638-0821**) offers a regular year-round service linking five Tusayan stops to Grand Canyon Village. To avoid parking problems inside the park, leave your car at Grand Canyon National Park Airport (or at your hotel) in Tusayan and take the shuttle into the park. Cost is $5 one way, $7 for a pass good all day. The shuttle schedule is posted at each stop.

From mid-April through mid-October, cars aren't allowed on the **West Rim Drive.** Instead you must ride the park's free shuttle service.

The shuttle operates daily (from mid-April through October), running every 15 minutes from 7:30am to sunset. You can board the bus at the **West Rim Interchange** bus stop, which is adjacent to the Bright Angel Lodge.

When the park shuttles aren't running, Fred Harvey offers a **hiker shuttle** (cost $3) to the South Kaibab Trailhead (at Yaki Point). The shuttle departs three times daily from the Bright Angel Lodge, Maswik Transportation Center (near the backcountry office), and the Yavapai Lodge. Call the **Bright Angel Transportation Desk** (☎ **303/297-2757**) for the schedule.

Getting Information Before Your Trip

ENTRANCE & CAMPING FEES

Admission to Grand Canyon National Park costs $20 per private vehicle and $10 for those on foot or bicycle. The receipt is good for a week and includes both rims. A **Grand Canyon Passport** ($40) entitles the holder to free admission to Grand Canyon for 1 calendar year. You can make advance reservations for campsites by calling ☎ **800/365-CAMP** (2267).

Permits are required for all overnight camping in the backcountry. This includes all overnight stays below the rims (except in the cabins and dorms at Phantom Ranch) and on park land outside of designated campgrounds.

Permits for the month desired go on sale on the first of the month, 4 months earlier. For example, permits for all of May go on sale January 1; permits for June go on sale February 1, and so on. You can get a **Backcountry Permit Request Form** by ordering the free Backcountry Trip Planner from the park by calling the park's main extension at ☎ **520/638-7888,** or writing to Grand Canyon National Park, P.O. Box 129, Grand Canyon, AZ 86023.

You can fax in your Permit Request Form to **520/638-2125** no earlier than the date the permits become available; or mail it with a postmark no earlier than the date the permits become available. No requests are taken by phone.

VISITOR CENTERS

There are four major visitor centers in Grand Canyon National Park. The **South Rim Visitor Center** is located in Grand Canyon Village and has displays, a free slide show on the park, and an information desk staffed by rangers. The **Yavapai Observation Station,** 1 mile east of the South Rim Visitor Center on Yavapai Point has an observation room where you can see and identify many of the monuments in the central canyon. Rangers here frequently lead interpretive programs.

The **Desert View Contact Station,** 26 miles east of Grand Canyon Village, is small and staffed by volunteers. It sells books and provides information on the canyon. The **North Rim Visitor Center** opened its doors in 1996. It has a small bookstore and information desk staffed by rangers and employees of the **Grand Canyon Association**.

SPECIAL REGULATIONS & WARNINGS

The following are some rules that visitors are required to follow for the good of the park:

◆ Grand Canyon is not the place for mountain bikers. Inside the park, bicycles must stay on roads.

◆ It's illegal to remove any resources from the park. These can be anything from flowers to potsherds. Even seemingly useless articles such as bits of metal from the canyon's old mining operations have historical value and are protected by law.

◆ Dogs must be leashed at all times and are not allowed on backcountry trails, buses, or in park lodging. The only exceptions are certified service dogs.

◆ Fires are strictly prohibited except at North Rim, Desert View, and Mather campgrounds. In the backcountry, use a small camp stove for cooking.

◆ An Arizona state fishing license is required for fishing. These are available at **Babbitt's General Store** in Grand Canyon Village.

SEASONS & CLIMATE

The climate at Grand Canyon varies greatly not only from season to season but from point to point. At 8,000 feet in elevation, the North Rim is by far the coldest, dampest part of the park. Its temperatures run about 30° cooler than at the canyon-bottom Phantom Ranch more than 5,000 feet below, and 7° cooler than the South Rim, roughly 1,000 feet below. It averages 25 inches of precipitation per year, compared to just 8 inches at Phantom Ranch and 16 inches on the South Rim.

The North Rim doesn't open until mid-May, so your only choice in early spring is the South Rim, where daily highs average 60° and 70° in April and May, respectively. Travelers should be prepared for late-winter storms, which occasionally bring snow to the rim. This is an ideal time to hike the inner canyon, with highs in April averaging 82 degrees.

In summer, the rims seldom become unbearably hot. Summer highs are usually in the 80s on the South Rim and in the 70s on the North Rim. The Inner Gorge, on the other hand, can be torrid, with highs in July averaging 106°. Localized monsoons frequently drench the park in late July and August, the wettest month of the year, when nearly 2.25 inches of rain falls on the South Rim. On the North Rim, nights can be nippy even during July, when low temperatures average a chilly 46°.

After the monsoons taper off in mid-September, fall is a great time to be anywhere in the park. Highs on the South Rim average 76° in September, 65° in October, and 52° in November. The North Rim has highs of 69° in September and 59° in October. (It closes in mid-October.) The Inner Gorge remains hot in September, but cools off considerably, to an average high of 84°, in October. The first winter storms can hit the North Rim as early as mid-October.

In winter, the North Rim is closed, and drivers to the South Rim should be prepared for icy roads and occasional closures as well. When the snow isn't falling, the South Rim warms up nicely, with average highs of 41° in January.

SEASONAL EVENTS

For 2 weeks every September, world-renowned classical musicians gather for the Grand Canyon Music Festival. Most of the offerings are chamber-music concerts, and all are at the **Shrine of the Ages Auditorium** next to the South Rim Visitor Center. Tickets for the 7:30pm concerts are available in advance through **Grand Canyon Chamber Music Festival,** P.O. Box 1332, Grand Canyon, AZ 86023 (☎ **800/997-8285** or 520/638-9215).

Kolb Studio houses special arts exhibits relating to the area. Also, actors occasionally stage historical dramas at the Shrine of the Ages Auditorium. For up-to-date information on special events, consult the park's newspaper, ***The Guide.***

USEFUL PUBLICATIONS

Among the hundreds of books written on the Grand Canyon, several in particular stand out. All of the following titles are available through the **Grand Canyon Association** (☎ **800/858-2808**).

For a general overview, try ***Grand Canyon: A Natural History Guide*** (New York: Houghton Mifflin Co., 1993), by Jeremy Schmidt. Here the author reveals the larger beauty of the canyon by exploring the smaller relationships between its dwellers—human and otherwise. If you're the type who leaves no stone unturned, you should buy ***An Introduction to Grand Canyon Geology*** (Grand Canyon Natural History Association, 1980) by Michael Collier. A graceful writer, Collier does more than make the canyon's geology accessible—he makes it beautiful. If people interest you most, look for ***In the House of Stone and Light: A Human History of Grand Canyon*** (Grand Canyon Natural History Association, 1978) by J. Donald Hughes. This meticulously researched book traces the canyon's human history from the prehistoric desert cultures through the 1970s.

Seeing the Highlights in a Day

After stopping at one of the **visitor centers** to get your bearings, hike a short distance down the **Bright Angel** or **North Kaibab trails** in the morning. (If the weather is hot or if your condition is not top-notch, a rim trail may be preferable.) During midday, attend a ranger presentation, for which times and locations are posted at the visitor centers. Later in the day, go on a scenic drive. On the South Rim, your best choice on the first day would be the **East Rim Drive,** which is open to cars year-round and has expansive views of the central and eastern canyon. On the North Rim, drive down the **Cape Royal Road.** To complete your scenic drive, watch sunset from **Lipan Point** on the South Rim or from **Cape Royal** on the North Rim.

Exploring the Park by Car

West Rim Drive

This 8-mile-long road from Grand Canyon Village to Hermit's Rest is open to private cars only when the shuttles aren't running, from mid-Oct to Mar. Allow a half day for this drive.

Your first stops are at **Trailview I and II.** From these view points, you can look back at Grand Canyon Village. Looking north across the canyon, you can see down the fault all the way to the North Rim. Below, look for the lush vegetation growing around the spring to find Indian Gardens.

The next stop, **Maricopa Point,** overlooks the old Orphan Mine, which produced some of the richest uranium ore anywhere during the 1950s. Below and to the west, you can see the metal framework from the tramway used to move ore to the rim from 1956 to 1959.

At the **Powell Memorial,** you'll find a memorial to John Wesley Powell, the one-armed Civil War veteran thought to be the first white person to float through the canyon. From atop the memorial, you can get an especially fine view 60 miles southeast to the San Francisco peaks, including Humphreys Peak,

9-0071A

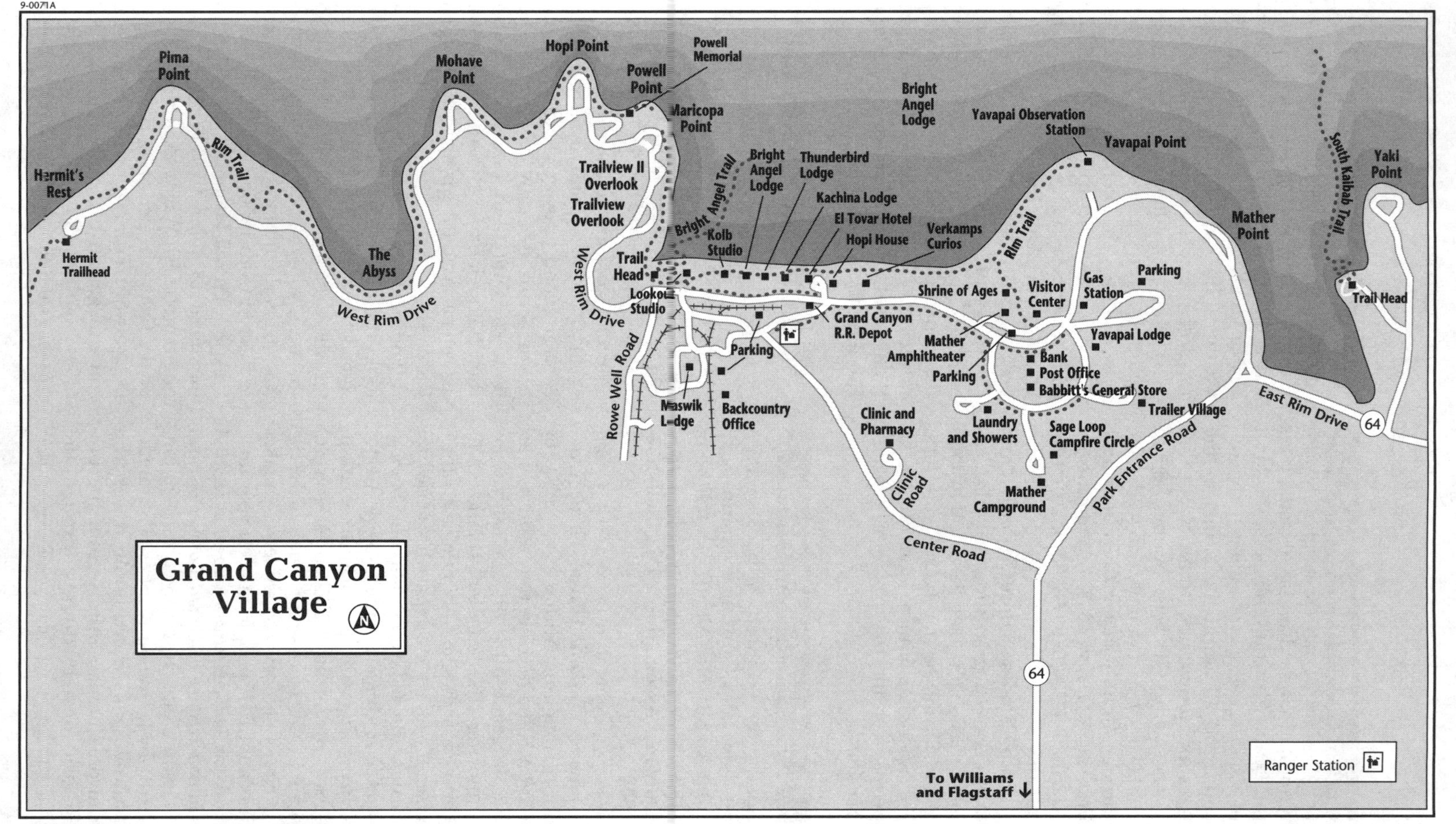
Grand Canyon Village
Hermit's Rest
Hermit Trailhead
Pima Point
Rim Trail
The Abyss
West Rim Drive
Mohave Point
Hopi Point
Powell Point
Powell Memorial
Maricopa Point
Trailview II Overlook
Trailview Overlook
Trail Head
Lookout Studio
Rowe Well Road
Bright Angel Trail
Kolb Studio
Bright Angel Lodge
Thunderbird Lodge
Kachina Lodge
El Tovar Hotel
Hopi House
Verkamps Curios
Bright Angel Lodge
Grand Canyon R.R. Depot
Parking
Maswik Lodge
Backcountry Office
Clinic and Pharmacy
Clinic Road
Center Road
Shrine of Ages
Mather Amphitheater
Parking
Visitor Center
Gas Station
Parking
Yavapai Lodge
Bank
Post Office
Babbitt's General Store
Trailer Village
Laundry and Showers
Sage Loop Campfire Circle
Mather Campground
Park Entrance Road
Yavapai Observation Station
Yavapai Point
Rim Trail
Mather Point
South Kaibab Trail
Yaki Point
Trail Head
East Rim Drive
64
64
To Williams and Flagstaff
Ranger Station

which at 12,643 feet is the highest point in Arizona.

Because the next stop, **Hopi Point,** projects far into the canyon, its tip is the best place on the West Rim Drive to watch the sunset. As the sun drops, its light will play across four of the canyon's loveliest temples. The flat mesa almost due north of the point is Shiva Temple. The temple to its left is Osiris; the one to its right is Isis. To the right of Isis is Buddha Temple.

The next stop, **Mohave Point,** is a great place to observe some of the Colorado River's most furious rapids. Furthest downstream (to your left) is Hermit Rapids. Above it, you can make out the top of the dangerous Granite Rapids. Just above Granite Rapids, you can make out the bottom of Salt Creek Rapids. As you look at Hermit Creek Canyon and the rapids below it, you can easily see how floods washed rocks from the side canyon into the Colorado River, forming the natural dam that creates the rapids.

Next you'll come to **The Abyss,** where the steep canyon walls drop 2,600 feet to the base of the Redwall Limestone.

Three thousand feet below the next stop, **Pima Point,** you'll see some of the foundations and walls from the old Hermit Camp, a tourist destination built in 1912 by the Santa Fe Railroad.

Before descending to Hermit Camp, tourists took a break at the next stop, **Hermit's Rest.** In this 1914 building, Mary Colter celebrated the "hermit" theme, by building what resembled a crude rock shelter, with stones heaped highest around the chimney. Inside, Colter covered the ceiling above the large fireplace with soot, so that the room had the look of a cave warmed by fire. Nearby are the only rest rooms on the drive and a snack bar selling sweets, chips, and soda. (Don't count on getting a meal.)

Highlights: Closed to cars during high season; the overlooks are much quieter than those on the East Rim drive and afford excellent river views.

Drawbacks: Occasional long waits for buses.

East Rim Drive

Allow a half day for this 25-mile-long scenic drive on Ariz. 64, which connects Grand Canyon Village with Desert View.

The first stop, **Yaki Point,** is accessible by car only when the shuttles aren't running. It's a great place to see the monuments of the central canyon, including Wotans Throne, Vishnu Temple, and Zoroaster Temple. Two trails are also easy to spot from here. To the north, the South Kaibab Trail descends in switchbacks below Skeleton Point. Meanwhile, the Tonto Trail meanders across the broad blue-green terrace known as the Tonto Platform.

The next stop, 7,406-foot-high **Grandview Point,** is one of the highest spots on the South Rim. In the 1890s, one of the canyon's early prospectors, Pete Barry built, and in some cases hung, a trail from Grandview Point to nearby Horseshoe Mesa, where he had a mining claim. He then built cabins and a dining hall on the mesa, and a hotel a short distance from Grandview Point. The hotel and the mine shut down in the early 1900s. Today only a trace of the foundation remains of the hotel, but the historic Grandview Trail is still in use.

Next you'll come to **Moran Point,** named for landscape painter Thomas Moran, whose sketches and oil paintings introduced America to the beauty of the canyon. Here is the best place from which to view the tilting block of rock known as "The Sinking Ship." Stand at the end of the point and look southwest at the rocks level with the rim. The "Sinking Ship" appears to be "submerged" in the horizontal layers of Coronado Butte (in the foreground). It's part of the Grandview Monocline, a place where rocks have bent in a single fold around a fault line.

Next comes **Tusayan Pueblo,** built in 1185 by the ancestral Pueblo people. It's the last known occupied pueblo among the 3,500 documented archaeological sites in and around the Grand Canyon. A self-guided tour takes you through it.

Built in 1932, the adjoining Tusayan Museum celebrates the traditions of the area's Native American tribes.

Don't miss the next stop, **Lipan Point.** With views far down the canyon to the west, it's a great place to catch the sunset. It also overlooks the Colorado River where the river makes two sweeping curves to form an enormous S. Just downstream of the S, the river begins cutting through the Vishnu Schist, and the steep-walled Inner Gorge begins.

Like Lipan Point, the next stop, **Navajo Point,** offers fine views of the Grand Canyon Supergroup, a formation of igneous and sedimentary rocks that has eroded altogether in many other parts of the canyon. The long, thin streaks of maroon, gray, and black, which tilt at an angle of about 10°, are layers of this formation.

The last stop on the East Rim Drive is **Desert View,** where you'll find the Watchtower, a 70-foot-high stone building designed by Mary Colter. Colter modeled it after towers found at ancient pueblos such as Mesa Verde and Hovenweep. Atop the Watchtower is an enclosed observation deck, which at 7,522 feet is the highest point on the South Rim. The rim at Desert View offers spectacular views of the east end of the canyon.

Highlights: Spectacular views of both the central and eastern canyon.

Drawbacks: Packed parking lots in summer.

North Rim: Cape Royal Drive

From the Grand Canyon Lodge on the North Rim, it's best to go the length of the scenic drive 23 miles directly to Cape Royal, on the Walhalla Plateau, and then to make your stops on the way back to the lodge. That way, you can do the short hikes near Cape Royal while your legs are fresh, then stop at the picnic areas, closer to the lodge, on your way back. Allow a half day to a day for this drive.

Start your driving tour at **Cape Royal,** where a gentle, paved 0.3-mile (each way) trail passes a natural bridge, Angel's Window, carved into a rock peninsula along the rim. The trail ends at the tip of Cape Royal, with views of the central and eastern canyon.

Your next stop may be at the **Cliff Springs Trail,** a 0.5-mile walk that ends at a small spring. (See "Day Hikes," below.)

From the next stop, **Walhalla Overlook and Walhalla Glades,** you can follow with your eyes the tan line of Unkar Creek as it snakes down toward Unkar Delta. The soil and abundant water at the delta made for excellent farming for the ancestral Pueblo people, who occupied the canyon through about A.D. 1175. Many of these people migrated seasonally to dwellings such as the two small pueblos across the street from this overlook.

The next stop, **Roosevelt Point,** is one of the best places in the Canyon to see the confluence of the gorge of the Little Colorado River with the Grand Canyon. They meet at nearly a right angle, unusual in that most tributaries enter at close to the same direction as the larger rivers.

By starting your driving tour of the Walhalla Plateau early in the day, you can reach the next stop, **Vista Encantadora,** in time for a late picnic. You'll find several tables with views of the canyon.

From there you can finish your driving tour by taking the 3-mile spur from the Cape Royal Road to **Point Imperial,** which at 8,803 feet is the highest point on the North Rim. It's also the best place on either rim to view the northeastern end of the park.

Highlights: Sparse crowds and lovely views of the eastern canyon.

Drawbacks: Has only one view point (Cape Royal) from which to see the central canyon; the Colorado River is not as visible on this drive as on the South Rim drives.

Organized Tours & Ranger Programs

The park offers a host of ranger programs whose schedule changes seasonally. A typical schedule includes guided hikes and walks, kids' programs, and discussions of geology, native species, and natural and cultural history. Evening programs are scheduled nightly. In winter, the South Rim cuts back on its programs and the North Rim is closed. For an up-to-date schedule, consult the park newspaper, ***The Guide.***

Guided Hikes & Trips. The nonprofit **Grand Canyon Field Institute** schedules dozens of backpacking trips, day hikes, and river trips, ranging in length from 1 to 8 days. Some explore broad subjects such as ecology; others hone specific skills such as orienteering or slot-canyon photography. Each is guided by experts on the topics covered. Because the courses vary greatly, the Field Institute assigns a difficulty level to each and attempts to ensure that participants find ones suited to their skill levels and interests. For more information call ☎ **520/638-2485** or write P.O. Box 399, Grand Canyon, AZ 86023.

Bus Tours. Fred Harvey schedules East Rim and West Rim tours ($12 and $19, respectively), sunset tours to Yaki or Mojave point ($8), and all-day outings ($20) that combine two of the shorter tours. Unlike the drivers on the free shuttles, Fred Harvey drivers narrate the tours. Kids 16 and under are free. For advance reservations, call ☎ **303/297-2757.** Once at the canyon, visit the Fred Harvey desks at Yavapei, Maswick, or Bright Angel lodges, or call ☎ **520/638-2631,** ext. 6015.

Nava-Hopi Tours (☎ **520/774-5003**) offers 1-day guided canyon tours that depart from Flagstaff at 8:30am and return by 5:30pm. Total cost is $42.

Historic & Man-Made Attractions

Most of the historic buildings on the South Rim are concentrated in **Grand Canyon Village,** a National Historic District. Hermit's Rest, on the West Rim Drive, and The Watchtower, on the East Rim Drive, are also of historical significance (see "Exploring the Park by Car," above).

More than a half dozen of these historic buildings were designed by Mary Colter, a Minneapolis schoolteacher who began decorating the shops that sold Indian art along the Santa Fe Railroad line in 1902. As both a decorator and a self-trained architect, Colter later designed these Grand Canyon landmarks: Hopi House (1905), The Lookout (1914), Hermit's Rest (1914), Phantom Ranch (1922), Watchtower (1932), and Bright Angel Lodge (1935). Colter's work drew heavily on the architectural styles of Native Americans and Spanish settlers in the Southwest. Another historic building, The El Tovar Hotel (1905), was designed by Charles Whittlesey.

On the North Rim, Grand Canyon Lodge, built in 1928, is included on the National Register of Historic Places.

Day Hikes

There's no better way to enjoy the canyon than by actually walking right down into it. The beauty and variety of the geology and the plant and animal life is vastly more impressive when you're seeing it all around you instead of looking down from the rims.

But although hiking below the rims is the best way to experience the canyon, it's not always a smart idea, especially at midday during summer. Changes in temperature and elevation can make hiking extremely difficult even in ideal conditions. The jarring descent can strain your knees; the climb back out will test your lungs. If it's hot out or you aren't up to climbing, consider walking on one of the rim trails, which can often be as pleasant as walks inside the canyon. They're especially nice in the forests on the North Rim.

First-time hikers in the canyon should consider one of the **corridor trails:** North Kaibab, South Kaibab, and Bright Angel. Well-maintained and clearly marked, these are regularly patrolled by park rangers. Each has at least one emergency phone and pit toilet. Drinking water is available at several sources along both the Bright Angel and North Kaibab trails, but not on the South Kaibab. Wherever you hike, carry plenty of water, and check with the rangers about the availability of water before leaving. Eat and drink regularly. Wear sunscreen, sunglasses, and protective clothing. If you hike into the canyon, allow yourself twice as much time for the trip out as for the descent.

RIM TRAILS: SOUTH RIM

South Rim Trail

8 miles to Hermit's Rest, 1 mile to Yavapai Point. Easy to moderate. Access: Grand Canyon Village, along the rim behind the El Tovar Hotel. Water sources at Grand Canyon Village, Hermit's Rest, Yavapai Point.

From Grand Canyon Village, you can follow the Rim Trail 8 miles west to Hermit's Rest or 1.5 miles northeast to Yavapai Observation Station.

West Rim Trail. Walking instead of driving is a great way to see the canyon without the crowds. This trail travels near the West Rim Drive and passes through all the same scenic overlooks, described in the driving tour (see "Exploring the Park by Car," above). The 1.3-mile stretch from the village to Maricopa Point is paved but climbs steeply. Past Maricopa Point, it planes off somewhat and the pavement ends. For the rest of the way to Hermit's Rest, the trail meanders through pinyon-juniper woodland along the rim (when not crossing overlooks). Roots and loose rocks make for tricky footing, but the scenery is lovely, and the crowds thin as you move west.

As 16 miles might be too much hiking for 1 day, I recommend hiking out on this trail from Grand Canyon Village and taking the shuttle back (mid-April through mid-October). By hiking out, you can avoid revisiting the same overlooks on the shuttle ride back. The shuttles stop at every turnout while en route to Hermit's Rest, but go nonstop on their way back to Grand Canyon Village.

South Rim Trail. This trail connects Grand Canyon Village and Yavapai Observation Station. Around the lodges, the path is a flat sidewalk teeming with people. The crowds dissipate somewhat between the east edge of the village and Yavapai Point. In this stretch, the trail is crudely paved and gently rolling.

Located 5 miles north of the park's South Entrance, **Yavapai** has a historic (1928) observation station with large windows overlooking the canyon. Below the largest window, a long interpretive panel identifies many of the landmarks in the central canyon, including Zoroaster Temple, Isis Temple, and Buddha Temple. You can also see the Kaibab Suspension Bridge, which spans the Colorado River at the base of the South Kaibab Trail. Parts of the Bright Angel, Plateau Point, and Tonto trails are also visible.

RIM TRAILS: NORTH RIM

Ken Patrick Trail

10 miles one way. Difficult. Access: From the south side of the parking area for Point Imperial or from the parking area for the North Kaibab Trail (on the North Rim entrance road, 2 miles north of Grand Canyon Lodge).

This 10-mile-long, steeply rolling trail travels through ponderosa pine and spruce-fir forest between the head of Roaring Springs Canyon and Point Imperial. Along the way, it poses a number of challenges. Beginning near the North Kaibab Trailhead, the trail rolls steeply in places and is often very faint. While challenging, the 3-mile section between the Cape Royal Road and Point Imperial is also the prettiest stretch, skirting the rim of the canyon above upper drainages of Nankoweap Creek. In these areas you'll see plenty of scarlet bugler, identifiable by tubular red flowers with flared lower petals, as well as a number of Douglas firs interspersed among the ubiquitous ponderosa pines.

Cape Final Trail

1.5 miles one way. Easy. Access: An unmarked dirt parking area off the Cape Royal Rd., 4.9 miles south of Roosevelt Point.

Because this trail is relatively flat and boulder-free, it's a good choice for a first hike in the backcountry. From an unmarked dirt parking area 4.9 miles south of Roosevelt Point, it meanders for 1.5 miles through ponderosa pine forest on an old jeep trail, ending at Cape Final, where you'll have nice views of the eastern canyon and of the Palisades of the Desert, the cliffs that form the eastern wall of Grand Canyon proper.

The Transept Trail & Bright Angel Point Trail

Bright Angel Point Trail 0.25 mile each way. Transept Trail 1.5 miles. Easy. Access: Behind North Rim General Store (near the campground), or by descending the back steps off the patios at Grand Canyon Lodge.

To familiarize yourself with the lay of the land on the North Rim, start with these trails, which are different sections of the same pathway. At the bottom of the stairs behind Grand Canyon Lodge, the Bright Angel Point Trail goes to the left, while the Transept Trail goes right.

The **Bright Angel Point Trail,** which is paved, travels 0.25 mile along a narrow peninsula dividing Roaring Springs and Transept canyons. It passes a number of craggy outcroppings of Kaibab Limestone, around which the roots of wind-whipped juniper trees cling like arthritic hands. The trail ends at 8,148-foot-high Bright Angel Point.

The **Transept Trail** travels 1.5 miles northeast along the rim of Transept Canyon, connecting the lodge and the North Rim Campground. Passing through old-growth ponderosa pine and quaking aspen, it descends into, then climbs out of, three shallow side drainages, with ascents steep enough to take the breath away from people unaccustomed to the altitude.

Cliff Springs Trail

0.5 mile one way. Moderate. Access: A small pullout 0.3 mile north of Cape Royal on the Cape Royal Rd.

Both scenic and fairly short, this hike, which begins at a small pullout 0.3 miles north of Cape Royal, is perfect for families. Although this dirt trail seems at first to head into forest *away* from the canyon, it quickly descends into a narrow, rocky side canyon that drains into the larger one—a reminder that the Walhalla Plateau is a peninsula. It hugs the north wall of the side canyon, passing under limestone overhangs, in light colored green by the canopies of box elder trees. The springs drip from one of these overhangs, where mosses carpet fissures in the rock. A waist-high boulder marks the end of the trail.

Widforss Trail

5 miles one way. Moderate. Access: A dirt road 0.25 mile south of the Cape Royal Rd. Follow this road about 1 mile to the parking area, which is well marked.

Named for landscape painter Gunnar Widforss, this 5-mile trail skirts the head of Transept Canyon before venturing south to Widforss Point. To reach it, drive on the entrance road to a dirt road 0.25 mile south of the Cape Royal Road. The clearly marked trailhead is a short distance down this road. For the first 2 miles, the trail undulates through ponderosa pine and spruce-fir forest, with spruce-fir on the shady side of each drainage. Past the head of Transept Canyon, the trail heads south through a stand of old-growth ponderosa. The trail reaches the rim again at Widforss Point, where you'll have a nice view of five temples. Near the rim are a picnic table and several good campsites.

CANYON TRAILS

Because of the huge elevation changes on the canyon trails, none should be called easy. (More people are rescued off the Bright Angel Trail, generally considered the "easiest" trail into the canyon than off any other trail.) In general, please note that rating a trail easy, moderate, or difficult oversimplifies the situation. For example, among the wilderness trails, the **Hermit Trail** is fine for day hikers going to Santa Maria Spring, but it's much more difficult beyond that point; the **Tonto Trail** is easy to walk on, but has almost no water. It's always a good idea to discuss your plans and your experience with a ranger before setting out on a hike.

SOUTH RIM CORRIDOR TRAILS

Bright Angel Trail

4.6 mile to Indian Garden, 7.8 miles to Colorado River, 9.3 miles to Bright Angel Campground. Access: Trailhead is just west of Kolb Studio, near Grand Canyon Village. 6,860 feet at trailhead; 3,800 feet at Indian Garden; 2,450 feet at Colorado River. Water sources at Mile-and-a-Half Rest House (seasonal), Three-Mile Rest House (seasonal), Indian Garden, Colorado River, Bright Angel Campground.

Both Native Americans and early settlers recognized this as a choice location for a trail. First, there's an enormous fault line, along which so much erosion has taken place that even the usually sheer Redwall Limestone holds vegetation. Then there's the water—more of it than anywhere on the South Rim.

On a day hike, follow the switchbacks below Grand Canyon Village to One-and-a-Half Mile House or Three-Mile House, each of which has shade, an emergency phone, and seasonal drinking water. The Park Service, which responds to hundreds of emergency calls on this trail every year, discourages many day-hikers from going past Mile-and-a-Half house.

If you continue on the trail past Three-Mile House, you begin a long descent to the picnic area near the spring at Indian Garden, where lush vegetation will surround you and large cottonwood trees provide shade. At 4.6 miles and more than 3,000 vertical feet from the rim, Indian Garden is dangerously deep for many people. However, a few well-prepared day-hikers may wish to hike an additional 1.5 miles past Indian Garden on the Plateau Point Trail. This relatively flat spur trail crosses the Tonto Platform to an overlook of the Colorado River 1,300 feet below.

South Kaibab Trail

6.3 miles to Colorado River, 7.3 miles to Bright Angel Campground. Trailhead at Yaki Point (Ariz. 64, East Rim Dr., 5 miles east of Grand Canyon Village). 7,260 feet at trailhead; 2,450 feet at Colorado River. Water sources at Colorado River and Bright Angel Campground.

Unlike the Bright Angel Trail, which follows natural routes into the canyon, this one was built using dynamite and hard labor. While the Bright Angel follows narrow side canyons below Indian Garden, the South Kaibab travels on ridge lines, with expansive views. And while the Bright Angel offers ample shade and water, the South Kaibab has no water and little shade. So the Bright Angel Trail is a better trail for most hikers.

For a good day hike, follow the South Kaibab Trail as it makes a series of switchbacks through the upper rock layers, down the west side of Yaki Point. Below the Coconino Sandstone, the trail heads north to Cedar Ridge, a platform that has pit toilets and a hitching post for mules. Shaded by pinyon and juniper trees, it affords expansive views down side canyons to the east and west. This is an excellent place for day-hikers to picnic and rest before hiking the 1.5 miles and 1,500 vertical feet back out.

NORTH RIM CORRIDOR TRAIL

North Kaibab Trail

2.7 miles to Supai Tunnel, 4.7 miles to Roaring Springs, 6.8 miles to Cottonwood Campground, 14.4 miles to the Colorado. Access: On North

Rim entrance road, 2 miles north of Grand Canyon Lodge. 8,250 feet at North Kaibab Trailhead; 5,200 feet at Roaring Springs; 4,080 feet at Cottonwood Campground; 2,400 feet at Colorado River. Water sources at Roaring Springs (seasonal), Bright Angel Creek, Cottonwood Campground (seasonal), Phantom Ranch, Bright Angel Campground. Maps: Bright Angel Point (7.5 minutes) and Phantom Ranch (7.5 minutes) quadrangles.

Less crowded than the South Rim corridor trails, this one begins at a parking area off the North Rim entrance road, 2 miles north of Grand Canyon Village. It starts with a long series of switchbacks through thickly forested terrain at the head of Roaring Springs Canyon. The first major landmark is Supai Tunnel. At 2.7 miles from the trailhead, and with seasonal water, shade, and rest rooms available, this is an excellent turnaround point for day-hikers. Beyond the tunnel, the trail descends in relatively gradual switchbacks through the Supai Group, then crosses a bridge over a creek bed. Past the bridge, the creek plummets. The trail travels along the south wall of Roaring Springs Canyon, on ledges above Redwall Cliffs.

A spire of Redwall Limestone known as "The Needle" marks the point where the trail begins its descent of the Redwall. Roaring Springs, the water source for both rims, becomes audible just above the confluence of Bright Angel and Roaring Springs canyons. A 0.2-mile-long spur trail descends to the springs. In the lush vegetation around it, you'll find drinking (seasonal) water, shade, and picnic tables. Roughly 5 miles and 3,000 vertical feet below the rim, this is the farthest a day-hiker will probably want to go.

WILDERNESS TRAILS

By hiking on corridor trails, you can acclimate yourself to the conditions in the canyon without having to negotiate the boulder-strewn and sometimes confusing **wilderness trails.** Rangers are seldom encountered on these trails, which are not maintained by the park. These trails have washed away in some places; in others, they descend steeply through cliffs.

Two South Rim wilderness trails, the Grandview and Hermit trails, work well for day hikes. Day-hikers often descend 3,000 vertical feet on the **Grandview Trail** to Horseshoe Mesa (avoid when wet or icy), or follow the **Hermit Trail** to Santa Maria or Dripping Springs. Other South Rim wilderness trails, poorly suited for day hikes, include the Tanner, New Hance, Boucher, and South Bass. North Rim wilderness trails include the Bill Hall, Thunder River, Deer Creek, North Bass, and Nankoweap.

Other Sports & Activities

Fishing. You're welcome to fish in the Colorado River, provided you have an Arizona fishing permit and trout stamp. Five-day nonresident permits are available for $18.50 at **Babbitt's Main Store** (☎ **520/638-2262**) on the South Rim. The trout fishing is best at the eastern end of the canyon, upstream of Phantom Ranch.

Biking. Inside the park, cyclists are required to stay on roads, many of them narrow and crowded. The best riding is on the West Rim Drive when the road is closed to cars. At these times, watch out for tour buses and shuttles.

Cross-Country Skiing. When snow sticks on the South Rim, you can cross-country ski at the **Grandview Nordic Center** in the Kaibab National Forest near Grandview Point. To get there, drive east toward Desert View on Ariz. 64. About 1.7 miles past the Grandview Point turnoff, turn right on the road to the Arizona Trail. The forest service has marked three loops in this area, each meandering through meadows and ponderosa pine forest. For more information call the **Kaibab National Forest Tusayan Ranger District Office** at ☎ **520/638-2443.**

White-Water Rafting. White-water raft trips inside the park generally last from

3 to 14 days and must be booked well ahead of time. While most trips begin at Lee's Ferry, Arizona, the end points vary. Some companies allow for partial trips by picking up or dropping off passengers at various points in the Canyon (most often at Phantom Ranch).

All the companies operating in the Grand Canyon are experienced and run excellent trips, though subject to the whims of the Colorado River and the storms that move through the canyon. For about $200 per day, all provide food, portable toilets, and some camping equipment, as well as access to parts of the Inner Canyon that are difficult, if not impossible, to reach on foot. Among them are some of the most beautiful places on earth.

The motorized trips are fastest, often covering the 277 miles from Lee's Ferry (above the Canyon) to Pierce Ferry (in Lake Mead) in 6 days, compared to as many as 19 for nonmotorized trips. Those who would rather savor the canyon's beauty at a more leisurely pace will prefer nonmotorized trips, which glide at close to the water's speed.

The following companies offer raft trips through the canyon: **OARS/ Grand Canyon Dories,** P.O. Box 216, Altaville, CA 95221 (☎ **800/346-6277** or 209/736-0805); **Aramark-Wilderness River Adventures,** P.O. Box 717, Page, AZ 86040 (☎ **800/992-8022** or 520/ 645-3296); **Arizona Raft Adventures,** 4050-F E. Huntington Dr., Flagstaff, AZ 86004 (☎ **800/786-7238** or 520/ 526-8200); **Arizona River Runners,** P.O. Box 47788, Phoenix, AZ 85068-7788 (☎ **800/477-7238** or 602/867-4866); **Canyon Explorations,** P.O. Box 310, Flagstaff, AZ 86002 (☎ **800/654-0723** or 520/774-4559); **Canyoneers,** P.O. Box 2997, Flagstaff, AZ 86003 (☎ **800/525-0924** or 520/526-0924); **Colorado River and Trail Expeditions,** P.O. Box 57575, Salt Lake City, UT 84157-0575 (☎ **800/ 253-7328** or 801/261-1789); **Diamond River Adventures,** P.O. Box 1316, Page, AZ 86040 (☎ **800/343-3121** or 520/ 645-8866); **Expeditions,** 625 N. Beaver, Flagstaff, AZ 86001 (☎ **520/779-3769**); **Grand Canyon Expeditions Co.,** P.O. Box O, Kanab, UT 84741 (☎ **800/ 544-2691** or 801/644-2691); **Hatch River Expeditions,** P.O. Box 1200, Vernal, UT 84078 (☎ **800/433-8966** or 801/789-3813); **High Desert Adventures, Inc.,** P.O. Box 40, St. George, UT 84771-0040 (☎ **801/673-1200**); **Moki Mac River Expeditions,** P.O. Box 21242, Salt Lake City, UT 84121 (☎ **800/284-7280** or 801/268-6667); **Outdoors Unlimited,** 6900 Townsend Winona Rd., Flagstaff, AZ 86004 (☎ **800/637-7238** or 520/ 526-4546); **Tour West,** P.O. Box 333, Orem, UT 84059 (☎ **800/453-9107** or 801/225-0755); **Western River Expeditions,** 7258 Racquet Club Dr., Salt Lake City, UT 84121 (☎ **800/453-7450** or 801/ 942-6669).

Two Tamer Alternatives. Aramark-Wilderness River Adventures, 50 S. Lake Powell Blvd., Page, AZ 86040 (☎ **800/ 528-6154** or 520/645-3279), offers a half-day smooth-water raft trip from the base of Glen Canyon Dam to Lees Ferry, where the companies floating into Grand Canyon *begin* their trips. **Fred Harvey** offers the same trip along with transportation from the South Rim. Cost for this 12-hour tour is $86 ($43 for 12 and under). For advance reservations call ☎ **303/297-2757.** Within 4 days, call ☎ **520/638-2631,** ext. 6015.

One- and two-day trips through the westernmost part of Grand Canyon are available through **Hualapai River Runners** (☎ **800/622-4409** or 520/769-2210), P.O. Box 246, Peach Springs, AZ 86434. These motorized trips begin with rapids in the lower Granite Gorge of Grand Canyon and end on Lake Mead. Costs range from $245 to $355 per person.

Overflights. Ten companies at Grand Canyon National Park Airport in Tusayan currently offer scenic airplane or helicopter rides over the canyon. With more than 250,000 people flying out of Tusayan alone every year, the flights, which generate a great deal of noise in parts of the park, have become a politically charged issue. Besides the noise pollution in what should be a pristine wilderness area, there have been a few crashes over the years.

The following companies offer air tours originating from Tusayan: **Papillon Grand Canyon Helicopters** (☎ **800/528-2418** or 520/638-2419); **Air Grand Canyon** (☎ **520/638-2686**); **AirStar Airlines and Helicopters** (☎ **800/962-3869**); **Eagle Canyon Airlines** (☎ **800/446-4584**); **Grand Canyon Airlines** (☎ **800/528-2413** or 520/638-2407); **Kenai Helicopters** (☎ **520/638-2764**); and **Windrock Aviation** (☎ **800/247-6259** or 520/638-9591).

Mule Rides. The prospect of descending narrow trails above steep cliffs on animals hardly famous for their intelligence might make you nervous. Once on the trail, however, you'll soon discover that the mules are no more enthralled by the idea of falling than you are. Although the mules walk close to the edges, accidents are rare.

From the South Rim, you can take a 12-mile round-trip day ride to Plateau Point, or purchase 1- or 2-night packages that go to the bottom of the canyon and include lodging and meals at Phantom Ranch. Because the rides are strenuous both for both riders and mules, the wranglers strictly adhere to the following requirements: you must weigh less than 200 pounds, be at least 4 feet, 7 inches tall, speak fluent English, and not be pregnant. *Be advised:* If the wranglers think you weigh too much, they won't hesitate to put you on the scale.

Costs range from $100 for the Plateau Point trip to $352.75 for the 2-night package. Trips to Phantom Ranch fill up months in advance, so make your reservations early. Reservations for the next 11 months (in addition to the current month) can be made beginning on the first of the month by calling ☎ **303/297-2757.** For reservations in the next 4 days, contact the **Bright Angel Transportation Desk** at ☎ **520/638-2631,** ext. 6015.

On the North Rim, mule rides are through a small, family run outfit, **Grand Canyon Trail Rides.** The company offers two types of rim rides and two canyon rides (none of which go to Phantom Ranch), at prices ranging from $15 to $85. Riders must be at least 12 to go on the all-day ride. No one over 200 pounds is allowed on the canyon rides; for the rim rides, the limit is 220 pounds. All riders must speak English.

The mule rides on the North Rim tend to fill up later than those on the South Rim. To sign up, visit the Grand Canyon Trail Rides desk (open daily from 7am to 6pm) at Grand Canyon Lodge, or call ☎ **520/638-9875.** The off-season number is ☎ 801/679-8665.

Horseback Riding. The only horseback riding near the South Rim is at **Apache Stables** (☎ **520/638-2891**), which operates at Moqui Lodge, just outside the park's South Entrance. The friendly horses make this a great family activity. Children as young as 6 are allowed on the 1-hour trail rides, which, like the 2-hour ones, loop through the Kaibab National Forest near the stables. Apache Stables also offers a 4-hour ride east through the forest to near Grandview Point. Prices for the rides, running mid-March through the end of November, range from $25 to $65.

On the North Rim, **Allen's Guided Tours** (☎ **801/644-8150**) offers horseback rides from 8am to 6pm Monday through Saturday. Departing from a corral 0.25 mile south of Jacob Lake on Ariz. 67, the tours travel on gentle terrain in the Kaibab National Forest. Prices range from $15 to $75.

Camping

INSIDE THE PARK

You can make reservations for campsites in the Mather and North Rim campgrounds by calling ☎ **800/365-CAMP** (2267).

Inside the park on the South Rim, 26 miles east of Grand Canyon Village on Ariz. 64, you'll find **Desert View Campground** (no phone; no advance reservations). At dusk, the yips of coyotes drift over this campground in pinyon-juniper woodland at the eastern edge of the park. Elevated, cool and breezy, the peaceful surroundings offer no clue that the bustling Desert View Overlook is within walking distance. The floor of the woodland makes for smooth tent sites, the most secluded being on the outside of the loop drive. The only drawback: The nearest showers are 26 miles away at Camper Services. During high season, this first-come, first-served campground usually fills up by noon.

Near Grand Canyon Village on the South Rim is **Mather Campground** (☎ **520/638-7851**). Despite having 319 campsites in a relatively small area, this remains a pleasant place. Pinyon and juniper trees shade the sites, spaced far enough apart to afford privacy to most campers. One area, however, should be avoided: Sites 150 to 171 on the Juniper Loop lie unpleasantly close to the entrance road. Also, it's good to be near, but not too near, the showers, located in the Camper Services building next to the campground. If you're too close, hundreds of campers tramp past.

For RV drivers, there's **Trailer Village** in Grand Canyon Village (P.O. Box 699), Grand Canyon, AZ 86023. Advance reservations: ☎ **303/297-2757;** same-day reservations, campground questions ☎ 520/638-2631, ext. 6035; fax 520/638-9247.

The neighbors are close, the showers far (0.4 mile) away, and the vegetation sparse. In surroundings like this, you might want to draw the curtains and stay in your RV. The beauty of a hookup is that it lets you do that. If, however,

Campground	Rim	Total Sites	RV Hookups	Dump Station	Toilets	Drinking Water
Cameron Trading Post RV Park	**South**	**48**	**48**	**Yes**	**No**	**Yes**
Demotte Park Campground	**North**	**23**	**No**	**No**	**Yes**	**Yes**
Desert View	**South**	**50**	**No**	**No**	**Yes**	**No**
Diamond Creek Campground	**South**	**open tent camping**	**No**	**No**	**Yes**	**No**
Flintstone Bedrock City	**South**	**unlimited tent sites**	**27**	**Yes**	**Yes**	**Yes**
Grand Canyon Camper Village	**South**	**300**	**250**	**Yes**	**Yes**	**Yes**
Jacob Lake Campground	**North**	**53**	**No**	**No**	**Yes**	**Yes**
Kaibab Lake Campground	**South**	**74**	**No**	**No**	**Yes**	**Yes**
Kaibab Camper Village	**North**	**130**	**70**	**Yes**	**Yes**	**Yes**
Mather Campground	**South**	**323**	**No**	**Yes**	**Yes**	**Yes**
North Rim Campground	**North**	**87**	**No**	**Yes**	**Yes**	**Yes**
Ten X Campground	**South**	**70**	**No**	**No**	**Yes**	**Yes**
Trailer Village	**South**	**84**	**84**	**Nearby**	**Yes**	**Yes**
Tuweep	**North**	**11**	**No**	**No**	**No**	**No**

* $12 two-person tent, $14 electric hookup, $16 water/electric, $1.50 each additional person

** $23 full hookup, $21 water/electric, $19 electric, $15 tent sites, $19 teepees

*** $22 hookups, $12 dry sites, $12 tent sites

you'd like to venture outside during your stay, scout the property before taking a site. A few sites at the end of the numbered drives have grass, shade trees, and one neighbor-free side. If you'd like to leave your RV altogether, you can catch a shuttle bus at a stop near the campground.

Inside the park on the North Rim, the **North Rim Campground** (☎ **520/638-2151**) is 44 miles south of Jacob Lake on Ariz. 67. Shaded by old-growth ponderosa pines and situated alongside Transept Canyon (part of Grand Canyon), this is a delightful place to spend a few days. The 1.5-mile-long Transept Trail links the campground to Grand Canyon Lodge, and the North Rim General Store is within walking distance. The nicest sites are the rim sites, which open onto the canyon. These cost an extra $5 but are worth it, being some of the prettiest anywhere. Showers (cost: $1.25 for 5 minutes) are within walking distance.

With only 83 sites, the North Rim Campground fills up for much of the summer. If you show up without a reservation when the campground is booked, you can put your name on the wait list in person after 8am. If spots come open, names on the list are called at 3pm sharp. The campground sometimes stays open on a limited basis after October 15, but few services are available in the park.

NEAR THE PARK

Just outside the park is **Grand Canyon Camper Village** in Tusayan, 1 mile

Showers	Fire Pits/ Grills	Laundry	Public Phone	Reserve	Fees	Open
No	No	No	Yes	Yes	$15	Year-round
No	Yes	No	No	No	$10	mid-May to mid-Oct
Yes	No	No	No		$12	mid-May to mid-Oct
No	Yes	No	No	No	$7 per person	Year-round
Yes	No	Yes	Yes	Yes	*	Feb–Nov
Yes	Yes	No	Yes	Yes	**	Year-round
No	Yes	No	No	No	$10	Year-round
No	Yes	No	No	No	$10	Apr–Oct
No	No	No	Yes	Yes	***	May 15–Oct 15
Yes	Yes	Yes	No	Mar–Nov	†	Year-round
Nearby	Yes	Nearby	Yes	Yes	‡	May 15–Oct 15
No	Yes	No	No	No	$10	Apr–Oct
Nearby	Yes	No	Nearby	Yes	$19	Year-round
No	Yes	No	No	No	free	when roads are passable

† $12 Mar–May and Sept–Nov, $15 June–Aug
‡ $15–$20 site, $4 tent only, no car

south of the park entrance on Ariz. 64 (P.O. Box 490, Grand Canyon, AZ 86023-0490, ☎ **520/638-2887**). This campground's advantage is its location, within easy walking distance of stores and restaurants on one side and of Kaibab National Forest on the other. Its disadvantages are its relatively narrow (average width: 27 feet) campsites and the noise from the nearby Grand Canyon National Park Airport, whose constant daytime helicopter takeoffs, together with the throngs of people at the campground itself, may bring back memories of Woodstock.

The tent sites are best. Shaded by ponderosa pines, they sit above the rest of the campground and border the national forest. The rest rooms are clean, the showers hot (25¢ for 2 minutes). There's also a playground and a gravel basketball court.

Ten X Campground (☎ **520/638-2443**) is 2 miles south of Tusayan on Ariz. 64. Large, wooded campsites make this the nicest campground within 20 miles of the South Rim. With plenty of distance between you and your neighbors, this is a great place to linger over a fire. All sites have fire pits and grills, and the campground host sells wood. Later, you'll find the soft, needle-covered floor perfect for sleeping. This campground does sell out. If you're driving up from Flagstaff or Williams, consider snagging a site before going to the canyon for the day.

Kaibab Camper Village is 0.5 mile west of Ariz. 67, just south of Jacob Lake, P.O. Box 3331, Flagstaff, AZ 86003 (☎ **520/643-7804** when open, 800/525-0924, or 520/526-0924 when closed). Compared to most South Rim RV parks, where sagebrush is often the largest plant in sight, this is like a fairy tale. The setting makes this easily the prettiest RV park in the Grand Canyon area. Tent campers will also be comfortable here, especially if they pay the extra $3 for one of the improved sites, which have sand rings and views of Jacob Lake. The use of generators is forbidden, so everyone can enjoy the quiet. Only two things are missing: showers—the nearest public ones are inside the park—and flush toilets.

DeMotte Park Campground (☎ **520/643-7298**) is a forest service campground 5 miles north of the park boundary on Ariz. 67. If you come here, bundle up for the night. It's 8,760 feet high, in spruce-fir forest, so you're sure to be cool. The road through the campground curves sharply and some of the spaces are small, so this place may not work for large RVs.

Just north of Jacob Lake on U.S. 89A is another Forest Service campground, **Jacob Lake Campground** (☎ **520/643-7298** or 520/643-7395). Nestled into rolling hills covered with ponderosa pine forest, this is a beauty of a Forest Service campground. Towering pines shade sites only a short drive from Jacob Lake. This campground has regular naturalist programs. Although it is open year-round, water is seasonal and during the winter unplowed roads are a major obstacle.

Accommodations

INSIDE THE PARK

Lodging inside the park is handled by **AMFAC Parks and Resorts,** 14001 E. Eliff, Aurora, CO 80014 (☎ **303/297-2757;** fax 303/297-31750). Beginning on the first of the month, you can reserve a room for the next 21 months (in addition to the current month). For example, on January 1, 1998, you could have reserved rooms through the end of October 1999. The only exception is Phantom Ranch, for which reservations are accepted only for the next 11 months. For reservations, only MasterCard or Visa are accepted. American Express, Diners Club, and Discover are acceptable upon arrival. AMFAC can take reservations up to the minute of your arrival.

The hotels themselves can be contacted through the same switchboard (☎ **520/638-2631;** fax 520/638-9247) and mailing address (P.O. Box 699, Grand Canyon, AZ 86023). The phone number for **Grand Canyon Lodge** is ☎ **520/638-2611.**

SOUTH RIM

The El Tovar

Reservations ☎ **303/297-3175;** fax 303/297-3175. Main switchboard ☎ **520/638-2631.** 65 rms, 10 suites. A/C TV TEL. $112–$169 double; $192–$277 suite. AE, DC, DISC, MC, V.

Designed by Charles Whittlesey as a cross between a Swiss Chalet and a Norwegian Villa, the El Tovar is a dark, cool counterpoint to the warm, pueblo-style buildings of Mary Colter. Completed in 1905 to accommodate the influx of tourists on the Santa Fe Railroad, the El Tovar, situated a few yards from the rim, casts a long shadow over Grand Canyon Village. Inside, moose and elk heads hang on varnished walls, dimly lit by copper chandeliers.

Take away the modern-day tourists and the El Tovar probably looks much as it did at its inception, when it offered guests all manner of luxury, including a music room, art classes, a barber, and roof garden. While many of these amenities have gone the way of the Flagstaff-to-Grand Canyon stagecoach, the hotel is still the most luxurious at the canyon and the only one to offer room service and a nightly turndown. You'll still find a pleasant upstairs sitting area (reserved for guests) and rooms with classic American furnishings.

Bright Angel Lodge

Reservations ☎ **303/297-3175;** fax 303/297-3175. Main switchboard ☎ **520/638-2631.** 34 rms (10 with sink only, 10 with sink and toilet, 14 with bath), 55 cabin rms. $40 hiker rm (double with sink only), $46 double (with sink and toilet), $56 standard rm (with bath); $66 historic cabin, $92–$227 rim cabin. AE, DC, DISC, MC, V.

In the 1930s, The Fred Harvey Co. sought to provide affordable lodging for the new visitors coming by train and automobile to the canyon. At the company's request, Mary Colter designed both the lodge and the cabins alongside it. The cabins were built around several historic buildings, including the park's old post office and the Bucky O'Neill Cabin, the oldest structure on the rim.

Low-end accommodations start with dormitory-style rooms in two long buildings adjacent to Bright Angel Lodge. At $40 a night, the hiker rooms are least expensive in the park. They have single beds and desks but no TVs or private bathrooms. Other rooms have double beds and toilets but no showers. Still others are appointed like standard motel rooms, only with showers instead of tubs.

Rooms in the historic cabins cost only $10 more than the nicest lodge rooms and are worth the extra money. These freestanding cabins, most of which house two guest rooms, tend to be bright inside, and the ones away from the rim are fairly quiet. At the high end of the price range are the four rim cabins, each of which has its own fireplace. These cabins cost $92, and the Bucky O'Neill Cabin goes for $227. They tend to fill up at least a year in advance.

Thunderbird and Kachina Lodges

Reservations ☎ **303/297-3175;** fax 303/297-3175. Main switchboard ☎ **520/638-2631.** 55 rms at Thunderbird, 49 rms at Kachina. A/C TV TEL. $102 double (park-side), $112 (canyon-side). AE, DC, DISC, MC, V.

The newest lodges inside the park, these are already slated for demolition in the new Grand Canyon master plan. It won't be any tragedy to see these buildings razed. Outside, they resemble '60s-era college dormitories, with flat roofs, decorative concrete panels, and metal staircases. Inside the rooms are pleasant enough, with Southwestern-style furnishings and windows as wide as the rooms themselves. Although AMFAC refuses to guarantee a canyon view, most of the upstairs rooms on the more expensive "canyon side" have at least a partial view of the canyon. Check-in for the Thunderbird is at the Bright Angel Lodge; for the Kachina, it's at the El Tovar.

Maswick Lodge

Reservations ☎ **303/297-3175;** fax 303/297-3175. Main switchboard ☎ **520/638-2631.** 278 rms. TV TEL. $59 cabin; $72 Maswick South, $107 Maswick North. AE, DC, DISC, MC, V.

Built in the 1960s, Maswick Lodge is in a wooded area, a 10-minute walk from the rim. If you're not up to walking, the Maswick Transportation Center, the hub for the canyon shuttles, is opposite the lodge. The lodge has a restaurant, sports bar, and gift shop.

Most of the guest rooms are in the two-story wood-and-stone buildings known as Maswick North and South. The rooms in Maswick North have nice furnishings and new carpets, and many have balconies overlooking the ponderosa pine forest. They're among the finest in the park. The ones in Maswick South are 5 years older, a bit smaller, and have less pristine views, but they also cost $35 less. Each of the cabin rooms has two double beds and a shower. Because of their proximity to the road and to festive off-duty employees, these may be a little noisier than the others. If staying here, bring a flashlight, as the area is dark at night.

Yavapai Lodge

Reservations ☎ **303/297-3175;** fax 303/297-3175. Main switchboard ☎ **520/638-2631.** 348 rms. TV TEL. $83 double (Yavapai West), $98 (Yavapai East). AE, DC, DISC, MC, V.

The largest lodge at the canyon, Yavapai is a mile from the historic district but close to Bank One, Babbitt's Store, and the park's visitor center. Built in 1970–72, the A-frame lodge has a large cafeteria and gift shop. Its rooms are in 10 single-story buildings known as Yavapei West and six two-story wood buildings known as Yavapei East. Most rooms in Yavapai West have cinder block walls, and all are compact. Yavapai East's rooms are larger, and many have good views of the forest. Most travelers would agree that they're worth the extra $15. There's more parking here than at the other lodges, since the lots were built to accommodate tour buses. The gravel paths connecting the buildings are very dark at night, so bring a flashlight.

CANYON BOTTOM

Phantom Ranch

Located inside the canyon, 0.5 mile north of the Colorado River on the North Kaibab Trail. Reservations ☎ **303/297-3175;** fax 303/297-3175. Main switchboard ☎ **520/638-2631.** Seven 4-person cabins, 2 cabins for up to 10 people each, 4 dorms of 10 people each. $22.27 dorm bed; $59.39 cabin (for 2 people); $11.70 for each additional person. AE, DC, DISC, MC, V.

The only park lodging below the canyon rims, the cabins at Phantom Ranch often sell out on the first day of availability, more than 11 months ahead. To reserve a spot, call as early as possible. (See directions above for AMFAC lodges.) If you arrive at the canyon without a reservation, contact the **Bright Angel Transportation Desk** (☎ **520/638-2631,** ext. 6015) for information about openings in the next 4 days.

Accessible only by mule or on foot, the ranch's nine specially cooled cabins are a simple pleasure. Mary Colter designed four of them—the ones with the most stone in the walls are hers—using rocks from the nearby Bright Angel Creek. Connected by dirt footpaths, they stand, natural and elegant, alongside picnic tables and under the shade of cottonwood trees. Inside each cabin, there's a desk, concrete floor, and 4 to 10 bunk beds, as well as a toilet and sink. A shower house for guests is nearby.

While most of Phantom Ranch was completed in the 1920s and '30s, four 10-person dorms, each with its own bathing facilities, were added in the early '80s. Used mostly by hikers, these are ideal for individuals and small groups looking for a place to bed down; larger groups are better served by reserving cabins, which provide both privacy and a lower per person price.

NORTH RIM

Grand Canyon Lodge

Reservations ☎ **303/297-3175;** fax 303/297-3175. Main switchboard ☎ **520/638-2631.** 201 cabin and motel rms. $95 double Rim Cabin, $85 Western Cabin, $84 Pioneer Cabin, $69 motel rm, $60 Frontier Cabin. AE, DC, DISC, MC, V.

Built in 1928, Grand Canyon Lodge seems to have grown into the landscape. Its roof of green shingles goes with the needles on the nearby trees, its log beams match their trunks, and its walls of Kaibab limestone blend with the rimrock itself. In its expansive lobby, a 50-foot-high ceiling absorbs sound like the forest floor. Beyond it, the octagonal "Sun Room" has three enormous picture windows opening onto the canyon. Two long decks with rocking chairs flank the sunroom, overlooking the canyon. The lodge also houses a saloon, a snack bar, a meeting room, and a full-service restaurant.

Made of the same materials as the lodge, 140 cabins have sprouted like saplings around it. There are four types, all with private bathrooms. With wicker furniture, bathtubs, and small vanity rooms, the Western Cabins and Rim Cabins are the most luxurious. The Western Cabins cost $85 per night, $10 less than the four Rim Cabins, which overlook the Bright Angel Canyon. The Rim Cabins generally fill up on their first day of availability, nearly 2 years in advance. The two other types, Pioneer and Frontier, are more rustic. Tightly clustered along the rim of Transept Canyon, they have walls and ceilings of exposed logs, upright gas heaters, and showers instead of bathtubs. The Frontier Cabins each have one guest room with a double bed and a twin bed. The Pioneer Cabins each have two guest rooms—one with a double bed and a twin bed, the other with two twins. For $84 ($24 more than the price of a Frontier Cabin), a family of five can stay in comfort in one of the Pioneer Cabins. If your reservations are for a Frontier or Pioneer Cabin, ask at check-in for one that overlooks Transept Canyon. The lodge may be able to accommodate you, and there's no extra charge for the view. A few motel rooms are also available. Although well maintained, their atmosphere doesn't compare to that of the cabins.

NEAR THE PARK

TUSAYAN

Best Western Grand Canyon Squire Inn

1.5 miles south of the park on Ariz. 64. P.O. Box 130, Grand Canyon, AZ 86023-0130. ☎ **800/622-6966** or 520/638-2681; fax 520/638-0162. 250 rms. AC TV TEL. Dec 21–31 $140 double; Mar 16–Oct 18 $135; Oct 19–Nov 30 $90; Dec 1–10 and Jan 1–Mar 15 $65. AE, DC, DISC, MC, V.

There's a lot to do at this hotel, which prides itself on being the only resort at Grand Canyon. You'll find two restaurants, two bars, tennis courts, a beauty [illegible] room, and an outdoor swimming pool. You can get a massage here, or pause to consider the three-story-high mural and waterfall in the lobby. The kids will love the Family Recreation Center, which features bowling, foosball, and video games. The rooms are no nicer than at the other places in town. But if you stay here, you probably won't spend as much time in them as you might elsewhere.

Grand Canyon Quality Inn and Suites

Ariz. 64, 1 mile south of the park entrance. P.O. Box 520 Grand Canyon, AZ 86023. ☎ **800/221-2222** reservations only, or 520/638-2673; fax 520/638-9537. 232 rms, including 56 suites. A/C TV TEL. $138 double (high season), $88 (off-season). AE, DC, DISC, MC, V.

In summer, guests here sun themselves around the large outdoor swimming pool and hot tub. In winter, they head for one of the hotel's two atriums, where tropical plants and palm trees shade an 18-foot-long spa with waterfalls. When they go back to their rooms, they find some of the nicest accommodations in town. All the rooms have refrigerators, and some have private decks. For guests who get thirsty in the spa, the hotel's bar is just a few yards away. The restaurant offers buffets that are especially popular with tour groups.

Grand Canyon Red Feather Lodge

Ariz. 64 in Tusayan, 1.5 miles south of the park entrance. P.O. Box 1460, Grand Canyon, AZ 86023. ☎ **800/538-2345** or 520/638-2414; fax 520/638-9216. 231 rms. A/C TV TEL. $108–$129 double (high season), $59–$109 (off-season). AE, DC, MC, V.

This is another mid- to high-priced hotel with amenities such as an exercise room, a small pool with spa, and free coffee around the clock. One building opened in 1995; another in 1960. In the new building, the first floor rooms are partway below the level of the parking lot. Avoid these if you're hoping for a view. The rooms in the old building, meanwhile, are smaller and darker than those in the new one, but are clean and have the same furnishings. At about $20 less per night, they're a good value.

Moqui Lodge

Ariz. 64, 0.25 mile south of Grand Canyon National Park. P.O. Box 369, Grand Canyon, AZ 86023. ☎ **303/297-2757** for reservations, local 520/638-2424; fax 520/638-2895. 136 rms. TV TEL. $98 double. MC, V for reservations. AE, DC, DISC, MC, V all acceptable upon check-in. Closed Nov 1–Mar 31.

Situated just outside the South Entrance gates, Moqui Lodge feels like part of the national park, only quieter. Built in the 1960s, the A-frame lodge took the place of an old trading post that first opened for business in the '20s. Inside the lobby, a chimney of flagstone and petrified wood climbs to a high ceiling supported by unpeeled logs. Opposite the fireplace, a colorful mural of Native American life decorates one wall.

Done in Southwestern styles, the rooms open onto parking lots and have ceiling fans instead of air conditioners. But they're well maintained, and you can lose the crowds instantly by walking into the national forest, just a few yards away. The Southwestern-style restaurant here is popular with locals, and the bar has been known to sell drafts for 75¢ during sporting events.

7-Mile Lodge

1.5 miles south of park entrance on Ariz. 64. P.O. Box 56, Grand Canyon, AZ 86023. ☎ **520/638-2291.** Reservations not accepted. 20 rms. A/C TV. $80 double (high season), $48 (off-season). AE, DISC, MC, V.

Instead of taking reservations, the owners of this motel start selling spaces at around 9am and usually sell out by early afternoon. If you need a place to stay, think about stopping here on your way into the park. Don't be put off by the motel's cramped office—surprisingly, the rooms are quite nice and large enough to hold two queen beds. Built in 1984, they have metal doors and walls thick enough to muffle the noise of planes from the nearby airport.

WILLIAMS

Best Western Inn of Williams

2600 Rte. 66, Williams, AZ 86046. ☎ **520/635-4400;** fax 520/635-4488. 79 rms. A/C TV TEL. $79–$135 double. Rates include continental breakfast. AE, DISC, MC, V.

The nicest rooms in Williams are at this hotel, atop a forested hill west of town. In addition to sofas, glass-topped coffee tables, and classic American furniture, the rooms offer smaller amenities such as coffeemakers and hair dryers. Outside, the pines grow to near the edge of the swimming pool.

Fray Marcos Hotel

235 N. Grand Canyon Blvd., Williams, AZ 86046. ☎ **800/843-8724;** fax 520/

635-2180. 89 rms. AC TV TEL. Apr–Aug $119 double; Sept–Oct, Nov 26–29, Dec 19–Jan 3, and Mar $99; Nov–Feb, except holidays, $69. AE, DISC, MC, V.

Named for a Franciscan monk believed to have been the first white person in the region, this luxurious hotel replaces the original Fray Marcos Hotel, which closed in 1954. In addition to the hotel, you will also find the Depot Cafe and the museum for the Grand Canyon Railway. In the lobby, original oil paintings of the Grand Canyon adorn the walls, and cushy chairs surround a large flagstone fireplace. Bellhops carry luggage to the spacious, comfortable Southwestern-style rooms. The lounge, Spenser's, features a 19th-century bar imported from Scotland. It offers simple dining and top-shelf liquor.

Norris Motel

1001 W. Rte. 66 (P.O. Box 388), Williams, AZ 86046. ☎ **520/635-2202;** fax 520/635-9202. 33 rms. A/C TV TEL. June–Aug $62 double; Nov–Mar $28; Sept–Oct and Apr–May $48. AE, DISC, MC, V.

In an era when many hotels regrettably advertise being "American owned," the sign at the Norris Motel heralds "British Hospitality," and the motel backs up the claim. Heather James, the British-born manager, does everything possible to make guests feel at home, even letting them walk her Great Dane. While all three buildings are pleasant, the newest, built in 1990, has the best view of the surrounding hills and is closest to the outdoor pool and spa. Its oversize rooms easily house two double beds, a desk, table, and refrigerator, all for a price lower than at most chain motels.

Red Garter Bed and Bakery

137 W. Railroad Ave. (P.O. Box 95), Williams, AZ 86046. ☎ **800/328-1484** or 520/635-1484. 3 rms with private baths. A/C TV. $65–$105 double. Rates include baked goods in morning. DISC, MC, V.

In the early 1900s this Victorian Romanesque building had a brothel upstairs, a saloon downstairs, and an opium den in the back. The innkeeper, John Holst, has worked hard to preserve both the building, built in 1897, and its colorful history. Each of the three guest rooms has custom-made (by Holst himself) moldings, a 12-foot-high ceiling, a ceiling fan, and antique furnishings. The nicest one, The Honeymoon Suite, overlooks Route 66 and is the largest and most luxurious of the three. Its two adjoining rooms were once reserved for the brothel's "best gals," who would lean out of the Pullman windows to flag down customers.

Mid-price chain hotels in Williams include **Ramada Inn Gateway to the Grand Canyon** (☎ **800/462-9381** or 520/635-4431), 642 E. Rte. 66. **Quality Inn Mountain Ranch** (☎ **520/635-2693**), 8 miles east of Williams on Route 1 (near I-40, Exit 171); **Day's Inn** (☎ **520/635-4051**), 2488 W. Rte. 66; **Comfort Inn** (☎ **520/635-4045**), 911 W. Rte. 66; **Fairfield Inn by Marriott** (☎ **520/635-9888**), 1029 N. Grand Canyon Blvd., off I-40, Exit 163; **Holiday Inn** (☎ **520/635-4114**), 950 N. Grand Canyon Blvd., off I-40, Exit 163. Inexpensive chain hotels include the **Travelodge** (☎ **520-635-2651**), 430 E. Rte. 66; **Motel 6** (☎ **520/635-9000**), 831 W. Rte. 66; and **Howard Johnson Express** (☎ **520/635-9561**), 511 N. Grand Canyon Blvd., off I-40, Exit 163.

FLAGSTAFF

Jeanette's Bed and Breakfast

3380 E. Lockett Rd., Flagstaff, AZ 86004-4043. ☎ **800/752-1912** or 520/527-1912; fax 520/527-1713. 4 rms with private baths. A/C. $95 double. Rates include breakfast. DISC, MC, V.

This B&B is as evocative, odd, and entertaining as the memories of a centenarian. Host Jeanette West (no centenarian, she) has stashed small antiques and curios throughout the house, and she encourages guests to find and share them with her. Most of the rooms are named for relatives of either Jeanette or her husband, Ray, and reflect the lives of those people. For example, Ray's grandmother, Icie Vean, had little money and owned metal furniture during her lifetime, so the room named for her has two metal hospital beds. The Amelia room, meanwhile, has antique oak furniture and a large fireplace.

With so many artifacts around, you could easily stay here without realizing that the house is new. Built in 1996, it's a replica of a 1912 Victorian, only with private bathrooms, each with an antique tub, in every room.

Birch Tree Inn Bed and Breakfast

824 W. Birch Ave., Flagstaff, AZ 86001-4420. ☎ **888/774-1042** or 520/774-1042; fax 520/774-8462. 5 rms. A/C. $60–$109 double. Rates include breakfast. AE, DISC, MC, V.

Two couples—Sandy and Ed Znetko and Donna and Rodger Pettinger—bought this 80-year-old country Victorian house in 1988. Now, thanks to them, this former fraternity house feels more like Grandma's than Animal House. A hanging chair turns in the breezes on a large wraparound porch, and a collection of china graces one set of dining-room shelves. Only a few things hint at the building's past: photos of fraternity brothers on the porch, and a slate billiard table, anchoring the game room.

Like the common areas, the guest rooms encourage repose. The Wicker Room features white wicker furniture and baskets. The Southwestern Room is the most luxurious, with a king-size bed and an oversize bathroom that has both a shower and a bathtub. In the Pella room, Sandy's Dutch heritage is celebrated with a colorful quilt, lace curtains, and handmade crafts.

Hotel Monte Vista

100 N. San Francisco St., Flagstaff, AZ 86001. ☎ **800/545-3068** or 520/779-6971; fax 520/779-2904. 47 rms. TV TEL. $25–$110 double. AE, DISC, MC, V.

Once in the lobby of the Hotel Monte Vista, you'll know you've left the chain hotels behind. Parakeets twitter in cages near the front desk, the Mills Brothers croon over the stereo, and relaxed voices filter in from the coffee shop next door. The rooms are a breath of fresh air, in more ways than one. There's still no air-conditioning in this 1926 hotel in historic downtown Flagstaff, so ventilation comes from open windows and ceiling fans. The corner rooms, each with two windows, are especially pleasing. There are no Southwestern patterns and pastel colors here, or, for that matter, flimsy prefabricated walls. You'll find plush carpeting on floors that feel rock-solid. It seems to have changed little since the days when movie stars such as Clark Gable and Humphrey Bogart stayed here while filming westerns.

Super 8 Motel

3725 N. Kasper Ave. (on Rte. 66, 1 mile west of I-40 Exit 201), Flagstaff, AZ 86004. ☎ **520/526-0818;** fax 520/526-8786. 90 rms. A/C TV TEL. May–Sept $64 double, Oct–Apr $52. Rates include donuts. AE, DISC, MC, V.

The beds here are comfortable and the rooms relatively quiet. If the hotel isn't full, ask for a place in the rear building. Slightly newer than the one in front, it has some of the largest rooms in the city and is farther from the highway and from the always-busy railroad tracks.

Good choices for expensive chain hotels in Flagstaff are **Embassy Suites Flagstaff,** 706 S. Milton Rd., ☎ **800/EMBASSY,** and **Best Western Woodlands Plaza Hotel**, 1175 W. Rte. 66, ☎ **800/528-1234** or 520/773-0597. Others include: **Amerisuites,** 2455 S. Beulah (north of I-40, Exit 195B); ☎ **520/774-8042;** and **Little America Hotel,** 2515 E. Butler (off I-40, Exit 198), ☎ **520/779-2741.**

A good mid-price chain hotel is **Econo Lodge West,** 2355 S. Beulah Blvd. (near I-40, Exit 195B), Flagstaff, AZ 86001, ☎ 520/774-2225. Others include: **Best Western Kings House Motel,** 1560 E. Rte. 66, ☎ 520/774-7186; **Best Western Pony Soldier Motel,** 3030 E. Rte. 66, ☎ 520/

526-2388; **Comfort Inn,** 914 S. Milton Rd. (near I-40, Exit 195B), ☎ 520/774-7326; **Days Inn,** 1000 W. Rte. 66, ☎ 520/774-5221; **Days Inn East,** 3601 E. Lockett (near I-40, Exit 201), ☎ 520/527-1477; **Days Inn I-40,** 2735 S. Woodlands Village Blvd. (near I-40, Exit 195B), ☎ 520/779-1575; **Fairfield Inn by Marriott,** 2005 S. Milton (near I-40, Exit 195B), ☎ 520/773-1300; **Holiday Inn Flagstaff Grand Canyon,** 2320 E. Lucky Lane (off I-40, Exit 198), ☎ 520/526-1150; **Howard Johnson,** 2200 E. Butler (off I-40, Exit 198), ☎ 520/779-6944; **Quality Inn Flagstaff,** 2000 S. Milton (near I-40, Exit 195B), ☎ 520/774-8771; **Ramada Limited,** 2755 S. Woodlands (near I-40, Exit 195B), ☎ 520/773-1111.

A good low-price chain hotel is the **Super 8 Motel,** 3725 N. Kasper Ave. (on Route 66, 1 mile west of I-40, Exit 201), ☎ **520/526-0818.** Others include: **Howard Johnson Inn,** 3300 E. Rte. 66, ☎ 520/526-1826; **Motel 6,** 2010 E. Butler (off I-40, Exit 198), ☎ 520/774-1801; **Motel 6,** 2440 E. Lucky Lane (off I-40, Exit 198), ☎ 520/774-8756; **Motel 6,** 2745 S. Woodlands Village Blvd. (near I-40, Exit 195B), ☎ 520/779-3757; **Ramada Limited,** 2350 E. Lucky Lane (off I-40, Exit 198), ☎ 520/779-3614; **Econo Lodge Lucky Lane,** 2480 E. Lucky Lane (off I-40, Exit 198), ☎ 520/774-7701; **Rodeway Inn East,** 2650 E. Rte. 66, ☎ 520/526-2200; **Rodeway Inn West,** 913 S. Milton (near I-40, Exit 195B), ☎ 520/774-5038; **Travelodge Flagstaff,** 801 W. Rte. 66, ☎ 520/774-3381.

NORTH RIM

Jacob Lake Inn

Junction of Ariz. 67 and U.S. 89A. (Mailing address: Jacob Lake Inn, Jacob Lake, AZ 86022.) ☎ **520/643-7232;** fax 520/643-7898. 12 rms, 26 cabins. May 14–Nov 31 $66 double rm or cabin, Dec 1–May 13 $49. AE, DC, DISC, MC, V.

In 1922 Harold and Nina Bowman bought a barrel of gas and opened a gas "stand" on the present-day site of the Jacob Lake Inn. Today this inn at the junction of Ariz. 67 and U.S. 89A is the main hub of activity between the North Rim and Kanab, Utah. To serve the growing summer crowds, many of the Bowmans' descendants travel south from their homes in Utah. They run the bakery, churning out excellent fresh-baked cookies; the soda fountain, whose milkshakes achieved international renown after being praised in a European guidebook; the gift shop, which features museum quality pieces by Native American artists; the restaurant; the motel; and the full-service gas station.

Lodgers can choose between motel rooms and cabins. The rooms in the front building are not nearly as peaceful as the rooms and cabins behind the lodge. Built in 1958, the motel rooms in back are solid and clean, if a bit threadbare in spots. The bathrooms have showers but no tubs. Most people prefer the cabins, even though the cabins cost more and are more rustic than the motel rooms. The cabin floors creak, their guest rooms (from one to three per cabin) are cramped, and most smell like soggy pine needles. In other words, they're exactly how cabins should be. (Unfortunately, two have been nicely restored and therefore ruined.) Each has its own private porch.

Kaibab Lodge

26 miles south of Jacob Lake on Ariz. 67. (Mailing address: HC 64, Box 30, Fredonia, AZ 86022.) ☎ **800/525-0924,** 520/638-2389 May 15–Oct 30, or 520-526-0924 rest of year; fax 520/527-9398. 24 cabinlike rms, with 2–4 separate rms per cabin building. $68 double. DISC, MC, V.

The main lodge here feels as warm and comfortable as a beloved summer camp. It has an upright piano, plastic trees, Christmas lights, wagon wheels, Indian rugs, watercolor paintings, board games, and portable heaters, all under a open-framed ceiling and enormous pine beams that date to its construction in the 1920s. Perhaps because the guest rooms lack phones and TVs, guests tend to congregate in the Adirondack-style chairs in front of the lodge's 5-foot-wide fireplace, in the small TV room, or at the tables across from the counter that doubles as front desk and beer bar. There's also a small gift shop, and a restaurant that serves breakfast and dinner.

Each cabinlike building houses two or more of the 24 guest rooms, which sleep from two to five people. The rooms are spare but clean, with paneling of rough-hewn pine. Because the walls are thin, stay across from friends here if you can. Located roughly 0.25 mile from the highway, the rooms open onto the broad expanse of DeMotte Park, one of the large, naturally occurring meadows on the Kaibab Plateau. At dawn and dusk, deer graze outside.

KANAB & FREDONIA

Best Western Red Hills

125 W. Center St., Kanab, UT 84741. ☎ **800/528-1234** reservations only, or 801/644-2675; fax 801/644-5919. 72 rms. A/C TV TEL. June 1–Jan 4 $82 double; Jan 5–Apr 21 $45 double. Rates include continental breakfast. AE, DISC, MC, V.

The best things about this hotel are its pool (with a deep end) and its roaring hot tub. It's also conveniently situated near the restaurants and shops in downtown Kanab. The rooms have large TVs and comfortable beds.

Blue Sage Motel and RV Park

330 S. Main (P.O. Box 701), Fredonia, AZ 86022. ☎ **520/643-7125.** 7 rms and 5 full hookups. A/C TV. May 16–Oct 31 $40 double; Nov 1–May 15 $35 double. $15 hookup. MC, V.

Small touches make this tiny, family run motel a pleasant stop. Petunias grace the patios, and clothesline-dried sheets freshen the beds. The rooms, which have swamp coolers instead of air conditioners, vary in size, as do the beds. Ask for queens instead of doubles—the cost is the same. Located behind the motel, the RV sites overlook a broad expanse of the Arizona Strip.

Grand Canyon Motel and Old Travelers Inn

175 Main St. (Box 456), Fredonia, AZ 86022-0456. ☎ **520/643-7646.** 15 rms, some with full kitchens. A/C TV. Old Travelers Inn $27.50 double; Grand Canyon Motel May 15–Oct 31 $32.50 double; Nov 1–May 14 $27 double. AE, MC, V.

Low prices make this hotel popular even during winter, when its occupancy still averages 80%. Four rooms are in the historic Old Travelers Inn, built in 1886. With high ceilings, original trim, and ceiling fans, they resemble B&B rooms, only without an innkeeper around. The others are in cabin-type buildings, built between 1936 and 1948. The cabin units, each with cable TV, refrigerators, and pine furniture, surround a grassy courtyard shaded by elm and spruce trees.

Holiday Inn Express

815 E. Hwy. 89, Kanab, UT 84741. ☎ **800/574-4061** reservations only, or 801/644-8888; fax 801/644-8880. 67 rms. A/C TV TEL. May 15–Oct 14 $85 double; Oct 15–Nov 1 and Apr 1–May 14 $59 double; Nov 2–Mar 31 $49 double. Rates include continental breakfast. AE, DC, DISC, MC, V.

One of the newest in town, this hotel features clean rooms in rich colors. It's located on the east end of town, across the street from the 9-hole Coral Cliffs Golf Course. For those who prefer hiking to golf, a trail leads into the red-rock canyon behind the golf course.

Parry Lodge

89 E. Center St., Kanab, UT 84741. ☎ **800/748-4104** or 801/644-2601; fax 801/644-2605. 89 rms. A/C TV TEL. Apr 15–Oct 31 $65 double; Nov 1–Apr 14 $51 double. AE, DISC, MC, V.

Many of the older rooms in this 1929 Colonial-style lodge display plaques bearing the names of stars who stayed here while filming Westerns. Room 131, for example, was built to house Frank Sinatra's mother-in-law while the famed crooner starred in *Sergeants Three.* (Sinatra stayed in an adjoining room.) Maple trees shade the older one-story buildings, making them look as if they were in the original colonies. If you want to spread out, though, bypass these historic buildings in favor of the two-story one. Completed in 1985, it has expansive (if somewhat drab) rooms. Open for all three meals, the lodge's restaurant serves breakfasts that are among the best in town.

EAST RIM

Cameron Trading Post Motel

On Ariz. 89 (P.O. Box 339), Cameron, AZ 86020. ☎ **800/338-7385** or 520/679-2231; fax 520/679-2350. 62 rms. 4 suites. A/C TV TEL. $74 double (high season); $59 (off-season). AE, DC, MC, V.

Renovated in the early '90s, the rooms in this motel are some of the nicest in the Grand Canyon area. Each features its own unique Southwestern-style furnishings, many of them handmade by the motel's staff. Some rooms open onto the gorge of the Little Colorado River, and a few afford views all the way down to the river (or dry riverbed) itself. The motel's Hopi building borders a small terraced garden with stone picnic tables, a fountain, and a large grill. There's a restaurant and an enormous trading post on the premises.

Lee's Ferry Lodge

4 miles west of Navajo Bridge on U.S. 89A (HC 67-Box 1), Marble Canyon, AZ 86036. ☎ **520/355-2230** or 520/355-2231; fax 520/355-2301. 11 units of all types, including 3 two-rm units. AC. $53 double. MC, V.

Some of the best porch-sitting anywhere can be enjoyed outside the low sandstone buildings of this sleepy roadside lodge, a popular stopping place for trout fishermen trying their luck above Lee's Ferry. Although the hotel sits close to the road, traffic is slow at night, and the overall effect is restful. Paintings of wildfowl, trout, and (oddly enough) flowers grace the rooms, which are small and rustic. The only thing not relaxing are the showers, which erupt like Old Faithful, only less faithfully.

Dining

INSIDE THE PARK

SOUTH RIM

Maswick and Yavapai Cafeterias

Located at Maswick and Yavapai lodges, respectively. ☎ **520/638-2631.** Reservations not accepted. AE, DC, DISC, MC, V. Breakfast $1.40–$4.70; lunch and dinner $3.75–$7. Maswick 6am–10pm daily. Yavapai 6am–9pm daily. CAFETERIA.

For the price of a burger, fries, and Coke at the Tusayan McDonalds, you can eat a full meal at either Maswick or Yavapai cafeterias. While the food at both is usually good, there are some key differences between them. Maswick serves full-dinner plates that can be ordered at any of four stations. Its Mexican station serves up burritos and tostadas with beans and rice on the side. The best value in town may be the bean-and-cheese burrito for just $3.75, a filling meal even after a day of backpacking. There's also a pasta station, a burger station, and another with fish and daily specials.

At Yavapai you can mix and match from a variety of stations, picking up a chicken leg from one, a slice of pizza from another, a dish of mashed potatoes from another. An attendant will follow your instructions to assemble a heaping dinner salad for under $2.

Arizona Steakhouse

At Bright Angel Lodge. ☎ **520/638-2631.** Reservations not accepted. Dinner $12–$20. AE, DC, DISC, MC, V. 5–10pm nightly. AMERICAN.

Lining up before this restaurant's 5pm opening isn't a bad idea. Instead of arriving after sunset to find an hour's wait, you can watch the sunset's colors through the long canyon-facing windows. Or, when the days are longer, finish the meal in time to step outside for the evening's colors.

Once you're seated, the service generally runs sluggishly. You'll have plenty of time for an appetizer—the sautéed mushroom caps are one good choice—or to choose from the restaurant's wine list. Entrees include hand-cut steaks and prime rib; chicken, swordfish, and salmon; and a daily vegetarian special. The food here tends to be inconsistent, but on a good night you can find a delicious meal.

El Tovar Restaurant

In the El Tovar Lodge. ☎ **520/638-2631,** ext. 6432. Reservations for dinner only. Breakfast $2.50–$9.50; lunch $6.20–$17; dinner $14.20–$24.75. AE, DC, DISC, MC, V. Breakfast 6:30–11am; lunch 11:30am–2pm; dinner 5–10pm. CONTINENTAL.

More than 90 years after opening its doors, this restaurant still seems to value good service and fine food. The dining experience starts with its lovely room—walls of Oregon pine graced with murals depicting the ritual dances of four Indian tribes.

At dinner, a Southwestern influence spices the continental cuisine. Appetizers include fennel-crusted soft-shell crabs with cilantro corn relish; Southwestern-style oysters Rockefeller; and lobster toast with jicama black bean salad and mango vinaigrette. For an entree, meat-eaters will enjoy the grilled filet mignon with a three-peppercorn sauce. Another nice choice is Florentine crepes with smoked mozzarella cream and blended rice pilaf.

The El Tovar accepts reservations for dinner only, but it's also open for breakfast and lunch. If you're on a budget, consider dining here during non-dinner hours, when you can get the same high-quality food for just a few dollars more than you'd spend at the other canyon restaurants. If you breakfast here, be sure to sample the coffee, the best inside the park.

Bright Angel Coffee Shop

In Bright Angel Lodge. ☎ **520/638-2631.** Reservations not accepted. Breakfast $1.95–$7; lunch and dinner $5.75–$12.20. AE, DC, DISC, MC, V. Breakfast 6:30–10:45am; lunch and dinner 11:15am–10pm. AMERICAN.

The burgers and patty melts here are tasty, as are some of the Southwestern dishes. This is also a good place for families, who can dine here without worrying too much about the children's behavior. The games on the kid's menu should distract the young ones until the french fries arrive.

Still, this restaurant doesn't merit high marks. It gets soiled from the throngs that tramp through it, and some of the staff members seem to care little about return business or even about tips. Besides, equally good food is available for less money at the Maswick and Yavapai cafeterias.

Babbitt's Delicatessen

In Babbitt's General Store (Mather Business Center). ☎ **520/638-2262.** Most items $2–$5. Cash only. 8am–7pm daily. DELI.

Many Park Service employees duck into this delicatessen for lunch. You can sit in a corner booth, read the paper, and watch the tourists pass. The deli serves sandwiches, salads, and fried chicken, but the best offerings are often the specials.

Desert View Trading Post Cafeteria

At Desert View, 25 miles east of Grand Canyon Village on Ariz. 64. ☎ **520/638-2360.** Most items $2–$5. Cash only. 8am–6pm (summer); 9am–5pm (rest of year). CAFETERIA.

The sandwiches, pizza, and burgers here will sustain you until you make it back to Grand Canyon Village. The breakfast offerings, including eggs and French toast, draw campers from nearby Desert View Campground.

INSIDE THE CANYON

Phantom Ranch

Inside the canyon 0.5 mile north of the Colorado River on the North Kaibab Trail. To order meals more than 4 days in advance, call ☎ **303/297-2757.** To order meals in the next 4 days, contact the Bright Angel Transportation Desk at ☎ **520/638-2631,** ext. 6015. $28.07 steak; $17.58 stew; $5.80 sack lunch; $12.33 breakfast. AE, DC, DISC, MC, V for meals; MC, V for advance reservations. AMERICAN.

At the bottom of the Grand Canyon, pretty much anything tastes good, so it's hard to say whether the food at Phantom Ranch would taste as great on the rim as it does here alongside Bright Angel Creek. If you want dinner served your way, however, bring a camp stove. Every evening two options are offered: a steak dinner at 5pm, and a hearty beef stew at 6:30pm. In the morning, heaping platters of eggs, bacon, and pancakes are laid out on the long blue tables. The only disappointment is the box lunch, whose meager offerings (bagel, summer sausage, juice, apple, peanuts, raisins, and cookies) don't seem worth the price.

Because the number of meals is fixed, hikers and mule riders must reserve them ahead of time through AMFAC (see number above) or at the Bright Angel Transportation Desk. As a last resort, inquire upon arrival at Phantom Ranch to see whether any meals remain. Up until 4pm this can be done in the canteen itself. After 4, ask at a side window behind the canteen. Between 8am and 4pm and 8 to 10pm, anyone is allowed in the canteen, which has snacks, soda, beer, and wine.

NORTH RIM

Grand Canyon Lodge Dining Room

At Grand Canyon Lodge. ☎ **520/638-2611,** ext. 160. Reservations required for dinner, not accepted for breakfast and lunch. Breakfast $1.85–$6.75; lunch $5.70–$7.45; dinner $12.25–$17.75. AE, DC, DISC, MC, V. Breakfast 6:30–10am; lunch 11:30am–2:30pm; dinner 5–9:30pm. CONTINENTAL.

Long banks of west- and south-facing windows afford views of Transept Canyon and help warm this room, where the high ceiling absorbs the clamor of diners. While it's unreasonable to expect gourmet dining in a place as remote as the North Rim, the food here is nearly as satisfying as the surroundings. The shrimp cocktail tastes about as good as one along the ocean. A good bet for a main course is the Pasta Lydia—fresh asparagus and potatoes tossed in pesto sauce with bow-tie pasta. Other choices include prime rib, steak, pork medallions, and dishes with fish or poultry. Lunch offerings include a variety of salads, sandwiches, and burgers. At breakfast, a full buffet costs under $8.

Grand Snack Shop

In the west wing of Grand Canyon Lodge. ☎ **520/638-2611.** Breakfast $1.95–$4.25; lunch and dinner $1.30–$3.80. Pizza: 14-inch supreme is $15.50. Cash only. 7am–9pm daily. SANDWICHES/LIGHT FARE.

The snack bar serves the best pizza on the North Rim, or so the joke goes—it's also, of course, the only pizza on the North Rim. In any case, a slice for $2.25 is an economical alternative to firing up the camp stove. The snack bar also serves burgers, premade salads, and breakfasts. If all you want is a cup of coffee and a muffin, stop by the saloon, where an espresso bar operates from 5 to 9:30am daily.

MARBLE CANYON

Lee's Ferry Lodge Vermilion Cliffs Bar & Grill

4 miles west of Navajo Bridge on Hwy. 89A, Marble Canyon. ☎ **520/355-2231.** Reservations for large groups only. Breakfast $2–$6.50; lunch $2.75–$6.25; dinner $5.95–$17.95. AMERICAN.

After rigging boats for trips down the Colorado, many river guides come here, and not just because the restaurant stocks 150 types of bottled beer. They also come for nicely prepared steaks, chicken, and fish, and for imaginative sandwiches. This restaurant, whose walls, tables, chairs, and bar all seem to have been cut from the same wood, frequently fills up on summer evenings. Most people come for dinner, but the breakfasts here are also excellent. If you don't want to bother "building" your own omelette, get all the ingredients together in a dish known as the Canyon Skillet: diced potatoes with ham, onion, green chile, and cheddar cheese topped with two eggs and toast.

TUSAYAN

Coronado Dining Room

At Best Western Grand Canyon Squire Inn, 1.5 miles south of the park on Ariz. 64, Tusayan. ☎ **520/638-2681,** ext. 4419. Breakfast buffet $8.95; dinner $10.95–$18.95. 6:30–11am (high season only), 5–10pm (year-round). SOUTHWESTERN.

The restaurant, which rates with the one at Moqui Lodge as best in Tusayan, serves the usual mix of Southwestern and American food, only prepared more expertly than in other area restaurants. Of the Southwestern dishes, the spinach enchiladas (marinated spinach wrapped in a soft corn tortilla and fried) and the pollo asada (charbroiled chicken breast with tomatoes and scallions) get high marks. The best time to eat here on summer nights is between 5 and 7pm, when entrees are discounted by $2 or more.

Moqui Lodge Dining Room

At Moqui Lodge, on Hwy. 64, 0.25 mile from the park's South Entrance, Tusayan. ☎ **520/638-2424.** Reservations not accepted. Breakfast $7.50; dinner $5.95–$18. No lunch. AE, DC, DISC, MC, V. 6:30–10am and 6–10pm. Lodge closed Nov 1–Apr 1. SOUTHWESTERN.

Bare as a country church, this restaurant occupies a wide, wood-paneled room with a ceiling that's high but humble. Electric candles and metal chandeliers flush the darkness from every corner. When the restaurant is crowded, voices resound off the woodwork like the din when a church lets out.

With no darkness to distract diners, the restaurant makes sure to serve appetizing food. While Moqui does offer American dinners such as fried chicken and rib-eye steak, it's best known for its Mexican fare, which rivals that of the Flagstaff restaurants and that regularly attracts park employees and Tusayan locals. These offerings include a variety of tostadas, enchiladas, and tacos. The fajitas—chicken, steak, or tofu served with peppers and onions in a flour tortilla—make a trip here worthwhile. For dessert, try the Derby Pie.

Steakhouse at Grand Canyon

1 mile south of the park entrance on U.S. 180/64, Tusayan. ☎ **520/638-2780.** Reservations for groups only. Main courses $6–$23. MC, V. 11am–11pm (summer); 5–10pm (winter). AMERICAN.

Tablecloths in the pattern of Holstein cowhides, steers' horns mounted on the walls, and waiters dressed like cowboys are reminders of this restaurant's devotion to beef. Most of the entrees are steaks or ribs, made from choice beef, filleted on site. The food tends to be fresh and tasty, and the service is prompt. If this restaurant has a shortcoming, it's that its service is *too* prompt—customers may feel as if they're being herded, in keeping with the beef motif. Still, the fresh food is more than enough to corral business.

We Cook Pizza and Pasta

On Ariz. 64, 1 mile south of the park entrance, Tusayan. ☎ **520/638-2274.** Reservations not accepted. Dinner $10–$20; lunch $7–$12. 11am–10pm (summer); noon–9pm (winter). ITALIAN.

In this restaurant's lengthy name, the owners forgot to mention how much they charge. The prices here are high even by Grand Canyon standards, especially for a place without table service. A large four-item pizza runs $20.50, and some pasta dishes cost over $10. After paying dearly for your food, you'll receive a number, then take a seat at one of the long picnic tables. At least the food is good when it comes. Pasta dishes such as the spicy shrimp linguini and the Cajun chicken fettucini taste especially delicious to the salt-deprived, and the pizza pleases most diners.

FLAGSTAFF

The Black Bean Burrito Bar and Salsa Company

12 E. Rte. 66, Gateway Plaza Suite 104, Flagstaff. ☎ **520/779-9905.** Reservations not accepted. $1–$6. No credit cards. Sun–Thurs 11am–9pm, Fri–Sat 11am–2am. MEXICAN.

The best burritos seem to turn up in the plainest environments. At the Black Bean, you'll eat out of plastic drive-in baskets while sitting at a counter that opens onto a pedestrian walkway. Sure enough, the burritos, which come with a choice of eight different salsas, are delicious. A favorite among Northern Arizona University students, the Black Bean offers 14 house specialty wraps (steamed or stir-fried food wrapped in tortillas), including exotic flavors such as peanut tofu and hummus, as well as traditional bean, chicken, and steak burritos. Wrapped in aluminum foil, the burritos have the heft of hand weights.

Charly's

Located in the historic Hotel Weatherford, 23 N. Leroux, Flagstaff. ☎ **520/779-1919.** Reservations accepted. Lunch $2.95–$8.95; dinner $6.50–$13.95. AE, DC, DISC, MC, V. Daily 11am–10pm. Closed for Sun lunch in winter. AMERICAN.

Charly's is spacious and cool, both inside, where the 12-foot-high ceilings of the Hotel Weatherford (built in 1897) provide breathing room, and on the sidewalk, a favorite place for summertime dining. Besides steaks and burgers, the restaurant offers a number of vegetarian dishes and salads perfect for light dining. Made with sun-dried tomatoes instead of anchovies, the blackened chicken Caesar salad is a cool pleasure. If you'd like to try Navajo fry bread but aren't up to eating a heavy meat stuffing, you can order it with sautéed vegetables instead. Most of the meals will leave you unencumbered enough to dance at the hotel bar, which features live entertainment nightly and has 20 beers on tap.

Dara Thai

1580 E. Rte. 66, Flagstaff. ☎ **520/774-0047.** Reservations accepted. Lunch and dinner $5.95–$11.95. DC, MC, V. Summer 11am–10pm; rest of year 11am–9pm. THAI.

Thai streamers, lights, and screens hang alongside steer's horns, wagon-wheel chandeliers, and horseshoes in this restaurant inside an old Route 66 hotel. In spite of the mixed signals sent by the decor, the food is entirely Thai, including curries, noodles, seafood, and vegetarian plates. If the 83 choices overwhelm you, try the medley of vegetables in oyster sauce.

Macy's

14 S. Beaver St., Flagstaff. ☎ **520/774-2243.** Reservations not accepted. Main courses $3.50–$6.25. No credit cards. Mon–Wed 6am–8pm; Thurs–Sat 6am–9pm; Sun 6am–6pm. VEGETARIAN/BAKED GOODS.

A nice breeze always seems to blow through this restaurant, skimming the dust off the elaborately drawn menus on the chalkboards and stirring aromas of patchouli, spices, and coffee. Macy's may not be able to save the world, but its fine vegetarian food, fresh pastries, and great coffee encourage people to slow down and smell the latte. It's a place where vegans are welcomed, where bikes lean against the building, and where the bathroom graffiti is life-affirming. A cashier here earnestly told me that she loves everything on the menu. In addition to the standard menu items such as meatless meatballs and breakfast couscous, Macy's serves daily specials, including a pasta of the day.

Pasto

19 E. Aspen Ave., Flagstaff. ☎ **520/779-1937.** Reservations accepted. Dinner $9.50–$13.95. MC, V. Sun–Thurs 5–9:30pm, Fri–Sat 5–10pm. ITALIAN.

Located in historic downtown Flagstaff, Pasto is one of the nicer rooms in town. Spacious and elegant, it has brick walls hung with old horns and trombones, a stamped tin ceiling, and a platform for the window-side tables. The restaurant bills itself as "fun Italian dining," perhaps referring to the learn-to-speak-Italian tapes that play in the rest rooms, or maybe to the crayons on the tables. Still, the dining is more delicious than fun. The Southwestern Black Bean Ravioli, which comes with a choice of sauces (try the "atomic"), is an outstanding dish, as is the Tortelloni Florentine (garlic lemon torts under cream sauce). There are a number of shrimp, chicken, and vegetarian dishes, many priced under $10.

WILLIAMS

Grand Canyon Coffee and Cafe

125 W. Rte. 66, Williams. ☎ **520/635-1255.** Prices for sandwiches: $3.50–$4.50. AE, MC, V. Summer Mon–Sat 8am–9pm. Low season Mon–Sat 9am–5pm. SANDWICHES.

For lunch, try this restaurant, which prominently displays Harley-Davidson T-shirts but traffics in food and drink that most bikers wouldn't touch, including Mocha Espresso Frappes, fruit smoothies, bottled waters, and Panini sandwiches served on Focaccia bread. Cooked on a cast-iron grill imported from Switzerland, the panini sandwiches are among the best I've tasted—and they're relatively inexpensive. One great choice is the "Chunky Cheese"—cheddar, mozzarella, and Swiss cheeses with tomato, grilled onion, and mayo.

Rod's Steakhouse

301 E. Rte. 66, Williams. ☎ **520/635-2671.** Reservations accepted. Lunch and dinner $7–$24. MC, V. 11:30am–9:30pm year-round. STEAKS.

If you're a steak lover, brake for the cow-shaped sign on Route 66. This landmark restaurant, sprawling across a city block between the highway's east- and west-bound lanes, has hardly changed since Rodney Graves, an early member of the U.S. Geological Survey, opened it in 1946. Printed on a paper cutout of a cow, the menu is still only about 6 inches across—more than enough space for its laconic descriptions of the restaurant's offerings. You can choose from deep-fried seafood such as "Filet of Cod tartar sauce" or "Jumbo Fantail Shrimp four pieces," all-time favorites such as "Bar-B-Que Ribs" and "Beef Liver grilled onions and bacon," or prime rib in three sizes, from the 9-ounce "Ladies lite cut" to the 16-ounce "Cattleman's hefty cut." Of course, the corn-fed, mesquite-broiled steaks that have kept this place in business for a half century are also available.

Pancho McGillicuddy's Mexican Cantina

141 Railroad Ave., Williams. ☎ **520/635-4150.** Reservations accepted. $2.50–$12.95. AE, DISC, MC, V. Summer daily 11am–10pm; winter daily 3–10pm. MEXICAN/AMERICAN.

The first tough decision at this restaurant is where to eat. Your choices are the outside deck, which receives some nice late-afternoon sun and features live entertainment in summer; the main dining room, done up like a courtyard in a Mexican Villa; and the historic barroom, site of the (1893) Cabinet Saloon. The next tough choice is which of the heavy but zesty Mexican dishes to order. The chicken flautas (deep-fried corn tortillas stuffed with tenderized chicken) are one good option. If, by chance, the food doesn't melt in your mouth, you can wash it down with a Dos Equis draft.

Red Garter Bakery

137 W. Railroad Ave., Williams. ☎ **520/635-1484.** Reservations not accepted. DISC, MC, V. Tues–Sun 7–11am and 4–8pm. BAKERY.

A talented pastry chef, Charlie McClain, came to the Red Garter from Flagstaff in the mid-1990s, bringing with him his mouth-watering scones, strudels, cinnamon rolls, and European-style bread. The pastries alone make a visit here worthwhile, but there's more to like. The fresh-ground coffee is rich and strong, and the bakery is in a historic building graced with its original wood floor, on which sits an enormous antique coffee grinder. If you're taking the train, you won't have to walk far to get here. It's right across the tracks from the Williams Depot.

Tiffany's Restaurant and Lube Room Lounge

233 W. Rte. 66. ☎ **520/635-2445.** Reservations accepted. Lunch and dinner $4.25–$14.95. AE, MC, V. 11am–10pm daily. AMERICAN.

The lounge and half of this restaurant occupy an old Route 66 gas station. Accordingly, the entire place is jammed with gas-station memorabilia, including stamped glass, filling-station signs, "Sky Chief" gas pumps, and photos of classic stations. Served up with plenty of napkins as well as drinks in unbreakable plastic mugs, the greasy roadhouse food at this restaurant will fuel you for days to come. The pizza, chicken, and hamburgers are all tasty, but the best choice, if you really want to fill up, is the baby-back ribs. Check on the daily specials in the bar, which attract many locals.

KANAB & FREDONIA

Best Friends Cafe

93 W. Center St., Kanab. ☎ **801/644-8843.** Breakfast $1.30–$5.50; lunch and dinner $3.95–$5.95. DISC, MC, V. Wed–Mon 7am–9pm, Tues 7am–2pm. Closed in winter. VEGETARIAN.

Best Friends Animal Sanctuary opened this cafe to serve vegetarian food to its employees. The cafe now attracts many travelers who come for excellent vegetarian sandwiches, salads, and pastas; for breakfast dishes such as eggless tofu scrambles; and for gourmet coffee. The servers seem a bit puzzled at times, as if they're filling in for the regular staff. If you're able to overlook an occasional blunder (such as being served a glass of half-and-half) and have a little time to spare, you'll enjoy the food.

Houston's Trails End Restaurant

32 E. Center St., Kanab. ☎ **801/644-2488.** Breakfast $2.75–$6.50; lunch $3.75–$6.25; dinner $5.25–$17.95. AE, DISC, MC, V. 6am–10:30pm daily. Closed Dec 1–Mar 1. STEAK/SEAFOOD/MEXICAN.

For a taste of Kanab's traditional fare, head for Houston's. While country music plays over the stereo, waitresses wearing toy (we hope) sidearms serve up meaty courses. The house special is chicken-fried steak. Other specialties include a chicken breast slathered in barbecue sauce, and baby-back ribs baked all day. The soup is made fresh daily, as are the enormous yeast rolls that come with each dinner. Breakfast includes a choice of omelettes, and lunch is mostly burgers and sandwiches.

Nedra's Cafe

U.S. 89A, Fredonia. ☎ **520/643-7591.** $2.75–$15.95. AE, DISC, MC, V. May 15–Oct 31 daily 7am–10pm; Nov 1–May 14 Thurs–Sun 11am–8pm. MEXICAN.

Because this restaurant serves tasty Mexican food at a moderate price, it's a great place to gorge after completing a North Rim backpacking trip. In addition to enchiladas, tostadas, burritos, and tacos, Nedra's serves less-common Mexican dishes such as carnitas (seasoned roast pork topped with fresh cilantro and green onions) and machaca (shredded beef cooked with tomatoes, onion, green chiles, cilantro, and egg). A few

American courses remain, including hamburgers, sandwiches, and steaks. In Kanab you'll find a similar restaurant, Nedra's Too.

Picnic & Camping Supplies

If possible, stock up on your camping items at a grocery store in a large city such as Flagstaff. In general, prices are lowest in Flagstaff and rise steadily as you near the canyon, peaking at Babbitt's inside the park. Inside the park, on the South Rim, you'll find **Babbitt's General Store,** in Grand Canyon Village (☎ **520/638-2262**); and **Babbitt Brothers Trading Co.,** at Desert View off Ariz. 64 (☎ **520/638-2393**). On the North Rim is the **North Rim General Store,** adjacent to North Rim Campground (☎ **520/638-2611,** ext. 270).

Outside the park, in Tusayan, is **Babbitt's Supermarket,** 1 mile south of park entrance on U.S. 89 and Ariz. 64 (☎ **520/638-2854**). In Williams: **Safeway,** 637 Rte. 66 (☎ **520/635-4381**). In Cameron: **Simpson's Market,** at the junction of U.S. 89 and Ariz. 64, next to the Chevron (☎ **520/679-2340**). In Kanab: **Glazier's Food Town,** 264 S. 100 E. (☎ **801/644-5029**). There are three in Flagstaff: **Albertson's,** 1416 E. Rte. 66 (☎ **520/773-7955**); **Basha's,** 2700 Woodlands Village Blvd. (☎ **520/774-3882**); and **Smith's,** 201 N. Switzer Canyon Dr. (☎ **520/774-2719**).

19

GRAND TETON NATIONAL PARK

By Ed Lawrence

THOUGH MUCH SMALLER THAN NEIGHBORING YELLOWSTONE, Grand Teton is equally impressive—inspiring, even—though in a more understated manner. Except for the towering mountains that made her famous, she's not as brassy as her cousin. You'll see wildlife—eagles and osprey along the Snake River, moose and, if you're lucky, a black bear in the vicinity of the Jackson Lake Junction, and pronghorn on the valley floor—but it is the landscape that makes this park.

Contrasted to the undulations of Yellowstone, Grand Teton presents two vistas: a long, wide valley, and straight-up peaks. If possible, once you enter the park make a beeline for the summit of Signal Mountain, near Jackson Lake. There you will have a commanding 360° view that will put the park and surrounding areas in perspective. It's also the spot that inspired the most famous photos of the park.

From the Jackson Point Overlook on Signal Mountain, you'll see a valley floor that was once covered with thousands of tons of ice and a freshwater sea; to the west are views of a mountain formation towering more than a mile overhead.

Consider this: The tops of the Tetons, which sit on a 40-mile long fault, were uplifted more than 30,000 feet from beneath the surface. The canyons and valleys that punctuate the mountains were carved during the Ice Age; glaciers also gouged out hundreds of lakes in the park.

One advantage of Grand Teton is that it's significantly easier to get around in than Yellowstone, in part because the park is smaller and activity centers are closer to each other. The lack of size doesn't reduce the park's appeal, though; it just makes her more accessible. Jackson Lake and the Snake River, prime recreational areas for fishers and boaters, are only short distances from the hiking trails and campsites. And though less imposing than the more famous Old Faithful Inn, Jackson Lake Lodge is every bit as appealing and comfortable.

The first homesteaders began arriving in the area in the 1880s. Many discovered, though, that the frigid winters and short growing season made it difficult—indeed, virtually impossible—to eke out a living, so they abandoned the area. However, by 1903 cattle ranchers discovered that wealthy eastern hunters were attracted to the area as a vacation site,

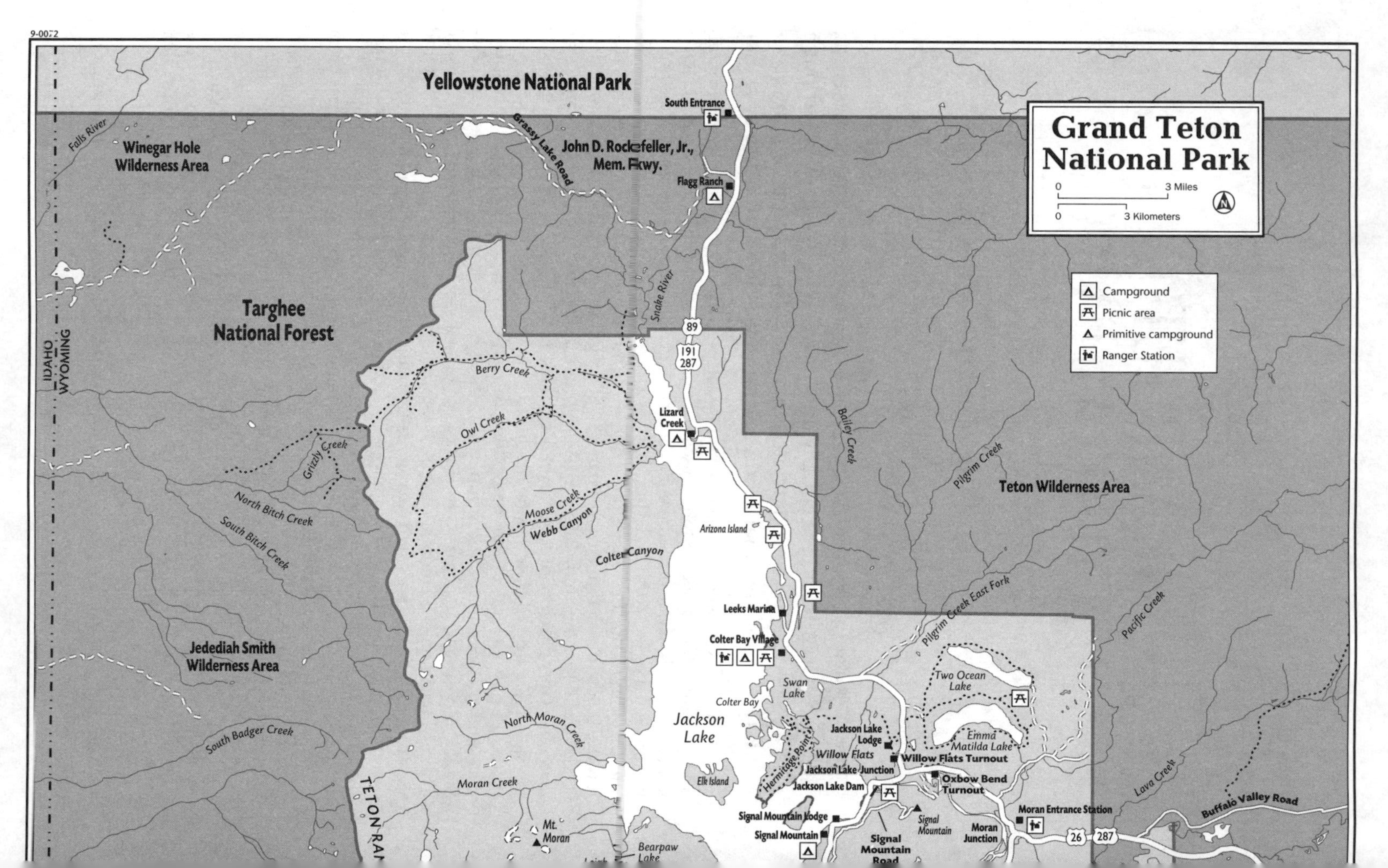

9-0072
Grand Teton National Park
0
3 Miles
0
3 Kilometers
Campground
Picnic area
Primitive campground
Ranger Station
Yellowstone National Park
South Entrance
John D. Rockefeller, Jr., Mem. Pkwy.
Grassy Lake Road
Flagg Ranch
Falls River
Winegar Hole Wilderness Area
IDAHO
WYOMING
Targhee National Forest
Snake River
89
191
287
Berry Creek
Owl Creek
Grizzly Creek
North Bitch Creek
South Bitch Creek
Moose Creek
Webb Canyon
Colter Canyon
Lizard Creek
Arizona Island
Bailey Creek
Pilgrim Creek
Teton Wilderness Area
Pilgrim Creek East Fork
Pacific Creek
Leeks Marina
Colter Bay Village
Jedediah Smith Wilderness Area
Swan Lake
Colter Bay
Jackson Lake
Two Ocean Lake
Emma Matilda Lake
Jackson Lake Lodge
Willow Flats
Willow Flats Turnout
Hermitage Point
Jackson Lake Junction
Jackson Lake Dam
Oxbow Bend Turnout
Elk Island
North Moran Creek
South Badger Creek
Moran Creek
TETON RAN
Signal Mountain Lodge
Signal Mountain
Signal Mountain Road
Moran Junction
Moran Entrance Station
Lava Creek
Buffalo Valley Road
26
287
Mt. Moran
Bearpaw Lake

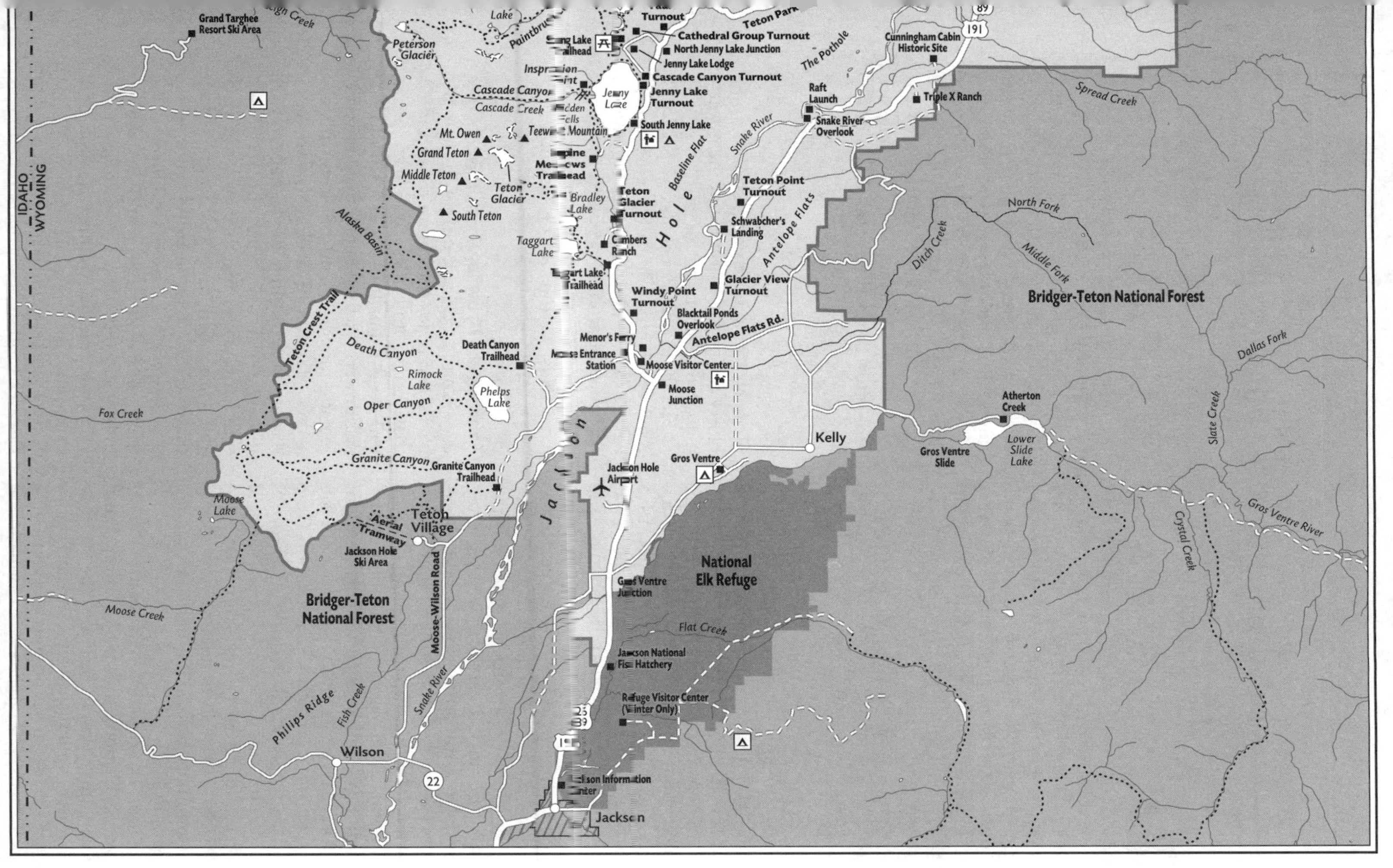

Grand Targhee Resort Ski Area
Peterson Glacier
Cascade Canyon
Cascade Creek
Mt. Owen
Grand Teton
Middle Teton
Teton Glacier
South Teton
IDAHO
WYOMING
Alaska Basin
Taggart Lake
Bradley Lake
Teton Crest Trail
Death Canyon
Rimock Lake
Phelps Lake
Death Canyon Trailhead
Fox Creek
Oper Canyon
Granite Canyon
Granite Canyon Trailhead
Moose Lake
Teton Village
Aerial Tramway
Jackson Hole Ski Area
Bridger-Teton National Forest
Moose Creek
Moose-Wilson Road
Snake River
Phillips Ridge
Fish Creek
Wilson
22
Teton Park
Turnout
Cathedral Group Turnout
North Jenny Lake Junction
Jenny Lake Lodge
Cascade Canyon Turnout
Jenny Lake Turnout
South Jenny Lake
Teton Glacier Turnout
Hole
Baseline Flat
Windy Point Turnout
Menor's Ferry
Station
Moose Visitor Center
Moose Junction
Blacktail Ponds Overlook
Antelope Flats Rd.
Glacier View Turnout
Schwabacher's Landing
Antelope Flats
Teton Point Turnout
The Pothole
Raft Launch
Snake River Overlook
Cunningham Cabin Historic Site
191
89
Triple X Ranch
Spread Creek
North Fork
Middle Fork
Ditch Creek
Bridger-Teton National Forest
Dallas Fork
Slate Creek
Atherton Creek
Lower Slide Lake
Gros Ventre Slide
Kelly
Gros Ventre
National Elk Refuge
Gros Ventre River
Crystal Creek
Flat Creek
Jackson
Jackson Hole

Tips from the Park Superintendent

Linda Olson, public affairs officer for Grand Teton National Park, has two suggestions for park visitors. The first is to do your homework and read about the park before you get here. "Getting to know the park ahead of your visit will help you understand these magnificent resources and make the most of your time here," she says. The second is to spend at least 2 days in the park. Too many visitors simply drive through on their way to Yellowstone, and miss many of the park's most spectacular attractions. "To really enjoy this area, you must get away from your car and hike the trails, sit by a beaver pond and watch a moose, float the Snake River at sunset, explore pioneer cabins, and much more," she says.

To beat the crowds, Olson recommends avoiding the most popular places, like Jenny Lake, at the busiest times, usually between 10am and 3pm. "Think like an elk," she says. "Do your activities in the early morning or the evening and bed down during the heat of midday." Morning and evening are also often the best times to see wildlife.

and the dude-ranching industry secured its first foothold in the area.

When cattle interests learned of a movement to convert privately owned grazing land on the valley floor to a national park, a rancorous tug-of-war began. Congress had designated the area outside Yellowstone Park the Teton Forest Reserve in 1897 and attempted to create a larger sanctuary in 1917; however, local opposition defeated the measure. In 1923, a more well reasoned and successful attempt was made to preserve the area for future generations when Maude Noble, a local environmentalist, and a group of other locals, aided by Yellowstone Superintendent Horace Albright, prepared a plan for setting aside a portion of the Jackson Hole (the great valley that runs the length of the Tetons on the east side) as a national recreation area. Congress first set aside 96,000 acres of mountains and forests (excluding Jackson Lake) as a national park in 1929.

John D. Rockefeller, Jr. got into the act by establishing the Snake River Land Company, which became the vehicle through which he accumulated more than 35,000 acres of land between 1927 and 1943. His goal was to donate the property for an enlarged park, but opponents in Congress prevented the government from accepting his gift.

Finally, in 1950, the feds and the locals reached a compromise: The government agreed to reimburse Teton County for revenue that would have been generated by property taxes, and to honor existing leaseholds. Grand Teton National Park was born.

Avoiding the Crowds. If you travel before the second week in June, you'll share the parks' two roads with more bison and elk than autos and RVs. In early spring, you'll be rewarded by an explosion of wildflowers as they begin to bloom, filling the meadows and hillsides with vast arrays of color. Traveling before peak season has economic advantages as well, since gateway city motel and restaurant rates are lower. Just because the park gates are open, though, doesn't mean that you'll have unimpeded access to the trails—some are closed until most of the snow melts—or that you'll be able to hike without getting your feet wet. Trails at higher elevations may be wet until early June.

The end of the season, after Labor Day weekend, is also a good time to visit.

Crowds begin to thin, and the roads become less traveled. In addition to more wildlife-viewing opportunities and improved fishing conditions in some areas, the fall foliage transforms the area into a calendar-quality image.

Unlike at Yellowstone, Grand Teton's activities are centered at three primary areas: Colter Bay, Jenny Lake, and the Moose visitor centers. They're often crowded. Nonetheless, it's always possible to escape the crowds simply by walking away—check out the overlooks, photograph the sites, then abandon the paved areas for unpaved trails. Except on the most popular and easily accessible trails, odds are good that once you're more than 0.25 mile from the pavement, your only company will be a handful of other hikers and the plants and wildlife of the park.

Getting There & Gateways

There are only three ways to enter the park. From the **north,** you must pass through Yellowstone National Park and exit at the park's South Entrance on the John D. Rockefeller, Jr., Memorial Parkway (U.S. 89/191/287), which leads right into Grand Teton National Park; there is no entrance station per se, but there is a park information station at Flagg Ranch, approximately 5 miles north of the park boundary.

You can enter from the **east,** via U.S. 26/287 and the Moran Entrance Station, but the next town along this road is Dubois, 55 miles east of the park (the road to Dubois is quite scenic, but the town is not considered a major "gateway").

You may also enter from the **south,** from Jackson, Wyoming, on the southern portion of the John D. Rockefeller, Jr., Memorial Parkway (U.S. 26/89/191); the first park facilities you will encounter are at Moose. The town of Jackson is probably the major gateway to the park.

The Nearest Airport. **Jackson Hole Airport** is inside the southern boundary of Grand Teton National Park and clearly the most convenient airport. It is served by **American, Continental Express, Delta, Skywest,** and **United Express.**

Renting a Car. Jackson is served by **Alamo, Avis, Budget, Thrifty, National,** and **Hertz.**

GETTING INFORMATION BEFORE YOUR TRIP

To receive park maps and information before your arrival, contact **Grand Teton National Park,** P.O. Drawer 170, Moose, WY 83012 (☎ **307/739-3300**). The Web site is **www.nps.gov/grte**.

The **Grand Teton Natural History Association** is a not-for-profit organization that provides information about the park through retail book sales at park visitor centers; you can also buy books about the park from them by mail. Contact the association at P.O. Drawer 170, Moose, WY 83012 (☎ **307/739-3403**).

VISITOR CENTERS

There are three visitor centers in the park. The **Colter Bay Visitor Center** (☎ **307/739-3594**), the northernmost of the park's visitor centers, offers information and publications, as well as a good Indian Arts Museum; you can pick up backcountry permits here as well. The center is open 8am to 5pm from mid-May to June, 8am to 8pm from June to Labor Day, and 8am to 5pm from Labor Day to October 1.

The **Moose Visitor Center** (☎ **307/739-3399**) is 0.5 mile west of Moose Junction on the Teton Park Road, at the southern end of the park, and offers a range of information and publications, audiovisual programs and exhibits, and issues permits; it is open 8am to 6pm daily from mid-May through early June, and 8am to 7pm daily from June through Labor Day, with reduced hours the rest of the year.

There is also **Jenny Lakes Visitor Center** (no phone), which is open 8am to 7pm daily from early June through Labor Day but closed for the rest of the year.

Finally, there is an information station at the **Flagg Ranch** complex (no phone), which is located approximately 5 miles north of the park's northern boundary.

ENTRANCE & CAMPING FEES

The cost to enter Grand Teton is $20 per vehicle for a 7-day period (no matter the number of occupants); your entrance permit is valid at both Yellowstone and Grand Teton national parks. **Single entrants** on foot or bicycle, or **skiers** pay $10 per person. The fee for **individual snowmobiles and motorcycles** is $15.

You can also purchase an **annual pass,** which is also valid in both parks, for $40. However, don't plan on sharing the pass with other travelers, since rangers at entry gates often request photo identification.

Fees for **camping** in Grand Teton are $12 per night at all the park campgrounds. You cannot make reservations.

SPECIAL REGULATIONS & WARNINGS

◆ **Collecting or defacing natural objects,** including picking wildflowers, is illegal.

◆ Motorcycles, motor scooters, and motor bikes are allowed only on park roads. **No off-road or trail riding** is allowed. Operator licenses and license plates are required.

◆ **Pets** must be leashed and are permitted only within 25 feet of roads and parking areas and may not be left unattended. Pets are prohibited in the backcountry and on trails.

◆ It is unlawful to approach within 100 yards of a bear or within 25 yards of other **wildlife.** Feeding any wildlife is illegal.

SEASONS & CLIMATE

Because of the high elevations and changing weather systems, the region is characterized by long, cold winters and short, though usually warm, summers.

Cold and snow may linger into April and May, though temperatures are generally warming. The average daytime readings are in the 40s and 50s, gradually increasing into the 60s and 70s by early June. So, during **spring** a warm jacket, rain gear, and water-resistant walking shoes may be welcome traveling companions.

Temperatures during the middle of the **summer** are typically 70° to 80°F in the lower elevations and are especially comfortable because of the lack of humidity. Nights, however, even during the warmest months, will be cool, with temperatures dropping into the low 40s, so you'll want to include a light jacket in your wardrobe. Summer thunderstorms are common.

As **fall** approaches you'll want to have an additional layer of clothing, since temperatures remain mild but begin to cool. The first heavy snows typically fall by November 1 and continue through March or April.

During **winter** months you'll want long johns, heavy shirts, vests and coats, warm gloves, and thick socks since temperatures hover in single digits, and subzero overnight temperatures are common.

Teton Park Road opens to conventional vehicles and RVs around May 1. The **Moose–Wilson Road** opens to vehicles about the same time. Roads close to vehicles on November 1 and open for snowmobiles in mid-December, though they never close for non-motorized use.

If you're planning on visiting Yellowstone as well as Grand Teton, and are considering making your trip to the parks prior to the middle of June, think about beginning your exploration in Grand Teton before working north to Yellowstone. Elevations here are slightly less and snow melts earlier so accumulations on trails are reduced, and temperatures are more moderate.

USEFUL PUBLICATIONS

The following books are interesting, informative, and easy to find: ***Teton Trails*** by Katy Duffy and Darwin Wile and

Grand Teton National Park, both available from the Grand Teton Natural History Association; ***A Guide to Exploring Grand Teton National Park,*** Linda Olson and Tim Bywater, RNM Press, Box 8531, Salt Lake City, UT 84108; ***An Outdoor Family Guide to Yellowstone and Grand Teton National Parks,*** Lisa Gollin Evans, The Mountaineers, 1001 SW Klickitat Way, Seattle, WA 98134; ***Yellowstone–Grand Teton Road Guide,*** Jeremy Schmidt and Steven Fuller, Free Wheeling Travel Guides, Box 7494, Jackson, WY 83001.

If you cannot find these publications in your local bookstore, you can order many of them by mail from the **Grand Teton Natural History Association,** P.O. Drawer 170, Moose, WY 83012 (☎ **307/ 739-3403**).

If You Only Have 1 Day

Loop roads lead to the major observation points and attractions. Although this 1-day itinerary assumes you are entering Grand Teton from the north, after visiting Yellowstone, you could just as easily begin your itinerary in Jackson, which is 8 miles south of the Moose Entrance Station.

Let's begin at the northern end of the **John D. Rockefeller, Jr., Memorial Parkway** (U.S. 89/181/287). **Flagg Ranch Information Station,** 2 miles beyond Yellowstone's South Entrance, is a sensible place to stop for supplies, maps, and answers to your questions. It's 5 miles further south to Grand Teton's northern boundary and another 11 miles to **Colter Bay Village.**

As you drive along the northern shore of Jackson Lake to Colter Bay, look across the lake to **Mt. Moran** and, in the distance, the spires of the **Cathedral Group.**

Colter Bay Village is one of the park's busiest spots. Several popular hiking trails start here, and there's also a **visitor center.** If you turn right at Colter Bay Junction and go another 0.5 mile, you'll be at the **Colter Bay Visitor Center;** stop here only if you wish to take in the **Indian Arts Museum.**

The **Lakeshore Trail** begins at the marina entrance and runs along the harbor for an easy, 2-mile round-trip. It's level, paved, and wheelchair accessible, offering you your best opportunity for a hike in this area if you don't have much time. The Douglas firs and pine trees here are greener and healthier than the lodgepole pines you see at higher elevations in Yellowstone.

A few minutes' drive south of Colter Bay is **Jackson Lake Junction,** the start of a 43-mile **loop road,** which takes you past the primary sites of the park. By traveling counterclockwise (to the west) to **Teton Park Road,** you'll drive beneath the shadows of the Grand Teton, an imposing 13,770-foot spire that is surrounded by an equally impressive group of mountains. You'll see lakes created by glaciers thousands of years ago, bordering a sagebrush valley inhabited by pronghorn and elk.

You should consider stopping at the **Jenny Lake Visitor Center,** 12 miles south of here, for an interesting geology exhibit and a relief model of the park. If you have time, take a walk around the lake (there are some great hiking trails in the area) or perhaps a boat ride before you get back in your car. Your best bet for a day hike in this area is the **Moose Ponds Trail.**

When you leave South Jenny Lake, you'll be driving over the relatively flat stretch of road to Moose, the southernmost of the park's service centers. One-half mile before Moose Junction is the **Moose Visitor Center,** which features exhibits of the Greater Yellowstone area's rare and endangered species, a video room, and an extensive bookstore. While you're in Moose, you might wish to visit the historic **Menor/Noble Historic District** and the **Chapel of the Transfiguration.**

As you return north along **U.S. 26/89/191** to Moran Junction, you'll travel alongside the Snake River as it bisects the valley, and have an opportunity to view the first sites inhabited by the valley's settlers. The best views along this road are the **Glacier View Turnout** and the **Snake River Overlook,** both of which are right off the road and well marked. At the Moran Junction, turn left for a final 5-mile drive back to Jackson Lake Junction, past **Oxbow Bend,** a great spot for wildlife viewing.

As the sun heads for the horizon at day's end, you can choose to sleep in a tent at one of several campgrounds, in luxury at one of the park's three resort hotels, or 13 miles south of the Moose Entrance in Jackson, Wyoming.

Touring Grand Teton

Though the park can be "done" in a few hours, your best bet is to allow at least 2 days for your visit. As with the short tour in the previous section, we begin at the northern end of the park. But you could just as easily start exploring from the southern end, near Jackson. From Jackson, it's 13 miles to the Moose Entrance Station, another 8 miles to the Jenny Lake Visitor Center, another 12 miles to the Jackson Lake Junction, and 5 more miles to Colter Bay.

The **John D. Rockefeller, Jr., Memorial Parkway** enters the park in the north and heads toward Jackson Lake Junction. Upon entering the Teton area, you'll immediately notice the dramatic way the landscape leaps up into your consciousness, especially in contrast with the comparatively more subtle topography of Yellowstone.

Approaching the park from the north, the first services you'll find are at **Flagg Ranch Resort,** a recently reconstructed lodging, information, and service center. The park's information station there is open 9am to 6pm from June through Labor Day. The ranch itself is open from May 15 to October 15 and from mid-December to mid-March.

Further south approximately 8 miles, at **Leek's Marina,** you'll find a casual restaurant that serves lighter fare and pizza during summer months. There are also five well-marked picnic areas along this route between Flagg Ranch Resort and Leek's Marina, and the views are spectacular, and unavoidable, at any of them.

It's a 16-mile drive from Flagg Ranch to the **Colter Bay Visitor Center (☎ 307/739-3594)**, which is open 8am to 5pm from mid-May to June; 8am to 8pm from June to Labor Day; and 8am to 5pm from Labor Day to October 1. In addition to an information desk and bookstore, the center houses the David E. Vernon collection of American Indian Art, which is worth a visit. Also on display are a range of clothing, implements, and weapons that provide a glimpse into 19th-century American Indian life. Several hiking trails are nearby. The **Lakeshore Trail** is a popular choice that almost anyone can do.

Four miles south of Colter Bay, turn east (left if you are traveling from the north) off the main road and follow an unpaved, mile-long road to **Grand View Point Trailhead.** The road is great for hikers, bikers, and people in cars; however, it is definitely not recommended for those towing trailers or for large RVs. A large, flat area at the end of the road offers a commanding view of the Grand Tetons, as well as an excellent picnicking spot.

The trailhead to **Christian Pond,** a short (0.5-mile, one-way) must-do hike, is some 200 yards south of the entrance to Jackson Lake Lodge, on the east side of the highway. It's unmarked, so look carefully. The hike is different than most since it's in a grassy, wet area that is prime habitat for waterfowl. However, in early months of the park year (May and June) it is also prime habitat for bears, so be sure and check with rangers before venturing onto the trail.

The next point of interest is a fraction of a mile further south from the Christian Pond Trailhead, and since there's no parking along the road, you should walk down. If not, it's back in the car for a short hop to **Willow Flats Turnout,** which presents views of the valley floor, where you may see moose, and across the valley to the Grand Teton itself. And, back in the car, it's approximately

0.5 mile further to the **Jackson Lake Junction** and the next leg of the journey.

When you get to Jackson Lake Junction, you should turn right onto **Teton Park Road,** following the signs toward Signal Mountain, Jenny Lake, and Moose. Keep your camera ready. You'll soon reach another turnout, a wide spot on the north (right) side of the road, a picnic area that offers stunning views across Jackson Lake to Mt. Moran and the northern section of the Teton Range.

Like its counterpart at Colter Bay, **Signal Mountain** offers visitors a place to camp, excellent accommodations in cabins and multiplex units, two restaurants, a lounge with TV (one of the few in the park), gasoline, and a small convenience store. Boat rentals are also available.

The paved **Signal Mountain Summit Road,** a 4-mile, one-way trip that terminates 1,000 feet above the valley floor is 1 mile south, but the road is so narrow and twisty that trailers and motor homes are not allowed. In summer, you'll see colorful wildflowers on this drive, including Indian Paintbrush, blue Lupine, and yellow pond lilies. Some 3 miles from the beginning of the road is the **Jackson Point Overlook,** reached by a paved, 100 yard path. It was here that the Hayden expedition's photographer William Henry Jackson shot his famous wet plate photos of Jackson Lake and the Tetons.

After heading down from the Signal Mountain Summit, continue south (left) on Teton Park Road. Look for the **Mt. Moran Turnout** on the west (right) side of the road approximately 4 miles south of the summit road. From here, you'll have a view of Skillet Glacier.

Looking for a hideaway? On the west (right) side of the road from Signal Mountain to the North Jenny Lake Junction, approximately 2 miles south of the Mt. Moran Turnout, is an unmarked, unpaved road that leads to **Spalding Bay.** (*Hint:* It's an unnamed gray line on the Park Service map.) You'll travel through a moose habitat before reaching the end of the road within 2 miles, or about 15 minutes of driving. There's a small campsite, boat launch with parking for trucks and boat trailers, and primitive rest room here. Use of the campsite requires a park permit, but it's an excellent place to find seclusion, with great views of the lake and mountains, even if you're not camping. The road is easily negotiable by an automobile or sport utility vehicle; we would not recommend it for an RV or towed trailer.

When you return to Teton Park Road and continue your descent from the summit, you'll find yourself traveling through a mostly flat, sagebrush- and pine-covered area that leads to one of the busiest spots in the park, the **Jenny Lake** area, which is about 11 miles from Jackson Lake Junction and 8 miles away from Moose, further down the road.

The **North Jenny Lake Junction** is the jumping-off point for a side trip to the shores of Jenny Lake, an area visited by elk, pronghorn, coyote, and bison. You'll make the trip via the one-way scenic drive (going south) that skirts the shores of Jenny Lake. At the junction, turn right. The road will become one way after the String Lake Turnoff.

Some say that the allure of the **Cathedral Group** comes from their Gothic appearance, other say its their majesty.

You can judge for yourself at the **Cathedral Group Turnout,** which offers the most spectacular views of peaks in the park. The turnout is located less than a mile beyond the North Jenny Lake Junction on the scenic road. From south to north, the three peaks are **Teewinot Mountain** (12,325 feet), **Grand Teton,** "the Grand" (13,770 feet), and **Mount Owen** (12,928 feet).

Cascade Canyon, which is easily identifiable on the horizon on the other side of Jenny Lake, was cut thousands of years ago by a large block of ice that flowed down from the mountains. When it retreated, it left the gem of the park, Jenny Lake. The road becomes one way when you reach **String Lake,** which has a popular picnic area that attracts crowds.

Perhaps the most popular of the glacial lakes, Jenny Lake sits nestled at the base of the tallest Teton peaks. A 6-mile **trail** that encircles the lake offers an excellent hike; however, parking is limited, so arrive early or late in the day. Between String and Jenny lakes you'll find the **Jenny Lake Lodge,** the best spot in the park for a fine dining experience.

After 2 miles, you'll rejoin the Teton Park Road; 1 mile farther on the right is the turnoff for **South Jenny Lake.**

Except for the Jenny Lake Lodge, which is not really on the lake at all, most of the services and facilities in the Jenny Lake area are located here, including the **Jenny Lake Visitor Center** (open 8am to 7pm, from June through Labor Day).

A boat shuttle leaves the Jenny Lake marina every half hour from 8am to 6pm during the summer season (June through mid-September) and costs $5 round-trip. Call the **Teton Boating Co.** (☎ **307/733-2703**) if you want to verify that the shuttle is running since snowmelt and the lake's level can affect the operating dates. Many hikers take this shuttle across the lake as a substitute for hiking on the Jenny Lake Trail.

The trailheads to **Hidden Falls, Inspiration Point,** and **Cascade Canyon** are also at the south end of Jenny lake, which creates an interesting dilemma. From the boat dock, the trip across the lake to the west side shortens the hike to the falls by some two-thirds. The alternative is a 2-mile hike around the south end of the lake. Either choice is a good one, but we'd take the long route. With Teewinot Mountain immediately overhead, this trail presents some of the best photo opportunities of either Yellowstone or Grand Teton.

From South Jenny Lake to Moose Junction is about 8 miles. This section of the road takes you along the **valley floor.** Look closely into the sagebrush for the shy pronghorn, often mistakenly called an antelope (they may be a distant cousin). You might also encounter a badger, one of the more mean-spirited creatures in the park.

Less than a mile from South Jenny Lake, a road leads off Teton Park Road to the right and the **Lupine Meadows Trailhead.** Should you be interested in a more taxing hike (and this is one of the most taxing in the entire valley), you might give this one a try.

The **Teton Glacier Turnout,** 1.5 miles south of the South Jenny Lake turnoff offers views of a glacier that had been growing for several hundred years until, within the past 100 years, it began a retreat.

After passing the **Taggart Lake Trailhead** on the west (right) side of the road, you'll soon reach the **Windy Point Turnout.** If you haven't done so already, or would like to do so again, this is a good place to wander in the sagebrush, perhaps looking for pronghorn. Just watch out for the badgers, too.

One of the most interesting historic sites in the park is **Menor/Noble Historic District,** which is identified by a large sign near the Moose Entrance Station. At this site, Bill Menor constructed the first homestead on the west side of the Snake River, in 1894, then later built and operated a ferry across the Snake River. He eventually sold the cabin to Maude Noble, who, at this same site in 1923, began hatching a plan to halt commercial development of the valley and create another recreation area. During the summer months, after the river has receded, visitors can ride a replica of the ferry across the river. Nearby is the **Chapel of the Transfiguration,** built in 1925 so settlers and visitors could avoid a long buckboard ride to church services in Jackson. Episcopal worship services are held on Sunday at 10:30am from June through August.

The Moose Visitor Center and Moose Village provide travelers with all of the requisites necessary for a tour of the park. The **visitor center** (open 8am to 5pm during winter, spring, and fall; 8am to 7pm during summer) offers permits for backcountry hiking, camping, and boating, and has a natural history display.

From Moose Junction, just across the Snake River, you can head south (right) to Jackson, Wyoming, or you can turn north (left) and start a **scenic drive** on U.S. 89 (also 26/191).

This scenic drive is the fastest route through Grand Teton National Park. The only drawback is that, while the drive along the Snake River is quite scenic and has dramatic views of the Tetons, you're away from the mountains, and there aren't as many overlooks and other attractions to take in along the way.

The junction of U.S. 26/89/191 with **Antelope Flats Road** is 1.2 miles north of the Moose Junction. The 20-mile route beginning here is an acceptable biking route. It's all on level terrain, passing by the town of Kelly and the Gros Ventre Campground before looping back to the Jackson Hole Highway at the Gros Ventre Junction, to the south. If you continue straight on Antelope Flats Road, you'll reach the **Teton Science School** at the road's end, about a 5-mile trip.

Less than a mile further along U.S. 26/89/191, on the left, **Blacktail Ponds Overlook** offers an opportunity to see how beavers build dams and the effect these ambitious creatures have on the flow of the streams. The area is marshy early in summer, but it's still worth the 0.25-mile hike down to the streams, where the beaver activity can be viewed more closely.

Two miles further along U.S. 26/89/191 brings you to the **Glacier View Turnout,** which offers views of an area that 140,000 to 160,000 years ago was filled with a 4,000-foot-thick glacier. The view of the gulch between the peaks offers vivid testimony of the power of the glaciers that carved this landscape. Lower **Schwabacher Landing** is at the end of a 1-mile, fairly well maintained dirt road that leads down to the Snake River; you'll see the turnoff 4.5 miles north of the Moose Junction. The road winds through an area filled with glacial moraine (the rocks, sand, gravel, and so forth that was left behind as glaciers passed through the area), the leftovers of the Ice Age. At the end of the road is a popular launch site for float trips and for fly-fishing. It's also an ideal place to retreat from the crowds. Don't be surprised to see bald eagles, osprey, moose, river otter, and beaver, which regularly patrol the area.

The **Snake River Overlook,** approximately 4 miles down the road beyond the Glacier View Turnout, is the most famous view of the Teton Range and the Snake River, immortalized by Ansel Adams. This overlook offers more than another view of the Grand Tetons, though it does provide that; you'll also see at least three separate, distinctive, 200-foot-high plateaus that roll from the riverbed to the valley floor, leaving a vivid example of the power of the glaciers and ice floes as they sculpted this area.

A half mile north of the Snake River Overlook, signs warn that the road to **Deadman's Bar Overlook,** which leads to a clearing on the riverbank, should only be negotiated by four-wheel-drive vehicles. Though the 1-mile road is unpaved and bumpy, it is maintained well enough to be handled by most sedans if there's no snow on the road and if it has not been raining.

The only views from here on will be in your rearview mirror, and since there are no further sites on this stretch of road, you will find the remaining 5 miles to the Moran Junction a chance to catch your breath.

The last leg of your loop tour (on U.S. 89/191/287) will lead you from Moran Junction back to Jackson Lake Junction and Teton Park Road. Upon reaching the Moran Junction, turn left.

One of the lesser-traveled trails in the park goes to the **Emma Matilda/Two Ocean Lake Area.** To get to the trailhead, turn onto Pacific Creek Road, 1 mile west of the Moran Entrance Station, and proceed 2.5 miles (past the Emma Matilda Trailhead, which you will see on the north (left) side of the road; turn left on Two Ocean Road and proceed to a small parking area, where you'll find the trailhead. Watch out for grizzly bears here.

A level path leads around the east end of Two Ocean Lake and secluded areas that provide excellent views across the lake to the Tetons; the round-trip around the lake is an easy 5.7 miles. If you have time, continue on to Emma Matilda

Lake, which was named after the wife of Billy Owen, reputedly the first climber to reach the peak of the Grand.

If you choose not to take this hike, return the way you came to the Moran–Jackson Lake Junction Road. This 5-mile stretch runs along meadows and wetlands that are popular picnic areas for moose. However, the highlight of this section is the **Oxbow Bend Overlook,** one of the best and most popular wildlife-viewing areas in the park. So load the camera and settle in to await the arrival of moose, mule deer, trumpeter swans, Canada geese, ducks, blue heron, bald eagles, osprey, white pelicans, beaver, muskrats, and river otter. Odds of viewing wildlife are best in the morning and evening.

It's only a hop, skip, or short jump back to the Jackson Lake Junction, roughly a mile. But keep your eyes peeled for moose in the woods on the north (right) side of the road.

Organized Tours & Ranger Programs

There are no regularly scheduled motorcoach tours at Grand Teton as there are at Yellowstone, but you will find several interesting ranger programs that range from sit-around-with-a-cup-of-coffee chats held daily at 8am at the Colter Bay Theater, to aggressive day and half-day hikes for serious trail buffs. You'll find the daily schedules in the park's paper, the ***Teewinot,*** which you can pick up at any visitor center.

At Colter Bay, a grand tour of the **Indian Arts Museum** is held daily at 9:30 am; a ranger-led **Swan Like Hike,** an easy, 1-hour stroll along a scenic path, is held daily at 4:30pm.

Jackson Lake Lodge overlooks one of the best moose and bird habitats in the park, so is an ideal spot for the **Wildlife Watch,** which is held between 6:30 and 8pm most evenings on the terrace of the hotel.

At Jenny Lake, the ranger-led **Inspiration Point Hike** begins with a boat ride across the lake ($4 adults, $2.25 children). From there, a 2½-hour hike takes you to this mountain overlook and back. Since you've skipped the first 2 miles of the hike by taking the boat, it's only 0.9 miles to the point, and this hike is achievable by most visitors in average shape and most youngsters, but we suggest you check with rangers regarding your personal circumstances. The hike begins at 8:30am.

Between South Jenny Lake and Moose, a ranger-led **wildflower hike** with moderate uphill climbs begins daily at the Taggart Lake Trailhead. From the trailhead, the 2-mile hike, with moderate uphill climbs, winds through a colorful valley area. *A caution:* This hike is conducted only during the height of the wildflower (and busy summer) season, between June 16 and July 28.

Day Hikes

COLTER BAY AREA

Lakeshore Trail

2 miles RT. Easy. Access: The trailhead is located at the Marina Entrance.

This short hike in the Colter Bay area starts at the marina and leads out to beaches on the west side of a point with views across Jackson Lake of the entire Teton Range. When you get to the point, the only sounds to distract you from your spectacular mountain views are of water lapping on the shore. This trip is interesting on an overcast day, when thunderclouds cover the peaks, the sky and lake turn dark gray, and the Tetons present the type of ominous setting seen in old black-and-white horror movies. This 2-mile loop can be completed in about 1 hour of brisk walking

TRAILS FROM THE HERMITAGE POINT TRAILHEAD

The **Hermitage Point Trailhead** located near the marina is the starting point for an interesting variety of trips that range in distance from 1 to 9 miles.

Heron Pond Trail

3 miles RT. Easy. Access: The trailhead is located at Hermitage Trailhead, Colter Bay.

This is bear territory, as well as a home for Canada geese, Trumpeter Swans, moose, and beaver. Wildflowers are part of the show, as well: The two most prominent flowers here are Heart Leaf Arnicas and the Indian Paintbrush, which are visible all summer. Don't be put off by the fact that the first 200 yards of the trail are steep; after reaching the top of a rise, it levels out and has only moderate elevation gains from that point on. Since three trails run through this same forested part of the Colter Bay area, the foliage and terrain for this, the Swan Lake and Hermitage Point trails are virtually identical.

Swan Lake Trail

3.9 miles RT. Easy. Access: The trailhead is located at Hermitage Trailhead, Colter Bay.

Finding swans at Swan Lake requires a trip around the lake to the south end, where a small island offers them isolation and shelter for nests. The distance from Swan Lake through a densely forested area to a sign at the Heron Pond intersection is 0.3 mile. Hermitage Point is 3 miles from this junction along a gentle path that winds through a wooded area that is a popular bear hangout. The total circumnavigation from the Colter Bay area is doable in 2 hours and is a favorite of everyone who has completed it.

Hermitage Point Trail: A Loop

6.5 RT. Moderate. Access: There are directional signs near the Swan Lake/Heron Pond Trail intersection.

It's a 6.5-mile loop from the previously mentioned trail intersection through a forested area to an isolated point on the end of land that looks across Jackson Lake to the Signal Mountain Lodge. If you're seeking solitude, this is an excellent place to find it, though you should check with rangers before leaving since this is bear country.

JACKSON LAKE LODGE AREA

Christian Pond Trail

1 mile RT. Easy. Access: The trailhead is some 200 yards south of the entrance to Jackson Lake Lodge, most easily accessed from the Lodge horse corrals. It's unmarked, so look carefully.

This trail goes through a grassy, wet area that is prime habitat for waterfowl. However, in early months of the park year (May and June) it is also prime habitat for bears, so be sure and check with rangers before venturing onto the trail. The 0.5-mile hike from the trailhead to the south end of the pond offers views of the entire pond and resident waterfowl. The south end of the pond is covered with little grassy knolls upon which the birds build their nests and roost, and beavers have constructed a lodge here too. In the warmer months, the area is covered with colorful wildflowers. It's a restful sanctuary, but one often infested by gnats and mosquitoes.

Willow Flats Trail

8.5 miles RT. Easy. Access: The trailhead is at Jackson Lake Lodge.

With careful planning, it's possible to start the day at the Jackson Lake Lodge, then hike across Willow Flats past Cygnet Pond to Colter Bay (for lunch). Willow Flats is a veritable haven for wildlife, especially moose, and offers tremendous views of Mt. Moran. After a lunch break at Colter Bay, you can take the path back to the lodge in time for dinner.

Signal Summit Mountain Trail

6 miles RT. Moderate. Access: The trailhead is located only footsteps from the entrance to the Signal Mountain Lodge.

The trailhead for this hike is well marked by a sign, but the trail itself, since it is not generally described in commercial trail books, is not well traveled since most visitors drive their cars up to the summit of Signal Mountain. The trail is in a beautiful forest with excellent Teton views. Allow 3 hours to complete the hike.

After negotiating a steep climb at the beginning of the trail, you'll come upon a broad plateau covered with lodgepole pines, grassy areas, and seasonal wildflowers. After crossing a paved road, you'll arrive at a large pond covered with lilies. The meadow beyond the pond is an excellent spot for listening to the sound of frogs and watching wildlife and waterfowl. The trail winds along the south and east rim of the pond before turning east and heading toward the summit of Signal Mountain. Shortly after leaving the pond, you'll find a fork in the road marked by a sign: The left (northern) route takes you along the rim of the mountain, meandering through sagebrush and pine trees to the summit. On the return from the summit, the southern trail skirts large ponds where you'll find waterfowl, moose, and, perhaps, black bear. Taking one route up and the other down does not increase the distance. Both trails offer excellent opportunities to observe the shy, red-headed, pileated woodpecker.

TWO OCEAN & EMMA MATILDA LAKE TRAILS

Access to Two Ocean Lake and Emma Matilda Lake trails is found in four different places: 1 mile north of Jackson Lake Lodge; at the Christian Pond Trailhead; and off the Pacific Creek and Two Ocean Lake roads, which are detailed below.

The Emma Matilda Lake Trailhead is on Pacific Creek Road; the Two Ocean Lake Trailhead is on Two Ocean Lake Road. To get there, drive 4 miles east of the Jackson Lake Junction on the road to the Moran Entrance, and turn left onto Pacific Creek Road. It's 2 miles to the Emma Matilda Lake Trailhead, which is at a turnout on the north side of the road, and less than a mile to Two Ocean Lake Road, where you turn left; the trailhead is at the end of this road, about 2 more miles. We prefer the latter two trailheads, since they are closer to the lakes by a mile, and farther from the crowds. Be especially on the lookout for grizzlies here.

Two Ocean Lake Trail

5.7 miles RT. Easy. Access: Two Ocean Lake Trailhead on Two Ocean Lake Rd.

This hike begins at the eastern end of the lake, which can be toured in either direction, and is an easy, flat hike with good footing. The largest elevation gain on the hike is at the southwest side of the lake, where it gains 100 feet. Look for swans and ducks, maybe a loon, in a bay at the north end of the lake, which also is a busy birding and butterfly area during summer months. The vegetation here includes geraniums, lupine, and asters. It's possible to branch off onto the Emma Matilda Lake Trail at the east end of Two Ocean Lake.

Emma Matilda Lake Trail

11.7 miles RT. Easy to moderate. Access: The trailhead is on Two Ocean Lake Rd. north of Jackson Lake–Moran Rd.

Emma Matilda Lake was named after the wife of Billy Owen, reputedly the first climber to reach the peak of the Grand Teton. The hike winds uphill for 0.5 mile from the parking area to a large meadow where you're likely to see mule deer. The trail on the northern side of the lake winds through a pine forest along a ridge 400 feet above the lake, then descends to an overlook where you'll have panoramic views of the Tetons, Christian Pond, and Jackson Lake. The south side of the lake trail is through a densely forested area populated by Englemann spruce and subalpine fir. It's possible to branch off onto the Two Ocean Lake Trail along the northeast and northwest shores of the lake.

JENNY LAKE AREA

Jenny Lake Loop Trail

7 miles RT. Easy to moderate. Access: The trailhead is at the East Shore Boat Dock.

This relatively easy hike on mostly flat terrain can be shortened by taking the Jenny Lake Boat Shuttle from the East Shore Boat Dock to the West Shore Boat Dock. The lake, which is 2.5 miles long, sits in a pastoral setting at the foot of the mountain range, so it presents excellent views throughout the summer. *A caution:* This is one of the most popular spots in the park, so plan accordingly; to avoid crowds travel early or late in the day. The trails to Inspiration Point and Hidden Falls and to the Moose Ponds branch off of this trail on the southwest shore of the lake. The trails to String and Leigh lakes branch off this trail on the north shore of Jenny Lake.

Hidden Falls/Inspiration Point Trail

1.8–5.8 miles RT. Moderate. Access: The trailheads are at the East Shore Boat Dock or at the West Shore Boat Dock of Jenny Lake (if you take the boat shuttle).

It is possible to take a boat ferry across Jenny Lake; from the West Boat Dock, it is a 0.9-mile hike up to Inspiration Point. We prefer to skip the boat trip and hike 2½ miles to the West Shore Boat Dock, then 0.9 mile to Inspiration Point, which is populated by marmots and squirrels and level enough to be manageable by children. The trail winds through a forest, with filtered views of the lake. You will hear Hidden Falls as it pours through a narrow gap in the rocks long before you see it. After crossing a small bridge over the creek and traveling uphill another 0.5 mile, you will arrive at Inspiration Point.

Whichever route you take to Inspiration Point, start early in the day so as to avoid the crowds. Then pace yourself. The last 0.4 mile to Hidden Falls, and the path beyond that to Inspiration Point, are steeper and require more strenuous activity than lower sections. However, they are well worth the effort. If you make it, you will be rewarded with a commanding view of the lake, the surrounding mountains, and the Jackson Hole—all in all, an excellent vantage point at which to catch your breath.

Cascade Canyon Trail

4.5 miles one way. Moderate to difficult. Access: The trail into Cascade Canyon begins at Inspiration Point.

Among knowledgeable hikers, the Cascade Canyon Trail is the most popular in park. However, depending upon your method of transport, it may be physically taxing. It is possible to reach the entrance to the canyon by taking a boat across Jenny Lake to the west shore boat dock, then hiking to Inspiration Point (see the "Hidden Falls/Inspiration Point Trail," above). From there it's a gentle ascent though a glacially sculpted canyon, the sides of which are metamorphic rock that is still being shaped by slides and the affects of snow, ice, and water. In summer, the area is filled with wildflowers, ducks nest along Cascade Creek, and moose and bear may be spotted. Because of changes in elevation and length (4.5 miles), the trip is rated as moderate by park rangers but it's one of the easiest long hikes in the park.

Moose Ponds Trail

3.5 miles RT. Easy. Access: The trailhead is the Jenny Lake Trailhead located at the East Shore Boat Dock.

A less taxing alternative to the Cascade Canyon trip is a detour to Moose Ponds, which begins on the Inspiration Point Trail. The ponds trail intersects the Inspiration Point Trail approximately 0.75-mile from the trailhead, and winds the balance of 2 miles to a habitat for a variety of waterfowl and wildlife. The area near the base of Teewinot Mountain, which towers over the region, is the home of a population of large animals, including elk, mule deer, black bears, and moose. The trail is at lake level, flat and short, and easy to negotiate in 60 to 90 minutes. The best times to venture forth are in early morning and early evening before sunset if you want to see wildlife.

String Lake Trail

1.8 miles one way. Easy. Access: The trailhead is located at the Leigh Lake Trailhead.

This easy hike along the eastern shore of String Lake has two attributes: It provides an easy access to Leigh Lake, and it's in a forest that is a better alternative for picnics than the crowded picnic area. You'll wander in the shade of a pine forest along the shore, with excellent views of Mt. Moran above. However, because this is a heavily trafficked area, you should not count on seeing much wildlife, if any.

Amphitheater Lake Trail

9.6 miles one way. Difficult. Trailhead: Use the Lupine Meadows Trailhead. From the Moose Entrance Station on Teton Park Rd. drive 6.6 miles to the Lupine Meadows Junction and follow signs to the trailhead; if you're coming from Jenny Lake, the trailhead is at the end of a road less than a mile south of South Jenny Lake.

This is a difficult hike, rangers say, and should not be attempted by any hiker not acclimated to the local altitude. The 4.8-mile hike to Amphitheater Lake gains over 3,000 feet. The payoff for making the trek is panoramic views of the valley below, as well as a close-up of the Grand Teton and Teton Glacier.

Taggart & Bradley Lakes Trail

5 miles RT. Moderate. Access: The trailhead is well marked and located west of Teton Park Rd., approximately 6 miles south of Jenny Lake.

Just down the road from South Jenny is the trailhead to Taggart Lake. This is a particularly interesting hike that winds through a burned out area quickly recovering, to a lake that was created by glacial movements. The hike from the parking lot to the lake, where you can fish from the shore, is only 1.6 miles along the southern (left) fork of the trail. Swimming, while not strictly prohibited, is definitely not recommended on account of water temperature. From the lake, you can return by the same trail or continue north to **Bradley Lake** for a round-trip of 5 miles. This route adds 1.8 miles to the trip, and the elevation gain is 467 feet, but the payoff is that at its highest point the trail overlooks all of Taggart Lake and the stream flowing from it. Like other hikes in Grand Teton, this one is best made during the early morning or early evening hours, when it's cooler and there's less traffic.

Exploring the Backcountry

You are required to secure a backcountry permit from the Park Service in order to use an overnight campsite; the good news is that for now the permits are free. The permit is valid only on the dates for which it is issued. There are two methods of securing permits: They may be picked up the day before you begin your trip, or you can make a reservation for a permit in advance of your arrival, which currently carries no fee. Reservations are only accepted from January 1 to June 1. *A caution:* The reservation is just that, a reservation; upon your arrival at the park, you'll need to secure the permit. Permits are issued at the Moose and Colter Bay visitor centers and the Jenny Lake Ranger Station; reservations may be made by writing the **Permits Office,** Grand Teton National Park, Box 170, Moose, WY 83012, or faxing 307/739-3438. A **Wyoming fishing license** is required to fish in Grand Teton.

The comfort level of your backcountry trip will be affected by how early in the season you make your hiking trip. Before all the snowmelt has cleared the area, flooding can be a problem.

Perhaps the most popular backcountry trail in Grand Teton, the 19.2-mile **Cascade Canyon Loop,** which starts on the west side of Jenny Lake, winds northwest 7.2 miles on the **Cascade Canyon Trail** to Lake Solitude and the Paintbrush Divide, then returns past Holly Lake on the 10.3 mile long **Paintbrush Trail.** Despite its shortness, it is one of the most rigorous hikes in either park because of gains in elevation—more than 2,600 feet—rocky trails, and switchbacks through scree that can become slippery, especially in years when snow remains until late June.

Rangers recommend the hike for several reasons, the most noteworthy of which is unsurpassed scenery. Wildlife, including moose and black bears, is in this part of the park, so hikers are cautioned to be diligent about making noise. There's also the possibility to sight a Harlequin duck, since they nest near the trail in Cascade Creek. You'll see many types of wildflowers, large stands of whitebark pine trees, and an almost unimaginable array of bird life.

Though it adds 5.1 miles to the trip (one way), a detour west from the Cascade Canyon Trail to **Hurricane Pass** will reward you with a view from the foot of **Schoolroom Glacier**. If you're feeling especially spunky, head west into the Jedediah Smith Wilderness on a trail that eventually reaches Alaska.

If you're unable to complete the hike in 1 day, you can trek 7.2 miles on the Cascade Canyon Trail to **Solitude Lake,** and return via the same trail. If you can afford a 2-day trip, camping zones are 6 miles west of the trailhead on the Cascade Canyon Trail, and 8.7 miles northwest on the Paintbrush Canyon Trail at Holly Lake.

The premier backcountry activity in Grand Teton is not hiking but rather **mountain climbing,** which you should not attempt alone unless you are expert (see "Mountaineering," below).

Other Summer Sports & Activities

Biking. The general consensus is that there are only two decent bike rides in the park, and one of them is on paved and gravel roads. Both are at the southern end of the park, near Moose, where (conveniently) you can also rent a bike if you haven't brought one along. Just remember that you'll have to bring your own bike; they can't be rented in the park.

The first route, called by some the **Antelope Flats and Gros Ventre Road,** is an easy, 13-mile trip on level terrain that begins at a trailhead 1 mile north of Moose Junction. The most interesting part of the ride may be its historical significance and photo opportunities as it winds through farm country past the remnants of an old ranch and what's left of the village of Kelly.

The **Shadow Mountain Loop Trail** is perhaps more picturesque, offering as it does a view of the Bridger-Teton National Forest. The trail climbs through the trees to the summit, offers views of the Teton Range along the way, then loops to the base of the mountain. Total distance is 7 miles, and the elevation gain is 1,370 feet. The trail is accessed from Antelope Flats Road, 1 mile north of the Moose Junction. From here, you'll ride 3 miles to a four-way intersection; Shadow Mountain is to the north (left).

Further details for bikers are available at visitor centers or at **Adventure Sports,** at Dornan's in the town of Moose (☎ **307/733-3307**), which is inside the boundaries of Grand Teton National Park. You can also rent mountain bikes here.

Boating. **Scenic cruises** of Jackson Lake are conducted daily, and floating steak-fry cruises are twice-weekly, both leaving from the **Colter Bay Marina** from May through September. Cruises cost $11 for adults, $6 for children; dinner cruises are $35 for adults, $23 for children.

Motorboats and canoe rentals, tackle, and fishing licenses are available at **Colter Bay Marina** and **Signal Mountain Resort.** Motorboats rent for $16 per hour, canoes for $8 per hour. (If you rent a boat, your boating permit is included.) Shuttles to the west side of Jenny Lake, as well as all the scenic cruises, are

Especially for Kids

Youthful visitors aged 8 to 14 are encouraged to explore and experience Grand Teton as members of the **Young Naturalist** program. To participate, pick up a copy of the Young Naturalist activity brochure at any visitor center, then complete projects outlined in the booklet during your stay. When you present the completed project and $1 to a ranger at the Moose, Jenny Lake, or Colter Bay visitor center, you'll be awarded a Young Naturalist patch!

There are two trails that most kids could do, both of which are at Jenny Lake. The **Inspiration Point** hike is less strenuous if you take the boat shuttle across Jenny Lake, which reduces the hiking distance to less than a mile; at 7 miles around, the Jenny Lake Loop Trail is a bit too long for kids, but the terrain is fairly level and doable if you stick to the portion along the eastern shore.

conducted by **Teton Boating Company** (☎ **307/733-2703**).

Additionally, you can rent kayaks and canoes at **Adventure Sports,** at Dornan's in the town of Moose (☎ **307/733-3307**), which is in the boundaries of Grand Teton National Park.

Float Trips. Though the Snake River runs full during spring runoffs, float trips here will not be confused with those on the Colorado River. However, one of the most effective and environmentally sound methods of viewing wildlife in Grand Teton is aboard a floating watercraft that silently moves downstream without disturbing the wildlife. Snake River float trips are offered by several park concessionaires, most of which operate between mid-May and mid-September, depending upon weather and river flow conditions. These companies offer 5- to 20-mile scenic floats, some with early morning and evening wildlife trips.

For an itinerary and prices contact the likes of **Barker-Ewing,** P.O. Box 100, Moose, WY 83012 (☎ **307/733-1800**); **Flagg Ranch Resort,** in the north part of Grand Teton National Park, P.O. Box 187, Yellowstone, WY 82190 (☎ **800/443-2311** or 307/543-2861); **Fort Jackson River Trips,** P.O. Box 1176, Jackson, WY 83001 (☎ **800/735-8430** or 307/733-2583); **Grand Teton Lodge Company,** P.O. Box 250, Moran, WY 83013 (☎ **307/543-2811**); **Lewis and Clark Expeditions,** at Snow King Ski Resort, P.O. Box 720, Jackson, WY 83001 (☎ **800/824-5375** or 307/733-4022); **O.A.R.S.,** Jackson, WY 83001 (☎ **307/733-3379**); **Signal Mountain Lodge,** in Grand Teton National Park, P.O. Box 50, Moran, WY 83013 (☎ **307/543-2831**); and **Triangle X Ranch with Osprey,** in Moose (☎ **307/733-5500**).

Horseback Riding. Horseback riding is popular in Grand Teton. The Grand Teton Lodge Company offers tours from stables next to popular visitor centers at Colter Bay and Jackson Lake Lodge. Choices are 1- and 2-hour guided trail rides daily aboard well-broken, tame animals. An experienced rider may find these tours too tame; wranglers refer to them as "nose-and-tail" tours. In Jackson, try **Bridger-Teton Outfitters** (☎ **307/739-4314** or 307/733-7745), **Green River Outfitters** in Pinedale (☎ **307/733-1044** or 307/367-2416), **Jackson Hole Trail Rides** (☎ **307/733-6992**), **Snow King Stables** (☎ **307/733-5781**), and the **Mill Iron Ranch** (☎ **307/733-6390**).

Mountaineering. If you're considering a challenging or technical climbing experience, head for the Teton Range, which offers opportunities for climbers of all skill levels. Experts are unable to resist the challenge of the Grand Teton, which towers 13,770 above sea level.

Two climbing schools in Jackson offer guided climbs to the summit each summer. **Exum Mountain Guides,** P.O. Box 56, Moose, WY 83012 (☎ **307/733-2297**), which has been around since 1931, offers guided climbs to the top of the Grand for $320. Group preparation classes run from $65 to $85. **Jackson Hole Mountain Guides and Climbing School,** 165 N. Glenwood St., Jackson, WY 83001 (☎ **307/733-4979**), offers advanced climbing courses for $125 and a Grand Teton summit climb for $465. Those who need to practice their moves on a rainy day should try the **Teton Rock Gym,** 1116 Maple (☎ **307/733-0707**). The Jenny Lake Ranger Station (☎ **307/739-3343**) is the center for climbing information (open only in summer); climbers are encouraged to stop in and obtain information on routes, conditions, and regulations. Registration for day climbs is not required, but overnight stays require a backcountry permit.

Winter Sports & Activities

Several park trails are open to cross-country skiers, but they are most suited to experienced shussers prepared to endure strenuous trips.

Additionally, the main park roads are open to snowmobiles. However, except for the Moose Visitor Center, which has rangers on duty to answer your questions and sell you a book, all Grand Teton facilities are closed during the winter months; you will have to purchase supplies at **Dornan's** in Moose, in Jackson, or at Teton Village, which has a small grocery store.

Teton Science School (☎ **307/733-4765**) offers a special winter natural history seminar, "Animal Track and Signs."

Camping

INSIDE THE PARK

Fees in all National Park Service campgrounds are $12 per night, and all have modern flush toilets, though other amenities vary. The two concessionaire-operated campgrounds are more expensive. Sites are the Colter Bay Trailer Village at $29 per night. Sites at Flagg Ranch are $25 per night with hookups, $17 for tents. The campground chart below lists amenities for each campground in the park. Note that where campgrounds accommodate RVs, they are not given a separate section from tent campers.

Gros Ventre, the largest campground in Grand Teton, has 360 sites in an isolated area on the valley floor 2 miles west of the general store in Kelly. There are no showers, but there is a tent-only section, as well as trailer dump station. It generally fills late in the day, if at all.

Jenny Lake Campground is a tent-only area with 49 sites. It's situated in a quiet, wooded area that fills by 9am most days.

Signal Mountain Campground, which also offers views of the lake and access to the beach, fills by 10am. It has 86 sites with views overlooking Jackson Lake and Mt. Moran, as well as a pleasant picnic area and boat launch.

Colter Bay Campground and **Colter Bay Trailer Village** has 462 total sites (112 with RV hookups at the trailer village), showers, and the only facility with a launderette, both of which are in the village. The area has access to the lake but is far enough from the hubbub of Colter Bay Village to offer a modicum of solitude; spaces are usually gone by noon. Just remember that there are two separate campgrounds in the Colter Bay area: The campground is operated by the Park Service and does not accept reservations; the trailer village is operated by the Grand Teton Lodge Company and has full RV hookups and a substantially higher fee.

Lizard Creek Campground, at the north end of Grand Teton National Park, offers an aesthetically pleasing wooded area near Jackson Lake with views of the Tetons, bird watching and fishing, and mosquitoes, so bring your repellent. (This is the only campground with a mosquito problem—it's also our favorite campground.) It is only 8 miles from facilities at Colter Bay and has 60 sites that fill by 2pm.

A final concessionaire-operated campground is located at the **Flagg Ranch Resort** complex on the John D. Rockefeller, Jr., Memorial Parkway. The area, situated in a wooded area next to the parkway, has 121 sites for RVs and campers, showers, and a launderette.

NEAR THE PARK

In Jackson, the **Wagon Wheel Campground** (☎ **307/733-4588**) is about 5 blocks north of Town Square at the Wagon Wheel Motel and has 42 sites for less than $20. The **Teton Village KOA** (☎ **307/733-5354**), 12 miles northwest of Jackson, has 148 sites; tent sites available for $25, RV sites for $33.

Astoria Mineral Springs, also known as Astoria Hot Springs, is at 12500 S. U.S. 89 (☎ **307/733-2659**) and has 110 tent and RV sites for around $20. It's located about 17 miles south of town toward Pinedale, *away from the crowds.*

Also away from the crowds, the **Snake River Park KOA Campground** is also on U.S. 89, 10 miles south of town (☎ **307/733-7078**), has 80 sites with prices similar to the KOA in Teton Village.

Accommodations

INSIDE THE PARK

To complicate matters, accommodations in Grand Teton come under the domain of three different concessionaires. Reservations at Jackson Lake Lodge, Jenny Lake Lodge, and Colter Bay Village should be made through the **Grand Teton Lodge Company,** P.O. Box 240, Moran, WY 83013 (☎ **307/543-2811**); reservations at Signal Mountain Lodge are made by contacting **Signal Mountain Lodge Co.,** P.O. Box 50, Moran, WY 83013 (☎ **307/543-2831**); reservations at **Flagg Ranch Resort** are made through Flagg Ranch, P.O. Box 187, Moran, WY 83013 (☎ **800/443-2311**).

Grand Teton National Park properties have in-room telephones, but none have in-room TVs or air-conditioning. You'll

Campground	Total Sites	RV Hookups	Dump Station	Toilets	Drinking Water
Inside the Park					
Colter Bay	350	No	Yes	Yes	Yes
Colter Bay Trailer Village	112	Yes	Yes	Yes	Yes
Gros Ventre	360	No	Yes	Yes	Yes
*Jenny Lake**	49	No	No	Yes	Yes
*Lizard Creek**	60	No	No	Yes	Yes
Signal Mountain	86	No	Yes	Yes	Yes
Near the Park					
Astoria Mineral Springs	110	Yes	Yes	Yes	Yes
Flagg Ranch	165	Yes	Yes	Yes	Yes
Snake River Park KOA	80	Yes	Yes	Yes	Yes
Teton Village KOA	148	Yes	Yes	Yes	Yes
Wagon Wheel	42	Yes	Yes	Yes	Yes

* Tents only are allowed here.

find TVs in the lounge areas at the Jackson Lodge, Signal Mountain Resort, and Flagg Ranch.

FLAGG RANCH VILLAGE AREA

Flagg Ranch offers travelers the full gamut of services: rooms in newly constructed cabins, tent and RV sites, an above-average restaurant, and gas station. It's also a popular jumping off spot for snowmobilers during winter months. However, since it's situated in a stand of pines in the middle of nowhere, there's not much to do here except watch the Snake River pass by.

Flagg Ranch Resort

P.O. Box 187, Moran, WY 83013. ☎ **800/443-2311** or 307/543-2861. 50 cabins and 54 motel units. $110–$120 cabin; $91–$110 motel rm. AE, DISC, MC, V. Open year-round.

The farthest thing from a ranch, this property is located on well-maintained grounds 5 miles from Yellowstone's South Entrance and 3 miles north of Grand Teton's northern boundary. The oldest operating guest facility in Jackson Valley, it recently completed a total facelift that transformed it from a so-so motel with low-priced cabins and a campground to an above-average resort. The lodge is the center of activity, having a restaurant, bar, convenience store, and gas station. New log cabins constructed in 1994 feature king-size beds, spacious sitting areas, wall-to-wall carpeting, and bathrooms with tubs and showers. The landscaping is a work in progress, though, so don't expect to lounge on inch-deep lawns. In the motel, the main attraction is a terrific view of the Snake River. However, we suggest you rent one of the newer cabins without river views and walk to the river, since the motel units are showing their age and there are no plans to refurbish them. Summer activities include float trips and fly-fishing. During winter months the lodge is popular with snowmobilers, who venture forth to Yellowstone trails, then return to the comfort of the bar,

Showers	Fire Pits/ Grills	Laundry	Public Phone	Reserve	Fees	Open
Yes	Yes	Yes	Yes	No	$12	Late May to Late Sept
No	Yes	Yes	Yes	Yes	$29	Late May to Late Sept
No	Yes	No	Yes	No	$12	Early May to Oct
No	Yes	No	Yes	No	$12	Late May to Late Sept
No	Yes	No	Yes	No	$12	Early June to Early Sept
No	Yes	No	Yes	No	$12	Mid-May to Mid-Oct
Yes	Yes	Yes	Yes	Yes	$20	Mid-May to Early Sept
Yes	Yes	Yes	Yes	Yes	$19/$25	Mid-May to Late Sept
Yes	Yes	Yes	Yes	Yes	$25/$33	Mid-Apr to Sept
Yes	Yes	Yes	Yes	Yes	$25/$33	May to Mid-Oct
Yes	Yes	Yes	Yes	Yes	$20	May to Sept

which serves hot drinks and offers football on a large-screen TV. The campground and RV facility are discussed under "Camping," above.

COLTER BAY VILLAGE AREA

Colter Bay Village Cabins

P.O. Box 240, Moran, WY 83013. ☎ **800/628-9988** or 307/543-2855. 274 units. $30–$109 cabin; $26 tent cabin. AE, DISC, MC, V. Open mid-May to late Sept.

This is the busiest full-service area in the park. Situated on the eastern shore of Jackson Lake, 38 miles north of Jackson, this full-fledged recreation center embraces a vast expanse of budget cabins, and is the least expensive of the three properties managed by Grand Teton Lodge Company. Guest accommodations are in roughly built but authentic-looking log cabins with tile floors perched on a wooded hillside; they are clean and simply furnished in a pioneer style. The simple baths have stall showers; some singles share baths. *A caution:* All cabins are not created equal. **Tent cabins** have rough log walls, canvas roofs, and concrete floors, share one common bath, and guests must bring their own sleeping bags. These are best if you are willing to rough it. The village provides an excellent base of operations for visitors since it has dining and other facilities, including a laundry. Scenic cruises and boat rentals can be arranged at the marina. There is also horseback riding.

Jackson Lake Lodge

P.O. Box 240, Moran, WY 83013. ☎ **800/628-9988** or 307/543-2855. 385 units. $99–$175 double; $113–$125 cottage; $315–$450 suite. AE, DISC, MC, V. Open late May to Oct.

The Jackson Lake Lodge is to Grand Teton what the Old Faithful Inn is to Yellowstone: the most famous of this park's properties. Situated on a bluff overlooking Willow Flats, 1 mile from Jackson Lake, it offers excellent accommodations, fine dining, and commanding views of the Teton Range and especially Mt. Moran. A self-contained resort and convention center, this is the only property in the park capable of handling large groups successfully, so don't be surprised to see gaggles of visitors wearing name tags and corporate attire. From the second-level lounge of the handsome, three-story main lodge, you'll be overwhelmed by views of the mountains framed in 60-foot windows. The lounge itself is an imposing area accented by two stone fireplaces, displays of oversized Native American art and sculptures, and comfortable conversation areas. The dining room, the Mural Room, is just off this area, as is the Pioneer Grill, which offers casual soda fountain–style dining in a 1950s atmosphere. A recent addition is the Blue Heron cocktail lounge, which is tucked off in its own corner of the building; it also offers views of the meadows and mountains, and live entertainment. Upscale shops selling Western clothing and jewelry are on the main level (there are also shops at the Signal Mountain Lodge). Guest rooms are in the main lodge and in cottages scattered about the property, some of which have balconies and mountain views. Lodge rooms are spacious and most offer double beds, electric heat, and newly tiled baths.

SIGNAL MOUNTAIN RECREATION AREA

Signal Mountain Lodge

P.O. Box 50, Moran, WY 83013. ☎ **307/543-2831.** 80 units. $72–$160 double. AE, DISC, MC, V. Open May–Oct.

This is the only resort located on the shores of Jackson Lake inside the park. In addition to offering spectacular views across the lake to the Tetons, it is centrally located on the main route from Moran Junction to Jenny Lake and close to several hiking trails. Of equal importance is the fact that you won't be disappointed by the accommodations, which come in several flavors. Most lodging is in freestanding cabins, motel-style rooms set amid the trees, and family bungalows, some of which enjoy beach frontage. There's also a full-size house that's large enough for a family reunion. The carpeted cabins feature handmade pine furniture, electric heat, covered porches, and tiled baths; and some have fireplaces and kitchenettes with microwave ovens and refrigerators. Once a fishing camp, this is now one of the park's independent lodgings. The recently refurbished registration building has a small TV-viewing area, a gift shop, and outdoor seating on a deck overlooking the lake. A restaurant and coffee shop serving average food share a separate building with a small lounge and gift shop. Recreational options include hiking, cycling, rafting, waterskiing, and fishing, but boat rentals are expensive here. A convenience store and gas station are on the property.

JENNY LAKE AREA

Jenny Lake Lodge

P.O. Box 240, Moran, WY 83013. ☎ **800/628-9988** or 307/543-2855. 37 units. $275 single; $350 double; $485–$500 double in suite. Rates include breakfast and dinner. AE, DISC, MC, V. Open late May to Oct.

This operation justifiably prides itself on seclusion, award-winning food, and comfortably furnished cabins. Located 19 miles from Jackson Airport and 13 miles from the Moose Entrance. The lodge's name is a misnomer, however, since it is not on the lake but rather sits away from the highway among forested glades, and the lodge functions primarily as a place to dine. Sofas are clustered around a fireplace to create a beautifully cozy sitting area, and the dining room is tastefully decorated with original works by local artists; a classical guitarist often accompanies the gourmet meals. The environment here is more formal than at most park properties (jackets are required at dinner, for instance). The atmosphere is subdued and charming, and the prices are appropriately high. The clientele tends to be mature and affluent, but lately there has been an increase in the number of couples with toddlers. Breakfast and dinner are included in the room charges, and are the finest in any of the park-operated restaurants. There is no lounge here, but the restaurant does serve liquor with meals. Accommodations are in beautiful log cabins, each having a traditional pitched shingle roof and a long, pillared porch; most have forest views. Inside are log furniture with cowhide upholstery, ample closet space, and tiled combination baths. Guided pack trips that leave from the lodge can be arranged with outfitters, and guests have the use of bicycles and can rent horses for the area's trails.

NEAR THE PARK

IN TETON VILLAGE

Alpenhof Hotel

3255 W. McCollister Dr., Teton Village, WY 83025. ☎ **800/732-3244** or 307/733-3242; fax 307/739-1516. 42 rms. A/C TV TEL. $63–$300 summer; $89–$379 winter. AE, DISC, MC, V. Closed Oct–Nov.

The Alpenhof continues to appeal to affluent guests interested in Wyoming's version of Bavaria. Only 50 yards from the tram, it offers excellent access to skiing, while in summer it is an excellent stopover for travelers negotiating the roads between Jackson, the Grand Tetons, and Yellowstone. With its pitched shingle roof, flower bedecked balconies, and flags flapping over an umbrella-dotted deck, the property resembles a Swiss chalet. The newly redecorated accommodations feature brightly colored alpine fabrics, new handcrafted European furnishings, excellent soundproofing, electric heaters, and tiled baths with big, soft towels. Two junior suites and four rooms with a shared deck are recent additions, as are five rooms with fireplaces; economy rooms offer double or queen beds, while deluxe units are larger. The most unique rooms are a quartet of fourth-floor rooms that can be reached only by an exterior staircase.

Your choices for dinner include award-winning and expensive continental fare that is served in The Alpenhof dining room, or pork, game, and pasta, which are staples in Dietrich's Bar and Bistro, a casual second-level dining area. After dinner, you can relax over cocktails by a stone fireplace, or on the outside deck.

Sojourner Inn

P.O. Box 348, Teton Village, WY 83025. ☎ **800/445-4655.** 100 rms. A/C TV TEL. $85–$260. AE, MC, V. Closed Nov and April–May.

Once a budget ski lodge, the Sojourner has been totally renovated in the past 8 years and attracts skiers during winter months and park visitors in summer. The reception area is accented by wood walls, stone floors, overstuffed furniture, and a stone fireplace. This is a lower-priced alternative to the high-end properties down the road. Standard guest rooms in the main lodge provide a comfortable place to hang your hat, especially in rooms with views of either the mountains or the valley floor. Larger rooms in the mountain lodge have living areas with sofa beds, various bed configurations, and tiled tub/shower baths. Four have kitchenettes. Two restaurants are on the mezzanine level: The Village Steak House serves steak and chicken meals, family style; the Fondue Pot offers a trendy menu in a casual environment during winter months. Visitors to the multilevel lounge are entertained by a big-screen TV, or they entertain themselves at the billiards table or on the patio. A recent addition is a pub. Summer visitors take advantage of swimming and sunning at the outdoor pool and whirlpools. Winter visitors can ski directly to a locker room with a whirlpool and sauna.

IN JACKSON

Days Inn of Jackson Hole

1280 W. Broadway (just off the junction of Wyo. 22 and U.S. 191), Jackson, WY 83001. ☎ **800/329-7466** or 307/733-0033. 91 rms, 13 suites. A/C TV TEL. $149 double; $159–$209 suite. Rates include continental breakfast. AE, DC, DISC, MC, V.

It's easily one of the nicer hotels on the west side of town, but it's on the high end of the price scale. In fall and spring, though, you'll pay less than half of the summer rates. What you can expect is an above-average Days Inn, an extremely helpful staff, a free continental breakfast (coffee, a wide variety of muffins, and fresh orange juice), and beautiful and spacious suites with fireplaces and hot tubs. This Days Inn would be a fine place to stay even if it weren't in Jackson.

Rusty Parrot Lodge

175 N. Jackson, Jackson, WY 83001. ☎ **800/458-2004** or 307/733-2000. 31 rms, 1 suite. TV TEL. $98–$215; $300 suite. Rates include full breakfast. AE, DISC, MC, V.

It might sound like an out-of-practice jungle bird, but since 1990 the Rusty Parrot has been one of the most finely tuned places to stay in Jackson. If it weren't right slap in the middle of town, you'd think it was a country lodge. Located across from Miller Park, the Parrot is decorated in the new-Western style of peeled log, with an interior appointed with pine furniture and river rock fireplaces. If you're going to spend this kind of money and not stay at a guest ranch, the Parrot is a good idea. Rooms are gigantic, and several have balconies. The suite is an incredible apartment with fireplaces in both the living area and the bedroom (it was the owner's personal residence while he was building his local mansion), perhaps the nicest suite in all of Jackson. Breakfast is more than an afterthought; a well-trained chef prepares omelettes and pastries, which accompany fresh fruits, juices, cereals, and freshly ground coffee. An added touch: therapeutic treatments by a staff masseuse.

Trapper Inn

235 N. Cache, Jackson, WY 83001. ☎ **800/341-8000** or 307/733-2648. 54 rms, 1 suite. A/C TV TEL. $85–$105 double; $195 suite. AE, DC, DISC, MC, V.

The location, 2 short blocks from the Town Square, is worth a gold mine, and the staff here are among the best you're going to find in Jackson. They know all the good deals, and they're not afraid to share. Based here, you can walk anywhere in downtown within minutes. Though the decor of the rooms is average, the space is not. In the newest building, erected in 1991, the rooms are larger than normal. Many come with minifridges. Laundry facilities and an indoor/outdoor hot tub are also on hand.

Virginian Lodge

750 W. Broadway, Jackson, WY 83001. ☎ **800/262-4999** or 307/733-2792. 135 rms, 12 minisuites, 11 suites. A/C TV TEL. $95–$105 double; $110 minisuite; $115–$155 suite. AE, DC, DISC, MC, V.

With its overhaul in 1995, the Virginian is attempting to earn its spurs as one of the better hotels in Jackson. It's not brand-new; it's not a resort; it doesn't have a golf course; and the highway is right outside the door. It is, however, more affordable than many of the other accommodations in Jackson. Under the same ownership since 1965, it's recently come alive with fresh coats of paint, new carpeting, and a hot tub. The nightmare of taxidermy that adorns the walls of the lobby and the bar remain in place and add to the hotel's Old West flavor. If prices were as high as many of the other places in Jackson, we'd have to say the place was tacky. But they aren't, so this is a good buy. The Virginian also has an outdoor heated pool, an average family style restaurant, an arcade for youngsters, and laundry facilities.

Wort Hotel

50 N. Glenwood, Jackson, WY 83001. ☎ **307/733-2190.** 55 rms, 5 suites. TV TEL. $145 double; $190–$295 suite. AE, DISC, MC, V.

This is an institution with real character, located 1 block south of the heart of town, an imposing two-story, Tudor building that was completely encased in stone and brick following a 1980 fire. The Wort's Tudor exterior, however, belies its location and major interior design elements—Western art and taxidermy. The lobby is graced by a warm and romantic fireplace, and a mezzanine sitting area provides a second hideaway. Comfortable, air-conditioned guest rooms have modern decor, thick carpeting, and tub/shower baths. Superior units face the street. The Governor's Suite boasts a traditional parlor. A gym and whirlpool have been added to a fitness center, but don't expect to build a body by Jake here. The dining areas were recently refurbished, but that hasn't changed the fact that these are noisy places to dine and there are several better alternatives nearby. The famous Silver Dollar Bar is a casual watering hole displaying 2,032 silver dollars inlaid in a bar. This was the first piece of furniture rescued during the fire.

Spring Creek Resort

P.O. Box 3154 (on top of the East Gros Ventre Butte), Jackson, WY 83001. ☎ **800/443-6139** or 307/733-8833. 117 units. A/C TV TEL. $120–$205; condo unit $200–$950 per night. AE, MC, V.

One of the most attractive and expensive resorts is situated atop Gros Ventre Butte, only 4 miles from the center of Jackson. Perched atop East Gros Ventre Butte, 1,000 feet above the Snake River, minutes from the airport, this resort commands 1,500 acres of land adjacent to a wilderness area populated by deer, moose, and other wildlife. Nearly every room is spacious and well appointed, with balconies offering views of the Teton Range. Guest rooms are in four buildings and feature fireplaces, Native American floor and wall coverings, refrigerators, and coffeemakers. Even the studio units boast kitchenettes. In addition to its own rooms, the resort arranges accommodations in privately owned condominiums on the butte, many of which are three-level homes, all lavishly furnished and featuring completely equipped kitchens. Specially designed rooms are reserved for travelers with disabilities. There's also swimming, two tennis courts, and a concierge who will arrange horseback rides and fishing excursions. Winter skiing at Teton Village is only 15 miles away.

Dining

INSIDE THE PARK

NEAR THE NORTHERN BOUNDARY

In addition to Flagg Ranch, fast food is available at **Leek's Marina,** which is located inside the park, a few miles north of Colter Bay.

Flagg Ranch Resort

5 miles north of Grand Teton's North Boundary, on the John D. Rockefeller, Jr., Parkway, Moran, WY. ☎ **800/443-2311.** Breakfast items $2–$6; lunch dishes $4–$7; dinner main courses $9–$14. DISC, MC, V. Summer daily 6am–10pm. TRADITIONAL AMERICAN.

The food at this oasis is better than what you'll find in a typical family restaurant, and servings are more generous. The dinner menu includes standard fish, chicken, and beef dishes, as well as home-style entrees like ranch beef stew and chicken pot pie. The ambience is down-home as well, both in winter and summer months—tables are covered with colorful upholstery in a newly constructed log building.

COLTER BAY

John Colter Chuckwagon and the **Cafe Court Pizza and Deli** are the two sit-down restaurants in the village, both of which are located across from the marina and visitor center. Both are open daily in summer from 6am to 10pm and serve all meals, but breakfast in the deli is a serve-yourself affair. Credit cards (AE, DISC, MC, and V) are accepted at both.

The **Deli** serves sandwiches, chicken, pizzas, salads, and soup, with prices that range from $3.50 for a tuna salad to $4.50 for an individual pizza, to $13 for a chicken dinner.

The **Chuckwagon** serves breakfast from a menu that includes everything from plain eggs to a Chuckwagon omelette. Lunch is soup, salad, and hot sandwiches. Dinner is a buffet with a nightly special. Expect to spend $6 to $8 for entrees of trout, lasagna, pork chops, and beef stew; New York strip steaks range in price from $10 to $14. The ambience is very casual and straightforward, since these restaurants cater to families.

In addition to the two sit-down restaurants here, there's also a **snack shop** located in the grocery store.

JACKSON LAKE JUNCTION

The casual dining choice at the Jackson Lake Lodge is the **Pioneer Grill,** complete with 1950s atmosphere and requisite soda fountain. Entrees are light and less expensive than at the Mural Room (described below), and a takeout menu is available. The restaurant serves three meals and is alone in offering a children's menu. The **Blue Heron** cocktail lounge is one of the two nicest spots in either park to enjoy a cocktail. The other is at Yellowstone Lake Hotel. The lounge here offers the same views as the dining room, as well as live entertainment.

The Mural Room

Jackson Lake Lodge. ☎ **307/543-2811.** Reservations recommended. Breakfast items $4–$7; lunch items $6–$9; dinner entrees $16–$20. AE, DISC, MC, V. Summer daily 6am–10pm. BEEF/FISH/PASTA.

The main dining room in the lodge is somewhat more formal than the Pioneer Grill, caters to a more sedate crowd, as well as corporate groups, and is also more expensive than most other park restaurants. Floor-to-ceiling windows provide lovely views of the lake and the Teton Range across a meadow where you might see moose. Walls are adorned with hand-painted, Western murals (what else?). Breakfast includes Belgian waffles, and vegetarian eggs Benedict. Lunch entrees range from the ordinary (a Teton burger) to a tasty smoked trout salad. Dinner may be a grand, five-course event that includes a shrimp cocktail, French onion soup, and Caesar salad, followed by Idaho trout, buffalo strip loin, vegetable lasagna, or rack of lamb.

SIGNAL MOUNTAIN

In addition to the main dining room, a **coffee shop** serves breakfast and lunch in an informal setting.

Aspens Dining Room

Signal Mountain Lodge. ☎ **307/543-2831.** Reservations recommended. Breakfast items $4–$6; lunch main courses $6–$8; dinner main courses $8–$21. AE, DISC, MC, V. Summer daily 6:30–10am, 11:30am–2:30pm, and 5:30–10pm. ECLECTIC AMERICAN.

Of the three locations to eat under this roof, only Aspens Dining Room serves full meals in a proper dining room overlooking the lake. Entrees include chicken pot pie, pasta, and veal saltimbocca. When the bargain-hunting folks who work for the park's concessionaires head out for dinner, though, chances are good they'll land here and order Nachos Supreme from the bar menu. This nutritionist's nightmare—melted cheddar and jack cheese with spicy beef or chicken served on a bed of corn chips topped with sour cream—will generally satisfy the appetite of two adults. Since the bar has one of three TVs in the park and is equipped with cable for sports nuts, the crowd tends to be young and noisy. As an alternative, snacks are served on the deck overlooking the lake.

JENNY LAKE

Jenny Lake Lodge

North of Jenny Lake. ☎ **800/628-9988.** Reservations required. Fixed-price dinner $38.50 (nonlodge guests only). AE, DISC, MC, V. Summer daily 7–9am, 11:30am–1:30pm, and 5:30–8pm. CONTINENTAL.

The finest meals in Grand Teton are served here, where a Cordon Bleu chef creates culinary delights for guests and, occasionally, a U.S. president. All three meals served daily are equally appetizing, but dinner is the bell-ringer. Guests choose from appetizers that may include chilled lobster salad or smoked sturgeon ravioli, as well as buffalo mozzarella and plum tomato salads. Entrees may include grilled salmon, rack of lamb, or prime rib of buffalo. Desserts are wonderfully decadent. Price is no object here for guests, since meals are included in the room charge. If you aren't a lodge guest, you'll have to call well in advance—and expect to get the second sitting for dinner.

NEAR THE PARK

IN TETON VILLAGE

Stiegler's

At the Jackson Hole Racquet Club, Teton Village Rd., Teton Village. ☎ **307/733-1071.** Reservations recommended. Main courses $14–$24. AE, MC, V. Tues–Sun 5:30–10pm. AUSTRIAN/CONTINENTAL.

People often wonder where the Von Trapps eat on vacation. I mean, Austrian cuisine isn't exactly lurking beyond every street corner. But in Jackson, there are two options: Steigler's Restaurant and Steigler's Bar. Since 1983, Steigler's has been confusing and delighting customers with such favorites as *Bauern Schmaus* for two (a "Farmer's Feast" that includes pork and bratwurst) and the less-perplexing venison filet mignon with morels. Peter Stiegler, the Austrian chef, invites you to "find a little *gemutlichkeit.*" Tyrolean leather breeches are, of course, optional.

Vista Grande

Teton Village Rd., Teton Village. ☎ **307/733-6964.** Main courses $9–$17. AE, MC, V. Daily 5–10pm. MEXICAN.

Since the late 1970s, the Vista Grande has been a crowd-pleaser. The food is great south-of-the-border cuisine (there are others in town, but this is one of the best), and the portions are plentiful. What also separates the Vista Grande from other Mexican restaurants is the variety of dishes: You'll find the requisite fajitas, burritos, chimichangas, and enchiladas, but also find chicken *asados*—grilled chicken on a bed of rice with *pico de gallo* (mild, table salsa), blackened tuna, and a vegetarian plate that makes no excuses for the fat grams.

IN JACKSON

Acadian House

170 N. Millward, Jackson. ☎ **307/739-1269.** Reservations recommended. Lunch dishes $3–$7; main dinner courses $9–$17. AE, DC, MC, V. Tues–Fri 11:30am–2pm; daily 5:30–10pm. CAJUN.

Formerly located at the junction of U.S. 89 and Wyo. 22 as you came into town from the west, the Acadian House has since moved to a downtown location, bringing its loyal following with it. Serving up some of the best flavors from the swamplands of southern Louisiana, this Cajun restaurant is Jackson's finest in the cayenne department. Traditional dishes like boudin—a sausage-and-rice dish—and shrimp étouffée, are offered alongside continental-style creations like crawfish fettucine. There are many other fish and seafood dishes, too. If you've never treated yourself to the South's most delicious bottom-feeder, try the catfish, a delicious delicacy blackened to perfection topped with almonds, pecans, and white wine.

Anthony's

62 S. Glenwood St., Jackson. ☎ **307/733-3717.** Main courses $10–$17. MC, V. Daily 5:30–9:30pm. PASTA.

Just south of the Wort Hotel is one of Jackson's two most notable downtown Italian restaurants, with dishes like fettucine with a heavy cream sauce, broccoli, and mushrooms. Though Anthony's is one of Jackson's mainstays, it's not by any stretch the finest restaurant in town. It is, however, the place to dine if you're looking for an Italian menu with plenty of pasta options.

The Blue Lion

160 N. Millward, Jackson. ☎ **307/733-3912.** Reservations recommended. Main courses $15–$26. AE, DC, MC, V. Daily 6–9:30pm. Closed Tues off-season. CONTINENTAL.

This quaint restaurant off the Town Square downtown, is filled offers a delicious array of creative entrees that reflect the restaurant's flair for rich foods. Rack of lamb, beef tenderloin medallions, and wild game, including elk loin grilled and served in a peppercorn sauce, are specialties. For every beef dish, there's a vegetarian entree prepared with zest. The pasta primavera is a delicious mixture of veggies sautéed in olive oil and served on a bed of fettucine with basil-walnut pesto.

The Granary

At the Spring Creek Resort, on top of the East Gros Ventre Butte, Jackson. ☎ **800/443-6139** or 307/733-8833. Reservations recommended. Lunch entrees $10–$15; dinner entrees $15–$25. AE, MC, V. Daily 11:30am–2pm and 5:50–8pm. STEAK/GAME.

Located 15 minutes from downtown Jackson atop the East Gros Ventre Butte, the Granary has been a standout choice since it opened in the 1980s, both for food and excellent views of the Tetons. Lunch is especially pleasant when weather allows dining outside on a wood deck. Special dishes include rabbit bratwurst and seafood quiche. Dinner entrees include crusted halibut, Colorado Lamb, and seared elk tenderloin.

Grille at the Pines

At the Teton Pines Resort, 3450 N. Clubhouse Dr., Jackson. ☎ **800/238-2223** or 307/733-1005. Reservations recommended. Lunch entrees $9–$14; dinner entrees $12–$20. AE, MC, V. Daily 11:30am–2pm and 5:30–10pm. STEAK/FISH/PASTA.

The Teton Pines Resort just happens to be home to what locals consider one of the finest restaurants in the valley. The Grille at the Pines overlooks a placid trout pond and Teton Pines golf course. The menu includes well-prepared steak and veal dishes, as well as the obligatory pasta dishes.

Gun Barrel Steak and Game Restaurant

862 W. Broadway, Jackson. ☎ **307/733-3287.** Main courses $11–$22. MC, V. Nightly 5–9:30pm. BEEF/GAME.

This restaurant has one of the most unique, and varied, wild game menus in the area. Appetizers include boar bratwurst and caribou quesadillas. Soups include game gumbo with smoked duck salad. Entrees are equally interesting, including bourbon baby-back ribs, red pepper fettucine, velvet elk, and buffalo tenderloin medallions. Try a game dish of buffalo or elk for a unique dining experience. The restaurant also has a first-class wine and beer menu. It was once a wildlife museum, so the heads of assorted animals stare down on diners as they eat.

Jedidiah's House of Sourdough

135 E. Broadway, Jackson. ☎ **307/733-5671.** Breakfast items $4–$8; lunch items $3–$7. AE, DC, MC, V. Daily 7am–2pm; in summer only, also 5–10pm. AMERICAN.

Though they get uppity and serve dinner in the summertime, Jedidiah's is known throughout the valley for its breakfast and its log-cabin atmosphere. This is the perfect spot to bring a big appetite for breakfast. The sourjacks are a stack of sourdough pancakes, served with blueberries if you like; the 'Diah's omelette is a big three-egg concoction stuffed with bacon, onions, and cheddar cheese and served with a side of potatoes. When open for dinner during summer months the staples are beef, chicken, trout, and, for the kids, a hot dog or hamburger for $3.50. The old photographs give customers a great excuse for staring at the walls while waiting for the food in a casual, western environment. During summer months, meals are also served on a patio.

Lame Duck

680 E. Broadway. ☎ **307/733-4311.** Most dishes $9–$17. AE, MC, V. Daily 5:30–10pm. CHINESE/JAPANESE.

You wouldn't think that a visit to the Wild West would yield good sushi prospects, but the Lame Duck is the only game in town for decent Japanese and Chinese cuisine. Favorite dishes include Samurai Chicken, otherwise known as the Oriental fajita, and Six Delicacies, a dish of duck, lobster, shrimp, snow peas, and mushrooms served with a secret sauce. To make fire alarms go off, try the Fireworks Shrimp: shrimp, snow peas, and bamboo shoots mixed with an incredible hot sauce. The Lame Duck also offers private tearoom seating for those who want to enjoy a more authentic sit-down, shoes-off Oriental experience.

Nora's Fish Creek Inn

5600 W. Wyo. 22, Wilson. ☎ **307/733-8288.** Reservations not accepted. Breakfast items $3–$7; lunch dishes $4–$6; dinner main courses $8–$14. DISC, MC, V. Daily 6am–9:30pm. AMERICAN.

This little place outside Wilson, which is 15 minutes from Jackson on Wyo. 22, is a great spot for a weekend breakfast, thanks to its all-you-can-eat pancakes. Locals have enjoyed it for years, and the place has achieved status as a Jackson Hole institution. The food isn't gourmet, and that's precisely why a lot of folks keep coming back. Prices are lower than anywhere else in town, and you still get as many coffee refills as you like. Dinner is fish, fish, and more fish, as in fresh Idaho trout.

Snake River Grill

Town Sq., Jackson. ☎ **307/733-0557.** Reservations recommended. Main courses $15–$30. AE, MC, V. Daily 5:30–10pm. Closed Nov and Apr. ECLECTIC.

Not just a favorite of the locals who consistently rate this one of the best restaurants in the valley, the Snake River Grill is also a popular spot with the local glitterati. Harrison Ford, Uma Thurman, and the like, as well as visiting politicians and dignitaries, have all dined here. The front dining room overlooks the Town Square, but there's a more private, romantic room in back. The menu changes seasonally, but you can expect eclectic entries like fresh fish (ahi tuna is a favorite), bourbon marinated pork chops, and venison. The wine list is equally noteworthy.

The Strutting Grouse

At Jackson Golf and Tennis Club, Wyo. 191, near Kelly, WY. ☎ **307/733-7788.** Reservations recommended. Lunch entrees $6–$14; dinner entrees $18–$24. AE, DISC, MC, V. Summer daily 11am–2pm and 5:30–9pm. BEEF/LAMB/FISH.

Though this restaurant, which overlooks the golf course on the valley floor 20 minutes from Jackson, caters primarily to local golfers, it enjoys an excellent reputation among nongolfers and valley visitors. The diet-conscious can order lunch from a menu that includes several salads, as well as mesquite-grilled chicken strips and a grouse pizza (actually, it consists of duck sausage and sun-dried tomatoes). The dinner menu includes the usual assortment of beef, lamb, and fish entrees, as well as a chef's special, typically a game dish. The Grouse is among the top-10 restaurants in the valley.

Picnic & Camping Supplies

You'll find a well-stocked general store at Moose Village; there are convenience stores at Flagg Ranch, Colter Bay Village, and at the Signal Mountain Resort.

Nearby Attractions

While snowbirds head south to Arizona for the winter, elk head for the **National Elk Refuge** (U.S. 26, P.O. Box C, Jackson, WY 83001, headquarters open Monday to Friday 8am to 4:30pm; ☎ **307/733-9212**), a spectacular expanse of land in the shadows of the Grand Tetons. There they hold a reunion of sorts—it's the largest gathering of elk in North America. Thinly timbered stretches of the Gros Ventre River roll into grassy meadows, sagebrush, and the outcroppings of rock along the foothills to form an ideal habitat for elk, moose, bighorn sheep, and more than 175 species of birds. Though wildlife viewing is excellent on the refuge throughout the year, winter is the best time to catch glimpses of the migrating elk herd. During the first snows of late autumn, the elk move from the higher elevations of the Tetons and Yellowstone National Park to the valley floor of the refuge in search of dwindling food. Each winter the Fish and Wildlife Service offers wonderful **horse-drawn sleigh rides** that provide up-close glimpses of the 8,000 elk. Rides early in the winter will find young energetic bulls playing and banging heads, while late winter visits (when the Fish and Wildlife Service begins feeding the animals) allow for looks at the rest of the herd. Tickets for the 45-minute rides ($10 for adults and $6 for children 6 to 12) can be purchased at the National Museum of Wildlife Art on Highway 26 across from the refuge. Ask about a combination pass for the sleigh ride and the museum.

20

GREAT BASIN NATIONAL PARK

by Don and Barbara Laine

A VAST AREA OF DESERT, VALLEYS, MOUNTAINS, LAKES, AND STREAMS, North America's Great Basin includes Nevada, Utah, and parts of California, Oregon, and Idaho. It received its name because the rainwater that falls here has no outlet to the sea.

Located along the Utah–Nevada border, Great Basin National Park provides an intimate glimpse into this vast, rugged section of America. Founded in 1986, the park not only looks out at the Great Basin's expanse of desert and mountains from the summit of 13,063-foot Wheeler Peak, but descends beneath the earth's surface for a fascinating tour among the intricately and delicately formed stalactites, stalagmites, and other exotic formations in the unreal world of Lehman Caves.

Hiking trails abound, through rugged pine and aspen forests, or above the tree line to a moonlike world of barren, windswept rocks. Camping in the park is a delight, with quiet campgrounds, plenty of trees, and splendid scenery. The park contains forests of bristlecone pine—trees that some scientists believe are the oldest living things on earth—as well as pinyon, juniper, spruce, fir, pine, and aspen. You'll see wildflowers such as yellow aster and Parry's primrose during the summer, and watch for mule deer, bighorn sheep, squirrels, and golden eagles.

Like most of the West's national parks, Great Basin offers ample activities to keep you busy for at least a week, and it is strongly suggested that you plan to spend at least 1 full day in the park. But for the best park experience, try to allow at least 3 full days, to provide enough time not only to tour Lehman Cave and explore the scenic drive, but also to hike to the delightful bristlecone pine forest and perhaps to one of the park's high-mountain lakes.

Because of its remoteness—Great Basin isn't near any other popular tourist destinations or even along a route to one—you'll find it relatively quiet and uncrowded, similar to what you would have found 30 or 40 years ago in America's loved-to-death parks such as Yosemite and Grand Canyon. Although Great Basin National Park is in Nevada, many visitors are Utah residents, on long-weekend excursions from Salt Lake City. Visitors to the national parks of Arizona and Utah who start their trips in Las Vegas, Nevada, can easily add Great Basin to their driving loop, either at the beginning or end.

Tips from a Park Ranger

Park ranger Anne Hopkins Pfaff, who has worked at Great Basin National Park on and off since 1988, enjoys both the park and the surrounding desert. "It's a gorgeous area," she says, "I like the remoteness."

Asked what she especially likes about the 77,000-acre park, Pfaff replies, "The variety of vegetation and habitats, and the views—especially the views that include both Wheeler Peak and out across the Great Basin, such as you get from Mather Overlook." This park, she says, "is one of America's real treasures, where you can get out on the trails and not see another human being." Pfaff says that as far as national parks go, Great Basin National Park campgrounds offer minimal services, and while many visitors thoroughly enjoy this aspect, others miss their creature comforts, such as hot showers and RV hookups.

Ranger Pfaff says she is impressed by the bristlecone pines—their age and their beauty—and considers a hike to the **bristlecone pine forest** among the park's top experiences. Also on her list of things all park visitors should try to do are touring **Lehman Cave** and taking the **Wheeler Peak Scenic Drive.** If she were to come to Great Basin National Park as a visitor it would be in September, she says, "when the crowds are gone and the weather is usually beautiful—not too hot at the lower elevations but not yet snow-covered in the upper elevations."

Avoiding the Crowds. Because Great Basin National Park is seemingly in the middle of nowhere, it receives far fewer visitors than most other national parks. However, it isn't deserted. During the **relatively busy summer season** you'll need to arrive at the visitor center early for your cave tour tickets (or purchase them in advance), and don't count on finding a campsite if you arrive late in the day, especially on weekends. The **busiest times** are from July through Labor Day, and although the park is quieter in spring, weather can be a problem, with snow in the higher elevations. The park has its **lowest visitation** in January and February, but that is also when it will be the coldest and snowiest. For those who can arrange it, the **best time** to visit is from the day after Labor Day through the end of September, when there are fewer people and the weather is beautiful—with warm days and crisp, cool nights. Early October is also usually nice, but check the weather reports—you could find yourself in an early winter snowstorm.

Just the Facts

GETTING THERE & GATEWAYS

Great Basin National Park is 5 miles west of the small town of Baker, Nevada; 70 miles southeast of Ely, Nevada; 385 miles east of Reno, Nevada; 286 miles north of Las Vegas, Nevada; 200 miles north of St. George, Utah; and 234 miles southwest of Salt Lake City, Utah.

From points in **west-central Utah,** take U.S. 50 west just across the state line into Nevada, go south on Nev. 487 to the village of Baker, and then west on Nev. 488 into the park. From St. George, take I-15 north to Cedar City, continue north on Utah 130 to Minersville, take Utah 21 west through Milford to the Nevada state line, where it becomes Nev. 487, which you follow to Baker, and then take Nev. 488 west to the park.

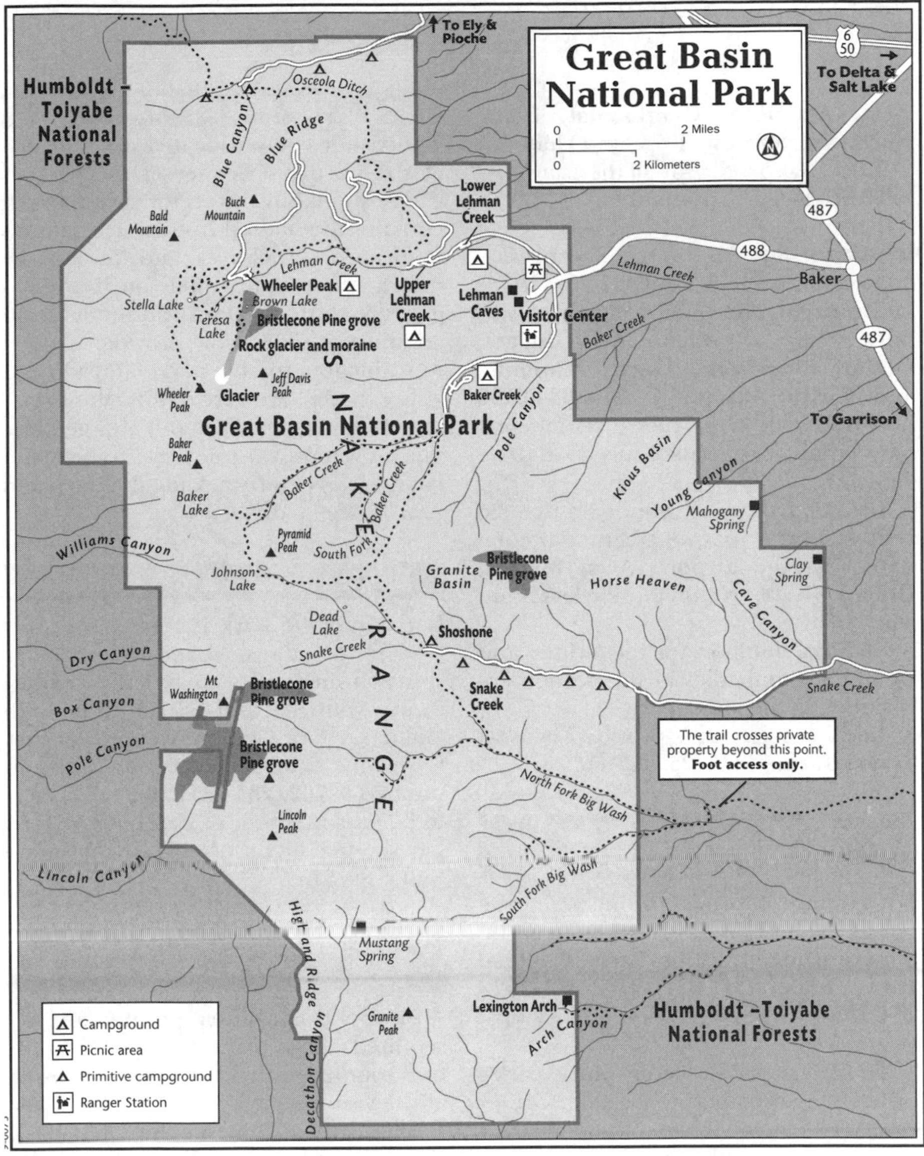

If coming from **Las Vegas, Nevada,** follow U.S. 93 north to U.S. 50, which you take east to Nev. 487, where you turn south to Baker, and then follow Nev. 488 into the park.

From **Ely** and **Reno, Nevada,** follow U.S. 50 east to Nev. 487, and follow directions above.

The Nearest Airports. The closest major airports are **McCarran International Airport** in Las Vegas (☎ **702/261-5743**) and **Salt Lake City International Airport** (☎ **801/575-2400**) in Salt Lake City, Utah.

Most airlines, including the following, have regularly scheduled flights into Las Vegas: **American, America West, Continental, Delta, Kiwi, Midway, Midwest Express, Northwest, Reno Air, Southwest, Sun Country, TWA, United,** and **US Airways.**

Salt Lake City is served by the following carriers, among others: **America**

West, American, Continental, Delta, Northwest, Skywest, TWA, and **United.**

See the appendix for all these airlines' toll-free reservations numbers.

Renting a Car. All the major car-rental companies are represented in Las Vegas at the airport. National companies with outlets here are **Alamo, Avis, Budget, Dollar, Enterprise, Hertz, National,** and **Thrifty. Allstate** (☎ **800/634-6186** or 702/736-6148) is a local rental company that also rents four-wheel-drive vehicles.

In **Salt Lake City,** you'll be able to rent from the following national companies at the airport: **Avis, Budget, Dollar, Hertz, National, Payless,** and **Thrifty.**

Toll-free numbers for the airlines and car rental companies in this section are included in the appendix.

Local taxi service is provided by **West Tracks Taxi** (☎ **435/259-2294**).

GETTING INFORMATION BEFORE YOUR TRIP

For advance information, including the park's color brochure, contact the **Superintendent, Great Basin National Park,** Baker, NV 89311-9702 (☎ **702/234-7331**). The Web site is **www.nps.gov/grba.**

Be sure to ask for a copy of the park's excellent newspaper-style guide, ***Bristlecone,*** which includes a map, current activities and costs, and nearby services. The Park Service can also provide current information on nearby lodging and dining possibilities and additional information on the park.

Those who want to buy maps and books can contact the **Great Basin Natural History Association** (☎ **702/234-7270**) at the park address above. Memberships ($10 individuals and $15 family) entitle you to a 15% discount on purchases.

The park is open every day of the year, but the visitor center and cave are closed Thanksgiving, Christmas, and New Year's Day.

VISITOR CENTER

The visitor center, located on Nev. 488 at the northeast corner of the park, is where you'll buy tickets for cave tours. It contains the natural history association's bookstore, brochures and other free information, and exhibits on the park's geology, history, flora, and fauna. In addition, a slide show provides a good introduction to the park. Outside the visitor center are rest rooms, the park's only public telephone, and a large parking lot where you can leave trailers and big vehicles before tackling the steep and narrow scenic drive.

ENTRANCE & CAMPING FEES

Entry into the park is free. Cave tours cost $4 for adults 16 and older, $3 for youths from 6 to 15, are free for children 5 and younger, and $2 for those with Golden Age or Golden Access passports. Cave tour tickets can be purchased by phone (☎ **702/234-7331**) from 24 hours to 30 days in advance. Camping costs $5 per site per night; use of the dump station costs $1.

SPECIAL REGULATIONS & WARNINGS

Although backcountry permits are not required, those planning to go into the backcountry are encouraged to **register** at the visitor center, where they will also receive information on the latest backcountry conditions and regulations. Hikers going to the top of 13,063-foot Wheeler Peak may develop symptoms of **altitude sickness** (headache, nausea), in which case they should turn back immediately. **Vehicles** are also sometimes affected by the elevation and steep roads, and the Wheeler Peak Scenic Drive, which leads to most trailheads, is not recommended for large motor homes and vehicles pulling trailers.

SEASONS & CLIMATE

Although open year-round, above-ground activities are limited during the winter by deep snow and bitter cold that make the higher elevations off-limits to all but the most rugged and skilled mountaineers. The cave can be visited at any time. Year-round temperature inside the cave is 50° and humidity is 90%, so a sweater or light jacket is advised. Outdoors, conditions are tied to elevation, which ranges from 6,825 feet at the visitor center to 13,063 at Wheeler Peak. Hiking trails at lower elevations are usually free of snow from late spring through early fall, but snow is possible at any time above 10,000 feet. **Summer thunderstorms** are common during the afternoon but can occur any time.

USEFUL PUBLICATIONS

Backcountry hikers will want to obtain detailed topographical maps, available at the visitor center.

Seeing the Highlights in a Day

In some ways, this is two parks: the caverns and the mountains. Because of the frequency of afternoon thunderstorms in the summer, it is usually best to do outdoor activities early in the day. Therefore, we recommend that those with only 1 day at the park should spend the morning on the **Wheeler Peak Scenic Drive,** possibly allowing time to hike at least part of one of the trails. Then, after a picnic lunch or sandwich from the cafe, take a **cave tour** (it's best to purchase tickets in advance; see "Entrance & Camping Fees," above), see the exhibits and programs in the **visitor center,** and take a walk along the **Mountain View Nature Trail.**

Those with 2 days might spend their first day as described above, and then, after a good night's sleep, tackle one of the tougher trails, such as the hike to the top of **Wheeler Peak.**

Exploring the Park by Car

The **Wheeler Peak Scenic Drive** runs 12 miles one way. The road is paved, but steep (about an 8% grade) and winding, as it ascends over 3,000 feet from the visitor center, at 6,825 feet elevation, to the base of Wheeler Peak, at almost 10,000 feet. Along the way there are pullouts where you can stop for views of the Great Basin and Wheeler Peak. At the first pullout, a short walk brings you to the remnants of an 18-mile aqueduct built in 1890 to carry water from Lehman Creek. The road ends at Wheeler Peak Campground, where several hiking trails begin. The road is not recommended for large motor homes or vehicles pulling trailers, and it is usually closed by snow (except for the first 3 miles) from fall through spring.

Organized Tours & Ranger Programs

The only way to see **Lehman Cave** is on a guided tour led by a park naturalist, who points out the intricately decorated stalactites, stalagmites, draperies, and shields that have been formed by the oozing and dripping of water. Far smaller than Carlsbad Caverns in New Mexico, Lehman Cave can be seen easily and fairly quickly. Although Lehman lacks the vastness of Carlsbad, it makes up for that in the number of beautiful cave formations it squeezes into this small space. In addition, Lehman Cave possesses formations called shields, rarely seen in other caves. These consist of two roughly circular halves that look like flattened clam shells. Scientists have yet to agree on how the shields are formed.

Cave tours begin near the visitors center and are given daily year-round (call for schedules), except on Thanksgiving, Christmas, and New Year's Day. A part of the tour is accessible to those in wheelchairs, with assistance. All children under 16 must be accompanied by adults; and because the cave temperature averages 50° year-round, warm clothing is suggested. Allow 60 to 90 minutes for the 0.75-mile walk.

The tours cost $4 for adults 16 and older, $3 for youths from 6 to 15, $2 for those with Golden Age or Golden Access passports, and are free for children 5 and under. Tickets can be purchased by phone from 24 hours to 30 days in advance.

Although the park's main ranger-led activity is the Lehman Cave tour, during the summer rangers are also busy leading **guided nature walks and hikes,** and presenting other programs. These change each year, but recent programs have included a 1.4-mile hike (one way) to the bristlecone pine grove. Rangers usually present **short talks** several times daily at the visitor center, and **evening campfire programs** at Wheeler Peak and Upper Lehman campgrounds, with subjects such as the night sky, gold prospecting, and the area's bat population. **One-hour programs for children,** who must be accompanied by adults, have also been scheduled in recent years.

Historic & Man-Made Attractions

Throughout the park are reminders of the region's mining days, and along several of the trails you will see the ruins of miner's cabins, some mining equipment, and mine shafts and tunnels (which are dangerous and should not be entered). Just outside the visitor center is the historic **Rhodes Cabin,** which dates from the period from 1920 to 1932 when Clarence Rhodes and his wife owned the property. The cabin, constructed of Englemann spruce and white fir, was one of nine tourist cabins built in the 1920s, along with a log lodge, a dining room, dance hall, and a swimming tank. This particular cabin was rented to tourists until 1933, and from then until 1936 was used as the home of the national monument custodian and his family. It was then used for storage before being restored by the Park Service.

Day Hikes

There's a wide variety of trails here, ranging from easy walks to challenging, high-altitude hikes. Higher-elevation areas may be closed by snow from late October until mid-June, and afternoon thunderstorms are common during July and August. Exposed ridges should be avoided during lightning storms. Hikers should also be aware that they may be sharing trails with rattlesnakes, which have the right-of-way.

Because of loose rock and steep grades on some trails, sturdy hiking boots with good ankle support are recommended. Hikers also need to carry plenty of water—usually 1 gallon per person per day. Park rangers emphasize that although the rocky alpine sections of the park at its highest elevations may appear rugged, they are actually quite fragile. Plants grow slowly and even under the best of conditions their survival rate is low. Therefore, hikers should be diligent about staying on trails, and having the least impact possible on the land.

SHORTER TRAILS

Mountain View Nature Trail

0.4 mile RT. Easy. Access: Outside the visitor center.

This is an easy self-guided loop, with a brochure available at the visitor center that provides information on plants, animals, and geology. The short trail is popular among those with 20 to 30 minutes to wait before their guided cave tour.

Alpine Lakes Loop

3 miles RT. Easy. Access: The trailhead is just north of Wheeler Peak Campground.

With an elevation gain of only about 400 feet, this is a relatively easy and accessible trail, especially popular with families. The loop can be hiked in either direction, passing through forests of spruce and pine trees, as well as meadows dotted with colorful wildflowers. The lakes—Teresa and Stella—are shallow and clear, and the reflections of snowcapped peaks are often seen in their smooth surfaces.

Bristlecone Pine Forest Trail

4.6 miles RT. Easy. Access: The trailhead is near the Wheeler Peak Parking Lot.

Those who want to take a relatively easy hike through a unique forest will enjoy this trail. It goes through a grove of bristlecone pine trees up to 3,000 years old, and then on to a view of an ice field and what is believed to be a **rock glacier**—a rock-covered permanent mass of ice moving very slowly downhill. Distance to the bristlecone pine grove is 1.4 miles one way, and the ice field is another 0.9 mile. During summer, rangers often lead hikes to the bristlecone grove.

Lexington Arch

1.7 miles one way. Moderate. Access: Located about 18 miles south of the visitor center off a dirt road; ask park rangers for specific directions and current road conditions.

This **six-story arch** is a bit out of the way, but the splendidly framed views through the arch's 75-by-120-foot opening are an ample reward for the necessary effort. After driving into Utah and then following a dirt road, you will find yourself hiking a sunny, moderately rated trail that takes you past wildflowers, mountain mahogany, fir, and pinyon. The easy-to-follow trail ends at the arch, unique because it has been carved from limestone, not sandstone as is usually the case in the American West. Also, some geologists believe it is not really an arch at all, but a natural bridge; the difference being that arches are formed by wind, rain, and ice; while bridges are created by the erosional forces of streams and rivers.

LONGER TRAILS

Baker Creek Trail

6 miles one way. Moderate to difficult. Access: The trailhead is at the end of Baker Creek Rd.

Following Baker Creek, this trail leads to Baker Lake, climbing from about 8,000 feet elevation to over 10,500 feet. The trail passes through meadows and forests, past pinyon, juniper, aspen, and pine, changing with the elevation. This trail is a good choice for **wildlife viewing,** where you are likely to see mule deer, rock squirrels, and a variety of birds. Anglers often stop to catch a trout or two in the creek, and the trail provides excellent views of the surrounding mountain peaks. Along the way you pass the remains of a miner's log cabin, before reaching picturesque **Baker Lake.**

Johnson Lake Trail

3.6 miles one way. Moderate to difficult. Access: The trailhead is at the end of Snake Creek Rd.

This rugged trail follows an old mining road, with an elevation gain of about 1,000 feet, before arriving at Johnson Lake, named for Alfred Johnson, who mined and processed tungsten here in the early part of the 20th century. The Johnson Lake Trail can be combined with the Baker Creek Trail to produce a loop, starting with the Baker Creek Trail and descending along Snake Creek. Parts of this loop are difficult to follow, and topographical maps and good mountaineering skills are recommended.

Lehman Creek Trail

3.3 miles one way. Easy. Access: Connects Upper Lehman Creek Campground with Wheeler Peak Campground.

Although there is a 2,100-foot elevation change along this trail, it's an easy downhill walk for those who start at Wheeler Peak Campground and have a vehicle waiting at Lehman Creek Campground. The trail mostly follows a bluff above **Lehman Creek,** crossing through several separate life zones and offering views of a wide variety of plant life, from sagebrush and cactus to forests of aspen, spruce, pinyon, and tall Douglas fir. Along the way you will also see mountain mahogany, and if your timing's right, an abundance of wildflowers.

Wheeler Peak Summit Trail

8.6 miles RT (from campground). Difficult. Access: Begins at Summit Trailhead, about 0.5 mile from Wheeler Peak Campground, or from the campground via Alpine Lakes Loop Trail, which intersects with Summit Trail.

Those looking for absolutely stupendous panoramic vistas will want to consider hiking this strenuous trail, which begins as a relatively gentle walk through a forest of pine, becoming considerably steeper as it reaches the tree line, until, rather abruptly, you find yourself on the summit, at an elevation of 13,063 feet, the second-highest point in Nevada. During its 3,000-foot ascent to the summit, the trail passes through several plant communities, including forests of Englemann spruce and pine, before climbing above the tree line. This is generally an all-day hike, and rangers advise starting early so you're off the summit by the time afternoon thunderstorms appear. Hikers are also advised to carry plenty of drinking water, extra clothing, and rain gear.

Exploring the Backcountry

There are numerous opportunities for backcountry hiking in the park, but few maintained trails. The most commonly used routes follow river valleys or ridgelines. **Topographical maps,** available at the visitor center, are essential, and although backcountry permits are not required, rangers strongly recommend that those planning to go into the backcountry **register** and discuss their plans with park staff before setting out.

> **Night found us back at camp completely exhausted.**
>
> **—Surveyor George Wheeler, for whom Wheeler Peak was named, in July 1869, after climbing the peak twice in 2 days.**

Backcountry camping is permitted in most areas, although not within 0.25 mile of most trails, in bristlecone pine forests, or within 100 feet of a water source. Backcountry campers are encouraged to use backpacking stoves; campfires are permitted below 10,000 feet elevation only, and you can not burn dead and down bristlecone pine. Trash, including toilet paper, should be packed out, and human waste should be buried at least a half foot deep and no less than 100 feet from water sources. Pets and bikes are prohibited in the backcountry, but horses, llamas, and mules are allowed. Check with rangers for applicable regulations.

Other Sports & Activities

Biking. Although biking is permitted only on designated motor vehicle roads, the park has miles of dirt roads, many of which receive little traffic. Bikers should check with rangers about which roads are open and their current condition.

Educational Programs. The **Great Basin Natural History Association** (see "Getting Information Before Your Trip," above) presents a series of programs for both adults and children, such as field trips to sketch wildlife, spot and identify raptors and other birds, learn about the park's plants, or explore the area's human history. Kids' activities in recent years have included a Saturday afternoon nature and drawing adventure at a park campground. Most of the adult programs last 1 day and cost $25 to $40, while the children's activities last several hours and cost about $10.

Fishing. The park's small, clear mountain streams provide good but somewhat difficult fishing for rainbow trout. All anglers over 11 will need a Nevada fishing license and trout stamp, available in Baker.

Horseback Riding. Some of the maintained trails plus the backcountry trails

Especially for Kids

The Great Basin Junior Ranger Program, for kids between the ages of 8 and 13, includes ranger-guided activities plus a number of projects outlined in a workbook. These include tree identification, plants and animals of the park, weather, and human influences on the Great Basin. Youths who attend the ranger-led program and complete at least seven of the workbook activities on their own become Junior Rangers.

Families are invited to stop at the visitor center and borrow a **Family Adventure Pack,** which offers activity ideas and equipment, such as a hand lens, compass, string, and pencils. Rangers also lead various walks, hikes, and other activities that are suitable for children, including some specifically geared to kids.

are open to horseback riding; check with park rangers.

Wildlife Viewing. Almost every visitor to Great Basin National Park will see wildlife, whether it be some of the many mule deer that frequent the campgrounds, meadows, and creek sides; or birds such as the pinyon jays, western tanagers, and Clark's nutcrackers. Park visitors should also watch for golden eagles, bighorn sheep, bobcats, and small mammals including rock squirrels and wood rats.

Winter Sports

Although there are no designated cross-country ski trails here, once snow falls—sometimes as early as October—the park becomes a winter playground, especially at higher elevations. You can use cross-country skis or snowshoes on many of the trails and several roads, although it's best to talk with rangers about your plans before setting out so you can avoid trails that might be too steep for your ability. In lean snow years you may have to hike a bit from parking areas to skiable snow, but there's almost always plenty of snow at the higher elevations.

One favorite cross-country ski trip is up **Baker Creek Road,** which leads to Baker Creek Campground, and then on up the Baker Creek Trail for a while before heading back. Those particularly skilled and in good physical condition might ski the 4-mile trail from **Upper Lehman Creek Campground** up to **Wheeler Peak Campground.** The trail climbs about 2,100 feet. Although Wheeler Peak Campground is technically closed from about mid-October through mid-June, skiers are welcome to spend the night.

There are no snowshoe or cross-country ski rentals available in the park or nearby, so be sure to pack your own if you're planning a winter trip.

Camping

INSIDE THE PARK

The park has four developed campgrounds—Lower Lehman Creek, Upper Lehman Creek, Baker Creek, and Wheeler Peak—with a total of just over 100 sites. They have lots of trees, pit toilets, picnic tables, and campfire grills. Those with large RVs will want to arrive as early in the day as possible, since there are only a limited number of sites that can easily accommodate rigs over 25 feet.

One campground, Lower Lehman Creek, with 11 sites, is open year-round, while the others are open from spring through fall, weather permitting. Some campsites are accessible to those in wheelchairs. There are also some primitive campsites available along **Strawberry Creek** in the far northern reaches of the park, and along **Snake Creek** in the southern half of the park. These sites have tables and pit toilets, but no drinking water.

Campground	Elev.	Total Sites	RV Hookups	Dump Station	Toilets	Drinkin Water
Lower Lehman Creek	7,500	11	No	No	Yes	Yes
Upper Lehman Creek	7,800	24	No	No	Yes	Yes
Baker Creek	8,000	32	No	No	Yes	Yes
Wheeler Peak	9,950	37	No	No	Yes	Yes

Backcountry camping is also permitted; see the section "Exploring the Backcountry," above. The park has an RV dump station (near the visitor center) but no hookups or showers (see "Accommodations," below). The park's only public telephone is at the visitor center, which is not within walking distance of any campgrounds. All campsites are on a first come, first-served basis.

NEAR THE PARK

At this writing there were no commercial campgrounds that were open on a consistent basis in the immediate park vicinity. However, one former campground was reportedly for sale, and other area business people have expressed interest in opening campgrounds. Check with the park office for current information.

Accommodations

There are no lodging facilities inside the park, but the tiny community of Baker, 5 miles east of the park entrance, has several lodging and dining opportunities. Otherwise, park visitors will find services in Ely, Nevada, 70 miles west; and Delta, Utah, about 100 miles east. Among franchise properties in Ely is the **Ramada Inn–Copper Queen Casino,** 815 7th St., Ely, NV 89301 (☎ **702/289-4884**), which has rates of $55 to $74 for a double. Motels in Delta include the **Best Western Motor Inn,** 527 E. Topaz Blvd., Delta, UT 84624 (☎ **800/354-9378** or 435/864-3882), with rates for two of $59 to $69 from May through September and $49 to $59 from October through April. Both Ely and Delta also have a variety of restaurants, plus fuel, groceries, and camping supplies.

NEAR THE PARK

The Border Inn

U.S. 50/6 at the Nevada–Utah border, 13 miles northeast of the national park (P.O. Box 30, Baker, NV 89311). ☎ **702/234-7300.** 29 units. A/C TV TEL. $30–$40 double. AE, DISC, MC, V.

This comfortable motel has basic rooms and 12 kitchenette units in Utah, and a restaurant with a bar and slot machines a few feet away in Nevada. The wood-paneled rooms are simply but attractively furnished and contain either one queen bed, two doubles, or two twins. There is a coin-operated laundry, VCRs and videotape rentals for movie buffs, and gasoline and diesel fuel are available. Pets are accepted. Campers can also come here for hot showers. Also see "Dining," below.

Silver Jack Motel and Gift Shop

Downtown Baker, 5 miles east of the national park (P.O. Box 166, Baker, NV 89311). ☎ **702/234-7323;** fax 702/234-7114. 7 rms plus 1 mobile home. A/C TV. $35–$45 double; mobile home $60 for up to 4. DISC, MC, V. Closed mid-Nov through mid-Mar.

This well-maintained family owned and operated motel is the closest lodging to the national park. Basic motel rooms have either one or two double beds, and one unit has two double beds plus a twin

Showers	Fire Pits/ Grills	Laundry	Public Phone	Reserve	Fees	Open
No	**Yes**	**No**	**No**	**No**	**$5**	**Year-round**
No	**Yes**	**No**	**No**	**No**	**$5**	**May 15–Oct 15**
No	**Yes**	**No**	**No**	**No**	**$5**	**May 15–Sept 15**
No	**Yes**	**No**	**No**	**No**	**$5**	**June 15–Sept 15**

bed in a separate room. Some units have shower-tub combinations, while others have showers only. There is an attractive patio with a fountain where guests sit, chat, and watch the hummingbirds. Animal-lovers will be pleased to know that pets are welcome. The attached gift shop offers local art and high-quality crafts, and the town's two restaurants (see below) are across the street. The separate mobile home, which has two bedrooms, a fully equipped kitchen, and a living room, is parked several blocks away.

Dining

INSIDE THE PARK

The only services in the park are the visitor center's cafe and gift shop, which are open from early April through October. Your choices here include light breakfasts, lunches, and snack items, along with the usual postcards and souvenirs plus American Indian crafts.

NEAR THE PARK

The Border Inn

U.S. 50/6 at the Nevada–Utah border, 13 miles northeast of the national park. ☎ **702/234-7300.** Breakfast and lunch $1.95–$5.95; full dinners $6.45–$10.95. AE, DISC, MC, V. Kitchen open daily 6am–10pm; bar open daily 24 hrs. Closed Christmas Day. AMERICAN.

Good burgers and chicken-fried steak are served at this roadside restaurant, which also specializes in homemade soups and baked items. Mexican food specials are the featured Friday night, and breakfast is usually available as long as the kitchen is open. There is also a children's menu. The room is large and open, with a bar along one side. There are also slot machines, video games, a pool table, a gift shop, a convenience store, an ATM, and a gas station with diesel fuel.

The Outlaw

Downtown Baker. ☎ **702/234-7302.** Breakfast $2.25–$4.95; lunch $3.95–$6.95; dinner $4.75–$18.95. DISC, MC, V. Summer daily 6am–9pm; bar open later. Winter hrs. shorter and may close for a couple of months in winter. AMERICAN.

The name conjures up an image of a rough Western bar, and the bar and pool table add to the decidedly Wild West saloon atmosphere. But this is actually a friendly family place, considered "Baker's living room," where locals come to sip coffee or beer and discuss the events of the day. Known for its hand-cut charbroiled steaks, The Outlaw wins over vegetarians as well with a garden burger and a garden dinner. It also serves pastas, ground buffalo steaks, baby-back ribs, and homemade burritos—and everything is made from scratch. A popular breakfast dish is The Scramble, which includes fried potatoes, onions, mild green chile, scrambled eggs, and cheddar cheese, with salsa on the side. The restaurant offers a children's menu. In addition to the pool table, you can try your luck on the slot machines or the video games.

T&D's Country Store & Restaurant

Corner of Elko and Main, downtown Baker. ☎ **702/234-7264.** Sandwiches and meals $2.25–$5.95; large pizzas $9.10–$15.10. AE, DISC, MC, V. Restaurant Sun–Thurs 11:30am–9pm, Fri–Sat 11:30am–10pm; store daily 8am–7pm. AMERICAN.

The restaurant is located in a bright and cheery sunroom attached to the small grocery store. It's known for its pizzas and deli sandwiches, but also serves burgers, steak sandwiches, pita sandwiches, and several more elaborate meals, including barbecued ribs and an Oriental chicken salad. There is a full bar, with several beers on tap, and a surprisingly good stock of wines available by the glass. There is also a large-screen TV, and plans were underway to add a separate sports bar. You can get your food items to go, and there is a full liquor store, gasoline and propane, videotape rentals, camping and fishing gear, plus hunting and fishing licenses.

Picnic & Camping Supplies

In addition to the snacks available at the cafe and gift shop in the park, you can find take-out food, ice, and packaged liquor at **The Outlaw.** Also in downtown Baker, **T&D's Country Store & Restaurant** has a good selection of groceries, plus ice, packaged liquor, camping and fishing supplies, hunting and fishing licenses, gasoline, and propane. At **The Border Inn,** along U.S. 50/6 at the Nevada–Utah border, there's a small convenience store, a 24-hour gas station with diesel fuel, a gift shop, and an ATM. All three properties are listed above.

21

GUADALUPE MOUNTAINS NATIONAL PARK

by Don and Barbara Laine

ONCE A LONG REEF POKING UP THROUGH THE OCEAN, THEN A DENSE forest, Guadalupe Mountains National Park is today a rugged wilderness of tall Douglas firs and lush vegetation rising out of a vast desert. Here you will find varied hiking trails, panoramic vistas, the highest peak in the state, plant and animal life unique in the Southwest, and a canyon that many believe is the prettiest spot in all of Texas.

As you approach from the north, the mountains seem to rise gradually from the landscape, but soon from the south they stand tall and dignified. El Capitan, the southern tip of the reef escarpment, watches over a sea of sand like a sentinel. In the south-central section of the park, Guadalupe Peak, at 8,749 feet the highest mountain in Texas, provides hikers with incredible views of the surrounding mountains and desert.

The 86,416-acre park has several separate sections. Park headquarters and the visitor center are at Pine Springs, along the park's southeast edge, where you'll also find a developed vehicle campground and several major trailheads, including one with access to the Guadalupe Peak Trail, the park's premier mountain hike. Nearby, a short dirt road leads to historic Frijole Ranch, with a museum and several trailheads. A horse corral is nearby. The McKittrick Canyon section of the park, near its northeast corner, may be the most beautiful spot in Texas, especially in fall, when its oaks, maples, and other trees produce a spectacular show of color unequaled in the Southwest. A day-use area only, McKittrick Canyon has a delightful stream, a wide variety of plant and animal life, several trailheads, and historic buildings. Along the park's northern boundary, practically in New Mexico, is the secluded and forested Dog Canyon.

Particularly impressive about Guadalupe Mountains National Park is its vast variety of flora and fauna. You'll find species here that don't seem to belong in west Texas, such as the maple and oak that produce the wonderful fall colors in McKittrick Canyon. Scientists say these seemingly out-of-place plants and animals are leftovers from a time when this region was cooler and wetter. As the climate changed and the desert spread, some species were able to survive in these mountains, where conditions remained somewhat cooler and more moist. At the base of the mountains, at

Tips from a Park Ranger

"This is essentially a hiking park," says Rich McCamant, the park's chief of interpretation and visitor services. He says the park's two main attractions, which he recommends to all visitors, are the hike to the top of Guadalupe Peak (Texas's highest mountain) and the colors in McKittrick Canyon, either the trees in fall or the wildflowers in spring.

McCamant says that those without the time or desire to hike the strenuous Guadalupe Peak Trail should consider hiking the moderately rated Smith Springs Loop Trail or Devil's Hall Trail.

"This is a park you can visit almost any time of year and have a good experience," McCamant says, although he adds that many consider October to have the best weather, while spring can be windy.

McCamant says there are five species of rattlesnakes in the park, but visitors probably won't see any, and in the history of the park there have been no reported rattlesnake bites. "The biggest threat here is the sun," he says. "Hikers really need to carry a gallon of water per day, and drink it."

He also warns that because many of the trails have a lot of loose rock, good hiking boots are essential. The other thing he wants park visitors to keep in mind is that there is no gasoline or other services close to the park, so they should bring plenty of fuel and everything else they might want.

lower elevations, you'll find desert plants such as sotol, agave, and prickly pear and other cacti; but as you start to climb, especially in stream-nurtured canyons, expect to encounter ponderosa pine, ash, walnut, oak, willows, and ferns. Numerous species of animals abound, include mule deer, elk, and all sorts of birds and snakes.

Avoiding the Crowds. Overall, Guadalupe Mountains National Park is one of America's lesser-visited national parks, with attendance of only about 225,000 each year. This is partly because it is primarily a wilderness park, where you'll have to tackle rugged hiking trails to get to the best vistas. But it's also out of the way and somewhat inconvenient—the closest lodging is 35 miles away from the park's main section. In fact, about the only time the park might be considered even slightly crowded is during spring break time at Texas and New Mexico colleges, usually in March, when students bring their backpacks and hit the trails. There are also quite a few families visiting during summer, although the park is not usually crowded even then, and visitation drops considerably once schools open in late August.

An exception is the **McKittrick Canyon** section of the park, renowned throughout the Southwest for its beautiful fall colors, at their best in late October and early November. The one road into McKittrick Canyon will be a bit busy then, but once you get on the trails you can usually walk away from the people.

Just the Facts

GETTING THERE & GATEWAYS

Located on the border of New Mexico and Texas, Guadalupe Mountains National Park is 55 miles southwest of Carlsbad, New Mexico, along U.S. 62/180. From Albuquerque drive east on I-40 for 59 miles to Clines Corners, and turn south on U.S. 285 for 216 miles to the city of Carlsbad, then head southwest 55 miles on U.S. 62/180 to the park entrance at Pine Springs. From El Paso

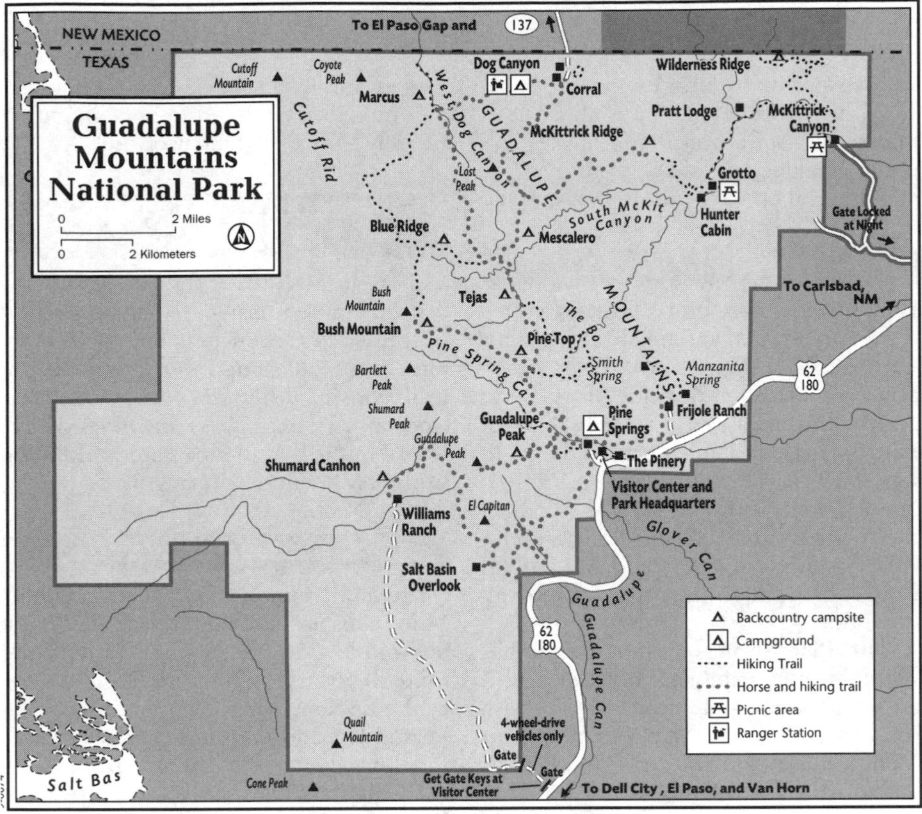

drive northeast 110 miles on U.S. 62/180 to Pine Springs.

The Nearest Airport. Air travelers can fly to **Cavern City Air Terminal** (☎ **505/885-5236**), 4 miles south of the city of Carlsbad, which has commercial service from Albuquerque. Taxi service is available at the airport, but there are no shuttle buses to the park.

The nearest major airport is **El Paso International** (☎ **915/772-4271**) in central El Paso just off I-10, with service from **American, America West, Continental, Delta, Southwest, Frontier,** and **Aero Litoral** (☎ 800/237-6639).

Renting a Car. Car-rental agencies at the El Paso airport include **Advantage, Alamo, Avis, Budget, Dollar, Hertz,** and **National.**

Toll-free reservations numbers for all the airlines and car-rental agencies listed in this section are given in the appendix.

GETTING INFORMATION BEFORE YOUR TRIP

For advance information contact the **Superintendent, Guadalupe Mountains National Park,** HC 60, Box 400, Salt Flat, TX 79847-9400 (☎ **915/828-3251;** fax 915/828-3269). The park's Web site is **www.nps.gov/gumo**. Books and maps can be ordered in preparation for your trip from the **Carlsbad Caverns–Guadalupe Mountains Association** P.O. Box 1417, Carlsbad, NM 88221-1417; (☎ **505/785-2232,** ext. 481). The association's Web site is www.caverns.com/~ccgma. An annual family membership in the nonprofit association costs $25, and provides a 15% discount at the bookstores at Guadalupe Mountains and Carlsbad Caverns national parks, plus at bookstores in many other national parks.

Those arriving in the city of Carlsbad before going to the park can get a variety of brochures, maps, and other information at the **National Park**

Service's administrative office and bookstore, at 3225 National Parks Hwy. (at its intersection with West Pecan Street). It's open Monday to Friday from 8am to 4:30pm, and on weekends in the summer.

VISITOR CENTERS

Park headquarters and the main visitor center are located at Pine Springs just off U.S. 62/180. There are three other access points along this side of the park: Frijole Ranch, about 1.5 miles east of Pine Spring and a mile north of the highway; McKittrick Canyon (day use only), about 7 miles east and 4 miles north of the highway; and Williams Ranch, about 8 miles south of Pine Spring and 8 miles north of the highway on a four-wheel-drive road.

The **Pine Springs Visitor Center** has natural history exhibits, a bookstore, and an introductory slide program. The visitor center is open 8am to 6pm from Memorial Day to Labor Day, and 8am to 4:30pm the rest of the year. It's closed Christmas Day.

McKittrick Canyon has a visitor contact station with outdoor exhibits and an outdoor slide program on the history, geology, and natural history of the canyon. The entrance gate opens at 8am daily, and closes at 4:30pm mountain standard time and at 6pm mountain daylight time.

On the north side of the park is **Dog Canyon Ranger Station,** at the end of N. Mex. 137, about 70 miles from Carlsbad and 110 miles from park headquarters. Information, rest rooms, and drinking water are available.

ENTRANCE & CAMPING FEES

Entry into the park is free. Camping costs $7 per individual site; group sites cost $2 per person with a 10-person minimum. Backcountry camping is also free, but a permit is required. Corrals are available for those who bring their horses to ride in the park; although use is free, permits are required. All permits are available at the Pine Springs Visitor Center and Dog Canyon Ranger Station, and must be requested in person, either the day before or the day of use.

SPECIAL REGULATIONS & WARNINGS

Visitors to McKittrick Canyon must stay on the trail; entering the stream is not permitted. Leashed pets are allowed in auto-accessible campgrounds but not on trails or in the backcountry. Neither wood nor charcoal fires are allowed anywhere in the park. Horses are prohibited in the backcountry overnight.

SEASONS & CLIMATE

In general, summers in the Guadalupe Mountains are hot (highs in the 80s and 90s and lows in the 60s) and winters are mild (highs in the 50s and 60s and lows in the upper 20s and 30s), but there can be sudden and extreme changes in the weather at any season. In spring and early summer, high winds can whip down the mountain slopes, sometimes reaching 100 m.p.h.; on hot summer days, thunderstorms can blow up quickly. The sun is warm even in winter, and summer nights are generally cool no matter how hot the afternoon. Clothing that can be layered is best, comfortable and sturdy walking/hiking shoes are a must, a hat and sunscreen are highly recommended, and plenty of drinking water is essential for hikers.

SEASONAL EVENTS

McKittrick Canyon's beautiful display of fall colors usually takes place between early October and mid-November. It varies, however, so call before going.

USEFUL PUBLICATIONS

Because the park's backcountry trails often crisscross each other and can be confusing, rangers strongly recommend that those planning any serious hiking bring topographical maps. An excellent book for hikers is ***Hiking Carlsbad***

Caverns and Guadalupe Mountains National Parks (Helena, Mont.: Falcon Press, 1996) by Bill Schneider, which was published in partnership with the Carlsbad Caverns–Guadalupe Mountains Association and is keyed to the Trails Illustrated topographical map of the park. Also very useful is a shorter and less expensive trail guide, ***Trails of the Guadalupes*** (Champagne, Ill.: Environmental Associates, 1992), by Don Kurtz and William D. Goran. These are available at the visitor center's bookstore or from the **Carlsbad Caverns–Guadalupe Mountains Association** (see the "Getting Information Before Your Trip" section, above).

A small seasonal publication, ***The Capitan Reef,*** contains pertinent up-to-the-minute information for visitors. It is available free at the visitor center.

Seeing the Highlights in a Day

This park is best experienced—*explored* would be a better word—over a period of 2 or 3 days, with at least 1 day devoted to the visitor center, historic attractions, and trails in the Pine Springs section; and another full day allotted to an exploration of McKittrick Canyon. Those with additional time could then head over to the park's third section, Dog Canyon.

Those who have only 1 day, however, can still see quite a bit, but they need to make a decision: Pine Springs or McKittrick Canyon?—there won't be time for both. If it's fall and the colors are right, drive to the **McKittrick Canyon Visitor Contact Station,** look at the exhibits, and hike the **McKittrick Canyon Trail** to the historic **Pratt Lodge.** If it's not fall, or if you don't care about fall colors, drive directly to the **Pine Springs Visitor Center**, see the exhibits, and hike one of the trails—the **Guadalupe Peak Trail** for the ambitious or the **Devil's Hall Trail** for those who prefer less physical exertion. If you've got 2 days, then do McKittrick Canyon on the first day, then drive to the Pine Springs Campground and attend the campfire program, and the next day hike a trail and explore the visitor center's exhibits.

Exploring the Park by Car

Guadalupe Mountains is not a good park for the vehicle-bound. There are no paved scenic drives traversing the park; roads here are simply means of getting to historical sites and trailheads.

Organized Tours & Ranger Programs

On summer evenings, rangers offer programs at the campground amphitheater. There are also frequent showings of geology videos daily at the visitor center.

Historic & Man-Made Attractions

The Pinery was one of 200 stations along the 2,800-mile Butterfield Overland Mail Coach Route. The stations could provide a fresh mule team every 20 miles and a new coach every 300 miles, in order to maintain the grueling speed of 5 miles an hour 24 hours a day. John Butterfield had seen the need for overland mail delivery between the eastern states and the West Coast, so he designed a route and the coaches and acquired a federal contract to deliver the St. Louis mail to San Francisco in 25 days. In March 1857 this was a real feat. The Pinery commemorates his achievement.

Named for nearby stands of pine, the Pinery had abundant water and good grazing. It was a high-walled rock enclosure with a wagon repair shop, blacksmith shop, corral for fresh horses and mules, and three mud-roofed rooms where passengers could get a warm meal, if they had time, and stretch their legs a bit. The first mail coach came through on September 28, 1858. Use continued for 11 months until August 1859, when this route was abandoned for a new road that better served the West's military forts.

Located in McKittrick Canyon, **Pratt Lodge** was built by Wallace E. Pratt in 1931–32, of stone quarried from the base of the Guadalupe Mountains, using heart-of-pine from east Texas for rafters, collar beams, and roof supports. Pratt, a geologist for the Humble Oil Co. (now Exxon), and his family came for summer vacations when the heat in Houston became unbearable. He finally retired here in 1945. Soon after, he and his family built a second house, Ship on the Desert, outside the canyon. In 1957, the Pratts donated 5,632 acres of their 16,000-acre ranch to the federal government to begin the national park. In addition to the grand stone lodge, there are several outbuildings, stone picnic tables, and a wonderful stone fence.

Williams Ranch house rests at the base of a 3,000-foot rock cliff on the west face of the Guadalupe Mountains. The 7.3-mile access road, navigable only by high-clearance 4X4s, follows part of the old Butterfield Overland Mail Route for about 2 miles. The road crosses private land and has two locked metal gates, for which you must sign out keys at the visitor center.

History is unclear on exactly who built the house and when, but it's believed to have been built around 1908, and it is fairly certain that the first inhabitants for any significant period of time were Henry and Rena Belcher. For almost 10 years, they maintained a substantial ranch here, at times with close to 3,000 head of longhorn cattle. Water was piped from Bone Spring down the canyon to holding tanks in the lowlands. James Adolphus Williams then acquired the property around 1917, and with the help of an Indian friend, ranched and farmed the land until moving to New Mexico in 1941. After Williams' death in 1942, Judge J.C. Hunter bought the property, adding it to his already large holdings in the Guadalupes.

Another historic site is **Frijole Ranch,** which was a working ranch from when it was built in the 1870s up until 1972. Inside the ranch house is a museum with exhibits on the cultural history of the Guadalupe Mountains, including prehistoric Indians, the later Mescalero Apaches, Spanish conquistadors, and ranchers of the 19th and 20th centuries. On the grounds are several historic buildings, including a schoolhouse.

Day Hikes

This is a prime hiker's park, with more than 80 miles of trails that range from easy walks to steep, strenuous, and sometimes treacherous adventures.

SHORTER TRAILS

Indian Meadow Nature Trail

0.6 mile RT. Easy. Access: Dog Canyon Campground, walk south from the water fountain.

This exceptionally easy stroll follows a series of numbered stops keyed to a free brochure, available at the trailhead. You'll learn about the native vegetation and cultural history of the area as you ramble along this virtually level dirt trail. The name comes from early settlers, who told of seeing Indian teepees in this lovely meadow.

McKittrick Canyon Nature Trail

0.9 mile RT. Easy. Access: McKittrick Canyon Visitor Center.

An ideal way to discover the variety of plants and animals that inhabit the canyon, this easy trail takes off to the left just past the visitor contact station. Read the numerous interpretive signs along the path, telling you all you wanted to know about, for example, why rattlesnakes are underappreciated and how the cactus supplies food and water to the environment.

Pinery Trail

0.75 mile RT. Easy. Access: The trailhead is in front of Pine Springs Visitor Center; or from parking area on U.S. 62/180, located 1 mile north of the park entrance road.

A paved trail, accessible by wheelchair, the Pinery Trail gives visitors a brief introduction to the low-elevation environment at the park. The interpretive signs discuss both the plants along the trail and the history of the area. About 0.25 mile from the visitor center the trail makes a loop around the ruins of an old horse-changing station, left over from the Butterfield Stage Route (see "Historic & Man-Made Attractions," above).

Smith Spring Loop

2.3 miles RT. Easy to moderate. Access: The trailhead for the counterclockwise direction is at the north edge of the Frijole Ranch and Museum.

The Smith Spring Loop begins in the dry desert and climbs 440 feet to the lush oasis of Smith Spring. The first part of the trail, which takes you to Manzanita Spring, is very easy and navigable by people with mobility impairments. If you take this walk in the evening, you might catch a glimpse of an elk, deer, or other wildlife coming to the spring for water. After Manzanita Spring, the trail begins the climb to Smith Spring, following a good example of a desert riverside zone along Smith Canyon. Look for the damage caused by a lightning fire in 1990, and observe the difficulty the desert environment has in repairing it. Smith Spring itself is a magnificent oasis, with enough water seeping out to form a waterfall and stream. Here you'll find maidenhair fern, bigtooth maple, chinquapin oak, and Texas madrone—all in the middle of the Chihuahuan Desert. Although lush, the area is fragile, so please remain in the designated area to preserve the ecosystem.

LONGER TRAILS

El Capitan Trail

9.4 miles one way. Moderate. Access: Williams Ranch.

This trail climbs over 1,500 feet and takes a full day to complete, plus the drive to Williams Ranch (requiring a four-wheel-drive vehicle; see "Historic & Man-Made Attractions," above). This is the only trail into the remote western part of the Guadalupe Mountains. The incredible scenery along the first 2 miles more than makes up for the long, slow climb up Shumard Canyon, a gain of over 1,300 feet. Stop occasionally to look back down the canyon to the west, and ahead toward Shumard Peak and the impressive escarpment of the Guadalupes. After Shumard Canyon the hike takes you 3 miles around El Capitan, keeping in the shadow of the escarpment and climbing another 200 feet. From some places you can look down to the highway below. After about 5 miles, the Salt Basin Overlook loop takes off to the right, and you stay to the left, gradually dropping down into Guadalupe Canyon, where you meet the other end of the lower Salt Basin Overlook loop. From here the last 3.4 miles of the trail is fairly easy, level walking to Pine Springs. The trail can also be hiked out and back from Pine Springs, an arduous 18.8-mile overnight hike, which is why most hikers get a lift from friends to the ranch and hike back to Pine Springs.

Guadalupe Peak Trail

4.2 miles one way. Difficult. Access: Pine Springs Campground.

This trail is strenuous, climbing almost 3,000 feet, but the views from the 8,749-foot high Guadalupe Peak are magnificent. The peak is the highest in the park and in all the state of Texas. If you have only 1 day to explore this park, and you are an average or better hiker, this is the hike you should choose. Start early, take plenty of water, and be prepared to work. When you've gone about halfway, you'll see what seems to be the top not too far ahead, but beware: This is a false summit. Study the changing life zones as you climb from the desert into the higher-elevation pine forests—this will take your mind off your straining muscles and aching lungs. A mile short of the summit, a campground lies in one of the rare level spots on the mountain. If you plan to spend the night, anchor your tent strongly since the winds can be ferocious up here, especially in spring.

From the summit, the views are stupendous. To the north are Bush Mountain and Shumard Peak, the next two highest points in Texas, with respective elevations of 8,631 and 8,615 feet. The Chihuahuan Desert stretches to the south, interrupted only by the Delaware and Sierra Diablo mountains. This is one of those "On a clear day you can see forever" spots—sometimes all the way to 12,003-foot-high Sierra Blanca, near Ruidoso, New Mexico, 100 miles north.

Lost Peak

3 miles one way. Moderate. Access: Dog Canyon Trailhead.

A moderate hike you can probably complete in a half day, Lost Peak is especially good near dawn or dusk when wild turkey, deer, and other wildlife are often seen. A lightning-caused fire scorched the area in 1994, and although many plants have been diligently recovering, the loss of the tall trees will be felt for a long time. After leaving the trailhead, follow the Tejas Trail up Dog Canyon on a gradual climb for about 1.5 miles. Just before reaching Dog Canyon Springs, the trail starts switchbacking up the west side of the canyon to a ridgeline, offering great views back to the campground. If you continue all the way to the peak, the next 1.5 miles climbs about 1,100 feet, the steepest section of the trail. There's no sign for the peak and it's easy to hike on by, so watch your topographical map carefully—the peak is just a bit to the right of the trail. After scrambling up to the summit for a panoramic view, head back down the trail. The total elevation change is 1,420 feet.

McKittrick Canyon

5.1 miles one way. Moderate to difficult. Access: McKittrick Canyon Trailhead.

McKittrick Canyon is one of the most famous scenic areas in Texas, and this trail explores the length of it. The first 2.3 miles to the Pratt Lodge are easy; the following 1.2 miles to the Grotto gain 340 feet in elevation and are considered moderate; and the final strenuous climb to the Notch rises 1300 feet in 1.6 miles. Even so, this is one of the most popular hikes in the park, though not everyone makes it to the Notch.

The canyon is forested with conifers and deciduous trees. In fall the maples, oaks, and other hardwoods burst into color, painting the world in bright colors set off by the rich variety of the evergreens. The stream in the canyon, which appears and disappears several times in the first 3 miles of the trail, is a unique, permanent desert stream, with reproducing trout. Hikers may not drink from, wade in, or disturb the stream in any way.

The first part of the trail is wide and seems quite flat, crossing the stream twice on its way to Pratt Lodge, which is wonderfully situated at the convergence of North and South McKittrick canyons. About a mile from the lodge a short spur veers off to the left to the Grotto, a recess with odd formations that look like they belong underground in a cave. This is a great spot for lunch at one of the stone picnic tables. Continuing down the spur trail to its end, you reach the Hunter Line Cabin, which served as temporary quarters for ranch hands of the Hunter family. Beyond the cabin, South McKittrick Canyon has been preserved as a Research Natural Area with no entry. Return to the main trail and continue toward the Notch, or head back down the canyon to your car. In another 0.5 mile, the trail begins switchbacking up the side of South McKittrick Canyon for the steepest ascent in the park, until it slips through the Notch, a distinctive narrow spot in the cliff. Sit down and rest while you absorb the incredible scenery. The view down the canyon is magnificent, and quite dazzling in autumn. You can see both Hunter Line Cabin and Pratt Lodge in the distance. Remember to start down in time to reach your car well before the gate closes.

Exploring the Backcountry

A variety of possibilities exist for backpacking. It's always best to discuss your plans with rangers before heading out into the backcountry, to find out about current trail conditions and to decide on the trail or combination of trails you want to take. The free backcountry campsite permits should be obtained no more than 24 hours in advance at the Pine Springs Visitor Center or Dog Canyon Ranger Station. Also, see "Camping," below.

The Bowl

13-mile loop. Difficult. Access: Pine Springs Campground.

This hike climbs 2,546 feet in elevation if you go to the top of Hunter Peak. Primarily an overnight hike, you'll camp either at Pine Top, about 4.2 miles down the trail and a bit off it to the left, or at Tejas Campsite about 5.5 miles along. The trail crosses a dry wash, follows the Tejas Trail up a hill, has a fairly level stretch, and then starts the climb up to Pine Top, rising 2,000 feet over 3 miles of switchbacks. The view from the top of the escarpment is breathtaking, so stop and rest a minute. The trail then continues through a magnificent pine forest—watch for elk along the way. There are some old water tanks and a pipe running along the trail in spots, left over from a water system used by ranchers years ago. You can take a side trip to the top of Hunter Peak for another incredible view before heading back down.

Other Sports & Activities

Horseback Riding. About 60% of the park's trails are open to horses for day trips, although horses are not permitted in the backcountry overnight. There are **corrals** at Frijole Ranch (near Pine Springs) and Dog Canyon (see "Entrance & Camping Fees," above). Each set of corrals contains four pens that can accommodate up to 10 horses. There are no horses or other pack animals available for hire in or near the park. Park rangers warn that horses brought into the park should be accustomed to steep, rocky trails.

Rock Climbing. Although climbing on the cliffs is permitted (a permit is required for all technical climbing), it is not recommended, as rangers say the rock is unstable. Contact rangers for additional information.

Wildlife Viewing & Bird Watching. Because of the variety of habitats here, and also because these canyons offer some of the few water sources in west Texas, Guadalupe Mountains National Park offers excellent wildlife viewing and bird-watching possibilities. **McKittrick Canyon** is considered among the best wildlife viewing spots, but a variety of species can be seen throughout the park. Those spending more than a few hours in the park will very likely see mule deer, and the park is also home to a herd of some 50 to 70 elk, which are sometimes seen in the higher elevations or along the highway in winter. Other **mammals** include raccoons, striped and hog-nosed skunks, gray foxes, coyotes, gray-footed chipmunks, Texas antelope squirrels, black-tailed jackrabbits, and desert cottontails. Bats are often spotted in the caves along the limestone cliffs in McKittrick canyon. Black bears and mountain lions are also known to live in the park, but are seldom seen.

About two dozen varieties of **snakes** make their home in the park, including five species of rattlesnakes. There are also numerous **lizards,** which are usually seen in the mornings and early evenings. These include the collared, crevice spiny, tree, side-blotched, Texas horned, mountain short-horned, and marbled whiptail. The most commonly seen is the prairie lizard, which is identified by the light-colored stripes down its back.

More than 200 species of **birds** are known to spend time in the park, including peregrine falcons, golden eagles,

Campground	Elev.	Total Sites	RV Hookups	Dump Station	Toilets	Drinking Water
Pine Springs	5,840	39	0	No	Yes	Yes
Dog Canyon	6,320	13	0	No	Yes	Yes
Carlsbad RV Park & Campground	3,110	136	95	Yes	Yes	Yes
Brantley Lake State Park	3,300	51+	51	Yes	Yes	Yes
White's City RV Park	3630	80+	80	No	Yes	Yes

turkey vultures, and wild turkeys. You are also likely to encounter rock wrens, canyon wrens, black-throated sparrows, common nighthawks, mourning doves, rufous-crowned sparrows, mountain chickadees, ladder-backed woodpeckers, solitary vireos, and western scrub jays.

Camping

INSIDE THE PARK

There are two developed vehicle-accessible campgrounds in the park. **Pine Springs Campground** is near the visitor center and park headquarters just off U.S. 62/180. There are 18 spaces for RVs (no hookups), one wheelchair-accessible site, 20 very attractive tent sites, and two group campsites. There is usually a campground host on duty. About 0.5 mile inside the north boundary of the park is **Dog Canyon Campground,** accessible from N. Mex. 137. Here there are nine tent sites and four RV sites (no hookups). Although reservations are not accepted, you can call ahead to check on availability of sites (☎ **915/828-3251**). Camp stoves are allowed, but wood and charcoal fires are prohibited.

The park also has 10 designated backcountry campgrounds, with from two to eight sites each. Be sure to pick up free permits at the Pine Springs Visitor Center or Dog Canyon Ranger Station the day of or the day before your backpacking trip. There is no drinking water available in the backcountry, and all trash, including toilet paper, must be packed out. Fires are strictly prohibited; use cookstoves only. You can only camp in designated campgrounds.

NEAR THE PARK

Nearby, you'll find commercial camping at **White's City RV Park** in White's City, and **Carlsbad RV Park** and **Brantley Lake State Park** in Carlsbad. For descriptions and information on these campgrounds, see "Camping" in chapter 10.

Accommodations

There are no accommodations within the park. The nearest are 35 miles northeast at **White's City,** New Mexico, and 55 miles northeast in Carlsbad, New Mexico. For more information on lodging in these locations, see "Accommodations" in chapter 10.

Dining

There are no restaurants within the park. Once again, the nearest dining possibilities are in **White's City,** New Mexico, 35 miles from the park, and in and near the city of **Carlsbad,** New Mexico, 55 miles from the park. For more information on restaurants in White's City and Carlsbad, see "Dining" in chapter 10.

Showers	Fire Pits/ Grills	Laundry	Public Phone	Reserve	Fees	Open
No	No	No	No	No	$7	Year-round
No	No	No	No	No	$7	Year-round
Yes	Yes	Yes	Yes	Yes	$15–$19	Year-round
Yes	Yes	No	Yes	No	$7–$11	Year-round
Yes	Yes	Yes	Yes	Yes	$15–$20	Year-round

Picnic & Camping Supplies

The closest grocery store to the national park is the convenience store located at the Texaco gas station in the **White's City complex,** at the intersection of U.S. 62/180 and N. Mex. 7, about 35 miles from the visitor center. You'll find a good variety of stores in the city of Carlsbad, including an **Albertson's** grocery store at 808 N. Canal St., at its intersection with West Church Street (☎ **505/885-2161**), which has a well-stocked deli and bakery, and is open daily 6am to 11pm.

22

JOSHUA TREE NATIONAL PARK

by Stephanie Avnet

At Joshua Tree National Park, the trees themselves are merely the starting point for exploring the seemingly barren desert. Viewed from the roadside, the dry land only hints at hidden vitality, but closer examination reveals a giant mosaic of intense beauty and complexity. From lush oases teeming with life to rusted-out relics of man's attempts to tame the wilderness, from low plains of tufted cacti to mountains of exposed, twisted rock, the park is much more than a tableau of the curious tree for which it's named.

The Joshua tree is said to have been given its name by early Mormon settlers traveling west, for its upraised limbs and bearded appearance reminded them of the prophet Joshua leading them to the promised land. It's not really a tree, though, but a variety of yucca, a member of the lily family.

Joshua Tree National Park's name is fitting, for here the peculiar tree reaches the southernmost boundary of its range. The park straddles two desert environments: First is the mountainous, Joshua tree–studded Mojave Desert forming the northwestern part of the park. Hotter, drier, lower, and characterized by a wide variety of desert flora like cacti, cottonwood, and native California fan palms, the Colorado Desert comprises the park's southern and eastern sections. Between them runs the "transition zone," displaying characteristics of each.

The area's geological timeline is fascinating, stretching back 8 million years to a time when the Mojave landscape was one of rolling hills and flourishing grasslands; horses, camels, and mastodons abounded, preyed on by saber-toothed tigers and wild dogs. Displays at the Oasis Visitor Center show how resulting climatic, volcanic, and tectonic activity have created the park's signature cliffs and boulders and turned Joshua tree into the arid desert you see today. Human presence has been traced back nearly 10,000 years with the discovery of Pinto Man, and you can see evidence of more recent habitation in the form of Native American pictographs carved into rock faces throughout the park. Miners and ranchers began coming in the 1860s, but the boom went bust by the turn of the 20th century. Then a Pasadena doctor, treating World War I veterans suffering from respiratory and heart ailments caused by mustard gas, prescribed the desert's clean, dry air—and modern interest in the area was born.

During the 1920s, a worldwide fascination with the desert emerged, and cactus gardens were much in vogue. Entrepreneurs hauled truckloads of desert plants into Los Angeles for quick sale or export, and souvenir hunters removed archaeological treasures. Incensed that the beautiful Mojave was in danger of being picked clean, Los Angeles socialite Minerva Hoyt organized the desert conservation movement and successfully lobbied for the establishment of Joshua Tree National Monument in 1936.

In 1994, under provisions of the federal California Desert Protection Act, Joshua Tree was "upgraded" to national park status and expanded to nearly 800,000 acres.

Flora. The eastern half of the park is mainly the lower Colorado Desert, dominated by the abundant and fragrant **creosote** bush, a drought-resistant survivor that even releases secretions into the surrounding soil to kill competing seedlings. Adding interest to the arid land are small stands of spidery, tenacious **ocotillo,** a split personality that drops its leaves in times of drought, appearing dry and spindly. But the ocotillo can sprout bushy leaves in a few days when the rains come, and its flaming blooms atop leafy green branches bear little resemblance to its dormant alter ego.

Most people associate desert plants with cacti, which are indeed here in abundance. One of the more unusual members of the cactus family is the **Bigelow cholla cactus** ("teddy bear" and "jumping" cactus). Cholla's fine needles appear soft and fluffy from afar, but anyone who has accidentally gotten a clump stuck to his or her skin or clothing knows the truth about those deceptive barbed spines. Most of the park's points of interest lie in the higher, slightly cooler and wetter Mojave desert, the special habitat of the burly **Joshua tree,** which displays huge white flowers following a good rainy season. Early pioneers (and many ignorant modern campers) tried to chop down the "trees" for firewood, only to discover that what resembled trunks were just toughened stalks that won't burn. Five **fan palm** oases (in both climate zones) flourish in areas where water occurs naturally at or near the surface.

Wildflower lovers, take note: The Joshua Tree area has traditionally been an excellent place to view nature's springtime bonanza. In addition to the flowering plants discussed above, the desert is home to sand verbena, desert dandelion, evening primrose, and dozens more varieties, some so tiny that you must crouch down to make out their brightly colored petals—veteran viewers call these "belly flowers." See below for more details.

Fauna. One of the more wonderful aspects of the Joshua Tree desert is the way this seemingly harsh and barren landscape slowly reveals itself to be richly inhabited. From the white-tailed **jackrabbits** abundant at the Oasis of Mara and throughout the park, to startling **bobcats** and **cougars** prowling around higher, less traveled elevations, the desert teems with life.

Some other frequently spotted residents: the **roadrunner,** a member of the cuckoo family with long, spindly legs and that telltale gait; the **coyote,** a fearless scavenger who'll openly trot along the road in search of food (*beware:* They'll eat tennis shoes or picnic trash as eagerly as rabbits or young tortoises); and **bighorn sheep,** most often seen atop the rocky hills they climb with sharp cloven hooves. Perhaps the most unusual animal is the **desert tortoise,** a slow-moving burrow dweller not often seen by casual visitors. The tortoises, which can live more than 50 years, are a protected endangered species, and you're prohibited from touching or interfering with them in any way. A poignant exception to this is if you encounter a tortoise on the road in danger of being hit—you're permitted

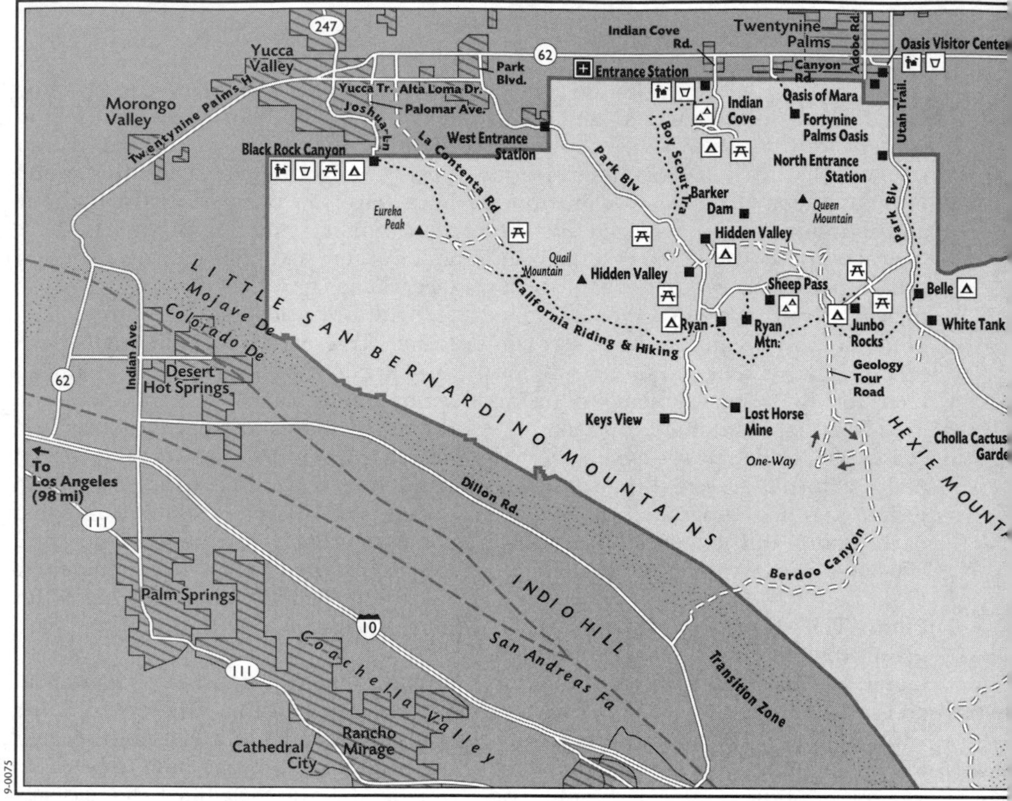

to pick it up gently with two hands and, holding it level, carry it off the road, placing it in the same direction as it was traveling.

Avoiding the Crowds. As Joshua Tree's chief of interpretation, Joe Zarki is usually consulted for advice on the park's natural flora and fauna. But he offers the following valuable tips for maximizing your enjoyment even during the most crowded months:

◆ Joshua Tree's greatest volume occurs in spring, when temperatures are moderate and wildflowers blooming. From March to May, monthly visitorship ranges from 150,000 up (the unofficial record is 233,000 in April 1995). Compared to summer, which sees 60,000 to 70,000 people each month, these figures are staggering. October and November are also popular, with numbers around 100,000. If you can, time your visit outside of these crowded periods—if not, try to visit during the week to avoid the crush of weekenders from nearby Los Angeles and stay away during spring break.

◆ Choose to enjoy the more popular activities (like designated nature trails and easy hiking routes) before 9 or 10am. Most people see the park between 10am and 4pm, so the evening hours can also offer some respite from crowds, and the sun sets after 7pm from May to September. In addition, you'll enjoy cooler temperatures during the morning and evening hours.

◆ Campers eager to stake their claim in the campground of their choice need to be diligent during springtime crowding, since it's first come, first served at all but one (Black Rock Canyon) of the park's campgrounds. Generally, it's best to arrive between 9am and noon to snatch an available space. The campsites near popular rock-climbing areas (Hidden Valley, Jumbo Rocks, Indian Cove)

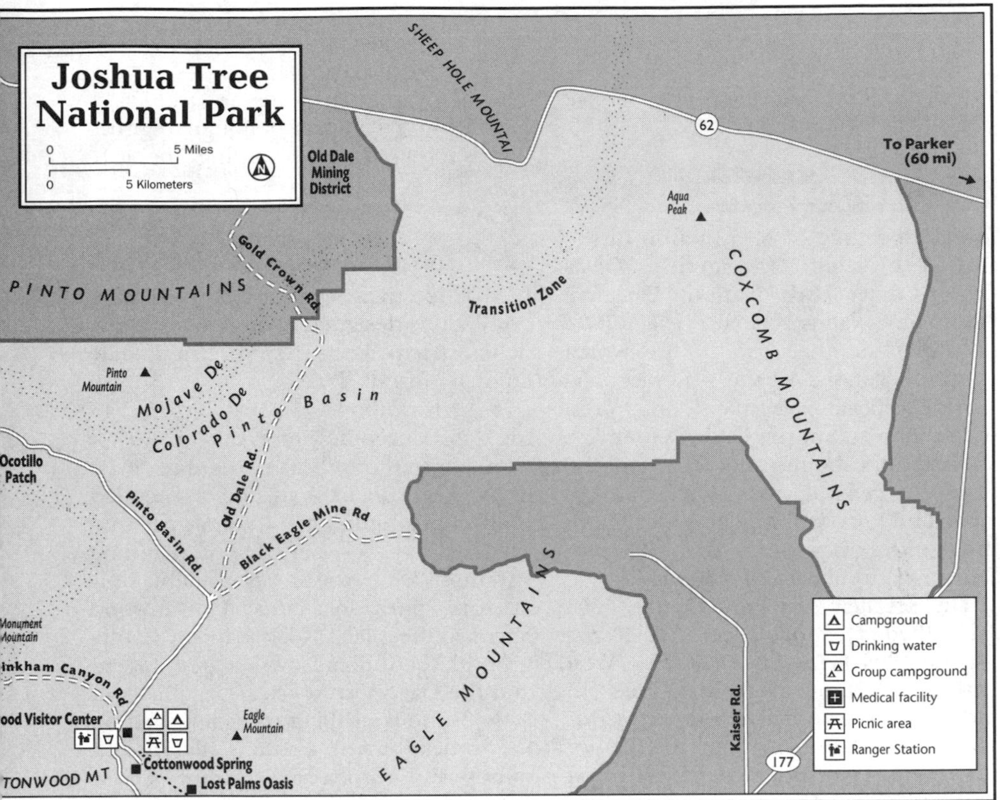

fill first. If you're staying over a weekend in peak season, try to claim your site Friday morning, before weekenders begin to arrive.

Just the Facts

GETTING THERE & GATEWAYS

There are three roads into the park. The most commonly used is the North Entrance Station at the end of Utah Trail in the town of Twentynine Palms, on Calif. 62, 40 miles north of its junction with I-10. Also along Calif. 62 is the West Entrance Station, on Park Boulevard in the town of Joshua Tree. On the southern side of the park is the Cottonwood Visitor Center, about 25 miles east of Indio along I-10.

The Nearest Airport. The nearest airport is the **Palm Springs Regional Airport,** 3400 E. Tahquitz Canyon Way (☎ **619/323-8161**). The airlines servicing the airport include **Alaska, American, America West, Delta/Skywest, United,** and **US Airways.** See the appendix for their phone numbers.

Renting a Car. **Avis, Budget, Dollar, Hertz,** and **National** have outlets at the Palm Springs airport. See the appendix for their phone numbers.

GETTING INFORMATION BEFORE YOUR TRIP

If you want to get information and a park map before you leave home, contact the **Superintendent, Joshua Tree National Park,** 74485 National Park Dr., Twentynine Palms, CA 92277 (☎ **760/367-5500**).

A terrific Internet Web site with abundant info on the park and several surrounding communities is at **www.desertgold.com**. It's also worth checking out the official National Park Service Web site at **www.nps.gov/jotr**.

VISITOR CENTERS

Your best source of information in the park is the large Park Service's **Oasis Visitor Center,** 74485 National Park Dr., Twentynine Palms, CA 92277 (☎ **760/367-7511**), on the road to the North Entrance Station. All the visitor centers provide official park maps, brochures, and schedules, but the Oasis Center also carries books about Joshua Tree and the desert in general, plus a selection of water- and tearproof topographical maps and guides. It's open daily (except Christmas) from 8am to 4:30pm.

The privately run **Park Center,** 6554 Park Blvd., Joshua Tree, CA 92252 (☎ **760/366-3448**), is near the West Entrance Station in Joshua Tree. In addition to providing official visitor materials and information, this center has a supply/gift shop, a deli, and an art gallery. The information desk, store, and deli are open Monday to Thursday from 9am to 5pm, Friday and Saturday from 8am to 6pm, and Sunday from 9am to 6pm. The art gallery is open Wednesday to Sunday from 10am to 5pm.

The **Cottonwood Visitor Center,** at the south end of the park, is really just a ranger shack with bare-bones information and camping directions. It's open daily (except Christmas) from 8am to 4pm.

ENTRANCE & CAMPING FEES

Admission to the park is $10 per car (valid for 7 days) and can be paid at any of the three entrances. Keep your receipt to show on exit and reentry.

Four of the nine developed campgrounds charge fees. Black Rock Canyon and Indian Cove charge $10 per night (the 13 group sites at Indian Cover cost $20 to $35 a night); Cottonwood charges $8 fee per night, $25 for one of the three group sites; Sheep Pass group camp charges $20 to $35 for one of its six sites. The other campgrounds are free, as is backcountry camping (though registration is required, see "Camping," below).

SPECIAL REGULATIONS & WARNINGS

In addition to the standard national park regulations designed to protect the fragile ecosystem, keep these in mind while enjoying Joshua Tree:

◆ Dehydration is a constant threat in the desert; even in winter, carry plenty of drinking water and drink regularly even if you don't feel thirsty. Recommended minimum supplies are 1 gallon per person per day or twice that if planning strenuous activity. Water is available only at four park locations: Cottonwood Springs, the Black Rock Canyon Campground, the Indian Cove Ranger Station, and the Oasis Visitor Center.

◆ Sections of the park (identified on the official map) contain abandoned mines and associated structures. Use extreme caution in the vicinity, watching for open shafts and prospect holes. Supervise children closely and never enter abandoned mines.

◆ There's potential flash flooding following even brief rain showers, so avoid drainage areas and be especially observant of road conditions at those times.

SEASONS & CLIMATE

Joshua Tree National Park's nearly 800,000 acres straddle two distinct desert climates—the eastern half of the park is hot, dry, lower Colorado Desert, while most points of interest lie in the higher, slightly cooler and wetter Mojave Desert. The Mojave will occasionally get a dusting of snow in winter, but neither section sees more than 3 to 6 inches of annual rainfall. Winter temperatures are in the comfortable 50s or 60s during the day and often approach freezing overnight; summer days can blaze past 100°F at noon and even nighttime offers little relief in August and September, when lows are still in the 80s. Though peak visitation occurs from October to May, particularly on weekends and during school vacations, summer's heat actually attracts many visitors, so even a sweltering August day might be a busy one around the park.

SEASONAL EVENTS

Best between February and May, the **springtime wildflower viewing** is dependent on rainfall, sunshine, and temperatures, but you can depend on seeing the brilliant blooms somewhere in the park each year. Rangers lead interpretive walks to the best displays, and 24-hour recorded information on prime viewing sites (updated at least weekly during the season) is available from the **Payne Foundation Wildflower Hotline** at ☎ **818/768-3533** or the **Living Desert Wildflower Hotline** at ☎ **760/340-4954.**

USEFUL PUBLICATIONS

In addition to the complimentary newspaper-style ***Joshua Tree Guide,*** printed by the Joshua Tree National Park Association and available throughout the area, the following publications might prove helpful: Robert Cates's *Joshua Tree National Monument: A Visitors Guide* (Chatsworth, Calif.: Live Oak Press, 1984), and John Krist's *50 Best Short Hikes in California Deserts* (Berkeley: Wilderness Press, 1995).

Or you can order them directly from the **Joshua Tree National Park Association,** 74485 National Park Dr., Twentynine Palms, CA 92277 (☎ **619/367-1488**).

Seeing the Highlights in a Day

An excellent first stop is the main **Oasis Visitor Center,** located alongside the Oasis of Mara, also known as the Twentynine Palms Oasis. For many generations the native Serrano tribe lived at this "place of little springs and much grass." Get maps, books, and the latest in road, trail, and weather conditions before beginning your tour and stroll the short, paved nature trail through the oasis behind the center—it provides an introduction to the park's flora, wildlife, and geology.

From the Oasis Center, drive south to **Jumbo Rocks,** which captures the complete essence of the park: a vast array of rock formations, a Joshua tree forest, and the yucca-dotted desert open and wide. Check out the many boulders that appear to resemble humans, dinosaurs, monsters, cathedrals, and castles; if you're visiting with kids, it's a great way to put their imaginations to work. Stroll among the giant rock piles and observe the rock climbers who travel from around the world to practice their craft here—they're one of the park's most distinctive features.

At Cap Rock Junction, the main park road swings north toward the **Wonderland of Rocks,** 12 square miles of massive jumbled granite. This curious maze of stone hides groves of Joshua trees, trackless washes, and several small pools of water. To the south is the road that deadends at mile-high **Keys View.** You get a panoramic view of the park from this wind-whipped overlook; several informative plaques explain the topography you're seeing and provide some insight into the delicate desert ecosystems found in the park.

Don't miss the contrasting Colorado Desert terrain found along Pinto Basin Road—to conserve time, simply plan to exit the park via this route, which ends up at I-10. You'll pass both the **Cholla Cactus Garden** and spindly **Ocotillo Patch** on your way to vast Pinto Basin, a barren lowland surrounded by austere mountains and punctuated by trackless sand dunes. Then continue to **Cottonwood Springs,** which has a cool, palm-shaded oasis and groves of mature cottonwood trees.

If you have only a day (or 2) in Joshua Tree National Park, try to participate in a ranger-led tour or hike (see below). You'll learn to appreciate the park in a short amount of time, for the rangers here are as exuberant about their patch of wilderness as they are well informed.

Exploring the Park by Car

There are two main roads through the park, and by driving them both you'll be able to see virtually every feature that distinguishes Joshua Tree; there are even a couple of easy opportunities to stop and stretch your legs while learning more about the region.

Park Boulevard loops through the high northern section between the North Entrance Station in Twentynine Palms and the West Entrance Station in Joshua Tree. Along the drive, which takes about 45 minutes one way, you'll get an eyeful of the spectacular rock formations and oddly shaped Joshua trees the park is best known for. Stop perhaps at one of the well-marked interpretive trails along the way (see "Day Hikes," below), but don't miss the detour to **Keys View,** the most visited spot in the park. A paved road leads to this mile-high mountain crest, where a series of plaques describe the land below and a panoramic view that encompasses both the highest (Mt. San Gorgonio) and the lowest (Salton Sea) points in southern California.

Pinto Basin Road bisects the park from top to bottom, forking away from Park Boulevard near the North Entrance Station and winding down to the Cottonwood Entrance off I-10. Driving it, you'll pass from the higher Mojave Desert into the lower Colorado Desert, across the "Transition Zone" snaking through the middle of the park; it's a fascinating melting pot where the two climates are both represented. Stop to marvel at the Cholla Cactus Garden (see "Day Hikes," below) or the Ocotillo Patch, where this spidery, tenacious desert shrub sports flaming red blooms following spring rains. At the park's southern end you can explore the lush Cottonwood Spring or see relics of World War II training maneuvers (see "Historic & Man-Made Attractions," below). From end to end takes between 45 and 60 minutes.

Organized Tours & Ranger Programs

A multitude of ranger-led seminars and guided hikes are offered. They include such topics as Photographing the Boulders, Birding for Beginners, Stars Over Joshua Tree (evening), and Wildlife Walk, as well as guided hikes on many of the park's popular trails. Throughout the wildflower blooming season, and especially during Easter week, special walks visit the most abundantly flowering areas.

The Park Service also conducts guided tours of the historic **Desert Queen Ranch** (see below). From approximately November to April, tours are at 10am and 1pm on Saturday and Sunday only. Contact the visitor center for a seasonal schedule; tours are given less frequently during the hot summer. Plan to arrive early, as these events are popular and groups are limited to 20.

Historic & Man-Made Attractions

Miners and ranchers began coming in the 1860s, including the McHaney brothers, who established the **Desert Queen Ranch.** It was later acquired by former Rough Rider Bill Keys, who lived there until his death in 1969. Though many of the ranch structures are now decrepit and overgrown, it's compelling to see how one hardy family made a home in the unforgiving desert. Admittance is limited to official Park Service tours (see above).

You can find Native American petroglyphs near **Barker Dam,** where an easy 1.1-mile loop hiking trail leads to a small man-made lake framed by the Wonderland of Rocks. After scrambling a bit to get atop the dam, you'll find a sandy path leading to the "Disneyland Petroglyph" site. Its wry name stems from the fact that a movie crew once retraced the ancient rock carvings to make them more visible to the camera, thus defacing them forever. If you investigate the cliffs along the remainder of the trail, however, you're likely to find some untouched drawings depicting animals, humans, and other aspects of desert life as interpreted by long-ago dwellers. You'll see additional petroglyphs along the 18-mile **Geology Tour Road,** a sandy and lumpy dirt road accessible only by four-wheel-drive vehicles or hardy mountain bikers.

During World War II, George S. Patton trained over a million soldiers in desert combat at several sites throughout the Mojave and Colorado deserts. Tank tracks are still visible in the wilderness around the former Camp Young, near Cottonwood Springs. The **Camp Young Memorial** marker is 1 mile east of Cottonwood Springs Road, just before the park entrance; an informational kiosk there gives details of the training maneuvers and daily camp life. To learn more, you can visit the **General Patton Memorial Museum** (☎ **760/227-3483**) in Chiriaco Summit, on I-10 about 5 miles east of the Cottonwood Entrance. The museum contains an assortment of memorabilia from World War II and other military glory days, as well as displays of tanks and artillery; it's open daily from 9am to 5pm (except Thanksgiving and Christmas).

Day Hikes

The good news about Joshua Tree: Its natural wonders are accessible to everyone, not just to the extreme outdoor adventurer. Nowhere is this more apparent than in the diversity of hiking and nature trails, which range from a 0.5-mile paved nature trail (ideal for even strollers and wheelchairs) to trails of 15-plus miles requiring strenuous hiking and backcountry camping.

SHORTER TRAILS

Barker Dam Nature Trail

1.1 miles RT. Easy. Access: The trailhead is located at the Barker Dam Parking Area.

This sandy path leads to a small lake—formed in a natural rock basin by a man-made dam—a relic of the ranchers who used such "tanks" to water their stock. Signs along the way describe some of the plant and animal life found here, including migratory wildfowl who use this as a watering hole on their journeys. After scrambling up the dam, you'll come to some Native American petroglyph sites (see "Historic & Man-Made Attractions," above). Allow 1 to 1½ hours.

Cap Rock Nature Trail

0.4 mile RT. Easy (paved). Access: The trailhead is located at the parking area for Cap Rock, an unusual rock formation resembling a Scottish tam perched atop a pile of boulders.

Climbers gather here, and they're as interesting to watch as the short, informative trail leading from the parking lot. In between identifying different desert plants along the path, test your footing on some of the rocks to get a feel for the climbing experience. Allow 30 to 40 minutes.

Cholla Cactus Garden Nature Trail

0.25 mile RT. Easy. Access: The trailhead is smack-dab in the middle of the park, about halfway between the North and South entrances.

This trail winds through an unusually dense concentration of Bigelow cholla, one of the desert's more fascinating residents. Often called "teddy bear cactus" for its deceptively fluffy appearance, cholla is also nicknamed "jumping cactus" for the ease with which its barbed spines stick to the clothing and skin of anyone who passes too close. Any ranger can tell you horror stories of people who've tripped into a cholla bush and emerged porcupine like and suffering—but please don't let that stop you from enjoying this pretty roadside diversion. Allow 20 to 30 minutes.

Cottonwood Springs Nature Trail

2 miles RT. Easy. Access: The trailhead is located at the Cottonwood Campground at the park's southern end.

The trail leads through rolling desert hills long inhabited by Cahuilla Indians. Signs along the way relate how they used native plants in their everyday lives; the trail culminates at lush Cottonwood Springs. The prolific underground water source supports thick groves of cottonwood and palm trees, plus the birds and animals who make them home. Allow 1 to 2 hours.

Desert Queen Mine

1.5 miles RT. Easy to moderate. Access: The trailhead is reached via a dirt road leading from Park Blvd., opposite the Geology Tour Rd.

The "trail" meanders and forks through the ruins of a gold mine that yielded several million dollars' worth of ore between 1895 and 1961. Building ruins, steel machinery parts, and sealed mine shafts dot the hillsides and ravine; there's a signboard at the overlook with more information about mine operations. Allow 1 to 3 hours.

Fortynine Palms Oasis

3 miles RT. Strenuous. Access: The trailhead is at the end of Canyon Rd. in Twentynine Palms (you have to access it by leaving the park boundaries and going down Canyon Rd).

This hike begins with a steep harsh ascent to a ridge fringed with red-spined barrel cacti. Down the other side, a rocky canyon contains the spectacular oasis whose fan palm and cottonwood tree canopy shades clear pools of green water. Plants, birds, and other wildlife are abundant in this miniature ecosystem, and the scorched trunks of trees bear witness to past fires that've nourished rather than destroyed the life here. Beware of rattlesnakes in the shaded brush around the oasis. Allow 2 to 3 hours.

Hidden Valley Nature Trail

1 mile loop RT. Easy. Access: The trailhead is a paved spur near the Hidden Valley picnic area.

This easy trail (allow 1 hour) is fun for kids and adults who like rock climbing and intrigue. You can see sport climbers surrounding the small valley, which is reputed to have been a hideout for 19th-century cattle rustlers. Signs posted along the trail talk about the area's geology and history. The trail is relatively level, though there's some easy boulder scrambling along the route.

High View Nature Trail

1.3 miles RT. Moderate. Access: The trailhead is reach via the dirt road turnoff immediately before the entrance to Black Rock Campground at the northwestern edge of the park.

This well-maintained and popular trail involves a steady, moderately steep climb to one of Joshua Tree's many spectacular vistas. Alternately rocky and sandy, the trail is marked by numbered signposts keyed to a leaflet often unavailable at the Black Rock Ranger Station. Benches are found at intervals and also at the summit. Allow 1½ to 2 hours.

Oasis of Mara Nature Trail

0.5 mile RT. Easy (paved). Access: The trailhead is located behind the Oasis Visitor Center.

Leading into a miniature ecosystem of palm trees, small ponds, and abundant animal life, this supereasy path (allow 30 to 40 minutes) is lined with interpretive signs. It's a great place to start your first visit to Joshua Tree and an excellent introduction to the centuries of human inhabitants who used the oasis to sustain life.

Pine City

3 miles RT. Easy. Access: Begin at the same trailhead for Desert Queen Mine.

This path takes you to a cluster of boulder formations and sandy washes. Pinyon pines thrive in the moisture provided by these natural drainage courses—the tree was exploited for food (pine nuts) by early inhabitants. Today birds gather in the trees and bighorn sheep are occasionally found among the rocks. Allow 1½ to 2 hours.

Ryan Mountain

3 miles RT. Strenuous. Access: The trailhead is located at a marked parking area along Park Blvd.

A constant, steep climb (almost 1,000 feet) leads to the best panoramic views in the park, encompassing snowcapped mountain peaks, broad tree-dotted valleys, and dark volcanic mounds. Ascending through a juniper and pinyon pine woodland, the trail is mostly rocky, well maintained, and easy to follow—you'll likely spot rock climbers to the west of the mountain. Allow 2½ to 3 hours.

Skull Rock Nature Trail

1.7 miles RT. Easy. Access: The trailhead is located at the Skull Rock Campground (Loop E).

Leading to another unusually anthropomorphic rock formation, the trail meanders through boulders, desert washes, and a rocky alleyway. Watch for the "ducks" (small stacks of rocks) that mark the pathway. Allow 2 hours.

LONGER TRAILS

Boy Scout Trail

16 miles RT. Moderate. Access: The trail is reached from the Wonderland of Rocks backcountry board, 6.4 miles east of the West Entrance Station.

From the trailhead, you progress downhill, through picturesque, sandy washes lined with oak and pine trees. Traveling through a variety of terrain, this trail can also be taken one way, either direction. The latter portion skirts a rocky mountainside, then finishes through open desert, ending up at the Indian Cove Ranger Station and backcountry board. Allow 1 to 2 days.

California Riding and Hiking Trail

35 miles RT. Easy to strenuous. Access: There are 6 access points along the trail's path; your best bet is to consult with park rangers and obtain a topographical map to help you stay on track.

In general, it's easier to travel from west to east since the western sections are at higher elevations. Marked by distinctive brown posts stenciled with "CRH," the many miles of this statewide trail pass through distinct areas of the park, from pinyon/juniper forests to flat, lower desert terrain. It takes 2 to 4 days to hike the trail in its entirety, but you can also hike it in sections ranging from 4.4 to 11 miles.

Lost Horse Mine

4 miles RT. Moderate. Access: The trailhead is at the end of a dirt road leading from Keys View Rd., 2.5 miles south of its junction with Park Blvd.

This trail leads to the ruins of the area's most successful mining operation. Well-preserved remnants include the steam engine that powered the machinery, a winch for lowering equipment into the mine, settling tanks, and stone building foundations. The trail, actually an old wagon road, winds up gradually through rolling hills; once there, you can take an additional short, steep hike to the hilltop behind the ruins for a fine view into the heart of the park. Hikers with children should keep a watchful eye around the mine ruins. Allow 3 to 4 hours.

Lost Palms Oasis

7.5 miles RT. Moderate. Access: Park at Cottonwood Spring, accessible by paved road just beyond the Cottonwood Campground.

This long trail leads through sandy washes and rolling hills to the oasis overlook, then a steep, rugged, and strenuous trail continues on to the canyon bottom. Whether or not you're up to the entire challenge, the beauty of birdsongs and rustling palms echoing through the canyon make this a special hike. Lost Palms is the park's largest oasis; look closely, for the remote canyon bottom is attractive to the elusive bighorn sheep. Allow 5 to 7 hours.

Other Sports & Activities

Biking. Because most of Joshua Tree National Park is designated wilderness, special care must be taken not to damage the fragile ecosystem. That means bicycles are restricted to roads, none of which have bike lanes. This effectively puts biking out of reach for most casual pedalers. If you're into mountain biking, though, and up to a challenge, there are miles of unpaved roads ripe for exploration. Distraction from autos is rare, particularly on four-wheel-drive roads like the 18-mile **Geology Tour Road,** which begins 2 miles west of Jumbo Rocks. Dry lake beds contrast with towering boulders along this downhill, sandy and lumpy dirt road; you can stop to see a Joshua tree woodland, abandoned mines, and Native American petroglyphs.

A short but rewarding ride starts at **Covington Flats,** accessible only by unpaved (two-wheel-drive OK) La Contentata Road in the town of Joshua Tree. From the picnic area, ride west to Eureka Peak, 4 miles away through lush high desert vegetation like extra-large Joshua trees, junipers, and pinyon pines. The road is steep near the end, but your reward will be a panoramic view of Palm Springs to the south, the Morongo Basin to the north, and the jagged mountain ranges of the park in between. For other bike-friendly unpaved and four-wheel-drive roads, consult the park map available at all visitor centers. There are no bike rentals available in the park, so you'll have to bring your own.

Rock Climbing. During most of the year, visitors to the park can observe rock climbers scurrying up, down, and across the many geological formations in the northwestern quadrant—or sometimes just stretching out, sunning themselves on flat rocks. Joshua Tree is one of the sport's premier destinations, with more than 4,000 individually rated climbs.

Spectacular geological formations have irresistible names like **Wonderland of Rocks** and **Jumbo Rocks**—lovers of Stonehenge and Easter Island will delight in bizarre stacks with names like **Cap Rock** (for the single flat rock perched atop a haphazard pile) or **Skull Rock** (where the elements have worn an almost-human countenance into a boulder arrangement). But human hands had nothing to do with nature's sculptural artistry here; these fantastic formations are made of quartz monzonite, once a molten liquid forced upward that cooled before reaching the surface. Groundwater seeped in and fractured the rocks, and as floods eventually washed away the ground cover and exposed the monzonite, natural erosion wore away the weakened sections, creating the bizarre shapes and piles you see today. Climbers of every skill level and many nationalities travel here from around the world, drawn by the otherworldly splendor of rock piles worn smooth by the elements.

Hidden Valley is another good place to watch enthusiasts from as far away as Europe and Japan scaling sheer rock faces with impossible grace. Climbers use the belay method of ascending a rock face using only their hands and feet (ropes are in place only to catch them in case of a fall); they also rappel, descending along a rope fixed at the top of a boulder. Climbers sometimes practice bouldering—working on strength and agility on smaller boulders within jumping distance to the ground. You can try some bouldering to sample the high-friction quartz monzonite; even tennis shoes seem to grip the rock surface.

If you'd like to learn the sport of rock climbing from scratch, it's easier than you think. The folks at (aptly named) **First Ascent** (☎ **800/325-5462**) have licensed, experienced climbing guides who'll orchestrate your entire excursion, starting with detailed instruction on rock-climbing basics. Later, the teacher will lead each climb, setting up ropes for belay and rappelling, then guiding students every step of the way. All-day excursions range from $75 per person in

Especially for Kids

Joshua Tree National Park is a great place for the kids—they'll see unusual plants and animals, learning just enough to stimulate their imaginations but not so much they zone out. From identifying familiar everyday shapes in rock formations to investigating the mysterious "teddy bear" cactus, the possibilities are endless. Parents must exercise caution, with regard to the weather and other dangers. Bring plenty of water, sunscreen, and protective clothing for children, and keep a close eye (if not grip) on them at all times to avoid their straying into perilous desert terrain (prickly cacti, steep rocks, or abandoned mine shafts).

Start by taking the kids on a designated nature trail (listed in the free *Joshua Tree Guide* and indicated by roadside signs). The park's 11 nature trails are interpretive, each providing numerous plaques along the way to help your family interpret the rocks, plants, and other characteristics you'll see in the context of their geological history and significance to animal and human desert dwellers. They're all short (0.25- to 2-mile loops) and relatively flat, making them ideal for most visitors. Two of these (**Oasis of Mara** and **Cap Rock**) are even paved and wheelchair-accessible.

The Park Service is eager for younger visitors to learn nature appreciation and conservation. Inside the complimentary *Joshua Tree Guide* are several "games" (thinly veiled educational activities) for kids, ranging from sketching rock formations and plants to quizzes on the park's facilities. If your youngster is interested enough to complete five of the activities, rangers at the Oasis Visitor Center will reward him or her with an official Junior Ranger badge.

groups of three or larger, $95 each for two people, or $165 for private instruction. The Oregon-based climbing school operates from October to May, and the prices include all necessary gear except special climbing shoes, which you must rent for $6 per day.

Camping

There are nine developed campgrounds in Joshua Tree National Park, as well as backcountry camping in the wilderness areas. Regulations are stringent for backcountry camping, including mandatory registration at 1 of 12 boards (see the Park Service map for locations). There are no showers or laundry facilities in the park, nor are there any RV utility hookups or an RV dump station. You can only make fires in the fire pits provided at each campsite. All campgrounds are open year-round.

At present, since the Park Service's vendor for camping reservations has been suspended, you cannot make reservations at any of the campgrounds (formerly, it was possible to make reservations at Black Rock Canyon). Officials say that there will be a new vendor in place by spring 1998 and that reservations will again be possible at that time.

You can make group camping reservations (sites accommodate from 10 to 70 people), but only by mail. You can write to the park headquarters in Twentynine Palms. You can also obtain a reservation application by phone (☎ **760/367-5500**), or download it from the Internet (**www.nps. gov/jotr**), but you can't actually make the reservation unless you send in the form.

Belle Campground, located on Pinto Basin Road 9 miles south of Twentynine Palms, has 18 sites. The only amenities are chemical toilets and fire pits (which you must use). There is no drinking water. This campground is free.

Black Rock Canyon Campground is in the northwest corner, at the head of the 35-mile California Riding and Hiking Trail (to reach it you have to leave the park boundaries), and is the most developed campground. It has 100 sites, flush toilets, and drinking water. Sites cost $10 per night. There is a visitor center here.

Cottonwood Campground, is in the southern portion of the park, near the Cottonwood Visitor Center. There are 62 individual sites ($10 per night) and three group sites ($25 per night). Drinking water is available, and there are flush toilets.

Hidden Valley Campground, located 14 miles south of Joshua Tree, California, is on the main park road. There are 39 sites, but no amenities (or drinking water). Camping here is free.

Indian Cove is just inside park boundaries west of Twentynine Palms; like at Black Rock, there are many hiking trails leading farther into Joshua Tree but no roads. The 101 individual sites ($10) and 13 group sites ($20 to $35) have chemical toilets but no drinking water.

Jumbo Rocks Campground, 11 miles south of Twentynine Palms on Utah Trace, has 125 sites with no amenities and is free.

Ryan Campground, 16 miles southeast of Joshua Tree, California, via Park Boulevard, has 31 sites with chemical toilets but no drinking water. It is free.

Sheep Pass group camp, a few miles east of Ryan Campground, has no individual sites; the group sites cost $20 to $35 per night. There are chemical toilets but no drinking water.

White Tank Campground, 2 miles beyond the Belle Campground on Utah Trace, has 15 sites with chemical toilets but no drinking water. It is free.

Accommodations

NEAR THE PARK

Aside from camping, there are no overnight accommodations available within the boundaries of Joshua Tree National Park.

Best Western Gardens Motel

71487 Twentynine Palms Hwy., Twentynine Palms, CA 92277. ☎ **800/528-1234** or 760/367-9141; fax 760/367-2584. 96 rms. A/C TV TEL. $65–$95 double. Corporate rates and AAA discounts are available. AE, DC, DISC, MC, V.

Located on the main highway at the western end of town, the Best Western Gardens might be a predictable

Campground	Total Sites	RV Hookups	Dump Station	Toilets	Drinking Water
Belle	18	No	No	Yes	No
Black Rock Canyon	100	No	No	Yes	Yes
Cottonwood	62 individual, 3 group	No	No	Yes	Yes
Hidden Valley	39	No	No	Yes	No
Indian Cove	101 individual, 13 group	No	No	Yes	No
Jumbo Rocks	125	No	No	Yes	No
Ryan	31	No	No	Yes	No
Sheep Pass	No individual, 6 group	No	No	Yes	No
White Tank	15	No	No	Yes	No

* Reservations can be made (by mail) for group sites only

representative of this motel chain, but it's also more reliable than many of the funky roadside places you'll pass. Kept sparkling clean and recently refurbished, the Best Western has nearly 100 rooms, including some one-bedroom efficiencies whose extra sleeping area and kitchenette are perfect for families. Many rooms have hot tubs, plus the motel has a heated outdoor pool and whirlpool. Continental breakfast is complimentary each morning, and all rooms have cable TV and in-room movies. If you're looking for a romantic retreat, pass this one up—but if you need a comfortable, affordable base from which to maximize your outdoor time, the Gardens fits the bill.

Joshua Tree Inn Bed & Breakfast

61259 Twentynine Palms Hwy., Joshua Tree, CA 92252. ☎ **800/366-1444** or 760/366-1188. 9 rms. A/C. $95–$150 double; $10 charge per extra person. Rates include breakfast. AE, DC, DISC, MC, V.

Not all local lore has to do with pioneering miners and ranchers—and one former motel, now a gracious B&B, boasts of a more recent rock 'n' roll history. Built in the 1950s, the Joshua Tree Inn has been the choice of the Rolling Stones, the Flying Burrito Brothers, and the cast of *Saturday Night Live*. The lobby is decorated with posters of folk singer/songwriter Gram Parsons, who died of a drug overdose here in 1973. Legends aside, the low-slung adobe-style inn and cottages are charming and near the West Entrance of Joshua Tree National Park, though set back far enough from the main highway to escape most of the traffic noise. Furnished in countrified florals and rustic antiques, all nine rooms have private baths, and many open onto a serene Japanese-style center courtyard. Full gourmet breakfast is served each morning, and chef Larry Gillette will also prepare (advance arrangements required) box lunches for the outdoor adventurer or candlelight dinners for the romantically inclined. If you visit midweek or during summer, the inn is likely to discount rates—it never hurts to ask.

Oasis of Eden

56377 Twentynine Palms Hwy., Yucca Valley, CA 92284. ☎ **760/365-6321;** fax 760/365-9592. 52 rms. A/C TV TEL. Feb–Apr $80–$180 double; May–Jan $65–$130 (higher costs are for "theme" rms). Inquire about AAA and senior discounts. AE, DC, DISC, MC, V.

It may look like plain motel on the outside, but the Oasis of Eden has surprises waiting behind its doors. If you think the name makes it sound like a good place

Showers	Fire Pits/ Grills	Laundry	Public Phone	Reserve	Fees	Open
No	Yes	No	No	No	No	Year-round
No	Yes	No	No	No	$10	Year-round
No	Yes	No	No	No*	$8–$25	Year-round
No	Yes	No	No	No	No	Year-round
No	Yes	No	No	No*	$10–$35	Year-round
No	Yes	No	No	No	No	Year-round
No	Yes	No	No	No	No	Year-round
No	Yes	No	No	No*	$25	Year-round
No	Yes	No	No	No	No	Year-round

for illicit liaisons, wait till you see one of the 13 "theme rooms," each with a whirlpool and VCR. The Oasis of Eden is a less-grand cousin to San Luis Obispo's famous Madonna Inn; here you can relive *The English Patient* in the white linen and khaki Safari Suite, revisit Caesar's Palace in the marble-pillared Roman Suite, or return to your club-wielding roots in the Cave Room. There are also 39 standard motel rooms, all with air-conditioning and some with kitchenettes. As motels go, this one's a cut above, offering 24-hour complimentary coffee and tea, a heated outdoor pool and spa, free local phone calls, and juice and breakfast breads at no extra charge.

29 Palms Inn

73950 Inn Ave., Twentynine Palms, CA 92277. ☎ **760/367-3505;** fax 760/367-4425. 19 rms. A/C TV. Feb–Apr $65–$95 double; May–Jan $60–$85 double. Midweek discounts sometimes apply, so inquire. AE, DC, DISC, MC, V.

The closest you can stay to the Joshua Tree National Park entrance is the 29 Palms Inn. This rustic, family run inn dates from the 1920s and consists of adobe cottages and old frame cabins scattered among 70 acres of the Oasis of Mara, the other side of which holds the main visitor center for the park. It has gradually become discovered by Hollywood celebrities who escape the stress of L.A. at this low-key resort dedicated to the art of relaxation. The grounds are quite lovely, including lawns strolled by geese from the nearby pond and shaded by the namesake 29 original palms. Behind the simple pool is the inn's restaurant, famed in its own right as one of the best in town (see "Dining," below). Included with the room is morning coffee and fresh-baked muffins around the pool patio. The cottages are all unique; some have a fireplace or wood stove and patio or deck, but all have evaporative coolers for the sweltering summer. There's also a three-bedroom, two-bath guest house available at $185 ($165 low season).

Dining

NEAR THE PARK

There are no concessions available within the boundaries of Joshua Tree National Park.

You can't be anywhere in the Southwest without seeing a Mexican restaurant, and the Morongo Basin is no exception. While none can compare to true south-of-the-border authenticity, you'll find tasty, traditional fare like saucy enchiladas, bulging burritos, layered tostadas, and plenty of crispy chips and salsa. The locals favor **Edchada's,** 56805 Twentynine Palms Hwy. in Yucca Valley (☎ **760/365-7655**), so well that they recently opened up a second restaurant in 29 Palms, at 73502 Twentynine Palms Hwy. (☎ **760/367-2131**). Both Edchada's are open daily from 11am to 9pm and have a full cocktail bar; they take credit cards (AE, DISC, MC, V). **Also in 29** Palms is **Ramona's,** 72115 Twentynine Palms Hwy. (☎ **760/367-1929**), a tiny family run place with vinyl tablecloths, pinãtas, and its own local following. Ramona's serves beer and wine only and is open Monday to Saturday from 11am to 8:30pm; credit cards are accepted (DISC, MC, V).

29 Palms Inn

73950 Inn Ave., Twentynine Palms. ☎ **760/367-3505.** Reservations recommended for dinner. Lunch entrees under $6; full dinners $8–$15. AE, DC, DISC, MC, V. Daily 11am–2pm and 5–9pm (until 9:30pm Fri–Sat). AMERICAN.

This restaurant is tucked away behind its namesake hotel's postage stamp–size pool and consists of a paneled dining room whose long, wide, hospitable bar sports a vaguely nautical Polynesian theme. Meals here enjoy their own fame, separate from the hotel's, and deservedly so. Starting with fresh vegetables from the inn's garden (which flourishes in this fertile oasis) and quality meat, poultry, and fish, the kitchen sends out simple meals accented with zesty condiment inventions (like their citrusy mustard/herb salad dressing). Lunch choices include fluffy quiche du jour, creamy soups, crunchy salads, and tostadas, plus a variety of hot and cold sandwiches. Dinner is more robust, featuring grilled meats and fish, seafood sautéd in butter and garlic, and whimsical specials like Cat Ballou Drunk Steak. The evening ambience is further enhanced by the white-plumed barn owls cavorting among the palm canopy. And the prices are very reasonable.

Don's American BBQ

72183 Twentynine Palms Hwy., Twentynine Palms. ☎ **760/367-0301.** Sandwiches/burgers $3–$4; full dinners $6–$23 (most under $15). AE, DISC, MC, V. Mon–Thurs 4–10pm, Fri–Sun noon–10pm. BARBECUE.

Local folks drive up from Palm Springs (1½ hours round-trip) just to get down 'n' dirty here. The tempting smell of tangy barbecue spices wafts through town from the giant grill outside the front door of this tiny shack decorated with beer-logo and military-insignia mirrors. Say hello to the grill master on your way in, then seat yourself at a wooden picnic table and roll up your sleeves. Regular- and oversized steaks, beef and pork ribs, chicken, and seafood are available, as well as some "exotic" fare like buffalo, kangaroo, alligator, and rattlesnake; every meal comes with a Paul Bunyan–size baked potato. The overhead must be low, because the prices are too. Don's is a fun choice if you've built up a hearty appetite with a day of hiking or rock climbing.

CAFES

Whether you crave the jolt of a cup of java or a fix of bohemian coffeehouse culture, you won't find the Morongo Basin lacking. In the heart of Twentynine Palms, **Casa de Java,** 73554 Twentynine Palms Hwy. (☎ **760/361-8823**), offers every imaginable variation on espresso, plus several pleasant indoor diversions—books, chess sets, and table tennis as well as live music, poetry readings, and performance art on Friday and Saturday nights. In addition to scattered comfy couches and armchairs, there's a computer/study room where you can play on the Internet for $8 an hour. Down the road in Joshua Tree is well-stocked **Jeremy's Cappuccino Bar,** 61597 Twentynine Palms Hwy. (☎ **760/366-9799**), where coffee drinks are only the beginning. They've got more than 70 varieties of imported and domestic beers; teetotalers can choose from around 35 teas, including yogi herbal blends, fruit infusions, and traditional English black teas. Deli snacks and baked treats are here for the noshing, and Jeremy's can even whip up a Häagen-Dazs milkshake. While inside walls boast a changing display of local art, the front windows are taped over with flyers, usually heralding live bands that play Friday and Saturday nights. Neither takes credit cards.

Picnic & Camping Supplies

General Stores. If there's camping (or climbing or hiking) gear that you left behind or suddenly decide you need, visit **Benton Bros. Family Center,** 73544 Twentynine Palms Hwy., Twentynine Palms (☎ **760/367-7814**), a general store carrying a limited selection of gear, including boots, cookstoves and fuel, ice chests, and hiking socks and hats. Or check out the **Park Center,** 6554 Park Blvd., Joshua Tree (☎ **760/366-3448**), near the West Entrance to the park; it carries a limited selection of common items like backpacks, water bottles, cookstove fuel, and clothing. A more comprehensive outfitter is 15 minutes away: **Jernigan's Sporting Goods,** 56867 Twentynine Palms Hwy., Yucca Valley (☎ **760/365-1828**), is in a shopping mall behind Denny's and can help you with everything from tents to lanterns to serious climbing gear and a dozen brands of heavy-duty hiking boots.

Serious Gear. Experienced climbers needing backpack or climbing equipment might want to step into **Nomad Ventures,** 61795 Twentynine Palms Hwy. (☎ **760/366-4684**), an outfitter conveniently located on the way to the park's West Entrance. Open daily, it rents and sells all kinds of shoes, packs, harnesses, and other necessities of the sport.

Picnic Supplies. Need provisions for picnicking or camping? You can stock up on the way in Yucca Valley, where **Kmart, Wal-Mart, Von's,** and **Stater Brothers** loom large along Highway 62, along with every fast-food joint you can imagine (like **Jack-in-the-Box, Taco Bell, Burger King,** and two **Del Taco's**). Once you're in Twentynine Palms, though, try the **Plaza Market** (☎ **760/367-3464**), across from the chamber of commerce in the Historic Plaza on the northwest corner of Adobe and Two Mile roads. This friendly local market in the original business center of town is convenient to the park's North Entrance. A good place to pick up sandwiches, salads, and other prepared lunch foods (including tempting brownies, muffins, and baked treats) is the **Finicky Coyote,** 73511 Twentynine Palms Hwy. (☎ **760/367-2429**), a downtown coffeehouse, deli, and gourmet food emporium popular among locals as a community hangout and purveyor of ultrarich fudge and truffles. You might also try the **Park Center** in the town of Joshua Tree. In addition to being the visitor center for the West Entrance Station, the Park Center has a deli/bakery/coffee bar ready to pack up easy lunchables.

23

LASSEN VOLCANIC NATIONAL PARK

by Matthew R. Poole

STASHED AWAY IN THE FAR NORTHEASTERN CORNER OF CALIFORNIA, Lassen Volcanic National Park is a remarkable reminder that North America is still forming and that the ground below is alive with the forces of creation and sometimes destruction. Lassen Peak is the southernmost peak in a chain of volcanoes (including Mount St. Helens) that stretches all the way from British Columbia.

Though it's dormant, 10,457-foot Lassen Peak is still very much alive. It last awakened in May 1914, beginning a cycle of eruptions that spit lava, steam, and ash until 1921. The eruption climaxed in 1915 when Lassen blew its top, sending up a 7-mile-high mushroom cloud of ash that was seen from hundreds of miles away. The peak itself has been dormant for nearly three quarters of a century, but the area still boils with ferocious intensity; hot springs, fumaroles, geysers, and mud pots are all indicators that Lassen hasn't had its last word. Monitoring of geothermal features in the park shows that they're getting hotter, not cooler, and some scientists take this as a sign that the next big eruption in the Cascades is likely to happen here.

Until then, the park gives you an interesting chance to watch a landscape recover from the massive destruction brought on by an eruption. To the north of Lassen Peak is the aptly named Devastated Area, a huge swath of volcanic destruction steadily repopulating with conifer forests. Forest botanists have revised their earlier theories that forests must be preceded by herbaceous growth after watching the Devastated Area immediately revegetate with a diverse mix of eight conifer species, four more than were present before the blast.

The Lassen area was inhabited by four groups of Native Americans before the arrival of whites. The Atsugewi, Maidu, Yana, and Yahi all used portions of the park as their summer hunting grounds. The white man's diseases and encroachment into their territory quickly decimated their population. By the turn of the 20th century, they were thought to be gone from the wilds of the Lassen area. In 1911, however, a nearly naked Native American man was discovered by butchers at a slaughterhouse in Oroville. When they couldn't communicate with him, the sheriff locked the man in a cell.

News of the "Wild Man" found a receptive audience among anthropologists at the University of California at Berkeley, who quickly rescued the man. Ishi, as he came to be known, turned out to be the last of the Yahi tribe and lived at the university's Museum of Anthropology for 5 years before succumbing to tuberculosis. Ishi, through sharing his knowledge with anthropologist Alfred Kroeber and others, is responsible for much of what's known about Native American culture in California.

The 108,000-acre park is a place of great beauty. The flora and fauna are an interesting mix of species from the Cascade Range, stretching north from Lassen, and species from the Sierra Nevada, stretching south. The resulting blend accounts for an enormous diversity of plants: 715 distinct species have been identified in the park. Though it's snowbound in winter, Lassen is an important summer feeding ground for transient herds of mule deer and numerous black bears.

In addition to the volcano and all its geothermal features, Lassen Volcanic National Park includes miles of hiking trails, 50 beautiful alpine lakes, large meadows, cinder cones, lush forests, cross-country skiing, and great backcountry camping. In fact, three quarters of the park is designated wilderness.

Avoiding the Crowds. Crowds? Forget it. Lassen is one of the least-visited national parks in the contiguous 48 states, so crowd control isn't a big consideration. Unless you're here on July 4 or Labor Day weekend, you won't encounter anything that could rightly be called a crowd. Even then you can escape simply by skipping the popular sites, like Bumpass Hell and the Sulphur Works, and heading a few miles down any of the backcountry trails.

Just the Facts

GETTING THERE & GATEWAYS

Part of the reason Lassen Volcanic National Park is one of the least visited national parks is its remote location. The most foolproof route is to take Calif. 44 east from Redding (via I-5), which leads directly to the Northwest Entrance to the park. A shortcut if you're coming from the south along I-5 is Calif. 36 in Red Bluff, which leads to the park's Southwest Entrance.

If you're arriving from the **east** via I-80, take the U.S. 395 turnoff at Reno and head to Susanville. Depending on which end of the park you're shooting for, take either Calif. 44 (to the Northwest Entrance) or Calif. 36 (to the Southwest Entrance) from Susanville.

Only one major road, Calif. 89 (also called the Park Road), crosses the park in a 39-mile half-circle with entrances and visitor centers at either end.

Most visitors enter the park at the Southwest Entrance Station, drive through the park, and leave through the Northwest Entrance, or vice versa. Two other entrances lead to remote portions of the park. **Warner Valley** is reached from the south on the road from Chester. **Butte Lake** entrance is reached by a cutoff road from Calif. 44 between Calif. 89 and Susanville.

The Nearest Airport. The nearest airport is the **Redding Municipal Airport,** 6751 Airport Rd. (☎ **916/224-4331**). The airport is serviced by **United Express** (see the appendix for the phone number).

GETTING INFORMATION BEFORE YOUR TRIP

To get information before you leave, contact the **Superintendent, Lassen Volcanic National Park,** P.O. Box 100, Mineral, CA 96063-0100 (☎ **916/595-4444**).

On the Web, the National Park Service's site has a page for Lassen at **www.nps.gov/lavo/**.

VISITOR CENTERS

The largest visitor center is just inside the **Northwest Entrance Station** at the Loomis Museum (open daily from late May to late September, 9am to 5pm).

There is also the **Southwest Information Center,** just inside the Southwest Entrance (with the same hours).

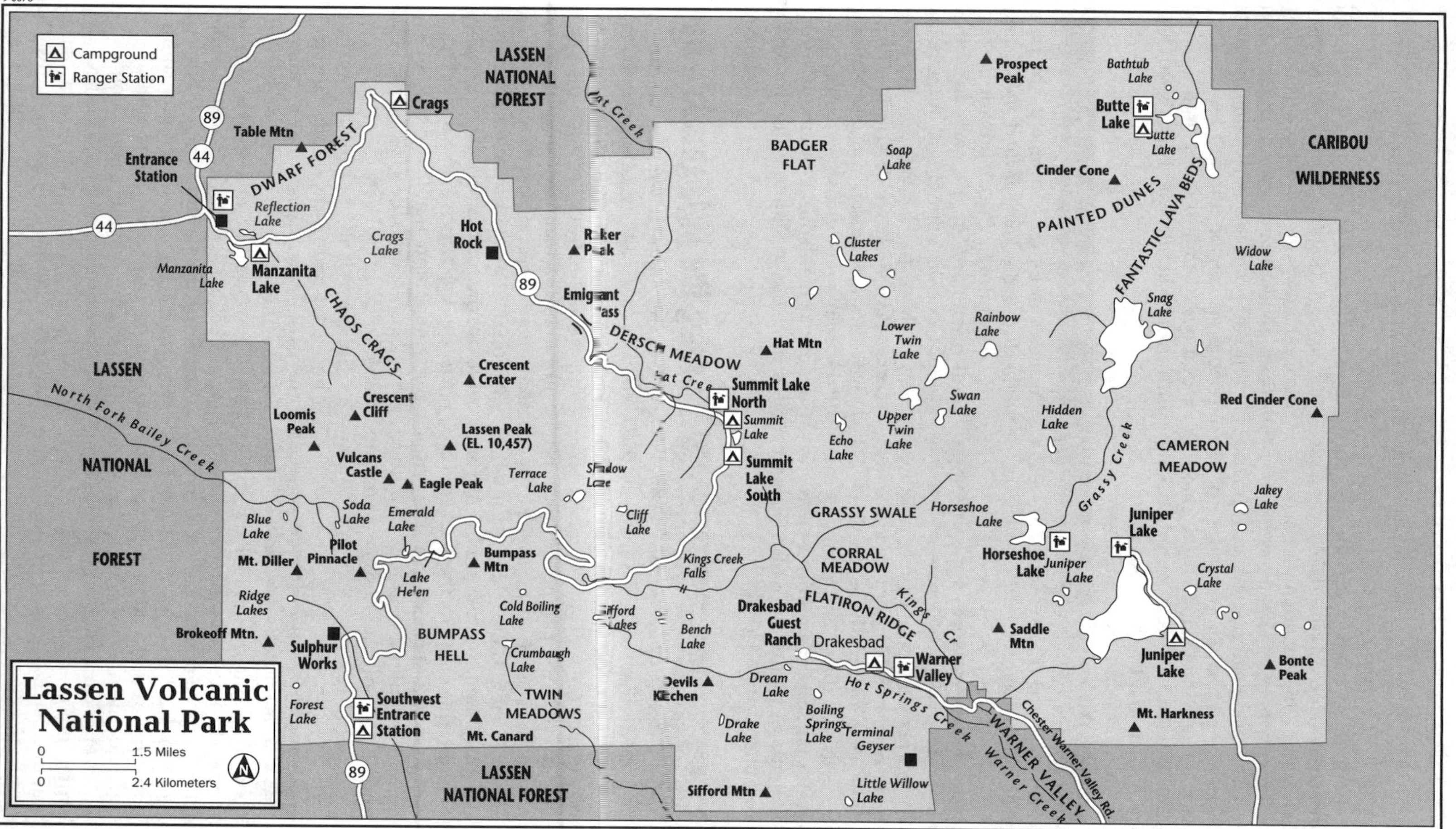
9-0076
Lassen Volcanic National Park
Campground
Ranger Station
0 1.5 Miles
0 2.4 Kilometers
LASSEN NATIONAL FOREST
CARIBOU WILDERNESS
LASSEN NATIONAL FOREST
North Fork Bailey Creek
Entrance Station
89
44
Table Mtn
DWARF FOREST
Reflection Lake
Manzanita Lake
Crags
Crags Lake
CHAOS CRAGS
Hot Rock
Crescent Crater
Crescent Cliff
Loomis Peak
Lassen Peak (EL. 10,457)
Vulcans Castle
Eagle Peak
Terrace Lake
Soda Lake
Emerald Lake
Blue Lake
Pilot Pinnacle
Mt. Diller
Lake Helen
Bumpass Mtn
Ridge Lakes
Brokeoff Mtn.
Sulphur Works
BUMPASS HELL
Cold Boiling Lake
Crumbaugh Lake
TWIN MEADOWS
Forest Lake
Southwest Entrance Station
Mt. Canard
DERSCH MEADOW
Hat Mtn
Summit Lake North
Summit Lake
Summit Lake South
Cliff Lake
Kings Creek Falls
Bench Lake
BADGER FLAT
Soap Lake
Cluster Lakes
Lower Twin Lake
Upper Twin Lake
Echo Lake
Swan Lake
Rainbow Lake
GRASSY SWALE
CORRAL MEADOW
FLATIRON RIDGE
Kings Cr
Drakesbad Guest Ranch
Drakesbad
Warner Valley
Dream Lake
Drake Lake
Boiling Springs Lake
Terminal Geyser
Hot Springs Creek
Sifford Mtn
Little Willow Lake
Prospect Peak
Bathtub Lake
Butte Lake
Cinder Cone
PAINTED DUNES
FANTASTIC LAVA BEDS
Widow Lake
Snag Lake
Hidden Lake
Horseshoe Lake
Grassy Creek
Red Cinder Cone
CAMERON MEADOW
Jakey Lake
Juniper Lake
Crystal Lake
Saddle Mtn
Bonte Peak
Mt. Harkness
WARNER VALLEY
Warner Creek
Chester Warner Valley Rd.

Both these centers provide the full spectrum of interpretive displays, ranger-led walks, informational leaflets, and emergency help.

The park headquarters in Mineral, located on Calif. 36, southwest of the park, offers information and publications Monday to Friday, 8am to 4:30pm from Memorial Day to Labor Day.

There are additional ranger stations at Summit Lake, and also in the more isolated reaches of the park in the Warner Valley, at Butte Lake, Horseshoe Lake, and Juniper Lake.

ENTRANCE & CAMPING FEES

The $5 per car entrance fee, valid for a week, comes with a copy of the *Lassen Park Guide,* a handy little newsletter listing activities, hikes, and points of interest. It's only $3 for an individual to enter the park on foot or on a bike. Camping fees range from $8 to $14.

SPECIAL REGULATIONS & WARNINGS

Because of the dangers posed by the park's thermal features, rangers ask that you remain on trails at all times. Fires are allowed in campgrounds only; please make sure that they're dead before leaving them. Mountain bikes are prohibited on all trails. Anyone spending the night in the backcountry must have a wilderness permit issued at the ranger stations. And don't forget to bring plenty of water, sunscreen, and warm clothing.

SEASONS & CLIMATE

Lassen Volcanic National Park resides in one of the coldest places in California. Winter begins in late October and doesn't release its grip until June. Even in summer, you should plan for possible rain and snow. Temperatures at night can drop below freezing at any time. Winter, however, shows a different and beautiful side of Lassen that more people are starting to appreciate. Since most of the park is over a mile high and the highest point is 10,457 feet, snow accumulates in incredible quantities (it's also a good thing to think about if you intend to stay in the area—some medical conditions can be affected by this high elevation). Don't be surprised to find snowbanks lining the Park Road into July.

USEFUL PUBLICATIONS

Available at either entrance to the park, Ellis Richard's ***Story Behind the Scenery*** (K.C. Dendoven Press) provides a general orientation to the park, as well as insight into its natural and human history. Robert and Barbara Decker's ***The Lassen Park Road Guide*** (Decker Press) gives a tour of Lassen Volcanic National Park from a motorist's view point, pointing out its highlights and natural history. It's available at either entrance to the park.

Seeing the Highlights in a Day

The highlight of Lassen is, of course, the volcano and all its offshoots: boiling springs, fumaroles, mud pots, and so on. You can see many of the most interesting sites in a day, making it possible to visit Lassen as a short detour from I-5 or U.S. 395 on the way to or from Oregon. Available at the park's visitor centers, the *Road Guide to Lassen Park* is a great traveling companion that'll explain a lot of the features you'll see as you traverse the park.

Bumpass Hell, a 1.5-mile walk off the Park Road in the southern part of the park, is the largest single geothermal site in the park—16 acres of bubbling mud pots cloaked in a stench of rotten egg–smelling sulfur. The name comes from an early Lassen traveler, Bumpass, who lost a leg after he took a shortcut through the area while hunting and plunged into a boiling pool. Don't make the same error.

Sulphur Works is another stinky, steamy example of Lassen's residual heat. Two miles from the southwest park exit, the ground roars with seething gases escaping from the ground.

Boiling Springs Lake and Devil's Kitchen are two of the more remote geothermal sites; they're in the Warner Valley section of the park, which you can reach by hiking from the main road or entering the park through Warner Valley Road from the small town of Chester.

Exploring the Park by Car

Only one major road, Calif. 89 (the Park Road), crosses the park in a half-circle with entrances and visitor centers at either end, and it is usually open from late May through much of October. Most visitors enter the park at the Southwest Entrance Station, drive through the park, and leave through the Northwest Entrance, or vice versa.

The 39-mile tour through this rugged yet captivating region should take no more than a few hours, though it's a good idea to factor in a few more hours to venture up Lassen Peak and explore the largest single geothermal site in the park, Bumpass Hell. If there's still time left, make an effort to stop at Sulphur Works near Mineral (about 2 miles from the southwest park exit), an acrid, noisy cauldron of steam vents that let off a mighty pungent odor.

Organized Tours & Ranger Programs

Free naturalist programs are offered daily in summer, highlighting everything from flora and fauna to geologic history and volcanic processes.

From January to March, a park naturalist gives free 2-hour ecoadventure snowshoe hikes across Lassen's snow-packed hills. The tours take place on Saturday afternoon at 1:30pm at the Lassen Chalet, located at the park's Southwestern Entrance. You must be at least 8 years old, warmly dressed, and wearing boots. Snowshoes are provided free of charge on a first-come, first-served basis, though a $1 donation is requested for upkeep. For more details, call park headquarters at ☎ **530/595-4444,** ext. 5133.

Day Hikes

Most Lassen visitors drive through in a day or two, see the geothermal hot spots, and move on. That leaves 150 miles of trails and expanses of backcountry to the few who take the time to get off-road. The *Lassen Trails* booklet available at the visitor centers (see above) gives good descriptions of some of the most popular hikes and backpacking destinations. Anyone spending the night in the backcountry must have a wilderness permit issued at the ranger stations. And don't forget to bring plenty of water, sunscreen, and warm clothing.

Bumpass Hell Trail

1.5 miles one way. Easy. Access: The well-marked trailhead is just off the Park Rd. in the southern part of the park.

This walk leads you through a quiet and peaceful meadow of wildflowers and chirping birds before depositing you in the middle of the largest single geothermal site in the park—16 acres of bubbling mud pots cloaked in a stench of sulfur. The name comes from an early Lassen traveler, Bumpass, who lost a leg after he took a shortcut through the area while hunting and plunged into a boiling pool. Stay on the wooden catwalks that safely guide you past the pyrite pools, steam vents, and noisy fumaroles and you won't make the same error.

Cinder Cone Trail

4 miles RT. Moderate. Access: The trailhead is located at the Butte Lake Campground at the far northeast corner of the park.

If 4 miles seems too short, you can extend this hike (and shorten the drive) by walking in about 8 miles from Summit Lake on the Park Road. Black and charred, Cinder Cone is bare of any sort of life and surrounded by dunes of multi-hued volcanic ash.

Lassen Peak Trail

2.5 miles one way. Moderate. Access: The trailhead is located 7.5 miles from the Southwest Entrance on the Park Rd.

This is probably the most popular hike in the park, a climb to the top of the peak. The trail may sound short, but it's steep and generally covered with snow until late summer. At 10,457 feet in elevation, though, you'll get a view of the surrounding wilderness that's worth every step of the way. On clear days you can see south all the way to Sutter Buttes near Yuba City and north into the Cascades. The round-trip takes about 4 to 5 hours.

Manzanita Lake Trail

1.5 miles RT. Easy. Access: The trailhead is located at the Northwest Entrance Station.

This trek runs along the shoreline of pretty Manzanita Lake, which is located at the Northwest Entrance to the park. It's easy to get to by car, and an easy hike for almost anyone. (If you want to do a bit more distance, continue around Reflection Lake as well.)

Nobles Emigrant Trail

10 miles RT. Easy. Access: The trailhead is located at the Northwest Entrance.

One of the park's easiest longer hikes is this scenic trail that passes though an old-growth forest, past Choas Crags (pink-hued rocks from an old weathered volcano), and into Lassen's Dwarf Forest, a bizarre region of stunted trees.

Pacific Crest Trail

17 miles one way. Moderate. Access: Get to the trail via the Warner Valley Rd. or by a long hike from Hat Lake.

The most interesting section of the trail for hikers who aren't trying to hike all the way through the park is the 5-mile segment south of Drakesbad that leads toward the park's boundary via Boiling Springs Lake and Terminal Geyser. This little-visited part of the park is actually one of the most spectacular geothermal displays this side of Yellowstone, and you're likely to have it all to yourself.

Paradise Meadow

3.5 miles RT. Moderate. Access: The trailhead is at the Hat Lake Overlook, which is right off Calif. 89 between Emigrant Pass and the Summit Lake Campgrounds.

This hike rises at a steady grade along a creek, eventually coming to a series of small waterfalls and a postcard-perfect meadow with outstanding wildflower displays during midsummer.

Summit Lake Loop

1.5 miles RT. Easy. Access: The loop can be accessed from either Summit Lake Campground.

This is another walk around a pristine alpine lake that's often frequented by deer in the evening.

Summit Lake Trailhead

8 miles RT. Moderate. Access: The longer version of the trail breaks off from the midpoint of the Summit Lake Loop (described above).

A popular day hike for campers at Summit Lake, this trek passes a myriad of lakes and wildflower-filled meadows on the way to Lower Twin Lake. After you pass the first moderately steep crest, the rest is cake.

Other Summer Sports & Activities

Biking. No mountain biking is allowed in Lassen. However, road bikers can test their stamina by tackling Lassen Volcanic National Park's Metric Century (100km/ 62 miles). Starting at the Lassen Chalet, you'll tour through beautiful wood countryside with occasional views of Lassen Peak. In the first 10 miles you'll climb almost 2,000 feet to crest the 8,512-foot summit. Eventually you'll reach Manzanita Lake, a good place to rest because from here you have to climb almost 3,000 feet back up to the Park Road summit before you can coast back to the chalet and your car.

Canoeing & Kayaking. Paddlers can take canoes, rowboats, and kayaks on any of the park lakes except Reflection, Emerald, Helen, and Boiling Springs. Motors, including electric motors, are strictly prohibited on all park waters. Lakes accessible from the Park Road include Manzanita and Summit. You can get to Butte Lake in the northeast section of the park on a gravel road from Calif. 44. Juniper Lake can be reached from a gravel road in the southeast section of the park.

Winter Sports & Activities

Cross-Country Skiing. The park road usually closes to cars in November due to snow, and most years it doesn't open until June, so cross-country skiers have their run of the park. Snowmobiles were once allowed but are now forbidden. Marked trails of all skill levels leave from Manzanita Lake at the north end of the park and Lassen Chalet at the south. There are heated bathrooms and running water at the chalet. Popular trips are the beginners' trails to Sulphur Works. More advanced skiers can make the trek to Lake Helen or Summit Lake.

You can also ski the popular 30-mile course of the Park Road in an overnight trek, but doing this involves a long car shuttle. For safety reasons, the park requires all skiers to register at the ranger stations before heading into the backcountry whether for an overnight or just the day. For details, call **Volcanic National Park Headquarters** at ☎ **530/594-4444.**

Sledding. During winter, heavy snows close Calif. 89 (the Park Road that passes through the park), but the southern entrance is kept open up to the ranger station. On weekends, those in the know bring their snow toys, kids, and picnic baskets and play on the gentle slopes that surround the station.

Camping

Car campers have their choice of seven park campgrounds with 375 sites total, more than enough to handle the trickle of visitors who come to Lassen every summer. In fact, so few people camp in Lassen that there's no reservation system except for the Lost Creek Group Campground, and stays are granted a generous 14-day limit. Sites do fill up on weekends, so your best bet is to get to the park early Friday to secure a place to stay. If the park is packed, there are 43 campgrounds in surrounding Lassen National Forest, so you'll find a site somewhere. There are also RV hookups at the Adam's Hat Creek Resort (see "Accommodations," below).

For information on how to make group camping reservations, call ☎ **530/595-4444,** ext. 5155.

By far the most "civilized" campground in the park is at **Manzanita Lake** (179 sites), where you can find hot showers, an RV dump station, flush toilets, a public pay phone, and a camper store. When Manzanita fills up, rangers open the **Crags Campground** (45 sites) about 5 miles away; it's much more basic (vault toilets and drinking water, but no showers). Farther in the park along Calif. 89 is **Summit Lake Campgrounds** (46 in the north portion, 48 in the south), on the north and south ends of Summit Lake, where you'll find flush toilets (in the north campground only). It's a pretty spot, often frequented by deer, and is a launching point for some excellent day hikes. On the southern end of the park you'll find **Southwest Campground** (21 sites), a walk-in camp directly adjacent to the Lassen Chalet parking lot; there are flush toilets and drinking water.

The two remote entrances to Lassen and Warner Valley have their own campgrounds. These are the **Warner Valley** (18 sites) and **Juniper Lake** (18 sites) campgrounds. Both are reached via dirt roads and are not recommended for trailers. However, they do have toilets, and the Warner Valley Campground has drinking water.

At press time, the **Butte Lake Campground** was closed for camping, though the area remains open for day use. If you wish to camp near Butte Lake, please inquire at park headquarters before your trip to see if the situation has changed.

Backcountry camping is allowed almost everywhere, and traffic is light. Ask about closed areas when you get your wilderness permit, which are issued at the ranger stations and required for anyone spending the night in the backcountry. There's one designated backcountry camping area at Juniper Lake, in the southeast section of the park.

Accommodations

INSIDE THE PARK

Drakesbad Guest Ranch

At the end of the Warner Valley Rd. from Chester, in the southern part of the park. (California Guest Services, 2150 N. Main St. no. 5, Red Bluff, CA 96080.) ☎ **530/529-1512.** 19 rms. $185 double. Rates include meals. MC, V. Open 1st week June to 3rd week Oct, weather permitting.

The only lodge operating in Lassen Park is Drakesbad, hidden in a high mountain valley and surrounded by meadows, lakes, and streams. Drakesbad is famous for its rustic cabins, lodge, and steaming thermal pool, fed by a natural hot spring and open 24 hours. The place is as deluxe as only a place with no electricity or phones can be, with handmade quilts on every bed and kerosene lamps to read by. Full meal service is available and very good. Since the lodge is extremely popular and open only for 5 months, reservations are booked as far as 2 years in advance (May and June are good times to call to take advantage of cancellations).

NEAR THE PARK

Adam's Hat Creek Resort

On Calif. 89, P.O. Box 15, Old Station, CA 96071. ☎ **530/335-7121.** 7 rms, 10 cabins. $45–$85 double. MC, V. Motel open year-round; cabins open May 1–Nov 1.

A haven for hunters and fishers (many of whom make their reservations years in advance), this small resort, 11 miles northeast of Lassen Volcanic National Park, features small housekeeping cabins and motel rooms situated alongside Hat Creek. The cabins come with kitchens where you can cook your catch. Otherwise, your main dining options are

Campground	Elev.	Total Sites	RV Hookups	Dump Station	Toilets	Drinki[ng] Wate[r]
Crags	5,700	45	No	No	Yes	Yes
Juniper Lake†	6,792	18	No	No	Yes	No
Manzanita Lake	5,890	179	No	Yes	Yes	Yes
Southwest	6,700	21	No	No	Yes	Yes
Summit Lake (North)	6,695	46	No	No	Yes	Yes
Summit Lake (South)	6,695	48	No	No	No	Yes
Warner Valley	5,650	18	No	No	Yes	Yes

† Not recommended for trailers since approach is via a dirt road.

* Campgrounds usually open in June or July and closed in September, but weather can affect these dates; call park headquarters for actual dates.

two nearby restaurants: Uncle Runt's Place and Indian John's Café. Also in the resort is an RV area with full hookups.

The Bidwell House

1 Main St., P.O. Box I790, Chester, CA 96020. ☎ **530/258-3338.** 14 rms (12 with bath), 1 cottage. $60–$65 double without bath, $78–$115 double with bath; $153 cottage for 6. Rates include full breakfast. MC, V.

In 1901, Gen. John Bidwell, a California senator who made three unsuccessful bids for the presidency, built a country retreat and summer home for his beloved young wife, Annie. Though he died before ever living in the house, Annie moved here and used it as a base for missionary work, converting scores of Native Americans to Christianity. After her death, when Chester had developed into a prosperous logging hamlet, the building, with its farmhouse-style design and spacious veranda, was converted into the headquarters for a local ranch.

Today, the house sits at the extreme eastern end of Chester, adjacent to a rolling meadow. The lake is visible across the road, and inside, Ian and Kim James maintain one of the most charming B&B inns in the region. Seven of the rooms have Jacuzzi tubs, and three offer wood-burning stoves; the cottage comes with a kitchenette. Breakfast is presented with fanfare and incorporates many gourmet touches, including home-baked breads and scrumptious omelettes. The Jameses also serve dinner Thursday to Saturday.

Lassen Mineral Lodge

On Calif. 36, P.O. Box 160, Mineral, CA 96063. ☎ **530/595-4422.** 20 rms. $60–$75 double.

A mere 9 miles south of the park's southern entrance, the Lassen Mineral Lodge offers motel-style rooms in a forested setting. In summer, the lodge is almost always bustling with guests and customers who venture into the gift shop, ski shop, general store, and full-service restaurant and bar. Also on the grounds is a pool and tennis court available during summer. For families, this is probably the best option in the Lassen area.

Mill Creek Resort

On Calif. 172 (3 miles south of Calif. 36), Mill Creek, CA 96061. ☎ **530/595-4449.** 9 cabins. $40–$60 cabin. No credit cards.

Set deep in the forest, the Mill Creek is that rustic mountain retreat you've always dreamed about while slaving away in the office. A homey country general store and coffee shop serve as the

Showers	Fire Pits/ Grills	Laundry	Public Phone	Reserve	Fees	Open
No	**Yes**	**No**	**No**	**No**	**$8**	**June–Sept***
No	**Yes**	**No**	**No**	**No**	**$8**	**June–Sept***
Yes	**Yes**	**No**	**Yes**	**No**	**$14**	**June–Sept***
No	**Yes**	**No**	**No**	**No**	**$10**	**June–Sept***
No	**Yes**	**No**	**No**	**No**	**$12**	**June–Sept**
No	**Yes**	**No**	**No**	**No**	**$10**	**June–Sept**
No	**Yes**	**No**	**No**	**No**	**$10**	**June–Sept**

resort's center, a good place to stock up on food while exploring Lassen Volcanic National Park. The housekeeping cabins, available on a daily or weekly basis, are clean, cute, and furnished in vintage 1930s and 1940s furniture, including kitchens (a good thing, since restaurants are scarce in this region). Pets are welcome, too.

St. Bernard Lodge

On Calif. 36 (10 miles west of Chester), P.O. Box 5500, Mill Creek, CA 96061. ☎ **530/258-3382.** 7 rms (none with bath). $52 double. MC, V.

This casual friendly lodge near the logging town of Chester has comfortable, attractively furnished rooms on the upper floor. The rustic country theme is enhanced by Andrew Wyeth prints and lonely landscapes that adorn the walls. The lodge's restaurant and bar are open to both guests and nonguests for breakfast, lunch, and dinner Thursday to Monday in summer and Friday to Monday in winter. For breakfast, try the large, fluffy pancakes with a side of honey ham. Top choice for dinner is a big ol' steak and side of fresh sweet corn. The baths are shared, but otherwise the St. Bernard Lodge comes with high recommendations.

Dining

INSIDE THE PARK

The only restaurant in the park (besides the Drakesbad Guest Ranch) is the **Summer Chalet Café** (☎ **530/595-3376**), which serves inexpensive, basic breakfasts, as well as sandwiches and burgers for lunch. At the park's South Entrance, it's open May to mid-October, daily from 8am to 6pm (the grill closes at 4pm, however).

NEAR THE PARK

When you're this far into the wilderness, the question isn't *which* restaurant to choose from, but *if* there is a restaurant to choose from. If bacon and eggs, sandwiches, steaks, chicken, burgers, pizza, and salads aren't part of your diet, you're in big trouble if you didn't pack your own grub.

Deciding where you're going to eat near Lassen Volcanic National Park depends mostly on which side you're on, north or south. Near the **Northwest Entrance** to the park in the town of Old Station (on Calif. 89; the town is small enough that street addresses aren't necessary) is **Uncle Runt's Place** (☎ **530/335-7177**), which serves your standard steaks, chicken, burgers, sandwiches, and such for lunch and dinner, and **Indian John's Café** (☎ **530/335-7177**), which serves basically the same stuff as Uncle Runt's, as well as pizza and your standard American breakfast.

At the South Entrance to the park, the closest restaurant is the **Lassen Mineral Lodge** (see "Accommodations," above) in the town of Mineral, which serves the usual uninspired mountain fare. A better bet is to head southeast along Calif. 36 to Chester and dine at the **St. Bernard Lodge** (see "Accommodations," above), which has one of the better restaurants in the Lassen region.

The best approach, however, is to either stay at a B&B or lodge that offers meals to its guests—such as the **St. Bernard Lodge, The Bidwell House,** or **Drakesbad Guest Ranch**—or at least provides a kitchen to cook your own meals, such as the **Adam's Hat Creek Resort** or **Mill Creek Resort.**

Picnic & Camping Supplies

The **Manzanita Lake Camper Store** (☎ **530/335-7557**), at the park's North Entrance, is a good place to stock up on groceries and basic outdoor gear. At the southern end of the park, you'll find just about every outdoor toy you'd ever want to play with in Lassen Park at the **Lassen Mineral Lodge,** on Calif. 36 in Mineral (☎ **530/595-4422**), including fishing and hunting supplies (this is big-time deer country) and the only cross-country ski rental in the area.

LITTLE BIGHORN BATTLEFIELD NATIONAL MONUMENT

by Ed Lawrence

Like the Revolutionary War battlefield at Lexington, Massachusetts, and Civil War battlefields at Gettysburg, Pennsylvania, and Appomattox, Virginia, the Little Bighorn Battlefield National Monument in eastern Montana presents visitors with an opportunity to immerse themselves in an area that is a microcosm of American history. The events that occurred on this battlefield reflected a series of events that began with an unstoppable push westward from the Atlantic seaboard, and which included what some call the unscrupulous behavior of a government, the politics of capitalism, and, ultimately, the final chapter in the traditional lifestyle of the American Indian. The events here represented the culmination of that chapter in American history.

Like many areas that have great significance for Indians—Devils Tower Monument in Wyoming and the Big Hole Battlefield in Montana, for instance—interest in the monument by visitors, Native Americans, and politicians has increased dramatically in recent years.

Until 1992, the battlefield was known as the Custer Battlefield in honor of the soldiers who fought there. However, when 20th-century activists protested that the battlefield recognized only one side of what occurred on its dusty soil, Congress changed the name. Since then, plans have been approved for the construction of a monument commemorating the Indians who fought to defend their homeland, though funds for its construction have not yet been raised.

The Prelude. The events leading to the battle reflect an era during which the westward expansion of the country dispossessed entire Indian nations. When Indians resisted the incursion of the settlers by attacking and killing them, the government decided it was cheaper to feed than to fight them, so much of the land in eastern Wyoming was permanently set aside for the tribes of the great plains—the Lakota, Cheyenne, and others—in the Fort Laramie Treaty of 1868.

However, when gold was discovered in the Black Hills of South Dakota in 1874 in the heart of the new reservation, a gold rush ensued, and the Indians found themselves again battling for their territory. The army was unable to stop the flow of immigrants. The Indians refused to sell the land back to the

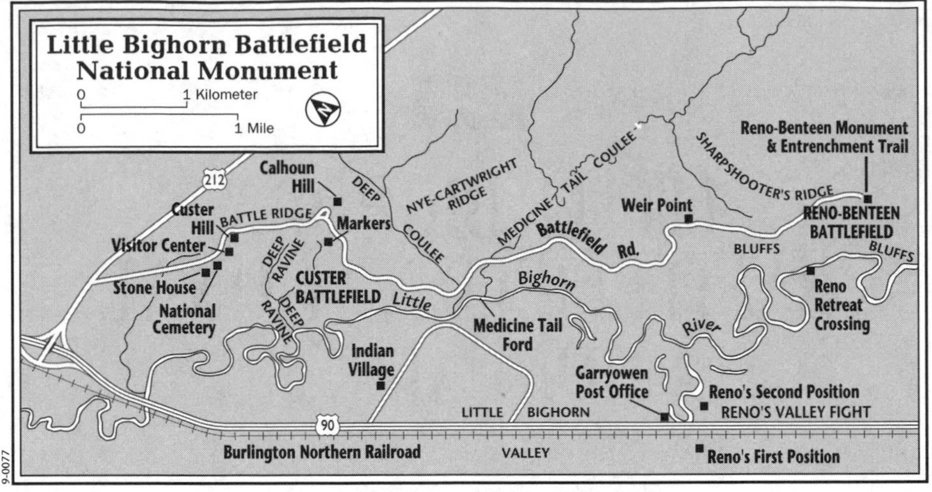

government. So, in defiance of government orders, they left the reservation and recommenced their attacks on the settlers and gold miners.

In December 1875, the government ordered the Indians to return to the reservation by the end of January 1876 or be treated as hostiles by military force, hunted and captured, or killed. Three separate expeditions were sent to carry out this mandate: One was led by Gen. George Crook from the Wyoming Territory, another by Col. John Gibbon from Montana Territory, the third by Gen. Alfred Terry from the Dakota Territory.

On June 25, 1876, on a small piece of flatland on the Bighorn River in eastern Montana, days after a skirmish on Rosebud Creek in which Crook's troops were knocked out of the campaign and forced to withdraw, the Indians drew the proverbial line in the sand, and stood united at a battlefield where they defended their rights to the land.

Following Crook's early defeat, Terry and Gibbon met on the Yellowstone River and decided to dispatch Gen. George Custer and the Seventh Cavalry to approach the Little Bighorn from the south and deal with the recalcitrant Indians.

The Battle. Custer was one of America's most fascinating military leaders. Known less for his brilliant tactics or his nerves of steel than his personality, he was one part genius and one part enigma. His life to that point had been an adventure in extremes: He graduated last in his class at West Point, yet became the youngest general in the history of the U.S. Army when Gen. Robert E. Lee surrendered to him during the Civil War. He was court-martialed for issuing an order to shoot army deserters in Kansas, yet later fought his way back up the military hierarchy to become commander of the Seventh Cavalry. He fancied himself a tamer of savages in the West but also had presidential aspirations, which may have affected his behavior during the last days of his life.

As the army closed in on the Indians, Custer, who was armed with information from his scouts about the location of the Indians' camp, divided his army. A battalion led by **Capt. Frederick Benteen** was assigned to scout the bluffs overlooking the southern end of the Indian encampment.

Maj. Marcus Reno, Custer's second in command, was ordered to cross the Bighorn River with his battalion and attack from the southwest, while Custer took his army to the northern end of the Indian village, which at that point included 1,000 lodges and 7,000 Indians, 1,500 of which were warriors.

Matters immediately went awry when Reno's men were ambushed in a surprise attack, beaten back, and forced to retreat to the top of a ridge where they hung on desperately against a constant onslaught for 48 hours.

At the same time, Custer had marched his troops through the night to the battlefield to attempt a surprise attack. The Indians weren't surprised; their scouts had been watching the general's actions for days and were prepared to do battle. His army outnumbered, as history records, Custer and his 260 soldiers and civilian personnel were routed by thousands of Indian warriors—Lakota, Cheyenne, Blackfeet, Oglala, and Northern Cheyenne, among them—under the leadership of **Sitting Bull, Crazy Horse,** and several other chiefs.

From Battlefield to Park. The battlefield was designated as a national cemetery in 1879 (though by that time, the bodies of Custer, his officers, and two civilians who had been killed in the battle had already been exhumed and buried elsewhere). The rest of the fallen troops' remains were reburied in a common grave at the same time. In the ensuing years, the cemetery became the final resting place for others killed in battles with Indians in the West. The battlefield was administered by the War Department until 1940, when the battlefield's upkeep was transferred to the National Park Service. It was designated as Custer Battlefield National Monument in 1946, and the name was later changed to Little Bighorn Battlefield National Monument in 1992.

Avoiding the Crowds. The national monument is popular, and visitation is busiest in the summer season between Memorial Day and Labor Day. The best advice if you wish to avoid crowds is to avoid these months, or arrive early in the morning or late in the day.

> **The best way to visit the Battlefield is to gain an understanding of what led to this famous battle. Start with a Little Bighorn Battlefield Handbook. Visit during the summer. And follow the brochure that is distributed at our entrance gate.**
>
> **—Superintendent Gerard Baker**

Just the Facts

GETTING THERE & GATEWAYS

Even given its importance in American history, Little Bighorn Battlefield will probably not be your primary destination in Montana. But you will find that it is a relatively easy detour on the way west or east if you are passing through this area, and is worth a trip if you are anywhere close by. Most people who visit the battlefield include it in their trip to Grand Teton or Yellowstone national park (see chapters 19 and 37, respectively), making the trip from the parks themselves or making the detour on the way from the Black Hills of South Dakota (see chapters 3 and 5).

If you are coming from the west, from **Billings,** Montana, take I-90 east 54 miles to the Little Bighorn Battlefield off-ramp at U.S. 212. If you are coming from the south, from **Sheridan,** Wyoming, take I-90 north (approximately 65 miles) to the same off-ramp at U.S. 212. If you are coming from the east, from the **Black Hills of South Dakota,** you will already be on U.S. 212. The battlefield is 42 miles west of Lame Deer, Montana.

The Nearest Airport. Billings is home to the busiest airport in Montana, **Logan International,** located on the rimrocks 2 miles north of downtown. Daily intrastate service is provided by **Big Sky Airlines,** and regional daily service is provided by **Delta, Frontier, Horizon, Northwest,** and **United.** Toll-free numbers of all of these can be found in the appendix.

Renting a Car. If you fly into Billings, you will have to rent a car, and you'll find several national rental chains at Logan International, including **Avis, Budget, Hertz,** and **National.** Their toll-free numbers are given in the appendix.

About the Superintendent

Since Baker was appointed superintendent of the park, a change has occurred that is resulting in a more balanced interpretation of the battle to visitors.

Baker is a full-blooded Mandan-Hidatsa Indian, raised at the Fort Berthold Reservation in North Dakota in a traditional Indian environment. Somewhat of a pioneer, Baker has opened the door to a different interpretation of the battle than historically presented by adding American Indians to the staff presenting interpretive talks.

"Our job is to tell the whole story of the events," he says. The major difference in information presented by Indian rangers is that "some have more personal insight based on stories passed from generation to generation by the families of warriors who were involved in the event."

Revisionist history?

"Not at all," Baker says, "we have merely 'humanized' the battle so that we aren't simply relating facts."

Baker's actions have not been without turmoil, since strong objections to his approach have been vocalized by "Custer buffs," who prefer the traditional methods of presenting the information.

GETTING INFORMATION BEFORE YOUR TRIP

You can get information before you leave by contacting the **Superintendent, Little Bighorn Battlefield National Monument,** P.O. Box 39, Crow Agency, MT 59022 (☎ **406/638-2622;** fax 406/638-2623). (The park has a page on the National Park Service Web site at **www.nps.gov/libi**; while many of these Web pages are filled with information, this one isn't, at least as of this writing.)

VISITOR CENTER

The visitor center is located just past the entrance and is an excellent starting point for a park tour. Visitors can view actual uniforms worn by Custer, read about his life, and see an eerie reenactment of the battles on a small-scale replica of the battlefield as dotted lights trace the movements of each army unit, as well as the Indian defenders. The park is open daily from 8am to 8pm from Memorial Day to Labor Day; spring and fall hours are 8am to 6pm; winter hours are 8am to 4:30pm.

ENTRANCE & CAMPING FEES

There is a $4 admission fee per vehicle. There is no camping available at the national monument.

SEASONAL EVENTS

Two celebrations commemorate the events of the battlefield. During **Little Bighorn Days,** an annual event in Hardin held in late June, the Battle of the Little Bighorn is reenacted for the public. The reenactment takes place 20 miles from the original battle site at a site 6 miles from Hardin. For information on specific dates, call ☎ **406/665-1672.**

The second, **Anniversary Days,** was first held at the monument in 1996 under the auspices of the Park Service and the park's new superintendent. This event brings together members of the five tribes that participated in the battle—some of whom were enemies of one another at the time, but shared a common disdain for the army—and members of the Seventh Cavalry, now based in Fort Hood, Texas. More than 7,000 visitors attended the last event.

USEFUL PUBLICATIONS

Available in the souvenir and gift shop at the visitor center are books proposing every imaginable theory on what actually took place, including the recently published book, ***Killing Custer*** (W.W. Norton and Co., 1994), by Montanan James Welch and Paul Stekler, which pieces together the battle from a Native American's perspective.

Seeing the Highlights in a Day

Since the road from the visitor center along the ridge overlooking the battlefield to the end of the park is only 4.5 miles long, it's possible to view the entire site in less time than passes during halftime of an NFL football game.

However, we think you'll shortchange yourself with that approach. Instead, plan to spend enough time to explore the visitor center, listen to interpretive historical talks presented by rangers there, and then tour the site. We think you'll leave with a greater appreciation for the monument and understanding of the history that led up to the battle.

After you've gotten a good dose of history at the visitor center to whet your appetite for exploration and put everything into context, the best way to explore the battlefield—and to see events in the sequence in which they occurred—is first to drive 4.5 miles from the visitor center to the **Reno-Benteen Monument Entrenchment Trail,** which is located at the end of the monument road, and double back.

Interpretive signs at the top of this bluff, which overlooks the encampment in which thousands of Indians had congregated, not to mention the Bighorn River, show the route followed by the armies of Custer, Benteen, and Reno as they approached the area from the south, and the position from which they defended themselves from their Indian attackers.

As you proceed north along the ridge, you'll pass **Custer's Lookout,** the spot from which the general first viewed the Indian village, which was populated by what may have been the largest gathering of Plains Indians in history. This was the spot at which Custer sent for reinforcements, though he continued marching north.

Capt. Thomas Weir lead his troops to **Weir Point** in hopes of assisting Custer, but was immediately discovered by the Indian warriors and forced to retreat to the spot held by Reno.

The **Medicine Trail Ford,** site no. 4 on the ridge, overlooks a spot well below the bluffs in the Medicine Trail Coulee on the Little Bighorn River, where hundreds of warriors who had been sent from the Reno battle pushed across the river in pursuit of Custer and his army.

Further north, the Cheyenne warrior Lame White Man led an attack up **Calhoun Ridge** (marker no. 5) against a company of the Seventh Cavalry that had charged downhill into the coulee. When Indian resistance overwhelmed the army, troops retreated back up the hill, where they were killed.

As you proceed to **markers no. 6 and 7,** you will find detailed descriptions of the events that occurred on the northernmost edges of the ridge, as well as **white markers** that indicate the places where army troops fell in battle.

Interestingly, regardless of which account of the battle you read, or which historian tells the tale, there is general agreement that no one knows where Custer died, or how. He was last seen on the ridge calling for the charge to battle, but his actions after that, including the cause and place of his death, are unrecorded. The bodies of the general, his brothers Tom and Boston, and nephew Autie Reed, all were found near marker no. 7 on **Custer Hill.**

Indian casualties during the rout are estimated at 60 to 100 warriors. Following the battle, which some say began early in the morning and ended within 2 hours, the Indians broke camp in haste and scattered to the north and south. Within a few short years they were all confined to reservations.

The bodies of Custer and his slain army were buried by the survivors of the Reno-Benteen armies in the place they fell. In 1881, the graves that could be located were reopened, and the bones reinterred at the base of a **memorial shaft** found overlooking the battlefield. Custer's remains were eventually reburied at the U.S. Military Academy at West Point in 1877.

Regardless of your personal view of the events that led to the battle, it is not possible to leave the Little Bighorn Battlefield without having a sense of the historical and cultural importance of the monument. While the battlefield commemorates the events of a tragic day in history, on a grander scale it presents a vivid reminder of the tumultuous events that characterized the West in the 19th century, some of which continue in the 20th century.

A GUIDED TOUR

If you want to get an insider's view that most of your fellow tourists will not have, immersing yourself in the history and culture of the area for a day, or a week, contact **Frontier Adventures,** P. O. Box 85, Colstrip, MT 59323 (☎ **800/684-5469**, PIN 2937), to arrange a comprehensive tour of the area led by a historian. During the trip you will trace the steps of the western expansion at several forts and along the Bozeman Trail, visit Native American campsites and petroglyphs, and find places unnoticed and undiscovered by most tourists. As you approach the end of the tour, you will travel south along the same routes followed by the Indians, who were retreating to the Little Bighorn in advance of Custer's army. You'll travel to the Crow's nest, a sight unseen by most visitors, along the same trail as Custer, Reno, and Benteen. Eventually reaching the southern end of the battlefield, you'll tour the area of the Indian encampment, and the battlefield ridge. The tour is possible in a long, but interesting, day. Rates start at $119 per day, and include lunch and transportation.

Accommodations

NEAR THE MONUMENT

There are no camping or picnicking facilities at the park.

The closest accommodations to the battlefield are in Hardin, 15 miles north of the battlefield on I-90.

The **American Inn,** 1324 N. Crawford Ave., Hardin, MT 59034 (☎ **800/582-8094**), has 42 units. A single costs $47, a double $65. The motel is located right off I-90 at Exit 495. This is definitely a one-stop shopping arrangement for families having, as it does, a 140-foot water slide for the kids, swimming pool and hot tub, and, just across the parking lot, a family-style restaurant, casino, and lounge. Room configurations include queen-size and double rooms, some with small refrigerators.

Just across the road, the **Super 8 Motel–Hardin,** 201 W. 14th St., Hardin, MT 59034 (☎ **800/800-8000** for reservations), with 49 rooms ranging in price from $46 to $52, is your next best alternative. This property offers no amenities except a room with a TV and bath, although the motel will provide you with a cup of coffee and a piece of toast in the morning.

Dining

NEAR THE MONUMENT

Little Bighorn Battlefield National Monument offers no dining facilities, so you are limited to places in Hardin as well. While not a culinary wasteland, it's close.

For the typical diner and things chicken-fried, try the **Purple Cow** (it's hard to miss), just east of the interstate at the Hardin Exit. For Indian tacos (cheese, ground beef, and veggies piled high), head 15 miles south where I-90 meets U.S. 212, and stop off at the **Custer Battlefield Trading Post** just across from the Little Bighorn Battlefield. Otherwise, don't expect much more than cafe food and fast-food restaurants.

25

MESA VERDE NATIONAL PARK

by Alex Wells

WITH MORE THAN 4,000 ARCHAEOLOGICAL SITES, MESA VERDE National Park is the largest archaeological preserve in the country and one of only 12 worldwide to be designated as a World Heritage Site by the United Nations Educational, Scientific, and Cultural Organization. Among the sites are some of the largest cliff dwellings in the world as well as mesa-top pueblos, pit houses, and kivas (subterranean rooms used for meetings and ceremonies)—all of which were built by the Ancestral Puebloans. The sites here tell the story of a 1,000-year period (A.D. 300–1300) during which these people shifted from a semi-nomadic hunter-gatherer lifestyle to a largely agrarian way of life centered around large communities in cliff dwellings. To protect these archaeological treasures, Congress established Mesa Verde National Park in 1906.

Mesa Verde must have looked inviting to the Ancestral Puebloans, whose descendants are the modern Pueblo tribes such as the Hopi, Zuni, and Acoma. On the mesa's north side, 2,000-foot-high cliffs form a natural barrier to invaders. The mesa slopes gently to the south, and from that slope erosion has carved numerous canyons, most of which receive abundant sunlight and have natural overhangs for shelter.

The Ancestral Puebloans became especially adept at surviving here. The mesa tops were covered with loess, a red, wind-blown soil good for farming. And while water was scarce, it could seep into the sandstone overhangs where the Ancestral Pueblo people eventually made their homes. For food, they farmed beans, corn, and squash; raised turkeys; foraged in the pinyon-juniper woodland; and hunted for game such as cottontail rabbits and deer. They wove sandals and clothing out of yucca fibers, and traded for precious stones and shells, which they used to make jewelry.

To the visitor today, however, their most impressive accomplishments are the multistoried cliff dwellings, which had been largely ignored until two ranchers, Richard and Charles Wetherill, discovered Cliff House while running cattle in the 1880s. The towers, kivas, and terraces of these dwellings, which were built between 1100 to 1300, seem to reveal an intelligence born of the earth itself. All have the shaped rectangular stones typical of Mesa Verde–style masonry, sophisticated ventilation systems, and, sometimes, painted walls.

Avoiding the Crowds. With 650,000 visitors annually, Mesa Verde seems packed at times. But John Sheek, a district ranger, points out that the numbers drop sharply in early and late summer. "June 15th to August 15th is our high summer visitation period," he says. "If people can come the first 2 weeks of June or the last 2 weeks of August, they'll hit less crowds."

Another way to beat the crowds, says Sheek, is to make the 12-mile drive to Wetherill Mesa. In 1996, only 8% of the park's visitors—just over 50,000 people—ventured to the mesa, which has some of the park's most interesting archaeological sites. The third and perhaps best way to beat the crowds, according to Sheek, is to hike one of the backcountry trails. "With our backcountry closed to camping, our hiking trails aren't used very much," he says. "These are great ways for people to get away."

Just the Facts

GETTING THERE & GATEWAYS

Mesa Verde National Park is in southeastern Colorado, about 200 miles southwest of Denver and 252 miles northwest of Albuquerque. The park entrance is located on U.S. 160, 10 miles east of the town of Cortez and 6 miles west of Mancos. The nearest lodging and restaurants are in Cortez, Mancos, and Dolores (10 miles north of Cortez on Colo. 145).

From Cortez, U.S. 666 runs north to Monticello, Utah (and on to Salt Lake City), and south to Gallup, New Mexico (on I-40). U.S. 160 runs east through Durango to Walsenburg, I-25, and west through the Four Corners area to the Grand Canyon region of Arizona. Colo. 145, north to Telluride and Grand Junction, intersects U.S. 160 at the east end of town.

The Nearest Airport. **Cortez–Montezuma County Airport** (☎ **970/565-7458**) is located on Country Road G, off U.S. 160/666, 1.5 miles southwest of Cortez. **United Express Airlines** (☎ **800/241-6522** or 970/565-9510) offers daily service between Cortez and Denver as well as limited service between Cortez and other cities in the Southwest. Rental cars are available at the airport through **U-Save Auto Rental** (☎ **970/565-9168**).

GETTING INFORMATION BEFORE YOUR TRIP

To receive a free planning guide for your trip to the park, contact **Mesa Verde National Park,** P.O. Box 8, Mesa Verde N.P., CO 81330 (☎ **970/529-4461**). For advance information on the area, contact the **Mesa Verde Country Visitor Information Bureau,** P.O. Box HH, Cortez, CO 81321-0990 (☎ **800/253-1616**); or the **Cortez Chamber of Commerce,** P.O. Box 968, Cortez, CO 81321 (☎ **970/565-3414**). The National Park's Web site is **www.nps.gov/meve**.

VISITOR CENTERS

The main visitor center is the **Far View Visitor Center,** 14 miles southwest of the Park entrance. This is the only place that sells tickets for the ranger-guided hikes. The center has an information desk, an impressive display of Native American art, and a small gift shop. It's open only during the summer from 8am to 5pm.

The volunteers at the small Morefield Ranger Station in Morefield Village share information on the hikes around the campground, on the campground itself, and on the Junior Ranger Program. It's open in summer only, usually during afternoon and early evening. A few books are sold here.

The Chief Ranger's Office is located at park headquarters near the Chapin Mesa Museum. It has the latest information on weather and can handle emergencies. Register here for the Petroglyph Point and Spruce Canyon trails.

The Chapin Mesa Archaeological Museum (open from 8am to 6:30pm in summer and 8am to 5pm the rest of the

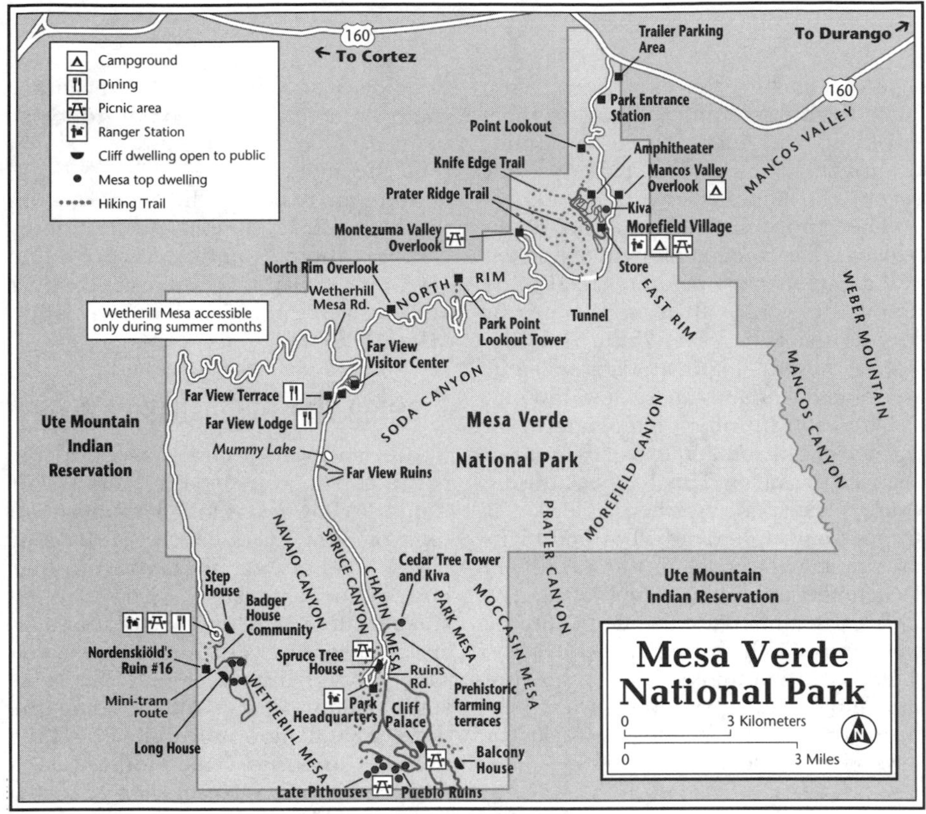

year) has dioramas and interpretive displays tracing the developments in the Pueblo culture. There's also a ranger-staffed information desk. The Mesa Verde Museum Association runs a bookstore here with over 400 titles on Native American and Southwestern subjects.

GETTING AROUND

The Park Service operates a minitram in the Wetherill Mesa area during the summer season. Leaving from the parking area, it will take you to the archaeological sites here. This is a real time-saver, since your only other choice is to hike; cars aren't permitted on the road in this area beyond the parking area.

SPECIAL REGULATIONS & WARNINGS

To protect the many archaeological sites, the Park Service has outlawed backcountry camping and off-trail hiking. It's also illegal to enter cliff dwellings without a ranger present. Similarly, all artifacts and archaeological sites are protected by federal law, so be very careful around the sites.

Driving at Mesa Verde takes time. The drive from the entrance gate to Far View Visitor Center takes roughly 45 minutes. From there, allow an additional 30 minutes to reach Cliff House or Balcony House and an hour to reach Wetherill Mesa. The Wetherill Mesa Road cannot accommodate vehicles longer than 25 feet. Cyclists must have lights to pedal through the tunnel on the entrance road.

SEASONS & CLIMATE

With an average annual precipitation of just 18 inches, Mesa Verde remains a dry place despite being between 6,000 feet and 8,572 feet high. For 10 months of the year, precipitation averages between

1 and 2 inches, the exceptions being June, the driest month with just .64 inches of rain, and August, when heavy rains dump 2.08 inches. The park typically receives 80 inches of snow in a season.

The Ancestral Puebloans no doubt learned that the mesa is a temperate place. Summer temperatures tend to be about 10° cooler than in the nearby Montezuma Valley. Even during July, the hottest month, highs average an easily bearable 87° and nighttime lows dip into the mid-50s. In winter, temperatures on the mesa can sometimes be 10° *warmer* than in the valley. This happens during calm, clear periods when cold air is trapped in the lowlands. Daytime highs on the mesa average in the low 40s in December, January, and February.

Because winter storms often continue well into March, spring tends to come late. Warm autumns, however, are not uncommon. In April, average temperatures are 5° cooler (60s for highs, 30s for lows) than in October.

SEASONAL EVENTS

◆ One weekend a month during summer, Native American artists demonstrate their crafts at various locations in the park.

◆ For 3 days in late July, Morefield Campground hosts the Mesa Verde Indian Arts and Crafts Sales Show.

◆ In August, Hopi dancers perform at Chapin Mesa Amphitheater. Contact the park for event dates.

USEFUL PUBLICATIONS

Written by Gil Wenger, a former chief archaeologist at the park, ***The Story of Mesa Verde*** (1980, Mesa Verde Museum Association) summarizes the natural and human histories of this area. Most of the book traces developments in the Ancestral Pueblo culture, frequently citing examples from the ruins at Mesa Verde.

In ***Indians of the Mesa Verde*** (Mesa Verde Museum Association), author Don Watson attempts to re-create a year (1268) in the life of the Ancestral Puebloans at Cliff Palace. The author draws on archaeology and anthropology to make an educated guess as to what their life might have been like.

You can purchase these books from the Mesa Verde Museum Association by calling their toll-free order line (☎ **800/305-6053**). Or you can visit their Web site at **http://mesaverde. org/EBP/MV/MV.html**.

Seeing the Highlights in a Day

If you have only a day to spend at the park, stop first at the Far View Visitor Center to buy tickets for a late-afternoon tour of either Cliff House or Balcony House—visitors are not allowed to tour both on the same day. Then travel to the Chapin Mesa Museum, where dioramas and interpretive displays will tell you some of the history behind the ruins you're about to see. After visiting the museum, walk down the trail behind the museum to Spruce Tree House. Lunch at Spruce Tree Terrace, then take the Ruins Road Drive. Cap your day with the guided tour. If time permits, you may wish to stop at Far View Ruins or the Cedar Tree Tower on your way out of the park.

If you have a second day at the park, stop at the visitor center to buy a ticket for the Long House Tour. Then travel to Wetherill Mesa. Either before or after your tour, visit the other sites on the mesa, including Step House and the Badger Community Trail. Upon returning to Chapin Mesa, you might take a walk on a backcountry trail.

Exploring the Park by Car

The main scenic drive in the park is the Mesa Top Ruins Drive. Each of the 10 stops along this 6-mile loop either overlooks cliff dwellings or is a short walk from mesa-top dwellings. The sites date from A.D. 675 to A.D. 1275 and include structures from the Basket Maker and three Pueblo periods. By reading the interpretive panels at each site, you can learn about the developments in architecture and the changes in Pueblo culture during those periods. Highlights include the Square Tower House Viewpoint, where you can use your binoculars to hunt for some of the 60 cliff dwellings in this canyon; Sun Point Pueblo, where a tunnel links a kiva—a subterranean room used in ceremonies—to a lookout tower; and the mysterious Sun Temple, a "D"-shaped structure that may have been a shrine.

On your way back to the Far View Visitor Center from the Mesa Top Ruins Road, consider stopping at Cedar Tree Tower, the first right after the four-way stop. There, you'll find another tower connected to a kiva by a subterranean tunnel. Southwest of this tower is the trailhead to the Farming Terrace Trail. (See "Day Hikes," below.) At the Far View Sites Complex, located 1 mile south of the Far View Visitor Center, six ruins are within walking distance, including what seems to be the remains of an ancient reservoir.

Organized Tours & Ranger Programs

Three of the park's spectacular cliff dwellings—Cliff Palace, Balcony House, and Long House—can only be visited during ranger-guided tours, for which there is a small charge. Tickets, which at this writing cost $1.35, go on sale at 8am every morning at the Far View Visitor Center. Visitors may tour Long House and either Cliff Palace or Balcony House on the same day, but may not tour both Cliff Palace and Balcony House in 1 day.

Departing every half-hour between 9am and 6pm, the Cliff Palace tour involves a 100-vertical-foot descent to the dwelling and a same-height climb to exit. In between, you'll have to scale a single 10-foot-high ladder. The work is well worth it. With 217 rooms and 23 kivas, Cliff Palace is the largest cliff dwelling in the Southwest and one of the largest in the world. Especially striking is the original red-and-white wall painting that remains inside a four-story tower.

Merely reaching the 45-room Balcony House, the most fortresslike of the Mesa Verde dwellings, will make you appreciate the agility of the Ancestral Puebloans, who used hand and foot holds and log ladders to scale the cliffs. During the tour, you'll descend 90 vertical feet of stairs, climb 32- and 20-foot-long ladders, and slip through a narrow 30-foot-long crawl space. When you do reach the dwelling, you'll be standing on a level stone floor 700 feet above the creek bed of Soda Canyon. The Puebloans dumped tons of fill inside 15-foot-high stone retaining walls below this floor, creating a level surface on which to build. Tours run every half-hour between 9am and 5pm.

Some people on the Long House tour will remember, above all, the 0.5-mile walk, the flight of 52 stairs, and the two 15-foot-high ladders they had to negotiate. Others will recall the dwelling itself, with its 21 kivas and 150 rooms stretching across a long alcove in Rock Canyon. At its center is a large plaza where the community gathered and danced. Granaries are tucked like mud dauber nests into two smaller alcoves (one above the other) to the rear of the large one. Tours meet at the minitrain depot on Wetherill Mesa and run every half-hour from 10am to 5pm.

The Cliff Palace tours run from mid-April to mid-November, a few weeks longer than the season for Balcony House. Wetherill Mesa, site of Long House, is open only from Memorial Day weekend through Labor Day. To replace these attractions during the off-season, the park offers ranger-guided tours of Spruce Tree House, a self-guided area in summer. Call the park to find out the exact opening and closing dates for its tours.

Day Hikes

SHORTER TRAILS

ON CHAPIN MESA

Spruce Tree House

0.25 mile one way. Easy. Access: Chapin Mesa Museum.

Open from 8:30am to 6:30pm daily during summer, this paved trail descends from behind Chapin Mesa Museum to Spruce Tree House, a dwelling with 114 rooms and eight kivas. Because Spruce Tree House sits in an 89-foot-deep alcove, this is the best-preserved dwelling at Mesa Verde. Rangers are here to answer questions during high season. Off-season, they guide tours here. The trail is accessible to the mobility-impaired, although they may require assistance on some of its grades.

Farming Terrace Trail

0.25 mile RT. Moderate. Access: The trailhead is just southwest of the parking area for Cedar Tree Tower.

This trail crosses over to a wash (dry riverbed) in which the Ancestral Puebloans built a series of check dams used to trap water and soil for farming. It goes a short distance down the wash before looping back to the trailhead.

ON WETHERILL MESA

Step House

0.5 mile RT. Easy. Access: Parking area on Wetherill Mesa.

This loop descends roughly 75 feet of stairs and switchbacks to Step House, a cliff dwelling that dates from A.D. 1226. Three Modified Basket Maker pithouses dating from A.D. 626 are found to the left of Step House (as you look toward it). A set of prehistoric stone stairs climbs from these ruins toward a break in the cliffs.

Badger House Community Trail

0.75 mile RT. Easy. Access: Wetherill Mesa Parking Area.

This handicapped-accessible tour visits mesa-top ruins on Wetherill Mesa. Usually uncrowded, the paved trail is accessible from one of three minitram stops or by making a longer walk from the parking area. The 12-stop self-guided tour details 600 years of history.

Nordenskiold's Site no. 16 Trail

2 miles RT. Easy. Access: Wetherill Mesa Parking Area.

Begin this quiet hike by taking the minitram to its trailhead, or by making a longer walk from the parking area. Mostly flat, the dirt trail descends over rocks for the last few yards before it reaches an overlook of Site no. 16, a 50-room cliff dwelling that was occupied for most of the 13th century. On the way, the self-guided tour identifies many of the plants in the area.

NEAR MOREFIELD CAMPGROUND

Knife Edge Trail

1.5 miles RT. Easy. Access: Near Morefield Village.

This trail follows the old Knife Edge Road, the only automobile route to the ruins until a tunnel was blasted between Prater and Morefield canyons in 1957. Now, during wet years, wildflowers brighten the old roadbed, which hugs the side of Prater Ridge on one side and drops off all the way to the Montezuma Valley on the other. A self-guided tour identifies many of the plant species along the trail. From the end of this trail, you can watch the sun set behind Sleeping Ute Mountain.

Point Lookout Trail

2.3 miles RT. Moderate. Access: Near Morefield Village.

This trail rises in tight switchbacks from the northeast corner of the campground to the top of Point Lookout, a monument conspicuous from near the park's entrance. It then traverses the top of this butte to a stunning overlook of the Montezuma Valley. Sheer drops in several places make this trail unsuitable for small children.

Prater Ridge Trail

7.8 miles RT. Moderate. Access: Near Morefield Village.

This loop rises 700 feet from the campground's west side to the top of Prater Ridge. Once atop the ridge, the trail forks, looping around the top of the mesa and opening onto views of the Montezuma and Mancos valleys and the La Plata Mountains. A cutoff trail halves the mesa-top loop, which zigzags around a number of side canyons. Because the trail is faint in places where it crosses the sandstone, some route-finding skills may be necessary here.

LONGER TRAILS

ON CHAPIN MESA

Three backcountry trails on Chapin Mesa are open to day hikers. Before hiking the Petroglyph Point and Spruce Canyon trails, register at the ranger station, where a booklet for the self-guided tour on the Petroglyph Point Trail can be borrowed or purchased for 25¢. No permit is required for the third one, the Soda Canyon Overlook Trail.

Petroglyph Point Trail

2.8 miles RT. Moderate. Access: A short distance down the paved trail to Spruce Tree House Ruin, just below the Chapin Mesa Museum and Chief Ranger Station.

This loop trail travels just below the rim of a side canyon of Spruce Canyon. It eventually reaches Petroglyph Point, one of the park's most impressive panels of rock art. Just past the petroglyphs, the trail climbs to the rim. It stays on the relatively flat rimrock on its return to Chapin Mesa Museum.

Spruce Canyon Trail

2.1 miles RT. Moderate. Access: Same as Petroglyph Point Trail.

This moderately difficult 2.1-mile loop trail descends 500 feet into a tributary of Spruce Canyon. Turning to the north, it travels up the bed of Spruce Canyon before climbing in steep switchbacks to the rim. It reaches the rim near the park's picnic area, a short walk from Chapin Mesa Museum. The vegetation along the bottom of the canyon includes Douglas firs and ponderosa pines, which flourish in the moist, cool canyon-bottom soil.

Soda Canyon Overlook Trail

1.5 miles. Easy. Access: The trailhead is located at a pulloff on the Cliff Palace Loop Rd.

This dirt trail crosses the rim from a parking area on the Cliff Palace Loop Road to overlooks of Soda Canyon and Balcony House. To view Balcony House, go right when the trail forks.

Camping

One campground in the park is impressive. **Morefield Campground** Aramark, 109 S. Main, P.O. Box 277, Mancos, CO 81328 (☎ **970/529-4474** in summer, 970/529-4421 in winter), located 4 miles past the entrance station on the park's entrance road, is the largest in the National Park System. Its 430 sites line four loop roads on the gently sloping floor of Morefield Canyon. For tent campers, the sites on Navajo Loop afford extra privacy. Though lower than the others, this loop is free of RVs and cuts into dense clusters of gambel oak.

If you'd rather look around, head for Hopi Drive, where the campsites are higher and less wooded than the others, affording views down the canyon. At dusk every night, mule deer browse in the bushes around many campsites. RV drivers will find 15 water-electric hookups. Showers cost 85¢ at Morefield Village, just outside the campground entrance, where laundry service is also available. The campground itself has public toilets, drinking water, and public phones. The fee is $17 for RV hookups, $10 for other sites. The campground is closed from mid-October until late April (call ahead for exact dates). Reservations are not accepted, but don't worry: This mammoth campsite has filled up only once in the last 5 years.

Accommodations

INSIDE THE PARK

Far View Lodge

Mesa Verde Company, Box 277, Mancos, CO 81328. ☎ **800/449-2288** or 970/529-4421. 150 rms. June 1–Sept 20 $94; Apr 24–May 31, Sept 21–Oct 25 $73. Closed Oct 26–Apr 23. AE, DISC, MC, V.

You can save nearly 2 hours each day by staying here and not commuting to the park. This should free up time for relaxing in the captain's chairs on the private deck of your room, from which you'll see as far as New Mexico on a clear day. Located in 17 buildings scattered across the hilltop, the rooms don't have phones or TVs, so there's little in the way of distractions. Each has a convex ceiling, Southwestern decor, and two double beds. Surprisingly, this lodge often has openings during high season.

NEAR THE PARK

Best Western Turquoise Motor Inn

535 E. Main, Cortez, CO 81321. ☎ **800/547-3376** reservations only, or 970/565-3778; fax 970/565-3439. 46 rms, 31 suites. A/C TV TEL. May 23–Aug 31 $73; Sept 1–May 22 $58. Rates include continental breakfast. AE, DC, DISC, MC, V.

This pleasant turquoise-and-peach-colored motor inn features 31 new two-bedroom suites in addition to the standard rooms in its older section, which dates from 1963. Recently remodeled, the older rooms feature coffeemakers and 25-inch TVs. Fountains in the courtyards and an indoor spa add to the ambience of this inn, which also has a heated pool.

Holiday Inn Express Cortez

2121 E. Main, Cortez, CO 81321. ☎ **800/626-5652** or 970/565-6000; fax 970/565-3438. 92 rms, 8 suites. A/C TV TEL. $96 (high season); $78 (off-season). Rates include continental breakfast. AE, DC, DISC, MC, V.

The 4,000 flowering plants on the grounds of this hotel draw tourists like nectar draws hummingbirds. Once on the hotel grounds, guests flit between luxuries—a 15-station fitness center, an indoor swimming pool, a hot tub, and the margaritas and Foster's drafts at Ko Ko's Friendly Pub—or they simply nest in one of the newly remodeled guest rooms, most of which have views of Mesa Verde or Sleeping Ute Mountain. Several suites have been specially designed for kids—in addition to having a king-size bed for the parents, each comes with a partitioned area modeled after a western fort, with bunk beds and a separate TV for the children.

Flagstone Meadows Ranch Bed & Breakfast

P.O. Box 1137, Mancos, CO 81328 (call for driving directions). ☎ **800/664-0719** or 970/533-9838; fax 970/533-9702. 8 rms with private bath. $75. Rates include full breakfast. MC, V.

Named for its flagstone facade and 40-foot-high flagstone chimney, this newly built log home sits at the end of a dirt road on 40 acres of pinyon-juniper woodland. The walls of the bright living room are covered with hunting trophies belonging to the host, former rodeo cowboy Harris Court. Though several rooms have private decks, most guests gravitate to the shared back porch and its views of the Mesa Verde and the La Plata Mountains. Come nighttime, however, the best view is straight up, through steam rising from the hot tub to the crystalline stars above. Breakfast is served on a 14-foot-long table of rough-hewn pine.

A Bed & Breakfast on Maple Street

102 S. Maple (P.O. Box 327), Cortez, CO 81321. ☎ **800/665-3906** or 970/565-3906. 4 rms with private bath. $59–$99; $59 all rms Nov–Mar. Rates include full breakfast. DISC, MC, V.

When not serving afternoon lemonade or a behemoth breakfast, hostess Nonnie Fahsholtz sews quilts for the beds, curtains for the windows, and napkins for the tables. She turns down the covers at night, then, shortly after sunrise, delivers coffee to the rooms. Like her husband, Roy, she seems to love the work. One group of guests felt so much at home here that they returned after checking out to see whether Nonnie had leftovers. Altered repeatedly since its construction in 1901, the house has the idiosyncrasies of a home. In the Pine Room, the ceiling barely clears 6 feet, and the adjoining kid's room is even lower. A vine-festooned spiral staircase leads to a loft room above the parlor.

Rio Grande Southern Bed & Breakfast

101 S. Fifth St. (P.O. Box 516), Dolores, CO 81323. ☎ **800/258-0434** or 970/882-7527. 8 rms, 3 with private bath. $50–$65. Rates include full breakfast. DISC, MC, V. Open Mar 1–Nov 30.

Although the Rio Grande Southern Railroad folded in 1893 after just 2 years in business, the hotel built for its customers has endured to become a National Historic Landmark. You'll check in at the old front desk, climb creaky stairs to the second floor, then drift down the hallway, passing Norman Rockwell prints, a tiny library, and the guest rooms themselves. Filled with antiques, they seem barely large enough to contain their own stories. If you're lucky, you'll be in Room 4, where Zane Gray is said to have stayed while writing "Riders of the Purple Sage." Breakfast is downstairs in a small cafe.

Anasazi Motor Inn

640 S. Broadway, Cortez, CO 81231. ☎ **800/972-6232** or 970/565-3773; fax 970/565-1027. 87 rms. A/C TV TEL. June 1–Sept 30 $62; Oct 1–May 31 $48. AE, DC, DISC, MC, V.

Groups in particular seem to enjoy this motor inn, which has a swimming pool, hot tub, volleyball court, restaurant, and lounge. Large murals—one of pueblo ruins, the other of Native American dances—add color to cinder-block buildings. Many of the ground-floor rooms have patios.

Outpost Motel, Cabins & R.V. Park

1800 Central Ave. (P.O. Box 295), Dolores, CO 81323. ☎ **800/382-4892** or 970/882-7271. 10 motel rms, 3 cabins, 14 full hookups. TV. $45.95 motel; $89 cabin; $16.50 hookup. AE, DISC, MC, V.

The motel rooms here are small and could use new mattresses, but the cabins, which sleep six to eight people, are an excellent value. Their full kitchens make them especially attractive to families who need accommodations for extended stays. A large wood deck overlooks the Dolores River, which borders the property on one side.

Dining

INSIDE THE PARK

Knife Edge Café

Morefield Village. Reservations not accepted. Breakfast and lunch $2.50–$3.57; dinner $6.95 ($3.50 for kids). AE, DISC, MC, V. 7:30am–8pm late May through Labor Day.

During summer, this cafe near Morefield Campground serves all-you-can-eat pancake breakfasts from 7:30 to 10am and dinners of baked chicken and barbecued beef from 5 to 8pm. The lunch menu is limited to a few sandwiches and hot dogs. Tables are outdoors on a sheltered porch, which is bordered on one side by a colorful mural.

Far View Terrace

Across from the Far View Visitor Center. Reservations not accepted. Breakfast $1.70–$5.25; lunch and dinner $2.50–$5.95. Daily 6:30am–9pm late Apr through late Oct. AE, DISC, MC, V. CAFETERIA.

This cafe serves a variety of foods, cafeteria-style, at stations with cryptic names such as "Easy Goes," "Cafe Features," and "Changing Scenes." The wide-ranging menu includes pancakes and eggs at breakfast; and salads, sandwiches, burgers, and Southwestern dishes at lunch and dinner. While eating, you can see as far as New Mexico through a long bank of windows.

Metate Room

Far View Lodge, across from Far View Visitor Center, 17 miles down the park entrance road. ☎ **970/529-4421.** Reservations not accepted. \$9.50–\$20.95. AE, DISC, MC, V. Nightly 5–9:30pm late Apr to late Oct. AMERICAN/ SOUTHWESTERN.

The nicest and by far most expensive restaurant in the park, the Metate Room serves American dishes such as roast turkey, leg of lamb, and steaks, as well as Southwestern meals like enchiladas, carne asada, and chicken stuffed with green chiles. Open for dinner only, the restaurant displays high-quality Indian rugs and pottery, which you might not notice, given the breathtaking views out the windows.

Spruce Tree Terrace

Across from Chapin Mesa Museum. \$1.90–\$3.25. AE, DISC, MC, V. Daily 8am–6pm mid-Apr through Oct; daily 10am–5pm Nov through mid-Apr. CAFETERIA.

Although hamburgers, cheeseburgers, and hot dogs dominate the menu, tossed salads, yogurt, and ice cream are also available. Sit in the Southwestern-style dining area, or take your food out onto the deck.

NEAR THE PARK

Main St. Brewery and Restaurant

21 E. Main, Cortez. ☎ **970/564-9112.** Reservations not accepted. Lunch \$4.75–\$5.75; dinner \$6.25–\$13.75. AE, MC, V. Mon–Sat 11am–closing; Sun 4pm–closing. AMERICAN.

Modern thin-bladed fans mince the air under a stamped-tin ceiling, and fanciful murals splash color above subdued wood paneling. The pleasant contrasts found in the decor carry over to the menu. In addition to beer-oriented food such as fish-and-chips, pizza, and bratwurst, it offers delicious light dining, including a vegetarian skewer plate and pasta primavera. The beers here go well with everything. Two especially fine choices are the hoppy, slightly bitter "Pale Export," and the Porter, perfected through a collaboration between the restaurant's owner, Rudi Baeumel, and several world-class brewmeisters in Milwaukee.

Francisca's

125 E. Main, Cortez. ☎ **970/565-4093.** Reservations not accepted. \$4.95–\$9.95. AE, DISC, MC, V. Summer Tues–Sat 11am–10pm; winter Tues–Sat 11am–9pm. NORTHERN NEW MEXICAN.

Owned by a Mexican American named Pete Montano, this restaurant feels festive in ways that chain restaurants like T.G.I. Friday's can only aspire to. Mexican paper flowers and garlands of chilies festoon the wicker gazebos at the center of the restaurant, where you can sip on a blue margarita and gaze out at the crowd usually waiting outside. The fresh northern New Mexican–style food, which features handmade tortillas and locally grown pinto beans, is worth celebrating. Vegetarians will love the veggie fajitas and meatless chile rellenos; carnivores can look forward to menudo (made of beef tripe), and red or green chile with roast pork.

Dusty Rose Café

200 W. Grand, Mancos. ☎ **970/533-9042.** Dinner reservations accepted. Breakfast \$1.75–\$5.25; lunch \$4.25–\$5.50; dinner \$7.50–\$16.50. Daily 7am–2pm and 4:30pm–closing. MC, V. ITALIAN.

Sun-catchers in the windows, a friendly staff, and low prices will remind you that you're still in rural Colorado. The handmade pastas and a number of delicious veal, chicken, and shrimp dishes seem to belong in northern Italy. For starters, you'll receive a hard Italian bread served with butter and cloves of juicy roasted garlic. Appetizers include deep-fried calamari, and grilled herb polenta with sherried mushrooms. If in the mood for pasta, try the Pasta Bella Vista—fettucine with shallots, bacon bits, sun-dried tomatoes, Parmesan cheese, and cream. After capping it off with cheesecake, cappuccino, and an after-dinner drink, you may agree that this is the best restaurant around.

Nero's

303 W. Main St., Cortez. ☎ **970/565-7366.** Reservations recommended. Dinner $6.95–$17.95. AE, MC, V. Summer daily 5–10pm, winter daily 5–9pm. ITALIAN.

A county named Montezuma doesn't sound like a place where you'd expect to find two great Italian restaurants. But the Dusty Rose is one, and Nero's, with food prepared by chef Richard Gurd, a graduate of the Culinary Institute of America, makes two. With just 11 tables in winter (and twice that when the deck opens in summer), Nero's is so small that even the six bar stools seem to jostle for space. The area that isn't crammed with furniture is dominated by Native American pottery, paintings, and sculptures. On a menu that features pasta, chicken, veal, seafood, and pork, the most popular item is the lasagna, made with spicy Italian sausage, hamburger, and four cheeses. If you can find room for an ultrarich desert, try the Bailey's Irish Cream Cheese Mousse.

The Dry Dock Restaurant and Pub

200 W. Main, Cortez. ☎ **970/564-9404.** Reservations accepted. Dinner $5.25–$26.95. AE, DISC, MC, V. Daily 5–10pm. SEAFOOD.

Miles from the nearest reservoir, this restaurant still manages to serve fish that tastes like today's catch. Perhaps due to the lack of water, parts of a fishing boat have been nailed to the restaurant walls. Although chicken, veal, and steak dishes are offered, this is the place to order seafood, whether it has legs (lobster), whiskers (blackened catfish), or a drinking problem (beer-batter shrimp). If you're still hankering for something Southwestern, try the fish burrito, which is delicious.

Old Germany Restaurant

200 S. 8th St., Dolores. ☎ **970/882-7549.** Reservations accepted. Main courses $5.50–$16.80. MC, V. Tues–Sat 4–9pm. GERMAN.

Come to this 1908 Victorian house when you're ready to trade "heart smart" for "hearty." Tuesday through Saturday nights, James Blount, a chef certified in his native Germany, cooks up a dozen rich, flavorful, and decidedly un-Pritiken entrees, including cordon bleu (breaded butterflied pork loin steak filled with ham and cheese); Hungarian chicken (a chicken breast covered with sliced bell peppers and onions in paprika sauce); and pork roast with purple cabbage. The menu does have at least one item that's said to be good for the heart: beer. Thirty-eight-ounce steins of Paulaner Oktoberfest go for $7.50.

Picnic & Camping Supplies

Inside the park, a general store in Morefield Village sells camping supplies and groceries from late April through mid-October. In nearby Cortez, **City Market**, 508 E. Main (☎ **970/565-6504**), sells everything you might want for a picnic or family outing.

26

MOJAVE NATIONAL PRESERVE

by Stephanie Avnet

To most Americans, the eastern Mojave is that vast, bleak, interminable stretch of desert to be crossed as quickly as possible while leaving California via I-15 or I-40. Few realize that these highways are the boundaries of what desert rats have long considered the crown jewel of the California desert.

This land is a hard one to get to know—unlike more developed desert parks, it has no lodgings or concessions, few campgrounds, and only a handful of roads suitable for the average passenger vehicle. But hidden within this natural fortress are some true gems—its 1.6 million acres include the world's largest Joshua tree forest; abundant wildlife; spectacular canyons, caverns, and volcanic formations; nationally honored scenic back roads and footpaths to historic mining sites; tabletop mesas; and a dozen mountain ranges.

It's ironic that the eastern Mojave owes much of its appearance to water—canyons carved by streams, mineral-encrusted dry lake beds, mountains whose colorful layers represent sandstone deposited in ancient oceans—for today the landscape is distinguished primarily by its extreme dryness. The climate changed most dramatically following the end of the last ice age, about 10,000 years ago; around this time the first human inhabitants are believed to have migrated into the Mojave area. Lakes fed by glacial runoff supported fish, large animals, and diverse vegetation. When traditional food like bison and antelope began to diminish, the Native Americans adapted a specialized lifestyle better suited to the arid climate, ultimately relying on small game and plant food like seeds and nuts. Petroglyphs in the region are testament to these early inhabitants.

The European invasion started in the 18th century, when Spanish missionaries and explorers began venturing north from Mexico. They found little use for this forbidding land, and it wasn't until the 19th century that American pioneers ventured into the Mojave. Trappers, adventurers, and settlers continued to cross the desert on their way west, fueling the dream of an overland passage to California that could bypass the daunting Sierra Nevada. The railroad arrived in 1883, boosting existing mining and ranching business; these two concerns still exist inside the modern-day preserve.

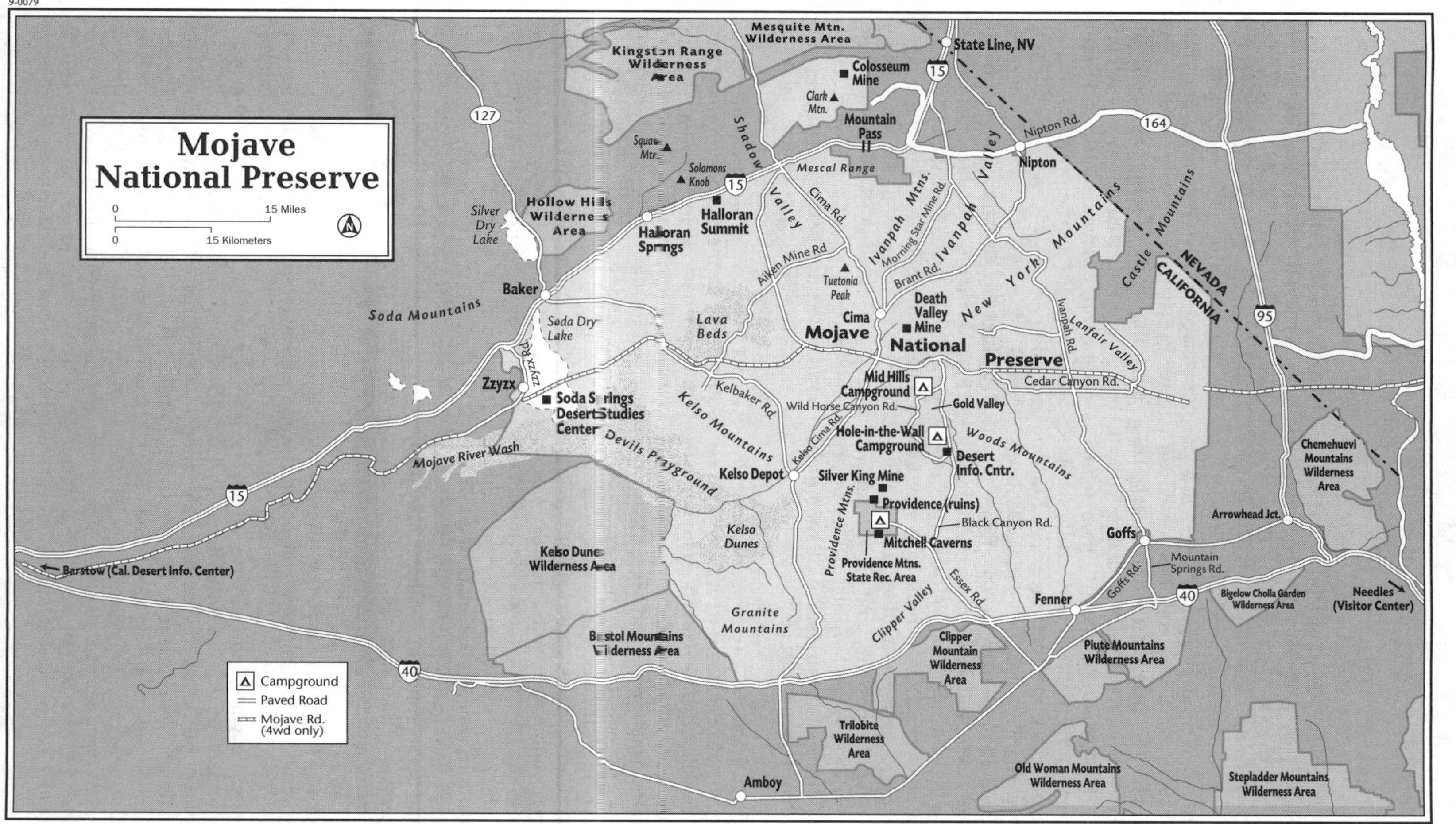
Mojave
National Preserve
0
15 Miles
0
15 Kilometers
Campground
Paved Road
Mojave Rd.
(4wd only)
Mesquite Mtn.
Wilderness Area
State Line, NV
Colosseum
Mine
Clark
Mtn.
Mountain
Pass
Nipton Rd.
Nipton
Shadow
Valley
Mescal Range
Solomons
Knob
Halloran
Summit
Silver
Dry
Lake
Baker
Soda Mountains
Soda Dry
Lake
Zzyzx
Zzyzx Rd.
Mojave River Wash
Devils Playground
Barstow (Cal. Desert Info. Center)
Cima Rd.
Aiken Mine Rd
Lava
Beds
Tuetonia
Peak
Ivanpah Mtns.
Morning Star Mine Rd.
Brant Rd.
Ivanpah
Valley
Cima
Mojave
National
Preserve
Death
Valley
Mine
New
York
Mountains
Castle
Mountains
NEVADA
CALIFORNIA
Ivanpah Rd.
Lanfair Valley
Cedar Canyon Rd.
Mid Hills
Campground
Wild Horse Canyon Rd.
Gold Valley
Kelbaker Rd.
Kelso Mountains
Kelso Cima Rd.
Hole-in-the-Wall
Campground
Desert
Info. Cntr.
Woods Mountains
Kelso Depot
Silver King Mine
Providence (ruins)
Black Canyon Rd.
Mitchell Caverns
Providence Mtns.
Providence Mtns.
State Rec. Area
Kelso
Dunes
Granite
Mountains
Clipper Valley
Essex Rd.
Clipper
Mountain
Wilderness
Area
Trilobite
Wilderness
Area
Amboy
Old Woman Mountains
Wilderness Area
Piute Mountains
Wilderness Area
Fenner
Goffs
Goffs Rd.
Mountain
Springs Rd.
Arrowhead Jct.
Chemehuevi
Mountains
Wilderness
Area
Bigelow Cholla Garden
Wilderness Area
Needles
(Visitor Center)
Stepladder Mountains
Wilderness Area
15
127
164
95
40

By the 1970s, naturalists and environmentalists had become gravely concerned with the protection of this unique area. Destructive off-road use, the theft of rare desert plants, the plunder of archaeological sites, and the killing of threatened desert tortoises all endangered the delicate ecological balance. Two decades of park politicking ended in 1994 when President Clinton signed into law the California Desert Protection Act, which created the new Mojave National Preserve. Thus far, the Mojave's elevated status hasn't attracted hordes of sightseers, and devoted visitors are happy to keep it that way. Unlike with a fully protected national park, the national preserve designation does allow hunting within its borders, and the continued grazing and mining in the preserve's boundaries are a sore spot for ardent preservationists.

Flora & Fauna. There's much more alive in the Mojave Desert than the human eye can immediately discern. Many animals are well camouflaged and/or nocturnal, but if you stay still and keep a sharp eye, the experience is rewarding. Wildlife includes the hopping **kangaroo rat, ground squirrels, cottontails** and **jackrabbits, bobcats, coyotes, lizards, snakes,** and the threatened **desert tortoise.** Consider yourself lucky to spot elusive **bighorn sheep** or shy **mule deer.** Migrating birds that stop off in the Mojave are met by permanent residents like **quail, pinyon jays, sparrows,** noisy **cactus wrens,** and the distinctive **roadrunner.**

You're certain to see familiar desert plants like the fragrant **creosote bush,** several varieties of **cacti** (including the deceptively fluffy looking **cholla "teddy bear" cactus**), and several strains of **yucca,** all relatives to the trademark high desert plant, the **Joshua tree.** On and around Cima Dome grows the world's largest and densest **Joshua tree forest.** Botanists say that Cima's Joshuas are more symmetrical than their cousins elsewhere in the Mojave. The dramatic colors of the sky at sunset provide a breathtaking backdrop for Cima's Joshua trees, some more than 25 feet tall and several hundred years old.

Other desert flora includes therapeutic **Mormon tea, cliff rose, aromatic blue sage, desert primrose,** and **catsclaw;** these flowering plants are among many that make the spring wildflower season a popular time to visit. **Junipers,** seed-bearing **pinyon pines,** and **scrub oaks** are found in the preserve's higher elevations.

Avoiding the Crowds. What crowds? Mojave National Preserve's unforgiving terrain and lack of visitor services discourages mass tourism, setting it apart from most national parks and thrilling the area's fans, most of whom believe that "roughing it" is the only way to appreciate the desert's natural beauty.

It makes sense, however, to be aware of general guidelines governing the California deserts. Peak visitation occurs during the springtime wildflower season (mid-February to May), when the preserve's limited campsites might fill up early in the day. This is particularly true on weekends and during school breaks. As temperatures rise, beginning in May and continuing to October, there's less traffic (if you can call it that) and greater opportunity to see the preserve in solitude.

Just the Facts

GETTING THERE & GATEWAYS

I-15, the major route between Los Angeles and Las Vegas, extends along the northern boundary of Mojave National Preserve. I-40, the major route between southern California and Arizona is the southern access route.

Common entry points include **Kelbaker Road,** which bisects the preserve from Baker at the north, through Kelso in the south. There are Kelbaker exits from both I-15 and I-40.

The **Essex Road** exit from I-40, 25 miles east of Kelbaker Road, is the access point for **Providence Mountains State Recreation Area** (Mitchell Caverns) and the two other campgrounds.

The town of **Nipton,** technically outside preserve boundaries but a common destination for Mojave travelers, is reached via Nipton Road from I-15, within visual range of the Nevada border.

The **Cima Road** exit from I-15 in Mountain Pass leads into the center of the preserve.

Since Mojave National Preserve is so large and the road access sometimes difficult, choose your access route based on the sites you wish to see.

The Nearest Airport. The nearest airport is Las Vegas's **McCarran International Airport,** 5757 Wayne Newton Blvd. (☎ **702/261-5743**). The following airlines have regularly scheduled flights into Vegas: Air Canada, Alaska Airlines, American/American Eagle, America West, American Trans Air, Canadian International, Condor, Continental, Delta/Skywest, Frontier, Hawaiian, Kiwi, Midway, Midwest Express, Northwest, Reno Air, Southwest, Sun Country, TWA, United, US Airways, and Western Pacific. See the appendix for phone numbers.

Renting a Car. All the major car-rental companies are represented in Las Vegas at the airport. National companies with outlets here are **Alamo, Avis, Budget, Dollar, Enterprise, Hertz, National,** and **Thrifty.** See the appendix for their phone numbers. Allstate (☎ **800/634-6186** or 702/736-6148) is a local rental company that also rents four-wheel-drive vehicles.

It's 91 miles (a 1½-hour drive) from Vegas to Baker on I-15, the westernmost point in the Mojave National Preserve. A four-wheel-drive vehicle is recommended for backcountry travel.

GETTING INFORMATION BEFORE YOUR TRIP

Before you leave, contact the **Superintendent, Mojave National Preserve,** 222 E. Main St., Suite 202, Barstow, CA 92311 (☎ **760/255-8801**).

There's some information on the preserve on the National Park Service's Web site at **www.nps.gov/moja.**

VISITOR CENTERS

The best source for up-to-date weather conditions and a free map is the **Mojave National Preserve-Baker Information Center,** 72157 Baker Blvd. (under the "World's Tallest Thermometer"), Baker, CA 92309 (☎ **760/733-4040**). It's open daily from 9am to 5pm and has a superior selection of books for sale.

Those approaching the preserve from I-40 will want to stop in **Needles,** where a brand new **Information Center,** 707 W. Broadway, Needles, CA 92363 (☎ **760/326-6322;** fax 760/326-4119) opened at the end of 1997. More than the Baker facility, this center has extensive exhibits and wall maps in addition to a fully stocked poster- and bookshop; all the official National Park Service publications on the preserve are available. The center is open Wednesday to Sunday; call for hours, which may be extended soon.

Additional information and maps are available inside the preserve at the **Hole-in-the-Wall Ranger Station** (☎ **760/928-2572**), which is open seasonally (as staffing allows).

There's also the **California Desert Information Center,** 831 Barstow Rd., Barstow, CA 92311 (☎ **760/252-6060**), operated by the Bureau of Land Management; it has a minimuseum and educational displays on the history and characteristics of the desert. The center is open daily from 9am to 5pm.

ENTRANCE & CAMPING FEES

At press time, there's no fee to enter Mojave National Preserve and no plans to institute one. For an update on the situation, contact one of the information centers listed above.

There are 69 campsites in the three developed campgrounds in the preserve.

Overnight fees range from $10 to $12. Backcountry camping is free and permits are not required.

SPECIAL REGULATIONS & WARNINGS

The desert can be a dangerous place, but there's little chance that you'll encounter any life-threatening situations, especially if you carefully follow some commonsense safety tips:

◆ Dehydration is a constant threat in the desert; even in winter, carry plenty of drinking water and drink regularly, even if you don't feel thirsty. Recommended minimum supplies are 1 gallon per person per day or twice that if you're planning strenuous activity. Within the preserve, reliable supplies of drinking water are available only at Providence Mountains State Recreation Area (Mitchell Caverns), Hole-in-the-Wall Campground, and Mid Hills Campground.

◆ Follow the National Park Service credo: "Leave only footprints, take only pictures, kill only time."

◆ There's potential flash flooding following even brief rain showers, so avoid drainage areas and be especially observant of road conditions at those times.

◆ Sections of the preserve contain abandoned mines and associated structures. Use extreme caution in the vicinity, watching for open shafts and prospect holes. Supervise children closely and never enter abandoned mines.

◆ The Mojave National Preserve is about 50 miles across from north to south and even longer from east to west; the distance can sneak up on you when you're traveling from one fascinating area to another, happily gazing out the window and not at the gas gauge. There are no service stations within the preserve, so it's wise to keep your tank at least half full, topping off whenever the opportunity presents itself. The nearest gasoline is available in Baker, Barstow, Needles, Amboy, Fenner, Ludlow, Mountain Pass (I-15), and Primm, Nevada.

SEASONS & CLIMATE

The Mojave National Preserve's 1.5 million acres lie in the high desert, with elevations ranging from 1,000 feet to 5,000 feet on average. While December to February can be windy and cold and the desert often gets a dusting of snow, June to September often sees blistering daytime temperatures exceeding 100°F. The best time to visit is between March and May, when temperatures are mild and wildflowers in bloom. October and November have comfortable weather and very few other visitors. The area gets precious little rainfall, but what does occur (usually during winter) can begin suddenly and cause flash flooding and difficult driving conditions.

SEASONAL EVENTS

Best between February and May, the **springtime wildflower viewing** is dependent on weather conditions like rainfall, sunshine, and temperatures, but you can depend on seeing the brilliant blooms somewhere in the preserve each year. The information centers can help direct you to the flowers currently in bloom, and 24-hour recorded information on prime viewing sites (updated at least weekly during the season) is available from the **Payne Foundation Wildflower Hotline** at ☎ **818/768-3533** or the **Living Desert Wildflower Hotline** at ☎ **760/340-4954.**

USEFUL PUBLICATIONS

You may want to check out John McKinney's *Walking the East Mojave: A Visitor's Guide to Mojave National Park* (Harper Collins, 1994), or John Krist's *50 Best Short Hikes in California Deserts* (Berkeley: Wilderness Press, 1995).

Seeing the Highlights in a Day

With careful planning, you can enjoy a good deal of Mojave National Preserve in a limited amount of time. When planning your route, consider the tour schedule at must-see **Mitchell Caverns** (see below) in order to allow time for the 1½- to 2-hour tour. Also remember that some areas are accessible from only one direction; either the north (I-15) or the south (I-40). The following itinerary assumes that you'll be embarking from Baker in the morning and taking the 1:30pm Mitchell Caverns tour.

An alternate itinerary would be to approach the preserve from the south, take the 10:30am tour (weekends and holidays only, excluding summer), drive to Baker for lunch, and then see the other highlights on your way back to I-40. With 2 days in the preserve, you can spread these activities out and add out-of-the-way treats like Soda Springs and the town of Nipton.

Begin in Baker by filling the tank, grabbing some breakfast and packing a picnic lunch, and then setting out on Kelbaker Road around 9am. Sixteen miles into the drive, the landscape darkens with volcanic ash and old lava flows. Dotting the lava beds is a series of **Cinder Cones,** left over from some of the area's volcanic eruptions.

The Kelso junction is about 16 miles farther; stop to explore the **Kelso Depot** (see below), once a bustling passenger/freight station complete with a restaurant and lodging for railroad workers.

If time allows, take the 19-mile trip up to **Cima** via the Kelso–Cima Road, which dips up and down like a roller coaster alongside the railroad tracks; if you're lucky a train will pass by—trains still run through the Mojave about four times daily. The main attraction here is **Cima Dome,** an almost perfectly rounded landform rising like a 75-square-mile mole 1,500 feet above the desert. The dome is a batholith, created by molten rock that, unlike its volcano cousin, stopped rising below the surface. This unusual formation is blanketed by majestic large Joshua trees, and you can further explore it via a marked hiking trail (see below).

Returning to Kelbaker Road, look for the spectacular **Kelso Dunes.** This 45-square-mile formation of magnificently sculpted sand is famous for its "booming," a low rumble emitted when small avalanches or blowing sands pass over the underlying layer. Geologists speculate that the extreme dryness of the East Mojave Desert, combined with the wind-polished, rounded nature of the individual sand grains, has something to do with the musicality. Sometimes the low rumbling sound resembles a Tibetan gong; other times it sounds like a 1950s doo-wop musical group. If you want to get closer or even hike the dunes (see "Day Hikes," below), there's a graded dirt spur about 7 miles south of the Kelso junction.

Continuing south from the dunes, you'll reach I-40 in about 16 miles, after passing through the jutting **Granite Mountains,** where erosion has removed all but resilient chunks of this extraordinarily hard rock. The piles of rosy-hued boulders that remain are alternately smooth and jagged, seeming to adopt familiar shapes when viewed from the right angles.

Take I-40 east to Essex Road; if there's time before the Mitchell Caverns tour, make your way to **Hole-in-the-Wall.** Today there's a ranger station, picnic area, and developed campground, but it's the kind of place that Butch Cassidy and the Sundance Kid would've chosen as a hideout. The twisted maze of rocks is rhyolite, a form of crystallized red lava rock; a series of iron rings aids descent into what is, literally, a "hole in the wall." If you're feeling adventurous (and nimble), scramble through for a glimpse of the canyon behind the rocks. For the extensive hike that begins here, see "Day Hikes," below.

Tucked into the Providence Mountains, in the southern portion of the preserve, is a treat everyone should try to see. The **Mitchell Caverns,** contained in a State Recreation Area in the National Preserve, are a geological oddity exploited for tourism but still quite fascinating. Rangers lead regular tours of these cool rock "rooms"; in addition to showcasing marvelous stalactites, stalagmites, and other limestone formations, the caves have proven to be rich in Native American archaeological finds. Tours are given daily between Labor Day and Memorial Day according to the following schedule: weekdays at 1:30pm and weekends/holidays at 10am and 1:30 and 3pm. In summer tours are Saturday and Sunday only at 1:30pm. They cost $6 for adults and $3 for kids 6 to 17; children under 6 are free. Each tour is limited to 25 people and fills quickly, so arrive early to ensure a spot. For more information, call ☎ **805/942-0662.** *Note:* Additional tours are often added without notice during periods of high demand. To check last-minute schedules or find out whether a particular tour is sold out, call the visitor center directly at ☎ **760/928-2586.**

The visitor center is filled with artifacts and photos of prospectors Jack and Ida Mitchell, who began offering lantern-lit tours of the caves in 1932 after failing to find silver on the property. There's ample opportunity for amateur geologists (young and old) to learn about the powerful forces that created this phenomenon.

Exploring the Park by Car

At the risk of discouraging you from leaving your car to really experience the Mojave, I must admit that **Kelbaker Road** provides an excellent opportunity to sample the preserve with a minimal expenditure of time or trouble. The well-paved two-lane road, bisecting the preserve north to south, between I-15 and I-40, takes about 1 hour one way without stopping.

You'll drive through the eerie blackened landscape of **lava beds** and **cinder cones,** visit the elegant but empty **Kelso Depot,** see the towering golden mounds of **Kelso Dunes,** and end with the dramatically sharp peaked piles of **Granite Mountains.**

Leading northeast from Kelso Depot, the Kelso–Cima Road provides another scenic diversion, running alongside railroad tracks to the tiny town of **Cima,** at the foot of a geological oddity called **Cima Dome.** Cima consists of a tiny U.S. Postal Service outpost and a ramshackle market (don't be fooled by its boarded-up appearance) carrying ice, chilled drinks and candy bars, and a few canned goods. Be prepared for the many heart-stopping dips in the Kelso-Cima Road; they're a favorite with young backseat passengers.

Visitors with four-wheel-drive vehicles or just unusually rugged passenger cars can drive the **Wildhorse Canyon Road,** looping from Mid Hills to Hole-in-the-Wall, at the preserve's heart. In 1989, this short route was declared the nation's first official "Backcountry Byway," an honor that federal agencies bestow on America's most scenic back roads. The 11-mile horseshoe-shaped road crosses wide-open country dotted with cholla and, in season, delicate purple, yellow, and red wildflowers. Dramatic volcanic slopes and flattop mesas tower over the low desert.

Organized Tours & Ranger Programs

The National Park Service ranger programs operate only on weekends between September and May, but they're worth planning a trip around. Organized by district interpreter Kirsten Talken, seasonal events range from 30 minutes to 3 hours and take place within the preserve. Examples of past programs are half-hour naturalist talks on the endangered desert tortoise or the area's violent geological history; expertly guided hikes of Kelso Dunes or the Hole-in-the-Wall petroglyph sites; photography tours with a pro along to give pointers; and evening excursions to stargaze or listen to stories. For more information, contact one of the information centers listed above.

The only organized attraction is Mitchell Caverns, and it's actually in a state park contained in the Mojave Preserve's boundaries. Everyone should try to visit this incredibly unique area (see above for details)—it's easily reached from the freeway, it's educational for kids and adults alike, and it offers a pleasant but not taxing amount of walking. The caves, which maintain an almost constant temperature of 65°F, provide a welcome respite during hot weather. Tours are given daily (see above).

Historic & Man-Made Attractions

In the days of steam engines, the town of Kelso was a critical watering spot for locomotives; elegant **Kelso Depot** was built by the Union Pacific in 1924 and served the railroad's desert run until 1985. The Spanish Revival–style structure was designed with a red-tile roof, graceful arches, and a brick platform. At its peak, during World War II, the town of Kelso supported 2,000 residents—the depot's diner, the Beanery, served customers 24 hours a day. Eventually diesel locomotives replaced the steam engines, and the nearby Vulcan Mine, so critical as a source of wartime iron, was closed. In the 1970s, the depot once again became a gathering place, as outdoor enthusiasts like the Audubon Society, the California Native Plant Society, and the Sierra Club flocked to Kelso's reliable springs to observe local wildlife. Once slated for demolition, Kelso Depot is boarded up and empty now, but the National Park Service is considering refurbishing the building for use as the preserve's visitor center.

Skirting the preserve's northern boundary is the charming whistle-stop town of **Nipton.** Founded in 1885, Nipton was a true ghost town nearly a century later, when Los Angeles transplants Jerry and Roxanne Freeman began restoring its dilapidated buildings and image. Once Nipton was at the center of Mojave industry, providing railroad access for miners and ranchers. Silent film star Clara Bow, who moved here from Hollywood with her rancher husband, Rex Bell, was a frequent visitor. Soon after the Freemans bought the town, they reopened the old trading post and hotel, which now operates as a B&B inn (see "Accommodations," below). The train still whistles by several times a day, greeting the nearly 70 current residents of Nipton.

At the western boundary of the preserve, on the shores of the stark white Soda Dry Lake, is **Soda Springs/Zzyzx.** Reached by taking the Zzyzx Road (a cryptic name that's puzzled generations of motorists) exit from I-15 and carefully negotiating a 4-mile rocky dirt road, the springs have a colorful history. In addition to being an important watering hole along the historic Mojave Road, the site was a Native American camp, a military outpost, a wagon station, the headquarters of a Hollywood radio evangelist, and a once-trendy health resort (sporting the fanciful name of Zzyzx Mineral Springs). The springs are still active, feeding the elegant pools left over from the resort's heyday and supporting an entire ecosystem of wildlife at the lakebed's edge. You can stroll among the buildings, now used by the California State University's Desert Studies Center, and learn more about the area's history—and the quasi-religious resort (which was closed in 1974 after it was determined that the builder had no claim to the land)—from the unmanned visitor center.

Day Hikes

In addition to the marked and maintained hiking trails in the preserve (like those between Mid Hills and Hole-in-the-Wall campgrounds), many hikers create their own routes using the abundant nonpaved roads crisscrossing the area. Some are so poor that they're passable only by sturdy off-road vehicles, so there's little or no traffic to disturb your hike.

There are several good hiking areas along **New York Mountains Road,** west of Ivanpah Road (itself unpaved). Mine ruins, ranch structures, and cool pine-studded canyons characterize the area; New York Mountains Road can be rough on standard passenger cars, so you'll see hikers and campers stopping wherever they can no longer advance. Several

The Mojave Road: A Desert Lifeline

There are scant reminders today of the once-vital **Mojave Road,** a desert lifeline passing through land now contained in the Mojave National Preserve. The Mojave tribe had lived along the Colorado River since the 10th century, cultivating the land and establishing an intricate network of trade stretching from Mexico to Santa Barbara. Friendly tribesmen even guided Spanish explorers and American settlers across the desert in the 18th and early 19th centuries. But by the 1850s, the U.S. government began surveying the land and declared the **Mojave Road** an official route west. As more settlers began staking claims on lands belonging to Paiute, Chemehuevi, Serrano, and Mojave tribes—and as plans were laid to bring the railroad through—the incidence of hostile Indian attacks rose dramatically.

The U.S. government responded by establishing army forts along the way for the protection of white travelers and mail carriers. Four of these lay within the boundaries of today's Mojave Preserve: **Piute Spring, Rock Spring, Marl Spring,** and **Soda Springs.** Only remnants of the Piute Spring fort are still visible; in addition to portions of the foundation and walls, you can also see wagon ruts in the earth. The road continued to flourish through the 1870s and 1880s as mining became important in the Mojave region, but the formerly indispensable Mojave Trail/Road went out with a whimper in 1893 with the completion of the second transcontinental railroad by the Atchison, Topeka and Santa Fe.

One popular legend of the Mojave Road involves Edward Beale, sent by the War Department in 1857 to construct a wagon road between New Mexico and the Colorado River. The overachieving Beale continued into California, bringing along imported camels as pack stock. After completion of the road, the camels were turned loose in the desert. Although the sad likelihood is they all died soon afterward, a popular element of desert folklore involves the apocryphal existence of elusive herds of camel descended from Beale's abandoned animals.

Today much of the road is barely discernable from the desert surrounding it, and because the unpaved trail tended to shift course to accommodate changing conditions, it's nearly impossible to pinpoint a precise path. But remnants can be seen at the four springs along its path, which were mandatory stops for any traveler; some substantial portions also became Cedar Canyon Road, a county-maintained, unpaved road in the eastern portion of the preserve.

If you want to try to navigate portions of the road, check with a park ranger for road conditions; you'll need at least a sturdy, high-clearance vehicle to drive Cedar Canyon Road and four-wheel-drive for most other portions. Some areas, like that around Piute Spring, are accessible only on foot.

Your best source for locating all identifiable remnants of the Mojave Road will be the National Park Service's official illustrated map of trails, a folding, waterproof guide currently in production. It is scheduled to be available at all the visitor centers (at a cost of roughly $8) by the end of 1998.

Also available at all the visitor centers is the "Recreational Map of Mojave National Preserve" ($6.95), which shows details of many roads within the preserve's boundaries, including portions of the Mojave Road that are passable by vehicles.

For additional history and tips on exploring this historic route, the hardcover *Mojave Road Guide* (Tales of the Mojave Road, 1986) by Dennis Casebier is the accepted authority; it's sold at the Baker and Needles visitor centers.

sections of the historic **Mojave Road** are also great for hiking but can be reached only by four-wheel-drive vehicles; remains of the wagon route stretch from Piute Wash beyond the eastern boundary of the preserve, through Cedar Canyon and past the lava beds, all the way to Zzyzx Springs on Soda Dry Lake at the western edge. When you're hiking in the backcountry, please respect private lands, which are usually well-marked.

SHORTER TRAILS

Kelso Dunes

3 miles RT (to the dunes). Moderate. Access: These golden dunes are located about 8 miles south of the Kelso Depot; the trailhead is located at the parking area.

These are the second-highest dunes in California, covering 45 square miles and reaching 700 feet high. The dunes are visible from Kelbaker Road, and 3 miles of graded dirt road leads to a parking area, where several interpretive signs give information on dunes ecology. There's no "trail"—just ramble to your heart's content trying to spot examples of the many plants and animals that live in the seemingly barren dunes. Among them are rodents, kit foxes, lizards, sand verbena, and desert primrose, which color the dunes with brilliant blooms of yellow, white, and pink in springtime. *Note:* Climbing the soft dunes requires some time and exertion, but tumbling back down is the fun reward. Of the 700-foot summit, it's been said, "Two hours up, 10 minutes down!"

Mary Beal Nature Trail

0.5 mile. Easy. Access: The trailhead is located at the Providence Mountains State Recreation Area Visitor Center, on Essex Rd., 16 miles from I-40.

Suitable for all ages, the path winds past examples of the diverse plant and animal life found in the Mojave; the trail is named for the prominent naturalist who spent 50 years in this desert collecting and studying botanical specimens. Numbered posts along the route are keyed to a brochure available for 25¢ inside the visitor center.

LONGER TRAILS

Cima Dome

4 miles RT. Moderate. Access: Start at the marked trailhead, on Cima Rd. between I-15 and the town of Cima (Spanish for "summit").

The well-maintained trail leads up Cima Dome, an unusual volcanic formation, to Teutonia Peak (600 feet elevation from the hike's starting point) and panoramic views of the surrounding desert. You'll walk through the abundant Joshua trees blanketing the dome, as well as Mojave yucca and prickly cholla "teddy bear" cactus. Near the summit, the trail is faint but marked with "cairns," small piles of stones left as signposts. This land is leased for grazing, and the hiking trail encounters two ranch gates: Be sure to close them as you pass through.

Mid Hills/Hole-in-the-Wall

2 miles RT to 8 miles one way. Easy to strenuous. Access: The trailhead is located at the Hole-in-the-Wall Picnic Area.

Stretching between the two campgrounds, this maintained trail can be hiked in part or full. The entire hike is a grand tour of canyons and tabletop mesas, large pinyon trees, and colorful cacti; it's an all-day, one-way undertaking if you can arrange a car shuttle and is much more enjoyable in the downhill direction from Mid Hills to Hole-in-the-Wall. If you're not up for a long day hike, the 2-mile hike from Hole-in-the-Wall Campground to Banshee Canyon offers an easier alternative. From Hole-in-the-Wall, the initial segment of the trail offers the most adventure; climbers descend through a vertical chute in the rock using a series of metal rings placed for this purpose. Even with handholds, the climb requires agility and concentration—don't try it if you have any doubts.

Especially for Kids

There's a lot for kids to enjoy in the Mojave, from scrambling on sandy Kelso Dunes to exploring Mitchell Caverns, which resemble an Indiana Jones movie set. You can show them lava beds so similar to the moon's surface that U.S. astronauts once trained here or make a contest of finding familiar shapes and profiles in the jagged Granite Mountains. Like other National Park Service properties, the Mojave Preserve participates in the **Junior Ranger Program;** kids earn their official Junior Ranger Badge by completing activities in a booklet. The puzzles, drawing exercises, and quizzes are thinly veiled tools to educate young visitors about desert history, wildlife, and ecology. Booklets are available at the Baker, Needles, and Hole-in-the-Wall information centers.

Other Sports & Activities

Biking. Opportunities are as extensive as the preserve's hundreds of miles of lonesome dirt roads. The 140-mile-long historic **Mojave Road,** a rough four-wheel-drive route, bisects the preserve east to west and visits many of the most scenic areas in the East Mojave; sections of this road make excellent bike tours, but you'll definitely need a mountain bike. Prepare well—the Mojave's dirt roads are rugged routes through desert wilderness. There are no bike rentals in the park, so you'll have to bring your own.

Camping

There are three established campgrounds within the Mojave National Preserve. None of the three campgrounds in the preserve has RV utility hookups, though the Hole-in-the-Wall Campground has a dump station. Similarly, no campgrounds have laundry facilities or showers.

The **Mid Hills Campground,** with 26 sites, is in a woodland of pinyon pine and juniper and offers outstanding views. It is located 35.5 miles northwest of Essex, off Black Canyon Road. This mile-high camp is the coolest in the East Mojave. There are no RV utility hookups or dump stations, but the campground's sites will accommodate RVs. Pit toilets, fire grates, and drinking water are provided, but there are no showers or public telephones. The fee for camping is $10 per site per night; the campground is open year-round; camping is on a first-come, first-served basis.

Nearby **Hole-in-the-Wall Campground** is perched above two dramatic canyons, 25.5 miles northwest of Essex, on Black Canyon Road, near the Mid Hills Campground. There are 37 sites available on a first-come, first-served basis year-round for $10 per site per night. You'll find pit toilets, drinking water, public phones, and fire grates, but no showers. There are no RV hookups, but there is a dump station, and the sites accommodate RVs.

Motorist warning: The washboard dirt road between the Mid Hills and Hole-in-the-Wall campgrounds might be too jarring for many two-wheel-drive passenger cars, but it is a good hiking trail (see "Mid Hills/Hole-in-the-Wall" under "Day Hikes," above).

The sites at **Providence Mountain State Recreation Area** (**☎ 805/932-0662** for park headquarters) are adjacent to the Mitchell Caverns Visitor Center. There are only six sites here, available on a first come, first served basis for $12 per night year-round. There are no RV utility hookups or a dump station, but you'll find pit toilets, drinking water, public telephones, and fire grates at each site. There are no showers.

One of the highlights of the East Mojave Desert is camping in the open desert all by your lonesome; at press time **backcountry camping** was fairly unregulated, requiring no registration. Campfires are prohibited outside of designated fire grates; backcountry campers need to pack out all trash; and take care not to set up in a gully or dry wash subject to flash flooding. It's advisable to contact an information center before establishing camp. And please respect private lands, which will marked.

Note: In addition to the campgrounds in the preserve, there will soon be spaces available in a privately owned campground in Nipton, in the open desert beyond the town's historic B&B inn. Amenities will include hot showers, potable water, easy access to the town's "trading post" market, and several RV hookups. For more information and reservations, call ☎ **760/856-2335.** At press time, these facilities were still being developed, but they should be available by the spring of 1998.

Accommodations

INSIDE THE PARK

Aside from camping, there are no overnight accommodations available within the boundaries of Mojave National Preserve.

NEAR THE PARK

Many visitors choose to stay in Barstow; though 1 hour from the preserve, this sizable community offers the greatest level of services, including several gas stations and a variety of dining options. Of the dozen motels in town, the most reliable are the reasonably priced **Best Western Desert Villa,** 1984 E. Main St., Barstow, CA 92311 (☎ **760/256-1781;** fax 760/256-9265), with 113 rooms; and **Holiday Inn,** 1511 E. Main St., Barstow, CA 92311 (☎ **760/256-5673;** fax 760/256-5917), which has 148 rooms. Both of these motels accept major credit cards (AE, CB, DC, DISC, MC, V), and rooms have all the expected amenities. Call for prices and reservations.

In nearby Baker, you'll find inexpensive lodging at a couple of unremarkable motels, including the **Bun Boy Motel,** at the junction of I-15 and Calif. 127 (P.O. Box 130, Baker, CA 92309; ☎ **760/733-4363**). On the Arizona border to the south, a 1-hour drive from the preserve, is **Needles,** which has its fair share of plain-Jane motels. Try the **Best Western Colorado River,** 2371 W. Broadway, Needles, CA 92363 (☎ **760/326-4552;** fax 760/326-4562), or the **Days Inn,** 1111 Pashard St., Needles, CA 92363 (☎ **760/326-5660;** fax 760/326-4002).

Primm, Nevada on the California–Nevada border features three hotel/casinos, each as large and garish as an amusement park. **Whiskey Pete's** (777 rooms), **Buffalo Bill's** (614 rooms), and **Primadonna** (661 rooms) are managed by the same company—the rooms here are pretty nice, really cheap, and (if you have a twisted sense of humor) an ironic counterpoint to the wilderness you came to the Mojave for. With a dozen restaurants, including those low-cost Vegas-style buffets, Stateline might also be your best dining bet. All of the Stateline hotels take major credit cards (AE, DC, DISC, MC, V) and have the expected amenities. For one-stop reservations call ☎ **800/FUN-STOP.**

The charming tiny town of **Nipton** boasts a "trading post" that stocks snacks, maps, ice, and Native American jewelry; and the **Hotel Nipton** (☎ **760/856-2335**), a B&B inn with a sitting room, two bathrooms down the hall, and four small guest rooms, each going for $50 a night. It takes credit cards (MC, V). The inn has an outdoor hot tub and a spectacular nighttime star show. Jerry Freeman, a former hard-rock miner who purchased the entire town in 1984, says hotel occupancy is up 80% since the East Mojave became a national preserve. He and his wife, Roxanne, moved from the famous sands of Malibu to the abandoned ghost town and have gradually brought it back to life; the restored turn-of-the-century adobe hotel is just the start of their plan to make the town a key component of the preserve. Nipton is located on Nipton Road along the northern border of the preserve, a few miles from I-15 near the Nevada state line.

Dining

INSIDE THE PARK

There are no dining facilities within the boundaries of Mojave National Preserve.

NEAR THE PARK

Bear in mind that *near,* when referring to the Mojave National Preserve, is a relative term. The places below range from 30 to 90 minutes from the preserve. The choices are limited; perhaps as the Mojave's increased profile stimulates tourism, visitor facilities like hotels and restaurants will follow. As it stands now, Mojave devotees tend to come for the appeal of raw nature and have little need for elegant (or even contemporary) restaurants.

The dining place nearest to the preserve's northern border is in **Baker** and has long been a beacon to motorists cruising this barren stretch of I-15. **The Mad Greek** (☎ **760/733-4354**), literally at the junction of I-15 and Calif. 127, is a roadside treasure and an ethnic surprise beloved by many. White tiles and Aegean-blue accents complement a menu of traditional Greek specialties like souvlaki, spinach-and-feta spanikopita, stuffed grape leaves, green salad with tangy feta, exquisite pastries, and even Greek beer. The mile-long menu also includes traditional road fare like hamburgers and hot sandwiches. The food is the main attraction, but travelers also know to "hold it" until they reach the Mad Greek's sparkling-clean rest rooms. Also in Baker is the **Bun Boy Restaurant,** at the Bun Boy Motel (see the section above for complete information), offering unimaginative but reliable diner food in a clean, calm setting.

Primm, Nevada, is also nearby on I-15. Over the years, this first exit across the border has grown and seems hell-bent on snatching an ever-increasing amount of business from Las Vegas. *Three* full-fledged hotel/casino developments are now clustered around the interstate; among them you can choose from **10 restaurants,** including 3 separate Vegas-style all-you-can-eat buffets. There's an all-day coffee shop in each resort, one Italian restaurant, one Mexican eatery, and the surprisingly good **Silver Spur Steak House** in Whiskey Pete's. At first the bright neon might seem in garish contrast to the subtle desert beauty all around; but folks with a sense of irony (and a pocketful of quarters) can definitely enjoy it here for a couple of hours. For more information see "Accommodations," above.

Other towns surrounding the preserve that have eating places are **Barstow, Needles, Newberry Springs, Searchlight** (Nevada), and **Yermo.**

Picnic & Camping Supplies

The most reliable source of supplies is in Barstow or Needles, which both have full-size supermarkets. There are small grocery stores and minimarts in Baker, Fenner, Nipton, and Searchlight; well stocked with beverages, ice, and snacks, their selection of canned goods and other supplies is limited.

27

MOUNT RAINIER NATIONAL PARK

by Tom Wells

On summer weekends, when the "mountain is out" or "putting on a show," as the locals say, busloads of tourists descend on Mt. Rainier, camcorders whirring, cameras clicking. Stuck trying to find a parking spot at Paradise, you can easily begin to wonder why you even bothered coming. Why deal with parking problems and traffic jams in the mountains after navigating Seattle or Tacoma's ungodly commuter traffic all week? Well, it's probably because beyond the designated view points, beyond the last no parking signs, beyond the visitor center where people crowd around videos to "experience" the mountain outside, there's an area that sums up the past, present, and future of the Cascades.

For anyone willing to expend a little bit of energy to get away from the roadside crowds, this mountain, which dominates the Puget Sound and western Washington skyline for miles around, has many secrets to share: mountain goats and marmots, streaming waterfalls, ominous walls of ice deep in the rain forest, and thousand-year-old trees set against alpine meadows teeming with summer wildflowers.

Should you visit on a dreary October day, despite what you may think, Mount Rainier was not named for its climatological proclivities. Rather, it was named in 1792 by Capt. George Vancouver for his friend Rear Adm. Peter Rainier (who never laid eyes on the mountain). The region's native people had known it as *Tahoma* for centuries, however, and the name remained (and some might say still remains) contentious up until the early 19th century. Nevertheless, the mountain remains Rainier to most people, while a sprawling city to the south, Tacoma, wound up with the Native American name for some reason.

Although the early peoples stayed away from the glacial peaks of the mountains out of a mixture of respect and fear, they hunted deer, elk, and mountain goats and gathered huckleberries on its lower slopes. Today's Puget Sound inhabitants see Mt. Rainier as a symbol of the wild Northwest, a land that lies in easy reach. Mount Rainier is a constant reassurance of the beauty that lies beyond the sprawl of suburbia.

While most of the mountains in the west were seen as obstacles to overcome by the early pioneers, 14,411-foot Mt. Rainier so captivated early settlers in the Puget Sound area that as early as the 1850s, less than a decade after Seattle was founded, aspiring mountaineers were heading for its snowcapped slopes with the hope of conquering it. In 1857, an army lieutenant, August Valentine Kautz, climbed to within 400 feet of the summit, and in 1870, Gen. Hazard Stevens and Philemon Van Trump made the first recorded complete ascent of the mountain (trapped near the summit at dark, they survived the night huddled in ice caves formed by sulfurous steam vents that kept the air temperature near 170°F). In 1884, James and Martha Longmire opened the mountain's first hotel, the Mineral Springs Resort, at a spot that now bears their name. In 1899, Mount Rainier became the nation's fifth national park, and by 1916, the trail system now known as the Wonderland Trail was completed, forming a loop nearly 100 miles long around the mountain.

Because of its massive system of glaciers and unpredictable weather, Mount Rainier is an unforgiving peak. Climbers throughout the years have died on its slopes for the same reasons the local peoples stayed away, yet each year more than 8,000 climbers set out for the summit of this dozing volcano. However, only 4,500 of them ever reach the top. The rest are turned back by bad weather, altitude sickness, exhaustion, and hazardous glacial crossings. This is not a mountain to be treated lightly, but because of its reputation for difficulty, Mt. Rainier often serves as a training ground for climbers planning expeditions to other famous peaks throughout the world.

Although the mountain is a magnet for climbers, these adventurers make up only a tiny fraction of the 2 million visitors who come to the park each year. This mountain is really all about hiking throughout the alpine meadows, and that is the main activity pursued by the vast majority of park visitors, most of whom visit during the short summer season that lasts only from July to September in the higher elevations.

The Cascades are not dead; they're just sleeping. This fact was driven home with cataclysmic finality with the eruption of Mount St. Helens on May 18, 1980. But what of Mt. Rainier? Could it do the same? Of course not; it's a national park.

Well, that's about as wrong as you can get.

Snow and glaciers notwithstanding, Rainier has a heart of fire. Steam vents at the mountain's summit are evidence of that, though this volcanic peak has been dormant for more than 150 years, it could erupt again at any time. However, scientists believe that Rainier's volcanic activity occurs in 3,000-year cycles, and luckily we have another 500 years (give or take) to go before there's another big eruption. So go ahead and plan that trip. Probably, only the scenery will blow you away.

Terrain. According to local legend, Martha Longmire, who helped found the first hotel in the area, was supposed to have exclaimed, "It looks just like paradise," upon her first visit to the subalpine meadows that now bear that name. It is these meadows, now the site of the seasonal Paradise Lodge and the Henry H. Jackson Memorial Visitor Center, that are the most popular spots in the park. Wildflowers cover the slopes here, and the vast bulk of the mountain rises so steeply overhead that it is necessary to strain one's neck to gaze up at the summit.

Mt. Rainier lies toward the southern end of the Washington Cascades. Here, the crags of the North Cascades are replaced by a volcanic landscape of rolling hills punctuated by Mount Rainier and Mount St. Helens and, to the east, two other volcanic landmarks—Mount Adams and Goat Rocks, the latter but a remnant of an ancient volcano, the former, a snow cone as impressive as Mt. Rainier.

It is said that Rainier makes its own weather, and more often than not, it isn't what people consider good weather. Because it rises more than a mile above the surrounding landscape, Mt. Rainier interrupts the eastward flow of moisture-laden air that comes in off the Pacific Ocean. Forced upward into the colder altitudes, this moist air drops its load of

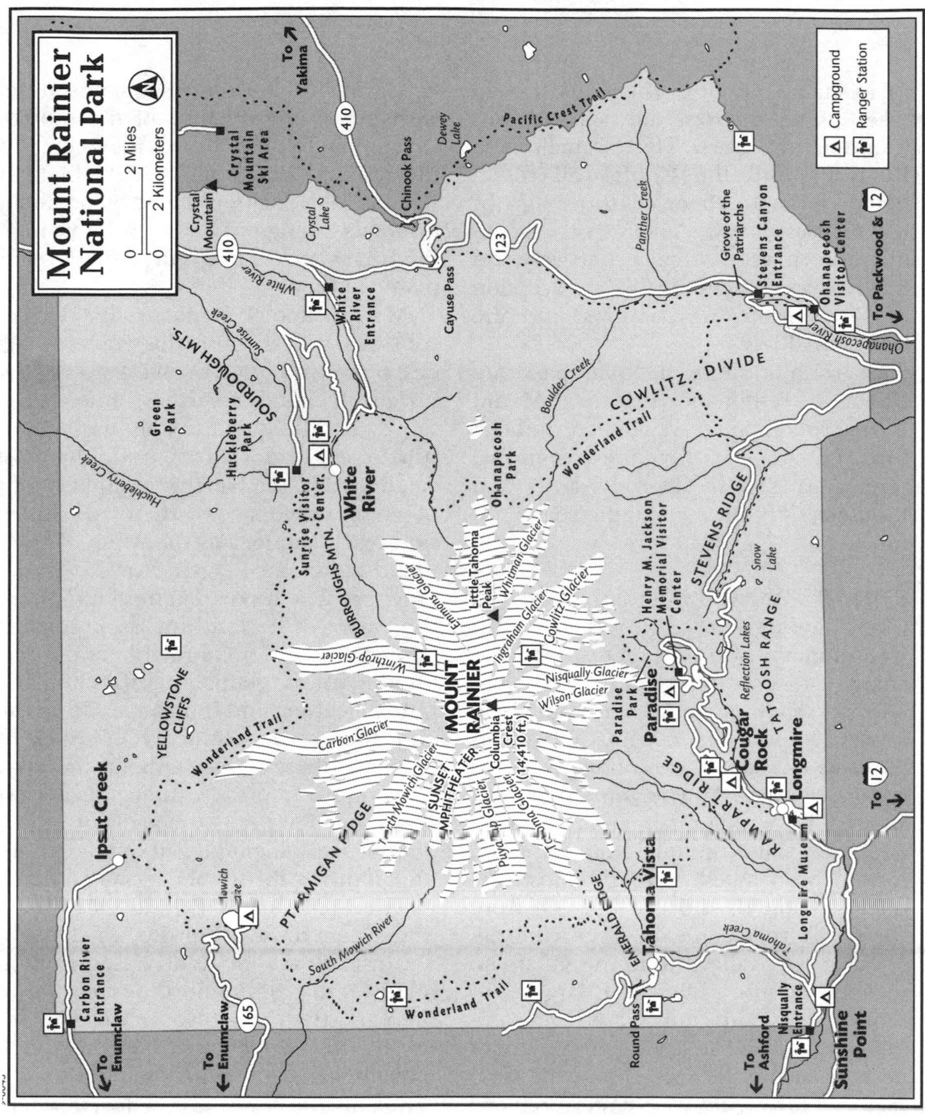

water on the mountain. At lower elevations on the west side this moisture falls as rain, which creates a rain forest in the Carbon River Valley. However, at higher elevations, the mountain's precipitation falls as snow. On average, more than 620 inches of snow fall each winter on Mt. Rainier, but in the winter of 1971–72, 1,122 inches (93.5 feet) of snow was recorded at Paradise, setting a world annual snowfall record.

Such massive amounts of snowfall are the reason that Mt. Rainier is the single most glaciated mountain in the contiguous 48 states. So much snow falls here each winter that it can't melt over the short summer months. Each year the snow accumulates, eventually compressing into ice that adds to the mountain's glaciers. There are 26 named glaciers on Mt. Rainier and another 50 unnamed ones. Among these are the largest (Emmons) and the lowest (Carbon) in the Lower 48.

These glaciers in turn feed a half dozen rivers. The Muddy Fork of the Cowlitz River and the White River take their names from the color that the glacial flour (silt) imparts to them. Fortunately, the Carbon River is not as black as its name implies. The river instead takes its name from the coal deposits found in the area. The Nisqually, the Puyallup, and the Cowlitz all retain names given to them centuries ago by the region's Native American tribes. All of these rivers eventually flow westward to the Puget Sound, with the exception of the Cowlitz, which flows into the Columbia River.

Surrounding the national park are three different national forests: Mount Baker, Snoqualmie, Wenatchee, and Gifford Pinchot. Within these national forests are seven wilderness areas and thousands of miles of logging roads and trails.

Flora & Fauna. In a national park, where animals need not fear death from humans, you often get unexpected chances to encounter wildlife up close and personal, sometimes whether you want to or not. Yes, cougars live in this park, as do black bears, but neither is seen very often. Much more commonly spotted large mammals are the park's deer, elk, and mountain goats. Deer, mostly black-tailed, are the most frequently spotted, and can be seen from the park's roads and on trails from the lowland river valleys up to the subalpine meadow country. Elk, much larger and more majestic in stature, are in less evidence than the deer, but can sometimes be seen in the Sunrise area in the summer and throughout the eastern regions of the park during the autumn. Mountain goats, which are actually not goats but rather a long-haired relative of the antelope, keep to the rocky slopes of alpine and subalpine meadows during the summer.

Perhaps the most entertaining and enviable of the park's wild residents are its marmots. These largest members of the squirrel family spend their days nibbling wildflowers in subalpine meadows, and stretching out on rocks to bask in the sun. In meadows throughout the park, these bloated sybarites seem oblivious to human presence, contentedly grazing only steps away from hikers.

Marmots share these subalpine zones with pikas, tiny relatives of the rabbits, that are more often heard than seen. Living among the jumbled rocks of talus slopes, pikas skitter about their rocky domains calling out warnings with a high pitched beep that is surprisingly electronic in tone.

Monkeyflowers, elephant's heads, parrot's beaks, bear grass; this grass menagerie represents just a small fraction of the variety of wildflowers to be found on the slopes of Mt. Rainier. This mountain's subalpine meadows are among the most celebrated in the Northwest. Bold swaths of color sweep across these mountainsides each summer as the white of snow melts away once again to reveal the greenery that lies hidden most months of the year. Although not as colorfully named as the flowers mentioned above, lupines, asters, gentians, avalanche lilies, phlox, heather, and Indian paintbrush all add their own distinctive splashes of color to these slopes. About the only thing more impressive than the flowers on Mount Rainier is the array of photographic equipment lugged out onto trails for capturing the floral displays on film.

The meadows at Paradise are much wetter than those at Sunrise, which lies in a rain-shadow zone and consequently is relatively dry. In the northwest corner of the park, the Carbon River Valley opens out to the Pacific Ocean and channels moisture-laden air into its depths. As a result, this valley is a rain forest where tree limbs are draped with mosses and lichens, and where Douglas firs and western red cedars grow to enormous proportions. However, it is in the southwest corner of the park, in the Grove of the Patriarchs near the Stevens Canyon Park Entrance, that some of the oldest trees stand—Douglas firs more than 1,000 years old and western cedars more than 25 feet in circumference.

Avoiding the Crowds. On a sunny summer weekend it is sometimes necessary to park more than a mile away from Paradise and walk on forest trails and the road to the meadows. Consequently, our best advice on how to avoid the crowds would be to travel to the mountain in the spring or fall. (May or October are probably the best months; before and after these months, respectively, the weather can be somewhat dicey and affect road conditions. Also, the rainy season starts in mid- to late October and can keep going until early spring.)

But you might consider avoiding the Sunrise and Paradise areas altogether, heading instead to the more remote sections of the park, such as the **Carbon River** area in the northwest section, or the **Denman Falls/Gobblers Knob** area in the southeast. Both of these areas are accessible by car and provide the same sorts of stunning vistas you get at Sunrise and Paradise. The **Westside Road,** which leads to the Denman Falls area, was closed right before the Tahoma Vista due to flood damage in 1997, so you might have to do some hiking (be sure and check at the ranger station for the latest info).

Otherwise, a good plan is to arrive at either Sunrise or Paradise *early* in the day—before 10am, spend an hour checking out the visitor center, and then hightail it out to your favorite hiking spot. Likewise, people generally leave the park between 4 and 6pm, so if you can arrange to arrive at a visitor center around 5pm (with the idea of staying put for an hour or so), you can avoid a lot of the unpleasant traffic.

Finally, you might try reversing this advice, hitting Sunrise at sundown. Most park visitors are leaving via the Southern Entrance toward Nisqually late in the day; you'll be heading in the opposite direction.

Just the Facts

GETTING THERE & GATEWAYS

Unlike its cousin across the Puget Sound, Olympic National Park, no roads completely encircle Rainier; the northwest corner of the park, for example, is only accessible through one entrance.

The **Nisqually Entrance** (also known as the Nisqually–Longmire Road) in the southwest corner of the park on Wash. 706, just east of **Ashford,** where most of the area's accommodations and services are to be found, is the park's main entrance. A few miles further east is **Elbe,** where a few more choices can be located.

However, at the northeast corner of the park, the **White River Entrance,** off Wash. 410, provides easier access from Seattle and points north if your goal is only the Sunrise area. The town closest to this entrance is **Greenwater,** which also provides some accommodations options.

In the northwest corner, the **Carbon River Entrance** is off Wash. 165. **Enumclaw** is the closest community to this entrance, though not much is to be found there.

At the southeast corner, the **Stevens Canyon Entrance,** off Wash. 123 from U.S. 12, provides access from Yakima. **Packwood** and **Randle,** both located south of the park on U.S. 12, are two of the largest towns in the nearby area. You'll find some recommendable accommodations in Packwood.

During the summer it is also possible to enter the park from the east on **Wash. 410,** which also leads to Yakima by way of Chinook Pass. Entering this way gives you the option of heading north to the White River Entrance or south to Stevens Canyon.

In winter, only the Nisqually Entrance is open.

The Nearest Airport. The nearest airport to Mount Rainier is the **Seattle-Tacoma International Airport** (☎ **206/431-4444**), 70 miles northeast of the park (the driving time to Mount Rainier is about 2 hours on I-5, Wash. 7, and Wash. 706 to the Nisqually Entrance. Sea-Tac Airport is served by about 30 airlines. The major carriers include **American Airlines, America West, Continental, Delta, Horizon, Northwest, Southwest, TWA, United,** and **US Airways.** Toll-free numbers for all these airlines are given in the appendix.

Renting a Car. Once you arrive, you'll be able to rent a car from all the major car-rental companies, including **Alamo, Avis, Budget, Dollar, Enterprise, Hertz, National,** and **Thrifty.** Their toll-free numbers are in the appendix.

GETTING INFORMATION BEFORE YOUR TRIP

To get information in advance of your visit, contact the **Superintendent, Mount Rainier National Park,** Tahoma Woods, Star Route, Ashford, WA 98304 (☎ **360/569-2211**).

Mount Rainier has a page on the National Park Service Web site at **www.nps.gov/mora** (and an expanded home page at www.nps.gov/mora/mora.html).

VISITOR CENTERS

When you arrive, you'll want to visit at least one of the park's four visitor centers.

The **Longmire Hiker Information Center and Museum** (☎ **360/569-2211,** ext. 3317) is located just inside the park beyond the Nisqually Entrance and is the welcoming center for the park.

The **Henry M. Jackson Memorial Visitor Center** (☎ **360/569-2211,** ext. 2328), near Paradise Meadows, is the park's main visitor center.

The **Ohanepecosh Visitor Center** (☎ **360/569-2211,** ext. 2352), off of Wash. 123 in the southeast corner of the park, is near the Stevens Canyon Entrance.

The **Sunrise Visitor Center,** off Wash. 410, past the White River Entrance (☎ **360/569-2211**, ext. 2357), is in the northeast section of the park.

ENTRANCE FEES

A **single-entry pass** is $10 per vehicle (not per person) for a 1-week pass. A **yearly pass** can be purchased for $20.

The park also honors the Golden Eagle Passport for entrance into all fee areas, as well as the Golden Age Passport for persons over 62 and the free Golden Access Passport for disabled persons. All three of these can be purchased at any of the visitor centers.

CAMPING FEES

Camping will cost you $10 per night at Sunshine Point, Cougar Rock, and White River; $12 per night at Ohanepecosh. Ipsut Creek is currently closed to vehicular traffic due to storm damage, but is open to backcountry campers. All camping in Mount Rainier is on a first-come, first-served basis; you cannot make reservations.

Backcountry camping is currently free with a permit obtained at any of the ranger stations. However, as early as 1998, Mount Rainier may begin charging a backcountry fee. You might want to call ahead to the ranger station located in the area you wish to visit.

SPECIAL REGULATIONS & WARNINGS

The main thing to remember in the heavily touristed spots in the subalpine portions of the park is to stay on the trails and stay off the wildflowers. Off-trail tramping has been the cause of erosion of the thin, loam topsoil that supports the fragile vegetation. Certain areas of the park are currently being restored to their natural, meadow state.

In 1994 alone, the waste off-flow from 42,000 hikers caused an overall decline in water quality, causing serious problems in some parts of the wilderness. To solve this problem, the National Park Service provides toilet facilities at all the major camping areas, and a blue-bag system for climbers going higher than 10,000 feet. They suggest backpackers use pit toilets at trailside camps. In addition, there is a recycling program in effect in the park, so look for the appropriately marked bins.

Be sure to boil any water taken from the park's rivers, as it has been known to carry Giardia, the little bug of the mighty intestinal disorder.

Obviously, don't even think about heading for a day climb anywhere near the upper altitudes of Rainier without checking in at a ranger station, or employing a guide. Steep snowfields can become slippery in the sun, and there are unstable ice bridges in others. Remember, people *die* in the high altitudes every year. Don't be another mind-numbing statistic!

SEASONS & CLIMATE

As might be expected, summer is the warmest and driest time of the year, with frequent fog banks rolling in late and early in the day, with temperatures ranging from the upper 40s to the low 70s. The spring and fall can be cool and drizzly, with occasional days of warm weather late in the spring and early in the fall. The greatest rainfall comes in January and December, with daytime temperatures in the 40s. Weather is generally going to get colder and nastier the higher up you go, and of course there is lots of snow in the higher elevations.

It's important that you dress in layers for a day visit, as you may encounter any type of weather. It can go from warm to cool very quickly as you climb in altitude, and rain can come in suddenly, so rain gear is a good thing to have.

USEFUL PUBLICATIONS

Mt. Rainier National Park publishes two free newspapers, the ***Tahoma*** and ***Snowdrift,*** available at all visitor centers, which give concise information about all activities at the park on a seasonal basis.

In addition, there is a free guide that includes both Mt. Rainier and Olympic national parks available from **American Park Network Publishing,** 100 Pine St., Suite 2850, San Francisco, CA 94111 (☎ **415/788-2228**). Or visit them on the Web at **www.AmericanParkNetwork.com**.

Park Highlights

Longmire, just inside the Nisqually Entrance, serves as welcoming center for the park. This is the park's oldest developed area, the site of the historic Mineral Springs Resort, which opened in 1899. Here you'll find the old Mt. Rainier National Park Headquarters, The National Park Inn, a museum, visitor center, general store, hiker information and permitting center, post office, and a year-round lodge and restaurant. Although it sounds as if this must be a small city, it is actually quite compact and rarely very crowded.

Paradise, in the south-central portion of the park, is a subalpine meadow and one of the most popular areas for visitors. Nearby you'll find the Henry M. Jackson Memorial Visitor Center, the park's main visitor center, a gracefully curving stone and concrete structure which houses a snack bar and the only public showers in the park. Interesting exhibits on geology, glaciers, and the local flora and fauna are here. Paradise is also the site of the seasonal (May to October) Paradise Inn, a historic mountain lodge. Rainier Mountaineering, which offers mountaineering classes and leads summit climbs, also has its facilities here at Paradise.

Ohanepecosh, off Wash. 123 in the park's southeast corner, offers scenic views of the Ohanepecosh River on the journey to the entrance of the small visitor center located here. Look for exhibits focusing primarily on the old-growth forest ecosystem that surrounds this particular area of the park. This is also the site of the 205-site Ohanepecosh Campground, as well as the site of several good, short hikes.

At 6,400 feet, **Sunrise,** in the northeast part of the park, is the highest point to which you can drive in Mount Rainier National Park. Next to the Henry Jackson Visitor Center, this is the second most popular spot in the park. You can find displays and naturalist-led walks here, a snack bar/restaurant, and programs on the subalpine and alpine zone ecosystems. You can also look at the glaciers up close with free telescopes. The visitor center here is open daily from July through mid-September.

The **Carbon River** area, in the northwest corner, provides access to the most heavily forested area in the park. The jury is still out as to whether the terrain is actually lowland forest or temperate rain forest. Trails here lead into the backcountry and connect with the **Wonderland Trail.** The **Mowich Lake** area is reached by a separate road (Wash. 165) than the Carbon River area, but they are in close proximity.

Seeing the Highlights in a Day

Most folks who make Mount Rainier a day trip are coming from the Seattle area, and they work their way around to Sunrise from the southwest corner of the park, driving first through Longmire to Paradise, then Ohanepecosh and on to Sunrise. But, Sunrise being named what it is, you might want to go the other way around to get the best daylight, in which case you'll want to enter on Wash. 410 at the park's northeast corner. If you're coming from the south or from Yakima, you'll want to adjust your entry point and itinerary accordingly. The single-day-tripper will not be able to visit the Carbon River area in the northwest.

It might be a bit pedestrian, but if you want to get the whole flavor of what Mt. Rainier is about, you will probably want to do the normal route and head into the park via the Longmire Entrance in late summer. You get old-growth forests, alpine meadows blooming with flowers, and a look at the rocky scree underneath the Emmons and Winthrop glaciers. Even if you can't see the Carbon River Rain Forest, you can at least read about it at one of the visitor centers. If you'd rather avoid lines of cars later in the day (and who doesn't?), get a jump on things early in the morning. By noon, Rainier is going to be packed.

For an 80-mile trip, start out at the **Nisqually Entrance** on Wash. 706, and check out the **Park Headquarters** and the **Longmire Museum** (open from 9am to 5:30pm daily in season) for exhibits on Native American culture, white exploration, and the natural history of the surrounding area, as well as the local flora and fauna. If you've already been driving a bit, take a walk on the excellent 1.8 mile **Trail of Shadows** across from the Longmire Lodge. The trail passes by the now cool hot springs which once hosted the famous Hot Springs Resort, as well as the cabin built by one of the Longmires in 1888.

Next, of course would be an up close and personal look at the fantastic burst of colors in **Paradise's** fields of brilliant paintbrush, anemones, and gentians. But first, visit the **Henry M. Jackson Memorial Visitor Center** and figure out what you're looking at. It might be the Nisqually or Wilson glacier hanging over your head. For a more up close view of the Nisqually Glacier, take the 1.2 mile (1-hour round-trip) **Nisqually Vista Trail** from the visitor center. Otherwise, there are numerous trails leading from the parking lot that will allow you to create your own designer wildflower stroll.

From Paradise, head east towards the **Stevens Ridge Entrance,** with your next goal a short hike along the **Grove of the Patriarchs** at Ohanepecosh. This 1.5-mile walk, one of the most popular in the park, is famous for its absolutely huge Douglas firs and cedars, located on a small island accessible by a bridge across the beautiful Ohanepecosh River. If you have time, take the **Ohanepecosh Nature Trail,** a quick 0.5-mile jaunt that will allow you to dip your feet in a shallow hot spring alongside the trail as you gaze down at a meadow of lush grass.

Finally, wind your way through forests of fir, cedar, and hemlock on the way to **Sunrise.** The big, whitecapped mountain in your rearview mirror to the south is Mt. Adams, equal in beauty, but more remote than Mt. Rainier.

Like we said, start this trip out early in the day. Be sure and get up to Sunrise before you lose the light. This side of the mountain is glacier-packed, so check out **Emmons Vista** for excellent views of the Little Tahoma and Emmons glaciers, or take the 1.5 mile **Sunrise Rim Trail,** which also leads away from the lodge. For a close up view, use the telescopes at the visitor center.

If You Have More Time

If you have more time, you'll want to do more hiking and other activities and not race from point to point so quickly. Just getting out into the park is something plenty of folks don't do, especially if they're only here on a day trip. But I have two specific suggestions if you want to exercise your adventure muscles.

The best way to explore the park is by foot. And the mother of all trails in the park is the **Wonderland Trail,** which, as it winds its labyrinthine route around the entire mountain (most folks plan 10 days to 2 weeks to do this one), takes you through any section of the park you might be interested in. There's no law that says you can't do a small portion of the Wonderland Trail, though, and since it's accessible from all the major park centers, you can do a piece as a day hike. (The trail is described in more detail under "Day Hikes," below.)

The least visited sections of the park are really some of the best, including the incredibly beautiful **Carbon River** area northwest of the mountain. But, like many things in life, the good things take a little more effort to get to. Still, if you have the time, go here. The Carbon River basin, depending on which biologist you talk to, contains either a very wet forest or a temperate rain forest. Either way, the only other temperate rain forest in the United States is on the Olympic Peninsula, making the Carbon River area is a unique jewel of an ecosystem.

Organized Tours & Ranger Programs

Gray Line Tours of Seattle offers regularly scheduled bus tours into the park from mid-spring through mid-fall. Call ☎ **800/426-7532** or 206/626-5208 for information or reservations. The tours depart daily from the Convention Center in downtown Seattle at 8am. The cost for the 1-day tour is $48.87 per person. There is also an overnight tour, including a night at the Longmire Inn (meals are not included). The cost for the overnight tour is $137.92 per person.

There are ranger-led tours, discussions, and seminars from Longmire, Ohanepecosh, Paradise, and Sunrise visitor centers.

At **Longmire,** there is a daily hike to Carter Falls, a Sunday-morning walk through Longmire Meadow, and an evening stroll on Fridays and Saturdays that focuses on the area's cultural history. Other walks and discussions are frequently scheduled.

At **Ohanepecosh,** there are several ranger-led hikes and walks along popular trails almost daily, as well as evening programs during July and August devoted to Mount Rainier's history.

From **Paradise,** there are daily walks to view wildflowers and glaciers, as well as a more strenuous ranger-led hikes on the weekends. Park naturalists also roam the area answering questions on a daily basis.

From the **Sunrise** area, there are daily ranger-led walks, weekend wildlife walks, and, on Saturday, a walk to the Emmons Glacier. During July and August there are evening campfire programs.

Day Hikes

If you're looking for solitude on the trails, then you've come to the wrong place. The trails in Mount Rainier National Park, especially those with views and meadows, are packed throughout the summer. On any trail leading out of Paradise or Sunrise, you're likely to see a lot of people.

If you feel trapped by the hordes and want to escape from what can feel like rush hour on the freeway, you'll have to work a bit harder. Trails in the northwest corner, near the Carbon River Entrance, are relatively quiet, though this road has been closed to motor vehicles since 1996 due to flood damage. Mowich Lake, however, sees more weekend foot traffic since the road there is still open.

We've classified hikes as "short" if they are 3 miles or under. Anything else is "longer." Levels of difficulty are also indicated for each hike. Just remember, a relatively short hike can still be moderate or even strenuous.

If you need information on trail availability or closures, call the **Hiker Information Line** (☎ **360/569-2211,** ext. 3317).

ALL THE WAY AROUND MOUNT RAINIER

Wonderland Trail

93 miles RT. Allow 10 to 14 days. Strenuous. 7,000-foot elevation gain. Access: This hike can be started form Longmire, Paradise, Sunrise, Mowich Lake, or Carbon River.

With varying degrees of difficulty, this 93-mile loop circles Mt. Rainier, with numerous connecting trailheads, and is the mother of all trails in the park. To some, it's a rite of passage in the northwest to make this loop through some of the most stunning vistas in the continental United States. Think hard and plan ahead before you try to take it all at once. You'll probably want to leave yourself about 2 weeks' time to make the whole loop, and you might want to cache some chow at various points along the path before you go that you can pick up later. There are more things to see on this trail than you can name. But, of course, expect to find yourself traveling through alpine meadows, glacial streams, mountain passes, valley forests, and an ultimate summit point of 6,500 feet at Panhandle Gap. There are many backcountry camping spots along the way that provide water in the summer, but in the off-season, things can get pretty dry, even though it's probably raining, so be sure to bring a good supply. In the interest of planning shorter trips, keep in mind that you can connect with this trail from any of the spokelike trails that crisscross and touch the trail throughout the park, allowing you to set up a hiking mileage and time schedule all your own.

LONGMIRE AREA

The **Lake George and Gobblers Knob Lookout Trail** is currently closed due to washout of entrance road. Call the **Hiker Information Line** (☎ **360/569-2211,** ext. 3317) for scheduled reopening.

SHORT HIKES

Trail of Shadows Nature Trail

0.7 mile RT. Easy. Access: The trailhead is located across the road from the Longmire Museum.

This short loop trail (with no elevation gains) is a highly enjoyable walk through the flowers of Longmire Meadow and takes you past the former site of the Longmire Springs Hotel, as well as an old log cabin that's the oldest man-made structure in the park. Don't drink out of the springs, say the many signs.

Carter Falls Trail

2 miles one way. Easy. Access: The trailhead is located 100 yards downhill from the Cougar Park Campground on the way to Paradise.

This trail passes a wooden pipeline that once served to help generate electricity for Longmire. Go past Carter Falls about 50 yards for a look at the second falls on your way, the zany Madcap Falls. Like many places in the park, this trail connects with the Wonderland Trail to take you to Paradise to the east, or Indian Henry's to the west.

Rampart Bridge Trail

4.6 miles RT. Easy to moderate. 1,339-foot elevation gain. Access: The trailhead is located across the road from the Longmire Museum.

This is a somewhat steep trail at first, before you arrive at the top of an ancient lava flow called the Ramparts, which offers panoramic views of the Nisqually

Valley to the south, Mt. Rainier to the north, and, to the west, the site of the massive Kautz Creek Mudflow of 1947. It's also your connection with many of the other trails in the area, including the Van Trump, Comet, and Christine Falls trails.

Van Trump Park & Comet Falls Trail

5 miles RT. Moderate. Access: The trailhead is located near Christine Falls Bridge on Wash. 123 to Paradise.

This steep (with a total elevation gain of 2,200 feet) trail leads through beautiful old growth to scenic Comet Falls, the second highest falls in the park at 320 feet. Another mile uphill takes you to beautiful views of the Nisqually, Van Trump, and Kautz glaciers. This is a popular trail in the summer, but there are often floods along its upper reaches; stop in at the ranger station and ask for information on trail conditions before heading up.

PARADISE AREA

Nisqually Vista Trail

1.2 miles RT. Easy. Access: The trailhead is at the Henry M. Jackson Memorial Visitor Center.

This easy interpretive trail leads upwards from the Henry M. Jackson Memorial Visitor Center to explore the high country flowers and the Nisqually Glacier.

Bench & Snow Lakes Trail

2.5 miles RT. Easy to moderate. Access: The trailhead is on Stevens Canyon Rd., with the trailhead located 1.5 miles east of Reflection Lakes.

You can catch both lakes on this trail of gradual ups and downs over low ridges before reaching Bench Lake after 0.75 mile, then continuing another 0.5 mile to Snow Lake, with beautiful views of beargrass and meadow flowers. The round-trip takes about an hour, with a 700-foot elevation gain.

Dead Horse Creek Trails

3 miles RT. Easy to moderate. Access: The trailhead is located at the northern end of the Jackson Visitor Center parking lot.

The Dead Horse Trails serve as conduits to the Moraine and Glacier Vista trails, as well as providing beautiful views of the Nisqually Glacier to your left as you head up the ridge, especially if you take the spur Moraine Trail to the left, 0.75 mile up the path.

Alta Vista Summit

1.5 miles RT. Easy. Access: Trailhead at Jackson Visitor Center parking lot.

This popular day hike, which leads off from the Jackson Visitor Center's parking lot, meanders through alpine meadows along a trail that leads to the top of an overlook of Paradise Meadows, Mount Adams, and Mount St. Helens to the south.

A LONGER HIKE

Skyline Loop Trails

5.8 to 6.5 miles RT. Moderate. Access: The trailhead is located to the left of the Paradise Ranger Station, next to the rest rooms.

You can't get much higher on Mt. Rainier without going to the top, at least on a day hike. These trails are sort of the extended versions of all the trails that surround Paradise; lots of beautiful alpine meadows, close-up views of the Nisqually Glacier, one of the most accessible and beautiful glaciers in the park. At Panorama Point, there are some rest rooms for a quick stop before the trail begins to loop back around to the southeast. At the top of this loop, you may have to traverse some snow, and if it's thick enough, you might have to take a detour around the top that adds about 0.75 mile to the loop; otherwise, it's a 5.8-mile round-trip (there's a 1,700-foot elevation gain). On the way back, check out the views of Mount Adams and Mount St. Helens.

SUNRISE & NORTHEASTERN AREAS

Sourdough Ridge Nature Trail

1.5 miles RT. Easy. Access: The trailhead is located at the parking lot of the Sunrise Visitor Center.

If you don't want to try the Sourdough Ridge Trail, this easy loop will provide you with a brief glimpse of what's on the larger path. It's a self-guided tour of the summer wildflowers and alpine meadows that's quite popular, and good for kids.

Sunrise Rim Trail

3 miles RT. Easy. Access: The trailhead is located at the Sunrise Visitor Center.

This is another nature trail with many interpretive signs to tell you what to look for as you gaze up at Mt. Rainier to the north. About 1.5 miles into the trail, you'll arrive at Shadow Lake, and just beyond, the walk-in Sunrise Campground. With a little more effort, you can hike south to the glacier overlook and be awed by the blue-white overhangs of Emmons Glacier.

Sourdough Ridge/Dege Peak Trail

4 miles RT. Easy to moderate. Access: The trailhead is at the Sunrise Visitor Center.

From the trailhead, climb to a ridgetop and turn east beneath the gaze of Antler Peak, after which you'll cruise along the ridge for wonderful views of Rainier to the south and the brilliant greens of the Yakima parklands below. At the top of Dege peak, look south for close-up views of the Cowlitz Chimneys, and farther off views of whitecapped Mt. Adams.

Naches Peak Trail

3.5 miles RT. Easy. Access: Take the Pacific Crest Trailhead located near Tipsoo Lake for a junction with the Naches Peak Loop Trail (there is also a wheelchair-accessible path at Tipsoo Lake, near the Pacific Crest Trailhead junction).

This is another popular one, and the views from the top of Naches Peak of the meadows and lakes stretching towards Rainier's icy summit will tell you why. From the Pacific Crest Trailhead, head south, traversing the east side of the Naches Peak, and the junction with the loop that can be taken at that point back to Tipsoo Lake, or continue ahead 0.5 mile to Dewey Lake, where there are good campsites.

Mt. Fremont Trail

5.5 miles RT. Moderate. Access: The trailhead is at the north end of the Sunrise Visitor Center parking lot.

From the trailhead you climb for about 0.33 of a mile along this popular trail through the surrounding meadows, then follow Sourdough Ridge to the left towards Frozen Lake. At the end of the lake, take the fork to the right for the easy 1.3-mile hike to the Fremont Lookout, from where you can get excellent glimpses of the surrounding Cascades and Olympics for miles around. You might even be able to see Seattle, on a clear day. The round-trip has a 1,200-foot elevation gain.

Burroughs Mountain Trail

7 miles RT. Moderate to difficult. Access: Branches off the Sunrise Rim Trail (described above).

If you can't handle the snow, you might not want to take this trail. It's ice-ax territory, sometimes until early August, so come prepared. Follow the Sunrise Rim Trail, which begins on the south side of the Sunrise Visitor Center parking lot, to Shadow Lake and Sunrise Campground, and a sharp upturn in slope toward the First Burroughs Peak at 7,000 feet. Beyond this point, you're in a delicate tundra climate, one of the few in the Lower 48. It's possible to take the Frozen Lake Trail at First Burroughs, and make a loop back to Sunrise, if you don't feel like climbing anymore. However, should you decide to head up the remaining 400 vertical feet, you'll be treated to fantastic views of Mt. Rainier, and the Emmons and Winthrop glaciers.

Berkely Park/Grand Park Trail

13 miles RT. Strenuous. Access: Branches off the Sourdough Ridge Trail (described above).

If the Fremont Lookout just isn't far enough west for you, head for the high tableland meadows and wildflower and green field bonanza at Grand Park. You can even hike across these, should you so choose, and picnic under the trees. But bring plenty of water—there's none up here. Head out of the Sunrise parking lot to the Sourdough Ridge Trail, where the view is the most scenic and the road the easiest. At 6,700-foot Frozen Lake, descend toward Berkely Park, keeping right with the trail to Mystic Lake. Berkely Camp is 4 miles from Sunrise, and it's another 2.5 miles, mostly uphill, to the Plateau of Grand Park.

Glacier Basin Trail

7 miles RT. Moderate to difficult. Access: The trailhead is located past the White River Campground Entrance Station, in the upper area of the White River Campground.

Watch out for rusting artifacts on this journey through a part of the park that wasn't always so protected. You'll see remnants of an old mining operation from the late 1800s in this glacial valley. Follow an old road up past the headwaters of the White River. After 1 mile, veer to the left for beautiful views of the Emmons Glacier. Beyond the junction of the trail with the Buroughs Mountain Trail, you'll arrive at Glacier Basin Camp. From here it's not far to Camp Schurman, in the crook of the Emmons and Winthrop glaciers. Look for climbers making the ascent to the summit here, along a secondary route.

Palisades Lake Trail

7 miles RT. Easy to moderate. Access: The trailhead is located at the Sunrise Visitor Center.

This is a pretty popular trail, so don't expect to get away from other hikers too often. However, if you're out for a fairly invigorating stroll through forest and meadowlands, this is a good one, with only small rises and falls in elevation overall as you wander past small alpine lakes towards a rock outcropping called, appropriately enough, the Palisades. There are also good campsites a little farther on at Dick's Lake and the Upper Palisades Lake, although they tend to be crowded in the summertime.

Summerland Trail

8.5 miles RT. Easy to moderate. Access: The trailhead is located past the White River Entrance, on the way to the Sunrise or the White River areas.

If you're into mountain goats, go ahead to Panhandle Gap, about 1.5 miles past the end of the 4-mile, one-way entrance into the Frying Pan Glacier area. This trail can host hundreds of hikers on a peak summer day, so beware. It's a 3.5-mile graded walk through mature forests before entering the Frying Pan Creek area, where the scenery opens up into the brushy upper Frying Pan Valley. From there it's a 0.5-mile steep climb to the spectacular Summerland Meadows. The total elevation gain is 1,500 feet.

OHANEPECOSH AREA

Silver Falls Trail

3 miles RT. Easy. Access: The trailhead is at the Ohanepecosh Visitor Center.

This trail, a fairly level one, is pretty popular with families as it winds its way through old-growth forests and over a bridge above the almost achingly pristine waters of the Ohanepecosh River facing the falls that give the area its name. The falls themselves drop 75 feet in a fine misting of spray. Across the bridge below the falls is the return trail to the Ohanepecosh Campground.

Grove of the Patriarchs Trail

2 miles RT. Easy. Access: The trailhead is located just west of the Stevens Canyon Entrance on Stevens Canyon Rd.

This short and incredibly popular trail follows the Ohanepecosh River before crossing over a bridge to an island of incredibly huge, thousand-year-old Douglas firs and western red cedars. Even though it's well traveled, it's still a pretty awe-inspiring place, if you can manage to find a little silence in which to meditate on the grandeur of the trees.

NORTHWESTERN RAINIER

In 1996, the Carbon River Road was closed due to storm damage, and unfortunately, it appears likely that 1998 will offer more of the same. For all trails listed below, remember that the road may end at a point approximately 5 miles before the entrance to the Ipsut Creek Campground. Be sure to call the **Park Information Line** (☎ **360/569-2211**) for information before taking any of the northwest Rainier trips.

Storm damage notwithstanding, all trails in the northwestern section of the park can best be reached by driving to the end of the Ipsut Creek Campground Road (or as close as possible) from the terminus of the Carbon River Road and connecting with the Wonderland Trail, or driving in on the Mowich River Road (Wash. 165). Junctions with the Wonderland Trail along this corner of the park by car, unlike those on the southern and northeastern side, are limited. The Carbon Glacier and Rainforest, Mystic Lake, Moraine Park, Mowich Lake, and Tolmie Peak trails can all be reached via the Carbon River Road and the Mowich Lake Road by car, or by the Wonderland Trail on an extended hike.

Tolmie Peak

6.5 miles RT. Moderate. Access: The trailhead is located at the end of Mowich Lake Rd. on the left side of the lake.

A hugely popular day hike this one is, with lots of traffic from weekenders and kids, but you know you can't really go that wrong anywhere around here. The trail proceeds gently through 1.25 miles of forested woodland to the junction at Ipsut Pass (elevation 5,100 feet). Stay left and proceed uphill another 1.75 miles to the subalpine meadows at Eunice Lake for a look at how far you're going to have to climb to Tolmie Peak. From this point on, the trail becomes moderate in difficulty on account of the elevation gain. *Note:* Tolmie Peak is closed to overnight backpackers. The entire hike has a 1010-foot elevation gain.

Spray Park Trail

6 miles RT. Moderate. Access: The trailhead is located on the southeast side of the Mowich Lake Walk-in Campground at the end of Mowich Lake Rd.

They say you should see Spray Falls at sunset if you want to see the light hit the spray action. Set amidst subalpine meadows, Spray Falls is a spectacular sight in the summer when the flowers are blooming, although most of the hike proceeds through forested terrain. The trailhead intersects the Wonderland Trail after a 0.25-mile descent. Follow the Spray Park Trail east for 2 miles, through the woods, across Lee Creek, and eventually to a junction with a spur trail to overlook the falls. The next 0.5 mile to the Spray Park Meadows is a steep climb up a series of switchbacks. Even more extensive meadows are found in another 0.5 mile. The whole trip has an elevation gain of 1,300 feet.

Carbon Glacier & Moraine Park Trails

7 to 11 miles RT (depending on route). Moderate to strenuous. Access: The trailhead is located at the end of the road at the Ipsut Creek Campground.

You begin this hike toward Moraine Park on the Wonderland Trail, the first 3 miles of which are a gentle uphill grade as they parallel the beautiful glacial waters of the Carbon River. Subsequently, the trail crosses the river on a suspension bridge just below the lower edge of the Carbon Glacier. Take a right turn on the Wonderland Trail at its junction with the Northern Loop, and the trail will lead you to the edge of this, the lowest and seemingly most monstrous glacier in the lower 48 states. The trail then becomes a series of steep switchbacks that lead you through the neighboring forest to Moraine Park. Along the way, you'll pass several campsites (Carbon River, Dick Creek, and further along, Mystic Lake).

Mystic Lake Trail

15.8 miles. Moderate to strenuous. Access: First, take the trail to Moraine Park, then continue to Mystic Lake.

To reach Mystic Lake, you must first hike to the narrow, subalpine valley of Moraine Park, a moderate to strenuous trip. When Mystic Lake is included in the hike, the entire round-trip distance becomes 15.8 miles with elevation gains of 3,900 feet. Beyond the park, the trail goes over two small, wooded ridges, and then descends a short distance to Mystic Lake. The trail was named by two early naturalists who claimed to have seen a mysterious whirlpool near the lake's outlet. many people use the campsites around Mystic Lake as base camps for exploring the Curtis Ridge area, for spectacular views of the Winthrop and Carbon glaciers.

Other Sports & Activities

Biking. It seems that wildflowers and bike tires don't mix. There currently aren't any trails open to mountain bikers in the Mount Rainier National Park. However, there are plenty of trails to ride at nearby **Crystal Mountain** and **White Pass** ski areas during the summer months. Crystal Mountain is by far the most popular of the two areas and is known for its grueling climbs and brake-turning downhills. Luckily, you can avoid much of the climbing by riding the lifts up. The lifts generally operate only on weekends, so come on a weekday only if you want a real workout. A good gravel road for biking is **Westside Road,** which you can access through the Nisqually Entrance of Mount Rainier National Park. This road used to provide access to campgrounds and picnic areas, but in 1967 a massive debris flow swept down the Tahoma Creek from the Tahoma Glacier and washed out not only a good chunk of the road, but the campground as well, and it is now completely closed to motorized vehicles. One of the best reasons to ride this road is the chance to get on some of the little-used west-side hiking trails (closed to bikes). Try strapping some hiking boots on your bike, though, because this is a great way to get away from the crowds and access some of the rare, less crowded areas of the park. However, you might want to call ahead for information on the usage of **Westside Road.** There was some damage in 1997, and it may not have been repaired by 1998.

Boating & Canoeing. Located in the northwest corner of the park, **Mowich Lake** is a pristine little lake with a peekaboo view of the mountain from its west side. The water is incredibly clear, and it's fun to paddle around gazing down into the deep at the large logs and boulders lying on the bottom. Early morning and late afternoon are particularly good times for a paddle. You might catch a glimpse of an otter, and in the evening, deer often feed in the meadows by the lake's edge. A walk-in campground beside the lake makes this a particularly great spot for a weekend camping and paddling trip. Yes, there are even a few fish in the lake if you want to try your luck.

Fishing. One of the best things about fishing in Mount Rainier National Park is that no fishing license is required. The bad thing is that the fishing isn't very good. However there are some fish out there, and you're welcome to try your hand at catching a few. Lots of people do. Just remember that only artificial lures and flies can be used within the park, and some posted waters are closed to fishing.

For the most part, glacial silt keeps Mt. Rainier's rivers too cloudy for fishing in the summer. The trout don't strike because they can't see anything. The **Ohanepecosh River** is one exception.

This river in the southeast corner of the park flows clear throughout the summer and is designated fly-fishing only. Anglers are also encouraged to release the more wild trout they catch. Most of the park's many lakes have one or another species of trout in them, but in most cases you're going to have to hike in to do your fishing. Some shorter hikes include **Sunrise Lake** below Sunrise Point, and **Louise, Bench, and Snow lakes,** east of Paradise off the road to the Stevens Canyon Park Entrance.

Horseback Riding. If you'd like to do some horseback riding, you've got a couple of choices in the area. In Elbe, you'll find **EZ Times Outfitters,** 18703 Wash. 706 (☎ **360/569-2449**), which leads rides into the Elbe State Forest. Over on the east side of the park, 19 miles east of Chinook Pass on Wash. 410, you'll find **Susee's Skyline Packers,** Bumping River Road (☎ **206/472-5558**). East of White Pass on U.S. 12, you'll find **Indian Creek Corral** (☎ **509/672-2400**) near the shore of Rimrock Lake. Horse rental rates start around $15 per hour.

Mountaineering. Each year, more than 8,000 people set out to climb the 14,411-foot summit of Mount Rainier. That only slightly more than half make it to the top is a testament to how difficult this climb is. Although the ascent does not require rock-climbing skills, the glacier crossings require basic mountaineering knowledge, and the 9,000-foot climb from Paradise is physically demanding. Also, the elevation often causes altitude sickness. This is not a mountain to be attempted by the unprepared or the untrained. Over the years, dozens of people have died attempting the summit. Because of the many difficulties presented by summit ascents at Mount Rainier, this mountain often serves as a training ground for expeditions headed to peaks all over the world.

The easiest and most popular route starts at Paradise at 5,450 feet and climbs to the stone climbers' shelter at 10,000-foot **Camp Muir.** From here, climbers, roped together for safety, set out in the middle of the night to reach **Columbia Crest,** the mountain's highest point. From the summit on a clear day, seemingly all of Washington and much of Oregon stretches below. The best way for most people to climb Mount Rainier is with **Rainier Mountaineering, Inc.,** 535 Dock St., Suite 209, Tacoma, WA 98402 (☎ **206/627-6242;** fax 206/627-1280), in winter, or Paradise, WA 98398 (☎ **360/569-2227**), in summer, which offers a variety of mountaineering classes as well as guided summer climbs. A 1-day basic climbing class combined with the 2-day summit climb costs a little more than $400.

White-Water Rafting. The Tieton River, which flows down the eastern slopes of the Cascades to the east of the national park is one of the state's most popular rafting rivers. However the rafting season lasts for only 3 weeks during the annual September drawdown of water from Rimrock Reservoir. Rafting companies offering trips on this river include **All Rivers Adventures** (☎ **800/74-FLOAT** or 509/782-2254), **Alpine Adventures** (☎ **800/926-RAFT** or 509/548-4159), and **River Riders** (☎ **800/448-RAFT** or 206/448-RAFT).

Wildlife Viewing. Hunting is prohibited in the Mount Rainier National Park, and consequently deer, elk, and mountain goats within the park have lost their fear of humans. Anyone hiking the parks trails in the summer can expect to encounter some of these large mammals. Deer are the most commonly spotted, although it is the park's mountain goats that seem to command the greatest interest. Look for goats on Goat Island Mountain across the White River valley from Sunrise (use binoculars) on the **Summerland Trail,** on **Mount Fremont** (5.5-mile roundtrip hike from Sunrise), and at **Skyscraper Pass** (7-mile roundtrip hike from Sunrise).

Undoubtedly, the most spotted mammals in the park are the marmots, which resemble beavers, but have round tails and live in the subalpine meadows. These big, shaggy squirrels are often seen lying on rocks and soaking up the sun. They often allow people to approach quite close, but when alarmed, will let loose with a shrill whistle.

Other Winter Sports & Activities

Cross-Country Skiing. There are several ungroomed cross-country trails around the **Paradise** area. Perhaps what's equally satisfying about this ski tour is the absence of crowds and cars that haunt these regions during the summer months. Peace and quiet abound here when snow covers the landscape. There is sometimes a threat of avalanches in this area (check at the Jackson Visitor Center or Paradise Ranger Station). The slopes above the Paradise Lodge usually stay covered with snow well into June. You can rent cross-country skis at Longmire at the National Park Inn (☎ **360/569-2411**). Skis, poles, and shoes will cost you $15 per day.

West of the park, the Mount Tahoma Trails Association Trail System maintains almost 90 miles of easy to difficult trails, which are accessed from Ashford (just follow the signs to the sno-parks). For information, maps, or hut reservations, contact the **Tahoma Trails Association,** P.O. Box 206, Ashford, WA 98304 (☎ **360/569-2451**), or stop by their headquarters in Ashford, which is usually open on winter weekends.

There are 10 miles of trails at **White Pass** (☎ **509/453-8731,** or 509/672-3106 for a snow report), which is located about 20 miles southeast of the park. There is also downhill skiing.

Outside the Northeast Entrance of the park, **Crystal Mountain** (☎ **360/663-2265**) offers good backcountry skiing possibilities, though there are no maintained trails. Only experienced skiers should attempt backcountry skiing here due to the difficult conditions and danger of avalanches. This is one of the best downhill ski areas in Washington.

Downhill Skiing. There are no downhill ski possibilities within Mount Rainier National Park. The nearby **White Pass** and **Crystal Mountain** ski areas (telephone numbers are given under "Cross-country Skiing," above) are very popular and highly recommended.

Snowmobiling. There is currently no snowmobiling allowed in the park. This was a recent decision and is under some dispute. You'll have to call ahead, if you're determined, since the situation could change.

Snowshoeing. If you've never tried snowshoeing and want to, visit Mount Rainier National Park on a winter weekend or holiday when free, ranger-led snowshoe walks lasting about 90 minutes are offered. If, after getting a taste for snowshoeing you want to do more, you can rent snowshoes by the day in Longmire at the gift shop beside the **National Park Inn** (☎ **360/569-2411**) for $12 per day.

One of the better snowshoeing routes in the park is the marked route from the Paradise parking lot behind the Jackson Visitor Information Center to the Nisqually Glacier Overlook. The **Nisqually Vista Trail** is only 1.25 miles long and twists and turns as it meanders up and down hills. At the turnaround, you're treated to a great view of the glacier and the rest of the mountain.

Lower down on the mountain, at Longmire, snowshoers can make a 4.6-mile loop up **Rampart Ridge.** This steep trail requires some route finding and the snow level is not always reliable, but if conditions are right, it makes for an enjoyable and rigorous hike. Another good snowshoeing trail in this same area is the trail to **Carter Falls,** which starts above Longmire just before the Cougar Rock Campground. This 2.2-mile round-trip trail follows a section of the Wonderland Trail, which goes all the way around the mountain. It's all uphill to Carter Falls.

Camping

There are almost 600 campsites in Mount Rainier in five drive-in campgrounds. Only one of these, **Sunshine Point,** is open year-round; all others are open seasonally (all are open by the end of June until mid-September, though specific opening and closing dates are dependent on weather). Fees range from $10 to $12 per night. There is a 14-day limit on camping during July and August. None of the campgrounds in the park have RV utility hookups, nor are there laundry or shower facilities.

You can't make reservations at any Mount Rainier campgrounds, so it's a first-come, first-served operation. However, you can make reservations for one of the 5 group sites at **Cougar Rock Campground** up to 90 days prior to your stay by phone or mail: Group Camping Reservations, Mount Rainier National Park, Tahoma Woods, Star Route, Ashford, WA 98304 (☎ **360/569-2211,** ext. 3301).

Ipsut Creek Campground is currently closed to vehicular traffic due to storm damage, but is open to backcountry campers.

Backcountry camping is currently free with a permit obtained at any of the ranger stations. However, as early as 1998, national parks may begin charging a backcountry fee. You might want to call ahead to the ranger station located in the area you wish to visit.

Cougar Rock, located 2.3 miles northwest of Longmire, has 200 individual sites and five group sites available for $12 per night; RVs and trailers allowed; drinking water and flush toilets are available. There is also an RV dump station here. You'll be able to listen to ranger programs in the amphitheater.

Ipsut Creek Camp Campground, 5.3 miles east of the park's Carbon River Entrance, is currently closed due to storm damage, so call park headquarters ahead of time for detailed information on camping in this area. A wilderness permit is currently required to camp here.

Ohanepecosh Campground, 11 miles north of Packwood, Washington, on Wash. 123, has 208 sites, all suitable for RVs and trailers for $12 per night. There are drinking water, flush toilets, an RV dump station, and an amphitheater for ranger programs.

Sunshine Point Campground, 0.33 mile from the Nisqually Entrance, has 18 sites available for $10 per night. RVs and trailers are allowed. There are pit toilets

Campground	Total Sites	RV Hookups	Dump Station	Toilets	Drinking Water
Cougar Rock	**200**	**No**	**Yes**	**Yes**	**Yes**
*Ipsut Creek**	**29**	**No**	**No**	**No**	**No**
La Wis Wis	**105**	**No**	**No**	**Yes**	**Yes**
*Mowich Lake**	**10**	**No**	**No**	**No**	**No**
Ohanepecosh	**208**	**No**	**Yes**	**Yes**	**Yes**
*Sunrise**	**8**	**No**	**No**	**No**	**No**
Sunshine Point	**18**	**No**	**No**	**Yes**	**Yes**
White River	**117**	**No**	**No**	**Yes**	**Yes**

* Camping here requires a Mount Rainier National Park backcountry permit.
*** Currently closed to car campers due to road washout; camping possible year-round with backcountry permit.

and drinking water available. This is the only campground open year-round.

White River Campground, 5 miles west of the White River Entrance, has 117 sites available for $10 per night; all are suitable for RVs and trailers. There are flush toilets and drinking water.

In addition to the drive-in campgrounds and the many backcountry camps, there are two walk-in campgrounds that often have spaces available even on weekends. **Mowich Lake Campground** (10 sites) is in the northwest corner of the park, not far from Ipsut Creek Campground, and the sites are only 100 yards from a parking lot. If you're prepared for a longer walk in, consider the **Sunrise Campground** (eight sites), which is about a mile from the Sunrise parking lot.

When the park campgrounds are full, try **La Wis Wis** (100 sites), a national forest campground on U.S. 12 and the Cowlitz River, near the Ohanepecosh Entrance to the park. There are also numerous unremarkable National Forest Service campgrounds along U.S. 12 east of White Pass and along Wash. 310 east of the park. These latter campgrounds are going to offer your best chance of finding a campsite on a Friday or Saturday night in summer. The campgrounds along Wash. 410 tend to be less crowded since they are harder to reach and are not near any fishing lakes.

Accommodations

For information or reservations at all of the lodgings inside the park, you can call or write **Mount Rainier Guest Services,** P.O. Box 108, Ashford, WA 98304 (☎ **360/569-2275**). The reservation office is open daily from April to October, from 8am to 4:30pm. Major credit cards and traveler's checks are accepted at all lodges and major visitors centers.

There are a number of places to stay in any of the surrounding communities in addition to those reviewed here. For a complete list, contact the **Seattle Visitor's Bureau** (☎ **206/461-5800**), the **Mount St. Helens Chamber of Commerce** (☎ **360/569-2339**), or the **Enumclaw Area Chamber of Commerce** (☎ **360/825-7666**).

INSIDE THE PARK

National Park Inn

Located at the Longmire Entrance, off Wash. 706 (P.O. Box 108, Ashford, WA 98304). ☎ **360/569-2275** reservations only, or 360/569-2411; fax 360/569-2770. 25 rms,

Showers	Fire Pits/ Grills	Laundry	Public Phone	Reserve	Fees	Open
No	Yes	No	Yes	No	$12	Late May to Mid-Oct
Yes	No	No	No	No	Free	***
No	Yes	No	No	No	$9–$12	Mid-May to Mid-Sept
No	Yes	No	No	No	Free	Year-round
No	Yes	No	Yes	No	$12	Late May to Late Oct
No	Yes	No	No	No	Free	Year-round
No	Yes	No	No	No	$10	Year-round
No	Yes	No	No	No	$10	Late June to Late Sept

18 with bath; 2 are wheelchair accessible. $64 double without bath, $88–$119 double with bath. AE, DC, DISC, MC, V.

Located in Longmire in the southwest corner of the park, this rustic lodge was opened in 1920 and fully renovated in 1990. With only 25 rooms and open year-round, the National Park Inn makes a great little getaway or base for exploring the mountain. The inn's front veranda has a view of Mount Rainier, and inside there's a guest lounge with a river-rock fireplace that's perfect for winter-night relaxing. The guest rooms vary in size, but come with rustic furniture, new carpeting, and coffeemakers. In winter this lodge is popular with cross-country skiers; skis and snowshoes can be rented here. The inn's restaurant has a limited menu that nevertheless manages to have something for everyone. There's also a small bar. Guests should note that this is a nonsmoking establishment. You'll need to book reservations well in advance during the summer months. If at first you don't succeed, keep trying because there are often plenty of cancellations.

Paradise Inn

Located just east of the Henry M. Jackson Memorial Visitor Center (P.O. Box 108, Ashford, WA 98304). ☎ **360/569-2275;** fax 360/569-2770. 126 rms, 95 with bath; 2 suites; 5 rms are wheelchair accessible. $68 double without bath, $95–$121 double with bath; $127 suite. AE, DC, DISC, MC, V. Closed early Oct to mid-May.

Built in 1917 high on the flanks of Mount Rainier in an area aptly known as Paradise, this rustic lodge offers breathtaking views of the mountain and the nearby Nisqually Glacier. Miles of trails and meadows make this the perfect spot for some relatively easy alpine exploring. Cedar-shake siding, huge exposed beams, cathedral ceilings, and a gigantic stone fireplace all add up to a quintessential mountain retreat. A warm and cozy atmosphere prevails. The guest rooms vary in size and amenities, so be sure to specify which type you'd like. The inn's large dining room serves three meals a day, and the Sunday brunch, served from 11am to 2:30pm, is legendary. There's also a snack bar, and after a long day hiking, you can relax with an adult beverage in the Glacier Lounge. Guests should note that this is a nonsmoking establishment.

OUTSIDE THE SOUTHWEST (NISQUALLY) ENTRANCE

Alexander's Country Inn

37515 Wash. 706 E., Ashford, WA 98304. ☎ **800/654-7615** or 360/569-2300; fax 360/569-2323. 7 rms; 5 suites. May 1–Oct 31 $89–$95 double; $115–$135 suite. Nov 1–Apr 30 $75 double; $85–$95 suite. Rates include full breakfast. Lower rates Nov–Apr. MC, V.

Located just outside the park's Nisqually Entrance, this large bed-and-breakfast first opened as an inn back in 1912. Today, as then, it is one of the preferred places to stay in the area, offering not only comfortable rooms but some of the best food for many miles around. Much care has been taken in restoring the interior. The first floor is taken up by the dining room, but on the second floor you'll find a big lounge where you can sit by the fire on a cold night. By far the best room in the house is the tower suite, which is in a turret and has plenty of windows looking out on the woods. After a hard day of playing on the mountain, there's no better place to relax than in the hot tub overlooking the inn's trout pond. The inn also rents two three-bedroom houses.

The Hobo Inn

Wash. 7 (P.O. Box 921), Elbe, WA 98330. ☎ **360/569-2500.** 8 rms. May–Oct $70–$85 double. Sept–Apr $50–$60 double. MC, V.

If you're a railroad buff, you won't want to pass up this opportunity to spend the night in a remodeled caboose. Each of the eight cabooses is a little bit different (one even has its own private hot tub). Though the oldest of the cars dates from 1916, they have all been outfitted with comfortable beds and bathrooms. Some have bay windows while others have cupolas. For the total railroad experience, you can dine in the adjacent Mount Rainier Dining Co. dining car restaurant and go for a ride on the Mount Rainier Scenic Railroad.

Mount Rainier Country Cabins

38624 Wash. 706 E., Ashford, WA 98304. ☎ **800/678-3942** or 360/569-2355. 11 cabins. $55–$80 double. AE, DISC, MC, V.

Located only 200 yards from the park's Nisqually Entrance, these cabins are set amid green lawns that attract deer throughout the year. These are not the most atmospheric of the cabins right outside the park entrance, but they are the cleanest and most up-to-date (aside from those at Wellspring and Stormking, which are both several miles farther down the road). Big picture windows let in plenty of light. Larger cabins have kitchens and fireplaces and sleep up to six people; smaller ones have microwaves and refrigerators; and one (no. 11) has a fireplace.

Mountain Meadows Inn Bed & Breakfast

28912 Wash. 706 E., Ashford, WA 98304. ☎ **360/569-2788.** 5 rms (all with private bath). $55–$95 double. Rates include full breakfast. MC, V.

Set beneath tall trees beside a small pond, this B&B was built in 1910 as the home of the superintendent for the lumber mill in the town of National, which was the site of the largest sawmill west of the Mississippi. When the mill shut down, much of the town was moved up the road to become present-day Ashford, but this impressive old home still stands and is today filled with antiques. The big front porch overlooks the pond, and there is room to roam on nearby trails through the National town site. An extensive model railroad collection is on display throughout the inn.

Stormking

P.O. Box 126, Ashford, WA 98304. ☎ **360/569-2964.** 1 cabin. $85–$105 double. MC, V.

Stormking started out as another hot tub and massage facility similar to the long-established Wellspring, and people enjoyed the setting and experience so much that they kept telling co-owner Deborah Sample that she should build a cabin and take overnight guests. That's just what she and co-owner Steven Brown did, and it's a gorgeous cabin. Set on the far side of a footbridge over a tiny pond, the modern cabin has a slate-floored entry hall, parquet floors, a woodstove, stereo system with plenty of relaxing music, and a high ceiling. In the big bathroom, which has a flagstone floor and is filled with plants, you'll find a double shower amid the greenery. Out on the back deck you'll find the hot tub. This place appeals primarily to young, active travelers.

Wellspring

54922 Kernahan Rd., Ashford, WA 98304. ☎ **360/569-2514.** 4 rms, 3 log cabins, 1 cottage. $75–$125 double. MC, V.

Billing itself a woodland spa, this rustic and relaxing hideaway more than lives up to its name and is an excellent choice for anyone wanting to be pampered and to have the chance to visit Mount Rainier. Private hot tubs and wood-fired saunas will take the chill off even the coldest night, while sore muscles will benefit from a massage by co-owner Sunny Thompson-Ward. Accommodations are an eclectic and fanciful mix. In the modern log cabins, which are tucked up against the edge of the forest, you'll find feather beds, woodstoves, and vaulted ceilings. In The Nest, you'll find a queen-size bed under a skylight and suspended from the ceiling by ropes. In the Three Bears Cottage, you'll find rustic log furniture and a full kitchen. In the

Tatoosh Room, you'll find a large stone fireplace, a whirlpool tub, and a waterfall shower. Want to sleep in a greenhouse with a cedar hot tub and wood-fired sauna? (You can, but you can't have the room to yourself until 9pm.) Several of the rooms and the cabins come with a breakfast basket. Hot tubs and saunas are an additional $5 per person per hour for guests. This New Age retreat isn't for everyone, but it is certainly the most unique accommodation in the area.

OUTSIDE THE NORTHEAST (WHITE RIVER) ENTRANCE

Alta Crystal Resort at Mt. Rainier

68317 Wash. 410 E., Greenwater, WA 98022. ☎ **800/277-6475** or 360/663-2500; fax 360/663-2500. 24 units. $89–$159 (1–4 people). AE, MC, V.

This is the closest lodging to the northeast (White River) park entrance and the Sunrise area. Though this condominium resort with wooded grounds is most popular in winter when skiers flock to Crystal Mountain's slopes (just minutes away), there's also plenty to do in summer, with an outdoor pool and nearby hiking trails. A hot tub is set in the woods. Accommodations are in one-bedroom and loft chalets. The former sleep up to four people and the latter have bed space for up to eight people. No matter what size condo you choose, you'll find a full kitchen and fireplace.

OUTSIDE THE SOUTHEAST (STEVENS CANYON) ENTRANCE

Hotel Packwood

104 Main St., Packwood, WA 98361. ☎ **360/494-5431.** 9 rms, 2 with bath. TV. $30 double without bath, $38 double with bath. MC, V.

Two stories tall with a wraparound porch and weathered siding, this renovated 1912 hotel looks like a classic mountain lodge even though it's right in the middle of this small town. The tiny rooms aren't for the finicky, but most guests spend their days traipsing around on park trails and come back to the hotel thoroughly exhausted. Though the hotel lacks much in the way of character, there are iron bed frames in some rooms, a fireplace in the lobby, and a hot tub. Packwood is about 10 miles from the Southeast Entrance to the park.

Dining

INSIDE THE PARK

In the park there are dining rooms at **Paradise Inn** (seasonal) and the **National Park Inn** (year-round). As the only formal dining options within the park, these restaurants tend to stay busy (the two inns are described in detail in the preceding section. For quick meals, there are snack bars at the **Henry M. Jackson Memorial Visitor Center,** at Paradise, and at **Sunrise Lodge.**

In Ashford you'll find a couple of places that bake great pies including the **Wild Berry Restaurant,** 37720 Hwy. 706 E., Ashford (☎ **360/569-2628**), which is one of the closest restaurants to the park's southwest (Nisqually) entrance, and, a bit farther west, the **Copper Creek Restaurant,** Wash. 706 East, Ashford (☎ **360/569-2326**).

One other interesting dining option in the area is the **Cascadian Dinner Train** (☎ **888/RRDINER**), which leaves from the town of Elbe, west of the park's Nisqually Entrance, and spends 4 hours meandering through the foothills. A vintage steam locomotive pulls the restored passenger cars, which include an observation lounge car. The dinner train costs $55 per person, and passengers have the option of prime rib, salmon, or ground ostrich steak.

Alexander's

37515 Wash. 706 E., Ashford. ☎ **360/569-2300.** Reservations recommended. Full dinners $16–$19; à la carte $11–$14. MC, V. AMERICAN.

Alexander's, which is also a popular B&B, is the best place to dine outside the Nisqually Entrance to the park. Fresh trout from the inn's pond is the dinner of choice here, but you'll also find beef stew, pork ribs, and pasta on the menu. Whatever you order, just be sure to save room for the wild blackberry pie.

Mt. Rainier Railroad Dining Co.

Wash. 7, Elbe. ☎ **360/569-2505.** Main courses $10–$17; lunch main courses $6–$11. DISC, MC, V. Mon–Fri 11am–7pm, Sat–Sun 8am–8pm. AMERICAN.

You can't miss this unusual restaurant in Elbe—just watch for all the cabooses of the adjacent Hobo Inn. Meals are basic, with steaks and fried seafoods the staples of the dinner menu, but the surroundings make this place worth a stop. You'll be dining in an old railroad dining car. Your car won't go anywhere while you dine, but you'll get a sense of being on a rail journey.

28

NORTH CASCADES NATIONAL PARK

by Tom Wells

VAST AND INACCESSIBLE ARE NOT WORDS OFTEN USED TO DESCRIBE the Cascade Range, but here in the northern reaches they are the only ones appropriate for a landscape that contains the largest wilderness in the state. The North Cascades, lying only 120 miles northeast of Seattle by road, are among the least visited and most inaccessible mountains in Washington. Here gray wolves and grizzly bears still roam, and human encroachment on their dominion is limited for the most part to the edges of the wilderness.

The North Cascades National Park Service Complex is at the heart of this region. Note the name; this is not just a park but a complex, which includes not only the national park itself but also Ross Lake and Lake Chelan national recreation areas. In 1988, by act of Congress, about 93% of the acreage of the entire complex was designated the "Stephen Mather Wilderness" under the 1964 Wilderness Act, so this can be called a wilderness in the strictest sense of the word. Unlike many national recreation areas, both Ross Lake and Lake Chelan are wild and remote, with minimal development or signs of human habitation outside a few areas.

A trip into this region is a true wilderness experience. With names like these—Mount Terror, Mount Despair, Mount Fury, Damnation Peak, Forbidden Peak, Phantom Pass, Jagged Ridge, Icy Peak, Rainy Pass—is it any wonder that North Cascades National Park Service Complex is one of the nation's least visited national parks (though, visitation to the entire complex runs about 400,000 per year)? It also doesn't help that there is only one paved road through the complex. Hiking here takes time and preparation. Although there are several shorter trails here and there in the park complex, most of them have been designed for the rugged few to take a few days or weeks at a time to get reacquainted with the natural state of things. If you're prepared, though, there's nothing else like it in the continental United States.

Geologically speaking, the North Cascades are some of the most complex and least understood mountains in North America. These peaks were formed over millions of years as a tectonic plate drifting northward from the South Pacific slammed into the North American coast, causing the area's sedimentary rocks to buckle, fold, and metamorphose. In some areas, the rock in the North Cascades is obviously the result of this collision and subsequent metamorphosis. However, in other areas, there is rock that predates the tectonic collision—one upthrust of mountain is believed to be 10 million years old.

Geologic complexity has been further augmented in the North Cascades by glaciation both past and present. In past ice ages both alpine glaciers and the continental ice sheet covered this region. The visual legacy of this intensive glaciation today can be seen in the wide U-shaped valleys carved out by the ice sheet. The single most fascinating legacy of this intensive glaciation today is Lake Chelan, which lies in the heart of the North Cascades southern section.

Avoiding the Crowds. Actually, it's not hard at all to avoid the crowds in the North Cascades. The lack of roads through the park, the weather, and the ruggedness of the terrain itself all work in concert to keep this one of the best kept secrets in the national park system.

But if it's true isolation you're looking for, head north. The Northern Unit of the national park has the least number of tourists (Lake Chelan, the Ross Lake Lodge, and Diablo Lake are all the more tourist-heavy spots due to the regular ferry service on Lake Chelan and their proximity to the Cascade Road) to deal with. But, considering that **Stehekin** (the cosmopolitan unit of the southern park section) has a permanent, year-round population of only around 70, it's a matter of avoiding the crowds or being absolutely alone. At least for the fall and winter.

In the summer, this park can be like many of the others in the system, and you're more likely to run into folks on the **Big Beaver Trail,** or on your way to **Hozomeen,** than in the fall, which is about the last part of the year in which you can easily get anywhere in the park. Ross Lake is thicker with boaters on summer holiday weekends, and the heaviest load of visitors all year can be found in Stehekin and the Cascade Pass during July and August. Of course, the deeper into the backcountry you go, the fewer people you are likely to encounter. Winter is not to be underestimated in this park, and remember the Cascade Road will almost certainly be closed.

Just the Facts

GETTING THERE & GATEWAYS

There's only one paved road that goes through the park complex, Wash. 20. Unless you want to loop up through Canada and come back in on the brief section of road (Hope Road, to be exact) that enters the park at the northern end of Ross Lake, this is the main artery.

There are a few unpaved alternatives, though. The Cascade River Road, which leaves Wash. 20 at Marblemount, enters the national park proper as an unpaved road. And the unpaved (and very rough) Stehekin Valley Road above High Bridge enters the national park proper. This road, however, does not connect with the outside world; to use it, vehicles must be barged up Lake Chelan from Chelan, Washington.

From Seattle on the west side, take the Wash. 20 exit off I-5 and head east, toward Rockport and Marblemount, into the park. From Spokane (the major metropolitan area on the east side) it's U.S. 2 West, linking up with U.S. 97 North, to Wash. 153 and finally, Wash. 20. And remember, in the winter, these roads could be closed any time from mid-October to May. Be sure to call ahead.

The Nearest Airport. **Seattle-Tacoma (Sea-Tac) International Airport** (☎ **206/626-6088**) is located 15 miles south of Seattle on I-5. It's served by **Alaska Airlines, America West, American Airlines, Continental, Delta, Horizon Air,**

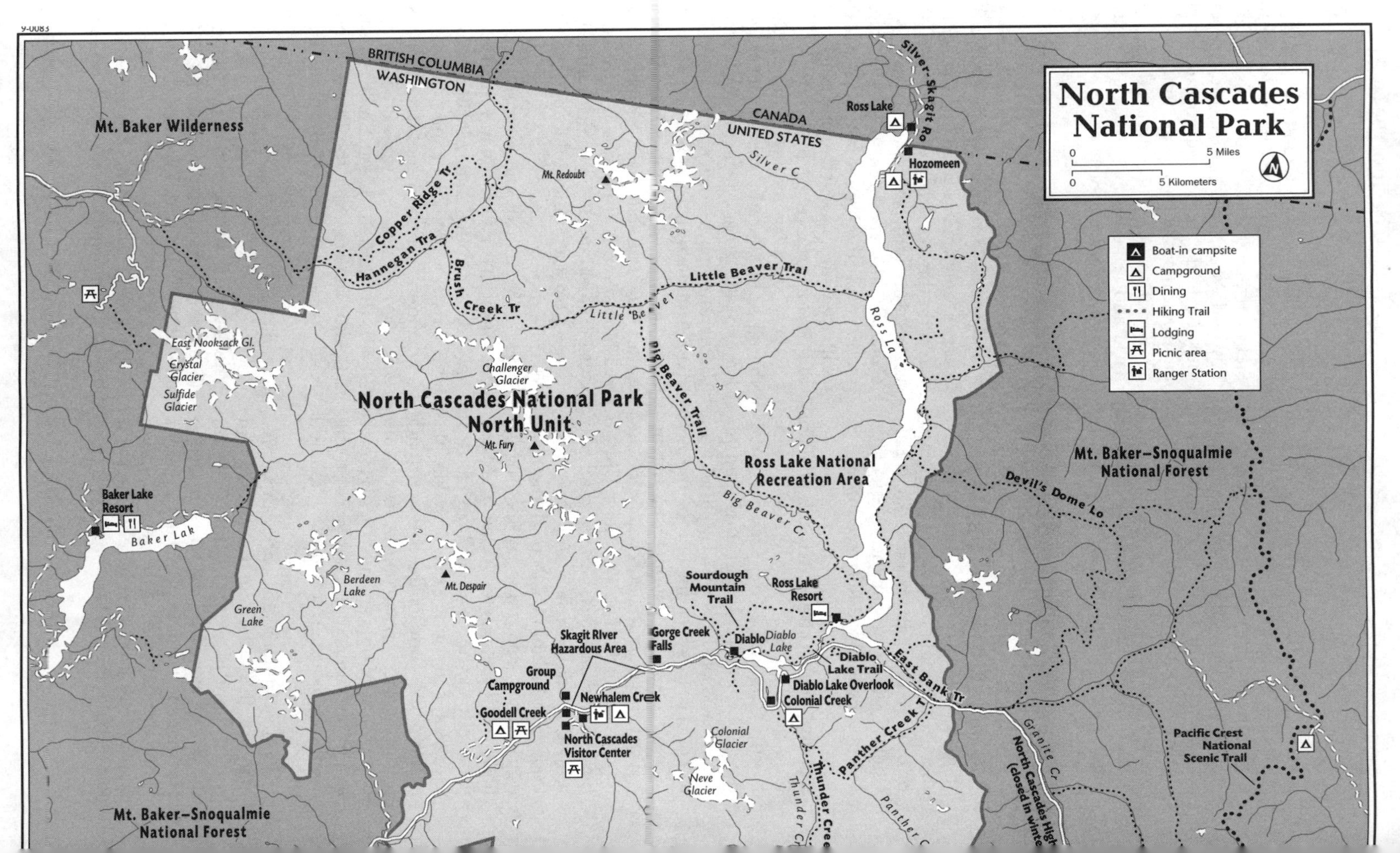

North Cascades National Park
0 5 Miles
0 5 Kilometers
Boat-in campsite
Campground
Dining
Hiking Trail
Lodging
Picnic area
Ranger Station
BRITISH COLUMBIA
WASHINGTON
CANADA
UNITED STATES
Mt. Baker Wilderness
Ross Lake
Hozomeen
Silver C
Mt. Redoubt
Copper Ridge Tr
Hannegan Tra
Brush Creek Tr
Little Beaver Trail
Little Beaver
Ross La
Big Beaver Trail
East Nooksack Gl.
Crystal Glacier
Sulfide Glacier
Challenger Glacier
North Cascades National Park North Unit
Mt. Fury
Ross Lake National Recreation Area
Mt. Baker–Snoqualmie National Forest
Devil's Dome Lo
Big Beaver Cr
Baker Lake Resort
Baker Lak
Berdeen Lake
Mt. Despair
Green Lake
Sourdough Mountain Trail
Ross Lake Resort
Diablo
Diablo Lake
Gorge Creek Falls
Skagit River Hazardous Area
Group Campground
Diablo Lake Trail
Diablo Lake Overlook
East Bank Tr
Newhalem Creek
Colonial Creek
Goodell Creek
North Cascades Visitor Center
Colonial Glacier
Neve Glacier
Panther Creek
Thunder Cr
Granite Cr
Pacific Crest National Scenic Trail
Mt. Baker–Snoqualmie National Forest

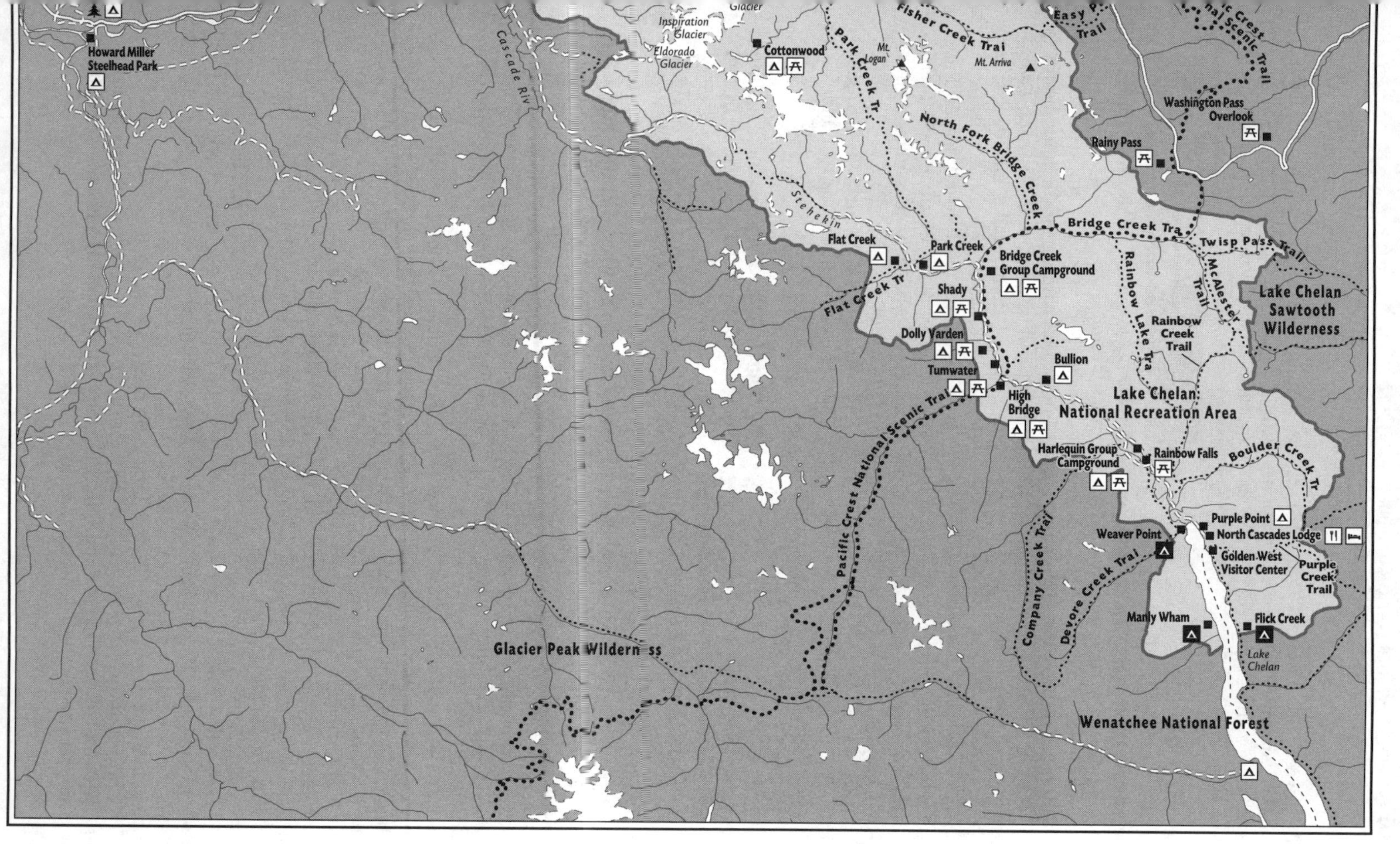

Howard Miller
Steelhead Park
Cascade Riv
Inspiration Glacier
Eldorado Glacier
Cottonwood
Mt. Logan
Mt. Arriva
Fisher Creek Trai
Park Creek Tr
North Fork Bridge Creek
Easy
Trail
Washington Pass Overlook
Rainy Pass
Stehekin
Flat Creek
Park Creek
Bridge Creek Tra
Twisp Pass Trail
Bridge Creek Group Campground
Rainbow Lake Tra
McAlester Trail
Lake Chelan Sawtooth Wilderness
Flat Creek Tr
Shady
Rainbow Creek Trail
Dolly Varden
Bullion
Tumwater
High Bridge
Lake Chelan National Recreation Area
Pacific Crest National Scenic Trail
Harlequin Group Campground
Rainbow Falls
Boulder Creek Tr
Purple Point
North Cascades Lodge
Weaver Point
Golden West Visitor Center
Purple Creek Trail
Company Creek Trail
Devore Creek Trail
Manly Wham
Flick Creek
Lake Chelan
Glacier Peak Wildern ss
Wenatchee National Forest

Northwest, Southwest, TWA, United, and **US Airways.** Toll-free reservations numbers for all of these are given in the appendix.

Renting a Car. Once you arrive, you'll be able to rent a car from all the major car-rental companies, including **Alamo, Avis, Budget, Dollar, Enterprise, Hertz, National,** and **Thrifty.** Their toll-free numbers are in the appendix.

GETTING INFORMATION BEFORE YOUR TRIP

For advance information, call or write **North Cascades National Park Service Complex,** 2105 Wash. 20, Sedro-Woolley, WA 98284 (☎ **360/856-5700**). You can also e-mail the park at NOCA_Interpretation@nps.gov, or check out the Web site at **www.nps.gov/noca**.

VISITOR CENTERS

The **North Cascades Visitor Center** (mile marker 120, Wash. 20, Newhalem ☎ **206/386-4495**), opened in 1993, is one of the more eco-oriented visitor information stations you'll find in the national park system. It's open daily in the summer, weekends only during winter. It focuses primarily on preservation, with some good exhibits, featuring slide shows and a walk-through environmental tour with placards and videos for a preview of the park. There is also a wheelchair-accessible trail leading from the back of the building that affords excellent views of the surrounding mountains; by June 1998 there will be another nearby accessible trail opening, to the Newhalem Creek Rockshelter archaeological site.

The **Golden West Visitor Center,** P.O. Box 7, Stehekin (☎ **509/856-5700,** ext. 340, then ext. 14), located on the banks of the northern tip of Lake Chelan, provides information on camping, hiking, and the local environs in general. There are several interpretive exhibits as well as a ranger or two to provide information. It's also the starting point for several trails. Nearby, you can rent bicycles.

GETTING AROUND INSIDE THE PARK

By Boat. On Lake Chelan in the spring and summer, both the *Lady Express* and the *Lady II* run to and from the Lake Chelan boat landing on the hour, but in the fall and winter, there's only the *Lady Express,* and then for the half day only. Both rides cost $22. It's wise to call ahead for reservations and schedules at the Lake Chelan Boat Company (☎ 509/682-4584). A third boat is planned for the 1998 season.

The **Ross Lake Resort** (☎ **206/386-4437**) operates water taxis to trailheads and campgrounds on Ross Lake.

By Shuttle Bus. Transportation up the Stehekin Valley Road is provided by two different shuttle buses.

One of these is operated by the **National Park Service** and costs between $5 and $10 depending on how far up the valley you go (currently Bridge Creek is the end of the bus route). Reservations for this bus should be made at least 2 days ahead of time (preferably much farther in advance) by calling the **Golden West Visitor Center** (☎ **360/856-5700,** ext. 340, then 14).

Between mid-June and the end of September, **another shuttle bus** runs several times a day between Stehekin Landing and High Bridge. No reservations are required for this bus, and the cost is $4. If you just want to ride as far as the Stehekin Pastry Company, the fare is only $1.

Taxi service is also available from the North Cascades Stehekin Lodge at the boat landing.

By Air. If you want to get to Stehekin in a hurry, you can make the trip by floatplane on **Chelan Airways** (☎ **509/682-5065** or 509/682-5555), which leaves from the dock next to the ferries. The fare is $120 round-trip. This company also offers flightseeing trips for between $80 and $150.

ENTRANCE & CAMPING FEES

There are currently no entrance fees for admission into the park itself, though there are fees for camping. Backcountry permits are required but free.

SPECIAL REGULATIONS & WARNINGS

Beware of the wintertime! Wash. 20 is usually closed from mid-November through mid-April. Call ahead to the park complex headquarters in Sedro-Woolley (☎ **360/852-5700**).

Check in at a **visitor center** for full details on trail info before you head in. Since this is bear and mountain lion country, you might want to pick up the free handout on hiking and camping safety.

Other than the general precautions that anyone would take when camping in a wilderness area, keep in mind that the North Cascades National Park Service Complex can be *extremely* remote for both the backcountry hiker and the mid-park driver. Even when day hiking only, remember to carry in enough water. And grab your food in Rockport, Marblemount, Twisp, or Winthrop—there's little to be had inside the park boundaries. Don't forget bug spray. There's a lot of water (not necessarily to drink), and consequently, lots of insects during some seasons at some locations.

Ten Essential Items

The Park Service considers the following ten items absolute essentials for even the day hiker in the North Cascades National Park Service Complex. Hikers should carry them and know how to use them.

◆ **Navigation** (a topographical map and compass)

◆ **Food and water** (boiling water can kill Giardia, but some treatment pills can't)

◆ **Clothing** (including rain gear, wool socks, a sweater, gloves, and hat)

◆ **Light** (a flashlight with spare bulb and batteries)

◆ **Fire** (waterproof matches and a fire starter, such as a candle)

◆ **Sun protection** (sunglasses and sunscreen)

◆ **First aid** (a kit including any special medications you might need)

◆ **Knife** (a folding pocket knife is best)

◆ **Signals** (both audible and visual: whistle and metal mirror)

◆ **Emergency shelter** (a plastic tube shelter or waterproof bivouac sack)

SEASONS & CLIMATE

The most pernicious of seasons for people visiting the North Cascades area is the winter, which begins creeping up in October in the upper elevations and mid-November in most other parts. It lasts until mid- to late April, and is accompanied by the regular closure of Wash. 20. The first snow at the upper elevations is often in September.

After the thaw, from April to September, things get pretty temperate, with daytime temperatures ranging from 50° to 70°F, depending on the elevation. However, this is a land of extremes: Trails at higher elevations are usually snow-covered into early July (though this varies considerably from year to year), and summer temperatures of 100°F are not unusual at Ross Lake and Lake Chelan. As can usually be expected in the northwest, rains arrive westerly from the Pacific in the spring and fall, with summer being the most pleasant all around. At any time, though, expect rain; it's always best to pack rain gear. The eastern side of the mountains is somewhat less wet than the western, though this is nothing to bank on.

In addition, with the extremes in altitude one is sure to find here, it's always good to bring something warm, even in the summer months.

SEASONAL EVENTS

There are several seasonal art shows and exhibits at the **Golden West Visitor Center** in the summertime. However, the only source for current listings is park headquarters in Sedro-Woolley, on Wash. 20 near I-5, west of the park (☎ **360/856-5700**).

USEFUL PUBLICATIONS

The park publishes a newspaper, the ***North Cascades Challenger,*** which can be obtained by writing park headquarters in Sedro-Woolley, and you can also get a copy of the park brochure with a map. (See "Getting Information Before Your Trip," above).

Seeing the Highlights in a Day

With the idea in mind that this is one of the most rugged wilderness areas in the United States, any attempt at seeing the park in a day must be made with the understanding that you're going to have to decide what section you want to be in, and you're going to have to consider what season of the year it is, because Wash. 20 gets shut down regularly from mid-November into April. For most folks, it's the summer cruise across the park via Wash. 20 (described in the next section) that becomes the ride of choice.

If You Have More Time

The road into the park is a beautiful cruise along the banks of the Skagit River, past the Mount Baker–Snoqualmie National Forest. Your last real connection with civilization, and the last chance to stock up on groceries, is Marblemount, the oldest town in the region. From here, you can head south or east. South is the Cascade River Road, and east is Wash. 20.

The **Cascade River Road** is a 25-mile stretch of unpaved road that leads to the Cascade Pass Trailhead, at the southern end of North Cascades National Park. The road passes near a fish hatchery and crosses the Skagit River before terminating at the Cascade Pass Trailhead. Many folks take the 3.5-mile trip to the top of the pass, which takes the hiker up a relatively modest set of switchbacks to beautiful views of glaciers and subalpine meadows.

If you're not up to the unpaved twistiness of the Cascade River Road, continue on Wash. 20 to **Newhalem,** where there is a visitor center that has some very good exhibits and regularly scheduled ranger-led walks and talks. This is a good place to get information about the many short walks and hikes that are in the immediate vicinity. You'll find some short, paved trails beginning behind the visitor center that afford beautiful views of the surrounding mountains. In addition, if you're there late enough in the day, check out the trail to **Ladder Creek Falls** (which is not on National Park Service property but rather that owned by Seattle City Light), which is fun in a most decidedly touristy manner. There's a hydroelectric dam at the end of trail that creates a minilight show on the falls at night, created by James Ross, the master dam builder of the area. It's worth the hike.

Next up on the route is the little town of **Diablo,** located at the foot of 389-foot-high **Diablo Dam,** which holds in the blue-green waters of Diablo Lake. There's a boat landing here, and several tours operated by Seattle City Light that take you around Diablo Lake. One particularly cheap ride takes you up the **Incline Railway,** a steep elevator-like trip up the hillside. There you can take walks across the top of Diablo Dam and the surrounding area. Call **Skagit Tours** (☎ **206/684-3030**) for more information.

As the road loops south from Diablo, look for fantastic views of **Neve Glacier.** In fact, there are beautiful views to be had from a plethora of turnouts along the road.

At the **Ross Lake Dam,** the lake begins its 24-mile dogleg up the eastern side of the park complex to the Canadian border. For views of the lake from the dam, stop the car and take the steep, 1-mile walk down the **Ross Dam Trail,** which leads over the top of the dam, eventually winding its way to the Ross Lake Resort and the North Cascades backcountry. Further along Wash. 20, take the turnout at the **Ross Lake Overlook,** where you can see the Ruby Arm (leading to Ruby Creek) as well as Ross Lake proper, heading north toward Canada.

The **Stehekin Area,** at the head of Lake Chelan, is not accessible by car. To get there, you have to either hike in, take a passenger ferry or floatplane up from the southern resort town of Chelan, or take the Cascade River Road from Marblemount to its southern terminus at the Cascade Pass Trailhead. From there, you can hike 11 miles over Cascade Pass to Flat Creek, along the Stehekin Valley Road, where you may be able to catch a shuttle bus to the Stehekin area, if the road is open (from approximately July 1 to mid-October). (Flood damage has closed the road from Flat Creek to its terminus 2 miles further at Cottonwood Camp.) Be sure to call ahead for up-to-date information and to reserve a seat on the **shuttle bus** (☎ **360/856-5700,** ext. 340, then ext. 14). A ferry ride up the lake from Chelan is the only quick way to the Stehekin Area. (A float plane is actually the quickest, though most expensive, option.)

Once you make it to Stehekin, you can rent a bike to ride the roads in the area, but bikes are not permitted on trails. Give yourself enough time and strength for the hike out, though.

If you wish to visit the **northern sections of the park,** there are a couple of options. From the Ross Dam area, park the car and hike the trail in to the Ross Lake Lodge landing. You can hike around the general area, or, better yet, catch a water taxi up the shores of the lake (arrange this at the resort). The taxis will drop you off at any of the trailheads that intersect both sides of the shores of this lake all the way to Hozomeen, the northernmost part of the lake in U.S. territory. **Ross Lake Resort** offers boat rentals (small outboards, canoes, and kayaks) for those who want to create their own itinerary along the lake.

The only real way to get near the **northwest section of the park** by vehicle is to head east from the Mount Baker Wilderness Area, which is popular and easily accessible because of the Mount Baker Ski Area. Beyond the Mount Baker area, take the Nooksack Road, which is accessible by four-wheel-drive regularly, and other vehicles semiregularly. As usual, it's a good idea to call ahead for road conditions. Beyond the end of the road lie the popular Hannegan Pass, Copper Ridge, and Chilliwack trails. These are popular trails in the summer season, but they are multiday hikes and require a permit for camping overnight. There are beautiful views all along the trails of glaciers spreading southward through the park, especially the Nooksack Glacier along the ridges overhanging the Nooksack River.

Organized Tours & Ranger Programs

For tours of Lake Diablo and Ross Dam, call **Skagit Tours** (☎ **206/684-3030**), which runs several boat and hiking trips along the southern stretches of Ross Lake and all over Diablo Lake. There's even a deluxe package that offers a fried chicken dinner after a cruise.

Seattle City Light (☎ **206/233-2709**) operates 4-hour **boat tours of Diablo Lake.** The tours start with a trip up an incline railway to the top of 389-foot-tall Diablo Dam. From there you board a boat for the 5-mile cruise to Ross Lake Dam, where you get a tour of the powerhouse. At the end of all this, you get a chicken or vegetarian spaghetti dinner. Tours are offered Thursday through Monday between mid-June and late September and cost $25 for adults, $22 for seniors, $12.50 for children 6 to 11. There are also 1½-hour tours of **Diablo Dam,** for $5, not including the boat ride or dinner.

Want to track radio-collared mountain caribou? Stalk newts, frogs, and salamanders in Heather Meadows? Learn about Lummi Indian basketry? Delve into the mysteries of mycology? Hang with some bats? You can do any of these things if you sign up for the right class through the North Cascades Institute. Offering more than 70 natural history field seminars each year, the **North Cascades Institute,** 2105 Wash. 20, Sedro-Woolley, WA 98284-9394 (☎ **360/856-5700,** ext. 209) is a non-profit educational organization that offers a wide range of courses each year. While these seminars, many of which involve camping out, focus on the North Cascades region, there are programs throughout the state. The institute has plans to open a North Cascades Environmental Education Center in 1999.

A variety of day trips are operated in conjunction with the two passenger ferries of the **Lake Chelan Boat Company** (☎ **509/682-4584**). Tours include the popular bus ride to 312-foot Rainbow Falls ($6 adults, $4 children ages 6 to 11), a bus ride up the valley and a bike ride back down ($12), and a narrated bus trip up the valley to High Bridge and then a picnic lunch ($20 adults, $10 children ages 6 to 11).

There are a limited number of ranger-led hikes in the park. These tours often start from the **North Cascades Visitor Center** or the Colonial Creek Campground, but this varies from year to year. Check in at the visitor center for a schedule of daily events.

Historic & Man-Made Attractions

The most famous man-made attractions in the park are the dams at Ross Lake and Diablo Lake, which together are responsible for all the popular water-sports activities in the Ross Lake area, as well as some of the lights you see in Seattle.

When it was completed in 1929, **Diablo Dam,** the lower of the two dams, was the tallest of its type at 389 feet. James Ross, the architect, engineer, and planner of the dam complex, overcame the remoteness of the area with a narrow-gauge railroad that cut through the surrounding mountains to its junction with Diablo Lake. From there, materials were lifted up the hillside by the **Incline Railway,** a famous little section of track that is really more of an elevator than anything else. Today, you can take a ride up the railway yourself for a nominal fee. There are tours and exhibits available at visitor centers located at both dams.

Day Hikes

Camping in the backcountry is free, but campers must obtain a free permit at one of the visitor centers, the National Park Service Complex **headquarters** in Sedro-Woolley, or the **Wildnerness Information Center** in Marblemount.

ROSS LAKE NATIONAL RECREATION AREA

Desolation Peak

8 miles RT. Moderate to difficult. Access: Desolation Landing on Ross Lake via the Ross Lake water taxi, or hike north along the East Bank Ross Lake Trail.

Calling all Kerouac fans! This is the peak that inspired Jack Kerouac's *Desolation Angels,* and it's no wonder that people (and in the middle of summer there are often quite a few of them) would be inspired to meditate on desolation after hiking up this steep hillside through alpine meadows. On the way to the top there are spectacular views of Mount Hozomeen, Jack Mountain, and below, beautiful Ross Lake. This can be a very hot and dry hike in the summer, however, and the full round-trip takes several days.

Thornton Lakes Trail

10.4 miles RT. Moderate. Access: The trailhead is reached via Wash. 20 to Thornton Lakes Rd., 3 miles west of Newhalem. The road climbs steeply to the trailhead.

Despite the fact that the first part of the trail is basically an old logging road that might remind you of resource-stripping, this trip is not to be missed. It's a moderately steep walk to the lakes, where the trail cuts to the right (north), for sublime views of the Picket Range at the top of Trappers Peak. Even if you don't take the side route, the sight of Mount Triumph's glaciers to the north, from the nestled valleys in which the lakes sit, is worth the hike.

Stetattle Creek

8 miles RT. Easy. Access: The trailhead is reached via the exit before the green bridge on Wash. 20, just before you reach the town of Diablo along Gorge Lake.

This is a good hike for fans of Diablo's power plant, (there are more than you think) who hike along this gentle, scenic path in the summertime along the creek. The trail meanders north for some 3-odd miles before hitting a stretch of giant, moss-hung trees, and finally petering out in the middle of the forest. The waters of Stetattle Creek often flow milky blue-white from the glacial silt that comes down from McMillan Spire and Mount Terror.

Sourdough Mountain

12.5 miles RT. Moderate to difficult. Access: The trailhead is located in the town of Diablo, or via water taxi on the West Bank Trail to the Pierce Mountain Trailhead.

From the west, the trail is easily accessible by car. But rest assured, either way, you're going to be doing some serious climbing; try a 3,000-foot climb from the Diablo direction, and in just 2 miles, too. And then there's the remaining 2,000 feet or so along the next 4 miles. It's a very densely forested walk over the first couple of miles. Be sure to take the right fork at the 3-mile mark to get to the summit for spectacular views of the lake and the glaciers that dot the horizon to the north. This area is hot and dry in the summer, so take extra water.

Diablo Lake Trail

7.6 miles RT. Easy. Access: The trailhead is at the end of the road, across from the Diablo Dam.

This is the Grand Central of the Diablo Lake area. You get views of Ross Dam and of the power lines, which the trail intersects, but you'll also see some larger old-growth trees and varied forests. The trail starts at Seattle City Light's power project dock, from where you can also pick up the tug for a ride to the base of upstream Ross Dam. Better to follow the trail as it winds along what was once the Skagit River, but is now Diablo Lake. In front of Ross Dam, however, you get a good idea of how well the dams really work by checking out the view as you cross the suspension bridge, which once traversed the Skagit River Gorge but now is part of the system of dams that make the Ross and Diablo lake areas.

Thunder Creek Trail

1.6 to 38 miles RT. Difficulty varies. Access: The 2 trailheads are south of Ross Lake; 1 is at the Colonial Creek Campground parking lot, the other at the amphitheater, though the 2 trails shortly join.

There are plenty of things to do if you decide to take the Thunder Creek Trail. You could amble past the Thunder Creek Arm of Diablo Lake to the intersection with the Fourth of July Pass Trail (also called the Panther Creek Trail) junction, head to the left, and make a loop around the hub of ever-looming (and it goes without saying, snowcapped and gorgeous) Ruby Peak. Or you could make a weekend trek through the rugged wilderness that lines the trail north to south on its way to its terminus in the Park Creek Area along the Stehekin River. Along the way, you can intersect with the Fisher Creek Trail, sloping left along the creek toward an intersection with a possible terminus over Easy Pass at Wash. 20.

From Diablo Lake, it's a broad and easily sauntered path for the first couple of miles, which then begin to slope upward for the next several miles, through the Panther Creek junction on the way to McAlester Creek Camp. This is the 6-mile mark, and a lot of day hikers head back the way they came at this point. Otherwise, it's off for the weekend camping trip in some of the most gorgeous country in the continental United States, through the rugged and lush valleys in the southern part of the North Cascades.

Pyramid Lake

4 miles RT. Moderate. Access: The trailhead is 1 mile east of Diablo, on the south side of the highway near the creek, close to mile marker 127.

This trail is like many in the park—steep. But it's not so steep that you want to leave it alone. The hike is a beautiful but relatively sharp climb, passing through pine and fir forests. It ends at a little pond of a lake, fed by the Colonial Glaciers looming above you along the southeast side of Pyramid Peak. You're liable to see climbers descending from the peaks at the end of the day, looking tired but happy after having ascended the 7,000 feet to the top of Pyramid.

Fourth of July Pass/Panther Creek

10 miles RT. Moderate. Access: Hike 1.8 miles up the Thunder Creek Trail to the junction with the trailhead.

For a day hike through some of the most astonishing country in the Lower 48, this section of trail isn't too shabby. It's a popular summer hike to the top of Fourth of July Pass, which shows off the ever-majestic Neve Glacier and Colonial Peak to the west. It ain't easy, though. It's a switchback-cursed climb from the bottomlands along Thunder Creek up to the 3,500-foot top of the pass. But that's the hardest part. You get to return via the beautiful drop down the Panther Creek Valley for 5 miles to the junction with Wash. 20 at the Panther Creek Bridge and the Ross Lake Trailhead.

East Bank Ross Lake Trail

0.5 to 34 miles one way. Easy to difficult. Access: Several points along the shore of the lake via the water taxi, or from Panther Creek Bridge to the terminus of the trail at Hozomeen Campground.

During the summer, this is one of the most popular trails in the whole park, with its plentiful and well-maintained campsites, the easy grade of its path, and its proximity to Wash. 20. To avoid crowds, you might want to wait until late in the season. The path serves as part of the eastern perimeter of the park, and borders the Pasayaten Wilderness and the Okanogan National Forest, from which several trails intersect the Ross Lake Trail. The highest point along the trail is the Desolation Peak Trail, near the north. Along the way, be prepared for black bears, beautiful fall foliage, and on the northern section of the trail, the possibility of sighting a member of one of the few remaining wolf packs in the Lower 48.

LAKE CHELAN NATIONAL RECREATION AREA

Coon Lake Trail

2.5 miles RT. Moderate. Access: The trailhead is at High Bridge, which is a stop on the shuttle bus up the valley.

This short trail leads to a pretty little lake that was created by beavers. Wildlife, especially waterfowl, is plentiful on and around the 15-acre lake. On the far side a waterfall on Coon Creek can be seen. Though forests surround the lake, there are views southwest to Agnes Mountain.

Rainbow Falls

7 miles RT. Easy. Access: The trailhead is at Stehekin Landing.

At 312 feet high, Rainbow Falls are among the most impressive falls in Washington and are a popular destination for a day-trippers who visit Stehekin on the *Lady of the Lake* or *Lady Express* (for more information, see "Getting Around Inside the Park" under "Just the Facts," above). The falls were created when a glacier scraped out the walls of the Stehekin Valley, leaving Rainbow Creek hanging high above the valley floor in much the same way that the famous waterfalls of the Yosemite Valley were formed. The falls are 3.5 miles from Stehekin landing by road and make a good day-hike destination if you are staying at the North Cascades Lodge; you get there by walking along the road. The lodge also offers a bus tour of the falls (although it's open to anyone and timed for the convenience of the "day-tripper"). Alternatively, if the shuttle bus is running, you can take it to and from the falls or just one way.

Rainbow Loop Trail

6 miles RT. Moderate to difficult. Access: The trail is reached at Rainbow Creek Trailhead, 5.5 miles from Stehekin.

While trails in the Stehekin area tend to be flat valley-bottom hikes or grueling climbs straight up the steep walls of the valley, this hike makes a good in-between choice. Not too easy, not too difficult. Views of the Stehekin Valley and Lake Chelan are the payoff. Start the hike from the Rainbow Creek Trailhead, which can be reached from the shuttle bus. From here climb 1,000 feet in 2.5 miles, along the way passing a bluff with a view of the valley, to a bridge over Rainbow Creek. Just before reaching the creek there is a trail junction. If you turn left here and hike up this trail 0.5 mile, you'll find views even more stunning than the ones along the main trail. The creek marks the midpoint of the trail, from which it is 2.5 miles down to the lower trailhead, which is at the bottom of a steep trail with more great views.

Agnes Gorge Trail

5 miles RT. Easy. Access: The trailhead is at High Bridge Campground; it can be reached via the park's shuttle bus.

This is an easy hike along the west-side cliffs of Agnes Gorge, with beautiful views of looming Mount Agnes above you. This is a good walk for a day visitor to the Stehekin area.

NORTH CASCADES NATIONAL PARK—SOUTHERN UNIT

The interior of the southern unit of the North Cascades National Park is remote. Most of the trails are concentrated on the northern or southern end. The northern trails are accessed via Wash. 20. The southern trails are accessed via the Cascade River Road, a winding, sometimes rugged stretch of unpaved craziness which will get you to the trail for Cascade Pass. Call ahead to Marblemount for road conditions because sometimes this is not easily accessible to the average vehicle. Hikers can take Thunder Creek Trail, an artery through the interior, for access to the Chelan/Stehekin area, but it's not a day hike.

Bridge Creek Trail

29 miles RT. Moderate. Access: The trailhead is at the Bridge Creek Bridge on the Stehekin Valley Rd.; the other end of the trail is at Rainy Pass on Wash. 20.

This backcountry hike steadily ascends to Wash. 20, though never steeply, through some beautiful valleys, after a short hike along a section of the Pacific

Crest Trail. There are beautiful views of Goode Mountain and Mount Logan, as well as the massive ice-hangs below Memaloose Ridge.

Cascade Pass/Sahale Arm Trail

11 miles RT. Difficult. Access: From Marblemount on Wash. 20, cross the bridge and drive east for 23.5 miles on the Cascade River Rd. to the trailhead.

This is one of the most popular hikes in the North Cascades National Park. Starting high above the valley of the North Fork Cascade River, the trail follows an ancient Indian trading route over the Cascades to Lake Chelan. Today the trail is popular as a day trip, an overnight trip, a climber's route to some challenging North Cascades rock, and as a through trail to Stehekin.

Park Creek Pass

8 miles one way. Moderate to difficult. Access: The trailhead is at Park Creek Campground on the Stehekin Valley Rd.

Though this hike is often crowded in the summer with people passing through Stehekin, it's still worth it to make your way up the steep, forested slopes towards the alpine meadows beyond the logistically named Five Mile Camp. From here on up it's glacier lilies and the cracking of calving glacier ice on the slopes of Goode Mountain. Huge chunks of ice have been known to crash into the valley below the slopes, so look for slabs as big as your average house crashing into the rocks below. Beyond the 6,000-foot Park Creek Pass, connect with the Thunder Creek Trail for a much longer hike to the Ross Lake Area.

NORTH CASCADES NATIONAL PARK—NORTHERN UNIT

The backcountry trails in this region, such as **Hannegan Trail, Chilliwack Trail,** and **Big Beaver Trail,** aren't easy to get to, but they're worth the effort. Here you'll find the most stupendous mountain views in the park complex. This is the most remote wilderness area in the state and may still be home to both wolves and grizzly bears. From virgin forests in glacial valleys to high meadows with head-on views of the park's jagged Picket Range, these hikes have everything.

Start from the trailhead from the Mount Baker Wilderness in the Mount Baker–Snoqualmie National Forest, near the northwestern section of the North Cascades National Park Northern Unit. From the town of Glacier drive 13 miles to F.S. 32 (Nooksack River Road), and continue to the trailhead at the Hannegan Campground at the road's end. You can also take a water taxi up Ross Lake and start your hike from the Big Beaver Landing. This ride will cost you $20 and must be arranged in advance.

Other Sports & Activities

Biking. Riding off the road is not allowed in the park, but there are still several good biking routes. Keep in mind that biking is usually best in late July and August, but even then, bad weather can descend suddenly to ruin the views and soak the riders.

The trip along **Wash. 20** through the park and also west of the park between Rockport and Marblemount is strenuous but beautiful. The road has a wide shoulder in many (though not all) places and several roadside campsites. Beware of some extremely steep stretches.

Mountain bikers will want to try the **Stehekin Valley Road** route, 21 miles from Flat Creek to the community of Stehekin, on Lake Chelan. The road parallels the glacier-fed Stehekin River and provides plenty of great views of the North Cascades peaks. The 312-foot-high Rainbow Falls is a required stop along the way.

Fishing. To fish inside the National Park Service Complex, you will need a Washington state fishing license.

Ross Lake contains naturally reproducing populations of both native rainbow and cutthroat trout, as well as eastern brook trout and a few bull trout. Fishing boats can be rented at the **Ross Lake Resort** (☎ **206/386-4437**).

Lake Chelan, although it looks like an awesome fishing hole, is so large, so deep, and so cold that it doesn't support a large fish population. However it does have quite a variety, including kokanee, land-locked chinook salmon, cutthroat, rainbow, Mackinaw trout, and freshwater ling cod (burbot). The **Stehekin River** and its tributary streams also offer excellent fly-fishing.

If you want to hire a guide to take you where the fish are biting, try **Fish'n Lake Chelan** (☎ **800/626-RUSH** or 509/682-2802) or **Graybill's Guide Service** (☎ **509/682-4294**).

Golf. Right on the edge of town, golfers will find the municipal **Lake Chelan Golf Course,** 1501 Golf Course Dr. (☎ **509/682-5421**). However, anyone out this way with golf clubs is probably headed to **Desert Canyon Resort,** 1201 Desert Canyon Blvd., Orondo (☎ **800/258-1173** or 509/682-2697), which is located 17 miles south of Chelan and has been voted the best public course in Washington.

Hang Gliding and Paragliding. In recent years, Lake Chelan has become one of the nation's hang gliding and paragliding meccas. Strong winds and thermals allow flyers to sail for a hundred miles or more from the Chelan Sky Park atop Chelan Butte, which is located on the outskirts of town. The top of Chelan Butte is now the Chelan Sky Park. Paragliding lessons are available here through **Chelan Paragliding School** (☎ **509/682-7777**).

Kayaking & Canoeing. Diablo Lake and Ross Lake both offer excellent flat-water paddling and are among the few inland waters in the Northwest with extensive boat-in campsites. However, there are two major drawbacks to paddling on Ross Lake: There is no road access to the lake in the U.S. (the unpaved Silver Skagit Road enters the park from British Columbia, leading to the north end of Ross Lake), and strong winds often blow in the afternoon. The first difficulty can be surmounted by calling the **Ross Lake Resort** (☎ **206/386-4437**), which offers a canoe and kayak shuttle service to transport boats from Diablo Lake (which is accessible by car) around Ross Dam to Ross Lake. The resort charges from $15 to $25 per canoe or kayak for this service and reservations must be made in advance for the shuttle at the beginning and end of your trip. You can also rent outboard motorboats, kayaks, and canoes at the Ross Lake Resort.

You'll also need a **backcountry permit** to overnight on Ross Lake. These permits are available at the North Cascades National Park Service Complex at the Wilderness Information Center in Marblemount. The permits allow you to stay at the many campsites along the shores of Ross Lake.

Because of the length of the lake and the difficulties of dealing with the wind, many paddlers stick to the lower end (unless they enter at Hozomeen at the lake's north end). Here you can explore the **Narrow Ruby Arm** using Green Point Campground (1 mile above the dam) as a base camp. Farther north are the Cougar Island (2 miles above the dam), Roland Point (4 miles above the dam), McMillan (5.5 miles above the dam), and Spencer's (6 miles above the dam) campgrounds.

If you aren't inclined to spend the money for the shuttle, you can have a similar experience paddling on **Diablo Lake,** which is an amazing turquoise due to the amounts of glacial flour suspended in the water. Diablo also has three boat-in campsites (Thunder Point, Hidden Cove, and Buster Brown) as well as a couple of small islands to explore. Alternatively, you can explore the lake from the drive-in Colonial Creek Campground on the Thunder Arm of the lake.

Snowshoeing. The **Stehekin Valley** makes an ideal snowshoeing destination. Not only are there quite a few miles designed for cross-country skiing, but many hiking trails offer opportunities for exploring slopes of the mountains surrounding the valley. The road is plowed to a point 9 miles north of Stehekin Landing. You can rent snowshoes at the North Cascades Stehekin Lodge.

Cross-Country Skiing. West of the park complex, the **Mount Baker Ski Area** is where most skiers end up. But if you're looking for someplace to do some cross-country skiing away from the crowds, consider Stehekin. In previous years, you would have found several groomed trails around the lower section of the Stehekin Valley, but this wasn't done in the 1997–98 season. The chance to ski past 312-foot-tall Rainbow Falls should not be missed.

Camping

Camping in the national park and recreation areas is on a first-come, first served basis, except for groups, who can call ☎ **360/873-4590,** ext. 16 for reservations. Camping in the backcountry is free, but hikers must obtain a free backcountry permit at a visitor center or the Wilderness Information Station in Marblemount. The only drive-in campsites are located along Wash. 20 through the Ross Lake area, except Hozomeen, which is accessible by car only through the Silver Skagit Road, 40 miles south of Hope, in British Columbia, Canada. All of the National Park Service campgrounds that follow (and most of the others) have toilet facilities (some flush, some vault) and drinking water available.

ALONG THE NORTH CASCADES HIGHWAY

Heading over the North Cascades Highway from the west side, you'll find a very nice campground, with walk-in sites, at **Rockport State Park** (62 campsites) just west of Rockport. This campground is set amid large old-growth trees. Right in Rockport itself, there are campsites in a large open field at **Howard Miller Steelhead Park** (59 campsites).

East of Marblemount, there are a couple of small National Forest Service campgrounds on the Cascade River Road, which leads to the trailhead for the popular hike to Cascade Pass. **Marble Creek** (24 campsites) is 8 miles east of Marblemount, and **Mineral Park Campground** (4 campsites) is 15 miles east of Marblemount. These, however, do not have drinking water; on the positive side, they are free.

Reservations at state park campgrounds can be made by calling **Reservations Northwest** (☎ **800/452-5687**). Some national forest campgrounds in the area also accept reservations. For more information call the **National Forest Reservation Service** (☎ **800/280-CAMP**).

IN ROSS LAKE NATIONAL RECREATION AREA

Goodell Creek ($7, 21 campsites, open year-round, but there is no drinking water in fall and winter) is just west of Newhalem and is popular with paddlers and anglers. It has a good view of the Picket Range from just across the highway. There are no showers, but there are pit toilets.

Newhalem Creek ($10, 107 campsites, open late May to October), one of the area's busiest campgrounds, is at the center of the action, near the North Cascades Visitor Center. It's wheelchair accessible and has a dump station. There are many short hiking trails nearby.

Colonial Creek ($10, 162 campsites, open mid-May to October) is on the banks of the Thunder Arm part of Diablo Lake. This is the largest campground on the highway and also the busiest. It has some nice sites on the water and access to boat ramps. Some sites are wheelchair accessible.

Hozomeen (free, 122 campsites, late May to October) is a more primitive campsite with no garbage facilities at the northern tip of Ross Lake.

IN LAKE CHELAN NATIONAL RECREATION AREA

At the north end of the lake, near Stehekin, there are nine campgrounds, most of which are served by the shuttle bus from Stehekin. **Purple Point Campground** is right in Stehekin and is the most convenient to the boat landing.

For information on campgrounds in the Stehekin Valley, contact the **Golden West Visitor Center,** P.O. Box 7, Stehekin, WA 98852 (☎ **360/856-5700,** ext. 340, then ext. 14).

Accommodations

There aren't a lot of choices for lodging in the park. To the west, along Wash. 20, you can find places in and near Marblemount and Rockport; to the east there's Mazama and Winthrop, also on Wash. 20.

INSIDE THE PARK

Ross Lake Resort

Rockport, WA 98283. ☎ **206/386-4437.** 17 cabins, $58–$140 double. MC, V.

There may not be another lodging of this type in the United States. All 13 of the resort's cabins are built on logs that are floating on Ross Lake. If you're looking to get away from it all, this place comes pretty close. There is no road to the resort. To reach it, you first drive to the Diablo Dam on Wash. 20, and then take a tugboat to the end of Diablo Lake, where a truck carries you around the Ross Dam to the lodge. Alternatively you can hike in on a 2-mile trail from mile marker 134 on Wash. 20. There is no restaurant or grocery store here, so be sure to bring enough supplies for your stay. What do you do once you get here? Rent a boat and go fishing, rent a kayak or canoe, do some hiking, or simply sit and relax.

North Cascades Stehekin Lodge

P.O. Box 457, Chelan, WA 98816. ☎ **509/682-4494.** 28 rms. $75–$105 double. MC, V.

Located right at Stehekin Landing, the North Cascades Stehekin Lodge is shaded by tall trees and overlooks the lake. There are a variety of room types ranging from basic rooms with no lake view to spacious apartments. The studio apartments, which have kitchens, are the best deal and all have lake views. Boat and bicycle rentals are available, and after a long day of pedaling, hiking, biking, or riding, you'll appreciate the hot tub.

Stehekin Valley Ranch

P.O. Box 36, Stehekin, WA 98852. ☎ **509/682-4677.** 3 cabins, 9 tent cabins. $60 per adult, $50 per child 7–12, $35 per child 4–6, $20 per child 3 and under. $10 more for cabins. Rates include all meals and transportation in lower valley. $5 off if you bring sleeping bag or sheets. No credit cards.

If you're a camper at heart, then the tent cabins at the Stehekin Valley Ranch should be just fine. With canvas roofs, screen windows, and no electricity or plumbing, these "cabins" are little more than permanent tents. Bathroom facilities are in the nearby main building. For slightly more comfortable accommodations, opt for one of the permanent cabins. Activities available at additional cost include horseback riding, river rafting, and mountain biking.

IN ROCKPORT

Clark's Skagit River Cabins & Resort

5675 Wash. 20, Rockport, WA 98283. ☎ **800/273-2606** or 360/873-2250; fax 360/873-4077; Web site www.northcascades.com. 23 cabins. TV. $47–$107 double. AE, DISC, MC, V.

The first thing you notice when you turn into the driveway to Clark's Skagit River Cabins is the rabbits. They're everywhere—hundreds of them in all shapes and sizes, contentedly munching the lawns or just sitting quietly. Today the bunnies are one of the main attractions at Clark's, but it's the theme cabins that keep people coming back. Western, nautical, Victorian, Native American, Adirondack, hacienda, and mill are the current choices of interior decor in these cabins. There are also other cabins that are equally comfortable, but the decor in the theme cabins is what makes Clark's just a bit different. These cabins are especially popular in winter when folks flock to the area to watch the bald eagles that congregate on the Skagit River. There's also a restaurant on the property.

IN MAZAMA

Freestone Inn

17798 Wash. 20, Mazama, WA 98833. ☎ **800/639-3809** or 509/996-3906; fax 509/996-3907. 12 rms, 15 cabins, 2 lodges. TEL. Summer $130–$225 double; $100–$195 cabin; $190–$300 lodge. Winter $110–$220 double; $90–$175 cabin; $170–$270 lodge. Lower rates in spring and fall. AE, DC, DISC, MC, V.

Located at the upper end of the Methow Valley outside the community of Mazama, the Freestone Inn is an up-and-comer. The inn's main building is a huge new log structure complete with massive stone fireplace in the cathedral-ceilinged great room that serves as lobby and dining room. The lodge sits on the shore of small Freestone Lake and has a superb view of the mountains rising beyond the far shore of the lake. Guest rooms are thoughtfully designed with gas fireplaces and double whirlpool tubs that open to the bedroom so you can lie in the tub and still see the fireplace. All in all, these are some of the most memorable rooms in the state. For more privacy, you can opt for one of the renovated Early Winters Cabins or one of the newly constructed cabins. Families may want to go all the way and rent one of the large lakeside lodges. Meals here are every bit as memorable as the rooms and setting. Northwest cuisine is the focus with prices in the $13 to $20 range.

The inn also offers tour arrangements, cross-country ski lessons, ski rentals, mountain-bike rentals, and sleigh rides. Nearby, there are ski trails and a lake for swimming (ice skating in winter).

The Mazama Country Inn

42 Lost River Rd., Mazama, WA 98833. ☎ **800/843-7951** or 509/996-2681; fax 509/996-2646; Web site www.mazama-inn.com. 14 rms. Summer $70–$95 double. Winter (including all meals) $150–$175 double. DISC, MC, V.

Set on the flat valley floor but surrounded by rugged towering peaks and tall pine trees, this modern mountain lodge is secluded and peaceful and offers an escape from the crowds in Winthrop. If you're out here to get some exercise, be it hiking, mountain biking, cross-country skiing, or horseback riding, the Mazama Country Inn makes an excellent base of operations. After a hard day of having fun, you can come back and soak in the hot tub and have dinner in the rustic dining room with its massive freestanding fireplace and high ceiling. The guest rooms are of medium size and simply furnished, but modern and clean. The inn also rents out six cabins ranging in size from one to five bedrooms.

IN WINTHROP

Hotel Rio Vista

P.O. Box 815, Winthrop, WA 98862. ☎ **509/996-3535.** 16 rms. A/C TV TEL. $65–$85 double. MC, V.

As with all the other buildings in downtown Winthrop, the Rio Vista looks as if it had been built for a Hollywood Western movie set. Behind the false front you'll find modern rooms with pine furnishings and an understated country decor. Step out onto your balcony and you'll have a view of the confluence of the Chewuch and Methow rivers. Guests often see deer, bald eagles, and many other species of birds. A hot tub overlooks the river.

Sun Mountain Lodge

P.O. Box 1000, Winthrop, WA 98862. ☎ **800/572-0493** or 509/996-2211; fax 509/996-3133. 102 rms, 13 cabins. Summer $145–$250 double; $145–$285 cabin. Winter $105–$205 double; $105–$240 cabin. Spring/fall, $105–$230 double; $105–$280 cabin. AE, MC, V.

If you're looking for resort luxuries and proximity to hiking, cross-country skiing, and mountain-biking trails, the Sun Mountain Lodge should be your first choice in the region. Perched on a mountaintop with grand views of the Methow Valley and the North Cascades, this luxurious lodge captures the spirit of the West in both its breathtaking setting and its rustic design. In the lobby, flagstone floors, stone fireplaces, and wagon-wheel tables all combine in a classically western style. Most guest rooms feature rustic Western furnishings and views of the surrounding mountains. The rooms in the Gardiner wing have balconies and slightly better views than those in the main lodge. The newest rooms are those in the Mount Robinson wing. If seclusion is what you're after, opt for one of the less luxurious cabins down on Patterson Lake.

A superb menu that focuses on Northwest cuisine makes the lodge's dining room the region's best restaurant, and the views will definitely take your breath away. Prices range from $18 to $25 for entrees.

The lodge offers ski rentals and ski school, horseback and sleigh rides, guided hikes, boat rentals, mountain-bike rentals, and ice-skate rentals. Guests can also use the outdoor heated pools, three whirlpools, tennis courts, exercise room, ski shop, children's playground, and ice-skating pond.

The Virginian

808 N. Cascades Hwy. (P.O. Box 237), Winthrop, WA 98862. ☎ **800/854-2834** or 509/996-2535. 40 rms, 7 cabins. A/C TV. $55–$85 double; $75 cabin. AE, DISC, MC, V.

Located just east of downtown Winthrop, the Virginian is a collection of small cabins and motel rooms on the banks of the Methow River. The deluxe rooms overlooking the river are our favorite rooms. These have high ceilings, balconies, and lots of space. The cabins, however, though quaint, don't have river views. The rooms and cabins are all lined with cedar, which gives them a rustic feel. A heated swimming pool, hot tub, horseshoe pit, and volleyball court provide recreational options. There's a restaurant and a bar popular with bicyclists.

Dining

Better stock up on the chow before you head into the park, Marblemount, Rockport, or Winthrop. In most places, including Ross Lake Resort, there's just no food to be had.

IN STEHEKIN

There are several dining options in Stehekin, but if you plan to stay in a cabin or camp out, be sure to bring all the food you'll need. Otherwise, simple meals are available at **North Cascades Stehekin Lodge** (☎ **509/682-4494**), which is located right at the boat dock in Stehekin. If you just have to have something sweet, you're in luck—the **Stehekin Pastry Company** (☎ **509/682-4677**), which is located 2 miles up valley from the boat landing, serves pastries and ice cream, as well as pizza and espresso.

IN MARBLEMOUNT

Buffalo Run Restaurant

5860 Wash. 20 (mile marker 106), Marblemount. ☎ **360/873-2461.** Main dishes $9.50–$30. AE, DISC, MC, V. Sun–Thurs 8am–9pm, Fri–Sat 8am–10pm. AMERICAN.

From the outside this looks like any other roadside diner, but once you see the menu, it's obvious this isn't just anyplace. The restaurant's owners have a buffalo ranch and feature buffalo meat on their menu here. There are buffalo burgers, buffalo chili, and buffalo T-bones. You'll also find venison and ostrich on the menu, as well as salmon and mussels. Of course there's a buffalo head (and skin) on the wall. You'll find the restaurant right in Marblemount.

IN THE WINTHROP AREA

The best meals in the Winthrop area are to be had at the dining rooms of **Sun Mountain Lodge,** where you'll also enjoy one of the most spectacular views in the state. See "Accommodations," above, for details.

The Duck Brand

Wash. 20 (Riverside Ave.). ☎ **509/996-2192.** Reservations recommended in summer. Main courses $6–$16. AE, MC, V. Daily 7:30am–9pm. MEXICAN.

Located across the street from the gas station and partially hidden by trees, the Duck Brand is a casual restaurant with a big, multilevel deck that's a great spot for a meal on a warm summer day. In cold or rainy weather, you can grab a table in the small dining room and order a plate of fajitas or ribs and a microbrew to wash it all down. The Duck Brand's muffins and cinnamon rolls make great trailside snacks.

Winthrop Brewing Company

155 Riverside Ave. ☎ **509/996-3183.** Main courses $5–$18. DISC, MC, V. Daily noon–midnight (shorter hrs in winter). AMERICAN.

Located in a tiny, wedge-shaped building in downtown Winthrop, this local watering hole is by far the liveliest restaurant/bar in town. The walls are covered with the owner's cigarette lighter collection, as well as old rifles and beer coasters from around the world. There's a deck out back overlooking the river and in summer, a beer garden. On weekends there's usually some kind of live music going on. The menu is typical pub fare—burgers, fish-and-chips, steaks, sandwiches, chicken, fish, and ribs.

29

OLYMPIC NATIONAL PARK

by Tom Wells

THERE PROBABLY AREN'T MANY OTHER PLACES IN THE UNITED STATES where one has a greater opportunity to develop sensory overload from experiencing rapidly changing ecological climates than in Olympic National Park. Where, other than here, can you go from enjoying views of white, chilled alpine glaciers to standing in a sopping-wet, green, rain forest to soaking in volcanically heated springs to resting thoughtfully on a misty Pacific coastline in a few hours' drive? Or, you could just as easily disappear from the outside world altogether by spending a few weeks exploring any section of this largely untouched, massively forested, and mountainous park.

There is still a sense of pervading mystery here that comes at you in so many different ways in these ancient mountains. Maybe it catches you deep in the middle of a grove of moss-draped, 15-foot thick, emerald-green trees reaching 200 feet into the sky, breathing air so moisture-laden and nutrient-rich that some plants draw in all the food they need just from the breeze. Maybe it hits you standing next to a glacier whose staggeringly massive ebb and flow has carved mountains for hundreds of thousands of years, and is still carving today.

In the mountains, remnants of 2-million-year-old glaciers that once crept northeast toward what are now the Straits of Juan de Fuca and the Hood Canal can still be seen today. The 60 glaciers inside the park continue to grind and sculpt the Olympic Mountains now as they did then, if only a bit more slowly. Farther down some of the steep coastal valleys traversing the peninsula lie the only temperate rain forests in the contiguous United States. In addition, the Olympic National Park contains the longest stretch of uninterrupted coastal wilderness area of any park south of Alaska. So, if variety is the spice of your life, you're in luck. You're sure to find more than you bargained for in Olympic National Park.

Water is serious business here. Rain is measured in feet, not inches, with some areas receiving up to 20 feet in a single season. Contrast this with some parts of the drier eastern side of the peninsula, which receive an average of a comparatively paltry 20 inches. Again, variety is the rule. If the crystalline, jade water of the many glacier-fed lakes feels a little too cold for comfort, there's always the opportunity to warm your bones in any of the hot springs that dot the western half of the park. (You have your choice of comfort levels, anywhere from 70° to 158°F.) Despite its inherent ruggedness, raininess and mysterious nature, the interior of the park began yielding its secrets

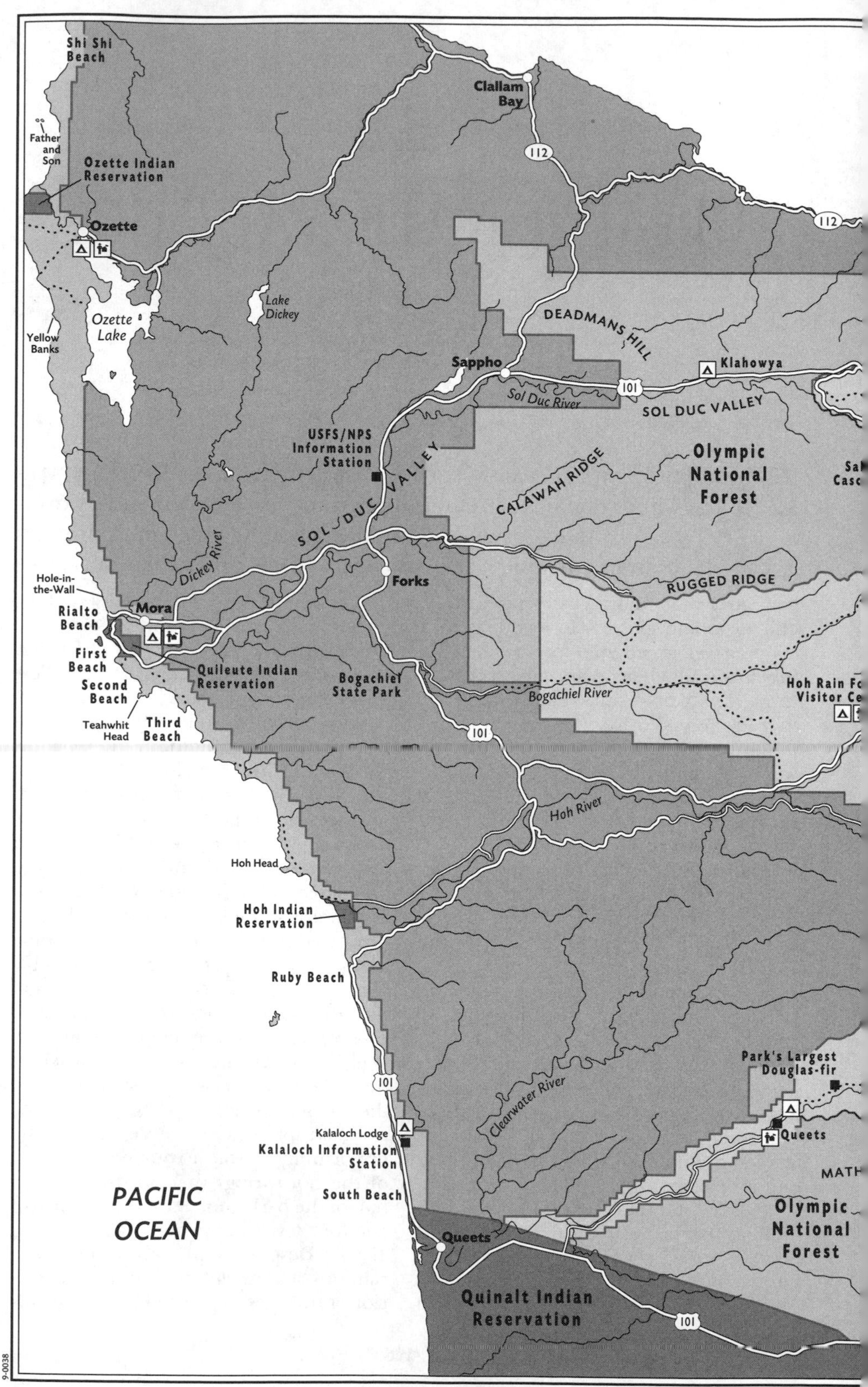

Shi Shi Beach
Father and Son
Ozette Indian Reservation
Ozette
Ozette Lake
Yellow Banks
Lake Dickey
Clallam Bay
112
DEADMANS HILL
Sappho
Klahowya
101
Sol Duc River
SOL DUC VALLEY
USFS/NPS Information Station
CALAWAH RIDGE
Olympic National Forest
SOL DUC VALLEY
Dickey River
Forks
RUGGED RIDGE
Hole-in-the-Wall
Rialto Beach
Mora
First Beach
Quileute Indian Reservation
Bogachiel State Park
Bogachiel River
Second Beach
Teahwhit Head
Third Beach
Hoh Rain Fo
Visitor Ce
Hoh River
Hoh Head
Hoh Indian Reservation
Ruby Beach
Clearwater River
Park's Largest Douglas-fir
Queets
Kalaloch Lodge
Kalaloch Information Station
South Beach
PACIFIC OCEAN
Queets
Quinalt Indian Reservation
Olympic National Forest
9-0038

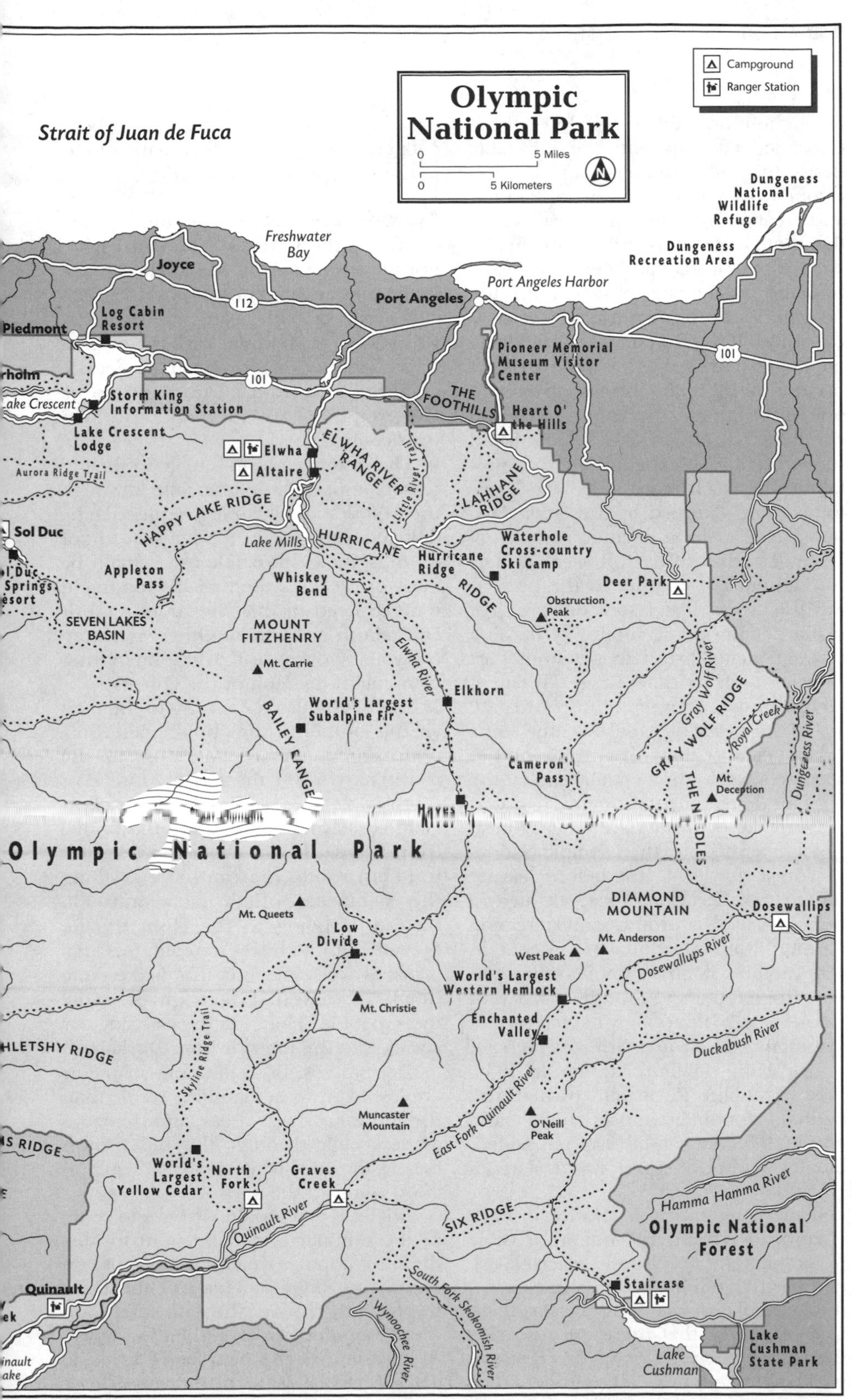

Olympic National Park
0
5 Miles
0
5 Kilometers
Campground
Ranger Station
Strait of Juan de Fuca
Dungeness National Wildlife Refuge
Dungeness Recreation Area
Freshwater Bay
Joyce
Port Angeles Harbor
Port Angeles
112
101
Log Cabin Resort
Piedmont
Pioneer Memorial Museum Visitor Center
Storm King Information Station
Lake Crescent
Lake Crescent Lodge
THE FOOTHILLS
Heart O' the Hills
Elwha
Altaire
ELWHA RIVER RANGE
Little River Trail
LAHHANE RIDGE
Aurora Ridge Trail
HAPPY LAKE RIDGE
Sol Duc
Lake Mills
HURRICANE
Waterhole Cross-country Ski Camp
Hurricane Ridge
RIDGE
Appleton Pass
Whiskey Bend
Deer Park
Obstruction Peak
SEVEN LAKES BASIN
MOUNT FITZHENRY
Elwha River
Mt. Carrie
Gray Wolf River
Elkhorn
World's Largest Subalpine Fir
BAILEY RANGE
GRAY WOLF RIDGE
Royal Creek
Dungeness River
Cameron Pass
THE NEEDLES
Mt. Deception
Olympic National Park
DIAMOND MOUNTAIN
Dosewallips
Mt. Queets
Low Divide
Mt. Anderson
West Peak
Dosewallups River
World's Largest Western Hemlock
Mt. Christie
Enchanted Valley
Duckabush River
Skyline Ridge Trail
Muncaster Mountain
East Fork Quinault River
O'Neill Peak
World's Largest Yellow Cedar
North Fork
Graves Creek
Hamma Hamma River
Quinault River
SIX RIDGE
Olympic National Forest
Quinault
South Fork Skokomish River
Staircase
Wynoochee River
Lake Cushman
Lake Cushman State Park

throughout the mid- to late 1800s. Both unbridled curiosity and the inevitable desire for timber, mineral, and tourism resources played a part in its exploration and creation by a citizenry fascinated by the thought of a last wilderness in the West. Homesteads had been established by westward-moving pioneers on the peripheries of the peninsula as early as the mid-1800s. However, the first documented exploration of the interior didn't occur until 1885, and the rush to explore one of the last great unknown territories completed itself around 1890 with a series of private expeditions, the most famous of which was dubbed the "Press Expedition." Funded by the *Seattle Press* newspaper, it was a documented chronicle of adventure followed widely throughout the country at the time. It was also no easy feat. It took one group of explorers a grueling month of hacking through dense brush to get from Port Angeles to Hurricane Ridge. Today, it takes approximately 45 minutes by car.

On the advice of these adventuresome explorers, who along the way found few feasible ways to commercially exploit the land for development, Congress declared most of the peninsula a national forest, which later became the Olympic National Forest. In 1909, just before leaving office, Pres. Theodore Roosevelt, an avid hunter, issued a proclamation creating Mount Olympus National Monument, in order to preserve the summer range and breeding grounds of dwindling herds of Roosevelt elk (flatteringly named for the president himself in a brilliant piece of prelegislative public relations). In 1938, Pres. Franklin Roosevelt turned the national monument into a national park, and in 1953 the coastal strip was added. Finally, in 1981, the park was declared a World Heritage Park.

Today the Olympic National Park encompasses some 1.5 million acres of mountains and rain forests, glacial lakes, and Pacific shoreline. It was either a fortunate stroke of planning, or fortunate lack of money, that there are no roads that divide the interior of this fantastic park. Consequently, large sanctuaries exist here for the elk, deer, eagles, bear, cougars, and any other fortunate inhabitants or visitors to its interior.

Avoiding the Crowds. Avoiding the crowds in the Olympic National Park is not the easiest task in the world. In fact, in the summer, it's fairly impossible. With easy access to both Seattle and Victoria, B.C., Olympic National Park is a magnet for visitors not only from the immediate area, but also from all over the world. However, there are a few options within your control.

The easiest solution is to go in the off-season, especially in the fall. Although the west side of Olympic is reputed to be deluged with rain in the fall and winter months, the eastern side can actually be fairly dry at the same time, so you might want to head in that direction, towards **Duckabush** or **Sequim.** Otherwise, strap on your snorkel and try some winter camping in the **Hoh** or the **Queets.**

You might also try getting to the park via the southern route, up the peninsula and through Aberdeen. Most of the tourists arrive on the ferries from Port Angeles and Port Townsend, or Port Gamble, having come across the bridge from Seattle. If you choose to take this southern route, you can see everything the peninsula offers in a nutshell. Instead of going to the Hoh, try the **Queets.** Although less traveled, this area is just as accessible and affords the same rain-forest views that you might get at the more popular Hoh. On the east side, try a walk into the interior from **Duckabush** or **Dosewallips.** Both jumping-off points are less likely to be handling traffic than the more northerly areas, and the views as you walk through the old growth beside the blue-white rivers are just as good as any in the park.

Finally, if you absolutely have to come in the summer and don't want to miss the most popular views, such as those on **Hurricane Ridge** or **Heart of the Hills,** try heading up in the late afternoon when everyone else is on their way down. At this time of the day, you're liable to get spectacular views of the sunset over the Straights of Juan de Fuca as the fog rolls in and the deer make their evening pilgrimage to the parking lot at the Hurricane Ridge Visitor Center.

As a further alternative, avoid Hurricane Ridge altogether and make the climb towards **Deer Park** to get the same views to the west as you get from the more popular vantage point.

Just the Facts

GETTING THERE & GATEWAYS

The main travel artery for all visitors to Olympic National Park is U.S. 101. This northernmost point of the famous coastal highway encircles and only briefly enters the park. Most of the traffic into and out of the park enters the northeastern side, from the major metropolitan points of Vancouver and Seattle.

If you're departing from **Seattle,** you can take either one of two ferries that run daily/hourly from the same downtown Seattle dock. The **Seattle–Bainbridge Island Ferry** takes you for a half-hour ride across the Puget Sound before arriving in Bainbridge Island. From there, take Wash. 305 north through Poulsbo to the Hood Canal Floating Bridge, and then Wash. 104 across to U.S. 101. The **Seattle–Bremerton Ferry** arrives in Bremerton after a 45-minute ride. From Bremerton, take Wash. 3 north to the Hood Canal Floating Bridge.

In addition, there are several smaller ferry services. The **Keystone Ferry** shuttles between Whidbey Island and Port Townsend. It's smaller, but in the off-season it can be a good bet for shorter lines. For information on all ferry schedules, call ☎ **800/843-3779** or 206/464-6400, or write care of **Washington State Ferries,** Colman Dock/Pier 52, 801 Alaskan Way, Seattle, WA 98104. You can also reach them on the Internet at **www.wsdot.wa.gov/ferries/current**.

If you'd rather drive your car over dry land only, head west from **Tacoma** via Wash. 16 over the Tacoma Narrows Bridge, which connects with the eastern shore of the Kitsap Peninsula just south of Gig Harbor. Drive north on Wash. 16 to Port Orchard and Bremerton. From Bremerton, take Wash. 3 to the Hood Canal Floating Bridge and across to U.S. 101.

To access the park from the south, take I-5 to **Olympia,** where you can connect with U.S. 101 North, or with Wash. 8 West to the other side of the U.S. 101 loop, to access the Pacific Ocean section of the park.

The Nearest Airport. **Seattle-Tacoma (Sea-Tac) International Airport** (☎ **206/626-6088**) is located 15 miles south of Seattle on I-5. It's served by **Alaska Airlines, America West, American Airlines, Continental, Delta, Horizon Air, Northwest, Southwest, TWA, United,** and **US Airways.** Toll-free reservations numbers for all these airlines are given in the appendix.

Fairchild International Airport is located in Port Angeles, where the park's main visitor center is. Fairchild is served by Horizon Air.

Renting a Car. All the major national car-rental companies have locations at Seattle-Tacoma International Airport. **Budget Rent-A-Car** has an office in Port Angeles. Their toll-free numbers are listed in the appendix.

GETTING INFORMATION BEFORE YOUR TRIP

For advance information, write to **Olympic National Park,** 600 E. Park Ave., Port Angeles, WA 98362-6798, or call ☎ **360/452-4501.** The park Web site is **www.nps.gov/olym**.

VISITOR CENTERS

There are three visitor centers in Olympic National Park, and several smaller ranger stations and information centers. All of the larger ones have exhibits, maps, guides, information, and rest room facilities. Many smaller ranger stations are located at popular trailheads and open only in summer. These offer maps, guides, and information.

The **Olympic National Park Visitor Center,** 600 E. Park Ave., Port Angeles, WA 98362 (☎ **360/452-4501**), located on the northern end of the park and within close proximity to Port Angeles, is a good jumping-off station before heading into the northwest part of the park. **The Pioneer Memorial Museum,** a cabin located behind the visitor center after being relocated from its original site, will leave you wondering how early settlers didn't go insane more frequently from claustrophobia. You can also rub a well-worn patch of elk hide here, if you've never felt an elk before.

It's a 30-minute drive from there to one of the most popular spots in the park, the **Hurricane Ridge Ranger/Information Center.** Here you'll find beautiful views (free telescopes!) of the many glaciers ringing this centrally located spot, of alpine meadows blooming in the summer, and in the middle of the day, of the wide variety of RVs available on the market today. It also has a snack bar, interpretive exhibits, and trails, and is a hub for several hiking trails. If you want to avoid the crowds, drive up in the late afternoon, as everyone else is leaving. Wait for sundown, and you might get a beautiful view of the mists coming in, and a visit from some surprisingly tame deer.

The **Hoh Rain Forest Visitor Center,** on the east side of the main part of the park, is some 15 miles off a turnoff from U.S. 101. This is an excellent spot for those who want to experience the amazing phenomenon that is the temperate rain forest without spending a soaking couple of days hiking. The information center is, like the Hurricane Ridge Observatory, a favorite spot for the tourists in the summer season. There are several interpretative trails and the beautiful Hall of Mosses nearby, as well as longer trails into the heart of the rain forest. Just remember that this visitor center is in the middle of the rain forest it gets unbelievably humid when full!

Smaller centers include the **Storm King Information Station,** on Crescent Lake in the northern section of the park, and the **Kalaloch Information Station,** on the south end of the beach section of the park. You can get food and some supplies near the **Sol Duc Ranger Station** at the **Hot Springs Resort.**

ENTRANCE & CAMPING FEES

Entrance into the park costs $10 per vehicle, or $5 per individual hiking or biking. If you plan to visit multiple times over the year, an Olympic National Park Annual Passport is available for $20.

There is a $1 per day parking charge at Ozette. There is a $2 per person per night charge for backcountry camping. For groups, there is a $5 fee for up to 12 people for up to 14 days' stay.

Camping in the park ranges from $8 to $12 a night. Fairholm, Hoh, Kalaloch, Mora, and Sol Duc campgrounds charge $3 for dump station usage.

SPECIAL REGULATIONS & WARNINGS

Follow all the usual rules. Pets are prohibited except in designated areas. Don't feed any animals. Vehicles are not allowed off the park roads.

Wilderness use permits, available at the **Wilderness Information Center** (located just behind the main visitor center in Port Angeles) and at all ranger stations, are required for overnight stays in the backcountry. During the summer, you may also need reservations for certain areas. Call the **Wilderness Information Center** (☎ **360/452-0300**) for information.

When hiking, be prepared for sudden and extreme weather changes.

SEASONS & CLIMATE

The climate of the entire peninsula is best described as varied, of the marine type. In the winter the temperatures stay in the 30s and 40s during the day, and 20s and 30s at night. At the lower elevations, near the water, there is rarely more than 6 inches of accumulated snow per season, and it melts quickly. However, on the upper slopes, the snowfall can become quite heavy.

The spring is the late half of the rainy season, mostly wet, mild, and windy. Temperatures range from 35° to 60°F, with lingering flurries of snow in the mountains.

Summer temperatures range from a low of 45° in the evening to 75° and up to 80° during the afternoons. In the latter half of the summer and early fall, fog and cloud banks drift into the valleys and remain until midday, burn off, and sometimes return in the evening. Thunderstorms may occur in the evening in the upper elevations.

The fall is moderately cold and blustery and ushers in the rainy season. Snow begins to fall in the mountains late in the season. Temperatures range from 30° to 65°.

Rainfall is varied throughout the Olympic Peninsula, but 76% of the precipitation falls during the 6-month period between October and March, primarily on the Pacific side of the peninsula.

SEASONAL EVENTS

There are seasonal events all over the place on the Olympic Peninsula, if not within the park itself. They include salmon cook offs; classical, jazz, and bluegrass festivals; boat races; light opera; arts and craft festivals; and many others. All events are seasonal and subject to change from year to year. For a full list, try the **Port Angeles Chamber of Commerce Visitor Center,** 121 E. Railroad Ave. (**☎ 360/452-2363**).

USEFUL PUBLICATIONS

There are several free publications that give a very good guide to the area. Pick up a ***North Olympic Peninsula Visitor's Guide,*** published by the *Peninsula Daily News* twice yearly. There's also a comprehensive guide (clearly a labor of love) crammed with facts both important and minuscule called ***Dan Youra's Olympic Peninsula Guide.*** It's available at several spots around the peninsula, either for free or for $1. You can get a copy through the mail via **Olympic Publishing,** 7450 Oaks Bay Rd., Port Ludlow, WA 98365.

Seeing the Highlights in a Day

First things first: Decide in advance what you would like to see. This is a big park, and no roads go completely through it. The roads that do venture inside (and they're major tourist attractions) are generally short and pleasant. It's no more than 15 miles from U.S. 101 to the Hoh Visitor Center, or Hurricane Ridge.

If you want to see the rain forests and the coastal strip, drive up from Olympia on U.S. 101 through the coastal region, perhaps stopping at the Kalaloch Information Station and Ruby Beach, and then head to the Hoh Rain Forest Visitor Center, from where you can explore further. To see the glaciers and the alpine meadows of the east side of the park, start by driving to the Pioneer Memorial Museum in Port Angeles, and from there head down to Hurricane Ridge, where you can take in a hike, or drive even further into the park. More details of these driving tours are given in the next section.

Exploring the Park by Car

THE RAIN FORESTS & THE COAST

If the rain forests are your destination, your best bet would be to drive north from Olympia along the western side of the peninsula. (Or, in reverse, southwest from Port Angeles or Port Townsend.) The first opportunity to see a bit of the rain forest is near the south shore of **Lake Quinault,** at the southern end of the main part of the park. If you plan to stay the night, this area is packed with lodges, motels, and campgrounds, so it might serve as a good base of operations.

From the ranger station on the south, there are several interpretive hikes along the shores. The view of the mountains here, across Lake Quinault, is quite spectacular on a sunny day, but save the rest of your day for the more hard-core rain forests. Lake Quinault serves as a good hors d'oeuvre more than anything.

Drive north on U.S. 101. At this point, you have an option—you can drive east to the **Queets Ranger Station** in the Queets River Valley for a rugged hike into some of the most beautiful (and remote) rain forests on the peninsula, or keep driving northwest to the **Kalaloch Information Station,** where you can enjoy views of the Pacific from Kalaloch to Ruby Beach. It's a tough call. You might get to see some elk in some of the former homestead meadows in the early morning or late afternoon on the 3-mile **Sam's River Loop Trail** in the Queets, but understand, it's the least accessible of the rain forests. The road to Queets is unpaved, but it's still a relatively decent gravel road. Despite the occasional pothole, it's highly navigable by your average light truck or utility vehicle, fairly navigable by your "beater" car, but occasionally intolerable for your Caddie. Watch out for seasonal closures during the winter and late fall, which you can find out about by calling park headquarters (☎ **360/452-4501**) before you set out.

After leaving the coastal area at Ruby Beach, continue your northward drive on U.S. 101 to the turnoff for the **Hoh Rain Forest Visitor Center.** It's a 15-mile drive from U.S. 101 to the center, with excellent views of the Hoh River along the way. If you wanted to, you could spend the rest of the afternoon hiking from the Hoh Visitor Center Parking Lot up to the **Olympus Ranger Station.** This moderate to heavy hike offers you the chance to go in just a few hours from temperate rain forest to alpine meadows with stunning views of Mount Olympus. If you're not feeling so ambitious, take the short **Hall of Mosses** or **Spruce Nature trails,** and get ready to head north again, to Sol Duc.

The last leg of our rain forest excursion takes you to one of the most commercially developed areas in the park, **Sol Duc** and the **Sol Duc Hot Springs Resort.** It might be a nice idea, before you head back down the coast to Olympia, or to sleep in your campsite or hotel room, to have a dip in these famous hot springs (open from late spring to early fall). The hot springs experience begins at $5 for a half-hour soak, but packages, including a sauna and a massage, can be purchased as well. But be forewarned: There's a resort here, and the springs can be crowded. Still, if you're into luxuriating after a long day hiking, it could be just the thing.

The area has more than hot springs. Try taking the 1-mile hike from the springs through some wonderfully dense forest to **Sol Duc Falls.** Or take the **Mink Lake Trail** through 2.5 miles of uphill grade and dense forest to get a look at one of the many higher altitude lakes that dot the Sol Duc region.

THE EAST SIDE OF THE PARK

Seen the rain forests? You could do a lot worse than spending a day seeing the glaciers and the alpine meadows of the east side of the park. This time, the jumping off point of convenience would probably be **Port Angeles.** First, visit the **Olympic National Park Visitor,** to get acquainted with what you're about to see. (It doesn't take all that long, as it's not very big, and it's not far from U.S. 101 in Port Angeles.)

As in our rain forest tour, this tour starts off with a choice: head back through Port Angeles for the **Elwha/ Altaire** area, or from the visitor center head to **Hurricane Ridge.** Either way, you're going to run into beautiful alpine meadows with endless varieties of wildflowers, views of blue-white glaciers, the whistles of marmots, and the panhandling of the local deer mobs. (Don't do it! Don't feed them!)

The **Elwha area** has a small ranger station beside Lake Mills, an alpine lake, and further up the road, a very nice observation point for viewing the surrounding hills. In addition, if you don't want to experience the crowds at Sol Duc, it is from Elwha that you can hike to the only other hot springs available inside the park. Located on the banks of Boulder Creek, the **Olympic Hot Springs** is not accessible by car, and don't expect amenities or guarantees of sanitation either. In other words, use at your own risk. But lots of people do just that each year.

Along the way to Hurricane Ridge from Port Angeles, stop at the **Heart of the Hills Ranger Station** for a beautiful view across the Strait of Juan de Fuca to Vancouver to the north. At **Hurricane Ridge,** one of the most popular spots in the park, there are a number of short interpretive trails, very good for seeing wildflowers, and many larger trails intersecting here as well. The visitor center has numerous interpretive exhibits and a snack bar if you get hungry from all that looking around.

Leaving Hurricane Ridge, Port Angeles, or the Elwha area, drive a little farther southeast, off a turnoff of U.S. 101, to the less crowded **Deer Park Ranger Station**, where you get the same sort of views as Hurricane Ridge and Elwha. The difference is that there are a lot less people here in general than either Elwha or Hurricane Ridge. It might be uncrowded when the other two areas are packed. The road to Deer Park is steep and graveled. It's open to all vehicles, but prepare to deal with steep inclines, turns, and potholes. In the wintertime the road may be closed due to excessive weather of the snow or rain type, so call ahead to park headquarters to check road conditions (☎ **360/452-4501**).

Outside Olympic National Park, consider visiting other communities along U.S. 101, such as Dungeness or Sequim Bay State Park on the northeastern tip of the peninsula, with their beautiful shorelines and views of the straits. As you travel further south, the Hood Canal will appear on your left—there are numerous places here to see seals on the rocks on a good day, especially at a place called, appropriately enough, Seal Point.

Organized Tours & Ranger Programs

You can't shake a stick in this park without finding an organized tour. There's something starting from practically every ranger station, for every reason, connected to any topic, at about any given time. The rangers really, really want you to know what's going on, and there's no end to the methods they'll employ, including films, discussions, lectures, walks, tours, or hikes.

You'll find **rain forest tours** originating from the Hoh, the Queets, the Quinault, or the Sol Duc ranger stations; **alpine wildflower walks** from the Elwha, Hurricane Ridge, or Deer Park areas; and **lakeside and waterfall walks** from the Storm King Ranger Station. Contact park headquarters for a seasonal schedule of day and evening events. Keep in mind that many of the ranger stations close from mid-fall to late spring.

Historic & Man-Made Attractions

There simply aren't a lot of man-made attractions within the park itself, unless you consider the Elwha River and Glines Canyon dams great attractions. But there are many old homestead sites scattered throughout the park, such as those found along the Geyser Loop Trail.

Day Hikes

There's a vast number of trails in the park, and it seems like they all connect somewhere. Consequently, it's very easy to tie several trails together to create your own, customized route. For a complete listing, write ahead for a free Olympic National Park map from the **Outdoor Recreation Information Center,** 915 Second Ave., Suite 442, Seattle, WA 98714 (☎ **206/220-7450**).

The following is a partial, though representative list of some of the many wonderful trails within the park. Most trails are hiker-only, with no dogs, horses, or mountain bikes allowed, as well as no wheelchair facilities. Backcountry permits are required for overnight trips. They're available at the **Wilderness Information Center** (located just behind the main visitor center in Port Angeles) and at all ranger stations. During the summer, you may also need reservations for certain areas. There is a $2 per person per night charge for backcountry camping. For groups, there is a $5 fee for up to 12 people for up to 14 days' stay. Call the Wilderness Information Center (☎ **360/452-0300**) for information.

COASTAL AREA

Cape Alava/Sand Point Loop

9.3 miles RT. Easy. Access: Ozette Ranger Station.

This loop begins with a stroll over a cedar-plank boardwalk through teeming coastal marsh and grasslands. (Careful! Boards are slippery when wet, which is most of the time.) The trail connects its second leg on a wilderness beach strip of the Pacific shoreline, the westernmost point on the Lower 48. Camping is permitted on the beach, but beware, it's a popular spot in the summer. Continue south 1 mile past the petroglyphs that can be seen from the rocks along the shore next to the high-tide line. Two miles south, the trail connects at the Sand Point leg, which is an easy stroll back to the Ozette Ranger Station.

Sand Point to Rialto Beach

17 miles one way. Easy to moderate. Access: Ozette Lake Ranger Station from the north or Mora Campground from the south.

This is a coastline famous for its shipwrecks, the memorials of which dot the beach at many points, along with an abandoned mine. Other than that, though, there's not a lot of man-made activity going on. Enjoy the sand and the mist, and the forests that come down to land's end, and get ready for the storms that visit here regularly.

Third Beach to Hoh River

17.1 miles one way. Moderate to difficult. Access: Third Beach Parking Area, 3 miles beyond the La Push Rd. left fork.

This trail is not your leisurely stroll. You'll be required to do a bit of inland skirting along some old oil company roads to avoid some of the more wicked headlands, and there are some sand ladders (contraptions constructed of cables and wooden slats) just beyond Taylor Point. In addition, there's a slightly treacherous crossing farther south at Goodman Creek. So what's the reward for the intrepid hiker? Toleak Point is located approximately 5.5 miles down the beach, where there is a sheltered campsite famous for its wildlife. The entire area is famous for its shipwrecks, wildlife, coastal headlands, and stacks. The trail ends at Oil City, north of the Hoh Indian Reservation.

Hoh River to Queets River

14.7 miles one way. Easy to moderate. Access: Ruby Beach Parking Lot.

The beaches here are wide and flat, the surf fishing is good, and with its proximity to U.S. 101, you can expect to see a lot of people here in the summer. This section, compared to the more northern trails, is fairly tame. Destruction Island Overlook is famous for its whale watching during March to April and November to December.

WESTERN PARKLANDS & RAIN FORESTS

Bogachiel River

Length varies. Easy to moderate in the lowlands, more difficult further inland. Access:

5 miles south of Forks, turn left across from Bogachiel State Park onto Undie Rd., and continue 5 miles to the trailhead.

This hike is as long or short as you want to make it, but it is an equally beautiful cousin to the often crowded Hoh River Trail. The beginning is loaded with rain forest extravaganza, huge Douglas firs, spruce, cedar, and big-leaf maples, including the world's largest silver fir, some 8 miles from the trailhead. Approximately 6 miles into the trail is the Bogachiel Shelter, and 8 miles in is Flapjack Camp, both of which provide good backcountry campsites. This is pretty much the end of the flatland; further up the trail begins to get steep.

Hoh River Valley

Up to 17 miles one way. Easy to moderate in the lowlands, more difficult further inland. Access: Hoh Rain Forest Visitor Center.

Start the valley trail from the trailhead at the visitor center. This is one of the most heavily traveled trails in the park, at least in the lower elevations, and it won't take you long to figure out why. Huge Sitka spruces hung with moss shelter the Roosevelt elk that wander among its lowlands. The first 13 miles, through the massive rain forests and tall grass meadows along the Hoh River Valley bottomlands, are relatively flat. Happy Four Camp (6 miles in) and Olympus Guard Station (9 miles in) provide excellent camp or turnaround sites. Continue eastward into the hills for the remaining 4 or 5 miles. If you connect with the Hoh Lake Trail, you can eventually find yourself at the edge of the famous Blue Glacier on Mount Olympus, elevation 7,965 feet. Be careful. After July, hiking near the park's glaciers can be dangerous because of snowmelt.

Sams River Loop Trail

3 miles RT. Easy to moderate. Access: Trailheads at the Queets River Ranger Station.

This short loop parallels both the Sams River and the Queets River, providing a view of some old homestead meadows, beautiful spruce trees, and perhaps an elk or two in the meadows in the evening.

Queets River Trail

Up to 16 miles one way. Moderate to difficult. Access: Trailhead at the Queets River Campground.

This is the trail for the serious rain forest/wilderness lover. Part of its charm lies in the fact that it requires a bit of effort from the average hiker to get to its payload of solitude and quietly majestic scenery. Be prepared to begin traversing the Queets River, about 50 yards from your car. Even on this first of several fords you will have to make across the river, the water can be treacherous if it's up. It's best to visit during the dry season in late summer, or you might be in for more than an atmospheric dunking. Alternatively, you can cross the Sams River to the right of the Queets, connecting and crossing the Queets River farther up. At 2.5 miles, gape in awe at the largest Douglas fir on the planet. After 5 miles of hiking through elk and giant fern territory, you'll arrive at Spruce Bottom, which is a common haunt for steelhead anglers and has several good campsites. The trail reaches its terminal point at Pelton Creek where there are also campsites available.

Maple Glade Rain Forest Trail

0.5 mile RT. Easy. Access: Trailhead located across the bridge from the Quinault Ranger Station.

Another beautiful, peaceful little trail with lots of exhibits. Take the kids, or just enjoy it yourself. As you meander, you'll pass through dense trees, open meadows, and an abandoned beaver pond. As usual, keep your eyes peeled for the ever-possible elk sighting.

Lake Quinault Loop

4 miles RT. Easy. Access: Trailheads located at various spots along the loop, including South Shore Rd., Quinault Lodge, Willaby

Campground, Quinault Ranger Station, and Falls Creek Campground. All access originates from the south shore of Lake Quinault.

This trail is easily accessible, well-maintained, and quite beautiful. Consequently, it's quite crowded in the summer. Elevation changes are gentle, making this an excellent walk for kids.

The trail wanders about the shore of Lake Quinault, past historic Lake Quinault Lodge as well as the adjacent campgrounds and other lakeside attractions before heading into its most popular section, the Big Tree Grove. Here you can wander among the huge trunks of 500-year-old Douglas firs. Watch for the interpretive signs. In addition, the Big Tree Grove can be experienced via a short, 1-mile loop trail, originating from the Rain Forest Nature Trail Parking Lot.

North Fork of the Quinault

Up to 15 miles one way. Moderate. Access: Trailhead located at the end of the North Shore Rd. Alternatively, if a washout has occurred at the trailhead, the trail is accessible from the South Shore Rd. as well.

This is either the end of the Skyline Ridge Trail or the beginning of the North Fork Trail, both of which could conceivably take you 47 miles all the way through the park to Altaire and Elwha on the north side, if you make the right connections and are maniacal enough. The trail is relatively benign for the first dozen miles as it winds its way inward along the river towards its source near Mount Seattle. Campsites are available at Wolf Bar (2.5 miles in), Halfway House (5.3 miles in), and in a gorge in Elip Creek (6.5 miles in). For the last several miles, the trail climbs steeply towards Low Divide, Lake Mary, and Lake Margaret, where you can get beautiful views of Mount Seattle, at an elevation of 6,246 feet. Snow can remain at this elevation until midsummer, so be ready. There's a summer ranger station at Low Divide, and many high-elevation campsites here as well.

NORTHERN PARK REGIONS

Sol Duc Falls

1.7 mile RT. Easy. Access: Trailhead at the Sol Duc Ranger Station.

One of the more popular spots on the peninsula, beautiful Sol Duc Falls is viewed from a bridge that spans the canyon just below the falls. On the way, check out the huge hemlocks and Douglas firs, some of which are 300 years old. This trail is wide, graveled, and level, making it great for kids.

Lovers Lane Loop

6 miles RT. Easy to moderate. Access: Trailhead next to Site 62 in Loop B of the Sol Duc Campground.

This trail extends a loop that begins just pass Sol Duc Falls. Cross the bridge at the falls and continue around on the Lovers Lane Trail, which will return you to the resort/campground area after taking you through beautiful spruce groves and fern glades. Portions of the trail are narrow and rocky, and can get muddy until things dry out in midsummer. Occasionally grouse are seen along the trail.

Mink Lake Trail

5 miles RT. Moderate. Access: Trailhead at the opposite end of the Sol Duc Resort Parking Lot from the pools.

This is a long climb up to Mink Lake, where herons are known to pursue an elusive trout or two. In late summer, brilliant buckbean flowers fill the marshy edges of the lake, and huckleberries are abundant.

Deer Lake

8 miles RT. Moderate. Access: Trailhead at the junction of Sol Duc Falls.

Yep. They got lots of deer here. The trail is a steady climb through beautiful woods to this tree-lined lake. Canada jays await to eat your food, but don't feed them. There are some switchbacks on this trail, and it can get pretty bumpy in spots.

North Fork of the Sol Duc

2.4 miles RT. Moderate. Access: North Fork Trailhead, 3.8 miles down the Sol Duc Rd. away from the resort.

On this trail you climb the ridge between the main and north forks of the river before descending into the North Fork Valley. The trail passes through old-growth forests, before arriving at the deep-green pools of the river. The curious can venture upriver for several more miles.

High Divide Loop

Up to 20 miles RT. Moderate. Access: Trailhead at the Sol Duc Ranger Station.

Like many trails in the park, this one gives you a chance to come up with your own designer trail. Take as short or as long a hike as you like. From the Sol Duc Ranger Station Trailhead, climb a relatively easy 0.8 wooded mile to Sol Duc Falls, and keep going. You can take a leg out to the Seven Lakes Basin Area, where you'll find many campsites (crowded in the summer), or toward Appleton Pass, some 14 miles inland. From Appleton Pass, pass nearby Heart Lake, and begin your climb toward Bogachiel Peak (elevation 5,474), which presents some of the most breathtaking views in the park. On clear summer days, you can enjoy the wildflowers along the slopes of Bogachiel, the view to the south of the glaciers of Mount Olympus, or the brilliant sunsets on the western Pacific horizon. Continue back down toward Sol Duc Trail through the Deer Lake area, and the final 4.6-mile leg back to the Sol Duc Trailhead.

Marymere Falls

2.2 miles RT. Easy. Access: Trailhead begins at the Storm King Ranger Station on the south shore of Lake Crescent.

This is one of the most popular hikes in the park. It's easy, well-maintained, close to U.S. 101, and has a definite goal: beautiful Marymere Falls. It's a popular trail for kids. The Barnes Creek Trail leads 0.7 mile through beautiful maples and conifers to the Marymere Trail turnoff. Continue up to the falls, where silvery water drops from a moss-covered outcropping some 100 feet to the basin below.

Spruce Railroad

8 miles RT. Easy. Access: Trailhead 4 miles from the Fairholm Campground, at the end of the North Shore Rd. along Lake Crescent.

This is the trail you want to take for a leisurely, hot summer-afternoon stroll. The trail does nothing but wander gently around the unbelievably blue-green, glacial-fed waters of Crescent Lake along an old stretch of abandoned railroad. Weather permitting, clamber down the bank and go for a swim, or simply enjoy the views of Mount Storm King. There are two abandoned railroad tunnels (don't go in!) and a much photographed arch bridge at Devil's Point. This flat, wide trail provides easy access to one of the parks most beautiful glacial lakes.

Geyser Valley Loop

5 miles RT. Moderate. Access: Drive just beyond the Elwha Ranger Station to Whiskey Bend Rd. Go past the Glines Canyon Dam, 1.5 miles up the road. Approximately 2 miles above the dam is the Whiskey Bend Trailhead, just beyond the Upper Lake Mills Trailhead.

From the Whiskey Bend Trailhead, hike 0.75 mile down the trail to the Eagles Nest Overlook for a view of the meadows that stretch from valley to valley. You may see an elk or black bear. Head back to the trail and proceed 0.5 mile to the Rica Canyon Trail for a view of Goblin's Gate, a rock formation in the Canyon Gorge that might look like a bunch of goblins' heads staring at you, if you stare back hard enough. The trail to Goblin's Gates drops 325 feet on the 0.5-mile walk to the viewing area. At this point, you can follow a riverside trail for another 0.5 mile to some prime fishing spots, or continue on to the Krause Bottom and Humes Ranch area. The Humes Ranch has been restored, although some of the wood is starting to get moldy. At any one of these points you can return north back to the Whiskey Bend Trail, or continue 0.8 mile northeast past Michael's Cabin, another old homestead.

Elwha River Trails

Up to 50 miles one way. Difficulty varies. Access: Drive just beyond the Elwha Ranger Station to Whiskey Bend Rd. Go past the Glines Canyon Dam, 1.5 miles up the road. Approximately 2 miles above the dam is the Whiskey Bend Trailhead, just beyond the Upper Lake Mills Trailhead.

The serious backpacker arranges a pickup car to be at the Dosewallips or the North Fork ranger districts and heads for a week or so along the trail that was fortuitously blazed for you by the famous Press Expedition in 1889, the expedition that essentially busted this park wide open to public knowledge. For a good distance, the trail follows the intense blue-green of the Elwha River to its beginnings at the sometimes snow-slushy peak at Low Divide (elevation 3,600 feet), which is also the junction of the head of the Quinault River. You can follow the trail blessedly downhill at this point to the North Fork of the Quinault.

What can you expect on such a monumental trip?

Old-growth forests, moist valley flatlands, and gently sloping hills appear around you as you explore the Elwha Valley before you begin your ascent towards the sometimes calf-busting walks up to Low Divide. As you might guess, Roosevelt elk, black bears, mountain lions, marmots, or a grouse or two might show up. At Low Divide, you're up pretty high, so enjoy the spectacular views of Mount Seattle to the north and Mount Christie to the south. From here, you begin your descent from the alpine environs to the deep, dense rain forests along the Quinault.

HURRICANE RIDGE AREA

Cirque Rim Trail and Big Meadow Loops

0.5 mile and 0.25 mile RT. Easy. Access: Parking lot of the Hurricane Ridge Visitor Center.

These trails provide a wonderful little taste of alpine meadows, deer, and the fireworks display of wildflowers that burst in the spring, along with excellent views of Port Angeles and the Straits of Juan de Fuca.

Hurricane Hill

2.75 miles RT. Easy to moderate. Access: From the Hurricane Ridge Visitor Center, drive 1.5 miles to the Hurricane Hill Trailhead.

This is a popular trail in the summertime, as it is a broad, easy climb along an abandoned work road up to the brilliant alpine meadows, with fantastic views of the Straits of Juan de Fuca and Port Angeles to the north.

High Ridge, Alpine Hills to Klahane Ridge

1 to 8 miles RT. Easy to moderate. Access: Hurricane Ridge Visitor Center.

You can take the short, paved 1-mile High Ridge Route (which is chock-full of interpretive exhibits) and then return to the parking lot, or you can proceed along the unpaved portion to Sunrise Ridge, a rocky little backbone of a view point off the High Ridge Trail, providing excellent panoramas of the Strait of Juan de Fuca, Port Angeles, and of course, the ever-present and ever-beautiful alpine glaciers and wildflowers. The rest of the 3.3-mile, somewhat strenuous walk climbs to the top of Klahane Ridge. As numerous signs mention, beware of the deer and marmots here! They're very unafraid, and some people have been mauled due to their own stupidity in trying to get a little too close.

Grand Ridge (Obstruction Point to Green Mountain)

11 miles RT. Moderate. Access: From Hurricane Ridge, turn left onto the dirt road to Obstruction Point, and continue 8.5 miles to the end of the road.

This is the highest section of trail in the park, a fact you might notice as you gaze out to Victoria, B.C. and the Strait of Juan de Fuca to the north, or to the south where you'll see the Grand Valley with its string of lakes and the numerous snow-clad peaks of the Olympic interior. There is both a shortage of trees and water on this hike.

From the parking lot, follow the trail to the left. (The right goes to Grand Valley.) In 2 miles you'll find yourself at the breathtaking top of Elk Mountain. Over the next 5.5 miles, you will pass through Roaring Winds Camp (not misnamed), up to Maiden Peak and finally Green Mountain. In late June the air is filled with the smell of Lyle's lupine, which grows amid the loose scree. This is a good turnaround point, unless you want to descend to Deer Park.

EASTERN & SOUTHEASTERN SECTION

Main Fork Dosewallips/ Constance Pass

11 miles one way. Moderate. Access: Trailhead located at the Dosewallips Campground and Ranger Station.

Take the Main Fork Dosewallips to the south, and you'll find yourself on a moderate climb through old-growth forests for 7.5 miles before the trail flattens out at Constance Pass. There are fields of wildflowers skirting the edge of Mount Constance. The trail ends in another 3.4 miles at Boulder Shelter in Olympic National Forest. You can also catch the Upper Big Quilcene Trail or the Upper Dungeness Trail here.

Main Fork of the Dosewallips

31 miles RT. Moderate. Access: The trailhead is located at the Dosewallips Ranger Station.

As usual, this is a versatile trail. You can catch a lot more of the inland trails from here, including Constance Pass Trail, the Gray Wolf Trail, and the Elwha River Trail. The Dosewallips side of the park sometimes seems like the neglected side. It's not as flashy as a glacial meadow or a rain forest. But the Dosewallips is one of the most beautiful rivers in the country, its jade-green water crashing down among narrow cliffs. And you might skirt some of the crowds.

Staircase Rapids

6.5 miles RT. Easy to moderate. Access: Trailhead located at the Staircase Ranger Station.

The Staircase Trail is one of the more popular hikes in the park, and once you get to Staircase Falls, you'll see why. Along the way you'll enjoy the sight of the North Fork Skokomish River through stands of huge cedar trees beside rapidly rushing white water. After the falls, the trail continues for another 1.5 miles, following in the footsteps of the 1890 O'Neil Expedition that named the area.

Other Sports & Activities

Biking. The first thing to know is that almost all trails in Olympic National Park are closed to mountain bikes. The only exception is the **Spruce Railroad Trail.** This trail was once a railroad grade that ran along the shore of the lake. It is quite flat and easy for its 4-mile length, and there is an additional 1.5-mile stretch of road past the North Shore Picnic Area. In the summer there are spots where you can get down the banks for a little dip in Lake Crescent. The highlight of the trail is a much photographed arched bridge across a rocky cove.

For road bikers, U.S. 101 can be somewhat treacherous, with eager tourists rubbernecking about and all. But if you get through all that, you can find some very nice rides on any of the roads that poke their way into the park. There's also a few dirt roads for mountain bikers available at the ends of paved roads, like the section from Hurricane Ridge to Obstruction Peak.

Llama Trips. It's llamas, llamas, llamas within the national park. Try **Wooley Packer Llama Co.,** 5763 Upper Hoh Rd., Forks, WA 98331 (☎ **360/374-9288**), which offers trips of up to 7 days within the park; or **Kit's Llamas,** P.O. Box 116, Olalla, WA 98539 (☎ **360/857-5724**), which offers day and overnight trips. And if you don't have enough llama selections already, there's **Olympak Llamas,** 3175 Old Olympic Hwy., Port Angeles, WA 98362 (☎ **360/452-4475**), which specializes in trips up the Elwha Valley and other areas within the national park.

Kayaking & Canoeing. On **Lake Crescent,** boat ramps can be found on U.S. 101 at Rosemary (near the middle of the lake) and at Fairholm (at the west end of the lake). On East Beach Road, on the lake's northeast shore there is a private boat ramp at the Log Cabin Resort.

Although large and often windy, glacier-carved Lake Crescent is a beautiful place to do a little paddling. Lush, green forests rise straight up from the shores of this 900-foot deep lake, giving these waters a fjord-like quality unmatched anywhere on the peninsula. If you launch at Rosemary, you can explore around Barnes Point, away from U.S. 101 traffic noise (but in view of the Lake Crescent Lodge). From Fairholm, you can paddle along the north shore, and from the Log Cabin Resort, you can explore the narrow bay that feeds the Lyre River, the lake's outlet stream. When winds blow down this lake, as they often do, the waters can be become very dangerous for small boats.

Canoes can be rented at **Fairholm General Store** (☎ **360/928-3325**) at the west end of the lake, or at the **Log Cabin Resort,** 3183 E. Beach Rd. (☎ **360/928 3325**), on the lake's northeast shore.

At **Ozette Lake,** there are three boat launches: at Swan Bay, on the Hoko-Ozette Road where it reaches the lake, and at the end of the Hoko-Ozette Road near the Ozette Ranger Station. Ozette Lake, 300 feet deep, nearly 10 miles long, and the third-largest natural lake in Washington, is a fascinating place to explore by sea kayak or canoe. Situated only a mile from the Pacific Ocean, the lake is indented by numerous coves and bays, both large and small, and holds three small islands. Campsites along the shore include the boat-in Erickson's Bay Campground.

The Swan Bay boat launch is probably the best choice for paddlers heading out on this large lake. For a leisurely half-day paddle, just explore the shores of this convoluted bay, in the middle of which is Garden Island. For a day-long paddle, try paddling down the lake to Tivoli Island. For an overnighter, head to the lake's western shore and the Erickson's Bay Campground. From here, you can explore up and down the west shore.

Both Lake Crescent and Ozette Lake are big lakes subject to quick changes of weather and wind. Whitecaps can come up suddenly, and cold waters can lead to hypothermia. Check the weather forecast before leaving, and keep an eye on the sky.

Snowshoeing. If the Olympic Mountains aren't very good for cross-country skiing, at least they're good for snowshoeing. Any one of the snow-covered roads leading into the mountains will offer some sort of winter walking. However, if it's views you seek, then head to **Hurricane Ridge** with the rest of the winter crowd and set out on any of the area's trails. Snowshoe rentals are available at the **Hurricane Ridge Lodge.**

White-Water Kayaking & Canoeing. Although the Olympic Mountains generate an astounding number of runnable rivers, the best of these are on the west side of the peninsula and along the southern slopes of the range. However, the east and north sides of the peninsula do offer some good runs. As elsewhere in the northwest, sweepers, strainers, and log jams are always a problem on the Olympic Peninsula's steep, narrow rivers. If you're interested in taking a white-water kayaking class, or obtaining any other information on local white-water action, contact the **Olympic Outdoor Center,** P.O. Box 2247, Poulsbo, WA 98370 (☎ **800/659-6095** or 360/697-6095), which offers a 5-day kayaking class on the Elwha River.

White-Water Rafting. There's some great white-water rafting on the Elwha, Hoh, and Queets rivers. The Hoh River trips last a couple of hours; trips on the Queets are overnight. Contact the **Olympic Raft & Guide Service,** 239521 U.S. 101 W., Port Angeles, WA 98363 (☎ **360/452-1443**). Rates begin at $35.

Camping

Currently, the only campsites that take reservations are the Kalaloch and Mora sites and then only for organized groups.

Campgrounds at Elwha, Heart O' the Hills, Hoh, July Creek, Kalaloch, Mora, Ozette, Queets, and Staircase are open **year-round;** other campgrounds are open only **seasonally,** and their exact schedules are subject to change. Campgrounds at higher elevations may be snow-covered (and closed) from early November to late June; seasonal campgrounds at lower elevations may open earlier. Be sure to call ahead to the park (☎ **360/452-4501**) to find out if the seasonal campground you are interested in is open. In the summertime, you can contact the ranger station nearest the place you want to go, and in the winter, contact the Olympic National Park headquarters to find out about trail and camping conditions.

You will have to pay $3 per use for the park's RV **dump stations.** There are no showers or laundry facilities inside the park, though both are available at the **Log Cabin Resort.**

There are no **RV utility hookups** at any of the national park campgrounds, though most can accommodate RVs of up to 21 feet. Note that RVs and trailers are prohibited at Deer Park and Dosewallips and that July Creek's campsites are all hike-ins. However, the **Log Cabin Resort,** on the north shore of Lake Crescent at the northern edge of the park, offers RV sites with hookups (see below).

NORTH- & EAST-SIDE CAMPGROUNDS

The six campgrounds on the northern edge of the park are some of the busiest in the park due to their proximity to U.S. 101.

Deer Park, a seasonal campground with 18 sites, is the easternmost of these campgrounds (to get there, take Deer Park Road from U.S. 101 east of Port Angeles); at 5,400 feet, it's also the only high-elevation campground in the park. Deer Park is reached by a winding one-way gravel road that will have you wondering how you're ever going to get back down the mountain (thus, RVs and trailers are prohibited). Deer frequent the campground, and hiking trails head out across the ridges and valleys.

Because of its proximity to Hurricane Ridge, **Heart O' the Hills,** a year-round campground with 105 sites, is very popular. It's located on Hurricane Ridge Road, 5 miles south of the Olympic National Park Visitor Center. Several trails start at or near the campground, which makes this a good choice if you want to do lots of day hikes.

Two campgrounds are located on Olympic Hot Springs Road, up the Elwha River, which is popular with kayakers and fly-fishers. **Elwha,** a year-round campground with 41 sites is the trailhead for a trail leading up to Hurricane Ridge. **Altaire,** a seasonal campground with 30 sites, has a boat ramp often used by rafters and kayakers. And, yes, there are hot springs up the road.

The only national park campground on Lake Crescent is **Fairholm,** a seasonal campground with 87 sites, located at the west end of the lake. This campground is popular with power boaters and tends to be rather noisy.

South of this area, nearby **Sol Duc,** a year-round campground with 80 sites, is set amid impressive stands of old-growth trees, adjacent to the Sol Duc Hot Springs (and the resort there). Not surprisingly, it is one of the most popular campgrounds in the national park.

Finally, you'll find RV sites with full hookups at the Log Cabin Resort, 3183 E. Beach Rd., on the north shore of Lake Crescent (☎ **360/928-3325;** fax 360/928-2088). Because there are no hookups at any of the national park campgrounds, this is a good choice. Unfortunately, they only accept RVs, so tent campers beware. Major credit cards (DISC, MC, V) are accepted, and the resort is open year-round.

SOUTHEAST-SIDE CAMPGROUNDS

At the end of F.S. 2610, which parallels the Dosewallips River and provides access to the Hayden Pass, Anderson Pass, and Lake Constance trails, you'll find **Dosewallips,** a seasonal campground with 30 sites. It's in a forested setting on the river's banks. RVs and trailers are prohibited.

The remote **Staircase,** a year-round campground with 59 sites, is located inland from the Hood Canal and is a good base for day hikes or as a starting point for a longer backpacking trip. It's located up the Skokomish River from

Campground	Elev.	Total Sites	RV Hookups	Dump Station	Toilets
Altaire	450	30	No	No	Yes
*Deer Park**	5,400	14	No	No	No
*Dosewallips**	1,540	30	No	No	Yes
Elwha	390	41	No	No	Yes
Fairholm	580	88	No	Yes	Yes
Graves Creek	540	30	No	No	Yes
Heart O' the Hills	1,807	105	Yes	No	Yes
Hoh	578	88	No	Yes	Yes
July Creek†	200	31	No	No	Yes
Kalaloch	50	175	No	Yes	Yes
Log Cabin Resort	580	40	Yes	Yes	Yes
*Mora***	0	94	No	Yes	Yes
North Fork	520	No	No	No	Yes
Ozette	0	13	No	No	Yes
Queets	290	20	No	No	No
Sol Duc	1,680	80	No	Yes	Yes
Staircase	765	59	No	No	Yes

* Trailer/RVs prohibited.
** Group Reservations Only (must be made directly through the ranger station).

Lake Cushman on F.S. 24 and is the trailhead for the Six Ridge, Flapjack Lakes, and Anderson Pass trails.

SOUTH- & SOUTHWEST-SIDE CAMPGROUNDS

If you want to say you've camped at the wettest campground in the contiguous U.S., head for **Hoh,** a year-round campground with 95 sites in the Hoh River Valley. Despite the damp, this is a very popular campground. It's located near the Hoh Rain Forest Visitor Center.

Queets, a year-round campground with 20 sites, is more off the beaten track and has good hiking and white-water kayaking nearby. This campground is located 14 miles up the Queets Road (unpaved) from U.S. 101.

Other rain-forest camping options include the park's campground on Quinault Lake, **July Creek,** a year-round campground with 29 sites. It's located on the north shore, and it's a walk-in.

East of Lake Quinault are two more rain-forest campgrounds. **North Fork,** a year-round campground with 7 sites, and **Graves Creek,** a year-round campground with 30 sites, provide access to a couple of the park's long-distance hiking trails. They are reached only by an unpaved road.

COASTAL CAMPGROUNDS

Along the peninsula's west side, there are also several beach campgrounds. One is **Mora,** a year-round campground with 91 sites, located on the beautiful Rialto

Drinking Water	Showers	Fire Pits/ Grills	Laundry	Reserve	Fees	Open
Yes	No	Yes	No	No	$10	Seasonal
Yes	No	Yes	No	No	$8	Seasonal
Yes	No	Yes	No	No	$10	Seasonal
Yes	No	Yes	No	No	$10	Year-round
Yes	No	Yes	No	No	$10	Seasonal
Yes	No	Yes	No	No	$10	Seasonal
Yes	Yes	No	No	No	$10	Year-round
Yes	No	Yes	No	No	$10	Year-round
Yes	No	Yes	No	No	$10	Year-round
Yes	No	Yes	No	Yes	$12	Year-round
Yes	Yes	Yes	Yes	Yes	$25	Year-round
Yes	No	Yes	No	Yes	$10	Year-round
No	Yes	No	No	No	Free	Seasonal
Yes	No	Yes	No	No	$10	Year-round
No	No	Yes	No	No	$8	Year-round
Yes	No	No	No	No	$12	Seasonal
Yes	No	Yes	No	No	$10	Year-round

† Walk-in sites.

Beach at the mouth of the Quillayute River west of Forks. You can make group reservations (only) here by contacting the ranger station; call the main park number (☎ **360/452-4501**) for more information.

The other national park campground in the coastal section of the park is the remote **Ozette,** a year-round campground with 14 sites on the north shore of Lake Ozette. It's a good choice for kayakers and canoeists, as well as people wanting to day-hike to the beaches on either side of Cape Alava. There is a designated swimming beach on the lake.

Accommodations

INSIDE THE PARK

Inside the park there are three lodges with rooms and cabins for rent. On the south side, near the coast, is Kalaloch Lodge. To the north, there's Lake Crescent and Sol Duc. There are plenty of signs leading to them all. Make reservations early!

Lake Crescent Lodge

416 Lake Crescent Rd., Port Angeles, WA 98363-8672. ☎ **360/928-3211.** 52 rms and cabins, 48 with bath. $67 double without bath, $99–$117.50 double with bath; $105–$126 cottage. AE, DC, DISC, MC, V.

This historic lodge is located 20 miles west of Port Angeles on the south shore of picturesque Lake Crescent and is the lodging of choice for those wishing to stay on the north side of the park. Wood paneling, hardwood floors, a stone fireplace, and a sunroom make the lobby a popular spot for just sitting and relaxing. The guest rooms in the main lodge building are the oldest and all have shared bathrooms. If you'd like more modern accommodations, there are a number of standard motel-style rooms, but these lack the character of the lodge rooms. If you have your family or some friends along, we recommend reserving a cottage. Those with fireplaces are the most comfortable (and are also the only rooms available between October 31 and late April), but the others are nice as well. All but the main lodge rooms have views of either the lake or the mountains. Rowboat rentals are available.

The Lodge Dining Room serves a limited menu of continental cuisine with an emphasis on local seafood. Prices are moderate. A lobby lounge provides a quiet place for an evening drink.

Log Cabin Resort

3183 E. Beach Rd., Port Angeles, WA 98363. ☎ **360/928-3325;** fax 360/928-2088. 4 rms; 24 cabins, 8 with bath; 1 chalet. $49 cabin for 2 without bath, $76–$90 cabin for 2 with bath; $106 double; $121 chalet. DISC, MC, V. Closed Christmas to Valentine's Day.

This log-cabin resort on the north shore of Lake Crescent first opened in 1895 and still has buildings that date from the 1920s. The least expensive accommodations are rustic one-room log cabins in which you provide the bedding and share a bathroom a short walk away (basically this is camping without the tent). More comfortable are the 1928 cabins with private bathrooms, some of which also have kitchenettes (you provide the cooking and eating utensils). The lodge rooms and a chalet offer the greatest comfort and best views. The lodge dining room overlooks the lake and specializes in local seafood. The resort also has a general store and RV sites.

Sol Duc Hot Springs Resort

Sol Duc Rd., U.S. 101 (P.O. Box 2169), Port Angeles, WA 98362. ☎ **360/327-3583;** fax 360/327-3593; Web site www.northolympic.com/solduc. 32 cabins. $85–$95 cabin for 2. AE, DISC, MC, V. Closed Oct to mid-May.

Located at the end of Sol Duc Road, The Sol Duc Hot Springs have for years been a popular family vacation spot. Campers, day trippers, and resort guests all spend the day soaking and playing in the hot-water swimming pools. The grounds of the resort are grassy and open, but the forest is kept just at arm's reach. The cabins are done in modern motel style and are comfortable if not spacious. There's an excellent restaurant here, as well as a poolside deli, espresso bar, and grocery store. Three hot spring–fed swimming pools are the focal point, and the pools are open to the public for a small fee. Massages are available.

Kalaloch Lodge

157151 U.S. 101, Forks, WA 98331. ☎ **360/962-2271;** fax 360/962-3391. 18 rms, 2 suites, 40 cabins. $56–$80 double; $99–$150 cabin for 2. Lower rates weekdays Nov–May. AE, MC, V.

This rustic, cedar-shingled lodge and its cluster of cabins perch on a grassy bluff. Below, the Pacific Ocean thunders against a sandy beach where huge driftwood logs are scattered like so many twigs. The breathtaking setting makes this one of the most popular lodges on the coast, and it's advisable to book rooms at least 4 months in advance. The rooms in the old lodge are the least expensive, but the ocean-view bluff cabins are the most in demand. The log cab ins across the street from the bluff cabins don't have the knockout views. For comfort you can't beat the motel-like rooms in the Sea Crest House.

A casual coffee shop serves breakfast and lunch while a more formal dining room serves dinner with an emphasis on salmon dishes. Dinner entree prices range from $10 to $18. The lodge also has a general store and gas station.

NEAR THE PARK

IN PORT ANGELES

Domaine Madeleine

146 Wildflower Lane, Port Angeles, WA 98362. ☎ **360/457-4174;** fax 360/457-3037; Web site www.northolympic.com/dm. 5 rms. TV TEL. $135–$165 double. Rates include full 5-course breakfast. AE, DISC, MC, V.

Located 7 miles east of Port Angeles, this B&B is set at the back of a small pasture and has a very secluded feel. Combine this with the waterfront setting and you have a fabulous weekend hideaway—you may not even bother exploring the park. The guest rooms are in several different buildings that are surrounded by colorful gardens, and all have views that take in the Strait of Juan de Fuca and the mountains beyond. There are also fireplaces and VCRs in the rooms, and whirlpool tubs in all but one. The breakfasts are superb.

Doubletree Hotel Port Angeles

221 N. Lincoln St., Port Angeles, WA 98362. ☎ **800/222-TREE** or 360/452-9215; fax 360/452-4734. 187 rms, 3 suites. A/C TV TEL. $99–$129 double; $165 suite. Lower rates off-season. AE, DC, DISC, MC, V.

If you're on your way to or from Victoria, there's no more convenient hotel than the Doubletree. Located on the waterfront, it's only steps from the ferry terminal. Most rooms have balconies and large bathrooms, and the more expensive rooms overlook the Strait of Juan de Fuca. There's a seafood restaurant adjacent to the hotel. Laundry/valet service is available, and an outdoor pool and hot tub provide recreational options.

The Tudor Inn

1108 S. Oak St., Port Angeles, WA 98362. ☎ **360/452-3138.** 5 rms. Summer $85–$125 double; other months $75–$110 double. AE, DISC, MC, V.

Located in a quiet residential neighborhood 13 blocks from the waterfront, this 1910 Tudor home is surrounded by a large yard and pretty gardens. On the ground floor you'll find a lounge and library, both with fireplaces that get a lot of use. Upstairs there are five rooms furnished with European antiques. Several rooms have good views of the Olympic Mountains.

WEST OF PORT ANGELES

Elwha Ranch Bed & Breakfast

905 Herrick Rd., Port Angeles, WA 98363. ☎ **360/457-6540;** Web sitewww.northolympic.

com/elwharanch. 3 rms. $85–$144 double. Rates include full breakfast. No credit cards.

Although it isn't located within the national park, this cedar-log inn, on a 72-acre ranch high above the Elwha River Valley, has a superb view up the valley into the park. Two of the rooms are in the main house, which has a casual western ranch feel and lots of windows to take in the views. If you're traveling with friends or family, opt for the two-bedroom suite. However, the nicest and most comfortable room here is a sort of modern cabin outside the front door of the main house. Be sure to get directions to the inn. Fresh pies are a specialty of innkeeper Margaret Mitchell.

IN THE FORKS AREA

Eagle Point Inn

380 Stormin' Norman Rd. (P.O. Box 546), Beaver, WA 98305. ☎ **360/327-3236.** 3 rms (all with private bath). $75–$85 double. Rates include full breakfast. No credit cards.

Located 10 miles north of Forks at milepost 202 on U.S. 101, this rustic B&B is housed in two log homes, one old and one new. Although the inn's 5 acres are surrounded by recently planted forest, the inn itself is in a beautiful parklike setting on the bank of the Sol Duc River. The guest rooms are everything the rooms in a log house should be—rustic, romantic, rugged—yet with antiques, down comforters, and private baths. Out in the yard you'll find a hot tub and a covered barbecue area should you want to fix your own meal.

Huckleberry Lodge

1171 Big Pine Way, Forks, WA 98331. ☎ **360/374-6008;** fax 360/374-5270. 4 rms (all with private bath). Summer $100–$160 double; other months $70–$95 double. MC, V.

Although ostensibly a modern hunting and fishing lodge, this place makes a great base of operations for anyone visiting the area. The lodge is down a gravel road on the edge of Forks and is set on 5 wooded acres adjacent to the Calawah River. In the living room, a moose antler table and trophy heads on the walls emphasize the hunting lodge aesthetic. Guest rooms are comfortable, though the private bathrooms are across the hall. For greater privacy, there's a cabin out behind the main house. Meals are available at additional cost, and fishing and hunting packages can be arranged.

Manitou Lodge

Kilmer Rd. (P.O. Box 600), Forks, WA 98331. ☎ **360/374-6295.** 7 rms. $75–$80 double. Rates include full breakfast. AE, MC, V. Take Wash. 110 west from north of Forks; turn right on Spur 110 and then right on Kilmer Rd.

This secluded B&B is set on 10 private acres and is only minutes from some of the most beautiful and remote beaches in the Northwest. The best room in the house is the Sacajawea, which has a marble fireplace and king-size bed. A separate cabin houses two of the rooms. Guests tend to gravitate to the comfortable living room, where a huge stone fireplace is the center of attention. Fires help chase away the chill and damp of this neck of the woods. Breakfasts are hearty and sometimes include huckleberry-apple-walnut pancakes. There's also a Native American art gallery on the premises.

Miller Tree Inn

654 E. Division St. (P.O. Box 953), Forks, WA 98331. ☎ **360/374-6806;** fax 360/374-6807. 6 rms, 3 with full bath. $60–$65 double without full bath, $70–$90 double with bath. Rates include full breakfast. MC, V.

Located just a few blocks east of downtown Forks, this large B&B is on the edge of the country and is surrounded by large old trees and pastures, with a hot tub on the back deck. There's nothing fussy or pretentious about this place—it's just a comfortable, friendly inn that caters primarily to outdoors enthusiasts and, during the winter months, anglers. Dinner is available if requested when you make your reservation.

SOUTH OF THE PARK

Lake Quinault Lodge

P.O. Box 7, Quinault, WA 98575. ☎ **800/562-6672** in Washington and Oregon, or 360/288-2900. 92 rms, 2 suites. June–Oct, $99–$140 double; $190–$220 suite. Sept–May, $65–$115 double; $150–$175 suite. AE, MC, V.

Located on the shore of Lake Quinault in the southwest corner of the park, this imposing grande dame of the Olympic Peninsula wears an ageless tranquillity. Huge old firs and cedars shade the rustic lodge, and Adirondack chairs on the deck command a view of the lawn. The accommodations range from small rooms in the main lodge to modern rooms with wicker furniture and little balconies to rooms with fireplaces. The annex rooms are the least attractive, but they do have huge bathtubs. None of the rooms has a TV or telephone. There's an indoor pool and a whirlpool. Canoe and paddleboat rentals are available, as are rain forest tours.

The dining room here is a large, dark place as befits such a lodge, and the menu reflects the bounties of the Olympic Peninsula, with seafood a specialty. A lounge provides big-screen TV for those who just can't give up the big game or music videos.

Dining

INSIDE THE PARK

Restaurant choices inside the park are slim. On the north side, there are dining rooms at Lake Crescent Lodge (open late April to late October) and the Log Cabin Resort (open Valentine's Day to Christmas), both of which are on the shores of Lake Crescent. On Lake Quinault, try the dining rooms at the Kalaoch Lodge and the Lake Quinault Lodge. (For more information on these, see "Accommodations," above.)

One other dining option on Lake Crescent is the **Fairholm General Store & Cafe,** 221121 U.S. 101 (☎ **360/928-3020**), which is at the west end of the lake and is open between April and October. Although all you'll get here are burgers, sandwiches, and breakfasts, the cafe has a deck with a view of the lake.

IN PORT ANGELES

If you're hit with a craving for something sweet while in town, check out **Bonny's Bakery,** 215 S. Lincoln St. (☎ **360/457-3585**), which is located in an interesting old building next door to the Port Angeles Library. Both French pastries and American favorites are baked here. For a good cup of espresso, try **Mombasa Coffee Co. Ltd.,** 113-A W. First St. (☎ **360/452-3238**).

Bella Italia

117-B E. First St. ☎ **360/457-5442.** Main dishes $7–$16. AE, DISC, MC, V. Mon–Sat 11am–11pm, Sun 11am–10pm. ITALIAN.

Located in the basement of a natural foods store in downtown Port Angeles, this restaurant has a sort of rathskeller feel, with heavy wood beams overhead. The menu, however, is strictly Italian and starts with a basket of delicious bread accompanied by an olive oil, balsamic vinegar, garlic, and herb dipping sauce. Local seafood makes it onto the menu in a few places, including a Dungeness crab ravioli, a smoked salmon fettucini, and steamed mussels and clams. There's a good selection of wines as well as an espresso bar and the Italian desserts are excellent. With its individual pizzas, and crayons and paper place mats, this is a good choice for families.

C'est Si Bon

23 Cedar Park Rd. ☎ **360/452-8888.** Reservations recommended. Main courses $20–$25. AE, CB, MC, V. Tues–Sun 5–11pm. FRENCH.

Located 4 miles south of town just off U.S. 101, C'est Si Bon is painted a striking combination of turquoise, pink, and purple that gives the restaurant a sort of happy elegance. Inside, the nontraditional paint job gives way to more classic decor—reproductions of European works of art, crystal chandeliers, and old musical instruments used as wall decorations. Most tables have a view of the restaurant's pretty garden. The menu is limited, which just about insures that each dish has been perfected. Desserts are limited, but rich and creamy.

The Coffee House Restaurant

118 E. First St. ☎ **360/452-1459.** Main courses $9–$13. MC, V. Mon–Sat 8am–9pm. INTERNATIONAL.

Before you can take a seat in this casual cafe in downtown Port Angeles, you'll have to walk past the pastry case, which should prompt you to not eat too much before it's time for dessert. Though the menu here draws on the cuisines of the world (Thai peanut stir-fry, jerked chicken, teriyaki salmon), the emphasis is on Mediterranean and Middle Eastern. There are always plenty of vegetarian offerings as well as lots of fresh local seafood.

Downriggers

115 E. Railroad Ave. ☎ **360/452-2700.** Reservations recommended. Main courses $10–$26. DISC, MC, V. Mon–Thurs 11:30am–9pm, Fri–Sat 11:30am–10pm, Sun 4–9pm. SEAFOOD.

At the back of the Landing Mall on the second level you'll find this large, casual restaurant, which is very convenient to the ferry landing. Walls of glass provide views of the ferries (so you don't miss yours) and take in some great sunsets. A long menu nearly guarantees that you'll find something you like, but just be sure to try the award-winning clam chowder. The appetizer menu includes quite a bit of good seafood. The salmon Wellington and a fettuccini made with smoked salmon, prawns, and scallops are just a couple of interesting main dishes.

Toga's International Cuisine

122 W. Lauridsen Blvd. ☎ **360/452-1952.** Reservations recommended. Main dishes $14–$27. MC, V. Tues–Sun 5–10pm. INTERNATIONAL/GERMAN.

Located on the west side of Port Angeles, this restaurant is an unexpected treat and serves some very unusual dishes the likes of which are not to be found anywhere else in the state. Chef Toga Hertzog apprenticed in the Black Forest and has brought to his restaurant the traditional *Jagerstein* style of cooking in which diners cook their own meat or prawns on a hot rock. With 24 hours notice you can also have traditional Swiss cheese fondue or a lighter seafood fondue. To start your meal, you might try the crabmeat Rockefeller or the sampler of house-smoked salmon, scallops, oysters, and prawns. For dessert nothing hits the spot like the Black Forest cake.

IN FORKS

The Smoke House Restaurant

U.S. 101 and La Push Rd. ☎ **360/374-6258.** Main dishes $5–$18. DISC, MC, V. Mon–Thurs 11am–9pm, Fri 11am–10pm, Sat 4–10pm, Sun 4–9pm. AMERICAN.

The name says it all here. This place smokes fish, and their salmon is just about the best we've ever had. It's got a good smoky flavor yet is tender and moist. If you're a fan of smoked salmon, don't miss this place. If you don't feel like sitting down for the smoked salmon dinner, smoked salmon salad, or smoked salmon and cheddar cheese tray appetizer, then consider getting some to go. It's great beach picnic food.

30

PETRIFIED FOREST NATIONAL PARK

by Alex Wells

THE FIRST THING YOU'LL PROBABLY NOTICE AT PETRIFIED FOREST National Park are the dozens of logs lying atop hills as if on display, many of them pointing in the same direction. Closer up you can see the colors in the wood—reds, greens, yellows, blues, and purples, all of them rich and moist-looking like wet paint. The colors might tempt you to touch the wood, and when you do you'll find it to be as cool and hard as stone.

About 225 million years ago these petrified trees were enormous conifers growing in a subtropical forest. Floods swept them into a large river, tearing off their branches in the process. Eventually the trees bottomed out in the shallow waters of the floodplain, where silt, mud, and volcanic ash buried them. Because almost no oxygen could reach the entombed trunks, they were slow to decay. Silica from the ash gradually permeated them. In a process not entirely understood, silica replaced or altered the wood's cells, eventually leaving quartz in its place. Minerals such as iron and manganese streaked the quartz with colors. The end result: The wood became precious, lovely rock.

Recognizing the financial value of this rock, early settlers began shipping it out on East Coast–bound trains. When the residents of the Territory of Arizona realized that the "wood" might soon be gone, they petitioned Congress to protect the "forests." Using the Antiquities Act, Pres. Theodore Roosevelt created Petrified Forest National Monument in 1906. It was designated a national park by Congress in 1962.

The same sediments that entombed the trees buried other plants and animals, preserving them as fossils as well. Today, erosion has exposed these clays and sandstones, collectively known as the Chinle Formation, throughout the park. With little or no vegetation to hold them in place, these rocks eroded quickly and unevenly, forming mesas, buttes, and furrowed, conical badlands, and unearthing thousands of fossils, including bones from some of the most remarkable creatures to inhabit the earth. In addition to the 225-million-year-old fossils, the grasslands here are full of artifacts of the Ancestral Pueblo people, the predecessors of the modern Pueblo tribes, who occupied this area in the 1100s and 1300s.

Even without these wonders, it would be worth coming here to see the rich red, gray, and maroon colors of the Painted

Desert. Shaped like a tusk (with the wider end near Cameron, Arizona), the desert spans from near Holbrook in the south to the Hopi mesas in the northeast to near the Grand Canyon in the west—far beyond the boundaries of the park. Its seemingly barren landscape is home to a rich diversity of plant and animal life: desert grasses; wildflowers, including Indian paintbrush and globemallow; juniper and other trees; mammals, including pronghorns, cottontails, and porcupines; reptiles, including collared lizards and prairie rattlesnakes; and birds, the most prominent being the raven.

Avoiding the Crowds. You can't lose the crowds simply by coming to Petrified Forest National Park. Cross-country travelers who might not otherwise visit this park pour into it because of its proximity to I-40, which passes within a few hundred yards of the park's north boundary. In 1996 roughly 940,000 people came to the park, and the numbers were up during the first months of 1997. Virtually all of these people travel down the same 27-mile scenic drive, stopping at its 20 pullouts. So these pullouts get crowded.

Michele M. Hellickson, the park's superintendent, offers three suggestions for avoiding the crowds, each of which involves extra effort. First, arrive early. "There aren't many visitors in the first few hours," she says. "It's also before the heat of the day, and the lighting on the rocks is spectacular." Second, stroll away from the parking areas. "Where there are pullouts, there are going to be people," Hellickson says. "But if you park at some of the pullouts and walk the length of the trails, you'll soon be away from the crowds. This will give you a chance to sit and hear the sounds of the desert and maybe get a picture that's different from everyone else's." Third, day-hike into the Painted Desert Wilderness. "That's the instant answer," says Hellickson. "I think it's relatively easy to do in this terrain. It's a landscape that lends itself to going out and exploring, with less fear involved."

Just the Facts

GETTING THERE & GATEWAYS

Petrified Forest National Park is located 90 miles east of Flagstaff, Arizona, 118 miles south of Canyon de Chelly National Park, and 180 miles north of Phoenix, Arizona. The North Entrance to Petrified Forest National Park is 25 miles east of Holbrook on I-40; the South Entrance is 20 miles east of Holbrook on U.S. 180. From Flagstaff, simply take I-40 west to Holbrook.

The Nearest Airport. Flagstaff's **Pulliam Airport** is serviced by America West Express (☎ **800/235-9292**).

By Train & Bus. Greyhound buses (☎ **520/524-3832**) make regular stops at the Circle K in Holbrook. **Amtrak** (☎ **800/872-7245**) offers train service to Winslow, 33 miles west of Holbrook.

Renting a Car. Car rentals are available through **Enterprise** (☎ **520/524-9143**) in Winslow, 33 miles west of Holbrook.

GETTING INFORMATION BEFORE YOUR TRIP

For advance information, contact **Petrified Forest National Park** (☎ **520/524-6228**), P.O. Box 2217, Petrified Forest National Park, AZ 86028. For information about lodging in the area, contact the **Holbrook Chamber of Commerce** (☎ **800/524-2459** or 520/524-6558), 100 E. Arizona, Holbrook, AZ 86025.

VISITOR CENTERS

The park has a visitor center at each end. Both sell books, videos, and park maps, and offer free bulletins on the park's geology, flora, and fauna. They also issue the free permits required for overnight backpack trips into the wilderness.

The **Painted Desert Visitor Center** is outside the park's North Entrance gate, so it's possible to visit here without paying the entrance fee. The main attraction

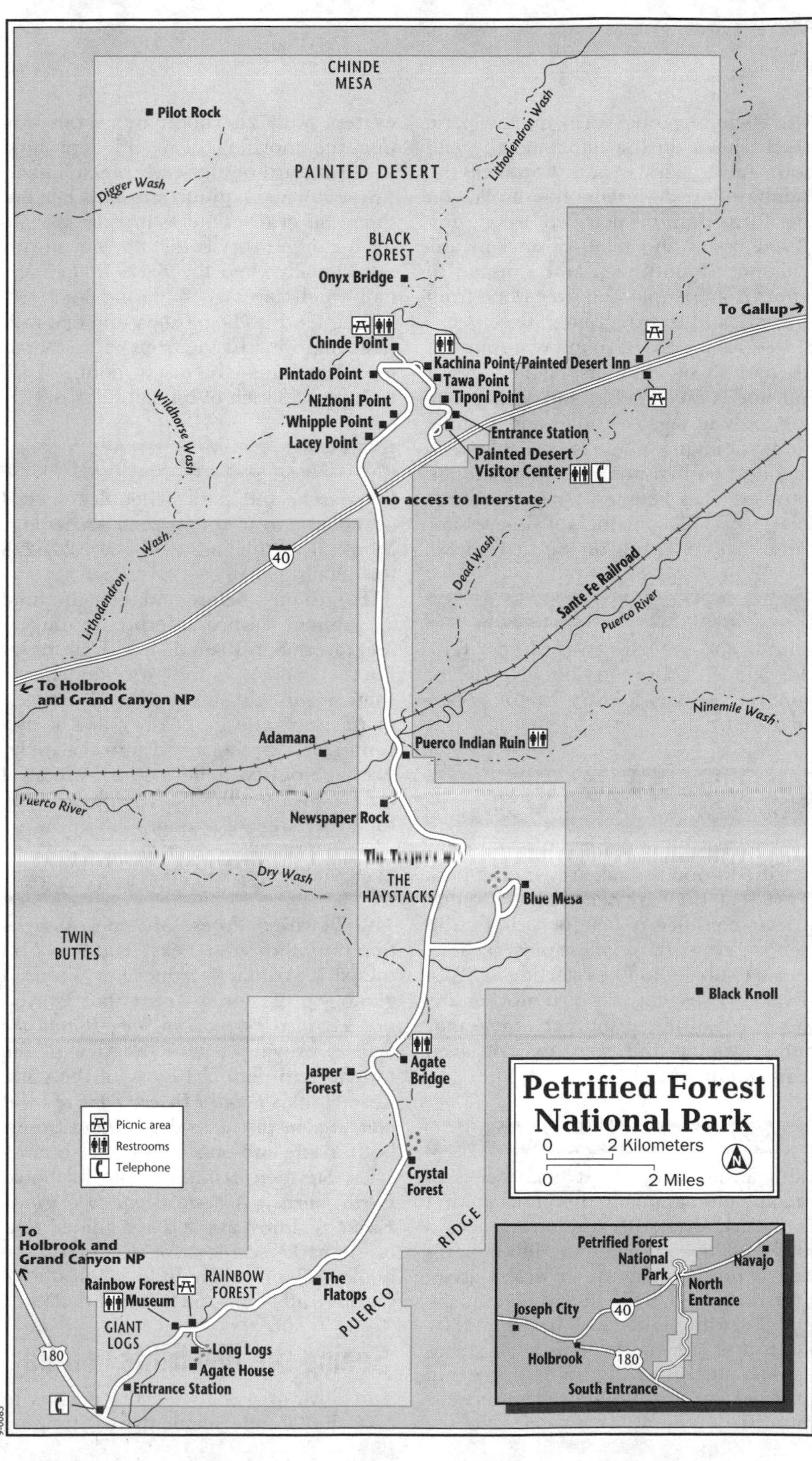
CHINDE
MESA
Pilot Rock
PAINTED DESERT
Digger Wash
Lithodendron Wash
BLACK
FOREST
Onyx Bridge
To Gallup
Chinde Point
Kachina Point/Painted Desert Inn
Pintado Point
Tawa Point
Nizhoni Point
Tiponi Point
Whipple Point
Lacey Point
Entrance Station
Painted Desert
Visitor Center
Wildhorse Wash
no access to Interstate
Wash
40
Lithodendron
Dead Wash
Sante Fe Railroad
Puerco River
To Holbrook
and Grand Canyon NP
Ninemile Wash
Adamana
Puerco Indian Ruin
Puerco River
Newspaper Rock
Dry Wash
THE
HAYSTACKS
Blue Mesa
TWIN
BUTTES
Black Knoll
Agate
Bridge
Jasper
Forest
Petrified Forest
National Park
0 2 Kilometers
0 2 Miles
N
Picnic area
Restrooms
Telephone
Crystal
Forest
RIDGE
To
Holbrook and
Grand Canyon NP
Rainbow Forest
Museum
RAINBOW
FOREST
The
Flatops
PUERCO
GIANT
LOGS
180
Long Logs
Agate House
Entrance Station
Petrified Forest
National
Park
Navajo
North
Entrance
Joseph City
40
Holbrook
180
South Entrance
9-0085

is a 20-minute-long video on the park, which shows on the hour and the half hour. At the park's South Entrance, the **Rainbow Forest Museum** has displays on the formation of petrified wood, fossilized bones and teeth of ancient animals once found here, and a display of letters from people who stole wood from the park and later regretted it.

Rest rooms can be found year-round at the park's visitor centers, Painted Desert Inn, and Puerco Pueblo, and during summer only at Agate Bridge and Chinde Point. Drinking water is available year-round at both visitor centers. There are long stretches between water sources at this park, so fill containers at either visitor center before starting on the scenic drive.

ENTRANCE & CAMPING FEES

Entrance to the park costs $10 per vehicle, $5 per visitor on foot, bicycle, or motorcycle. Backcountry camping permits are free.

SPECIAL REGULATIONS & WARNINGS

Because an estimated 25,000 pounds of petrified wood are taken from the park every year, the Park Service has adopted a zero-tolerance policy for visitors who remove even the smallest pieces. Violators are subject to fines starting at $275. If rangers suspect you of removing any wood or other resources, they may detain you at the park exit or even search your car.

SEASONS & CLIMATE

With an average of just 9.65 inches of precipitation annually, this park couldn't get much drier. Because it averages a lofty 5,400 feet in elevation, however, it's not as hot as many other desert areas. Even in July, daily highs average in the mid-80s, with nightly lows in the low 50s. Of course, the park occasionally heats up—temperatures in the 100s are not unusual in midsummer. The hottest months, July and August, are also the wettest, with afternoon monsoons cutting the morning heat and depositing nearly a third of the yearly precipitation. These storms continue into early fall, but the weather dries out as it cools. By winter it can get very cold, and snowstorms occasionally close the park. In January, daily highs average 42°F and lows 19°. Spring tends to be blustery and dry, with daily highs increasing from 54° in March to 80° in June—the driest month of all, with just .33 inch of rainfall.

SEASONAL EVENTS

In March, the park schedules special events as part of the **Arizona Archeology Month.** Call the park at ☎ **520/524-6228** for details.

For 10 days before and after the June 21 **summer solstice,** interpretive rangers meet from 8 to 10am daily with visitors at Puerco Pueblo. As the group watches, a shaft of sunlight shines through a notch in the rock and gradually crawls to the center of a circle carved into the rocks. Archaeologists believe the Ancestral Puebloans used this petroglyph to monitor the change of seasons.

USEFUL PUBLICATIONS

The **Petrified Forest Museum Association** publishes several excellent books on the park. Written by Sidney Ash, a retired geology professor at Weber State University, ***Petrified Forest: The Story Behind the Scenery*** provides a nice overview of the human and natural history of the park. Rose Houk's ***Painted Desert: Land of Light and Shadow*** discusses the Painted Desert both inside and outside the park boundaries. Stephen Trimble's colorful book, ***Earth Journey: A Road Guide to Petrified Forest,*** is almost as good as a guided tour of the park's scenic drive. To order these books, all of which have color photographs, call ☎ **520/524-6228,** ext. 239.

Seeing the Highlights in a Day

The obvious way to see the park is to take the 27-mile **scenic drive.** Stopping at all the pullouts will make for a long, enjoyable day. If you can free up another day, a walk into the **Painted Desert Wilderness** might be in order (see "Day Hikes," below). In summer, you probably won't want to spend a whole day in the Painted Desert, since there's virtually no shade or water. However, hiking in the early morning or late afternoon is a great way to absorb its colors and lighting. Combine this with a pre- or post-hike picnic at the **Chinde Point Picnic Area.**

Exploring the Park by Car

The direction you choose for the scenic drive depends on which way you're traveling on I-40. If coming from the west, take U.S. 180 east from Holbrook to the park's South Entrance, drive through the park, then rejoin I-40 at the park's North Entrance. If coming from the east, do the opposite, driving through the park from the North Entrance and exiting on to U.S. 180 in the south.

1. If you travel from the south, you'll start at **The Rainbow Forest Museum.** Behind the museum is the Giant Logs Self-Guided Trail (see "Day Hikes," below), the first of several easy trails through the petrified forests.

2. Just past the museum you'll see a spur road, open 12:30 to 4pm daily, to the **Long Logs** and the **Agate House** trailheads. If you'd like to hike these trails when the road is closed, park at Rainbow Forest Museum and walk the 0.5 mile to the trailhead. The Agate House Trail, which goes to the right from the parking area, ends at an prehistoric pueblo made of petrified wood. Forking to the left, the Long Logs Trail loops through some of the longest and most spectacular petrified trees in the area (see "Day Hikes," below).

3. As you continue along the drive, you'll pass the **Flat Tops,** small mesas capped by hard, erosion-resistant sandstone. If you'd like to enter this small wilderness, check with park personnel for instructions.

4. Several miles past the Flat Tops is the **Crystal Forest,** where visitors in the late 1800s came across ground covered with sparkling bits of petrified wood. At that time, the petrified logs in this area were flecked with quartz and purple amethyst crystals. These crystals attracted gem hunters, some of whom went so far as to dynamite the trees. Although many crystals and the smaller pieces are gone, some very colorful logs remain (see "Day Hikes," below).

5. Next comes **Jasper Forest,** an overlook from atop a 150-foot-high bluff. This is a great place to observe the various effects of erosion. Looking downhill, you'll notice that large chunks of sandstone and petrified wood have tumbled from the bluff to the desert floor. Soft clay eroded out from under the harder wood and sandstone, undermining it and eventually sending it downhill. Because erosion continues, someday the rocks underfoot will tumble downhill as well.

6. The first thing you'll notice at **Agate Bridge** is the remarkable bridge itself. With each end firmly embedded in sandstone, a petrified log forms a natural bridge across an arroyo that cuts through the ground underneath its midsection. The next thing you'll probably notice is the concrete span that "supports" it. In 1917, workers who wanted to preserve the bridge as a tourist attraction buttressed it with concrete. If you think the concrete detracts from the bridge, be thankful those same well-meaning people never saw Delicate Arch in Arches National Park.

7. Next, a 2-mile spur goes to **Blue Mesa.** Like all the badlands in the park, Blue Mesa is made up of soft rocks that are now eroding away by as much as 3 inches a decade—fast enough to change appreciably in the span of a human lifetime. The layers represent different times. The gray and white clay was once part of a floodplain; the sandstone was in streambeds. The Blue Mesa Trail, one of the prettiest walkways in the park, descends from the fourth and last overlook on the spur road (see "Day Hikes," below).

8. Next comes the turnoff for conical badlands known as the **Teepees.** These sit in one of the most fossil-rich areas in the park. Paleontologists have unearthed well-preserved imprints of ancient ferns, as well as dozens of fossilized bones, including many from metoposaurs—6- to 10-foot-long amphibians whose wide jaws were perfect for trapping fish.

9. From an overlook 2 miles past the Teepees, you can look down on **Newspaper Rock,** into which the Ancestral Pueblo people pecked dozens of petroglyphs—rock art carved out of the dark patina on the stone. Among them is an image of the famous humpbacked flute player, Kokopelli. The petroglyphs in this area aren't limited to Newspaper Rock, so be sure to scan the surrounding rocks with your binoculars.

10. With so many petroglyphs around Newspaper Rock, it seems inevitable that a prehistoric dwelling be nearby. Sure enough, a mile down the road is **Puerco Pueblo,** the remains of a 100-room pueblo occupied in the 1100s and again in the 1300s by the Ancestral Puebloans. To see this dwelling, walk the easy 0.5-mile loop trail (see "Day Hikes," below).

11. The remaining stops between Puerco Pueblo and the Painted Desert Visitor Center are overlooks of the Painted Desert. Each one affords a unique view, but the panorama from the hilltop at **Pintado Point** may be most spectacular. Just past Pintado Point is **Chinde Point,** where you'll find sheltered picnic tables, rest rooms (open seasonally), and another nice overlook.

12. A quarter of a mile past Chinde Point is the turnoff for **Kachina Point** and the **Painted Desert Inn National Historic Landmark.** Here, you can descend into the desert on the Painted Desert Wilderness Trail, or, if the drop seems a bit imposing, hike to Tawa Point on the Painted Desert Rim Trail (see "Day Hikes," below). After hiking, be sure to visit the landmark itself, which has displays on the history of the area.

Organized Tours & Ranger Programs

Because the park's rangers change the topics, locations, and times of their lectures, you'll need to check at either visitor center to see what's on tap on a given day. Typically, the schedule might include archaeology lectures at Puerco Pueblo, geology talks at the Painted Desert overlooks, and paleontology discussions at either the Rainbow Forest Museum or on Long Logs Trail. When the rangers aren't lecturing, they're usually chatting with visitors.

Historic & Man-Made Attractions

The **Painted Desert Inn,** which overlooks the desert from Kachina Point, once served as a lunch counter and trading post for early travelers on Route 66. After the Park Service purchased the inn from private owners in 1936, workers in the Civilian Conservation Corps (CCC) rebuilt it in the Southwestern style, covering the building's original petrified-wood walls with stucco. Inside, they installed oak floors and hand-painted glass ceiling tiles, and added six new guest rooms, each with a fireplace. Upon completion in 1940, the 28-room inn became an immediate hit with travelers. It was closed again, however, during the last years of World War II. After the war, the Fred Harvey Company took control of the building, using it as a visitor center and restaurant until 1963, when the new Painted Desert Visitor Center opened.

In 1947, Fred Kabotie, the renowned Hopi artist whose work also graces the Desert Watchtower at the Grand Canyon, painted several murals inside, including one that depicted the annual journey of the Zuni to their sacred salt mines. Kabotie's murals may have helped save the building, which has severe structural problems caused by expansion and contraction of the clay underneath it. When it was threatened with demolition in the 1960s, preservationists cited the value of Kabotie's art as they called for protecting the building. The Painted Desert Inn was declared a National Historic Landmark in 1987.

Today it houses the **Painted Desert Inn Museum,** which celebrates the area's cultural heritage. Open daily 8am to 4pm, the museum displays Native American artifacts found in and around the park. Among them is a famous petroglyph of a mountain lion—an image reproduced in contemporary art throughout the Southwest. The building itself is also worth admiring. Kabotie's famous mural still adorns one wall, and the wood floors and glass ceiling tiles are intact. To the rear of the building, one of the original petrified-wood walls has been exposed. Park crews continue to work on the exterior, but a more significant renovation is on hold, pending an appropriation from Congress.

Day Hikes

SHORTER TRAILS

Giant Logs Trail

0.4 mile RT. Easy. Access: Rainbow Forest Museum.

This paved trail loops past some of the park's largest petrified logs, including "Old Faithful," which spans nearly 9 feet at its base. The trail has 11 stops, each corresponding to a page in the guide (free to borrow, 50¢ to keep) at the trailhead. At each stop, you'll find out about the trees or the area's geology. Constructed in the '30s by the CCC, the trail has some steps, making access difficult for people in wheelchairs.

Agate House

0.9 mile RT. Moderate. Access: 0.5 mile down spur road from Rainbow Forest Museum.

An enjoyable walk takes you to Agate House, a pueblo that archaeologists believe was briefly occupied between A.D. 1100 and 1300. (Archaeologists suspect a brief occupation because very little "trash" was found in the area.) Colorful bits of petrified wood dot the ground on the way to the eight-room pueblo, which sits atop a knoll overlooking a vast expanse of desert. Made from petrified wood and mortar, Agate House must have been one of the prettiest dwellings anywhere in its time—a house of jewels, on a hill. The pueblo's largest room was reconstructed by workers in the '30s. That's how it acquired a window, something the Ancestral Pueblo dwellings never had.

Long Logs Trail

0.6 mile RT. Easy. Access: 0.5 mile down spur road from Rainbow Forest Museum.

This relatively flat, paved loop will give you an idea of the immensity of the Araucarioxylon trees that grew in this area during the Triassic period. Many of the longest, including one that measures 116 feet, lie alongside the trail on the north end of the loop. You'll see places where these petrified logs protected the softer clay underneath them and prevented it from eroding. The trail also takes you within a few feet of badlands. The different colored layers are caused by mineral deposits in the clay.

Crystal Forest Trail

0.8 mile RT. Moderate. Access: Crystal Forest stop on scenic drive.

This paved trail, which includes a few steep grades, reminds us of why it's important to leave the petrified wood in place. Look carefully and you can see where gem hunters hacked at or even dynamited logs. The wood that's left is still lovely, though, and a few smoky quartz crystals remain. Still, it's hard not to wonder what this area looked like before the thieves came.

Blue Mesa Trail

1 mile RT. Moderate to difficult. Access: Blue Mesa turnoff on scenic drive.

This paved loop trail descends steeply to the floor beneath the blue-, gray-, and white-striped badlands at Blue Mesa—some of the prettiest land in the park. You may notice that it's hard to determine the size of the hills. Because they lack vegetation, there is little to provide a sense of scale. At the bottom, you can observe how the different colors of these hillsides streak and blend where the clay has washed into drainages. Look for small fossils, abundant in the area. The trail has numerous interpretive panels, spaced to give you a chance to catch your breath as you walk.

Puerco Pueblo Trail

0.5 mile RT. Easy. Access: Puerco Pueblo.

This relatively flat loop travels around the 100-room Puerco Pueblo. The 30 excavated rooms hint at the floor plan of the buildings—a trapezoid around an outdoor plaza where most of the activity in the community took place. As you walk, you'll observe places where the rooms were one, two, or three deep around the plaza. Where they were two deep, the rooms on the outside may have been used to store crops harvested from the floodplains below. The inside rooms, which opened onto the plaza, were probably used for sleeping or shelter from inclement weather. Three kivas—ceremonial rooms dug into the ground—were located inside the plaza, and one is obvious alongside the trail. Part way around the loop, a short trail leads down to an overlook from which you can see numerous petroglyphs.

Painted Desert Rim Trail

1.2 miles RT. Easy. Access: Kachina Point stop on scenic drive.

As this cinder trail meanders along the Painted Desert rim between Kachina and Tawa points, it affords stunning views of the desert itself, where gray, pink, and red badlands stand out against the green grasses at their bases. The trail is atop the basalt of the Bidahochi formation, which at 8 million years old is much younger than most other rocks in the park. This layer has disappeared in many areas of the park but is widespread in other parts of northern Arizona. Here, it provides fertile soil for a diversity of vegetation, including juniper, Mormon tea, sagebrush, and cliffrose.

LONGER TRAILS

Painted Desert Wilderness Trail

About 0.5 mile one way. Moderate to difficult. Access: Kachina Point.

This trail descends in switchbacks down the face of the badlands below Kachina Point, then follows Lithodendron Wash for a short distance before petering out in the grasslands on the floor of the Painted Desert. You won't find water or shade here, but you will have a chance to experience firsthand the colors and landforms of this desert. Before wandering far, be sure to identify landmarks you can use to retrace your steps. (The Painted Desert Inn is a good one.) If you carry a topographical map and plenty of water and sunscreen, you should have few problems in this desert, which has excellent sight lines and few insurmountable obstacles. Walk on the dry stream beds when possible. Besides being easier, this minimizes the damage to the fragile plant life.

It's worth spending the night here just to watch the sun dip below the red sands of the desert. Before bedding down, you must first obtain a backcountry permit at one of the visitor centers, then walk at least 0.5 mile into the 43,000-acre Painted Desert Wilderness, which starts on the other side of Lithodendron Wash. The direction you take from the bottom of the wash will depend on which "use area" you sign up for on your permit. You'll find spots smooth enough for camping near many of the mesas and badlands. (Keep in mind, however, that runoff can create problems during storms.) Don't forget to pack insect repellent; in spite of its dry climate, the park has been known to host an unusually active population of no-see-ums.

Rainbow Forest Wilderness

No marked trails, so distances are at the discretion of the hiker. Moderate to difficult. Access: Rainbow Forest Museum.

The park's other wilderness area is the Rainbow Forest Wilderness, which at 7,240 acres is less than one-seventh the size of the Painted Desert Wilderness. Although this area of desert prairie remains open to hiking and camping, the Park Service prefers to send people to the Painted Desert Wilderness, which is more colorful and spacious than this one. If you do wish to enter this area, ask a ranger about the best places to go.

Camping

There are no campgrounds within the park boundaries. Visitors with backcountry permits are allowed to stay in the park after it closes for the evening, but they must hike at least 0.5 mile into the wilderness before camping. Those interested in car camping can choose between two campgrounds in Holbrook, 25 miles west of the park on I-40.

The best thing at the **KOA Campground,** 102 Hermosa Dr., Holbrook, AZ 86025 (☎ **520/524-6689**), is the large swimming pool, which shimmers like a mirage on sunny days. The 24 sites and 100 RV hookups themselves are exposed to the sun and wind, as the owners try to grow new trees in an unforgiving landscape. The tent sites, which are grassy, are nicest. The cost is $17.95 for tents, $21.95 for full hookups ($2 cheaper in winter). Reservations are accepted. The campground offers public phones, toilets, drinking water, laundry, showers, and a dump station. It's open year-round. During the high season, the campers can feast at relatively inexpensive evening cookouts and all-you-can-eat pancake breakfasts.

Located just 3 blocks south of the KOA Campground, **OK RV,** 1576 Roadrunner Rd., Holbrook, AZ 86025, (☎ **520/524-3226**), charges a bit less for its 150 hookups than its neighbor. Electric, water, sewer, and cable are included in the rates, which run $15 to $17. There's no pool here, though, and the 6 tent sites aren't as plush as at the KOA. OK RV offers public phones, toilets, drinking water, laundry, showers, and a dump station. It's open year-round. Reservations not accepted.

Accommodations

No accommodations are available inside the park.

NEAR THE PARK

The place to get a bed for the night is Holbrook, 25 miles west of the park. A number of chain motels line its two main thoroughfares, West Hopi Drive (off I-40 Exit 285) and Navajo Boulevard (off I-40 Exit 286 or 289). The moderately priced chains include: **Adobe Inn Best Western,** 615 W. Hopi Dr. (☎ **800/528-1234** or 520/524-3948); the **Arizonian Best Western,** 2508 E. Navajo (☎ **800/528-1234** or 520/524-2611); **Days Inn,** 2601 E. Navajo Blvd. (☎ **800/329-7466** or 520/524-6949); **Econo Lodge,** 2596 E. Navajo (☎ **800/424-4777** or 520/524-1448); **Ramada Limited,** 2608 E. Navajo (☎ **800/272-6232** or 520/524-2566); and **Super 8,** 1989 E. Navajo (☎ **800/800-8000** or 520/524-2871). Inexpensive lodging can be found at **Travelodge,** 2418 E. Navajo (☎ **800/578-7878** or 520/524-6815).

Holiday Inn Express

Holbrook, AZ 86025. ☎ **800/465-4329** or 520/524-1466; fax 520/524-1788. 55 rms, 4 suites. A/C TV TEL. May 21–Aug 19 $66; Aug 20–Oct 31 $59; Nov 1–Feb 28 $53. Rates include continental breakfast. AE, DC, DISC, MC, V.

Everything here merits praise, from the lobby, which features sculptures by Utah artist Gary Price, to the rooms, which seem even newer than their age—the hotel was built in 1992. Plum-colored carpeting and off-white walls freshen the rooms, and the beds are firm and comfortable.

Rainbow Inn

2211 E. Navajo Blvd., Holbrook, AZ 86025. ☎ **800/551-1923** or 520/524-2654. 40 rms. A/C TV TEL. June–Sept $47; Oct–May $37. AE, DC, DISC, MC, V.

"Rainbow" might not be the best word to describe this small two-story motel, where gray is the color of choice. But although it's a bit less colorful than other motels in the area, the Rainbow Inn's rooms are immaculate, and each comes with a small refrigerator. There's also free popcorn at night.

Wigwam Motel

811 W. Hopi Dr. (P.O. Box 788), Holbrook, AZ 86025. ☎ **520/524-3048.** 16 wigwam rms. A/C TV TEL. $30 for 1 bed; $35 for 2.

Even if you don't stay here, the Wigwam Motel makes for a great photo. Each of the motel's 15 rooms is inside its own 75-foot-high wood-and-concrete wigwam, built for kicks during Route 66's glory days in the 1940s. The motel's owners have done a good job of preserving this bit of Americana. The wigwams are clean and well maintained, and each is furnished with the motel's original hand-carved hickory furniture. The only drawbacks are the undersized bathrooms and windows.

Comfort Inn

2 blocks south of I-40 Exit 289 (2602 Navajo Blvd., Holbrook, AZ 86025). ☎ **800/221-2222** or 520/524-6131; fax 520/524-2281. 60 rms. A/C TV TEL. May–Sept $70; Oct–Apr $54. Rates include continental breakfast. AE, DISC, MC, V.

The rooms at this moderately priced motel are just as well-kept as the flower patch out front, where not a single weed is growing. In addition to being pleasant, the Comfort Inn is surprisingly quiet for being a few hundred yards from the interstate. If you feel like a bit of light recreation, you can play Ping-Pong in a poolside gazebo.

Motel 6

2514 Navajo Blvd., Holbrook, AZ 86025. ☎ **520/524-6101;** fax 520/524-1806. 126 rms. A/C TV TEL. Mid-May to mid-Dec $33; mid-Dec to mid-May $31. AE, DISC, MC, V.

With double-occupancy rates at around $30, the Motel 6 is a great value. The rooms, while small, are solid and clean. There's also a large swimming pool inside a courtyard sheltered from the desert winds.

Dining

INSIDE THE PARK

Cougar Café

Next to the Painted Desert Visitor Center. ☎ **520/524-3756.** Breakfast $.80 to $4.75; lunch and dinner $2.75 to $4.50. AE, DC, DISC, MC, V. Summer daily 8am–6pm, winter daily 8am–5pm. CAFETERIA.

The cafe serves hot breakfasts, including eggs and pancakes. At lunch, Navajo tacos and a variety of sandwiches and burgers are available, as well as daily specials. *Note:* In addition to the Cougar

Cafe, a small fountain serves up sandwiches and snacks at the park's South Entrance.

Mesa Italiana Restaurant

2318 E. Navajo Blvd., Holbrook. ☎ **520/524-6696.** Lunch $3.50–$8.95; dinner $6.50–$14.95. MC, V. Tues–Sun 11am–9pm. ITALIAN.

Generally regarded as the best restaurant in Holbrook, Mesa Italiana serves traditional Italian dishes, including baked ziti, stuffed shells, lasagna, linguine, and pizza, at reasonable prices. The Italiana Mushrooms (mushrooms stuffed with chicken, spinach, and fresh herbs, all topped with a garlic white-wine sauce) may deceive you into thinking that you've left the land of the green chile hamburger steak. The restaurant's owner, Margaret Belasco, recommends the Chicken Jerusalem (a chicken breast sautéed with butter, garlic, artichoke hearts, mushrooms, and shrimp, all under a white-wine and lemon sauce). Mesa Italiana has a nice wine list, but if you're traveling on a budget beware the cost of alcohol here: A bottle of Bud goes for $2.75, and prices climb from there.

Mandarin Beauty Restaurant

2218 E. Navajo Blvd., Holbrook. ☎ **520/524-3663.** Reservations accepted. Lunch entrees $4.25–$5.25; dinner entrees $5.95–$10.95. AE, MC, V. Daily 11am–9pm. CHINESE.

This restaurant, which opened in 1997, would be a good choice for Mandarin food even in a major city. The 73 choices include shrimp, beef, scallops, chicken, and pork dishes as well as vegetarian fare such as eggplant or tofu. Two fine dishes are the chicken with mixed vegetables, and the bean curd with black mushrooms.

Joe and Aggie's

120 W. Hopi, Holbrook. ☎ **520/524-6540.** Breakfast $1–$4.55; lunch and dinner $2.25–$9.95. No credit cards. Mon–Sat 8am–8pm. AMERICAN.

For more than 40 years at the same Route 66 location, Joe Montano has cooked Mexican and American food while his wife, Aggie, has waited tables. Business has slowed since I-40 was built, but then, so have Joe and Aggie, who pass the spare time playing cards with friends in the front booth. At breakfast, the chile cheese omelette and the egg burro (scrambled eggs with hash browns and cheese rolled in a flour tortilla) are great choices. At lunch and dinner you can select from Mexican platters, traditional American dishes, and combinations of both, such as a Mexican hamburger steak with red or green chile.

El Rancho

867 Navajo Blvd., Holbrook. ☎ **520/524-3332.** Reservations accepted. Breakfast $2.25–$4.75; lunch and dinner $2.50–[illegible] AE, MC, V. Tues–Sun 7am–10pm. MEXICAN.

This is the place to go to get copious amounts of Mexican or American food at reasonable prices. Don't fill up on the free chips and salsa, because the restaurant's main courses are more than a meal. You can order heavy (a sour cream cheese enchilada) or heavier (an El Rancho burger with chile strips).

Picnic & Camping Supplies

In Holbrook, picnic supplies are available at **Safeway,** 702 W. Hopi Dr. (☎ **520/524-3313**), and **Basha's,** 1519 Navajo Blvd. (☎ **520/524-2607**).

31

POINT REYES NATIONAL SEASHORE

by Matthew R. Poole

POINT REYES IS A 100-SQUARE-MILE PENINSULA OF DARK FORESTS, wind-sculpted dunes, endless beaches, and plunging sea cliffs. Aside from its beautiful scenery, it also boasts historical treasures that offer a window into California's coastal past, including lighthouses, turn-of-the-century dairies and ranches, and the site of Sir Francis Drake's 1579 landing, plus a complete replica of a Coast Miwok Indian village.

The national seashore system was created to protect rural and undeveloped stretches of the coast from the pressures of soaring real estate values and increasing population, preserving both the natural features and unique culture of the coast. And nowhere is the success of the system more evident than at Point Reyes. Layers of human history coexist peacefully here with one of the world's most dramatic natural settings. Residents of the surrounding towns—Inverness, Point Reyes Station, and Olema—have steadfastly resisted runaway development. You won't find any strip malls or fast-food joints here—just laid-back coastal towns with cafes and country inns where gentle living prevails. The park, a 71,000-acre hammer-shaped peninsula jutting 10 miles into the Pacific and backed by Tomales Bay, is loaded with wildlife, ranging from tule elk, birds, and bobcats to gray whales, sea lions, and great white sharks.

Though the peninsula's people and wildlife live in harmony above the ground, the situation beneath the soil is much more volatile. The infamous San Andreas Fault separates Point Reyes, the northernmost landmass on the Pacific Plate, from the rest of California, which rests on the North American Plate. Point Reyes is making its way toward Alaska at a rate of about 2 inches per year, but there have been times when it has moved much faster. In 1906, Point Reyes jumped north almost 20 feet in an instant, leveling San Francisco and jolting the rest of the state. The 0.5-mile Earthquake Trail, near the Bear Valley Visitor Center, illustrates this geological drama with a loop through an area torn by the slipping fault. Shattered fences, rifts in the ground, and a barn knocked off its foundation by the quake illustrate that the earth is alive here. If that doesn't convince you, a seismograph in the visitor center will.

Avoiding the Crowds. Though the park is heavily visited, crowds are only a problem at a few places and only during certain times. If you visit the lighthouse on a

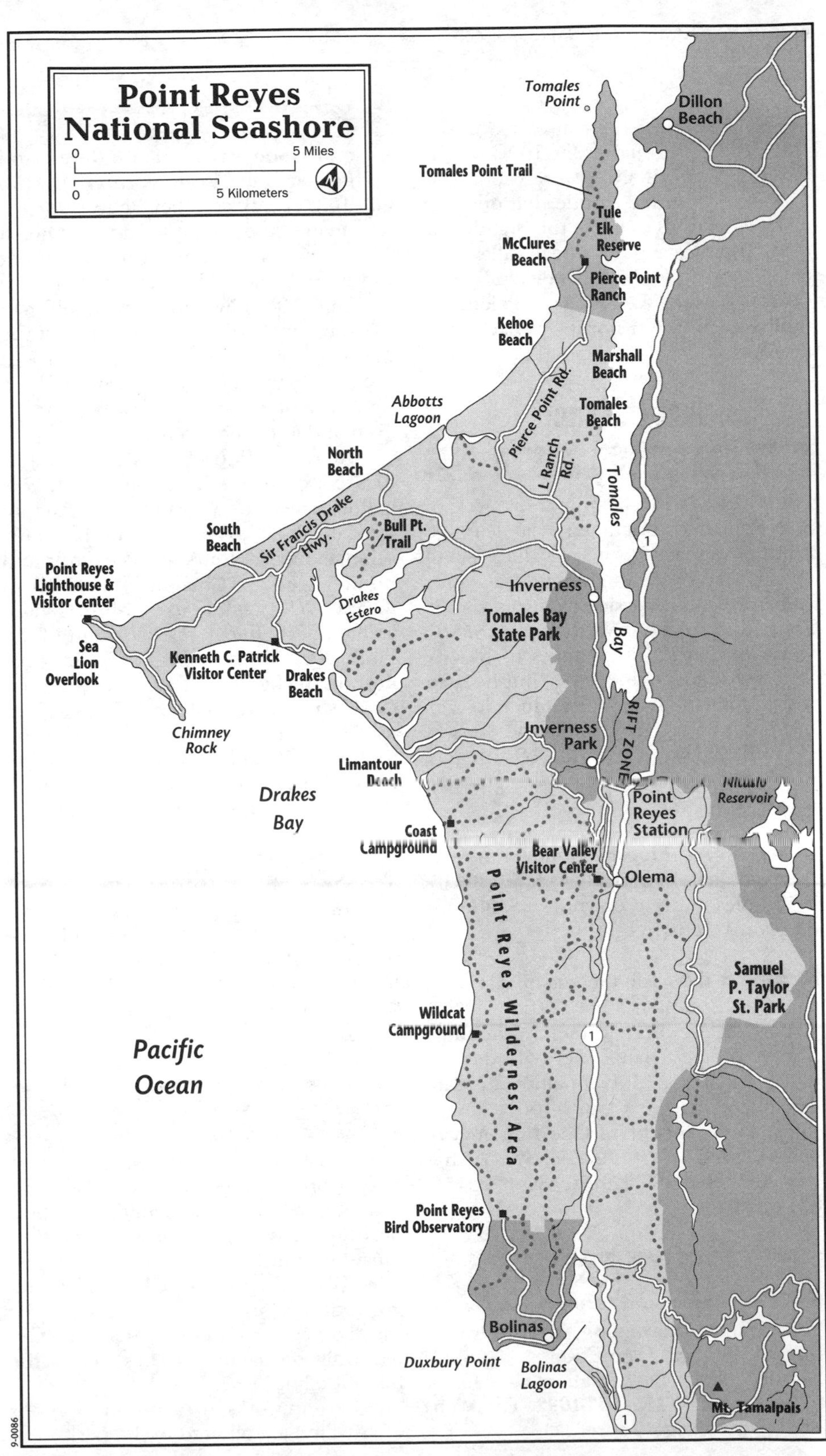
Point Reyes
National Seashore
0
5 Miles
0
5 Kilometers
N
Tomales
Point
Dillon
Beach
Tomales Point Trail
Tule
Elk
Reserve
McClures
Beach
Pierce Point
Ranch
Kehoe
Beach
Marshall
Beach
Pierce Point Rd.
Abbotts
Lagoon
Tomales
Beach
North
Beach
L Ranch
Rd.
Tomales
South
Beach
Sir Francis Drake
Hwy.
Bull Pt.
Trail
1
Point Reyes
Lighthouse &
Visitor Center
Inverness
Drakes
Estero
Tomales Bay
State Park
Bay
Sea
Lion
Overlook
Kenneth C. Patrick
Visitor Center
Drakes
Beach
RIFT ZONE
Chimney
Rock
Inverness
Park
Limantour
Reservoir
Drakes
Bay
Point
Reyes
Station
Coast
Bear Valley
Visitor Center
Olema
Point Reyes Wilderness Area
Samuel
P. Taylor
St. Park
Wildcat
Campground
1
Pacific
Ocean
Point Reyes
Bird Observatory
Bolinas
Duxbury Point
Bolinas
Lagoon
Mt. Tamalpais
1
9-0086

weekend or holiday during whale season (December through March), be prepared for crowds and realize you'll have to wait for the free shuttle that operates from Drakes Beach to the lighthouse area. Trails leaving from Bear Valley tend to be more crowded on weekends than others. Try the **Five Brooks** or **Palomarin trailheads** to avoid hordes of backcountry tourists.

Just the Facts

GETTING THERE & GATEWAYS

Point Reyes is only 30 miles northwest of San Francisco, but it takes at least 90 minutes to reach by car (it's all the small towns, not the topography, that slows you down). The easiest route is via Sir Francis Drake Boulevard from U.S. 101 south of San Rafael; it takes its bloody time getting to Point Reyes, but does so without any detours. For a much longer but more scenic route, take the Stinson Beach/Highway 1 exit off U.S. 101 just south of Sausalito and follow Highway 1 north.

The Nearest Airport. **San Francisco International Airport** (☎ **415/761-0800**) is 14 miles south of downtown San Francisco on U.S. 101.

Renting a Car. All the major national car-rental companies have offices at the airport or elsewhere in the city. In addition to the big chains, there are dozens of regional rental companies in San Francisco, many of which offer lower rates. These include **A-One Rent-A-Car,** 434 O'Farell St. (☎ **415/771-3977**), and **Bay Area Rentals,** 229 7th St. (☎ **415/621-8989**).

GETTING INFORMATION BEFORE YOUR TRIP

For advance information, write to Information Request, Point Reyes National Seashore, Point Reyes Station, CA 94956-9799, or call ☎ **415/663-1092.** The Web site is **www.nps.gov/pore**.

VISITOR CENTERS

As soon as you arrive at Point Reyes, stop at the **Bear Valley Visitor Center** (☎ **415/663-1092**) on Bear Valley Road (look for the small sign posted just north of Olema on Highway 1) and pick up a free Point Reyes trail map. The rangers here are extremely friendly and helpful, and can answer any questions you have about the national seashore. Be sure to check out the great natural history and cultural displays as well. Hours are weekdays 9am to 5pm and weekends 8am to 5pm.

The **Ken Patrick Visitor Center,** located at Drakes Beach, houses a 250-gallon saltwater aquarium and a 16-foot minke whale skeleton, among many other exhibits. Hours are weekends and holidays (except Christmas) from 10am to 5pm. The **Lighthouse Visitor Center,** located at the most westerly point of the Point Reyes Peninsula, offers information on the lighthouse and lifesaving services performed over the 125 years of its use as well as natural history exhibits on whales, seals, and wildflowers. Hours are from 10am to 5pm. It is closed Tuesday, Wednesday, and December 25.

ENTRANCE & CAMPING FEES

Entrance to the park is free. Camping is $10 per site per night, and permits are required. Reservations can be made up to 2 months in advance by calling ☎ **415/663-8054** Monday to Friday, 9am to 2pm.

SPECIAL REGULATIONS & WARNINGS

- Dogs and other pets are not permitted on trails, in campgrounds, or on beaches that are seal habitats or bird nesting areas. On other beaches they must be leashed.
- Wood fires are prohibited in campgrounds. Use only charcoal, gas stoves, or canned heat. Driftwood fires are permitted only on sandy beaches below the high-tide line.
- No fireworks, firearms, or weapons of any kind are allowed in the park.

◆ Bicycles are only permitted on roads or designated bike trials.

◆ Check the tide tables before walking on the beaches. Rising water can trap you against a cliff with no possibility of escape.

◆ For your safety, sleeping on the beach is prohibited; it can be really dangerous. High tide frequently comes to the base of the cliffs and can trap the unwary.

◆ Do not climb cliffs—they can crumble easily. Your foothold may vanish, leaving you in thin air. Walking or sitting below cliffs is also dangerous due to falling rock.

◆ In wooded areas keep an eye out for poison oak's waxy three-leaf clusters. Also be sure to check for ticks as the Lyme-disease-carrying black-legged tick is common here.

◆ The pounding surf and rip currents are treacherous, especially at McClures Beach and Point Reyes Beaches, north and south. Stay away from the water.

◆ Don't disturb any abandoned baby seals or sea lions you may encounter on the beach. The mother may be preoccupied with finding lunch, and she won't come back until you leave. In fact, you could be fined up to $10,000 for your good intentions. However, if a pup looks injured or in danger, call the **Mammal Center** at ☎ **707/465-MAML.**

SEASONS & CLIMATE

Weather at Point Reyes is very fickle. The seasons here generally reverse expectations: Summer tends to be cold and foggy until the afternoon (the point itself is the foggiest place on the West Coast), while winter is clear and, if not exactly warm, often more tolerable. But these are generalizations at best—winter storms can rage for weeks and sometimes the summer fog miraculously holds off for days. Spring and fall usually see the best weather (that is, little fog, warm temperatures).

There are no hard-and-fast rules about the weather, though—it varies not only from day to day, but hour to hour. To make matters more frustrating, the clearing of fog often signals the onset of strong winds. So, if you are planning to explore the park on foot, prepare yourself for cool weather, dampness, and wind (*lots* of wind, winds that have reached up to 133 m.p.h., the highest wind speed recorded on the Pacific Coast). The best plan is to take advantage of variations in local weather by being flexible with your itinerary: Save indoor sightseeing for rainy or foggy days, and hit the beach or go hiking when the sun comes out.

SEASONAL EVENTS

In July, Point Reyes National Seashore hosts an annual **Native American Celebration.** Every third Saturday in July, Native American basket-makers, wood- and stone-carvers, singers, and dancers convene at Point Reyes for an annual public celebration at Kule Loklo, an authentic reconstruction of a village of the indigenous Coast Miwok Indian tribe. Classes in Native American crafts and skills are also offered intermittently throughout the year. Call ☎ **415/479-3281** for more information.

USEFUL PUBLICATIONS

A comprehensive guide book to the National Seashore, ***Point Reyes National Seashore: A Hiking and Nature Guide,*** by Don and Kay Martin, covers the history, geology, tide pools, climate, and other natural aspects of Point Reyes. Also included are 37 round-trip trial descriptions with relief maps, and 80 illustrations of local flora and fauna. To order write to Martin Press, P.O. Box 2109, San Anselmo, CA 94979.

The ***Natural History of the Point Reyes Peninsula,*** by naturalist Jules G. Evens (Point Reyes National Seashore Association, 1993), is a comprehensive and sometimes anecdotal overview of Point Reyes's natural history, ranging from the cycle of seasons and natural science to the native and introduced animals—

such as gray whales, salmon, elk, cougars, newts, and migrating birds—living in and around the peninsula.

Seeing the Highlights in a Day

The first thing you should do is stop in at the **Bear Valley Visitor Center** and pick up the free Point Reyes map, which lists all the trails and roads open to cars, bikes, horses, and hikers. While you're here, spend some time at **Kule Loklo,** an authentic reconstruction of a village of the indigenous Coast Miwok Indian tribe, and **Morgan Horse Ranch,** the only working horse-breeding farm in the national park system. Afterward, take a short stroll along the **Earthquake Trail,** an informative 0.7-mile walk along the infamous San Andreas Fault, and, time permitting, the 0.7-mile self-guided **Woodpecker Nature Trail.**

By far the most popular, and crowded, attraction at Point Reyes National Seashore is the venerable **Point Reyes Lighthouse,** located at the westernmost tip of Point Reyes. The drive along on the **Sir Francis Drake Highway** is worth the trip, a 45-minute, 20-mile scenic excursion through rolling, windswept meadows and working dairy ranches (watch out for cows on the road). When the fog burns off, the lighthouse and the headlands provide a fantastic lookout point for spying common mures, basking sea lions, and gray whales as they make their southward and northward migration along the coast from December through March.

If there's still some time left in your day, the **Point Reyes Bird Observatory**—an ornithological research organization located at the southeast end the park—is a must for bird-watchers, or you can rent a mountain bike in Olema and pedal the popular **Olema Valley Trail.** And don't think your day ends at nightfall, either, because **Tomales Bay Kayaking** offers sunset and full-moon guided paddle trips on placid Tomales Bay (see "Other Sports & Activities," below).

Some of the park's best, and least crowded, highlights can only be approached on foot through hiking trails, such as **Alamere Falls,** a freshwater stream that cascades down a 40-foot bluff onto Wildcat Beach, or **Tomales Point Trail,** which passes through the Tule Elk Reserve, a protected haven for roaming herds of tule elk that once numbered in the thousands. These trails usually end up being all-day outings, however, so they're best for those who plan to spend a day simply hiking in the park.

Exploring the Park by Car

The main scenic road in the park is the Sir Francis Drake Highway (described above in "Seeing the Highlights in a Day"). An excellent turnoff on this road is Mount Vision Road, which winds its way up to the Mount Vision Overlook for a panoramic view of the entire peninsula.

There are two other major roads within the park. Pierce Point Road forks north from the Sir Francis Drake Highway toward Tomales Point, passing Tomales Bay State Park (a popular picnicking area that offers relatively warm and safe waters) and Abbotts Lagoon (a bird-watchers' paradise) before ending at McClures Beach. The other major road is Limantour Road, which bisects the park before ending at Limantour Beach, a popular spot for beachcombing, picnicking, and bird watching at nearby Estero de Limantour. Both these roads are primarily used to access trailheads and beaches, but can also double as scenic alternatives to touring Sir Francis Drake Highway.

Organized Tours & Ranger Programs

Rangers lead special programs within Point Reyes National Seashore year-round, including wildlife hikes, local history lessons, and habitat restoration. All tours are free, but you'll need to call the **Bear Valley Visitor Center** (☎ **415/663-1092**) for up-to-date schedules. It's open weekdays 9am to 5pm and weekends 8am to 5pm.

Other groups such as the **Golden Gate Audubon Society** (☎ **510/843-2222**) and **Oceanic Society Expeditions** (☎ **415/474-3385**) run special excursions and outings to the park. During whale season the Oceanic Society takes naturalist-led whale-watching boats from the San Francisco Marina to Point Reyes every weekend that the weather permits. The 6-hour trip costs $50 for adults and $48 for kids and senior citizens. No children under 10 are allowed.

Historic & Man-Made Attractions

One of the two most popular man-made attractions at Point Reyes National Seashore is **Kule Loklo,** a restored Coast Miwok Indian village, which often hosts displays of dancing, basket-making, Native American cooking, and indigenous art. The other is the Park Service's **Morgan Horse Ranch,** the only working horse-breeding farm in the National Park System. Both are located near the **Bear Valley Visitor Center** on Bear Valley Road and are open year-round.

But if you really want to escape the crowds and have some stinky man-made entertainment, head to **Johnson's Oyster Farm** (☎ **415/669-1149**), off Sir Francis Drake Boulevard, about 6 miles west of Inverness (open Tuesday to Sunday 8am to 4pm). Located in the park, right on the edge of Drakes Estero (a large saltwater lagoon within the Point Reyes Peninsula that produces nearly 20% of California's commercial oyster yield), Johnson's may look and smell like a dump, with its cluster of trailer homes, shacks, and oyster tanks surrounded by huge piles of oyster shells, but those tasty bivalves don't come any fresher or cheaper. The popular modus operandi is 1) to buy a couple of dozen, 2) head for an empty campsite along the bay, 3) fire up the barbecue pit (don't forget the charcoal), 4) split and barbecue the little guys, 5) slather them in Johnson's special sauce, and then 6) slurp 'em down.

Day Hikes

There's a little of everything for hikers here—32,000 acres, crisscrossed by 70 miles of trails, are set aside as wilderness where no motor vehicles or bicycles are allowed. The principal trailheads are Bear Valley, Palomarin, Five Brooks, and Estero. All have adequate parking. I strongly advise that you pick up a free trail map at the visitor center before shoving off.

Bear Valley Trail

8 miles RT. Easy. Access: Bear Valley Trailhead south of the visitor center parking area.

This well-worn trail leads through wooded hillsides until it reaches the shore at Arch Rock, where Coast Creek splashes into the sea through a "sea tunnel" (actually the arch of Arch Rock). This is your best bet for an easy, beautiful walk through the woods to the beach.

Estero Trail

4.5 miles one way. Easy to moderate. Access: Estero Parking Area.

A favorite with birders, this mellow 4.5-mile trail meanders along the edge of Drakes Estero and Limantour Estero (*Estero* is the Spanish word for estuary). The brackish waters here draw flocks of waterfowl and shorebirds as well as many raptors and smaller species. Along the way you cross a dam and a bridge over Home Bay.

Coast Trail

7 miles RT. Easy to moderate. Access: Palomarin Trailhead, just off Mesa Rd. at the southern tip of the park.

Recommended by locals, this trek is one of Point Reyes's prettiest. This section of the trail skirts a cliff offering stunning views and then passes several small lakes and meadows before it reaches Alamere Falls, a freshwater stream that cascades down a 40-foot bluff onto Wildcat Beach.

Easily the longest trail at the national seashore, the Coast Trail continues on for a 15-mile one-way hike along the coast that is usually done in 2 days, camping a third of the way through at Wildcat Beach. (There's another campground at Santa Maria Beach.) The trail ends at the American Youth Hostel. You'll need a second car, however, to shuttle you back to the trailhead where you began.

Tomales Point Trail

4.5 miles one way. Easy to moderate. Access: Parking lot at the end of Pierce Point Rd.

This trail gives hikers a tour of the park's rugged shoreline and also passes through an elk reserve, home to the park's 400-strong herd of tule elk. Watch for their V-shaped tracks on the trail. About halfway through, you come to the highest spot on Pierce Point, where on a clear day you can see over the bay to the Sonoma Coast and Mt. Saint Helena to the northeast.

Stewart Trail

9 miles RT. Moderate. Access: Five Brooks Parking Area.

This trail to Wildcat beach is one of the few unpaved trails in the park open to mountain bikes and is also quite popular with horseback riders. It's quite steep and not nearly as scenic as most other trails.

Abbotts Lagoon Trail

3 miles RT. Easy. Access: Abbotts Lagoon Trailhead Parking Area on Pierce Point Rd.

If you're looking for a short, easy trail located well away from the masses, this is the one. After climbing a small ridge, you're led down to Abbotts Lagoon, a popular watering hole for migratory birds.

Mount Wittenberg Trail

2 miles one way. Difficult. Access: Bear Valley Trailhead.

For the Rambo in your bunch, this huffer-puffer weeds out the weenies due to its steep elevation, peaking at 1,407 feet rather abruptly. Start at the Bear Valley Trailhead, south of the parking area, and turn right on to the Mount Wittenberg Trail after 0.2 mile. The trail up the ridge is steep but rewards hikers with great views back east across the Olema Valley. Instead of turning around directly, if you still have the gas you can loop back along Baldy Trail and take an alternative path such as the Meadow Trail back to Bear Valley Trail, the main route home.

Beaches

The **Great Beach** is one of California's longest. It is also one of the windiest, and home to large and dangerous waves. You can't swim here, but the beachcombing is some of the best in the world. Tide poolers should go to lonely **McClure's Beach** at the end of Pierce Point Road during low tide or hike out to **Chimney Rock,** east of the lighthouse. Swimmers and dog owners will want to stick to **Limantour Beach,** located in the protected lee of Point Reyes. **Kehoe Beach,** in the northwest of the park, is known for its spring wildflower blooms, while **Hearts Desire Beach** at Tomales Bay State Park has the warmest, safest swimming (as well as a $5 per vehicle fee).

Sir Francis Drake reputedly landed the *Pelican* (later rechristened the *Golden Hind*) on the sandy shore of Drakes Bay in June 1579, to replenish supplies and make repairs before sailing home to England. **Drakes Beach** is now home to the Kenneth C. Patrick Visitor Center and **Drakes Beach Cafe** (Thursday to Monday 10am to 6pm; ☎ **415/669-1297**), the only food concession in the park, famous for its great oysters. This beach is good for swimming and beach fires.

Other Sports & Activities

Whale Watching. Each year, gray whales (it's the barnacles that make them appear gray) migrate from their winter breeding grounds in the warm waters off the Baja Coast to their summer feeding grounds in Alaska. You can observe them as they undertake this enormous

10,000-mile journey from just about anywhere within Point Reyes National Seashore, though the most popular vantage point is at the Point Reyes Lighthouse.

During peak season (December to March), you might see dozens of whales from the lighthouse, where the **Lighthouse Visitor Center** (☎ **415/669-1534,** closed Tuesday, Wednesday, and Christmas) offers great displays on whale migration and maritime history. During this period, the Park Service runs a shuttle from Drakes Beach to the **Point Reyes Lighthouse,** where watchers have been known to see as many as 100 whales in a single afternoon. Even if the whales don't materialize, the lighthouse itself, a fabulous old structure teetering high above the sea at the tip of a promontory, is worth a visit. Two other spots, Chimney Rock, to the east of the lighthouse, and Tomales Point, at the northern end of the park, offer just as many whales without the crowds.

If you're lucky, you'll catch the whales performing a few of their classic moves. You may see their powerful flukes rising out of the water in preparation for a dive. You'll certainly see their spouts, formed by the condensed moisture of their exhalation, which can rise 10 to 15 feet in the air and be seen from 10 miles away. Occasionally you may see their heads popping out above the surface for a look around (in a maneuver whale watchers call "spyhopping"), or their whole bodies lurching right out of the water in what's called a breach. Why they perform the last two is a mystery. Some speculate that when they spyhop they're actually checking coastal landmarks.

Biking. As most ardent Bay Area mountain bikers know, Point Reyes National Seashore has some of the finest mountain-bike trails in the region—narrow dirt paths winding through densely forested knolls and ending with spectacular ocean views. A trail map is a must (available for free at the Bear Valley Visitor Center) since many of the park trails are off-limits to bikes. *Note:* Bicycles are forbidden on the wilderness area trails, and plotting a course exclusively on the bike trails can be tricky, so plan your route well in advance. The Abbotts Lagoon Trail, the Stewart Trail, the Estero Trail, the Olema Valley Trail, and part of the Bear Valley Trail are all open to bikes.

If you didn't bring your own rig, you can rent a mountain bike at **Trail Head Rentals** in Olema (☎ **415/663-1958**), which rents nice Fisher mountain bikes for about $24 a day and also is a good source of trail information.

Bird Watching. During Audubon's annual Christmas bird count, Point Reyes is regularly found to have the largest concentration of diverse bird species in the continental United States—approximately 350. Popular bird-watching spots are Abbotts Lagoon and Estero de Limantour, or you can hang out with the pros at the **Point Reyes Bird Observatory** (☎ **415/868-1221**), one of the few full-time ornithological research stations in the United States, located at the southeast end of the park on Mesa Road. This is where ornithologists keep an eye on approximately 350 feathered species. Admission to the visitor center and nature trail is free, and visitors are welcome to observe the tricky process of catching and banding the birds. (Open daily 15 minutes after sunrise to sunset. Banding hours vary, call for exact times; ☎ **415/868-0655.**)

Kayaking. Kayak trips, including 3-hour sunset outings, 3½-hour full-moon paddles, yoga tours, day trips, and longer excursions, are organized by **Tomales Bay Kayaking** (☎ **415/663-1743**), open Friday to Sunday, 9am to 6pm, and by appointment. Instruction, clinics, and boat delivery are available, and all ages and levels are welcome. Prices start at $45 for tours. Rentals begin at $25 for one person, $35 for two. Don't worry: The kayaks are very stable and there are no waves to contend with because you'll be paddling through placid Tomales Bay, a haven for migrating birds and marine mammals. The launching point is located on Highway 1 at the Marshall Boatworks in Marshall, 8 miles north of Point Reyes Station.

Camping

Camping within the park is limited to four hike-in camps. Wildcat Camp, near Alamere Falls, is a 6.5-mile hike from Bear Valley Trailhead. Coast Camp is on an open bluff, 2.3 beach miles west of the Limantour beach parking lot. These camps near the sea are often foggy and damp, so bring a good tent and sleeping bag. Sky Camp (1.7 miles from Sky Trailhead on Limantour Road) and Glen Camp (4.6 miles from the Bear Valley Trailhead) are set in the woods away from the sea, more protected from the coastal elements.

In all camps, individual sites hold up to eight people and have picnic tables and food lockers. Pit toilets and drinking water are available. Camping is $10 per site per night; permits are required and stays are limited to 4 days. Sites can be reserved up to 2 months in advance by calling ☎ **415/663-8054** Monday to Friday 9am to 2pm. Dogs are not permitted on any trails or in the campgrounds.

Just outside the park is the **Olema Ranch Campground** (☎ **415/663-8001**), which has 200 sites for tents or motor homes, as well as rest rooms, showers, a Laundromat, and nearby restaurants and a grocery store. Expect to pay about $18 per couple a night for this prime Marin property, located about 0.5 mile north of downtown Olema on Highway 1. Reservations recommended.

Accommodations

INSIDE THE PARK

Point Reyes Hostel

Off Limantour Rd., P.O. Box 247, Point Reyes Station, CA 94956. ☎ **415/663-8811.** 44 bunks, 1 private rm. $12 per person. MC, V. Reception hrs daily 7:30–9:30am and 4:30–9:30pm.

Located deep inside Point Reyes National Seashore, this beautiful old ranch-style complex has 44 dormitory-style accommodations, including one room that's reserved for families (though at least one child must be 5 years old or younger). There are also two common rooms, each warmed by wood-burning stoves during chilly nights, as well as a fully equipped kitchen, barbecue (bring your own charcoal), and patio. If you don't mind sharing your sleeping quarters with strangers, this is a $12 per person deal that can't be beat. Reservations (and earplugs) are strongly recommended. The maximum stay is 3 nights.

NEAR THE PARK

There are four towns in and around the Point Reyes National Seashore boundary—Olema, Point Reyes Station, Inverness Park, and Inverness—but they are all so close together that it really doesn't matter where you stay, because you'll always be within a stone's throw of the park. While the accommodations in Point Reyes are excellent, they're also expensive, with most rooms averaging

Campground	Total Sites	RV Hookups	Dump Station	Toilets	Drinking Water
Coast Camp	12	No	No	Yes	Yes
Glen Camp	12	No	No	Yes	Yes
Olema Ranch Campground	203	Yes	Yes	Yes	Yes
Sky Camp	12	No	No	Yes	Yes
Wildcat Camp	12	No	No	Yes	Yes

$100 per night. Be sure to make your reservation far in advance during the summer and holidays, and dress warm: Point Reyes gets darn chilly at night.

Note: If you're having trouble finding a vacancy in Point Reyes, call the **West Marin Network** (☎ **415/663-9543**) for information on available lodgings.

Bear Valley Inn

88 Bear Valley Rd., Olema, CA 94950. ☎ **415/663-1777.** 3 rms, none with bath. $75–$135 double. Rates include breakfast. AE, MC, V.

Ron and JoAnne Nowell's venerable two-story 1899 Victorian has survived everything from a major earthquake to a recent forest fire—which is lucky for you, because you'll be hard pressed to find a better B&B for the price in Point Reyes. Granted, the Bear Valley Inn isn't perfect: The rooms lack private baths and the main highway is a tad too close. But it's loaded with Victorian charm, right down to the profusion of flowers and vines outside and comfy chairs fronting a toasty-warm wood stove inside. It's in a great location, too, with three good restaurants only a block away, and the entire national seashore at your doorstep. Ron, who also runs a mountain-bike rental shop next door, can set you up wheel-wise for about $25 a day and point you in the right direction.

Blackthorne Inn

266 Vallejo Ave. (off Sir Francis Drake Blvd., south of Inverness), P.O. Box 712, Inverness, CA 94937. ☎ **415/663-8621.** 5 rms (3 with bath). $105–$195 double without bath, $155–$195 double with bath. Rates include buffet breakfast. MC, V.

This elaborate redwood home, with its octagonal widow's walk, spiral staircase, turrets, and multiple decks, looks more like a superdeluxe tree house than a B&B. My favorite, and the most expensive, unit is the Eagle's Nest, an octagonal room enclosed by glass and topped with a private sundeck with a catwalk leading to the private outhouse. The largest room is the Forest View Studio, virtually a suite with a deck, while the smallest room is the Hideaway, which has a private entrance and a sitting area facing the woods. Both are furnished with wicker and decorated with floral fabrics and modern lithographs. The main sitting room in the house features a large stone fireplace, skylight, and stained-glass windows and is surrounded by a huge deck. Guests have use of the hot tub on the top deck.

Manka's Inverness Lodge & Restaurant

P.O. Box 1110, on Argyle St. (off Sir Francis Drake Blvd., 3 blocks north of downtown Inverness), Inverness, CA 94937. ☎ **800/58-LODGE** or 415/669-1034. 8 rms, 2 cabins. $115–$200 rm; $185–$225 cabin. MC, V.

This immediately lovable old hunting lodge is one of my favorite places to stay and dine on the coast. Every room resembles the sort of rustic old mountain cabin you read about in Jack London novels, and the restaurant has that perfect balance of countrified charm and

Showers	Fire Pits/ Grills	Laundry	Public Phone	Reserve	Fees	Open
No	**Yes**	**No**	**No**	**Yes**	**$10**	**Year-round**
No	**Yes**	**No**	**No**	**Yes**	**$10**	**Year-round**
Yes	**Yes**	**Yes**	**Yes**	**Yes**	**$10–$18**	**Year-round**
No	**Yes**	**No**	**No**	**Yes**	**$10**	**Year-round**
No	**Yes**	**No**	**No**	**Yes**	**$10**	**Year-round**

polished refinement. In addition to the standard rooms in the main lodge (which are anything but standard with their tree-limb bedsteads, billowy down comforters, and bucolic furnishings), there are two luxuriously appointed cabins adjacent to the inn, and a quartet of smaller, less expensive rooms in the redwood annex.

For the ultimate romantic splurge, inquire about their three secluded guest houses: Grizzly Lodge, Boat House, and Chicken Ranch. The lodge's reputation is built on its restaurant, which dominates the bottom floor (see "Dining," below).

Point Reyes Country Inn & Stables

12050 Hwy. 1 (P.O. Box 501), Point Reyes Station, CA 94956. ☎ **415/663-9696;** fax 415/663-8888. 5 rms, 2 studios. $85–$160, $25 additional guest; $10–$15 per horse. Rates include breakfast. MC, V.

Are you and your horse dreaming of a country getaway to the Point Reyes National Seashore? Then book a room at Point Reyes Country Inn & Stables, a five-bedroom, ranch-style home on 4 acres that offers pastoral accommodations for two- and four-legged guests (horses only). Each room has a private bath, either a balcony or a garden, and plenty of hiking and riding trails. The innkeepers have also added two new studios with kitchens above the stables, and rent out two cottages on Tomales Bay equipped with decks, stocked kitchens, fireplaces, and a shared dock. Breakfast is included with all rooms.

Dining

The Gray Whale

12781 Sir Francis Drake Blvd., Inverness. ☎ **415/669-1244.** Main courses $5–$10. MC, V. Daily 11am–8pm. ITALIAN.

For more than a decade The Gray Whale cafe has been a popular pit stop for Bay Area residents heading to the lighthouse at Point Reyes. Why so popular? First off, it's cheap: Sandwiches such as the roasted eggplant with pesto and mozzarella are only $5, as are most of the salads and pastas. Second, it's pretty good: Personal favorites are the specialty pizzas, such as the Californian (artichoke hearts, fresh basil, and tomatoes) and the Vegetarian (baked eggplant, roasted onions and romas, broccoli, and piles of freshly grated Parmesan cheese). Veteran hikers and mountain bikers stop by for an espresso booster, sipped on the small patio overlooking the block-long town of Inverness.

Manka's Inverness Lodge & Restaurant

On Argyle St. (off Sir Francis Drake Blvd., 3 blocks north of downtown Inverness), Inverness. ☎ **415/669-1034.** Main courses $18–$22. MC, V. AMERICAN.

The specialty of this fine restaurant is game and fish, including oysters from Tomales Bay. The limited menu might feature pheasant with a Madeira jus, mashed potatoes and a wild huckleberry jam, black buck antelope chops with sweet corn salsa, or everybody's favorite, pan-seared elk tenderloin. It's open for dinner Thursday through Monday with a brunch on Sunday.

Station House Cafe

11180 Main St., Point Reyes Station. ☎ **415/663-1515.** Reservations recommended. Breakfast $4.45–$7.50; lunch $5.50–$9.50; dinner $6–$19. DISC, MC, V. Daily 8am–10pm. AMERICAN.

A local favorite, the Station House Cafe is known for its good food and animated atmosphere, particularly when the live music fires up on weekends. For breakfast, try the fritatta with asparagus, goat cheese, and olives, which always seems to taste better while sitting outside on the shaded garden patio. Luncheon specials might include two-cheese polenta served with sautéed fresh spinach and grilled garlic-buttered tomatoes. The menu changes every week, but always features locally grown beef and a good selection of fresh fish. For dinner, start with a platter of local oysters and mussels, followed by a braised lamb shank (made with Guinness Stout) or one of their old standbys such as meat loaf with garlic mashed potatoes or fish-and-chips with country fries and coleslaw. Rounding out the menu are homemade chili, steamed clams, and fresh soup made daily. The cafe has an extensive list of fine California wines, plus local and imported beers.

Taqueria La Quinta

11285 Hwy. 1 (at 3rd and Main sts.), Point Reyes Station. ☎ **415/663-8868.** Main courses $4–$6. No credit cards. Wed–Mon 11am–9pm. MEXICAN.

Fresh, good, fast, and cheap: What more could you ask for? Taqueria La Quinta has been one of my favorite lunch stops in downtown Point Reyes for years and years. A huge selection of Mexican-American standards are posted above the counter, but those in the know inquire about the seafood specials. Since it's all self-serve, you can skip the tip, but watch out for the salsa—it's *hot.*

32

REDWOOD NATIONAL & STATE PARKS

by Matthew R. Poole

WHEN HE WAS GOVERNOR OF CALIFORNIA, RONALD REAGAN once said that if you've seen one redwood, you've seen them all. He couldn't have been more wrong. Redwood National and State Parks is living proof. While he was right that a 366-foot-tall coast redwood (the world's tallest, located in the Tall Trees Grove) does in fact look pretty much like the next one, Reagan was guilty of not seeing the forest for the trees.

It's impossible to explain the feeling you get in the old-growth forests of Redwood National and State Parks without resorting to Alice-in-Wonderland comparisons. Like a tropical rain forest, the redwood forest is a multistoried affair, the tall trees being only the top layer. Everything is big, misty, and primeval; flowering bushes cover the ground, 10-foot-tall ferns line the creeks, and the smells are rich and musty. It's so Jurassic Park that you can't help but half-expect to turn the corner and see a dinosaur.

When Archibald Menzies first noted the botanical existence of the coast redwood in 1794, more than 2 million acres of redwood forest carpeted California and Oregon. By 1965 heavy logging had reduced that to 300,000 acres and it was obvious something had to be done if any redwoods were to survive. The state created several parks around individual groves in the 1920s, and in 1968 the federal government created Redwood National Park. In May 1994, the National Park Service and the California Department of Parks and Recreation signed an agreement to manage the four contiguous redwood parks cooperatively, hence the name Redwood National *and* State Parks.

The 105,516-acre park offers a lesson in bioregionalism. When the park was first created to protect the biggest coast redwoods, logging companies continued to cut much of the surrounding area, sometimes right up to the park boundary. Unfortunately, redwoods in the park began to suffer as the quality of the Redwood Creek drainage declined from upstream logging, so in 1978 the government purchased a major section of the watershed, having learned that you can't preserve individual trees without preserving the ecosystem they depend on.

Though logging of old-growth redwoods in the region is still a major bone of contention between the government, private landowners, and environmentalists, it's an auspicious sign that there *is* contention, a sign that perhaps we have all learned to see the forest *and* the trees for what they are: the undisputed monarchs of all living things, thriving links to the Age of Dinosaurs and humble reminders that the era of mankind is but a hiccup in time to the venerable *Sequoia sempervirens.*

Avoiding the Crowds. The parks include three major features—the ocean setting, old-growth forests, and the prairies. Not many people discover the latter. These bald hills (called "prairies," here) offer excellent views over the tops of the redwoods and down to the ocean. Plus, if you are chilled by the coastal environment and hiking in the shade of the redwoods, the bald hills in contrast are hot and sunny in the summertime. The prairie region also offers many opportunities to explore the park by either hiking to the historic barns used during the ranching days before the park's establishment, or visiting the School House Peak Firelook to check out the view, or hiking to the valley bottom along the Dolason Prairie Trail.

Just the Facts

GETTING THERE & GATEWAYS

The parks are located on a narrow strip near the coast in northern California, about 375 miles north of San Francisco. There are three major routes to the Redwood Coast. U.S. 101 travels up from San Francisco and down from Brookings, Oregon, to traverse much of the length of the parks. U.S. 199 leads from the north of the park to Grants Pass, Oregon, to the northeast. The main route to the east is Calif. 299, which goes from Redding, California, to meet up with U.S. 101 south of the park.

If you're heading from the south, you'll want to stop in Orick. If you're heading from the north (Oregon), you'll want to stop in Crescent City. Why? Because both towns have excellent information centers crammed with useful (and important) information about the Redwood National and State Parks, including free maps.

The Nearest Airports. **Eureka-Arcata Airport** is located in McKinleyville, 28 miles south of the Redwood Information Center near Orick. **Crescent City Airport** is located in Crescent City, at the north end of the park. Both are served by United Airlines. Much further afield, **San Francisco International Airport** (☎ **415/761-0800**) is located 14 miles south of downtown San Francisco on U.S. 101.

Renting a Car. All major national car-rental chains have offices at San Francisco International Airport. Rentals are also available at both Eureka-Arcata and Crescent City airports.

GETTING INFORMATION BEFORE YOUR TRIP

For advance information, contact **Redwood National and State Parks,** 1111 Second St., Crescent City, CA 95531 (☎ 707/464-6101), or visit their Web site at **www.nps.gov/redw**.

VISITOR CENTERS

The southern gateway to the Redwood National and State Parks is the town of Orick, on U.S. 101. You can't miss it: Just look for the dozens of burl stands alongside the road. Here you'll find the sleek **Redwood Information Center,** P.O. Box 7, Orick, CA 95555 (☎ **707/464-6101,** ext. 5265), one of California's rare examples of well-placed tax dollars (though some may dispute this since it is near a floodplain and within a tsunami zone). If you plan to spend any amount of time exploring the park, stop here first and pick up a free map; the displays of fauna and wildlife aren't too bad, either. It's open daily from 9am to 5pm year-round. If you missed the Redwood Information Center, don't worry: About 7 miles further north on U.S. 101 is the **Prairie Creek Visitor Center,** which carries all

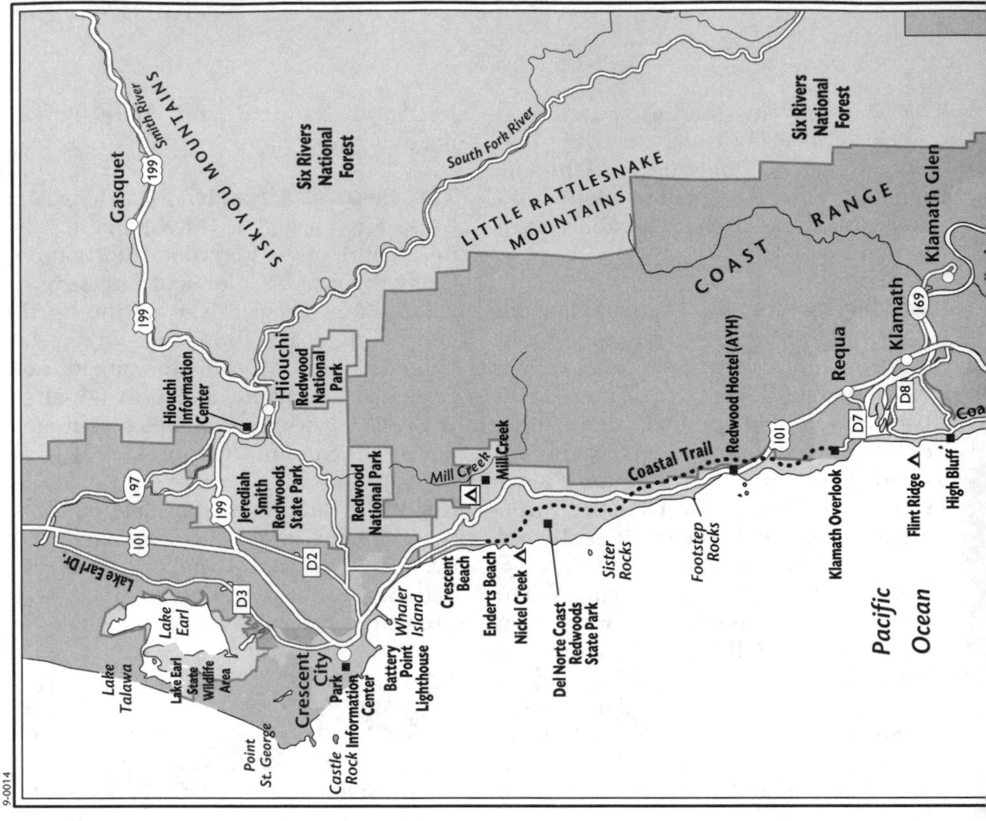

the same maps and information. It's open daily from 9am to 5pm in the summer, daily 10am to 2pm in winter; ☎ **707/464-6101,** ext. 5300.

The northern gateway to the Redwood National and State Parks is Crescent City. This "city" is a real eyesore (at least along U.S. 101), but it's your best bet for a cheap motel, gas, fast food, and outdoor supplies. Before touring the park, pick up a free guide at the **Redwood National and State Parks Headquarters and Information Center,** 1111 2nd St. (at K Street), Crescent City, CA 95531 (☎ **707/464-6101,** ext. 5064). It's open daily 8am to 5pm.

If you happen to be arriving via U.S. 199 from Oregon, the rangers manning the **Hiouchi Information Station** (☎ **707/464-6101,** ext. 5067) and **Jedediah Smith Visitor Center** (☎ **707/464-6101,** ext. 5113) can also supply you with the necessary maps and advice. Both are open daily in the summer months from 9am to 5pm and when staffing is available in the spring and fall months.

ENTRANCE & CAMPING FEES

Admission to the national park is free, but to enter any of the three state parks (which contain the best redwood groves), you'll have to pay a $5 day-use fee, which is good at all three.

Camping fees range from $12 to $16 for drive-in sites. Walk-in sites are free, though a backcountry permit is required.

SPECIAL REGULATIONS & WARNINGS

The north coast used to be one of those places where people left their keys in the ignition in case someone had to move their car. But no more. Lock your car and put valuables in the trunk or take them with you.

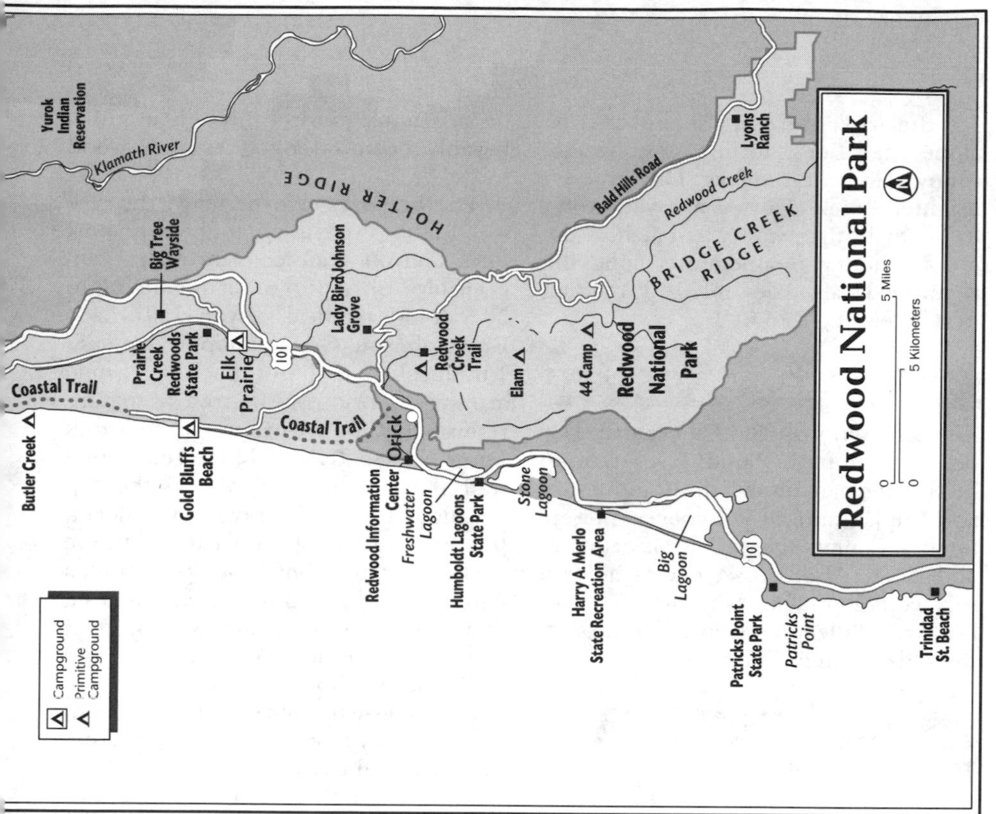

◆ Don't disturb any abandoned baby seals or sea lions you may encounter on the beach. The mother may be preoccupied with finding lunch, and she won't come back until you leave. In fact, you may be fined up to $10,000 for your good intentions. However, if a pup looks injured or in danger, call the **Mammal Marine Center** at ☎ **707/465-MAML.**

◆ On the beach, be aware of tidal fluctuations. Swimming is hazardous because of cold water and strong rip currents.

◆ Watch for poison oak, particularly in coastal areas.

◆ Follow park regulations regarding bears and food storage; all food and scented personal care items should be secured and hidden from view in vehicles, placed in bear-proof lockers (located at each drive-in campsite), or hung from trees. Never feed bears or wild animals (remember: A fed bear is a dead bear). Roosevelt elk are wild and unpredictable; do not approach them on foot.

◆ Water from natural sources should be treated before drinking.

◆ Tree limbs can fall during high winds, especially in old-growth forests.

SEASONS & CLIMATE

Frankly, all those huge trees and ferns wouldn't have survived for 1,000 years if it didn't rain one heck of a lot. Count on rain or at least a heavy drizzle during your visit, then get ecstatic when the sun comes out—it can happen anytime. Spring is the best season for wildflowers. Summer is foggy (it's called "the June gloom" but often includes July and August). Fall is the warmest, sunniest (relatively) time of all, and winter isn't bad, though it is cold and wet (try 69 inches of rain on the average), and some park facilities are closed. A storm can provide the most introspective time to see the park, since you'll probably be alone. And after a storm passes through, sunny days often follow. On an even brighter note, chances are you won't freeze to death or wither and melt, as the average annual temperature along the Redwood Coast varies only 16°F, ranging from a low of 45° to 61°F.

SEASONAL EVENTS

Annual events include an Earth Day beach cleanup, the Smith River cleanup in May, the banana slug derby in August, and the Jammin' at Jed concert in September. Contact the park for exact dates and times. Also, Crescent City holds a surf contest in October, and the park holds a candlelight celebration through the old growth in December.

USEFUL PUBLICATIONS

The Visitor Guide published each summer describes all the activities taking place throughout the parks, including stories on elk, bear, cougars, and resource management issues, plus a list of summer programs, from kayaking to guided walks and evening talks.

Seeing the Highlights in a Day

Before you venture into the Redwood National and State Parks, first stop by the **Redwood Information Center** in Orick (or the **Redwood National and State Parks Headquarters and Information Center** in Crescent City, depending on which direction you're coming from) and pick up a free official map and guide, which will clue you in to all the parks' main attractions.

Next, take the don't-miss detour along U.S. 101 called the **Newton B. Drury Scenic Parkway,** which passes through dazzling groves of redwoods and elk-filled meadows before leading back onto the highway 8 miles later. Two other spectacular drives are the **Coastal Drive,** which winds through stands of redwoods and offers grand views of the Pacific, and **Howland Hill Road,** an unforgettable journey through an unbelievably beautiful old-growth redwood forest.

The best way to experience the redwoods, however, is on foot. The short **Fern Canyon Trail** leads through a fantastically lush grotto of ferns clinging to 50-foot-high vertical canyon walls. **Lady Bird Johnson Grove Loop** is an easy, 1-hour self-guided tour that loops 1 mile around a glorious lush grove of mature redwoods. Closer to shore is the **Yurok Loop Nature Trail,** a 1-mile self-guided trail that gradually climbs to the top of rugged sea bluff (with wonderful panoramic views of the Pacific), but the best trail of all is **Boy Scout Tree Trail,** a 6-mile round-trip trail through a lush, cool, damp forest brimming with giant ferns and majestic redwoods.

If you are more of a type A person, take a **Jet-Boat Tour** up the Klamath River Estuary to view bear, deer, elk, and more along the river banks, or a half day ranger-led **kayak tour** around the Klamath River Estuary (there is a fee for this, and reservations are required).

But the real reason you came here is to see the world's tallest tree, right? To do this you'll first have to get a permit from the Redwood Information Center near Orick to travel the Tall Trees Trail. This 4-hour drive/hike expedition is limited to the first 50 permits each day, so get yours early. It's an experience you'll never forget.

Exploring the Park by Car

A number of scenic drives cut through the park. Steep, windy **Bald Hills Road** (located a few miles north of Orick on U.S. 101) will take you back into the Redwood Creek watershed and up to the shoulder of 3,097-foot Schoolhouse Peak. Don't even think of driving a motor home up here or pulling a trailer. A few miles further north is the **Lost Man Creek Trail,** a short, unpaved scenic drive through the redwood forest. The 1.5-mile trip leads past the World Heritage Site dedication area and on to a cascade on Lost Man Creek. Again, anyone with a motor home or pulling a trailer can forget this one.

A don't-miss detour along U.S. 101 is the **Newton B. Drury Scenic Parkway,** which passes through dazzling groves of redwoods and elk-filled meadows before leading back onto the highway 8 miles later. While you're cruising along, take the **Cal-Barrel Road** turnoff, a narrow, packed-gravel road located just north of the Prairie Creek Visitor Center off the Newton B. Drury Scenic Parkway. It offers a spectacular 3-mile tour through an old-growth redwood forest (no trailers or motor homes).

One of the premier coastal drives on the Redwood Coast starts at the mouth of the Klamath River and runs 8 miles south toward Prairie Creek Redwoods State Park. The narrow, partially paved **Coastal Drive** winds through stands of redwoods, with spectacular views of the Pacific and numerous pullouts for picture-taking (sea lions and pelicans abound) and short hikes. Keep an eye out for the World War II radar station, disguised as a farmhouse and barn. If you're heading south on U.S. 101, take the Alder Camp Road exit just south of the Klamath River Bridge and follow the signs to the Mouth of Klamath. North-bound travelers should take the Redwood National and State Parks Coastal Drive exit off the Newton B. Drury Scenic Parkway. Campers and cars with trailers are not advised.

The most amazing car-friendly trail in all of the Redwood National and State Parks, however, is the hidden, well-maintained gravel road called **Howland Hill Road** that winds for about 12 miles through Jedediah Smith Redwoods State Park. It's an unforgettable journey through a spectacular old-growth redwood forest—considered by many one of the most beautiful areas in the world. To get there from U.S. 101, keep an eye out for the BP gas station at the south end of Crescent City; just before the station, turn right on Elk Valley Road, and follow it to Howland Hill Road, which will be on your right. After driving through the park, you'll end up at U.S. 199 near the town of Hiouchi, and from there it's a short jaunt west to get back to U.S. 101. Plan at least 2 to 3 hours for the 45-mile round-trip, or all day if you want to do some hiking or mountain biking in the park. Trailers and motor homes are not recommended.

Organized Tours & Ranger Programs

The parks run interpretive programs—ranging from trees to tide pools, legends to landforms—at the Hiouchi and Redwood information centers and in the Crescent Beach area during summer months, as well as year-round at the park headquarters in Crescent City (☎ **707/464-6101,** ext. 5064). Park rangers lead campfire programs and numerous other activities throughout the year as well. Call the **Parks Information Service** for both the national and state parks (☎ **707/464-6101,** ext. 5265) to get current schedules and events. There's also a ranger-led **kayaking tour** in the summer (see "Other Sports & Activities," below).

Day Hikes

Regardless of how short or long your hike may be, dress warm and bring plenty of water and sunscreen. Backpackers along the Redwood Creek Trail must get a free backcountry permit for an overnight stay at any information center in the parks. *Note:* Pets are prohibited on all of the parks' trails.

Fern Canyon Trail

1.5 miles RT. Easy. Access: From U.S. 101, take the Davison Rd. exit (at Rolf's Park Cafe), which follows along Gold Bluffs Beach to the Fern Canyon parking lot. Day-use fee is $5. No motor homes or trailers more than 24 feet long.

This short, heavily traveled trail leads to an unbelievably lush grotto of lady, deer, chain, sword, five-finger, and maidenhair ferns clinging to 50-foot-high vertical walls divided by a babbling brook. It's only about a 1.5-mile walk from Gold Bluffs Beach, but be prepared to scramble across the creek several times on your way via small footbridges.

Lady Bird Johnson Grove Loop

1 mile RT. Easy. Access: Lady Bird Johnson Grove. Take the Bald Hills Rd. exit off U.S. 101, 0.5 mile north of Orick.

Here's an easy, self-guided tour that loops around a glorious lush grove of mature redwoods. It's the site at which the national park was dedicated by Lady Bird Johnson in 1968. The following year it was named for her.

Yurok Loop Nature Trail

1 mile RT. Easy. Access: The trailhead is 6.5 miles north of the Klamath River Bridge on U.S. 101 at Lagoon Creek.

This self-guided trail gradually climbs to the top of rugged sea bluff (with wonderful panoramic views of the Pacific) before looping back to the parking lot. If someone's willing to act as shuttle driver, have him or her meet you at the Requa Trailhead and take the 4-mile coastal trail to the mouth of the Klamath.

Big Tree Trail

0.25 mile RT. Easy. Access: Take the Big Tree turnoff along the Newton B. Drury Scenic Parkway.

For the nonhiker in your group, this is a short paved trail leading to a really big tree.

Enderts Beach Trail

1.2 miles RT. Easy. Access: The trailhead is at the end of Enderts Rd. at the south end of Crescent City (about 3 miles south on U.S. 101 from downtown, across from the Ocean Way Motel).

This short 1.2-mile round-trip trail leads down to Enderts Beach. In the summer, free 1½- to 2-hour ranger-guided tide pool and seashore walks are offered when the tides are right. You start at the beach parking lot, descend to the beach, and explore rocky tide pools at its southern end. For specific tour times, call ☎ **707/464-6101,** ext. 5064. *Here's a tip:* Also along Enderts Road is one of the prettiest picnic sites on the California coast: the **Crescent Beach Overlook.** Pack a picnic lunch at Good Harvest Cafe (see "Picnic & Camping Supplies," below), park at the Overlook, lay your blanket on the grass, and admire the ocean view atop your personal 500-foot bluff.

Tall Trees Trail

1.3 miles one way. Moderate. Access: The trailhead is at the end of Tall Trees Access Rd., off Bald Hills Rd. Permit required.

To see the world's tallest tree—some 365.5 feet tall, 14 feet in diameter, and more than 600 years old—you'll first have to go to the Redwood Information Center near Orick to obtain a free map and permit to drive to the Tall Trees Grove Trailhead. (*Note:* Only 50 permits are issued per day on a first-come, first-served basis.) After driving to the trailhead, you have to walk a steep 1.3 miles down into the grove, but what a small price to see tallest tree in the world. By the way, the average time spent gawking at the world's largest tree is 1 minute 40 seconds, even though the whole expedition takes about 4 hours.

Boy Scout Tree Trail

3 miles RT. Easy. Access: Ask for directions and a map at the Jedediah Smith Information Center.

After taking this 3-mile round-trip trail through Jedediah Smith Redwoods State Park, you'll understand why an activist like Woody Harrelson would chain himself to the Golden Gate Bridge to protest logging old-growth forest. This is nature primeval, a lush, cool, damp forest brimming with giant ferns and majestic redwoods. It's truly an emotional experience just being here.

Friendship Ridge, Coastal Loop Trail

7.5 miles RT. Moderate. Access: Fern Canyon Trailhead on Davison Rd.

This is possibly the most varied and beautiful hike in Redwood National Park. Beginning at the Fern Canyon Trailhead, you'll follow the Coastal Loop Trail north, then veer right and follow the Friendship Ridge Trail. For the next 3 miles you'll walk through a magical fern and redwood forest, then join the West Ridge Trail through old-growth forest to Butler Creek Camp and back south along the Coastal Loop Trail.

Exploring the Backcountry

The long, beautiful **Coastal Trail,** which runs the entire length of the parks' coastal section and as near the ocean as possible, can either be hiked in a day in small segments, or as a great 3- or 4-day trip using several backcountry camps on the route. One of the nicest runs is from Crescent Beach south into the Del Norte Coast Redwoods State Park. A permit is required if you stay overnight at Butler Creek or along Redwood Creek.

Redwood Creek Trail

16 miles RT. Moderate to difficult. Access: The trailhead is at the end of Redwood Creek access road, off Bald Hills Rd.

This hike is a beauty, passing through Tall Trees Grove (where the tallest trees in the world grow on the banks of Redwood Creek), periodic meadows, new-growth forests, and awesome vantage points overlooking the Grove. You'll camp along the fine sandbars of Redwood Creek. The bridges on Redwood Creek are only installed from May 15 to September 15, and from the end of October to the beginning of April heavy rains make creek crossings extremely dangerous.

Other Sports & Activities

Wildlife Viewing. One of the most striking aspects of **Prairie Creek Redwoods State Park** is its herd of **Roosevelt elk,** usually found in the appropriately named Elk Prairie in the southern end of the park. These gigantic beasts can weigh up to 1,000 pounds. The bulls carry huge antlers from spring to fall. Elk are also sometimes found at Gold Bluffs Beach—it's an incredible rush to suddenly come upon them out of the fog or after a turn in the trail. Nearly 100 black bears also call the park home but are seldom seen. Unlike those at Yosemite and Yellowstone, these bears are still afraid of people. Keep them that way by giving them a wide berth, observing food storage etiquette while camping, and disposing of garbage properly.

Fishing. The Redwood Coast's streams are some of the best steelhead trout and salmon breeding habitat in California. Park beaches are good for surf casting but be prepared for heavy wave action. A California fishing license is required, and you should check with rangers about any special closures before wetting a line.

Beaches. The park's beaches vary from long white-sand strands to cobblestone pocket coves. The water temperature is in the high 40s to low 50s year-round, and it's often rough out there. Swimmers and surfers should be prepared for adverse conditions.

Crescent Beach is a long sandy beach just 2 miles south of Crescent City that's popular with beachcombers, surf fishers, and surfers.

Just south of Crescent Beach is **Endert's Beach,** a protected spot with a hike-in campground and tide pools at its southern end.

Whale Watching & Bird Watching. High coastal overlooks (like Klamath Overlook and Crescent Beach Overlook) make great whale-watching outposts during the December/January southern migration and the March/April return migration.

The northern sea cliffs also provide valuable nesting sites for marine birds like auklets, puffins, murres, and cormorants. Birders will also love the park's coastal freshwater lagoons, which are some of the most pristine shorebird and waterfowl habitat left and are chock-full of hundreds of different species.

Bicycling. Unfortunately, most of the hiking trails throughout the Redwood National and State Parks are off limits to mountain bikers. However, **Prairie Creek Redwoods State Park** has a fantastic 19-mile mountain-bike trail through dense forest, elk-filled meadows, and glorious mud holes. Parts of it are real thigh burners, though, so beginners should sit this one out. Pick up a 25¢ trail map at the Elk Prairie Campground Ranger Station.

There are a few other mountain-bike loops in the 20-mile range, but they are *serious* thigh burners and make the one above look easy. These loops are the Holter Ridge Trail and Little Bald Hills. Also, there is mountain biking available on the old U.S. 101, now the Coastal Trail within Del Norte Coast Redwoods State Park.

Horseback Trail Rides. Tall Trees Outfitters, located at the Orick Rodeo Grounds just outside of downtown Orick on U.S. 101, offers interpretive trail rides through the parks. Trail rides are available every day during the summer for various lengths of time, including overnight trips. Riders should be at least 5 years old. For more information, call ☎ **707/488-5785.**

Jet-Boat Tours. Tours aboard a jet boat take visitors upriver from the Klamath River Estuary to view bear, deer, elk, osprey hawks, otters, and more along the riverbanks. It's about $20 for a 30-mile trip, $28 for a 45-mile lunch or dinner cruise. Schedules run May 1 through October 30. For more information, contact **Klamath River Jet Boat Tours,** Klamath (☎ **800/887-JETS** or 707/482-7775).

Kayaking. A more serene alternative to exploring the Klamath River than bumping around in a jet boat is to take a ranger-led **kayak tour.** Offered only during the summer months, the half-day trip costs only $20 and includes all the requisite kayak gear. For more information or to make reservations, call the **Redwood National Park Information Center** at ☎ **707/464-6101,** ext. 5265.

Camping

Five small campgrounds are located in the national park. Four of the walk-in (more like backpack-in) camps—Little Bald Hills, Nickel Creek, Flint Ridge, and DeMartin—are free, and only one (the Redwood Creek Gravel Bar) requires a permit from a visitor center in advance.

Most car campsites are in the Prairie Creek and Jedediah Smith state parks, all at $14 to $16 per night. **Elk Prairie Campground** is located 5 miles north of Orick on U.S. 101. It has 75 sites and is near fishing and hiking trails. There's a dump station but no RV hookups. **Gold Bluffs Beach Campground** is 3 miles north of Orick on U.S. 101, then 7 miles west on Davison Road. It has 25 sites and cold showers. **Jedediah Smith Campground,** located on U.S. 199 at Hiouchi, has 106 tent or RV sites. There's an RV dump station, but no hookups. You'll find rest rooms and pay showers. Fees range from $12 to $16 per night.

If the camping areas above are filled, try the **Mill Creek Campground,** in Del Norte Coast Redwoods State Park, located 7 miles south of Crescent City on U.S. 101. It has 145 tent or RV sites. There's a dump station but no hookups. The walk-in tent sites are actually quite nice, situated amid the forest. Fees range from $14 to $16 per night.

Farther from the park attractions but also farther from the crowds are four national forest campgrounds (**Panther Flat, Grassy Flat, Patrick Creek,** and **Big Flat**) in the mountains above the park. All of these are located along U.S. 199, east of the parks in the Smith River

Recreation Area. Sites are $7 to $17 per night and can be reserved by calling ☎ **800/280-2267**—where an actual person can help you make decisions.

Another camping alternative is the relatively unknown **Clifford Kamph Memorial Park,** located 1 mile south of the Oregon border off U.S. 101. It has several grassy campsites with picnic tables, perched on a bluff overlooking the ocean. At $5 per night for beachfront access, it's a steal.

Accommodations

A number of bed-and-breakfasts and funky roadside motels are available in the surrounding communities of Crescent City, Orick, and Klamath. **The Crescent City/Del Norte Chamber of Commerce** (☎ **800/343-8300**) can steer you toward a good match.

If you're bringing along the family or traveling in a group along the Redwood Coast, then consider dropping the motel idea and instead renting a fully furnished home on the ocean or river's edge for as little as $80 a night. Call **Redwood Coast Vacation Rentals** for a free brochure at ☎ **707/487-8008.**

INSIDE THE PARK

Redwood AYH Hostel–Demartin House

14480 U.S. 101 (across from Wilson Creek Beach, about 7 miles north of Klamath) Klamath, CA 95548. ☎ **707/482-8265.** 30 bunks, 1 family rm. $12. MC, V.

The only lodging actually within the park, this turn-of-the-century logger's mansion was remodeled in 1987 to accommodate 30 guests dormitory-style (bunks and shared baths). What it lacks in creature comforts it makes up for in location—a mere 100 yards from the beach, surrounded by hiking trails leading along the Redwood Coast (the staff leads nature walks and is well versed in local history). Family rooms are available with advance notice, and the hostel even takes reservations by credit card (strongly recommended in the summer). Showers, common room, redwood deck, country kitchen, dining room, wood stove, and bicycle storage are included in the $12 nightly rate.

NEAR THE PARK

Crescent Beach Motel

1455 Redwood Hwy. S. (2 miles south of downtown on U.S. 101), Crescent City, CA 95531. ☎ **707/464-5436.** 27 rms. TV. Summer $64–$68 double; winter $49–$52 double. AE, DISC, MC, V.

Crescent City has the dubious distinction of being the only city along the coast without a fancy hotel or bed-and-breakfast. There is, however, an armada of cheap motels, the best of which is the Crescent Beach Motel. Near the highway, about 1 mile south of town, this single-story structure is the only local motel set directly on the beach. The newly remodeled and refurbished rooms are clean and simple; most have queen-size beds and color TVs. Four of the units face the highway; try to get one of the others, all of which have sliding glass doors opening onto decks and a small lawn area overlooking the bay. There's no restaurant or bar on the premises, but one of the city's most popular restaurants, the Beachcomber (see "Dining," below), is located next door.

Curly Redwood Lodge

701 Redwood Hwy. S., Crescent City, CA 95531. ☎ **707/464-2137.** 36 rms. TV TEL. Summer $60–$65 double; winter $37–$39 double. AE, DC, MC, V.

This is a blast from the past, the kind of place where you might have stayed as a kid during one of those cross-country vacations in the family station wagon. It was built in 1959 on grasslands across from the town's harbor, and completely trimmed with lumber from a single ancient redwood. Although they're not full of the latest high-tech gadgets, the bedrooms are among the largest and best-soundproofed in town, and certainly the most evocative of a bygone, more innocent age. In winter, about a third of the bedrooms (the ones upstairs) are locked and sealed. Overall, the aura is more akin to Oregon than anything you might imagine in California.

Requa Inn

451 Requa Rd. (from U.S. 101 take the Requa Rd. exit and follow the signs), Klamath, CA 95548. ☎ **707/482-8205.** 10 rms. Summer $59–$95 double; winter $49–$85 double. DISC, MC, V.

Established in 1885, the venerable Requa Inn, a two-story charmer located on the banks of the lower Klamath River, offers ten spacious guest rooms, each modestly decorated with antique furnishings; eight come with private baths with showers or claw-foot tubs, four offer views of the lower Klamath River. The inn's main attraction is the cozy parlor downstairs, where guests bury themselves in the plump armchairs to read beside the wood-burning stove. There are plenty of enticements just outside, including sandy riverside beaches, numerous hiking trails in nearby Redwood National Park, and, of course, fishing. Breakfast is included in the room rate, lunch is offered in the summer, and dinner is served daily (see "Dining," below).

Dining

Beachcomber

1400 U.S. 101, Crescent City. ☎ **707/464-2205.** Reservations recommended. Main courses $6–$15. MC, V. Thurs–Tues 5–9pm. SEAFOOD.

The decor is as predictably nautical as its name implies: rough-cut planking, a scattering of artfully arranged driftwood, fishnets, and buoys dangling above a dimly lit space. The restaurant lies beside the beach, 2 miles south of Crescent City's center. Its fans cite it as one of the two best restaurants in town. The cuisine is a joy to fish-lovers who prefer not to mask the flavor of their seafood with complicated sauces. Most of the dishes are grilled over madrone-wood barbecue pits, a technique perfected since this place was established in 1975. Pacific salmon, halibut, lingcod, Pacific snapper, oysters, and steamer clams are house specialties, dishes for which visitors line up, especially on Friday and Saturday nights.

Harbor View Grotto Restaurant & Lounge

150 Starfish Way, Crescent City. ☎ **707/464-3815.** Reservations recommended. Lunch main courses $6–$9; dinner $8–$35. MC, V. Daily 11:30am–10pm. SEAFOOD/STEAKS.

This is the best-established nonchain restaurant in town, specializing in fresh seafood at market prices since 1961. Completely renovated in December 1995, it has pleasant views of the ocean and harbor from both the dining room and lounge. It's capped with a miniature lighthouse inspired by Crescent City's Battery Point Lighthouse. The "light eaters" menu includes a cup of white chowder (made fresh daily), salad, a main course, and vegetables; heavy eaters can choose from three different cuts of prime rib. Menu items include fresh fish from local fishing fleets, such as Pacific snapper or salmon. Crab or shrimp Louis, as well as crabmeat or shrimp sandwiches, are perpetually popular.

Requa Inn Restaurant

451 Requa Rd., (from U.S. 101 take the Requa Rd. exit and follow the signs), Klamath. ☎ **707/482-8205.** Reservations required. Main courses $10–$28. DISC, MC, V. Lunch Fri–Mon 10am–2pm (summer only), dinner daily 5–9pm. SEAFOOD/STEAKS.

This simple yet dignified restaurant—one of only two in the greater Klamath area—serves a no-nonsense double-digit menu of steak, chicken, and fresh seafood. On Friday and Saturday summer nights, go with the seasoned prime rib and baked potato; the grilled salmon and halibut are also good bets, as is the fresh-baked blackberry cobbler and a side of vanilla ice. Be sure to request a table overlooking the Klamath River. After dinner, retire to the parlor for an after-dinner drink by the fireplace.

Rolf's Park Café

On U.S. 101 (about 2 miles north of town), Orick, CA 95555. ☎ **707/488-3841.** Main courses $5–$13 lunch; $9.50–$17.50 dinner. MC, V. Lunch daily 10am–4pm, dinner daily 4–9pm. Possibly closed Dec–Mar, so call ahead. SEAFOOD/STEAKS/WILD GAME.

Rolf Rheinschmidt, a talented chef who has worked around the world, decided it was time to semi-retire, so he opened up his own restaurant in the small town of Orick. Now he wows redwood visitors with his tried-and-true versions of bratwurst, Wiener schnitzel, and crêpes Suzette, as well as his specialty, a marinated rack of spring lamb. He also offers more exotic choices such as buffalo, wild boar, and elk steak (if you're truly adventurous, get a combo of all three). Each dinner entree includes lots of extras: hors d'oeuvres, a salad, vegetables, farm-style potatoes, and bread. If you're a big breakfast eater, Rheinschmidt's German Farmer Omelet—an open-faced concoction of ham, bacon, sausage, mushrooms, cheese, potatoes, and pasta, topped with sour cream and salsa and garnished with a strawberry crepe—is guaranteed to fill your tank.

Picnic & Camping Supplies

You can purchase sandwiches and other light fare at the **Good Harvest Cafe,** 700 Northcrest Dr., in Crescent City (☎ **707/465-6028**).

Groceries are available at **Safeway,** 475 M St. (☎ **707/465-3353**), and at **Ray's Supermarket,** 625 M St. (☎ **707/465-4045**). Both are in Crescent City. Or you might try the **Orick Market,** 121175 Hwy. 101 in Orick (☎ **707/488-3225**).

Both **Wal-Mart** and **Kmart** are good sources of camping supplies and are located in Crescent City.

33

ROCKY MOUNTAIN NATIONAL PARK

by Don and Barbara Laine

SNOW-COVERED PEAKS STAND WATCH OVER LUSH VALLEYS AND SHIMmering alpine lakes, creating the perfect image of America's most dramatic and beautiful landscape: the majestic Rocky Mountains. Here, the pine- and fir-scented forests are deep, the air is crisp and pure, and the rugged mountain peaks reach up to grasp the deep-blue sky. The views are simply spectacular.

But what makes Rocky Mountain National Park unique is not only its breathtaking scenery, but also its variety. In relatively low areas, about 7,500 to 9,000 feet, ponderosa pine and juniper cloak the sunny southern slopes, with Douglas fir on the cooler northern slopes. The thirstier blue spruce and lodgepole pine cling to the banks of streams, along with occasional groves of aspen. Elk and mule deer thrive. On higher slopes, forests of Engelmann spruce and subalpine fir dominate, interspersed with wide meadows vibrant with wildflowers in spring and summer. This is also home to bighorn sheep, which have become a symbol of the park. Above 11,500 feet the trees become increasingly gnarled and stunted, until they disappear altogether and alpine tundra takes over. Fully one-third of the park is in this bleak, rocky world, many of its plants identical to those found in the Arctic.

Within the 415 square miles (265,727 acres) protected by the national park are 17 mountains above 13,000 feet. Longs Peak, at 14,255 feet, is the highest.

Trail Ridge Road, which cuts west through the middle of the park from Estes Park, then south down its western boundary to Grand Lake, is one of America's great alpine highways. Consistently rated among the most scenic highways in America, in 1996 Trail Ridge Road was designated an All-American Road, one of the first six in the nation. Climbing to 12,183 feet near Fall River Pass, it is the highest continuously paved highway in the United States. The road is usually open from Memorial Day into October, depending on snowfall. The 48-mile scenic drive from Estes Park to Grand Lake takes about 3 hours, allowing for stops at numerous scenic view points. Exhibits at the Alpine Visitor Center at Fall River Pass, 11,796 feet above sea level, explain life on the alpine tundra.

Fall River Road, the original park road, leads from Estes Park to the Fall River Pass via Horseshoe Park Junction. West of the Endovalley Picnic Area, the

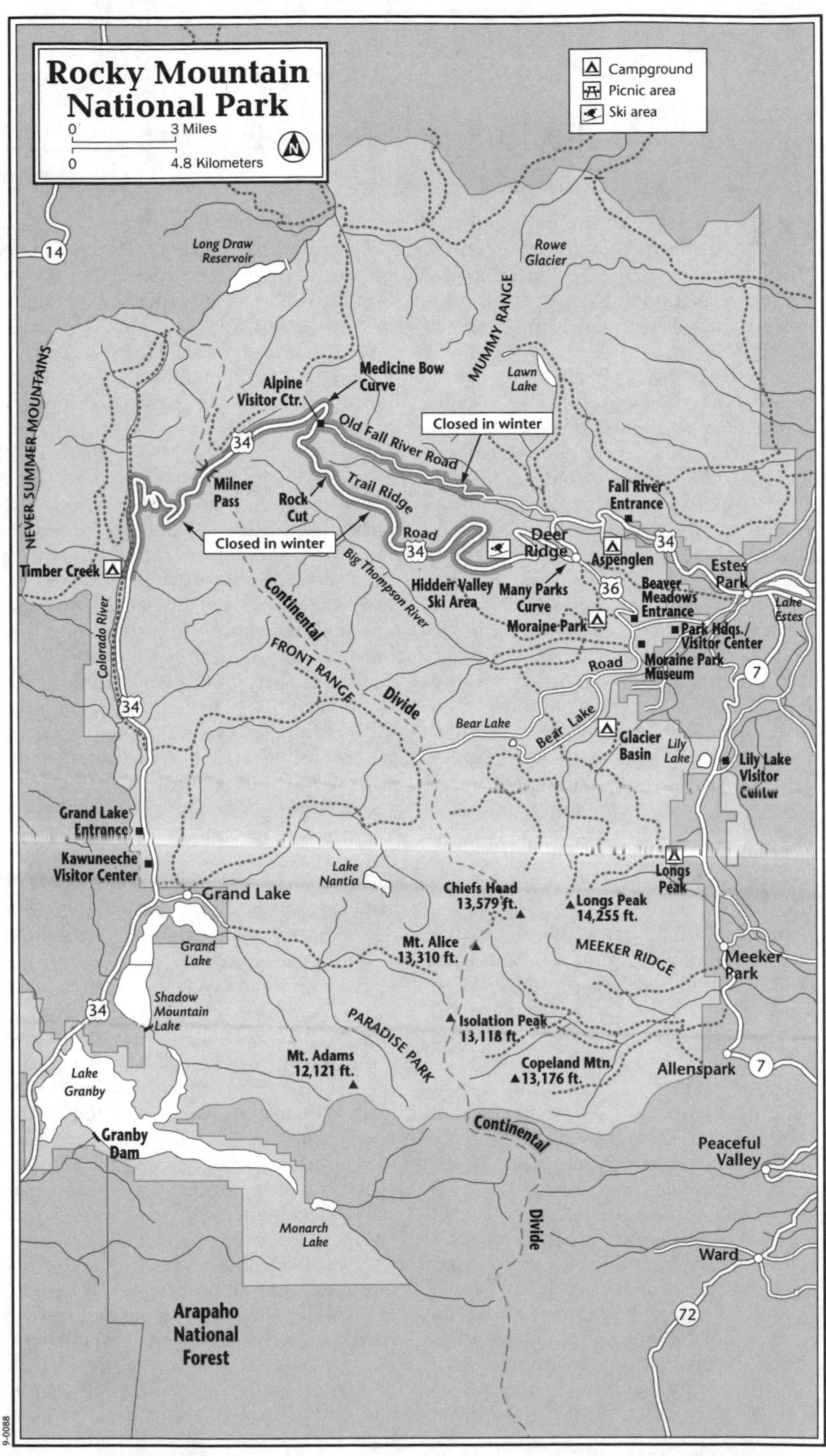
Rocky Mountain National Park
0 3 Miles
0 4.8 Kilometers
N
Campground
Picnic area
Ski area
14
Long Draw Reservoir
Rowe Glacier
MUMMY RANGE
NEVER SUMMER MOUNTAINS
Lawn Lake
Alpine Visitor Ctr.
Medicine Bow Curve
Old Fall River Road
Closed in winter
34
Milner Pass
Rock Cut
Trail Ridge Road
Closed in winter
Fall River Entrance
Deer Ridge
Aspenglen
Estes Park
Lake Estes
Timber Creek
Big Thompson River
Hidden Valley Ski Area
Many Parks Curve
36
Beaver Meadows Entrance
Moraine Park
Park Hdqs./ Visitor Center
Continental Divide
FRONT RANGE
Moraine Park Museum
Road
Colorado River
7
Bear Lake
Bear Lake
Glacier Basin
Lily Lake
Lily Lake Visitor Center
Grand Lake Entrance
Kawuneeche Visitor Center
Lake Nantia
Longs Peak
Grand Lake
Chiefs Head 13,579 ft.
Longs Peak 14,255 ft.
Grand Lake
Mt. Alice 13,310 ft.
MEEKER RIDGE
Meeker Park
Shadow Mountain Lake
Isolation Peak 13,118 ft.
PARADISE PARK
Mt. Adams 12,121 ft.
Copeland Mtn. 13,176 ft.
Allenspark
Lake Granby
Granby Dam
Continental Divide
Peaceful Valley
Monarch Lake
Ward
72
Arapaho National Forest
9-0088

Tips from a Park Ranger

The diversity of the park and the ease in which visitors can experience its many facets make Rocky Mountain National Park special, says Doug Caldwell, the park's information officer.

"There are other alpine tundra areas in the United States, but you usually have to do a lot of hard hiking," Caldwell says. "What makes Rocky Mountain National Park unique is that Trail Ridge Road takes you up to the tundra, above tree line, in the comfort of your car; you can see plant and animal communities that if not for this park you would have to go to the Arctic Circle to see."

Those willing and able to hike can see plenty of tundra country, according to Caldwell, who suggests having a friend drop you off at the Ute Trail turnout on Trail Ridge Road, and hiking the 6 miles down through Forest Canyon to Upper Beaver Meadows. "This canyon is among the wildest in the park," says Caldwell, "and the hike along its steep side provides spectacular views of the canyon and Longs Peak, the park's tallest mountain."

Another hike that Caldwell recommends is the 2-mile (one way) **Gem Lake Trail,** on the park's east side. "When you're going up that trail there are several places to look across the Estes Valley to Longs Peak, and the lake is a wonderful spot for a picnic." Those who want to work a bit harder will be well rewarded on another of Caldwell's favorites. "One that I really enjoy on the west side of the park is the East Inlet Trail," Caldwell says. "Once you get up there a couple of miles, and gain some elevation, you look back toward Grand Lake and think you're in Switzerland."

Longs Peak, at 14,255 feet elevation, is the northernmost of Colorado's famed "fourteeners" (mountains that exceed 14,000 feet elevation), and it's a popular hike, says Caldwell. "You don't need technical climbing gear once the ice is gone, usually by mid-July," Caldwell says, adding that hikers may have some physical problems with the altitude at first. "It's wise to give yourself a couple of days to acclimate before tackling Longs Peak," Caldwell says. He also recommends that high-elevation hikers drink more fluids, eat regularly, carry energy bars, and take it slow. "Listen to your body," he advises. Another bit of advice he gives backpackers is to spend time discussing their plans with rangers in the park's backcountry office before setting out. "We'd much rather spend time with them beforehand to try to get to know their abilities and expectations and advise them where to go than be called out on a search and rescue mission."

One activity that many visitors miss out on is viewing the night sky, says Caldwell. He suggests taking a picnic supper and stopping at the Trail Ridge Road **view points** after dark, when most park visitors are in their motel rooms or their campsites. "We don't have any light pollution here," he says. "You think you can just reach up and touch the Milky Way. You can see satellites, and the Perseid meteor shower in August is something you won't soon forget."

Asked how to avoid the crowds, Caldwell says that since most visitors remain close to the roads, the easiest way to find a bit of solitude even during the park's busiest times is to take off down a hiking trail. "The farther you go up the trail the fewer people you'll encounter." He adds that another sure way to escape humanity is to visit in winter, and explore the park on snowshoes or cross-country skis.

But when would he visit?

"Fall, from September through mid-October, is the best time," he says. "Days are warm and comfortable, nights are cool and crisp, there are fewer people than in summer, and the aspens are changing. You can see hundreds of elk, and watch the bulls bugle as they protect their harems from the other bulls."

road is one way uphill, and closed to trailers and motor homes. As you negotiate its gravely switchbacks, you get a clear idea of what early auto travel was like in the West. This road, too, is closed in winter.

One of the few paved roads in the Rockies that leads into a high, mountain basin is Bear Lake Road, which is kept open year-round, with occasional half-day closings to clear snow. Numerous trails converge at Bear Lake, southwest of park headquarters via Moraine Park.

Avoiding the Crowds. The park is only fully accessible for half the year, so few people come in the off-season. The very busiest time in the park is from mid-June through mid-August—essentially during school vacation—so just before or just after that period is best. But winter is gaining in popularity too, even though you won't be able to drive the entire Trail Ridge Road, because it is the quietest time, and although the park can be bitterly cold, it is also beautiful. Regardless of when you visit, the best way to avoid crowds is by putting on a backpack or climbing onto a horse.

Just the Facts

GETTING THERE & GATEWAYS

Entry into the park is from either the east (through the town of Estes Park) or the west (through Grand Lake). East and west sides of the park are connected by Trail Ridge Road, open during summer and early fall, but closed because of snow the rest of the year. Most visitors enter the park from the Estes Park side. The Beaver Meadows Entrance, west of Estes Park via U.S. 36, is the national park's main entrance and the best way to get to the visitor center and headquarters. It is also the most direct route to Trail Ridge Road. U.S. 34 West from Estes Park takes you to the Fall River Entrance (north of the Beaver Meadows Entrance), and from there you can access Old Fall River Road or Trail Ridge Road.

Estes Park is about 71 miles northwest of Denver, 44 miles northwest of Boulder, and 42 miles southwest of Fort Collins.

The most direct route from Denver is via U.S. 36 through Boulder. At Estes Park, that highway joins U.S. 34, which runs up the Big Thompson Canyon from I-25 and Loveland, and continues through Rocky Mountain National Park to Grand Lake. An alternative scenic route to Estes Park is Colo. 7, the "Peak-to-Peak Scenic Byway" that transits Central City (Colo. 119), Nederland (Colo. 72), and Allenspark (Colo. 7) under different designations.

Heading south from Estes Park on Colo. 7 you can access two trailheads in the southeast corner of the national park, but there are no connecting roads to the main part of the park from those points. These are Longs Peak Trailhead—the turnoff is 9 miles south of Estes Park and the trailhead about another mile; and Wild Basin Trailhead—another 3.5 miles south to the turnoff and then 2.2 miles to the trailhead.

In summer, a free national park **shuttle bus** runs from the Glacier Basin parking area to Bear Lake, with departures every 15 to 30 minutes.

Those who want to enter the national park from the west can take U.S. 40 north from I-70 through Winter Park and Tabernash to Granby, and then follow U.S. 34 north to the village of Grand Lake and on into the park.

The Nearest Airport. Visitors arriving by plane will fly into **Denver International Airport** (☎ **303/342-2000**) and either rent a car or continue to Estes Park with **Charles Tour and Travel Service** (☎ **800/586-5009** or 970/586-5151), which also provides tours into Rocky Mountain National Park during the summer.

Denver is a major airline hub. The following carriers have daily service: **American, America West, Continental, Delta, Frontier, Northwest, Sun Country, TWA, United,** and **US Airways.**

Renting a Car. Most major car-rental companies have offices at Denver's airport, including **Alamo, Avis, Budget, Dollar, Enterprise, General, Hertz,** and **National.**

Toll-free reservations numbers for all the airlines and car-rental companies mentioned in this section will be found in the appendix.

Getting Information Before Your Trip

Contact **Rocky Mountain National Park,** Estes Park, CO 80517-8397 (☎ **970/586-1206**), for brochures and information on current conditions. The park's Web site is **www.nps.gov/romo**.

Visitor Centers

Entering the park from Estes Park, it's wise to stop first at **park headquarters,** U.S. 36 west of Colo. 66 (☎ **970/586-1206**). There's a good interpretive exhibit here, including a relief model of the park, an audiovisual program, a wide choice of books and maps for sale, and knowledgeable people to answer questions and give advice. A self-guided nature trail just outside the building identifies many of the park's plants. The headquarters is open in summer, daily from 8am to 9pm; in winter, daily from 8am to 5pm.

The **Kawuneeche Visitor Center** (open in summer daily from 7am to 7pm; winter, daily from 8am to 4:30pm) is located at the Grand Lake end of Trail Ridge Road (☎ **970/627-3471**). In addition to exhibits on the geology, plants, animals, and human history of the park's west side, there is a small theater where films and video programs are shown, and a short self-guided nature trail. The **Alpine Visitor Center** (open in summer daily from 9am to 5pm) at Fall River Pass, has exhibits that explain life on the alpine tundra and a viewing platform from which you are almost certain to see elk. Next door is the Fall River Store, open in summer only, with a snack bar and gift shop. The **Moraine Park Museum** (open mid-June to mid-September, daily from 9am to 5pm) is located on Bear Lake Road in an historic log building that dates from 1923. It has full visitor facilities, in addition to excellent natural-history exhibits that describe the creation of the park's landscape, as well as the plants and animals of the park. There's also a nature trail outside.

Entrance & Camping Fees

Park admission costs $10 per vehicle for up to 1 week; $5 for bicyclists, motorcyclists, and pedestrians. An annual park pass costs $20. Campers in the park's developed campgrounds will pay $12 to $14 per night during the summer and $10 in the off-season when the water is turned off, usually from late September to May. Permits are required at all times for overnight trips into the backcountry, and include camping at the park's designated backcountry and bivouac campsites. Cost is $15 from May through October; the rest of the year, the permits are free. Campground reservations can be made by calling **Biospherics, Inc.** (☎ **800/365-CAMP** [2267]).

Special Regulations & Warnings

Rocky Mountain National Park's high elevation and extremes of climate and terrain are among its most appealing features, but also its greatest hazards. Hikers should try to give themselves several days to acclimate to the altitude before seriously hitting the trails, and hikers with respiratory or heart problems would do well to discuss their plans with their physicians before leaving home. Hikers also need to be prepared for rapidly changing conditions, including sudden afternoon thunderstorms in July and August. If lightning threatens, everyone is well advised to stay clear of ridges and other vulnerable high points.

Seasons & Climate

Even though the park is open year-round, **Trail Ridge Road,** the main east-west thoroughfare through the park, is always closed in winter. It's safest to assume that you will not be able to drive clear across the park from mid-October until Memorial Day—even into June it's quite possible that the road will be closed for hours or even a day or more by snow. That's not to say that intrepid travelers can't enjoy the park in winter. All park entrances are open, trails are open to snowshoers and cross-country skiers, and roads to a number of good view points and trailheads are plowed. Snowmobiling is also permitted, but only on the west side of the park, accessible from Grand Lake. Those with the proper skills and equipment can cross-country ski into the high country, although they need to be aware of storm and avalanche dangers and should always check with rangers before setting out.

Weather is a key factor that will affect your trip to the park in any season. In summer, temperatures typically climb into the 70s during the day and drop into the 40s at night, but because of the park's high elevation—and range of elevations—you'll find that temperatures vary greatly. The higher into the mountains you go the cooler it gets. Rangers say that for every 1,000 feet in elevation gain, the climate changes the equivalent of traveling 600 miles north. Tree line in the park—the elevation at which trees can no longer grow—varies, but is at about 11,500 feet.

Winters usually see high temperatures in the 20s and 30s and lows from 10° below zero to 20° above. Spring and fall temperatures can vary greatly from pleasantly warm to bitterly cold and snowy. For this reason, spring and fall are when you need to be flexible and adjust your itinerary to suit current conditions. Particularly at higher elevations, windchill factors can be extreme, and hypothermia can be a problem at any time, even in summer, when afternoon thunderstorms sometimes occur without warning, causing temperatures to drop dramatically and suddenly.

SEASONAL EVENTS

The elk rutting season in September and October brings hundreds of elk to the lower elevations, where you can often hear the macho bulls bugle and watch them trying to keep other bulls away from their females.

USEFUL PUBLICATIONS

The park's visitor centers have U.S. Geological Survey topographical maps for sale. Also available is an excellent guidebook, ***Hiking Rocky Mountain National Park*** (Old Saybrook, Conn.: The Globe Pequot Press) by Kent and Donna Dannen, which gives detailed trail descriptions; and the informative ***Rocky Mountain National Park Road Guide*** (Jackson Hole, Wy.: Free Wheeling Travel Guides) by Thomas Schmidt, which provides thumbnail sketches of virtually everything you'll see along the park's roadways. These and other trip-planning tools can be obtained from the **Rocky Mountain Nature Association** at the park (☎ **800/816-7662** or 970/586-1258), which sells a variety of maps, guides, books, and videos (including some in PAL format). Those who want to help the nonprofit association, and get a 15% discount on purchases at Rocky Mountain and many other national parks and monuments, can become members at an annual cost of $15 for individuals and $25 for families.

Seeing the Highlights in a Day

This park simply begs for an extended visit—4 to 7 days would be ideal, allowing time to stop at view points, see the exhibits, and hike at least several trails. But it also has the advantage of offering a wonderful experience to visitors who have only a short amount of time, or who are not able or willing to hike.

Those arriving in summer or early fall with only 1 day to see the park will want to stop at one of the visitor centers, and then drive the fantastically scenic **Trail Ridge Road,** described below. Stop at the view points and take the half-hour walk along the **Tundra World Nature Trail** to get a close-up view of the plants, animals, and terrain of the tundra.

Those returning to the east or west sides will have time for little else, since it takes about 3 hours each way for the 48-mile drive, but those passing through the park on their way to somewhere else might want to take another short hike, described under "Day Hikes," below.

Exploring the Park by Car

Although Rocky Mountain National Park is generally considered the domain of hikers and climbers, ideal for those who want to leave the crowds behind and head into the backcountry, it's surprisingly easy to enjoy this park thoroughly without working up a sweat. For that we thank **Trail Ridge Road,** built in 1932 and undoubtedly one of America's most scenic highways, providing expansive and sometimes dizzying views in all directions. This remarkable 48-mile road rises to over 12,000 feet in elevation and crosses the Continental Divide. Along the way it offers spectacular vistas of snowcapped peaks, deep forests, and meadows of wildflowers full of browsing bighorn sheep, elk, and deer. Allow at least 3 hours for the drive, and consider a short walk or hike from one of the many vista points.

To get a close-up look at the tundra, pull off Trail Ridge Road into the **Rock Cut Parking Area** (elevation 12,110 feet), about halfway along the scenic drive. You'll have splendid views of glacially carved peaks along the Continental Divide, and on the 0.5-mile **Tundra Nature Trail** you'll find signs identifying and discussing the hardy plants and animals that inhabit this region.

Trail Ridge Road is closed by winter snows. In recent years it has usually been clear by late May and closed again between mid- and late October. But even well into June, the road can be closed for snow for hours or even days at a time.

There are two other roads within the park. **Old Fall River Road,** 9 miles long and unpaved, is one way uphill only. It's usually open from July 4 through mid-October. **Bear Lake Road** is the access road to Bear Lake and is open year-round.

Organized Tours & Ranger Programs

Campfire talks and other programs are offered at each visitor center between June and September. Consult the "High Country Headlines" newspaper (free at visitor centers) for scheduled activities, which vary from talks on the park's wildlife and geology to photo walks, fly-fishing, and orienteering programs. At night, rangers periodically lead night-sky programs using the park's computerized telescopes, and also nightly talks during the elk's rutting season. Winter visitors will find a variety of activities, including moonlight hikes and snowshoe and cross-country ski trips.

Historic & Man-Made Attractions

Remnants from the area's mining and ranching days of the late 1800s and early 1900s still persist in the park. Hikers will encounter the ruins of several historic cabins on the Lulu City and Eugenia Mine trails (see "Day Hikes," below). The **Moraine Park Museum** on Bear Lake Road contains exhibits mainly on natural history, but the building itself—a log structure built as a social center in 1923—is listed on the National Register of Historic Places. A 0.5-mile walk from Trail Ridge Road on the west side of the park stands **Never Summer Ranch,** a preserved dude ranch dating from the 1920s. It was started as a cattle ranch by Denver saloon owner John Holzwarth after Prohibition began, but Holzwarth soon discovered that it was more pleasant and profitable to take in paying guests (at $11 per week including room, meals, and a horse) than to do the hard work of actual ranching. The ranch buildings contain many of their original furnishings. Check at the visitor centers for tours run by the park.

Day Hikes

Rocky Mountain National Park contains more than 350 miles of hiking trails, ranging from short, easy walks to extremely strenuous and difficult hikes that require climbing skills. Trail difficulty can also vary by time of year—the higher elevations usually have snow until at least mid-July. Many of the park's trails, such as Longs Peak, can be done either as day hikes or overnight backpacking trips. Hikers are strongly advised to discuss their plans with park rangers before setting out. The following are some of our favorite trails; there are many more.

SHORTER TRAILS

Alberta Falls Trail

0.6 mile one way. Easy. Access: Glacier Gorge Parking Area.

With an elevation change of only 160 feet, this is an easy and scenic walk along Glacier Creek to pretty Alberta Falls. Along the sunny trail you'll see beaver dams and an abundance of golden-mantled ground squirrels.

Bierstadt Lake Trail

1.4 miles one way. Moderate. Access: North side of Bear Lake Rd., 6.4 miles from Beaver Meadows.

This trail climbs 566 feet through an open forest of aspen to Bierstadt Lake. From there you'll find good views of Longs Peak from the northwest side of the lake. This trail also connects with several other trails, including one that leads to Bear Lake.

Tundra World Nature Trail

0.5-mile loop. Easy. Access: Near Rock Cut Parking Area on Trail Ridge Rd.

This wheelchair-accessible nature trail has exhibits identifying various tundra plants and animals, and describing how they have adapted to the harsh tundra environment.

Eugenia Mine Trail

1.4 miles one way. Moderate. Access: Longs Peak Ranger Station.

This walk to an abandoned mine follows the Longs Peak Trail for about 0.5 mile and then forks off to the right, heading through groves of aspens and then evergreens before arriving at the site of the mine, where you'll see hillside tailings, the remnants of a cabin, and abandoned mine equipment. The trail has an elevation gain of 508 feet.

Emerald Lake Trail

1.8 miles one way. Easy to moderate. Access: Bear Lake.

This trail offers spectacular scenery on its route past Nymph and Dream lakes to its destination of Emerald Lake. The 0.5-mile hike to Nymph Lake is easy, climbing 225 feet; then the trail is rated moderate to Dream Lake (another 0.6 mile) and Emerald Lake (another 0.7 mile), which is 605 feet higher than the starting point at Bear Lake. In addition to the mountain lakes, you'll see the surrounding mountains, which are especially pretty when seen reflected in the surface of Nymph Lake, or towering over Dream Lake. In summer there's an abundance of wildflowers along the path between Nymph and Dream lakes.

Gem Lake Trail

2 miles one way. Moderate. Access: Trailhead on Devil's Gulch Rd., north of Estes Park.

This is a relatively low-elevation trail, starting at only 7,740 feet, but has an elevation change of 1,090 feet. It offers good views of the town of Estes Park and Longs Peak, and delivers hikers to a pretty lake.

Ouzel Falls Trail

2.7 miles one way. Moderate. Access: Wild Basin Ranger Station.

This hike climbs about 950 feet and crosses Cony Creek on two bridges before delivering you to a picture-perfect waterfall, among the park's prettiest. The trail passes through areas that were burned in a 1978 fire—usually good spots to see wildlife—and also offers fine views of Longs Peak and Mount Meeker.

Mills Lake Trail

2.5 miles one way. Moderate. Access: Glacier Gorge Junction.

This trail leads to a picturesque mountain lake, nestled in a valley among towering mountain peaks. Among the best spots in the park for photographing dramatic Longs Peak (the best lighting is usually in late afternoon or early evening), this is also the perfect place for a picnic. The trail has an elevation change of about 700 feet.

LONGER TRAILS

Lulu City Trail

3.7 miles one way. Moderate. Access: Colorado River Trailhead near the western boundary of the park.

This trail gains just 350 feet in elevation, as it winds along the river floodplain, through lush vegetation, past an 1880s mine and several mining cabins, and then along an old stage route into a subalpine forest before arriving at the site of Lulu City. Founded in 1879 by prospectors hoping to strike gold and silver, it was abandoned within 10 years, and little remains today except for the ruins of a few cabins.

Ute Trail

6 miles one way. Moderate. Access: Ute Trail turnout on Trail Ridge Rd.

An excellent way to see the tundra, this moderate hike is really fairly easy if you can get a ride to the top from a friend and walk down the 3,300-foot descent. The hike down the side of a canyon provides great views.

East Inlet Trail

6.9 miles one way. Moderate to difficult. Access: The west portal of Adam's Tunnel, southeast of the town of Grand Lake.

This trail is an easy walk the first 0.3 mile to scenic Adams Falls. It then wanders along some marshy areas, crosses several streams, and then, becoming more strenuous, climbs sharply in elevation to Lone Pine Lake, about 5.5 miles from the trailhead. It is another 1.4 miles, partly through a subalpine forest, to Lake Verna. The trail continues after the lake, but it is not maintained. Total elevation gain to Lake Verna is 1,809 feet.

Timber Lake Trail

4.8 miles one way. Difficult. Access: East side of Trail Ridge Rd., 9.6 miles north of the Grand Lake Entrance.

You'll work hard on this strenuous hike but be amply rewarded with views of timberline lakes and alpine tundra. With an elevation change of 2,060 feet, this hike takes you through a forest of lodgepole pines, follows a creek lined with subalpine wildflowers, and then arrives at the lake, surrounded by rocks, tundra, snow, and a few trees.

Lawn Lake Trail

6.2 miles one way. Difficult. Access: Lawn Lake Trailhead on Fall River Rd.

This strenuous hike, with an elevation gain of 2,249 feet, follows the Roaring River through terrain dotted with ponderosa pine. Along the way you can see all too plainly the damage done by a massive flood that occurred when the Lawn Lake Dam broke in 1982, killing three campers. At higher elevations there are scenic views of Mummy Mountain.

East Longs Peak Trail

8 miles one way. Difficult. Access: Longs Peak Ranger Station.

This strenuous trail is recommended only for experienced mountain hikers and climbers in top physical condition. It climbs some 4,855 feet along steep ledges and through a narrows to the top of 14,255-foot Longs Peak, the highest point in the park. The trek takes most hikers about 15 hours to complete and can be done in 1 or 2 days. Those planning a 1-day hike should consider starting out extremely early, so they will be well off the peak before the summer afternoon thunderstorms arrive. For a 2-day hike, go 5 or 6 miles the first day, stay at a designated backcountry campsite, and complete the trip the following day. Those making the hike in early summer (usually up until mid-July) should be prepared for icy conditions.

Exploring the Backcountry

There are numerous opportunities in the park for backpacking and technical climbing, and hikers and climbers will generally find that the further they go into the backcountry, the fewer other humans they will see. Some of the day hikes discussed above can also be done as overnight hikes; for example, the East Longs Peak Trail, which takes most people about 15 hours round-trip, is often completed over 2 days. Hikers can also combine various shorter trails to produce loops that can keep them in the park's backcountry for up to a week.

The park has well over 100 small **backcountry campsites,** which must be reserved beforehand. Backpackers should carry portable stoves, since wood fires are permitted at only a few sites with metal fire rings. In addition to the designated backcountry campsites there are two dozen cross-country zones, in some of the least accessible sections of the park, which are recommended only for those with good map and compass skills.

The park's **Backcountry Office** should be the first stop for those planning backpacking trips. Rangers there know the trails and camping areas well and are happy to advise hikers on the best choices for their abilities and expectations. Backcountry permits are required for all overnight hikes. Technical climbers who expect to be out overnight usually set up a bivouac, a temporary, open-air encampment that is normally at or near the base of a route or on the face of a climb. Designated bivouac zones have been established; permits are required.

Backcountry and bivouac permits are obtained at park headquarters and ranger stations. They cost $15 from May through October but are free from November through April. For information call ☎ **970/586-1242.** Only seven campers are allowed in any backcountry campsite at the same time, and there are also limits for some bivouac areas. In addition, there is a 7-night backcountry camping and bivouac limit from June to September, with no more than 3 nights in any one spot. Tents are not permitted in the backcountry in summer, or in bivouac zones at any time.

Other Sports & Activities

Biking. As in most national parks, bikes are not permitted off established roads, and here bicyclists will in most cases be sharing roadways with motor vehicles along narrow roads with 5% to 7% grades. However, bicyclists still enjoy the challenge and scenery. One popular 16-mile ride is the **Horseshoe Park/Estes Park Loop,** which goes from Estes Park west on U.S. 34 past Aspenglen Campground and the park's Fall River Entrance, and then back east at the Deer Ridge Junction, following U.S. 36 through the Beaver Meadows Entrance. There are plenty of beautiful mountain views. A free park brochure provides information on safety, regulations, and suggested routes.

Tours, rentals, and repairs are available at **Colorado Bicycling Adventures,** 184 E. Elkhorn Ave., Estes Park (☎ **800/607-8765** or 970/586-4241). Rentals are $5 to $7 for 1 hour, $15 to $25 for a half day, and $21 to $40 for a full day, depending on type of bike, with discounts for multiday rentals. They also have child carriers, car racks, and locks. The company offers both road trips in the national park (downhill on paved roads), for around $50 to $70, and off-road mountain-bike tours outside the park for experienced riders for about $45 per person.

Climbing & Mountaineering. **Colorado Mountain School,** P.O. Box 2062, Estes Park, CO 80517 (☎ **970/586-5758**), is a year-round guide service and a national park–sanctioned technical rock climbing and mountaineering school (including ice climbing and ski mountaineering) that caters to all ages and abilities. The most popular climb is **Longs Peak** (the highest mountain in the park). It can be ascended by novice climbers in good physical condition via the "Keyhole," but its north and east faces are for experts only. Colorado Mountain School offers both half- and full-day excursions, with rates per person ranging from $75 to $300. The school also operates a small store, and offers lodging in a hostel-type setting, at about $20 per night per person. For information stop at the ranger station at the Longs Peak Trailhead.

Educational Programs. The **Rocky Mountain Nature Association,** Rocky Mountain National Park, Estes Park, CO 80517 (☎ **970/586-1258**), offers a wide variety of seminars and workshops, ranging from half-day to several days. Subjects vary but might include songbirds, flower identification, edible and medicinal herbs, painting, wildlife photography, tracking park animals, astronomy, human history, and edible mushrooms. Programs are scheduled year-round, although the greatest number are held during July and August. Rates range from $25 to $50 for half- and full-day programs, and $65 to $175 for multiday programs. Nature Association members get 10% discounts.

Fishing. Four species of **trout** are fished in the park streams and lakes: brown, rainbow, brook, and cutthroat. Anglers must get a state fishing license, and are only permitted to use artificial lures or flies. A number of lakes and streams, including Bear Lake, are closed to fishing; a list of open and closed waters plus regulations and other information are available in a free park brochure. Anglers might also try the abundant opportunities for fishing in the nearby national forests.

Horseback Riding. Many of the national park's trails are open to those on horseback, and several outfitters provide guided rides, both within and outside the park. Typical prices are $18 for a 1-hour ride, $32 for 2 hours, $40 for 3 hours, $50 for a half day, and $70 for a full day. Highly recommended is the Sombrero Ranch Stables' breakfast ride, running from March through December and including a 2-hour ride and all-you-can eat full breakfast, for $32. Sombrero has stables on the east side of the park opposite Lake Estes Dam, at 1895 Big Thompson Hwy. (U.S. 34) (☎ **970/586-4577**). The company also offers horseback rides on the west side of the park in the Grand Lake area (☎ **970/627-3514**).

Hi Country Stables operates two stables inside the park, with similar rides and rates—**Glacier Creek Stables** (☎ **970/586-3244**) and **Moraine Park Stables** (☎ **970/586-2327**). **National Park Village Stables** at the Fall River Entrance of the national park on U.S. 34 (☎ **970/586-5269**) and the **Cowpoke Corner Corral,** at Glacier Lodge 3 miles west of town, 2166 Colo. 66 (☎ **970/586-5890**), both offer similar rides and rates from May through September.

Photography. To get those calendar-quality photos of spectacular snow-capped mountains, you'll want to get up early. Most of the best views face east, and early-morning light is usually best.

Skiing & Snowshoeing. A growing number of people have been discovering the joys of exploring the park on cross-country skis and snowshoes, which are conveniently available for rent at area sporting goods stores (see "Picnic & Camping Supplies," below). Snowshoes are an often overlooked means of travel. Made of lightweight materials with anti-slip surfaces, they have become a great way for nonskiers to explore the outdoors in winter.

If you're headed into the backcountry for cross-country skiing or snowshoeing, stop by park headquarters for maps, information on where the snow is best, and a free backcountry permit if you plan to stay out overnight. Keep in mind that trails are not groomed. On winter weekends, rangers often lead guided snowshoe walks on the east side of the park and guided cross-country ski trips on the west side, starting in February. Participants must supply their own equipment.

Popular winter recreation areas include Bear Lake, south of the Beaver Meadows Entrance. A lesser-known part of the park in Wild Basin, which is south of the park's east entrances, off Colo. 7 about a mile north of the community of Allenspark. A 2-mile road, closed to motor vehicles for the last mile in winter, winds through a subalpine forest to the Wild Basin Trailhead, which follows a creek to a waterfall, a rustic bridge, and eventually to another waterfall. Total distance to the second falls is 2.7 miles. Chances are good for spotting birds along the trail, such as Clark's nutcrackers, Steller's jays, and the American dipper. On winter weekends, the Colorado Mountain Club often opens a warming hut at the Wild Basin Ranger Station.

Snowmobiling. Several areas on the park's west side are open to snowmobiles, including all of Trail Ridge Road to the west of Milner Pass. There is also a snowmobile trail that leads from the park into the adjacent Arapaho National Forest. Snowmobilers are required to register at the Kawuneeche Visitor Center, near Grand Lake.

Especially for Kids

The park offers a variety of special hikes and programs for children, including an especially popular trip to the park's beaver ponds. A ranger-led program for kids from 6 to 12 years old, called **"A Child's View,"** concentrates on the park's geology and wildlife through hands-on activities. The park's **Junior Ranger Program** lets kids earn badges by completing activities that teach them about the park's plants and animals and environmental concerns. Most of the kids activities are scheduled during the summer; check on schedules at any park visitor center.

Wildlife Viewing & Bird Watching. Rocky Mountain National Park is a premier wildlife-viewing area, especially in fall, winter, and spring. Look for large herds of elk in meadows and on mountainsides. During the fall rutting season a group of park volunteers called the **Rocky Mountain National Park Elk Bugle Corps** are stationed at elk-viewing areas in the evenings to help people get the best views while not disturbing the animals—elk are often just 30 or 40 feet away.

Park visitors also often see mule deer, beavers, coyotes, and river otters. Watch for moose among the willows on the west side of the park. In the forests there is an abundance of songbirds and small mammals; particularly plentiful are gray and Steller's jays, Clark's nutcrackers, chipmunks, and golden-mantled ground squirrels. You also have a good chance of seeing bighorn sheep, marmots, pikas, and ptarmigan along Trail Ridge Road. For detailed and current wildlife-viewing information, stop by one of the park's visitor centers and check on the many interpretive programs, such as bird walks. Local wildlife-watching suggestions can be heard on radio at 530AM.

Camping

INSIDE THE PARK

The park has five campgrounds with a total of 589 sites, with nearly half at Moraine Park. Moraine Park and Glacier Basin require reservations Memorial Day through early September. For reservations call **Biospherics, Inc.** (☎ **800/365-CAMP** [2267]). In summer, arrive early if you hope to snare one of the first-come, first-served campsites. Campsites cost $12 to $14 per night during the summer; $10 in the off-season. No showers or RV hookups are available. Camping is limited to 3 days at Longs Peak and 7 days at other campgrounds.

NEAR THE PARK

THE EAST SIDE

Choices on the east side include the **Estes Park KOA,** 1 mile east of Estes Park on U.S. 34, at 2051 Big Thompson Ave., Estes Park, CO 80517 (☎ **800/KOA-1887** for reservations, or 970/586-2888). Scenically located across the street from Lake Estes and within walking distance of the Big Thompson River, this KOA lacks a swimming pool, but makes up for it with cable TV hookups and miniature golf. It also sells LP gas.

On Mary's Lake Road about 1.5 miles from its intersection with U.S. 36, you'll find **Mary's Lake Campground,** 2120 Mary's Lake Rd. (P.O. Box 2514), Estes Park, CO 80517 (☎ **800/445-6279** or 970/586-4411). This campground has beautiful mountain views and campsites for everything from tents to 40-foot RVs. There's also a playground and basketball court. Pick up fishing licenses and bait and tackle here for shore fishing at the lake and streams in the national park.

The **National Park Resort,** 3501 Fall River Rd., Estes Park, CO 80517 (☎ **970/586-4563**), is a wooded campground on

Campground	Elev.	Total Sites	RV Hookups	Dump Station	Toilets	Drinkin[g] Water
In the Park						
Aspenglen	8,230	54	0	No	Yes	Yes
Glacier Basin	8,600	150	0	Yes	Yes	Yes
Longs Peak	9,400	26	0	No	Yes	Yes
Moraine Park	8,150	247	0	Yes	Yes	Yes
Timber Creek	8,900	100	0	Yes	Yes	Yes
Near Park's East Side						
Estes Park KOA	7,500	62	62	Yes	Yes	Yes
Mary's Lake	8,200	150	90	Yes	Yes	Yes
National Park Resort	8,200	100	80	Yes	Yes	Yes
Spruce Lake RV Park	7,622	110	110	Yes	Yes	Yes
Near Park's West Side						
Elk Creek	8,400	33	33	Yes	Yes	Yes
Green Ridge	8,500	81	0	Yes	Yes	Yes
Stillwater	8,350	127	20	Yes	Yes	Yes
Willow Creek	8,300	35	0	No	Yes	Yes

* Fees are winter/summer.

the border of the park that can accommodate both tents and RVs. Full hookups include electricity, water, sewer, and cable TV. A coin-operated laundry is nearby. Cabins, available year-round, cost $90 to $130.

The most luxurious camping is at **Spruce Lake R.V. Park,** U.S. 36 and Mary's Lake Road (P.O. Box 2497), Estes Park, CO 80517 (☎ **970/586-2889**), located about a mile west of the intersection of U.S. 34 and Business U.S. 36. Here you'll be pampered with miniature golf, a large playground, stocked private fishing lake, and large sites. Ground tents are not permitted.

THE WEST SIDE

Covering more than 36,000 acres along the western edge of Rocky Mountain National Park in Arapaho National Forest, the **Arapaho National Recreation Area** contains excellent fishing lakes (several with boat ramps) and opportunities for hiking, mountain biking, cross-country skiing, snowshoeing, snowmobiling, hunting, and camping in a mountain forest.

The recreation area's campgrounds offer shaded campsites plus the usual picnic tables and fire pits. These include its most developed, **Stillwater Campground,** located off U.S. 34 on the west bank of Lake Granby, about 6 miles south of the community of Grand Lake. Stillwater has showers plus water and electric hookups, available only in summer; a limited number of sites are open in winter, although water is then turned off.

Also located in the Arapaho National Recreation Area, south of Grand Lake, are **Green Ridge Campground** (about 4 miles south on U.S. 34 and then 1 mile south on County Road 66); and **Willow Creek** (about 9 miles south on U.S. 34 and then about 4 miles west on County Road 40). All three are located on lakes with fishing and boat ramps. For

Showers	Fire Pits/ Grills	Laundry	Public Phone	Reserve	Fees*	Open
No	Yes	No	Yes	No	$12	May–Sept
No	Yes	No	Yes	Yes	$14	June–Sept
No	Yes	No	No	No	$10–$12	Year-round
No	Yes	No	Yes	Yes	$10–$14	Year-round
No	Yes	No	Yes	No	$10–$12	Year-round
Yes	No	Yes	Yes	Yes	$19–$25	Apr 25–Oct 19
Yes	Yes	Yes	Yes	Yes	$20–$25	May–Sept
Yes	Yes	No	Yes	Yes	$19–$22	May–Sept
Yes	Yes	Yes	Yes	Yes	$17–$26	Apr–Oct 15
Yes	Yes	Yes	Yes	Yes	$15–$19	Year–round
No	Yes	No	Yes	Yes	$10	May–Oct
Yes	Yes	No	Yes	Yes	$12–$17	Year-round
No	Yes	No	No	No	$8	May–Oct

information, contact the **Arapaho National Recreation Area office** (☎ **970/887-4100**). For campsite reservations (Stillwater and Green Ridge only), call ☎ **800/280-CAMP.**

There are also several commercial campgrounds in the community of Grand Lake, just outside the national park's West Entrance. They all combine modern conveniences with a forest-camping feel. **Elk Creek Campground,** P.O. Box 549, Grand Lake, CO 80447 (☎ **800/355-2733** or 970/627-8502), is located on Golf Course Road, off U.S. 34 on the north side of the village. It has tent and RV sites in a wooded setting, a pond with license-free trout fishing, a playground, a family room, and a convenience store.

Accommodations

There is no lodging or dining inside the national park.

NEAR THE PARK

ESTES PARK AREA (EAST SIDE OF THE NATIONAL PARK)

For help finding accommodations in and around Estes Park, contact the **Estes Park Area Chamber of Commerce Lodging Referral Service,** P.O. Box 3050, Estes Park, CO 80517 (☎ **800/443-7837** or 970/586-4431; fax 970/586-6336; Web site www.estesnet.com).

Among national chains here are **Best Western Lake Estes Resort,** 1650 Big Thompson Hwy. (U.S. 34) (P.O. Box 1466), Estes Park, CO 80517 (☎ **800/292-8439** or 970/586-3386), rates of $92 to $115 single or double, $145 to $200 suite from mid-June to mid-September; and $50 to $85 single or double and $92 to $150 suite the rest of the year; and **Holiday Inn of Estes Park,** U.S. 36 and Colo. 7 (P.O. Box 1468), Estes Park, CO 80517 (☎ **800/80-ESTES** or 970/586-2332), charging $59 to $100 single or double and $100 to $200 suite in summer, and $50 to $75 single or double and $89 to $155 suite in winter.

Aspen Lodge at Estes Park

6120 Colo. 7, Longs Peak Rte., Estes Park, CO 80517. ☎ **800/332-6867** from outside Colorado (reservations only), or 970/586-8133; direct from Denver 303/440-3371; fax 970/586-8133. 36 rms, 23 cabins. Late May through Aug: 3-day minimum, packages include 3 meals, children's program, entertainment, and recreation (horseback riding extra). 3 days shared rm $389 each adult, $225 each child 3–12 years, children under 3 free; single adult $560. 4 days shared rm $499 each adult, $295 each child 3–12 years, children under 3 free; single adult $740. 7 days shared rm $799 each adult, $510 each child 3–12 years, children under 3 free; single adult $1170. For horseback riding, add $295 to the weekly rate. Sept to late May $79–$169 double per night, including full breakfast. Holiday rates higher. AE, DISC, DC, MC, V.

Among Colorado's top dude ranches, Aspen Lodge is a full-service western-style resort, offering horseback riding, tennis, hiking, mountain biking, fishing, cross-country skiing, ice-skating, snowshoeing, snowmobiling, and a myriad of other activities. Guests stay in the handsome log lodge, with a commanding stone fireplace in the lobby, or in cozy one-, two-, or three-room cabins nestled among the aspens. All lodge rooms have balconies, and most rooms and cabins have splendid views of Longs Peak, the national park's tallest mountain. Trails on the lodge's 82 acres of grounds lead directly into Rocky Mountain National Park. Guests can also enjoy an outdoor heated swimming pool and hot tub, and the sports center, which has racquetball, a weight room, and a sauna. Meals are varied and delicious. The lodge also schedules numerous activities to entertain both children and teens.

Baldpate Inn

4900 S. Colo. 7 (P.O. Box 4445), Estes Park, CO 80517. ☎ **970/586-6151.** 12 rms (2 with full bath, 1 with half bath), 3 cabins (all with full bath). $70–$125 double. Rates include full breakfast. DISC, MC, V. Closed Oct–Apr.

Built in 1917, the Baldpate was named for the novel *Seven Keys to Baldpate,* a murder mystery in which each of seven visitors believes he or she possesses the only key to the hotel. In 1996 the Baldpate was added to the National Register of Historic Places. Guests today can watch several movie versions of the story, read the book, and add their keys to the inn's collection of more than 20,000.

The inn is located 7 miles south of Estes Park, at an elevation of 9,000 feet. It offers its guests several prime areas for relaxation: the comfortable lobby, with an impressive fireplace; the library, with a VCR and free use of the inn's video collection; the covered front porch; and the sunny open deck, at the site of the inn's former dance hall, where big bands led by Tommy Dorsey and Lawrence Welk once performed. The early 20th-century–style rooms are each unique, with handmade quilts on the beds. An excellent soup-and-salad buffet is served for lunch and dinner daily during summer (see "Dining," below). The inn is completely smoke free.

Boulder Brook

1900 Fall River Rd., Estes Park, CO 80517. ☎ **800/238-0910** or 970/586-0910; fax 970/586-8067. 16 suites. TV TEL. $89–$169 double; $129–$199 spa suite. Rates vary by season. AE, DISC, MC, V.

It would be hard to find a more beautiful setting among the tall pines for a lodging establishment. All suites face the Fall River, have private riverfront decks, and full or partial kitchens. Spa suites contain two-person spas, plus fireplaces, sitting rooms with cathedral ceilings, and king-size beds. One-bedroom suites offer king-size beds, window seats, two TVs, fireplaces, and baths with oversized whirlpool tub and shower combinations. There's also a year-round outdoor hot tub. Movie buffs will love the VCRs in every suite and the extensive movie library. The Boulder Brook is popular with those celebrating wedding anniversaries and other events; special occasion packages are available year-round.

Estes Park Center/ YMCA of the Rockies

2515 Tunnel Rd., Estes Park, CO 80511-2550. ☎ **970/586-3341,** or from Denver direct 303/448-1615. 530 rms (490 with bath), 201 cabins. Lodge rm summer $46–$87, winter $32–$61; cabin year-round $51–$207. No credit cards.

Extremely popular, this conference and family center is an ideal place to get away from it all or to use as home base while exploring the Estes Park area. The spacious mountain cabins have two to four bedrooms that sleep up to 10, complete kitchens, and telephones. Some have fireplaces. Lodge units are basic. YMCA membership is required, but the underprepared can buy it here at a nominal charge. The center occupies 860 wooded acres, and offers hiking, horseback riding, miniature golf, a heated swimming pool, fishing, bicycling, three tennis courts, and cross-country skiing. Pets are permitted in cabins, but not lodge rooms.

Glacier Lodge

Colo. 66 (P.O. Box 2656), Estes Park, CO 80517. ☎ **800/523-3920** or 970/586-4401. 26 cottages. TV. Summer $95–$160; spring and fall $80–$130. DISC, MC, V. Closed Nov–Apr.

Deer and elk frequently visit these lovely cottages, spread across 15 acres of woodland along the Big Thompson River. Poolside chalets sleep up to six; cozy, homey river duplexes have outside decks overlooking the stream; and river triplexes are similar, with western-style decor. Almost all have kitchens and fireplaces, with a bundle of wood delivered daily. There are also four group lodges that sleep from 12 to 30—rates range from $395 to $775 in summer; lower in the spring and fall. Guests can use a swimming pool, sport court, playground, fishing area, lending library, and stables. Children will enjoy storytelling on Monday evenings and assorted kids' activities on Friday evenings in summer ($7). Everyone will enjoy the free breakfasts on Thursday.

H-Bar-G Ranch Hostel

3500 H-Bar-G Rd., off Dry Gulch Rd. (P.O. Box 1260), Estes Park, CO 80517. ☎ **970/586-3688;** fax 970/589-5004. 100 beds (20 cabins with bath; lodge baths "down the hall"). Memorial Day–Labor Day, $9 per bed; call for cabin rates. Hostelling International membership required (available at the hostel). Closed Labor Day–Memorial Day. MC, V.

Bring a sleeping bag to throw on your dorm bunk, and be prepared to pitch in with daily chores—that's the hosteler's way. You can also make advance reservations for a family cabin with private bath, by advance reservation. Men and women in the lodge sleep in separate rooms. Everyone shares the kitchen and game room. You'll also find tennis and volleyball courts, barbecues, a piano, and hiking trails leading into the national park. Check in between 5:15 and 9pm. Pickup is available at 5pm at the Estes Park Tourist Information Center. The hostel is 4.5 miles northeast of Lake Estes, in the Roosevelt National Forest at an elevation of 8,200 feet, close to Rocky Mountain National Park.

Romantic Riversong Inn

Lower Broadview Dr. off Mary's Lake Rd. (P.O. Box 1910), Estes Park, CO 80517. ☎ **970/586-4666;** fax 970/577-1961. 9 rms. $135–$250 double. Rates include breakfast. MC, V.

A 1920 Craftsman mansion on the Big Thompson River, this elegant bed-and-breakfast is at the end of a country lane, the first right off Mary's Lake Road after it branches off U.S. 36 south. Its grounds include 27 forested acres with hiking trails and a trout pond, as well as abundant wildlife. The cozy bedrooms are decorated with a blend of antique and modern country furniture; some have ornate brass beds and claw-foot tubs, several have jetted tubs for two, and all have fireplaces. Smoking is not permitted. Hosts Sue and Gary Mansfield prepare gourmet candlelight dinners by advance arrangement for the romantically inclined.

Streamside Cabins

1260 Fall River Rd. (P.O. Box 2930), Estes Park, CO 80517. ☎ **800/321-3303** or 970/586-6464; fax 970/586-6272. 19 units. TV. $115–$165 double; $145–$175 suite. AE, DISC, MC, V.

These cabin suites, on 17 acres along the Fall River, about a mile west of Estes Park on U.S. 34, are surrounded by woods and meadows of wildflowers. Deer, elk, and occasional bighorn sheep are such regular visitors that many have been given names. Inside the cabins, everything is top-drawer. They all have king- or queen-size beds, fireplaces, cable TV, VCRs, and decks or patios with gas grills. Most also have full kitchens, and many have beamed cathedral ceilings, skylights, and whirlpool tubs or steam showers. Guests can also use the indoor hot tub/swim spa.

GRAND LAKE AREA (WEST SIDE OF THE NATIONAL PARK)

For a complete listing of lodging and dining choices in the Grand Lake Area, contact the **Grand Lake Area Chamber of Commerce,** P.O. Box 57, Grand Lake, CO 80447 (☎ **800/531-1019** or 970/627-3372 for the chamber, 970/627-3402 for the visitor center; fax 970/627-8007; Web site www.grandlakecolorado.com).

Daven Haven Lodge

604 Marina Dr. (P.O. Box 1528), Grand Lake, CO 80447. ☎ **970/627-8144;** fax 970/627-5098. 16 cabins. TV. $68–$140. DISC, MC, V.

Set among pine trees about 1 block's distance from the lake, this group of cabins offers secluded and quiet lodging. The cabins vary in size, sleeping from two to nine people. Six have fireplaces. You'll also find a heated swimming pool, a volleyball court, horseshoes, a bonfire pit, and a barbecue area. The Back Street Steakhouse, open nightly during the summer (call for winter schedule), offers steaks, pastas, and house specialties such as crab-stuffed trout and Jack Daniels pork chops.

Driftwood Lodge

12255 U.S. 34 (P.O. Box 609), Grand Lake, CO 80447. ☎ and fax **970/627-3654.** 17 units. TV TEL. Summer rm $60–$75 double; suite $95; lower rates in winter. DISC, MC, V.

Located 3 miles south of town, this comfortable and well-maintained motel offers basic rooms plus suites. It has a swimming pool, sauna, whirlpool, playground, and volleyball court.

The Inn at Grand Lake

1103 Grand Ave. (P.O. Box 1590), Grand Lake, CO 80447. ☎ **800/722-2585** or 970/627-9234. 17 rms. Summer $55–$65 double; lower rates in winter. DISC, MC, V.

This restored historic building, constructed about 1890, was originally Grand Lake's courthouse and jail. Now the western-style inn offers comfortable, modern lodging with an Old West feel. Rooms have a variety of bed combinations, and several sleep up to six; most are decorated with antiques. Some rooms have refrigerators, and two have kitchenettes. About half have shower-tub combinations, and the rest have showers only. The inn is located in the center of town, about a half block from the lake.

Dining

OUTSIDE THE PARK

ESTES PARK AREA (EAST SIDE OF THE NATIONAL PARK)

Baldpate Inn

4900 S. Colo. 7. ☎ **970/586-6151.** Reservations recommended. Buffet $10 adults, $7 children under 10. DISC, MC, V. Memorial Day–Sept, daily 11:30am–7pm. SOUP AND SALAD.

Don't be misled by the simple cuisine—the buffet is deliciously filling and plentiful. Everything is made fresh for the meal, and the cooks barely stay one muffin pan ahead of the guests. The two soups of the day could include hearty stews, chili, a marvelous chicken rice, garden vegetable, and classic French onion. The salad bar provides fresh greens and an array of toppings, plus chunks of cheese, and fruit and vegetable salads. Honey wheat bread is a staple, plus wonderful rolls, muffins, and cornbread. To top off the meal there are fresh homemade pies and cappuccino. For the history of the Baldpate Inn, see its listing under "Accommodations," above.

The Dunraven Inn

2470 Colo. 66. ☎ **970/586-6409.** Reservations highly recommended. Main courses $8–$27. AE, DISC, MC, V. Sun–Thurs 5–10pm, Fri–Sat 5–11pm; closed slightly earlier in winter. ITALIAN.

The eclectic decorations here include various images of the *Mona Lisa,* from a mustachioed lady to opera posters, plus autographed dollar bills posted in the lounge area. Smokers and nonsmokers alike will be pleased with the new separate smoking room, which leaves the main dining room entirely smoke-free. House specialties are scampi, linguine with white clam sauce, veal parmigiana, chicken cacciatore, and Dunraven Italiano, which is a charbroiled sirloin steak in a sauce of green, red, and yellow peppers, with black olives, mushrooms, and tomatoes. Fresh fish is served most evenings, and prime rib, New York strip, fettuccini Alfredo, and vegetarian plates are also available. The restaurant offers a children's menu.

Estes Park Brewery

470 Prospect Village Dr. ☎ **970/586-5421.** $5–$7. AE, DC, DISC, MC, V. Summer daily 11am–midnight; closes earlier in winter. AMERICAN.

Pizzas, burgers, sandwiches—including meatball and grilled turkey—and bratwurst made with the brewery's own beer are the fare here. Vegetarians can order a veggie burger and a variety of salads; kids can choose from a children's menu. The brewery here specializes in Belgian-style ales, such as Longs Peak Raspberry Wheat, and also produces an excellent India pale ale. You can try to learn the process yourself on a free tour, or just purchase beer at the brewery to go. Even children are welcome in the tasting room, where they can sample the brewery's own root beer and cream soda—on tap, of course. There are also video games and pool tables.

La Casa Del Estorito

222 E. Elkhorn Ave. ☎ **970/586-2807.** Reservations recommended in summer. Main courses $5–$20. AE, DC, DISC, MC, V. Daily 11am–9:30pm; Sun champagne brunch 10:30am–1:30pm. MEXICAN/CAJUN/AMERICAN.

One thing that Mexican and Cajun cuisine have in common, besides the Gulf of Mexico, is a high level of spiciness—that's the emphasis at the Estorito family's restaurant in downtown Estes Park. This establishment is also known for its generous portions, as well as great views of the Big Thompson River from its banquet room, used often during the busy summer season. Try the blackened swordfish, mesquite chicken, or the very popular fajitas. There are also burgers and sandwiches.

Molly B's

200 Moraine Ave. ☎ **970/586-2766.** Reservations recommended for dinner. Breakfast $2.50–$7; lunch $4–$7; dinner $6–$17. AE, MC, V. Thurs–Tues 6:30am–3pm and 4–9pm. Closed mid-Oct to mid-Apr. AMERICAN.

The friendly staff make you feel right at home in this casual, popular restaurant. Menu items include vegetarian entrees, fresh seafood, pasta, prime rib, steak, and homemade desserts. Beer and wine are available, as is a children's menu. In summer there's patio seating. Molly B's also offers catering year-round.

GRAND LAKE AREA (WEST SIDE OF THE NATIONAL PARK)

Chuck Hole Cafe

1131 Grand Ave. ☎ **970/627-3509.** $2–$6. No credit cards. Memorial Day–Labor Day 6:30am–3pm; shorter hours rest of year. AMERICAN.

This small cafe, decorated with historic photos and prints, has a very western feel. It serves traditional breakfasts such as omelettes and pancakes, and quick lunches including burgers and sandwiches. There is a children's menu.

EG's Garden Grill

1000 Grand Ave. ☎ **970/627-8404.** Main courses $7–$11 at lunch; $10–$20 at dinner. AE, DISC, MC, V. Summer daily 11am–10pm; open year-round but call for hours at other times. NEW AMERICAN/SEAFOOD.

With its large stone fireplace, trellised ceiling, and spacious outdoor beer garden, this restaurant has a warm and comfortable atmosphere. The menu offers innovative variations on traditional American dishes, such as mustard catfish and chicken breast stuffed with sun-dried tomato pesto and mushroom sauce. There are also daily seafood specials and a children's menu.

Picnic & Camping Supplies

In Grand Lake, the **Mountain Food Market,** 400 Grand Ave. (☎ **970/627-3470**), and the **Circle D,** 701 Grand Ave. (☎ **970/627-3210**), have good selections of groceries and picnic supplies. The **Boardwalk Deli,** 826 Grand Ave. (☎ **970/627-5029**), makes sandwiches and also sells deli meats and cheeses by the pound. You can also get picnic and fishing supplies, plus almost anything else you might want, at **Grand Lake Pharmacy,** 1123 Grand Ave. (☎ **970/627-3465**).

Just 0.75 mile from the main east entrance to the park, **Country Supermarket** is located in a small shopping center at 900 Moraine Ave. in Estes Park (☎ **970/586-2702**). The store has a good stock of groceries, including fresh meats and produce, a deli and ATM, ice and firewood, and a large RV-accessible parking lot. It's open 7am to 10pm in summer; 7am to 9pm the rest of the year.

Those looking for camping and outdoor sports supplies and equipment should stop at **Outdoor World,** downtown at 156 E. Elkhorn Ave. (☎ **970/586-2114**), which sells all sorts of backpacking equipment, including hiking boots, outdoor clothing, maps, and supplies. It also rents equipment, such as backpacks, day packs, hikers' baby carriers, sleeping bags, tents, and snowshoes. Outdoor World is open daily 9am to 9pm in summer, and 9am to 5:30pm the rest of the year.

Another good choice is **Colorado Wilderness Sports,** 358 E. Elkhorn Ave. (☎ **800/504-6642** or 970/586-6548), which has a store with sales and rentals and an indoor climbing gym. The retail sales department sells hiking and camping equipment, winter-sports items, fishing supplies and licenses, and outdoor clothing. You can also rent camping gear such as tents, sleeping bags, snowshoes, cross-country skis, and downhill skis. This complete establishment also offers fly-fishing and climbing instruction and guided trips both in and near the national park, as well as a kids' outdoor adventure program in half- and full-day sessions. Hours are 9am to 9pm daily year-round.

Nearby Attractions

Both the communities of Estes Park and Grand Lake can be destinations of their own, offering a variety of outdoor activities on public lands outside Rocky Mountain National Park. You can get details from the **Estes Park Chamber Resort Association,** P.O. Box 3050, Estes Park, CO 80517 (☎ **800/443-7837** or 970/586-4431; fax 970/586-6336; Web site www.estesnet.com); and the **Grand Lake Area Chamber of Commerce,** P.O. Box 57, Grand Lake, CO 80447 (☎ **800/531-1019** or 970/627-3372 for the chamber, 970/627-3402 for the visitor center; fax 970/627-8007; Web site www.grandlakecolorado.com).

One stop every outdoors-lover should consider is a visit to **Enos Mills Cabin,** Colo. 7 opposite Longs Peak Inn in Estes Park (☎ **970/586-4706**). Enos Mills was an innkeeper, self-taught naturalist, author, and an enthusiastic advocate for the outdoors in general and the Rocky Mountains in particular. He was also a major force behind the establishment of Rocky Mountain National Park, lobbying extensively for the creation of the park at the behest of Pres. Theodore Roosevelt. His 1885 cabin and homestead, still operated by Mills's family, are open to the public. Memorabilia in the cabin includes copies of Mills' 15 books and the cameras he used to take thousands of photos of the mountains he loved. There's also a bookshop, photo gallery, and nature center. Call for hours and fees.

34

SAGUARO NATIONAL PARK

by Don and Barbara Laine

THE STATELY SAGUARO CACTUS, SYMBOL OF THE AMERICAN SOUTHwest, is the king here, dominating the entire landscape. One of America's few national parks dedicated to protecting one specific plant, Saguaro National Park also preserves an impressive area of Sonoran Desert. Saguaros are plants with personalities. They often look human, as they stand tall and proud, their arms reaching toward the sky or pointing the way. Though some achieve heights of 50 feet and weigh up to 8 tons, saguaros grow slowly. It usually takes them 15 years to reach 1 foot in height, and they don't flower or produce fruit until they're about 30. They take about 100 years to reach a height of 25 feet. Their maximum lifetime is about 200 years.

One of the hottest and driest parts of North America, the Sonoran Desert also, somewhat ironically, has an amazing variety of life, more than any other of the continent's deserts. Although the saguaro towers above the landscape, and is consequently the first thing we notice here, this desert is home to dozens of other cacti, grasses, shrubs, flowers, and trees, as well as several hundred species of birds, mammals, and reptiles. Many of them are uniquely adapted to the demanding environment of this dry land. For instance, javelinas, those odd-looking piglike animals, have mouths so tough they can bite through prickly pear cactus pads in search of moisture; and kangaroo rats never need to drink at all—they extract all the water they need from seeds.

Saguaro National Park is composed of two separated sections. The Tucson Mountain District, also called Saguaro West, covers 32 square miles of Sonoran Desert west of the city of Tucson; while the Rincon Mountain District, also called Saguaro East, covers 104 square miles of saguaro forest, desert, foothills, and mountain terrain on the east side of Tucson. The two sections are about 30 miles apart.

Both districts offer visitor centers with exhibits, scenic drives, and trails open to hikers and horseback riders. Other park activities include wildlife viewing and bird watching. When the rain cooperates at the right time of year, there are also spectacular shows of wildflowers and cactus blooms. Saguaro East has backcountry camping, but the park has no campgrounds accessible by motor vehicle.

Avoiding the Crowds. Annual visitation is about 2.9 million people, with Saguaro West receiving the most visitors. The park's busiest time is from Christmas through Easter. Those wanting to avoid

Tips from a Park Ranger

For those who have not experienced the Southwest's deserts, and particularly the Sonoran Desert of southern Arizona, Saguaro National Park can be a very unusual experience, according to Tom Danton, the park's chief of interpretation.

"Many visitors are petrified," he says. "It's essential they stop at the visitor center to learn about the park before going out into it." The park environment, with its extreme heat and forests of saguaro, is alien to most people's experiences. Visitors can be even more frightened, Danton says, when they learn there are rattlesnakes, Gila monsters, and other poisonous creatures in the park.

Among his suggestions for enjoying Saguaro West are hiking the 5.5-mile Hugh Norris Trail. "Within 30 minutes you feel like you're on the top of the world," he says. "You get a tremendous sense of accomplishment." For those with less ambition or time, he suggests the short Valley View Overlook Trail and the Desert Discovery Nature Trail, both also in the western district.

On the east side, he suggests the easy Freeman Homestead Trail, which passes by the site of a historic homestead, and the challenging Tanque Verde Ridge Trail, which, he says, is "steep and rugged, but gives you great views of Tucson and the mountains." To really be alone, he recommends trying some of the backcountry trails, where you'll be hiking from desert up into forests of Douglas fir and ponderosa pine.

The prettiest time at the park is in spring when the wildflowers and cacti are in bloom; but Danton himself would visit in midwinter, because the weather is best for hiking. He says that other pluses for winter are that there are a large number of interpretative programs, such as moonlight walks, and that you seldom see any poisonous reptiles.

Danton says that one problem for visitors going to Saguaro East is the lack of parking, even at the visitor center. He suggests that those with recreational vehicles use a smaller vehicle in the park, if they have one, or check with rangers about where to park their big rigs. There are pullouts just inside the Cactus Forest Drive where motor homes can be parked when there's no room in the parking lot.

crowds should visit at other times, although all visitors who plan on hiking will want to avoid summer because of the extreme heat. Fall through mid-December can offer the best of both worlds: fewer crowds and lower temperatures on the trails.

The other way to avoid crowds, even at the busiest times, is to hike. While the park gets a lot of visitors during the first 3 months of the year, many confine their activities to scenic drives, short walks, and looks at the exhibits in the visitor centers. Within 15 minutes you can easily leave the crowds behind.

Just the Facts

GETTING THERE & GATEWAYS

Saguaro National Park is located in southern Arizona near Tucson, about 116 miles southeast of Phoenix. There are two parts to the park: the Rincon Mountain District (Saguaro East) and the Tucson Mountain District (Saguaro West), each about 15 miles from downtown Tucson. To get to Saguaro East from Tucson, head east on Broadway Boulevard and turn right on Old Spanish Trail, which meanders in a southeast

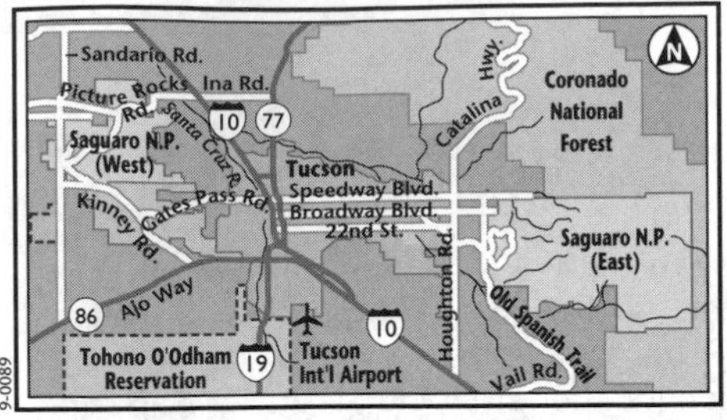

direction to the park. Watch for signs for the park as you go.

To get to Saguaro West from Tucson, go west on Speedway Boulevard, which first becomes Gates Pass Road and then ends at Kinney Road, where you turn right and continue to the park entrance.

From Phoenix, follow I-10 southeast towards Tucson and watch for signs directing you to the park.

The Nearest Airport. Located 6 miles south of downtown, **Tucson International Airport** (☎ **520/573-8100**) is served by many airlines, including **America West, American, Continental, Delta, Northwest, Southwest,** and **United.**

Renting a Car. At the Tucson airport, you'll be able to rent a car from **Alamo, Avis, Budget, Dollar, Hertz,** and **National.**

Toll-free reservations numbers for all the airlines and car rental agencies listed in this section are given in the appendix.

GETTING INFORMATION BEFORE YOUR TRIP

For advance information, contact the **Superintendent, Saguaro National Park,** 3693 South Old Spanish Trail, Tucson, AZ 85730-5699 (☎ **520/733-5153** for the east side, **505/733-5158** for the west side; fax 520/733-5183). The Web site is **www.nps.gov/sagu**. For information on other area attractions and services, contact the **Tucson Convention and Visitors Bureau,** 130 S. Scott Ave., Tucson, AZ 85701 (☎ **800/638-8350** or 520/624-1817).

VISITOR CENTERS

The park has two visitor centers, one in each district. On the west side of the park, in the Tucson Mountain District, the **Red Hills Visitor Center** contains a museum, an information desk, and a bookstore. The museum offers exhibits on desert life and a 15-minute slide program on the uniqueness and importance of deserts.

On the park's east side, in the Rincon Mountain District, the **visitor center** has similar facilities on a somewhat smaller scale. It has an excellent 15-minute video presentation on the flora and fauna of the park and also exhibits on saguaro, cacti, and the world's deserts. Both visitor centers are open daily 8:30am to 5pm year-round except Christmas Day.

ENTRANCE FEES

Entry into the east district costs $4 per private vehicle, or $2 per individual entering the park on foot, bicycle, or motorcycle. Entry into the west district is free.

SPECIAL REGULATIONS & WARNINGS

Extreme heat, cactus spines, and poisonous reptiles are the main safety hazards at Saguaro National Park. Temperatures that soar to 115°F in summer make hiking not only uncomfortable but often dangerous. Those who insist on hiking in the warmer months can minimize the dangers by starting very early in the day, perhaps by 4am, and getting off the trails by noon. Hikers should carry plenty of water and drink it even if they do not feel thirsty.

The heat isn't the only hazard outdoors. Cactus spines can be very painful, as anyone who's inadvertently backed into one while trying to line up a photo can tell you. The bites of rattlesnakes, Gila monsters, and various types of scorpions are poisonous. Park rangers recommend that you always look before putting your hands or feet under rocks or in other hidden spots, and that you use a flashlight at night to help avoid unwanted encounters. Weather-related dangers include lightning (stay off exposed ridges during thunderstorms) and flash floods (avoid drainages during rain).

The usual national park regulations apply here. For overnight hikes, free backcountry camping permits are required. They are available at the Rincon Mountain District Visitor Center or by writing to the park.

SEASONS & CLIMATE

Here in the desert the summers are hot and the winters comfortable, so the best time to visit, especially for hikers, is between October and April. Summer high temperatures are routinely between 100° and 115°F, with lows generally in the 70s. Visitors should also beware of the occasional torrential thunderstorms in July, August, and September, which bring dangers from lightning and flash floods.

During winter, high temperatures are usually in the 60s and low 70s, with lows dropping into the upper 30s and 40s. Occasionally it snows, but it's almost always light and melts quickly. Winters are also known for periodic gentle rains, but most of the time it's sunny.

SEASONAL EVENTS

The best wildflower displays are from mid-March through mid-April. Cacti bloom a bit later—some kinds flower from mid-April through September, although the saguaro usually bloom from late April through June.

USEFUL PUBLICATIONS

Those particularly interested in the plants, animals, and geology of the park can get additional information from two books, both titled ***Saguaro National Monument.*** The larger, more detailed was written by Napier Shelton and published by the National Park Service in 1985. The other, shorter version was written by Doris Evans and published in 1993 by the Southwest Parks and Monuments Association. Detailed descriptions of hikes both in and near the national park will be found in ***Tucson Hiking Guide*** (Boulder, Colo.: Pruett Publishing Co., 1997) by Betty Leavengood.

Seeing the Highlights in a Day

Because Saguaro National Park is composed of two separate sections—the Rincon Mountain District on the east side of Tucson and the Tucson Mountain District on the west side—visitors should ideally spend at least a day or two at each district, starting with the visitor centers, then the short interpretative walks, and finally a serious hike or two. Those with only a day can either see a bit of each district or choose to explore one of them more thoroughly.

To see both sections of the park in 1 day, start in the **Tucson Mountain District** at the impressive new **Red Hills Visitor Center,** where you can examine the exhibits and try to get a handle on life in the Sonoran Desert. Check the bulletin board for the schedule of ranger-led activities; if your timing is right you can join a short guided walk on the **Cactus Garden Trail,** just outside the visitor center, which serves as an excellent introduction to the park. You can also take this short walk on your own. Then drive the 9-mile **Bajada Loop Drive** through a thick stand of saguaro, taking time for a short hike along the **Valley View Overlook Trail.** Those interested in early American Indians will want to take a slight detour off the Bajada Loop Drive to ponder the meaning of the rock art on the **Signal Hill Petroglyph Trail.**

By now it should be lunchtime, so you can stop in one of the picnic areas if you happened to bring food, or at a restaurant in Tucson as you drive through on your way to the **Rincon Mountain District.** Stop at the visitor center as you enter the park—by now you may have a few questions for the rangers, such as, "What were those two big eyes staring out at me from a hole in that old saguaro?" (probably an elf owl). Then head out onto the 8-mile **Cactus Forest Drive** for an easy close-up look at a forest of saguaro. About a third of the way into

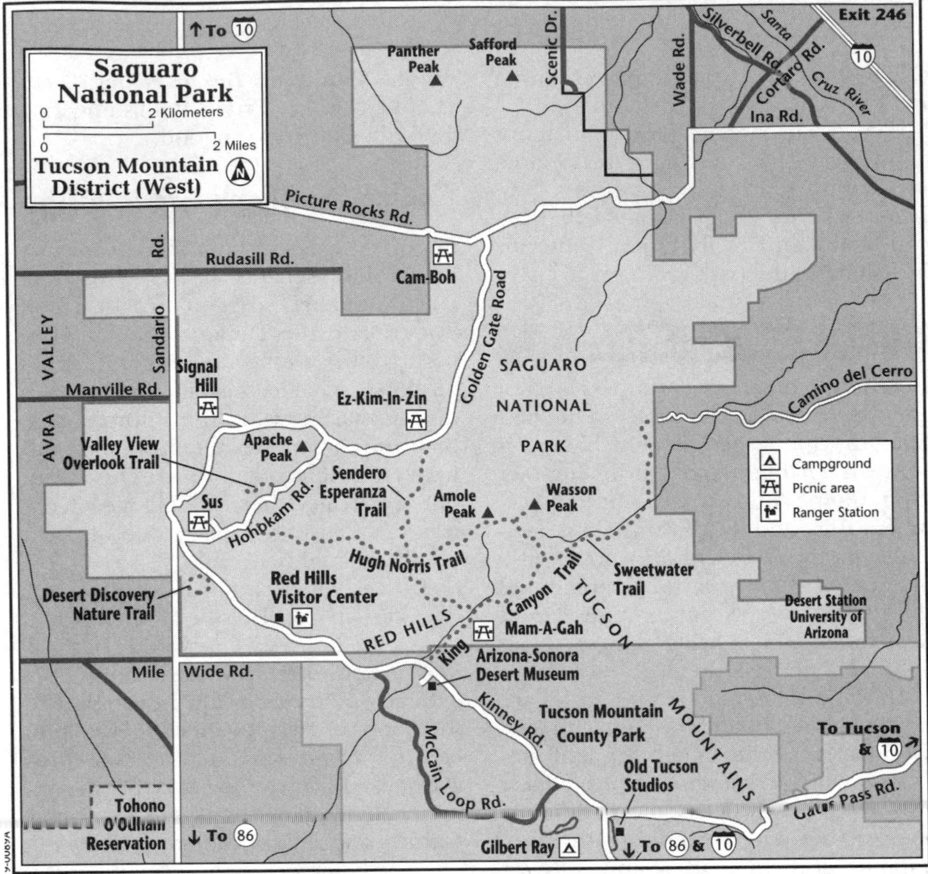

the drive the road crosses the Cactus Forest hiking trail, where you can get out of your vehicle, stretch your legs, and walk a short way into the saguaro forest. If time remains, pull off at the Javelina Picnic Area access road and take a walk along the **Freeman Homestead Trail,** which offers good scenic views and a look at the remains of an old homestead.

Exploring the Park by Car

Each section of the park has its own scenic drive. Before you set out on one, consider buying one of the inexpensive booklets discussing the park's terrain and vegetation at the visitor centers. The 9-mile **Bajada Loop Drive** in the western section begins at the Red Hills Visitor Center and proceeds through a dense forest of saguaro cacti, offering scenic views. There are pullouts where you can get out of your vehicle for a close-up view of the saguaro, and a trailhead for the very worthwhile **Valley View Overlook Trail** (see "Day Hikes," below). Because 6 miles of the loop is gravel, those driving low clearance vehicles or towing trailers should check on current conditions before starting.

In the eastern section of the park, the **Cactus Forest Drive** is a somewhat hilly and twisting 8-mile loop that wanders through a forest of saguaro, which are here more numerous and closer to the road than those in the Bajada Loop Drive. This one-way road is paved, and also provides access to picnic areas, several hiking trails, and short walks.

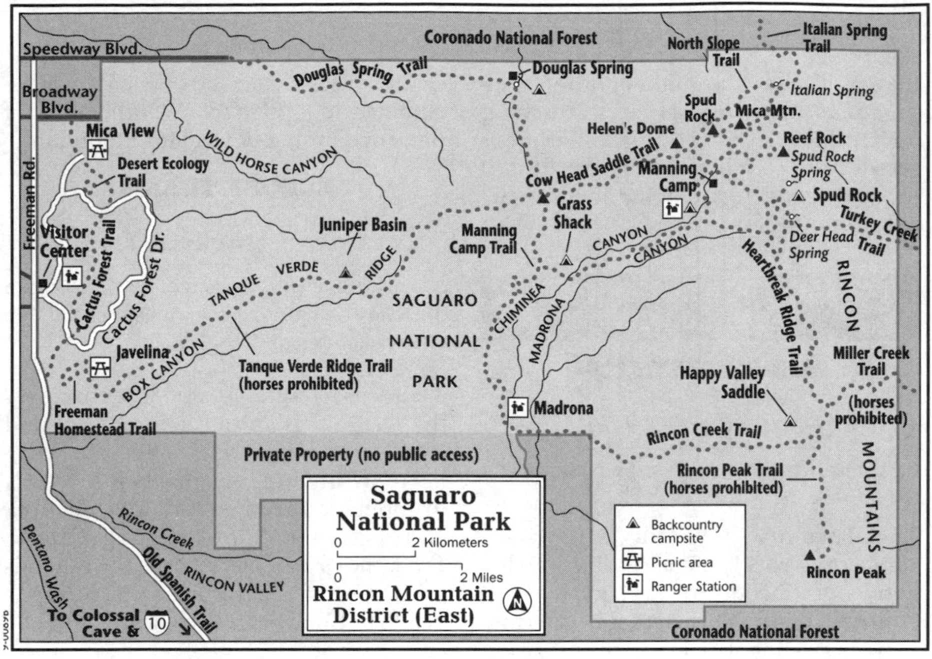

Organized Tours & Ranger Programs

Ranger-led guided walks, hikes, and talks take place year-round, although most occur from December through April. Activities vary, but might include an easy cactus or bird identification walk, a 4-mile hike through the desert, a video program on desert life, or slide shows on wildflowers or bats. Check at the visitor centers for schedules.

Historic & Man-Made Attractions

Both sections of the park contain impressive **rock art** believed to have been created by the Hohokam people, who lived here from about A.D. 700 to A.D. 1500. The best and easiest place to see rock art is on the Signal Hill Petroglyphs Trail, though you'll also find petroglyphs along the King Canyon Trail. Both trails are in the Tucson Mountain District. These petroglyphs (a type of rock carving) usually depict figures of humans and animals plus many abstract designs, such as wavy lines and combinations of circles and spirals.

The park also contains reminders of the miners and settlers who arrived in the late 1800s. The remains of the **Gould Mine,** active in the early 1900s, can be seen along the Sendero Esperanza Trail, in the Tucson Mountain District. In the Rincon Mountain District you can see what's left of an **adobe house** built in 1929 on the Freeman Homestead Trail, and several **lime kilns,** built in about 1880, along the Cactus Garden Trail. See "Day Hikes," below.

Day Hikes

Desert hiking can be a killer, literally. Those planning to do any serious hiking at Saguaro National Park are strongly advised to talk with rangers about their plans before setting out, and then to carry at least a gallon of water per day per person. Rangers do not recommend hiking at all in the summer, when temperatures frequently reach a scorching 115°F. Because some of the longer trails are difficult to follow, hikers are advised to carry good topographic maps, available at the visitor centers.

TUCSON MOUNTAIN DISTRICT (SAGUARO WEST)

SHORTER TRAILS

Cactus Garden Trail

0.15 mile RT. Easy. Access: Red Hills Visitor Center.

A level nature walk just outside the visitor center, this wheelchair-accessible trail is a good introduction to the park and the Sonoran Desert environment. Interpretative signs identify a variety of desert plants.

Signal Hill Petroglyphs Trail

0.25 mile RT. Easy. Access: North of Signal Hill Picnic Area, off Golden Gate Rd., 5 miles northwest of the Red Hills Visitor Center.

This short trail zigzags up the side of a small hill to an area containing dozens of examples of American Indian rock art, believed to have been left by the Hohokam people between 500 and 1,300 years ago (see "Historic & Man-Made Attractions," above).

Desert Discovery Nature Trail

0.5 mile RT. Easy. Access: Kinney Rd., 1 mile northwest of the Red Hills Visitor Center.

This mostly level wheelchair-accessible trail has signs describing the plants, animals, and ecology of the Sonoran Desert. It also provides panoramic views of the Tucson Mountains.

Valley View Overlook Trail

1.5 miles RT. Easy. Access: Bajada Loop Dr., 3.5 miles north of the Red Hills Visitor Center.

Built by the Civilian Conservation Corps in the 1930s, this trail passes through cactus forests and two washes before climbing to a ridge for splendid views of the surrounding desert and mountains.

LONGER TRAILS

Sendero Esperanza Trail

3.2 miles one way. Moderate. Access: Golden Gate Rd., about 6 miles northeast of the Red Hills Visitor Center.

There are several steep switchbacks as the trail leaves an old mining road and climbs to a ridge, which offers spectacular views in all directions, before finally dropping to the Mam-A-Gah Picnic Area and a junction with the King Canyon Trail. Along the way it passes the remains of the Gould Mine, which was enthusiastically but unproductively worked in the early part of the 1900s.

King Canyon Trail

3.5 miles one way. Moderate to difficult. Access: On Kinney Rd., directly across from the Arizona–Sonora Desert Museum, about 2 miles southwest of the Red Hills Visitor Center.

This trail combines with the last 0.3 mile of the Hugh Norris Trail to take you from 2,800 feet elevation to the top of Wasson Peak, at 4,687 feet, the highest point in the Tucson Mountains. Along the trail are petroglyphs believed to have been created by the Hohokam people, some open mine shafts that you'll want to avoid, and panoramic views once you get to the higher elevations. The trail is rocky in spots so good hiking boots are recommended.

Hugh Norris Trail

4.9 miles one way. Difficult. Access: Bajada Loop Dr., 2.5 miles north of the Red Hills Visitor Center.

The longest and most difficult in the park's Tucson Mountain District, this trail begins with a series of switchbacks that lead to a ridge overlooking a huge forest of saguaro cactus. From there it offers good panoramic views and passes old mines and intriguing rock formations. The trail climbs another series of switchbacks before finally making its way to the top of Wasson Peak, at 4,687 feet, from which you generally have spectacular views of Tucson and the surrounding mountains. The trail has a total elevation gain of 2,087 feet.

RINCON MOUNTAIN DISTRICT (SAGUARO EAST)

SHORTER TRAILS

Desert Ecology Trail

0.25 mile RT. Easy. Access: Cactus Forest Dr., east of the Mica View Picnic Area.

Interpretive signs along this paved wheelchair-accessible walkway explain how plants and animals of the Sonoran Desert make the most of the limited amount of water available.

Freeman Homestead Trail

1 mile RT. Easy. Access: Off Cactus Forest Dr., on the Javelina Picnic Area access road.

This walk through gently rolling desert terrain offers good panoramic views as well as close-up views of saguaro, ocotillo, and other desert plants. Along the way, you'll find several interpretative signs describing desert life and the remains of the Freeman Homestead, a three-room adobe house built by Safford Freeman in 1929. All that's left now is a mound of sand from the adobe bricks and a portion of the foundation.

LONGER TRAILS

Cactus Forest Trail

5 miles one way. Easy. Access: Near the east end of Broadway Blvd., just east of Freeman Rd.

This sandy, level trail, which can also be accessed from two points on the Cactus Forest Drive, is simply a very pleasant walk though a forest of cactus, primarily saguaro, where you'll also see a variety of other desert plants, such as paloverde and mesquite, as well as large beehive-shaped lime kilns, dating from about 1880.

Douglas Spring Trail

6 miles one way (to Douglas Spring Campground). Difficult. Access: East end of Speedway Blvd.

This trail through the foothills of the Rincon Mountains is considered strenuous, starting off fairly level but gradually becoming steeper, and then alternating between steep and flat sections all the way to Douglas Spring Campground. Along the way you'll find lots of cactus, especially prickly pear, and some interesting rock formations. Signs of damage from a devastating 1989 fire can still be seen here, as well as the results of revegetation. The trail continues beyond the campground, providing access to other backcountry trails. You need a backcountry permit to stay overnight at the campground (see "Camping," below).

Tanque Verde Ridge Trail

6.9 miles one way (to Juniper Basin Campground). Difficult. Access: Javelina Picnic Area off Cactus Forest Dr.

This trail offers splendid panoramic views as it follows a ridgeline northeast into the wilderness area. You'll see saguaro, cholla, prickly pear, and other cactus for a while, and then pinyon, juniper, and some oak as you climb higher into the foothills. The Juniper Basin Campground, at a 6,000 foot elevation, is 2,900 feet higher than the trailhead. Although the trail continues, this is a good spot for day hikers to turn around. See "Exploring the Backcountry," below, for information on forging ahead.

Exploring the Backcountry

All the park's backcountry hiking and camping opportunities are in the Rincon Mountain District (the eastern section), which includes the 59,930-acre **Rincon Mountain Wilderness.** Varying

Especially for Kids

Kids will enjoy the "Please Touch" table in the **Red Hills Visitor Center.** The park also has several **Junior Ranger Programs,** in which children complete a variety of projects and activities to earn Junior Ranger badges and certificates.

considerably in elevation, this area contains both hot desert sprinkled with saguaro and other cacti, and relatively cool forests of pine and mixed conifer. The main access routes into the backcountry are the **Douglas Spring Trailhead** and **Tanque Verde Ridge Trailhead,** which are discussed above. From these two trails you can access more than 100 miles of interconnecting trails, as well as the park's six backcountry campgrounds (see "Camping," below). Dirt roads lead to several other trailheads; check with park rangers for directions and current conditions. Rangers strongly suggest that those going into the backcountry carry topographical maps, which can be purchased at either visitor center.

Other Sports & Activities

Biking. Bikes are permitted on the scenic drives in both districts. In addition, mountain bikes are allowed in the Rincon Mountain District on the section of the Cactus Forest Trail within the loop drive.

Horseback Riding. Horseback riding is permitted on most trails in both districts of the park, although horses are not allowed off-trail. Horses may be kept overnight in the backcountry campgrounds in the Rincon Mountain District. At Manning Camp there's a corral; at the other backcountry campgrounds, riders should secure horses with a picket rope slung between two trees. Get details from park rangers.

Wildlife Viewing & Bird Watching. Both sections of the park offer abundant opportunities for wildlife and bird watching, although because Saguaro East has a greater range of elevations, and therefore climates, you'll see a larger variety of animals there.

In both sections of the park, look for holes punched in saguaro cacti by Gila woodpeckers and gilded flickers. These finicky birds sometimes make several cavities before settling on one as home for the year, and they always punch out a new home when they return the following year. The extra holes are taken over by other desert inhabitants, including cactus wrens, Lucy's warblers, and cute little elf owls.

Among other birds you're likely to see in both sections of the park are black-throated sparrows, brown towhees, verdin, brown-crested flycatchers, Costa's hummingbirds, roadrunners, mourning doves, white-winged doves, Gambel's quail, American kestrels, and red-tailed hawks. In the eastern part of the park you'll also see rufous-crowned sparrows, olive warblers, yellow-rumped warblers, solitary vireos, American robins, pygmy nuthatches, Steller's jays, mountain chickadees, violet-green swallows, broad-tailed hummingbirds, and Cooper's hawks.

Mammals commonly seen in the park include desert cottontails, Harris ground squirrels, round-tailed ground squirrels, striped skunks, javelina, mule deer, and southern long-nose bats, which pollinate saguaro flowers while feeding on their nectar. You may also spot white-tailed deer in the higher elevations of Saguaro East. Reptiles commonly seen include zebra-tailed and western whiptail lizards, gopher snakes, and king snakes. In the desert and foothill areas, watch out for the many western diamondback rattlesnakes, which are poisonous.

Camping

INSIDE THE PARK

There are no drive-in campgrounds within the national park, but backpackers will find six backcountry campgrounds in the Rincon Mountain Wilderness. All the campgrounds have three sites each except Manning Camp, which has six. Water is available at Manning year-round, but water availability at the other campgrounds is spotty—ask a ranger. Campers who don't want to get sick must treat backcountry water before drinking. Backcountry camping is permitted only in designated campsites. Pick up the required (but free) permit at the Rincon Mountain District Visitor Center or by writing to the park.

NEAR THE PARK

Four miles south of the park's Tucson Mountain District is **Gilbert Ray Campground,** just off Kinney Road on McCain Loop Road, operated by the Pima County Parks and Recreation Department (☎ **520/883-4200**). It offers an attractive desert mountain environment of saguaro, prickly pear, cholla, mesquite, and paloverde, with well-maintained gravel sites.

Convenient for visitors to the national park's Tucson Mountain District, the campground at **Catalina State Park,** 9 miles north of Tucson on Ariz. 77 (☎ **520/628-5798**), has nicely spaced, well-shaded sites, an abundance of rock squirrels, and splendid views of the Santa Catalina Mountains to the southeast.

There are also campgrounds in the Santa Catalina District of the **Coronado National Forest** (☎ **520/749-8700**), to the north of the national park's Rincon Mountain District. Located along the Catalina Highway, they include **Molino Basin,** about 18 miles northeast of Tucson, which has virtually no facilities and can accommodate trailers up to 22 feet only; **Rose Canyon,** about 33 miles northeast of Tucson, which offers fishing at Rose Canyon Lake; and **Spencer Canyon,** located near the top of Mount Lemmon about 39 miles northeast of Tucson, which can accommodate trailers up to 18 feet only.

Among commercial campgrounds in the area are **Cactus Country RV Resort,** 10195 S. Houghton Rd. (☎ **800/777-8799**), at I-10 Exit 275, which has large spaces, some shade trees, and attractive desert landscaping. All RV sites have full hookups including cable TV. There are only a small number of tent sites. Campers have access to a convenience store with RV supplies and propane, a game room, a playground, shuffleboard, and horseshoes.

Accommodations

There are no accommodations inside the park.

NEAR THE PARK

Best Western Inn at the Airport

7060 S. Tucson Blvd., Tucson, AZ 85706. ☎ **800/528-1234** or 520/746-0271; fax 520/889-7391. 147 rms. A/C TV TEL. Mid-Sept to Jan $59–$79 double; Feb to Mar $95–$129 double; Apr to mid-Sept $49–$75 double. Rates include continental breakfast. AE, DC, DISC, MC, V.

This hotel is about the first you'll come to as you leave the airport. Not only does it offer a good range of amenities at surprisingly reasonable rates, but it's also amazingly quiet—all rooms are soundproofed to cut out the nearby airport noise. Guests save money on complimentary evening beer and wine, as well as the free breakfast buffet. The rooms are all comfortable and have small refrigerators. There's also a restaurant, lounge, whirlpool, and a tennis court.

Bienestar Bed & Breakfast

10490 E. Escalante Rd., Tucson, AZ 85730. ☎ **800/293-0004** or 520/290-1048; fax 520/290-1367. 2 rms, 1 suite. Oct–May $85 double, $125 suite; June–Sept $62 double, $93 suite. DISC, MC, V.

Located on the east side of Tucson, this hacienda-style home convenient to the Rincon Mountain District of Saguaro National Park is set amid spacious grounds, complete with stables (handy if you happen to be traveling with your

Campground	Elev.	Total Sites	RV Hookups	Dump Station	Toilets	Drinking Water
Cactus Country R.V. Resort	3,300	246	246	Yes	Yes	Yes
Catalina State Park	2,700	48	23	Yes	Yes	Yes
Gilbert Ray	2,600	160	142	Yes	Yes	Yes
Molino Basin	4,500	49	0	No	Yes	No
Rose Canyon	7,000	75	0	No	Yes	Yes
Spencer Canyon	8,000	68	0	No	Yes	Yes

horses). The hillside setting provides far-reaching views of mountains and valley, and the desert landscaping gives the inn a solid sense of place. Friendly innkeepers have provided refreshingly tranquil lodging. The one suite is huge, with a complete entertainment center, a beautiful large bathroom, a little garden patio area, two fireplaces, and a custom-made bed. The smaller Santa Rita room is equally comfortable, if somewhat oddly designed—its bathroom is across the hall, though it's designated for this room only. The Garden room features hand-forged Mexican twin beds and has an adjoining private bath. Breakfasts here feature natural foods, including organic coffee and eggs from free-range hens. Outside there's a swimming pool and a whirlpool spa.

Casa Tierra

11155 W. Calle Pima, Tucson, AZ 85743. ☎ **520/578-3058;** fax 520/578-3058. 3 rms. $75–$95 double. Rates include a full vegetarian breakfast. No credit cards. Closed June–Aug.

If you've come to Tucson to be in the desert and you really want to be a *part* of the desert, then this is where you should stay. Casa Tierra, a modern adobe home surrounded by 5 acres of cacti and paloverde, is situated on the west side of Saguaro National Park's Tucson Mountain District, and has fabulous views of a landscape filled with saguaros. Guests also enjoy stunning sunsets and views of the mountains to the north. The owners are a young couple who designed this inn to resemble homes from the days of Spanish rule. Surrounding a central courtyard with a desert garden is a covered seating area where guests congregate. The rooms have queen beds, brick floors, and private patios. The outdoor whirlpool spa makes a perfect stargazing spot at night.

Doubletree Guest Suites Tucson

6555 E. Speedway Blvd., Tucson, AZ 85710. ☎ **800/222-TREE** or 520/721-7100; fax 750/721-1991. 304 suites. A/C TV TEL. Feb–Apr $95–$140 suite for 2; May–Sept $59–$79 suite for 2; Oct–Jan $79–$99 suite for 2. Rates include full breakfast. AE, DC, DISC, MC, V.

With reasonable rates throughout the year, this all-suite hotel is a good choice both for those who need plenty of space and those who want to be in the upscale east side of Tucson near restaurants and shopping. The five-story brick building is arranged around two long courtyards, one of which has a large pool and whirlpool. The lobby is small but attractively decorated in contemporary southwestern style. The guest rooms also feature contemporary furnishings, with the glass blocks over the wet bars adding an art deco touch. All suites have refrigerators, coffeemakers, irons, and ironing boards. The hotel's restaurant serves primarily Italian dishes. The hotel also offers room service, a complimentary 2-hour cocktail reception, valet/laundry

Showers	Fire Pits/ Grills	Laundry	Public Phone	Reserve	Fees	Open
Yes	No	Yes	Yes	Yes	$15–$25	Year-round
Yes	No	No	Yes	No	$9–$15	Year-round
No	No	No	Yes	No	$6–$9	Year-round
No	No	No	No	No	$6	Oct–May
No	No	No	No	No	$10	Apr–Oct
No	No	No	No	No	$10	Apr–Oct

service, an exercise room, a business center, and access to a nearby health club, tennis courts, and golf.

El Adobe Ranch

4630 N. El Adobe Ranch Rd., Tucson, AZ 85745. ☎ **520/743-3525;** fax 520/297-2080. 5 casitas. Oct–Apr $175 double; May–Sept $110 double. Rates include continental breakfast. AE, MC, V.

Sort of a cross between a bed-and-breakfast and a guest ranch, this unusual lodging offers seclusion amid saguaros and accommodation in contemporary southwestern-style casitas. Staying here is a bit like having your own modern home down a dirt road out in the desert, with the Tucson Mountain District of Saguaro National Park practically in your backyard. Three casitas—Spanish-style cabins—have their own kitchens, and two have kitchenettes and whirlpool tubs. All have fireplaces in both the living room and bedroom.

Hotel Congress

311 E. Congress St., Tucson, AZ 85701. ☎ **800/722-8848** or 520/622-8848; fax 520/792-6366. 40 rms. TEL. $31–$45 double. Student discount available. Lower rates for shared hostel rms. AE, MC, V.

Located in the heart of Tucson's downtown arts district, the Hotel Congress once hosted John Dillinger. Today it operates as a youth hostel and budget hotel. Conveniently located near the Greyhound and Amtrak stations, this hotel is especially popular with students and European backpackers. The lobby has been restored to its original southwestern elegance, and most of the hostel rooms have been recently renovated, though the building is still far from luxurious. Some bathrooms have tubs only and others have showers only. There's a popular cafe off the lobby, as well as an appropriately Western bar. At night the Club Congress is a popular and loud dance club. Guests can pick up free earplugs at the front desk if they want to sleep through the noise.

Smuggler's Inn

6350 E. Speedway Blvd. (at Wilmot), Tucson, AZ 85710. ☎ **800/525-8852** or 520/296-3292; fax 520/722-3713. 121 rms, 28 suites. A/C TV TEL. Jan to mid-May $109–$119 double, $125–$135 suite; mid-May to Sept $56–$63 double, $96 suite; Oct–Dec $66–$73 double, $96 suite. AE, DC, DISC, MC, V.

The Smuggler's Inn is a comfortable and economically priced hotel built around an attractive garden and pond. Neatly trimmed lawns and tall palm trees give the garden a tropical look. The recently renovated guest rooms are spacious, and all have modern furnishings and a balcony or patio. The decor of the inn's restaurant has a Caribbean nautical theme, though the food doesn't reflect this. There's also a cocktail lounge. The inn offers room service, a complimentary morning newspaper, and health club privileges. Its facilities include a pool, whirlpool, and putting green.

Dining

There are no restaurants inside the park.

NEAR THE PARK

Anthony's in the Catalinas

6440 N. Campbell Ave. ☎ **520/299-1771.** Reservations highly recommended. Main courses $7.50–$12 at lunch, $16–$28 at dinner. AE, DC, MC, V. Mon–Fri 11:30am–1:30pm and 5:30–10pm; Sat–Sun 5:30–10pm. SOUTHWESTERN/CONTINENTAL.

If you head north on Campbell Avenue up into the foothills of the Catalinas, you'll come to this modern hacienda-style building overlooking the city. Anthony's exudes southwestern elegance from the moment you drive under the portico and let the valet park your car. The waiters are smartly attired in tuxedos and the guests are almost as well dressed. Quiet classical music plays in the background, and the lights of the city below twinkle through the window of the main dining room. In such a rarefied atmosphere you'd expect only the finest meal, and that's what you get. Smoked salmon is a fitting beginning, followed by lamb Wellington, baked in puff pastry with pâté and prosciutto. At 78 pages, the wine list may be the most extensive in the city. The pastry cart may tempt you, but, if it's available, don't miss out on the best part of a meal: the day's soufflé (order early).

El Charro Cafe

311 N. Court Ave. ☎ **520/622-1922.** Reservations recommended for dinner. Main courses $4.25–$15.50. AE, DISC, MC, V. Sun–Thurs 11:30am–10pm, Fri–Sat 11:30am–11pm. MEXICAN.

Located in an old stone building in El Presidio Historic District, El Charro claims to be Tucson's oldest family operated Mexican restaurant—it's been serving authentic Tucson-style Mexican food for 75 continuous years. A porch has been glassed in for a greenhouselike dining area overlooking the street, and there's also dining downstairs. Look at the roof of El Charro as you approach, and you might see a large metal cage containing beef drying in the sun. This is the main ingredient in *carne seca,* El Charro's well-known specialty, rarely found outside the Tucson area.

Other El Charro branches can be found in the Tucson International Airport (☎ 520/573-8222) and at 6310 E. Broadway (☎ 520/745-1922). Adjacent to all locations is the family run Toma!, a colorful bar/cantina.

Little Anthony's Diner

7010 E. Broadway Blvd. ☎ **520/296-0456.** Burgers and sandwiches $4–$5.50. MC, V. Mon–Thurs 11am–10pm, Fri 11am–11pm, Sat 8am–11pm, Sun 8am–10pm. AMERICAN.

This is a great place for kids, although kids-at-heart will also enjoy the 1950s music and decor. The staff is good with children, and there's a video-game room and a rocket ship outside to ride. How about a Jailhouse Rock Burger or Hound Dog Hot Dog with a tower of onion rings? Daily specials and bottomless soft drinks make feeding the family fairly inexpensive. Beer and wine are also served. Most nights after 5pm there's a DJ along with the dinner.

Pronto

2955 E. Speedway Blvd. ☎ **520/326-9707** (take-out line). $2.50–$7.50. MC, V. Mon–Thurs 11am–9pm, Fri–Sat 11am–10pm, Sun 4–9pm. INTERNATIONAL.

A good example of what can be done to recycle a fast-food establishment, Pronto retains the walk-up counter, but now boasts an international menu and hip decor. Come here for fast, affordable food in an informal setting. You'll discover gourmet twists on old standards such as burgers, sandwiches, tacos, salads, pizzas, and pastas—plus more exotic creations such as Mediterranean-style vegetarian dishes and chicken satay. Beer, wine, and espresso are available. Sit at the collage-topped cafe-style tables or get your order to go—Pronto is consistently voted Tucson's best take-out restaurant by readers of a local newspaper.

Scordato's

4405 W. Speedway Blvd. ☎ **520/792-3055.** Reservations highly recommended. Main courses $16–$25. AE, DC, DISC, MC, V. Tues–Sat 5–9pm, Sun 4–9pm. ITALIAN.

Located near Saguaro West, this restaurant looks a bit like a lost Italian villa searching for the Mediterranean Coast, with saguaros standing next to cypresses out front. Inside, plush carpets, comfortable brocade chairs, and big windows allow diners to enjoy desert views in comfort. Despite the crystal chandeliers and tapestries on the walls, you don't have to dress up for dinner here, where you'll find both families and business types. The menu contains many tempting choices, although it's difficult to move beyond the variety of veal dishes. Veal stresa is a favorite—it's stuffed with prosciutto and mozzarella and then sautéed in marsala and white wine sauce. There's an extensive wine list.

The Tack Room

7300 E. Vactor Ranch Trail (off Sabino Canyon Rd., about 0.5 mile north of Tanque Verde Rd.). ☎ **520/722-2800.** Reservations recommended. Main courses $24.50–$34. AE, DC, DISC, MC, V. May to mid-Jan Tues–Sun 6–11pm; late Jan–Apr daily 6–11pm. SOUTHWESTERN/AMERICAN.

The Tack Room is Tucson's most prestigious restaurant, and dining here is a very special experience. Housed in an older southwestern-style hacienda with an atmosphere of casual elegance, The Tack Room has a bevy of tuxedoed waiters who attend to your every need, with service that is both attentive and discreet. Diners are pampered from the time they sit down and taste the little bites of marinated salads to the moment the last bit of dessert is savored. Particularly tasty are the plump guaymas shrimp subtly seasoned with orange zest and garlic, the perfectly grilled salmon with papaya salsa, and the crisp yet succulent duck, topped with pistachios and resting on a mound of not-too-sweet fig-and-orange chutney. Coffee comes with a condiment tray that includes whipped cream and crumbled Belgian chocolate.

Picnic & Camping Supplies

Although there are no stores within the park's boundaries, you'll find plenty of places to stock up on supplies in the Tucson area. Recommended for basic groceries are the numerous **Safeway** supermarkets, including the one at 7110 N. Oracle Rd., Tucson (☎ **520/575-0949**), which has a deli, bakery, pharmacy, and liquor department in addition to a good selection of groceries. You'll also find pretty much whatever you need food- and beverage-wise at the area's several **Albertson's Food & Drug Stores,** including the outlet at 6363 E. 22nd St. (☎ **520/571-9091**).

For camping, hiking, backpacking, and mountain-biking gear, as well as tips on outdoor recreation locations, stop at **Summit Hut,** 5045 E. Speedway Blvd., Tucson (☎ **800/499-8696** or 520/325-1154), open 7 days a week and offering both sales and rentals. Another good bet for supplies and equipment for camping and other outdoor recreation is **Popular Outdoor Outfitters,** 6315 E. Broadway Blvd. (☎ **520/290-1644**), also open 7 days a week.

35

SEQUOIA & KINGS CANYON NATIONAL PARKS

by Stacey Wells

In the heart of the Sierra Nevada, just south of Yosemite, are Sequoia and Kings Canyon national parks, home to the largest Giant Sequoia trees in the world and a deep gorge of a canyon that rivals Yosemite Valley. Sequoia and Kings Canyon are separate parks snuggled next to one another and managed as a single entity. Combined, they outsize Yosemite. Their peaks stretch across 1,350 square miles and include the 14,494-foot Mount Whitney, the tallest point in the continental United States. The parks are also home to the Kaweah Range, a string of dark, beautiful mountains nestled amid the Sierra, and three powerful rivers: the Kings, Kern, and Kaweah. Despite their size, these two parks attract less than half the number of Yosemite's annual visitors, making them an appreciated alternative for those looking to avoid huge crowds.

In fact, visitors from Yosemite might find the contrast shocking. You won't find four dozen ranger-led hikes here, or a shuttle bus with drivers pointing out landmarks like tour guides. There are no special events, nothing aimed at bringing more folks in than would otherwise come just to see the beauty and majesty of the largest living things on earth. None of this is likely to change any time soon. The Park Service here is determined to learn from Yosemite's mistakes and so are residents in nearby towns. This is nature, not Disneyland. Expect far fewer people, far less to entertain, and far more to explore at your leisure.

The parks owe their existence to a small band of determined conservationists in the mid-1800s. Alarmed by the wholesale destruction of the region's sequoia forests, these farsighted people pushed to make the area a protected park. Finally, Sequoia National Park was created in 1890, along with the tiny General Grant National Park, which was established to protect Grant Grove. But the move was too late to spare the Converse Basin from the profiteers. Once the largest stand of Giant Sequoias in the world, today it's a cemetery of tree stumps, the grave markers of fallen giants.

In 1926, the park was expanded eastward to include the smaller Kern Canyon and Mount Whitney. But rumblings continued over the fate of Kings Canyon itself. For awhile, its future lie as a reservoir. It wasn't until the 1960s that Kings Canyon was finally protected for good. In 1978, Mineral King was added to Sequoia's half of the park and since then, the boundaries have stayed put. The parks have been managed jointly since World War II.

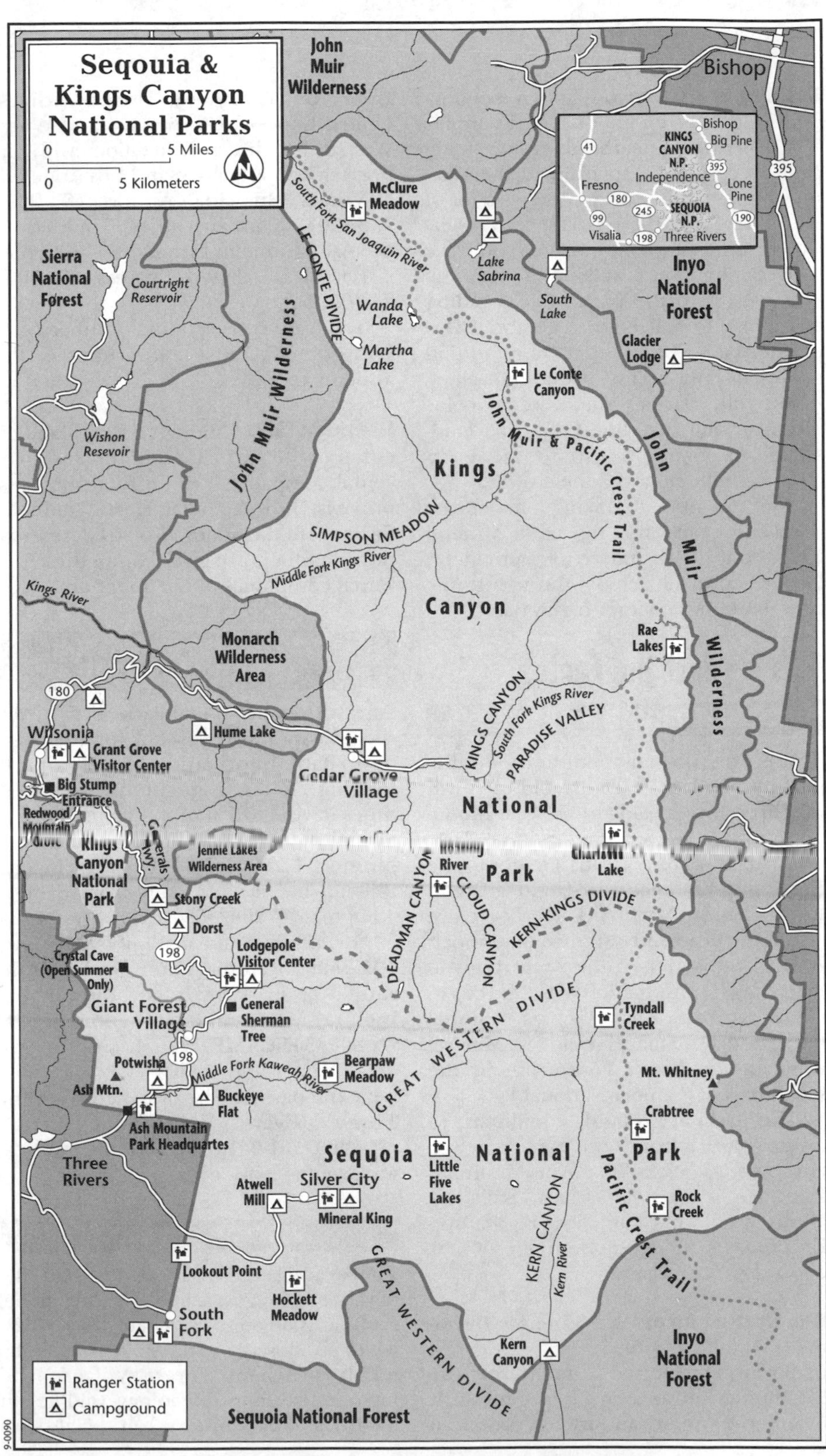
Sequoia & Kings Canyon National Parks
0
5 Miles
0
5 Kilometers
N
John Muir Wilderness
Bishop
Big Pine
KINGS CANYON N.P.
Independence
Lone Pine
Fresno
SEQUOIA N.P.
Visalia
Three Rivers
41
395
180
245
99
198
190
McClure Meadow
South Fork San Joaquin River
LE CONTE DIVIDE
Lake Sabrina
South Lake
Inyo National Forest
Sierra National Forest
Courtright Reservoir
Wanda Lake
Martha Lake
Glacier Lodge
Le Conte Canyon
John Muir Wilderness
John Muir & Pacific Crest Trail
Wishon Resevoir
Kings
SIMPSON MEADOW
Middle Fork Kings River
Kings River
Canyon
Monarch Wilderness Area
Rae Lakes
KINGS CANYON
South Fork Kings River
PARADISE VALLEY
Wilsonia
Grant Grove Visitor Center
Hume Lake
Cedar Grove Village
Big Stump Entrance
National
Redwood Mountain Grove
Kings Canyon National Park
Jennie Lakes Wilderness Area
River
Park
Lake
Stony Creek
DEADMAN CANYON
CLOUD CANYON
KERN-KINGS DIVIDE
Dorst
Crystal Cave (Open Summer Only)
Lodgepole Visitor Center
Giant Forest Village
General Sherman Tree
GREAT WESTERN DIVIDE
Tyndall Creek
Potwisha
Middle Fork Kaweah River
Bearpaw Meadow
Mt. Whitney
Ash Mtn.
Buckeye Flat
Ash Mountain Park Headquartes
Crabtree
Three Rivers
Sequoia
National
Park
Little Five Lakes
Atwell Mill
Silver City
Mineral King
Rock Creek
KERN CANYON
Kern River
Pacific Crest Trail
Lookout Point
Hockett Meadow
GREAT WESTERN DIVIDE
South Fork
Kern Canyon
Inyo National Forest
Ranger Station
Campground
Sequoia National Forest
9-0090

Avoiding the Crowds. Though Sequoia and Kings Canyon national parks are far less visited than nearby Yosemite, it still can get crowded, especially in the summer high season. Luckily, there's a lot of empty space in these parks, so it's relatively easy to find solitude once you leave your car and start walking. To get the most access to the park while avoiding traffic, try to visit before Memorial Day or after Labor Day, keeping in mind that snow can limit access in the high elevations. Fall provides some scenic color often missing from the California landscape. As always, a trip to the backcountry will help avoid the crowds.

You can also try taking one of the dead-end roads into the park. Mineral King, South Fork and, to a lesser extent, Cedar Grove, all lack the through traffic prevalent on the larger highways.

Just the Facts

GETTING THERE & GATEWAYS

There are two main entrances to the parks. Calif. 198 via Visalia and the town of Three Rivers leads to the **Ash Mountain Entrance** in Sequoia National Park. Calif. 180 via Fresno leads straight to the **Big Stump Entrance** near Grant Grove in Kings Canyon National Park. There are also three dead-end entrance roads open only in the summer: the Kings Canyon Highway (a continuation of Calif. 180) to **Cedar Grove** in Kings Canyon National Park, and two smaller roads to **Mineral King** and to **South Fork,** both in the south part of Sequoia National Park.

The parks are roughly equidistant (5 hours by car) from both San Francisco and Los Angeles. The Ash Mountain Entrance is 36 miles from Visalia, or about an hour away. The Big Stump Entrance is 53 miles from Fresno, or about 1½ hours away.

The Nearest Airports. Fresno Air Terminal (☎ **209/498-4095**) is the nearest major airport, located 53 miles from the Big Stump Entrance in Kings Canyon. It is served by **American Airlines, American Eagle, Delta, Skywest, United Airlines, United Express, US Airways,** and **Wings West.** It has direct connections with airports in San Francisco and Los Angeles.

Visalia Municipal Airport (☎ **209/738-3201**), a tiny airstrip, is 36 miles from the Ash Mountain Entrance. The airport is served by **United Express** (☎ **800/241-6522**).

Toll-free reservations numbers are also given for all these airlines in the appendix.

Renting a Car. Although not available in either of the parks, most of the major car rental companies can be found in Fresno: **Avis, Budget, Dollar, Hertz, National, Sears,** and **Standard.** Toll-free reservations numbers are given for all these car-rental companies in the appendix.

GETTING INFORMATION BEFORE YOUR TRIP

Start with the National Park Service Web site at **www.nps.gov/seki/** for the most up-to-date information on the park, lodging, hikes, regulations, and best times to visit. Much of the same information plus road conditions are available by phone (☎ **209/565-3341**). A live operator can be reached daily from 8am to 4:30pm at ☎ **209/565-3134**.

For lodging information call ☎ **209/335-5500.** Campground reservations should be made by calling **Biospherics, Inc.,** a Maryland-based company, at ☎ **800/365-CAMP** (2267). Information on lodging and activities outside but near the park can be obtained from the **Three Rivers Reservation Centre** (☎ **209/561-0410**) or on the Web at **www.sequoiapark.com**.

VISITOR CENTERS

There are three visitor centers in the parks. The biggest is in Sequoia National Park at **Lodgepole** (☎ **209/565-3782**), which is closed in winter. It's 4.5 miles north of Giant Forest Village, and includes exhibits on geology, wildlife, air quality, and park history. You can also buy books and maps here. The **Foothills Visitor Center** (☎ **209/565-3134**), open year-round, is just inside the Ash Mountain Entrance on Highway 198 and includes exhibits on the chaparral region's ecosystem. The visitor center in **Grant Grove,** Kings Canyon National Park (☎ **209/335-2856**), includes exhibits on logging and the role of fire in the forests.

ENTRANCE & CAMPING FEES

It costs $10 per car to enter the park or $5 for individuals walking in or arriving by bicycling. Camping in the park costs $6 to $14 a night.

SPECIAL REGULATIONS & WARNINGS

The roads in the park are particularly steep and winding. Those in RVs will find it easiest to come from Calif. 180 from Fresno.

Do not feed any animals, even the cutest of ground squirrels. Piped water is safe, but all groundwater should be boiled for 3 minutes before drinking. Rattlesnakes are common; look where you step and touch. In the foothills, check your clothes frequently for ticks. Beware also of black bears. When camping, store all food in lockers and put all garbage in bear-proof containers.

Backcountry permits are required for all overnight hikes. Make reservations by mail to the park 14 days in advance, but no earlier than March 1. A few permits are available on the day of departure on a first-come, first-served basis.

Motorbikes and mountain bikes are not permitted on any park trails.

SEASONS & CLIMATE

Sequoia and Kings Canyon, for the most part, share a climate that varies considerably depending on the region of the park. A good rule of thumb throughout the park is to remember that the higher you go, the cooler it gets. So pack a parka on any trip that climbs above the valley floor or ventures into the backcountry.

During the summer, temperatures at lower elevations can climb into the 90s and higher, and plummet into the 50s at night. Afternoon temperatures average in the 60s and 70s in spring and fall, and again, evenings are usually cool. Afternoon showers are fairly common year-round. Winter days average in the 40s and 50s, and seldom drop below zero, although much of the land is buried beneath several feet of snow. Remember, a particularly wet winter often leads to an incredibly stunning and powerful spring.

Seeing the Highlights in a Day

Eighty percent of park visitors come here on day trips—an amazing statistic considering the geography of this place. Three to four days will do the park justice, but it is possible to take a short walk through a grove of big trees in one afternoon. Day-trippers should stick to Grant Grove if possible—it's the most accessible. Coming from the south, Giant Forest is a good alternative as well, although the trip takes some time on the steep and narrow Generals Highway. Cedar Grove and Mineral King, two other destination points, are a bit farther afield and require an early start or an overnight stay.

If you only have 1 day, we recommend driving from Giant Forest to Grant Grove, or vice versa. It's about 2 hours through the park, plus whatever additional time is necessary to resume your route outside its entrances. Get your bearings by starting at a park visitor center—either the **Foothills Visitor Center** near the Ash Mountain Entrance or the **Grant Grove Visitor Center.** Whether traveling this route from the north or south, you'll see the varied climate within the park as you pass through dense forest to exposed meadows and then through scrubby foothills covered in oaks and underbrush. In spring and summer, much of the route is dotted by wildflowers and the southern portion runs along the Kaweah River. This route also passes near two large stands of Giant

Sequoias, one at Grant Grove and the other at Giant Forest. Both have easy trails looping through the majestic stands. At Grant Grove, a footpath passes lengthwise through a fallen sequoia.

If You Have More Time

SEQUOIA NATIONAL PARK

The best-known stand of sequoias in the world can be found in **Giant Forest,** part of Sequoia National Park. Named in 1875 by explorer and environmentalist John Muir, this park consists mostly of huge meadows and a large grove of giant trees. At the northern edge of the grove, you can't miss the **General Sherman Tree,** considered the largest living thing on the planet, although it is neither the tallest nor the widest. It is believed to be between 2,300 and 2,700 years old, *and it's still growing*. Every year, it adds enough new wood to make another 60-foot-tall tree. The tree is part of the 2-mile **Congress Trail,** a foot trail that includes groups of trees with names such as The Senate and The House.

Another interesting stop in Giant Forest is **Tharp's Log,** a cabin named after the first non–Native American settler in the area, Hale Tharp, who grazed cattle among the Giant Sequoias and built a summer cabin in the 1860s from a fallen sequoia hollowed by fire. It is the oldest cabin remaining in the park.

You'll also encounter two kitschy items in the Giant Forest vicinity. **Tunnel Log** is a toppled tree that you can drive *through,* and **Auto Log** is a tree that you can drive *on.*

Nearby **Crescent Meadow** is a pristine clearing dotted with wildflowers and tall grasses. A trail wraps around the meadow. This is also the trailhead for several backcountry hikes.

Also in the area is **Moro Rock,** a large granite dome that offers one of the most spectacular views in the Sierra. From atop the rock, the high-elevation, barren mountains in the Kaweah Range appear dark and ominous. Snow caps the ridgeline throughout the year. While the cliffs appear towering and steep, they are actually smaller than the summit of the Sierra, which is obscured from view. The walk to the top takes visitors up hundreds of stairs and requires about a half hour to get up. At the top is a narrow, fenced plateau with endless views. During a full moon, the mountain peaks shimmer like silver.

South of the Giant Forest is the turnoff for **Crystal Cave,** one of more than 100 caves in the park and one of just two in the area that offer guided tours (Boyden Cavern in the neighboring national forest is the other). The cave is composed of limestone that has turned to marble, and is full of stalactites and stalagmites. To reach the entrance, drive 7 miles down the narrow, winding road (RVs, trailers, and buses are prohibited), and the cave entrance is an additional 15-minute walk down a steep path. The Sequoia Natural History Association conducts 45-minute tours daily between 11am and 4pm from June to Labor Day, and less often in May and late September. Tickets are not sold at the cave, but rather at the Lodgepole and Foothills visitor centers. Cost is $5 for adults, $2.50 for children and seniors with a Golden Eagle Pass, and free for children under age 6. Information is also available by telephone (☎ **209/565-3759**). It gets cold underground, so bring a sweater or jacket.

Giant Forest also has a market, restaurant, and lodging, but only through 1998. All amenities here are being phased out, with the last of them expected to close in October 1998. They will eventually be replaced at the Wuksachi Village.

Lodgepole, the most developed area in both parks, lies just northeast of the Giant Forest on the Generals Highway. Here, you'll find the largest visitor center in either park. There is a large market, several places to eat, the **Walter Fry Nature Center** (see "Especially for Kids," below), a laundry, and a post office.

South of Giant Forest about 16 miles is the region of the park known as the **Foothills.** Located near the Ash Mountain Entrance, the Foothills has a visitor center, several campgrounds and **Hospital Rock,** a large boulder with ancient pictographs that are believed to have been painted by the Monache Indians that once lived here. Nearby are about 50 grinding spots once used to smash acorns into flour. A short trail leads down to a beautiful spot along the Kaweah River where the water gushes over rapids into deep, clear pools. Hospital Rock also has a nice picnic area.

Mineral King is a pristine, undeveloped region in the southern part of the park. This high-mountain valley was carved by glaciers and is bordered by the tall peaks of the Great Western Divide. To reach this area, patient drivers must follow the marked highway sign 3 miles outside Sequoia National Park's Ash Mountain Entrance. From the turnoff to Mineral King, it's a 28-mile trip that makes many tight turns and takes 1.5 hours to drive. Trailers, RVs, and buses are not allowed. The road is closed in winter.

The rocky landscape in Mineral King is as colorful as a rainbow—red and orange shales mix with white marble and black metamorphic shale and granite. In winter, this area is prone to avalanches. The most prominent point in the area is **Sawtooth Peak,** which reaches 12,343 feet. Sawtooth and other peaks in this region resemble the Rocky Mountains more than the rest of the Sierra Nevada because they are made of metaphoric rocks. The trails in Mineral King begin at 7,500 feet and climb from there. Park rangers sometimes conduct hikes around here. The best way to experience Mineral King is to stay overnight in one of two nearby campgrounds.

KINGS CANYON NATIONAL PARK

With its rugged canyon, huge river, and desolate backcountry, Kings Canyon is considered a hiker's dream. It consists of Grant Grove and Cedar Grove, as well as portions of the Monarch Wilderness and Jennie Lakes Wilderness. *One other point of note:* Between Grant Grove and Cedar Grove is a stretch of land not in the park, but in Sequoia National Forest instead. This region includes Hume Lake, Boyden Cavern, and several campgrounds.

Grant Grove is the most crowded region in either park. Not only is it located just a few miles from a main entrance, but the area is also a thoroughfare for travelers heading from Giant Forest to the south or Cedar Grove to the east. The grove was designated as General Grant National Park in 1890, and was incorporated when Kings Canyon National Park was formed in 1940.

Here you'll find the towering **General Grant Tree** amid a grove of spectacular Giant Sequoias. The tree was discovered by Joseph Hardin Tomas in 1862 and named 5 years later to honor Ulysses S. Grant. It measures 267.4 feet tall, 107.6 feet around, and is thought to be the world's third-largest living thing, possibly 2,000 years old. This tree has been officially declared "The Nation's Christmas Tree" and is the cornerstone of the park's annual Christmas tree ceremony.

Two and a half miles southwest of the grove is the **Big Stump Trail,** an instructive hike that can be slightly depressing as it winds among the remains of logged sequoias. Since sequoia wood decays slowly, you'll see century-old leftover piles of sawdust that remain from the logging days. Nearby, **Panoramic Point** visitors can stand atop a 7,520-foot ledge and see across a large stretch of the Sierra, and across Kings Canyon. **Grant Grove Village** also has a restaurant, market, gift shop, and visitor center.

Although in the same park, **Cedar Grove** seems a world away. That this region is around today is sheer luck. There were plans to flood Kings Canyon by damming the Kings River. Today it's an incomprehensible move and one that would have buried Cedar Grove beneath a very deep lake. With that future thwarted, the region stood to become another Yosemite, but people fought hard to prevent that fate and eventually everyone agreed that there are better uses for the Sierra than to convert it to a giant parking garage. Even after the park was established, Cedar Grove was excluded due to the controversy over how this region would be developed. It was finally annexed in 1965 and under a master plan for the area, will remain as it is today. One look and you'll see why any other alternative would have been foolish.

Cedar Grove is covered with lush landscape, tumbling waterfalls and miles upon miles of solitude. Half the fun is driving through **Kings Canyon** as its sheer granite walls close around you and the wild South Fork of the Kings River races by. One mile east of the Cedar Grove Village turnoff is **Canyon View,** where visitors can see the glacially carved U shape of Kings Canyon. Easily accessible nature trails in Cedar Grove include Zumwalt Meadow, Roaring River Falls, and Knapp's Cabin. Zumwalt Meadow is dotted with ponderosa pine and has good views of two rock formations, the **Grand Sentinel** and **North Dome.** The top of Grand Sentinel is 8,504 feet above sea level while North Dome, which some say resembles Half Dome in Yosemite, towers over the area at 8,717 feet. The mile-long trail around the meadow is one of the prettiest in the park. The best place to access this walk is at a parking lot 4.5 miles east of the turnoff for Cedar Grove Village.

Roaring River Falls is a 5-minute walk from the parking area 3 miles east of the turnoff to the village. Even during summer and dry years, water crashes through a narrow granite chute into a cold, green pool below. During a wet spring, these falls are powerful enough to drench visitors who venture too close. **Knapp's Cabin** can be reached via a short walk from a turnoff 2 miles east of the road to Cedar Grove Village. Here, during the 1920s, Santa Barbara businessman George Knapp commissioned lavish fishing expeditions. This tiny cabin was used to store tons of expensive gear.

Ten miles west of Cedar Grove, in the national forest and back toward Grant Grove, is the entrance to **Boyden Cave,** the only other cave in the area to host tours. Boyden Cave hosts visitors in summertime only (☎ **209/736-2708**). Cost is $6.50 for adults and children age 14 and up, and $3.25 for children ages 3 to 13. Children under age 3 are admitted free. Tickets can be purchased at the entrance. The cave is open May to October from 11am to 4pm daily.

Cedar Grove also hosts a small village with a store and gift shop, restaurant, laundry, showers, lodge, and campgrounds. This region of the park is often less crowded than others because it is at the end of the road. It is closed from mid-November to mid-April.

The **Monarch Wilderness** is a 45,000-acre region protected under the 1984 California Wilderness Act. Part of it lies on the grounds of Sequoia National Forest and it adjoins wilderness in Kings Canyon National Park. It's small, tough to reach, and so steep that hikers practically need to be roped in to climb. You're near the wilderness area when you pass Kings Canyon Lodge and Boyden Cave.

The **Jennie Lakes Wilderness** is even smaller at 10,500 acres. Although tiny enough to hike through in a day, it exhibits a variety of wilderness features, including the 10,365-foot Mitchell Peak and several wide, lowland meadows. This region lies between the Generals Highway and Highway 180, east of Grant Grove.

Organized Tours & Ranger Programs

Once again, Sequoia and Kings Canyon national parks are not Yosemite—there aren't a lot of organized activities. Those programs that are offered are seasonal and apt to change at whim. Pick up the park newspaper, ***The Sequoia Bark,*** or ask at a visitor center for details.

Day Hikes

NEAR GIANT FOREST

Congress Trail

2 miles RT. Easy. Access: Start at the General Sherman Tree, just off the Generals Hwy., 2 miles northeast of Giant Forest Village.

This self-guided nature walk circles some of Sequoia National Park's most well known and loved giants. The trail is a paved loop with a 200-foot elevation gain. Here you'll find the General Sherman Tree, considered to be the largest living thing on earth. Other Giant Sequoias along this loop include the President, Chief Sequoyah, General Lee, and McKinley trees. The Lincoln tree is nearby. Several groups of trees include The House and The Senate. Try standing in the middle of these small clusters of trees to gain the perspective of an ant at a picnic. The walk is dotted with inviting benches as well.

Crescent Meadow Loop

1.8 miles RT. Easy. Access: Begin at the Crescent Meadow Parking Area.

The meadow is a large, picturesque clearing dotted with high grass and wildflowers, encircled by a forest of firs and sequoias. The park's oldest cabin (Tharp's Log) is along this route as well. This is a particularly nice hike in early morning and at dusk, when the indirect sunlight allows those with a camera to take the best pictures.

Hazelwood Nature Trail

1 mile RT. Easy. Access: Begin on the south side of the Generals Hwy., across from the road to Round Meadow.

Follow the signs for a good, educational walk with exhibits that explain the relationship between trees, fire, and humans while winding among several stands of sequoias.

High Sierra Trail

9 miles RT. Moderate. Access: The trailhead is near the rest rooms at the Crescent Meadow Parking Area.

This is one gateway to the backcountry, but the first few miles also make a great day hike. Along the way are spectacular views of the Kaweah River's middle fork and the Great Western Divide. The trail runs along a south-facing slope and is therefore warm in spring and fall. Get an early start in summer. From the trailhead, cross two wooden bridges over Crescent Creek until you reach a junction. Tharp's Log is to the left, the High Sierra Trail to the right. Hike uphill and a bit further on through the damage done by the Buckeye Fire of 1988, a blaze ignited by a discarded cigarette 3,000 feet below near the Kaweah River. After 0.75 mile you'll reach Eagle View, which offers a picturesque vision of the Great Western Divide. To the south are the craggy Castle Rocks.

Continue on to see Panther Rock, Alta Peak, and Alta Meadow. At 2.75 miles is a sign to the Wolverton Cutoff, a trail used as a stock route between the Wolverton Corrals and the high country. A bit further on is Panther Creek and a small waterfall. At 3.25 miles is another fork of Panther Creek and above is the pink and gray Panther Rock. Follow a few more creeks to reach the last fork of Panther Creek, down a steep, eroded ravine.

Huckleberry Trail

4 miles RT. Moderate. Access: Begin at the Hazelwood Nature Trail Parking Area, 0.3 mile east of Giant Forest Village on the Generals Hwy.

This is a great hike with a lot of beauty and not a lot of people. It passes through forest and meadow, near a 100-year-old cabin and an old Indian village. The first mile of this hike takes you along the Hazelwood Nature Trail. Head south at each junction until you see a big sign with blue lettering that marks the start of the Huckleberry Trail. You pass a small creek and meadow before reaching a second sign to Huckleberry Meadow. The next mile is steep and there's a cross beneath sequoias, dogwood, and white fir. At the 1.5-mile point is a Squatter's Cabin, a log building built in the 1880s. East of the cabin is a trail junction. Head north (left) up a short hill. At the next junction, veer left along the edges of Circle Meadow for about a quarter mile before you reach another junction. The right is a short detour to Bear's Bathtub, a pair of sequoias hollowed by fire and filled with water. Legend has it that an old mountain guide named Chester Wright once surprised a bear taking a bath here, hence its name. Continue on the trail heading northeast to the Washington Tree, almost as big as the General Sherman Tree, then on to Alta Trail. Turn west (left) to Little Deer Creek. On both sides of the creek are Indian mortar holes. Some of the largest are 3 feet in diameter and it's unknown what they were used for. At the next junction, head north (right) to return to the Generals Highway and the last leg of the Huckleberry Trail to the parking area.

Moro Rock

0.25 mile one way. Moderate. Access: Begin at the Moro Rock Parking Area.

This walk climbs 300 feet up 400 steps that twist along this gigantic bolder perched perilously on a ridge top. Take it slow. The view from the top is breathtaking. It stretches to the Great Western Divide, which looks barren and dark, like the end of the world. Mountains are often snowcapped well into summer. During a full moon, the view is even stranger, and more beautiful.

Moro Rock and Soldiers Loop Trail

4.6 miles RT. Moderate. Access: The trailhead is 30 yards west of the cafeteria at Giant Forest Village.

This hike cuts cross-country from the village to Moro Rock. Part of the early trail is parallel to a main road, but the hike quickly departs from the traffic and heads through a forest dotted with Giant Sequoias. A carpet of ferns occasionally hides the trail. It pops out at Moro Rock, and then it's just a quick heart-thumper to the top.

Trail of the Sequoias

6 miles RT. Moderate. Access: The trailhead is at the northeast end of the General Sherman Tree Parking Area.

This trail offers a longer, more remote hike into Giant Forest, away from the crowds and along some of the more scenic points of this plateau. The first quarter mile is along the Congress Trail before heading uphill at Alta Trail. Look for signs that read TRAIL OF THE SEQUOIAS. After 1.5 miles, including a 0.5-mile steep climb among Giant Sequoias, is the ridge of the Giant Forest. Here are a variety of specimens, young and old, fallen and sturdy. Notice the shallow root system of fallen trees, and the lightning-blasted tops of others still standing. The trail continues to Log Meadow, past Crescent Meadow and Chimney Tree, a sequoia hollowed by fire. At the junction with Huckleberry Trail, follow the blue and green signs north toward the General Sherman Tree and back to Congress Trail.

NEAR GRANT GROVE

Azalea Trail

3 miles RT. Easy. Access: The trailhead begins at the Grant Grove Visitor Center.

From the visitor center, walk past the amphitheater to the Sunset Campground and cross Calif. 180. The first mile joins the South Boundary Trail as it meanders through Wilsonia and crisscrosses Sequoia Creek in a gentle climb. After 1.5 miles is the third crossing of Sequoia Creek, which may be dry in late summer, but the banks are lush with ferns and brightly colored azaleas. But, azaleas contain a toxin that can cause convulsions and paralysis if they are ingested. Return the way you came.

Big Stump Trail

1 mile RT. Easy. Access: Begin at the picnic area near the entrance to Grant Grove from Kings Canyon.

This trail meanders through what was once a grove of Giant Sequoias. All that's left today are the old stumps and piles of

100-year-old sawdust. A brochure available at visitor centers (and at the trailhead during the summer) describes the logging that occurred here in the 1880s. To continue onward, see the Hitchcock Meadow Trail described below, which leads to Viola Fall.

Dead Giant Loop

2.25 miles RT. Easy. Access: The trailhead is at the lower end of the General Grant Tree Parking Area. It begins near a locked gate with a sign that reads NORTH GROVE LOOP.

The Dead Giant Loop and the North Grove Loop (described below) share the first 0.75 mile. The trail descends a fire road and after a quarter mile hits a junction. Take the lower trail. After another half mile you'll break off from the North Grove Loop and head south around a lush meadow. It's another quarter mile to a sign that reads "Dead Giant." Turn west to see what's left of this tree. The trail climbs slightly as it circles a knoll and comes to Sequoia Lake Overlook. The lake was formed in 1899 when the Kings River Lumber Company built a dam on Mill Flat Creek. The water was diverted down a flume to the town of Sanger. During logging, millions of board feet of Giant Sequoias were floated down that flume to be finished at a mill in Sanger. The lumber company went bankrupt in a few years and sold the operation to new owners who moved it over to Converse Basin. The lumber company clear-cut Converse Basin, once the world's largest stand of sequoias. Continue around the loop back to the Dead Giant sign, then head back to the parking area.

General Grant Tree Trail

0.5 mile RT. Easy. Access: Begin at the Grant Tree Parking Area a mile northwest of the visitor center.

The walk leads to the huge General Grant Tree, which is also the nation's only living national shrine. The walk includes signs to help visitors interpret forest features.

Hitchcock Meadow Trail

3.5 miles RT. Easy. Access: Begin at the picnic area near the entrance to Grant Grove from Kings Canyon.

This trail arrives at the pretty Viola Fall. The first half mile mirrors the Big Stump Trail described above. From there, hike another quarter mile to Hitchcock Meadow, a large clearing actually in Sequoia National Forest that is surrounded by sequoia stumps. Notice the small sequoias in this area, these are the descendants of the Giant Sequoias logged in the last century. From here the trail climbs slightly to a ridge, where it reenters Kings Canyon National Park before descending a short series of steep switchbacks to Sequoia Creek. Cross the creek and look for a sign directing you to Viola Falls, a series of short steps that join into one fall when the water level is high. It is very dangerous to venture down the canyon, but above it are several flat places that make great picnic spots.

North Grove Loop

1.2 miles RT. Easy. Access: Begin at the lower end of the General Grant Tree Parking Area.

The trail follows an abandoned mill road from long ago. It cuts through stands of dogwood, sugar pine, sequoia, and white fir. A large dead sequoia shows evidence of a fire.

Park Ridge Trail

4.7 miles RT. Easy. Access: Begin at the Panoramic Point Parking Area, a 2.5-mile drive down a steep road from Grant Grove Village.

This hike begins by walking south along the ridge, where views of the valley and peaks dominate. On a clear day, you can see Hume Lake in Sequoia National Forest, the San Joaquin Valley and occasionally, the coast range 100 miles away. Return the same way.

Sunset Trail

6 miles RT. Moderate to strenuous. Access: Begin across the road from the Grant Grove Visitor Center.

The hike climbs 1,400 feet past two waterfalls and a lake. After crossing the highway, the trail heads left around a campground. After 1.25 miles, follow the South Boundary Trail toward Viola Falls. You'll reach a paved road where you can head to the right to see the park's original entrance. Return the way you came, or follow the road to the General Grant Tree parking area and walk to the visitor center.

NEAR CEDAR GROVE

Bubbs Creek Trail

8 miles RT. Moderate to strenuous. Access: The trailhead is at the east end of the parking area at Road's End.

The trail begins by crossing and recrossing Copper Creek. This site was once an Indian village and shards of obsidian can still be found on the ground in this area. After the first mile you'll enter a swampy area that offers a good place to watch for wildlife. The trail here closes in on the river, where deer and bear drink. At 2 miles, you'll come to a junction. The trail to Paradise Valley heads north (left), while the hike to Bubbs Creek veers right and crosses Bailey Bridge, over the South Fork of the Kings River.

Continue hiking east over four small, wooden bridges that cross Bubbs Creek. The creek was named after John Bubbs, a prospector and rancher who arrived here in 1864. The trail will climb on the creek's north side, throwing in a few steep switchbacks to keep you alert. The switchbacks also provide nice, alternating views of the canyon of Paradise Valley and Cedar Grove. At 3 miles is a large, emerald pool with waterfalls. Far above is a rock formation known as the Sphinx. John Muir named the feature after Egypt's famous likeness. At 4 miles you enter Sphinx Creek, a nice place to spend the day or night (with a wilderness permit). There are several campsites nearby. Hike back the way you came or along the Sentinel Trail described below.

Mist Falls

8 miles RT. Moderate to strenuous. Access: Begin at the short-term parking area at Road's End, past Cedar Grove Village and follow the signs.

This is one of the more popular trails leading to the backcountry, but it's also a nice day hike. The first 2 miles are dry, until you reach Bubbs Creek Bridge. Take the fork to the left and head uphill. The first waterfall is not your destination point, although it is a pretty spot to take a break. From here, the trail meanders along the river, through forest and swamp areas before it comes out at the base of Mist Falls, a wide expanse of a fall that flows generously in spring. There are dozens of great picnic spots here, and along the way up. Return along the same route, or at Bubbs Creek Bridge, cross over and head back on the Sentinel Trail described below. This will add a mile to the hike. From Mist Falls, you can also continue on to Paradise Valley, described below.

Muir's Rock

100 yards RT. Easy. Access: The rock is 100 yards from the parking area at Road's End, along the trail to Zumwalt Meadow.

OK, so you can't walk too far, don't have time, and so on. Well now there's no excuse. This level, simple, short stroll takes you to one of the most historically significant spots in the park's modern-day history. From this wide, flat rock, John Muir used to deliver impassioned speeches about the Sierra.

Paradise Valley

12 miles RT. Moderate to strenuous. Access: Begin at the short-term parking area at Road's End, past Cedar Grove Village and follow the signs.

This is a great overnight hike because the valley is so pretty and there's much to explore. But it can also be accomplished as an ambitious day hike. Follow the above trail to Mist Falls and then head up 3 miles of switchbacks to Paradise Valley. The valley is 3 miles long, relatively flat, and beautiful. Hike through the valley to connect with the John Muir Trail and the rest of the backcountry, or return the way you came.

River Trail

5.5 miles RT. Easy. Access: From the Cedar Grove Ranger Station, drive 3.1 miles to the Roaring River Falls Parking Area.

The trail hugs the river and can be shortened if you just want to walk to the waterfalls (a half mile round-trip), or Zumwalt Meadows (3 miles round-trip; a shorter version is listed below). The waterfalls are 0.25 mile along the trail. The falls are short, but powerful. Do *not* attempt to climb them. Just north of the falls, back toward the parking area, is a sign that reads ZUMWALT MEADOW—ROAD'S END. Take this trail, which initially hugs the highway before breaking off into a beautiful canyon.

At 1.5 miles is the Zumwalt Bridge. If you cross the bridge you'll be a quarter mile from the Zumwalt Meadow parking area. Do not cross the bridge; continue onward up the canyon for another quarter of a mile to Zumwalt Meadow. From here there's a slight incline. In a half mile you'll reach a fork; head uphill. The rest of the hike follows the riverbank, which sports plenty of swimming and fishing holes. After 2.5 miles you'll come to another footbridge. Cross over and it's a short half-mile walk back to the Road's End parking area, where you can try and catch a ride. Otherwise, retrace your steps back to your car.

Sentinel Trail

4.6 miles RT. Easy. Access: The trailhead mirrors the hikes to Bubbs Creek, Mist Falls, and Paradise Valley described above.

Essentially what this hike does is encircle a small length of the South Fork of the Kings River. After hiking 2 miles on the river's north side, the trail splits and heads north to Mist Falls and Paradise Valley or east across Bailey Bridge toward Bubbs Creek. Follow the eastern trail but instead of hiking on to Bubbs Creek, follow a sign that reads ROAD'S END—2.6 MILES. This will take you through dense groves of pine and cedars, with occasional views of Grand Sentinel. You'll cross Avalanche Creek before emerging into a huge meadow and returning near the riverbank. At 2 miles, you can see Muir's Pulpit, the huge boulder described above. At 2.25 miles, you'll find a footbridge that points back to the parking area.

Zumwalt Meadows

1.5 miles RT. Easy. Access: The trail begins at the Zumwalt Meadows Parking Area, 1 mile west of Road's End, on Calif. 180 past Cedar Grove Village.

Cross the bridge and walk left for 100 yards to a fork. Take the trail that leads right for a bird's-eye view of the meadow below before descending 50 feet to the ground below. The trail leads along the meadow's edge, where the fragrance of ponderosa pine, sugar pine, and incense cedar fill the air. The loop around returns along the banks of the South Fork of the Kings River. Grand Sentinel and North Dome rise in the background.

OTHER HIKES

Cold Springs Nature Trail

2 miles RT. Easy. Access: Begin at Mineral King's Cold Springs Campground, across from the ranger station.

This easy loop illustrates the natural history and beauty of the region. It passes near private cabins left over from the days prior to 1978 and the area's addition to Sequoia National Park. The walk offers views of the Mineral King Valley and surrounding peaks. It can get hot and dry in summer, so carry additional water.

Deer Cove Trail

4 miles RT. Strenuous. Access: The trailhead is in the Monarch Wilderness, on Calif. 180, about 2.7 miles west of the Cedar Grove Village turnoff. The parking area is on the north side of the road.

This hike in the Monarch Wilderness, officially maintained by the U.S. Forest Service, starts at 4,400 feet and climbs to 5,600. It follows short, steep switchbacks that climb through bear clover and manzanita. After the first 0.5 mile, it passes above a large spring. Deer Cove Creek is in a steep drainage area at the 2-mile mark. This area is heavily wooded with cedar, fir, and Jeffrey pine. To continue on, see the Wildman Meadow Trail below.

Kings River National Recreation Trail

6 to 10 miles RT. Easy to Spring Creek; strenuous to Garlic Meadow Creek. Access: On Calif. 180, 6 miles below Big Stump Entrance, turn north on F.S. 12S01 (a U.S. Forest Service road), a dirt road marked MCKENZIE HELIPORT, DELILAH LOOKOUT, CAMP 4½. Drive 17.5 miles to the Kings River. Turn west and drive another 2.5 miles to Rodgers Crossing. Cross the bridge and turn east, following signs to Kings River Trail. The trailhead is at the east end of a parking lot another 7 miles ahead, at the road's end.

So it's a long drive, but after hiking in upper Kings Canyon, this is a great place to see what it looks like from the bottom. The views here rival anything in the park, with peaks towering overhead and the river rushing nearby. The hike cuts through the Monarch Wilderness along the belly of Kings Canyon although this trail, too, lies in the national forest, not the park. The trail starts along a dirt road but soon departs and follows the river, which is broad and powerful at this point. The first mile alternates between rapids and pools that sport great fishing. At 1.5 miles is a view up Converse Creek and its rugged canyon.

At 3 miles you'll find Spring Creek, a short but pretty waterfall and good place to rest. You can turn around here for a total hike of 6 miles, or proceed for the 10-mile option. The trail from here ascends the steep Garlic Spur, a ridge that ends suddenly at the ledge of the canyon. The trail above Spring Creek is flecked with obsidian. The nearest source of this rock is the Mono Craters, more than 100 miles to the north. For that reason, many believe this trail was used for trading by the Monache Indians. After the long, steep ascent, the trail heads down to Garlic Meadow Creek. A short way upstream are large pools and wide resting areas. Beyond the creek, the trail is not maintained.

Marble Fork Trail

6 miles RT. Strenuous. Access: Follow the dirt road at the upper end of Potwisha Campground, which is 3.8 miles east of the Ash Mountain Entrance. There is a small parking area past campsite no. 16.

This is one of the most scenic hikes in the Foothills area. The walk leads to a deep gorge where the roaring Marble Falls spills in a cascade over multicolored boulders. From the parking area, begin hiking north up the Southern California Edison flume. After crossing the flume on a wooden bridge, watch for a sign to the trail and head east uphill. The trail crosses some steep switchbacks and near some large poison oak bushes with stems 3 inches wide. Watch out for these bare sticks in late fall and winter.

The trail will begin to flatten out and settle into a slight slope for the rest of the hike up to the waterfalls. Look for large yuccas and California bay along the way. After 2 miles, you can see the waterfalls as the hike cuts through white and gray marble, a belt of the rock that is responsible for seven caves in the park, including Crystal Cave near Giant Forest. Once you reach the falls, it's almost impossible to hike any further and only very experienced hikers should attempt a walk downstream. The marble slabs break very easily. Boulders in the area can get very slick. Be extra careful when water is high. This is a good hike year-round, but can be very hot during summer afternoons.

Potwisha & River's Edge

0.5 mile RT. Easy. Access: From the Ash Mountain Entrance, take the highway to the Potwisha Campground. At the campground entrance (which will be to your left) turn right down a paved road toward an RV dump station. Take the paved road until it hits a dead-end at a parking area. Continue toward the river on a footpath to open bedrock.

This was once the site of an Indian village known as Potwisha, home to a tribe of Monache Indians. The main village was just about where the dump station is now (another modern-day reminder of the respect shown Native Americans). On the bedrock are mortar holes where the women squatted nearby to grind acorns into meal. From here the trail continues above the river to a sandy beach and a good swimming hole. The trail turns east upstream before the suspension bridge, then northward up a short but steep hill. Near the top of the hill you'll run into Middle Fork Trail. Turn west (left) and hike the short distance back to the parking area.

Wildman Meadow

14 miles RT. Strenuous. Access: The trailhead for the Deer Cove Trail, with which this trail connects, is in the Monarch Wilderness, on Hwy. 180, about 2.7 miles west of the Cedar Grove Village turnoff. The parking area is on the north side of the road.

This hike through the Monarch Wilderness mirrors the first 2 miles of the hike to Deer Cove. After reaching Deer Cove, it's a steep ascent to 7,500 feet—a 1,900-foot gain in 5 miles. From Deer Cove, hike 3.5 miles to a sandy knoll, from where there is a good view into the rugged canyon drainage area of Grizzly Creek. At 6.5 miles, you'll top the ridge and cross over to the north-facing slope. A quick drop lands you in Wildman Meadow, where a large stock camp occupies the edge of the clearing.

Exploring the Backcountry

Be aware of bears that frequent these regions. In the summer months, mosquitoes and sunburn are real pests. Stay off of high peaks during thunderstorms and don't attempt any climb if it looks as if a storm is rolling in. Exposed peaks are often struck by lightning. And finally, many of these routes are buried under snow in winter.

Backcountry permits are required for all overnight hikes. Make reservations only by mail to the park at least 14 days in advance, but no earlier than March 1. A few permits are available on the day of departure on a first-come, first-served basis.

Note: There are 15 ranger stations in the wilderness of the park. There are seven along the John Muir and Pacific Crest trails. Another seven are in the southern part of the park in the Sequoia backcountry. Most are not staffed from fall to spring. To find which ranger station is closest to your trailhead, consult the park map handed out free at all entrances.

Alta Peak–Alta Meadow

16 miles RT. Strenuous. Access: From Giant Village, drive about 3 miles north on the Generals Hwy. and then turn right on the Wolverton Rd. turnoff. Look for the trail at the southeast end of the parking area at Wolverton Creek.

From Wolverton, hike on the Lakes Trail toward the Panther Gap Trail. Head right on the Panther Gap Trail, up through the 8,400-foot gap to Alta Trail. Turn left on Alta Trail, hike past the junction with Seven-Mile Hill Trail and the junction with Alta Peak Trail. Left takes you up Alta Peak, a 2,000-foot ascent in 2 miles that offers spectacular vistas. If climbing isn't your idea of fun, plow straight ahead to Alta Meadow, which also has a nice view and good places to camp.

High Sierra Trail

10 miles RT. Moderate to strenuous. Access: Take Calif. 198 to Giant Village and proceed to Crescent Meadow Rd. Bear right at the Y, passing the signed parking area for Moro Rock to the road's end and the Crescent Meadow Parking Area.

This trail is a popular route into the backcountry. Some utilize this as a one-way passage to Mount Whitney. This trail gets a lot of sun, so begin early. From the parking area, head out on a paved trail to the south, over several bridges and to a junction. Turn right onto the High Sierra Trail. You will pass Eagle View, the Wolverton Cutoff and Panther Creek. Hike at least 3 miles before setting up camp.

Jennie Lakes Trail

12 miles RT. Moderate to strenuous. Access: From Grant Grove, drive about 7 miles south on the Generals Hwy. to the turnoff for Big Meadows Campground. The trailhead and parking are on the south side of the road next to a ranger station.

This is a nice overnight hike that's not too demanding, and can be further extended into the Jennie Lakes Wilderness Area. From the parking area, cross through the campground and across Big Meadow Creek. From here the trail climbs. At Fox Meadow, there is a wooden trail sign and register for hikers to sign. At the next junction, head right toward Jennie Lakes (left goes toward the Weaver Lake Trail) and up to Poop Out Pass. From here it's a drop down to the Boulder Creek drainage area and on to emerald-green Jennie Lakes. This hike can be combined with a second day hike to Weaver Lake. Just retrace your steps to the Weaver Lake turnoff. Weaver Lake is a relatively warm mountain lake that reportedly is surrounded by blueberry bushes that weigh heavy with fresh fruit in July.

Lakes Trail

12.5 miles RT. Moderate to strenuous. Access: From Giant Forest, drive north on the Generals Hwy. to the Wolverton Parking Area. The trailhead is on the left of the parking lot as you enter from the highway.

This trail hikes along a string of tarns, high-mountain lakes created by the scouring action of glaciers thousands of years ago. Heather Lake and Pear Lake are popular destinations along this route. From the trailhead head east, avoiding the Long Meadow Trail. Climb up a moraine ridge and soon you'll be hiking above Wolverton Creek, which darts through small meadows strewn with wildflowers. At a junction with the Panther Gap Trail head left toward Heather Lake. At a second junction you have to choose. To the right is Hump Trail, a steep but always open trail. Left is the Watchtower Trail, which leads along a granite ledge blasted in the rock with dynamite. With the Tokopah Valley far below, this hike is not for those who suffer vertigo. Both trails wind up at Heather Lake. Camping is not allowed here, but is OK further up the trail at Pear Lake.

Other Summer Sports & Activities

Rock Climbing. There is no rock climbing school in Sequoia–Kings Canyon, but Mountain and River Adventures (☎ **619/232-4234**) teaches rock climbing and can point experienced climbers to the best rocks in the vicinity.

Fishing. Easily accessed waters are limited to Kings and Kaweah rivers. High-country lakes have a few non-native trout.

Kayaking. The Kaweah and Upper Kings rivers inside the parks are not open for boating, but there are companies that run trips just outside the parks. Trips on the Kings are only for the very brave and

Especially for Kids

The Walter Fry Nature Center in Sequoia, located at the Lodgepole Campground, is a fun place for children to visit during the summer months. They can look through a microscope, watch water bugs, and generally get entertained, albeit briefly.

experienced as it is one of the steepest, wildest rivers in the West.

White-Water Rafting. If you want the thrill without the fear, try white-water rafting. **Kaweah White Water Adventures** is a local outfit that runs Class III, IV, and V trips for beginners and intermediate paddlers. Trips usually last 5 hours, are run in inflatable kayaks or rafts, and are offered from April through August. Cost is $35 to $100 Monday to Thursday, $40 to $110 Friday to Sunday (☎ **800/229-8658** or 209/561-1000). Half the fee is due when you make a reservation, but often, walk-in bookings are available too. There are also a few other companies in the area that run trips down the Kaweah and Kern rivers. Call **Sierra South** (☎ **619/376-3745**), **Outdoor Adventures** (☎ **800/232-4234**), or **Whitewater Voyages** (☎ **800/488-RAFT**).

Winter Sports & Activities

Two **cross-country ski** areas operate in Sequoia and Kings Canyon national parks. Sequoia Ski Touring (☎ **209/565-3435**) is at Wolverton, just north of Giant Forest Village. It offers rentals, instruction, and trail maps for 35 miles of marked backcountry trails. The same company operates in Kings Canyon, in Grant Grove (☎ **209/335-2314**). You'll find the same services here, but the selection of trails is wider. Skiers with their own equipment can ski free. Trail maps are available at visitor centers.

On winter weekends, rangers lead introductory **snowshoe** hikes in **Grant Grove** (☎ **209/335-2856**) and in **Giant Forest** (☎ **209/565-3135**). Snowshoes are provided, but a $1 donation is requested.

Camping

Camping reservations for Sequoia/Kings Canyon should be made with **Biospherics, Inc.** at ☎ **800/365-2267.** Twelve of the fourteen campsites in the parks are on a first-come, first-served basis and do not accept reservations in advance. Only Lodgepole and Dorst require advanced reservations, and then only from Memorial Day to mid-October. Grant and Cedar Grove group campsites must be made by mail-in reservation. Mail requests to either **Sunset Group Sites** at Grant Grove, or **Canyon View Group Sites** at Cedar Grove, at P.O. Box 926, Kings Canyon National Park, CA 93633.

There is a 14-day camping limit in the park from June 14 to September 14, with a 30-day maximum per year. Unless otherwise noted, campgrounds are open year-round. Many campgrounds at higher elevations close in late fall. There is a limit of one vehicle and six people per campsite, except at Potwisha, which allows two vehicles. Group campsites are available at Dorst, Sunset, and Canyon View. Trailers are permitted at 11 of the 14 campgrounds, but there are no hookups at any of the campgrounds. Pets are allowed in all campgrounds, but must be on a leash.

IN SEQUOIA NATIONAL PARK

To get to **Buckeye Flat** (The Foothills, Sequoia National Park, ☎ **209/565-3341**) from the Ash Mountain Entrance, drive about 6 miles northeast on the Generals Highway to the Hospital Rock Ranger Station. Then follow signs to the campground, which is several miles down a narrow, windy road. This is a small campground in a park where large campgrounds dominate. It's set along

Campground	Elev.	Total Sites	RV Hookups	Dump Station	Toilets	Drinking Water
Inside Sequoia National Park						
Atwell Mill	6,650	21	0	No	Yes	Yes
Buckeye Flat	2,800	28	0	No	Yes	Yes
Cold Springs	7,500	40	0	No	Yes	Yes
Dorst	6,700	218	0	Yes	Yes	Yes
Lodgepole	6,700	250	0	Yes	Yes	Yes
Potwisha	2,100	44	0	Yes	Yes	Yes
South Fork	3,650	13	0	No	Yes	No
Inside Kings Canyon National Park						
Azalea	6,600	114	0	Yes	Yes	Yes
Crystal Springs	6,600	66	0	Yes	Yes	Yes
Moraine	4,600	120	0	Yes	Yes	Yes
Sentinel	4,600	83	0	Yes	Yes	Yes
Sheep Creek	4,600	111	0	Yes	Yes	Yes
Sunset	6,600	119	0	Yes	Yes	Yes
Outside the Parks						
Big Meadows	7,600	15	0	No	Yes	No
Buck Rock	7,500	5	0	No	Yes	No
Hume Lake	5,200	40	0	No	Yes	Yes
Landslide	5,800	9	0	No	Yes	No
Upper Ten Mile	5,800	10	0	No	Yes	No
Horse Creek	300	80	0	Yes	Yes	Yes
Lemon Cove	300	55	30	Yes	Yes	Yes

the Middle Fork of the Kaweah River and offers lots of shade and privacy, though it still gets toasty in summer.

Potwisha (The Foothills, Sequoia National Park, ☎ **209/565-3341**) is 3 miles northeast of the Ash Mountain Entrance on the Generals Highway. This is one of the smaller campgrounds in the park, located along the Marble Fork of the Kaweah River. Sites are nestled beneath oak trees, but it can get very hot in the summer.

To reach **South Fork** (The Foothills, Sequoia National Park, ☎ **209/565-3341**) take Calif. 198 from Visalia to Three Rivers and turn east on South Fork Road, where you then drive 23 miles to the campground. The smallest and most remote campground in the park, South Fork is just inside Sequoia's southwestern border. It is set along the South Fork of the Kaweah River. A ranger station nearby has hiking maps and information.

Atwell Mill (Mineral King, Sequoia National Park, ☎ **209/565-3341**) is located on the winding Mineral King Road, 25 miles east of Calif. 198 in Three Rivers. This road is not recommended for trailers or RVs. Mineral King is a beautiful area to stay in, just not easy to get to. This small,

Showers	Fire Pits/ Grills	Laundry	Public Phone	Reserve	Fees	Open
No	Yes	No	Yes	No	$6	May–Oct
No	Yes	No	Yes	No	$12	Apr–Oct
No	Yes	No	Yes	No	$6	May–Oct
No	Yes	Yes	Yes	Yes	$14	May–Oct
Yes	Yes	Yes	Yes	Yes	$14	May–Oct
No	Yes	No	Yes	No	$12	Year-round
No	Yes	No	Yes	No	$6	Year-round
No	Yes	No	Yes	No	$12	Year-round
Yes	Yes	No	Yes	No	$12	May–Oct
Yes	Yes	Yes	Yes	No	$12	May–Oct
Yes	Yes	Yes	Yes	No	$12	May–Nov
Yes	Yes	Yes	Yes	No	$12	May–Oct (as needed)
Yes	Yes	Yes	Yes	No	$12	May–Oct (as needed)
No	Yes	No	Yes	No	Free	June–Oct
No	Yes	No	Yes	No	Free	June–Oct
No	Yes	No	Yes	No	$12	May–Sept
No	Yes	No	Yes	No	Free	May–Oct
No	Yes	No	Yes	No	Free	May–Oct
No	Yes	No	Yes	No	$14	Year-round
Yes	Yes	Yes	Yes	Good idea	$15-$19	Year-round

pretty campground is located near the East Fork of the Kaweah River, at Atwell Creek. Its elevation is about 6,500 feet.

Cold Springs (Mineral King, Sequoia National Park, ☎ **209/565-3341**) is a few miles east of Atwell Mill on the Mineral King Road—it's also not recommended for trailers or RVs. This campground is at an elevation of 7,500 feet, the highest car camping available in the park. It's also a good starting point for many backcountry hikes.

Dorst (Giant Forest, Sequoia National Forest, ☎ **800/365-2267**) is 14 miles northwest of Giant Forest on the Generals Highway. This is one of the larger campgrounds in the park and, at 6,700 feet, one of the highest. It's near some nice backcountry trails and Muir Grove. A grocery, dump station, and laundry are nearby. There are also evening ranger programs.

Lodgepole (Giant Forest, Sequoia National Park, ☎ **800/365-2267**), 5 miles northeast of Giant Forest Village, is the park's largest campground and one of the most popular. It's pretty, but crowded. In summer, you'll find a grocery, showers, restaurant, laundry, dump station, gift shop, horseback riding facilities, you name it. Evening ranger talks are also held here. The campground is near some spectacular big trees and enough backcountry trails to offer some solitude.

IN KINGS CANYON NATIONAL PARK

There are three campgrounds located near Calif. 180 in Grant Grove. All three have evening ranger programs, a grocery, a dump station, horseback riding facilities, and showers nearby. **Azalea** (Grant Grove, Kings Canyon National Park, ☎ **209/565-3341**) is one of the nicest large campgrounds in the park. It's set at 6,600 feet, near the privately owned Lake Sequoia (available for sightseeing only). **Crystal Springs** (Grant Grove, Kings Canyon National Park, ☎ **209/565-3341**) and **Sunset** (Grant Grove, Kings Canyon National Park, ☎ **209/565-3341**) both offer a pretty spot to relax near the big trees.

There are three campgrounds in Cedar Grove, all within a short walk of Cedar Grove Village near Calif. 180. In the village, you'll find a grocery, dump station, and laundry, as well as bicycle rentals and horseback-riding facilities. **Sentinel** (Cedar Grove, Kings Canyon National Park, ☎ **209/565-3341**) is one that fills up fast. If this is full, nearby **Sheep Creek** (Cedar Grove, Kings Canyon National Park, ☎ **209/565-3341**) opens to catch the overflow. The third, **Moraine** (Cedar Grove, Kings Canyon National Park, ☎ **209/565-3341**) also opens on an as-needed basis. This is the furthest from the crowds and the noise.

IN SEQUOIA NATIONAL FOREST

There are several campgrounds in Sequoia National Forest, roughly between Grant Grove and Cedar Grove. None of them accept reservations, but call ☎ **209/338-2251** for information. **Big Meadows** and **Buck Rock** are located about 5 miles down Big Meadows Road, which is off the Generals Highway. Big Meadows, set at 7,600 feet, is close to trails to the Jennie Lakes Wilderness. Buck Rock, about 2 miles further down the Big Meadows Road, is a good place to go to beat the crowds.

Hume Lake, set on the banks of (appropriately enough) Hume Lake, has fishing spots nearby and is close to a grocery store. To get there from Grant Grove, drive 6 miles northeast on Calif. 180 to Hume Lake Road, then turn south and drive 3 miles to the lake.

To get to **Landslide,** drive south on Hume Lake Road 7 miles around the lake, and then go up Ten Mile Road to the campground. This hidden gem is set along Ten Mile Creek, 2 miles from Hume Lake. **Upper Ten Mile** is another primitive campsite a few miles further along Ten Mile Road.

Accommodations

INSIDE THE PARKS

If you aren't camping, there are just four places to stay inside the park. Call ☎ **209/335-5500** to make reservations at Cedar Grove, Grant Grove, or Stony Creek. Other numbers are listed below.

Cedar Grove Lodge

Calif. 180, Cedar Grove, Kings Canyon National Park. ☎ **209/335-5500.** 18 rms. A/C. $90 double. MC, V. Closed in winter.

The motel offers comfortable rooms on the bank of the Kings River. There are communal decks with river views. Rooms are standard motel fare. Getting here is half the fun. It's a 36-mile drive down a winding highway that provides beautiful vistas along the way. It has a sundeck and is near nature trails.

Giant Forest Lodge

Calif. 198, Giant Forest, Sequoia National Park. ☎ **209/535-5500.** 83 rms, 1 suite. $109 double; $272 suite . MC, V. Closed in winter, and will close permanently in Oct 1998.

Motel-style rooms with either two double or two queen-size beds. All rooms are carpeted with minimal furnishings. There are two restaurants nearby described below in "Dining."

Grant Grove Lodge

Calif. 180, Grant Grove, Kings Canyon National Park. ☎ **209/335-5500.** 52 cabins and rms; 9 with private bath. $40–$80 double. MC, V.

Amenities are in scarce supply at this rustic lodge. Nine cabins have electricity, indoor plumbing, and private baths. The other 43 are cabins with kerosene lan-terns for light, wood-burning stoves for heat, and communal bathrooms. Some are rustic, wooden cabins; others are made of canvas. Still, rooms and tents provide comfortable places to stay. Some cabins have outdoor stoves for cooking. There's a 30-room modern unit being added now that will be ready by the fall of 1998.

Silver City Resort

Mineral King, Sequoia National Park. ☎ **209/561-3223,** in winter call 209/724-4109. 15 cabins. 8 with shared bath. $55–$175 double. MC, V. Closed Sept–May. Take Hwy. 198 through Three Rivers to the Mineral King turnoff. Silver City is a little more than halfway between Lookout Point and Mineral King.

This place fills up fast. Reservations are accepted in January for the year. Call the winter line listed above. Most of the cabins have kitchens or wood-burning stoves. Less expensive rooms can sleep two to five people. More expensive units have three bedrooms, private bathrooms, and living area.

IN SEQUOIA NATIONAL FOREST

Kings Canyon Lodge

Calif. 180, Sequoia National Forest. ☎ **209/335-2405.** 11 cabins and rms, 2 with shared bath. $65–$150 double. MC, V. Sometimes closed in winter. Take Calif. 180 from Grant Grove toward Cedar Grove. The lodge is at the halfway point, about 15 miles from both locations.

Built in the 1930s, this lodge is practically a historic landmark. It's also one of the only places to buy gasoline near the parks, and uses double gravity pumps that are worth seeing even if you don't need to fill up. The lodge is a mixture of cabins and rooms. All were built out of knotty pine. Each has either one or two double beds. There is also a bar and grill on-site that serves breakfast, lunch, and family-style dinners.

Montecito-Sequoia Lodge

8000 Generals Hwy., Sequoia National Forest. ☎ **800/227-9900,** 800/843-8667, or 209/565-3388; fax 209/565-3223. 36 rms and suites, plus 13 cabins that share a bathhouse. $88–$128 double; $8–$59 for each extra person. Lower rates available off-season. Special weeklong packages available. Rates include breakfast and dinner. AE, DC, DISC, MC, V. Take Calif. 180 into the park, turn right at the fork and drive 8 miles south to the lodge entrance, turn right and follow the road about 0.5 mile to the parking lot.

The Montecito offers comfortable rooms in a well-stocked resort that caters to families with children and large groups, though it does just as well at providing for guests of all ages. It's also the only sizable lodge open year-round in the Sequoia–Kings Canyon area. The lodge itself is in Sequoia National Forest, between Grant Grove and Lodgepole. Rooms are located in four separate buildings. Another 13 individual cabins share a bathhouse. The main building and many private rooms overlook the Kaweah Range. Meals are served buffet-style. There is also a bar on the premises. A large lake accommodates sailing and canoeing. During winter, guests can also go cross-country skiing, snowshoeing, and ice-skating. Facilities include a heated outdoor pool, a Jacuzzi, a sundeck, two outdoor tennis courts, watersports equipment, nature trails, game room, children and teen programs, conference rooms, and a laundry.

Stony Creek Lodge

Generals Hwy., Sequoia National Forest. ☎ **209/335-5500** or 209/561-3314. 11 rms. $100 double. Lower rates available off-season. MC, V. Closed Sept–May. Take the Stony Creek Village exit off the Generals Hwy. between Grant Grove and Giant Village.

This is the plushest place to stay in the Sequoia–Kings Canyon area. Rooms are cozy and large. The lodge itself is in Sequoia National Forest, between Grant Grove and Lodgepole. A restaurant is nearby. There's a tour desk inside.

OUTSIDE THE PARKS

Of the two entrances to the parks, Calif. 198 offers the bulk of accommodations. *One important note:* As the highway bisects the town of Three Rivers, its name changes to Sierra Drive. The **Three Rivers Reservation Centre** offers one-stop shopping (☎ **209/561-0410**) for guests looking for a place to stay in the Three Rivers and Lemon Cove areas. Visalia is another option, as are a few motels along Calif. 180.

Ben Maddox House

601. N. Encina St., Visalia. ☎ **800/401-9800** or 209/739-0721. 4 rms. TV TEL. $85 double. Rates include breakfast. AE, DISC, MC, V.

The house is set on a Victorian-lined street, 4 blocks from downtown. Large palm trees grace the front yard and the house itself is impressive, with a large, triangular gable. Built of redwood in 1876, the owners of the Ben Maddox House have worked to retain the home's original charm. Rooms are trimmed in dark oak trim and white oak floors. Furnishings date from the 1700s and 1800s. Two front rooms have a small porch, accessed through French doors. Breakfast is cooked to order from a menu. There's a swimming pool and a Jacuzzi.

Best Western Holiday Lodge

40105 Sierra Dr., Three Rivers. ☎ **800/528-1234** or 209/561-4119; fax 209/561-3427. 50 rms, 4 suites. 3 rms with shower only. A/C TV TEL. $67–$85 double. AE, DC, DISC, MC, V.

Standard motel fare in a nice location. Most rooms look out on the Kaweah River. Rooms come with two double beds, two queens, one king or one queen. Suites have a separate living area, two televisions, and sofas that fold out for sleeping. Some rooms have fireplaces. If an agent at the toll-free number says the motel is full, call the front desk directly. Outside there's a pool and a playground for children.

Buckeye Tree Lodge

46000 Sierra Dr., Three Rivers. ☎ **209/561-5900;** fax 209/561-4611. 11 rms and 1 cottage, 8 with shower only. A/C TV TEL. $47–$114 double. AE, DC, DISC, MC, V.

This lodge looks pretty average from the outside, but its rolling lawns that end at the riverbank are picturesque. This is a relaxing place to stay, with rear porches off of every room. Rooms are standard, but come equipped with a refrigerator and VCR. Pets are allowed as well and should be mentioned when making reservations.

Lake Elowin Resort

43840 Dineley Dr., Three Rivers. ☎ **209/561-3460;** fax 209/561-1300. 10 cabins; showers only. A/C. $60–$92 double. AE, DC, DISC, MC, V. From eastbound Sierra Dr. in Three Rivers, about 2.5 miles before the park entrance, turn left on Dineley Dr. (the street sign says DINLEY) and drive across a bridge. Bear right, and it's less than 1/2 mile to the resort's driveway.

Undoubtedly one of the best places to stay in the Sierra, this 70-year-old resort is as a resort should be: a place to get away from it all. No phones, no televisions, just rustic but clean cabins nestled under huge trees, all looking out at Lake Elowin, a small body of water above the Kaweah River. Brothers Milton and Dennis Melkonian have owned it for years. All guests must sign a contract upon check-in saying they'll abide by the rules: no smoking, no littering, no car alarms, no pets, no guests. Guests who break the rules are fined $150. But they're easy rules to abide by, more in place to ward off those with an uncooperative attitude.

Cabins can accommodate two to six people. Cabin no. 1 sits close to the lake, with a nice view from the kitchen window. It also has a bedroom, ample-size living room, and bath. Cabin no. 10 has a bedroom that sleeps five, a family room, and a dining area. All cabins include linens and towels, kitchen utensils, and pots and pans. Some have fireplaces and barbecues. You bring the food, sunblock, and good attitude. Visit it on the Web at www.resorts@lake-elowin.

Mesa Verde Plantation Bed & Breakfast

33038 Calif. 198, Lemon Cove. ☎ **800/240-1466** or 209/597-2555; fax 209/587-2551. 8 rms, 4 with full bath, 2 with shower only, 2 with shared bath. A/C. $70–$125 double. Rates include full breakfast. AE, DC, DISC, MC, V. On Calif. 198, 16 miles west of the park entrance.

A cross between the Southwest and the Old South, with enough *Gone with the Wind* theme rooms to fulfill a schoolgirl's, or movie buff's, fantasies. The rooms are named for characters in the film. Scarlett's Room is like a bridal suite with a large bath. Rhett's Room is dim and dark, Belle's looks like a bordello (one of our favorites), and Prissy's Room is painted a hot pink apt to cause minor brain hemorrhaging. Another slightly uncomfortable point: The *phrase private* bath here sometimes means not only will you be sharing facilities with other guests, but in several rooms, toilets are sequestered behind a curtain, which may provide your roommate with a little more information than he or she needs to know. The best part about this place is the large swimming pool and oversize Jacuzzi out back. Visit it for yourself on the Web at www.plantationbnb.com.

Organic Gardens Bed & Breakfast

44095 Dineley Dr., Three Rivers. ☎ **209/561-3652.** 2 rms. A/C. $104 double, $20 per extra person. Rates include full breakfast. 2-night minimum stay on weekends. MC, V. From eastbound Sierra Dr. in Three Rivers, about 2.5 miles before the park entrance, turn left on Dineley Dr. (the street sign says DINLEY) and drive across a bridge. Bear right again and drive about a mile. The driveway will be on your left.

This B&B is a tiny jewel tucked into the Sierra. The two large guest rooms are enhanced by the obvious attention to detail that went into their design (for example, both have private entrances and solariums). The tile floors were laid by the innkeepers. There's a Jacuzzi (guests can request private hours), a photography/looming studio, and an impressive organic garden on the premises. The best part of all of this is the hospitality of owners Brenda Stoltzfus and Saundra Sturdevant, who moved here from the Bay Area. Breakfasts are vegetarian and served on the deck, weather permitting. Times are flexible. The menu may include crepes, pumpkin-walnut scones, fried potatoes, homemade bread, and homemade granola with yogurt, seasonal fruits, and fresh coffee. You can visit their Web site at www.theworks.com/~eggplant. The house is nonsmoking.

Sierra Lodge

43175 Sierra Dr., Three Rivers. ☎ **800/367-8875** or 209/561-3681; fax 209/561-3264. 17 rms plus 5 suites; 8 rms with shower only. A/C TV TEL. $49–$155 double. AE, DC, DISC, MC, V.

Built to resemble a Swiss chalet, this is a rather funky place to stay. Rooms all enter from double, sliding glass doors. They're spotless, but tend to be snug, and some even have fireplaces. All rooms contain a small refrigerator. The bathtubs are tiny. And outside there's a small pool.

Sierra Inn

37692 E. Kings Canyon (Calif. 180), Dunlap. ☎ **209/338-2144.** 8 rms and 1 suite. TV. $50–$150 double in summer, $45–$100 in winter. DISC, MC, V.

The best thing about this place is its choice location just 11 miles from the Big Stump Entrance to Kings Canyon. Rooms come with either one double or two twin beds, and the suite has a kitchen and room to sleep at least four people. There's an inviting restaurant and bar on the premises that hops in the summertime, and serves breakfast, lunch, and dinner. There is no dress code, but dinner reservations are suggested during peak-season.

The Spalding House

631 N. Encinal St., Visalia. ☎ **209/739-7877;** fax 209/625-0902. 3 suites. $85 double. Rates include breakfast. MC, V.

This turn-of-the-century Colonial Revival house offers only suites, each with a private bath and sitting room. Guests always enjoy the library, which contains more than 1,500 books, and the music room with its 1923 Steinway grand piano. The owners have restored the entire home themselves, decorating it with oriental rugs, antiques, and reproductions. It is totally nonsmoking.

Dining

INSIDE THE PARKS

Cedar Grove Cafe

Cedar Grove, Kings Canyon National Park. $4–$6 breakfast and lunch; $6–$12 dinner. MC, V. Daily 8am–8pm. Closed Oct–May. DINER.

From May through September, this is a fine place to grab a quick bite. The menu is simple and the prices are affordable by national park standards. Breakfasts include eggs, cereals, fruit, and pastries, and lunch is mostly burgers and sandwiches. Dinner features specials that rotate nightly and may include pasta, chicken, and so on. There's a nice outdoor seating area near the river.

Lodgepole Deli & Pizza

Lodgepole, Sequoia National Park. $4–$12 for breakfast, lunch, and dinner. MC, V. Daily 8am–8pm. SANDWICHES/PIZZA.

One of the few year-round places to grab a quick sandwich, salad, calzone, or pizza. Ice-cream dishes are available.

Giant Forest Village Cafeteria

Giant Forest, Sequoia National Park. $4–$10 for breakfast, lunch, and dinner. MC, V. Daily 7am–9pm from May–Sept; frequently closes earlier in winter. Closes permanently in Oct 1998. ECLECTIC CAFETERIA.

All meals are served cafeteria-style. A good place to bring the kids with a wide selection of munchables and a very laid-back atmosphere. Breakfasts include cereals, egg and meat dishes, and fruit and pastries. Lunch is burgers, sandwiches, salads, and various hot entrees. Dinner selections include three different entrees.

Fireside Pizza

Giant Forest, Sequoia National Park. $8–$16. MC, V. Daily 11am–10pm. Closes permanently in Oct 1998. PIZZA.

Specialties include your basic pizza and calzones. Nothing too fancy, but enough to satisfy the craving for a pizza.

Kings Canyon Lodge Bar and Grill

Calif. 180, Sequoia National Forest. ☎ **209/335-2405.** $6–$12 for weekend barbecue dinners. MC, V. Daily 8am–8pm. Sometimes closed in winter, so call ahead. DINER/BARBEQUE.

This place tucked off the road between Grant Village and Cedar Grove is privately owned. The restaurant is a short-order fare for breakfast, with burgers, soups, and salads for lunch and dinner. All the food is prepared in a small kitchen and served piping hot. On weekends, try the barbecue dinner special for $12. It includes all the trimmings and is a sort of tradition. The actual dining room here is tiny, and an antique bar occupies the main portion of the lodge. The atmosphere is very kid-friendly around mealtime.

Grant Grove Restaurant

Grant Grove, Kings Canyon National Park. $4–$6 for breakfast and lunch, $8–$20 for dinner. MC, V. May–Sept daily 7am–10pm; Oct–Apr 7am–8pm. AMERICAN.

This restaurant is nothing fancy or spectacular, but if you're hungry, this is the place. It offers a simple menu with something for everyone. Breakfast ranges from omelettes and pancakes to simple cereal or fruit. Lunch offers sandwiches, hot entrees and an all-you-can-eat buffet. Dinner meals include New York steak, chicken cordon bleu, and nightly specials. There's also a tasty dinner buffet available. Prices are a little steep, but lower than most national park restaurants.

Stony Creek Restaurant

Generals Hwy., Sequoia National Forest. Reservations suggested. $5–$10 breakfast and lunch; $8–$22 for dinner. MC, V. Daily 7am–3pm and 5–9pm. AMERICAN.

This is the nicest restaurant nearby and the closest you'll get to fine dining without traveling to Visalia or Fresno. All three meals are available. Breakfast includes the staples, plus a variety of delicious homemade muffins. Salads and sandwiches are served for lunch, and the dinner specials change nightly.

NEAR THE PARKS

Michael's on Main

123 W. Main St., Visalia. ☎ **209/635-2686.** Reservations required. Entrees $15–$22. AE, DC, MC, V. Mon–Thurs 11am–3pm and 5–10pm, Fri 11am–3pm and 5–11pm, Sat 5–11pm. CALIFORNIA.

The great debate in the town of Visalia is whether Michael's or Vintage Press (see below) serves better food. Main dishes here at Michael's range from fresh seafood to grilled items, such as pork tenderloin with a sauce of port and wild mushrooms, or fillet of rabbit. There are also several good pastas.

Noisy Water Cafe

41775 Sierra Dr., Three Rivers. ☎ **209/561-4517.** Breakfasts and lunches $4–$7; dinners $8 and up. AE, MC, V. Daily 6:30am–10pm in summer, 6:30am–9pm in winter. AMERICAN.

A great place to eat. Prices are reasonable and the food is high quality, but the best part about this cafe is the selection. Breakfasts include a choice of omelettes, pancakes, French toast, steak and eggs, or south-of-the-border specialties. Lunch includes dozens of hot and cold sandwiches. And dinner entrees include fish, pasta, beef, and chicken specialties, plus vegetarian dishes. The restaurant also has an extensive wine and beer selection, and offers a $140 bottle of champagne, should you be in the mood to celebrate. The restaurant includes a large main dining room and a smaller anteroom with huge windows overlooking the Kaweah River. The service is friendly, fast, and knowledgeable.

Squaw Valley Restaurant

30910 Calif. 180, Squaw Valley. ☎ **209/332-2011.** $3–$7. AE, DISC, MC, V. Daily 7am–2pm; Tues–Sun 2–9pm.

This restaurant gets the area's best-buy award: Meals are inexpensive if not downright cheap, and the portions are healthy. Breakfasts include a selection of special egg scrambles, omelettes, griddle selections, and steak and eggs. Most entrees come with potatoes, biscuits and gravy, or toast. Lunch and dinner selections include hamburgers, barbecue beef, burritos and tacos, salads, and club sandwiches. Everything is quite good. The atmosphere is reminiscent of a diner and the staff is friendly, patient, and helpful. This place doubles as a stained-glass gallery for a local artist, whose works (most for sale) hang in the windows.

The Vintage Press

216 N. Willis St., Visalia. ☎ **209/733-3033.** Reservations recommended. Main courses $12–$25. AE, DC, MC, V. Mon–Thurs 11:30am–2pm and 6–10pm, Fri–Sat to 11pm. AMERICAN/ CONTINENTAL.

This is the best place to eat within 100 miles. The interior was designed to replicate a gin mill in gold rush San Francisco. The bar was imported from that city and made by Brunswick of bowling alley fame. This place seats 250 amid a host of antiques and leaded mirrors. The menu features a dozen meat and fish selections, including steak; red snapper with lemon, almonds, and capers; and pork tenderloin with Dijon mustard, red chile, and honey. The menu also includes ambitious daily selections. A piano player twinkles the keys in the bar from 5 to 9pm Thursday to Saturday.

Picnic & Camping Supplies

Markets throughout the park may have that forgotten flashlight, tarp, or lantern mantle—then again, they may not. It's very hit and miss here, but persistence pays off. Some also have limited backcountry equipment, and of course, antibear canisters.

The **Cedar Grove Market** is open 7am to 8pm daily May to September; closed September to May. The **Grant Grove Market** is open from 8am to 9pm May to September and 8am to 7pm September to May. The **Giant Forest Market** is open from 8am to 8pm May to September, but will close for good in October 1998. The **Lodgepole Market,** which has the widest selection available, is open from 8am to 8pm May to September. During the winter, a small variety of goods is available in Wolverton.

36

THEODORE ROOSEVELT NATIONAL PARK

by T. D. Griffith

NESTLED IN THE NORTH DAKOTA BADLANDS, FAR FROM THE BANTER of Washington politics, stands a park named for a president who is remembered as being, among other things, one of the great conservationists of his or any other time. In western North Dakota, where many of his early experiences gave rise to his later environmental efforts, Theodore Roosevelt is honored with a national park that pays tribute to the memory of this great conservationist.

When he became president in 1901, Roosevelt pursued his love of natural history by creating the U.S. Forest Service and by signing the 1906 Antiquities Act, under which he proclaimed 18 national monuments. He also obtained Congressional approval to establish five national parks and 51 wildlife refuges, as well as set aside millions of acres of land as national forests. As a conservationist, Roosevelt is arguably without equal among American presidents. So it is understandable that he should be the only president for whom a national park has been named.

Roosevelt first traveled to the North Dakota badlands in September 1883. Before returning home to New York, he became interested in the cattle business and joined two other men as partners in the Maltese Cross Ranch. The following year, Roosevelt came back to North Dakota and established a second open-range ranch, the Elkhorn, which became his principal residence in the area.

During his frequent visits, "T.R." led the "strenuous life" that he loved. When he wasn't studying botany or herding cattle, Roosevelt hunted, fished, and enjoyed the camaraderie of fellow Dakotans, some of whom would later form the nucleus of his Rough Riders.

Roosevelt arrived in the badlands soon after the last of the bison herds had been slaughtered, and he spent much time pondering what was being done to the animals and land around him. He carried those thoughts and convictions, borne on the Dakota prairie, into his later political life.

Badlands & Buffalo. The colorful moonscape of the North Dakota badlands provides the scenic backdrop for Theodore Roosevelt National Park. Carved over millions of years by the natural forces of the wind and rain, and the tireless waters of the Little Missouri River, this land is home to a variety of animals and plant life.

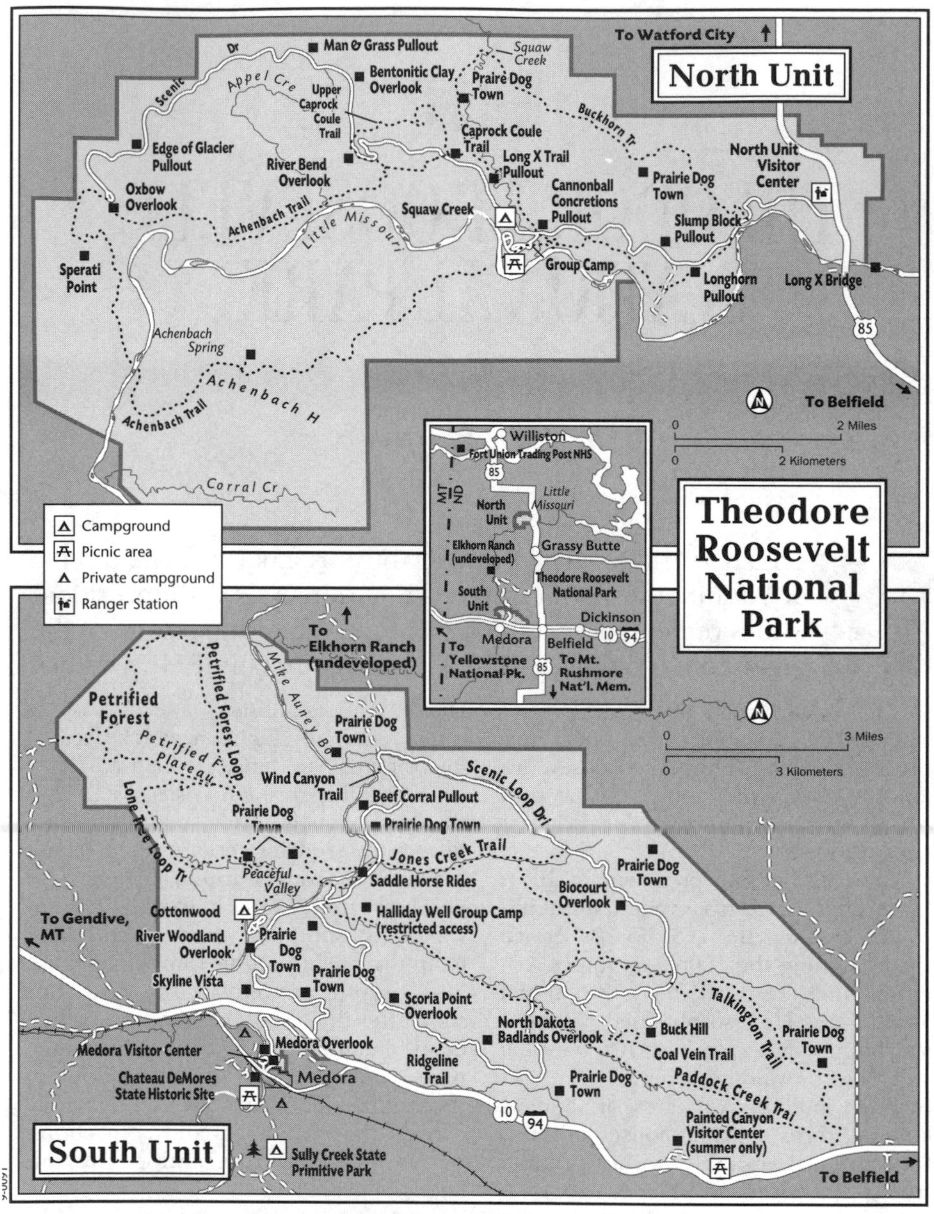

Some 60 million years ago, streams carried eroded materials eastward from the young Rocky Mountains, then deposited them on a vast lowland, today's Great Plains. During the warm, rainy periods that followed, dense vegetation grew, fell into swampy areas, and was later buried by new layers of sediment. Eventually this plant material turned into lignite coal. Some plant life became petrified.

Even as layers of sediment were being deposited, streams were starting to carve through the soft strata and to sculpt the infinite variety of buttes, tablelands, and valleys that make up the badlands today.

As inhospitable and barren as this land looks, it is home to a large variety of

Tips from the Chief of Interpretation

After a decade at Theodore Roosevelt National Park and a dozen years with the National Park Service in Alaska, Chief of Interpretation Bruce Kaye likes to think he knows something about weather and safe travel.

"The best month to be without crowds at Theodore Roosevelt National Park, yet do the things you want to do in view of the weather, is September," Kaye says. "But even at the height of the summer season," he added, "most visitors won't reach critical mass due to overcrowding."

"Summertime is not all that busy," Kaye says. "You can still go out into the backcountry and not see people. You can even drive one of the loop roads and not be inundated with people."

Kaye encourages visitors to view Roosevelt's two ranch sites—the Maltese Cross, whose ranch house was relocated from the state capital in Bismarck to a site near the visitor center in 1959, and the Elkhorn Ranch site, located 35 miles north of Medora. Kaye said visitors should check with rangers before traveling to the Elkhorn site, to ensure that high water will not impede their progress.

While visiting the park, Kaye says travelers should keep their eyes out for a wide variety of wildlife, including bison, elk, wild horses, mule and white-tailed deer, coyote, antelope, 200 species of birds, and the ever-abundant prairie dog.

He added that, since the park is open every day of the year, hiking, camping, and cross-country skiing are ideal experiences in the off-season.

creatures and plants. Rainfall supports an abundance of prairie grasses and wildflowers, and more than 200 species of birds inhabit the North and South units of the park.

Mule deer and white-tailed deer inhabit the park, and prairie dogs have built their tunnel "towns" in the grasslands. Through careful management, some animals that nearly became extinct in the 19th and early 20th centuries are once again thriving on the Great Plains. Bison and elk, for example, were reintroduced into the area in 1956 and 1985, respectively.

> **I never would have been president if it had not been for my experiences in North Dakota.**
>
> **—Theodore Roosevelt**

The wealth of wildlife that first attracted T.R. and thousands of other avid sportsmen to this area still exists. Bands of wild horses roam in the park's South Unit, just as they did when Roosevelt rode over this land and tended his cattle a century ago.

Avoiding the Crowds. Since the park has 70,000 acres, two spread-out units, and less than a half million visitors per year, avoiding crowds at Theodore Roosevelt National Park is not a difficult task. In general, you'll see fewer visitors in early morning and evening hours, particularly during the high-visitation months of June, July, and August. Early fall is especially appealing to those seeking a more contemplative experience. But even during the height of the summer season, those enjoying backcountry treks and scenic drives are not likely to encounter throngs of camera-clad vacationers: This national park is just too big, and visitation too low, to make that occur.

Just the Facts

GETTING THERE & GATEWAYS

The park's **South Unit** is located 130 miles west of **Bismarck** and 7 miles east of **Medora** (Exit 27 on I-94). The **North Unit** is located near Watford City. From I-94, take Exit 42 (Belfield), then you must continue north on U.S. 85 another 50 miles to the North Unit Entrance. The park also includes Theodore Roosevelt's **Elkhorn Ranch,** which is located between the North and South units, but visitors should ask rangers about road conditions before attempting to go there.

The Nearest Airport. **Bismarck Municipal Airport** (☎ **701/222-6502**), the nearest airport to Theodore Roosevelt National Park, is in the capital of North Dakota, 117 miles away. It is served by only two airlines, **Northwest** and **United Express.**

Renting a Car. **Avis** and **Enterprise** have outlets in the airport.

The toll-free numbers for these airlines and car-rental agencies are in the appendix.

GETTING INFORMATION BEFORE YOUR TRIP

You can request an informational package before your trip by contacting the **Superintendent, Theodore Roosevelt National Park,** P.O. Box 7, Medora, ND 58645 (☎ **701/623-4466** for the South Unit, the main number; or 701/842-2333 for the North Unit). The park has a page on the National Park Service Web site at **www.nps.gov/thro**.

For information about the area, contact the **Medora Chamber of Commerce,** P.O. Box 186, Medora, ND 58645 (☎ **701/623-4910**).

VISITOR CENTERS

The park has three visitor centers. The **Medora Visitor Center** (for the South Unit) is located just inside the park entrance at Medora and is open daily, mid-June through Labor Day, 8am to 8pm, and daily the remainder of year from 8am to 4:30pm.

The **Painted Canyon Visitor Center** is about 7 miles east of Medora and open daily mid-June through Labor Day, 8am to 6pm; from April to mid-June and September to mid-November, it is open daily 8:30am to 4:30pm. The **North Unit Visitor Center,** located at the eastern end of the North Unit, just off U.S. 85, is open daily from Memorial Day through September, 9am to 5:30pm; it is open weekends and most weekdays the rest of the year.

In addition to the North and South units, the park also consists of the **Elkhorn Ranch** site, the location of Roosevelt's second cattle ranch, located 35 miles north of the Medora Visitor Center, but it is undeveloped and may not be accessible on account of road and weather conditions.

Hikers and horseback riders should inquire at a visitor center for information about the backcountry trails that cover the park and to obtain a free backcountry camping permit.

ENTRANCE & CAMPING FEES

Entrance fees of $10 per vehicle or $5 per person for a 7-day pass are collected during the summer months; camping fees may be collected throughout the year.

All campgrounds cost $10 per site per day, plus $1 per horse if you use the horse-camping site in the South Unit. Group camps cost $2 per person, with a minimum of $20.

You'll need a backcountry permit to hike or camp overnight in the backcountry of either unit; you can get this permit at the Medora or North Unit Visitor Center, and it's free, but you can't send off for it in advance.

SPECIAL REGULATIONS & WARNINGS

The animals in the park are wild and should be viewed from a safe distance (even the prairie dogs can bite). Drinking water should be obtained from approved sources; water in the backcountry is not recommended for human consumption unless boiled. Watch out for ticks in late spring and early summer. Climbing on the steep, barren slopes of the badlands can be dangerous due to slippery clays and soft sediments that may yield underfoot, so stay on designated trails. Motor vehicles and bicycles are permitted only on park roads. Off-road use is prohibited. Horses are prohibited in campgrounds, picnic areas, and on self-guided nature trails.

SEASONS & CLIMATE

The climate in the badlands can be extreme (bitter cold and snow in the winter and intense heat in the summer), with high or low temperatures and sudden violent storms. Prepare yourself for a variety of conditions.

SPECIAL EVENTS

The **50th anniversary** of the establishment of the park was held during 1997, but in 1998 the park will continue celebrating with a celebration of the 50th anniversary of the North Unit. Call the park for more details about scheduled events. The **Maah Daah Hey Trail** will also be finished by the fall of 1998, establishing a 120-mile link between the North and South units through the rugged North Dakota badlands. (See "Exploring the Backcountry," below, for more information on this trail.)

USEFUL PUBLICATIONS

The National Park Service has a variety of brochures that explore the cultural and natural resources of Theodore Roosevelt National Park. A **road log guide,** sold in the visitor center, gives detailed information about the landscape and may enhance the quality of your visit. For a list of publications, contact the Park Superintendent, Theodore Roosevelt National Park, P.O. Box 7, Medora, ND 58645 (☎ **701/623-4466**).

Finally, the Theodore Roosevelt Nature and History Association produces *Frontier Fragments,* one of the finest park newspapers we've found in the national park system. The publication is updated annually and is filled with relevant stories on the park's history, wildlife, interpretive offerings, and visitor services. It also includes a "Kid's Corner," with appropriate activities and articles for youngsters. It's available at any of the visitor centers.

Seeing the Highlights in a Day

If you only have 1 day, you'll probably want to limit yourself to either the North or South Unit. Since it's more accessible from I-94, it's usually the South Unit that people concentrate on.

If you're coming from the east, stop first at the Painted Canyon Overlook and Visitor Center to get a sweeping, panoramic view of the North Dakota badlands, then continue 7 miles west to the Medora Visitor Center. Here, you'll be able to view a film and listen to one or more ranger talks. There's also a museum here you can poke through to see some of Theodore Roosevelt's personal effects. Be sure to stop in at the Maltese Cross cabin, behind the visitor center. Take the 36-mile scenic driving loop around the park, stopping at the overlooks (be sure to stop at one of the prairie dog towns), and stop along the way to take in a scenic interpretive trail, such as Skyline Vista Trail. All these are described more fully in the section below. All in all, you can pack a lot into a visit of just a few hours until you're off on your way to the next destination.

Exploring the Park by Car

You might be able to see many of the highlights of Theodore Roosevelt

National Park in 1 day. But we wouldn't recommend it. To truly experience the natural attractions that lured Roosevelt and thousands of other outdoor enthusiasts to this region of the world, you'll want to see it close-up, rather than through some bug-splattered windshield. Camp the night away under clear skies and twinkling stars, or stop by a bed-and-breakfast, motel, or hotel in a neighboring community. Take a hike or two on some of the park's nature trails, or enjoy a walking tour or a campfire program led by a park ranger.

THE SOUTH UNIT

If you're traveling west on I-94, your first introduction to Theodore Roosevelt National Park is the **Painted Canyon Overlook** and **Visitor Center,** about 7 miles east of Medora. Here, on the upper ridge of the badlands, is an unparalleled panorama of ragged ridges and colorful hues. The visitor center sports rest rooms, picnic shelters, tables, and water from April through October. The visitor center here is closed sometimes during the winter months, when visitation is lower, but that shouldn't stop you from dropping in to take a look. Watch especially for **wild horses,** the descendants of former domestic ranching stock; you might even see bison grazing.

The **museum** housed in the **Medora Visitor Center** features personal items that once belonged to Theodore Roosevelt, ranching artifacts, and natural history displays. Tours are conducted (free, about 20 minutes) through the **Maltese Cross cabin** from mid-June through Labor Day; if there are no scheduled tours, you can still take a self-guided tour. T.R. used this cabin, which was relocated to its new home behind the visitor center after a detailed restoration program. It's helpful to see these, if only to put the landscape in a historical context.

One of the most impressive man-made features of the South Unit is a paved **36-mile scenic loop road** with interpretive signage that explains some of the park's historical and natural phenomena. The scenic drive is best accessed from the Medora Visitor Center and turning right onto the loop in Peaceful Valley. If you've bought the road log, as we recommend (see "Useful Publications," above), which will give you more detailed information about the park and what you'll see, you'll want to travel counterclockwise around the loop road. Descriptions of the shorter interpretive trails are incorporated into the driving tours for the North and South units; for more information on longer hiking opportunities, please see "Exploring the Backcountry," below.

South Unit Scenic Drive. In any season, the South Unit Scenic Drive can take you into some of the most remote and miraculous areas of North Dakota. When Lt. Col. George Armstrong Custer traveled through these badlands he described them as "hell with the fires burned out." In reality, they are teeming with wildlife, wildflowers, and bird life. The South Unit is comprised of 46,158 acres, of which 10,510 acres are designated as wilderness.

Scoria Point is the first overlook you'll come to. Strictly speaking, scoria is volcanic in origin, but in the badlands, wherever a seam of coal has caught fire and baked the surrounding sand and clay, it's called scoria. You'll see it from this view point, where the topsoil has been stripped away by erosion and the harder material underneath is exposed.

About a mile farther, you'll come to the **Ridgeline Nature Trail.** If you choose to take this very short (0.6 mile one way) hike, you'll learn more about the badlands and their ecology. This is an easy trail, suitable for most people.

The overlook you'll come to is the **North Dakota Badlands Overlook.** The view here is over Paddock Creek, and what you'll see is a bleak, almost lunar landscape. This is because erosion has worn away the top soil, leaving behind only the rocks and harder materials underneath the thin, top layer.

After crossing Paddock Creek, you'll come to the turnoff for the **Coal Vein**

Trail, a short (0.8-mile) loop that winds through an area where a fire burned in a coal seam from 1951 through early 1977. After 25 years, the fire had baked the clay and soil here, thus changing both the appearance of the terrain and altering the vegetation patterns. Here, you'll be walking around the scoria (the same kind of formations you viewed from a distance at the Scoria Point Overlook earlier). You must drive down a short, unpaved road to reach the trail.

After returning to the main loop road, you'll next come to the turnoff for **Buck Hill.** It's only a short walk to the hill itself from the end of the road. The hill (at 2,855 feet) has two very different slopes. On the south side, the slopes are hot and dry, and you'll see only shrubs and small plants. On the north side, which is wetter and cooler, you'll see trees.

Several miles farther will bring you to the **Boicourt Overlook,** which affords one of the best views of the badlands in the South Unit.

At the next stop, you'll be able to take the **Wind Canyon Trail.** This is a very short walk up to the ridge here, where you'll have a great view of the Little Missouri River, which did much to create the landscape here. Beyond the river, to the west, is the virtually untouched wilderness of the South Unit.

After passing the **Beef Corral Pullout** and a **prairie dog town,** which is just beyond on your left, you'll pass the parking lot for the **Jones Creek Trail.** This is one of two trailheads for the Jones Creek Trail on Scenic Loop Drive. (You passed the other one earlier; it was at the parking area between the Boicourt Overlook and the Wind Canyon Trail pullout.) The trail itself is 3.7 miles and leads into the heart of the badlands.

The final stop on the Scenic Loop Drive is in **Peaceful Valley,** shortly before you reach the intersection where you turned off onto the loop. The Peaceful Valley Ranch here, which is on National Historic Register, was established originally during the heyday of cattle ranching in the 1880s. The tall central section of the ranch house was constructed about 1885. Today, the ranch offers **trail rides** for a fee from May through the end of September (details are given under "Horseback Riding in the Park," below).

THE NORTH UNIT

Fewer visitors take the time to travel to the park's North Unit, and much of it is not served by paved roads, so this is the place to go to avoid some of the crowds (though even the South Unit of the park rarely becomes "crowded"). There are 24,070 acres in the North Unit, of which 19,410 acres are designated as wilderness. Stop at the visitor center at the entrance to the unit, and the rangers will help you plan your time.

North Unit Scenic Drive. The 14-mile **scenic drive** travels from the entrance station to the **Oxbow Overlook** with plenty of turnouts and interpretive signs along the route. Keep your eyes open for longhorns on the prairie between the entrance and Squaw Creek Campground—these are the same type of cattle raised by ranchers here during Roosevelt's time. At the Oxbow Overlook, you must double back along the same route.

Since less of the North Unit is developed, the thing to do here is to get out of the car at one of the scenic pullouts and take a hike. Whether you go a long or a short distance, you'll be able to see dramatic scenery populated with many bison, elk, and bighorn sheep but few people.

The **Little Mo Nature Trail,** which starts at Squaw Creek Campground, offers a comfortable, leisurely walk through the Little Missouri River bottom. The trail cuts through woodlands near the river as well as badlands formations and gives you two options. The shorter portion of the loop is only 0.7 mile, paved, and wheelchair accessible. But you can also extend your hike by 0.4 mile and take the unpaved portion. If you're more adventurous, you'll see some additional formations and cross some wildlife trails that (mostly) bison use.

The **Caprock Coulee Nature Trail,** which is located 1.5 miles west of Squaw Creek Campground, is another easy, self-guiding nature trail that winds through badlands, dry water gulches, across breaks, then finds a welcome interruption in the grassy plains of the park. The total length of the round-trip is 1.6 miles.

If you want to do something more ambitious, then combine the self-guiding nature trail with the **Upper Caprock Coulee Trail.** Together, they run a distance of 4.1 miles (this portion is 3.3 miles). You'll go farther into the wilderness this way if you have the stamina; it also brings you back to the trailhead so that you don't have to double back over the same route.

It's at this point where the North Unit Scenic Drive is closed for the winter. If you continue, you'll end up at the **Oxbow Overlook,** another sweeping panoramic view of the badlands.

The **Sperati Point Trail** can be accessed from the Oxbow Overlook. This is the spur of the Achenbach Trail that leads to the Oxbow Bend Overlook and makes a less strenuous alternative if you want something shorter than the Achenbach's 16 miles. (The length of this trail is 1.5 miles round-trip.) The trail leads to the narrowest gateway in the badlands. The flow of the Little Missouri River once continued north to Hudson Bay. Blocked during the Ice Age, the river was forced to find a new course and finally broke through the gap between this point and the Achenbach Hills on the other side. The Little Missouri now drains into the Gulf of Mexico via the Missouri-Mississippi system.

Exploring the Backcountry

If you wish to explore some of the wilderness the park has to offer, you'll need a free **backcountry permit** from the Medora or North Unit visitor center to do any overnight camping. You can also explore the backcountry on horseback. If you do bring a horse, you must camp either in the backcountry or at the group campsite in the South Unit. You can also board your horse at the Peaceful Valley Ranch (see "Horseback Riding in the Park," below, for more information). Your stay in the Theodore Roosevelt National Park backcountry is limited to 14 consecutive days.

Special Regulations. You cannot have a campfire in the backcountry due to the possibility of wildfires, so you must bring a self-contained camp stove. You must pack out what you pack in (no burying of trash). Groups entering the backcountry are limited to 10 persons (or 8 persons with 8 horses). Finally, don't drink the water in the backcountry; there are no safe, approved water sources here.

The mother of all trails in the area will be the **Maah Daah Hey Trail** when it is finished by fall 1998. (By the end of 1997, 90 miles of the trail's entire length of 120 miles were finished.) The finished trail will stretch from the U.S. Forest Service campground in McKenzie County in the north (it is located 20 miles south of Watford City off U.S. 85) to Sully Creek State Park, south of Medora, its southern terminus. There will be seven fenced camping sites for overnighters, including hitching posts for your horses, vault toilets, and fire rings, but those won't all be finished until 1999. The trail will pass through and connect the South and North units of Theodore Roosevelt National Park and will be open to hikers, horseback riders, and mountain bikers.

If you would like to get more information about this particular trail, contact the **U.S. Forest Service, Medora District,** at 161 21st St. W., Dickinson, ND 58601 (☎ **701/225-5151**); or the **McKenzie District** office at HC02, Box 8, Watford City, ND 58854 (☎ 701/842-2393).

SOUTH UNIT TRAILS

Petrified Forest Trail

16 miles RT (from the east). Moderate. Access: You can get on the trail at the parking area for the Jones Creek Trail on its eastern end; from the west, the trailhead is located at the end a dirt road (ask park rangers for directions).

Pieces of petrified wood are scattered throughout this national park, but the greatest concentration can be reached only on foot or horseback along this lengthy trail. The trail leads up along Petrified Forest Plateau. Just don't take any souvenirs.

NORTH UNIT TRAILS

Achenbach Trail

16 miles RT. Moderate. Access: The trailhead is located at the Squaw Creek Campground.

This route climbs from the river bottomlands up through the Achenbach Hills, drops down to the river again, climbs to the Oxbow Overlook on a spur trail, then returns along the river bottom to the campground. Before departing, ask a ranger about the condition of river crossings. The "spur" trail is the Sperati Point Trail that is described in "The North Unit," above.

Buckhorn Trail

11 miles RT. Moderate. Access: This loop trail is accessible from the Caprock Coulee Nature Trail (see its description under "The North Unit," above).

About a mile from the trailhead, hikers discover a large prairie dog town. Of the seven varieties of prairie dogs, only the black-tailed variety inhabits Theodore Roosevelt National Park.

Organized Tours & Ranger Programs

Ranger programs are offered at all visitor centers and campgrounds during the summer seasons. These include nature walks and longer hikes. The seasons runs from mid-June through the early part of September. The self-guided tours of the Maltese Cross cabin at the Medora Visitor Center are offered in the summer as well. If snow conditions permit, rangers may conduct ski tours in winter, but call ahead if you are interested in this option.

Historic & Man-Made Attractions

In addition to the Maltese Cross cabin, which is described more fully under "The South Unit," above, there are several other options in the area.

At the **Elkhorn Ranch** site, where Theodore Roosevelt started his second cattle ranch in the area, no buildings remain (save the foundation from the main ranch house). To get there, you must take the dirt road that goes north out of the South Unit (its turnoff is at the top of the Scenic Loop Drive) and drive another 20 miles, but you must cross the river to get to the actual ranch site. You should inquire at the Medora Visitor Center about river conditions before attempting this trip.

Chateau DeMores State Historic Site, near the town of Medora, is a 27-room chateau that the Marquis DeMores built for his wife in 1884 and that still stands. The wealthy French nobleman owned a number of businesses in early-day Medora, including a slaughterhouse, the chimney of which still dominates the town. The marquis named the town for his wife and persuaded the Northern Pacific Railroad to locate a station there. He was a casual acquaintance of Theodore Roosevelt. Guided tours of the chateau are generally offered from late May through September.

Knife River Indian Villages National Historic Site, consisting of five villages along the Knife River in North Dakota, was inhabited by the Mandan, Hidatsac and later the Arikara from the early 1500s to 1860. Today, it's located 0.5 mile north of Stanton, North Dakota, east of Grassy Butte via S. Dak. 200 (then via County Road 37), and offers insights into early life on the North Dakota plains. The site is open from 8am to 6pm daily from Memorial Day through Labor Day, to 4:30pm daily the rest of the year. The exhibits and 15-minute audiovisual program depict life in the villages before and after Euro-American contact. Earthlodge tours are conducted daily, June through August, and other activities are planned throughout the year. Check the visitor center for scheduled times and dates.

Trails, from 0.5 mile to 2 miles in length, lead to three village sites. Other trails meander through prairie and woodland ecosystems. All trails are open during visitor center hours and some are wheelchair accessible.

For more information, contact the **Superintendent, Knife River Indian Villages NHS,** P.O. Box 9, Stanton, ND 58571 (☎ **701/745-3309**).

Fort Union Trading Post National Historic Site was, for nearly 4 decades in the early 19th century, known as Fort Union, a bastion of John Jacob Astor's American Fur Company, which dominated the fur trade in the region of modern-day North Dakota, Montana, and Saskatchewan. Now, as then, the focal point of the historic site is Fort Union's Indian Trade House. The house served as the primary setting for the exchange of valued trading goods between the fur company and Assiniboines, Crows, Crees, and Lakotas. In this, the farthest reaches of the Missouri River country, the National Park Service and the Fort Union Association have meticulously restored and refurnished the Trade House to its appearance in 1851. The site is located about 2 hours north of Theodore Roosevelt National Park via U.S. 85 at Belfield, North Dakota; N. Dak. 16 at Beach, North Dakota; or Mont. 16 at Glendive, Montana. The Bourgeois House Visitor Center is open from 8am to 8pm from Memorial Day through Labor Day, from 9am to 5:30pm the remainder of the year. The Indian Trade House is open from 9:45am to 5:45pm daily during the summer only. Ranger tours are offered from noon to 3:30pm daily during the summer, with self-guided tours the remainder of the year.

For scheduled dates of special programs, or for more information, contact the **Superintendent, Fort Union Trading Post NHS,** RR 3, Box 71, Williston, ND 58801 (☎ **701/572-9083**).

Horseback Riding in the Park

Most people in Theodore Roosevelt National Park hike, but a large number enjoy horseback riding on many of the trails since backcountry trails are open to both those on foot and on horse. If you don't bring your own animal, you can go on a guided trail ride organized by one of the park's concessionaires. In the South Unit, contact **Peaceful Valley Trail Rides,** P.O. Box 8, Medora, ND 58645 (☎ **701/623-4496**); they offer rides from May 1 to October 1 and have regularly scheduled rides lasting from 1¼ to 2½ hours, or they will organize special, extended rides for you. They also board horses. From 10am to 2pm daily during the season, they'll also give you a 1-hour lesson in horseback riding. In the North Unit, the concessionaire is **Little Knife Outfitters,** R.R. 1, Box 116, Stanley, ND 58784 (☎ **800/438-6905** or 701/842-2631).

Camping

Cottonwood Campground in the South Unit and **Squaw Creek Campground** in the North Unit are operated on a first-come, first-served basis; neither has RV utility hookups, nor are there any dump stations in Cottonwood Campground (there is a dump station at the entrance to Squaw Creek Campground). Camping fees are $10 per night for each campground.

You'll find drinking water, flush toilets, public telephones, and fire grates in both campgrounds, but no showers or other facilities. Campgrounds are open year-round, but the availability of water is limited during the winter.

Camping for organized groups is available at the **Halliday Well Campground** in the South Unit and in part of the **Squaw Creek Campground** in the North Unit. Groups must have a written reservation from the park superintendent.

Riding groups with their own horses should write the superintendent to make special arrangements. It's possible to camp with a horse, but only in the South Unit campground; the cost is additional.

Other privately run and Forest Service campgrounds are located near both units of the park, and you can get a list of them when you write for park info.

Accommodations & Dining

There are no accommodations or dining facilities in the park (either unit), but you will find hotels, motels, bed-and-breakfasts, as well as a variety of modest eating establishments year-round at **Medora, Belfield,** and **Beach** near the South Unit, and at **Watford City** near the North Unit. Most are open year-round but some close seasonally in the winter, so call ahead to make sure and to check the prices, which also tend to be seasonal and, due to the isolation, somewhat higher than average.

In Medora. The **AmericInn,** the most luxurious choice, is located at 75 E. River Rd. S., 1 block south of the Medora Community Center (☎ **800/634-3444** or 701/623-4800). It has seasonal rates, ranging from $40.90 for a double room in the winter (going up to $60 in the summer) to $160.90 for a suite in the summer high season; AE, DC, DISC, MC, and V are accepted.

The **Badlands Motel,** on Pacific Avenue, and the **Rough Riders Motel,** at 3rd and 3rd, both in Medora, charge $45 for a double in the winter, $77 in the summer. They both take AE, DISC, MC, and V. For reservations, call ☎ **800/MEDORA-1** or 701/623-4444.

Custer's Condos, located at 156 East River Rd. S. in Medora, have full kitchens, large living rooms, cable TV, up to four bedrooms, and are open year-round (☎ **800/783-6366,** PIN 0749 or 701/623-4378); prices range from $40 to $95 during the summer, and $34 to $68 during the winter. Credit cards are not accepted for payment but may be used to reserve a room.

In Belfield. The **Bel-Vu Motel** is located west of U.S. 85 on U.S. 10 (☎ **701/575-4245**). A double costs $36 to $40 in the winter, $40 to $45 in the summer; MC and V are accepted.

The **Trapper's Inn** is located at I-94 and U.S. 85 North (☎ **800/284-1855** or 701/575-4261); a double costs $44.50 in winter, $54.50 from May through early June, and $64.50 the rest of the summer; AE, DC, DISC, MC, and V are accepted.

In Beach. The **Buckboard Inn** is located at I-94 and N. Dak. 16 South (☎ **701/872-4794**); a double costs $37.05 to $42.35 during the summer; AE, DISC, MC, and V are accepted.

In Watford City. The **McKenzie Inn** is located on U.S. 85 West (☎ 701/842-3980); the year-round rate is $32 for a double; AE, DISC, MC, and V are accepted.

The **Watford City Inn** is on U.S. 85 West (☎ **701/842-3686**); rates are $29.95 to $44.95 for a double during the summer, $26.95 to $42.95 during the winter; AE, DISC, MC, and V are accepted.

37

YELLOWSTONE NATIONAL PARK

by Ed Lawrence

THINK ABOUT THIS: WHAT OTHER NATIONAL PARK BOASTS SUCH AN assortment of thermal geysers and hot springs that their total exceeds the number found on the rest of the planet? On top of which there's a waterfall that's twice as tall as Niagara Falls. Not to mention a canyon deep and colorful enough to fall into the "grand" category. Sure, other parks have great hiking trails and beautiful geologic formations, but virtually all of the geology in Yellowstone is reachable by anyone in average shape.

Wildlife? Ever focus your telephoto lens on a wild, untamed grizzly bear? Or a bald eagle? What about a wolf? Thousands of visitors have these experiences here every year.

And the park doesn't appeal solely to the visual senses; you'll smell it, too. By one biologist's estimate, Yellowstone has more than 1,100 species of plants, so when wildflowers cover the meadows in spring, you won't just see them, you'll be overpowered by their fragrances. The mud pots and fumaroles have their own set of odors, though many are less pleasing than a wild lily.

Your ears will be filled with the sounds of geysers noisily spewing forth thousands of gallons of boiling water into the blue Wyoming sky. After sunset, coyotes break the silence of the night with their high-pitched yips.

You can spend weeks hiking its backcountry or fishing its streams, or spend a day or two seeing the park from behind the windshield.

What was that? Yes, it's possible to see the highlights of Yellowstone without ever leaving your car. *Really.* Park roads lead past most of the key attractions and are filled with wildlife commuting from one grazing area to another. There's no doubt you will return home with vivid memories if you take just this approach to your visit of the park, but of course there's so much more to see by actually getting out of your vehicle.

And Yellowstone's season is year-round: It's just as active even well after summer, when the park is open for snowmobiling and skiing for 3 months during the winter.

The beauty of Yellowstone's natural architecture comes from its geology. The area experienced three separate volcanic periods beginning 600,000 years ago. During major eruptions, thousands of square miles of land mass were blown skyward, leaving enormous calderas (volcanic depressions). This process repeated itself several times—there is geologic evidence of 27 layers of lava in some areas. The volcanic mountains were subsequently glaciated during the ice ages. The powerful glacial bulldozing caused by the movement of these gigantic blocks of ice shaped the valleys and canyons of the park.

Yellowstone National Park was officially created in 1872, when Pres. Ulysses Grant signed legislation making it the first national park in the world. In the years afterward it suffered from incompetent superintendents and shortages of cash until at last, in 1886, the U.S. Army took possession. In 1916, control of the park was transferred to the newly created National Park Service. Yellowstone became the first park to come under its stewardship.

Avoiding the Crowds. The best way to avoid the majority of the crowds in Yellowstone is to avoid the busy summer season (July and August). Between May and mid-June and after Labor Day, crowds are greatly diminished and the park's attractions are much more accessible. A downside to this approach is the risk of inclement weather; at these elevations spring weather can be spotty, cool at the least. May hikes to geysers are occasionally through patches of snow, or on muddy trails. Another downside is that all of the park's facilities and trails may not be open because of snow or, most often, early season bear activity.

If you travel during peak season, the best alternative is to park your vehicle as quickly as possible and venture along trails into the lesser-traveled areas of the park. Except on the most popular and easily accessible ones, odds are good that once you're more than a quarter of a mile from the pavement, your only company will be a handful of other hikers and the plants and wildlife of the park.

Another strategy is to travel at times of day when others are eating. You'll also avoid the lines at restaurants. Better yet: Pick up a sack lunch at one of the Hamilton stores and head for a scenic overlook, or one of the park picnic areas.

Of course, the best way of distancing yourself is to head for the backcountry wilderness areas. Though this requires a greater physical commitment, you will discover that you have huge expanses of the park to yourself. With a backcountry permit, you can experience the essence of the wilderness without having to crawl over the tourists in front of you. You'll also see many of the most beautiful sections of the park, which tourists typically miss.

Just the Facts

GETTING THERE & GATEWAYS

To get to Yellowstone from **Bozeman,** Montana (91 miles), take U.S. 191 south to its junction with U.S. 287 and head straight to the park's West Entrance.

Billings, Montana, is 95 miles from Yellowstone's Northeast Entrance (closed from October 15 to Memorial Day). It's a 65-mile drive south on U.S. 212 to Red Lodge, then 30 miles on the Beartooth Highway to the park.

Cody, Wyoming, is 52 miles to Yellowstone's East Entrance, which is closed from November 1 to April 30, via U.S. 14/16/20. To Yellowstone's Northeast Entrance, it's 53 miles via Wyo. 120/296 to the Beartooth Highway (which is closed from October 15 to Memorial Day) intersection, and 14 miles beyond that to the entrance.

The Nearest Airports. The most convenient airports are in Bozeman or West Yellowstone.

Bozeman's airport, **Gallatin Field,** has daily service via **Delta, Northwest,** and **United,** as well as **Horizon** and **Skywest** (☎ **800/453-9417**) commuter flights.

The **West Yellowstone Airport** (☎ **406/646-7631**), U.S. 191, 1 mile north of West Yellowstone, provides commercial air service seasonally, from June through September only, on Delta's commuter service, **Skywest.**

The airport in Billings, **Logan International,** is the busiest in Montana and is located on the rimrocks 2 miles north of

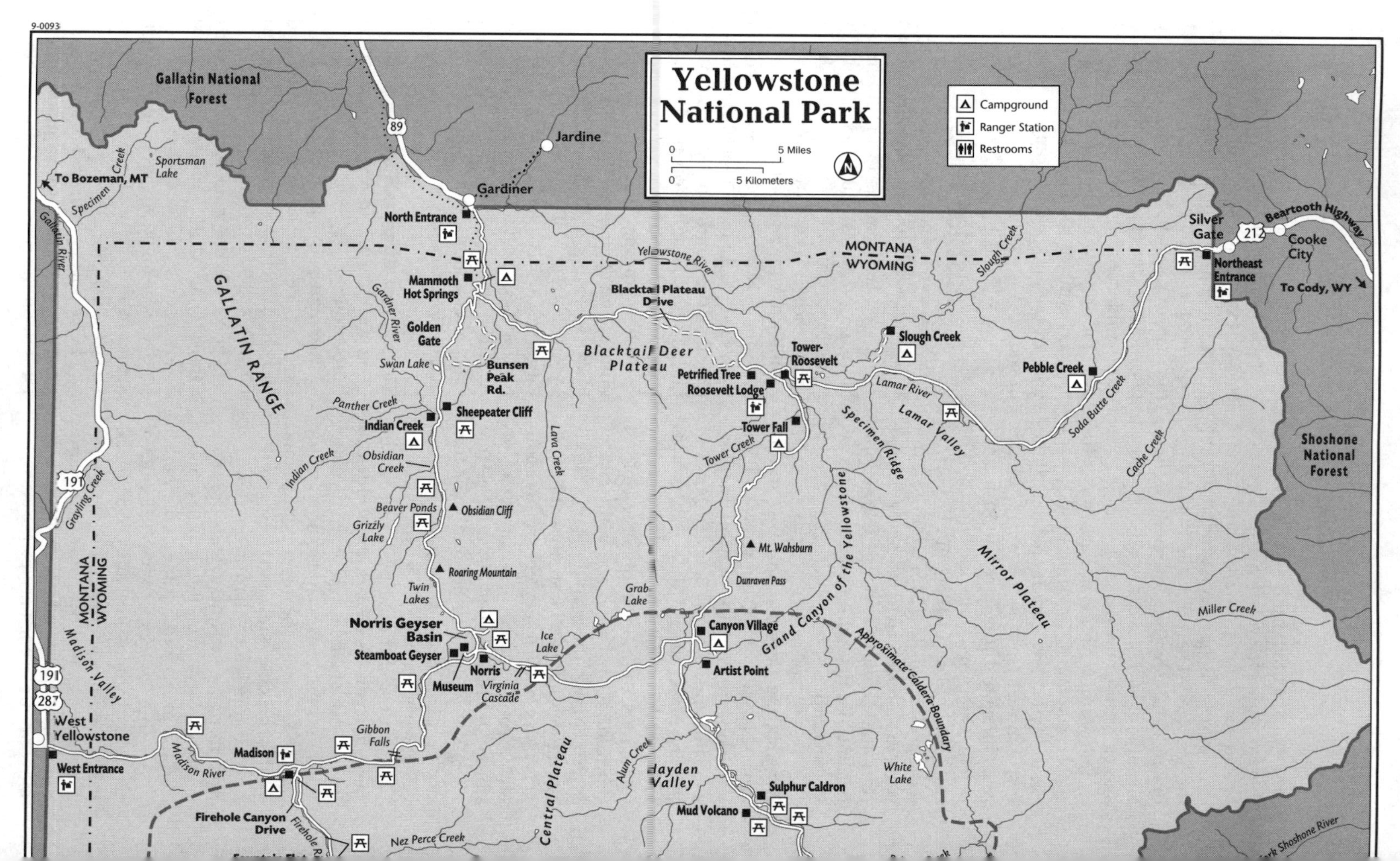
9-0093
Yellowstone National Park
0
5 Miles
0
5 Kilometers
Campground
Ranger Station
Restrooms
Gallatin National Forest
To Bozeman, MT
Specimen Creek
Sportsman Lake
Gallatin River
89
Jardine
Gardiner
North Entrance
MONTANA
WYOMING
Yellowstone River
Slough Creek
Silver Gate
212
Beartooth Highway
Cooke City
Northeast Entrance
To Cody, WY
GALLATIN RANGE
Mammoth Hot Springs
Gardner River
Golden Gate
Swan Lake
Bunsen Peak Rd.
Blacktail Plateau Drive
Blacktail Deer Plateau
Tower-Roosevelt
Petrified Tree
Roosevelt Lodge
Slough Creek
Pebble Creek
Lamar River
Lamar Valley
Soda Butte Creek
Specimen Ridge
Tower Fall
Tower Creek
Panther Creek
Sheepeater Cliff
Indian Creek
Lava Creek
Shoshone National Forest
Cache Creek
Obsidian Creek
191
Grayling Creek
Indian Creek
Beaver Ponds
Obsidian Cliff
Grizzly Lake
Mt. Wahsburn
Grand Canyon of the Yellowstone
Mirror Plateau
Roaring Mountain
Dunraven Pass
Twin Lakes
Grab Lake
MONTANA
WYOMING
Madison Valley
Norris Geyser Basin
Steamboat Geyser
Norris
Museum
Ice Lake
Virginia Cascade
Canyon Village
Artist Point
Approximate Caldera Boundary
Miller Creek
191
287
West Yellowstone
West Entrance
Madison
Madison River
Gibbon Falls
Central Plateau
Alum Creek
Hayden Valley
White Lake
Sulphur Caldron
Mud Volcano
Firehole Canyon Drive
Firehole R
Nez Perce Creek
Shoshone River

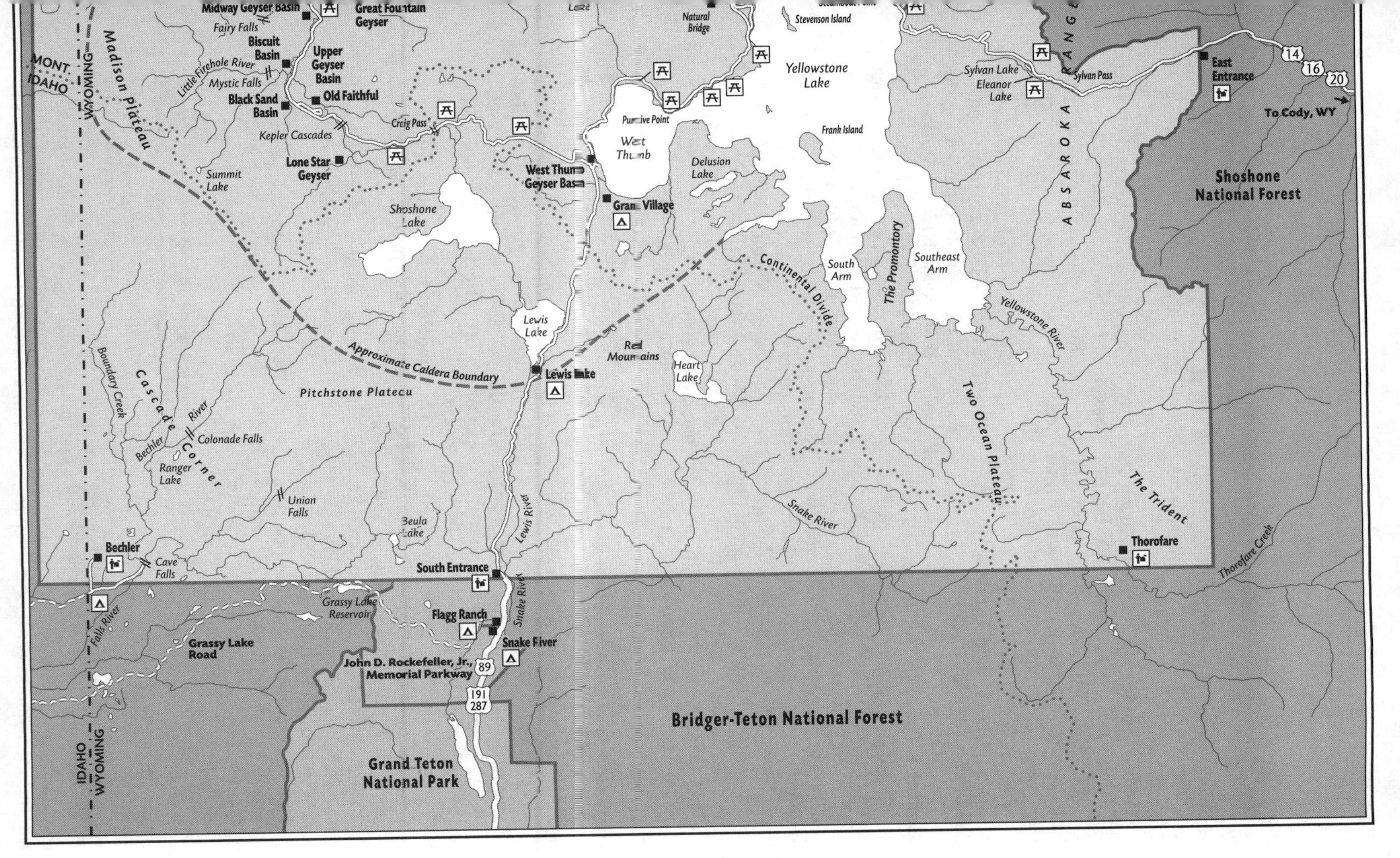

Midway Geyser Basin
Great Fountain Geyser
Fairy Falls
Biscuit Basin
Upper Geyser Basin
Little Firehole River
Mystic Falls
Black Sand Basin
Old Faithful
MONT.
IDAHO
WYOMING
Madison Plateau
Kepler Cascades
Craig Pass
Lone Star Geyser
Summit Lake
Shoshone Lake
Natural Bridge
Stevenson Island
Yellowstone Lake
Frank Island
West Thumb
Delusion Lake
Grant Village
South Arm
The Promontory
Southeast Arm
Sylvan Lake
Eleanor Lake
Sylvan Pass
East Entrance
14
16
20
To Cody, WY
ABSAROKA
Shoshone National Forest
Continental Divide
Yellowstone River
Lewis Lake
Red Mountains
Heart Lake
Approximate Caldera Boundary
Pitchstone Plateau
Boundary Creek
Cascade Corner
River
Bechler
Colonade Falls
Ranger Lake
Union Falls
Beula Lake
Lewis River
Two Ocean Plateau
Snake River
The Trident
Thorofare
Thorofare Creek
Bechler
Cave Falls
South Entrance
Grassy Lake Reservoir
Flagg Ranch
Snake River
Falls River
Grassy Lake Road
John D. Rockefeller, Jr., Memorial Parkway
89
191
287
Bridger-Teton National Forest
IDAHO
WYOMING
Grand Teton National Park

downtown. Daily intrastate service is provided by **Big Sky Airlines** (☎ **800/237-7788** or 406/245-2300). Regional daily service is provided by **Delta, Horizon** (☎ **800/547-9308**), **Northwest,** and **United.**

Cody's **Yellowstone Regional Airport,** 3001 Duggleby Dr., Cody, WY 82414 (☎ **307/587-5096**), serves the Northeast Entrance of Yellowstone National Park with year-round commercial flights via **Skywest** (☎ **800/453-9417** or 307/587-9740) and **United Express** (☎ **800/241-6522** or 307/527-6443).

Renting a Car. Most of the major car-rental agencies have operations in the gateway cities. In **West Yellowstone,** Avis is open from May to September, and Budget is open year-round. In **Bozeman** and **Billings,** Avis, Budget, Thrifty, National, and Hertz all have operations. Billings is also served by Alamo. **Cody** is served by Thrifty, Avis, Hertz, and Budget.

The toll-free numbers for these airlines and car-rental agencies are in the appendix.

GETTING INFORMATION BEFORE YOUR TRIP

To receive maps and information prior to your arrival, contact the **Superintendent, Yellowstone National Park,** WY 82190 (☎ **307/344-7381**). The park's Web site is located at **www.nps.gov/yell.**

Information regarding lodging, tours, boating, and horseback riding is available from **Amfac Parks and Resorts,** P.O. Box 165, Yellowstone National Park, WY 82190 (☎ **307/344-7311**).

The Yellowstone Association operates bookstores in park visitor centers, museums, and information stations. To order a catalog listing books they offer, contact **The Yellowstone Association,** P.O. Box 117, Yellowstone National Park, WY 82190 (☎ **307/344-2293**).

VISITOR CENTERS

There are five major and three minor visitor and information centers in the park, and each has something different to offer.

The **Albright Visitor Center** (☎ **307/344-2263**), at Mammoth Hot Springs, is the largest of all the visitor centers. It provides visitor information, publications about the park, exhibits depicting park history from prehistory through the creation of the National Park Service, and a wolf display on the second floor.

The **Old Faithful Visitor Center** (☎ **307/545-2751**) is one of the park's largest. An excellent film describing the geysers, *Yellowstone, A Living Sculpture,* is shown throughout the day in an air-conditioned auditorium. Various park publications and an informative seismographic exhibit are added attractions. Rangers also post projected geyser eruption times here.

The **Canyon Visitor Center** (☎ **307/242-2550**), located in Canyon Village, is the place to go for books and an interactive exhibit on bison.

The **Fishing Bridge Visitor Center** (☎ **307/242-2450**), located near Fishing Bridge on the north shore of Yellowstone Lake, has an excellent wildlife display, as well as information and publications.

The **Grant Village Visitor Center** has information, publications, a slide program, and a fascinating exhibit that examines the effects of fire in Yellowstone.

The **Madison Information Station & Bookstore** has information and publications.

The **Norris Information Station** is located in the Norris Geyser Basin Museum.

The **West Thumb Information Station** can give you maps and information about the area.

ENTRANCE & CAMPING FEES

The cost to enter Yellowstone is $20 per **vehicle** for a 7-day period (no matter the number of occupants); your entrance permit is valid at both Yellowstone and Grand Teton national parks. **Single entrants** on foot, bicycle, or skis pay $10 per person. The fee for individual **snowmobiles** and **motorcycles** is $15.

If you're planning to visit the parks more than once in a calendar year, consider purchasing an **annual pass,** which is also valid in both Yellowstone and Grand Teton, for $40. However, don't plan on sharing the pass with other travelers, since rangers at entry gates often request photo identification.

Fees for **camping** in Yellowstone are $10, $12, or $14.50 per night, depending on the number of amenities the campground offers. The RV campground at Fishing Bridge charges $25.20 per night and has full hookups; while other campgrounds have sites suitable for RVs, this is the only one with hookups, and only RVs are allowed here.

SPECIAL REGULATIONS & WARNINGS

◆ **Defacing park features** Picking wildflowers, or collecting natural or archaeological objects, is illegal.

◆ **Climbing** Because of the loose, crumbly rock in Yellowstone, climbing is discouraged throughout the park, and prohibited in the Grand Canyon of the Yellowstone.

◆ **Motorcycles** Motorcycles, motor scooters, and motorbikes are allowed only on park roads. No off-road or trail riding is allowed. Operator licenses and license plates are required.

◆ **Pets** Pets must be leashed and are permitted only within 25 feet of roads and parking areas and may not be left unattended. Pets are prohibited in the backcountry, on trails, on boardwalks, and in thermal areas for obvious reasons.

◆ **Swimming** Swimming or wading is prohibited in thermal features or in streams whose waters flow from thermal features in Yellowstone. It is dangerous and therefore not recommended in Yellowstone Lake because of the low water temperature.

◆ **Wildlife** It is unlawful to approach within 100 yards of a bear or within 25 yards of other wildlife. Feeding any wildlife is illegal.

SEASONS & CLIMATE

For general information on seasons and climate in the area, see "Seasons & Climate," in the Grand Teton National Park chapter. Keep in mind that nearby Grand Teton is actually a bit lower in elevation that Yellowstone, so snows melt later in Yellowstone and temperatures are slightly lower.

Traveling Yellowstone's roads during spring months can be a roll of the dice, since openings can be delayed for days (sometimes weeks) at a time, especially at higher altitudes. The combination of a massive road improvement project (in progress at this writing) and heavy spring snowstorms may cause lengthy delays.

The only road open year-round is the **Mammoth Hot Springs–Cooke City Road.**

Plowing in Yellowstone begins in early March. The first roads open to motor vehicles usually include **Mammoth–Norris, Norris–Canyon, Madison–Old Faithful,** and **West Yellowstone–Madison.** The latter may open by the end of April. If the weather cooperates, the East and South entrances, as well as roads on the east and south sides of the park, will open early in May. Opening of the **Tower–Roosevelt** to **Canyon Junction Road,** however, may be delayed by late season snowfall on Dunraven Pass.

The **Sunlight Basin Road** (which is also called the **Chief Joseph Highway**), connecting the entrance at Cooke City, Montana, with Cody, Wyoming, often opens by early May. The **Beartooth Highway** between Cooke City and Red Lodge, Montana, is generally open by Memorial Day weekend.

Road closures begin occurring in mid-October, when the Beartooth Highway closes. Depending upon weather, most other park roads remain open until the park season ends on the first Sunday in November.

The road between **Gardiner and Cooke City, Montana,** remains open year-round to serve the needs of the inhabitants of that small, isolated community. The good news is that this presents late-season travelers with an opportunity to see the northeast area of the park and some of its wildlife during spectacularly beautiful winter months.

USEFUL PUBLICATIONS

The following books are interesting, informative, and easy to find: ***The Yellowstone National Park,*** Hiram Chittenden (Norman, Okla.: University of Oklahoma Press); ***Yellowstone Trails,*** Mark C. Marschall (Yellowstone National Park, Wyo.: The Yellowstone Association); ***Yellowstone and Grand Teton,*** Matt Harding/Freddie Snalam (Boulder, Colo.: All Points Publishing, P.O. Box 4832, 80306); ***An Outdoor Family Guide to Yellowstone and Grand Teton National Parks,*** Lisa Gollin Evans (Seattle: The Mountaineers, 1001 SW Klickitat Way, 98134).

If you cannot find these publications in your local bookstore, you can order many of them by mail from the **Yellowstone Association,** Box 117, Yellowstone National Park, WY 82190 (☎ **307/344-2293**).

If You Only Have 1 Day

If you are so pinched for time that you have only 1 or 2 days to tour Yellowstone, the recommended approach is to take advantage of the park's loop roads and create a limited itinerary for yourself.

For either loop, you first have to enter the park at West Yellowstone and drive to the Madison junction, 14 miles inside the park. Along the way, you'll see most of the wildlife that lives in the park, and much of the park's topography. Buffalo, elk, and deer predominate this area, and the scenery's spectacular—you'll see National Park Mountain before arriving at the Junction, trumpeter swans in the Madison River, and signs of the fire that ravaged the park in 1988. Both loops allow you to explore the Norris Geyser Basin.

For the **upper loop** (84 miles from Madison Junction), drive north to Norris, proceed north to Mammoth Hot Springs, east to Tower-Roosevelt, south to Canyon Village, and west again to Norris, finally returning to Madison Junction and West Yellowstone or to wherever you are staying. A **lower loop** (96 miles from Madison Junction) also begins by leading you north to Norris, but then you would travel east to Canyon Village, south to Lake Village and West Thumb, west to Old Faithful, and then back to the Madison Junction.

The Upper Loop. If you're pressed for time, the Norris Geyser basin is a major concentration of **thermal attractions** and has a nice **museum.** It's not Old Faithful, but you'll still have plenty of photo ops. Mammoth has one of the park's major attractions, the ever growing **terraces** of Mammoth Hot Springs. In addition to the natural attraction, the **Albright Visitor Center** provides excellent historical background for everything you'll see in the park. From Mammoth the route winds through forested areas that lead to the edge of the **Lamar Valley,** the region called the Old West area of Yellowstone Park. Then, as you continue south, you'll arrive at the **Grand Canyon,** one of the most dramatic sights in park.

The Lower Loop. This is a better way to go, in our opinion. You'll also see the two largest geyser areas in Yellowstone: **Norris** to the north and the park's signature attraction, **Old Faithful,** to the south. On the eastern side of this route, you'll find the **Grand Canyon of Yellowstone,** and **Hayden Valley,** where you'll find resident herds of buffalo. Farther south, the **Yellowstone Lake** area is a haven for water-lovers: There's fishing, boating, and places for picnicking on the shore of the lake.

If you have 2 days, then do both loops. Whether you have 1 day or 2, we recommend that you spend a night in one of the park hotels, and you'll find yourself minutes from all of the major attractions.

If You Have More Time

Stretching your visit to several days will let you get the most out of the park.

Since the roads in Yellowstone are organized into a series of interconnecting loops, it doesn't really matter where in the park you begin a more wide-ranging exploration. It's really a function of your particular interests and your convenience. To simplify things, we will discuss attractions and activities going clockwise along each section of the **Grand Loop Road** (which combines the Upper and Lower loops), beginning at the **Madison Junction.** But you can enter the loop at any point, and follow our tour as long as you are traveling clockwise.

WEST YELLOWSTONE TO NORRIS

Since the largest percentage of visitors to Yellowstone enter at the **West Yellowstone Entrance,** we'll use that as a jumping-off point to begin your extended tour of the park. As you travel the 14 miles from the gate to **Madison Junction,** you will find the **Two Ribbons Trail,** which offers an opportunity to walk through and inspect the effects of the 1988 fire.

The 0.5-mile round-trip **Harlequin Lake Trail,** located 1.5 miles west of the Madison Campground on the West Entrance Road, offers an excellent, easy opportunity to explore the area. It winds through the burned forest to a small lake that is populated by various types of waterfowl.

An alternative hike, one of the best in the area, is up the **Purple Mountain Trail,** which begins 0.25 mile north of the Madison Junction on the Norris Road. This hike requires more physical exertion, as it winds 6 miles (round-trip) through a burned forest to the top of what many consider only a tall hill, with an elevation gain of 1,400 feet.

Madison Junction is where you'll enter the northern loop toward Norris Junction, along a windy 14-mile section of road that parallels the **Gibbon River.** At **Gibbon Falls,** which is 84 feet tall, you'll see water bursting out of the edge of a caldera in a rocky canyon, the walls of which were hidden from view for several hundred years until being exposed by the fire of 1988. There's a delightful **picnic area** just below the falls, on an open plateau overlooking the Gibbon River. Before arriving at Norris Junction, you'll discover the **Artist Paint Pot Trail** in Gibbon Meadows 4.5 miles south of the Norris Junction, an interesting, worthwhile, and easy half-mile stroll. Across the road from the trailhead is **Elk Park,** where you can expect to see a large resident herd of elk.

NORRIS GEYSER BASIN

Perhaps more than any other area in Yellowstone, this basin presents living testimony to the park's unique thermal activity. It is the location of one of the park's highest concentration of thermal features, including the most active geysers, with underground water temperatures that reach 459°F.

There are two loop trails here, both mostly level with wheelchair access, to the Porcelain Basin and the Back Basin. If you take in both of them, you'll see most of the area's interesting thermal features. If you're pressed for time, take the shorter, **Porcelain Basin Trail,** a boardwalk that takes only 45 minutes. To me, this area is especially spectacular on summer days when thermal activity takes place on the ground with thunder and lightning storms overhead.

The 1.5-mile **Back Basin Loop** is easily negotiable in 1 hour and passes by **Steamboat Geyser,** which has been known to produce the world's highest and most memorable eruptions. However, these 400-foot waterspouts occur infrequently, so it will take some luck to see one. Conversely, **Echinus Geyser** erupts several times a day.

Check out the **Norris Geyser Basin Museum** and the **Museum of the National Park Ranger** while you're here. Hours vary by season, but you can expect the museums to be open from 8am to 6pm during the busiest times (roughly Memorial Day to Labor Day, but again weather is a factor here).

NORRIS TO MAMMOTH HOT SPRINGS

From Norris Geyser Basin, it's a 21-mile drive north to Mammoth Hot Springs, past the **Twin Lakes,** beautiful, watery jewels surrounded by trees. During the spring and early summer, the water is milky green because of the runoff of ice and snow. This is an excellent place to call time-out and do some bird watching.

On the east (right, if you are traveling north) side of the road 4 miles from Norris is **Roaring Mountain,** a patch of ground totally devoid of brush and plant life, covered with trees and stumps of trees from the 1988 fire.

Just up the road 2 miles is the **Beaver Lake Picnic Area,** an excellent little spot right on Beaver Lake for a snack. It's also a good place to keep an eye out for moose.

As you wend your way half a mile to Obsidian Cliff, across the road from the picnic area the terrain changes quickly, you'll find yourself driving through a narrow valley bisected by a beautiful green stream. **Obsidian Cliff** is where ancient peoples of North America gathered to collect obsidian, a hard, black rock that was used to make weapons and implements.

Traveling the final few miles to Mammoth Hot Springs, you're in an area that is especially interesting because of its geologic diversity. You'll see evidence of the fire, large springs and ponds, and enormous glaciated rock terraces and cliffs.

Exit the valley and head north onto a high plateau, where you'll find **Swan Lake,** which is surrounded by Little Quadrant Mountain and Antler Peak to the west, and Bunsen Peak to the north.

At the northernmost edge of the Yellowstone Plateau, you'll begin a descent through **Golden Gate.** This steep, narrow stretch of road was once a stagecoach route constructed of wooden planks anchored to the mountain by a massive rock called the **Pillar of Hercules,** the largest rock in an unmarked pile that sits next to the road.

MAMMOTH HOT SPRINGS

This area may offer the best argument for getting off the roads, out of your car, and into the environment. Stop first at the large **Albright Visitor Center** (☎ **307/344-2263**), located near park headquarters, which has more visitor information, exhibits, and publications than the other centers.

One of Yellowstone's most unique, beautiful, and fascinating areas are the **Upper** and **Lower Terraces.** The mineral-rich hot waters that flow to the surface here do so at an unusually constant rate, roughly 750,000 gallons per day, which results in the deposit of almost 2 tons of limestone on these ever-changing terraces. Contours are constantly undergoing change in the hot springs, as formations are shaped by large quantities of flowing water, the slope of the ground, and trees and rocks that determine the direction of the flow.

On the flip side of the equation, nature has a way of playing tricks on some of her creatures: **Poison Spring** is a sinkhole on the trail, so named because carbon dioxide collects there, often killing creatures that stop for a drink. The **Lower Terrace Interpretive Trail** is one of the best ways to see this area.

After passing **Palette Spring,** where bacteria create a collage of browns, greens, and oranges, you're on your way to **Cleopatra** and **Minerva terraces.** Minera is a favorite of visitors because of its bright colors and travertine formations, the product of limestone deposits.

The hike up the last 150 feet to the Upper Terrace Loop Drive is slightly steeper, though there are benches at frequent intervals. From here you can see all the terraces and several springs—**Canary Spring** and **New Blue Spring** being the most distinctive—and the red-roofed buildings of **Fort Yellowstone,** which is now the park headquarters.

MAMMOTH HOT SPRINGS TO TOWER JUNCTION

Heading east from Mammoth on the Tower Road, a 6-mile drive will bring you to the **All Person's Fire Trail,** so named because this flat and easy stroll along a boardwalk offers an excellent opportunity to educate yourself about the affects of the fire on the environment.

Two miles later is **Blacktail Plateau Drive,** a 7-mile, one-way dirt road that offers great wildlife-viewing opportunities and a bit more solitude. You'll emerge back onto the Mammoth–Tower Road, about a mile west of the turnoff to the Petrified Tree.

Turn right onto this half-mile-long road that dead-ends at the **Petrified Tree,** a redwood that, while standing, was burned by volcanic ash more than 50 million years ago.

TOWER-ROOSEVELT

Just beyond the Petrified Tree, you'll come to **Tower-Roosevelt,** the most relaxed of the park's villages and a great place to take a break from the more crowded attractions. Even if you aren't going to stay, you might want to take a look at the **Tower Soldier Station,** now the ranger residence at Tower Junction, one of three surviving outposts from the era of U.S. Cavalry management of the park. Also here is **Roosevelt Lodge,** a rustic building that commemorates Pres. Teddy Roosevelt's camping excursion to this area of the park in 1903.

At **Specimen Ridge,** 2.5 miles east of the Tower Junction on the Northeast Entrance road, you'll find a ridge that entombs one of the world's most extensive fossil forests.

FROM TOWER JUNCTION TO THE GRAND CANYON OF THE YELLOWSTONE

A few minutes' drive from the Tower area is the **Calcite Springs Overlook.** A short loop along a boardwalk leads to the overlook at the rim of **The Narrows,** the narrowest part of the canyon. You can hear the river raging through the canyon some 500 feet below, and look across at the canyon walls comprised of rock spires and bands of columnar basalt. Just downstream is the most prominent feature in the canyon, **Bumpus Butte.**

Continuing south, you will travel through the **Washburn Range,** an area in which the 1988 fire ran especially hot and fast. The terrain changes dramatically as the road climbs, as well as along some major hills toward **Mount Washburn.** There are trailheads for the **Mount Washburn Trail,** one of my favorites, on each side of the summit.

As you approach **Dunraven Pass** (8,859 feet), keep your eyes peeled for the shy mountain sheep, since this is one of their prime habitats.

One mile further south is the **Washburn Hot Springs Overlook,** which offers sweeping views of the Grand Canyon. On a clear day, you can see 50 to 100 miles south, beyond Yellowstone Lake.

CANYON VILLAGE

You're in for yet another eyeful when you reach the **Grand Canyon** of Yellowstone National Park. Compared to the Grand Canyon of Arizona, the Yellowstone canyon is relatively narrow; however, it's equally impressive because of the steepness of the cliffs, which descend hundreds of feet to the bottom of a gorge where the Yellowstone River flows. It's also equally colorful, with displays of oranges, reds, yellows, and golds. You won't find thermal vents in Arizona, but you will find them here, a constant reminder of ongoing underground activity.

You should plan on encountering crowds when you reach **Canyon Village.** The **Canyon Visitor Center** (☎ **307/242-2550**) is the place to go for books and a new exhibit on bison. It's also staffed with friendly rangers used to dealing with the crowds here.

An auto tour of the canyon follows **North Rim Drive,** a two-lane, one-way road that begins in Canyon Village, to your first stop, **Inspiration Point.** On the way, you'll pass a **glacial boulder** estimated to weigh 500 tons that was deposited by melting ice more than 10,000 years ago.

At Inspiration Point, a moderately strenuous descent down 57 steps takes you to an overlook with views of the Lower Falls and canyon. There are several other view points you can stop at along North Rim Drive before you reconnect with the main Canyon Village–Yellowstone Lake road, which will take you down to South Rim Drive.

For the adventurous, an alternative to driving from one overlook to another is to negotiate the **North Rim Trail,** which is slightly more than 2.25 miles long, beginning at Inspiration Point. Unfortunately, the North Rim Trail is not a loop, so if you take the hike, you'll have to backtrack to get your car at Inspiration Point. The footpath brings you closer to what you want to see, and you won't be fighting for elbow room, as you will at the overlooks that are only accessible to cars.

Whether you drive or walk, you should go down to the **Upper Falls View,** where a 0.25-mile trail leads down from the parking lot to the brink of the **Upper Falls** and an overlook within splashing distance of the rushing river and the waterfall. At this point you won't just hear, you'll feel the power of the river as it begins its course down the canyon.

The **South Rim Drive** leads to several overlooks and better views of the Lower Falls. The most impressive vantage point is from the bottom of **Uncle Tom's Trail,** a steep, 500-foot route to the river's edge that begins at the first South Rim parking lot.

South Rim Road continues to a second, lower parking lot and a trail that leads to **Artist Point.** The view here is astounding, one of my favorites in the park, and is best in the early morning.

CANYON VILLAGE TO FISHING BRIDGE

The road winds through the **Hayden Valley,** which is a vast expanse of beautiful green meadows accented by brown cuts where the soil is eroded along the banks of the Yellowstone River. The valley is now a wide, sprawling area where bison and antelope play and where trumpeter swans, white pelicans, and Canada geese float along the river. This is also a prime habitat for the grizzly, so during early spring months pay close attention to binocular-toting visitors grouped beside the road.

Nature is working at her acidic best at the **Sulphur Caldron** and **Mud Volcano** areas, 12 miles south of the Canyon Junction, which were described by the frontier minister Edwin Stanley as "unsightly, unsavory, and villainous." I think he was right on the money, so you'll certainly not want to miss this area. There's certainly nothing like the sound of burping mud pots.

At **Dragon's Mouth Spring,** turbid water from an underground cavern is propelled by escaping steam and sulfurous gases to an earthside exit where it colors the earth with shades of orange and green. The belching of steam from the cavern and the attendant sound, which is due to the splash of 180°F water against the wall in a subterranean cavern, creates a medieval quality; hence, the name of the spring.

Nearby **Mud Volcano** is an unappetizing mud spring, the product of vigorous activity caused by escaping sulfurous gases and steam. The youngest feature in the area is **Black Dragon's Caldron,** which is often referred to as the demon of the backwoods, and rightly so. The caldron emerged from its subterranean birthplace for the first time in 1948 when it announced its presence by blowing a hole in the landscape, scattering mature trees hundreds of feet in all directions. Since then, continual seismic activity and intermittent earthquakes in the area have caused it to relocate 200 feet south of its original position.

The road across the Yellowstone River at **Fishing Bridge** was once the only eastern exit in the park, the route leading over Sylvan Pass to Cody, Wyoming. The bridge, which was built in 1902, spans the Yellowstone River as it exits Yellowstone Lake, and is another prime spawning area for native trout. The **Fishing Bridge Visitor Center** (☎ **307/242-2450**), which is open from 8am to 6pm, has an excellent wildlife display. You'll find an excellent hiking trail, **Elephant Back Loop Trail,** leading off the short strip of highway between Fishing Bridge and the Lake Village area.

YELLOWSTONE LAKE AREA

As if the park didn't have enough record-setting attractions, at 7,773 feet **Yellowstone Lake** is North America's largest high-altitude lake. The lake exhibits its multifaceted personalities every day, which range on the emotional scale from a placid, mirrorlike surface to a cauldron whipped by southerly winds that create 3- to 4-foot waves. Because the lake has the largest population of native cutthroat trout in North America, it makes an ideal fishing spot during the summer.

Lake Village, on the northwest shore of the lake, offers a wide range of amenities, the most prominent of which is the majestic 100-year-old **Lake Yellowstone Hotel,** perhaps the most beautiful structure in the park.

Just south of Lake Village is the **Bridge Bay Marina,** the center of the park's water activities. Here you can arrange for guided fishing trips or small boat rentals, or learn more about the lake during an informative and entertaining 1-hour narrated boat tour. The marina is usually open from mid-June to mid-September.

Though the **Natural Bridge,** near Bridge Bay, is well marked on park maps, it's one of the park's best-kept secrets, and you may end up enjoying it by yourself. The mile-long path down to the bridge, a geologic masterpiece consisting of a massive rock arch 51 feet overhead, spanning Bridge Creek, is an excellent bike route.

The **West Thumb** area along the western shoreline, is the *deepest* part of Yellowstone Lake. Because of its suspiciously craterlike contours, many scientists speculate that this 4-mile-wide, 6-mile-long, water-filled crater was created during volcanic eruptions approximately 125,000 years ago.

The **West Thumb Geyser Basin** is notable for a unique series of geysers. Some are situated right on the shores, some overlook the lake, and some can be seen *beneath* the lake surface. Three of the shoreline geysers, the most famous of which is **Fishing Cone,** are occasionally marooned offshore when the lake level rises. Fortunately, the area is surrounded by half a mile of boardwalks, so it's easy to negotiate.

Maps and details about the area are available in the **West Thumb Information Station,** which is housed in a log structure that functioned as the original West Thumb Ranger Station. The center is open daily from May through September from 9am to 5pm.

As you depart the West Thumb area, you are presented with two choices: either to head south toward Grand Teton National Park or to head west across the **Continental Divide** at Craig Pass, en route to Old Faithful.

GRANT VILLAGE TO THE SOUTH ENTRANCE

In contrast to the forgettable village of Grant is the beautiful 22-mile drive to **Grand Teton** along high mountain passes and **Lewis Lake.** After the lake loses its winter coat of ice, it is a popular spot for early season anglers who are unable to fish streams that are clouded by the spring runoff.

Beyond the lake, the road follows the Lewis River through an alpine area and along the **Pitchstone Plateau,** a pile of lava more than 2,000 feet high and 20 miles wide that was created some 500,000 years ago. A high gorge overlooking the river provides views that are different from, but equally spectacular to, those in other sections of the park.

WEST THUMB TO OLD FAITHFUL

The most interesting phenomenon on the Old Faithful route is **Isa Lake** at Craig Pass. Unlike most lakes and streams in the park, it drains into both eastern and western drainages and ends up in the Pacific Ocean and the Gulf of Mexico. Amazingly, as a consequence of a gyroscopic maneuver, the outlet on the *east* curves *west* and drains to the Pacific, and the outlet on the *west* curves *east* and drains to the Gulf.

Before you reach the Old Faithful geyser area, two additional detours are recommended. Two and one-half miles southeast of Old Faithful is an overlook at the spectacular **Kepler Cascades,** a 150-foot, stair-step waterfall on the Firehole River that is footsteps from the parking lot.

Near that parking lot is the trailhead for the second detour, a 5-mile roundtrip to the **Lone Star Geyser** (on the eponymous trail), which erupts every 3 hours, sending steaming water 30 to 50 feet from its 12-foot cone.

OLD FAITHFUL GEYSER AREA

Despite the overwhelming sight of the geysers and steam vents that populate the Old Faithful area, I suggest you resist the temptation to explore until you've stopped at the **Old Faithful Visitor Center** (☎ **307/545-2751**). It's larger and has more staff and facilities than most other park visitor centers. You will also want to check the information board for estimated times of geyser eruptions, and plan your time accordingly.

The Old Faithful area is generally divided into four sections: **Upper Geyser Basin,** which includes Geyser Hill, **Black Sand Basin, Biscuit Basin,** and **Midway Geyser Basin.** All of these areas are connected to the Old Faithful area by paved trails and roads. If time allows, hike the area; it's fairly level, and distances are relatively short. Between the Old Faithful area and Madison Junction, you'll also find the justifiably famous **Lower Geyser Basin,** including Fountain Paint Pot and the trails surrounding it. You can see some of these geysers on Firehole Lake Drive.

Though **Old Faithful** is not the largest or most regular geyser in the park, its image has been seen on everything from postage stamps to whiskey bottles. It acquired its name when the Washburn Expedition of 1870 observed its predictable pattern of eruptions, which hasn't changed in more than a century. Like clockwork, the average interval between eruptions is 79 minutes, though it may vary 20 minutes in either direction. A typical eruption lasts 1½ to 5 minutes, during which 3,700 to 8,400 gallons of water are thrust upward to heights of 180 feet. For the best views and photo opportunities of the eruption in the boardwalk area, plan on arriving at least 15 minutes before the scheduled show to assure a first-row view.

An alternative to a seat on the crowded boardwalk is a stroll from the Old Faithful Geyser up the **Observation Point Trail** to an observation area that provides better views of the entire geyser basin. The path up to the observation point is approximately 0.5 mile, and the elevation gain is only 200 feet, so it's an easy 15-minute hike. The view of the eruption of the geyser is more spectacular from here and the crowds less obtrusive.

Accessible by walkways from Old Faithful Village, the **Upper Geyser Basin Loop** is referred to as Geyser Hill on some maps. The 1.3-mile loop trail winds among several thermal attractions. **Anemone Geyser** may offer the best display of the various stages of a typical eruption as the pool fills and overflows, after which bubbles rising to the surface begin throwing water in 10-foot eruptions, a cycle that is repeated every 7 to 10 minutes.

Two other stars of the show in the Upper Geyser Basin are **Castle Geyser** and **Grand Geyser.** Castle Geyser, which has the largest cone of any geyser in the park, currently erupts for 20 minutes every 10 to 12 hours, after which a noisy steam phase may continue for half an hour. Grand Geyser, the tallest predictable geyser in the world, usually erupts every 7 to 15 hours with powerful bursts that produce streams of water that may reach 200 feet in height.

The **Riverside Geyser** is situated on the bank of the Firehole River, near **Morning Glory Pool.** One of the most picturesque geysers in the park, its 75-foot column of water creates an arch

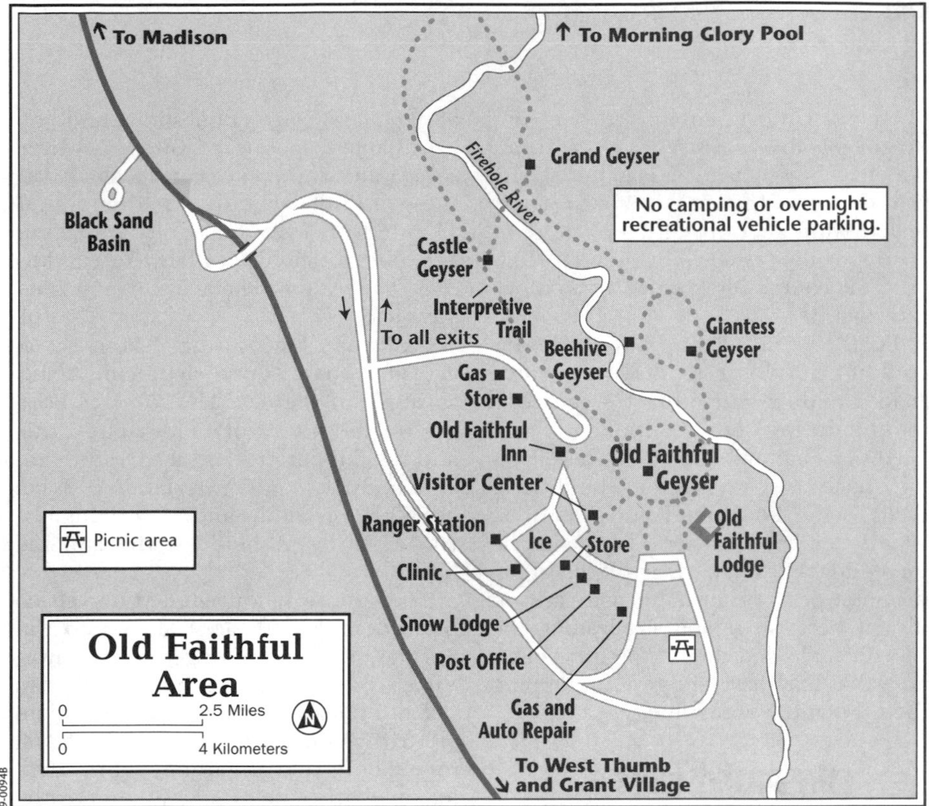

over the river. **Morning Glory Pool** was named for its likeness to its namesake flower in the 1880s, but has since lost its bloom. Vandals have tossed so much debris into its core over the years that it now suffers from poor circulation and reduced temperatures, which are causing unsightly brown and green bacteria to grow on its surface.

The **Black Sand Basin** is a cluster of especially colorful hot springs and geysers located a mile north of Old Faithful. It is interesting primarily because of its black sand, a derivative of obsidian. **Biscuit Basin,** located 2 miles further up the road, was named for biscuitlike deposits that surrounded colorful **Sapphire Pool** until a 1959 earthquake caused the pool to erupt, sending them skyward. Both the Black Sand Basin and the Biscuit Basin can be viewed from flat, interpretive boardwalks.

The **Midway Geyser Basin** extends for about a mile along the Firehole River. The major attractions here are the **Excelsior Geyser,** the third-largest geyser in the world and once the park's most powerful geyser, and the well-known **Grand Prismatic Spring,** the largest hot spring in Yellowstone, and the second largest in the world.

OLD FAITHFUL TO MADISON JUNCTION

Believe it or not, there are other superb geysers and hot springs on **Firehole Lake Drive,** all viewable without leaving your vehicle, along a 3-mile, one-way road that passes several of them. The turnoff for Firehole Lake Drive is about 8 miles north of Old Faithful area. There are three geysers of particular interest on this road. The largest is **Great Fountain Geyser,** which erupts every 8 to 12 hours, typically spouting water some 100 feet high for periods of 45 to 60 minutes. However, the lucky visitor may see the occasional "superburst" that reaches heights of 200 feet or more.

Estimates are that **White Dome Geyser** has been erupting for hundreds of years. Unfortunately, the age and height of this massive cone are not matched by spectacular eruptions. The vent on top of the cone has been nearly sealed with deposits of "geyserite," so eruptions now reach only 30 feet. However, the cone itself is worth a trip down this road.

Further on, **Pink Cone Geyser** couldn't be closer to the road, since road builders cut into the geyser's mound during construction.

About a half mile north of where Firehole Lake Drive rejoins the Grand Loop Road is the **Fountain Paint Pots** area. This is a very popular spot, so you may be forced to wait for a parking place. All the various types of thermal activity are on display here, so as you stroll along the easy, 0.5-mile boardwalk, you'll be in an area that may have six geysers popping their lids at the same time.

Organized Tours & Ranger Programs

Self-guided car audio tours are a great way to get the most out of a drive through the park in your own vehicle. Just rent an audiocassette player that plugs into your vehicle's cigarette lighter and plays through your FM radio, sit back, and listen as prerecorded messages describe park routes and attractions, and provide historical and environmental information. There's even a section that addresses the interests of younger travelers. The system, which rents for $25 for a full day or $16 for a half day, is available from **Amfac Parks and Resorts** at all hotel activity desks and is highly recommended.

Like many of the other services and activities in Yellowstone, organized tours are spearheaded for the most part by **Amfac Parks and Resorts** (☎ **307/344-7311** for tour reservations).

Motorcoach tours are available from all of Yellowstone's villages. Itineraries follow the Upper (North) Loop, Lower (South) Loop, and the best of both. Drivers provide interesting facts and stories along the way, answer questions, and stop at all major points of interest, where short guided walks are conducted. All of these are full-day tours. Children under 11 ride free. Fares for adults are $23 to $29; fares for children 12 to 16 are $11 to $13. You cannot make reservations in advance.

At Bridge Bay Marina, 1-hour **scenicruiser boat tours** are conducted throughout the day. The tours explore the northern part of Yellowstone Lake, and the skipper presents a narrative that is interesting and entertaining. Fares are $7.50 for adults and $4 for children (those under 2, held on the lap, are free).

One- and two-hour **guided horseback trail rides** are available at Mammoth Hot Springs, Roosevelt Lodge, and Canyon Village corrals. Children must be 8 years old and at least 48 inches tall. Tour prices are $18.50 for a 1-hour ride and $28.50 for a 2-hour ride. Check any activity desk for times and dates. Reservations are recommended, and may be made at **Amfac** activity centers in the hotels, though not before you leave home.

Despite budget cutbacks, the park continues to offer free ranger-led educational programs that will significantly enhance your experience of the parks. Programs usually begin early in June and continue until Labor Day.

Evening **campfire programs** (bring a flashlight and warm clothing) are presented nightly at campgrounds at Mammoth Hot Springs, Norris, Madison, Grant, Bridge Bay, and Canyon; three times weekly at Lewis Lake Campground, and twice a week at Tower. Anyone can attend these free programs. Here are some sample titles: "The National Park Idea," "Greater Yellowstone Ecosystem," "History of Yellowstone," "Explore Yellowstone," "Wildlife of Yellowstone," and "The Aquatic World of Yellowstone." Many of these activities are wheelchair-accessible.

Rangers also conduct **walking** and **hiking programs** throughout the park that are chronicled in the park newspaper, which you'll receive when you enter.

Day Hikes

WEST YELLOWSTONE TO MADISON

Two Ribbons Trail

0.75 mile RT. Easy. Access: The trailhead is located 3 miles east of the West Entrance at a turnout on the north side of the road.

This trail offers an opportunity to walk through and inspect the effects of the 1988 fire. Along this 0.75-mile loop trail, you'll see a mosaic of blackened, singed, and unburned trees—charred snags and green trees side by side among boulders shattered by the heat. The scraggly, deformed branches and piles of rock are surrounded by bushes and fresh, bright green tree shoots that are only now emerging from the soil.

Harlequin Lake Trail

0.5 mile RT. Easy. Access: The trailhead is located 1.5 miles west of the Madison Campground on West Entrance Rd.

This trail offers an excellent, easy opportunity to explore the area by following a half-mile trail that winds through the burned forest to a small lake that is populated by various types of waterfowl.

Purple Mountain Trail

6 miles RT. Easy. Access: The trailhead is located 0.25 mile north of the Madison Junction on the Madison–Norris Rd.

This hike requires more physical exertion as it winds 3 miles through a burned forest to the top of what many consider only a tall hill, with an elevation gain of 1,400 feet.

Artist Paint Pot Trail

0.5 mile RT. Easy. Access: The trailhead is located 4.5 miles south of Norris Junction in Gibbon Meadow.

This interesting and worthwhile (and easy) half-mile stroll along a relatively level path winds through a lodgepole pine forest in Gibbon Meadows, to a mud pot at the top of a hill. This thermal area contains some small geysers, hot pools, and steam vents.

NORRIS GEYSER BASIN

Porcelain Basin Trail

0.75 mile RT. Easy. Access: The trailhead is located at Norris Geyser Basin.

This short trail, which can be completed in 45 minutes, is on a level boardwalk that, like the Back Basin Loop, is in a concentration of thermal attractions that may change every year.

Back Basin Loop

1.5 miles RT. Easy. Access: The trailhead is located at Norris Geyser Basin.

This level boardwalk is easily negotiable in 1 hour and passes by **Steamboat Geyser,** which has been known to produce the world's highest and most memorable eruptions. However, these 400-foot waterspouts occur infrequently, so it will take some luck to see one. Conversely, Echinus Geyser erupts several times a day.

MAMMOTH HOT SPRINGS AREA

Lower Terrace Interpretive Trail

1.5 miles RT. Easy. Access: The well-marked trailhead is located south of the village on the road to Norris.

This interpretive trail is one of the best ways to see this area. The trail starts at 6,280 feet and climbs another 300 feet along marginally steep grades, through a bare, rocky, thermal region to a flat alpine area and observation deck at the top, but it's not a difficult climb. A park guide says the 1.5-mile round-trip walk to the Upper Terrace and back takes 2 hours, but it can be done in less.

All Person's Fire Trail

0.5 mile RT. Easy. Access: The trailhead is located on Tower Rd., 8 miles east of Mammoth Hot Springs.

This flat and easy stroll along a boardwalk presents an excellent opportunity to educate people to the affects of the fire on the environment.

Bunsen Peak Trail

4.2 miles RT. Moderate. Access: The trailhead is across the road from the Glen Creek Trailhead, 5 miles south of Mammoth on the Mammoth–Norris Rd.

This trail leads to a short but steep 2.1-mile trip to the 8,564-foot summit, with a 1,300-foot gain in elevation. Park rangers say this is a favorite for watching the sunrise behind Electric Peak, off to the northwest, which glows with a golden hue. At the top of the peak, you will be 3,000 feet above the valley.

GRAND CANYON OF THE YELLOWSTONE RIVER AREA

North Rim Trail

2 miles one way. Easy. Access: The trailhead is at Inspiration Point.

This trail, which is described more fully in the Grand Canyon section above, has as its primary attractions better views than you'll see from the paved overlooks.

South Rim Trail

3.2 miles one way. Easy. Access: The trailhead is at the parking lot just beyond South Rim Dr. Bridge.

Like the North Rim Trail, there are more and better views of the canyon and river than you can see from a vehicle, and you're away from the crowds.

Uncle Tom's Trail

500 feet one way. Moderate. Access: The trailhead is located at the South Rim Parking Lot.

The short trip is down 328 stairs and paved inclines that lead to the river. The trail is rather steep, but can be negotiated in an hour, though it will be challenging for the neophyte hiker.

Mount Washburn Trail

6 miles RT. Moderate. Access: The trailhead is at the end of Old Chittenden Rd. and at Dunraven Pass.

The Mount Washburn Trail falls into the "If you can only do one hike, do this one" category. The rises are fairly gradual, and they're interspersed with long, fairly level stretches. At this elevation, however, the best method of attacking the mountain is to pace yourself, which has its own rewards: You have time to appreciate the views to the east of the Absaroka Mountains, south to Yellowstone Lake, and west to the Gallatin Mountains. Odds are good that you'll see mountain sheep, since it's a popular summer grazing area for them, as well as yellow-bellied marmots and the wily red fox. The hike to the summit is an easy 90-minute walk at a steady pace, or 2 hours with breaks. At this elevation, where weather changes quickly, it's always a good idea to bring several layers of clothing. Fortunately, there's a warming hut in the base of the ranger lookout, viewing telescopes, and rest rooms, but, alas, no hot chocolate machine.

YELLOWSTONE LAKE AREA

Elephant Back Loop Trail

2 miles RT. Easy. Access: From the east, the trailhead is on the right side of the road, just before the turnoff for the Lake Yellowstone Hotel.

The hike is to an overlook that provides photographers with panoramic views of Yellowstone Lake and its islands, the Absaroka Range, and Pelican Valley.

Storm Point Trail

2 miles RT. Easy. Access: The trailhead is located 3.5 miles east of Fishing Bridge, directly across from the Pelican Valley Trailhead (on the lake side of the road).

The Storm Point Trail follows a level path that terminates at a point jutting into the lake with panoramic views. It begins near Indian Pond. During spring months, this is a popular spot with grizzlies, so the trail may be closed; however, even when it's open, check with rangers regarding bear activity.

OLD FAITHFUL AREA

Lonestar Geyser Trail

5 miles RT. Easy. Access: The trailhead is at the parking lot opposite Kepler Cascades.

This is another trail that falls into the "Gotta do it" category, and its popularity is its only disadvantage. Despite the probability that you'll be sharing the territory with others, there are several compelling reasons to give it a go. From the trailhead you'll wend your way through a forested area along a trail that parallels the Firehole River. The payoff for your effort is the arrival at the geyser, though it will not be found in the *Guinness Book of Records*. It sits alone, a vanilla chocolate ice cream cone near the middle of a vast meadow partially covered by grass and trees, exposed rock, gravel, and volcanic debris. Surrounding it are small, bubbling geysers and steam vents. The 5-mile hike is easily doable in 2 hours.

Observation Point Trail–Solitary Geyser

2.1 miles RT. Easy. Access: The trailhead is at the Old Faithful boardwalk.

This trail leads to an observation area that provides better views of the entire geyser basin. The path up to the observation point is approximately 0.5 mile, and the elevation gain is only 200 feet, so it's an easy 15-minute hike. The view puts the entire Upper Geyser Basin into a different perspective; it is possible to see most of the major geysers, as well as inaccessible steam vents located in the middle of wooded areas. From the top of the boardwalk continue to the Solitary Geyser on a downhill slope that leads past the geyser, through the basin, and back to the inn, which completes the loop.

Geyser Hill Basin Loop

1.3 miles RT. Easy. Access: The trailhead is at the Old Faithful boardwalk.

One of the most interesting, and easiest, loops in the area, this trail winds among several thermal attractions. Anemone Geyser may offer the best display of the various stages of a typical eruption as the pool fills and overflows; the Lion Group consists of four geysers that are interconnected beneath the surface; Doublet Pool is especially popular with photographers who are attracted by a complex series of ledges and deep-blue waters. Giantess Geyser is known for its violent eruptions.

Mystic Falls Trail

1.1 miles one way. Easy. Access: The trailhead is located at Imperial Meadows in Biscuit Basin.

This is a favorite of park rangers. The trail leads to a waterfall on the Little Firehole River that drops more than 100 feet, one of the steepest in the park. The trail starts at Biscuit Basin, crosses the river, then disappears into the forest. The total distance to the falls is only 1.1 miles; there's a trail to take you to the top.

To make your return more interesting, continue 0.2 mile to the Little Firehole Meadows Trail, which has an overlook that offers a view of Old Faithful in the distance. Best estimates are that the total time for the hike is an easy 2 hours, with an elevation gain of only 460 feet.

Fairy Falls Trail

12 miles RT. Moderate. Access: The trailhead is located at Imperial Meadows in Biscuit Basin.

Though considerably longer than the Mystic Falls Trail, the Fairy Falls Trail is equally popular with the park staff because it leads to a taller waterfall. The easy 6-mile hike begins at the Imperial

Meadows Trailhead, 1 mile south of the Firehole River Bridge on Fountain Flat Drive. It winds through an area populated by elk along Fairy Creek, then past the Imperial Geyser. From here, it joins Fairy Creek Trail and travels east to the base of the falls. The total gain in elevation is only 100 feet.

Fountain Paint Pot Trail

0.5 miles RT. Easy. Access: The trailhead begins at Fountain Paint Pot Parking Lot.

This area is a very popular attraction, so you may be forced to wait for a parking place. All of the various types of thermal activity are on display here, so as you stroll along the easy 0.5-mile boardwalk you'll be in an area that may have six geysers popping their lids at the same time.

Exploring the Backcountry

Most park trails are in snow country, 6,000 to 9,000 feet above sea level, and many areas will be covered with snow until late May or early June. As a consequence, some of what are described as intermittent creeks and streams during summer months may be filled with melting snowpack that converts them to impassable, swiftly running rivers. Trails become temporary creek beds, and campsites may be damp as well.

You are required to secure a backcountry permit from the Park Service in order to use an overnight campsite; however, the good news is that the permits are free. There are two methods of securing permits: They may be picked up the day before you begin your trip, or you can make a reservation for a permit in advance of your arrival, which carries a $20 fee. *A caution:* The reservation is just that, a reservation; upon your arrival at the park, you'll need to secure the permit.

Reservations in Yellowstone must be made more than 48 hours in advance, and may be requested by writing the **Backcountry Office,** P.O. Box 168, Yellowstone National Park, WY 82190, or checking with a ranger station; telephone reservations are not being accepted. Permits are issued at the following ranger stations: Bechler, Canyon, Mammoth, Old Faithful, Tower, West Entrance, Lake, and South Entrance. They are also available at the Grant Village Visitor Center and, occasionally, at the East and Northeast entrances, and the Bridge Bay Ranger Station.

The Yellowstone Backcountry. If you just can't get your fill of geysers, several trails lead to backcountry thermal areas that are unlikely to be populated with tourists. The **Shoshone Geyser Basin** and **Heart Lake Geyser Basin** contain active geysers, as do **Ponuntpa Springs** and the **Mudkettles** in the Pelican Valley Area, **Imperial Geyser** in the Firehole area, and the **Highland Hot Springs** on the Mary Mountain Trail. If you head in these directions, be careful: A young man died in 1988 when he fell into a superheated pool.

Shoshone Lake. Shoshone Lake is the park's largest backcountry lake, and a popular spot for backcountry hikers. The shortest route to the lake is via the **Delacy Creek Trail,** which begins 8 miles east of Old Faithful on the Old Faithful–West Thumb Road. From here, the trail winds 3 miles along Delacy creek through moose country and the edge of the forest at the lake. From here it's a toss-up: You can head around the lake in either direction. Assuming you take a clockwise track around the lake, a distance of 18 miles, you'll take the **East Shore Trail** to its intersection with **Dogshead Trail,** then head west on the **South Shore Trail** until it intersects with the **North Shore Trail** and returns to your starting point.

As you travel the lake's loop trail along the **East Shore Trail** you'll have views of the lake at the top of a 100-foot rise. Then, on the **South Shore Trail,** you'll cross the Lewis Channel, which may have thigh-high water as late as July. Beyond that, the trail is a series of rises that are easily negotiable by the average hiker, passes across shallow Moose Creek, and through meadows where you may spot deer or moose early in the morning or evening.

The **North Shore Trail,** 7 miles long, is a mostly level path that winds through a lodgepole pine forest, though there is one 200-foot-tall ridge. The best view of the lake is from cliffs on this trail.

The loop trail is especially popular with overnighters, since there are 26 campsites on the loop, the largest of which has space for eight campers.

The Bechler Region. This area in the park's southwest section is often referred to as the Cascade Corner because it contains a majority of the park's waterfalls. It was not scarred by the fires of 1988 and offers great opportunities to view thermal features. Many backpacking routes cut through this region, including one that leads to Old Faithful on the **Bechler River Trail.**

To begin your hike, drive into the park from Ashton, Idaho, and check in at the Bechler Ranger Station, where you'll find yourself far from the maddening crowds. To reach the ranger station, drive east 26 miles from Ashton on the Cave Falls Road; 3 miles before reaching Cave Falls you'll find the ranger station turnoff. The ranger station is 1.5 miles down the gravel road.

The most adventurous, and scenic, route is from the ranger station 30 miles to the end of the trail at the **Lone Star Trailhead** near Old Faithful. If you take this route along the Bechler River Trail then cross the Bechler River, which will be knee-deep in water until July, at the 5.5-mile mark. (The only bridge on the trail was removed years ago.) Beyond the crossing, you'll pass Collonade Falls 5 miles later, then Iris and Ragged falls before reaching a patrol cabin at Three Rivers Junction at the 13-mile marker, a popular camping area with room for 12 people. There are a total of 10 campsites between the ranger station and Three Rivers.

If you continue toward Old Faithful, you'll intersect the **Shoshone Lake Trail** at the 23.5-mile marker, and exit 6.5 miles later.

As an alternative, begin a loop tour from the ranger station. Hike 3.5 miles along the **Bechler River Trail** past the waterfalls to the **Boundary Creek Trail,** then return to the station via the **Bechler Meadows Trails,** a round-trip of 7 miles.

Thorofare Area. The Thorofare area in the southeast corner of the park has one-way hikes ranging in length from 4 to 50 miles. The area is popular because of its drop-dead scenery, access to remote areas of Yellowstone Lake, and the summits of some of the park's tallest peaks; however, its remote location also deters many hikers. Once used by Indians as the main highway between Jackson Hole and points north, remnants of their presence are seen in teepee rings and lean-tos that are visible to the explorer today.

It is best known for the **Thorofare Trail,** which covers nearly 70 miles on a round-trip through some of the most isolated and pristine wilderness in the lower 48 states, while tracing Yellowstone Lake's southern and eastern boundaries. The cutthroat trout fishing is phenomenal in the early summer. There are several campsites on the trail.

The trail, which provides the easiest access to the Upper Yellowstone Valley, begins at the **Nine Mile Trailhead** (also called the **Thorofare Trailhead**), which is located 9 miles east of Fishing Bridge on the East Entrance Road. Since this is grizzly bear country, you'll want to check with rangers before heading off during the spring spawning season. From here, the trail travels across Cub Creek (1.5 miles) and Clear Creek (3 miles), both of which may have high, swift water early in the season. The **Park Point Campsites** (with room for 12) are located 6.5 miles from the trailhead; they are a favorite with campers since they provide unimpaired views of the sunset across Yellowstone Lake. The next 9 miles of the trip are in trees, so don't count on spectacular views; however at **Terrace Point,** 15.5 miles from the trailhead, you'll have 180° views of the Yellowstone River Valley.

Aside from the grizzlies, the major obstacle to early-season trips in the

Thorofare is water; you'll encounter knee-deep water at **Beaverdam Creek,** and at **Trapper Creek,** which is knee deep until late July. However the views are spectacular: You'll have views of Turret and Trident mountains, and of the Yellowstone River. When you reach the Thorofare Ranger Station at the 32-mile marker you will have arrived at the spot rangers say is one of the most remote in the Lower 48—you're 32 miles from the nearest road of any kind.

The Sportsman Lake Trail. This trail, which begins near Mammoth Hot Springs and extends west toward U.S. 191 to Sportsman Lake, is a moderate, 14-mile trail which displays a diverse combination of flora and fauna. From the Glen Creek Trailhead 5 miles south of Mammoth Hot Springs, spend 2 miles on the Glen Creek Trail as you traverse a mostly level, wide-open plateau covered with sagebrush that is the home of herds of elk and a bear management area. At the **Sepulcher Mountain Trail** at the 3-mile mark the terrain increases in steepness as you continue northwest on the **Sportsman Lake Trail;** the elevation gain is approximately 2,300 feet to the Sepulcher summit (though you don't go to it on this route).

The trail eventually enters the forest and descends to a log that is used to cross Gardner River. Then, it's uphill for another 4 miles to **Electric Divide,** another 2,000-foot gain in elevation. From there, the trail descends 2,100 feet in 3 miles to Sportsman Lake, which is located in one of the areas that burned in 1998. Two campsites provide overnight spaces for a total of 30 visitors.

Other Summer Sports & Activities

Biking. Yellowstone's narrow and twisty roads, crowded with motorized traffic, make life difficult for bikers. Off-road opportunities are limited because of the small number of trails on which bikes are allowed. The following trails are available to mountain bikers, but you should be aware that you will share the roads with hikers. The Mount Washburn Trail, leaving from the Old Chittenden Road, is a very strenuous trail that climbs 1,400 feet. The Lone Star Geyser Trail, which is accessed at Kepler Cascade near Old Faithful, is an easy 1-hour ride on a user-friendly road. Near Mammoth Hot Springs, Bunsen Peak Road and Osprey Falls Trail provide a combination ride: For the first 6 miles you travel around Bunsen Peak on a bike trail; getting to the top requires a 3-mile, uphill ride. A hike down to Osprey Falls adds 3 miles to the journey.

There is one place to rent bikes in West Yellowstone: **Yellowstone Bicycles** (☎ **406/646-7815**).

Boating. The best place to enjoy boating in Yellowstone is on Yellowstone Lake, which has easy access and beautiful, panoramic views. The lake is also one of the few areas where powerboats are allowed. Rowboats and outboard motorboats can be rented at **Bridge Bay Marina** (☎ **307/344-7381**).

Horseback Riding. After hiking, perhaps the second-best method of touring the park is on the back of a trusty cayuse, though some would rank horseback riding first. Visitors may take two approaches to this Western experience: **Amfac Parks and Resorts** offers riding tours from stables situated next to popular visitor centers in Canyon Village, Roosevelt Lodge, and Mammoth Hot Springs. Roosevelt Lodge also offers evening rides from June into September. Choices are daily 1- and 2-hour guided trail rides aboard well-broken animals.

For experienced riders these tours may prove to be too tame; even wranglers call them "nose-and-tail" tours. If you're looking for a more serious riding experience, contact the parks and request a list of approved concessionaires that lead backcountry expeditions. These will be on approved trails, but will

Especially for Kids

You may find that several of the ranger programs will appeal to kids. And don't forget the **All Person's Fire Trail,** an interpretive trail leading through a burned-out area of the park with signs to teach the young ones about forest fires. It's located on Tower Road, just east of Mammoth Hot Springs (see "If You Have More Time," above).

Like many national parks, Yellowstone has a **Junior Ranger Program** for kids ages 5 to 12. For $2, you get a special activity paper, *Yellowstone's Nature.* (Sign up at any visitor center). Kids receive a Junior Ranger badge for completing certain activities.

travel deeper into the park, especially the overnight trips.

Fishing. Since there's no rule of thumb to follow when it comes to fishing the park, before venturing to the rivers or streams, pick up a copy of the park's fishing regulations at a ranger station. Different stretches of the same river may have different regulations regarding the use of lures and tackle, for example. The same holds true for bank fishing, as compared to using drift boats; except for the Lewis River channel, all the park's rivers are closed to boats. Your best bet may be to check with one of the fishing shops in the gateway cities, since they'll know where the fish are biting and the type of gear best suited to the conditions.

With 136 square miles of surface and a fleet of boats available for rent, **Yellowstone Lake** is the most popular fishing hole. It's also perhaps the easiest place to catch fish. Fishing from the shore is allowed and wading is popular, but the most successful fishing is done aboard a boat, which can be rented at Bridge Bay Marina (see "Boating," above). The lake is most accessible from the north end at Bridge Bay, Fishing Bridge, Mary Bay, West Thumb, and Lake Lodge.

Winter Sports & Activities

During winter months, Yellowstone is transformed into a surreal wonderland of snow and ice. The landscape is blanketed with a glistening cloak of powdery snow. The geyser basins take on a more dominant role, with the air's temperature in stark contrast to their steaming waters. Nearby trees are transformed into "snow ghosts" by frozen thermal vapors. Bison become frosted shaggy beasts, easily spotted as they take advantage of the more accessible vegetation on the thawed ground surrounding the thermal areas. If you're fortunate enough to experience a Yellowstone winter, the memories will stay with you forever.

Transportation into the park is mainly by snowmobiles and tracked vehicles called snow coaches. Only two of the park's hostelries, **Mammoth Hot Springs Hotel** and the **Old Faithful Snow Lodge,** provide accommodations from December through March, as does **Flagg Ranch.** The only road that's open for cars is the **Mammoth Hot Springs–Cooke City Road.** Yellowstone may be accessed from the west or south by snow coach or snowmobile.

For additional information on all of the following winter activities and accommodations, contact **Amfac Parks and Resorts (☎ 307/344-7311)**. There are also many activities, outfitters, and rental shops in the park's gateway towns.

Cross-Country Skiing. Yellowstone's light, powdery snow is a skier's dream. Whatever your level of expertise, there are backcountry and ski-in trails suitable for you. Whether gliding through a forested trail or striding past grazing elk and bison on the 40-plus miles of trails surrounding the Old Faithful Geyser area, the experience is unparalleled. The best cross-country ski trails in Yellowstone may be the **Lone Star Geyser Trail,** an 8-mile trail in a remote setting that starts at the Old Faithful Snow Lodge; the **Fern Cascades Trail,** which winds for 3 miles through a rolling woodland landscape on a loop close to the Old Faithful area; and the **Upper Geyser Basin and Biscuit Basin Trail,** which some say is the best in Yellowstone, though it may take an entire day to negotiate. The trail, which begins near the Old Faithful Visitor Center, winds 5 miles through flat terrain.

Equipment rentals (about $12 per day), ski instruction, ski shuttles to various locations, and guided ski tours are all available at the park's two winter lodging options: the **Old Faithful Snow Lodge** and the **Mammoth Hot Springs Hotel.** Discounts are available for multiday rentals of skis or snowshoes. Ski instruction costs $17 per person for a 2-hour group lesson. A half-day guided excursion (two-person minimum) is around $32 per person; a full day is $69 per person. For groups of three or more, the cost is $21 per person for a half day, $48 per person for a full day.

Ski rentals are available in West Yellowstone at **Bud Lilly's,** 39 Madison Ave. (☎ **406/646-7801**).

Ice-Skating. The Mammoth Skating Rink is located behind the Mammoth Hot Springs Recreation Center. On a crisp winter's night you can rent a pair of skates ($4) and glide across the ice while seasonal melodies are broadcast over the PA system. It's cold out there, but there's a warming fire at the rink's edge.

Snowmobiling. An excellent way to winter sightsee at your own pace is by snowmobile. There are roads groomed specifically for snowmobile travel throughout the park. A driver's license is required for rental ($130 per day for two riders at Mammoth Hot Springs Hotel or Old Faithful Snow Lodge), and a quick lesson will put even a first-timer at ease.

Snow Coach Tours. It is possible to enjoy the sights and sounds of Yellowstone without raising a finger, except to write a check or sign a credit card voucher, by taking one of the scenic snow coach tours that are available at various locations in the park for about $12.

If you've never seen a snow coach, you're in for a treat. Don't be fooled into thinking that this distinctively Yellowstone mode of transportation is merely a fancy name for a bus that provides tours during winter. Imagine instead an Econoline van with tank treads for tires and water skis extending from its front, and you won't be surprised when you see this unusual looking vehicle. The interiors are toasty warm, with seating for a large group, and they usually allow each passenger two bags. They aren't the fastest, smoothest, or most comfortable form of transportation, but they do allow large groups to travel together, and they're cheaper and warmer than snowmobiles. They're also available for rent at many snowmobile locations.

Guides provide interesting and entertaining facts and stories of the areas as you cruise the park trails, and give you opportunities to photograph scenery and wildlife.

They are also available for hire by groups at most snowmobile locations.

In West Yellowstone, contact **Three Bear Lodge** (☎ **800/221-1551**), **Yellowstone Arctic** (☎ **800/646-7365**), or **Yellowstone Alpen Guides** (☎ **406/646-7242**).

For **Flagg Ranch** or **Jackson** snow coach information, contact **Flagg Ranch** (☎ **800/443-2311**) or **Amfac Parks and Resorts** (☎ **307/344-7311**).

Camping

Of the 12 campgrounds in Yellowstone, seven are operated by the **National Park Service;** these are located at Indian Creek, Lewis Lake, Mammoth, Norris, Pebble Creek, Slough Creek, and Tower Fall. The remaining five campgrounds are operated by **Amfac Parks and**

Resorts; these are located at Bridge Bay, Canyon, Grant Village, Madison, and Fishing Bridge. The only campground equipped with RV hookups is at **Fishing Bridge RV Park,** and it accepts hard-sided vehicles only (no tents or tent trailers); however, though there are no hookups at the other campgrounds, RVers can be accommodated at any of them. Campgrounds begin opening early in May and some remain open until November 1, though this changes from year to year, depending on the weather. Dates vary with weather and road conditions, however, so the wise traveler will double-check by calling the park's main telephone number (☎ **307/344-7381**).

You may make reservations at the five campgrounds run by Amfac Parks and Resorts, which is the only advantage the concessionaire-run campgrounds offer. They're located at Bridge Bay, Canyon, Grant Village, Madison, and Fishing Bridge. **Same day** and **advance reservation** may be made by calling ☎ **307/344-7311** (TDD 307/344-5395) or by writing to **Amfac Parks and Resorts,** P.O. Box 165, Yellowstone National Park, WY 82190, but reservations must be made either over the phone or in writing. Sites are not preassigned; it's all first-come, first-served—you're reserving a space, not a *particular* site.

Camping is allowed only in designated areas and is limited to 14 days between June 15 and Labor Day, and to 30 days the rest of the year. Checkout time for all campgrounds is 10am. Quiet hours are strictly enforced between the hours of 8pm and 8am. No generators, radios, or other loud noises are allowed during these hours.

INSIDE THE PARK

These are campgrounds created for hardy souls in the great outdoors, so don't be surprised to find that the Park Service has taken a minimalist approach to providing amenities. To avoid disappointment with the facilities, check the chart below to determine the level of comfort at each campground. Public showers and laundry facilities are available at Canyon Village, Fishing Bridge, Grant Village, and Lake Lodge; showers only are available at the Old Faithful Lodge. Plan on arriving at most campgrounds by 8am to be certain to secure a site; since it's larger, the **Canyon Campground** fills later.

Camping fees in Yellowstone vary from $10 to $25.20 per night. At Indian Creek, Lewis Lake, Pebble Creek, Slough Creek, and Tower Fall the per-night cost is $10; at Mammoth and Norris it is $12; at Canyon, Bridge Bay, Grant Village, and Madison it is $14.50; at Fishing Bridge RV Park, the most expensive of the campgrounds since it offers electrical, water, and sewer hookups for RVs, it is $25.20.

The **Tower Falls Campground** is near a convenience store, restaurant, and gas station at Roosevelt Lodge and has 32 **forested** sites; it is located 19 miles north of Canyon Village and 18 miles east of Mammoth.

Slough Creek Campground is located in a remote section of the Lamar Valley, near the Northeast Entrance, where there are fewer people, good fishing, and the possibility of wolf sightings; however, rest room facilities are in pit toilets. There are 29 sites here.

Canyon Campground, with 271 sites, is the busiest in the park, so it generally requires an earlier check-in. Sites are assigned and are in a heavily wooded area. (This is the only campground where campsites are assigned.) There's a store, restaurants, visitor center, and laundry nearby at Canyon Center.

Fishing Bridge RV Park, with 340 sites, may open later in the season than projected because it is situated in an area with heavy spring bear activity; as a consequence, only hard-sided camping vehicles are allowed.

Bridge Bay Campground has 429 sites near the shores of Yellowstone Lake, offering tremendous views, especially at sunrise and sunset. Unfortunately, though surrounded by the forest, the area has been clear-cut, so it offers no privacy. It is close to boat launching facilities and the boat rental operation.

The **Madison** and **Norris campgrounds** are situated near the heart of the park. Madison, with 280 sites, is a partly-wooded area that is close to wildlife activity and near the river, so it offers excellent opportunities for fishing and hiking. Norris is smaller, with 116 sites, but offers similar amenities in a wooded site and is on the Gibbon River, close to fishing and the Norris Geyser Basin, and only 12 miles from Canyon Village.

NEAR THE PARK

There are three National Forest Service campgrounds in the **West Yellowstone** area, all located in the Gallatin National Forest (see the campground chart in the preceding section for amenities). Bakers Hole and Rainbow Point accommodate RVs only; Lonesomehurst accommodates RVs and tent campers. They are all open seasonally, from Memorial Day through Labor Day, cost $12.50 per night, and are convenient to the park entrance at West Yellowstone. For reservations, call ☎ **800/280-2267. Bakers Hole,** just 3 miles north of West Yellowstone on U.S. 191, is popular and has only 72 sites, so reserve early. Only RVs are accepted, but there are no hookups. **Lonesomehurst,** 8 miles west of the park on U.S. 20, then 4 miles north on Hebgen Lake Road, is only one-third the size of Bakers Hole and fills up quickly in summer, so reservations are strongly advised. It has tent and RV sites. **Rainbow Point** is reached by driving 5 miles north of West Yellowstone on U.S. 191, then 3 miles west on F.S. 610, then north for

Campground	Total Sites	RV Hookups	Dump Station	Toilets	Drinking Water
In the Park					
*Bridge Bay**	429	No	Yes	Yes	Yes
*Canyon**	271	No	Yes	Yes	Yes
*Fishing Bridge**	340	Yes	Yes	Yes	Yes
*Grant Village**	425	No	Yes	Yes	Yes
Indian Creek	75	No	No	Yes	Yes
Lewis Lake	85	No	No	Yes	Yes
*Madison**	280	No	Yes	Yes	Yes
Mammoth	85	No	No	Yes	Yes
Norris	116	No	No	Yes	Yes
Pebble Creek	32	No	No	Yes	Yes
Slough Creek	29	No	No	Yes	Yes
Tower Fall	32	No	No	Yes	Yes
Near the Park					
Bakers Hole	72	No	No	Yes	Yes
Lonesomehurst	26	No	No	Yes	Yes
Rainbow Point	85	No	No	Yes	Yes

* Reserve through Amfac Parks and Resorts.
Fishing Bridge, Bakers Hole, and Rainbow Point accept hard-sided vehicles only.

2 miles on F.S. 6954. It accommodates only RVs, but there are no hookups.

Accommodations

INSIDE THE PARK

To book a room within Yellowstone, you need to contact **Amfac Parks and Resorts,** P.O. Box 165, Yellowstone National Park, WY 82190 (☎ **307/344-7311**). Yellowstone accommodations are normally open from early summer to late October. The winter season begins in mid-December and runs through mid-March, offering snowmobilers and cross-country skiers accommodations and meals at either Mammoth Hot Springs or Old Faithful Snow Lodge and Cabins.

And don't forget to consider **Flagg Ranch Resort,** which is described in accommodations in Grand Teton, in chapter 19. Only 2 miles from Yellowstone's South Entrance, it's a convenient jumping-off point for exploring the southern reaches of the park and for snowmobiling in Yellowstone during the winter months.

It's easier to find a vacant room before June 15 and after September 15. They're typically fully booked during the peak season, so reservations should be made at least 6 months in advance. But there is no "off-season" in Yellowstone, so don't expect to find reduced rates at any time of the year.

MAMMOTH HOT SPRINGS AREA

This area is popular because of its diversity. You'll find the park's best visitor center here; colorful, Travertine limestone terraces; a historic hotel with one of the park's three finest restaurants; and a campground.

Showers	Fire Pits/ Grills	Laundry	Public Phone	Reserve	Fees	Open
No	Yes	No	Yes	Yes	$14.50	Late May to Sept
Yes	Yes	Yes	Yes	Yes	$14.50	Late May to Sept
Yes	Yes	Yes	Yes	Yes	$25.20	Late May to Labor Day
Yes	Yes	Yes	Yes	Yes	$14.50	Late May to Sept
No	Yes	No	No	Yes	$10	Late May to Sept
No	Yes	No	No	No	$10	Mid-June to Oct
No	Yes	No	Yes	Yes	$14.50	Late May to Sept
No	Yes	No	Yes	No	$12	Year-round
No	Yes	No	Yes	No	$12	Mid-May to Sept
No	Yes	No	No	No	$10	Mid-June to Sept
No	Yes	No	No	No	$10	Late May to Oct
No	Yes	No	No	No	$10	Late May to Mid-Sept
No	Yes	No	Yes	Yes	$12.50	Late May to Sept
No	Yes	No	No	Yes	$12.50	Late May to Sept
No	Yes	No	Yes	Yes	$12.50	Late May to Sept

Mammoth Hot Springs Hotel and Cabins

At Mammoth Hot Springs, P.O. Box 165, Yellowstone National Park, WY 82190. ☎ **307/344-7311** for reservations. 96 rms, 126 cabins. TEL. $47–$70 rm; $305 suite; $38–$69 cabin. AE, DISC, MC, V. Open late May to late Sept and Dec–Mar.

On the site of old Fort Yellowstone, 5 miles from the North Entrance, is this old-fashioned hotel surrounded by thick lawns that attract hungry elk most summer afternoons (the oldest part of the hotel dates from 1937). This is the only hotel that is open during both summer and winter seasons in the northern part of the park. The high-ceilinged lobby gleams with the luster of natural wood floors. A winsome woodstove and soft sofas add to the room's warmth. The adjacent Map Room is a monstrous space set aside for reading on overstuffed sofas, writing at undersized desks, and admiring the scenery through huge windows; it also doubles as a lecture area. Suites measure up to those of Old Faithful Inn and Lake Yellowstone Hotel. Standard rooms and cabins, arranged around three grassy areas, offer minimal but apt appointments. If you need a tub, make your request when you fix your reservation; otherwise, you be showering in a tiny, old-fashioned stall. The cottage-style cabins are a viable alternative, some having private hot tubs and sundecks. A formal dining room and a fast-food restaurant are both located in a separate building.

CANYON VILLAGE AREA

Canyon Village's location in the middle of the park and the many attractions nearby make it one of the busiest areas in the park, which may be its biggest drawback. The Grand Canyon, though, is a short walk from the center of the village.

Canyon Lodge and Cabins

P.O. Box 165, Yellowstone National Park, WY 82190. ☎ **307/344-7311** for reservations. 37 rms, 572 cabin units. $97 double; $49–$90 cabin. AE, DISC, MC, V. Open June–Sept.

This new lodge is located 0.5 mile from the Grand Canyon of the Yellowstone and Inspiration Point, one of the busiest spots in the park. The lodge offers tastefully appointed but ordinary motel-style accommodations in the three-story lodge building, and in cabins that are scattered throughout Canyon Village. You won't find any surprises in the motel units, which have five sleeping configurations, to accommodate the needs of couples and families. The cabins are single-story duplex and fourplex structures with private baths that are among the largest in the park; these units are much nicer than their rustic counterparts in other areas.

TOWER-ROOSEVELT AREA

In addition to cash, the price you pay for staying at this out-of-the-way location is that accommodations are the least modern in the park and the restaurant's food is, at best, average. The payoff is Tower-Roosevelt's proximity to hiking trails and the Lamar Valley and River.

Roosevelt Lodge Cabins

P.O. Box 165, Yellowstone National Park, WY 82190. ☎ **307/344-7311** for reservations. 80 cabins. $29–$69 cabin. AE, DISC, MC, V. Open June–Oct.

The lodge was built in the wake of one of Teddy Roosevelt's legendary treks west, though he didn't sleep here (he opted instead for a tent in the woods). It is a rugged but charming stone edifice with a building-long porch. The inside is one, long common room, similar to the Lake Lodge but significantly nicer. A dining area is at one end and a lounge at the other; the registration desk is in the middle. Services here include horseback riding, western trail cook-outs, and stagecoach rides. The bare-bone cabins, called **Roughriders,** are aptly named; they provide two beds, clean linens, a writing table, and that's about it. Showers are footsteps up a nearby trail. More attractive **Frontier** cabins have showers. The cabins are isolated from crowds at larger hotels and campgrounds, so the appeal here is clearly to budget-conscious, dedicated outdoor types.

LAKE VILLAGE AREA

Though it suffers the same isolation as the Tower-Roosevelt area to the north, the Yellowstone Lake area has enough other attractions to make up for that deficiency. In addition to providing access to the lake's recreational opportunities and the proximity of hiking trails, you'll find accommodations in a historic hotel as well as motel and cabin units, not to mention lakeside camping sites.

Lake Lodge Cabins

On Lake Yellowstone, P.O. Box 165, Yellowstone National Park, WY 82190. ☎ **307/344-7311** for reservations. 186 cabins. $45–$90 double. AE, DISC, MC, V. Open June–Sept.

These cabins, which surround Lake Lodge, face the lake 0.25 mile from the Lake Yellowstone Hotel and Cabins. The lodge is an old Western longhouse fronted by a porch and rockers that invite visitors to sit and gaze out across the waters. The floors inside the lodge gleam like a gymnasium, which is exactly what this building brings to mind. Eating and drinking take place at a small, uninviting bar area and a cafeteria that serves inexpensive meals, so your best bet is to make the quarter-mile trek to the hotel for a decent meal or, if nothing else, a better environment. There's also an undernourished gift shop. Freestanding cabins are well preserved, clean, and situated near a trout stream that threads through a wooded area; chances are good that access to it will be restricted early in the summer when the grizzlies emerge from hibernation. **Western** cabins provide electric heat, paneled walls, two double beds, and tub/shower combinations; **Frontier** cabins are smaller and have only one double bed and a small, shower-only bathroom. The cabins are most suitable for outdoor types.

Lake Yellowstone Hotel and Cabins

Grand Loop Rd. (on the north side of the lake), P.O. Box 165, Yellowstone National Park, WY 82190. ☎ **307/344-7311** for reservations. 194 rms, 102 cabins, 1 parlor suite. TEL. $90–$131 double; $69 cabin; $357 parlor suite. AE, DISC, MC, V. Open mid-May to late Sept.

Dating from 1891 the hotel is the oldest here, and one of the most attractive in the park. This colonial-style building is still glistening following a major renovation project that was completed in 1991. A large sitting area looks out on the lake. Though not as famous as Old Faithful Inn, this hotel has a distinctive air of elegance. Accommodations are in the hotel, in a motel-style annex, and in cabins. The upper-end rooms here are among the nicest in the park. Smaller rooms in the annex are decorated in a typical motel style; as a low-priced alternative, I'd opt for one of the freestanding cabins decorated with knotty-pine paneling. If you stay here, request a single cabin, rather than a duplex, since walls are paper thin; or, bring earplugs. The dining room is capable of feeding busloads, which is a daily occurrence. A recent addition is a take-out deli on the first floor, which serves ordinary finger food at a snail's pace. (A better option for a light meal is the snack bar at the nearby Hamilton store.)

GRANT VILLAGE AREA

Though it does not lack services—there's a visitor center, motel, and two restaurants here—I think Grant Village has less character than any other center in the park.

Grant Village Lodge

On the West Thumb of Yellowstone Lake, P.O. Box 165, Yellowstone National Park, WY 82190. ☎ **307/344-7311** for reservations. 300 rms. TEL. $74–$90 double. AE, DISC, MC, V. The village is open May–Sept.

The southernmost of the major overnight accommodations in the park, Grant Village was completed in 1984 and is one of the more contemporary choices in Yellowstone. The lodge consists of six rather ordinary looking, motel-style two-story chalets that are set back from the water's edge, and a reception area and gift shop that are in a separate building near the village entrance. Rooms are tastefully furnished, most being outfitted with light wood furniture, track lighting, and laminate counters. Nicer, and more expensive, rooms have lake views. Mid-range rooms are set farther back from the lake and overlook drab, unlandscaped grounds. Considering that this is one of the few places where you will find a private bath with a shower (albeit without a tub), prices are relatively reasonable. Since Grant Village is isolated from other park centers, plan on drinking in a tiny lounge and eating in one of two restaurants that overlook the lake. Other guest services located here include a self-service laundry, service station, and convenience store.

OLD FAITHFUL AREA

Ignore the crowds. Block out the frenzied pace. At the Old Faithful area you'll spend a night in the midst of the most famous and largest geyser basin in the world, by itself reason enough to visit Yellowstone. You'll also have more choices of rooms, restaurants, and services, including a visitor center, gas station, and Hamilton store, than anywhere else in the park.

Old Faithful Inn

P.O. Box 165, Yellowstone National Park, WY 82190. ☎ **307/344-7311** for reservations. 359 rms. TEL. $47–$210 double; $305 suite. AE, DISC, MC, V. Open May–Oct.

The crown jewel of this area's hotels is located 30 miles from West Yellowstone and 39 from the South Entrance. This stately turn-of-the-century log palace towers six stories over the geyser basin. The striking lobby boasts a lofty, vaulted ceiling. Sitting areas overlook the lobby, surrounding a three-story stone fireplace from which hangs a massive, noisy clock. The lazy geyser-watcher can avoid the crowds by watching the show from a comfortable second-floor terrace with excellent views of eruptions. Guest rooms are in the main building and in wings that flank the main lodge. The original rooms are well appointed but may not have private baths, so the wing rooms offer better facilities and more privacy. If you want to watch the geyser erupt from your room, ask for Suite 3014 or Room 229. The main dining room, a masterpiece in its own right, is warmed on cool evenings by a fieldstone fireplace. The lobby also houses a fast-food outlet, a bar, and gift shop.

Old Faithful Lodge Cabins

Old Faithful, P.O. Box 165, Yellowstone National Park, WY 82190. ☎ **307/344-7311** for reservations. 122 cabins (some without private bath). $25–$41 double. AE, DISC, MC, V. Open May–Oct.

If you're looking for a dirt-cheap geyser view that's close to a cafeteria and a snack bar, these rustic and economical cabins will fit the bill, and they'll suit the tightest of budgets. The **Frontier** cabins are a cut below the Western cabins you'll find at the Canyon Lodge, but here they are the most expensive units, and you'll still have the privacy of your own full bath. The next step down is the **Economy** cabin, which has a toilet and sink but no bath and costs $4 less. The **Budget** units are furnished with beds and sinks, and that's about it, but they do have harder sides than tents. For Economy and Budget cabins, showers and rest rooms are located nearby. Perhaps the busiest spot in the geyser area, the lodge offers visitors several snack shops and a huge cafeteria. Just off the lobby is one of the largest gift shops in the park and a gymnasium that occasionally hosts square dancing and movies.

Old Faithful Snow Lodge and Cabins

Old Faithful, P.O. Box 165, Yellowstone National Park, WY 82190. ☎ **307/344-7311** for reservations. 65 rms, 34 1-bedrm cabins. $47–$56 double; $69–$90 cabin. AE, DISC, MC, V. Open June–Oct and Dec–Mar.

Note: Plans are underway for the replacement of the Snow Lodge structure with a "new" Old Faithful Snow Lodge near the original location that may be open by midsummer 1998. The 34 cabins will remain; the new Snow Lodge will also will have 65 rooms.

The third property at the famous geyser is a nondescript two-story facility that offers low-cost shelter in a motel-style environment. Rooms are clean, spartan, converted dormitory units, only one of which has a private bath. Frontier cabins with showers and Western cabins with tub-shower combinations have been added to the property since the 1988 fire. Other facilities include a family style restaurant that serves up traditional (average quality, average priced) meals and bar service, and a postage-stamp-size gift shop that is located in the lobby. This is only one of two facilities in the park that are open during winter months. It's an inexpensive alternative to higher priced accommodations in the gateway cities.

NEAR THE PARK

WEST YELLOWSTONE

Best Western owns a large portion of the lodging market in West Yellowstone, with four different motels around town. The **Best Western Desert Inn** at 133 Canyon (☎ **800/528-1234** or 406/646-7376) has 57 rooms. In season, a double room goes for $96 per night; in winter, the rate drops to $57 per night. The **Best Western Executive Inn** at 236 Dunraven (☎ **800/528-1234** or 406/646-7681) is by far the largest Best Western property in West Yellowstone with 82 rooms. Its summer rates are $85 per night, lower in winter. The **Best Western Weston Inn** at 103 Gibbon (☎ **800/528-1234** or 406/646-7373) has 55 rooms. In summer, rates are $95 per night, double, with a king bed.

Firehole Ranch

11500 Hebgen Lake Rd., West Yellowstone, MT 59758. ☎ **406/646-7294** in summer, or 307/733-7669 year-round. 10 cabins, each sleeps up to 6. $200–$290 per person per day, double occupancy. Rate includes all meals, airport transfers, and activities (except guided fishing). 4-day minimum stay required. No credit cards.

Recently named Orvis's Lodge of the Year, the ranch is a perennial favorite among serious fly-fishers who challenge rainbow, German brown, and cutthroat trout on six streams near the West Entrance of the park. Located approximately 20 miles from West Yellowstone, the resort is surrounded by thousands of acres of national forest and has 1 mile of private shoreline on Hebgen Lake, thus affording guests an enormous wilderness area in which to ride horses, hike, canoe, and make use of the ranch's supply of mountain bikes. Cocktails are served in a cozy nook prior to the serving of exquisite meals prepared by a French chef. Breakfast is served buffet style, and box lunches are prepared for the midday repast. Lodging is in 10 cabins, most suitable for two guests, though several have sofa beds. The nicest units have separate living quarters, complete with wood-burning stoves, bedrooms furnished with king-size beds, and private baths with tub-shower combinations. There are no TV sets on the property, and telephone service is limited; kids under age 12 are not allowed without the prior approval of the management. The ranch's reputation for offering an excellent outdoor experience, top-drawer meals and service, and high-class accommodations is well deserved.

Stagecoach Inn

209 Madison (at Dunraven), West Yellowstone, MT 59758. ☎ **800 842/2882** or 406/646-7381. 88 rms. TV TEL. $55–$121. AE, DISC, MC, V.

The lobby area is very tastefully done with a Western flair that includes large stuffed animals from the park hanging on the walls. Walls and the ceilings are all wood, and an enormous wooden staircase leads to second-level rooms. Guest accommodations are in well-appointed rooms with modern baths, so this is a comfortable choice for an overnighter. The Coachman restaurant serves three meals of traditional, well-prepared Western fare. The lounge is a popular spot, equipped as it is with a large-screen TV for sporting events, a fireplace that warms the room during winter months, and several video poker gambling games. This is clearly one of the nicer properties in town.

West Yellowstone Conference Hotel Holiday Inn SunSpree Resort

315 Yellowstone Ave., West Yellowstone, MT 59758. ☎ **800/HOLIDAY** or 406/646-7365. 123 rms and suites. A/C TV TEL. $70–$130 double; $90–$200 suite. Special snowmobile/snow coach packages available during winter. AE, DISC, MC, V.

The wordy name of West Yellowstone's newest hotel says it all, and a little bit more. Though their conference facilities are first-rate, those not on business will also be pleased. The extra amenities that warrant the SunSpree name make this a fine resort. Being brand new, the rooms are particularly welcoming, with lush carpeting and polished appointments, as well as coffeemakers, hair dryers, minifridges, microwaves, and sofas. The king spa suites are especially popular with snowmobilers in winter and feature an in-room Jacuzzi. The Oregon Short Line Restaurant is a decent place to sample regional and international cuisine. A heated indoor pool, exercise area, and laundry round out the amenities. All things considered, there is no finer hotel in West Yellowstone.

GARDINER

Absaroka Lodge

U.S. 89 at the Yellowstone River Bridge. ☎ **800/755-7414** or 406/848-7414. 41 rms. A/C TV TEL. $50–$100. AE, MC, V.

The lodge is well situated on a bank overlooking the river canyon only 3 blocks from the village center. Well-appointed rooms have private balconies with views into Yellowstone Park and queen-size beds. As in all the properties in town, the staff will assist in arrangements with outfitters for fly-fishing, rafting, and, in the fall, hunting.

Best Western by Mammoth Hot Springs

U.S. 89, P.O. Box 646, Gardiner, MT 59030. ☎ **800/828-9080** or 406/848-7311. 85 rms. A/C TV TEL. Summer $84–$94 double; winter $47–$57 double. AE, MC, V.

Though half a mile farther south of the center of the town, the Best Western also has nicely furnished rooms with spectacular views, and is adjacent to the Mine, one of the better restaurants. During winter months you can rent cross-country skiing and snowmobile equipment; winter packages are available.

COOKE CITY

If you choose to spend the night in Cooke City, you have several options, although none of them includes modern facilities, gourmet dining, or valet parking. Rooms at each of the properties listed below are clean and comfortable, but that's about all lodgings in Cooke City offer. Expect to pay from $50 to $65 for a room, regardless of the season.

The 32-room **Soda Butte Lodge** on Main Street (☎ **406/838-2251**) is Cooke City's largest, with a restaurant, lounge, and heated pool. The somewhat smaller **Alpine Motel,** also on Main Street (☎ **406/838-2262**), is a bare-bones operation, but it accepts pets. The **High Country Motel,** Main Street (☎ **406/838-2272**), has 15 rooms.

CODY

Buffalo Bill Village Resort: Comfort Inn, Holiday Inn & Buffalo Bill Village

17th and Sheridan Ave., Cody, WY 82414. ☎ **800/527-5544. Comfort Inn:** 75 rms. A/C TV TEL. $50–$130 double. AE, DC, DISC, MC, V; **Holiday Inn:** 190 rms. A/C TV TEL. $50–$130 double. AE, DC, DISC, MC, V;

Buffalo Bill Village: 85 rms. TV TEL. $65–$120 double. AE, DC, DISC, MC, V. Buffalo Bill Village is only open May–Sept.

Blair Hotels of Wyoming operates these three downtown Cody lodgings. Though the term *resort* is hardly appropriate, the central grouping of two chain motels and a set of Western cabins (Buffalo Bill Village) is certainly convenient. The complex houses four restaurants, a swimming pool, and shops at the Ol' West Boardwalk, where you can even book a local rafting trip to complete your Cody experience.

The Irma Hotel

1192 Sheridan Ave. (at 12th St.), Cody, WY 82414. ☎ **307/587-4221.** 40 rms. A/C TV TEL. $35–$85 double. AE, DC, DISC, MC, V.

Named for Buffalo Bill's daughter, The Irma is considered a tourist attraction in its own right because Buffalo Bill himself built it. An imposing brick structure in the heart of town, the Irma is just as popular today as it was at the turn of the century (largely because it's still the first hotel travelers come across after miles of driving). The 15 suites from the original hotel have been refurbished with a mixture of Victorian elegance and Wild West flamboyance not soon forgotten. The floors aren't exactly flat, but they are well carpeted. The rooms are decorated with antiques, the beds with new bed coverings, and baths are modern. The Buffalo Bill suite has two bedrooms, one with twin beds, one with a queen. The Irma Suite, which sits on the corner of the building, has a queen-size bed, writing table, and vanity in the bedroom area, which is enclosed by a sliding door, a small sitting area with TV, telephone, and old-fashioned bathroom with a tub-shower combination. The hotel's large dining room is furnished with old oil paintings, memorabilia from Cody's collection, and taxidermy. Prime rib is the specialty of the house. The large bar area is very popular with both locals and tourists, especially early on summer evenings when a shoot-out takes place on the street outside.

Dining

INSIDE THE PARK

The major hotels in Yellowstone—Mammoth Hot Springs Hotel, Old Faithful Inn, and Lake Yellowstone Hotel—offer excellent meals that are served in comfortable, semiformal environments. Actually, semiformal here means a shirt with a collar; shoes are required, socks aren't. Considering the task that faces an executive chef attempting to produce hundreds of meals a day at these busy resorts, the food is quite appetizing. The alternative is larger crowds, lower prices, and fewer meal selections at the restaurants and cafeterias at Mammoth Hot Springs, Roosevelt Lodge, Canyon Village, Grant Village, and the Lodge at Lake Yellowstone.

The main dining rooms at the major hotels—Old Faithful Inn, Lake Yellowstone Hotel, Mammoth Hot Springs Hotel, Grant Village, and Canyon—have specific hours during which meals are served, and require reservations, which can be made in person, or by phone (☎ **307/344-7901**). The second-tier restaurants and cafeterias at the hotel complexes are less formal, the fare lighter, and the prices lower, so you may have to wait for a table or wait in a cafeteria line for up to 30 minutes.

MAMMOTH HOT SPRINGS

Mammoth Hot Springs Hotel Dining Room

At Mammoth Hot Springs. ☎ **307/344-5314.** Dinner reservations required; not accepted for lunch or breakfast. Breakfast dishes $2–$6; main lunch courses $6–$9; main dinner courses $8–$21. AE, DISC, MC, V. Summer daily 6:30–10am, 11:30am–2pm, and 5:30–10pm. STEAK/SEAFOOD.

The breakfast buffet includes the usual scrambled eggs, French toast, and muffins. Delicious omelettes are served with home fries and toast. The midday meal includes sandwiches: teriyaki chicken breast, grilled vegetarian, and grilled bratwurst. Dinner is standard park fare.

One specialty is shrimp and scallops served over linguine and topped with a curry sauce.

CANYON VILLAGE AREA

Like restaurants in the other park centers, the eating options at Canyon Village consist of three choices: a casual, soda fountain–style restaurant; a fast-food restaurant; and a conventional dining room.

The **Canyon Glacier Pit Snack Bar,** which is operated by Hamilton Stores, is situated in the same building as the convenience store and souvenir shop, so it's possible to buy a souvenir ashtray even while you're eating. Seating is on stools in the fashion of a '50s soda fountain, so you can expect to wait up to 30 minutes for a stool during peak hours. Breakfast consists of egg dishes, lunch is soup and sandwiches, and dinner is traditional Western food. The snack bar is open from 6:30am to 10pm daily from May 18 to September 24.

The **Canyon Lodge Cafeteria** is a fast-food alternative managed by Amfac Parks and Resorts and is located across the parking lot in the Canyon Lodge area. Hours are the same as at the snack bar, and the menu bears some striking similarities, but you may get through the cafeteria line faster than you would get a stool at the soda fountain. The cafeteria is open from June 1 to September 8.

Canyon Lodge Dining Room

In the Canyon Lodge, at Canyon Village. ☎ **307/344-7901.** Reservations required. Breakfast items $2–$6; lunch entrees $5–$7; dinner entrees $12–$17. AE, DISC, MC, V. 6:30–10:30am, 11:30–2pm, and 5:30–10pm. Open June–Sept only. STEAK/SEAFOOD.

Though this is the best restaurant in the Canyon area, the environment doesn't measure up to its counterparts at Yellowstone Lake or Old Faithful, for instance. The Canyon area is populated more by visitors spending longer periods of time at the park than those on whirlwind tours—as well as campers and hikers—so the crowd is less formal and lower-key. Since the same company manages the kitchens of all the major park hotels, you can expect a similar menu and food quality as are offered in the other major centers: steak, chicken, fish, and pasta dishes that are, if not outstanding, not bad.

TOWER-ROOSEVELT AREA

Roosevelt Lodge

Tower-Roosevelt area. No phone. Reservations not accepted. Breakfast items $4–$7; main lunch courses $6–$12; main dinner courses $8–$21. AE, DISC, MC, V. Summer daily 6:30–10am, 11:30am–2:30pm, and 5:30–10pm. STEAK/SEAFOOD/BARBECUE.

Perhaps because of its location, away from the busiest park centers, and the casual attitude of guests who choose to stay in the low-priced cabins in this area, the environment at Roosevelt is more lighthearted than at its counterparts. The menu is similar to that found in the park's other second-tier dining rooms, and prices are identical.

YELLOWSTONE LAKE

At the simple end of the spectrum, a recently opened **deli** in the Lake Yellowstone Hotel serves lighter fare—sandwiches and the like—in an area that is slightly larger than a broom closet from 11am to 9pm. Just down the road the **Hamilton Store** offers three meals in a section of the store that is shared with tourist items; the best bet here is breakfast or a burger. It's open from 7am to 9pm. Inexpensive meals served cafeteria-style are available at the **Yellowstone Lake Lodge and Cabins** from 7am to 8pm.

Lake Yellowstone Hotel

On the north side of the lake. ☎ **307/242-3899.** Dinner reservations required; not accepted for lunch or breakfast. Breakfast items $2–$6; main lunch courses $5–$7; main dinner courses $8–$21. AE, DISC, MC, V. Summer daily 6:30–10am, 11:30am–2:30pm, and 5:30–10pm. PASTA/STEAK/SEAFOOD.

At the Lake Yellowstone Hotel, breakfast is a touch nicer than the breakfast buffet that is standard fare at most Amfac restaurants in the park. While enjoying lake views, complete with sunrise for early risers, you can greet the day with bacon, eggs, and home fries, or a Southwestern pan breakfast seasoned with chiles and salsa. For guests with less hearty appetites, there's a wide selection of fresh fruit, juices, pastries, and cereals. The dinner menu is equally inviting. Appetizers include duck quesadillas and spanikopitas (a tasty Greek pastry stuffed with spinach and cheese). Quality entrees include fettucine with smoked salmon, breast of duck, and, of course, several beef dishes.

GRANT VILLAGE

The casual choice here is the **Lake House,** footsteps away from the Grant Village Restaurant. It specializes in less-expensive fish entrees, including fried clam strips ($7), blackened halibut ($12), burgers, and beer. Meals are served from 5:30 to 9pm. Reservations cannot be made here.

Grant Village Restaurant

At Grant Village. ☎ **307/242-3899.** Dinner reservations required; not accepted for lunch or breakfast. Breakfast items $2–$6; main lunch courses $6–$9; main dinner courses $11–$21. AE, DISC, MC, V. Summer daily 6:30–10am, 11:30am–2:30pm, and 5:30–10pm. STEAK/SEAFOOD.

Breakfast and lunch at the Grant Village Restaurant are much as they are in other park restaurants, though the chef occasionally surprises diners with interesting dishes that stray from the norm. Lunch may include panfried trout covered with toasted pecans and lemon butter, cheese steak, and a ⅓-pound burger. Dinner choices range from honey lemon chicken to swordfish with lemon dill beurre, and blackened prime rib. Quality and ambience here are comparable to that of the better dining rooms at the major park hotels.

OLD FAITHFUL AREA

Choices abound here. The **Snow Lodge** serves three meals, but the lower prices definitely reflect a lower quality and less refined ambience than the Old Faithful Inn. Reservations are not accepted here. The **Old Faithful Lodge** cafeteria serves lunch and dinner in a fast-food environment that fits the mood of a crowd on the move; an ice-cream stand in the lobby is your best choice for dessert. Lines tend to be short, and move quickly in any case.

Old Faithful Inn

Near Old Faithful. ☎ **307/545-4999.** Dinner reservations required. Breakfast items $3–$6; main lunch courses $5–$9; main dinner courses $8–$21. AE, DISC, MC, V. Summer daily 6:30–10am, 11:30am–2:30pm, and 5:30–10pm. STEAK/SEAFOOD.

It's worth coming here for the architecture, if not the food, so I suggest making reservations for at least one meal during your stay, even if only for a buffet breakfast. Meals are reasonably priced, if you include the atmosphere in the bill. The all-you-can-eat breakfast bar is a deal at $7. The lunch menu is about the same as at other places in the park. Dinner choices range from chicken taco salad to the requisite barbecued shrimp served at the other park hotels. On the whole, a worthwhile experience.

NEAR THE PARK

WEST YELLOWSTONE

Bullwinkle's Saloon, Gambling and Eatery

19 Madison. ☎ **406/646-7974.** Lunch entrees $5–$8; dinner entrees $9–$18. MC, V. Summer daily 11am–2am. TRADITIONAL AMERICAN.

Bullwinkle's is the newest restaurant in town and some say the best. Both the lunch and dinner menus are filled with traditional choices: burgers and salads for lunch, chicken, steaks, and ribs at dinner. The atmosphere here is lively and sometimes noisy, since the saloon also features video poker machines. If you're faced with a 20-minute wait—a possibility during peak summer months—you can relax in the bar.

The Canyon Street Grill

22 Canyon Ave. ☎ **406/646-7548.** Most meals $5–$9. No credit cards. Daily 7am–10pm. TRADITIONAL AMERICAN.

One reason to like this delightful, '50s-style spot that serves breakfast, lunch, and dinner is its motto: "We are not a fast food restaurant, we are a cafe reminiscent of a bygone era when the quality of the food meant more than how fast it could be served." They aren't kidding: The food here is hearty and reasonably priced, as in steak, mashed potatoes, and veggies, which go for $8.95.

Eino's Tavern

8955 Gallatin Rd. ☎ **406/646-9344.** Most items $3 and up. No credit cards. Daily noon–8pm. Closed first 2 weeks of Dec. AMERICAN.

You're in for a unique experience at Eino's, where, in winter, locals snowmobile out (there's a trail that follows U.S. 191 from West Yellowstone) just to have the opportunity to pay for grilling their own food. Sound unusual? It's certainly a novel concept, but one that keeps people coming back. If you want to blend in with the locals, go up to the counter and place your order for a steak, teriyaki chicken, hamburger, or hot dog—just don't gasp when you're handed an uncooked piece of meat. Simply drop your drink off at the nearest available table and head for the grill room like you've been there before. Stand around and shoot the breeze with other patrons until your food is exactly the way you like it, and enjoy. Steaks and chicken come with a choice of baked potato or garden salad. Hamburgers come with chips. It's not exactly a fine dining experience, but it's a lot of fun and the views of Hebgen Lake are spectacular.

The Outpost Restaurant

115 Yellowstone Ave., in the Montana Outpost Mall. ☎ **406/646-7303.** Lunch entrees $5–$8. AE, MC, V. Daily 7am–10pm. AMERICAN.

This end-of-the-hallway eatery is difficult to find—it's in the center of the mall—but it's definitely worth the trouble. The menu is more varied than elsewhere in town, the place has more atmosphere than the typical tourist spot, and there's an excellent salad bar.

GARDINER

Bear Country Restaurant

232 Park St. ☎ **406/848-7188.** Breakfast $2–$5; lunch $5–$8; dinner $9–$12. DISC, MC, V. 7am–2pm and 4:30–8pm. TRADITIONAL AMERICAN.

There's nothing fancy about this family oriented restaurant; it's an old-fashioned place the chains are attempting to duplicate, usually unsuccessfully. The owners have been serving standard fare here, across from the park entrance, for some time, and don't have any plans to change the menu or the way they serve traditional American fare.

Montana Blues Chuckwagon Dinner Theater

Yellowstone Village Motel, U.S. 89. ☎ **800/424-445.** Reservations required. Fixed price $14.50 adults, $6.50 children. AE, DISC, MC, V. Nightly 6:30pm. Closed Mon. AMERICAN.

Montana Blues offers an Old West experience by combining a chuck-wagon dinner—meat, potatoes, and salads—with a vocal group consisting of a father and his three sons, who specialize in harmonic renditions of Western favorites. You can expect a combination of average food coupled with down-home entertainment.

The Yellowstone Mine

In the Best Western by Mammoth Hot Springs, U.S. 89. ☎ **406/848-7336.** Reservations not accepted. Breakfast items $4–$6; main dinner courses $10–$20. AE, DISC, MC, V. Daily 6–11am and 5–9pm. AMERICAN.

The old-time mining atmosphere may not spark your appetite, but the meals come in healthy portions, and the prices are, like the hotel's, reasonable. Steaks and seafood are the restaurant's specialty. There's also a lounge and casino known as the Rusty Rail. Inside you'll find live poker, machine poker, keno—whatever you need for a fix before you head into gambling-free Wyoming.

CODY

La Comida

1385 Sheridan Ave. ☎ **307/587-9556.** Main courses $5–$11. AE, DISC, MC, V. Daily 11am–10pm. MEXICAN.

The Mexican fare is not to be confused with the beef-and-cheese combos found in the fast-food chains. A favorite entree is *pechuga* over rice (tasty bites of chicken breast baked in cream with green chiles and Swiss cheese) and a spinach-filled enchilada baked with blue corn tortillas. Though the atmosphere here is supercasual, and meals are served on a deck overlooking the town's main drag, the final product reflects the serious approach to good preparation taken by a veteran chef.

Maxwell's Restaurant

937 Sheridan Ave. ☎ **307/527-7749.** Daily 7am–9pm. AE, DISC, MC, V. Lunch dishes $7–$10; dinner entrees $8.75–$16.50. ECLECTIC AMERICAN.

Maxwell's specialties are vegetarian salads and sandwiches: Philly steak, veggie, mesquite chicken. Dinner runs the gamut from pasta to chicken, seafood, pork, and beef. The wine list includes labels from California, Washington, Italy, and Australia. Clearly a family-oriented operation, seating is in upholstered booths and at highly varnished wooden tables. Adjacent to the restaurant is **Maxwell's Bakery and Coffee,** a morning spot for fresh pastries, bagels, muffins, cinnamon rolls, and the like. The baker is a master whose specialty is Hungarian sourdough.

Silver Dollar Bar & Grill

1313 Sheridan Ave. ☎ **307/587-3554.** Most items $4–$6. No credit cards. Mon–Sat 11am–9pm. BURGERS.

If you're looking for locals, the Silver Dollar is where you'll find them. Located on Cody's main street, the restaurant makes its home in what was once the town's first post office. Though their claim to world-famous burgers may be stretching the truth a bit, the food is hearty, and the occasional live entertainment makes for a fun night of music and dancing. Expect a mixed crowd at this Cody standard; the Silver Dollar has been around since 1960.

Stefan's Restaurant

1307 Sheridan Ave. ☎ **307/587-8511.** Lunch dishes $5–$7; main dinner courses $11–$20. AE, DISC, MC, V. Mon–Sat 11am–10pm, Sun 10am–2pm. ECLECTIC AMERICAN.

Stefan's has quickly joined the handful of restaurants that occupy the town's culinary center stage. The southwestern interior decor gives off intimations of enchiladas and tamales, but the favorite entree among locals is filet mignon stuffed with mushrooms, dried tomatoes, and Gorgonzola cheese. Other dishes include fresh seafood, meat loaf, and house pasta. A "little bites" menu offer's children's meals for $3.

Picnic & Camping Supplies

Pick up your food and camping supplies at the ubiquitous Hamilton stores, located in all the park villages.

38

YOSEMITE NATIONAL PARK

by Stacey Wells

YOSEMITE'S SKY-SCRAPING GEOLOGIC FORMATIONS, LUSH MEADOWS, swollen rivers, and spectacular waterfalls make it a tourist destination for travelers from around the world. It's home to three of the world's 10 tallest waterfalls and the largest single piece of exposed granite anywhere, not to mention one of the world's largest trees and the most recognized rock formation.

The greatest thing about all this is you don't have to be a mountaineer to enjoy this beauty. Yosemite's most popular attractions are accessible to everyone, whether they want to hike around or just stand and stare. No matter where you go, you'll see a view worth remembering. In the span of a mile here, you can behold the quiet beauty of a forest, walk into a pristine meadow, observe a sunset from a towering granite cliff, hike a half-mile-high waterfall, enjoy a moonlit night as bright as day, climb a rock, and eat a gourmet meal before falling asleep, be it under the stars or in a luxurious bed in a four-star hotel.

Yosemite Valley, where 95% of tourists head, is just a small sliver of the park, but it holds the bulk of the region's jaw-dropping features. An estimated 4.1 million people visit here each year. This is the place of record-setting statistics: the highest waterfall in North America and three of the tallest in the world (Upper Yosemite, Sentinel, and Ribbon falls); the biggest and tallest piece of exposed granite (El Capitan); and stands of the Giant Sequoia.

In spite of its beauty, recent years have brought a disquieting sense of foreboding to this wilderness haven. One trip during peak season and you'll understand why. Traffic backs up for miles, trees and branches along the Merced River become clotheslines, and candy wrappers, cigarette butts, and discarded soft drinks litter the valley. Songbirds can barely be heard over the din of voices yelling and hooting. At times like these, New York's Central Park offers more respite. Preserving the wild beauty of the park despite the hordes of visitors is the biggest challenge facing Yosemite today. Big changes are expected in the next 5 years as the Park Service grapples with the best way to permit access without causing more irreparable damage to this natural wonderland.

Visitors should also know that Yosemite is still living with the aftereffects of the devastating floods of January 1997. What began as a torrential downpour during one of the park's swankier events turned into one of the worst winter storms on record. When the rain stopped several days later, Yosemite

Valley was Yosemite lake. Swollen streams and creeks swept tons of debris—trees, rocks, brush—into the valley, clogging the Merced River. Campgrounds were submerged, employees' quarters flooded, and much of Yosemite Lodge was under 2 feet of water. Despite frantic attempts at sandbagging, hundreds of people were forced onto higher ground—the top floor of buildings—and everyone was stuck. The water was so high and ferocious that it washed out roads and stranded about 2,000 people in the valley, including the several hundred on hand to celebrate New Year's Eve. So much was damaged that the valley closed for almost 3 months, and even after it was reopened, travel was restricted on the park's all-weather highway.

Even now, a year later, much remains lost. While park workers managed to clean most of the fallen trees, boulders, and rocks out of the heavily populated parts of the valley by mid-1997, some backcountry trail bridges remain unrepaired, half of the campsites in the valley are gone. The folks who live here now do so with a measure of understanding: They're living at the mercy of Mother Nature.

Avoiding the Crowds. In Yosemite, we recommend avoiding holiday weekends in spring and summer if possible—during the busiest times, the park has often had to turn people away due to overcrowding. Until a more elaborate system is in place to reduce the traffic in Yosemite Valley, the park will continue to institute a policy of closing entrances when a certain number of vehicles have been admitted and, in their estimation, a maximum density of visitors has been reached. The campgrounds are usually full from June through August, and expect some crowds in late spring and early fall as well. Winter is a great time to visit Yosemite—not only is the park virtually empty, but there are a number of activities from skiing at Badger Pass to sledding, ice-skating, and snowshoeing. Keep in mind, however, that the high country along Calif. 120 and Tioga Pass Road is inaccessible to vehicles from mid-fall to early June, depending on snow levels.

Just the Facts

GETTING THERE & GATEWAYS

Yosemite is a 3½-hour drive from San Francisco and a 6-hour drive from Los Angeles. Many roads lead to Yosemite's four entrances. From the west, the **Big Oak Flat Entrance** is 88 miles from Manteca via Calif. 120, and passes through the towns of Groveland, Buck Meadows, and Big Oak Flat. **Arch Rock Entrance** is 75 miles northeast of Merced via Calif. 140, which passes through Mariposa and El Portal. The **South Entrance** from Wawona is 64 miles north of Fresno and passes through Oakhurst, Bass Lake, and Fish Camp. From the east, the **Tioga Pass Entrance** is the only option. It is 10 miles west of Lee Vining via Calif. 120.

The Nearest Airports. Fresno Air Terminal is the nearest major airport, located 90 miles from the South Entrance at Wawona (☎ **209/498-4095**). It is served by **American Airlines, American Eagle, Delta, Sky West, United Airlines, United Express, US Airways** and **Wings West.** It has direct connections with airports in San Francisco and Los Angeles.

Merced Airport, in the city of Merced, is 73 miles southwest of the Arch Rock Entrance. It is served by United Express (☎ **800/241-6522**).

Mariposa Airport (☎ **209/966-2143**), in Mariposa, has a tiny airstrip with space for 50 private planes.

Renting a Car. Most of the major car-rental companies can be found in Fresno: **Avis, Budget, Dollar, Hertz, National, Sears,** and **Standard.**

The toll-free numbers for these airlines and car rental agencies are in the appendix.

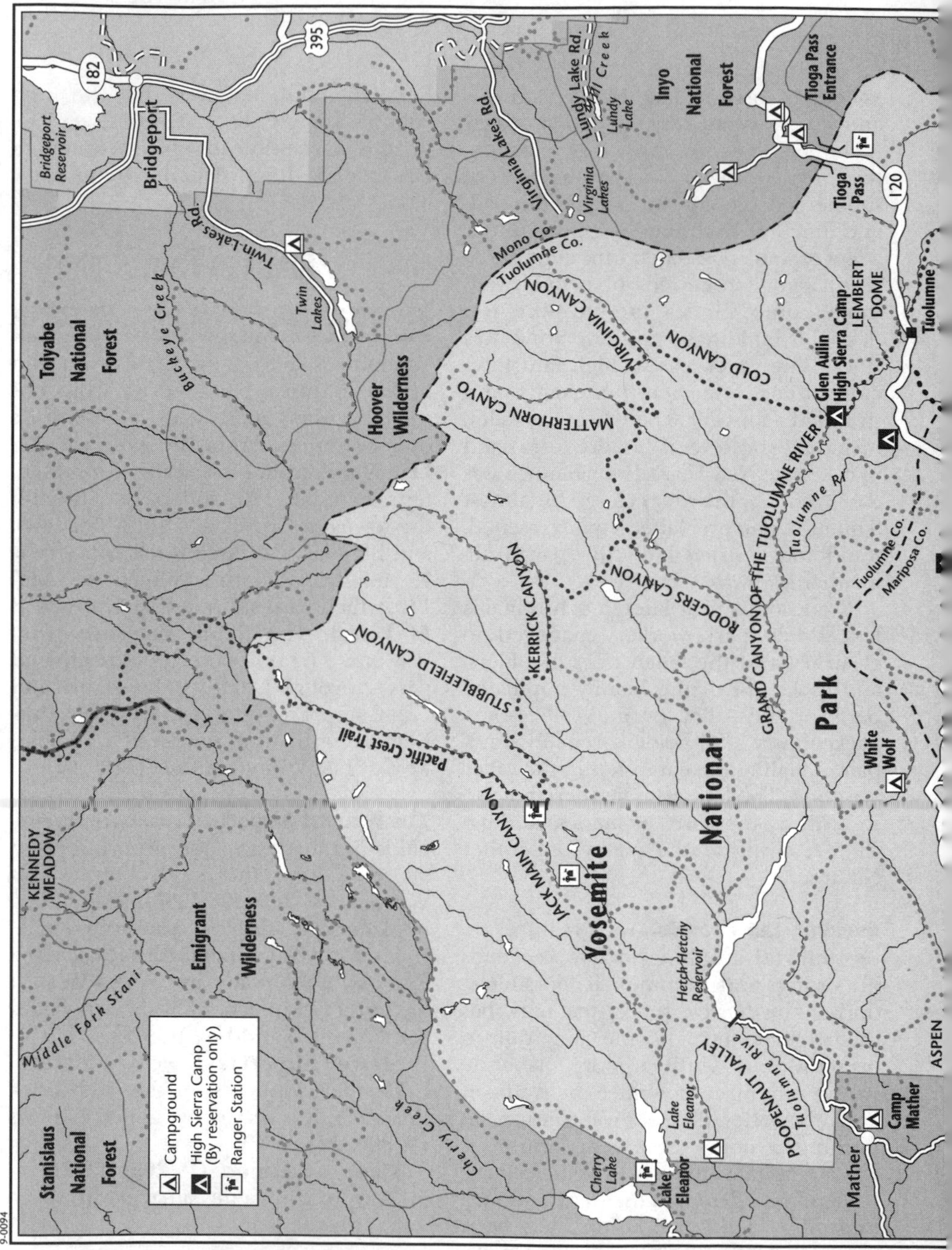

GETTING INFORMATION BEFORE YOUR TRIP

If you're planning a visit to Yosemite National Park, you can get general information on accommodations, weather, and permits from their Touch-Tone phone menu at ☎ **209/372-0200** or on-line at **www.nps.gov/yose/**. A live operator is available weekdays from 8am to 4:30pm at ☎ **900/454-YOSE.** The hearing impaired can obtain information by calling ☎ **209/372-4726.**

Campground reservations can be made by calling **Biospherics, Inc.** at ☎ **800/436-PARK** (7275).

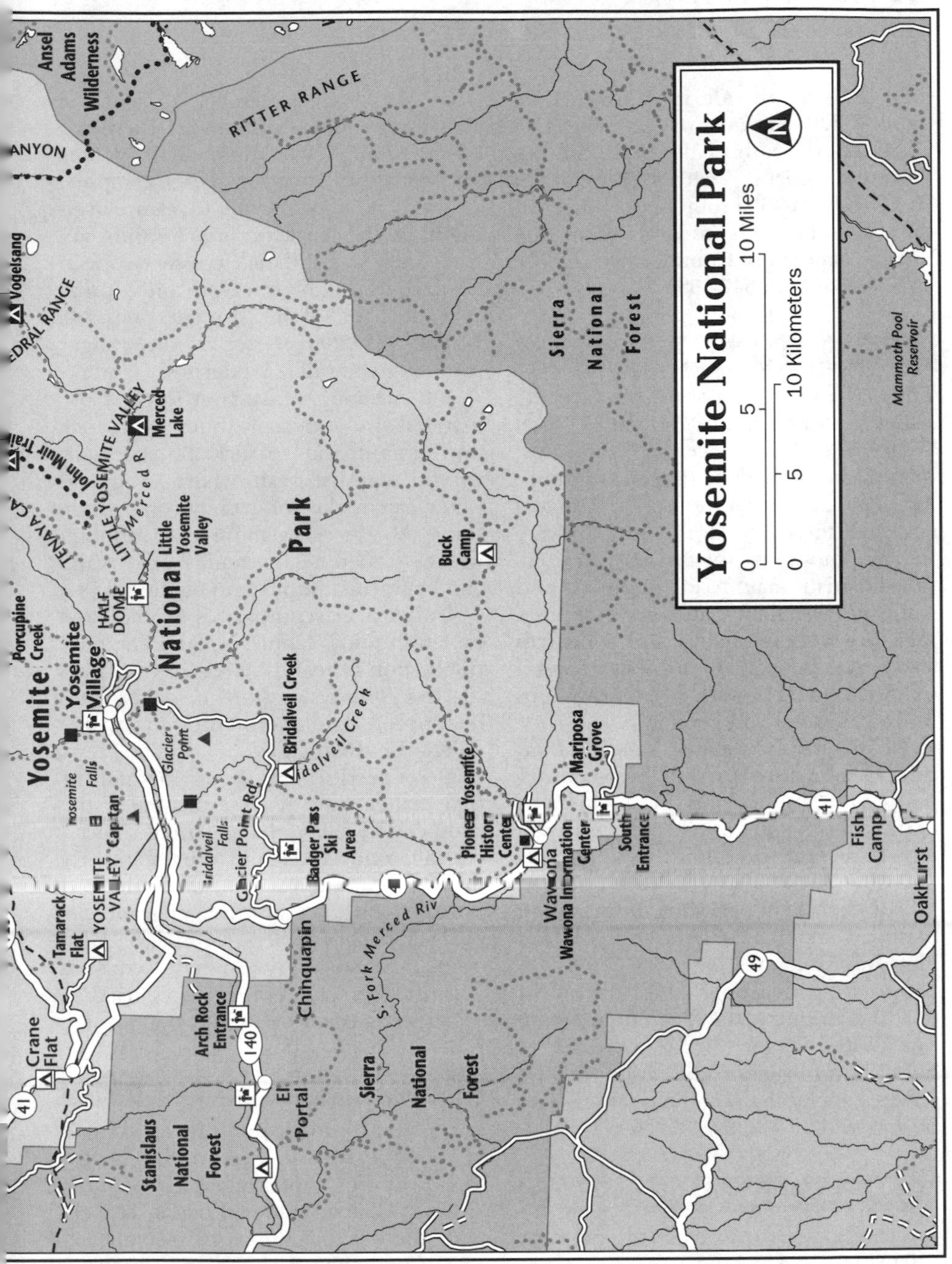

Another great resource is **YATI,** or the Yosemite Area Travelers Information, ☎ **209/723-3153** or **www.yosemite.com**. Also, the **Yosemite Association** is a nonprofit organization that publishes books and interpretive information for visitors ☎ **209/379-2646** or online at **www. yosemite.org**.

Information on lodging and activities outside the park is available from visitor centers and chambers of commerce in surrounding cities. If you're coming from the west on Calif. 120, call the **Tuolumne County Visitor Center** at ☎ **800/446-1333** or the **Chinese Camp Visitor Center** at ☎ **800/446-1333.** On

Calif. 140, call the **Mariposa Town Center** at ☎ **800/208-2434** or 209/966-2456. On Calif. 41 south of the park, call the **Yosemite Sierra Visitors Bureau** at ☎ **209/683-4636.** From Lee Vining on the park's eastern boundary, call the **Lee Vining Chamber of Commerce** at ☎ **760/647-6629** or 760/647-6595.

VISITOR CENTERS

The best and biggest visitor center is the **Valley Visitor Center** in Yosemite Village, ☎ **209/372-0299.** The center offers information on tours, daily ranger programs, lodging, and restaurants. The rangers who staff the center are helpful, insightful, and knowledgeable. Inside, information boards update road conditions and campsite availability, and serve as message boards. Maps, books, and videos can also be purchased. There are also several exhibits on the park's environment, wildlife, history, and geology.

Nearby is the **Yosemite Valley Wilderness Center,** a room with high-country maps and information on equipment and trails. A ranger at the desk can answer all your questions, issue permits and offer advice about the high country.

Elsewhere, the **Wawona Information Station** (☎ **209/375-9501**) and **Big Oak Flat Information Center** (☎ **209/379-1899**) give general park information. In the high country, the **Tuolumne Meadows Visitor Center** (☎ **209/372-0263**) is helpful. Information on visitor-related services, including accommodations, can be accessed at ☎ **209/372-1000.**

ENTRANCE & CAMPING FEES

It costs $20 per car to enter the valley, or $10 per person if arriving on bicycle, motorcycle, or on foot. Camping in a Yosemite campgrounds costs $3 to $15 a night.

SPECIAL REGULATIONS & WARNINGS

In Yosemite National Park, there is a 7-day **camping limit** in the valley and in Wawona and a 14-day limit elsewhere, from May 1 to September 15. For the remaining months of the year, there is a 30-day limit. A maximum of six people and two vehicles may stay at each campsite.

You'll need a permit to **camp overnight** in the backcountry. Permits are free, but it's a good idea to reserve one in advance during high season, and for that there's a fee of $3. To get one, call ☎ **209/372-0200** or stop by any ranger station or the valley Wilderness Center.

When **hiking,** make your safety a priority. Trails, especially ones over rock and granite, can be slick. Be especially careful on Mist Trail, where wind and water can make for treacherous conditions. Always carry more than enough water—sometimes 1- and 2-mile walks can easily turn into 5- and 6-mile hikes.

Under no circumstances should food be left in tents, cabins, or cars. The **bear** population is healthy and, in some cases, fearless. There are storage lockers and bear-proof containers throughout the park—use them.

Never feed a bear, or any animal for that matter. Sure it's a thrill, but if the prospect of being bitten by a squirrel doesn't send shivers up your spine, try this: When animals become dependent on human food, they quit foraging and begin harassing travelers for meals. Most often, this results in the animal's demise as park rangers take a dim view of troublesome pests, which are quickly put down.

SEASONS & CLIMATE

For general information on the climate of Yosemite, see the "Seasons & Climate" section of the chapter on nearby Sequoia & Kings Canyon national parks. The climate there is very similar to Yosemite's.

The high country in Yosemite receives up to 20 feet of snow, and visitors who plan a winter trip should be well-experienced in winter travel.

SEASONAL EVENTS

January to February: Chefs' Holidays. Yosemite hosts nationally renowned chefs, who share their secrets with participants. Each session concludes with a banquet in The Ahwahnee Dining Room. Cost is $75 per person, including gratuity but excluding alcohol. Two-, three- and five-day packages that include overnight accommodations at The Ahwahnee and admission to two banquets are available for $580 to $1,200 plus tax, based on double occupancy.

November to December: Vintners' Holiday. California's finest winemakers hold tastings in The Ahwahnee Great Lounge. Each session concludes with a Vintners' Banquet. The four-course gala event held in The Ahwahnee Dining Room pairs four wines with a specially selected food. Cost is $80 per person, including gratuities and wine.

December 22, 24 & 25: The Bracebridge Dinner. This event transports diners to 17th-century England. Servers wear costumes and the dining room is filled with music and song course upon course of delectable dishes. This popular dinner requires reservations, which are secured by lottery. Applications are available December 1 to January 15 and are due February 15 for the following year. Cost is $200 per person.

December 31: New Year's Eve Dinner. On New Year's Eve, the tenor for the night is set by a swing band and dinner dance. The same reservations system applies here as with the Bracebridge Dinner. The cost is also $200.

Seeing the Highlights in a Day

If you're like most visitors to Yosemite, you'll stick to the valley and not stay long. It's ironic, considering the immensity and grandeur of the property, but if you have limited time, don't despair—there's a lot to see and do. The following are some attractions that will give you the most Yosemite flavor in just a little time.

Most importantly, learn two very important words: ***shuttle bus.*** Dump your car and pick up a bus schedule; it will quickly become your friend. *Note:* If you don't plan to stay overnight, use the Curry Village day-use parking lot to catch the shuttle. The bus is free, easy and operates year-round, with fewer stops in winter. For that reason, we've included shuttle bus stop numbers wherever possible throughout the valley sections in this book. Bus stops are well marked and within easy walking distance from all parking lots.

The **Valley Visitor Center** (shuttle bus stop nos. 6 and 9) is your logical starting point. Here, you'll see and hear an orientation on how the valley was created, learn about Yosemite's unique granite landscaping, and gain an appreciation and understanding of the park. More importantly, you can see what there is to see and orient yourself.

If you're not apt to take off on your own, one of the best ideas to spend your time wisely is taking one of the **guided tours** (see "Organized Tours & Ranger Programs," below). But if group activities aren't really your bag, try the following sites on your own.

The base of **Lower Yosemite Fall** (shuttle bus stop no. 7) is an easy walk from the parking lot across from Yosemite Lodge. From here, you will be able to see a portion of the magnificent water show. During peak runoff, it's not uncommon to get wet as the force of the fall sends spray in every direction. In winter, a huge snow cone caused by freezing water rises to heights of up to 300 feet at the base of this fall.

Happy Isles (shuttle bus stop no. 16) is another major attraction. Located at the convergence of several inlets, it's the site of the valley's new nature center. This is also the trailhead for Vernal and Nevada falls, two picturesque staircase waterfalls that can be reached on foot.

Next, we recommend a visit to **Mirror Lake** (shuttle bus stop no. 17), a small lake named for the near-perfect way it reflects the surrounding scenery. It's slowly filling up with silt and is less dramatic and mirrorlike than it used to be, but its shore still offers a beautiful view of Half Dome. This short stroll is well marked.

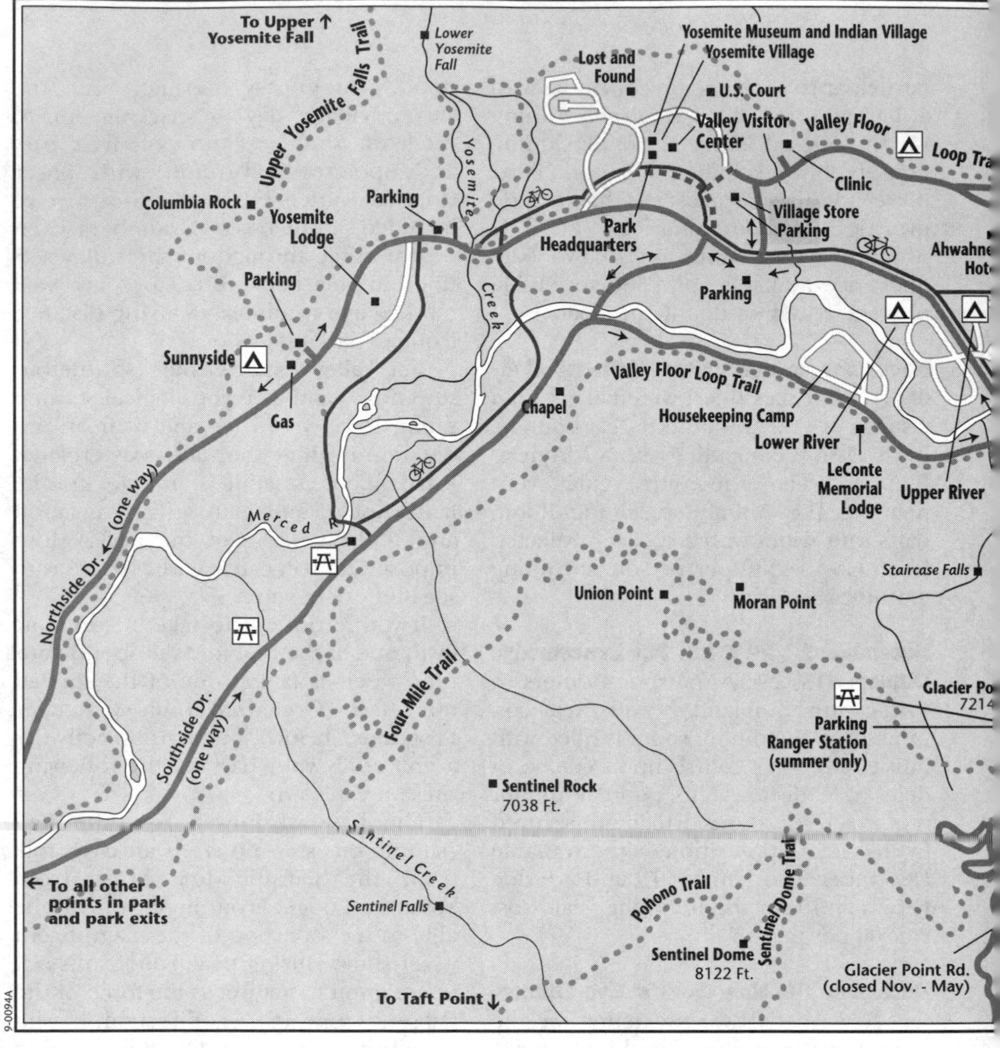

From there, if you have more time, there's a variety of hikes and activities at your disposal. Make the most of your time, and choose from our recommendations.

If You Have More Time

It's relatively easy to find your way around Yosemite. All road signs are clear and visible. Although at first Yosemite Valley may appear a confusing series of roadways, you'll soon realize that everything leads to a one-way road that hugs the valley's perimeter. To get from one side to the other, you can either drive the entire loop or travel one of the few bridges over the Merced River. It is, however, easy to find yourself heading in the wrong direction on the one-way road, so be alert whenever you merge and just follow the signs.

In addition to the year-round shuttle bus in Yosemite Valley, Wawona and Tuolumne Meadows offer a similar service during summer months only. Driving in any of these places during peak season—or even off-season in the valley—is a surefire way to ensure that you'll miss important sights, get stuck in traffic, and hate your vacation. Summer months are particularly bad and you'd have to be nuts to want to try and navigate around all the crazy tourists (of

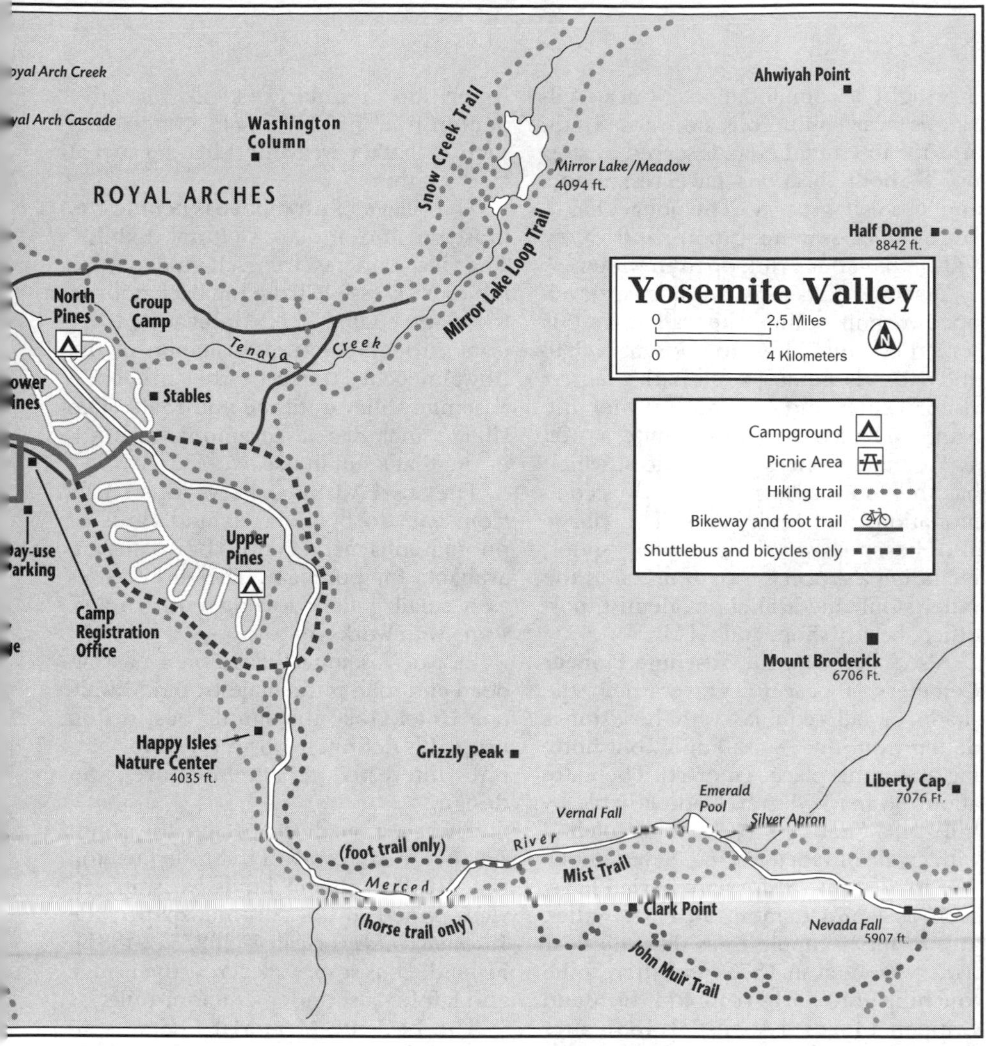

course not you), cyclists, and other road warriors, so be bright and park the car whenever possible.

A second benefit to parking is that almost as soon as you're out of eyesight of your vehicle, you have ceased to become a typical Yosemite tourist. Most park visitors never get very far from their car.

YOSEMITE VALLEY

Face it, most people come to Yosemite to see this giant study in shadow and light. In spring, after winter snow begins melting in the high country, waterfalls encircle Yosemite Valley, shimmering like a diamond necklace. Careful observers can watch rock climbers inch up the massive granite face of El Capitan or Half Dome. There are wide, beautiful meadows, towering trees, and the ever present sound of rushing water in the background. The great irony is that the original park boundaries, established in 1890, excluded the valley.

Yosemite Valley consists of three developed areas. All the hotels, restaurants, and shops can be found in **Yosemite Village, Yosemite Lodge,** and **Curry Village,** and all campgrounds are within walking distance of these places. Curry Village (also called Camp Curry) and Yosemite Lodge offer the bulk of the park's overnight accommodations. Curry Village is near shuttle bus stop nos. 1, 13, and 14. Yosemite Lodge is served by stop no. 8. Both locations have restaurants and a small grocery. The lodge has a large public swimming pool, and Curry Village has an ice rink open in winter.

Yosemite Village is the largest developed region within the valley, and is served by shuttle bus stop nos. 3, 5, 6, 9, and 10. It is home to the park's largest visitor center and headquarters for the National Park Service in Yosemite, as well as Yosemite Concession Services, which has the contract to run all park accommodations and restaurants. The village also has a host of stores and shops, including a grocery, restaurants, and the valley's only medical clinic, dentist, post office, beauty shop, and ATM.

Also, check out the **Yosemite Pioneer Cemetery,** a peaceful graveyard in the shade of tall sequoias with headstones dating from the 1800s. Funny, but nothing about this place is morbid. There are about 36 marked graves, identifiable by horizontal slabs of rock, some etched with crude or faded writing. Several notables in Yosemite history are buried here, such as James Lamon, an early settler, known for his apple trees that still bear fruit, who died in 1875. And there's the touching grave of 14-year-old Effie Maud Crippen, who died August 31, 1881, after "she faltered by the wayside and the angels took her home."

Next door, you'll find the **Yosemite Museum and Indian Cultural Exhibit.** Both are free and provide a historic picture of the park, before and after it was settled and secured as a national treasure. The museum entrance is marked by a crowd-pleaser, the cross-section of a **1,000-year-old sequoia** with memorable dates identified on the tree's rings. Highlights include the signing of the Magna Carta in 1215, the landing of Columbus in the New World, and the Civil War. The ring was cut in 1919 from a tree that fell in the Mariposa Grove south of the valley in Wawona. The **Indian Cultural Exhibit** strives to explain the life of Native Americans who once lived here, and Native Americans regularly speak or give demonstrations in long-forgotten arts such as basket weaving. Kids get a real kick out this.

The village of **Ahwahnee** is behind the museum and Indian Cultural Exhibit. The village offers a free, self-guided walking tour accessible from the back door of the visitor center. This exhibit accepts visitors through the transformation of the Ahwahneeche, the tribe that inhabited Yosemite Valley until the mid-1850s. The village includes a ceremonial roundhouse that's still in use.

The **Ansel Adams Gallery** is open daily from 9am to 6pm. Prints and cards of photographs made famous by Adams are available for purchase. The shop serves as a small gallery for current artisans, some with works for sale.

East of Yosemite Village on a narrow, dead-end road is the majestic old **Ahwahnee Hotel.** Take the shuttle bus to stop no. 4. It's definitely worth a visit for anyone interested in architecture and design.

There's a small **chapel** on the south side of the Merced River, shuttle bus stop no. 11. The chapel holds worship services posted in the park newspaper, the ***Yosemite Guide*** (or call ☎ **209/372-4831**). From the bus stop, walk across the bridge and left for just under a quarter mile.

The **LeConte Memorial Lodge** is an educational center and library at shuttle bus stop no. 12. Built in 1903 in honor of a University of California geologist named Joseph LeConte, the Tudor-style granite building provide talks free of charge. They are listed in the *Yosemite Guide.*

One of the park's highlights is **The Mist Trail** to Vernal Fall. The trail itself can be slick and treacherous, but it is a pretty walk up 500 steps to the top of the waterfall. Miniature rainbows dot the trail as mist from the waterfall splashes below and ricochets back onto the trail. This walk is frequently closed in winter due to snow.

At the valley's far east end beyond Curry Village is the **Happy Isles Nature Center,** shuttle bus stop no. 16. The center is closed in the winter. Summer hours are 9am to 5pm daily, with spring and fall hours as posted. This new structure was built after a deadly rock slide damaged the previous quarters. A huge slab of granite high up on a wall behind the building crashed to earth in late 1996 with such force that it created a 120 m.p.h. gust of wind that flattened about 500 trees. While some of the trees are gone, the remnants of the rock slide remain. Happy Isles is named for three nearby inlets labeled by Yosemite's guardian in 1880. It serves as the trailhead for some great hikes (see "Day Hikes," below). The nature center offers exhibits and books on the various animal and plant life found in Yosemite. There are exhibits on park animals, a night display, and more. It's a super place for children to explore, and we know a couple of 30-something kids who had a great time here too. This is also the location of the park's Junior and Senior Ranger programs.

NORTH OF THE VALLEY

Hetch Hetchy and Tuolumne Meadows are remarkably different regions on opposite sides of the park. **Hetch Hetchy** is on the park's western border and can be reached by taking the turnoff just outside the park's Big Oak Flat Entrance. **Tuolumne Meadows** is on the park's eastern border, just inside Tioga Pass. Both places are inaccessible by motor vehicle in the winter. In summer, Hetch Hetchy gets hot and Tuolumne Meadows gets crowded.

Hetch Hetchy is home to the park's reviled **reservoir,** one fought for years by the famed conservationist John Muir. In the end, Muir lost and the dam was built ensuring water for the city of San Francisco. Many believe the loss exhausted Muir and hastened his death in 1914, a year after a bill was signed to fund the dam project. Construction began in 1919.

South of Hetch Hetchy, inside the park, are two large stands of **Giant Sequoias.** The Merced and Tuolumne groves offer a quiet alternative to the Mariposa Grove of Big Trees in Wawona. The two groves are accessible only on foot. The **Merced Grove** is a 4-mile round-trip walk that begins on Calif. 120 about 4.5 miles beyond the Big Oak Flat Entrance. While the trees don't mirror the majesty of the Mariposa Grove, the solitude here makes this a real treat for hikers. The **Tuolumne Grove** of about 25 trees can be reached by a 1-mile hike (2 hours round-trip) on a trail located near Crane Flat.

About 1½ hours east along Calif. 120 is Yosemite's **high country.** This primitive region is low on amenities, which makes it a frequent haunt of those who enjoy roughing it—but even cushy-soft couch potatoes can enjoy the beauty up here. Glistening granite domes tower above lush green meadows, cut by silver swaths of streams and lakes. Many of Yosemite's longer hikes begin or pass through here. There are some worthwhile sights for anyone willing to venture away from the valley masses.

A drive toward the high country on Calif. 120, also known as Tioga Road and Tioga Pass Road, offers other breathtaking views of granite landscaping. There are nearby picnic spots at the picturesque Tenaya Lake.

Olmsted Point, located midway between White Wolf and Tuolumne Meadows, offers one of the most spectacular vistas anywhere in the park. Here you can see the enormous walls of the Tenaya Canyon and an endless view all the way to Yosemite Valley. In the distance are Cloud's Rest and the rear of Half Dome. To the east Tenaya Lake glistens like a sapphire. One of the park's larger lakes, Tenaya is easily accessible, but the water is freezing.

About 8 miles east of Tenaya Lake is **Tuolumne Meadows,** a huge high-country flat surrounded by domes and steep granite mountains that themselves offer exhilarating climbs. The meadow is a beautiful place to hike and fish, or just stand and gape. To the north of the meadow is Lembert Dome, at about 2 o'clock, and then working clockwise,

Johnson Peak at 7 o'clock, Unicorn Peak and Fairview Dome at 10 o'clock, and Pothole Dome. Up the road is the central region of **Tuolumne,** a crowded conglomerate of buildings that include a visitor center, campground, canvas tent cabins, and grocery. The real draw here is the scenery and lack of valley crowds. But in July and August, the small confines make it just as intolerable. Continue east to reach Tioga Lake and Tioga Pass.

SOUTH OF THE VALLEY

This region, which includes Wawona and the Mariposa Grove of Big Trees, is densely forested. There are a handful of granite rock formations, but nothing like those found elsewhere. En route to Wawona from Yosemite Valley on Calif. 41, you'll come across several wonderful views of the valley. **Tunnel View,** a turnout just before passing through a long tunnel en route to Wawona, provides one of the park's most recognizable vistas—it was memorialized on film by photographer Ansel Adams. To the right is Bridalveil Fall, opposite El Capitan. Yosemite Falls and Half Dome lie straight ahead.

Between Yosemite Valley and Wawona is Glacier Point Road, the thoroughfare to the spectacular **Glacier Point.** From the parking area 16 miles down the road, it's a short hike to an amazing overlook that provides a view of the glacier-carved granite rock formations all along the valley and beyond. From here, you are eye-level with Half Dome, which looks close enough to reach out and touch. Far below, Yosemite Valley resembles a green-carpeted ant farm. There are also some pretty sights of more obscure waterfalls not visible from the valley floor. Glacier Point also has a geology hut and a new lodge for wintertime cross-country skiers that doubles the rest of the year as a snack shack. To reach Glacier Point, take one of the buses (check at tour desks for information) or drive south of the valley on Calif. 41 to the turnoff for Glacier Point Road (closed in winter). Follow the winding road to the parking lot and walk a few hundred yards to the lookout. This is an excellent spot for pictures.

Continue south on Calif. 41 to reach **Wawona,** a small town 30 miles from the valley that runs deep with history. It was settled in 1856 by homesteader Galen Clark, who built a rustic way station for travelers en route from Mariposa to Yosemite. The property's next owners, the Washburn brothers, built much of what is today the Wawona Hotel, including the large, white building to the right of the main hotel, which was constructed in 1876. The two-story hotel annex went up 3 years later. When Congress established Yosemite National Park in 1890 and charged the U.S. Army with managing it, Wawona was chosen as the army's headquarters. Every summer, soldiers would camp in what today is the Wawona Campground.

As Yosemite grew in popularity, so did the **Wawona Hotel** and the town itself. When the Wawona Hotel was added to the park in 1932, Section 35 (the number assigned to the plot in its legal description) was allowed to remain in private ownership. It remains so today, just east of the hotel off of Calif. 41. Unless you're hiking or staying here in a private home or cabin, there is no real reason to venture along the narrow road that leads to the town. In fact, the number and collection of buildings can be depressing.

The public Wawona is much more enjoyable. The **Mariposa Grove** is a stand of Giant Sequoias, some of which have been around for 3,000 years. They stretch almost 300 feet tall, are 50 feet in circumference and weigh an average of 2 million pounds. The 500 trees here are divided into the Upper Grove and Lower Grove. The easiest way to see the trees is on an open-air tram that runs during summer. The cost is $8 for adults, $7.25 for seniors, $4 for children. Kids under age 4 are free. A family pass costs $24 and admits 2 adults and all the kids in the crew age 4 to 15. Trams leave every 20 minutes. The trip is narrated by a ranger and lasts about an hour. It makes regular stops at the Grizzly Giant, Wawona Tunnel Tree, and Mariposa Grove Museum. It's worth hopping out and walking around as often as possible. Just take the next tram back. All of this is also accessible on foot. It's an uphill walk to the groves, 2.5 miles each way.

The **Grizzly Giant** is the largest tree in the grove. At "just" 200 feet it is shorter than some of its neighbors, but its trunk measures more than 30 feet in diameter at the base. A huge limb halfway up measures 6 feet in diameter and is bigger than many of the "young" trees in the grove. Some say that limb is larger than any tree east of the Mississippi.

The **Wawona Tunnel Tree** had a tunnel 10 feet high and 26 feet long cut through it in 1881. Thousands of visitors were photographed driving through the tree before it toppled in the winter of 1968–69—its death was caused by heavy snowfall. (The tree had been weakened by the tunnel and its shallow root system.) No one saw the tree fall. Another tunnel tree, the California Tree, cut in 1895, still stands near the Grizzly Giant.

The **Mariposa Grove Museum** was the first building built by Galen Clark. It was last refurbished in 1981. During the summer, it displays exhibits and sells books and educational material.

Near the Wawona Hotel are the **Thomas Hill Studio** and **Pioneer Yosemite History Center.** The studio, which keeps sporadic hours that are impossible to pin down but are frequently listed in the park newspaper, the *Yosemite Guide,* is the former work space of noted 19th-century painter Thomas Hill. Hill painted a number of award-winning landscapes, including some recognizable ones of Yosemite.

The Pioneer Center offers a self-guided walking tour of cabins and buildings moved to this site in 1961 from various locations in the park. Each represents a different time in Yosemite's short history. During the summer, the National Park Service interpreters dress in period clothing and act out characters from the park's past. To reach the Pioneer Center, walk across the covered bridge. An entertaining, 10-minute stagecoach ride is offered from here for a small fee.

Organized Tours & Ranger Programs

If you're staying in the valley, the Park Service and Yosemite Concession Services present nearly a dozen **evening programs** that explore all aspects of the park's history and culture. In past summers, programs have included a discussion on early expeditions to Yosemite, the park's flora and fauna, and legends of Native Americans who once lived here. Other programs have focused on the courageous ascent of paraplegic Mark Wellman up El Capitan, and the global ecology and major threats to Yosemite's environment.

Inquire about current programs upon check-in at your hotel or at the information booth outside the Valley Visitor Center. While most programs are held in the valley, all major campgrounds in the park offer **campfire programs** throughout the week.

A number of **guided walks** are also available. Check at one of the visitor centers or in the *Yosemite Guide,* the park newspaper, for current topics, start times, and locations. Walks may vary from week to week, but you can always count on nature hikes, evening discussions, and the sunrise photography program aimed at replicating some of Ansel Adams's works. Most do not require advance registration—just show up at the appointed time and place. The sunrise photo walk always gets rave reviews from the early risers who venture out at dawn. The living history evening program outside at Yosemite Lodge is great for young and old alike.

Guided backpacking tours range from simple walks to multiday excursions into Yosemite's backcountry and can be arranged by calling ☎ **209/372-8344.** Techniques and skills are taught along the way. Meals are included on longer trips. The instructor-to-student ratio does not exceed 7-to-1. Private trips are available, as is transportation to and from the trailhead. Three-day trips ascend Mount Lyell or hike from Young Lakes to Mount Conness. Four-day excursions travel from Ten Lakes to Tuolumne Meadows, or from Tuolumne Meadows to Yosemite Valley.

A host of **guided bus tours** is also available. You can buy tickets at tour desks at Yosemite Lodge, The Ahwahnee, Curry Village, or beside the Village Store in Yosemite Village. Advance reservations are suggested for all tours, and space can be reserved in person or by calling ☎ **209/372-1240.** Double-check at tour desks for updated departure schedules and prices. Most of the tours leave from Yosemite Lodge.

The **Valley Floor Tour** is a great way to get acclimated. It's a 2-hour ride in either an open-air tram or an enclosed motor coach, depending on the weather. The cost is $17 per person, $8.50 for children, and $15 for seniors. Trams depart from Yosemite Village, the Ahwahnee, Yosemite Lodge, and Curry Village every half hour daily (hours vary by season). The trip includes a good selection of photo ops, including El Capitan, Tunnel View, and Half Dome. A guide leads a historical, geological, and informative discussion from a pulpit at the head of the tram. This ride is also available on nights when the moon is full or near full. It's an eerie but beautiful scene. Moonlight illuminates the valley's granite walls and gives visitors a rare picture of Yosemite. Dress warmly, though, because it can get mighty chilly after the sun goes down, though blankets and hot cocoa are provided. On the other hand, if you take this trip during the day, wear sunscreen.

The **Glacier Point Tour** is a 4-hour scenic bus ride through the valley to Glacier Point. The round-trip cost is $20 for adults, $19.25 for seniors, and $10.25 for children. Buses depart Yosemite Lodge, the Ahwahnee, Yosemite Village, and Curry Village daily at 10am and 1:30pm. One-way trips are also available for hikers interested in returning to the valley on foot. Cost is $10 for adults and seniors, and $5 for children. One-way fares leave Yosemite Lodge at 8:30am, 10am, and 1:30pm daily. Buses depart Glacier Point at 10am, noon, and 3:30pm. Reservations must be made at least 1 day ahead of time. All Glacier Point buses are available spring through fall only.

Tours also depart from Yosemite Valley to the **Mariposa Grove.** The trip takes 6 hours and costs $34 for adults and $18 for children. Buses depart Yosemite Lodge at 9:30am daily. The trip includes the Big Trees tram tour that winds through the grove and stops for lunch at Wawona (lunch is not provided). You can combine the trip to Glacier Point and Mariposa Grove in an 8-hour bus ride that costs $44.50 for adults and $25 for children. Buses depart Yosemite Lodge at 9:30am daily.

Buses also depart Yosemite Valley for **Tuolumne Meadows,** although they don't allow for much time to explore, unless you arrange to stay overnight. It's an all-day trip, with stops along the way. Cost is $20 for adults and seniors, $10.25 for children. You can also jump off at any point along the way and the fare will be reduced.

Several organizations host tours to the valley from surrounding cities. Most go out of their way to accommodate guests, who benefit from not having to drive, skirting traffic jams and learning from experienced tour guides along the way.

Bass Lake–Yosemite Tours (☎ **209/877-8687**) conducts scheduled as well as customized trips. Cost range from $34 to $48, depending on the tour. Tours are operated on small, air-conditioned buses with huge picture windows. The sightseeing includes Mariposa Grove, Yosemite Valley, and Glacier Point. Geology, flora, and fauna are pointed out along the way. Stops are scheduled for lunch, shopping, and photo opportunities. Pickup can be arranged from various motels throughout Oakhurst and Bass Lake.

From spring through fall, the Yosemite Theater offers inexpensive theatrical and musical programs designed to supplement Park Service programs. These tend to repeat from year to year, but old favorites include a conversation with John Muir, a film on Yosemite's future, and sing-alongs. Inquire at the Valley Visitor Center.

Day Hikes

Remember that you'll need a permit to camp overnight in the backcountry (see "Special Regulations & Warnings," above).

IN & NEAR THE VALLEY

Mirror Lake

2.6 miles RT. Easy. Access: Take the shuttle bus to stop no. 17 or 18 and follow the signs.

A 0.5-mile paved trail climbs about 60 feet along the west side of Tenaya Creek to Mirror Lake, aptly named because the still surface reflects the overhanging granite above. A beautiful 3-mile loop around the lake may be accessible by 1998. The trail, which once traveled across Tenaya Creek via a picturesque rock footbridge, was washed out in 1997. The rush of water in Tenaya Creek broke the bridge in three and left part of it toppled in the creek bed.

Lower Yosemite Fall

0.5 mile RT. Easy. Access: Take the shuttle bus to stop no. 7. Follow the paved path from the Yosemite Fall Parking Area to the base of this waterfall.

Be prepared to get damp. Lower Yosemite Fall reaches 320 feet, but it packs the accumulated punch of the entire 2,425-foot waterfall. You can also take this trip from Yosemite Village by following the path from the Valley Visitor Center to the Yosemite Fall Parking Area. Add another 0.5 mile or 40 minutes each way. This walk is wheelchair-accessible with assistance.

Upper Yosemite Fall

7.2 miles RT. Strenuous. Access: Take the shuttle bus to stop no. 8. The trailhead is next to Sunnyside Walk-in Campground, behind Yosemite Lodge.

Up, up, and away. Climbing 2,700 feet and offering spectacular views from the ledge above, this hike is really not for the faint of heart. Take it slow, rest often, and absorb the scenery as you climb higher and higher above the valley. One mile up, you'll reach Columbia Point, which offers a panoramic view. The rest of the trail dips and climbs, with ample opportunity for cooling off beneath the spray from the fall above. The last quarter mile is a series of torturous, seemingly endless switchbacks which ascend through underbrush before opening at a clearing near the top of the fall. The view from here inspires vertigo. It's a worthwhile walk upstream to see the creek before it takes a 0.5-mile tumble to the valley floor below. You can also stay overnight up here, with proper permits and equipment.

Columbia Rock

2 miles RT. Moderate. Access: Use the trailhead for Upper Yosemite Fall.

The hike mirrors the beginning ascent of the waterfall trail, but stops at Columbia Rock, 1,000 feet above the valley. There's no valley view from here, but the sights are still impressive. Because it's on the sunny side of the valley, it's also less likely to get an accumulation of snow.

Base of Bridalveil Fall

0.5 mile RT. Easy to moderate. Access: Drive or walk to the Bridalveil Fall Parking Area, about 3 miles west of Yosemite Village. Follow trail markers.

Bridalveil Fall drops 620 feet from top to bottom. In the spring, expect to get wet. This walk is wheelchair accessible with assistance.

Mist Trail to Vernal Fall

3 miles RT. Moderate to strenuous. Access: Take the shuttle bus to stop no. 16 and walk to

the Happy Isles Bridge. Cross the bridge and follow the signs to the trail.

This hike begins on the famous 211-mile John Muir Trail to Mount Whitney in Sequoia and Kings Canyon national parks. From the Happy Isles Bridge, the trail climbs 400 feet to the Vernal Fall Bridge, which has a good view of what lies ahead, as well as water and rest rooms. The rest of the climb requires a choice. You can either take a series of switchbacks along the side of the mountain and come out above the fall, or ascend the Mist Trail (our suggestion), which is a steep climb with 500 steps—it's wet, picturesque, and refreshing. The Mist Trail is so named because the spray from the fall drenches anyone who tackles this route, especially in spring. *Be warned:* It's slick and requires cautious steps. Once you reach the top, you can relax on a series of smooth, granite benches and soak in the cool, refreshing water before hiking back down.

Onward to Nevada Fall

6.8 miles RT. Moderate to strenuous. Access: Use the trailhead for Vernal Fall.

This trip mirrors the Vernal Fall climb for the first 3 miles. From Vernal Fall, hike to Nevada Fall on either side of the river. Along the south side, you'll walk the John Muir Trail. The north side is the extension of the Mist Trail. Either way, it's a climb. For variety, you can descend on the opposite trail.

Four-Mile Trail to Glacier Point

9.6 miles RT. Strenuous. Access: The trailhead is 1.25 miles from Yosemite Village, at the Four Mile Parking Area, post V-18, or take the shuttle bus to the Yosemite Lodge stop no. 8 and walk behind the Lodge over the Swinging Bridge to Southeast Dr. The trailhead is 0.25 mile west.

This trail climbs 3,200 feet and has some terrific views (OK, so does every trail climbing out of Yosemite Valley). This trail ends at Glacier Point, but if you'd like to extend, it connects with the Panorama Trail at the end. However, if you plan to hike both simultaneously, it may require an overnight stay and advanced preparation—the combined round-trip distance is 14 miles.

Panorama Trail

9 miles one way. Moderate to strenuous. Access: The hike begins at Glacier Point, at the east end of the parking area.

From Glacier Point, this trail drops 3,200 feet, but somehow it still feels like a climb. At one of the prettiest points, it crosses Illilouette Fall about 1.5 miles from Glacier Point. It continues along the Panorama Cliffs and eventually winds up at Nevada Fall, where it's a straight descent to Yosemite Valley via the Mist or John Muir trails. You can hike this trail in conjunction with the Four-Mile Trail, but it might entail an overnight stop. It's also possible to take the bus to Glacier Point and hike only one way.

Half Dome

16.5 miles RT. Moderate to strenuous. Access: Take the shuttle bus to stop no. 16 at Happy Isles.

This long, steep trip climbs 4,900 feet. From Happy Isles, take the John Muir Trail past Vernal and Nevada falls, and through Little Yosemite Valley. Leave the John Muir Trail for the Half Dome Trail and look for a natural spring atop a short spur. Fill up here because this is the last water on the way up. The last 200 feet of hiking up the back of Half Dome require the use of cables. And a strong heart wouldn't hurt.

Hiking this rock is a divisive issue. Some question why humans are so compelled to conquer every summit. Others say because it's there. A lot of people agree. An estimated 600 people climb Half Dome every day in the summer. It's possible to cut the length by beginning in Little Yosemite Valley (you'll need a wilderness permit to camp here).

SOUTH OF THE VALLEY

Chilnualna Falls from Wawona

8 miles RT. Strenuous. Access: Enter Yosemite National Park on Calif. 41 and continue north. Turn right on Chilnualna Rd., just north of the Merced River's south fork. Stay on this road until it dead-ends at "The Redwoods," about 1.3 miles. This is the trailhead.

One of the tallest outside Yosemite Valley, this fall cascades down two chutes. The one at the bottom is narrow and packs a real punch after a wet winter. A series of switchbacks leads to the top fall, and from here you can hike to Bridalveil Campground, or continue on to Chilnualna Lakes. If you plan to hike to the lakes, this is a great place to stay overnight, but don't forget your wilderness permit. Also remember to pack a swimsuit—there are a few swimming holes at the base of the waterfall.

Chilnualna Falls from Bridalveil Fall

18.8 miles RT. Moderate to strenuous. Access: Take Calif. 41 to Glacier Point Rd. and turn east. Take Glacier Point Rd. to the trailhead at Bridalveil Campground.

The trail goes along gentle grades through forests at first, then turns up toward Turner Meadows. It's a scenic trip without Yosemite's summer crowds. It offers pretty views as the trail wanders near overlooks along the route to the falls.

Grizzly Giant

1.6 miles RT. Easy. Access: The trail begins at a sign near the map dispenser at the east end of the Mariposa Grove parking lot.

This is the walking alternative to the tram tour. It's a nice stroll to see an impressive tree and the hike only climbs 400 feet.

The Mariposa Grove

13 miles RT. Moderate to strenuous. Access: Park at the Wawona Store Parking Area and walk east 0.25 mile to Forest Dr. The trailhead is on the right.

It sounds long, but there is a one-way option in the summer that uses the Wawona shuttle bus service on the return trip. This hike is a nice alternative to the crowded drive to the Mariposa Grove. It climbs through a forest, then ascends the Wawona Dome and Wawona Basin, both of which provide excellent views.

Ostrander Lake

12.8 miles RT. Moderate to strenuous. Access: Take Calif. 41 to Glacier Point Rd. and turn east. Take Glacier Point Rd. to the trailhead about 1.3 miles past Bridalveil Campground, on the right-hand side of the road.

The trail begins on an abandoned road. It winds through evidence of a forest fire until it reaches Bear Meadow. It begins to climb after crossing Bridalveil Creek and crosses several ridges before reaching the lake. The best camping is reportedly on the lake's west end. Ostrander Lake is popular in summer and during winter as a cross-country ski spot. The Sierra Club also manages the nearby Ostrander Hut.

Sentinel Dome

2.2 miles RT. Moderate. Access: Take Glacier Point Rd. to the Sentinel Dome Parking Lot, about 3 miles from Glacier Point.

You'll be able to see Sentinel Dome on your left. At the first fork, bear right. The trail winds through manzanita and pine before beginning its ascent. It's a steep scramble to the top of Sentinel Dome and you have to leave the trail on the north side in order to scramble up. The view from the top offers a 180° panorama of Yosemite Valley that includes a host of impressive and recognizable geologic landmarks.

Taft Point

2.2 miles RT. Easy. Access: The trailhead begins at the same point as the hike to Sentinel Dome. At the fork, head left.

The walk to Taft Point is undemanding. It crosses a broad meadow dotted in early summer by wildflowers. Near Taft Point, note the deep chasms in the rock, known as the "fissures." Some of the cracks are 40 feet long and 20 feet wide at the top and 100 feet deep. The wall of Yosemite Valley actually overhangs the narrow ravine below and if you carefully peer over the cliff, note that your head is on the opposite side of a stream running far beneath you. A small pipe railing further on marks the 6-by-3-foot Taft Point Overlook hanging over Yosemite Valley.

Wawona Meadow Loop

3.5 miles RT. Easy. Access: Take the paved road through the golf course on the west side of Calif. 41, and walk about 50 yards to the trail.

This relaxing stroll encircles Wawona Meadow, curving around at its east end and heading back toward the road. It crosses the highway and winds through forest until it returns at the Wawona Hotel. Some cars still use this road, so watch out.

Wawona Point

1 mile RT. Easy. Access: Take the tram tour at the Mariposa Grove to the Wawona Tunnel Tree and exit.

Hike back to the north, toward Wawona and follow a spur road at the Galen Clark Tree. From here you can see the entire Wawona Basin, a view only available to those who venture out on foot.

NORTH OF THE VALLEY

Cathedral Lakes

8 miles RT. Moderate. Access: The trailhead is at the west end of Tuolumne Meadows, west of Budd Creek. Take the shuttle bus in summer to avoid parking problems.

These lakes are set in granite bowls cut by glaciers. The peaks and domes around both Lower and Upper Cathedral lakes are worth the hike alone. Lower Cathedral Lake is next to Cathedral Peak, and is a good place to stop for a snack before heading up the hill to enjoy the upper lake.

Cloud's Rest

14 miles RT. Moderate. Access: Take Calif. 120 to Tenaya Lake. The trailhead begins at a campground parking lot down a closed road that crosses an outlet of the lake.

This hike descends through a wooded area. Head toward Sunrise Lake. Ascend out of Tenaya Canyon and at a junction, bear right (this part of the trail is usually well signed). Views begin almost at once. Your destination is clear, which is a good thing since the trail is sketchy at this point. The last scramble to the top is a little spooky, with sheer drops on each side. Yosemite River is on the right and the Little Yosemite on the left. Bravery is rewarded with spectacular views of the park's granite domes. Overnight stays are rewarded with beautiful sunrises.

Dog Lake

3 miles RT. Easy. Access: Take Calif. 120 to the access road for Tuolumne Lodge. Pass the Ranger Station and park at a parking lot on the left. Walk north up an embankment and recross the highway to find Dog Lake Trail.

This is an easy climb through forests with great views of Mount Dana. Dog Lake is warm, shallow, and great for swimming.

Elizabeth Lake

6 miles RT. Moderate. Access: Take Calif. 120 to the group camping area of Tuolumne Meadows Campground, where the trail begins.

This popular day hike attracts a slew of people, which can be a bummer, but it's magnificent nonetheless for its beauty. Elizabeth Lake glistens like ice. Don't forget your camera and some extra film—the entire route is one long Kodak moment.

El Capitan (the back way)

14.4 miles RT. Strenuous. Access: Take Calif. 120 to the Tamarack Flat Campground. Turn right and follow the road to the east end of the campground, where you'll see an abandoned road. The trail begins here.

Trek along the abandoned road to Cascade Creek and then along a roadbed to the North Rim Trail. Prepare for switchbacks. The trail climbs and climbs and climbs to a summit, where it hits a spur trail. Take the spur to the summit to enjoy the views. (The main trail heads to Eagle Peak.) *Be careful:* Punishment for carelessness is a poorly rated, one-way trip to the valley floor.

Gaylor Lakes

6 miles RT. Moderate. Access: Take Calif. 120 to Tioga Pass. The trailhead is on the northwest side of the road.

This trail begins with a climb, then descends to the alpine lake. It's a particularly pretty hike in early summer, when the mountainsides are dotted with wildflowers.

Glacier Canyon to Dana Lake

4.6 miles RT. Moderate to strenuous. Access: Take Calif. 120 to Tioga Lake. The trailhead is on the west side of the lake, about a mile east of the pass.

This is a less-crowded alternative to the above hike to Mount Dana that doesn't top the mountain, although that alternative is available for experienced hikers. The trail begins at the Ansel Adams Wilderness and is not maintained, although it is fairly visible. This area is easily damaged so make sure to tread lightly. The route leads through the headway of Glacier Canyon to Dana Lake, which is fed by glaciers. Mount Dana looms large from the lake's shore.

Glen Aulin

10.4 miles RT. Moderate to strenuous. Access: Take Calif. 120 toward Tuolumne Meadows, about 1 mile east of the Tuolumne Meadows Visitor Center and just a few yards east of the bridge over the Tuolumne River. Follow a marked turnoff and take the paved road on your left. The trailhead begins about 0.3 mile ahead, at a road that turns right and heads up a hill toward the stables.

Start hiking across a flat meadow toward Soda Springs and Glen Aulin. The trail is well marked and signs along the way do a good job of pointing out the area's history. This was once the old Tioga Road, which was built in 1883 to serve the Great Sierra Mine in Tioga Pass.

This walk offers a view to the landmarks of Tuolumne Meadows. Lembert Dome rises behind you almost 900 feet above the meadow. About 0.4 mile from the trailhead the road forks; head right up a grassy slope. In less than 500 feet is a trail that leaves the road on the right and a steel sign that says Glen Aulin is 4.7 miles ahead. Along the way you'll pass Fairview Dome, Cathedral Peak, and Unicorn Peak. The crashing noise you hear is Tuolumne Falls, a cascade of water that drops 12 feet and then 40 feet down a series of ledges. From here you can see a nearby High Sierra camp. There's also a hikers' camp if you want to spend the night.

Lembert Dome

2.8 miles RT. Moderate. Access: The trailhead is at a parking lot north of Calif. 120 in Tuolumne Meadows at road marker T-32. Follow the nature trail that starts here and take off at marker no. 2.

This hike offers a bird's-eye view of Tuolumne Meadows and it's a great vista. A well-marked trail leads you to the top, and from there you'll see the peaks that encircle the valley, plus get a pretty good idea of how the meadow system is laid out. It's a great place for sunrises and sunsets.

May Lake

2.5 miles RT. Easy. Access: Take Calif. 120 east past White Wolf. Turn off at road marker T-21 and drive 2 miles to the May Lake Parking Area.

Winding through forests and granite, this picturesque hike offers ample opportunities to fish, but swimming is not allowed.

May Lake is in the center of Yosemite National Park and is a good jumping-off point for other high-country hikes. There are numerous peaks surrounding the lake, including the 10,855-foot-high Mount Hoffman, which rises behind the lake. There is a High Sierra camp here as well, and a hikers' camp on the south side of the lake.

Mono Pass

8.5 miles RT. Moderate to strenuous. Access: The trailhead for this hike is on the south side of Calif. 120 as you enter the park from Lee Vining. Drive about 1.5 miles from the park entrance to Dana Meadows, where the trail begins on an abandoned road and alongside Parker Creek Pass.

You'll pass some historic cabin sites, then hike down to Walker Lake, and return via the same route. The hike loops into the Inyo National Forest and the Ansel Adams Wilderness, and climbs to an altitude of 10,600 feet.

Mt. Dana

5.8 miles RT. Strenuous. Access: The trailhead is on the southeast side of Calif. 120 at Tioga Pass.

This climb is an in-your-face reminder that Mount Dana is Yosemite's second-highest peak. The mountain rises 13,053 feet and the trail gains a whopping 3,100 feet in 3 miles. The views at the top are wonderful, once you're able to stand upright after catching your breath. You can see Mono Lake from the summit. In summer, the wildflowers add to this hike's beauty.

North Dome

10 miles RT. Easy to moderate. Access: Take Calif. 120 east to the Porcupine Flat Campground, past White Wolf. About 1 mile after the campground is a sign for Porcupine Creek at a closed road. Park in the designated area.

Walk south down the abandoned road toward the Porcupine Creek Campground. A mile past the campground the trail hits a junction with the Tenaya Creek and Tuolumne Meadows Trail. Pass a junction toward Yosemite Falls and head uphill toward North Dome. The ascent is treacherous due to loose gravel, but from the top you'll catch an all-encompassing view of Yosemite Valley, second only to the view from Half Dome.

Polly Dome Lake

12.5 miles RT. Easy to moderate. Access: Take Calif. 120 past White Wolf to Tenaya Lake. Drive about 0.5 mile to a picnic area midway along the lake. The trailhead is across the road from the picnic area.

This hike is easily the road least traveled. The trip to Polly Dome Lake is a breeze and you'll find nary another traveler in sight. There are several lakes beneath Polly Dome that can accommodate camping. The trail fades in and out so watch for markers. It crosses a rocky area en route, then skirts southeast at a pond just after the rocky section. Polly Dome Lake is at the base of Polly Dome, a visual aide to help hikers stay the course.

Soda Springs

1.5 miles RT. Easy. Access: 2 trailheads—1 is at a crosswalk just east of the Tuolumne Meadows Visitor Center. The other leaves from a parking lot north of Calif. 120 at road marker T-32. Follow the gravel road around a locked gate.

This trail crosses Tuolumne Meadows, then Tuolumne River on a wooden bridge. It's peaceful and beautiful, the sound of the river gurgling along as it winds slowly through the wide expanse of Tuolumne Meadow. The trail heads to a carbonated spring where you can taste the water, although it gets mixed reviews. For years, the spring was administered and owned by the Sierra Club, which operates the nearby Parsons Lodge, now an activity center. Also nearby is the historic McCauley Cabin, which is now a ranger's residence.

Sunrise Lakes

7 to 8 miles RT. Moderate to strenuous. Access: Take Calif. 120 to Tenaya Lake. The

trail begins in the parking area on the east side of the road near the southwest end of the lake.

Look for a sign that says SUNRISE. Follow the level road to Tenaya Creek. Cross the creek and follow the trail to the right. The hike parallels Tenaya Creek for about 0.25 mile, then moves away through a wooded area and climbs gently up a rocky rise. After a while the trail descends quickly to the outlet of Mildred Lake. You'll be able to see Mount Hoffmann, Tuolumne Peak, and Tenaya Canyon.

At the halfway mark, the trail passes through a hemlock grove and then comes to a junction. Head left. (The trail on the right goes toward Cloud's Rest.) About 0.25 mile from the junction you'll reach Lower Sunrise Lake, tucked into the slope of Sunrise Mountain. The trail climbs past Middle Sunrise Lake and continues upward along a cascading creek coming from Upper Sunrise Lake. From there it follows the lake's shore and opens in less than 0.5 mile onto a wide, bare sandy pass. It's all downhill from here. Before you is the snowcapped Clark Range. The trail then begins its descent, sharply switching back and forth in some places. There is a High Sierra camp and backpackers' camp here as well.

Vogelsang

14.4 miles RT. Moderate to strenuous. Access: Take Calif. 120 to Tuolumne Meadows and watch for the signed trailhead for the John Muir Trail and Lyell Fork.

The trail goes south through the woods to a footbridge over the Dana Fork. Cross the bridge and follow the John Muir Trail upstream. Go right at the next fork. The trail crosses the Lyell Fork by footbridge. Take the left fork 200 feet ahead. Continue onward and just before crossing the bridge at Rafferty Creek, you'll reach another junction. Veer right and prepare for switchbacks up a rocky slope. The trail climbs steeply for about a quarter mile then levels off as it darts toward and away from Rafferty Creek for the next 4 miles.

The trail then gradually ascends to Tuolumne Pass, crossing many small creeks and tributaries en route. Two small tarns mark the pass. One drains south and the other north. Just south of the tarns the trail splits. Veer left. (The right fork offers a 2-mile round-trip jaunt to Boothe Lake.) You'll climb to a meadow with great views, and here, at 10,180 feet, reach the highest of Yosemite's High Sierra camps. It's very pretty, with a great location—the base of Fletcher Peak, on the banks of Fletcher Creek and close to Fletcher Lake.

Other Summer Sports & Activities

About the only thing you can't do in Yosemite is surf. In addition to sightseeing, Yosemite is a great place to bike, ski, rock climb, fish, even golf. All of which serves as a reminder that while here, you really aren't getting away from it all.

Biking. Bikes may be rented by the hour ($5.25) or the day ($20) at Curry Village or Yosemite Lodge. Both shops are open 8am to 7pm daily, but the Curry Village shop closes in winter. Hours may vary slightly depending on weather and the season. Information is also available by calling ☎ **209/372-8367** or 209/372-8319. Helmets are required for all riders under age 18 and provided to riders of all ages free of charge. Cyclists benefit from having access to special bikeways, as well as shuttle bus roads and thoroughfares for general traffic.

Fishing. General information is available from the **California State Department of Fish and Game** (☎ **209/222-3761**) or the **U.S. Army Corps of Engineers** (☎ **209/689-3255**). **Yosemite Creek Outfitters** leads fly-fishing trips in Yosemite (☎ **209/962-5060**). This Groveland-based organization offers everything from 1-day fly-fishing lessons to multiday excursions on horseback or by white-water raft. You can also make custom arrangements.

Especially for Kids

Yosemite offers a number of children's programs that make adults envious. Since everything in the park is huge beyond comprehension, park staff have planned activities that attempt to bring the park down to kids' size. Children ages 8 to 12 can sign up for the **Junior and Senior Rangers Program,** which hooks them up with a national park ranger who helps the children discover nature and the secret places in the valley. Kids receive a patch after completion of the program. Registration is at the **Happy Isles Nature Center** (shuttle bus stop no. 16). The program is offered June through August.

Other programs of interest to children include ranger-led walks, which begin at the Yosemite Valley Visitor Center (shuttle bus stop nos. 6 and 9). These vary by season. Check the visitor center for information. The Indian Cultural Museum (shuttle bus stops nos. 6 and 9) has exhibits and brief lectures conducted by descendants of Yosemite's first residents. The Happy Isles Nature Center (shuttle bus stop no. 16) has displays and dioramas of park animals that children will enjoy.

Golf. Wawona sports a 9-hole golf course designed in 1917 by noted course designer Walter G. Fovarque, who laid out many courses in Japan. The par-35 course is 3,050 yards long and alternates between meadows and fairways. You can book your tee time by phone (☎ **209/375-6572**).

There are several other courses just outside the park. **The River Creek Golf Course** (☎ **209/683-3388**) is in the small hamlet of Ahwahnee (not the hotel). And just to add to the confusion, the **Ahwahnee Golf Course** (☎ **209/642-1343**) is in Oakhurst.

Horseback Riding. Yosemite Valley phased out its stables in 1997, although pack animals and private stock may still board there. Stables remain at Wawona, and at Tuolumne Meadows in summer only. Reservations can be made by phone (☎ **209/372-8427** or 209/372-8348).

Guided backcountry pack trips are also available with advanced reservations from May to September. These 4- to 6-day saddle trips lead to Yosemite's High Sierra camps. Meals are included. The cost is $550 to $900. **Yosemite Trails Pack Station** (☎ **209/683-7611** or 209/683-9122) offers riding just south of Wawona. **Minarets Pack Station** (☎ **209/868-3405**) is in the High Sierra and leads day trips to Yosemite and the Ansel Adams Wilderness. You may also try the horses at the **Bohna Arena** (☎ **209/683-2817**).

Rafting. A raft rental shop is located at Curry Village (☎ **209/372-8341**). Daily rental fees are $12.50 for adults, $10.50 for children under 13. Fees include a raft, paddles, mandatory life preservers, and transportation from El Capitan back to Curry Village.

Rock Climbing. No guide would be complete without mentioning Yosemite's famous rock-climbing school. The park is considered one of the world's premier climbing grounds. The **Yosemite Mountaineering School** (☎ **209/372-8344**) provides experienced instruction for beginning, intermediate, and advanced climbers in the valley and Tuolumne Meadows. Classes last anywhere from a day to a week. Private lessons are also available. All equipment is provided. Rates vary according to the class or program.

Winter Sports & Activities

A winter visit offers unique beauty plus the peace and quiet that must have once been commonplace in Yosemite. Snow dusts the granite peaks and valley floor, bends trees, and creates a wonderland for visitors. Accommodation is cheaper and slightly easier to find, but even a day trip can be very rewarding. Though many animals hibernate during the cold months, this is the best time of year to see the valley as it was before it became such a popular place.

Cross-Country Skiing. Excursions are led from Badger Pass and Glacier Point. Information is available by phone (☎ **209/372-8444**). Learn to telemark, snow camp, or take an overnight expedition.

Downhill Skiing. Yosemite's **Badger Pass** is open from Thanksgiving through Easter Sunday. Year-round information is available by phone (☎ **209/372-1446**). Twenty-two miles from the valley, Badger Pass was established in 1935. It's a small resort with nine runs, four lifts, and a chair tow. It's geared toward intermediate skiers and is reputed to be an excellent place to learn to ski.

Ice-Skating. The ice rink at Curry Village is open early November to March, weather permitting. One session costs $5 for adults and $4.50 for children. Skate rental is another $2. Sessions are at noon to 2:30pm, 3:30 to 6pm, and 7 to 9:30pm daily. The rink also offers morning sessions from 8:30 to 11am on weekends.

Camping

Campground reservations can be made 3 months in advance by calling **Biospherics, Inc.** at ☎ **800/436-PARK** (7275). Payment can be made by check, money order, or credit card (DISC, MC, V).

In Yosemite National Park, there is a 7-day camping limit in the Valley and Wawona, and a 14-day limit elsewhere from May 1 to September 15. For the remaining months of the year, there is a 30-day limit. Some campgrounds are closed in winter, so call in advance. Some sites are first-come, first-served. A maximum of six people and two vehicles may stay at each campsite. Checkout time is noon. Pets are allowed in some campgrounds. General campground information is available by Touch-Tone phone at ☎ **209/372-0200.**

Now for the really bad news: The Valley lost half of its roughly 800 campsites during a flood in early 1997. The lost campsites will eventually be replaced further away from the Merced River, but no one's predicting when construction will begin.

Outside the park, campgrounds range from $9 to $11 in national forests, and are first-come, first-served. Private campgrounds are also available.

Note: Wilderness permits are required for all overnight backpacking trips in the park. No wilderness camping is allowed in the valley.

INSIDE THE PARK

There are several campgrounds in Yosemite Valley. All of them are near parking, a grocery, and a laundry, as well as raft, bicycle, and ski rentals. Campers will have to pay $2 for showers at Camp Curry. The small **Sunnyside Walk-in** (shuttle bus stop no. 7) is the most bohemian gathering in the valley, a magnet for hikers and climbers taking off or just returning from trips. It's situated behind Yosemite Lodge, near the trailhead for Yosemite Falls and near rocks frequently used by beginning rock climbers.

Lower Pines (bus stop no. 19), like most campgrounds in Yosemite Valley, is wide open with lots of shade but limited privacy. Still, it's a nice place, with clean bathrooms, and a nice meadow to the north. **North Pines** (bus stop no. 18) is beautifully situated beneath a grove of pines trees that offer little privacy but big shade. It's also near the river and roughly a mile from Mirror Lake. **Upper Pines** is the only valley campground that allows pets and the valley's only campground open in winter. Pets must be on a leash and are allowed only in the campground, not on trails. This site is closest

Campground	Elev.	Total Sites	RV Hookups	Dump Station	Toilets	Drinki Wate
Inside Yosemite National Park						
Bridalveil Creek	7,200	110	0	No	Yes	Yes
Crane Flat	6,200	116	0	No	Yes	Yes
Hodgdon Meadow	4,900	195	0	No	Yes	Yes
Lower Pines	4,000	60	0	Nearby	Yes	Yes
North Pines	4,000	85	0	Nearby	Yes	Yes
Porcupine Flat	8,100	52	0	No	Yes	No
Sunnyside	4,000	35 (tent only)	0	No	Yes	Yes
Tamarack Flat	6,200	52 (tent only)	0	No	Yes	No
Tuolumne Meadows	8,600	314	0	Nearby	Yes	Yes
Upper Pines	4,000	238	0	Yes	Yes	Yes
Wawona	4,000	100	0	Nearby	Yes	Yes
White Wolf	7,900	100	0	No	Yes	Yes
Yosemite Creek	6,200	75 (tent only)	0	No	Yes	No
Outside the Park						
Lumsden	1,500	10 (tent only)	0	No	Yes	No
Lumsden Bridge	1,500	9 (tent only)	0	No	Yes	No
The Pines	3,200	21	0	No	Yes	Only to C
Indian Flat	1,500	35	0	No	Yes	Yes
Lee Vining	8,000	129	0	No	Yes	No
Tioga Lake	9,700	13	0	No	Yes	Yes
Yosemite-Mariposa	2,000	40	30	Yes	Yes	Yes

to the Happy Isle Nature Center. The property is pretty and shady, but there's no seclusion or peace and quiet in the summer.

Campers near Wawona can try the **Wawona Campground,** 1 mile north of Wawona on Calif. 41. Once again, there's not much seclusion, but it's a pretty place to stay beneath towering trees. The campground is near both the Mariposa Grove of Giant Sequoia and the Merced River, which offers some of the better fishing in the park. Pets are permitted. Wawona has a grocery store, disposal station, and horseback-riding facility.

About 8 miles down Glacier Point Road, you'll come to **Bridalveil Creek.** Near the beautiful Glacier Point, this campground is away from the valley crowds, but within a moderate drive to the valley sights. The campground is set along Bridalveil Creek, which flows to Bridalveil Fall, a beauty of a waterfall, especially after a heavy winter or wet spring. Pets are accepted.

North of the valley, **Hodgdon Meadow,** near the Big Oak Flat Entrance, is located along North Crane Creek and near the Tuolumne River's south fork. A grocery store is nearby, and pets are permitted. The Big Trees are 3 miles southeast.

Several campgrounds are located on or near Calif. 120.

Crane Flat, about 20 miles east of the town of Buck Meadows, is near the Big Trees and away from valley crowds. It's is a large but nice campground with the essential comforts nearby, such as a

Showers	Fire Pits/ Grills	Laundry	Public Phone	Reserve	Fees	Open
No	Yes	No	Yes	No	$10	June–Oct
No	Yes	No	Yes	Yes	$15	June–Oct
No	Yes	No	Yes	May–Sept	$15	Year-round
Nearby	Yes	Nearby	Yes	Yes	$15	Mar–Oct
Nearby	Yes	Nearby	Yes	Yes	$15	Apr–Oct
No	Yes	No	Yes	No	$6	July–Sept
Nearby	Yes	Nearby	Yes	No	$3	Year-round
No	Yes	No	Yes	No	$6	July–Sept
Nearby	Yes	No	Yes	For 1/2 the spaces	$6	June–Sept
Nearby	Yes	Nearby	Yes	Yes	$15	Year-round
No	Yes	No	Yes	May–Sept	$15	Year-round
Nearby	Yes	No	Yes	No	$10	July–Sept
No	Yes	No	Yes	No	$6	July–Sept
No	Yes	No	Yes	No	Free	Apr–Oct
No	Yes	No	Yes	No	Free	Apr–Oct
No	Yes	No	Yes	No	$9	Year-round
No	Yes	No	Yes	No	$9	Year-round
No	Yes	No	Yes	No	$5	May–Oct
No	Yes	No	Yes	No	$7	June–Oct
Yes	Yes	Yes	Yes	A good idea	$18–$30	Year-round

grocery and a gas station. Yosemite Valley is about 20 miles away. **Tamarack Flat** is about 2.5 miles down a side road off Calif. 120 past Crane Flat Campground.

A bit off the beaten path, this little-known campground is more secluded than most, which means fewer folks rest their heads here. It's equidistant from the valley and Tuolumne Meadows.

White Wolf Campground is on White Wolf Road, just off Tioga Road. Secluded in a forest, this is a nice place to stay for several days with easy access to nearby hiking. The trails here lead to several lakes, including Grant Lake and Lukens Lake. There's a dirt road to Harden Lake, and beyond that, a trail to Smith Peak, which overlooks the Hetch Hetchy Reservoir. Mosquitoes are fierce in the summer. Beware the sometimes neglected bathrooms. A grocery is nearby, and pets are accepted.

Just pass the turnoff for White Wolf Road is the road to **Yosemite Creek Campground,** about 5 miles down. This quaint place set along Yosemite Creek is a good place to check if the park is full and you need a place to stay. It's a lesser-known campground where you do everything yourself, and for that reason, it frequently has space available. Near Yosemite Creek is **Porcupine Flat,** a few more miles east on Calif. 120. This is another great campground that may have space if you're in a pinch. It has lots of shade, shrubs, and trees.

Tuolumne Meadows Campground, near the Tuolumne Meadows Visitor Center, is the biggest campground in Yosemite, and, amazingly, often the least crowded. Its location in the high country makes it a good spot from which to head off with a backpack. It's also near the Tuolumne River, hence good for fishing.

NEAR THE PARK

Yosemite is surrounded by national forests that offer campgrounds comparable to the ones in Yosemite, albeit less crowded. There are also private campgrounds, which will cost you.

To get to the campgrounds in **Stanislaus National Forest** (☎ **209-962-7825**), take Calif. 120 from Groveland about 8 miles east (about a mile east of the turn for County Road J20). There you'll find to the right the entrance road for **The Pines,** about 1.5 miles from the Tuolumne River. This campground gets scorching hot here during the summer. If you turn left instead and drive 1 mile, then turn right onto a dirt road and drive 6 more miles, you'll come to **Lumsden,** along the Tuolumne River, on a scenic stretch between the Hetch Hetchy and Don Pedro reservoirs. It's at an elevation of about 1,500 feet and also very hot in summer. **Lumsden Bridge** is another 1.5 miles down the dirt road. This is a fave of rafters because the location is close to the Tuolumne River's best stretches, which are some of California's most awesome stretches of white water.

West of the park, 7 miles northeast of Mariposa on Calif. 140, is **Yosemite-Mariposa KOA Campground,** 6323 Calif. 140, Mariposa (☎ **209/966-2201**), which comes complete with a swimming pool, playground, store, and laundry. This is another good save if Yosemite if full. The campground is 28 miles from the park entrance and near the Merced River.

Indian Flat, in the Sierra National Forest (☎ **209/683-4665**), is 4 miles south of El Portal on Calif. 140, and 24 miles north of Mariposa. This is a pretty place next to the Merced with several good swimming holes.

The Lee Vining Creek Campgrounds, 4 to 5 miles west of Lee Vining along Calif. 120, are four campgrounds clustered in a group. They're basically just places to rest your head for a fee. The campgrounds are set along Lee Vining Creek.

Tioga Lake, 10 miles west of Lee Vining on Calif. 120, is located in the Inyo National Forest (☎ **760/872-4240**). A pretty camp set at 9,700 feet in the eastern Sierra, it's a good place to stay if Tuolumne Meadows is full.

Accommodations

There are accommodations to fit every budget and every taste in or near Yosemite. Yosemite Valley itself caters to families and offers everything from campgrounds to the opulent Ahwahnee Hotel where every room has a view on the sheer granite greatness of the valley. All sites are located at or near shuttle bus stops and have parking nearby. A more narrow scope of choices is available outside the valley but still within the park.

INSIDE THE PARK

Lodging in the park is under the auspices of **Yosemite Concession Services Corp. (YCS).** Rooms can be reserved up to 366 days in advance (☎ **209/252-4848**). Reservations are also accepted by mail at **Yosemite Reservations,** 5410 E. Howe Ave., Fresno, CA 93727.

The exception to all of this is Wawona. While YCS operates the Wawona Hotel, there are several dozen private homes that are rented seasonally through **Redwood Guest Cottages** (☎ **209/375-6666**). It's a real hodgepodge and appears fairly hit-and-miss in terms of quality, which may be why these places are seldom mentioned in guidebooks. But it's an option.

Housekeeping Camp

Yosemite Valley. ☎ **209/252-4848.** 266 units, all with shared rest room and shower facilities. Reservations required. $44.50 per site (up to 4 people; $4 for every extra person). CB, DC, DISC, MC, V. Shower house open summer only.

This place is funky. It's the closest thing to camping without pitching a tent. The sites are fence-enclosed shanties built on concrete slabs, each with a table, cupboard, electrical outlets, shelves, a mirror, and lights. The sleeping areas have two single-size fold-down bunks and a double bed. The park is slowly eliminating sites, with the idea of eventually getting the number of units down to 232. There's a Laundromat nearby.

Curry Village

Yosemite Valley. ☎ **209/252-4848.** 427 canvas tent cabins with central shared bath and about 100 wooden cabins, some with bath. Reservations suggested. $42 per tent cabin, double, with additional charge for extra adults or children. Cabins range from $59.25–$75.25 with bath, double, with an additional charge extra adults. Lower rates Nov–Mar. DC, DISC, MC, V. Parking is available or take the shuttle bus to stop nos. 1, 13, and 14.

Curry Village is a mass of white canvas tents that dot the valley's south slope. It was founded in 1899 as a cheaper alternative for valley visitors at a mere $2 a day, but guests can kiss those days goodbye. Today, it's often condemned as a kiddie hellhole, filled in the summer with crying and roughhousing. I found it tolerable and the easiest place to crash. It's also home to a decent pizza parlor with beer by the pitcher and a large-screen TV, a hamburger shack, a sports shop, a general store with the valley's best wine selection (still meager), one grossly overpriced cafeteria, and an ice-cream stand. It also has a main tour desk where guests can book events throughout the valley. Canvas tents have wood floors, sleep two to four people, and are equipped with beds, dressers, and an ample supply of wool blankets. Tents have electrical outlets and daily maid service. In short, convenience usually makes this worth the noisy toddler next door. Outside there's a swimming pool and sundeck.

Yosemite Lodge

Yosemite Valley. ☎ **209/252-4848.** 249 motel rms and suites. Reservations suggested. Some with A/C TEL. $70.50–$107.25 double, with additional charge for extra adults. Lower rates Nov–Mar. DC, DISC, MC, V. Parking available or take the shuttle bus to stop no. 8.

This is a conglomerate of cabins, regular motel rooms, and suites. Most rooms offer one or two double or king-size beds. They are unremarkable, but comfortable and clean. Some look out onto Yosemite Falls, and some have patios or terraces. It's not uncommon to see deer and other wildlife scamper through this area. Spring mornings offer a wonderful orchestra of songbirds and some stunning views of Yosemite Falls at sunrise. The complex contains an overpriced cafeteria; the new Mountain Room Restaurant, which has great views and wonderful desserts; and the Garden Terrace, which serves an awesome salad bar. There is also a swimming pool, lounge, general store, and tour desk where guests can book events throughout the valley. Baby-sitting is available.

The Ahwahnee

Yosemite Valley. ☎ **209/252-4848.** 95 rms, 4 suites, 24 cottages. A/C TEL. $229.50 for all regular rms and cottages; up to $485 for suites. Lower rates Dec–Jan. DC, DISC, MC, V. Rates include coffee and pastries for breakfast. Parking available or take shuttle bus to stop no. 4.

The hotel's accommodations are fit for a king or queen, and it has hosted both. Queen Elizabeth slept here, as did Pres. John F. Kennedy, actor Clint Eastwood, poet Alfred Noyes, and quarterback Steve Young. It's tough to top the Ahwahnee, a six-story rock structure that offers beautiful views from every window. The hotel has a number of common rooms on the ground floor. There are three fireplaces large enough to stand in, and the rooms are furnished with large, overstuffed sofas and chairs on which to read or play games. Guest rooms are upstairs, with suites located on the top floor, accessible only by special elevator key. Suites include a pair of rooms, one for sleeping and another for sitting. The Sun Suite is a bright pair of rooms in lime and yellow with comfy lounges and floor-to-ceiling French windows that open out onto the valley. The library room's rich decor includes a fireplace and walls of books. Regular rooms offer a choice of two double or one king-size bed, with a couch and plush towels and snuggly comforters. Rooms have original stencils on the walls dating from 1927, when the hotel was built. The entire hotel received a $1.5 million renovation in January 1997. VCRs are available upon request. Outside there's a swimming pool.

Wawona Hotel

Calif. 41, Wawona, Yosemite National Park. ☎ **209/252-4848.** 104 rms, 50 with shared bath. $70.75–$97.50 double, additional charge for extra adults. DC, DISC, MC, V. From Yosemite Valley, take Calif. 41 south 27 miles toward Fresno.

This is a classic, Victorian-style hotel composed of six stately white buildings set near towering trees in a green clearing. Don't be surprised if a horse and buggy round the driveway by the fishpond—it's that kind of place. Maybe it's the wide porches, the nearby nine-hole golf course, or the vines of hops cascading from one veranda to the next. The entire place was designated a National Historic Landmark in 1987. Clark Cottage is the oldest building, dating from 1876. The main hotel was built in 1879. Rooms are comfortable and quaint with a choice of a double and a twin, a king, or a double bed (most of the latter share baths). All rooms open onto wide porches and overlook green lawns. Clark Cottage is the most intimate. The main hotel has the widest porches and plenty of Adirondack chairs, and at night, the downstairs sunroom hosts a pianist. Check out the whistling maintenance man who hits every high note in the "Star Spangled Banner" while the American flag is hoisted each morning. Outside there's an outdoor pool and two tennis courts.

White Wolf Lodge

Calif. 120, White Wolf, Yosemite National Park. ☎ **209/252-4848.** 24 canvas tent cabins, 4 cabins. All canvas cabins share bath and shower house. $44–$80 double, with an additional charge of $7.50 per adult and $3.50 per child. DC, DISC, MC, V. Parking available across a 2-lane road. Closed in winter. From Yosemite Valley, take Calif. 120 east 33 miles toward Tioga Pass.

Imagine a smaller, quieter, cleaner Curry Village with larger tents, each equipped with a wood-burning stove. This small outpost was bypassed when Tioga Road was rebuilt. White Wolf Lodge is not a lodge but a cluster of canvas tent cabins, a few wooden ones out front, and a general store/restaurant. It's located halfway between the valley and the high country, and generally isn't overrun with visitors. It's a popular spot for midweek hikers and weekend stopovers. Though this place gets crowded, it still retains a homey feeling—maybe because there's no electricity after 11pm when the generator shuts off. Wood cabins all have a private bath and resemble regular motel rooms, with neat little porches and chairs out front. Canvas cabins beat the Curry Village style by a mile. Each sleeps four in any combination of twin and double beds. Helpful staff will show guests how to work the wood-burning stove. Benches outside give guests someplace to rest their weary feet and watch the stars. Bathrooms are clean and access is controlled to guests, with the exception of a few midday hours when nearby campers can pay for showers.

Tuolumne Meadows Lodge

Calif. 120, Tuolumne Meadows, Yosemite National Park. ☎ **209/252-4848.** 69 canvas tent cabins, all with shared bath and shower house. $44, double, with additional charge of $7.50 per adult or $3.50 per child. DC, DISC, MC, V. Parking available in an adjacent lot. Closed in winter. From Yosemite Valley, take Calif. 120 east 55 miles toward Tioga Pass.

Not a lodge, but another group of canvas tent cabins. Like White Wolf, these also have wood-burning stoves and sleep up to four. The crowds get thicker here as this is prime territory for backcountry trekkers and campers. There's also a tiny general store, tour desk, and restaurant.

Yosemite West Cottages

P.O. Box 36, Yosemite National Park, CA 95389. ☎ **209/642-2211.** A fluctuating number of cabins and private homes. TV. $85–$150 and up. Take Calif. 41 for 12 miles north of Wawona.

Yosemite West rents private homes and cottages in the park that range in size and accommodate families as well as couples. All cabins have kitchenettes, and the vacation homes have full kitchens. It's just like living in the park. Homes are equipped with oversize beds and are ready and warm upon arrival. From here it's 10 miles to the valley and 8 miles to Badger Pass.

OUTSIDE THE PARK

If you strike out in the park, or prefer to stay outside, there are a plethora of choices. Each gateway community has built up a strong tourist trade catering to travelers.

ALONG CALIF. 120 (EAST OF THE PARK)

Groveland Hotel

18767 Calif. 120, Groveland. ☎ **800/273-3314** or 209/962-4000; fax 209/962-6674. 17 rms, including 3 suites. A/C TEL. $95–$175 double, $25 for each extra person. All with private bath, 4 with shower only. Rates include continental breakfast and wine in the evening. AE, DC, DISC, MC, V.

This is a great place to stay, picked as one of the nation's top 10 inns in 1997 by *Country Inns* magazine. The rooms are spacious, the hosts are gracious, and there's enough history, good food, and conversation to give travelers pause before heading into Yosemite. Peggy and Grover Mosley have poured their heart into making their hotel an elegant but comfortable place to stay. Vacant for years and on the verge of tumbling down, the Mosely's decided to forgo a quiet retirement from very interesting careers (you'll have to ask for yourself) to renovate and reopen the hotel. It is now a historic landmark. Most of the rooms are upstairs and many have large spa bathtubs. Most rooms are named after women of the Sierra. One exception is Lyle's Room, named for the hotel's resident ghost. Lyle's disdain for clutter atop one bureau was vouched for by a patron who swears her makeup case was moved to the sink. Then there's Charlie's Room, named for a hard-driving, tobacco-spitting resident who drove a stage, then started a trucking company. When he died, the townspeople learned he was a she. All rooms are filled with antiques, have thick down comforters, beds you want to jump on, and plush robes. Suites have fireplaces.

Hotel Charlotte

18736 Calif. 120, Groveland. ☎ **800/961-7799** or 209/962-6455. 11 rms, 3 with shared bath, 2 with shower only. A/C in summer only. $56.70–$124.20 double. Rates include continental breakfast. AE, MC, V.

Walking into the Charlotte is like stepping back in time. Built in 1918 by an Italian immigrant, it's warm, comfortable, and no-nonsense. You'll be greeted by a lobby filled with antiques and red velvet-covered furnishings. The rooms are all upstairs. The hotel offers twin, double, and queen beds. Several rooms adjoin one another and have connecting bathrooms (perfect for families). Rooms are quaint and have the basics, but nothing more. There is also a common game/TV room. The continental breakfast is great: strong coffee, fresh warm muffins, and juices. Casual dining is offered downstairs.

The Inn at Sugar Pine Ranch

21250 Calif. 120, Groveland. ☎ **888/800-7823** or 209/962-7823. 12 rms and cottages. All with private bath, 8 with shower only. A/C. $110–$150 double, $25 for each extra person. Rates include a full breakfast. MC, V.

This whitewashed inn, just outside of Groveland headed toward the park, is a new addition along the route to Yosemite. The main building is an old farmhouse built in 1860. There are also separate cottages. Everything is laid out beneath tall pine trees. Rooms are comfortable and plush. Some cottages have whirlpool bathtubs and fireplaces. Some rooms have balconies. All have nice views. Outside there's a pool.

ALONG CALIF. 140

Best Western Yosemite Way Station

4999 Calif. 140, Mariposa. ☎ **800/528-1234** or 209/966-7545; fax 209/966-6353. 76 rms. A/C TV TEL. $79–$85 double, $6 for each additional person. Rates include continental breakfast. AE, DC, DISC, MC, V.

Typical motel accommodations. Clean and comfortable, but nothing fancy. It is within walking distance of restaurants and shops and is near public transportation to Yosemite. There's a pool and Jacuzzi.

Cedar Lodge

9966 Calif. 140, El Portal. ☎ **800/321-5261** or 209/379-2612; fax 209/379-2712. 206 rms, some family units, one 3-bedroom suite with private pool and Jacuzzi. A/C TV TEL. $85–$125 double; 275–$375 suite. AE, MC, V.

Eight miles outside the park, this lodge offers big rooms, some with kitchenettes, in a wooded setting. It is owned by Yosemite Motels, which operates six motels outside the park. Variety makes this place an attractive option for visitors. It can accommodate every size group, from couples to families and large groups. Conference room seating is available for 250. There are two restaurants and a lounge on the premises. Public buses to the park are available from here. Guests have access to VCRs, video rentals, indoor and outdoor swimming pools, and a Jacuzzi.

Comfort Inn

4994 Bullion St., Mariposa. ☎ **800/321-5261** or 209/966-4344; fax 209/966-4655. 78 rms; suites with full kitchens. A/C TV TEL. $79–$85 double, $180–$350 suite. Rates include continental breakfast. AE, DC, DISC, MC, V.

Regular motel-style accommodations. Large, clean rooms and conveniently located within walking distance of restaurants and near public transportation to Yosemite. There's a pool and Jacuzzi.

Mariposa Hotel-Inn

5029 Calif. 140, Mariposa. ☎ **800/317-3244** or 209/966-4676; fax 209/742-5963. 5 rms. A/C TV. $75–$89 double, $10 for each additional person. Rates include continental breakfast. Rates 15% lower Nov–Mar. AE, DISC, MC, V.

A former stage stop, this building was converted to a hotel in 1901. It has undergone several renovations since, each in an effort to expand the size of its rooms, but the charm of this historic building has been preserved. Guests enter from a large oak door at street level and climb an interior flight of stairs to the foyer, from which a long hall leads to individual rooms. All the rooms are large with sitting areas. The Marguerite Room has the hotel's original claw-foot bathtub. Della's Room is named after a Native American whose hand-woven baskets hang on the walls. Check out Nana's Room—a bright, well-lit room that gets the morning sun. The veranda at the rear of the hotel often serves as a gathering point for patrons to meet or eat breakfast. The hotel is close to shopping and restaurants.

Miners Inn

5181 Calif. 49 N., Mariposa. ☎ **800/321-5261** or 209/742-7777; fax 209/742-4655. 76 rms. A/C TV TEL. $75–$159 double, $6 for each additional person. AE, DC, DISC, MC, V.

A standard motel in a rustic setting that strives to recapture the Old West. Deluxe rooms include spa tubs and fireplaces. There's a pool, Jacuzzi, on-site restaurant and lounge, and public transportation to Yosemite nearby.

Mother Lode Lodge

5052 Calif. 140, Mariposa. ☎ **800/398-9770** or 209/966-2521. 14 rms, including a suite and family unit. TV. $39–$65 double. Lower rates in off-season. Rates include continental breakfast in summer. DISC, MC, V.

Best on the budget. The no-frills rooms here are sparse but clean. Basic rooms have one or two queen-size beds, a small desk, and mirror. The bathrooms are tiny, and the TVs have very few channels. Outside there's a pool.

Poppy Hill Bed & Breakfast

5218 Crystal Aire Dr., Mariposa. ☎ **800/58-POPPY** or 209/742-6273. 3 rms, 2 with shared bath. A/C. Apr–Sept $85–$100 double, Oct–Mar $75–$90. $20 each additional person. Rates include full breakfast. AE, DC, DISC, MC, V. Take Calif. 140 past Mariposa 3 miles, turn left on Whitlock Rd. and right on Crystal Aire Dr.

This restored country home filled with antiques offers queen-size beds, down comforters, bathrobes, sitting areas, and scenic views. There's also an above-ground pool and a Jacuzzi.

Yosemite View Lodge

11156 Calif. 140, El Portal. ☎ **800/321-5261** or 209/379-2681; fax 209/379-2704. 158 rms and kitchenettes. A/C TV TEL. $129–$169 double. MC, V.

Just outside Arch Rock Entrance, this lodge offers guests accommodations on the river, which can turn wet and wild during the spring. All rooms have refrigerators and microwaves, some have spa tubs and fireplaces. A new restaurant is under construction. Public buses to the park are available. There are two outdoors pools and three outdoor Jacuzzis.

ALONG CALIF. 41

Comfort Inn

40489 Calif. 41, Oakhurst. ☎ **800/321-5261** or 209/683-8282; fax 209/658-7030. 113 rms, 2 suites. A/C TV TEL. $80–$120 double. Lower rates off-season. Rates include continental breakfast. AE, DC, DISC, MC, V.

Regular motel-style accommodations. Rooms are large and clean. There's a pool and a Jacuzzi.

Ducey's on the Lake

Pines Village, North Shore, Bass Lake, P.O. Box 109, Bass Lake. ☎ **800/350-7463** or 209/642-3902. 20 rms and suites. A/C TV. Summer $168–$298 double; winter $105–$210. $300–$350 suite. DC, DISC, MC, V. From Calif. 41, take Rd. 222 to the north shore of Bass Lake.

This historic country inn offers a variety of leisure activities. Guests stay in chalets and rooms that boast Native American decor and comfortable furnishings. Vaulted ceilings and beams were built with trees from the 44-acre property. Large bathrooms have plush towels and thick bathrobes. All units have terraces and fireplaces, and some have whirlpools. Guests have access to VCRs, tennis courts, a jogging track, nature trails, and laundry. Baby-sitting is available.

Oakhurst Lodge

40302 Calif. 41, Oakhurst. ☎ **800/655-6343** or 209/683-4417; fax 209/683-4417, ext. 171. 60 rms. A/C TV TEL. $57–$63 double. Lower rates off-season. AE, CB, DC, DISC, MC, V.

This place offers clean rooms with small refrigerators and one or two queen-size beds. The motel is within walking distance of numerous restaurants and adjacent to a nice picnic area. Outside there's a pool.

Rose Pine Inn

41703 Rd. 222, Oakhurst. ☎ **209/642-2800.** 9 rms, 7 with full bath, 1 with shower only. A/C TV. $55–$95 in summer, cheaper in winter. Rates include expanded continental breakfast. MC, V. Take Calif. 41 through Oakhurst 3 miles to Rd. 222, turn right and drive exactly 2 miles. The inn is on your left.

Rooms range from single bedrooms to split-level family cottages, nestled in a picturesque canyon. The Garden Room is pretty, with a separate entrance, private bath, kitchenette, and nice porch. The family units are spacious. One includes a deep bathtub, slate tile, nice patio, living room, and full kitchen. The Hidden Rose Room is small, but romantic, with a spa perfect for a massage while relaxing in front of the TV. The owners are helpful and unobtrusive. Guests benefit from the Rose Pine Inn's off-the-beaten-path location—these accommodations are a bargain. Try the yummy homemade cinnamon rolls for breakfast.

Tenaya Lodge

1122 Calif. 41, Fish Camp. ☎ **800/635-5807** or 209/683-6555; fax 209/683-8684. 244 rms, 20 suites. A/C MINIBAR TV TEL. Summer $159–$239 double, winter $69–$209. Add $20–$80 for suite. Buffet breakfast $11 per couple. Children stay free in parents' rm. AE, DC, DISC, MC, V.

Whoever built this place had one foot in the Adirondack Mountains and another in the southwest. This three- and four-story resort opened in 1990 on 35 acres full of hiking trails. The rest of the lodge includes a gas station and general store. The lobby has an impressive fireplace towering three-stories and built of river rock. The staff is nice, helpful, and accommodating. The rooms are ultramodern with multiple phones and a built-in safe. On the site are three restaurants, which comprise all after-hours activity between Oakhurst and Yosemite. Guest can enjoy indoor and outdoor swimming pools, on-site massage specialists, health club, game room, and sleigh and hay rides depending on season.

Dining

We're not sure much proper "dining" goes on around these parts, but there are a dozen places to please your palate in the valley and a handful in the rest of the park. Some are good, a few are wonderful, and all are overpriced. Ah, but what price can be put on feasting in the wilderness, in the shadow of granite giants, in one of the most popular places on the planet?

Finding great food outside Yosemite isn't impossible, but it'll take some work. More common are the average restaurants and cafes, where you can grab something in a pinch and again, pay more than it's worth. These places are everywhere, particularly along Calif. 140 and Calif. 41. However, there are some good buys, quirky places, and excellent establishments along each route.

IN THE VALLEY

The Ahwahnee Dining Room

The Ahwahnee Hotel, Yosemite Valley. ☎ **209/372-1489.** Dinner reservations required. Breakfast $6–$15; lunch $9–$13; dinner $10–$25. DC, DISC, MC, V. Daily 7–10:30am, 11:30am–3pm, and 5:30–9pm. Shuttle bus stop no. 4. AMERICAN.

Dining here takes your breath away. Even if you are a died-in-the-wool, down-to-earth, sleep-under-the-stars backpacker, the Ahwahnee Dining Room will not fail to make an impression. This is where the great outdoors meets four-star cuisine. With understated elegance, the cavernous dining room, its candelabra chandeliers hanging from the 34-foot-tall beamed ceiling, seems intimate once you're seated at a table. Don't be fooled—this place seats 450. As for the menu, how about Salmon Ahwahnee, which comes with Dungeness crab with béarnaise sauce and wild rice? Or rack of lamb with rosemary polenta? Grilled stuffed quail? New York steak buried under a trio of mushrooms and served with herb-roasted potatoes? That represents a sliver of the selections offered on various dinner menus, which shift frequently. Don't forget dessert. The crème de bole is to die for. Breakfast includes a mouth-watering selection of omelettes, frittatas, and house specialties, such as a thick apple crepe filled with raspberry puree. Lunch sandwiches range from a portabello mushroom sandwich to pasta salad with tomato and fresh mozzarella. The Ahwahnee also has a tremendous wine list. If you're feeling generous, try the Silver Oak Cabernet. An evening dress code requires men to wear a coat and tie, but the tie is often forgiven.

Curry Cafeteria

Curry Village. No phone. $4–$12. DC, DISC, MC, V. Daily 7–10am and 5:30–8pm. Shuttle bus stop nos. 1, 14, and 15. ECLECTIC CAFETERIA.

Starving? Eat here. Otherwise, go to great lengths to stay away. The food's not bad, but the prices are extreme. While there's something here for everyone—big breakfast, small nibble, you name it—the shell shock of paying $20 for breakfast for two (and meager breakfasts they were) requires advanced preparation. This place is short on atmosphere and long on dollar signs. Yosemite Concession Services, with all its know-how, should be ashamed.

Curry Hamburger Stand

Curry Village. No phone. $3–$4.50. Daily 11am–4pm. Closed in winter. Shuttle bus stop nos. 1, 14, and 15. SANDWICHES.

Your basic burger joint. This burger stand also offers chicken sandwiches and outdoor seating. It's a quick place for a quick bite. Try an order of fries; they're huge.

Curry Village Pizza Patio

Curry Village, Yosemite Valley. No phone. $8–$14. DC, DISC, MC, V. Mon–Fri 5–9pm; Sat–Sun noon–9pm. Shuttle bus stop nos. 1, 14, and 15. PIZZA.

Need to watch ESPN? This is the place, but you may have to wait in line. The alternative to the big-screen room is the scenic outdoors with its large umbrellas, table service, and Mother Nature, plus or minus a hundred kids. But one of the park's few big screens waits inside, and if you're a sports buff, this is the place to be. The lounge also taps a few brews—nothing special but a mix aimed to please. This is a great place to chill after a long day.

Degnan's Deli

Yosemite Village. No phone. $4–$5. DC, DISC, MC, V. Daily 8am–6pm. Shuttle bus stop nos. 3, 5, and 10. SANDWICHES/LIGHT FARE.

A solid delicatessen with a large selection of sandwiches made to order as well as incidentals. It's half market, half deli. The sandwiches are generous. Sometimes the line to order gets long, but it moves quickly. There's also a selection of premade stuff—salads, sandwiches, desserts—in addition to snacks to stuff in a knapsack before heading out for the day. Degnan's also has a decent beer and wine selection.

Degnan's Pizzeria and Ice Cream

Yosemite Village. No phone. Pizza $7–$13. DC, DISC, MC, V. Daily 11:30am–5:30pm. Shuttle bus stop nos. 3, 5, and 10. PIZZA/ICE CREAM.

Adjacent to Degnan's Deli, this place offers pizza and ice cream. The pizza is definitely not baked in a brick, wood-fired oven, but it's pizza. The ice-cream scoops are small, but it's ice cream.

Degnan's Pasta

Yosemite Village. No phone. Entrees $4–$7. DC, DISC, MC, V. Mon–Fri 11am–2pm and 5–8pm; Sat–Sun 11:30am–8pm. Shuttle bus stop nos. 3, 5, and 10. ITALIAN.

Adjacent to Degnan's Deli and Degnan's Pizzeria and Ice Cream (a gastronomic monopoly in Yosemite?), this is one of the valley's newest editions. Formerly the Loft Restaurant, Degnan's Pasta is a good family place, with a cheery atmosphere.

There's a central fireplace and high-beamed ceilings. The pasta menu features a variety of pasta sauces that frequently rotate. Hot bread sticks, salads, and desserts are made fresh daily.

Garden Terrace

Yosemite Lodge. No phone. $7.75 flat price, $5.50 for children age 5–15, $1.50 for children ages 1–5. DC, MC, V. Daily 11am–9pm. Shuttle bus stop no. 8. SOUP/SALAD/PASTA.

This all-you-can-eat soup, salad, and pasta bar may be the best deal in the valley. It includes 30 selections of homemade soups, fresh salads, and baked goods. Pasta selections vary and can range from spaghetti to manicotti. Carved meats are also available for an additional $3.75. A double-pane skylight and windows allow plenty of sunlight. The restaurant just opened in mid-1997 and has received good reviews from visitors as convenient and a good deal.

Mountain Room Restaurant

Yosemite Lodge. No phone. Entrees $12–$20. DC, DISC, MC, V. Daily 6–9pm. Shuttle bus stop no. 8. AMERICAN.

The best thing about this restaurant is the view. The food's good, too, but the floor-to-ceiling windows overlooking Yosemite Falls are spectacular. The restaurant opened in 1997 and is a worthy alternative to the prices charged at the Ahwahnee. We spent $55 on dinner for two, including wine. The grilled chicken breast was flavorful and moist, as was the Idaho trout, but watch out for a few bones. Meals come with vegetables and bread. Soup or salad is extra. There is a children's menu, entrees for vegetarians, and an amazing dessert tray. The Mountain also has a good wine list.

Village Grill

Yosemite Village. No phone. Burgers and sandwiches $3–$4.50. Daily 7:30am–4pm (summer only). Shuttle bus stop nos. 3, 5, and 10. SANDWICHES.

This is a no-frills burger joint. The Village Grill also offers chicken sandwiches and outdoor seating. It's a good place for a quick bite.

Yosemite Lodge Cafeteria

Yosemite Lodge. No phone. Entrees $4–$12. DC, DISC, MC, V. Daily 6:30–10am, 11:30am–2pm, and 5–8:30pm. Shuttle bus stop no. 8. ECLECTIC CAFETERIA.

Breakfast, lunch, and dinner, all thoroughly mediocre. This cafeteria is convenient, but the prices are high—though that don't seem to bother the hundreds of people who eat here every day. On the plus side, there's enough room here to accommodate a family, and kids love the place.

ELSEWHERE IN THE PARK

Tuolumne Meadows Lodge

Tuolumne Meadows, Calif. 120. ☎ **209/372-8413.** Reservations required for dinner. Breakfast $2–$6; dinner $4–$16. DC, DISC, MC, V. 7–9am and 6–8pm. AMERICAN.

One of the two restaurants in Yosemite's high country, the lodge offers something for everyone. The breakfast menu offers eggs, pancakes, fruit, and granola. The Meadow Scramble is a mouthful of eggs, ham, and veggies served with potatoes and toast. Lighter fare is also available. Granola, yogurt, and oatmeal are staples. Dinners always include a beef, chicken, fish, pasta, and vegetarian specialty, all of which change frequently. The quality can swing, but the prime rib and New York steak are consistently edible. There's also a children's menu.

Wawona Hotel Dining Room

Wawona, Calif. 41, Wawona. ☎ **209/375-1425.** Breakfast and lunch $4–$7; dinner $12–$20. DC, DISC, MC, V. Daily 7:30–10am, noon–1:30pm, and 5:30–8:30pm; Sun brunch 7:30am–1:30pm. AMERICAN.

The Wawona Dining Room mirrors the hotel's ambience—wide open, lots of windows, and sunlight. And the fare is great. For breakfast choose from a variety of items, including the Par Three, a combo of French toast or pancakes, eggs, and bacon or sausage—just what you need before hitting the golf course. Lunch is a buffet that changes seasonally. Dinner is delectable. In addition to some amazing entrees, such as roast duckling with cranberry orange glaze, grilled polenta, and Indian Tom's South Fork Trout, there are some delicious appetizers, particularly the stuffed mushroom caps, grilled artichokes, and gulf shrimp cocktail.

White Wolf Lodge

White Wolf, Calif. 120. ☎ **209/372-8416.** Reservations required for dinner. Breakfast $4–$7; dinner $10–$17. DC, DISC, MC, V. Daily 7–9am and 6–8:30pm. AMERICAN.

For breakfast there's a choice of eggs, pancakes, omelettes, or biscuits and gravy. Dinner always includes a beef, chicken, fish, pasta, and a vegetarian dish. The actual menu items vary. The portions are large, the staff is wonderful and enthusiastic, but alas, the food is mediocre.

OUTSIDE THE PARK

The Branding Iron

640 W. 16th St., Merced. ☎ **209/722-1822.** Reservations suggested. Entrees $13–$20. AE, MC, V. Mon–Fri 11:30am–2pm and 5:30–9pm; Sat–Sun 5:30–9pm. STEAK/SEAFOOD.

Merced's most popular steak house, The Branding Iron is in the heart of town, beyond big, green awnings. The prime rib is a house favorite, but the rest of the menu gets rave reviews as well. Entrees come with soup, salad, vegetables, and potatoes.

Castillo's Mexican Food

4995 5th St., Mariposa. ☎ **209/742-4413.** Reservations recommended in summer. Entrees $8–$15. MC, V. Daily 11am–9pm. From eastbound Calif. 140, turn right on 5th St. Drive 1 block. The restaurant is on your right. MEXICAN.

Established in 1955, this cheerful, cozy cantina serves breakfast, lunch, and dinner all day. The food is good and portions are plentiful. Entrees come with salad, rice, and beans, and can also be ordered à la carte. The house specialty, the Tostada Compuesta, fills a hungry belly. A children's menu is available. The service is great. Chips, salsa, and guacamole arrived before we'd removed our coats.

Charles Street Dinner House

5043 Calif. 140, Mariposa. ☎ **209/966-2366.** Reservations recommended in summer. Entrees $15–$50. AE, DISC, MC, V. Tues–Sat 5–9pm. Closed Jan. STEAK/SEAFOOD.

The owner here likes to describe this place as "gourmet." Let's just say it's a hearty place with hearty (if sometimes mediocre) food, and leave it at that. Whatever it is, the Charles Street Dinner House is straight out of the Old West. The huge wagon wheel in the front window makes that clear. Inside is a kitschy compilation of family photos and plastic flowers. The menu covers everything American food is supposed to be, in an attempt to appeal to international travelers. There is a wide selection of steak and seafood dishes, plus nightly specials. All entrees come with soup, salad, and bread. The New York steak was unimpressive and the Scallone—the chef's concoction of abalone and scallops—lacked flavor. At an average of $20 a meal, it seems customers deserve a little more. It didn't help that the selection of wines and beers was weak. The service is quite good, however.

Hotel Charlotte

18736 Calif. 120, Groveland. ☎ **800/961-7799** or 209/962-7872. Reservations suggested in summer. Entrees $11–$16. AE, MC, V. Summer daily 6–10pm; winter 5–9pm. AMERICAN.

Casual dining is offered in the small dining room of this quaint hotel. The menu includes mostly meat and fish dishes. Daily specials range from halibut with lemon to barbecue baby-back ribs. Vegetarians can chose from pasta primavera or stir-fry. All meals include soup, salad, veggies, potato or rice, and bread. There is also a full bar and a healthy wine list.

The Groveland Hotel's Victorian Room

18767 Calif. 120, Groveland. ☎ **800/273-3314** or 209/962-4000; fax 209/962-6674. Reservations suggested. Entrees $13–$20. AE, DC, DISC, MC, V. Summer daily 6–11pm; winter 6–8:30pm. CALIFORNIA CUISINE.

With a unique combination of four-star food and a one-star dress code, this restaurant offers casual dining at its finest. The menu has something for everyone and is constantly changing to reflect what's fresh and in season. Your choices may include a sumptuous rack of lamb marinated in rosemary and garlic, salmon with fresh cucumber and dill, chicken breast with fresh fruit salsa, and more. The menu usually has a fresh seafood and pasta special as well as an innkeeper's special. All entrees are served with soup or salad and fresh, warm bread. There's an adjacent bar and what has to be one of the most extensive wine lists in the Sierra. That may not be saying much, but this one is solid and reflects innkeepers Peggy and Grover Mosely's attention to detail. The restaurant is wheelchair accessible. The Groveland Hotel is also an excellent place to stay the night.

The Iron Door Saloon and Grill

Calif. 120, Groveland. ☎ **209/962-6244.** Entrees $4–$14. DISC, MC, V. Daily 11am–9pm. BURGERS.

You'll miss this place if you blink. Groveland is about 3 blocks long, and this is the best watering hole in town. It's a funky, fun, comfortable place to hang out for a few hours if you're sick of traffic or lines. The saloon and grill are in adjacent rooms. The bar is stocked with history, from the hunting trophies on the walls to the dollar bills pinned to the ceiling (go ahead, ask). Kids are welcome, so long as they steer clear of the bar. The food is strictly burgers, fries, and shakes, and it's all good. There are 27 burger variations to chose from, including buffalo meat and veggie tofu. There are also kids' offerings and salads. The milkshakes are dreamy. You'll hear live music most Fridays and Saturdays. Watch out for Thursday night—the family karaoke night that for some unknown reasons compels hoards of teens to take to the stage and belt out tunes from the 1970s and '80s (think *Saturday Night Fever*).

Lenny's

1052 W. Main St., Merced. ☎ **209/722-0350.** Entrees $10–$16. AE, MC, V. Mon–Fri 7am–9:30pm, Sat 7am–10pm, Sun 9am–9pm. ITALIAN.

A popular Merced restaurant that serves old world favorites. Recipes on the menu here have been passed down for generations, but the owner has added a few American twists of his own. The lunch buffet, loaded with pastas and at least 15 other dishes, seems the best bargain in town. Dinners are more elaborate, with all sauces and sausages made on the premises. Lenny's also serves 150 kinds of beer and has an espresso bar.

Meadows Ranch Cafe

5024 Calif. 140, Mariposa. ☎ **209/966-4242.** Reservations recommended on summer weekends. Breakfast $3–$6; lunch $4–$6; dinner $6–$16; pizza $7.95. MC, V. Mon–Sat 7am–10pm in summer, 7am–9pm in winter; Sun 9am–noon. AMERICAN.

A great place for a quick bite or a full meal. The food is wholesome and fresh and the coffee is great. Breakfasts include a variety of egg dishes, omelettes, and breakfast burritos—a toss of eggs, meat, veggies, and cheese rolled in a warm tortilla. Lunch includes a selection of more than two dozen sandwiches on a variety of breads. For dinner, you can choose from pizzas, pasta, and a few grilled items, including grilled lemon herb chicken breast and barbecued beef. The owners recently began a much-anticipated Sunday brunch. The 100-year-old dining room is adjacent to the cafe's new brew pub, where patrons can watch the brewing process.

PJ's Cafe and Pizzeria

18986 Calif. 120, Groveland. ☎ **209/ 962-7501.** Entrees $3–$7; pizza $5–$15. No credit cards. Daily 7am–8pm. PIZZA/LIGHT FARE.

Best known as a pizzeria and burger house, PJ's serves a hearty breakfast with an eye toward helping all of us lower our fat and cholesterol intake. That being said, you can still order bacon and eggs without getting the evil eye. Breakfast comes with potatoes and toast. All meat and egg dishes use a special low-cholesterol oil. PJ's also uses only lean ground chuck in its chili, taco meat, and meat sauces, which are available for lunch and dinner. The pizzas are interesting, ranging from a create-your-own to the yummy pesto-chicken-artichoke-heart-tomato combination.

Picnic & Camping Supplies

If you've forgotten something, chances are you'll be able to get it in the valley. But elsewhere in the park it's tough to find equipment. The same goes for gateway cities, which have little more than mom-and-pop stores. The best place to get supplies in the valley is the **Yosemite Village Store,** which has food as well as backpacking and camping equipment. The **Yosemite Lodge Gift Shop** and **Curry Village General Store** also stock some supplies. The **Mountaineering Shop** at Curry Village sells clothing and equipment for day hikes as well as back-country excursions. The staff here is incredibly helpful and surprise, the prices seem pretty competitive with what's available on the outside. A small selection of necessities can be bought at White Wolf and Tuolumne Lodge.

39

ZION NATIONAL PARK

by Don and Barbara Laine

IT'S NOT HARD TO CONJURE UP A SINGLE DEFINING IMAGE OF MOST national parks, but Zion, a collage of images and secrets, is impossible to pin down. Zion National Park is not simply the towering Great White Throne, the deep Narrows Canyon, or all the cascading waterfalls and emerald green pools. There's an entire smorgasbord of experiences and sights here, from massive stone sculptures and monuments to lush forests and rushing rivers.

Today, 150 years after the Mormon settler Isaac Behunin named his homestead here "Little Zion," the park still casts a spell over you as you gaze upon its sheer multicolored walls of sandstone, explore its narrow canyons, hunt for hanging gardens of wildflowers, or listen to the roar of the churning, tumbling Virgin River. Take time to walk its trails, visit view points at different times of the day to see the changing light, and let the park work its magic.

Because of its extremes in elevation (from 3,700 feet to almost 9,000 feet) and climate, Zion harbors a vast array of flora and fauna. Wild animals here include pocket gophers, mountain lions, hundreds of birds (including golden eagles), and dozens of snakes. As for plants, about 800 native species have been found: cactus, yucca, and mesquite in the hot, dry desert areas; ponderosa pine trees on the high plateaus; and cottonwoods and box elders along the rivers and streams. Watch for the red claret cup cactus, which has spectacular blooms in the spring, and for wildflowers such as the manzanita, with its tiny pink blossoms, and the bright red hummingbird trumpet, sometimes called the "Zion Lily." And don't miss the hanging gardens of plant life clinging to the sides of the sandstone cliffs.

Zion National Park is many things to many people: a day hike down a narrow canyon, a rugged climb up the face of a massive stone monument, or the quiet appreciation of the red glow of sunset over majestic peaks. To some degree, each of these experiences is possible only because of rocks—their formation, uplifting, shifting, breaking, and eroding. The most important of Zion's nine rock layers in creating its colorful formations is Navajo sandstone, the thickest rock layer in the park, at up to 2,200 feet. Millions of years ago a shallow sea covered the sand dunes here, causing minerals, including lime from the shells of sea creatures, to glue sand particles together to form sandstone. Later, movements in the earth's crust lifted up the land, draining away the sea but leaving rivers that gradually carved the soft sandstone into the spectacular shapes we see today.

But where do the marvelous colors of the rocks come from? Essentially, from plain old rust. Most of the rocks at Zion are colored by iron, or hematite (iron oxide), either contained in the original stone or carried into the rocks by groundwater. Although iron often creates red and pink hues, seen in much of Zion's sandstone faces, it can also result in blacks, browns, yellows, and even greens. Sometimes the iron seeps into the rock, coloring it through, but often it just stains the surface in vertical streaks. Rocks are also colored by bacteria that live on their surfaces. The bacteria ingest dust and expel iron, manganese, and other minerals, which stick to the rock and produce a shiny black, brown, or reddish surface called desert varnish.

Avoiding the Crowds. The park is open year-round (visitor centers are closed Christmas Day), 24 hours a day, although weather conditions may limit some activities at certain times. If possible, try to avoid the peak summer months of June, July, and August, when temperatures are hot and Zion receives almost half its annual visitors. The quietest months are December, January, and February, but of course it's cold and you may have to contend with some snow and ice.

A good time to visit, if your schedule permits, is in April, May, September, or October, when the weather is still good and the park is less crowded than in the summer.

As usual, once in the park, the best way to avoid crowds is simply to walk away from them, either on the longer and more strenuous hiking trails or into the backcountry. It's sad but true: Most visitors in Zion never bother to venture far from their cars, and their loss can be your gain. You can also avoid the hordes by spending time in Kolob Canyons, in the far northwest section of the park; it's spectacular and receives surprisingly little use, at least in comparison to Zion Canyon.

> **Nothing can exceed the wondrous beauty of Zion . . . in the nobility and beauty of the sculptures there is no comparison.**
>
> **—Geologist Clarence Dutton, 1880**

Just the Facts

GETTING THERE & GATEWAYS

Zion National Park is located in the southwestern corner of Utah, 83 miles southwest of Bryce Canyon National Park and 120 miles northwest of the north rim of Grand Canyon National Park in northern Arizona. It's 309 miles south of Salt Lake City, 42 miles northwest of Kanab, and 158 miles northeast of Las Vegas, Nevada. It's composed of two parts: Zion Canyon, the main section of the park, and the less visited Kolob Canyons, in the park's northwest corner. The closest towns with airport service are St. George (46 miles southeast of the park), and Cedar City (60 miles north).

The easiest way to get to the park is to approach from the west on I-15, which runs north to Salt Lake City and southwest through Arizona to Nevada. From I-15, go east on Utah 9 if approaching from the south, or go south on Utah 17 and then east on Utah 9 if approaching from the north; Utah 9 then continues east to the park's South Entrance. The western approach is the easiest route into the park—it's more direct, avoids possible delays at the Zion–Mt. Carmel Tunnel, and delivers you to Springdale, just outside the park's South Entrance, where most of the area's lodging and restaurants are located.

The Kolob Canyons section, in the park's northwest corner, is reached on the short Kolob Canyons Road off I-15, Exit 40.

Tips from a Ranger

"Overpowering, but also intimate" is how backcountry ranger Dave Rachlis sees Zion National Park. "These are some of the highest vertical rock walls that some people will ever see." Rachlis explains that the Navajo sandstone that forms Zion's walls is one of the thickest sedimentary formations in the world, at 2,200 feet, which can be seen in the West Temple just behind the visitor center.

Rachlis says that one of the best aspects of the park, from the visitor's point of view, is its trail system, mainly constructed in the 1920s and 1930s. "The park has a sense of grandeur, but then it also has access—you can go up the West Rim Trail or you can go up the East Rim Trail, and you can get into these narrow canyons, and really experience the park pretty easily."

Most visitors to Zion, according to Rachlis, stay only a short time and see only a small part of the park—what's visible from the view points—but he recommends that visitors stay at least a full day, preferably more. "In two or three days you can see most of the major regions of the park and get a chance to get out on the trails a bit for day hikes," he says.

Hikers should keep in mind that they can see the park from two perspectives. "You need to decide what experience you want—to climb to a high plateau and gaze down into the canyons; or to descend into a canyon and look up. I think the West Rim Trail is probably our most scenic trail in terms of getting you up onto the plateau where you can look down into the canyons." He also recommends the La Verkin Creek Trail, which leads to Kolob Arch, believed to be the world's largest freestanding arch. "This trail is very intimate, very colorful—the rock is a little more orange to red than it is in the main canyon. It's just a really magnificent area."

A hike through the Narrows is "the ultimate slot canyon experience," according to Rachlis. "You're following a river drainage, wading or swimming in spots. In summer, it's one of the cooler areas of the park." He adds, "One of the unique aspects of the Narrows is that the river runs year-round."

One mistake that some park visitors make, Rachlis says, is to downplay the dangers of the easy and moderate hiking trails, where most injuries occur. He says that people understand the hazards on difficult trails such as Angels Landing, where you're inching along a knife-edge ridge; but that you also need to be careful on trails with less-obvious dangers. "Sandstone is slippery, and a 20-foot fall can kill you as easily as a 1,000-foot fall," he says.

As for when to visit, Rachlis says the trails can be hot in summer, so the best time for hiking is probably spring and fall—from April through June and from September through November. The park is also less crowded at those times. But he adds that the park has unpredictable weather, so it's best to call to check on current conditions before showing up.

The eastern approach to the park is less direct but far more beautiful. From either the south or the north take U.S. 89 to Utah 9 at Mount Carmel, then go east on Utah 9 for a spectacularly scenic 24-mile drive. However, be aware that this route into the park drops over 2,500 feet in elevation, passes through the mile-long Zion–Mount Carmel Tunnel, and winds down six steep switchbacks.

Oversized vehicles are charged $10 to use the tunnel (see "Special Regulations & Warnings," below).

GETTING INFORMATION BEFORE YOUR TRIP

For advance information on the park, including hiking trails, camping, and lodging, contact the **Superintendent, Zion National Park,** Springdale, UT 84767-1099 (☎ **435/772-3256**). It's best to write at least a month before your planned visit, and specify what type of information you need. Officials ask that those needing advance information write instead of call, leaving the phone lines open for those in or near the park needing current and changeable information such as hiking trail conditions and closures. The park's Web site is **www.nps.gov/zion**.

You can purchase books, maps, and videos from the nonprofit **Zion Natural History Association,** Zion National Park, Springdale, UT 84767 (☎ **800/635-3959** or 435/772-3264). Some publications are available in foreign languages, and videos can be purchased in VHS or PAL formats. Major credit cards are accepted. Becoming a member of the association ($15 single or $25 family annually) gets you a 20% discount on purchases. See "Useful Publications," below.

VISITOR CENTERS

The park currently has two visitor centers. The more comprehensive **Zion Canyon Visitor Center** (☎ **435/772-3256**), near the South Entrance to the park, has an orientation video program and a museum with exhibits on the geology and history of the area. Rangers here can answer questions and provide backcountry permits. You can also buy books, maps, videos, postcards, and posters, and pick up free brochures. The smaller **Kolob Canyons Visitor Center** (☎ **435/586-9548**), in the northwest corner of the park off I-15, provides information, permits, books, and maps. Plans are also underway for construction of another visitor center, to be located at the edge of **Watchman Campground,** expected to open by 2000.

ENTRANCE & CAMPING FEES

Entry into the park (for up to 7 days) costs $10 per private vehicle or $5 per motorcycle, bicycle, or pedestrian. Frequent visitors might prefer the $20 annual pass. On the way there, oversized vehicles approaching from the east (see "Special Regulations & Warnings," below) are charged $10 for use of the Zion–Mount Carmel Tunnel on the east side of the park.

Permits required for overnight trips into the backcountry can be picked up at the visitor centers for $5 per person per night. Camping in either of the park's two campgrounds costs $10 per night.

SPECIAL REGULATIONS & WARNINGS

The mile-long Zion–Mount Carmel Tunnel was not built for oversized vehicles. The tunnel is too narrow for two-way traffic involving anything larger than passenger cars and pickup trucks. Therefore, any vehicle over 7 feet, 10 inches wide (including mirrors) or 11 feet, 4 inches tall (including luggage racks) can only pass by driving down the center of the tunnel after all other traffic has been stopped. Large vehicles can accomplish this feat only from 8am to 8pm daily from March to October; during other months arrangements can be made at park entrances or by calling park headquarters (☎ **435/772-3256**). The charge is $10, good for two trips through the tunnel during a 7-day period.

All vehicles over 13 feet, 1 inch tall and certain other particularly large vehicles are prohibited from driving anywhere on the park road between the East Entrance and Zion Canyon. Furthermore, from March to October, all vehicles over 21 feet long are prohibited from parking at the Temple of Sinawava

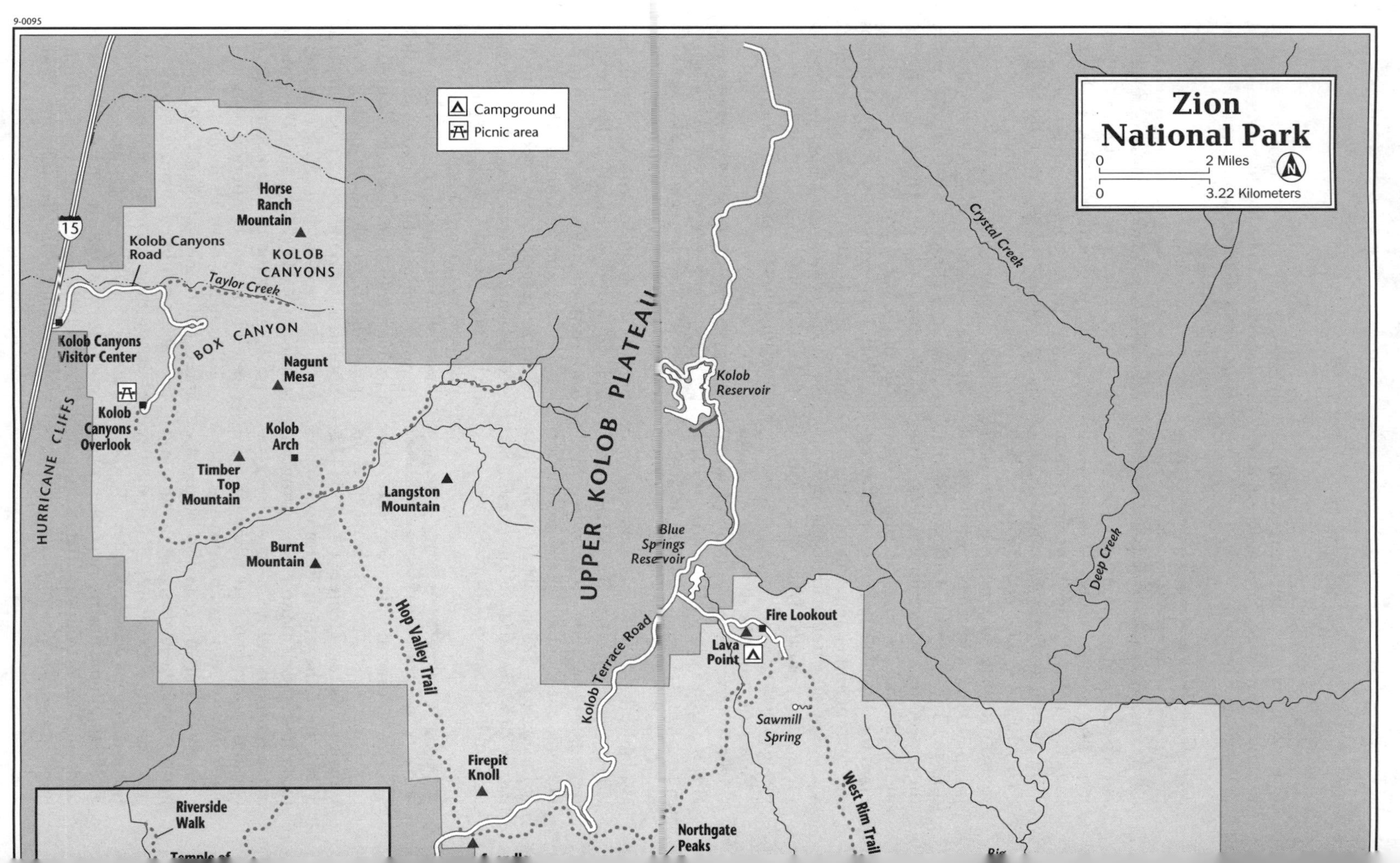
9-0095
Zion
National Park
0
2 Miles
0
3.22 Kilometers
Campground
Picnic area
15
Kolob Canyons Road
Horse Ranch Mountain
KOLOB CANYONS
Taylor Creek
BOX CANYON
Kolob Canyons Visitor Center
Nagunt Mesa
Kolob Canyons Overlook
Kolob Arch
HURRICANE CLIFFS
Timber Top Mountain
Langston Mountain
Burnt Mountain
Hop Valley Trail
Firepit Knoll
Riverside Walk
UPPER KOLOB PLATEAU
Kolob Reservoir
Blue Springs Reservoir
Kolob Terrace Road
Fire Lookout
Lava Point
Sawmill Spring
Northgate Peaks
West Rim Trail
Crystal Creek
Deep Creek

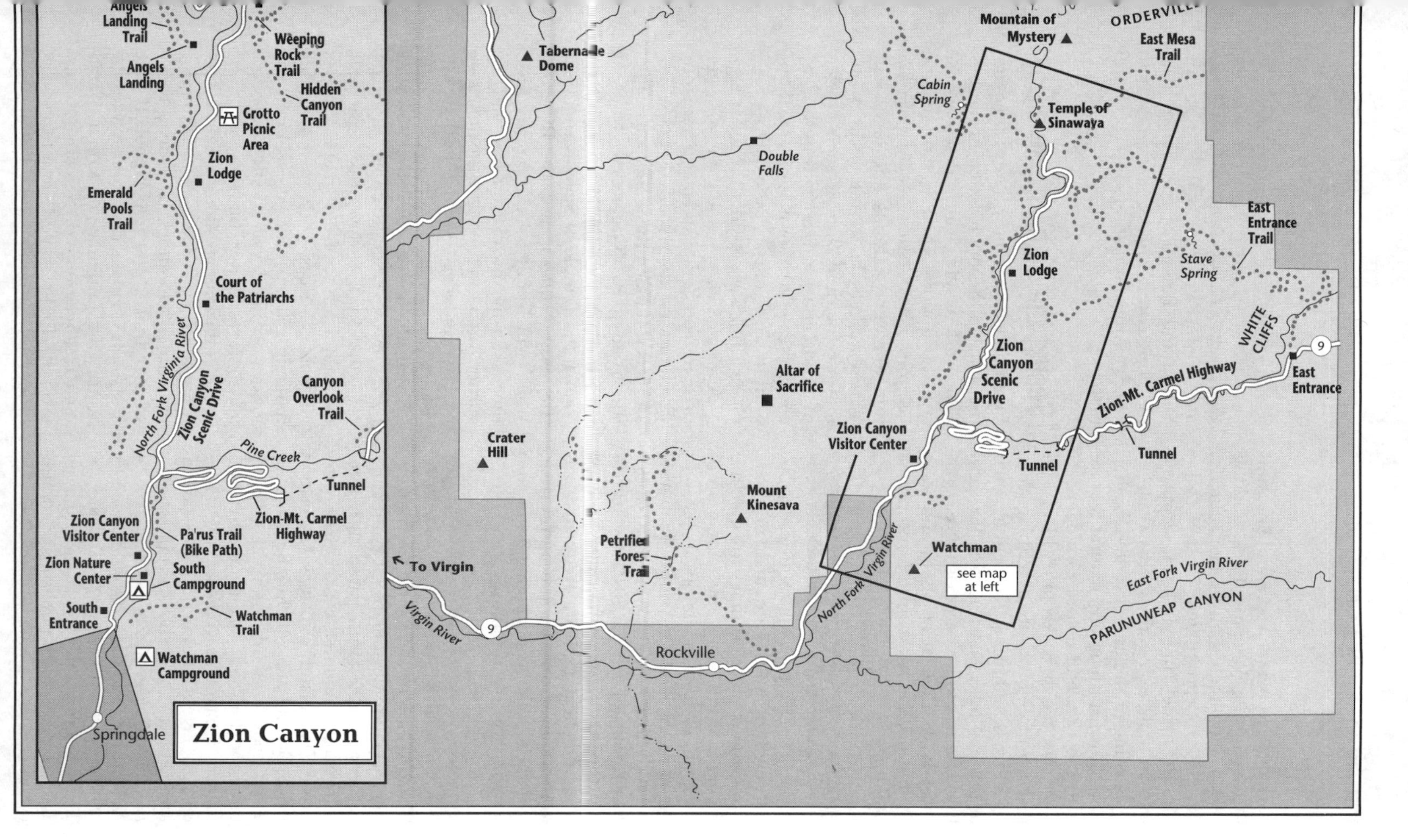

Zion Canyon
Angels Landing Trail
Angels Landing
Weeping Rock Trail
Hidden Canyon Trail
Grotto Picnic Area
Zion Lodge
Emerald Pools Trail
Court of the Patriarchs
North Fork Virginia River
Zion Canyon Scenic Drive
Canyon Overlook Trail
Pine Creek
Tunnel
Zion-Mt. Carmel Highway
Zion Canyon Visitor Center
Pa'rus Trail (Bike Path)
Zion Nature Center
South Campground
South Entrance
Watchman Trail
Watchman Campground
Springdale
Tabernacle Dome
Double Falls
Crater Hill
To Virgin
Virgin River
9
Rockville
Petrified Forest Trail
Mount Kinesava
Altar of Sacrifice
Mountain of Mystery
ORDERVILLE
East Mesa Trail
Cabin Spring
Temple of Sinawava
Zion Lodge
Zion Canyon Scenic Drive
Zion Canyon Visitor Center
Tunnel
Watchman
see map at left
North Fork Virgin River
Stave Spring
East Entrance Trail
WHITE CLIFFS
East Entrance
Zion-Mt. Carmel Highway
East Fork Virgin River
PARUNUWEAP CANYON

Parking Area between 9am and 5pm and from entering Weeping Rock Parking Area at any time. As for smaller vehicles, bicycles are prohibited in the Zion–Mount Carmel Tunnel, the backcountry, and on trails, except the Pa'rus Trail.

Feeding or molesting wildlife, vandalism, and disturbing any natural feature of the park are of course forbidden. At the visitor center, backcountry hikers can pick up a free brochure describing close to 20 trails and listing regulations, such as prohibitions against lighting fires and traveling in groups of 12 or more. Dogs must be leashed at all times and away from trails, the backcountry, and public buildings.

SEASONS & CLIMATE

Zion experiences all four seasons, although the winters are mild and rarely bring snow. The best times to come are spring and fall, when the temperatures range from lows in the 40s to pleasant highs in the 80s. Remember that summer daytime highs often soar above 100°F, with lows in the 70s. Do your hiking then in the early morning to avoid both the heat and the frequent afternoon thunderstorms in July and August, which can change a babbling brook into a raging torrent in minutes.

USEFUL PUBLICATIONS

The Zion Park Guide, a small free newspaper-format guide available at both visitor centers, is packed with extremely helpful information about the park. The nonprofit **Zion Natural History Association** (see "Getting Information Before Your Trip," above) published several excellent books, including the colorful and informative 55-page *Zion National Park, Towers of Stone,* by J. L. Crawford; the easy-to-understand 22-page booklet *An Introduction to the Geology of Zion National Park,* by Al Warneke; and *Exploring the Backcountry of Zion National Park: Off-trail Routes,* by Thomas Brereton and James Dunaway. The association also publishes a very useful pocket-size hiking guide, *Zion: The Trails,* compiled by Bob Lineback. For detailed trail descriptions, try *Hiking Zion & Bryce Canyon National Parks* (Helena, Mont.: Falcon Press, 1997) by Erik Molvar and Tamara Martin. Those planning backcountry hikes should purchase a copy of the association's topographical map.

Seeing the Highlights in a Day

If you only have a short time at the park, first make a thorough review of the free **Zion Park Guide,** which describes the available options. Then head to the **Zion Canyon Visitor Center** to see the orientation video and exhibits, and finally talk with a ranger about your abilities and interests. Because Zion has such a variety of landscapes and activities, you can easily create your own itinerary. If you want to see as much of the park as possible in 1 full day, consider the following:

After a quick stop at the visitor center, drive to Zion Lodge and take a **tram tour,** which hits the major roadside view points and lets you watch the scenery instead of the road (see "Organized Tours & Ranger Programs," below). Get off the tram at the **Temple of Sinawava** and take the easy 2-mile round-trip **Riverside Walk,** which follows the Virgin River through a narrow canyon past hanging gardens. You can then take the next tram back to the lodge for lunch in the lodge restaurant.

Near the lodge you'll find the trailhead for the **Emerald Pools.** Especially pleasant on hot days, this easy walk through a forest of oak, maple, fir, and cottonwood trees leads to a waterfall, hanging garden, and the shimmering lower pool. This walk should take about an hour, round-trip, but those with a bit more ambition may want to add another hour and mile to the loop by taking the moderately strenuous hike on a rocky, steeper trail to the **upper pool.** If time and energy remain, drive back toward the South Park Entrance and stop at **Watchman Trailhead** (east of Watchman Campground), for its 2-mile, 2-hour round-trip, moderately strenuous hike leading to a plateau with beautiful views of several rock formations and the town of Springdale. In the evening, try to take in the campground amphitheater program.

Exploring the Park by Car

If you enter the park from the east, along the steep 13-mile **Zion–Mount Carmel Highway,** you'll pass Checkerboard Mesa, a massive sandstone rock formation covered with horizontal and vertical lines that make it look like a huge fishing net. Once in the park, you'll view a fairyland of fantastically shaped rocks of red, orange, tan, and white, as well as the Great Arch of Zion, carved high in a stone cliff.

Once inside, almost all Zion National Park visitors guide their cars along the 14-mile round-trip **Zion Canyon Scenic Drive,** which starts at the Zion Canyon Visitor Center and stops at view points and trailheads. The drive is both beautiful and convenient, letting visitors see what they want at their own pace. But it won't be around forever. Traffic congestion, damage to roadside vegetation, noise, pollution, and parking hassles are all making the park experience less and less pleasant, especially during the busy summer months. Park officials expect to replace the scenic drive with a mandatory shuttle-bus service operating in Zion Canyon by 2000. In the meantime, motorists can still drive themselves, *but be forewarned:* Especially in the summer, traffic is awful, and the parking situation seems more appropriate to New York or Los Angeles than a national park. In summer, save yourself the headache: leave your car at the Zion Lodge parking lot, and take the open-air **tram** (see "Organized Tours & Ranger Programs," below).

A better choice for a self-guided scenic drive is in the northwest corner of the park. The **Kolob Canyons Road** (about 45 minutes from Zion Canyon Visitor Center at I-15 Exit 40) runs 5 miles among spectacular red and orange rocks, ending at a high vista. There and back, the trip takes about 45 minutes, including stops at numbered view points. Be sure to get a copy of the *Kolob Canyons Road Guide* at the Kolob Visitor Center. Here's what you'll pass along the way:

Leaving **Kolob Canyons Visitor Center,** you'll drive along the Hurricane Fault to **Hurricane Cliffs,** a series of tall, gray limestone cliffs, and then onward to **Taylor Creek,** where a pinyon-juniper forest clings to life on the rocky hillside. Your next stop is **Horse Ranch Mountain,** which, at 8,726 feet, is the national park's highest point. Then after a series of colorful rock layers, where you might be lucky enough to spot a golden eagle, you come to **Box Canyon,** along the south fork of Taylor Creek, with sheer rock walls soaring over 1,500 feet high.

Then you continue to a canyon exposing a rock wall that likely began as a sand dune before being covered by an early sea. Next stop is a side canyon, with large, arched alcoves boasting delicate curved ceilings. Then head on to a view of **Timber Top Mountain,** which at its base is a sagebrush-blanketed desert, but at its peak is covered with stately fir and ponderosa pine. You might see mule deer on the brushy hillsides, especially just after sunrise or before sunset between October and March. From there continue to **Rockfall Overlook,** to see the large scar on the mountainside where a 1,000-foot chunk of stone crashed down in July 1983, the victim of erosion. And finally, stop along the way to examine the canyon walls themselves, colored orange-red by iron oxide and striped black by mineral-laden water running down the cliff faces.

Organized Tours & Ranger Programs

An excellent introduction to the park is the **tram tour,** which starts at Zion Lodge and takes you to all the major roadside view points along the Zion Canyon Scenic Drive. The 1-hour ride goes from the lodge to the Temple of Sinawava and back and includes an informative and entertaining commentary by the tram driver, who points out prominent formations, historic sites, and other things you might have missed on your own, such as daring climbers scaling the seemingly sheer rock walls. There are several stops where passengers can get off for better views or connect with trailheads; afterwards, they can return to the stop to catch another tram going back. Buy your tram tickets in the lodge at a charge of $3 for adults and $2 for children under 12. The tram operates on the hour from 10am to 4pm daily from April to October. Tickets are good for round-trip journeys and permit you to get off at trailheads or view points and complete the trip on later trams.

Park rangers present a variety of free programs and activities. **Amphitheater programs,** which sometimes include a slide show, take place most evenings at campground amphitheaters. Topics vary, but could include the animals or plants of the park, geology, humans' role in the park, or something more unique to Zion, such as its slot canyons. Rangers also give short **talks** on similar subjects several times daily at the Zion Canyon Visitor Center and other locations. **Ranger-guided hikes and walks,** which may require reservations, might take you to little-visited areas of the park, or on a trek to see wildflowers, or out at night for a hike under the full moon. Schedules of the various activities are posted on bulletin boards at the visitor centers and campgrounds.

Getting a Bird's-eye View of the Park. **Scenic Airlines** (☎ **800/634-6801**) offers combination air tours over Bryce Canyon and Zion national parks, plus the North Rim of the Grand Canyon. Tours operate year-round, with prices starting at $275 for adults and $225 for children.

Historic & Man-Made Attractions

There are no major historic sites in Zion National Park, but there is some evidence of the early peoples who inhabited the area. Lucky hikers with sharp eyes may see potsherds, pieces of ancient stone tools, rock art, and other archaeological objects. Park officials ask that you do not touch these artifacts (skin oils can damage them), but report their location to rangers.

Day Hikes

Zion offers a wide variety of hiking trails, ranging from easy half-hour walks on paved paths to grueling overnight hikes over rocky terrain. Several free brochures on hiking trails are available at the visitor centers, and the **Zion Natural History Association** publishes several good booklets describing established trails and off-trail routes (see "Useful Publications," earlier in this chapter). Hikers with a fear of heights should be especially careful when choosing trails; many include steep, dizzying, and potentially fatal drop-offs. Water found in streams in the park is not safe to drink. Smoking is prohibited on all trails.

Guided hikes in the park and nearby areas are offered by **Bike Zion,** 1458 Zion Park Blvd., Springdale (☎ **800/4-SLIKROK** or 435/772-3929). Hikers can choose anything from a 2½-hour hike for $35 to multiday backpacking trips, including rugged excursions through slot canyons with a qualified rappelling instructor. The company also has a hiker and backpacker shuttle service.

SHORTER TRAILS

Weeping Rock Trail

0.5 mile RT. Easy. Access: Weeping Rock Parking Lot on the scenic drive.

This is among the park's shortest and easiest rambles. A self-guiding nature trail, it leads to a rock alcove with a spring and hanging gardens of ferns and wildflowers. Although paved, the trail is relatively steep (gaining 98 feet) and slippery, and not suitable for wheelchairs.

Canyon Overlook

1 mile RT. Moderate. Access: East side of Zion–Mt. Carmel Tunnel.

This self-guided trail takes you to an overlook with a magnificent view of lower Zion Canyon and Pine Creek Canyon. There are some long drop-offs, but the fences will reassure nervous walkers. Trail guides are available at the visitor center and at the trailhead.

Emerald Pools Trails

1.2–2.5 miles RT. Easy to moderate. Access: Across from Zion Lodge.

This can be either an easy 1-hour walk or a moderately strenuous 2-hour hike with steep drop-offs, depending on how much you choose to do. A 0.6-mile paved path (suitable for those in wheelchairs, with assistance) leads from the Emerald Pools Parking Area through a forest of oak, maple, fir, and cottonwood, to several waterfalls, a hanging garden, and the picturesque Lower Emerald Pool.

From here, a steeper, rocky trail (not appropriate for wheelchairs) continues 0.25 mile to Middle Emerald Pool, and then climbs another 0.33 mile past cactus, yucca, and juniper to Upper Emerald Pool, with another waterfall. Total elevation gain is 69 feet to Lower Emerald Pool, 150 feet to the middle pool, and 400 feet from the trailhead to Upper Emerald Pool.

Riverside Walk and the Gateway to the Narrows

2 miles RT. Easy. Access: Temple of Sinawava at the end of the scenic drive.

This paved trail follows the Virgin River upstream to the Zion Canyon Narrows, past trailside exhibits and hanging wildflowers in spring and summer. Accessible to those in wheelchairs with some assistance, the trail has an elevation change of only 57 feet. At the Narrows, the pavement ends, and here you have to decide whether to turn around or to continue upstream into the Narrows itself (yes, you will get wet), where the canyon walls are only 24 feet apart and more than 1,000 feet high. Before entering the Narrows you'll want to have checked the weather forecast and discussed your plans with park rangers, since being at the bottom of a very narrow slot canyon is definitely not a place you want to be in a rainstorm, when flash floods are a serious threat. Permits required for longer treks in the Narrows but not for short day hikes (see "The Narrows," below).

Watchman Trail

2 miles RT. Moderate. Access: The service road east of Watchman Campground Registration Station.

This moderately strenuous but relatively short hike gets surprisingly light use, possibly because it can be very hot in the middle of the day. Climbing to a plateau near the base of the Watchman formation, it offers splendid views of lower Zion Canyon, Oak Creek Canyon, the Towers of the Virgin, the West Temple formations, and the town of Springdale. The trail takes about 2 hours to complete and has an elevation gain of 368 feet.

Hidden Canyon Trail

2 miles RT. Moderate. Access: Weeping Rock Parking Lot along the scenic drive.

A particularly scenic hike, this trail climbs 850 feet through a narrow water-carved canyon, ending at the canyon's mouth. Those wanting to extend the hike can go another 0.6 mile to a small natural arch. Hidden Canyon Trail includes long drop-offs, and is not recommended for anyone with a fear of heights.

Pa'rus Trail

3.5 miles RT. Easy. Access: Entrance to South Campground, near the amphitheater parking area.

This easy, paved trail (fully accessible to wheelchairs) follows the Virgin River, providing views of the rock formations in lower Zion Canyon. Unlike other park trails, this one is open to bicycles and leashed pets. The elevation gain is only 50 feet.

LONGER TRAILS

Taylor Creek Trail

5.4 miles RT. Moderate. Access: Kolob Canyons Rd., about 2 miles from Kolob Canyons Visitor Center.

This is a 4-hour hike along the middle fork of Taylor Creek—you might get your feet wet fording the creek. The trail leads past two historic cabins to Double Arch Alcove, with an elevation gain of 450 feet.

Angels Landing Trail

5 miles RT. Difficult. Access: Grotto Picnic Area along the scenic drive.

This 4-hour hike is most certainly not for anyone with even a mild fear of heights. The trail climbs 1,488 feet to a summit that offers spectacular views into Zion Canyon. *But be prepared:* The final half mile follows a narrow, knife-edge trail along a steep ridge, where footing can be slippery even under the best of circumstances. Support chains have been set along parts of the trail.

Hop Valley Trail

13.4 miles RT. Moderate to difficult. Access: Trailhead on Kolob Terrace Rd.

This backcountry trail loses about 1,000 feet as it meanders through sunny fields and past Gambel oak, partly following an old jeep road and then a stream, before taking you to La Verkin Creek. Some hikers connect with the La Verkin Creek/ Kolob Arch Trail to see Kolob Arch.

East Rim Trail

8 miles RT. Difficult. Access: Weeping Rock Parking Lot along the scenic drive.

This strenuous hike takes all day and climbs over 2,000 feet to Observation Point. But if you can manage it, the incredible views down into the canyon make all the exertion worthwhile. This trail also gives access to other east rim trails: Cable Mountain and Deertrap Mountain.

La Verkin Creek/Kolob Arch Trail

14 miles RT. Difficult. Access: Kolob Canyons Rd. at Lee Pass.

Although there are no drop-offs, this backcountry trail is quite strenuous. Descending almost 700 feet, it follows Timber and La Verkin creeks, ending at Kolob Arch, which, at 310 feet long, just may be the world's largest freestanding arch.

The Narrows

16 miles one way. Moderate. Access: Chamberlain's Ranch (outside the park).

Hiking the Narrows is not hiking a trail at all, but walking or wading along the bottom of the Virgin River, through a spectacular 1,000-foot-deep chasm that, at a mere 21 feet wide, definitely lives up to its name. Passing fanciful sculptured sandstone arches, hanging gardens, and waterfalls, this moderately strenuous hike is recommended for those in good physical condition who are up to fighting sometimes-strong currents. Those who want a taste of the Narrows can walk and wade in from the end of the Riverside Walk (see above), but more than a short trip will involve a long full- or 2-day trek, which involves arranging a shuttle to the starting point at Chamberlain's Ranch and then transportation from the Temple of Sinawava, where you'll leave the canyon.

The Narrows is subject to flash flooding, and can be very treacherous. Park service officials remind hikers that they are responsible for their own safety, and should check on current water conditions and weather forecasts. This hike is *not* recommended when rain is forecast or threatening. Permits ($5) are required for full-day and overnight hikes, and must be purchased at the visitor center the day before your hike.

Exploring the Backcountry

There are numerous backpacking opportunities in the park, and a number of the day hikes discussed above are actually more comfortably done in 2 or more days. In addition to the park's established trails and the famous Narrows, there are a number of off-trail routes for those experienced in using topographical maps—get information at the Backcountry Desk in the Zion Canyon Visitor Center. Backcountry permits ($5 per person per night) are required for all overnight hikes in the park.

West Rim Trail

26.6 miles RT. Difficult. Access: Grotto Picnic Area on the scenic drive.

This trail climbs over 3,500 feet into the high country, with a view point overlooking the Right Fork of North Creek Canyon (at 12.8 miles) and then continuing to Lava Point. There are striking views from most points on the trail.

Especially for Kids

Kids from 6 to 12 years old can join the **Junior Rangers,** participate in a variety of programs, and earn certificates, badges, and patches. Morning and afternoon sessions, each lasting 2½ hours, meet daily from Memorial Day through Labor Day at the Nature Center in the South Campground. There's a one-time fee of $2 per child, and the age range is strictly enforced.

Other Sports & Activities

Biking & Mountain Biking. With one notable exception, bikes are prohibited on all trails, as well as forbidden to travel cross-country within the national park boundaries. This leaves only the park's established roads (except for the Zion–Mount Carmel Tunnel, where bikes are also prohibited), which are often clogged with motor vehicles.

But there's hope. The **Pa'rus Trail,** opened in late 1994, is the first phase of a new transportation plan for Zion National Park. It runs a little under 2 miles along the Virgin River from the entrance to Watchman Campground to the beginning of the Zion Canyon Scenic Drive, crossing the river and several creeks, and providing good views of Watchman, West Temple, the Sentinel, and other lower-canyon formations. The trail is paved, and open to bicyclists, pedestrians, and those with strollers or wheelchairs, but closed to cars, motorcycles, and other motor vehicles. The future looks even brighter: Plans call for allowing only shuttle buses, bicyclists, and hikers on the scenic drive, making the park truly bike-friendly.

Although mountain bikers will find they are generally not welcome on the trails of Zion National Park, just outside the park, mostly on Bureau of Land Management and state-owned property, are numerous rugged Jeep trails that are great for mountain biking, plus more than 70 miles of slickrock cross-country trails and single-track trails. Gooseberry Mesa, above the community of Springdale, is generally considered the best mountain-biking destination in the area, but there are also good trails on nearby Wire and Grafton mesas.

Talk with the knowledgeable staff at **Bike Zion,** 1458 Zion Park Blvd., Springdale (☎ **800/4-SLIKROK** or 435/772-3929), about the best trails for your interests and abilities. This full-service bike shop also offers maps, a full range of bikes and accessories, repairs, shuttle service for you and your bike, and rentals ($23 per day for a 21-speed mountain bike). Bike Zion offers guided mountain-bike trips, starting at $35 for a 2½-hour tour, and a variety of multiday excursions, including some with catered gourmet meals or educational themes.

Horseback Riding. Guided rides in the park are available March through October from **Canyon Trail Rides,** P.O. Box 128, Tropic, UT 84776 (☎ **435/679-8665**), with ticket sales and information at Zion Lodge. A 1-hour ride along the Virgin River costs $12 and a half-day ride on the Sand Beach Trail costs $35. Riders must weigh no more than 220 pounds, and children must be at least 5 years old for the 1-hour ride and 8 years old for the half-day ride. It's best to make reservations.

Rock Climbing. Expert technical rock climbers love the tall sandstone cliffs in Zion Canyon, although rangers warn that much of the rock is loose, or "rotten," and climbing equipment and techniques suitable for granite are often less effective here. Permits (free at this writing) are required for overnight climbs, and because some routes may be closed at times, such as during peregrine falcon nesting from early spring through July, climbers should check at the visitor center before setting out. Less-experienced climbers not yet ready for Zion should try nearby Snow Canyon State Park (see "Nearby National Monuments & State Parks," at the end of this chapter).

Wildlife Viewing & Bird Watching. It's a rare visitor to Zion who doesn't spot a critter of some sort, from mule deer—often seen along roadways and in campgrounds year-round—to the many varieties of lizards seen from spring through fall, including the park's largest lizard, the chuckwalla, which can grow to 20 inches. The ringtail cat, a relative of the raccoon, prowls Zion Canyon at night, and is not above helping itself to your camping supplies. Along the Virgin River you'll see bank beaver, so named because they live in burrows instead of building dams. The park is also home to coyotes, black-tailed jackrabbits, cottontails, chipmunks, several types of squirrels, voles, skunks, porcupines, gophers, and a variety of bats.

The rare peregrine falcon, among the world's fastest birds, sometimes nests in the Weeping Rock area, where you're also likely to see the American dipper, canyon wren, and white-throated swift. Bald eagles sometimes winter in the park, and you might also see golden eagles. Snakes include the poisonous great basin rattlesnake, usually found only below 8,000 feet elevation, as well as nonpoisonous king snakes and gopher snakes. Tarantulas, those large, slow-moving hairy spiders, are often seen in the late summer and fall. Contrary to popular belief, the tarantula's bite is not deadly, although it may be somewhat painful.

Camping

INSIDE THE PARK

The absolute best place to camp is at one of the **national park campgrounds,** if you can find a site. Reservations are not accepted, and the campgrounds often fill by noon in the summer, so get there early in the day to claim a site. Some campers stay at nearby commercial campgrounds their first night in the area, then hurry into the park the next morning, circling like vultures until a site becomes available.

Both of Zion's main campgrounds—**South** and **Watchman**—are located just inside the park's South Entrance. They

Campground	Elev.	Total Sites	RV Hookups	Dump Station	Toilets	Drinking Water
Lava Point	7,900	6	0	No	Yes	No
South	4,000	126	0	Yes	Yes	Yes
Watchman	4,000	231	50+	Yes	Yes	Yes
Mukuntuweep	6,000	150	30	Yes	Yes	Yes
Zion Canyon	4,000	180	180	Yes	Yes	Yes

have paved roads, well-spaced sites, lots of trees, and that national park atmosphere you came here to enjoy. There are rest rooms with flush toilets but no showers, and sites for those with disabilities. Although there are no RV hookups at either national park campground as of this writing, work was underway to install electric hookups in one loop of Watchman Campground. It was expected that there would be at least 50 sites with electric hookups available by summer of 1998; check with park officials on the project's status and fees. **Lava Point,** located on the Kolob Terrace, is somewhat primitive.

NEAR THE PARK

Just outside the park entrances, on both the east and south sides, are commercial campgrounds with hot showers and RV hookups. Keep in mind that the park's visitor center, campgrounds, and most of its developed attractions are closer to the South Entrance than the East.

Mukuntuweep RV Park & Campground, located about 0.25 mile east of the East Entrance to Zion National Park on Utah 9 (P.O. Box 193, Orderville, UT 84758; ☎ **435/648-2154**), has great views of the surrounding rocks. There are some shade trees, grassy tent sites, a fishing pond, a playground, and a game room. Across the street, under the same management, is a store, restaurant (see "Dining," below), curio shop, and gas station. In addition to campsites, there are six log cabins, a hogan, and a teepee, all of which share the campground's bathhouse and cost $25 for two persons.

Just outside the South Entrance to the park is **Zion Canyon Campground,** on Zion Park Boulevard 0.25 mile south of the park's South Entrance, P.O. Box 99, Springdale, UT 84767 (☎ **435/772-3237;** fax 435/772-3844). It has tree-shaded sites and grassy tent areas, and although quite crowded in summer, the campground is clean and well-maintained. On the premises is a store with groceries, souvenirs, and RV supplies, plus a restaurant.

In addition to the two commercial campgrounds discussed here, there is also camping at Cedar Breaks National Monument and Snow Canyon State Park, which are discussed at the end of this chapter in the section "Nearby National Monuments & State Parks."

Accommodations

Room tax is about 10% in Springdale; 9% in the park. Pets are not accepted unless otherwise noted.

INSIDE THE PARK

Zion Lodge

In Zion National Park. ☎ **435/772-3213;** fax 435/772-2001. Information and reservations: AmFac Parks & Resorts, 14001 E. Iliff Ave., Suite 600, Aurora, CO 80014. ☎ 303/29-PARKS; fax 303/338-2045. 121 units. A/C TEL. Motel rm $80–$90 double; suite $113–$120 double; cabin $85–$95 double. AE, DISC, MC, V.

The charming cabins on the forested grounds here offer spectacular views of the park's rock cliffs. Each contains a

Showers	Fire Pits/ Grills	Laundry	Public Phone	Reserve	Fees	Open
No	**Yes**	**No**	**No**	**No**	**Free**	**May–Oct**
No	**Yes**	**No**	**Yes**	**No**	**$10**	**Apr–Sept**
No	**Yes**	**No**	**Yes**	**No**	**$10+**	**Year-round**
Yes	**Yes**	**Yes**	**Yes**	**Yes**	**$14–$18**	**Mar–Oct**
Yes	**Yes**	**Yes**	**Yes**	**Yes**	**$15–$20**	**Year-round**

private porch, a stone (gas-burning) fireplace, two double beds, pine board walls, and log beams. The comfortable motel units are basic, with two queen-size beds and all the usual amenities except televisions. Suites each have one king-size bed, a separate sitting room, and refrigerator. At the gift shop you can get everything from postcards and T-shirts to top-quality silver and turquoise American Indian jewelry. The lodge's restaurant (see "Dining," below) offers wonderful views with its three daily meals.

NEAR THE PARK

The properties listed here are either in Springdale, a village of some 350 people at the park's South Entrance, or between Springdale and the nearby community of Virgin, to the west.

Bumbleberry Inn

97 Bumbleberry Lane, Springdale, UT 84767. ☎ **800/828-1534** or 435/772-3224; fax 435/772-3947. 23 rms. A/C TV TEL. Apr–Oct $54–$59 double; Nov–Mar $49–$54 double. DISC, MC, V.

Set back from the main highway, the Bumbleberry offers large, quiet rooms at a good price. Most rooms have two queen-size beds and tub/shower combinations, although five rooms each have one queen bed and shower only. Prints depicting the area's scenery decorate the walls. There's also indoor racquetball, an arcade, indoor whirlpool tub, heated outdoor pool, and an adjacent restaurant. Pets are sometimes accepted at the discretion of the management, so make sure they behave.

Canyon Ranch Motel

668 Zion Park Blvd. (P.O. Box 175), Springdale, UT 84767. ☎ **435/772-3357;** fax 435/772-3057. 21 units. A/C TV. Mar–Oct $58–$68 double; Nov–Feb $44–$54 double. AE, DISC, MC, V.

Consisting of a series of two- and four-unit cottages set back from the highway, this motel has the look of an old-fashioned auto camp on the outside while providing modern motel rooms inside. Rooms are either new or newly remodeled, and options include one queen- or king-size bed, two queens, or one queen and one double. Some rooms have showers only, while some have shower/tub combinations. Kitchen units are also available. Room 13, with two queen-size beds, offers spectacular views of the Zion National Park rock formations through several large picture windows; views from most other rooms are almost as good. The units surround a lawn with trees and picnic tables, and there is also an outdoor heated swimming pool and whirlpool tub. Pets are accepted at the discretion of the management.

Cliffrose Lodge & Gardens

281 Zion Park Blvd. (P.O. Box 510), Springdale, UT 84767. ☎ **800/243-UTAH** or 435/772-3234; fax 435/772-3900. 30 rms, 6 suites. A/C TV TEL. Summer $88–$145 double. Lower rates in the winter. AE, DISC, MC, V.

With river frontage and 5 acres of lawns, shade trees, and flower gardens, the Cliffrose offers a beautiful setting just outside the entrance to Zion National Park. The modern, well-kept rooms have all the standard motel appointments, with wood furnishings, floral-print bedspreads, and unusually large bathrooms with shower/tub combinations. On the lawns you'll find comfortable seating, including a lawn swing, plus a playground and large outdoor heated pool. Guests have use of a self-service laundry.

Desert Pearl Inn

707 Zion Park Blvd., Springdale, UT 84767. ☎ **888/828-0898** or 435/772-8888; fax 435/772-8889. 61 units. A/C TV TEL. $70–$150 double. AE, DISC, MC, V.

This handsome brand-new property, which opened late in 1997, offers luxurious and comfortable accommodations with beautiful views of the area's scenery. Spacious rooms have either two queen-size beds and a queen sleeper, or one king and a queen sleeper. Units also have comfortable seating, refrigerators, microwave ovens, wet bars, and bidets. The grounds are nicely landscaped. The inn also has a huge outdoor heated pool and whirlpool. Plans call for construction of a restaurant and additional units.

El Rio Lodge in Zion Canyon

995 Zion Park Blvd. (P.O. Box 204), Springdale, UT 84767. ☎ **888/772-3205** or 435/772-3205. 11 rms, including 1 suite. A/C TV. Summer $47–$52 double, $60 suite; lower in winter. AE, DISC, MC, V. Pets accepted with $10 fee.

A mom-and-pop operation built in the early 1960s, El Rio has five rooms upstairs and five downstairs, all with private baths and tub/shower combos. Although small, the rooms are very clean and comfortable, with simple but attractive decor. The upstairs rooms have two double beds and an outdoor walkway and porch affording terrific views of Zion Canyon. The downstairs rooms have one queen bed each, though roll-aways are available. The suite has its own private parking area, refrigerator, extra-large bath, and use of the yard, with great views of the rock walls of Zion Canyon. Although there are no phones in the rooms, a public phone is available outside. There's no pool on premises.

Flanigan's Inn

428 Zion Park Blvd. (P.O. Box 100), Springdale, UT 84767. ☎ **800/765-RSVP** or 435/772-3244; fax 435/772-3396. 39 units. A/C TV TEL. Mid-Mar to Nov $79–$89 double; Dec to mid-Mar $49–$69 double. All rates include continental breakfast buffet. AE, DISC, MC, V.

A mountain lodge atmosphere pervades this very attractive complex of natural wood and rock, set among trees, lawns, and flowers just outside the entrance to Zion National Park. Parts of the inn date from 1947, but all rooms were completely renovated in the early 1990s, and have Southwest decor with wood furnishings and local art. Some units also have whirlpool tubs and bidets, and one room has a fireplace. Flanigan's has its own nature trail leading to a hilltop vista, and a heated outdoor swimming pool. Kitchenettes are available, but if you don't want to cook, the on-site restaurant serves dinner, in addition to a continental breakfast for guests only (see "Dining," below).

Harvest House Bed & Breakfast at Zion

29 Canyon View Dr. (P.O. Box 125), Springdale, UT 84767. ☎ **435/772-3880;** fax 435/772-3327. 4 rms. A/C. $80–$100 double. Rates include full breakfast. DISC, MC, V.

This Utah territorial–style house was built in 1989. It has a cactus garden out front and a garden sitting area in back with a koi (Japanese carp) pond and spectacular views of the national park rock formations. The rooms are furnished with an eclectic mixture of contemporary and wicker items, and decorated with original art and photography. One upstairs room faces west and has grand sunset views, and the other two have private decks facing Zion's impressive rock structures. The suite can accommodate up to five adults. The full, gourmet, yet low-fat, breakfasts are sumptuous, and include fresh baked sweet breads, fresh-squeezed orange juice, granola, fruit, yogurt, and a hot main course that changes daily. Facilities include an outdoor whirlpool. Children under 7 are not permitted.

O'Tooles Bed & Breakfast

980 Zion Park Blvd. (P.O. Box 29), Springdale, UT 84767. ☎ **435/772-3457;** fax 435/772-3324. 5 rms. (2 with shared bath), 1 suite. A/C. Apr–Oct $60–$79 double; suite $125 double plus $15 for each additional person; lower rates off-season. Rates include full breakfast. DISC, MC, V.

This lovely two-story bed and breakfast, built in 1929, is furnished mostly with antiques, many from the families of owners Rick and Michelle O'Toole. On the first floor there are two cheerful rooms, decorated in early-20th-century style. They share a bath (shower only), and each has one double bed and a private sink. Upstairs the large suite takes up the entire floor, and has a vaulted ceiling, a wood-burning stove in the sitting room, and its own kitchen. In addition, the cute Garden Cottage, which was moved here from inside the national park, contains three rooms, two on the main floor and one in the basement. The homemade breakfast generally includes home-baked breads, fresh fruit, and a hot main dish such as an omelette or pancakes. The kitchen is available for guest use for lunch and dinner. Children under 8 are not permitted.

Snow Family Guest Ranch

633 E. Utah 9 (P.O. Box 790190), Virgin, UT 84779. ☎ **800/308-SNOW** or 435/635-2500; fax 435/635-2758. 9 rms. A/C. $85–$150 double; additional person $20. AE, DISC, MC, V.

This delightful horse ranch is nestled in the shadow of Zion National Park on 12 acres of green pastures, all enclosed in white rail fences. The location is peaceful and quiet, just 12 miles west of the South Entrance to Zion and about 30 miles east of St. George. Inside, the rooms have handsome log furnishings, and either one or two queen-size beds, a king, or two twins; most also feature comfortable window seats. Views look out across the ranch to the red rock mesas and canyons beyond. Guests can fill up on the full breakfast served each morning, and then snack on light refreshments offered in the afternoon. There is also a living room with piano, a separate TV room with a big-screen TV, and a swimming pool, hot tub, gazebo, and a pond. Guided scenic trail rides are offered for an additional charge.

Zion Park Inn and Conference Centre

1215 Zion Park Blvd., Springdale, UT 84767. ☎ **800/934-7275** or 435/772-3200; fax 435/772-2449. 120 units. A/C TV TEL. Mid-Mar to mid-Oct $80–$95 double, $110–$160 suite and family unit; mid-Oct to mid-Mar $58–$68 double, $85–$125 suite and family unit. AE, DC, DISC, MC, V.

This new, casually elegant two-story complex is located 1.5 miles from the South Entrance of Zion National Park. Rooms are tastefully appointed in Southwest style. The grounds are beautifully landscaped, with phenomenal views of the area's red rock formations. There's also a heated outdoor swimming pool and hot tub, plus a restaurant (see "Dining," below), gift shop, country market store, guest laundry, and a liquor store. Pets are accepted, but at management's discretion and for an extra fee.

Dining

INSIDE THE PARK

Zion Lodge

Zion National Park. ☎ **435/772-3213.** Dinner reservations required in the summer. Breakfast items $2.95–$5.95; lunch items $4.75–$8.95; main dinner courses $8.95–$16.25. AE, DC, DISC, MC, V. Daily 6:30–10am, 11:30am–3pm, and 5:30–9pm. AMERICAN.

A mountain lodge atmosphere prevails here, complete with large windows that look out toward the park's magnificent rock formations. House specialties at dinner include an excellent slow-roasted prime rib au jus, and the very popular Utah red mountain trout. The menu also includes several chicken dishes, such as a skinless chicken breast basted with a spicy Caribbean sauce and served with a red-onion relish. Vegetarians have several choices, such as pasta marissa and black-bean ragout. Ask about the lodge's specialty ice creams and other exotic desserts. At lunch you'll find the trout and barbecued pork ribs, plus burgers, sandwiches, and salads. Breakfasts offer all the usual American selections. The restaurant will pack lunches to go and offers a children's menu and full liquor service.

NEAR THE PARK

All of the following restaurants, except the Zion Mt. Carmel Restaurant, are located in Springdale, just outside the park's South Entrance.

Bit & Spur Restaurant & Saloon

1212 Zion Park Blvd., Springdale. ☎ **435/772-3498.** Reservations recommended. Main courses $7–$15. MC, V. Mar–Oct 5–10pm (bar open until 1am); Nov–Feb Thurs–Mon 5–10pm. Closed Christmas holidays. MEXICAN/SOUTHWESTERN.

This may look like an Old West saloon, with its rough wood-and-stone walls and exposed beam ceiling, but it's an unusually clean saloon with a family dining room, patio dining, and original oil paintings on the walls. The food here is also a notch or two above what might be expected, closer to what you'd expect in a good Santa Fe restaurant. You'll find generous portions of Mexican standards such as burritos, flautas, chile rellenos, and a traditional chile stew with pork; but you'll also find more exotic creations, such as the pollo relleno—a grilled breast of chicken stuffed with cilantro pesto and goat cheese and served with smoked pineapple chutney. Also good are the smoky chicken—a smoked, charbroiled game hen with sourdough stuffing and chipotle sauce—and the deep-dish chicken enchilada, with scallions, green chiles, and cheese. The Bit & Spur has full liquor service and an extensive wine list.

Flanigan's Inn

428 Zion Park Blvd., Springdale. ☎ **435/772-3244.** Reservations recommended. Main course grills $5.50–$14.95. AE, DISC, MC, V. Mon–Thurs 3–9:30pm, Fri–Sun until 10pm. Shorter hrs in the winter. AMERICAN/REGIONAL.

This restaurant makes the most of the area's spectacular scenery with large windows for inside diners plus an outdoor patio. The menu includes items such as burgers, grilled vegetable burritos, chicken breast sandwiches, mesquite smoked chicken marinated in herbs, broiled beef tenderloin, and broiled fresh Atlantic salmon with melted dill butter. Flanigan's uses fresh local ingredients and herbs from the inn's garden in many of its dishes. Beer-lovers can order microbrewed draft beers.

Shonesburg Restaurant

897 Zion Park Blvd. ☎ **435/772-3522.** Reservations accepted. Breakfast $3.53–$6.25; lunch $4.65–$6.45; dinner $5.45–$17.95. DISC, MC, V. Daily 7am–10pm; shorter hrs in winter. AMERICAN.

This establishment consists of a comfortable coffee shop in front, and a more formal restaurant in back. Everything in the restaurant is made from scratch. Breakfasts include a variety of egg dishes—there's even a vegetarian omelette—plus Bumbleberry crepes, pancakes, and stuffed French toast. For lunch you'll find fish-and-chips, sandwiches, and burgers. Dinner entrees include fettucine Alfredo, marinated breast of chicken, trout, salmon, shrimp, and broiled New York strip steak. All dinners come with the popular "tossed at the table" house salad, fresh-baked bread, and vegetable of the day. The homemade pies for dessert are local legends, especially the bumbleberry pie, with its secret mixture of berries. Espresso, lattes, and cappuccinos are popular accompaniments.

The restaurant's playhouse hosts live musical theater each summer; see "Entertainment in Nearby Springdale," below.

Switchback Grille

1149 Zion Park Blvd. ☎ **435/772-3777** or 435/772-3888. Reservations recommended. Main courses $7.95–$21.95. AE, DC, DISC, MC, V. Daily 7am–10pm year-round. CONTINENTAL.

The Switchback is located at the Zion Park Inn and Conference Centre. The well-designed, 150-seat room offers spectacular views of Zion National Park's famed red rock formations from every table. Diners also get to see the restaurant's open-oven rotisserie, where the house specialty flame-broiled chicken is prepared. Pizzas are wood-fired in a kiln, and steaks and a variety of pastas are also offered. Outdoors you'll find patio dining and barbecues on special occasions. The Switchback also features a children's menu, box lunches to go, and full liquor service, including imported beer and wine.

Zion Mt. Carmel Restaurant

0.25 mile east of the East Entrance to Zion National Park. ☎ **435/648-2829.** Reservations for large groups a day in advance. Breakfast $3.25–$5.95; sandwiches $3.50–$5.50; Mexican dishes $2.95–$7.95. AE, DISC, MC, V. Daily 9am–5pm. AMERICAN/MEXICAN.

This is a down-home coffee shop, with great homemade pies, spicy New Mexican–style Southwest dishes, burgers, sandwiches, shakes, and sundaes. Locals love the green chile beef and bean burrito and the enchilada-style burrito, smothered in chile sauce. The breakfast menu includes the standards: ham and eggs, omelettes, pancakes, and French toast. No alcoholic beverages are served.

Zion Pizza & Noodle

868 Zion Park Blvd., Springdale. ☎ **435/772-3815.** Reservations not accepted. Main courses lunch $3.95–$11.95; dinner $7.95–$11.95. No credit cards. Mar–Thanksgiving noon–10pm; shorter hrs late Nov to Dec. Closed Jan–Feb. PIZZA/PASTA.

Located in a former Mormon church with a turquoise steeple, this busy cafe has small, closely spaced tables and walls decorated with black-and-white photos. Patrons order at the counter and help themselves at the beverage bar while waiting for their food. The 12-inch pizzas, baked in a slate-stone oven, have plenty of chewy crust and are quite good, though New York–style pizza purists might be put off by oddly topped specialty pies, such as the Southwestern burrito pizza or barbecue chicken pizza. But have no fear: You can still get a basic cheese pizza, or add any of the 15 extra toppings from pepperoni to green chiles to pineapple. Pasta choices include fettucine with roma tomatoes, fresh mushrooms, pesto sauce, cream, and grated Parmesan; stromboli; and very often the popular special of manicotti marinara. Take out and delivery are available, but alcohol is not.

Picnic & Camping Supplies

You'll find most of the supplies you want in Springdale, just outside the park's South Entrance. The **Canyon Super Market,** 65 Zion Park Blvd. (☎ **435/772-3402**), just outside the park entrance, sells groceries, camping supplies, ice, and firewood. In downtown Springdale, the **Zion Park Market,** 855 Zion Park Blvd. (☎ **435/772-3251**), has groceries and also video rentals. Just north of Zion Park Market is a coin-operated laundry. On the south end of Springdale on Utah 9 (the opposite side of town from the national park), the **Springdale Fruit Company** (☎ **435/772-3222**) sells fresh organic fruits, vegetables, and juices, plus trail mixes and baked goods. It also has a picnic area. Those short on cash will find an ATM at the **Zion Canyon Cinemax Theatre Complex,** just outside the South Entrance to Zion National Park, at 145 Zion Park Blvd. (☎ **435/772-2400**).

ENTERTAINMENT IN NEARBY SPRINGDALE

Virtual nature and live music and theater attract national park visitors to swinging Springdale.

"The Grand Circle: A National Park Odyssey," a multimedia production presented on a 24-by-40-foot screen in the outdoor Obert C. Tanner Amphitheater, is an excellent introduction to the national parks and monuments of southern Utah and northern Arizona. Using a state-of-the-art sound and projection system, the 1-hour program gives a brief look at the geology of the area, but devotes most of its time, sounds, and sights to the awe-inspiring scenery. Showings are scheduled at dusk nightly from late May through early September. Tickets are $4 for adults, $3 for students and children under 12, or $10 per family.

The amphitheater, located just off Zion Park Boulevard, is also the venue for about 18 **concerts** each summer, ranging from the annual Utah Symphony pops concert in late June or early July, to bluegrass, country, and acoustic. Tickets cost $5 to $9, depending on the performer (most are $7). For information on the multimedia production or concert series contact **Dixie College in St. George** (☎ **435/652-7994**).

You'll find an even bigger screen—some six stories high by 80 feet wide—at **Zion Canyon Cinemax Theatre,** just outside the South Entrance to Zion National Park at 145 Zion Park Blvd. (☎ **435/772-2400**). Here you can see the dramatic film *Treasure of the Gods* with thrilling scenes of the Zion National Park area, including a hair-raising flash flood through Zion Canyon's Narrows and some dizzying bird's-eye views. Also shown is *The Great American West,* in which the Old West comes alive through the words of pioneers, Indian chiefs, and explorers. Admission is $7 for adults, $4.50 for children 3 to 11. Films are shown hourly, 365 days a year; March through October from 9am to 9pm, and November through February from 11am to 7pm. The theater complex also includes a tourist information center, ATM, picnic area, gift and souvenir shops, a food emporium, a 30-minute photo processor, bookstore, and art gallery.

For live shows head to downtown Springdale and **Grandma Ruby's Playhouse** at the Shonesburg Restaurant, 897 Zion Park Blvd. (☎ **435/772-3522**), which presents musicals such as *The Unsinkable Molly Brown, Oklahoma,* and *Seven Brides for Seven Brothers* each summer from Memorial Day to Labor Day. The summer stock company includes area college students majoring in theater. Performances take place Tuesday through Saturday evenings, with preshow entertainment at 7:30pm, followed at 8pm by the main production. Call for current information.

Nearby National Monuments & State Park

The area surrounding Zion National Park offers a variety of scenic wonders and recreational opportunities. In addition to other nearby national parks, which are discussed elsewhere in this book, there are several excellent national monuments and state parks within 90 minutes of Zion National Park's South Entrance.

CEDAR BREAKS NATIONAL MONUMENT

This is a delightful little park, a wonderful place to spend a few hours or several days, gazing down from the rim into the spectacular natural amphitheater, hiking the trails, and camping among the spruce, firs, and summer wildflowers.

The park forms a natural coliseum, which looks a lot like Bryce Canyon National Park, more than 2,000 feet deep and over 3 miles across, filled with stone spires, arches, and columns shaped by the forces of erosion and painted in ever-changing reds, purples, oranges, and ochers. Why the name Cedar Breaks? Well, the pioneers who came here called such badlands "breaks," and they mistook the juniper trees along the cliff bases for cedars.

JUST THE FACTS

At over 10,000 feet elevation, it's always pleasantly cool at Cedar Breaks. At night it actually gets downright cold, so take a jacket or sweater, even if the temperature is scorching just down the road in St. George. The monument opens for its short summer season only after the snow melts, usually in late May, and closes in October, unless you happen to have a pair of cross-country skis or a snowmobile, in which case you can visit anytime.

Getting There. Cedar Breaks National Monument is 85 miles north of the main section of Zion National Park. From Zion's South Entrance head west on Utah 9, then north on Utah 17 to I-15. Then follow I-15 north to Exit 57 for Cedar City, turn and head east on Utah 14, then north on Utah 148, which goes straight into the monument. From the Kolob Canyons section of Zion, which is off Exit 40 of I-15, it is only 40 miles to Cedar Breaks.

The national monument is 23 miles east of Cedar City, 56 miles west of Bryce Canyon National Park, and 247 miles south of Salt Lake City. If you're coming from Bryce Canyon or other points east, the park is accessible from the town of Panguitch via Utah 143. If you're coming from the north, take the Parowan Exit off I-15 and head south on Utah 143. It's a steep climb from whichever direction you choose, so take care, especially if your vehicle is prone to vapor lock or (like many motor homes) to loss of power on hills.

Information & Visitor Center. One mile from the South Entrance gate is the visitor center, open daily June to late September, with exhibits on the geology, flora, and fauna of Cedar Breaks. You can purchase books and maps there, and ask rangers for help in planning your visit. For advance information, contact the **Superintendent, Cedar Breaks National Monument,** P.O. Box 749, Cedar City, UT 84720 (☎ **435/586-9451**). The monument's Web site is **www.nps.gov/cebr**.

Fees & Regulations. Admission is $4 per vehicle or $2 per person on foot, bike, or motorcycle; there is no charge for those passing through the park on Utah 143. Mountain bikes are not allowed on hiking trails. Dogs, which must be leashed at all times, are prohibited on all trails, in the backcountry, and in public buildings.

Health & Safety Concerns. The high elevation—10,350 feet at the visitor center—is likely to cause shortness of breath and tiredness. Those with heart or respiratory conditions should consult their doctors before making the trip to Cedar Breaks. During thunderstorms you need to avoid overlooks and other high, exposed areas—they're often targets for lightning.

Ranger Programs. During the monument's short summer season, rangers offer nightly **campfire talks** at the campground; **geology talks** at Point Supreme, a view point near the visitor center, every day at 2:30pm and Monday through Friday also at 10am; and **guided hikes** on Saturday and Sunday mornings. A complete schedule is posted at the visitor center and the campground.

EXPLORING CEDAR BREAKS BY CAR

The 5-mile road through Cedar Breaks National Monument offers easy access to the monument's scenic overlooks and trailheads. Allow 30 to 45 minutes to make the drive. Start at the visitor center and nearby **Point Supreme** for a panoramic view of the amphitheater. Then drive north, past the campground and picnic ground turnoff, to **Sunset View** for a closer look at the amphitheater and its colorful canyons. From each of these overlooks you'll be able to see out across Cedar Valley, over the Antelope and Black mountains and into the Escalante Desert.

Continue north to **Chessman Ridge Overlook,** so named because the stone hoodoos directly below the overlook seem like massive chess pieces. Watch for swallows and swifts soaring among the rock formations. Then get back into your car and head north to **Alpine Pond,** to walk among the wildflowers on the self-guided nature trail (see "Hiking," below). Finally, proceed to **North View,** which offers perhaps your best view of the amphitheater and its stately rock statues.

SUMMER SPORTS & ACTIVITIES

Hiking. Unfortunately, there are no trails into the bottom of the amphitheater, but the monument does have two high-country trails. The fairly easy 2-mile **Alpine Pond Trail** loop leads to a picturesque forest glade and pond surrounded by wildflowers, and offers panoramic views of the amphitheater along the way. A trail guide is available at the trailhead.

A somewhat more challenging hike, the 4-mile **Spectra Point Trail** (also called the Ramparts Trail) follows the rim more closely than the Alpine Pond Trail. It also takes you through fields of wildflowers and groves of bristlecone pines more than 1,500 years old. You'll need to be especially careful of your footing along the exposed cliff edges.

Wildlife Watching. Because of its relative remoteness, Cedar Breaks is a good place for spotting wildlife. You're likely to see mule deer grazing in the meadows along the road early and late in the day. Marmots make their dens near the rim, and are often seen along the Spectra Point Trail. You'll spot ground squirrels, red squirrels, and chipmunks everywhere. Pikas, related to rabbits, are here too, but it's unlikely you'll see one. They're small, with short ears and stubby tails, and prefer the high, rocky slopes.

Birders should have no trouble spotting the Clark's nutcracker in the campground, with its gray torso and black-and-white wings and tail. The monument is also home to swallows, swifts, blue grouse, and golden eagles.

WINTER SPORTS & ACTIVITIES

The monument is essentially shut down from late October through mid-May, but though the snow-blocked roads will keep cars out, they're perfect for snowmobilers and cross-country skiers, who usually come over from nearby Brian Head Ski Area. Keep in mind, though, that all facilities are closed and the only people you're likely to see will be an occasional park ranger patrolling on a snowmobile.

Camping. A 30-site campground in a beautiful high-mountain setting, **Point Supreme,** just north of the visitor center, is open from June to mid-September, with sites available on a first-come, first-served basis. It has rest rooms, drinking water, picnic tables, grills, and an amphitheater for the ranger's evening campfire programs; but there are no showers or RV hookups. Camping fee is $9 per night. Keep in mind that, even in midsummer, temperatures can drop into the 30s at night at this elevation, so bring cool-weather gear.

PIPE SPRING NATIONAL MONUMENT

Located in the Kaibab-Paiute Indian Reservation in northwestern Arizona, this national monument preserves the stone headquarters of a 19th-century cattle ranch operated by the Church of Jesus Christ of Latter-day Saints (Mormons). Nicknamed Winsor Castle for early ranch superintendent Anson Perry Winsor, it was built in 1870 ostensibly as a fort to protect Mormon settlers from Navajo raiders. Fortunately, the thick rock walls, made from stone quarried from the red sandstone cliffs just west of the fort, never had to withstand an attack. The real purpose of the structure was to be a ranch for the church's southern Utah tithing herd—the cattle contributed by Mormon families as one-tenth of their incomes.

JUST THE FACTS

Pipe Spring National Monument is about 65 miles—though less than 30 miles as the crow flies—south of Zion National Park. Follow Utah 9 east to U.S. 89, turn right (south) to Kanab, then follow U.S. 89A to Fredonia, Arizona, and finally turn right (west) onto Ariz. 389 to the monument.

A **visitor center** and **museum,** at the entrance to the monument, has exhibits depicting the lives of both the American Indians of the area and Mormon settlers. Nearby, you'll find a bookstore, gift shop, and snack bar. There are no other dining, lodging, or camping facilities at the monument.

The monument is open daily, 8am to 4:30pm. Admission is $2 per person. For information write **Pipe Spring National Monument,** Moccasin, AZ 86022 (☎ **520/643-7105**). The monument's Web site is **www.nps.gov/pisp**.

EXPLORING THE PARK

From the visitor center, follow the walkway by the orchards, gardens, and irrigation ponds to the massive fort—actually two stone houses sharing a spring and joined by high walls with sturdy wooden gates. In summer you can take a guided tour, which lasts about 45 minutes; or at any time you can explore the fort and grounds on your own, following a map and descriptive brochure provided free at the visitor center.

Inside the fort you'll see the restored bedrooms, meeting room, parlor, cheese-making room, and kitchen, with the table set in Mormon fashion, the plates upside down and chairs facing away from the table to facilitate kneeling for before-meal prayers. You can also step inside the telegraph room, with the original telegraph stand and a photograph of the first operator, Luella Stewart. Outside, you'll find the blacksmith shop, with a display of pioneer tools; a bunkhouse that was used by explorer John Wesley Powell's survey crew in 1871; a harness room with ranch equipment; and a 0.5-mile loop trail that leads up the sandstone cliffs behind the house.

During the summer you'll also see demonstrations of pioneer life, such as weaving, cheese-making, and cooking.

SNOW CANYON STATE PARK

Among Utah's most scenic state parks, sometimes called a "vest pocket Zion," Snow Canyon offers an abundance of opportunities for photography, hiking, rock climbing, and horseback riding. The park is surrounded by rock cliffs and walls of Navajo sandstone in every imaginable shade of red, layered with white and black from ancient lava flows. Hike the trails to discover the shifting sand dunes, mysterious lava caves, colorful desert plants, and variety of rock formations. There's also an attractive cactus garden and several ancient petroglyphs (ask park rangers for directions). By the way, don't come here looking for snow—Snow Canyon was named after the pioneers Lorenzo and Erastus Snow, who discovered it.

JUST THE FACTS

It's best to avoid summers here—temperatures are often well over 100°F. Winters are mild, though nights can be chilly. Spring and fall usually have perfect weather, and are therefore the busiest times for the park.

Getting There. The park is located 11 miles northwest of St. George, off Utah 18. From Zion it is about 60 miles west. Follow Utah 9 to I-15, Exit 16; then head south to St. George (Exit 8); and finally take Utah 18 northwest to the park's entrance road.

Information, Fees & Regulations. For a copy of the park's brochure, contact **Snow Canyon State Park Headquarters,** P.O. Box 140, Santa Clara, UT 84765-0140 (☎ **435/628-2255**). Day-use fee is $4 per vehicle, or $1.50 per person on foot, bike, or motorcycle. Like most state parks, dogs are welcome, even on the trails, but must be leashed.

SPORTS & ACTIVITIES

Hiking. The best way to see Snow Canyon is on foot or horseback (see below). Several short trails make for easy full- or half-day hikes. The **Hidden Pinyon Trail** is a 1.5 mile round-trip self-guided nature trail that wanders among lava rocks, through several canyons, and onto rocky flatlands, along the way offering panoramic views of the surrounding mountains. The trail begins across the highway from the campground; you can pick up a brochure at the park office/ entrance station. It's an easy walk, but allow at least an hour, especially if you're planning to keep an eye out for Mormon tea, cliffrose, prickly pear cactus, and banana yucca.

An easy 0.75-mile (one way) trail leads to **Johnson Arch.** It begins just south of the campground and passes by the popular rock-climbing wall (see below), some low sand dunes, and then a small canyon with a view of Johnson Arch high above.

Also popular is the **Lava Caves Trail,** a 1.5-mile round-trip hike that starts just north of the campground. The caves are about a half mile along the trail, but watch carefully—it's easy to miss them. They were formed from liquid lava, and have at times been occupied by American Indian tribes. Another quarter mile past the caves is the West Canyon Overlook, with a breathtaking view into West Canyon.

Several longer and steeper trails lead to spectacular views of the canyons and distant vistas; check with park rangers.

Horseback Riding. **Snow Canyon Stables,** P.O. Box 577, Santa Clara, UT 84765 (☎ **435/628-6677**), offers horseback rides of various lengths into some of the more inaccessible and beautiful parts of the park, year-round. Prices start at $15 for a 1-hour ride; an overnight camping trip, including dinner and breakfast, is $125.

Rock Climbing. Snow Canyon State Park is a popular destination for rock climbers, especially those looking to polish their skills a bit before tackling the "experts only" rock walls of Zion National Park. Climbers especially like the tall wall of rock on the east side of the road just south of the campground, but it has become so popular that the park has issued a moratorium on bolting. Check with the park office for information.

Wildlife Watching. You're likely to see cottontail rabbits, ground squirrels, and songbirds; luckier visitors may also spot desert mule deer, bobcats, coyote, kit foxes, eagles, and owls. Although you probably won't spot them, desert tortoises (a federally listed threatened species) and Gila monsters also live in the park. There are also some rattlesnakes, which you'll want to avoid.

CAMPING

The 36-site campground (☎ **800/322-3770**) is one of the best in the state park system. One section has electric hookups; but those who don't need electricity can set up camp in delightful little side canyons, surrounded by colorful red rocks and Utah juniper. The views are spectacular no matter where you camp. The campground offers hot showers, modern rest rooms, and an RV sewage dump station. Campsites with electricity cost $13; those without are $11. Reservations are recommended from February to May and September to November. There's a $5 nonrefundable reservation fee.

Appendix

USEFUL TOLL-FREE NUMBERS & WEB SITES

◆ Airlines ◆

Air Canada
☎ 800/776-3000
www.aircanada.ca

Air Nevada
☎ 800/634-6377

Alaska Airlines
☎ 800/426-0333
www.alaskaair.com

America West Airlines
America West Express
☎ 800/235-9292
www.americawest.com

American Airlines
☎ 800/433-7300
www.americanair.com

American Trans Air
☎ 800/543-3708

Big Sky Airlines
☎ 800/237-7788

British Airways
☎ 800/247-9297
☎ 0345/222-111 in Britain
www.british-airways.com

Canadian Airlines International
☎ 800/426-7000
www.cdair.ca

Carnival Airlines
☎ 800/824-7386
www.carnivalair.com

Condor
☎ 800/524-6975

Continental Airlines
☎ 800/525-0280
www.flycontinental.com

Delta Air Lines
☎ 800/221-1212
www.delta-air.com

Eagle Canyon Airlines
☎ 800/446-4584

Frontier
☎ 800/432-1359

Hawaiian Airlines
☎ 800/367-5320
www.hawaiianair.com

Horizon Air
☎ 800/547-9308

Kiwi International Air Lines
☎ 800/538-5494
www.jetkiwi.com

L.A.B. Flying Service
☎ 800/426-0543

Mesa Airlines
☎ 800/637-2247

Midway Airlines
☎ 800/446-4392

Midwest Express
☎ 800/452-2022

Northwest Airlines
☎ 800/225-2525
www.nwa.com

Reno Air
☎ 800/736-6247

Scenic Airlines
☎ 800/634-6801

Skywest
☎ 800/453-9417

Southwest Airlines
☎ 800/435-9792
www.iflyswa.com

Sun Country
☎ 800/359-6786

Tower Air
☎ 800/34-TOWER
☎ 800/348-6937 outside New York
☎ 718/553-8500 in New York
www.towerair.com

Trans World Airlines (TWA)
☎ 800/221-2000
www2.twa.com

United Airlines
United Express
☎ 800/241-6522
www.ual.com

US Airways
☎ 800/428-4322
www.usair.com

Virgin Atlantic Airways
☎ 800/862-8621 in the continental U.S.
☎ 0293/747-747 in Britain
www.fly.virgin.com

Western Pacific
☎ 800/930-3030

◆ Car-Rental Agencies ◆

Advantage
☎ 800/777-5500
www.arac.com

Alamo
☎ 800/327-9633
www.goalamo.com

Avis
☎ 800/331-1212
in the continental U.S.
☎ 800/TRY-AVIS
in Canada
www.avis.com

Budget
☎ 800/527-0700
www.budgetrentacar.com

Dollar
☎ 800/800-4000

Enterprise
☎ 800/325-8007

General
☎ 800/327-7607

Hertz
☎ 800/654-3131
www.hertz.com

National
☎ 800/CAR-RENT
www.nationalcar.com

Payless
☎ 800/PAYLESS
www.paylesscar.com

Rent-A-Wreck
☎ 800/535-1391
www.rent-a-wreck.com

Sears
☎ 800/527-0770

Standard
☎ 800/953-2277

Thrifty
☎ 800/367-2277
www.thrifty.com

Value
☎ 800/327-2501
www.go-value.com

Index

Abbotts Lagoon, 506
Achenbach Hills, 590, 591
Acoma Indians, 399
Adams, Ansel, 323, 640, 641
  Gallery, 638
  Wilderness, 647, 648, 650
Adams Falls, 532
Agate House, 493, 495
Agnes Gorge, 457
Agua Canyon, 93
Ahwahnee, 638, 650
Ahwahnee, The, 655, 660–61
Airlines, 690
Airports. *See specific destinations*
Air tours
  Badlands, 35–36
  Black Hills, 76
  Bryce Canyon, 93
  Canyonlands, 125
  Denali, 221
  Glacier, 249
  Glacier Bay, 270, 273
  Grand Canyon, 292–93
  Talkeetna, AK, 232
Alamere Falls, 504, 505
Alaska Railroad, 211–12, 231
Alberta Falls, 531
Allenspark, CO, 535
Alpine, TX, 54
Alpine Visitor Center, 524, 528
Alta Peak, 571–72
Altitude sickness, 8
Amphitheater Lake, 328
Anacapa Island, 162–68
Ancestral Puebloan Indians. *See* Pueblo Indians
Anchorage, AK, 210–11, 212
Annie Creek Canyon, 185
Ansel Adams Wilderness, 647, 648, 650
Antelope Flats, 329
Antelope House, 112
Antelopes, 65, 68, 122, 585, 604
Apgar Lake, 253
Apgar Village, 259, 261
Appistoki Falls, 251
Arapaho National Forest, 535, 537–38
Arapaho National Recreation Area, 537–38
Archaeological sites, 125, 139, 171, 173, 285–86. *See also* Mesa Verde National Park
Arches National Park
  accommodations, 21–24
  attractions, 15
  avoiding crowds, 10, 12
  camping, 13, 21
  for children, 20
  hiking, 15–18
  restaurants, 24–26
  scenic drives, 13–15
  sports and activities, 18–20
  supplies, 26
  tours and programs, 15
Arch Rock (Channel Islands), 166
Arch Rock (Point Reyes), 505
Artist Paint Pot, 609
Ashford, WA, 427
  accommodations, 442, 443–44
  restaurants, 444–45
Astoria Hot Springs, 332

Babb, MT, 266
Backcountry. *See also specific parks*
  driving. *See* Four-wheeling
  permits, 3, 8
  planning a trip, 8
Badger Pass, 631, 651
Badlands, 583–85. *See also* Theodore Roosevelt National Park
Badlands National Park
  accommodations, 37–38
  attractions, 32, 38
  avoiding crowds, 30
  camping, 36–37
  hiking, 33–35
  restaurants, 38
  sports and activities, 35–36
  tours and programs, 32–33
Bainbridge Island, 469
Baker, CA, 206, 207, 413
  accommodations, 421
  restaurants, 207, 422
Baker, NV, 344, 354
  accommodations, 352–53
  restaurants, 354
Baker Creek, 349, 351
Baker Lake, 349
Baker National Forest, 426
Balanced Rock, 14, 15
Bald Crater Peak, 186
Bald eagles. *See* Eagles
Ballooning, 36, 76
Baring Falls, 250
Barker Dam, 372–73
Barstow, CA, 422
Bartlett Cove, 270, 271, 274, 275
Bartlett Cove National Park, 274
Bartlett Lake, 273
Barton Warnock Environmental Education Center, 56–57
Bass Lake, 642–60, 659
Bats, 51, 153, 157, 194, 363, 552, 678
Beaches
  Channel Islands, 162, 166, 172
  Crater Lake, 190
  Glacier Bay, 274
  Olympic, 474, 483, 484
  Point Reyes, 500, 506
  Redwood, 515, 518, 519
Beal, Mary, 419
Beardslee Islands, 274
Bear Lake (Rocky Mountain), 527, 530, 535
Bears
  Big Bend, 43, 53
  Denali, 208, 220, 223
  Glacier, 254, 266
  Grand Teton, 325, 328, 329
  Guadalupe Mountains, 363
  Mount Rainier, 426
  Olympic, 468
  Redwood, 520
  safety tips, 7, 43, 250, 515, 561, 634

Sequoia and Kings Canyon, 571
Yellowstone, 604, 613
Bear Valley Visitor Center (Point Reyes), 500, 502, 504–5
Beatty, NV, 206, 207
Beaver, WA, 486
Beaver Lake, 602
Beaver Meadows Entrance, 527, 533, 535
Beavers
Big Bend, 51
Bryce Canyon, 104
Canyonlands, 122
Denali, 208, 220
Grand Teton, 316, 323, 324, 325
North Cascades, 457
Rocky Mountain, 531, 535
Zion, 678
Bechler Region (Yellowstone), 613
Belfield, ND, 593
Belle Fourche River, 234, 235
Bench Lake, 433
Benteen, Frederick, 394
Berkely Park, 435
Bierstadt Lake, 531
Big Beaver Trail, 447, 458
Big Bend National Park
accommodations, 54–55
attractions, 46–47
nearby, 56–57
avoiding crowds, 39–40
camping, 42, 52–54
for children, 52
hiking, 47–50
restaurants, 55–56
scenic drives, 42, 44–45
sports and activities, 50–51
supplies, 55
tours and programs, 45–46
Big Bend Ranch State Park, 56
Bighorn River, 394
Bighorn sheep
Badlands, 30
Canyonlands, 122
Death Valley, 194
Glacier, 266
Great Basin, 343, 351
Joshua Tree, 367
Mojave, 412
Rocky Mountain, 524, 535
Big Room (Carlsbad Cavern), 149, 150, 151, 153, 154, 157
Big Spring Canyon, 128
Biking. *See also* Mountain biking
Arches, 20
Badlands, 36
Bryce Canyon, 96–97
Canyonlands, 132
Crater Lake, 188
Death Valley, 203
Denali, 223
Glacier, 245
Grand Staircase–Escalante, 104
Grand Teton, 329
Great Basin, 350
Gustavus, AK, 273–74
Joshua Tree, 376
Lassen, 388–89
Mojave, 420
Mount Rainier, 437
North Cascades, 458
Olympic, 479–80
Point Reyes, 506, 507
Saguaro, 552
Yellowstone, 614
Yosemite, 649
Zion, 677
Billings, MT, 395, 595, 598
Bird watching. *See also specific birds*
Badlands, 34
Big Bend, 51–52
Bryce Canyon, 97
Capitol Reef, 143–44
Carlsbad Caverns, 157
Cedar Breaks, 687
Channel Islands, 162, 166, 171, 173, 175
Grand Staircase–Escalante, 106
Grand Teton, 325
Great Basin, 349, 351
Guadalupe Mountains, 363, 364
Jewel Cave, 76
Mojave, 412
Point Reyes, 507
Redwood, 519–20
Rocky Mountain, 535
Saguaro, 551
Snow Canyon, 689
Zion, 666, 678
Bismarck, ND, 586
Black Dragon's Caldron, 604
Black Elk Wilderness Area, 64
Black Hills, 27, 30, 31, 36, 37, 58–86, 234–40, 393, 395
Black Hills National Forest, 38, 77, 80
Black Rock Canyon, 378
Blue Mesa, 493–94, 496
Boating. *See also* Canoeing; Cruises; Jet boating; Kayaking; Rafting
Arches, 19–20
Canyonlands, 129
Denali, 223
Glacier, 253
Glacier Bay, 272
Grand Teton, 322, 329
Mount Rainier, 437
permits, 3
Talkeetna, AK, 232–33
Yellowstone, 614
Bobcats, 194, 351, 367, 412, 500
Bogachiel River, 474–75
Boquillas, Mexico, 56
Boquillas Canyon, 48
Borax Flats, 200
Borax Museum, 197
Borglum, Gutzon, 61–62, 64, 65
Boulder, CO, 104
Boundary Springs, 186
Bow, Clara, 417
Bowman Lake, 252, 253, 255–56
Box Canyon, 673
Boyden Cavern, 563, 564
Boy Scout Tree, 516, 518–19
Bozeman, MT, 595
Bradley Lake, 328
Brantley Lake State Park, 158, 364
Brian Head Ski Area, 687
Bridalveil Falls, 643, 645, 652
Bridge Creek, 457–58
Bridger-Teton National Forest, 329
Bright Angel Lodge, 281, 287, 297, 306
Bright Angel Point Trail, 289
Bright Angel Trail, 283, 290
Bristlecone pines, 344, 349, 350
Broken Arch, 14, 15, 16
Bryce, Ebenezer, 87
Bryce, UT
accommodations, 100
restaurants, 102–3
Bryce Amphitheater, 88, 92, 93, 95
Bryce Canyon Country Rodeo, 103
Bryce Canyon Lodge, 93, 94, 96, 99, 101

Bryce Canyon National Park, 104, 137
  accommodations, 99–101
  attractions, 92, 94
    nearby, 103–7
  avoiding crowds, 88, 90
  camping, 92, 98–99
  for children, 97
  hiking, 88, 94–96
  restaurants, 101–3
  scenic drives, 92–93
  sports and activities, 96–98
  supplies, 103
  tours and programs, 93–94, 96
Bryce Pioneer Village, 98, 100
Bubbs Creek, 568
Buffalo (bison), 30, 67, 68, 72, 583, 585, 589, 600
Buffalo Gap National Grasslands, 30, 38
Bumpass Hell, 384, 386, 387
Bunsen Peak, 610
Burro Mesa Pour-Off, 47–48
Burroughs Mountain, 434
Butch Cassidy and the Sundance Kid, 141, 415
Butte Lake, 384, 386, 389, 390
Butterfield Overland Mail Coach Route, 359, 360

Cabrillo, Juan Rodriguez, 162–63, 169
  Monument, 174
Cactus Flat, SD, 30
Cactus Forest, 551
Cactus Forest Drive, 547–48
Cactus Garden, 550
Calf Creek, 104, 106
Calf Creek Recreation Area, 104, 105, 106
California Riding and Hiking Trail, 375, 378
Camarillo, CA, 164, 165
Cameron, AZ, 305
  supplies, 312
Camping. *See also specific national parks*
  Arapaho National Forest, 537–38
  Black Hills, 77–81
  Calf Creek Recreation Area, 106
  Cedar Breaks, 687
  Dixie National Forest, 99
  etiquette, 8
  fees, 3–4
  Grand Staircase–Escalante, 106–7
  regulations, 8
  reservations, 3–4
  Sequoia National Forest, 576
  Snow Canyon State Park, 689
  Stanislaus National Forest, 654
Camp Young Memorial, 373
Canoeing
  Arches, 19–20
  Big Bend, 50–51
  Canyonlands, 129
  Glacier, 253
  Lassen, 389
  Mount Rainier, 437
  North Cascades, 459
  Olympic, 480–81
Canyon de Chelly National Monument
  accommodations, 116–17
  attractions, 111–12
  avoiding crowds, 109, 110
  camping, 115–16
  hiking, 114–15
  restaurants, 117–18
  scenic drives, 112–15
  supplies, 118
  tours and programs, 114–15
Canyon del Muerto, 108, 110, 112
Canyonlands National Park, 20
  attractions, 124, 125
  avoiding crowds, 120, 122
  camping, 21, 123, 132–33
  for children, 132
  hiking, 123, 125–28
  scenic drives, 124
  sports and activities, 128–32
  tours and programs, 124–25
Canyon Village (Yellowstone), 603–4, 620, 626
  visitor center, 598, 603
Cape Alava, 474
Cape Final Trail (Grand Canyon), 289
Cape Royal Drive (Grand Canyon), 286
Capitol Dome, 139
Capitol Gorge, 139, 140
Capitol Reef National Park, 90, 104
  accommodations, 145–47
  avoiding crowds, 136–37
  camping, 137, 144–45
  for children, 143
  hiking, 136, 140–42
  historic attractions, 138, 139–40
  restaurants, 147
  scenic drives, 138–39
  sports and activities, 142–44
  tours and programs, 139–40
Carbon Glacier, 436–37
Carbon River, 425–26, 427, 430, 431, 436
Caribou, 454
  Denali, 208, 210, 211, 219, 220
Carlo Creek, 210
Carlsbad, NM, 150, 356, 357
  accommodations, 158–59
  camping, 158, 364
  restaurants, 160, 364–65
  supplies, 160
Carlsbad Cavern, 150, 153–55
Carlsbad Caverns National Park
  accommodations, 158–60
  attractions, 153–54
  avoiding crowds, 149
  camping, 157–58
  for children, 157
  ranger programs, 153
  restaurants, 159–60
  scenic drives, 153
  sports and activities, 156–57
  tours, 152, 153, 154–55
Car rentals, 691
Carson, Kit, 112
Carter Falls, 432, 439
Cascade Canyon, 327
Cascade Range, 384, 446–47. *See also* North Cascades National Park
Cassidy Arch, 141
Castolon, TX, 42, 51, 55
Castolon Historic District, 46
Cathedral Group (Grand Teton), 319, 321
Cathedral Lakes (Yosemite), 646
Cedar Breaks National Monument, 679, 685–87
Cedar City, UT, 667, 686
Cedar Grove (Kings Canyon), 560, 561, 563–64, 576, 582
  camping, 576
  restaurants, 580
Cedar Pass (Badlands), 31, 36
Cedar Pass Lodge, 37, 31, 32, 38
Center Lake, 77, 80
Channel Islands National Park
  attractions, 166–76
  avoiding crowds, 164
  camping, 165, 168, 171, 172, 174, 176
  hiking, 168–72, 174, 175–76

sports and activities, 176
supplies, 178
tours and programs, 168
traveling to, 164–65
Chapel of the Transfiguration, 322
Chapin Mesa Museum, 400–401, 405
Chateau DeMores State Historic Site, 591
Chelan, Lake, 446, 447, 450, 451, 459, 461. *See also* Lake Chelan National Recreation Area
boating, 450, 454
ferries, 453
fishing, 459
Chelan, WA, accommodations, 461
Cherry Canyon, 172
Chester, CA, 391
Chihuahuan Desert, 44, 45, 47, 56, 57, 149, 153, 361, 362
Children. *See also specific parks*
traveling with, 6
Chilicotal Mountain, 45
Chilnualna Falls, 645
Chimney Rock, 141
Chinle, AZ, 108, 110, 115, 118
accommodations, 116–17
restaurants, 117–18
Chisos Basin, 44–45, 48, 52, 54, 55
Chisos Mountain Lodge, 55, 54, 55
Chisos Mountains, 41, 43, 44, 45, 49–50
Cholla cactus, 367, 373, 412, 416, 419, 551, 553
Cholla Cactus Garden, 371, 373
Christian Pond, 320, 325
Christy Ranch, 169, 177
Chumash Indians, 162, 163, 166, 169, 171, 172, 173, 175
Cima, CA, 415, 416
Cima Dome, 415, 416, 419
Cinder Cones (Lassen), 387
Civilian Conservation Corps, 47, 49, 54
Clams, 271
Cleetwood Cove, 185
Cliff House (Mesa Verde), 399, 401, 402, 403
Clifford Kamph Memorial Park, 521
Cliff Shelf (Badlands), 32, 34
Cliff Springs Trail (Grand Canyon), 289
Climbing. *See* Mountain climbing; Rock climbing
Clinton, Bill, 103, 105, 193, 412
Coastal Drive, 516, 517
Coast Miwok Indians. *See* Miwok Indians
Cody, WY, 595, 598
accommodations, 624–25
restaurants, 629
Cohab Canyon, 141
Colorado River, 106, 119, 120, 126, 277, 279, 280, 286, 418
rafting, 19–20, 129, 291–92
Colorado River Overlook, 132
Colter, Mary, 278, 285, 287, 297, 298
Colter Bay Village, 317, 319, 331, 334, 338
Colter Bay Visitor Center, 317, 320, 324, 328, 330
Columbia River, 426
Columbia Rock (Yosemite), 643
Comet Falls, 433
Constance Pass, 479
Continental Divide, 247, 530, 605
Cook, Frederick, 214
Cooke City, MT, 599
accommodations, 624
Coolidge, Calvin, 83, 269
Coon Lake, 456–57
Copper Creek, 568
Cortez, CO, 400, 409
accommodations, 406–7
restaurants, 407, 408, 409
Cottonwood Canyon (Bryce Canyon), 106
Cottonwood Canyon (Death Valley), 203
Cottonwood Springs (Joshua Tree), 371, 372, 373–74
Cottonwood Visitor Center (Joshua Tree), 369, 370, 378
Cougars, 143, 367, 426, 468, 504, 516
Coyotes
Black Hills, 67, 76
Bryce Canyon, 97
Canyonlands, 122
Death Valley, 194
Devils Tower, 238
Joshua Tree, 367
Mojave, 412
Rocky Mountain, 535
Theodore Roosevelt, 594
Zion, 678
Craggy Igloo Mountain, 219
Crater Lake, 179–80, 186–87
cruises, 183, 185
Rim Drive, 184
swimming, 188
Crater Lake Lodge, 182, 183, 184, 185, 189, 190
Crater Lake National Park
accommodations and restaurants, 189–91
attractions, 182–84, 185
avoiding crowds, 180
camping, 182, 189
hiking, 180, 183, 184–88
sports and activities, 188–89
tours and programs, 184–85
Crazy Horse, 395
Memorial, 38, 58, 60, 61, 66
Creosote bush, 367, 412
Crescent Beach, 518, 519
Crescent City, CA, 513, 514, 516, 523
accommodations, 521–22
restaurants, 522
Crescent Lake, 477, 479, 480, 481–82, 484
Crescent Meadow, 562, 565
Cross-country skiing
Bryce Canyon, 97–98
Cedar Breaks, 687
Crater Lake, 188–89
Glacier, 254
Grand Canyon, 291
Great Basin, 351
Lassen, 389
Mount Rainier, 3, 439
North Cascades, 460
Rocky Mountain, 534–35
Sequoia and Kings Canyon, 573
Yellowstone, 615–16, 651
Crow Agency, MT, 396
Cruises
Crater Lake, 183, 185
Glacier, 248–49, 253
Glacier Bay, 270, 272–73
Grand Teton, 322, 329–30
North Cascades, 450
Crystal Cave, 562
Crystal Forest, 495–96
Crystal Mountain, 437, 439
Cuba (shipwreck), 173
Curry Village, 637, 638, 649, 650, 651, 655, 661, 665
Custer, George Armstrong, 80, 394–95, 397–98, 588
Custer, SD, 59, 60, 61
ballooning, 36, 76
camping, 80–81
horse-packing trips, 77
Custer Battlefield. *See* Little Bighorn Battlefield National Monument

Custer State Park, 38, 58–59, 60, 65–67
accommodations, 81, 83
attractions, 66
camping, 77–80
restaurants, 84
scenic drives, 66–67
sports and activities, 76–77
Cuyler Harbor, 173, 174

Dana Lake, 647
Dawson Pass, 253
Dead Horse Creek, 433
Dead Horse Point State Park, 125, 133
Deadman's Bar Overlook, 323
Deadwood, SD, 71
accommodations, 82–83
camping, 81
restaurants, 86
Death Valley National Park
accommodations, 204–6
attractions, 197, 198–99
avoiding crowds, 194
camping, 194, 196, 203–4
for children, 203
hiking, 197, 200–202
restaurants, 206–7
scenic drives, 197–98
sports and activities, 203
supplies, 207
tours and programs, 199
Deer, 143, 426, 438, 468, 520, 552, 585, 600. *See also* Mule deer
Deer Cove (Sequoia), 571
Deer Creek (Bryce Canyon), 107
Deer Lake (Olympic), 476–77
Deer Park (Olympic), 469
Delicate Arch, 12, 14, 16–17
Delta, UT, 352
Denali Highway, 210
Denali National Park
accommodations, 216–17, 225–30
wilderness lodges, 216, 229–30
avoiding crowds, 210, 213
camping, 213, 215–17, 219, 222, 224–25
evening entertainment, 230–31
hiking, 215, 221–23
restaurants, 230
scenic drives, 213
shuttle buses, 216, 217–20
sports and activities, 223–24
tours and programs, 215, 220–21
Denali State Park, 211
Denman Falls, 427
Denver, CO, 527–28
Desert pupfish, 194, 201
Desert Queen Mine, 374
Desert Queen Ranch, 372
Desert tortoises, 199, 367–68, 412, 416, 689
Desolation Peak, 454–55
Devastated Area, 383
Devil's Cornfield (Death Valley), 197
Devils Garden (Arches), 12, 14, 17, 20, 21
Devil's Rock Garden (Bryce Canyon), 106
Devils Tower National Monument
accommodations and restaurants, 240
avoiding crowds, 237
camping, 238, 239–40
climbing the tower, 238
hiking, 239
tours and programs, 239
Diablo Dam, 452–53, 454
Diablo Lake, 452–54, 456, 459
hiking, 455
Diamond Lake, 190
Dinosaurs, 129
Disabled travelers, 6–7
passes for, 3
Dixie National Forest, 97, 99
Dog Canyon, 355, 359, 362, 363
Dog Canyon Ranger Station, 358, 364
Dog Lake, 646
Dogsledding, 221
Dolores, CO, 407
restaurants, 409
Double Arch (Arches), 14, 15
Dragon's Mouth Spring, 604
Drakes Beach, 506
Druid Arch, 127–28
Drury, Newton B., Scenic Parkway, 516, 517
Ducks (Harlequin), 329
Dunlap, CA, 580
Dutton Creek, 187

Eagle Borax Works, 199
Eagles
Black Hills, 67, 76
Bryce Canyon, 97, 106
Canyonlands, 122
Capitol Reef, 143
Devils Tower, 238
Grand Teton, 313
Great Basin, 343, 351
Guadalupe Mountains, 364
Olympic, 468
Yellowstone, 594
Zion, 678, 689
Earthquake Trail, 500, 504
East Anacapa Island, 166–68
East Glacier, MT, 244, 247, 258
accommodations, 261
restaurants, 264–65
East Rim Drive (Grand Canyon), 285–86
Eielson, AK, 212
Elbe, WA, 427, 444–45
accommodations, 442–43
Elbe State Forest, 438
El Capitan, 355, 361, 646–47
Elephant Hill, 127, 132
Elephant Seal Cove, 175, 176
Elizabeth Lake, 646
Elk
Black Hills, 60, 67, 68, 72
Bryce Canyon, 97
Glacier, 266
Grand Canyon, 277
Grand Teton, 328, 342
Guadalupe Mountains, 356
Mount Rainier, 426, 438
Olympic, 468
Point Reyes, 500, 504
Redwood, 515, 519, 520
Rocky Mountain, 524, 526, 529, 535
Theodore Roosevelt, 585
Yellowstone, 600
Elkhorn Ranch, 583, 585, 586, 591
Elk Mountain (Wind Cave), 72, 77–78
Elk Park (Yellowstone), 601
Elk Prairie (Redwood), 519
El Paso, TX, 40–41, 150–51, 357
El Portal, CA, 658, 659
El Tovar (Grand Canyon), 287, 297, 306
Elwha River, 478, 481
Ely, NV, 344, 345
accommodations, 352
Emerald Lake (Rocky Mountain), 531
Emerald Pools (Zion), 672, 675
Emma Matilda Lake, 324, 326
Emmons Glacier, 435
Endert's Beach, 518, 519
Environment, protecting the, 8
Escalante, UT, 104
Escalante National Monument. *See* Grand Staircase–Escalante National Monument
Escalante Natural Bridge, 104–5

Escalante River, 104–5
Escalante River Canyon, 103
Essex, MT, 261–62
Estes Park, CO, 524, 527, 528, 533, 534, 543
  accommodations, 538–40
  camping, 536–37
  restaurants, 541–42
  supplies, 542–43
Eugene, OR, 180–81
Eugenia Mine, 531
Eureka Dunes, 200

Fairbanks, AK, 211, 212, 214
Fairview Point, 93
Fairy Falls, 611–12
Fairyland Canyon, 95, 97
Falcons. *See* Peregrine falcons
Fall River Pass, 524, 528
Far View Visitor Center, 400, 407–8
Fees, 2–3
Fern Canyon, 516, 517–18
Ferries
  Bainbridge Island, 469
  Channel Islands, 164–65
  Glacier Bay, 270
Fiery Furnace, 14, 17
Firehole Lake, 607, 609
Firehole River, 611
Fish Camp, CA, 660
Fishing
  Black Hills, 77
  Bryce Canyon, 97
  Glacier, 245, 253
  Glacier Bay, 272
  Grand Canyon, 282, 291
  Grand Teton, 329
  Great Basin, 349, 350
  Mount Rainier, 437–38
  North Cascades, 458–59
  permits, 3
  Redwood, 519
  Rocky Mountain, 534
  Sequoia and Kings Canyon, 572
  Yellowstone, 615
  Yosemite, 649–50
Fishing Bridge Visitor Center, 598, 604–5
Flagg Ranch, 318, 319, 330, 332, 333–34, 338, 619
Flagstaff, AZ, 110, 280, 281, 490
  accommodations, 301–3
  restaurants, 309–10
  supplies, 312
Flathead Lake, 253
Flathead River, 247, 253–54
Flat Tops, 493
Flightseeing. *See* Air tours
Float trips. *See also* Canoeing; Rafting
  Grand Teton, 330
Flowers. *See* Wildflowers
Foothills, 562–63
Foothills Visitor Center, 561, 562
Forks, WA
  accommodations, 485, 486
  restaurants, 488
Formation Room (Jewel Cave), 73
Fort Leaton State Historical Park, 56
Fortress Rock, 112
Fort Union Trading Post National Historic Site, 592
Fortynine Palms Oasis, 374
Fossil Exhibit (Badlands), 33
Fountain Paint Pots, 606, 608, 612
Four-wheeling
  Arches, 20
  Big Bend, 50
  Canyon de Chelly, 114
  Canyonlands, 124, 129, 131, 132
  Capitol Reef, 142–43
  Death Valley, 194, 195
  Grand Staircase–Escalante, 105–6
Foxes (Island), 162, 171
Fredonia, AZ
  accommodations, 304
  restaurants, 311–12
Freeman Homestead, 545, 548, 551
Fremont Gorge, 141
Fremont River, 134, 140–41, 143, 144
Frenchy's Cove, 166
Fresno, CA, 560, 631
Friendship Ridge, 519
Frijole Ranch, 355, 358, 360, 363
Fruita, UT, 134, 138, 139–40
  camping, 144
Fruita Schoolhouse, 139–40
Fry, Walter, Nature Center, 562, 573
Furnace Creek, 195, 197, 198, 202, 204
Furnace Creek Creek Visitor Center, 195, 197, 203
Furnace Creek Ranch, 205, 206, 207

Gallup, NM, 110
Gardiner, MT, 599
  accommodations, 624
  restaurants, 628–29
Garfield Peak, 184, 187, 189
Gates of the Arctic National Park, 222
Gaylor Lakes, 647
Gem Lake, 526, 531
General Grant Tree, 563, 567
General Sherman Tree, 562, 565
Geyser Valley, 477–78
Giant Forest (Sequoia), 561, 562, 576–77, 582
  camping, 575–76
  hiking, 564–66
  restaurants, 580
Giant Logs (Petrified Forest), 495
Gibbon Meadows, 601
Gibbon River, 601
Gifford Farmhouse, 138, 140
Gifford Pinchot National Forest, 426
Gillette, WY, 237
Glacier Basin, 435, 536
Glacier Bay Lodge, 270, 272, 273, 275
Glacier Bay National Park
  accommodations and restaurants, 275–76
  attractions, 272
  avoiding crowds, 270
  camping, 271, 272, 274–75
  hiking, 273
  sports and activities, 273–74
  tours and programs, 272–73
Glacier Institute, 249
Glacier National Park
  accommodations, 258–64
  attractions, 246–47
  avoiding crowds, 242
  camping, 244–45, 255–58
  hiking, 249–53
  restaurants, 264–66
  scenic drives, 247–48
  sports and activities, 253–55
  tours and programs, 248–49
Glacier Park Lodge, 247, 259, 264
Glacier Point, 640, 642, 644
Glaciers, 220, 247, 269–70, 323, 329, 425, 433, 435, 436–37, 465. *See also* Glacier Bay National Park; Glacier National Park
Glen Aulin, 647
Glen Canyon National Recreation Area, 104, 106, 137
Glenn Springs, TX, 46

Goat Island Mountain, 438
Goat Lick, 247
Gobblers Knob, 427
Godfrey Glen, 185–86
Gold Bluffs Beach, 519
Golden Canyon (Death Valley), 202
Golden Throne (Capitol Reef), 142
Golden West Visitor Center, 450, 452
Gold Rush, 192, 196, 231
Golf, 459, 650
Gooseberry Canyon, 126
Gordon Stockade, 66
Gould Mine, 549, 550
Government Springs, 50
Granby Lake, 537
Grand Canyon Field Institute, 287
Grand Canyon Lodge, 295, 297, 299, 307
Grand Canyon National Park. *See also* North Rim; South Rim
  accommodations, 296–305
  attractions, 283, 287
  avoiding crowds, 280
  camping, 281, 293–96
  hiking, 283, 287–91
  restaurants, 305–12
  scenic drives, 283, 285–86
  shuttle bus, 281
  sports and activities, 291–93
  supplies, 312
  tours and programs, 286–87, 292–93
Grand Canyon of Yellowstone, 600, 603–4, 610
Grand Canyon Village, 280, 281–82, 287, 293–95
Grand Junction, CO, 10, 137
Grand Lake, CO, 524, 527, 529, 543
  accommodations, 540–41
  camping, 537, 538
  restaurants, 542
  supplies, 542
Grand Park, 435
Grand Sentinel, 564
Grand Staircase–Escalante National Monument, 103–7
Grand Teton National Park
  accommodations, 332–38
  attractions, 319–24
    nearby, 342
  avoiding crowds, 316–17
  camping, 318, 331–32
  for children, 330
  hiking, 322, 324–29, 330
  restaurants, 338–42
  scenic drive, 319, 321, 322–24
  sports and activities, 329–31
  supplies, 342
  tours and programs, 324
Grandview Point, 285
Granite Mountains, 415, 416
Grant Grove (Kings Canyon), 558, 560–63, 573, 576, 577, 582
  camping, 576
  hiking, 566–69
  restaurants, 581
  visitor center, 561
Grant Village, 598, 627
Grant Village Lodge, 621–22
Grapevine Hills, 48
Great Basin National Park
  accommodations, 352–53
  attractions, 348
  avoiding crowds, 344
  camping, 343, 344, 351–52
  for children, 348, 351
  hiking, 343, 346, 348–50
  restaurants, 353–54
  scenic drives, 347
  sports and activities, 350–51
  supplies, 354
  tours and programs, 347–48
Great Beach (Point Reyes), 506
Great Bear Adventure, 254
Great Falls, MT, 242, 243
Great horned owls, 97
Great white sharks, 176, 500
Green River, 119, 120, 125, 126, 129
Greenwater, 427
Grinnell, George Bird, 241
Grizzly Bear Creek, 77
Grizzly Giant, 641
Grosvenor Arch, 106
Gros Ventre, 331
Gros Ventre River, 342
Grotto Canyon (Death Valley), 202
Groveland, CA
  accommodations, 657–58
  restaurants, 663–64, 665
Guadalupe Mountains National Park, 151, 153
  accommodations and restaurants nearby, 364–65
  attractions, 359–60
  avoiding crowds, 356
  camping, 358, 363, 364
  hiking, 358–59, 360–63
  sports and activities, 363–64
  tours and programs, 359
Guadalupe Peak, 355, 356
Guadalupe Peak Trail, 355, 356, 359, 361–62
Gustavus, AK, 270, 272–74
  accommodations, 275–76
  restaurants, 275–76

Haines, AK, 273
Half Dome, 635, 640
  hiking, 644–45
Hang gliding, 459
Happy Isles Nature Center, 635, 638–39, 650
Hardin, MT, 398
Harlequin ducks, 329
Harlequin Lake, 601, 609
Harmony Borax Works, 199
Harney Peak, 67, 80
Harvey, Fred, 287
Hatch, Orrin, 105
Hat Shop (Bryce Canyon), 94
Havasupai Indians, 277
Hayden Valley, 604
Health concerns, 7–8, 91
Healy, AK, 210
  accommodations, 227–28
  camping, 228–29
Heather Lake, 572
Hebgen Lake, 623
Hell Canyon, 73, 76
Hermitage Point Trailhead, 324–25
Hermit's Rest, 285, 287
Heron Pond, 325
Hetch Hetchy, 639, 654
Hickman Bridge, 139
Hickman Natural Bridge, 141
Hidden Canyon, 675
Hidden Falls, 327
Hidden Lake, 247, 250
Hidden Valley (Joshua Tree), 374, 376, 378
High Sierra Trail, 565, 572
Hiking, 8. *See also specific parks*
  maps for, 4–5
  safety tips, 7–8, 43
Hill, Thomas, Studio, 641
Hill City, SD, 84
Hitchcock Meadow, 567
Hohokam Indians, 549, 550
Hoh Rain Forest, 470, 472
Hoh River, 474, 481
Hoh River Valley, 475
Holbrook, AZ, 490
  accommodations, 497–98
  camping, 497
  restaurants, 499
  supplies, 499
Hole-in-the-Rock Scenic Backway, 106
Hole-in-the-Wall, 415, 416, 419, 420

Hood Canal, 465, 469
Hood Canal Floating Bridge, 469
Hoover, Herbert, 109, 192
Hopi Indians, 108–9, 277, 278, 399, 402, 495
Hopi Point, 285
Horseback riding
  Badlands, 36
  Big Bend, 50
  Black Hills, 77
  Bryce Canyon, 96
  Canyon de Chelly, 115
  Capitol Reef, 143
  Carlsbad Caverns, 156–57
  Denali, 223–24
  Glacier, 245, 253
  Grand Canyon, 293
  Grand Staircase–Escalante, 104
  Grand Teton, 330
  Great Basin, 350–51
  Guadalupe Mountains, 358, 363
  Mount Rainier, 437
  Redwood, 520
  Rocky Mountain, 534
  Saguaro, 551
  Snow Canyon State Park, 689
  Theodore Roosevelt, 502
  Yellowstone, 614–15
  Yosemite, 650
  Zion, 677–78
Horse Ranch Mountain, 673
Horses, wild, 585, 588
Horseshoe Canyon, 122, 125, 128
Horsethief Lake, 77, 80
Hospital Rock, 563
Hot-air ballooning, 36, 76
Hot Springs, SD, 60
  restaurants, 86
Hot Springs, TX, 45, 46, 48, 52
Hozomeen, 447
Hualapai Indians, 277
Huckleberry Meadow, 565
Hulett, WY, 240
Hume Lake, 576
Hunter Peak, 363
Hunting, 3
Hurricane Ridge, 468–69, 470, 472, 473, 478–79

Ice-skating, 616, 651
Incline Railway, 453, 454
Indian Arts Museum (Grand Teton), 319, 320, 324
Indian Cultural Museum (Yosemite), 638, 650
Indian Meadow (Guadalupe Mountains), 360
Indian Museum of North America at Crazy Horse, 66
Indians. *See* Native Americans; *and specific tribes*
Information sources, 2, 4. *See also* Web sites
Inspiration Point (Bryce Canyon), 88, 92, 93
Inspiration Point (Grand Teton), 327, 330
Inspiration Point (Yellowstone), 603, 604
Interior, SD, 37–38
Inverness, CA
  accommodations, 509–10
  restaurants, 510
Inyo National Forest, 648, 654
Ipsut Creek, 440
Iron Mountain Road, 67
Isa Lake, 605–6
Island fox, 162, 171
Island in the Sky District, 119, 120, 123, 124, 131, 132, 133
  hiking, 126–27
Island in the Sky Visitor Center, 122, 123, 124

Jackrabbits, 14, 52, 97, 157, 363, 367, 412, 678
Jackson, William Henry, 321
Jackson Glacier, 247
Jackson Hole, WY, 316, 317, 330, 331
  accommodations, 336–38
  camping, 332
  restaurants, 340–42
Jackson Lake, 313, 319, 320, 324, 325, 329, 334
Jackson Lake Lodge, 313, 320, 324, 325, 330, 332, 334, 338
Jackson Memorial Visitor Center, 428, 429, 430, 433, 439, 444
Jackson Point Overlook, 321
Jacob Lake, 296, 303
Janesville WI, 35–36
Jasper Forest, 493
Javelinas, 544, 552
Jayhawker Canyon, 202
Jedediah Smith Redwoods State Park, 517, 518
Jeep tours. *See* Four-wheeling
Jefferson, Thomas, 58, 62
Jennie Lake Wilderness Area, 563, 564, 572
Jenny Lake, 316, 317, 321–22, 324, 327, 329–30, 335
  camping, 331
  cruises, 329–30
  hiking, 322, 327–28, 330
  visitor center, 317–18, 319, 322
Jenny Lake Lodge, 322, 335, 339
Jet boating
  Arches, 19–20
  Canyonlands, 129
  Redwood, 520
  Talkeetna, AK, 232
Jewel Cave National Monument, 38, 58, 60, 61, 72–77
  attractions, 75
  avoiding crowds, 73–74
  for children, 74
  hiking, 76
  ranger programs, 75–76
  restaurants, 83–84
  tours, 75, 76
John D. Rockefeller, Jr., Memorial Parkway, 317, 319, 320
John Muir Trail, 569, 571, 644
Johns Lake, 246
Johnson Arch, 689
Johnson Creek, 106
Johnson Lake, 349
Joshua Tree National Park
  accommodations near, 378–80
  attractions, 371–73
  avoiding crowds, 368
  camping, 368–69, 370, 377–78
  for children, 377
  hiking, 373–75
  restaurants near, 380–81
  scenic drives, 372
  sports and activities, 376–77
  supplies, 381–82
  tours and programs, 372
Joshua trees, 366, 367, 371, 410, 412, 419
Jumbo Rocks, 371, 376, 378
Juneau, AK, 270
Juniper Lake, 386, 389, 390

Kabotie, Fred, 495
Kaibab National Forest, 291
Kaibab-Paiute Indian Reservation, 687
Kaibab Plateau, 277
Kaiparowits Plateau, 103
Kalispell, MT, 242, 243
Kanab, UT, 104, 280
  accommodations, 303–5
  restaurants, 311
  supplies, 312
Kantishna District (Denali), 210, 213, 216–19, 229–30

Kaweah River, 558, 561, 563, 565, 572–75
Kawuneeche Visitor Center, 528, 535
Kayaking
  Arches, 19
  Big Bend, 50–51
  Channel Islands, 176
  Glacier, 253
  Glacier Bay, 274
  Grand Teton, 330
  Lassen, 389
  North Cascades, 459
  Olympic, 480–81
  Point Reyes, 504, 507–8
  Redwood, 516, 517, 520
  Sequoia and Kings Canyon, 572–73
Keane Wonder Mine, 200
Keane Wonder Spring, 200
Kelbaker Road, 412–13, 416
Kelso Depot, 415, 416, 417
Kelso Dunes, 415, 416, 419
Ken Patrick Trail (Grand Canyon), 288–89
Kepler Cascades, 606
Kern River, 558, 573
Kerouac, Jack, 454–55
Keystone, SD, 60
  restaurants, 84
  tours, 76
Keystone Ferry, 469
Kings Canyon, 558, 564, 569, 570, 572
Kings Canyon National Park. *See* Sequoia and Kings Canyon National Parks
King's Palace, 154, 157
Kings River, 558, 563, 564, 567, 568, 570, 572–73
Kings River National Recreation Trail, 570
Kintla Lake, 252, 256
Klamath, CA
  accommodations, 522
  restaurants, 522–23
Klamath Falls, OR, 180
Klamath River, 516, 517, 520, 522
Knapp's Cabin, 564
Knife River Indian Villages National Historic Site, 591–92
Kodachrome Basin State Park, 93, 99, 104, 106
Kolb Studio, 283
Kolob Arch, 676
Kolob Canyons, 667, 673, 676
Kolob Canyons Visitor Center, 669, 673
Kule Loklo, 503, 504, 505
Ladder Creek Falls, 452
Lady Bird Johnson Grove, 518
La Harmonia Store, 46
Lajitas, TX, 51
Lake Chelan National Recreation Area, 456–57, 461
Lake Crescent Lodge, 484, 487
Lake McDonald Lodge, 250, 259–60, 264
Lake Quinault Lodge, 487
Lake Village (Yellowstone), 605, 621
Landscape Arch, 12, 14–15, 17
La Sal Mountains, 14, 18, 21
Lassen Peak, 383, 387, 388
Lassen Volcanic National Park
  accommodations, 390–92
  attractions, 386–87
  avoiding crowds, 384
  camping, 389–90
  hiking, 387–88
  restaurants, 392
  scenic drives, 387
  sports and activities, 388–89
  supplies, 392
  tours and programs, 387
Las Vegas, NV, 90, 195, 280, 343, 344, 345, 413, 667
Lathrop Canyon, 127
La Verkin Creek, 676
La Wis Wis National Forest, 441
Lawn Lake, 532
LeConte Memorial Lodge, 638
Lee's Ferry, AZ, 292, 305
Lee Vining, CA, 631, 634
  camping, 654
Legion Lake, 76, 80, 83
Lehman Cave, 343, 344, 347–48
Lehman Creek, 349
Leigh Lake, 328
Lembert Dome, 647
Lemon Cove, CA, 579
Lester Ranch, 174
Lewis River, 605
Lexington Arch, 349
Lighthouse Visitor Center (Point Reyes), 502
Limantour Beach, 506
Lincoln, Abraham, 61, 62
Lithograph Canyon, 76
Little Bighorn Battlefield National Monument
  accommodations near, 398
  attractions, 397–98
  avoiding crowds, 395
  history of battle, 393–95
  restaurants near, 398
  special events, 396
  tours, 398
Little Bighorn Days (Hardin), 396
Little Missouri River, 583, 589, 590
Lizards, 17, 53, 97, 143, 363, 412, 490, 552, 678
Llama trips, 480
Lobo Canyon, 172
Lodgepole (Sequoia), 560–61, 562, 573, 575, 580, 582
Logan Pass, 244, 247, 252
Lone Pine, CA, 206
Lone Star Geyser, 606, 611
Longhorn cattle, 56
Long Logs (Petrified Forest), 495
Longmire Hiker Information Center and Museum, 428–32
Longs Peak, 524, 526, 532
  hiking, 531, 532–33
  mountaineering, 534
Loomis Museum, 384
Lost Horse Mine (Joshua Tree), 375
Lost Mine (Big Bend), 47, 49
Lost Palms Oasis, 375
Lost Peak, 362
Lower Calf Creek Falls, 104
Lower Yosemite Fall, 643
Lumsden, CA, 654

McClure's Beach, 503, 506
McDonald, Lake, 246, 248, 249, 250, 253, 255, 256, 259–60
McKinleyville, CA, 513
McKittrick Canyon, 355, 356, 358, 359–60, 362–63
Madison Junction, 601, 607
Main Fork Dosewallips, 479
Maltese Cross Cabin, 587, 588, 591
Mammoth Hot Springs (Yellowstone), 600, 602
  accommodations, 619–20
  hiking, 609–10
  restaurants, 625–26
  visitor center, 598, 602
Mancos, CO, 405, 406
  accommodations, 406
  restaurants, 408–9
Many Glacier Lake, 248, 249, 250–51, 253
Manzanita Lake, 388, 389
Manzanita Spring, 361
Maple Glade Rain Forest, 475
Maps, 4–5
Marble Canyon, AZ, 305, 307–8
Marble Falls, 570–71
Marblemount, WA, 463–64

Maricopa Point, 283
Mariposa, CA, 634
  accommodations, 658–59
  restaurants, 663, 664–65
Mariposa Grove Museum, 641
Mariposa Grove of Big Trees, 640–41, 642, 645
Marmots, 143, 426, 438–39, 472, 535, 687
Marsical Mine, 46–47
Marymere Falls, 477
Massacre Cave, 113
Mather Overlook, 344
May Lake, 647–48
Mazama, WA, 462
Mazama Village, 182–83, 185, 186, 187, 189, 190
Maze District (Canyonlands), 120, 122, 124, 128
Medford, OR, 180
Medora, ND, 586, 592, 593
  accommodations, 593
Medora Visitor Center, 586, 587, 588, 591
Menor/Noble Historic District (Grand Teton), 319, 322
Merced, CA, 631
  restaurants, 663, 664
Merced Grove, 639
Merced River, 630–31, 638
Mesa Arch (Canyonlands), 126
Mesa Top Ruins Drive, 402–3
Mesa Verde National Park
  accommodations, 406–7
  attractions, 402
  avoiding crowds, 400
  camping, 405
  hiking, 403–4
  restaurants, 407–9
  scenic drives, 402–3
  tours and programs, 403
Mill Creek, CA, 391–92
Mills, Enos, Cabin, 543
Mills Lake, 532
Mineral, CA, 386, 391
Mineral King, 558, 560, 561, 563, 574–75, 577
Miners Mountain, 142
Mink Lake, 476
Mirror Lake, 635, 643
Mist Falls, 568, 569
Mitchell Caverns, 415–17
Miwok Indians, 500, 503, 504, 505
Moab, UT, 10, 12, 122, 133
  accommodations, 21–24
  bike rentals, 20
  camping, 21, 133
  outfitters, 18–19, 129, 130–31
  restaurants, 24–26
  supplies, 26
Mohave Point, 285
Mojave Desert, 366, 367, 370–73, 410, 412
Mojave Indians, 418
Mojave National Preserve, 410–22
  accommodations, 421
  attractions, 414–16, 417
  avoiding crowds, 412
  camping, 413–14, 420–21
  for children, 420
  hiking, 417, 419
  restaurants near, 422
  scenic drives, 416
  sports and activities, 420
  tours and programs, 416–17
Mojave Road, 418, 419, 420
Monache Indians, 563, 571
Monarch Wilderness, 563, 564, 570–71
Mono Pass, 648
Monticello, UT, 133, 400
Monument Canyon, 108
Moorcroft, WY, 237
Moose
  Denali, 208, 211, 218, 219, 225
  Glacier, 241, 246, 254, 266, 267
  Grand Canyon, 297
  Grand Teton, 316, 325, 328, 329
  Talkeetna Moose Dropping Festival, 232
Moose, WY, 319, 330, 331
Moose Ponds, 327
Moose Village, 322
Moose Visitor Center, 317, 319, 322, 331
Moraine Park Museum, 528, 530, 534
Moran, Thomas, Point, 285
Moran, WY, 317, 319–20, 330
Morefield Village, 400
Morgan Horse Ranch, 504, 505
Mormon settlers, 106, 126, 134, 138, 140, 366, 666, 687–88
Moro Rock, 562, 566
Mosaic Canyon, 201
Mossy Cave, 94
Mount Adams, 430, 433, 434
Mountain biking. *See also* Biking
  Big Bend, 50
  Bryce Canyon, 96–97
  Canyonlands, 129, 131–32
  Capitol Reef, 142–43
  Custer State Park, 76–77
  Denali, 223
  North Cascades, 458
  Olympic, 479–80
  Point Reyes, 506, 507
  Prairie Creek Redwoods State Park, 520
  Rocky Mountain, 533–34
  Talkeetna, AK, 232
  Zion, 677
Mountain climbing
  Glacier, 253
  Grand Teton, 329, 330–31
  Mount Rainier, 438
  Rocky Mountain, 534
  Yosemite, 650
Mountaineering, 216, 429, 438, 534, 650, 665. *See also* Mountain climbing; Rock climbing
Mountain goats, 426, 438
Mountain lions, 43, 52, 363, 666
Mount Baker Ski Area, 460
Mount Carmel, UT, 668–69
Mount Constance, 479
Mount Dana, 647, 648
Mount Fremont, 434
Mount McKinley, 208–11, 214, 216, 220, 221, 232
Mount Mazama. *See* Crater Lake
Mount Moran, 319, 321, 328
Mount Owen, 321
Mount Rainier, 423–24, 426, 432, 438
Mount Rainier National Park
  accommodations, 441–44
  attractions, 429–31
  avoiding crowds, 426–27
  camping, 428, 440–41
  hiking, 430, 431–37
  restaurants, 444–45
  sports and activities, 437–39
  tours and programs, 431
Mount Rushmore National Memorial, 38, 58, 60, 61–65
  attractions, 63, 65
  avoiding crowds, 62
  hiking, 65
  restaurants, 83, 84
  scenic drives, 63–64
  tours and programs, 64–65
Mount St. Helens, 424
Mount Scott, 187
Mount Storm King, 477
Mount Washburn, 603, 610, 614
Mount Whitney, 558, 572, 644

Mount Wittenberg, 506
Mowich Lake, 430, 437, 441
Mud Volcano, 604
Muir, John, 249, 269, 568, 569
  Rock, 568, 569
  Trail, 569, 571, 644
Muldrow Glacier, 220
Mule deer
  Badlands, 30
  Big Bend, 52
  Black Hills, 67, 76
  Bryce Canyon, 97
  Carlsbad Caverns, 157
  Glacier, 266
  Grand Teton, 328
  Great Basin, 343, 349, 351
  Guadalupe Mountains, 356
  Mojave, 412
  Rocky Mountain, 524, 535
  Saguaro, 552
  Theodore Roosevelt, 585
  Zion, 687
Mule Ears Spring, 48
Mule rides, at Grand Canyon, 293
Mummy Cave, 112–13
Mummy House, 112
Mussels, 271
Mystic Falls, 611
Mystic Lake, 437

Naches Peak, 434
Narrows, the (Zion), 666, 668, 675, 676
National Elk Refuge, 342
Native American Celebration (Point Reyes), 503
Native Americans. *See also* Petroglyphs; *and specific tribes*
  Big Bend, 46
  Black Hills, 67
  Devils Tower, 236, 239
  Lassen Volcanic, 383–84
  Little Bighorn, 393–95, 397–98
  Mojave, 410, 418
  Mount Rainier, 426, 430
  Theodore Roosevelt, 591–92
  Yosemite, 638
Natural Bridge (Bryce Canyon), 93
Natural Bridge (Death Valley), 201
Navajo Indians, 108–13, 277
Navajo Point, 286
Navajo Reservation, 110–11
Needles, CA, 123, 413, 422
  accommodations, 421
Needles District (Canyonlands), 119, 120, 123, 124, 125, 132, 133
  hiking, 127–28
Needles Highway, 66, 67, 72, 80
Needles Visitor Center, 122, 123, 125, 132
Nemo, SD, 82
Nenana River, 210, 223, 228
Nevada Fall, 644
Never Summer Ranch, 530
Newcastle, WY, 81
Newhalem, 452
Newspaper Rock, 494
Nipton, CA, 413, 417, 421
Nisqually Glacier, 433
Noble Historic District (Grand Teton), 319, 322
Norris Geyser Basin, 598, 600, 601–2, 609
Norris Geyser Basin Museum, 601
North Cascades Institute, 454
North Cascades National Park
  accommodations, 461–63
  attractions, 452–53, 454
  avoiding crowds, 447
  camping, 451, 460–61
  hiking, 454–58
  restaurants, 463–64
  sports and activities, 458–60
  tours and programs, 453–54
North Dakota badlands, 583–85. *See also* Badlands National Park; Theodore Roosevelt National Park
North Dakota Badlands Overlook, 588–89
North Dome (Kings Canyon), 564
North Dome (Yosemite), 648
North Fork Cascade River, 458
North Kaibab Trail (Grand Canyon), 290–91
North Rim (Grand Canyon), 280, 286, 293, 312
  accommodations, 299, 303
  camping, 295–96
  hiking, 288–89, 290–91
  restaurants, 307
  visitor center, 282
North Umpqua River, 191
North Unit Scenic Drive, 589–90

Oakhurst, CA, accommodations, 659–60
Oasis of Mara, 367, 371, 374, 377
Oasis Visitor Center, 366, 370, 371, 377
Ogle Cave, 156
Ohanepecosh Nature Trail, 430
Ohanepecosh River, 429, 435–36, 437
Ohanepecosh Visitor Center, 428, 429, 431, 435
Old Faithful, 600, 606–7
  accommodations, 622–23
  hiking, 611–12
  restaurants, 627
  visitor center, 598, 606
Old Faithful Inn, 622, 627
Olema, CA, 502
  accommodations, 509
Olema Valley, 504
Olmsted Point, 639
Olympia, WA, 469
Olympic Hot Springs, 473
Olympic National Forest, 479
Olympic National Park, 427
  accommodations, 484–87
  attractions, 471, 473
  avoiding crowds, 468–69
  camping, 470, 481–84
  hiking, 472, 473–79
  restaurants, 487–88
  scenic drives, 471–73
  sports and activities, 479–81
  tours and programs, 473
Orick, CA, 513, 520, 523
  restaurants, 523
Ostrander Lake, 645
Ouzel Falls, 531–32
Owls (Great horned), 97
Oxbow Bend (Grand Teton), 320, 324
Oxbow Overlook (Theodore Roosevelt), 589, 590, 591
Oysters, 505
Ozette Lake, 480

Pacific Crest Trail, 180, 187–88, 388, 434, 457–58, 571
Packwood, WA, 427, 444, 445
Page, AZ, 292
Painted Canyon Visitor Center, 586, 587, 588
Painted Desert, 489–90
  visitor center, 490, 492, 494–95, 498–99
Painted Desert Inn, 494–95
Painted Desert Rim Trail, 496
Painted Desert Wilderness, 490, 493, 497
Painted Desert Wilderness Trail, 494, 496–97

Paiute Indians, 87, 134, 277
Palisades Lake, 435
Palm Springs, CA, 369
Panguitch, UT, 101
Panther Creek, 456
Parade of Elephants, 14, 15–16
Paradise Meadow, 388
Paradise (Mount Rainier), 429, 430, 433, 439
Paradise Valley, 568–69
Paragliding, 459
Park Avenue, 14, 16
Park Creek, 458
Patton, George S., Memorial Museum, 373
Peaceful Valley Ranch, 589
Peach Springs, AZ, 292
Peak-to-Peak Scenic Byway, 527
Peary, Robert, 214
Peek-a-boo Canyon, 105
Peregrine falcons, 97, 106, 364, 678
Permits, 2, 3, 8
Petrified Forest National Park
  accommodations near, 497–98
  attractions, 492–93, 494–95
  avoiding crowds, 490
  camping, 492
    nearby, 497
  hiking, 495–97
  restaurants, 498–99
  scenic drives, 493–94
  supplies, 499
  tours and programs, 494
Petrified Tree (Yellowstone), 603
Petroglyph Point (Mesa Verde), 405
Petroglyphs
  Arches, 14, 15, 16
  Big Bend, 46, 49
  Capitol Reef, 134, 138, 139, 140
  Joshua Tree, 372, 373
  Little Bighorn, 398
  Mesa Verde, 405
  Mojave, 410
  Olympic, 474
  Petrified Forest, 492, 494, 495
  Saguaro, 549, 550
  Zion, 688
Pets, traveling with, 7
Phantom Ranch, 282, 287, 298–99, 307
Phipps Wash, 105
Phoenix, AZ, 280
Piedmont, SD, 85–86
Pierre, SD, 31, 60, 61, 77
Pine Canyon (Wind Cave), 48–49
Pine City (Joshua Tree), 374
Pine Creek Canyon (Zion), 675
Pinery, The (Guadalupe Mountains), 359, 360–61
Pine Springs, 356, 358, 359, 361, 364
Pine Springs Visitor Center, 355, 358, 359, 363
Pintado Point, 494
Pioneer Memorial Museum (Olympic), 470, 471, 641
Pioneer Yosemite History Center, 641
Pipe Spring National Monument, 687–88
Pitamakan Pass, 252–53
Piute Spring, 418
Point Bennet, 174
Point Lookout (Mesa Verde), 404
Point Reyes Bird Observatory, 504, 507
Point Reyes Lighthouse, 504, 507
Point Reyes National Seashore
  accommodations, 508–10
  attractions, 504, 505
  avoiding crowds, 500, 502
  beaches, 506
  camping, 502, 508
  hiking, 504, 505–6
  restaurants, 510–11
  sports and activities, 506–8
  tours and programs, 504–5
Point Reyes Station, CA, 502, 508, 510–11
Polebridge, MT, 242, 248, 252, 253
  accommodations, 262
  restaurants, 265
Polly Dome Lake, 648
Polychrome Pass, 220
Ponderosa Canyon, 92–93
Port Angeles, WA, 469, 471, 472
  accommodations, 485–86
  restaurants, 487–88
Port Townsend, WA, 469
Potato Harbor Overlook, 170
Potwisha, 571
Powell, John Wesley, 87, 119–20, 122, 688
  Memorial, 283
Powell Lake, 106
Prairie Creek Redwoods State Park, 519, 520
Prairie Creek Visitor Center, 513–14
Prairie dogs, 30, 32, 60, 67, 91, 97, 238, 585, 589, 591
Prairie grasslands, 29–30, 34, 67, 68, 72, 237
Prater Ridge (Mesa Verde), 404–5
Pratt Lodge, 359–60, 362
Presidential Trail (Mount Rushmore), 64, 65
Primm, NV, 422
Prince Island, 173
Prisoner's Harbor, 169
Pronghorns, 30, 67, 72, 97, 490
Prospect, OR, accommodations, 190–91
Providence Mountains State Recreation Area, 413, 414, 415, 420
Pueblo Indians. *See also* Mesa Verde National Park
  Canyon de Chelly, 108, 110, 112, 113–14
  Canyonlands, 127
  Grand Canyon, 285–86, 286
  Petrified Forest, 489, 492, 494, 495, 496
Puerco Pueblo, 494, 496
Puget Sound, 423, 469
Pumice Desert, 183, 184, 186
Pumice Flat, 188
Pyramid Lake, 456

Quartz Lake, 252
Queen's Garden (Bryce Canyon), 92, 93, 94–95
Queets River, 474, 475, 481
Quinault, Lake, 471–72, 475–76, 487

Rabbits. *See* Jackrabbits
Rafting
  Arches, 19–20
  Big Bend, 50–51
  Canyonlands, 129
  Denali, 223
  Glacier, 253–54
  Grand Canyon, 291–92
  Grand Teton, 330
  Mount Rainier, 438
  Olympic, 481
  Talkeetna, AK, 232–33
  Yosemite, 650
Rainbow Falls (North Cascades), 457, 458
Rainbow Forest Museum (Petrified Forest), 492
Rainbow Forest Wilderness, 497

Rainbow Point Overlook (Bryce Canyon), 92
Rain forests, 470, 472. *See also* Olympic National Park
Rampart Bridge, 432–33, 439
Randle, 427
Rankin Ridge, 72
Rapid City, SD, 30, 32, 38, 60, 61, 237
  accommodations, 82
  camping, 81
  restaurants, 84–85
  tours, 76
Rattlesnakes, 30, 53, 97, 138, 238, 490, 545, 546, 552, 678, 689
Rattlesnake Springs, 150
Reagan, Ronald, 512
Red Bluff, CA, 384
Redding, CA, 384
Red Hills Visitor Center, 546, 547, 548, 550, 552
Redwood Creek, 519
Redwood Information Center, 513, 516
Redwood National and State Parks
  accommodations, 521–22
  attractions, 516
  avoiding crowds, 513
  camping, 514, 520–21
  hiking, 516, 517–18
  restaurants, 522–23
  scenic drives, 516–17
  sports and activities, 517–18
  supplies, 523
  tours and programs, 517
Reifel, Ben, Visitor Center, 31, 32, 35, 36
Reno, Marcus, 394
Reno, NV, 344, 345
Rhodes Cabin (Great Basin), 348
Rialto Beach, 474
Riggs Spring, 96
Rim Drive (Crater Lake), 184, 189
Rim Trail (Bryce Canyon), 88, 92, 94, 95
Rim Village (Crater Lake), 182, 183–84, 187, 189
  hiking, 186–87
  visitor center, 182, 183
Rincon Mountain District (Saguaro), 544–47, 551, 552
Rincon Mountain Wilderness, 551–53
Rio Grande River, 39, 45, 50–51, 52, 56
Rio Grande Village, 45, 47, 52–55
River running. *See* Canoeing; Kayaking; Rafting
Roadrunners, 194, 199, 367, 412, 552
Roaring Mountain, 602
Roaring River Falls, 564
Roaring Springs Canyon, 291
Roberts Prairie Dog Town, 32
Rock climbing
  Arches, 20
  Badlands, 31
  Devils Tower, 238, 239
  Joshua Tree, 376–77
  Sequoia and Kings Canyon, 572
  Snow Canyon State Park, 689
  Zion, 678
Rockefeller, Jr., John D., Memorial Parkway, 317, 319, 320
Rockerville, SD, 85
Rockport, WA, 461–61
Rocky Mountain National Park
  accommodations, 538–41
  attractions, 525, 529–30
    nearby, 543
  avoiding crowds, 527
  camping, 528, 533, 536–38
  for children, 535
  hiking, 525, 531–33
  restaurants near, 541–42
  scenic drives, 530
  sports and activities, 533–35
  supplies, 542–43
  tours and programs, 530
Rogue River Gorge, 191
Roosevelt, Franklin D., 163, 468
Roosevelt, Theodore, 58, 62, 68, 73, 234, 279, 468, 489, 543, 583, 585, 587, 588, 591, 620
  Elkhorn Ranch, 583, 585, 586, 591
Roosevelt elk. *See* Elk
Roosevelt Lodge, 608, 614, 620–21, 626
Roosevelt National Park. *See* Theodore Roosevelt National Park
Rosa Island, 161–62
Roseburg, OR, 180
Ross Lake, 446, 450, 453, 454, 456, 459, 461
Ross Lake Dam, 453, 454, 459
Ross Lake National Recreation Area, 454, 460
Roubaix Lake, 80
Ruby Beach, 471, 472
Running Eagle Falls, 251
RVs (recreational vehicles), 5–6
Ryan Mountain, 375

Sable Pass, 220
Saddle Pass, 35
Safety tips, 7–8
Sage Creek, 36
Saguaro East, 544–47, 551, 552
Saguaro National Park, 544–57
  accommodations near, 553–56
  attractions, 547–48, 549
  avoiding crowds, 544–45
  camping, 552–53
  for children, 552
  hiking, 545, 546, 547, 549–52
  restaurants near, 556–57
  scenic drives, 548
  sports and activities, 552
  supplies, 557
  tours and programs, 549
Saguaro West, 544–47, 549, 550–51
St. George, AZ, 667
St. Mary, MT, 244, 255, 257, 258
  accommodations, 262
St. Mary Lake, 248–49, 253
St. Mary Lodge, 264, 262
Salt Creek, 201
Salt Lake City, UT, 343, 345–46
Sams River, 475
San Andreas Fault, 500
Sand Dune Arch, 14, 15, 16
Sand Dunes (Death Valley), 201
San Francisco, CA, 502, 513, 560, 631
San Miguel Island, 161–65, 167, 173–74
Santa Barbara ice plant, 175
Santa Barbara Island, 161–65, 167, 175–76, 176
Santa Cruz Island, 161–62, 163, 165, 166, 167, 169–71, 177
Santa Elena, Mexico, 56
Santa Elena Canyon, 44, 45, 47, 51
Santa Rosa Island, 161–62, 163, 165, 167, 171–72, 176
Savage River Bridge, 219
Sawtooth Peak, 563
Schoolroom Glacier, 329
Schwabacher Landing, 323
Scorpion Canyon, 170
Scorpion Ranch, 169–70, 171
Scotty's Castle, 195, 197, 199

Scuba diving, Channel Islands, 176
Sea kayaking. *See* Kayaking
Sea lions, 162, 167, 173, 174, 175, 503, 515
Seals, 162, 167, 173, 175, 503, 515
Seattle, WA, 423–24, 427–28, 447, 450, 469
Senior citizen travelers, 2–3
Sentinel Dome, 645
Sequoia and Kings Canyon National Parks, 558–82. *See also* Cedar Grove; Giant Forest; Grant Grove
  accommodations, 576–80
  attractions, 561–64
  avoiding crowds, 560
  camping, 560, 573–76
  for children, 573
  hiking, 562, 563, 564–72
  restaurants, 580–82
  sports and activities, 572–73
  supplies, 582
  tours and programs, 564
Sequoia Lake, 567
Sequoia National Forest, 563, 576, 577–78, 580–81
Serrano Indians, 371
Sharks, great white, 176, 500
Sheep, 219, 610. *See also* Bighorn sheep
Sheep Creek, 95–96
Sheridan, WY, 395
Shoshone Lake, 612–13
Sierra National Forest, 654
Signal Hill Petroglyphs, 549, 550
Signal Mountain, 313, 321, 325–26, 331, 334–35, 339
Signal Mountain Lodge, 325, 330, 332, 334–35, 339
Sioux Falls, SD, 33, 435
  tours, 76
Sioux Indians, 28, 31, 66
Sir Francis Drake Highway, 502, 504
Sitting Bull, 395
Skagit River, 452, 461
Skiing. *See also* Cross-country skiing
  Mount Rainier, 439
  Rocky Mountain, 534–35
  Yellowstone, 651
Skokomish River, 479
Skull Rock, 375
Skyline Arch, 14, 16
Slaughter Canyon Cave, 150, 154–57
Sledding, 389
Slickrock Canyon, 49
Sliding House, 114
Smith Redwoods State Park, 517, 518
Smith River, 516
Smith River Recreation Area, 520–21
Smith Spring, 361
Smugglers Cove, 170
Snake Creek, 351
Snake River, 313, 319, 322–23, 330
Snake River Overlook, 320
Snakes, 194, 552, 666, 678. *See also* Rattlesnakes
Snoqualmie National Forest, 426
Snow Canyon State Park, 678, 679, 688–89
Snow coach tours, at Yellowstone, 616
Snow Lake, 433
Snowmobiling
  Black Hills, 77
  Cedar Breaks, 687
  Crater Lake, 189
  Grand Teton, 331
  Rocky Mountain, 535
  Yellowstone, 615, 616
Snowshoeing
  Bryce Canyon, 97
  Crater Lake, 189
  Glacier, 254
  Mount Rainier, 439
  North Cascades, 460
  Olympic, 480
  Rocky Mountain, 534–35
  Sequoia and Kings Canyon, 573
  Yellowstone, 616
Soda Canyon, 405
Soda Dry Lake, 417, 419
Soda Springs, 417, 418, 648
Sol Duc Falls, 472, 476
Sol Duc Hot Springs, 472, 484
Solitary Geyser, 611
Solitude Lake, 329
Sonoran Desert, 103, 544, 545, 550, 551
Sourdough Mountain, 455
Sourdough Ridge, 434
South Rim (Grand Canyon), 280, 291, 292, 293, 312
  accommodations, 297–99
  attractions, 287
  camping, 293–95
  hiking, 288, 290, 291
  restaurants, 305–7
  visitor center, 281–82, 283
South Unit Scenic Drive (Theodore Roosevelt), 588–89
Spalding Bay, 321
Specimen Ridge, 603
Spider Cave, 150, 154, 156
Spirit of Adventure (tour boat), 272, 273, 274
Spooky Canyon, 105
Sportsman Lake, 614
Springdale, UT
  accommodations, 680–82
  entertainment, 684–85
  restaurants, 683–84
  supplies, 684
Spruce Canyon, 405
Spruce Railroad, 477
Spruce Tree House, 403–4
Squaw Canyon, 128
Squaw Valley, CA, 581–82
Staircase Falls, 479
Stanislaus National Forest, 654
Star watching, 92
Steamboat, OR, 191
Steamboat Geyser, 601
Stehekin, WA, 447, 450–51, 461
Stehekin Lodge, 460, 461, 463
Stehekin River, 456, 458, 459
Stehekin Valley, 460, 461
Stella Lake, 348
Step House, 404
Stetattle Creek, 455
Stevens Canyon, 427
Stockade Lake, 77, 80
Stovepipe Wells, 195, 203, 204, 206, 207
Straits of Juan de Fuca, 465, 469, 479
Strawberry Creek, 351
String Lake, 321, 328
Stuart Falls, 188
Sully Creek State Park, 590
Sulphur Creek Canyon (Capitol Reef), 141
Sulphur Works (Lassen Volcanic), 384, 386, 387, 389, 604
Summit Lake, 386–89
Sundance, WY, 240
Sun Point, 247
Sunrift Gorge, 247
Sunrise Lakes (Yosemite), 648–49
Sunrise Point (Bryce Canyon), 93
Sunrise Visitor Center (Mount Rainier), 428–31, 434
Surfing, 516, 519
Susanville, CA, 384
Susitna River, 232–33
Swamp Canyon, 93
Swan Lake, 325, 602
Swiftcurrent Lake, 260

Swimming, 188. *See also* Beaches
Sylvan Lake, 80, 83
Syncline Valley, 127

Tacoma, WA, 469
Taft Point, 645–46
Taggart Lake, 328
Tahoma Indians, 423
Take-Out Beach, 20, 129
Talkeetna, AK, 210, 216, 231–33
Talkeetna River, 232–33
Tall Trees Grove, 518, 519
Tanque Verde Ridge, 551
Tarantulas, 678
Tattler Creek, 220
Taylor Creek, 676
Teepees (Petrified Forest), 494
Teewinot Mountain, 321, 327
Teklanika River, 219
Telescope Peak, 202
Tenaya Creek, 643, 649
Teresa Lake, 348
Terlingua, TX, 50, 51
  accommodations, 54–55
Teton Village, WY, 331, 332
  accommodations, 335–36
  restaurants, 339–40
Tharp's Log, 562
Theodore Roosevelt National Park
  accommodations and restaurants, 593
  attractions, 587, 591–92
  avoiding crowds, 585–86
  camping, 586, 592–93
  hiking, 588, 589, 590–91
  scenic drives, 587–90
  sports and activities, 592
  tours and programs, 591
Thornton Lakes, 455
Thorofare Area (Yellowstone), 613–14
Thorofare Pass (Denali), 220
Thor's Hammer, 93
Three Rivers, CA, 560, 578
  accommodations, 578, 579
  restaurants, 581
Thunderbird Lodge, 111, 113, 114, 116, 117, 118
Thunder Creek, 455–56
Tieton River, 438
Timber Lake, 532
Timber Top Mountain, 673
Tioga Lake, 654
Titus Canyon, 201, 203
Toklat, AK, 212
Toklat River, 220
Tolmie Peak, 436
Tomales Bay, 500, 504, 507–8
Tomales Point, 504, 506
Torrey, UT, 137
  accommodations, 145–47
  camping, 144–45
  restaurants, 147
  supplies, 147
Torrey Pines State Reserve, 162
Tortoises. *See* Desert tortoises
Tourist information. *See* Information sources
Tower Arch, 12, 18
Tower Junction, 602, 603
Trail Ridge Road, 524, 526–30, 535
Transept Trail (Grand Canyon), 289
Tropic, UT, 98
  accommodations, 100, 101
  restaurants, 102
Tropic Reservoir, 97, 99
Tsaile, AZ, 117
Tsegi Overlook, 113
Tucson, AZ, 545, 546
  accommodations, 553–56
  restaurants, 556–57
  supplies, 557
Tucson Mountain District (Saguaro), 544–47, 549, 550–51
Tuff Canyon, 47
Tundra World Nature Trail, 531
Tunnel Log, 562
Tuolumne Grove, 639–40
Tuolumne Meadows, 639–40, 642, 647, 650
  accommodations, 656–57
  camping, 653–54
  hiking, 648
  restaurants, 662
  visitor center, 634
Tuolumne Pass, 649
Tuolumne River, 654
Turkeys, wild, 364
Tusayan, AZ
  accommodations, 299–300
  air tours, 293
  restaurants, 308–9
Tusayan Pueblo, 285–86
Twentynine Palms, CA, 369, 378, 381–82
  accommodations, 378–80
  restaurants, 380–81
  supplies, 381–82
Twin Falls (Glacier), 251
Twin Lakes (Yellowstone), 602
Two Medicine Lake, 248, 249, 251, 255
Two Ocean Lake, 323–24, 326
Two Ribbons Trail, 601

Ubehebe Crater, 201–2
Upheaval Dome, 126
Upper Kintla Lake, 252
Upper Yosemite Fall, 643
Ute Indians, 14, 16

Vail and Vickers Company, 163, 167, 171, 172
Valdez Cave (Channel Islands), 169
Valley View Overlook (Saguaro), 550
Vancouver, George, 163, 423
Ventura, CA, 164, 165, 176
  accommodations, 177
  restaurants, 177–78
  supplies, 178
Vernal Fall, 638, 643–44
Viola Falls, 568
Virgin, UT, 682
Virgin River, 672, 676, 678
Visalia, CA, 560
  accommodations, 578, 580
  restaurants, 581, 582
Visitor information. *See* Information sources
Volcanoes, 383, 424, 604
  Crater Lake, 179, 186–87

Walhalla Glades, 286
Wall, SD, 30, 37
  accommodations, 38
Wall Drug Store (Wall, SD), 37
Walnut Canyon, 153
Walter Fry Nature Center, 562, 573
Warner Valley, 384, 386, 389
Washburn Hot Springs, 603
Washington, George, 58, 62, 63
Wasson Peak, 550, 551
Watchman, the (Crater Lake), 186
Watchman Trail (Zion), 672, 675
Watchtower, the (Yellowstone), 286, 287
Water, drinking, 7–8
Waterton Lakes National Park, 241, 266–68
  camping, 267
  hiking, 267

Waterton Village (Glacier), 267–68
Watford City, ND, 586, 593
 accommodations, 593
Wawona, 638, 640, 641, 645, 646, 650, 652, 656, 662–63
Wawona Meadow, 646
Wawona Tunnel Tree, 641
Weatherill Mesa, 400, 402, 404
Web sites, 2, 4, 5, 690–91
Weeping Rock, 674
Weeping Wall, 246–47
Wenatchee National Forest, 426
West Glacier, MT, 242, 243, 246, 247, 249, 251, 254, 258
 accommodations, 262–64
 restaurants, 266
West Rim Drive (Grand Canyon), 283, 285
West Thumb Geyser Basin, 605
West Yellowstone, MT, 595, 598, 601, 609
 accommodations, 623–24
 bike rentals, 614
 camping, 618–19
 restaurants, 627–28
Whale watching
 Channel Islands, 162, 166, 170
 Gustavus, AK, 274
 Point Reyes, 506–7
 Redwood, 519–20
Wheeler Peak, 343, 344, 346, 347, 350
Wheeler Peak Scenic Drive, 344, 347
Whidbey Island, 469
White, Georgie, 279
White City, OR, 190
Whitefish, MT, 254
White Giant, 155
White House Ruin, 112, 114, 115
White Pass, 437, 439
White River, 425, 441
White River Visitor Center, 31, 32, 38
White's City, NM, 157–58, 160, 364, 365
White-water rafting. *See* Rafting
White Wolf, 653, 656, 663
Widforss Trail (Grand Canyon), 289
Wildcat Beach, 505–6
Wildflowers
 Badlands, 30
 Crater Lake, 185
 Grand Teton, 325, 326
 Great Basin, 343, 348, 349
 Guadalupe Mountains, 356
 Joshua Tree, 368, 371
 Lassen Volcanic, 388
 Mojave, 412, 414
 Mount Rainier, 426, 428, 435
 Olympic, 473, 479
 Petrified Forest, 490
 Point Reyes, 502
 Redwood, 515
 Saguaro, 545, 547
 Yellowstone, 594
 Zion, 687
Wildlife. *See also specific animals*
 safety tips, 7, 43
Wildlife Museum (West Glacier), 254
Wildman Meadow, 571
Wildrose Peak, 202
Williams, AZ, 278, 280, 281
 accommodations, 300–301
 restaurants, 310–11
Williams Ranch, 358, 360, 361
Willow Flats, 325
Wind Cave National Park, 38, 58–60
 attractions, 70
 avoiding crowds, 68
 camping, 68, 70, 77–78
 hiking, 72
 ranger programs, 72
 restaurants, 83
 scenic drives, 71–72
 tours, 70–71
Window View (Big Bend), 44, 47
Winfield Scott (shipwreck), 168
Winslow, AZ, 490
Winsor Castle, 687
Winthrop, WA
 accommodations, 462–63
 restaurants, 463, 464
Winthrop Glacier, 435
Wizard Island (Crater Lake), 179–80, 183, 185, 186, 188
Wolfe Ranch, 14, 15, 16
Wolverton, CA, 565, 571, 573, 582
Wolves, 208, 219, 220, 446, 458, 594
Wonder Lake, 212, 219, 220
Wonderland of Rocks (Joshua Tree), 371, 372
Wonderland Trail, 424, 431, 432, 436, 439
Wood River, 230
Wounded Knee, SD, 38
Wrangell–St. Elias National Park, 210, 222

Yahi Indians, 383–84
Yavapai Observation Station, 282
Yavapai Point, 288
Yellowstone Lake, 600, 605, 621
 boating, 614, 615
 hiking around, 610–11
 restaurants, 626–27
Yellowstone National Park, 317. *See also* Canyon Village; Mammoth Hot Springs; Old Faithful
 accommodations, 619–25
 attractions, 600–608
 avoiding crowds, 595
 camping, 599, 616–19
 for children, 615
 hiking, 601, 602, 603, 609–14
 restaurants, 625–29
 scenic drives, 600–603
 sports and activities, 614–16
 supplies, 629
 tours and programs, 608
Yellowstone River, 604, 610
 Grand Canyon of, 600, 603–4, 610
Yosemite Falls, 630, 643
Yosemite Lodge, 631, 635, 637, 638, 641, 642, 649, 655, 662
Yosemite Museum, 638, 650
Yosemite National Park
 accommodations, 654–60
 attractions, 635–41
 avoiding crowds, 631
 camping, 634, 651–54
 for children, 650
 hiking, 638, 643–49
 restaurants, 660–65
 shuttle bus, 635, 636
 sports and activities, 649–51
 supplies, 665
 tours and programs, 641–43
Yosemite Pioneer Cemetery, 638
Yosemite River, 646
Yosemite Valley, 630–31, 637–39, 650
 accommodations, 654–56
 camping, 651–52
 floor tour, 642
 hiking, 643–45
 restaurants, 660–62

Yosemite Valley Wilderness Center, 634, 635
Yosemite Village, 638, 661–62, 665
 visitor center, 634
Yovimpa Overlook, 92
Yucca Cave, 113
Yurok Loop Nature Trail, 516, 518

Zabriskie Point, 197, 198, 202
Zion Canyon, 667, 673, 678
 hiking, 675–76
Zion Canyon Cinemax Theatre, 685
Zion Canyon Scenic Drive, 673
Zion Lodge, 673, 678, 679–80
Zion–Mount Carmel Tunnel, 668–69, 672
Zion National Park
 accommodations, 679–82
 attractions, 672–73, 674
  nearby, 685–89
 avoiding crowds, 90, 667
 camping, 669, 678–79
 for children, 677
 hiking, 668, 672–73, 674–77
 restaurants, 682–84
 scenic drives, 673
 sports and activities, 677–78
 supplies, 684
 tours and programs, 673–74
Zumwalt Meadows, 417, 419, 564, 569
Zzyzx Mineral Springs, 668–69, 672